CANADIAN TORT LAW

Allen M. Linden
A Justice of the Federal Court of Canada

Seventh Edition

Butterworths
A Member of the LexisNexis Group

The Butterworth Group of Companies

Canada:
75 Clegg Road, MARKHAM, Ontario L6G 1A1
and
1721-808 Nelson St., Box 12148, VANCOUVER, B.C. V6Z 2H2
Australia:
Butterworths Pty Ltd., SYDNEY, ADELAIDE, BRISBANE, CANBERRA, HOBART, MELBOURNE and PERTH
Ireland:
Butterworth (Ireland) Ltd., DUBLIN
Malaysia:
Malayan Law Journal Sdn Bhd, KUALA LUMPUR
New Zealand:
Butterworths of New Zealand Ltd., WELLINGTON and AUCKLAND
Singapore:
Butterworths Asia, SINGAPORE
South Africa:
Butterworth Publishers (Pty.) Ltd., DURBAN
United Kingdom:
Butterworth & Co. (Publishers) Ltd., LONDON and EDINBURGH
United States:
LEXIS Publishing, CHARLOTTESVILLE, Virginia

National Library of Canada Cataloguing in Publication Data

Linden, Allen M., 1934-
    Canadian tort law

7th ed.
First ed. published under title:
Includes bibliographical references and index.
ISBN 0-433-43100-8 (bound). —ISBN 0-433-43101-6 (pbk.)

1. Torts - Canada.   I. Linden, Allen M., 1934- Canadian negligence law.   II. Title.

KE1232.L56 2001   346.7103   C2001-903798-8

Printed and bound in Canada

To
my grandchildren,

Adam and Benji Wiseman,

Sarah and Danya Firestone,

Julia and Ethan Weinberger,

and any other precious grandchildren yet to come,

in the hope that tort law will furnish them
with some measure of protection
in this sometimes dangerous world.

Preface

This book, like its six earlier editions, seeks to furnish an overview of most of the Canadian law of torts. It now seems strange that the original edition of this book in 1972 was the first torts textbook written in Canada. Perhaps it was understandable, because, in those days, the Canadian law of torts was really just the British law of torts and there were already in existence a number of acceptable English tort texts. Perhaps, at that time, the work of the Canadian judiciary was not thought to be distinctive enough to merit separate treatment. Perhaps there were too few full-time teachers of tort law then who were able to undertake such an enormous task.

In any event, the so-called common law of torts has lost its commonality in recent years. Canadian courts, and courts in the other Commonwealth countries, have finally begun to travel along paths of their own choosing. The decision of the Privy Council in *Invercargill* has accelerated this phenomenon, as has the increasing independence of thought among the Commonwealth judiciary. The law of torts is now being rewritten so as to reflect the varying needs of each jurisdiction.

In some areas of tort law, Canadian courts and legislatures have been in the vanguard. Led by an increasingly independent and scholarly Supreme Court of Canada, Canadian judges, at all levels, have made unique contributions to the corpus of tort law. Our judges have frequently developed novel and wise solutions to thorny tort problems. They have contributed many a perceptive and even literary analysis. In the last few years the Canadian law reports have begun to crackle with new life as our judiciary becomes more confident, more profound, more creative. So significant has been the Canadian contribution that it is now commonplace to see British and other Commonwealth courts referring to Canadian authorities in their analysis. This book seeks to focus on the Canadian contribution to the development of the law of torts, but, of course, also deals to a certain extent with the U.K. material, the other Commonwealth material and, where helpful, the U.S. jurisprudence. I have not analyzed every single decision that is available on every topic, preferring to concentrate instead only on the more significant ones.

This seventh edition, as usual, has described many new cases that have added to or altered the existing law, some of them quite significant. For example, the expiry of *res ipsa loquitur*, the new developments in compensation for economic loss, the current views on prenatal injuries, and alterations in the law of vicarious liability are among the many matters explained.

The major innovation of this new edition is the incorporation of the modern structure for analysis of pure economic loss cases recently articulated by the Supreme Court of Canada, which was based on the outstanding book, *Economic Negligence*, by Dean Bruce Feldthusen. I am delighted that Dean Feldthusen, the Commonwealth's leading scholar in this field, has kindly agreed to co-write with me a new chapter 12, into which we have placed all of the pure economic loss material in order to reflect the recent effort by the Supreme Court to rationalize its approach to these matters. I am truly grateful to Dean Feldthusen for his major contribution in drawing together and rewriting with me the material which has heretofore appeared in different parts of this book.

Another significant new feature of this seventh edition is the inclusion of a new chapter 20, The Civil Law of Delict in Quebec, which is based on the work of Justice Jean-Louis Baudoin of the Quebec Court of Appeal, who is the author of Quebec's leading torts text in French, *La Responsibilité Civile Delictuelle*. My law clerk, Charles Tingley, a graduate of McGill University Law School and now at Davies Ward Phillips & Vineberg in Toronto, assisted me greatly in revising one of Justice Baudoin's monographs written in English, summarizing briefly the Quebec law. I hope this new chapter will be of assistance to English-speaking Canadian lawyers and judges who have tended to ignore the many interesting and useful torts cases in French that emerge from the Quebec courts.

There has also been a major updating in this edition of the material on medical law, nuisance law, occupiers' liability law and products liability based on the superb research contribution of my daughter, Lisa Linden Wiseman, formerly of the Toronto law firm of Goodman and Carr, who thoroughly researched these areas and offered much valuable advice.

I should also like to thank Stephen Jarvis for his valuable suggestions about psychiatric damage, a subject that is now considered important enough to merit its own chapter 11 in this edition.

An enormous vote of thanks go to Aija Carisse, my devoted long-time Judicial Assistant, who slaved over my messy notes throughout the long, hot summer of 2001, miraculously transforming those scratchings into a readable manuscript. In addition, my current Judicial Assistant, Glenda Gourlay, generously pitched in helping to prepare parts of the manuscript as well.

My gratitude must be expressed to Pepperdine University, School of Law, where I have served as Adjunct Professor these last two winters, to my colleagues and students there and to Dean Richardson Lynn and Associate Dean Shelley Saxer for honouring me by allowing me to teach there.

The people at Butterworths — Caryl Young, Shaun Johnson, and Lorraine Kirby — also deserve my thanks for their support and for transforming the manuscript into this most attractive book.

I want also to thank my wonderful wife, Marjorie, who forewent much of our summer vacation time these last two years so that I could complete this project. Her steadfast encouragement and abiding love makes it all possible and worthwhile.

This volume is dedicated to my grandchildren — Adam and Benji Wiseman; Sarah and Danya Firestone; and Julia and Ethan Weinberger; and any other precious grandchildren yet to come — in the hope that tort law will furnish them with some measure of protection in this sometimes dangerous world.

Allen M. Linden
Ottawa
October 7, 2001

Table of Contents

Table of Cases

A

B

D

E

F

I

J

K

L

M

N

O

P

Q

R

T

U

V

W

Chapter 1

Introduction: The Functions of Tort Law

The law of torts hovers over virtually every activity of modern society. The driver of every automobile on our highways, the pilot of every aeroplane in the sky, and the captain of every ship plying our waters must abide by the standards of tort law. The producers, distributors and repairers of every product, from bread to computers, must conform to tort law's counsel of caution. No profession is beyond its reach: a doctor cannot raise a scalpel, a lawyer cannot advise a client, nor can an architect design a building without being subject to potential tort liability. In the same way, teachers, government officials, police, and even jailers may be required to pay damages if someone is hurt as a result of their conduct. Those who engage in sports, such as golfers, hockey-players, and snowmobilers, may end up as parties to a tort action. The territory of tort law encompasses losses resulting from fires, floods, explosions, electricity, gas, and many other catastrophes that may occur in this increasingly complex world. A person who punches another person on the nose may have to answer for it not only in a tort case but also in the criminal courts. A person who says nasty things about another may be sued for defamation. Hence, any one of us may become a plaintiff or a defendant in a tort action at any moment. Tort law, therefore, is a subject of abiding concern not only to the judges and lawyers who must administer it but also to the public at large, whose every move is regulated by it.

Although it is relatively easy to point to the activities within the compass of tort law, it is not so simple to offer a satisfactory definition of a tort. The term itself is a derivation of the Latin word, *tortus*, which means twisted or crooked. The expression found its way into the early English language as a synonym for the word "wrong". It is no longer used in everyday language, but it has survived as a technical legal term to this day.[1]

Many authors have striven to define tort law and to mark it off from criminal law, contract law and quasi-contract law, but none of them has been entirely

---

[1] See *Lawson v. Wellesley Hospital* (1975), 9 O.R. (2d) 677, at p. 681 (*per* Dubin J.A.). Affd on another point, [1978] 1 S.C.R. 893.

successful. Perhaps the best working definition so far produced is "A tort is a civil wrong, other than a breach of contract, which the law will redress by an award of damages."[2] But even this formulation does not tell us very much. It merely asserts that a tort consists of conduct for which the courts will order compensation, which is almost as circular as saying that a tort is a tort. Nevertheless, it is true that "A 'tort' is a legal construct . . . , [which] only exists where the law says it exists."[3]

A more promising description of tort law can be obtained by focussing on function. In tort litigation, the courts must decide whether to shift the loss suffered by one person, the plaintiff, to the shoulders of another person, the defendant.[4] The principles and rules of the law of torts, which have been developed over the centuries, assist the courts in this task. No definition could possibly depict the richness and variety of the subject matter of tort law. In order to know what tort law is, it is necessary to study in some detail what it aims to do and what it does in fact, as well as the basic principles incorporated within it. Only at the end of this book will the reader possess an accurate picture of the terrain of tort law.

Tort law is not one-dimensional; it serves several functions.[5] It is "pluralistic".[6] The purpose of this chapter is to identify in a preliminary and tentative way the main aims of modern tort law. Not all of its goals are harmonious, indeed some may be in conflict with others. Not all the purposes of tort law are expressed openly in the case law. On the contrary, some of them are unrecognized or dimly perceived, or even vehemently denied. Some are achieved only indirectly and some not at all. Thus tort law serves a potpourri of objectives, some conscious and some unconscious.

Some reject the idea that tort law serves any particular instrumental function. Professor Ernest Weinrib,[7] for example, has argued that "goals have nothing to do with tort law". Those instrumentalists who believe the contrary, he contends, are not advancing a theory of tort law but rather a "theory of social goals" into

---

[2]   Fleming, *The Law of Torts,* 9th ed. (1998), p. 1; *Prosser and Keeton on the Law of Torts*, 5th ed. (1984), pp. 1-2, reproduces several definitions; Williams and Hepple, *Foundations of the Law of Torts* (1976); for an excellent treatise on the Quebec law, see Baudouin, *La Responsabilité Civile*, 5th ed. (1998); see Dobbs, *The Law of Torts* (2000), p. 1.

[3]   See in *Angus v. Hart* (1988), 52 D.L.R. (4th) 193, at p. 199 (S.C.C.) (*per* La Forest J.). See also Cory J.'s definition of a tort in *Hall v. Hebert*, [1993] 2 S.C.R. 159, 15 C.C.L.T. (2d) 93, at p. 118.

[4]   Wright, *Cases on the Law of Torts*, 4th ed. (1967), Introduction.

[5]   See Williams, "The Aims of the Law of Tort", [1951] Current Legal Problems 137; Fleming, "The Role of Negligence in Modern Tort Law" (1967), 53 Va. L. Rev. 815; R. Keeton, "Is There a Place for Negligence in Modern Tort Law?" (1967), 53 Va. L. Rev. 886. See also Klar, "The Role of Fault and Policy in Negligence Law" (1996), 35 Alta. L. Rev. 24, at p. 29. These are not "purposes" but only "incidental consequences".

[6]   See England, *The Philosophy of Tort Law* (1993).

[7]   "Understanding Tort Law" (1989), 23 Valp. L.J. 485. See also Weinrib, *The Idea of Private Law* (1995); Coleman, *Risks and Wrongs* (1992).

which tort law may or may not fit. Professor Weinrib charmingly opines that tort law, like love, has no ulterior ends:

> Explaining love in terms of ulterior ends is necessarily a mistake, because a loving relationship has no ulterior end. Love is its own end. In that respect, tort law is just like love.[8]

Professor Weinrib asserts that it is as unfair to criticize tort law for not achieving certain social goals as it is to "criticize a turtle for failing to fly". Tort law is non-instrumentalist, he insists, being concerned merely with the "propriety of activity".[9]

It is true that tort law, like love, is valuable for its own sake, but there are many aspects of love and many facets of tort law. Professor Weinrib, by maintaining that there are no pragmatic ends of love and of torts, undervalues them both. There is more to love and to torts that just their intrinsic unpolluted merit, however splendid that may be. Neither should be sold short. True, the greatest thing about love is love itself, but love also inspires song, animates poetry, builds new families, encourages new enterprises, etc. Love can take credit for some of the good things that happen in our world, even though lovers may not start out with these effects in mind. Similarly, tort law may achieve beneficial effects, without necessarily setting out to do so, things like compensation, deterrence and education. Thus, whether by design or not, tort law, like love, is valuable not only intrinsically but also for its other contributions to a better world.

Like so many social institutions, tort law is being re-evaluated in the context of our times. It is often assailed as a relic of a bygone age which has no purpose in contemporary society.[10] If it is true that tort law no longer serves us, it should be buried along with the other fossils of the legal system. Reports of the death of torts have been greatly exaggerated, however.[11] The mere assertion that tort law is useless does not establish the truth of that indictment. There is a disturbing paucity of data relevant to the aims and efficacy of tort law. We are debating in the dark. What is more disconcerting is that we do not possess reliable techniques of measurement upon which to base valid conclusions. Unsubstantiated claims and counterclaims are no basis for rational choice. It may be that our society will ultimately choose to jettison tort law, but it should not be done until we have evaluated *all* of its benefits and *all* of its costs. It is too early for such a decision to be taken because our information is still fragmentary. We have barely begun to analyze the aims and functions of tort law. Empirical studies should be undertaken to measure the efficacy of tort law in achieving its goals.

---

[8] *Ibid.*, at p. 526. See generally Cooper-Stephenson and Gibson, *Tort Theory* (1993).
[9] "The Special Morality of Tort Law" (1989), 34 McGill L.J. 403, at p. 412.
[10] Sugarman, "Doing Away With Tort Law" (1985), 73 Calif. L. Rev. 555.
[11] Fridman, *The Law of Torts in Canada*, (1989), at p. iv.

Only after these studies are concluded will we be able to make an informed decision about the destiny of tort law.[12]

A. Compensation

First and foremost, tort law is a compensator. A successful action puts money into the pocket of the claimant. This payment is supposed to reimburse the claimant for the economic and psychic damages suffered at the hands of the defendant.[13]

The reparation function of modern tort law is so fundamental that some commentators have asserted that it is tort law's *only* legitimate task. The late Dean C.A. Wright, for example, contended simply that the "purpose of the law of torts is to adjust [the] losses [arising out of modern living] and to afford compensation for injuries sustained by one person as the result of the conduct of another".[14] Another scholar has argued that justice requires, most of all, the reparation of wrongs.[15] Indeed, he thought that penal sanctions might well be replaced by civil ones, once the latter "acquired a sufficient efficacy".

This view is inaccurate. If the sole role of tort law were universal compensation, it would have become extinct long ago. The truth is that only certain victims, "the deserving", win damages in tort. The "undeserving" are denied recovery. In other words, only those who are able to prove that they were injured through another's fault or negligence receive reparation, and those who cannot go without. "A loss must lie where it falls", asserted Oliver Wendell Holmes,[16] unless there is a good reason to shift it. That good reason was fault. Holmes argued that the state's "cumbrous and expensive machinery ought not to be set in motion unless some clear benefit is to be derived from disturbing the status quo. State interference is an evil, where it cannot be shown to be a good." Such a benefit was derived when a loss was shifted from an innocent plaintiff to a wrong-doing defendant.

This theory had its heyday prior to the advent of the welfare state and widespread liability insurance. The interaction of these two factors changed the face of tort law. Increased social awareness coupled with liability insurance led to an increase in the incidence of tort liability. Devices such as *res ipsa loquitur*, negligence *per se*, and contributory negligence legislation were employed to

---

[12] An impressive start on such an exercise is Fleming, *The American Tort Process* (1988). For a survey of the state of tort research in Canada, see McLaren, "The Theoretical and Policy Challenges in Canadian Compensation Law" (1985), 23 Osgoode Hall L.J. 609. For a study of criminal law's effect see Friedland, *Securing Compliance* (1988).

[13] See Cory J., quoting this paragraph in *Hall v. Hebert, supra*, n. 3, at p. 118.

[14] "Introduction to the Law of Torts" (1944), 8 Camb. L.J. 238. See also Lord Reid in *Cassell & Co. Ltd. v. Broome*, [1972] 2 W.L.R. 645, at p. 682. For a superb analysis of Wright's contribution to torts scholarship, see Brown, "Cecil A. Wright and the Foundations of Canadian Tort Law Scholarship" (2001), 64 Sask. L.R. 169.

[15] Del Vecchio, *Justice* (1924), p. 216.

[16] See *The Common Law* (1881), p. 96.

compensate more and more claimants.[17] Eventually, in opposition to Holmes, scholars began to contend that "worthwhile 'social gain' *is* achieved by shifting losses from innocent victims".[18]

A new rationale for tort law — loss distribution — was devised to reflect these developments and to spur further growth along these lines.[19] According to this theory, accident losses are no longer shifted from one individual to another. Rather, the costs are transferred to industrial enterprises and insured activities which generate most accidents. These activities do not bear these costs themselves but spread them throughout the community *via* price increases or insurance premiums. Thus, the expense is borne by the segment of society participating in the activity. Consequently, a massive loss that might bankrupt a defendant, if shifted to that individual, can be divided into infinitesimal portions to be exacted from many people without undue hardship to any of them. Pursuant to this reasoning, if tort law fails to compensate everyone, it is not performing its loss distribution task adequately. It is somewhat unsporting, however, to criticize tort law for not doing something it was never designed to do: the new criterion of loss-spreading was never taken into account by the architects of tort law.

When one begins to advocate that *all* accidental losses should be recompensed, one departs from the territory of tort law and enters the regime of social welfare. The logical extension of loss-distribution is social security. It is a mere "palliative," a temporary stopping-place on the way to a complete social insurance system.[20] For tort law could not perform the role of social welfare adequately, even if its basis were strict liability rather than fault. Tort recovery certainly helps to cushion the financial blow of accidental injury. It is welcome enough if there is nothing else available, but if full and swift compensation is the only task of tort law, it should be replaced by something else less costly and less dilatory.

The loss-distribution theory was an admirable attempt by tort scholars to expand the incidence of tort reparation. It was a disguised movement toward increased social welfare by sincere reformers who were impatient with the sluggish advance of progressive legislation. Through this humane theory a few more accident victims may have won compensation, but it was still limited to

---

[17] See generally Fleming, *op. cit. supra*, n. 2, pp. 12 *et seq.*

[18] Franklin, "Replacing the Negligence Lottery: Compensation and Selective Reimbursement" (1967), 53 Va. L. Rev. 774, at p. 782.

[19] See generally Ehrenzweig, *Negligence Without Fault* (1951), also at (1966), 54 Calif. L. Rev. 1422; Ehrenzweig, "Assurance Oblige — A Comparative Study" (1950), 15 Law & Cont. Prob. 445; Fleming, *op cit. supra*, n. 2; Harper, James and Gray, *The Law of Torts*, 2nd ed. (1986); Priest, "The Invention of Enterprise Liability: A Critical History of the Intellectual Foundations of Modern Tort Law" (1985), 14 J. Leg. Stud. 461; Lang, "The Activity Risk Theory of Tort; Risk, Insurance and Insolvency" (1961), 39 Can. Bar Rev. 53. See also *Nettleship v. Weston*, [1971] 3 All E.R. 581 (*per* Denning M.R.); White, *Tort Law In America* (1980).

[20] Ison, *The Forensic Lottery* (1967). See also Atiyah, *Accidents, Compensation and The Law*, 5th ed. (1993).

those "lucky" enough to be hurt by activities in which the tort remedy and liability insurance operated. Its main contribution was that a private type of social welfare could be supplied to some of those who needed it, without any necessity for a dramatic break from the free enterprise system.

There is less need for loss-distribution in tort law today. Modern societies have begun to recognize an obligation toward their sick, their aged, and their poor. Hospital and medical care plans have been enacted. Workers' compensation, unemployment insurance, sick pay, disability, old age, and survivorship payments are becoming increasingly common. These benefits are available to individuals injured by tortious conduct as well as to those who are unable to establish any tort liability. One study has revealed that 40 per cent of all the money received by automobile accident victims came from non-tort sources such as these, and the proportion of this type of aid is steadily rising.[21] As a consequence of these developments, a denial of tort recovery is no longer the tragedy it used to be.

We have erected a complex three-level system to furnish compensation for injured Canadians.[22] At the bottom level are social insurance measures which provide hospital and medical care and some income replacement to all, regardless of the cause of injury or illness. On top of this are several schemes which provide fuller compensation on a no-fault basis for special groups in society such as workers and crime and auto accident victims.[23] At the pinnacle is tort law, which provides more complete reparation for those who are able to prove that they were hurt through the fault of another person.

It has been urged that this complex structure should be unified and forged into a single enriched social welfare scheme which would treat all the sick and injured alike.[24] This debate, however, cannot be divorced from a more general discussion about the guaranteed annual income[25] and other anti-poverty measures.[26] No one denies that both tort law and the present patchwork of welfare schemes need better co-ordination. The disagreement is over whether tort law should survive as an "additional or supplemental remedy,"[27] over and above the floor of social insurance. The key issue is whether the resources used to run the tort system would be more wisely spent if they were distributed through the

---

[21] *The Report of the Osgoode Hall Study on Compensation for Victims of Automobile Accidents* (1965); Klar, "The Osborne Report: 'No' to No-Fault" (1989), 68 Can. Bar Rev. 301.

[22] See Linden, "Automobile Accident Compensation in Ontario — A System in Transition" (1967), 15 Am. J. Comp. L. 301, for a fuller description. See also Conard et al., *Automobile Accident Costs and Payments* (1964).

[23] See Linden and Firestone, *Butterworths Ontario Motor Vehicle Insurance Practice Manual* (1995).

[24] Ison, *op cit. supra*, n. 20; *Report of the Royal Commission of Inquiry on Compensation for Personal Injury in New Zealand* (1967) (Woodhouse Report); Ison, *Accident Compensation: A Commentary on the New Zealand Scheme* (1980).

[25] Theobald, *The Guaranteed Income* (1967).

[26] Blum and Kalven, *Public Law Perspectives on a Private Law Problem — Auto Compensation Plans* (1965), also in (1964), 31 U. Chi. L. Rev. 641.

[27] James, "The Future of Negligence in Accident Law" (1967), 53 Va. L. Rev. 911, at p. 912.

social welfare system. Before attempting any conclusion on this position, the other functions of tort law have to be considered.

B. Deterrence

The second historic function of tort law is deterrence or the prevention of accidents. Such legal luminaries as Bentham, Austin, and Salmond believed that the purpose of tort law was not much different from that of the criminal law.[28] Lord Mansfield once wrote that damages acted "as a punishment to the guilty, to deter from any such proceedings in the future . . . ".[29] This should surprise no one in view of the common roots of tort and criminal law.[30]

Judges often express their desire to deter future torts in holding defendants liable, especially when an award of punitive damages is involved. For example, Mr. Justice La Forest, in awarding punitive damages in *Norberg v. Wynrib* declared that "the exchange of drugs for sex by a doctor in a position of power is conduct that cries out for deterrence".[31] Mr. Justice Major in *Stewart v. Pettie*,[32] recently articulated the deterrent role of negligence law as follows:

> One of the primary purposes of negligence law is to enforce reasonable standards of conduct so as to prevent the creation of reasonably foreseeable risks. In this way, tort law serves as a disincentive to risk-creating behaviour.

In *Galaske v. O'Donnell*,[33] a case in which a driver was held liable for failing to buckle in a child passenger, Mr. Justice Cory indicated his desire to foster safety when he explained:

> If the fixing of responsibility on a driver to ensure that young passengers wear seat belts saves one child from death or devastating injury then all society will have benefited.

So, too, Mr. Justice La Forest has indicated in *Winnipeg Condominium Corporation No. 36 v. Bird Construction Co.*,[34] a negligence case, that:

> Allowing recovery against contractors in tort for the cost of repair of dangerous defects thus serves an important preventative function by encouraging socially responsible behaviour . . . tort law serves to encourage the repair of dangerous defects and thereby to protect the bodily integrity of inhabitants of buildings.

---

[28] Williams, "The Aims of the Law of Tort", [1951] Current Legal Problems 137, at p. 144.
[29] *Wilkes v. Wood* (1763), 19 State Tr. 1153, 98 E.R. 489. See also Holt C.J. in *Ashby v. White* (1703), 2 Ld. Raym. 938, 92 E.R. 126.
[30] Malone, "Ruminations on the Role of Fault in the History of the Common Law of Torts" (1970), 31 La. L. Rev. 1; also in Malone, *Essays in Torts* (1986); Hall, "Interrelations of Crime and Tort" (1943), 43 Colum. L. Rev. 753 and 967.
[31] *Norberg v. Wynrib*, [1992] 2 S.C.R. 226, at p. 268.
[32] [1995] 1 S.C.R. 131, at p. 150.
[33] [1994] 1 S.C.R. 670, at p. 690.
[34] [1995] 1 S.C.R. 85, at pp. 118 and 120.

It may be said, therefore, that judges view tort law as a "whip that makes industry safer and saner".[35]

The admonitory function of tort law operates in two ways. Firstly, individuals who are required to pay damages for losses caused by their substandard conduct will try to avoid a recurrence. Secondly, tort judgments against transgressors are meant to warn others. The threat of tort liability is supposed to deter wrongful conduct and to stimulate caution on the part of those who wish to avoid civil liability for their conduct.[36] In other words, the lesson being taught to society is that tort, like crime, does not pay.[37]

Deterrence has been one of the fundamental assumptions of tort law, but assumptions do not necessarily correspond with reality. On the empirical evidence so far collected, it is hard to tell whether the civil sanction has any sting left in it. Some scholars contend that tort law's deterrent role is a myth,[38] while more charitable authors suggest that the possibility of deterrence is "of a low order".[39]

Certainly, there are impediments in the way of successful deterrence through tort law. Firstly, some individuals are unwilling to conform to the behaviour patterns prescribed by tort law. Some motorists, for example, persist in driving too fast or with their ability impaired, in spite of legal prohibitions. This is not unique to tort law. There are many citizens in our society who knowingly violate the criminal law. Other branches of the law are similarly flouted by some members of our society. All that can be done with these wilful offenders is to impose whatever legal sanction is appropriate and hope that this attitude does not spread throughout society. Tort law and the other legal norms can have little influence on these people.

Secondly, certain persons may be willing to conform to the standard of care expected of them, but they may be unable to live up to it. The awkward, the accident-prone, and those of limited intelligence are sometimes incapable of performing reasonably, however hard they may try.[40] Fortunately, most people are not inadequate to the demands of modern living and will act cautiously in order to avoid mishaps.

---

[35] Little, "Up With Torts" (1987), 24 San Diego L. Rev. 861, at p. 868.

[36] *Prosser and Keeton on the Law of Torts*, 5th ed. (1984), p. 25.

[37] See *Rookes v. Barnard*, [1964] A.C. 1129 (*per* Lord Devlin). See also *Cassell & Co. Ltd. v. Broome*, [1972] 2 W.L.R. 645, at p. 671 (*per* Hailsham L.C.). See generally Zimring and Hawkins, *Deterrence* (1973); *Swanson Estate v. R.* (1991), 7 C.C.L.T. (2d) 186, at p. 198 (Fed. C.A.) (*per* Linden J.A.), "negligence, like crime, does not pay".

[38] For example, Ison, *The Forensic Lottery* (1967). See also U.S. D.O.T. study by Klein and Waller, *Causation, Culpability and Deterrence in Highway Crashes* (1970). See Klar, *op. cit. supra*, n. 5, at p. 13.

[39] Morris, "Negligence in Tort Law — With Emphasis on Automobile Accidents and Unsound Products" (1967), 53 Va. L. Rev. 899, at p. 900. See also Bruce, "The Deterrent Effects of Automobile Insurance and Tort Law: A Survey of the Empirical Literature" (1984), 6 Law & Pol. 67; see Klar, *supra*, note 21, at p. 308, describing White Study for Osborne Report.

[40] James and Dickson, "Accident Proneness and Accident Law" (1950), 63 Harv. L. Rev. 769.

Thirdly, someone willing and able to live up to the standards of tort law may be totally ignorant of them. People cannot change their conduct to comply with directions of which they are not apprised. Fortunately, most everyday activities can be performed in a right way or in a wrong way. In most instances one can tell the difference between responsible and risky conduct. Juries have had to pass judgment upon these acts for centuries and they have not met with any major difficulties. In any event, the rules of the road are in statutory form and are known to drivers. Speed limits must be posted. Professional people and entrepreneurs learn the customs of their trades, which are relied upon as important indicators of due care.[41] Of course there are borderline cases, but those individuals should realize that their conduct is at least questionable in these circumstances. People may sometimes investigate the risks inherent in a particular course of conduct and may even hire experts to advise them how to proceed. Another point to consider is that there are a substantial number of people who know more about tort law than the average person. Because of this, the behaviour of certain people, such as doctors, lawyers, law students, police officers, insurance people, adjusters, court officials, and service station employees may be affected more by tort law than that of the general public. In addition, there are many citizens who have been involved in tort litigation as parties, witnesses or jurors and have learned something about the operation of tort law.

Fourthly, an even graver deficiency plagues tort law. The advent of liability insurance has removed some of its prophylactic power because the civil sanction is rarely applied against the tortfeasors themselves. When a judgment against an individual is paid by the individual's insurer, whatever preventive force tort law retains is further enfeebled. Some scholars have argued, therefore, that there is no sting left in tort law in the motor vehicle accident area because liability insurance coverage for motorists is almost universal.[42] This position is too simplistic Despite compulsory insurance laws, a tiny percentage of Canadian motorists are still uninsured.[43] These individuals remain subject to the full deterrent lash of tort law, since they have to pay personally for the consequences of their negligence. Of course, many of the uninsured drivers are judgment-proof and cannot pay damages awarded against them. However, when judgments are rendered against uninsured motorists they may lose their licences and be taken off the road altogether, if an unsatisfied judgment fund is forced to pay the awards on their behalf.[44] Removal of such drivers from the highways is the most stringent deterrent of them all, and occurs as an indirect result of tort liability. There are, moreover, many motorists who carry only the minimum limits of liability insurance required by law. These people are personally responsible if a damage award against them exceeds this figure. Furthermore,

---

[41]   See Chapters 6 and 7.

[42]   See, for example, Fleming, *supra*, n. 2.

[43]   Lofchik, "The Ontario Motor Vehicle Accident Claims Act" (1970), 28 U.T. Fac. L. Rev. 94, suggests only 2% lack coverage in Ontario.

[44]   *Ibid.*, at p. 96.

the loss in question may not be covered by the terms of the insurance policy at all. For example, the person injured by the driver may be some person excluded by the provisions of the policy. Another possibility is that the motorist may have forfeited the right to be indemnified by violating one of the conditions of the policy. For instance, if the motorist drives while drunk, he or she is not covered by the policy, even though the insurer is initially responsible by statute to any third person who has suffered loss. Lastly, even if the insurer stands behind the motorist, the motorist must still undergo the inconvenience of being involved in a civil suit, something no one enjoys. Despite all these potentially unpleasant repercussions, one survey revealed that 58 per cent of the respondents felt that civil liability did not affect careful driving, whereas only 14 per cent thought that it did.[45] It is hard to assess the reliability of this study, but it does seem to reveal the public's perception of the problem.

In addition to imposing civil liability for negligence, the common law courts withhold or reduce the recovery of anyone who is contributorily negligent with regard to their own safety.[46] Contributory negligence is still being used to encourage care by plaintiffs. The knowledge that one will be denied compensation in whole or in part as a result of one's own negligence should spur one to use caution. This rule may be doubly influential, because the negligence of a driver may be imputed to passengers and to family.[47] Thus, not only is the contributorily negligent actor waiving the right to recover but may also impede friends and relatives from receiving full damages for their injuries. The application of the seat belt defence is an example of the use of contributory negligence law as a deterrent to dangerous conduct.[48]

1. INSURANCE COMPANY INFLUENCE

Whereas liability insurance dulls the financial incentive of *drivers* to use care, it sharpens the motivation of insurance *companies* to prevent accidents. The more mishaps occur during an activity, the less profit is earned and the higher the cost of insurance coverage for those who engage in it. Whenever insurance premiums rise, dissatisfaction with the insurance industry intensifies. This is turn stimulates pressure for the state to nationalize the business. Since insurance companies want to avert this fate and to maximize profits, they try to reduce accidents.

One technique employed by insurance companies is the linking of each individual's premium to his or her accident record. A claim-free driver pays less than one who has been responsible for an accident. That cannot help but remind some motorists of their duty to exercise care. Indeed, Professor Fleming has indicated that an increase in premiums could be an even more effective deterrent

---

[45] Bombaugh, "The Department of Transportation Auto Insurance Study and Auto Accident Compensation Reform" (1971), 91 Colum. L. Rev. 207, at p. 233.

[46] See *infra*, Chapter 13.

[47] No longer in Ontario, though, as it was under the Negligence Act, R.S.O. 1970, c. 296, s. 2, am. by S.O. 1977, c. 59 [now R.S.O. 1990, c. N.1].

[48] *Yuan v. Farstad* (1967), 66 D.L.R. (2d) 295 (B.C.).

than personal liability, since the former has to be paid if the motorist wishes to continue driving whereas a tort judgment probably could not be paid at all.[49] A recent survey in the United States has shown that only 21 per cent of the respondents thought that their insurance premiums would be raised if they were involved in an accident.[50] This figure certainly casts doubt on the efficacy of such a sanction. Nevertheless, if 21 per cent are deterred by this threat, *some* benefit may be derived from it. If the public were better informed about their rights and duties in relation to insurance coverage, this sanction might become more influential.

Another tool at the disposal of an insurer is the cancellation of a policy or refusal to provide coverage. In Canada, this is not as disastrous as it is elsewhere, because of the existence of a pooling mechanism which guarantees that insurance is available to all, regardless of how bad a risk they are. Strangely, an American study disclosed that only 2 per cent of the people interviewed expected the cancellation of their policy after an accident. Since an "unperceived penalty cannot deter future deviant conduct," the force of this sanction is minimal.[51]

Insurers can stimulate their insureds to institute safer practices. One product liability insurance company was suddenly confronted by a series of claims against its insured arising from breaking ketchup bottles. Upon investigation, the company discovered that its insured had recently changed the design of its bottles. When the insurer suggested that this new type of container be abandoned, the insured complied. Another insurance company provided coverage for a well-known music composer, who had the dangerous habit of writing music at the same time that he was driving his automobile. As a result, he was frequently involved in accidents because of his inattention. His premium rates soared. Eventually, his insurance company informed him that his policy would have to be cancelled if he did not terminate this practice. Instead of giving up his music-writing while travelling, the composer hired a chauffeur to operate his car for him.[52]

The insurance industry has also undertaken driver education campaigns, supported safety organizations, advocated defensive driving, combatted drunken driving, urged the use of seat belts and other worthwhile endeavours. More recently, these efforts have been stepped up, but there is still much more that can be done. Pressure from insurers for such measures as crashworthy vehicles, safer highways, tougher licensing laws, and stricter enforcement of traffic laws will accelerate their introduction.

To be sure, these efforts aimed at accident reduction are indirect and hardly of major significance. Direct government intervention would be far more

---

[49] "The Role of Negligence in Modern Tort Law" (1967), 53 Va. L. Rev. 815, at p. 825.

[50] U.S. D.O.T., *Public Attitudes Towards Auto Insurance* (1970), p. 67.

[51] See Bombaugh, *supra*, n. 45, at p. 233.

[52] Other examples are mentioned in Klar, *op. cit. supra*, n. 5, at p. 14, *i.e.*, I.U.D., drugs, sports equipment, etc., discontinued.

effective. Unhappily though, most governments lack the courage to do the things necessary to cut accidents appreciably. The minimal efforts of the insurance industry are better than nothing.

2. PARTNERSHIP WITH CRIMINAL LAW

Tort law may act as a partner of the criminal law. The civil sanction may reinforce the efforts of penal enforcement authorities, which are occasionally ineffectual.[53] Criminal penalties are often so insignificant that they do not deter anyone. A highway traffic offence, for instance, may produce a fine of only $50, an amount that frightens no one. Demerit point schemes provide the additional threat of licence suspension, but most infractions cost only one or two points out of the 12 or 15 needed to revoke a driver's permit.[54] A serious violation like drunk driving may lead to the loss of a licence, but such offences are less common than the minor ones that often precede collisions. Another reason for the inefficacy of the criminal law is that its enforcement is sporadic. Millions of highway infractions are reported each year but a far greater number are never detected. Every motorist has contravened some traffic law without having been prosecuted for it.

Tort law can assist penal law in this area. Evidence of the violation of a criminal statute may be relied upon by a civil court in a suit by a person injured thereby.[55] There are, of course, limitations on civil enforcement. Some harm to an individual is necessary for an action to lie. Moreover, private citizens rather than the police are left to administer the sanction. Normally this would hamper its effectiveness, but because plaintiffs prosecuting their own claims have a financial incentive to succeed, they may well do a more thorough job than a prosecutor.[56] Tort law adds to the list of potential law enforcement officers an entire army of zealous assistants. This additional sanction renders the criminal law "more effective".[57] Lord Justice Goddard once concluded that "the real incentive for the observance by employers of their statutory duties under [certain statutes] is not their liability to substantial fines, but the possibility of heavy claims for damages".[58] In addition, punitive damages are available in certain extreme cases, providing extra force to the civil sanction.

The decision of *Menow v. Honsberger and Jordan House Ltd.* is a good example of a tort action assisting in criminal law enforcement.[59] The plaintiff was served alcoholic beverages by the employees of the defendant hotel after he

---

[53]   Williams, *supra*, n. 28, at p. 150; Morris, "The Relation of Criminal Statutes to Tort Liability" (1933), 46 Harv. L. Rev. 453, at p. 458.

[54]   See Highway Traffic Act, R.S.O. 1990, c. H.8, s. 56.

[55]   See *infra*, Chapter 7.

[56]   Williams, *supra*, n. 25, at p. 148; Posner, "A Theory of Negligence" (1972), 1 J. Leg. Stud. 29, at p. 48.

[57]   Fricke, "The Juridical Nature of the Action Upon the Statute" (1960), 76 L.Q. Rev. 240, at p. 255.

[58]   *Hutchinson v. London & North Eastern Ry. Co.*, [1942] 1 K.B. 481, at p. 488 (C.A.).

[59]   [1970] 1 O.R. 54; affd [1971] 1 O.R. 129; affd [1974] S.C.R. 239.

had become intoxicated, in violation of the Liquor Control Act of Ontario. He was then ejected from the hotel into a situation of danger near a busy highway. Shortly thereafter, as he was staggering along the road, he was struck by a negligently driven vehicle. At trial, Mr. Justice Haines stated that "by committing this unlawful act, the corporate defendant has not only committed an offence under the relevant liquor statutes, but it has also breached a common law duty to the plaintiff not to serve him liquor when he was visibly intoxicated".[60] This decision should put some teeth into the penal legislation, which is woefully under-enforced. Despite frequent arrests of drunken drivers who have visited bars, one rarely hears of prosecutions or cancelled tavern licences because of the violation of this statute. Mr. Justice Haines did not allude to this difficulty in his reasons, but this case cannot help but alert innkeepers to the risks they run not only from penal enforcement but also from civil proceedings against them. Mr. Justice Haines pointed out that he did not want every tavern owner "to act as a watch dog for all patrons who enter his place of business and drink to excess",[61] but he was prepared to countenance it in certain circumstances. Even a caution such as this should foster increased discretion by tavern owners.

There arc, of course, numerous other statutes, the violation of which may yield tort liability.[62] Violators of food and drug laws may be subjected to tort liability as well as penal fines. Anyone who fails to install or inspect a gas furnace according to the legislative requirements risks not only a penal prosecution but also civil liability. The availability of the tort remedy may act as a prod where the criminal law has become a dead letter.

One recurrent complaint about our society is that whenever we want to eradicate some nasty activity, we pass a law making it a crime. Consequently, we may have overloaded our police forces and oppressed some of our citizenry. As a result, the Law Reform Commission of Canada has called for restraint in the use of the criminal law.[63] The sanction of tort law may be more attractive in combatting some of this anti-social conduct because it operates *only* at the behest of a victim. The increasing use of tort actions by rape and child abuse victims can never replace criminal law remedies, but it has some advantages, for example, discovery is available, it is more private, the claimant is more in control of the process and the burden of proof is less onerous. Although the stigma is not as powerful as that of criminal law, it does nevertheless express some public disapproval of the wrongful activity, it may supply a modicum of social control,[64] and it allows for awards for damages for the victims, something that is more useful to them than a fine or jail sentence.

---

[60] *Ibid.*, at p. 60.
[61] *Ibid.*, at p. 63.
[62] See *infra*, Chapter 7.
[63] Law Reform Commission of Canada, *Our Criminal Law* (Report 3, 1976).
[64] See Linden, "Torts in the 80's: A Canadian Perspective", in Law Society of Upper Canada, Special Lectures, *Torts in the 80's* (1983), p. 399, *Myers v. Haroldson* (1989), 48 C.C.L.T. 93 (Sask. Q.B.), rape; *M.(M.) v. K.(K.)* (1989), 61 D.L.R. (4th) 392 (B.C.C.A.), child abuse.

C. Education

Tort law is an educator. Along with criminal prosecutions, coroners' inquests, royal commissions and the like, a tort trial is a teacher.[65] It educates the public,[66] not just potential tortfeasors but all of us. Indeed, Glanville Williams has suggested that making someone pay compensation may be "educationally superior to a fine" in that "it teaches a moral lesson".[67] The communications explosion has magnified the importance of this didactic role of tort law. Malpractice, libel, and product liability cases in particular attract the attention of the press. Doctors, journalists, and manufacturers closely observe the outcomes of these disputes, which concern them so vitally. Their trade journals often report the results of litigation involving fellow professionals. Each annual report of the Canadian Medical Protective Association, for example, contains a summary of the medical malpractice suits that go to trial each year in Canada. Advice may be given. Conferences may be convened to discuss the problems dealt with in the litigation. Members of the public may become more alert in their dealings with these professionals. They may become less trusting and ask more questions. To be sure, this is not the most efficient way of curtailing substandard practices; other forms of regulations would undoubtedly be preferable. The sad fact is, however, that professional groups are reluctant to police their own professions strenuously, and manufacturers are often largely immune from government supervision. Until our society is prepared to use more effective weapons, the educational force of tort law may be all there is.

Tort law is also a reinforcer of values. Like the criminal law, tort law enshrines many of the traditional moral principles of Anglo-American society. This is a mixed blessing for many of these values are in need of reassessment. Tort law may well impede the birth of new moral principles through its conservation of the older values. If, however, any new moral ideals catch hold, they will infiltrate the principles of tort law. At worst, tort law slows down their acceptance and permits some sober second thoughts.

By dramatizing in open court certain acts of "wrong-doing", tort law may condemn "anti-social elements" and at the same time "exalt the good".[68] Slipshod manufacturers, inadequate drivers, and careless doctors are subject to judicial disapproval in open court. Even if a defendant is insured, could not care less about the outcome, or refuses to alter future conduct, the law publicly marks

---

[65]   See generally on the criminal law, Andenaes, "Deterrence and Specific Offences" (1971), 38 U. Chi. L. Rev. 538; Andenaes, "The Moral or Educative Influence of Criminal Law" (1971), 27 J. Soc. Issues 17; Hawkins, "Punishment and Deterrence: The Educative, Moralizing and Habituative Effects", [1969] Wis. L. Rev. 550; Thurman Arnold, "The Criminal Trial as a Symbol of Public Morality" in *Criminal Justice in Our Time*, Howard (ed.), (1965), pp. 141 *et seq.*

[66]   See Cory J. in *Hall v. Hebert*, [1993] 2 S.C.R. 159, 15 C.C.L.T. (2d) 93, at p. 119.

[67]   "Aims of the Law of Tort", [1951] Current Legal Problems 137, at p. 149.

[68]   *Ibid.*, at p. 143. See also *Prosser and Keeton on the Law of Torts*, 5th ed. (1984), p. 21.

the defendant as a "wrong-doer" and vindicates the plaintiff's complaint.[69] In this way tort law, like criminal law, furnishes an opportunity to foster community feeling about common moral values.[70] Obviously, failure to conform to the standards of tort law is not as morally reprehensible as murder, rape, robbery or arson. Nevertheless, all of these acts are torts as well as crimes. Under either legal categorization, such conduct is unacceptable to right-thinking individuals. Under either description, it should be, and is, publicly denounced.

Tort law may occasionally be *more* effective than criminal law for this purpose. A victim of a criminal assault might prefer to sue the attacker in tort rather than call the police, because the former course may provide some monetary gain while the latter will not. Further, such aggrieved persons may wish to take some action against their aggressors, but may not want them to end up in jail. Another benefit of tort proceedings is that they may be easily settled when the claimant's ardour cools, whereas criminal cases do not lend themselves to such efficient disposal.[71] Some offensive conduct deserves public disapproval, but at the same time is too trivial for the criminal sanction. For example, such distasteful conduct as spitting in someone's eye can lead to official condemnation if the victim launches a tort suit. It is a costly and time-consuming avenue of redress, but it is available to those who feel outraged by such conduct. Such actions are permitted even though they may yield the winner only nominal damages.

One value at the heart of tort law is the notion of individual responsibility, something that is central to Western civilization. If people act responsibly, they should be rewarded; if they act irresponsibly, they should be punished. There is no need to disguise the fact that this is the underlying morality of the fault system. No one denies that the fault system is riddled with imperfections; it is costly, difficult to administer, denies compensation to many injured people, and is replete with delays. Nevertheless, it is also a mark of nobility when a society directs its members to conduct themselves reasonably in their relations with their fellow citizens, or pay for the consequences. A concomitant of this is that people must also look after themselves, or be denied compensation if they are hurt. There are some exceptions made for children and the mentally disabled, but none for the dull-witted or the awkward. Many people seem to feel that it is "just and fair" to make the "guilty" pay, not the "innocent", and that the "innocent" *should* receive compensation, but not the "guilty".[72] Philosophers call

---

[69] Morris, "Negligence in Tort Law — With Emphasis on Automobile Accidents and Unsound Products" (1967), 53 Va. L. Rev. 899, at p. 905.

[70] Erickson, *The Wayward Puritans* (1966), p. 4; Mead, "The Psychology of Primitive Justice" (1918), 23 Am. J. Soc. 577; see also White, "The Function of Deterrence in Motor Vehicle Accident Compensation Schemes", Osborne Report (1988), p. 436.

[71] Williams, *supra*, n. 67, at p. 148.

[72] *The Report of the Osgoode Hall Study on Compensation for Victims of Automobile Accidents* (1965) indicated that 42% of the injured respondents favoured the fault system, whereas 48% opposed it. One might expect that the attitudes of society generally would be more favourably disposed to fault. See Chapter VIII, Table VIII-1.

this corrective justice.[73] The philosophy of the age of reason, not determinism, still permeates tort law. The fundamental goal is individual restraint and respect for one's fellow creatures, something which is required more than ever in mass urban societies.

Tort law also demonstrates abiding respect for the dignity of the individual. It treats every claimant as unique, special, and different to everyone else in the world. In assessing damages under tort theory, each person is supposed to recover what each *personally* has lost. Not only does the person with a large salary or heavy medical costs receive full compensation, but the non-pecuniary or psychic losses are also recompensed. Pain and suffering is assessed. The music-lover, if deprived of hearing, receives more than one who is not interested in music. The golfer who is incapacitated gets more than a sedentary individual. Tort trials go to great lengths to calculate these individuals' losses. This is certainly one of the reasons why the tort system is so expensive and dilatory. There is also considerable doubt about how accurate this exercise is. Certainly lawyers and judges frequently encounter difficulty deciding what a case is "worth". Judges and juries may differ. Awards may vary from place to place and from time to time. Despite these demerits, however, a system that endeavours to achieve these aims manifests a rare concern for human beings, an attitude that deserves nourishment. In one way, those who argue that everyone should receive compensation for injuries are being more humane, because everyone is to be looked after, but they are also being less humane, because the special qualities and unique losses of each individual are ignored. Only tort law is tailored to deal with each person as an individual entity. This is unquestionably one of its weaknesses, but it is also one of its greatest strengths.

Tort law is, therefore, performing some of the functions of the school and, to an extent, the church. The moral principles upon which tort law is based are constantly being reiterated for the benefit of those who are involved and those who observe. This is a healthy thing, for these principles are useful guidelines for individuals to follow in ordering their relations with their fellow human beings.

D. Psychological Function

Tort law may perform certain psychological functions.[74] For example, the tort action, like the criminal law, may provide some appeasement to those injured by

---

[73]   See Epstein, "Nuisance Law: Corrective Justice and Its Utilitarian Constraints" (1979), 8 J. Leg. Stud. 49; Posner, "The Concept of Corrective Justice in Recent Theories of Tort Law" (1981), 10 J. Leg. Stud. 187; Weinrib, "Toward a Moral Theory of Negligence Law" (1983), 2 J. Law & Phil. 37; Chapman, "Ethical Issues in the Law of Tort" (1982), 2 U.W.O.L. Rev. 1; Bayles and Chapman, *Justice, Rights and Tort Law* (1983); Weinrib, *The Idea of Private Law* (1995).

[74]   Ehrenzweig, "A Psychoanalysis of Negligence" (1953), 47 Nw. U.L. Rev. 855. See, generally, Ehrenzweig, *Psychoanalytic Jurisprudence* (1971).

wrongful conduct.[75] Lord Diplock has contended that no one would suggest using tort law for the purpose of vengeance.[76] Nevertheless, though it is distasteful to most of us, this has always been one of the unexpressed uses of tort law and criminal law. Too many human beings still seem to have need of such an outlet for their desire for revenge. The sad fact is that there is in many of us something primitive which tort law may satisfy.[77]

This questionable service that tort law performs can be put in a more positive and acceptable form. It gives some psychological comfort to the injured. It can be said that tort law helps to keep the peace by providing a legal method of quenching the thirst for revenge. It will be recalled that this was the historical rationale for the creation of tort law.[78] Money damages were paid to the victims of tortious conduct in the hope of curtailing blood feuds. If these legal avenues to revenge were closed today, some victims of wrongful conduct might once again take up clubs and axes to "get even" with their aggressors.[79] It is better to pursue a wrongdoer with a writ than with a rifle.

There is some support for this view in the experience of the Soviet Union.[80] Shortly after the revolution the tort action was abolished, but it soon had to be resurrected. Even Communists, purified as they were supposed to be from economic avarice, apparently obtained some psychological satisfaction from tort suits. It should also be pointed out that liability insurance was not permitted in the U.S.S.R. so that the tort sanction operated directly on the tortfeasors and their pocketbooks.[81] Another clue to the personal revenge element in tort law is our insistence on defendants being sued personally, even though there is insurance against the loss. True, we say that we are playing this cat-and-mouse game to avoid distorting the deliberations of the jury, but in reality we may be doing it to permit victims to obtain a semblance of personal retribution.

Tort law may counteract the feeling of alienation and despair which pervades our society. Governments, corporations, unions, and universities have grown too large and impersonal. A feeling of helplessness and personal insignificance grips too many of our people. Many individuals feel that they have lost control over their lives. No one seems to care about them anymore. A protest march, a sit-in

---

[75] Keeton, "Is There a Place for Negligence in Modern Tort Law?" (1967), 53 Va. L. Rev. 886, at p. 888. See Cory J. in *Hall v. Hebert, supra*, n. 66, at p. 119, C.C.L.T., "appeasing the victim".

[76] See *Cassell & Co. Ltd. v. Broome*, [1972] 2 W.L.R. 645, at p. 721.

[77] Morris, "Liability for Pain and Suffering" (1959), 59 Colum. L. Rev. 476, at p. 478. See also Morris, "Punitive Damages in Tort Cases" (1951), 44 Harv. L. Rev. 1173. This is so, even if some victims express no "desire for retribution against anyone", see Ison, *Accident Compensation* (1980), p. 179.

[78] See generally Malone, "Ruminations on the Role of Fault in the History of the Common Law of Torts" (1970), 31 La. L. Rev. 1; also in Malone, *Essays in Torts* (1986).

[79] See Prosser, Wade and Schwartz, *Cases and Materials on Torts*, 9th ed. (1994), p. 1, prevent parties from taking "the law into their own hands".

[80] Gray, "Soviet Tort Law: The New Principles Annotated", [1964] U.Ill.L.F. 180. See also McLaren, "The Origins of Tortious Liability: Insights from Contemporary Tribal Societies" (1975), 25 U. of T.L.J. 42.

[81] Fleming, "The Role of Negligence in Modern Law" (1967), 53 Va. L. Rev. 815, at p. 824.

or some other dramatic act can change all this. For a time, people *do* seem to care about the protestors. The media takes notice of them. They seem to matter more. They become "relevant". There seems to be a psychological need for personal recognition, which may contribute something to the popularity of this type of activity. A tort suit may likewise provide some psychological satisfaction. Instead of rebelling or demonstrating with a picket sign,[82] an aggrieved individual may begin a law suit. The tort trial is an institution that displays great concern for the individual, especially if there is a jury. The parties have the undivided attention of everyone in the court — judge, jury, counsel, witnesses, spectators and occasionally, the press and the public. The award of damages for pain and suffering clearly manifests "fellow feelings".[83] As much time as is necessary to conclude the case is allocated to it, whether it be a day, a week, a month or a year. Without doubt this is a lavish process, but each accident victim is entitled to demand such an exhaustive hearing.

Of course, a litigant must be able to afford the elaborate psychiatric treatment. It is not provided to everyone as a matter of right. Moreover, there must be some legitimate grievance recognized by tort law, or the action can be snuffed out at an early stage. In addition, the promiscuous use of litigation is discouraged by the offer to settle technique.[84] If someone wants the psychological satisfaction of dragging the defendant into court, even after an admission of liability and an offer to pay, this may be done, but the defendant's subsequent costs must be paid if the trial award is less than was offered in settlement by the defendant. Fortunately, not everyone demands a full-scale trial of his or her case. Most tort suits are settled. Nevertheless, the thought that this *is available*, if needed, should give some comfort to the alienated.

Tort trials enrich our society with ritual and symbolism.[85] The solemnity, the formality, and the language of tort litigation contribute to a sense of mystery. This is something all societies seem to require.[86] As agnosticism supplants religion in the modern world, rituals such as court proceedings are gaining in importance. More and more of us, suffering from "future shock", are searching for bridges with the past, points of stability, to comfort us as the world races by.[87] The traditions of litigation may supply some medicine for this ailment.

Our society will never rid itself of disputes and quarrels.[88] Indeed, it may not be wise to eliminate them even if we could. It is natural to seek a human resolution to these omnipresent human disagreements. Tort law, despite its manifold inadequacies, provides a forum for this symbolic quest for human

---

[82] See Friedman, *The Republic of Choice* (1990), p. 191, if someone has "a sense of entitlement", they do not "feel left out", they have a "stake in society", referring to civil rights.

[83] Morris, *supra*, n. 69, at p. 905.

[84] See Ontario Rules of Civil Procedure, Rule 49.

[85] Edelman, *The Symbolic Uses of Politics* (1964).

[86] Freud, *Totem and Taboo* (1918).

[87] See Toffler, *Future Shock* (1970).

[88] Christie, "A Living Society is a Quarreling Society", in Ziegel (ed.), *Law and Social Change* (1973).

justice. We do not know very much about the psychological reasons for the mystique surrounding the dispensation of human justice according to law. We do know, however, that for most people the process exudes an aura of dignity, humanity and impartiality. There is little danger that it will ever be replaced by computers providing mathematical answers to our problems.[89]

E. Market Deterrence

The law of tort may reduce accidents through market deterrence.[90] This must be distinguished from the type of deterrence discussed above, whereby tort law *directly* attacks the specific occasions of danger. Market or general deterrence functions *indirectly*. It lowers accident costs by making those activities that are accident-prone more expensive by requiring them to bear the full costs of the mishaps they produce. This renders safer substitutes more attractive, because they cost less.

There are certainly more effective ways of reducing accidents. The criminal law and administrative regulation are widely used to cut accidents. We prohibit certain activities altogether if they are too dangerous, even if they could pay their way in the market. For example, we forbid dynamite blasting or the firing of guns in the centre of the city. Further, we regulate the way in which certain activities are conducted. Automobiles, although they are allowed on the highways, may not be driven in excess of the speed limit and drivers must comply with the rules of the road.

There are, however, many types of activities we do not wish to prohibit altogether nor to supervise too closely. Market deterrence can function here as a useful adjunct to criminal and administrative law. We permit these activities to be carried on with only the minimum of control — tort law's general guideline of reasonable care. Thus businesspeople may carry on business as long as they do not negligently injure anyone. If they do hurt someone, they are required to pay the costs incurred by the victim. As the total of damage costs rises, the price of products or activities will increase accordingly. Eventually, businesspeople would have to institute safer practices or be driven out of business as their customers switch to less costly substitutes. This is accomplished automatically

---

[89] Tribe, "Trial by Mathematics: Precision and Ritual in the Legal Process" (1971), 84 Harv. L. Rev. 1329, at pp. 1391 *et seq.*

[90] The argument in this section is a superficial summary of the elaborate and penetrating analysis developed by Professor Calabresi in a series of articles through the 1960s, which culminated in the publication of his book *The Costs of Accidents: A Legal and Economic Analysis* (1970). A fine description and critique of this theory can be found in Atiyah, *Accidents, Compensation and the Law*, 5th ed. (1993). See also Calabresi, "Fault, Accidents and the Wonderful World of Blum and Kalven" (1965), 75 Yale L.J. 216; Blum and Kalven, "The Empty Cabinet of Dr. Calabresi: Auto Accidents and General Deterrence" (1967), 34 U. Chi. L. Rev. 239. See also Posner, *Economic Analysis of Law*, 3rd ed. (1986); Shavel, *Economic Analysis of Accident Law* (1987); Landis and Posner, *Economic Structure of Tort Law* (1987). For a superb judicial application of these economic theories see Justice La Forest's reasons in *Norsk Pacific Steamship Co. Ltd. v. Canadian Nat'l Railway*, [1992] 1 S.C.R. 1021.

through the ordinary forces of the market, without any help from politicians and bureaucrats.

Only a fool would be content with market deterrence as the *only* tool for keeping accidents in check. Nevertheless, as a *subsidiary* technique the idea has some allure because it is founded on respect for individual choice in a free market economy. It permits people to decide whether they will engage in any activity and pay its full costs including the accident expenses, or whether they will engage in safer alternative activities which are less costly.

The foundation of this doctrine is simply economics, the theory that individuals know what is best for themselves. Because of this, we should permit them to make their own decisions about how to spend their money. In other words, the way a society allocates its resources should be a reflection of the individual choices made by all its members. If people want automobiles rather than schools, they should have automobiles rather than schools. As long as the prices of the various goods and services available reflect the full costs of providing them, the buyers will be able to make informed decisions.

If the full costs of accidents are not borne by the activity that produced them, the market process will be distorted. More individuals will choose a particular activity than should do so, because it is subsidized to the extent that it is relieved from any portion of its accident costs. The result would resemble the government paying part of the cost of the steel that goes into automobiles. Such a subsidy reduces the cost of and increases the demand for the product, which generates more accidents. Consequently market deterrence works best when the entire price of all accidents is loaded onto the activities generating it. It operates more effectively under an absolute liability system than it does under a fault-based regime. Nevertheless, it can function to a degree within a negligence system. The theory can also be utilized by government-operated social insurance schemes and even by loss insurance measures.

This market or general deterrence approach reduces accident costs in two ways. Firstly, it creates a financial incentive for people who are engaged in dangerous activities to switch to safer activities. If the participants in a risky activity have to pay for its full cost, some of them may transfer to a safer activity which is cheaper. Whenever someone decides to substitute a less hazardous activity for a more dangerous one, society benefits. Of course, any such decision would take into account not only the cost differential but also the quality of the substitute activity.

An example will illustrate the way this theory works. Let us say that someone is considering the purchase of a new automobile. Assume further that the expense of owning a car is $1,000 per year, which includes $200 for insurance. Without a car, annual transportation costs on bus, taxi and train would be $500. This $500 annual cost differential may help one to decide that it is not worth it to buy the car. This is good, because the fewer cars on the road, the fewer automobile collisions will result. If one were not required to pay the $200 for insurance, as would be the case if the accident costs were borne by some government scheme financed out of general revenue, the smaller cost differential of $300 might make vehicle ownership more attractive, and one might buy the car. Consequently, market deterrence can foster the use of public transportation, which is less accident-prone than private motor-car traffic.

Market deterrence may also curtail the number of accidents in which youthful drivers are involved. It is established that younger drivers are far more accident-prone that older ones. Insurance costs, which reflect this propensity, are therefore higher for young people. Many youths who could afford to buy an old jalopy cannot pay the high insurance premiums exacted from them. Thus there may be fewer teenagers in old jalopies on the highways than there would be if the costs of accidents were paid out of government funds.

The second way in which general deterrence diminishes the expenses of accidents is to encourage people to alter the *way* in which they conduct their activities, rather than changing the *type* of activities altogether. Perhaps another example will be of assistance. Let us assume that a motorist spends an average amount of $200 per year on accident costs. Further, suppose that the motorist were to adopt a different kind of braking system on the car, the accident expenses would total only $100. The safer brakes are available at a cost of $50. The motorist might well decide to spend the $50 for the new brakes, cut the accident costs to $100, and thereby save $50 annually in accident costs. If the $200 accident costs were paid by the state, there would be no cost incentive to switch to the new brakes.

The market deterrence theory has not yet been empirically tested. We do not know how efficiently it operates, or indeed if it functions at all. It may work only with some activities, but not with others. Its effectiveness will partially depend upon the elasticity of the demand for the product or activity. It will also hinge on the proportion of the price made up by accident costs. In many activities the proportion of accident costs compared with labour and material costs will be so infinitesimal that the additional burden placed upon the activity by tort liability tends to keep these costs down. Market or general deterrence would tend to have more bite if *all* the costs of accidents — fault-caused as well as non-fault-caused — were included in the price of the activity. Even if this were the case there might not be sufficient price incentive to foster changes in the way activities are conducted. In any event, little harm is done by shifting the loss to the enterprise, because this course can also be supported on the ground that it is "just and fair" that accident costs be borne by those who engage in certain activities.[91] It can also be justified by the theory of loss-distribution.

Another serious shortcoming of the market deterrence approach is that it discriminates heavily against the poor. By placing the full costs of accidents on the activities which generate them, we are permitting the rich to engage in dangerous activities which the poor cannot afford. In short, this "works like a

---

[91] Keeton, "Is There a Place for Negligence in Modern Tort Law?" (1967), 53 Va. L. Rev. 886, at p. 891. See also Weiler, "Defamation, Enterprise Liability and Freedom of Speech" (1967), 17 U. of T.L.J. 278, at p. 282.

regressive tax".[92] This argument would have more force if market deterrence were used exclusively to curtail accidents. The fact is, however, that most really dangerous activities are prohibited for rich and poor alike by the criminal law. Furthermore, it is only in the marginally risky situations that market deterrence operates. It must be admitted that if the market is going to be used at all, it must *necessarily* discriminate against the less affluent members of our society. This is what the market system is all about. But this should not discourage us unduly. The overwhelming majority of Canadians earn salaries which are relatively similar. There are only a few lucky ones at the top and a few unlucky ones at the bottom. For most people each expenditure involves a question of their priorities and how they wish to spend their limited resources.

In conclusion, tort law would probably never survive if market deterrence were its *only* aim. However, market deterrence may be achieved *in addition* to the other objectives of tort law, as a kind of bonus. In this context it is merely another factor to consider in deciding whether tort law deserves continued life.

F. Ombudsman

Tort law is an ombudsman. It can be used to apply pressure upon those who wield political, economic or intellectual power; in short, it empowers the injured.[93] This is rarely the expressed aim of a tort suit, but it can be an important side-effect.

The burgeoning regulatory activities of modern government have been much discussed in recent years. Some people complain about excessive governmental intrusion into their affairs. Others advocate the complete regulation of nearly every aspect of our daily lives. By and large we have adopted a middle course; we regulate only certain activities and to varying degrees. Some government agencies are zealous in the enforcement of their mandates, whereas others are rather somnolent. The history of some agencies has revealed that instead of diligently pursuing their legislative mandate, administrators often try to win the approval and support of those they must regulate.[94] To some extent this may be

---

[92] Morris, *supra*, n. 69, at p. 903.

[93] Linden, "Empowering the Injured" in *Torts Tomorrow* (1998); Shapo, "Changing Frontiers in Torts: Vistas for the 70's" (1970), 22 Stan. L. Rev. 330, at pp. 333 *et seq.*; Page, "Of Mace and Men: Tort Law as a Means of Controlling Domestic Chemical Warfare" (1969), 57 Geo. L.J. 1238; Linden, "Tort Law as Ombudsman" (1973), 52 Can. Bar Rev. 155; Linden, "Reconsidering Tort Law as Ombudsman" in Steel and Rodgers-Magnet, *Issues in Tort Law* (1983); Linden, "Public Law and Private Law: The Frontier from the Perspective of a Tort Lawyer" (1976), 17 Cahiers de Droit 831; Williams and Hepple, *Foundations of the Law of Tort*, 2nd ed. (1984); Gellhorn, *Ombudsmen and Others* (1966); Wade, "Tort Law as Ombudsman" (1986), 65 Oregon L. Rev. 309; *contra*, Fridman, *Introduction to the Law of Torts* (1978), it is a "monstrous idea" to allow tort law to act as a "legitimized busybody" or as a "new-fangled inquisitor" but permissible to let it act as a method of keeping officials from "straying away from the path of valid righteous conduct".

[94] See generally Leiserson, *Administrative Regulation: A Study in Representation of Interests* (1942), p. 14; Truman, *The Governmental Process* (1951), Chapter 5; Redford, *Administration of*

necessary, since conflict and antagonism should be held to a minimum. But without some conflict and antagonism, the job cannot be done effectively. Too often personnel are exchanged between a regulated industry and the board supposed to supervise it. In such circumstances the public interest may be sacrificed.

Tort law can be of service here. Individuals victimized by conduct violating legislative provisions may initiate civil proceedings. The civil courts will utilize the statutory directives in evaluating the offending conduct.[95] The illegal activity may be penalized by civil sanctions, even where the administrative or criminal ones are not applied. The legislative policy can be advanced by tort law even where those responsible for promoting the policy fail to do so. The damages sought in such a case may not be of primary concern to the plaintiff; the main goal may be to stimulate administrative action.

Through the actions of false imprisonment, assault, battery, and negligence, tort law spurs police forces to act more responsibly in their dealings with citizens.[96] The law reports contain several cases in which undue police interference with liberty has yielded a tort judgment. *Christie v. Leachinsky*,[97] for example, is a classic case in which civil liberties were granted judicial precedence over the convenience of the police. The plaintiff, arrested on a contrived charge so that he could be kept in custody, was awarded damages for false imprisonment. Lord Simonds asserted that a man is "entitled to know why he is deprived of his freedom". He proclaimed, "Blind, unquestioning obedience is the law of tyrants and of slaves. It does not yet flourish on English soil."[98] Further, he added, "The liberty of the subject and the convenience of the police or any other executive authority are not to be weighed in the scales against each other . . . a man is not to be deprived of his liberty except in the due course and process of law."[99]

Another landmark case is *Koechlin v. Waugh*,[100] where two teenagers were stopped by the police, who thought they looked suspicious because they were "sauntering along the street", one wearing rubber-soled shoes and a windbreaker. One of the teenagers refused to answer some questions, a scuffle ensued and the boys were arrested. Their tort action against the police was successful. Although the court indicated that it would have been wiser for the boys to have co-operated with the police, it held that they had a right to know what they were suspected of or charged with. The police acted on insufficient evidence. Since

---

National Economic Control (1952), p. 385; Bernstein, *Regulating Business by Independent Commissions* (1955), Chapter 3; Edelman, *The Symbolic Uses of Politics* (1964), p. 24.

[95] See *infra*, Chapter 7.

[96] See Weiler, "The Control of Police Arrest Practices: Reflections of a Tort Lawyer" in A.M. Linden (ed.), *Studies in Canadian Tort Law* (Toronto: Butterworths, 1968), at p. 416. Even police commissions have been challenged for inadequate training of police officers, see *Johnston v. Adamson* (1982), 34 O.R. (2d) 236 (C.A.); leave to appeal to S.C.C. refused 35 O.R. (2d) 64n.

[97] [1947] A.C. 573.

[98] *Ibid.*, at p. 591.

[99] *Ibid.*, at p. 595.

[100] [1957] O.W.N. 245.

no one must "submit to restraint on his freedom unless he [knows] the reason why that restraint should be imposed",[101] the boys had the right, in the circumstances, to resist the officers. Police officers are similarly limited by the law of negligence in the way they may conduct a chase or use their firearms. An officer cannot shoot at a petty thief when the thief is running away,[102] whereas the officer may shoot to kill a violent bank robber. In *Priestman v. Colangelo and Smythson*,[103] a tragic accident occurred because of the use of a gun by a police officer during an automobile chase. Although the tort suit against the officers was ultimately dismissed, the incident was followed by the promulgation of a set of new and stricter rules for gun use by the police.[104] The tort suit, even though it was unsuccessful, may have contributed to closer supervision of the employment of firearms during law enforcement.

Perhaps the most spectacular success of tort law as a weapon of social reform has been in the products liability area. The captains of industry have at last been made accountable to ordinary people.[105] Irate consumers have deployed the tort action in their battle against the manufacturers of shoddy goods. The producers of thalidomide have been required to pay millions of dollars in damages to the children deformed by that drug. The manufacturers of automobiles have had to pay a fortune to motorists injured by their substandard products. Even the design of motor vehicles has come under judicial attack. One court has criticized automakers for making papier-mâché cars.[106] It has been held that liability could be imposed for a roof that collapsed,[107] a gas tank rupture that caused a fire,[108] and for a steering assembly that was not crashworthy.[109] In *Phillips v. Ford Motor Co.*,[110] Mr. Justice Haines decided that the fail-safe system of a set of power brakes in a Lincoln Continental was inadequate. On the other hand, the manufacturers of a car which crashed into someone at 115 m.p.h. were relieved of responsibility although a dissenting judge felt that this reckless and abnormal use of the car was foreseeable.[111] Now cigarette-makers[112] and providers of tainted blood[113] are being forced to pay for the medical costs they cause.

This capacity of tort law to challenge industrial decision-making opens up exciting possibilities for consumer democracy. Although Professor Fleming has

---

[101] *Ibid.*, at p. 247.

[102] *Beim v. Goyer*, [1965] S.C.R. 638, accidental shooting of escaping car thief. See *infra*, Chapter 5.

[103] [1959] S.C.R. 615. See generally B. McDonald, "Use of Force by Police to Effect Lawful Arrest" (1966-67), 9 Crim. L.Q. 435.

[104] See Weiler, *supra*, n. 96.

[105] See *infra*, Chapter 16.

[106] *Badorek v. Rodgers*, C.C.H. Prod. Liab. Rep. §5899 (Cal. Supr. Ct.) referred to in Shapo, *supra*, n. 93, at p. 333.

[107] *Dyson v. General* Motors (1969), 298 F. Supp. 1064 (Pa.).

[108] *Grundmanis v. British Motors* (1970), 308 F. Supp. 303 (Wisc.).

[109] *Larsen v. General Motors* (1968), 391 F. 2d 495 (U.S.C.A. 8th Cir.).

[110] [1970] 2 O.R. 714; revd on procedural grounds by [1971] 2 O.R. 637.

[111] *Schemel v. General Motors* (1967), 384, F. 2d 802.

[112] Cupp, (1998) 46 U. Kan. L. Rev. 465.

[113] *Walker Estate v. York-Finch General Hospital* (2001), 198 D.L.R. (4th) 193 (S.C.C).

questioned the capacity of negligence trials to second-guess experts,[114] this watch-dog function, especially if performed by a jury, is vital in a world increasingly run by distant bureaucrats. Damage suits can be effectively deployed in technology assessment, in that they can provide a "special therapeutic kind of deterrence aimed at stimulating positive constructive alternatives".[115] The courts can examine not only whether the producers utilized *known* technology properly, but whether they were sufficiently resourceful in their research to discover *new* technology.[116] As the bar grows bolder and more socially conscious, and as class actions make them potentially more profitable, we can expect more of these tort suits in the area of technology assessment.[117] It is a tool of immense potential in the movement for a more humane society.

The struggle for the environment provides new opportunities for tort law. Professor Joseph Sax contends that tort litigation provides an "additional source of leverage in making environmental decision-making operate rationally, thoughtfully, and with a sense of responsiveness to the entire range of citizen concerns".[118] Although he agrees that courts alone cannot do an adequate job, he says they can help to "open the doors to a far more limber governmental process", since the "more leverage citizens have, the more responsive and responsible their officials and fellow citizens will be".[119]

The virtues of tort action in this area are many.[120] Firstly, the judiciary is independent and not amenable to political pressure. Secondly, the tort route permits ordinary citizens to take the initiative instead of making them wait for civil servants to make up their minds to move. Thirdly, the judicial process reduces these controversies to specific cases; it eliminates reliance upon vague generalities such as potential loss of jobs and tax revenue and the danger of world competition. Of course judicial intervention does not remove the need for other more systematic considerations of environmental issues. It merely encourages the extra effort by administrators to take into account citizen concerns. Tort law, therefore, serves as a catalyst, not as a usurper, of the legislative process.

The various professional groups in society are not immune to attack by negligence action.[121] A medical malpractice action has repercussions not only for the

---

[114] See "The Role of Negligence in Modern Tort Law" (1967), 53 Va. L. Rev. 815, at p. 821.

[115] Katz, "The Function of Tort Liability in Technology Assessment" (1960), 38 U. Cinc. L. Rev. 582, at p. 607.

[116] *Ibid.*, at p. 655.

[117] *Ibid.*, at p. 640. See *contra*, Henderson, "Expanding the Negligence Concept: Retreat from the Rule of Law" (1976), 51 Ind. L.J. 467, labelling the proponents of this theory "irresponsible".

[118] *Defending the Environment: A Strategy for Citizen Action* (1971). See review by Jaffe (1971), 84 Harv. L. Rev. 1562. See also Estrin and Swaigen, *Environment on Trial* (1974), p. 236.

[119] *Ibid.*

[120] *Ibid.*, at pp. 108 *et seq.*

[121] See Chapter 5, *infra*. Even a law society can be challenged for inadequate supervision, see *Calvert v. L.S.U.C.* (1981), 32 O.R. (2d) 176 (H.C.); *Edwards v. Law Society of Upper Canada* (2000), 1 C.C.L.T. (3d) 193 (Ont. C.A.), no duty owed; affd [2001] S.C.J. No. 77 (S.C.C.).

doctor involved but also for the entire medical profession whose procedures can be challenged thereby. Medical decisions in treatment and in experimentation are increasingly under judicial eyes for approbation or condemnation. Although this may strike terror into the hearts of some doctors, a healthy and vibrant profession must constantly justify its stewardship. So too the conduct of lawyers, architects, accountants and other skilled groups may be subject to examination in courts at the behest of any unsatisfied customer who has suffered loss at their hands.

1. PUBLICITY

Tort law provides a wronged individual with a weapon to direct unfavourable publicity against a tortfeasor.[122] Because of the communications revolution this publicity sanction can be a powerful force for social reform. Of course it can also be abused. Modern governments have at their disposal various methods of exposing activities they wish to condemn or praise. Public hearings about subversive activities may provide powerful sanctions even in the absence of criminal prosecution. Official statements, invitations to individuals to "discuss" matters, or intimations that government action is "being considered" may attract headlines. Radical groups also have become experts in the manipulation of the media to publicize their various causes; in the same way a tort suit can attract enormous publicity for the causes of the ordinary citizen.

The media have focussed considerable attention on civil suits against auto manufacturers, drug producers, polluters, and over-enthusiastic police officers. Consequently, by commencing a tort action a claimant may be able to cast a spotlight upon the defendant. This may act as a deterrent to the defendant and to other potential transgressors in three ways. Adverse publicity can cost the defendant money. A tort claim over an exploding Coca-Cola bottle may be broadcast to millions of potential customers, some of whom may switch to Pepsi-Cola. Profits may sink. Even if the impact of this unfavourable publicity is only temporary, considerable financial loss may be incurred. Similarly, following an air crash, passenger claims and the attention given to them, may spur other passengers to travel on different carriers. Moreover, the value of a corporation's shares may be reduced by adverse publicity arising from civil law suits. When a number of tort actions were launched in the early 1960s against the Richardson-Merrell Company, the North American producers of thalidomide and Mer/29, their stock, which had been selling at 25-35 times the earnings, plunged to 15-20 times the earnings.[123] This was a massive paper loss to the stock-holders, one that was not justified by the actual threat to the company's financial health.

---

[122] Rourke, "Law Enforcement Through Publicity" (1957), 24 U. Chi. L. Rev. 225; Fisse, "The Use of Publicity as a Criminal Sanction Against Business Corporations" (1971), 8 Melb. U.L. Rev. 107.

[123] See Wright, Linden and Klar, *Canadian Tort Law: Cases, Notes and Materials*, 9th ed. (Markham: Butterworths, 1990), Chapter 16, pp. 16-57 (not in later editions).

Secondly, the defendant can suffer a loss of prestige. Although this too may result in monetary loss, it is important for its own sake. Everyone, even corporate managers and bureaucrats, is anxious to be held in public esteem. Businesses spend millions on public relations campaigns to polish their corporate images. This may be ruined by civil suits that tarnish their reputation for quality goods and services.

Thirdly, negative publicity may induce government intervention. Public officials may become apprised of dangerous or improper activities. Criminal prosecutions or administrative sanctions may follow. Where legislative jurisdiction for administrative action is lacking, public opinion may be aroused to such an extent that the politicians respond with new legislation to control the perceived abuse.

The power of the publicity sanction is difficult to measure, since it depends upon the reactions of individuals to information. This is both its weakness and its strength.[124] It is a weakness because there is no way to ensure that a law suit will receive any media attention at all. Most ordinary actions do not. Moreover, the public may not think the conduct complained of is reprehensible, or the defendant may be largely impervious to bad publicity by virtue of being a monopoly or a government agency. Lastly, the defendant may take steps to neutralize the negative effect of the publicity by launching an expensive counter-publicity campaign.[125] On the other hand, the indefinite nature of the publicity sanction may render it *more* powerful than a civil suit or a criminal prosecution, because damage awards and fines are relatively easy to forecast, whereas the result of bad publicity is impossible to prophesy. A civil trial may drag on for months under the glare of publicity. The public may become incensed; the firm may be driven to insolvency; the government may react decisively. If a class action has been launched, the publicity pressure is amplified. It is this very unpredictability of the publicity sanction that makes tort litigation so fearsome to corporate managers.[126]

Another advantage of the publicity sanction is that it is both triggered and imposed by ordinary citizens. Any individual who is injured by another's wrongful conduct may institute civil proceedings. One does not have to wait until a prosecutor or civil servant decides to act. Public servants are reluctant to move. Their resources may be limited. Politics may enter into the picture. An aggrieved person labours under no such burdens; aided by a lawyer, anyone may commence proceedings at any time, even if the case is by no means ironclad. Of course, there is the hazard of unfair legal attacks upon innocent defendants. To an extent this is controlled by awarding costs against those who lose law suits, by motions to strike out claims if they are frivolous or vexatious, and similar

---

[124] See Rourke, *supra*, n. 122, at p. 238.

[125] As the General Motors Corporation did, following the much-publicized U.S. Senate hearings on automobile safety. For counter-publicity purposes, they coined the slogan "Mark of Excellence".

[126] See Plant, "Strict Liability of Manufacturers for Injuries Caused by Defects in Products — An Opposing View" (1957), 24 Tenn. L. Rev. 938.

measures. The danger is not removed, but it is contained. The publicity sanction is also administered by ordinary people, whose personal reactions to the stimuli of the media do the damage. Government officials and judges who normally impose sanctions are involved here only indirectly.

2. INSTITUTIONAL LIMITATIONS

There are institutional limitations on the effectiveness of tort law as a tool for social reform. Firstly, the substantive law may be incapable of producing an acceptable decision. For example, present negligence law may dictate a dismissal of a defective product claim, nuisance law may be unavailable against certain polluters, and an erroneous police arrest may be held to have been reasonable in the circumstances. Our judges are understandably reluctant to reformulate the law. As a consequence, the content of the law may lag behind the popular will. Paradoxically, a harsh decision in a well-publicized tort case may stimulate legislative reform, whereas a decision that corresponds with our sense of justice may lull us into a false sense of security. Progressive scholars who assert that negligence liability has become strict because of *res ipsa loquitur* and other such devices may be impeding rather than accelerating the movement towards tougher controls on government and business. Legislators may think all is well, when it is not. Thus a plaintiff who loses a tort case after a trial in the glare of the media may be more help to future victims than one who wins. A judge who says no may do more good than one who says yes.

A second fetter on the effective use of tort law as an ombudsman stems from the economics of litigation. Lawyers usually work for fees, not for principles; litigants usually sue for money, not for ideals. Investigation of accidents is expensive. Expert witnesses must be paid for their work. In short, tort trials cost money. Lots of it. Unless there is a good chance of winning, litigants are unwise to sue, for losers must pay not only their own legal costs but also those of the winning parties. The allure of a quick settlement dulls the crusading ardour of many a claimant. Because of this, law suits that test the frontiers of tort law are difficult to finance. Only the rare case, the rare litigant and the rare lawyer become involved in such litigation.

These economic restraints may be overcome in various ways. The contingent fee,[127] for example, which is available as an alternative method of financing litigation in several provinces and in the United States, may ease the financial burden of potential claimants. Under a contingent fee system, plaintiffs can get lawyers to represent them without risking anything. If the case is won, the award is shared with the lawyer. If it is lost, the lawyer goes without a fee. The existence of this system may have been a factor in the rapid growth of tort law in the United States.[128] The availability of class actions has made some of these cases

---

[127] Williston, "The Contingent Fee in Canada" (1968), 6 Alta. L. Rev. 184; Arlidge, "Contingent Fees" (1974), 6 Ottawa L.J. 374.

[128] See R. Keeton, *Venturing to Do Justice: Reforming Private Law* (1969), for a description of some of these changes.

more attractive to litigants. Claimants in these cases may also be assisted by legal aid, consumer advocates, neighbourhood law offices and other such services. There is a reservoir of trained legal talent which is ready to undertake this ombudsman role as it is rendered more economically feasible.

The third restraint on bold intrusions into the conduct of government, business, and the professions stems from the nature of the judicial process itself. Judges cannot decide cases the way they, personally, would prefer. *Stare decisis* forbids this. The only paths upon which judges may travel are well-worn ruts. They cannot take wing on flights of fancy. That is not the judicial way. There is also some question about the capacity of judges to make expert decisions for which they may be ill-equipped. A *fortiori* this would apply to civil jury cases. But somehow the idea of review of expert decisions by lay people, if it is wisely exercised, is most appealing. One might well argue that the role of the jury in these cases should be enlarged rather than contracted if we really want to have decision-makers accountable to the people. The adversary system may not be the ideal way of determining some of these questions. One problem with it is the lack of any official public representation in these disputes. Another difficulty stemming from this is that all the information available may not be adduced in court. The rules of evidence may place blinkers on the court and prevent certain facts from being considered. Despite the problems, however, judicial review of these decisions is a worthwhile activity. There is no usurpation of the legislative role by the courts. Their contribution is largely restricted to increments and to filling in gaps. The legislatures are, after all, the final arbiters who can undo anything the courts have wrought.

If we wish to render this ombudsman function of tort law more potent, we could enact strict liability in products cases, we could statutorily shift the onus of proof to the defendants, we could allow contingent fees, we could allow more class actions, we could limit the number of tort trials, we could allow for more third party interventions, we could improve the quality of media coverage and other similar measures.[129] The judiciary will nevertheless remain central to the continued vitality of tort law.

Thus, tort law may be used as an ombudsman, as an empowerer of the injured and as an instrument of social reform. In the absence of a legislative or administrative response, it can exert some influence. No one would ever dream of replacing legislative control with the sporadic thrusts of tort law. But it would also be risky to abandon the tort action completely, because it may be the only recourse available to an aggrieved person, other than a protest march or an act of violence.

---

[129] See Linden, "Reconsidering Tort Law as Ombudsman", *supra*, n. 93, at p. 16; see also White, *Tort Law in America* (1980).

G. The Future of Tort Law

These are some of the functions of modern tort law which any cost-benefit analysis of the system will have to consider. The compensation aim of tort law is still significant, even though its importance is waning, because it recompenses in full the losses of victims, including general damages. The deterrence element may still be helpful, though its therapeutic power has been eroded, because individual defendants remain responsible, in theory at least, for their conduct. Market deterrence may influence accident cost, although we cannot be sure of this until it has been empirically tested. These matters can and should be measured over the next few years.

The other functions of tort law are more difficult to analyze because they cannot be quantified. They lie more in the ephemeral realm of values. They are directed at the tone and the quality of life. It is hard to tell whether the educational function of tort law has any impact on our citizenry. We do not know whether the moral beacon which emanates from tort principles enlightens anyone. We cannot know whether the psychological impact of tort law draws people closer together or whether it alienates them further from their society. The use of tort law as an ombudsman and as a weapon of social reform may turn out to be its most promising function in the decades ahead. It may well become its primary *raison d'être* in the future.

We must keep in mind the fact that tort law, like all law, changes to meet altering conditions. Legal rules which are established with one goal in mind may change their character and begin to service other needs. Oliver Wendell Holmes has described the process as follows:

> The customs, beliefs or needs of a primitive time establish a rule or a formula. In the course of centuries the custom, belief or necessity disappears but the rule remains. The reason that gave rise to the rule has been forgotten and ingenious minds set themselves to inquire how it is to be accounted for. Some ground of policy is thought of, which seems to explain it and to reconcile it with the present state of things; and then the rule adapts itself to the new reasons which have been found for it, and enters on a new career. The old form receives a new content, and in time even the form modifies itself to fit the meaning which it has received.[130]

Tort law has undergone such metamorphoses in its time. It began its career primarily as a deterrent. Its role was gradually transformed to that of a compensator predominantly. As the task of reparation becomes increasingly superfluous in the modern welfare state, it may well be that the ombudsman function may dominate the future evolution of tort law. It is clear, however, that its role will require redefinition if it is not to end up on the ash-heap.

Tort law is certainly not indispensable to our society. Very few things are. It does, nevertheless, serve a mixture of worthy objectives. None of them are met completely, and each could be advanced more effectively by other instruments. The trouble is that we have not yet invented such mechanisms. Nor is there any guarantee that they would be introduced if discovered. We do, however, possess

---

[130] *The Common Law* (1881), p. 5.

tort law which is aimed at "maximizing service and minimizing disservice to multiple objectives".[131] This description may not stir excitement in our hearts, but it should make us pause before we conclude that tort law is "doomed to irrelevance".[132]

It should also concern us when a leading scholar like Professor Klar, a self-proclaimed "tort law enthusiast", opines "ironically" that "the success of tort threatens its survival in the 21st Century".[133] If tort has been successful over the years, this should not be a reason for its demise. On the contrary, it should be a reason to preserve it, and even strengthen it, while at the same time seeking to improve it when it is in need of reform as has been done in the area of auto accident compensation.

For the present, at least, tort law is "far from dead or moribund".[134] One day we may fashion alternative institutions more responsive to all of our needs. Hopefully, it will not be too long before our social welfare programmes are integrated and rationalized, but this would not necessitate discarding tort law. We may choose to let it live in peaceful coexistence with social insurance. By opting for such a solution, tort law could continue to serve society, alongside whatever new techniques are devised. Individuals should not be prevented from suing cigarette-makers, movie and music producers, professionals, educators,[135] alcohol and gun manufacturers and drug distributors when they have been damaged by them in the hope of obtaining compensation and of altering their careless conduct, if that can be proven.

Eventually, tort law may become very much like a Gothic cathedral — a rather elaborate structure, but one that continues both to function and to uplift the human spirit. We certainly would not want, nor could we afford, a society where everyone had to pray in a cathedral. Similarly, it would be unthinkable for tort law to be the *only* source of compensation, deterrence, moral guidance, and psychological satisfaction. But this does not mean that tort law cannot remain as *one* such mechanism. No society enriches itself by destroying its architectural, intellectual, and artistic achievements; such needless waste impoverishes our existence, without adding anything to the quality of our lives.

---

[131] R. Keeton, "Is There a Place for Negligence in Modern Tort Law?" (1967), 53 Va. L. Rev. 886, at p. 897.

[132] Fleming, "The Role of Negligence in Modern Tort Law" (1967), 53 Va. L. Rev. 815, at p. 815; Fleming, "Is There A Future For Torts?" (1984), 58 Aust. L. J. 131, also at 44 La. L. Rev. 1193.

[133] "The Role of Fault and Policy in Negligence Law" (1996), 35 Alta. L. Rev. 24, at p. 29.

[134] James, "The Future of Negligence in Accident Law" (1967), 53 Va. L. Rev. 911, at p. 912. The Supreme Court of Canada has revitalized Canadian tort law, see A. Linden and W. Linden, "The Supreme Court of Canada and Canadian Tort Law" in Beaudoin, *The Supreme Court of Canada* (1986); Alexander, "Bora Laskin and The Law of Torts" (1985), 35 U. of T.L.J. 591; Irvine, "Chief Justice Dickson and the Evolving Law of Torts" (1991), 20 Man. L.J. 330, part of "The Dickson Legacy" issue. For the United States situation, see Schwartz, "The Beginning and The Possible End of The Rise of Modern American Tort Law" (1992), 26 Georgia L. Rev. 601.

[135] *Phelps v. Hillingdon London Borough Council,* [2000] 4 All E.R. 504 (H.L.), liability for educational negligence.

Finally, tort law can constantly underscore our dedication to individual autonomy, individual dignity, individual responsibility and individual worth. It can also remind us that there are more important values than dry efficiency and icy rationality.

Before reaching any conclusion about the destiny of tort law, we shall have to ponder the present quality of life in Canada, what it has been, and what we want it to become.

Chapter 2

Intentional Interference with the Person

The first basis of tort liability is the intentional infliction of harm. Where one person deliberately causes damage to another, tort law generally requires that person to make good the loss so inflicted.

In rendering civilly responsible all intentional wrong-doers, tort law seeks to advance its various aims. Individuals whose interests are deliberately interfered with must be compensated for their losses. Those who inflict losses on purpose must be made to pay for them to deter repetition both by the wrongdoers themselves and by others in the community. This serves to educate society about acceptable and unacceptable conduct. It also offers psychological gratification to victims and to people in general.

These costs must be borne by the activities that produce them, causing them to be more expensive and thus, perhaps, reducing reliance upon them. Lastly, holding intentional wrong-doers liable focusses attention on their acts and enables citizens and government officials to react to them, if they choose to do so.

To date, several nominate torts have evolved, which have been used for these purposes, but liability for intentional conduct has not been limited to these alone. Occasionally tort law, responding to the needs of the times, has furnished new theories of liability for intentional conduct. There is every reason to believe that it will react similarly in the future where convincing arguments are advanced for the creation of a new tort.

The bulk of this chapter examines the nominate torts available for the intentional interference with the person. Before that, however, the concept of intention is briefly explained.

A. Intention

Conduct is intentional if the actor desires to produce the consequences that follow from an act.[1] Thus, if one person swings a fist at another's nose, hoping

---

[1]   Glanville Williams, *Criminal Law*, 2nd ed. (1961), §§16, 18, 19; *Restatement, Torts, Second,*

to strike it, and succeeds in connecting with it, the result has been intended. On the other hand, if someone shoots at a tree, but accidentally hits a person, there is no intention to hit the person even though there was an intention to hit the tree. No responsibility will be borne for the intentional infliction of harm to the person, even though liability may follow on another theory. Intention, therefore, is a concept which connects conduct with its results.

Certain results of conduct may be intended, whereas others are not. A motorist who drives a vehicle at 60 miles per hour in a 50-mile-per-hour zone may be violating the law intentionally, but if the car collides with something the motorist will not be considered to have intended that consequence unless actually wishing to achieve it. The motorist may be liable for the loss in negligence, but that is another story altogether. Similarly, one may drive one's car intending to get to work, but if a collision results during the course of the trip, it is not a legally relevant intention in deciding the liability issues. The significant matter is whether an injury complained of has been intended by the actor, not whether some other intention unrelated to the loss was in the actor's mind.

1. CONSTRUCTIVE INTENTION

Conduct may be treated as intentional even though its results are not actually desired, if the consequences are known to be substantially certain to follow.[2] In *Garratt v. Dailey*,[3] for example, the defendant pulled a chair out from under the plaintiff as she was about to sit down on it. It was held that the injuries suffered by the plaintiff could be considered intentional if the defendant knew with substantial certainty that she would attempt to sit where the chair had been. Consequently, the terrorist who throws a bomb at the King, who is riding in a carriage beside the Queen, is treated as though the intent was to injure the Queen as well, even if the terrorist was fervently praying all the while that the bomb would hurt only the King and not the Queen. In these circumstances it is sometimes said that the intention is "constructive", or that it has been "imputed" to the defendant. In other words, the conduct is treated as though it were intentional, while strictly it is not, because the law will not tolerate anyone being dealt with less leniently on such facts. This is not unlike the criminal law principle which holds that individuals are deemed to intend the natural and probable consequences of their acts.[4]

2. TRANSFERRED INTENT

Another situation where courts impute intention is the fiction called "transferred intent". If A strikes at B who ducks, and A hits C instead, this result is treated as

---

§8A. See generally Atrens, "Intentional Interference with the Person" in Linden (ed.), *Studies in Canadian Tort Law* (1968).

[2] *Restatement, Second*, §8A.

[3] (1955), 46 Wash. 2d 197, 279 P. 2d 1091.

[4] Atrens, *supra*, n. 1, at p. 381; *D.P.P. v. Smith*, [1961] A.C. 290, altered by Criminal Justice Act, 1967, s. 8; *cf.*, *Parker v. R.* (1963), 111 C.L.R. 610 (H.C. Aus.); revd [1964] A.C. 1369 (P.C.).

though it were intended by A.[5] What is important to the court is not the identity of the plaintiff, but the fact that the defendant desired to strike another person unlawfully. Such a malefactor, even if someone is hit unintentionally, can be no better off than if the chosen target was hit successfully. In law the malefactor is equally blameworthy and either injured victim is entitled to compensation. This resembles the notion of "transferred malice" in criminal law, which also penalizes an accused who punches at one person, hits some glass which shatters and injures a second person.[6]

Not only can intention be transferred from one person to another, it can also be shifted from one intentional tort to another. For example, if one person intends to batter another, but misses and merely frightens the victim, there is sufficient intention present to constitute an assault, even though a battery and not an assault was desired.[7] Similarly, if one person shot at another, intending only to frighten the other person, the shooter could be held liable for battery if the bullet struck the victim, or even if it hit a stranger.[8] Prosser has contended that intent will be transferred from any one of the five intentional torts which descended from the old trespass action (battery, assault, false imprisonment, trespass to land and trespass to chattels) to any one of the others.[9] In the criminal law also, wrongful intent is often transferred from one person to another[10] and from one type of crime to another.[11] It may be that the Canadian courts would not wish to transfer intent indiscriminately from any of these torts (and crimes) to all of the others, regardless of their comparative severity. Perhaps they should be reluctant to transfer intent from a minor wrong to a more serious one, for the wrongful intent may be trivial in comparison with the result achieved. The courts could always fall back and consider the loss from the perspective of negligence liability, which might be a more balanced approach in some situations.

3. INTENTION, VOLITION AND MOTIVE

Intention should be distinguished from volition, even though courts sometimes use the terms "intentional" and "voluntary" interchangeably.[12] The courts do not have to consider whether conduct is intentional unless there has been a voluntary act committed by the defendant. There can be no intentional conduct without

---

[5] Prosser, "Transferred Intent" (1967), 45 Tex. L. Rev. 650; *Carnes v. Thompson* (1932), 48 S.W. 2d 903; *Bunyan v. Jordan* (1937), 57 C.L.R. 1 (H.C. Aus.).

[6] *R. v. Deakin* (1974), 16 C.C.C. (2d) 2 (Man. C.A.) (*per* Matas J.A.); *R. v. Saunders and Archer* (1576), 2 Plowd. 473, 75 E.R. 706.

[7] *I de S. & Wife v. W. de S.* (1348), Year Book, 22 Liber Assisarum, folio 99, p. 60.

[8] *Randall v. Ridgley* (1939), 185 So. 632; *Weistart v. Flohr* (1968), 67 Cal. Reptr. 114.

[9] *Prosser and Keeton on the Law of Torts*, 5th ed. (1984), p. 37.

[10] *R. v. Chapin* (1909), 22 Cox. C.C. 10; see s. 212(b) Criminal Code.

[11] *R. v. Kundeus* (1975), 32 C.R.N.S. 129; *R. v. Ortt*, [1969] 1 O.R. 461 (C.A.); *R. v. Crawford* (1970), 1 C.C.C. (2d) 515 (B.C.C.A.).

[12] For example, *Morriss v. Marsden*, [1952] 1 All E.R. 925; *Tillander v. Gosselin*, [1967] 1 O.R. 203.

volition, although there can certainly be voluntary conduct which is not intentional. The onus is on a defendant to establish absence of volition.[13]

Tort liability will never be imposed if the conduct complained of is involuntary. In other words, a voluntary act is a prerequisite of any tort responsibility. One might say that there is no act at all, in tort law as well as in criminal law, without a conscious contraction of the muscles which brings about the bodily movement.[14] The defendant's mind must prompt or direct bodily movements before any tort liability will be imposed.[15] Thus, if the defendant's muscles contract while asleep,[16] or unconscious because of a sudden illness,[17] there can be no tort liability because the defendant has not acted voluntarily. When a person intrudes upon another's land while sleepwalking,[18] or is carried onto another's property,[19] no trespass is committed. In the latter case, the trespass is that of those who carried the defendant, as it was their will and not the defendant's that operated. Another illustration occurs when A swings B's arm, which slaps C. B is not liable, although A would be, for it is A's act and not B's which causes the contact.[20]

Intention must also be differentiated from motive. Intent is the word used to describe the desire to bring about certain consequences; motive is the term utilized to describe the underlying objective which inspired the intentional conduct.[21] A person may intend a given result, such as the death of another, for any number of motives including revenge, financial gain, or self-defence. The motive for any tortious act is not usually important in tort law. Conduct may be tortious even though the actor is acting in order to benefit the plaintiff's health.[22] Similarly, it is intentional if the conduct is merely playful,[23] part of an initiation ceremony,[24] a practical joke,[25] or meant to be complimentary, for instance, kissing a person. It may be that damages awarded for minor invasions committed under these circumstances will only be nominal, but they can be actionable invasions

---

[13] *Boomer v. Penn*, [1966] 1 O.R. 119.

[14] Holmes, *The Common Law* (1881), p. 91; Glanville Williams, *Criminal Law*, 2nd ed. (1961), §§16, 18, 19. The criminal defence of automatism is relevant here, *R. v. K.*, [1971] 2 O.R. 401; *Bleta v. R.*, [1964] S.C.R. 561.

[15] *Lawson v. Wellesley Hospital* (1975), 61 D.L.R. (3d) 445, at p. 452 (*per* Dubin J.A.); affd on another ground, [1978] 1 S.C.R. 893.

[16] *Stokes v. Carlson* (1951), 240 S. W. 2d 132.

[17] *Gootson v. R.*, [1948] 4 D.L.R. 33; *Boomer v. Penn*, [1966] 1 O.R. 119; *Slattery v. Haley* (1922), 52 O.L.R. 95; affd 52 O.L.R. 102 (C.A.).

[18] Fridman, "Mental Incompetency" Part II (1964), 80 L.Q. Rev. 84.

[19] *Smith v. Stone* (1647), Sty. 65, 82 E.R. 533.

[20] *Weaver v. Ward* (1616), Hob. 134, 80 E.R. 284.

[21] See Cook, "Act, Intention and Motive in the Criminal Law" (1917), 26 Yale L.J. 644.

[22] *Boase v. Paul*, [1931] O.R. 625 (C.A.); *Mulloy v. Hop Sang*, [1935] 1 W.W.R. 714 (Alta. C.A.); *Malette v. Shulman* (1990), 2 C.C.L.T. (2d) 1 (Ont. C.A.).

[23] *Hawryluk v. Otruba* (1987), 42 C.C.L.T. 306 (Ont. H.C.).

[24] *Kinver v. Phoenix Lodge I.O.O.F.* (1885), 7 O.R. 377 (C.A.).

[25] *Wilkinson v. Downton*, [1897] 2 Q.B. 57.

nevertheless. It is the interest of the plaintiff, not the secret motivation of the defendant, that is most significant to the court.

It is possible, however, for certain intentional injuries to be excused if the reasons for them are recognized as legitimate defences by tort law. For example, if self-defence or the protection of a third person is the motive for a battery or an arrest, they may be considered acceptable excuses.[26]

4. MISTAKE

Conduct may be considered to be intentional even where the defendants act by mistake. If defendants desire to produce a particular result which they mistakenly believe to be innocent, they may nevertheless be held liable for intending the consequence.[27] Thus, individuals who intrude on another's land in the mistaken belief that they are authorized to enter,[28] or that they are the owners themselves,[29] cannot plead their mistake in justification. Those who exercise control of another's personal property, in the erroneous belief that they have legally purchased it, are liable for conversion.[30] If one person shoots at another person's dog, mistakenly believing it to be a wolf,[31] the shooter may be civilly liable for the result, even though it would be excusable under the criminal law. Nor will liability be excused if, in the "sincere yet mistaken belief . . . in the propriety of his illegal action", one person ejects another from land,[32] an employer forcefully disciplines an employee,[33] a man whips a youth who has insulted his daughter,[34] or a restauranteur imprisons someone for non-payment of a debt,[35] although the amount of damages awarded may be less than it would be otherwise.

These cases must all be distinguished from those where the result is truly "accidental" and not "intended" at all. If one cuts down a tree expecting it to fall on one's own land, there is no liability for intentional trespass if by miscalculation the tree falls on a neighbour's land. It would be otherwise if the tree fell where expected, but without the person's knowledge this turned out to be on the land of a neighbour. The latter case is considered to be one of intentional intrusion, albeit under mistake, and is nevertheless actionable.[36] Another

---

[26] See *infra*, Chapter 3.

[27] Atrens, "Intentional Interference with the Person" in Linden (ed.), *Studies in Canadian Tort Law* (Toronto: Butterworths, 1968), p. 393.

[28] *Turner v. Thorne*, [1960] O.W.N. 20.

[29] *Basely v. Clarkson* (1681), 3 Lev. 37, 83 E.R. 565 (C.P.).

[30] *Hollins v. Fowler* (1875), L.R. 7 H.L. 757.

[31] *Ranson v. Kitner* (1888), 31 Ill. App. 241.

[32] *Hodgkinson v. Martin*, [1928] 3 W.W.R. 763, at p. 764 (B.C.C.A.) (*per* Martin J.A.). The quantum of damages may be reduced, however.

[33] *Mitchell v. Defries* (1846), 2 U.C.Q.B. 430 (C.A.).

[34] *Slater v. Watts* (1911), 16 B.C.R. 36, 16 W.W.R. 234 (C.A.).

[35] *Bahner v. Marwest Hotel Co.* (1969), 6 D.L.R. (3d) 322; affd 12 D.L.R. (3d) 646 (B.C.C.A.).

[36] Whittier, "Mistake in the Law of Torts" (1902), 15 Harv. L. Rev. 335, at p. 337; Fleming, *The Law of Torts*, 8th ed. (1992), p. 77; *cf. Shewish v. MacMillan Bloedel Ltd.* (1990), 3 C.C.L.T. (2d) 291 (B.C.C.A.).

example of "accident" occurs when someone shoots at a wolf, but the bullet goes astray and hits a dog which also happens to be in the vicinity.[37] This result (which should be contrasted with the result of shooting at a dog believing it to be a wolf[38]) is not intended, although it might be found to be negligent in appropriate circumstances.

At first blush these principles seem to be at variance with the fault rationale, and so they are. Nevertheless, people who deliberately interfere with the persons or properties of others without making adequate investigation of their rights should bear the burden of their own mistakes, however innocent they may be. In property cases, this result can be justified on the ground that it clarifies property rights.[39] In other cases, since one of two innocent persons must bear the loss, the courts have concluded that the one who intrudes by mistake is the one who should pay rather than the totally innocent victim,[40] however anomalous and unreasonable this may seem to some.[41] Although the defendant may be morally blameless, it is felt to be preferable to hold liable the person who sought to produce the physical results accomplished, rather than the passive and helpless victim.

5. YOUTH

There is no general immunity from liability for intentional torts in favour of children, but youth may be taken into account by the courts during their consideration of liability for intentional conduct,[42] despite the older authority to the contrary.[43] Youth in itself is not the significant factor, but rather how it affects the defendant's capacity to form the requisite intention for liability. Children may be excused from liability for intentional torts if they are incapable of forming the specific intent required to commit the tort in question, but they will be held liable if they are capable.[44] There is no age specified under which children are immune from liability, as there is in the criminal law,[45] but children under four are probably beyond the reach of tort liability.[46]

Occasionally children are held liable for their intentional torts. A child of five, for example, who pulled a chair out from under someone who was about to

---

[37]   *Stanley v. Powell*, [1891] 1 Q.B. 86.

[38]   See *Ranson v. Kitner, supra*, n. 31.

[39]   Fleming, *The Law of Torts,* 9th ed. (1998), p. 45 *et seq.*

[40]   *Prosser and Keeton on the Law of Torts*, 5th ed. (1948), p. 110; Atrens, *supra*, n. 27, at p. 387.

[41]   Whittier, *supra*, n. 36.

[42]   Atrens, *supra*, n. 27, at p. 387; Bohlen, "Liability in Tort of Infants and Insane Persons" (1942), 23 Mich. L.R. 9. As for the negligence liability of children, see *infra*, Chapter 5.

[43]   *Jennings v. Rundell* (1799), 8 Term Tep. 335, 101 E.R. 1419 (*per* Lord Kenyon).

[44]   *Prosser and Keeton, op. cit. supra*, n. 40, p. 1071; Fleming, *op. cit. supra*, n. 39, p. 21; Alexander, "Tort Liability of Children and Their Parents", in D. Mendes da Costa (ed.), *Studies in Canadian Family Law* (Toronto: Butterworths, 1972), at p. 852.

[45]   See Criminal Code, R.S.C. 1985, c. C-46, s. 13, 12 years of age.

[46]   See Alexander, *supra*, n. 44, at p. 854.

sit down on it was held liable in battery.[47] A child of six, who pushed a four-year-old down and fractured her arm, was also held liable for assault and battery.[48]

More often, however, children are excused from liability. For example, a child of five who shot a playmate in the eye with an arrow during a game of cowboys and Indians was relieved of liability for both negligence and trespass.[49] It was agreed that trespass did not lie because "the infant defendant did not intend to injure the infant plaintiff"[50] and further, because "the shooting of an arrow from a bow without wrongful intent is in itself an innocent act".[51] This case may be criticized for focussing on the desire to injure, rather than on the intention of causing offensive contact, which is normally all that is required for liability.[52]

One of the leading Canadian cases is *Tillander v. Gosselin*,[53] where a child just under three years old pulled another child out of its carriage and dragged it along the ground, seriously injuring it. He was nevertheless relieved of liability both in negligence and assault. Mr. Justice Grant explained as follows:

> In this action, the defendant's tender age at the time of the alleged assault . . . satisfies me that he cannot be said to have acted deliberately and with intention when the injuries were inflicted upon the infant plaintiff.
>
> I do not believe that one can describe the act of a normal three-year-old child in doing injury to the baby plaintiff in this case as a voluntary act on his part . . . . The defendant child, however, would not have the mental ability at the age of three to appreciate or know the real nature of the act he was performing. A child of that age emulates or imitates the actions of those about him rather than making his own decisions. In the present case there could be no genuine intent formulated in his mind to do harm to the child plaintiff or to perform whatever act he did that caused the injury.[54]

Although the decision may be supported on its facts, its language is less than satisfactory. First, the use of the word "voluntary" was inappropriate, since the child was clearly conscious and its mind was directing its bodily movements. Secondly, the language imparts the impression that there must be an intention to do harm, whereas it is enough to desire to cause offensive contact.

Children have been treated relatively leniently by the law, but their victims have had to bear the losses caused by them, which can be harsh at times. It might well be that, despite our compassion for youthful wrongdoers, the law should move toward more stringent standards for children in order to instill

---

[47] *Garratt v. Dailey* (1955), 46 Wash. 2d 197, 279 P. 2d 1091.

[48] *Baldinger v. Banks* (1960), 201 N.Y.S. 2d 629; see also *Ellis v. D'Angelo* (1953), 253 P. 2d 675, 4-year-old liable for attack on babysitter.

[49] *Walmsley v. Humenick*, [1954] 2 D.L.R. 232 (B.C.).

[50] *Ibid.*, at p. 240.

[51] *Ibid.*, at p. 249.

[52] See *Baldinger v. Banks*, *supra*, n. 48, at p. 631.

[53] [1967] 1 O.R. 203; affd 61 D.L.R. (2d) 192 (C.A.).

[54] *Ibid.*, at p. 210, O.R.

greater responsibility in them and to encourage their parents to supervise them more closely.[55]

6. MENTAL ILLNESS

Mental illness itself furnishes no general immunity from liability for intentional torts, but may provide a basis for excusing certain defendants from responsibility,[56] even though there is early authority to the contrary.[57]

It is clear now that if defendants whose minds are totally blank, by reason of mental illness, conduct themselves like robots or automatons, they will be exonerated because they have not committed a voluntary act.[58] Similarly, those who are unconscious by reason of a heart attack or other sudden illness cannot be responsible for their actions.[59]

It is also established law that mental illness will render a person immune from intentional tort liability if it is "so extreme as to preclude any genuine intention to do the act complained of".[60] Consequently, "if a mentally ill person is by reason of his illness incapable of the intent to assault a person, he is not liable in an action founded upon that assault".[61]

Another matter which is undisputed is that the onus of proving that a defendant is mentally ill, and therefore entitled to special consideration, rests on the defendant.[62] As was declared by Eberle J. in *Gerigs v. Rose*,[63]

> [T]he onus lies upon the defendant to establish the defence of insanity . . . [that is] . . . to prove, by a balance of credible evidence, a lack of intention on the part of the defendant to apply force to the person of another.

Beyond these simple propositions there is considerable confusion, which reflects society's ambivalence toward the mentally ill. On one hand, courts are

---

[55] See generally, *infra*, Chapter 5. Some jurisdictions make parents statutorily liable for the damages caused by their children up to certain limits; see Parental Responsibility Act, S.O. 2000, c. 4.

[56] See generally, Robins, "Tort Liability of the Mentally Disabled" in Linden (ed.), *Studies in Canadian Tort Law* (1968), at p. 76; Sharpe, "Mental State as Affecting Liability in Tort" (1975), 23 Chitty's L.J. 46; "The Liability of Lunatics in the Law of Tort" (1952), 26 Aus. L.J. 299; Bohlen, "Liability in Tort of Infants and Insane Persons" (1924), 23 Mich. L. Rev. 9; Fridman, "Mental Incompetency" Part II (1964), 80 L.Q. Rev. 84; Picher, "The Tortious Liability of the Insane in Canada" (1975), 13 Osgoode Hall L.J. 193.

[57] *Weaver v. Ward* (1616), Hob. 134, 80 E.R. 284, "if a lunatic hurt a man, he shall be answerable in trespass"; *Taggard v. Innes* (1862), 12 U.C.C.P. 77, at p. 78; *Stanley v. Hayes* (1904), 8 O.L.R. 81.

[58] Robins, *supra*, n. 56, at p. 87; *Lawson v. Wellesley Hospital* (1975), 61 D.L.R. (3d) 445, at p. 452 (Ont. C.A.); affd on another point, [1978] 1 S.C.R. 893.

[59] *Slattery v. Haley* (1922), 52 O.L.R. 95; affd 52 O.L.R. 102 (C.A.).

[60] *Tindale v. Tindale*, [1950] 4 D.L.R. 363, at p. 366 (B.C.) (*per* Macfarland J.), see also *Wilson v. Zeron*, [1941] O.W.N. 353, at p. 354 (*per* Greene J.); affd [1942] O.W.N. 195 (C.A.).

[61] *Lawson v. Wellesley Hospital, supra*, n. 58, at p. 450.

[62] *Tindale v. Tindale, supra*, n. 60, at p. 366; *Baron v. Whalen*, [1938] 1 D.L.R. 787 (B.C.) *Phillips v. Soloway* (1956), 6 D.L.R. (2d) 570 (Man. Q.B.).

[63] (1979), 9 C.C.L.T. 222, at p. 227 (Ont.).

sympathetic to the plight of the mentally ill and want to remain faithful to the notion of liability only for fault. On the other hand, courts would like to assist the injured victims of the mentally ill and encourage greater care by the guardians of the mentally ill. In addition, the courts would prefer to avoid importing into tort law the complexities associated with the mental illness defence in criminal law, if possible.

The tests of mental illness employed by various common law courts range all the way from the adoption of the *M'Naghten* test of the criminal law, which excuses defendants if they do not understand either what they were doing or that it was wrong,[64] down to the refusal to grant any immunity whatsoever, except for the absence of voluntariness.[65]

The Canadian courts have fashioned a compromise position, halfway between the criminal law test and the complete denial of immunity — mentally ill persons will be relieved of liability if they are incapable of appreciating the nature and quality of their act. It is not an excuse if the person understood this but did not realize his or her act was wrong.[66] As Galligan J. has stated:

> . . . regardless of whether or not a person because of insanity did not know that his act was wrong, if he intended to kill and appreciated the nature and quality of his acts, the defence of insanity is not available to him.[67]

It is, therefore, entirely possible under this test for defendants, who are mentally ill according to the criminal law test, to be rendered civilly liable for their conduct.[68] This principle, which incorporates the first branch of the criminal law test but not the second branch, has recently been embraced in *Lawson v. Wellesley Hospital*, where a psychiatric patient in a hospital attacked another patient. In allowing the case to proceed to trial, Mr. Justice Dubin, for the majority of the Ontario Court of Appeal, explained: "Where a person, by reason of mental illness, is incapable of appreciating the nature or quality of his acts, such a person has committed no tort since the intention, which is an essential element of the cause of action, is missing."[69]

Using this test, a mother who attacked her daughter with an axe,[70] a man who

---

[64] *White v. Pile* (1951), 68 N.S.W.W.N. 176; *cf.* Civil Code of Lower Canada, Art. 1053, which held liable for their faults only those who were "capable of discerning right from wrong". Now Art. 1457, "endowed with reason", that is, with the "ability to discern right from wrong".

[65] *Donaghy v. Brennan* (1901), 19 N.Z.L.R. 289, damages limited to actual loss only; see also *White v. White*, [1950] P. 39 (*dictum* of Denning L.J.); *Stanley v. Hayes* (1904), 8 O.L.R. 81, *dictum*, since defendant knew what he was doing.

[66] *Phillips v. Soloway* (1956), 6 D.L.R. (2d) 570 (Man.); see also *Morriss v. Marsden*, [1952] 1 All E.R. 925; *Hanbury v. Hanbury* (1892), 8 T.L.R. 559 (C.A.).

[67] *Squittieri v. de Santis* (1976), 15 O.R. (2d) 416, at p. 417. See also *Gerigs v. Rose, supra*, n. 63, at p. 228 (*per* Eberle J.).

[68] *Baron v. Whalen*, [1938] 1 D.L.R. 787 (B.C.), arteriosclerosis causes car accident.

[69] *Supra*, n. 58, at 452. Mr. Justice Eberle has explained that the word "or" in this formulation of the test was a "slip" and was meant to be an "and", see *Gerigs v. Rose, supra*, n. 63, at p. 229.

[70] *Tindale v. Tindale, supra*, n. 60.

attacked another with a knife[71] and one who shot a police officer[72] were held liable. A person who burned down a barn was held responsible because the court was not convinced that he did not know or appreciate what he was doing.[73] So too, a person who attacked a hotel manager with a blunt instrument was held liable, on the ground that he knew the nature and quality of the act and his lack of knowledge of wrongdoing was immaterial.[74] A mental patient's estate, however, was not held liable when he killed his attendant because the jury found that he was "by reason of mental illness incapable of appreciating the nature and consequences of his act".[75]

This position, although certainly not devoid of problems, seems to be about as good a compromise as we can expect for the time being. In the years ahead we may see a trend toward dealing with the mentally ill in the same way as other defendants in the hope that this may foster better supervision of them.

Now that we have briefly considered what is meant by the word "intention", let us examine the nominate torts involving deliberate conduct.

B. Battery

A person who intentionally causes a harmful or offensive contact with another person is liable for battery.[76] This nominate tort protects the interest in bodily security from deliberate interference by others. It seeks to reduce the incidence of violence in our society.

The most typical situation of battery arises when someone punches or kicks another person.[77] Similarly, if a policeman grabs someone unnecessarily roughly, "beyond generally acceptable standards of conduct", it is battery.[78] It is also a battery if a weapon or missile is the instrument of contact. Thus, if someone stabs,[79] or shoots,[80] or strikes another person with a stick,[81] or a rock,[82] it is actionable. So too, to push someone off a hayride cart is a battery.[83] Such clearly direct invasions of bodily security give rise to liability, but so do certain indirect

---

[71] *Phillips v. Soloway, supra*, n. 66; *Squittieri v. de Santis, supra*, n. 67, stabbing to death.

[72] *Gerigs v. Rose, supra*, n. 63.

[73] *Stanley v. Hayes, supra*, n. 65, at p. 83.

[74] *Morriss v. Marsden, supra*, n. 66, at p. 928; see also *Whaley v. Cartusiano* (1990), 68 D.L.R. (4th) 58 (Ont. C.A.).

[75] *Wilson v. Zeron, supra*, n. 60, at pp. 353-54. See also *Fiala v. Cechmanek*, [2001] A.J. 823 (Alta. C.A.), no liability for attack during unforeseen manic episode.

[76] Fleming, *The Law of Torts*, 9th ed. (1998), p. 29; *Beals v. Haywood*, [1960] N.Z.L.R. 131; *Norberg v. Wynrib*, [1992] 2 S.C.R. 226, at p. 246 (*per* La Forest J.); at p. 303 (*per* Sopinka J.).

[77] *Johnston v. Burton* (1971), 16 D.L.R. (3d) 660 (Man.); *Karpow v. Shave*, [1975] 2 W.W.R. 159 (Alta.), punch; *Roundall v. Brodie* (1973), 7 N.B.R. (2d) 486.

[78] *Collins v. Wilcock*, [1984] 1 W.L.R. 1172, at p. 1177 (D.C.).

[79] *Reid v. Davison* (1972), 7 N.S.R. (2d) 563.

[80] *Cook v. Lewis*, [1951] S.C.R. 830; *Loomis v. Rohan* (1974), 46 D.L.R. (3d) 423 (B.C.).

[81] *Fagan v. Metropolitan Police Commissioner*, [1969] 1 Q.B. 439, at p. 444, [1968] 3 All E.R. 442.

[82] *Fillipowich v. Nahachewsky* (1969), 3 D.L.R. (3d) 544 (Sask.).

[83] *Hawryluk v. Otruba* (1978), 42 C.C.L.T. 306 (Ont. H.C.).

intrusions, such as pulling a chair out from under someone who is about to sit down and causing that person to fall to the ground,[84] throwing someone against a door,[85] secretly putting poison into someone's food[86] or firing a gun so close that someone is burned.[87] Blowing pipe or cigar smoke at someone can be a battery.[88] It is suggested that a battery can be committed by intentionally causing physical harm, however indirectly it is brought about.[89]

It is not necessary that the skin of the plaintiff be touched. Battery includes offensive contact with the plaintiff's clothing,[90] with an object that the plaintiff is carrying,[91] or with the horse the plaintiff is riding,[92] because such contact is regarded as serious enough to generate a violent response.

Nor is it necessary that a battery cause any actual harm to the plaintiff.[93] Offensive contact is enough, however trivial it may seem, for it may trigger retaliatory measures by persons whose dignity and self-respect are threatened thereby. Better to permit an action for these seemingly minor intrusions than to invite violent counter-attacks by the aggrieved victims. Thus, it is a battery to jostle someone rudely,[94] to grab a person by the nose,[95] to pull off someone's hat,[96] or a flower someone is wearing,[97] or to cut off someone's hair.[98] It has been held that to pour water on someone,[99] or to spit on another person is also a battery,[100] because such conduct is "highly provocative of retaliation by force".[101]

A battery can be committed even though no harm or insult is intended by the contact.[102] If the contact is offensive to the recipient, even if a compliment was

---

[84]   *Garratt v. Dailey* (1955), 46 Wash. 2d 197, 279 P. 2d 1091; see also *Hopper v. Reeve* (1817), 7 Taunt. 698, 129 E.R. 278.

[85]   *MacDonald v. Hees* (1974), 46 D.L.R. (3d) 720 (N.S.).

[86]   *Commonwealth v. Stratton* (1873), 114 Mass. 303; *Snouffer v. Snouffer*, 621 N.E.2d 829 (Ohio 1993); *MacDonald v. Sebastian* (1987), 42 C.C.L.T. 213 (N.S.), poison in well.

[87]   *R. v. Hamilton* (1891), 12 N.S.W.L.R. 111. See *contra*, Trindade, "Intentional Torts: Some Thoughts on Assaults and Battery" (1982), 2 Oxford J.L. S. 211.

[88]   *Richardson v. Hennly*, 434 S.E.2d 772 (1993), revd on other ground, 444 S.E.2d 317, pipe; *Leichtman v. W.L.W.*, 634 N.E.2d 697 (1994), cigar.

[89]   But see Klar, *Tort Law*, 2nd ed. (1996), p. 26.

[90]   *Piggly Wiggly v. Rickles* (1925), 212 Ala. 585, 103 So. 860.

[91]   *Morgan v. Loyacomo* (1941), 190 Miss. 656, 1 So. 2d 510; *Fisher v. Carrousel Motor Hotel* (1967), 424 S.W. 2d 627 (Tex.); *Green v. Goddard* (1702), 2 Salk. 641, 91 E.R. 540.

[92]   *Dodwell v. Burford* (1669), 1 Mod. Rep. 22, 86 E.R. 703.

[93]   The action arises, therefore, for purposes of the limitation period, when the acts are done, *Nicely v. Waterloo Regional Police Force* (1991), 7 C.C.L.T. (2d) 61 (Ont. Div. Ct.).

[94]   *Cole v. Turner* (1704), Holt. K.B. 108, 90 E.R. 958, N.P.

[95]   *Stewart v. Stonehouse*, [1926] 2 D.L.R. 683 (Sask. C.A.).

[96]   *Seigel v. Long* (1910), 160 Ala. 79, 53 So. 753.

[97]   *Humphries v. Connor* (1864), 17 I.C.L.R. 1.

[98]   *Forde v. Skinner* (1830), 4 C. & P. 239, 172 E.R. 687.

[99]   *Pursell v. Horn* (1838), 8 Ad. & El. 602, 112 E.R. 966; *Soon v. Jong* (1968), 70 D.L.R. (2d) 160.

[100]   *Scott v. R.* (1975), 24 C.C.C. (2d) 261 (Fed. C.A.), beer spit on police officer.

[101]   *Alcorn v. Mitchell* (1872), 63 Ill. 553 (*per* Sheldon J.); see also *R. v. Cotesworth* (1704), 6 Mod. Rep. 172, 87 E.R. 928; *Draper v. Baker* (1884), 61 Wis. 450, 21 N.W. 527.

[102]   *Wilson v. Pringle*, [1986] 2 All E.R. 440, at p. 445 (C.A.).

intended, it is tortious, as where one person hugs[103] or kisses another person without consent.[104] In the same way, if someone interferes with another as a joke,[105] or even where it is done to assist another,[106] it may amount to a battery if it is unwelcome. Where a nurse in good faith administers a vaccination believing wrongly that there has been consent, that is battery.[107]

This does not mean that every insignificant touching of another person amounts to a battery. A line must be drawn between those contacts which are regarded as normal everyday events, which people must put up with in a crowded world, and those which are considered to be offensive and, therefore, unacceptable.[108] No liability will follow when one taps another person on the shoulder to get attention,[109] or jostles someone while passing in a narrow passage.[110] It would be otherwise if the tap on the shoulder was a violent one or if the jostling was done roughly and rudely. Liability might also be found if the plaintiff warned the defendant in advance that the plaintiff would not tolerate any contact at all. The difference between the trivial and the actionable might be illustrated by this example. If one touches another person's thigh on a crowded subway in order to prevent that other person or oneself from falling, this would not be a battery. If the same external act were done merely for the pleasure of the defendant, however, liability would ensue.

Improper sexual contact, in addition to being a crime, is a tort. Consequently, criminal conduct such as rape, child sexual abuse and incest are batteries that are actionable civilly. As Mr. Justice La Forest stated, in relation to incest, in *M. (K) v. M. (H)* :[111]

> Although assault and battery can only serve as a crude legal description of incest . . . there is no question . . . that incest constitutes an assault and battery.

There seems to be an epidemic of these law suits in recent years. One explanation for this may be the need for "therapeutic jurisprudence".[112] Other

---

103   *Spivey v. Battaglia* (1972), 258 So. 2d 815 (S.C. Fla.).

104   *Ragsdale v. Ezell* (1989), 49 S.W. 775 (Ky.). *Cf.*, *Wilson v. Pringle*, [1986] 2 All E.R. 440 (C.A.), where the Court wrongly required pleading of "hostility" in battery case. See Reynolds, "Tortious Battery: Is 'I Didn't Mean Any Harm' Relevant?" (1984), 37 Okla. L. Rev. 717.

105   *Newman v. Christensen* (1948), 39 N.W. 2d 417 (Nb.).

106   *Clayton v. New Dreamland Roller Skating Rink* (1951), 82 A. 2d 458, manipulation of broken arm.

107   *Teows v. Weisner* (2001), 3 C.C.L.T. (3d) 293 (B.C.S.C.). See also, *infra,* Chapter 3.

108   Devlin, *Samples of Lawmaking* (1962), p. 85

109   *Coward v. Baddeley* (1859), 4 H. & N. 478, 157 E.R. 927.

110   *Cole v. Turner* (1704), Holt. K.B. 108, 90 E.R. 958, N.P.

111   [1992] 3 S.C.R. 3, 14 C.C.L.T. (2d) 1, at p. 16 (S.C.C.). It also amounts to a breach of fiduciary duty, see p. 39. See also *Y. (S.) v. C. (F.G.)* (1996), 30 C.C.L.T. (2d) 82 (B.C.C.A.), cap on damages does not apply in these cases.

112   See Feldthusen, "The Civil Action for Sexual Battery: Therapeutic Jurisprudence?" (1993), 25 Ottawa L. Rev. 203. See also "The Canadian Experiment with the Civil Action for Sexual Battery", in *Torts in the Nineties* (1997). See also Grace and Vella, *Civil Liability For Sexual Abuse and Violence in Canada* (Butterworths 2000).

explanations are the avoidance of criminal trials, in which plaintiffs have no control and which can be particularly brutal; the availability of damages; the lighter burden of proof; the ability to obtain discovery of the defendant; and favourable limitation periods.[113]

So important an interest is bodily security that a battery is actionable even if, at the time, the victim is totally unaware of the interference. Consequently, to kiss someone while they are asleep,[114] or to interfere with someone while anaesthetized,[115] is a battery and an action lies when this is discovered upon awakening. Such an invasion is no less serious when the victim is asleep than when awake.

So seriously is the tort of battery viewed by the courts, that, unlike the situation in negligence, a defendant will be held liable for all of the consequences of wrongful conduct, whether they were intended or not and whether they were foreseeable or not. As Borins C.C.J. explained in *Bettel v. Yim*:[116]

> If physical contact was intended, the fact that its magnitude exceeded all reasonable or intended expectations should make no difference. To hold otherwise . . . would unduly narrow recovery where one deliberately invades the bodily interests of another with the result that the totally innocent plaintiff would be deprived of full recovery for the totality of the injuries suffered as a result of the deliberate invasion of his bodily interests . . . the intentional wrongdoer should bear the responsibility for the injuries caused by his conduct and the negligence test of "foreseeability" to limit, or eliminate, liability should not be imported into the field of intentional torts.

C. Assault

Assault is the intentional creation of the apprehension of imminent harmful or offensive contact. The tort of assault furnishes protection for the interest in freedom from fear of being physically interfered with. Damages are recoverable by someone who is made apprehensive of immediate physical contact, even though that contact never actually occurs. The underlying policy thrust of the tort of assault, like that of battery, is the reduction of violence. Because threatening to inflict harm is apt to attract retaliation in the same way as causing harm, it must also be discouraged by tort law.[117]

---

[113] See Klar, *Tort Law*, 2nd ed. (1996), p. 45; *P.(V.) v. Canada (Attorney General)* (1999), 47 C.C.L.T. (2d) 249 (Sask. Q.B.), native resident school case containing summmary of decisions; *A.(C.) v. C. (J.W.)* (1997), 36 C.C.L.T. (2d) 224 (B.C.S.C.); *T.(L.) v. T. (R.W.)* (1997), 36 C.C.L.T. (2d) 207 (B.C.S.C.).

[114] *Restatement, Torts, Second*, §18, Comment D.

[115] *Schweizer v. Central Hospital* (1974), 6 O.R. (2d) 606; *Mohr v. Williams* (1905), 95 Minn. 261, 104 N.W. 112.

[116] (1978), 20 O.R. (2d) 617, at pp. 628-29; see also *Allan v. New Mount Sinai Hospital* (1980), 28 O.R. (2d) 356, at p. 365 (*per* Linden J.); revd on procedural point 33 O.R. (2d) 603n; *Mahal v. Young* (1986), 36 C.C.L.T. 143 (B.C.S.C.); *Manning v. Grimsley* (1981), 643 F. 2d 20.

[117] See Fleming, *The Law of Torts*, 9th ed. (1998), p. 31.

Assault should be distinguished from battery, although the two are often blurred together and called "assault".[118] This does not usually matter very much because in most cases both assault and battery are committed in rapid succession. If a battery occurs, the assault tends to be ignored since the quantum of damages for it will be rather small. An assault can be committed without a battery and battery can occur without an assault preceding it. For example, swinging at someone and missing is an assault but not a battery; striking someone from behind, without his or her knowledge, is a battery but not an assault.

Conduct which intentionally arouses apprehension of an imminent battery constitutes an assault. Shaking a fist at another person,[119] lunging at someone in an effort to attack,[120] and swinging an axe at another person,[121] are actionable assaults. An assault may also be committed if a person is surrounded by a group of people in a hostile manner,[122] or if a loaded gun is pointed threateningly at someone.[123] Unleashing a growling dog in order to frighten someone can be an assault. Tailgating another car, intentionally putting the other driver in fear of an imminent collision, can also amount to assault.[124] Blocking another person's progress has also been said to amount to an assault, but this is questionable.[125]

Frightening or threatening someone, however, does not constitute an assault unless the event feared is imminent. To threaten to do harm to someone at some future time, because this is not as likely to spur retaliation, does not amount to an assault, although it may give rise to other tortious or even criminal responsibility.[126] Hence, shaking one's fist at someone who is out of reach, making a threat over the telephone, or reaching for someone who is standing safely behind a counter, lack the required immediacy for assault liability.[127]

Words may transform an apparent assault into innocent behaviour and, conversely, they may render actionable conduct which would otherwise be harm-

---

[118] See *Bruce v. Dyer* (1966), 58 D.L.R. (2d) 221, at p. 216; affd [1970] 2 O.R. 482n (C.A.); *MacDonald v. Hees* (1974), 46 D.L.R. (3d) 720, at p. 730 (N.S.); *Mann v. Balaban*, [1970] S.C.R. 74. See also, for the purposes of criminal cases, Criminal Code, R.S.C. 1985, c. C-46, s. 265.

[119] *Bruce v. Dyer*, [1970] 1 O.R. 482n (C.A.).

[120] *Stephens v. Myers* (1830), 4 C. & P. 349, 172 E.R. 735, N.P.

[121] *I. de S. & Wife v. W. de S.* (1348), Year-Book, 22 Liber Assisarum, folio 99, p. 60. See Wright, Linden and Klar, *Canadian Tort Law, Cases, Notes and Materials*, 10th ed. (Markham: Butterworths, 1994), Chapter 2, p. 46.

[122] *Read v. Coker* (1853), 13 C.B. 850, 138 E.W. 1437.

[123] *R. v. Hamilton* (1891), 12 N.S.W.L.R. 111.

[124] *Herman v. Graves* (1998), 42 C.C.L.T. (2d) 250, at p. 266 (Alta. Q.B.) (*per* Mason J. quoting this statement).

[125] *Ibid.*

[126] *Criminal Code*, R.S.C. 1985, c. C-46, ss. 372 and 423.

[127] *Western Union Telegraph v. Hill* (1933), 150 So. 709. *Prosser and Keeton on the Law of Torts*, 5th ed. (1984), p. 44.

less.[128] For example, if one person draws a sword and points it at another person within range, this would be an assault. If at the same time, however, the person utters words that make it clear that there is no intention to use the sword, it will not amount to an assault.[129] Conversely, innocuous conduct such as putting one's hand in one's pocket is not an assault, but if at the same time one proclaims that one is reaching for one's gun and will shoot, it would constitute an assault. In the same way, to make a lewd suggestion to someone is not an assault, but if the speaker then advances threateningly, it may become actionable.[130]

Another problem involving the use of words is the question of "conditional assault". If one person points a gun at another and says, "Your money or your life!", it might be argued that it is not an assault because the plaintiff may avoid any harm by complying with the condition and parting with the money. It could be contended that the requirement of immediacy is absent. Such an argument is fallacious, however, for one cannot impose conditions upon another, when one has no legal right to do so.[131] It would be otherwise if a landowner said to a trespasser, "Get off my land or I'll throw you off," for in such a case, the landowner is only threatening to do that which the landowner is entitled to do.

It is sometimes said that words alone cannot constitute an assault.[132] Normally, this is correct, but it is not invariably so. This notion is a variant of the requirement of immediacy; in other words, a mere threat unaccompanied by some conduct indicating that it is to be executed immediately lacks the element of imminence necessary for liability. A responsible plaintiff in these circumstances need not be fearful and need not take defensive measures, for mere menacing words are cheap and all too common. Threats must normally be combined with action before they become so dangerous as to invite a response. It is possible, however, to arouse apprehension of imminent harm by words alone and, if this transpires, it is actionable.[133] One example of such a threat would be telephoning someone and announcing that their telephone receiver has dynamite in it and is being detonated immediately. Anyone hearing such words would be reasonably apprehensive of imminent physical harm and should be entitled to recover for assault. Another situation where words alone might amount to assault would be if a motionless highwayman, standing with a gun in hand pointed at a person, shouted "Stand and deliver!"[134]

The actual ability to execute a threat need not be present, as long as it appears to a reasonable plaintiff that it is there. If a person is reasonably apprehensive of imminent physical contact, even though in no real danger, there may still be recovery for assault. Therefore, to point an unloaded gun at someone who

---

[128] See generally, Handford, "Tort Liability for Threatening or Insulting Words" (1976), 54 Can. Bar Rev. 563.

[129] *Tuberville v. Savage* (1699), 1 Mod. Rep. 3, 86 E.R. 684.

[130] *Fogden v. Wade*, [1945] N.Z.L.R. 724.

[131] *Prosser and Keeton, op. cit., supra*, n. 127, at p. 45.

[132] *Read v. Coker, supra*, n. 122.

[133] See Handford, *supra*, n. 128, at p. 570.

[134] *R. v. Wilson*, [1955] 1 All E.R. 744, at p. 745; *Restatement, Torts, Second*, §31.

reasonably believes it to be loaded is assault.[135] To reach for someone's throat
with a choking motion, even in jest, is assault if the person reasonably believes
the threat is serious.

The emotion of fear is not required for assault; it is enough if there is an
apprehension of unpleasant contact.[136] If a pipsqueak holds a fist up to Shaquille
O'Neal and threatens to knock his block off, Shaq may sue for assault, even
though he is not in the least frightened. Tort law protects even the brave from
offensive threats. It also seeks to curtail acts of retaliation which could be
vicious.

Because the interest being protected by the law of assault is that of mental
security, there can be no assault if the plaintiff is not conscious that there is any
danger. Thus, to point a loaded gun at a sleeping person is probably not an
assault, though if the person were actually shot while asleep, it would be a
battery.[137]

1. TORT, CRIME, AND COMPENSATION FOR VICTIMS OF CRIME

Conduct which amounts to the tort of battery or assault would also usually
constitute a criminal assault. A defendant who punches someone on the nose is
liable both for the tort of battery and the crime of assault. The victim may sue
for damages, and in addition the defendant may be prosecuted by the Crown in
the criminal courts. The outcome in each proceeding is largely irrelevant to the
other since the parties, issues, and burdens of proof are somewhat different. One
who is convicted of a criminal assault is not immune from a later civil action for
the damages resulting from that assault,[138] but may be excused from paying
punitive damages to the victim.[139] The victims of these civil batteries and
criminal assaults are theoretically able to secure tort compensation, but are
rarely successful in practice.[140] Similarly, the right to restitution provided for in

---

[135] *Kennedy v. Hanes*, [1940] O.R. 461, at p. 469 (*dictum* of Urquhart J.); affd [1941] S.C.R. 384,
liability in negligence for air gun going off; *Allen v. Hannaford* (1926), 138 Wash. 423, 244 P.
700; *Brady v. Schatzel*, [1911] Q.S.R. 206; *McClelland v. Symons*, [1951] V.L.R. 157, at p. 163;
R. v. St. George (1840), 9 C. & P. 483, 173 E.R. 921, at p. 926 (*per* Parke B. *dictum*); see also
Criminal Code, R.S.C. 1985, c. C-46, s. 86, pointing a firearm; *cf.*, *R. v. Cleary* (1870), 9
N.S.W.S.C.R. 75; *Blake v. Barnard* (1840), 9 C. & P. 626, 173 E.R. 985, at p. 986 (*per* Abinger
C.B.).

[136] *Restatement, Torts, Second*, §24, comment B; *Brady v. Schatzel*, *supra*, n. 132.

[137] *State v. Barry* (1912), 45 Mont. 598, 124 P. 775.

[138] *Nelson v. Sneed*, [1976] 1 W.W.R. 360 (Alta.); *Stevens v. Quinney*, [1979] 5 W.W.R. 284 (Sask.
Q.B.). The civil case may be stayed, see *Stickney v. Trusz* (1973), 45 D.L.R. (3d) 275; affd
(1974), 46 D.L.R. (3d) 80 and 82; *Demeter v. Occidental Inc. Co. of California* (1975), 11 O.R.
(2d) 369 (H.C.); Klar and Elman, "Annotation to *Loedel v. Eckert*" (1977), 3 C.C.L.T. 145.

[139] See *infra*, Section G.

[140] Only 1.8% of Ontario crime victims collected anything from their attackers, see Linden,
"Victims of Crime and Tort Law" (1969), 12 Can. Bar J. 17, summarizing *The Report of the
Osgoode Hall Study on Compensation for Victims of Crime* (1968). One incest victim won an
award, see *The Globe & Mail*, April 3, 1987.

the Criminal Code[141] is seldom employed,[142] and woefully inadequate in any event.

To remedy this problem legislation has been enacted to furnish compensation for innocent victims of violent crime and, incidentally, the victims of these torts. Beginning in 1964 in New Zealand and in the United Kingdom, this type of scheme has been established in almost all the provinces of Canada, several American states, and Australia.[143] Although outside the scope of this book, these crime compensation benefits may be available to many people who would be entitled to tort recovery for assault and battery, and reference should be made to the appropriate provincial legislation, and to the two fine books on the topic by Burns[144] and Miers.[145]

D. False Imprisonment

Anyone who intentionally confines another person within fixed boundaries is liable for the tort of false imprisonment. This tort protects the interest in freedom from restraint within particular limits. Its name is something of a misnomer. Firstly, there is no need for any prison to be involved. Although one can certainly imprison someone by incarceration behind prison walls, it can also be accomplished in other ways. Secondly, the confinement cannot be "false" in the sense of being unreal. The word "false" is intended to impart the notion of unauthorized or wrongful detention. Because this tort is a descendant of the trespass action, no actual loss is required as a pre-requisite of recovery.[146] Nor is fault an element of an action; to keep someone in prison illegally beyond the authorized period is, as a matter of law, actionable. "False imprisonment is a tort of strict liability."[147]

There can be no false imprisonment without a total confinement. The restraint must be complete within definite boundaries; for example, to block

---

[141] R.S.C. 1985, c. C-46, ss. 738 to 741. See *R. v. Zelensky* (1978), 20 Crim. L.Q. 272 (S.C.C.); Chasse, "Restitution in Canadian Criminal Law" (1977), 36 C.R.N.S. 201.

[142] See generally Linden, "Restitution, Compensation for Victims of Crime and Canadian Criminal Law" (1977), 19 Can. J. Crim. L. 49, also in Law Reform Commission of Canada, *Community Participation in Sentencing* (1976).

[143] See, *e.g.*, Compensation for Victims of Crime Act, R.S.O. 1990, c. C.24; Linden, *Report of the Osgoode Hall Study on Compensation for Victims of Crime* (1968); Burns and Ross, "A Comparative Study of Victims of Crime Indemnification in Canada, B.C. as Microcosm" (1973), 8 U.B.C.L. Rev. 105; Miers, "The Ontario Criminal Injuries Compensation Scheme" (1974), 24 U. of T.L.J. 347; Eremko, "Compensation of Criminal Injuries in Saskatchewan" (1969), 19 U. of T.L.J. 263; Bryan, "Compensation to Victims of Crime" (1968), 6 Alta. L. Rev. 202; Samuels, "Compensation for Criminal Injuries in Britain" (1967), 17 U. of T.L.J. 20.

[144] *Criminal Injuries Compensation*, 2nd ed. (1991).

[145] *Responses to Victimization* (1978).

[146] *Prosser and Keeton on the Law of Torts*, 5th ed. (1984), p. 47. See Trindade, "The Modern Tort of False Imprisonment" in *Torts in the Nineties* (1997).

[147] *R. v. Governor of Brockill Prison, Ex Parte Evans (No. 2)*, [2000] 4 All E.R. 15 (H.L.), at p. 20 (*per* Lord Steyn).

another person's way is insufficient if another route can be taken.[148] One, however, can be imprisoned in a room,[149] in an automobile,[150] or in a boat set adrift on the water.[151]

The restraint is not total if there is a reasonable means of escape left open to plaintiffs. If shut in a room from which they can easily exit without danger, there is no imprisonment, even if they must commit a minor trespass to escape.[152] If a person must leap into the sea or jump out of a speeding car to be free, however, the restraint is considered to be complete.[153]

Restraint may be accomplished by direct force or by the threat of force to which the plaintiff submits.[154] A plaintiff, who reasonably perceives that force may be employed is imprisoned if deciding to submit and not to risk violence.[155] It will also be an imprisonment if the plaintiff goes along with another, in a suspected shoplifting case for example, in order to avoid a "scene which would be embarrassing".[156] This has been described as a type of psychological imprisonment,[157] but it is as real as if one were physically overpowered. It is also possible to confine someone by retaining control of that person's valuable property,[158] or perhaps even by holding hostage someone's child or a beloved pet.[159] If, as a result of the defendant's intentional conduct, a person reasonably feels totally restrained, however that result is obtained, it amounts to an imprisonment and is actionable unless it is justifiable.

It was once thought that a touch was required for an arrest,[160] but this is no longer the case.[161] The key today is whether there has been an assertion of and submission to control. If a police officer shouts at someone, "You are under arrest!", and that person refuses to submit and runs off, there has been no arrest. This may be so even if that person feigns submission in order to facilitate a

---

[148] *Bird v. Jones* (1845), 7 Q.B. 742, 115 E.R. 668.
[149] *Meering v. Grahame-White Aviation Co. Ltd.* (1919), 122 L.T. 44 (C.A.).
[150] *Burton v. Davies*, [1953] Q.S.R. 26; *Jacobson v. Sorenson* (1931), 183 Minn. 425, 236 N.W. 922.
[151] *R. v. Macquarrie and Budge* (1875), 13 N.S.W.S.C.R. 264.
[152] *Wright v. Wilson* (1699), 1 Ld. Raym. 739, 91 E.R. 1394; *Restatement, Torts, Second*, §36, comment A.
[153] See *Whittaker v. Sanford* (1912), 110 Me. 77, 85 A. 399.
[154] *Martin v. Houck* (1906), 141 N.C. 317, 54 S.E. 295; *Prosser and Keeton, op. cit. supra*, n. 146, at p. 49.
[155] *Lebrun v. High-Low Foods Ltd.* (1968), 69 D.L.R. (2d) 433 (B.C.); *Bahner v. Marwest Hotel Co.* (1969), 6 D.L.R. (3d) 322; affd (1970), 12 D.L.R. (3d) 646 (B.C.C.A.).
[156] *Campbell v. S.S. Kresge Co. Ltd.* (1979), 74 D.L.R. (3d) 717, at p. 719 (N.S.) (*per* Hart J.); *Sinclair v. Woodward's Store Ltd.*, [1942] 2 D.L.R. 395 (B.C.); *Conn v. David Spencer Ltd.*, [1930] 1 D.L.R. 805 (B.C.).
[157] *Chaytor v. London, New York and Paris Assoc. of Fashion Ltd.* (1961), 30 D.L.R. (2d) 527 (Nfld.).
[158] *Ashland Dry Goods v. Wages* (1946), 302 Ky. 577, 195 S.W. 2d 312, purse.
[159] *Cf., Herring v. Boyle* (1834), 1 Cr. M. & R. 377; 149 E.R. 1126 (N.P.).
[160] *Russen v. Lucas* (1824), 1 C. & P. 153, 171 E.R. 1141 (N.P.); *Genner v. Sparks* (1704), 1 Salk. 79, 87 E.R. 928.
[161] *Warner v. Riddiford* (1858), 4 C.B.N.S. 180, 140 E.R. 1052.

getaway. There is a criminal law decision to the effect that, when a police officer grabs someone, who then shakes the officer off, an arrest has been completed.[162] Although such a principle might be helpful in the criminal law context, it is preferable to refuse to extend it into tort law, where damages should be payable only if there has been a restraint that is more than a fleeting one.

It is not necessary for a plaintiff to be conscious of confinement in order to be imprisoned. Like battery and unlike assault, the interest in freedom from restraint is so prized that it is protected even when the plaintiff is unaware of being interfered with.[163] In the case of *Meering v. Grahame-White Aviation Co. Ltd.*, Lord Justice Atkin explained:

> [a person could be] imprisoned without his knowing it. I think a person can be imprisoned while he is asleep, while he is in a state of drunkenness, while he is unconscious, and while he is a lunatic. . . . So a man might in fact . . . be imprisoned by having the key of a door turned against him so that he is imprisoned in a room in fact although he does not know that the key has been turned.[164]

The House of Lords recently reaffirmed this principle in *Murray v. Ministry of Defence*[165] where Lord Griffiths declared:

> The law attaches supreme importance to the liberty of the individual and if he suffers a wrongful interference with that liberty it should remain actionable even without proof of special damage . . . [that is, awareness of the imprisonment.]

Such a principle should serve to protect from unlawful confinements, vulnerable people such as small children and the mentally disabled, who might be unable to demonstrate the requisite awareness. It would also render civilly accountable all those who choose to confine others because the conduct is equally unacceptable whether the victim is aware of it or not.

Confinement can be caused not only by positive conduct but also by the failure to act. To neglect to free a prisoner at the end of a term in jail, for example, can amount to imprisonment.[166] If a prisoner is held in a cell under intolerable conditions, however, this may amount to negligence but not false imprisonment since the conditions of his confinement cannot alter the nature of his confinement and he has no liberty capable of false imprisonment.[167] However, if a prisoner is placed in solitary confinement without justification, this deprivation

---

[162] *R. v. Whitfield*, [1970] S.C.R. 46.

[163] Prosser, "False Imprisonment — Consciousness of Confinement" (1955), 55 Colum. L. Rev. 847.

[164] (1919), 122 L.T. 44, at p. 53 (C.A.), *cf.*, *Herring v. Boyle, supra*, n. 159, *dictum*; see also, *Restatement, Torts, Second*, §35, where compromise reached, to the effect that consciousness is required, unless harm results.

[165] [1988] 2 All E.R. 521, at p. 529 (H.L.), dictum since plaintiff aware.

[166] *Morriss v. Winter*, [1930] 1 K.B. 243; *R. v. Governor of Brockill Prison, ex parte Evans (No. 2)*, [1998] 4 All E.R. 993 (C.A.).

[167] See *Hague v. Deputy Governor of Parkhurst Prison: Weldon v. Home Office*, [1991] 3 All E.R. 733, [1991] 3 W.L.R. 3 (H.L.).

of "residual liberty" can be actionable, as it is a "prison within a prison".[168] If someone goes on board a ship expecting to go ashore at the end of the journey, the refusal to release the person as agreed will amount to an imprisonment.[169] If, however, a person enters into a situation of confinement on certain understood terms, that person cannot insist on being released whenever so choosing. Consequently, a miner cannot demand to be hauled to the surface before the expiry of the work day,[170] a passenger cannot expect to leave a train at a stop signal between stations,[171] and a person who uses a ferry dock under posted conditions which require the payment of the fare before leaving, cannot complain when restrained until paying.[172] In the same way, one might be taken to have agreed to be detained in order to undergo a search at an airport or at a discount store, if that is the normal procedure or if a reasonable notice to that effect is posted.

This does not mean that imprisonment can be used as a method of enforcing a civil debt. An innkeeper cannot detain someone for non-payment of an account,[173] nor can a restauranteur hold someone in custody in order to force payment of a disputed bill,[174] or even, for that matter, a clearly legitimate account. In such situations, creditors should resort to the civil courts for their remedies, or even to criminal prosecution if it is warranted. They must not take the law into their own hands by arresting or by ordering a police officer to make an arrest.[175] In some circumstances a citizen's arrest is permitted, but if there is an excess of force used, liability will be imposed.[176]

1. MALICIOUS PROSECUTION

One must also take care not to institute a groundless prosecution deliberately, for if one does one may be rendered tortiously liable for malicious prosecution, which involves the use of the agency of the criminal process, rather than the exercise of direct physical control, to cause the imprisonment of another. The tort of malicious prosecution, though closely related to false imprisonment, is somewhat different, requiring the presence of four elements. First, criminal

---

[168] *Hill v. British Columbia* (1997), 38 C.C.L.T. (2d) 182, at p. 188 (B.C.C.A.) (*per* Newbury J.A.).

[169] *Whittaker v. Sanford* (1912), 110 Me. 77, 85 A. 399.

[170] *Herd v. Weardale Steel, Coal & Coke Co. Ltd.*, [1915] A.C. 67; see also *Burns v. Johnston*, [1916] 2 I.R. 144; affd [1917] 2 I.R. 137; See Amos, "Contractual Restraint of Liberty" (1928), 44 L.Q. Rev. 464.

[171] Fleming, *The Law of Torts*, 9th ed. (1998), p. 35; *Martin v. Berends*, [1989] O.J. No. 2644, refusal to let person off bus not imprisonment.

[172] *Balmain New Ferry Co. Ltd. v. Robertson* (1906), 4 C.L.R. 379; affd [1910] A.C. 295 (P.C.). See *contra*, Tan, "A Misconceived Issue in the Tort of False Imprisonment" (1981), 44 Mod. L. Rev. 166.

[173] *Sunbolf v. Alford* (1838), 3 M. & W. 248, 150 E.R. 1135.

[174] *Bahner v. Marwest Hotel Co.*, *supra*, n. 151; *Perry v. Fried* (1972), 32 D.L.R. (3d) 589 (N.S.S.C.).

[175] Poirier, "Economic Analysis of False Imprisonment in Canada: A Statistical and Empirical Study" (1985), 34 U.N.B.L.J. 104.

[176] *Briggs v. Laviolette* (1994), 21 C.C.L.T. (2d) 105 (B.C.S.C.).

proceedings must have been instituted by the defendant against the plaintiff; second, those proceedings must have been concluded favourably to the plaintiff; third, there must have been a lack of reasonable and probable cause for the defendant's conduct, and fourth, there must have been an improper purpose underlying the defendant's conduct, not an honest belief in guilt.[177]

False imprisonment and malicious prosecution are available against the Attorney General or Crown prosecutors who are not immune from tort liability in respect of their prosecutorial functions.[178] A malicious failure to prosecute may even be actionable.[179]

There are other tort actions available for interference with the judicial process, such as abuse of process,[180] maintenance and champerty[181] and spoliation,[182] but they are beyond the scope of this book.[183]

E. Intentional Infliction of Mental Suffering

Anyone who intentionally causes another person severe mental suffering may be liable in tort.[184] This basis of liability, which was established relatively recently, is not the progeny of the trespass action, but a descendant of the action on the case. Consequently, it is not actionable without proof of actual harm. There must be a "visible and provable illness" resulting from the conduct of the defendant.[185]

It will be recalled that the assault action was deficient in that a wrongdoer might frighten another person out of his wits without incurring tort liability, as long as the wrongdoer did not arouse apprehension of immediate harmful or offensive contact. It was no credit to tort law that one would not be civilly liable for threatening to chop another person up into little pieces in the future, even though this caused the plaintiff severe emotional distress. The courts, because of

---

[177] See Fleming, *op. cit. supra*, n. 171, pp. 579 *et seq.*; *Prosser and* Keeton, *op. cit. supra*, n. 146, at p. 870. See also *Nelles v. Ontario* (1989), 60 D.L.R. (4th) 609 (S.C.C.); *Hinde v. Skibinski* (1994), 21 C.C.L.T. (2d) 314 (Ont. Gen. Div.) (*per* Lederman J.).

[178] *Nelles, supra*, n. 178. See also *Proulx v. Quebec (A.G.)*, 2001 S.C.C. 66, 2001 S.C.J. No. 65, 2001 Can. Sup. Ct. LEXIS 70. See Klar, *Tort Law*, 2nd ed. (1996), p. 55.

[179] *P.(K.) v. Desrochers,* [2000] 5 C.C.L.T. (3d) 24 (Ont. S.C.J.) (*per* MacKinnon J.).

[180] See Irvine, The "Resurrection of Tortious Abuse of Process" (1989), 47 C.C.L.T. 217; see also *Canadian Pacific International Freight Services Ltd. v. Starber International Inc.* (1992), 12 C.C.L.T. (2d) 321 (Ont. Gen. Div.) for good outline of the tort.

[181] See Klar, *op.cit. supra*, n. 178, at p. 61.

[182] See *Spasic Estate v. Imperial Tobacco Ltd.* (2000), 2 C.C.L.T. (3d) 43 (Ont. C.A.), action not struck out by Borins J.A.; see Sommers and Siebert, "Intentional Destruction of Evidence: Why Procedural Rules are Insufficient" (1999), 78 C.B.R. 38; but see *Endean v. Canadian Red Cross Society* (1998), 42 C.C.L.T. (2d) 222 (B.C.C.A.), no such tort.

[183] See generally Klar, *op.cit. supra*, n. 178, at p. 59 *et ff.*

[184] See Prosser, "Insult and Outrage" (1956), 44 Calif. L. Rev. 40; Glasbeek, "Outraged Dignity: Do We Need a New Tort?" (1968), 6 Alta L. Rev. 77; Handford, "Tort Liability for Threatening or Insulting Words" (1976), 54 Can. Bar Rev. 563.

[185] See *Frame v. Smith*, [1987] 2 S.C.R. 99, at p. 128 (*per* Wilson J.); but see, *contra,* Molloy J. in *Tran v. Financial Debt Recovery Ltd.* (2000), 2 C.C.L.T. (3d) 270 (Ont. S.C.J.), at p. 283, "emotional harm" enough, need not be "psychiatric condition" to be compensable.

their fear of false claims and the difficulties of proving mental suffering, limited the scope of the assault action and were reluctant to expand the protection afforded thereby.

That bleak period in the history of tort law was abruptly ended in 1897 with *Wilkinson v. Downton.*[186] As a practical joke, the defendant told the plaintiff that her husband had been hurt in an accident and needed her help. As a result the plaintiff suffered shock, entailing weeks of incapacity. On a deceit theory, there was no legal problem in allowing tort recovery for the cost of the railway fare she had spent to send people to the assistance of her husband because that was financial harm. Her claim for the resulting nervous shock, however, was without legal precedent.[187] That did not prevent Mr. Justice Wright from awarding damages. The court's legitimate concern about false claims had to be set aside when the conduct of the defendant was "plainly calculated to produce some effect of the kind which was produced".[188] His Lordship offered another example of a situation in which he thought tort liability should result; if a person who is seriously ill is told, wrongly, that his doctor has said that he has only one day to live, and the shock causes the person's death, the person who informed him incorrectly should be responsible. Such flagrant cases as these clearly demanded a remedy, and tort law responded.

There are other situations of liability for intentional conduct causing severe emotional distress. The American cases,[189] which are much more numerous than the Canadian and Commonwealth ones, have drawn a line between mere insult, which is not actionable, and "extreme and outrageous" conduct, which is.[190] The latter type of conduct is not only more reprehensible, and therefore more deserving of sanction, but there is also a greater likelihood that the mental suffering is not feigned in such a case. Hence, where someone posed as a military police officer and accused a foreign person of corresponding with a German spy during World War I, recovery was allowed.[191] Similarly, flagrant conduct such as spreading a false rumour that the plaintiff's son had hanged himself,[192] or beating a man in the presence of his wife,[193] or doing an unauthorized autopsy on a spouse's body[194] would attract liability. So too, a finance company which bombards one of its debtors who is ill (to the company's

---

[186] [1897] 2 Q.B. 57.

[187] See *infra*, Chapter 11.

[188] *Wilkinson v. Downton*, [1897] 2 Q.B. 57, at p. 59.

[189] Now subject to constitutional protection if statements not malicious, see *Falwell v. Hustler* (1988), 485 U.S. 46 (S.C. U.S.); *Dworkin v. Hustler* (1989), 567 F. (2d) 1188.

[190] *Restatement, Torts, Second*, §46; Magruder, "Mental and Emotional Disturbance in the Law of Torts" (1936), 49 Harv. L. Rev. 1033; Giveler (1982), 82 Colum. L. Rev. 42; see McLachlin J. in *Rahemtulla v. Vanfed Credit Union* (1984), 29 C.C.L.T. 78, at p. 94 (B.C.S.C.), adopting this distinction in a brutal firing case. See also *Frame v. Smith, supra*, n. 175, at p. 127 (*per* Wilson J.), family situation.

[191] *Janvier v. Sweeney*, [1919] 2 K.B. 316 (C.A.).

[192] *Bielitski v. Obadiak*, (1922), 65 D.L.R. 627 (Sask. C.A.).

[193] *Purdy v. Woznesensky*, [1937] 2 W.W.R. 116 (Sask. C.A.).

[194] *Edmonds v. Armstrong Funeral Home Ltd.*, [1931] 1 D.L.R. 676 (Alta. C.A.).

knowledge) with offensive and threatening letters may be required to compensate for the mental suffering so caused.[195] If a government erroneously informs a woman that her husband has been placed in a mental health facility, damages are payable, even where malice is absent.[196] If a husband tells his wife that he is homosexual, causing her to worry about exposure to AIDS, he may be liable on this theory and others.[197] Cases of government customs officers harassing yacht owners[198] and R.C.M.P. officers harassing a female fellow officer[199] have led to damage awards against the Crown on this theory. A newspaper that contravenes a press ban and identifies a victim of sexual abuse can be held liable in damages, but the theory underlying this is the statutory violation.[200]

Not every insult hurled will yield tort liability. The courts cannot protect us from every practical joke or unkind comment. It is not yet tortious to embarrass or to swear at another person, even if it upsets that person.[201] Free speech requires that individuals be permitted to express unflattering opinions about one another. It is better for humans to develop tougher hides than to seek damages for every insult. Besides, no court would believe a claimant who alleged psychiatric damage from being sworn at by the defendant, at least without evidence of aggravated circumstances. Consequently, to invite a person to engage in sexual intercourse is not normally actionable,[202] because apparently, tort law took the view that "there is no harm in asking".[203] As humiliating as this may be to a plaintiff, the courts have not felt that such conduct was sufficiently outrageous to warrant tort liability. If the circumstances are aggravated, however, damages may be forthcoming, as where the plaintiff is married, to the knowledge of the defendant, and the invitations are persistent and accompanied by abuse and threats.[204] Similarly, if such an illicit invitation were issued to a particularly vulnerable person, such as a child, an older person, or perhaps to a pregnant woman, it might well be actionable.[205] The quality of outrageousness

---

[195] *Clark v. Associated Retail Credit* (1939) 105 Fed. 2d 62 (U.S.C.A.D.C.); see also *Robbins v. C.B.C.*, [1985] Que. S.C. 152; *Timmermans v. Buelow* (1984), 38 C.C.L.T. 136 (Ont. H.C.), landlord threatened "fragile" tenant; *cf.*, *Hasenclever v. Hoskins* (1988), 47 C.C.L.T. 225 (Ont. Div. Ct.), harrassing telephone calls, not enough in circumstances.

[196] *Barnes v. Commonwealth* (1937), 37 S.R.N.S.W. 511; see *infra*, Chapter 11.

[197] *Bell-Ginsburg v. Ginsburg* (1993), 17 C.C.L.T. (2d) 167 (Ont. Gen. Div.) (*per* Rosenberg J.).

[198] *Rollinson v. Canada* (1994), 20 C.C.L.T. (2d) 92 (F.C.T.D.) (*per* Muldoon J.).

[199] *Clark v. Canada* (1994), 20 C.C.L.T. (2d) 241 (F.C.T.D) (*per* Dubé J.).

[200] *C. (P.R.) v. Canadian Newspaper Co.* (1993), 16 C.C.L.T. (2d) 275 (B.C.S.C.); *R. (L.) v. Nyp* (1993), 16 C.C.L.T. (2d) 281 (Ont. Gen. Div.); *cf. Cox Broadcasting v. Cohn* (1975), 420 U.S. 469 (U.S.S.C.), privacy theory, no liability on constitutional grounds.

[201] *Brooker v. Silverthorne* (1919), 99 S.E. 350, South Carolina, swearing and threats; carriers and innkeepers in the United States are held to higher standards, however, see Prosser, *supra*, n. 174, at p. 54.

[202] Magruder, *supra*, n. 190, at p. 1055.

[203] *Ibid.* Nowadays, of course, the sexual harrassment remedy in human rights legislation is available to victims of this unacceptable type of conduct in some situations.

[204] *Samms v. Eccles* (1961), Utah 2d 289, 358 P. 2d 344; Prosser, *supra*, n. 184, at p. 56.

[205] Prosser, *supra*, n. 184, p. 58. Racial insults may be actionable, see *Contreras v. Crown-Zellerbach* (1977), 565 P. 2d 1173 (Wash.); Delgado, "Words That Wound: A Tort Action for

might also be based on the special position of authority of the defendant. If a landlord,[206] a police officer, or a school principal uttered insults or threats to someone over whose future well-being they had some control, these acts might be considered beyond the bounds of decency, and consequently actionable.[207]

Sometimes courts require a substantial degree of self-possession. A defendant who announced that he was going to shoot someone, and then went into a neighbouring room and fired a revolver, was held not liable to the plaintiff, who overheard these threats and was taken ill.[208] It is hard to believe that similar conduct would not be actionable in Canada today, for it is almost certain to cause distress to any normal witness and is without any social utility whatsoever. The courts have also refused to extend this action into the family law area where it might serve as a "weapon for spouses . . . to injure one another", with hurtful effects on the children.[209]

F. Privacy

Although the right to privacy is well-entrenched in American tort law,[210] the Canadian and English courts have been reluctant to recognize a separate right to privacy.[211] Even the great innovator Denning M.R. has declared, "[W]e have as yet no general remedy for infringement of privacy."[212] This statement may not be as accurate as it once was. At least one Canadian court has recognized a general right to privacy.[213] Several trial judges have refused to dismiss actions for the invasion of privacy at the pleading stage on the ground that it has not been shown that our courts will not create a right to privacy.[214] Recently Chief Justice

---

Racial Insults, Epithets and Name-calling" (1982), 17 Harv. C.R.-C.L. L. Rev. 133. See also *Timmermans v. Buelow, supra,* n. 195.

[206] *Stevenson v. Bagham,* [1922] N.Z.L.R. 225, threat to burn house down.

[207] Prosser, *supra,* n. 184, at p. 56.

[208] *Bunyan v. Jordan* (1937), 57 C.L.R. 1 (H.C. Aus.).

[209] *Frame v. Smith, supra,* n. 185, at p. 129.

[210] *Nader v. G.M.* (1970), 307 N.Y.S. 2d 647.

[211] Winfield, "The Right to Privacy" (1931), 47 L.Q. Rev. 23; Gibson (ed.), *Aspects of Privacy Law* (1980); Gibson, "Common Law Protection of Privacy: What To Do Until the Legislators Arrive" in Klar (ed.), *Studies in Canadian Tort Law* (Toronto: Butterworths, 1977); Burns, "The Law and Privacy: The Canadian Experience" (1976), 54 Can. Bar Rev. 1; Todd, "Protection of Privacy" in Mullany, *Torts in the Nineties* (Sydney: LBC Information Services, 1997).

[212] *Re X,* [1975] 1 All E.R. 697, at p. 704 (C.A.). See also *Bingo Enterprises Ltd. et al. v. Plaxton et al.* (1986), 26 D.L.R. (4th) 604, at p. 608 (Man. Q.B.) (*per* Barkman C.J.M.), "the tort of violation of privacy in regard to disclosure of private information has not been recognized in Canada". affd 41 Man. R. (2d) 19 (C.A.). Leave to appeal to S.C.C. refused December 8, 1986, 46 Man. R. (2d) 160*n*.

[213] *Roth v. Roth* (1991), 4 O.R. (3d) 740 (Ont. Gen. Div.) (*per* Mandel J.); see also *Lipiec v. Borsa* (1996), 31 C.C.L.T. (2d) 294 (Ont. Gen. Div.).

[214] *Krouse v. Chrysler Canada Ltd.* [1970] 3 O.R. 135 (H.C.) (*per* Parker J.); *Burnett v. Canada* (1979), 94 D.L.R. (3d) 281 (Ont. S.C.) (*per* Driscoll J.); *Capan v. Capan* (1980), 14 C.C.L.T. 191 (Ont. S.C.) (*per* Osler J.). In *Saccone v. Orr* (1981), 34 O.R. (2d) 317 (Co. Ct.), Jacob C.C.J. recognized a "right to privacy" where the defendant taped a private conversation and published it against the plaintiff's will.

Carruthers has stated "the Courts in Canada are not far from recognizing a common law right to privacy if they have not already done so".[215] Furthermore, courts have been willing to protect privacy interests under the rubric of nuisance law.[216] We seem to be drifting closer to the American model.[217]

In the United States, a separate right to privacy has existed for many years.[218] Dean Prosser has argued that privacy is not one tort, but a complex of four: (1) intrusion on the plaintiff's seclusion or private affairs; (2) public disclosure of embarrassing private facts about the plaintiff; (3) publicity that places the plaintiff in a false light in the public eye; and (4) appropriation of the plaintiff's name or likeness for the defendant's advantage.[219]

The first three types of privacy invasion have not found favour with Canadian courts,[220] but the fourth has, under the description of the tort of "appropriation of one's personality". In *Krouse v. Chrysler Canada Ltd.*,[221] an action photograph of a football game was used in some advertising material. The plaintiff could be identified as one of the players depicted in the photo. Because he had not consented to this use of his photo, he claimed damages. Mr. Justice Estey recognized that there was a tort of appropriation of one's personality, but he dismissed the claim because the usefulness of the player's name had not been diminished and, therefore, there had been no infringement of the player's legal right.[222] In a similar case, where a photograph of the plaintiff waterskiing was used by the defendant to promote its business without the plaintiff's consent, damages of $500, the commercial value of the photo, were awarded.[223] Rather

---

[215] *Dyne Holdings Ltd. v. Royal Insurance Co. of Canada* (1966), 431 A.P.R. 318, at p. 334 (P.E.I. C.A.); leave to appeal to S.C.C. refused 148 Nfld. & P.E.I.R. 359*n*.

[216] *Motherwell v. Motherwell* (1976), 73 D.L.R. (3d) 62 (Alta. C.A.); *Pateman et al. v. Ross* (1988), 68 Man. R. (2d) 181 (Q.B.); *cf.*, *Hasenclever v. Hoskins* (1988), 47 C.C.L.T. 225 (Ont. Div. Ct.).

[217] Irvine, "The Invasion of Privacy in Ontario — A 1983 Survey", Law Society of Upper Canada, Special Lectures, *Torts in the 80's* (1983).

[218] See Warren and Brandeis, "The Right To Privacy" (1980), 4 Harv. L. Rev. 193.

[219] See Prosser, "Privacy" (1960), 48 Calif. L. Rev. 383; *cf.*, Bloustein, "Privacy As An Aspect of Human Dignity: An Answer to Dean Prosser" (1964), 39 N.Y.U. L.J. 962. See also Fried, "Privacy" (1968), 77 Yale L. Rev. 475; Kalven, "Privacy in Tort Law — Were Warren and Brandeis Wrong?" (1966), 31 Law & Contemp. Probs. 325.

[220] The tort of "false light invasion of privacy", which exists in the United States, was rejected in Manitoba, see *Parasuik v. Canadian Newspapers Co.* (1988), 53 Man. R. (2d) 78 (Q.B.).

[221] [1974] 1 O.R. 225 (C.A.); revg. [1972] 2 O.R. 133 (H.C.).

[222] In *Gould Estate v. Stoddart Publishing Co.* (1996), 30 O.R. (3d) 520, Lederman J. of the Ontario Court General Division dismissed a claim for appropriation of personality on the basis of a "sales vs. subject" distinction, finding that Glenn Gould's personality was not being used for the purpose of "commercial exploitation" but rather to respond to " . . . public interest in knowing more about one of Canada's musical geniuses". Affd (1998), 39 O.R. (3d) 545 (C.A.); leave to appeal refused (1999), 82 C.P.R. (3d) vi (S.C.C.).

[223] See *Athans v. Canadian Adventure Camps Ltd.* (1977), 4 C.C.L.T. 20 (Ont. H.C.) (*per* Henry J.); *cf. Gould Estate v. Stoddart Publishing Co.* (1998), 43 C.C.L.T. (2d) 1 (Ont. C.A.), no liability for printing photo in book.

than this being an invasion of privacy, it has been suggested that it is a form of "publicity piracy".[224]

Various aspects of the right to privacy have been protected in Canada and the Commonwealth under different legal theories, such as trespass, contract and defamation.[225] In Quebec, Art, 1053 of the Civil Code (now 1457) was utilized to award damages to someone who was bothered by phone calls for three days.[226] The theory of "passing off" has been used to protect what might be considered an aspect of privacy.[227] In business situations, breach of confidence actions may be used.[228]

Legislation has been enacted in five provinces, making it a "tort, actionable without proof of damage, for a person, wilfully and without a claim of right, to violate the privacy of another".[229] In addition, the federal government has forbidden the interception of private communications by electronic or mechanical devices unless judicial authorization has been obtained.[230] Violators of this legislation may, *inter alia*, be required to pay punitive damages to the person aggrieved. Printing a photograph of a young offender in violation of legislation forbidding this permits courts to award damages.[231] There are other legislative provisions as well.[232]

Although legislative protection of privacy interests has not significantly advanced this area of the law, it has generated some activity. According to the courts, the nature and degree of privacy to which an individual is entitled is that

---

[224] See Gibson, "A Comment on *Athans v. Canadian Adventure Camps Ltd.*" (1977), 4 C.C.L.T. 37, at p. 42.

[225] See, for example, *Green v. Minnes* (1892), 22 O.R. 177 (C.A.) and see Gibson, *supra*, n. 224.

[226] See *Robbins v. C.B.C. (Que.)* (1957), 12 D.L.R. (2d) 24 (Que. S.C.). See also *Aubry v. Editions Vice Versa Inc.* (1998), 45 C.C.L.T. (2d) 119 (S.C.C.), photo printed without consent.

[227] See *Lord Byron v. Johnston* (1816), 2 Mer. 29; *cf.*, *Clark v. Freeman* (1848), 11 Beav. 112, 50 E.R. 759; *Dackrell v. Dougall* (1899), 80 T.R. 556. See also *Sim v. J.H. Heinz Co. Ltd.*, [1959] 1 W.L.R. 313 (C.A.); Mathieson, "Comment" (1961), 39 Can. Bar Rev. 409.

[228] *Pharand Ski Corp. v. Alberta* (1991), 7 C.C.L.T. (2d) 225 (Alta. Q.C.), relying on *International Corona Resources Ltd. v. L.A.C. Minerals Ltd.*, [1989] 2 S.C.R. 574.

[229] See Privacy Act, R.S.B.C. 1996, c. 373, s. 1(1); Privacy Act, R.S.S. 1978, c. P-24, s. 2; Privacy Act, R.S.M. 1987, c. P-125, s. 2(1); and Privacy Act, R.S.N. 1990, c. P-22, s. 3. Violation must be wilful, *Hollinsworth v. BCTV* (1998), 44 C.C.L.T. (2d) 83 (B.C.C.A.).

[230] Manning, *The Protection of Privacy Act* (Toronto: Butterworths, 1974). See also Privacy Act, R.S.C. 1985, c. P-21.

[231] *F. (P.) v. Ontario* (1989), 47 C.C.L.T. 231 (Ont. Dist. Ct.); *F.(J.M.) v. Chappell* (1998), 41 C.C.L.T. (2d) 26 (B.C.C.A.).

[232] See, e.g., Consumer Reporting Act, R.S.O. 1990, c. C.33; Telephone Act, R.S.O. 1990, c. T-4, s. 112; Canada Post Corporation Act, R.S.C. 1985, c. C-10, s. 48 [rep. & sub. R.S.C. 1985, c. 1 (2nd Supp.), s. 172] forbidding interception of mail. See also Access to Information Act, R.S.C. 1985, c. A-1; Freedom of Information and Protection of Privacy Act, R.S.B.C. 1996, c. 165; Freedom of Information and Protection of Privacy Act, S.C. 1994, c. F-18.5; The Freedom of Information and Protection of Privacy Act, S.M. 1997, c. 50 (C.C.S.M., c. F175); Freedom of Information and Protection of Privacy Act, R.S.O. 1990, c. F.31; Act respecting Access to Documents held by Public Bodies and the Protection of Personal Information, R.S.Q., c. A-2.1; Right to Information Act, S.N.B. 1978, c. R-10.3; Freedom of Information and Protection of Privacy Act, S.N.S. 1993, c. 5; Freedom of Information Act, R.S.N. 1990, c. F-25.

which is "reasonable in the circumstances, due regard being given to the lawful interests of others".[233] Therefore, the actions of a "peeping Tom"[234] and a person listening to and recording a telephone conversation with the consent of only one of the participants[235] may be violations of privacy, though the inadvertent showing of a topless photo[236] and the publication of a list that identifies a person as a carrier of a communicable disease for internal hospital use[237] are not.

A potential catalyst for further movement in this area is the Canadian Charter of Rights and Freedoms. An earlier draft of the Charter had expressly recognized a "right to be secure against arbitrary invasion of privacy" along the lines of the International Declaration of Human Rights, but this was not included in the final draft of the Charter. There are two sections, however, that lend weight, albeit imperfectly, to a right of privacy. Section 7, which guarantees the right to "life, liberty and security of the person", according to one scholar is "only meaningfully guaranteed if privacy is an implicit condition in the grant of such rights".[238] In *R. v. O'Connor*,[239] L'Heureux-Dubé J. acknowledged this logic by stating that the Supreme Court of Canada " . . . has on many occasions recognized the great value of privacy in our society. It has expressed sympathy for the proposition that section 7 of the Charter includes a right to privacy."[240] More directly, the purpose of section 8, which guarantees the right to be secure against unreasonable search and seizure, is to protect individuals from unjustified " . . . intrusions upon their privacy".[241] In *R. v. Dyment*,[242] La Forest J. wrote that " . . . privacy is essential for the well-being of the individual. For this reason alone, it is worthy of constitutional protection." Despite the importance of privacy, its constitutional protection has been generally limited to criminal and quasi-criminal contexts in which the threat to privacy is state-sanctioned.[243] The Supreme Court has also expounded upon the relevance of constitutional

---

[233] *Davis v. McArthur* (1970), 10 D.L.R. (3d) 250 (B.C.S.C.); revd [1971] 2 W.W.R. 142, 17 D.L.R. (3d) 760 (B.C.C.A.). In the words of the Manitoba Court of Appeal, the invasion of privacy must be "substantial", *Bingo Enterprises Ltd.*, *supra*, n. 212, at p. 612.

[234] *Lee v. Jacobson* (1994), 120 D.L.R. (4th) 155 (B.C.C.A.), no actual finding of invasion of privacy was made in this case as a new trial was ordered because of factual errors made by the trial judge.

[235] *Ferguson v. McBee Technographics Inc.*, [1989] 2 W.W.R. 499 (Man. Q.B.), Jewers J. refused to accept the Criminal Code's requirement that only one person consent to the interception as a defence to the civil action for violation of privacy under the Manitoba Privacy Act.

[236] *Milton v. Savinkoff* (1993), 18 C.C.L.T. (2d) 288 (B.S.C.S.).

[237] *Peters-Brown v. Regina District Health Board.* (1995), 26 C.C.L.T. (2d) 316 (Sask. Q.B.); affd (1996), 31 C.C.L.T. (2d) 302 (Sask. C.A.).

[238] Cohen, "Invasion of Privacy: Police and Electronic Surveillance in Canada" (1992), 27 McGill L.J. 619, at p. 665.

[239] [1995] 4 S.C.R. 411, at p. 482.

[240] See, for example, *R. v. Mills*, [1986] 1 S.C.R. 863, at 919-20; and *R. v. Morgentaler*, [1988] 1 S.C.R. 30, at p. 55.

[241] *Hunter v. Southam*, [1984] 2 S.C.R. 154, at p. 160. For a discussion of privacy in the context of the Charter see Ehrcke, "Privacy and the Charter of Rights" (1985), 43 Adv. 53.

[242] [1988] 2 S.C.R. 417, at p. 427.

[243] *Ibid.*, at p. 431.

protection of privacy to the common law. In *Hill v. Church of Scientology of Toronto*,[244] a Charter challenge involving the tort of defamation, Cory J. wrote that " . . . reputation is intimately related to the right of privacy which has been accorded constitutional protection . . . the publication of defamatory comments constitutes an invasion of the individual's personal privacy and is an affront to that person's dignity". Additional encouragement to those advocating a right of privacy can be gleaned from Art. 5 of the Quebec Charter of Human Rights and Freedoms that provides that "every person has a right to respect for his private life".

The law of privacy has become a complex field with a voluminous literature that can only be touched on here.[245]

G. Damages: Compensatory, Aggravated and Punitive

The perpetrator of an intentional tort is liable to pay not only compensatory damages but also aggravated and/or punitive damages. There are now three different types of damages available in Canadian tort cases. The first is general or compensatory damages, which are meant to reimburse a victim of wrongdoing for any losses suffered, both pecuniary and non-pecuniary. The principles of damage assessment are to be found in works devoted to the subject.[246]

The second type is aggravated damages, which are also compensatory, but which may be awarded only in cases where a defendant's conduct has been "particularly high-handed or oppressive, thereby increasing the plaintiff's humiliation and anxiety".[247] To allow such damages there must be a finding that a defendant was "motivated by actual malice, which increased the injury to the plaintiff . . . by increasing the mental distress and humiliation of the plaintiff". Aggravated damages express the "natural indignation of right-thinking people arising from the malicious conduct of the defendant". Mr. Justice La Forest has recently explained[248] that "[a]ggravated damages may be awarded if the battery has occurred in humiliating or undignified circumstances". They are not awarded in addition to general damages, but are awarded as part of the general damages. The "aggravating features" are taken into account by the court and the award of general damages is increased accordingly. Although these types of

---

[244] [1995] 2 S.C.R. 1130 and 1179.

[245] See generally, Westin, *Privacy and Freedom* (1967); Miller, *The Assault on Privacy* (1971); Neill, "The Protection of Privacy" (1962), Mod. L. Rev. 393; Pedrick, "Publicity and Privacy: Is It Any of Our Business?" (1970), 20 U. of T. L.J. 391; Williams, "Invasion of Privacy" (1973), 11 Alta. L. Rev. 1; Ont. Law Reform Commission, *Report on Protection of Privacy in Ontario* (1968); Marshall, "The Right to Privacy: A Skeptical View" (1975), 21 McGill L.J. 242; Rankin, "Privacy & Technology: A Canadian Perspective" (1984), 22 Alta. L. Rev. 323.

[246] See Waddams, *The Law of Damages*, 3rd ed. (1997); Cooper-Stephenson and Saunders, *Personal Injury Damages in Canada*, 2nd ed. (1996); Cassels, *Remedies: The Law of Damages* (Irwin 2000).

[247] See *Hill v. Church of Scientology of Toronto*, [1995] 2 S.C.R. 1130, at pp. 1205-06 (*per* Cory J.).

[248] *Norberg v. Wynrib*, [1992] 2 S.C.R. 226, at pp. 263-64.

damages may overlap, they are distinguishable in that "punitive damages are designed to punish whereas aggravated damages are designed to compensate".

The third, punitive or exemplary damages, unlike general and aggravated damages, are not compensatory; their aim is "to punish" a defendant and to express "outrage at the egregious conduct of the defendant".[249] They are akin to a civil fine that is meant to "act as a deterrent to the defendant and to others from acting in this manner". Exemplary damages may be awarded only "where the combined award of general and aggravated damages would be insufficient to achieve the goal of punishment and deterrence". In addition, it is necessary for such an award to "serve a rational purpose"; that is, the Court must ask: "was the misconduct of the defendant so outrageous that punitive damages were rationally required to act as deterrence?"

Exemplary damages are necessary, for, according to Cory J.,[250] without them the wealthy and powerful might regard awards of general damages as a "licence fee" to continue harming "vulnerable victims". The most effective means of protection will be supplied by the knowledge that fines in the form of punitive damages may be awarded in cases where the defendant's conduct is truly "outrageous". In the words of La Forest J.[251] punitive or exemplary damages are "awarded to punish the defendant and to make an example of him or her in order to deter others". In short, punitive damages are meant to "teach a wrongdoer that tort does not pay".[252]

MacIntyre J.[253] has listed the adjectives describing the type of conduct that would warrant an award of punitive damages as "harsh, vindictive, reprehensible and malicious"; in other words, the conduct must be so "extreme in its nature and such that by any reasonable standard it is deserving of full condemnation and punishment". Cory J. has written[254] that the conduct has to be so "malicious, oppressive and high-handed that it offends the court's sense of decency". Other common words used to identify the conduct of the wrongdoer are "callous", "outrageous", "evil", "scandalous", "high-handed", and "wanton".[255]

The Canadian law relating to punitive or exemplary damages has diverged sharply from that of the United Kingdom in recent years. As MacIntyre J.

---

[249] See *Hill, supra*, n. 247, footnote 215, at pp. 1208-209. See generally Fridman, "Punitive Damages in Tort" (1970), 48 Can. Bar Rev. 373; Atrens, "Intentional Interference with the Person" in Linden (ed.), *Studies in Canadian Tort Law* (1968); Morris, "Punitive Damages in Tort Cases" (1931), 44 Harv. L. Rev. 1173; Cherniak and Morse, "Aggravated, Punitive and Exemplary Damages in Canada", Law Society of Upper Canada, Special Lectures, *Torts in the 80's* (1983); Ontario Law Reform Commission, *Report on Exemplary Damages* (1991), recommending retention and reform. This concept has been incorporated into Quebec law by Mr. Justice Rothman in *Papadatos v. Sutherland* (1987), 42 C.C.L.T. 184 (Que. C.A.), defendant "merited denunciation".

[250] See *ibid.*, at p. 1209.

[251] See *Norberg v. Wynrib*, [1992] 2 S.C.R. 226, at pp. 263-64.

[252] *Rookes v. Barnard*, [1964] A.C. 1129, at p. 1227 (H.L.) (*per* Lord Devlin).

[253] *Vorvis v. Insurance Corporation of British Columbia*, [1989] 1 S.C.R. 1085, at pp. 1107-108.

[254] See *Hill, supra*, n. 247, at p. 1208.

[255] See *Denison v. Fawcett*, [1958] O.R. 312, at p. 312 (C.A.).

pointed out in *Vorvis*,[256] the Courts of Australia, New Zealand and Canada have all "rejected" the narrower British approach as expressed in *Rookes v. Barnard*,[257] adopting instead a "wider scope for the application of punitive damages". The Ontario Law Reform Commission has encouraged this manifestation of independence in this country.[258] The law of Quebec also permits exemplary damages in appropriate situations.[259]

The standard of proof in punitive or exemplary damage cases is the civil standard of proof — on the balance of probabilities — not the criminal standard of proof — beyond a reasonable doubt. Nevertheless, an award of exemplary damages "should always receive the most careful consideration and the discretion to award them should be most cautiously exercised".[260] Furthermore, according to Wilson J., the quantum awarded should not be "excessive" but should be "reasonable", in keeping with the Canadian experience in the award of relatively modest punitive damages.[261]

In recent years, there have been many awards of punitive or exemplary damages made by Canadian courts. Most of the awards have been made in cases of intentional torts, such as battery,[262] rape,[263] assault and unlawful arrest,[264] trespass to land,[265] trespass to goods,[266] trespass to a ship,[267] abuse of

---

[256] *Supra*, n. 253, at p. 1105.

[257] [1964] A.C. 1129 (H.L.).

[258] See Ontario Law Reform Commission, "Report on Exemplary Damages" (Toronto: 1991).

[259] *Patenaude v. Roy* (1994), 26 C.C.L.T. (2d) 237 (Que. C.A.); leave to appeal to S.C.C. refused 187 N.R. 239n. See Pauline Roy, "les dommages exemplaires en droit québécois" (Doctoral Thesis, University of Montreal, 1996). Intentional wrongdoing needed, see *Augustus v. Gosset*, [1996] 3 S.C.R. 268.

[260] See MacIntyre J. in *Vorvis*, *supra*, n. 253, at pp. 1104-105.

[261] See *Vorvis*, *supra*, n. 253, at p. 1131. See also Schwartz in *Re MacDonald Estate* (1993), 89 Man. R. (2d) 161 (Q.B.); revd in part (1994), 95 Man. R. (2d) 123, at p. 149 (C.A.) — awards should "conform with the restraint that Canadian courts have exercised".

[262] *Norberg v. Wynrib*, *supra*, n. 251; *Karpow v. Shave*, [1975] 2 W.W.R. 159 (Alta. T.D.) (*per* D.C. McDonald J.), spectator attacking hockey player; *Delta Hotels v. Magrum* (1975), 59 D.L.R. (3d) 126 (B.C.S.C.).

[263] *W. v. Meah*, [1986] 1 All E.R. 935 (Q.B.); *Myers v. Haroldson* (1989), 48 C.C.L.T. 93 (Sask. Q.B.).

[264] *Basil v. Spratt* (1918), 44 O.L.R. 155 (C.A.); *Eagle Motors (1958) Ltd. v. Makaoff* (1970), 17 D.L.R. (3d) 222 (B.C.C.A.), false imprisonment.

[265] *Pollard v. Gibson* (1924), 55 O.L.R. 424 (C.A.); *Pafford v. Cavotti* (1928), 63 O.L.R. 171 (C.A.); *Patterson v. De Smit*, [1949] O.W.N. 338 (C.A.); *Carr-Harris v. Schacter*, [1956] O.R. 944 (H.C.); *Starkman v. Delhi Court Ltd.*, [1961] O.R. 467 (C.A.); *Cash & Carry Cleaners v. Delmas* (1973), 44 D.L.R. (3d) 315 (N.B.C.A.); *Townsview Properties Ltd. v. Sun Construction Equipment Co. Ltd.* (1974), 7 O.R. (2d) 666 (C.A.); *Austin v. Rescon Constn. (1984) Ltd.* (1987), 48 C.C.L.T. 64 (B.C.C.A.), profit taken into account in arriving at award; *Horseshoe Bay Retirement Society v. S.I.F. Development Corp.* (1990), 3 C.C.L.T. (2d) 75 (B.C.S.C.); *Nantel v. Parisien* (1981), 18 C.C.L.T. 79 (Ont. S.C.), landlord.

[266] *Owen and Smith (Trading as Nuagin Car Service) v. Reo Motors (Britain) Ltd.*, [1943] All E.R. Rep. 734 (C.A.); *Taylor v. Ginter* (1979), 108 D.L.R. (3d) 223 (B.C.S.C.).

[267] *Fleming v. Spracklin* (1921), 50 O.L.R. 289 (C.A.); *Mackay v. Canada Steamship Lines Ltd.* (1926), 29 O.W.N. 334.

process,[268] defamation,[269] conversion,[270] fraud,[271] breach of copyright[272] and patent infringement.[273] They have not been limited to intentional tort situations, however, but they may be awarded in contract cases,[274] fiduciary relationship cases,[275] charter violation cases,[276] and other situations where the court, in a civil case, feels that it is necessary to condemn the outrageous conduct of a defendant. It may be said that "the categories that describe the conduct that attracts an award of punitive damages are not closed".[277]

Although not normally awarded for negligent conduct,[278] a court may permit exemplary damages in a negligence case where the "negligence consisted in a course of conduct, deliberately undertaken and persisted in, which was directed solely against the plaintiff" by denying him appropriate medical care.[279] Exemplary damages were granted in a medical malpractice case, where the doctor showed callous disregard for his patient[280] and in a product liability case, where the defendant "merited condemnation".[281]

It is necessary for the court to assess the general damages and any aggravated damages before turning to the matter of punitive damages, because it cannot know until after that time whether the defendant's conduct is so outrageous that punitive damages are rationally required to act as a deterrent. In other words, punitive damages can be awarded only if the combined award of general and aggravated damages are thought to be insufficient to achieve the goal of deterrence.[282]

When a defendant has been convicted of a criminal offence and punished for it, the civil court is less likely to make an award of punitive damages because courts do not wish to punish a wrongdoer twice.[283] It depends, however, on the adequacy of the penalty imposed by the criminal court. In an appropriate case an

---

[268] *Flame Bar-B-Q Ltd. v. Hoar* (1979), 106 D.L.R. (3d) 438 (N.B.C.A.).
[269] *Ross v. Lamport*, [1975] O.R. 402 (C.A.); *Gillett v. Nissen Volkswagen Ltd.* (1975), 58 D.L.R. (3d) 103 (Alta. T.D.); *Hill*, *supra*, n. 247.
[270] *Grenn v. Brampton Poultry Co.* (1959), 18 D.L.R. (2d) 9 (Ont. C.A.).
[271] *McKenzie v. Bank of Montreal* (1975), 7 O.R. (2d) 521 (H.C.); affd 12 O.R. (2d) 719 (C.A.); *Barthropp v. West Vancouver* (1979), 17 B.C.L.R. 202, a municipality's arrogant failure to issue a building permit.
[272] *Pro Arts Inc. v. Campus Crafts Holdings Ltd.* (1980), 50 C.P.R. (2d) 230, at p. 250 (Ont. H.C.).
[273] *Lubrizol Corp. v. Imperial Oil Limited*, [1996] 3 F.C. 40 (C.A.).
[274] See *Vorvis*, *supra*, n. 253.
[275] See *Norberg v. Wynrib*, *supra*, n. 251 (*per* McLachlin J.); *Huff v. Price* (1990), 51 B.C.L.R. (2d) 282 (C.A.); *Re MacDonald Estate* (1994), 95 Man. R. (2d) 123 (C.A.).
[276] *Collin v. Lussier* (1983), 6 C.R.R. 89 (Fed. T.D.).
[277] See *R. (G.B.) v. Hollett* (1996), 30 C.C.L.T. (2d) 215 (N.S.C.A.) (*per* Pugsley J.A.); leave to appeal refused (1997), 145 D.L.R. (4th) vii.
[278] *Kaytor v. Lion's Driving Range Ltd.* (1962), 35 D.L.R. (2d) 426 (B.C.)
[279] *Robitaille v. Vancouver Hockey Club Ltd.* (1979), 19 B.C.L.R. 158 (*per* Esson J.); affd (1981), 16 C.C.L.T. 225 (B.C.C.A.).
[280] *Coughlin v. Kuntz* (1989), 2 C.C.L.T. (2d) 42 (B.C.C.A.).
[281] *Vlchek v. Koshel* (1988), 44 C.C.L.T. 314, at p. 320 (B.C.S.C.).
[282] See *Hill*, *supra*, n. 247, at p. 1208 (*per* Cory J.).
[283] *Willington v. Marshall* (1994), 21 C.C.L.T. (2d) 198 (Prowse J.) (B.C.S.C.).

award for punitive damages may be made, for example, against a robber who has been criminally punished, because a criminal conviction is not an absolute bar to punitive damages.[284] It is merely *one* of the factors to consider in deciding whether to award punitive damages and, of course, the amount thereof. It is uncommon, therefore, to see punitive damage awards in cases where there has been a criminal conviction, but it is not precluded.[285] In most of the cases, no punitive damage award has been made, as, for example, in *Loomis v. Rohan*,[286] a plaintiff was shot four times by the defendant and rendered a paraplegic, but no punitive damages were allowed because the defendant had been sent to prison for his conduct. Similarly, where a five-year-old child was brutally raped, no punitive damages were permitted because the defendant had already been jailed for the offence.[287]

It is possible to win punitive damages from a wrongdoer who has been convicted of a criminal offence if the wrongdoer obtains a conditional discharge since "there has been no conviction or punishment imposed upon the accused" and hence no "mitigating circumstances".[288] Punitive damages, however, will not be awarded against the estate of a wrongdoer who committed suicide after killing the deceased, because it is unlikely that others "similarly motivated might be intimidated by the imposition of punitive damages".[289] If the plaintiff provokes the assault, this may be taken into account in mitigation of the punitive damages awarded, but not the compensatory damages.[290] Such cases clearly demonstrate that there is a punitive element in awarding extra exemplary damages in these tort cases which supplements the work of the criminal law. Where the criminal process has been utilized, however, tort law usually withdraws, except to the extent of ordinary compensation.

Finally, it is possible to obtain punitive damages against the employer of someone who has personally been guilty of the outrageous conduct, for instance, where an employee of the Crown seduced the plaintiff while she was incarcerated in an institution for young women.[291] There must usually be some evidence

---

[284] *Joanisse v. Y. (D.)* (1995), 27 C.C.L.T. (2d) 278 (B.C.S.C.).

[285] *Willington v. Marshall, supra,* n. 283, Prowse J. refused to strike out claim for punitive damages in case of criminal conviction.

[286] (1974), 46 D.L.R. (3d) 423 (B.C.).

[287] *Radovskis v. Tomn* (1957), 9 D.L.R. (2d) 751 (Man.).

[288] *Loedel v. Eckert* (1977), 3 C.C.L.T. 145, at p. 151 (B.C.) (*per* Lander L.J.S.C.); *cf.,* when the action is brought by the father of the victim after a conditional discharge, *Kenmuir v. Huetzelmann* (1977), 3 C.C.L.T. 153 (B.C. Co. Ct.).

[289] *Breitkreutz v. Public Trustee* (1978), 6 C.C.L.T. 76, at p. 79 (*per* McClung J.); *cf., Flame Bar-B-Q v. Hoar* (1979), 106 D.L.R. (3d) 438, punitive damages awarded against estate of deceased accountant who abused the legal process in order to wreck a company.

[290] *Check v. Andrews Hotel Co. Ltd.* (1974), 56 D.L.R. (3d) 364 (Man. C.A.) (Matas J.A.); *Shaw v. Gorter* (1977), 2 C.C.L.T. 111 (Ont. C.A.); *Landry v. Patterson* (1978), 22 O.R. (2d) 335 (C.A.); *cf., Mason v. Sears* (1979), 31 N.S.R. (2d) 521; *Holt v. Verbruggen* (1981), 20 C.C.L.T. 29 (B.C.S.C.); *Hurley v. Moore* (1993), 18 C.C.L.T. (2d) 78 (Nfld. C.A.).

[291] *R. (G.B.) v. Hollett* (1996), 30 C.C.L.T. (2d) 215 (N.S.C.A.), Crown employee liable as well as Crown. Leave to appeal refused (1997), 145 D.L.R. (4th) vii.

of complicity or blameworthiness on the part of the employer, for there is no warrant to levy punitive damages against a truly innocent employer.[292]

---

[292] *Peeters v. Canada* (1993), 18 C.C.L.T. (2d) 136, at p. 147 (F.C.A.) (*per* MacGuigan J.A.), Crown liable for beating of inmate.

Chapter 3

Defences to the Intentional Torts

Conduct that would ordinarily result in liability for an intentional tort may be excused. There are a variety of reasons, sometimes called privileges, that might lead a court to absolve defendants from civil responsibility they would otherwise be required to bear. For example, individuals who consent to an invasion of one of their interests, will not be allowed by the courts to claim the protection of tort law. Similarly, those who act in self-defence or in defence of their property or another person may be relieved of tort liability. The defences of necessity and legal authority are also invoked by courts to justify damage intentionally inflicted. Here as elsewhere the courts must balance the interest being invaded and the interest being advanced by the conduct of the defendant. Needless to say, the solutions are not without difficulty. Moreover, the issues raised are often of considerable social importance.

This chapter will examine the main defences to intentional torts including consent, self-defence, defence of third persons, defence of property, necessity and legal authority.

A. Consent

If individuals consent to the intentional invasion of their interests, they will be precluded from recovering tort damages for any loss suffered as a result. Individuals are the masters of their own bodies and properties, and free to forego their rights if they choose to do so. Tort law will not force its protection on anyone who chooses to waive it. In part, this is a manifestation of the historic individualism of the common law which allows people to work out their own destiny even if they do so foolishly. Moreover, when defendants, as a class, are allowed to rely on consenting plaintiffs, this enlarges the freedom of plaintiffs, as a class, to order their own affairs by securing the co-operation of potential future defendants.[1] In other words, holding these defendants liable would inhibit them in future co-operative efforts with willing plaintiffs. Consent is

---

[1]   Mansfield, "Informed Choice in the Law of Torts" (1961), 22 La. L. Rev. 17.

based on "presumption of individual autonomy and free will. It is presumed that the individual has freedom to consent or not to consent."[2]

The defence of consent may also be justified in terms of economic efficiency. As Posner and Landes explain, consent "transforms coercion into a mutually desired and, therefore, a value maximizing transaction; it transforms the brawl into the boxing match".[3]

Consent may be either express or implied by conduct. An express consent may be given orally or in writing.[4] In determining whether there has been an express consent and what its scope has been, the normal contract principles apply.[5] It should be noted that a written consent is not the consent itself, but merely evidence of consent, which can be undermined with evidence of fraud, duress, lack of capacity, and other similar circumstances.[6] A valid consent can be given without uttering a word. For example, a person standing in a line of people being vaccinated and holding up an arm to be inoculated has indicated consent by behaviour. Unexpressed private feelings if not communicated do not govern, whereas the objective manifestation of consent does.[7] When people reasonably rely on such conduct by plaintiffs, they must be protected from tort liability.[8] But silence cannot normally be relied upon as a manifestation of consent, unless it is reasonable to do so. Thus, one who defiantly but silently stands one's ground after being threatened with a punch, cannot be taken to have consented to the blow.[9]

One may consent to certain invasions of bodily security by entering into situations where it is generally understood that one has waived one's right to remain free from bodily contact. One who participates in certain sports, for example, agrees to permit whatever bodily contact is allowed by the rules. Thus, a hockey player cannot complain about a body check, even a good stiff one, but might recover if hit in the face with a hockey stick by another player.[10] In the same way, those who play games in which opponents throw mud balls and lumps of clay at one another consent to being hit by one of these objects,[11] but

---

[2]   *Norberg v. Wynrib*, [1992] 2 S.C.R. 226, at p. 247 (*per* La Forest J.).

[3]   See Landes and Posner. "An Economic Theory of Intentional Torts", 1 Intl. Rev. of Law and Economics 127, at p. 143.

[4]   Rozovsky and Rozovsky, *The Canadian Law of Consent to Treatment*, (Toronto: Butterworths, 1990).

[5]   See *infra*, Chapter 13. If a notice is posted that may be a term of the agreement, see *Robinson v. Balmain New Ferry Co. Ltd.*, [1910] A.C. 295, voluntary assumption of risk.

[6]   See *Schwiezer v. Central Hospital* (1974), 6 O.R. (2d) 606.

[7]   *O'Brien v. Cunard Steamship Co.* (1891), 154 Mass. 272, 28 N.E. 266.

[8]   *Restatement, Torts, Second*, §50, someone asking for a kiss, receiving mixed signals.

[9]   *Prosser and Keeton on the Law of Torts*, 5th ed. (1984), p. 113.

[10] *Agar v. Canning* (1965), 54 W.W.R. 302; affd 55 W.W.R. 384 (Man. C.A.); See also *Martin v. Daigle* (1969), 6 D.L.R. (3d) 634 (N.B.C.A.); *Pettis v. McNeil* (1979), 8 C.C.L.T. 299 (N.S.). Criminal liability is also possible for outrageous attack with hockey stick as a weapon, see *R. v. McSorley*, [2000] B.C.J. No. 1993.

[11] *Wright v. McLean* (1956), 7 D.L.R. (2d) 253 (B.C.).

do not agree to rocks being thrown at them. One who enters a fist fight manifests a willingness to be punched, but not stabbed.[12]

Two recent cases are instructive. In *Matheson v. Governors of Dalhousie University*[13] a participant in a game of borden ball was injured when tackled during a game in which it had been agreed that there would be no bodily contact. Despite this, recovery was denied because the court was of the view that the incident was "not such an act to be considered 'unexpected, unusual, infrequent or out of the ordinary' during a game of borden ball as played at this institution and with which the plaintiff was familiar". In contrast is the case of *Colby v. Schmidt,*[14] where the plaintiff was struck in the jaw during a game of rugby some time after he had parted with the ball. Mr. Justice Oppal awarded damages and explained that the plaintiff had not consented to the "type of conduct and actions exhibited by the defendant". The court stated:

> By playing a sport which involves physical contact, a player does not assume any and all risks. There must be a realistic limit as to that risk. Similarly, a person who engages in a sport in which violence and injuries prevail is not rendered immune from legal liability. [This conduct] was clearly beyond the scope of any consent given. . . either expressed or implied. It is agreed that a player's conduct in a game involving physical contact should not be judged by "standards suited to polite social intercourse". [These] acts were unusual and beyond the scope of the ordinary standards of the game.

In sum, therefore, consent is given to the ordinary risks and contacts involved in sports, possibly even to the extent that rules are violated, if that is common, but no consent is given when the conduct of the defendant is beyond the bounds of fair play or when it is malicious and out of the ordinary.[15]

Consent is a defence. Mr. Justice Laskin has said that "consent, on the principle of *volenti,* may be a defence to an intentional tort".[16] The onus, therefore, is on the defendant to establish facts which prove valid consent.[17] This is especially true if there is no written consent where the law requires one.[18] The earlier authority to the effect that the plaintiff had to prove lack of consent is now eclipsed.[19] The law of consent to intentional torts should be consistent with the principles governing voluntary assumption of risk in negligence cases, which places the onus of proof on the defendant.[20] Moreover, it should also correspond

---

[12] *Teolis v. Moscatelli* (1923), 119 Atl. 161 (R.I.); *Lane v. Holloway,* [1968] 1 Q.B. 379 (C.A.).

[13] (1983), 25 C.C.L.T. 91, at p. 104 (N.S.T.D.) (*per* MacIntosh J.).

[14] (1986), 37 C.C.L.T. 1, at p. 6 (B.C.S.C.) (*per* Oppal J.).

[15] *Wright v. McLean, supra,* n. 11, quoting 6 L.Q. Rev. 111.

[16] *Hambley v. Shepley* (1967), 63 D.L.R. (2d) 94, at p. 95 (Ont. C.A.), *dictum.* See also *Norberg v. Wynrib, supra,* n. 2, at p. 246 (*per* La Forest J.).

[17] *Kelly v. Hazlett* (1976), 1 C.C.L.T. 1 (Ont.) (*per* Morden J.). See also *Reibl v. Hughes* (1977), 16 O.R. (2d) 306 (*per* Haines J.); revd (1978), 6 C.C.L.T. 227 (C.A.); revd (1980), 14 C.C.L.T. 1 (S.C.C.).

[18] *Schweizer v. Central Hospital, supra,* n. 6.

[19] *Christopherson v. Bare* (1848), 11 Q.B. 473, 116 E.R. 554, at p. 556; *Ford v. Ford* (1887), 143 Mass. 577, at p. 578, 10 N.E. 474, at p. 475 (*per* Holmes J.).

[20] *Infra,* Chapter 13.

with the rules in connection with the action for trespass, whereby the onus of proof rests on the defendant to establish lack of intention and negligence.[21] In addition, it seems needlessly unfair to place the burden on a plaintiff who has been punched or imprisoned to prove there was no consent, rather than calling on the offender to furnish an explanation for apparently tortious conduct.

In a sexual battery case, the onus is also on the defendant to prove consent.[22] In *Scalera,* the issue was whether an insurance policy excepting "any intentional or criminal act" covered certain acts of sexual assault. The Court was unanimous in deciding that it did not, but there was a disagreement about the onus of proof. For the majority, McLachlin J. (as she then was) held that the onus in sexual battery, like that in other battery cases, rested on the defendant, explaining:

> These arguments persuade me that we should not lightly set aside the traditional rights-based approach to the law of battery that is now the law of Canada. The tort of battery is aimed at protecting the personal autonomy of the individual. Its purpose is to recognize the right of each person to control his or her body and who touches it, and to permit damages where this right is violated. The compensation stems from violation of the right to autonomy, not fault. When a person interferes with the body of another, a *prima facie* case of violation of the plaintiff's autonomy is made out. The law may then fairly call upon the person thus implicated to explain, if he can. If he can show that he acted with consent, the *prima facie* violation is negated and the plaintiff's claim will fail. But it is not up to the plaintiff to prove that, in addition to directly interfering with her body, the defendant was also at fault.

For the minority, Justice Iacobucci wrote:

> While it is not necessary in this appeal to decide whether the burden of proving non-consent will always rest on the plaintiff, I believe that it should for sexual battery. To repeat, sexual contact is only "harmful or offensive" when it is non-consensual. To succeed in an action for intentional battery, one must prove both that (a) the defendant intended to do the action; and (b) the reasonable person would have perceived that action as being harmful or offensive. For sexual activity, an action is harmful or offensive if it is non-consensual. Therefore in sexual battery, the trier of fact must be satisfied that the defendant intended to engage in sexual activity which a reasonable person would have perceived to be non-consensual.

1. REALITY OF CONSENT

An apparent consent is invalid if it has been obtained by fraud, duress, undue influence, or from someone who is legally incapable of consenting.[23]

---

21   *Cook v. Lewis,* [1951] S.C.R. 830.

22   *Non-Marine Underwriters, Lloyd's of London v. Scalera,* [2000] 1 S.C.R. 551, at pp. 565-66 and 610. See also Sullivan, "Trespass to the Person in Canada" (1987), 19 Ottawa L. Rev. 533.

23   Fleming, *The Law of Torts,* 8th ed. (1992), p. 80. *Norberg v. Wynrib, supra,* n. 2, at pp. 246-47.

a) Fraud

Fraud vitiates a consent if it goes to the nature and quality of the act. If the deceit relates only to some collateral matter, however, the consent will remain operative. Consequently, a choir-master who had sexual intercourse with one of his female students who was not yet aware of the facts of life, under the pretense that it would improve her singing, did not obtain a valid consent.[24] Similarly, a woman who engaged in sexual intercourse under the fraudulently induced belief that it would cure certain physical disorders, did not consent, for she thought the act was "pathological and not carnal".[25] So too, a man who falsely told a woman that he was a bachelor and went through a form of marriage and then cohabited with her was liable to her for damages.[26] The courts view sexual intercourse with someone believed to be one's lawful spouse as an entirely different act than it is with someone who is not one's spouse. In the past, it was held that engaging in sexual intercourse without disclosing that one had a venereal disease did not nullify the consent,[27] but, today, someone with herpes or AIDS who knowingly infects another without disclosing their infection, would be liable.[28]

On the other hand, someone who consents to sex because of a fraudulent promise to marry or to pay for the favour would probably be unable to recover for battery, since there has been no fraud as to the nature of the act, but only as to the likely benefits flowing therefrom.[29] If someone poses as a doctor and watches a qualified doctor perform a vaginal examination on a patient, this is not a fraud which goes to the nature and quality of the act, although it might yield liability if the imposter touched the patient.[30] The Supreme Court of Canada has indicated that someone, even a prostitute, infected with AIDS by a carrier who knew, or should have known, about it can recover, subject to a possible reduction in damages because of contributory negligence.[31]

It is sometimes extremely difficult to draw the line between deceit that goes to the nature and quality of the act and deceit that is only collateral. It seems that the courts are distinguishing between gross and serious frauds, on one hand, and minor and less fundamental deceits, on the other. It may be acceptable to excuse

---

[24] *R. v. Williams*, [1923] 1 K.B. 340.

[25] *R. v. Harms*, [1944] 2 D.L.R. 61 (Sask. C.A.).

[26] *Graham v. Saville*, [1945] O.R. 301, [1945] 2 D.L.R. 489 (C.A.). But see also *Smythe v. Reardon*, [1949] Q.S.R. 74; *Papadimitropoulos v. R.* (1958), 98 C.L.R. 249.

[27] *Hegarty v. Shine* (1878), 14 Cox C.C. 145; *R. v. Clarence* (1888), 22 Q.B.D. 23. Doubted by Sopinka J. in *Norberg v. Wynrib, supra*, n. 2, at p. 316.

[28] *Prosser and Keeton on the Law of Torts*, 5th ed. (1984), p. 120. See *Kathleen K. v. Robert B.* (1984), 198 Cal. Rptr. 273, battery liability for herpes transmission; Alexander, "Liability in Tort for the Sexual Transmission of Disease: Genital Herpes and the Law" (1985), 70 Cornell L.R. 101; see also *Barbara A. v. John G.* (1983), 193 Cal. Reptr. 422, fraud re sterility, liable for pregnancy.

[29] *Ibid.*

[30] *Bolduc and Bird v. R.*, [1967] S.C.R. 677; see also *R. v. Rosinski* (1824), 1 Mood. C.C. 19, 1 Lew. C.C. 11 (C.C.R.).

[31] See *Hall v. Hebert*, [1993] 2 S.C.R. 159, 15 C.C.L.T. (2d) 93, at p. 127 (*per* Cory J.).

the perpetrators of minor frauds from criminal responsibility in these cases, but tort law need not adopt the test of the criminal law. In a civil action the courts should be less ready to relieve these liars and cheats from tort liability for the consequences of their frauds. Even a minor deceit, if it is reasonably relied on by someone and leads to contact that would not otherwise have been allowed, should lead to tort liability.

b) Duress

Consent secured by force or threat of force is not acceptable,[32] nor is consent extracted from someone who is under the influence of drugs.[33] Mere economic duress, however, was not sufficient in the past to obliterate an otherwise valid consent,[34] but this conclusion is increasingly under attack.[35]

c) Undue Influence

There has been a dramatic expansion of the concept of undue influence vitiating consent. In *Norberg v. Wynrib*,[36] the Supreme Court of Canada held liable for battery a doctor who gave painkilling drugs to one of his addicted female patients in return for sexual favours. Mr. Justice La Forest, for the majority (Gonthier, Cory JJ.), explained that a consent cannot stand where a "position of relative weakness. . . interfere[s] with the freedom of a person's will".[37] The validity of a consent depends on the "power relationship between the parties".[38] "[A] two step process is involved in determining whether or not there has been legally effective consent."[39] If there is proof of a "power dependency" relationship, that is a "marked inequality in the respective power of the parties" and proof of "exploitation" of the weaker by the stronger, the consent is not genuine.[40] A promising alternative approach to this problem was advanced by Madam Justice McLachlin, who suggested that the principles of fiduciary relationship could better resolve issues such as these without the need to distort the tort principles of consent. Building on the authority of Madam Justice Wilson in *Frame v. Smith*[41] Her Ladyship held that there was a breach of a

---

[32] *Lebrun v. High-Low Foods Ltd.* (1968), 69 D.L.R. (2d) 433; *Norberg v. Wynrib, supra*, n. 2.

[33] *Beausoleil v. La Communauté des Soeurs de la Charité et al.* (1964), 53 D.L.R. (2d) 65. *Cf.* sedated person who understood nature and consequences of treatment, *Kelly v. Hazlett* (1976), 1 C.C.L.T. 1 (Ont. H.C.J.).

[34] *Latter v. Braddell* (1881), 50 L.J.Q.B. 488; *Prosser and Keeton, op. cit. supra*, n. 28, at p. 121.

[35] Bankier, "The Avoidance of Contracts for Economic Duress: Threats to Employment: American Developments and Anglo-Canadian Prospects" (1974), 22 Chitty's L.J. 73.

[36] *Supra*, n. 2, relying on the contact idea of 'unconscionability' and the criminal law idea of 'authority'.

[37] *Ibid.*, at p. 247.

[38] *Ibid.*

[39] *Ibid.*, at p. 256.

[40] *Ibid.*, at pp. 256 *et ff.*

[41] [1987] 2 S.C.R. 99, at p. 136; Ellis, *Fiduciary Duties in Canada* (1988).

fiduciary relationship that existed between the parties here, as one vulnerable party placed her trust in someone with superior power to exercise utmost good faith on behalf of the person reposing that trust.[42] Although the majority did not feel that it had to deal with this analysis, it has some advantages, and we can expect to see it employed again in the future.[43]

In addition to this sex-for-drugs case, the courts have also nullified consents in other situations of people in authority exercising control over vulnerable individuals. For example, where a school teacher was sued for taking advantage of a 15-year-old student he induced to engage in homosexual relations with him, the court held him liable for the first encounter (but not the later ones over a period of years).[44] The court found that there was no "genuine consent" because the teacher had "such a greater amount of power or control over the [youth] as to be in a position to force compliance".[45] In another case,[46] a foster father who engaged in sexual intercourse with his 15-year-old foster daughter was held liable, despite an apparent consent, because the court felt it was unthinkable that the defence could be allowed in what amounted to a case of incest. There will undoubtedly be more cases where, in the circumstances of various other relationships, such as lawyers, professors, police and employers, the court will be prepared to invalidate what may appear to be a consent. Thus, one might say that "no means no" and, in certain situations, "yes" may also mean no.

d) Youth

Young children cannot give a valid consent. Their parents must do so on their behalf. Young people generally acquire the power to consent when they reach the age of majority, and may exercise it even before they reach the age of majority. In *Johnston v. Wellesley Hospital*,[47] a 20-year-old underwent an acne treatment by a dermatologist when the age of majority was 21 years. The court held that the consent was operative because the plaintiff was capable of fully appreciating the nature and consequences of the treatment and could, therefore, validly agree to it. Similarly, a 16-year-old was held to have the requisite maturity and intelligence to validly consent to heart surgery.[48] Thus it may well be that youthful persons are able to consent to intrusions to their interests,

---

[42]   *Canson Enterprises Ltd. v. Boughton & Co.,* [1991] 3 S.C.R. 534, at p. 543.

[43]   See Oppal J. at trial, Sopinka J. used contract theory.

[44]   *Lyth v. Dagg* (1988), 46 C.C.L.T. 25 (B.C.S.C.).

[45]   *Ibid.,* at p. 32.

[46]   *M.(M.) v. K.(K.)* (1989), 61 D.L.R. (4th) 392 (B.C.C.A.), father had pleaded guilty to crime of sex with foster child, s. 153(1)a.

[47]   [1971] 2 O.R. 103; see also *Booth v. Toronto General Hospital* (1910), 17 O.W.R. 118, 19-year-old consented validly. See *infra*, Section 2a) Children.

[48]   *Van Mol v. Ashmore* (1999), 444 C.C.L.T. (2d) 228 (B.C.C.A.); leave to appeal dismissed [1999] S.C.C. No. 117.

even though they may still be minors, if they fully understand what is happening.[49]

e) Criminal Behaviour

There are some early authorities to the effect that consent to a criminal act is null and void,[50] but those cases are unlikely to be followed today.[51] It is unwise to permit a wrongdoer who engages in a fight, and loses, to complain later in a civil court.[52] People who agree to an illegal fight are normally denied access to civil courts on the ground of consent and on the doctrine of *ex turpi causa non oritur actio*,[53] unless one of them employs excessive force or a weapon.[54] For example, in *Dolson v. Hughes*[55] the plaintiff, a large man, was about to strike the defendant, a small man, with his fist, when the defendant thrust a broken beer glass in his face, causing a wound which required 64 stitches to repair. The action was dismissed. The defence of consent was found to be "inappropriate" since the plaintiff consented only to a fist fight, not to being struck by broken glass. However, Mr. Justice Taylor refused to permit the plaintiff to "seek assistance of the Court as arbiter or referee of this unlawful conduct". His Lordship indicated that the doctrine of *ex turpi causa* would "bar any action for damages in respect of a tort committed in the course of criminal conduct to which the plaintiff is a party, provided that the criminal conduct concerned is of an inherently reprehensible nature and that the injury complained of occurred as a natural consequence of the commission of the offence", because the court must not be "used as a means of securing compensation in respect of reprehensible conduct which the law forbids and seeks to punish".

In a similar vein, if a woman consents to an illegal abortion, she will not be successful in recovering civil damages from the abortionist,[56] despite the argument that liability might encourage public disclosure of the criminal practice. If a woman under the age of consent agrees to engage in sexual intercourse, however, the court will nullify her consent and recognize that these

---

[49]   *C.(J.S.) v. Wren*, [1987] 2 W.W.R. 669 (Alta. C.A.), parents could not stop abortion that young woman, 16 years old, consented to. See also *Gillick v. West Norfolk and Wisbech Area Health Authority*, [1985] 3 All E.R. 402 (H.L.), doctor can treat minor without parental consent; on the issue of consent for the mentally disabled, see *Eve v. Mrs. E.*, [1986] 2 S.C.R. 388.

[50]   *Matthew v. Ollerston* (1963), Comb. 218; *Boulter v. Clark* (1747), Bull. N.P. 16.

[51]   Fleming, *op. cit. supra*, n. 23, at p. 82.

[52]   Bohlen, "Consent as affecting Civil Liability for Breaches of the Peace" (1924), 24 Colum. L. Rev. 819.

[53]   See *Hartlen v. Chaddock* (1957), 11 D.L.R. (2d) 705 (N.S.); *Tomlinson v. Harrison*, [1972] O.R. 670.

[54]   *Lane v. Holloway*, [1968] 1 Q.B. 379 (C.A.); *Hartlen v. Chaddock, supra*, n. 51. For criminal law situations, see *R. v. Jobidon*, [1991] 2 S.C.R. 714; Stalker (1994), 32 Alta. L. Rev. 484.

[55]   (1979), 107 D.L.R. (3d) 343, at p. 348 (B.C.).

[56]   *Sayadoff v. Warda* (1954), 125 Cal. App. 2d 626, 271 P. 2d 140; *cf., Joy v. Brown* ((1953), 173 Kan. 833, 252 P. 2d 889.

statutes are meant to protect her from her own lack of judgment,[57] even though it may wrongly appear to some that she is being rewarded for abandoning her virtue.[58]

2. CONSENT IN THE MEDICAL CONTEXT

A doctor must not treat or even touch a patient without the patient's consent.[59] Any person may refuse to accept medical attention, however foolish it may be to do so,[60] and even if it means death as a result.[61] An intoxicated person who refuses to consent, however, may have to be treated against his expressed will for he lacks the capacity to refuse.[62] A doctor generally must not furnish medical care against a person's will, no matter how beneficial or necessary it may be.[63] As was explained in *Allan v. New Mount Sinai Hospital et al.*:[64]

> While our Courts rightly resist advising the medical profession about how to conduct their practice, our law is clear that the consent of a patient must be obtained before any surgical procedure can be conducted. Without a consent, either written or oral, no surgery may be performed. This is not a mere formality; it is an important individual right to have control over one's own body, even where medical treatment is involved. It is the patient, not the doctor, who decides whether surgery will be performed, where it will be done, when it will be done and by whom it will be done.

Moreover, the onus is on the doctor to prove there has been a consent, not on the patient to show there has not.[65] Where there is a language barrier, for example, a doctor must show the patient understood what was being consented to.[66]

---

[57] *M.(M). v. K.(K.), supra*, n. 46; *Bishop v. Liston* (1924), 199 N.W. 825 (Neb.); *cf., Barton v. Bee Line* (1933), 238 App. Div. 501, 265 N.Y.S. 284.

[58] *Morris on Torts* (1953), p. 32.

[59] This common law has been codified and expanded by provincial legislation; see, for example, Ontario's Health Care Consent Act, 1996, S.O. 1996, c. 2, Schedule A, as amended; see also R.S.B.C. 1996, c. 181. If a doctor reasonably believes he has consent under the Act he is not held liable; see s. 29 of the Ontario Act.

[60] *Mulloy v. Hop Sang*, [1935] 1 W.W.R. 714 (Alta. C.A.). See generally Picard, *Legal Liability of Doctors and Hospitals in Canada*, 3d ed. (1996), p. 63.

[61] *Masny v. Carter-Halls-Aldinger Co.*, [1929] 3 W.W.R. 741, at p. 745 (Sask.). The wishes of the mentally ill with regard to invasive treatment must also be respected, see *B.(M.) v. Alberta (Minister of Health)* (1997), 40 C.C.L.T. (2d) 35 (Alta. Q.B.).

[62] *Fortey (Guardian ad litem) v. Canada (A.G.)* (1999), 46 C.C.L.T. (2d) 271 (B.C.C.A.), duty of police to get medical treatment for intoxicated detainee despite repeated refusals.

[63] See generally Rozovsky and Rozovsky, *supra*, n. 4; McCoid, "A Reappraisal of Liability for Unauthorized Medical Treatment" (1957), 41 Minn. L. Rev. 381.

[64] (1980), 28 O.R. (3d) 356, at p. 364 (*per* Linden J.); revd on pleading issue 33 O.R. (2d) 603*n* (C.A.). On the other hand, consent to shock therapy, in 1960 at least, excused a doctor from liability, see Rothman J.A. in *Morrow v. Hôpital Royal Victoria* (1989), 3 C.C.L.T. (2d) 87 (Que. C.A.).

[65] *Ibid.*, at p. 363; *Kelly* and *Reibl*, both *supra*, n. 17. See also Picard, *supra*, n. 60, pp. 48 *et seq.*

[66] *Adan v. Davis*, [1998] O.J. No. 3030, 43 C.C.L.T. (2d) 262 (Ont. Gen. Div.).

The dramatic case of *Malette v. Shulman*[67] sheds light on these issues. The plaintiff was a Jehovah's Witness, who, in accordance with her religious belief, carried a signed card on her person indicating that she was to be given "NO BLOOD TRANSFUSION!" A nurse found the card, showed it to the doctor, but in good faith he still administered a transfusion, saving the patient's life. The patient's daughter arrived and insisted that the blood transfusion be ended, but it was nevertheless continued. The court held that once the doctor was aware of the card he was no longer able to rely on the emergency exception. The card clearly expressed the patient's withdrawal of consent, and it did not matter that the doctor was unable to advise the patient as to the possible results of her decision.

The motivation behind the common law was eloquently summed up by the trial judge, Donnelly J. :

> However sacred life may be. . . certain aspects of life are properly held to be more important than life itself. Such proud and honourable motivations are long entrenched in society, whether it be for patriotism in war, duty by law enforcement officers, protection of the life of a spouse, son or daughter, death before dishonour, death before loss of liberty, or religious martyrdom. Refusal of medical treatment on religious grounds is such a value.[68]

On appeal, Mr. Justice Robins summarized the law as follows:

> The right of a person to control his or her own body is a concept that has long been recognized at common law. The tort of battery has traditionally protected the interest in bodily security from unwanted physical interference. Basically, any intentional nonconsensual touching which is harmful or offensive to a person's reasonable sense of dignity is actionable. Of course, a person may choose to waive this protection and consent to the intentional invasion of this interest, in which case an action for battery will not be maintainable. No special exceptions are made for medical care, other than in emergency situations, and the general rules governing actions for battery are applicable to the doctor-patient relationship. Thus, as a matter of common law, a medical intervention in which a doctor touches the body of a patient would constitute a battery if the patient did not consent to the intervention. Patients have the decisive role in the medical decision-making process. Their right of self-determination is recognized and protected by the law.[69]

Following the *Malette* decision, legislation was enacted to give legal effect to advance medical directives by authorizing individuals to nominate someone to make medical decisions on their behalf, if they become unable, by reason of disability, to do so themselves. Where such a proxy or substitute decision maker has been named, doctors and other health professionals, made aware of this, must abide by their directions.[70]

---

[67] (1987), 63 O.R. (2d) 243; affd (1990), 72 O.R. (2d) 417 (C.A.).

[68] *Ibid.,* at p. 272, 63 O.R.

[69] *Ibid.,* at p. 423, 72 O.R.

[70] See, for example, Substitute Decisions Act, 1992, S.O. 1992, c. 30, as amended.

a) Withdrawal of Consent

It has also been decided that a patient has the right to withdraw consent at any time during a surgical procedure. Mr. Justice Cory explained this in *Ciarlariello v. Schacter*:[71]

> An individual's right to determine what medical procedures will be accepted must include the right to stop a procedure. It is not beyond the realm of possibility that the patient is better able to gauge the level of pain or discomfort that can be accepted or that the patient's premonitions of tragedy or mortality may have a basis in reality. In any event, the patient's right to bodily integrity provides the basis for the withdrawal of a consent to a medical procedure even while it is underway. Thus, if it is found that the consent is effectively withdrawn during the course of the proceeding then it must be terminated. This must be the result except in those circumstances where the medical evidence suggests that to terminate the process would be either life threatening or pose immediate and serious problems to the health of the patient.

It is always a question of fact whether the consent has been withdrawn in the circumstances and whether it has been given again, but as Justice Cory observed in *Ciarlariello*, "generally if there is any question as to whether the patient is attempting to withdraw consent, it will be incumbent upon the doctor to ascertain whether the consent has in fact been withdrawn."

b) Emergencies

An exception to this principle of individual autonomy is the emergency situation. A doctor is privileged to provide medical attention in order to save the life or preserve the health of the patient if it is impracticable to obtain a consent from the patient, a substitute decision maker, or the family.[72] Mere convenience, however, is not enough to create the privilege. If a doctor discovers a diseased testicle during a hernia operation, the doctor may remove it if there is a strong likelihood that it will become gangrenous, endangering the life or health of the patient, and if it is unreasonable to postpone its removal.[73] On the other hand, a doctor cannot tie off a woman's Fallopian tubes during a Caesarian operation where there is no urgency, even though it would be convenient to do so.[74] Unless a woman's life or health is in immediate danger, or unless a further operation would endanger her life or health, a surgeon should leave her Fallopian tubes alone.[75] The decision about medical treatment is for the patient to make, not the doctor, and doctors must act accordingly.[76]

---

[71] [1993] 2 S.C.R. 119, at p. 136 and p. 135, consent withdrawal, but no liability since patient later agreed to continue with procedure.

[72] *Marshall v. Curry,* [1933] 3 D.L.R. 260 (N.S.). See also ss. 18(4), Health Care Consent Act, *supra,* n. 59.

[73] *Ibid.*

[74] *Murray v. McMurchy,* [1949] 2 D.L.R. 442 (B.C.); *Parmley v. Parmley,* [1945] S.C.R. 635.

[75] *Tabor v. Scobee* (1952), 254 S.W. 2d 474.

[76] *Parmley v. Parmley, supra,* n. 74, at p. 89.

Another situation where consent is not required is where the health of the public may be endangered. In such a case medical care may be mandated regardless of a patient's consent. For example, persons with communicable diseases may be required to undergo treatment.[77]

In Canada, hospitals are required to obtain written consent before surgery[78] and usually secure the signatures of all surgery patients on consent forms which are drawn very widely. The wording used not only authorizes the planned surgery, but also permits the doctor to "carry out such additional or alternative operative measures as in his opinion may be found advisable".[79] Provisions such as these are so vague that some American courts have rendered them virtually inapplicable.[80] Our courts, on the other hand, seem to be relying on them to permit doctors some considerable leeway to deal with unforeseen difficulties that arise during operations. Mr. Justice Marshall of the Newfoundland Court of Appeal has explained the position in this way:

> [The] inviolable right [of a person to decide about treatment] must be interpreted in relation to the overall social interest of precluding undue hindrance of the physician legitimately act-ing within the scope of the consent actually given by adopting too narrow a view of its ambit. The full extent of that consent must be gained by looking at all of the circumstances arising from the relation of doctor and patient, against the background of which the formal consent will be viewed.[81]

c) Children

In the case of a child consent for medical treatment must usually be given by a parent unless the young person is 16 years old or married.[82] Doctors who supply medical attention to a young person under 16, without a parent's consent, may be civilly liable and may be disciplined,[83] but it is unlikely that they will be guilty of a criminal offence if they act reasonably and for the benefit of the patient.[84]

If parents refuse to consent to necessary medical treatment on behalf of their child, there is a statutory mechanism which permits a court to authorize it.[85]

---

[77] Health Protection and Promotion Act, R.S.O. 1990, c. H.7; Communicable Diseases Act, R.S.N. 1990, c. C-26.

[78] Section 32, Regulations enacted pursuant to Public Hospitals Act, R.S.O. 1990, c. P.40.

[79] See St. Joseph's Hospital, Toronto, Consent Form.

[80] *Rogers v. Lumberman's Mutual* (1960), 119 So. 2d 649 (La.); *Baldez v. Percy* (1939), 35 Cal. App. 2d 485, 96 P. 2d 142.

[81] *Brushett v. Cowan* (1990), 3 C.C.L.T. (2d) 195, at p. 202 (Nfld. C.A.), consent to biopsy included bone biopsy; see also *Goodwin v. Brady* (1991), 7 C.C.L.T. (2d) 319 (B.C.C.A.).

[82] See the Public Hospitals Act Regulations.

[83] See *Re "D" and the Council of the College of Physicians and Surgeons of B.C.* (1970), 11 D.L.R. (3d) 550, unprofessional conduct.

[84] See Criminal Code, R.S.C. 1985, c. C-46, s. 45.

[85] Child and Family Services Act, R.S.O. 1990, c. C-11, s. 62; see *Re B.(R.) v. C.A.S. of Metro Toronto* (1988), 63 O.R. (2d) 385 (C.A.); *Children's Aid Society of Hamilton-Wentworth v. K.(L.)* (1989), 70 O.R. (2d) 466 (U.F.Ct.). See *Superintendent of Family and Child Service and Dawson*

There are decisions in the United States where courts have ordered that medical attention be furnished to pregnant mothers, over their protest, in order to protect their unborn children,[86] but, in Canada, this has been forbidden.[87]

d) Scope of Consent

When one consents to an operation it normally includes permission to do whatever is usually done in connection with the surgery being performed. Consequently, the surgeon is authorized to engage another doctor to administer the anaesthetic,[88] and perhaps even to do the surgery itself.[89] The routine cleaning, shaving, and administration of drugs is also encompassed in the consent, unless of course patients object, which they are entitled to do at any time. Thus, if a patient instructs an anaesthetist not to inject the anaesthetic into the patient's left arm and the doctor does so nevertheless, the doctor will be held liable for battery.[90]

Consent to perform a particular operation, however, does not give doctors carte blanche to do whatever they feel is advisable, unless of course the consent form grants such a general power. Hence, the consent to remove one tooth does not permit a dentist to remove all of a patient's upper teeth.[91] Neither does consent to a tonsillectomy allow the surgeon to authorize a dentist to extract some teeth while the patient is under anaesthetic, however rotten and in need of extraction they may be.[92] Nor does a patient who agrees to an operation on a toe thereby consent to a spinal fusion.[93] A person may consent to a limited operation only and forbid anything beyond a certain point. Thus, if a patient agrees to an exploratory stomach operation in order to ascertain the nature of an unidentified lump, expressly insisting that nothing more be done, and the doctor removes part of the stomach as a result of the findings, and without further consent, the doctor will be held liable.[94] In a recent case,[95] a woman altered the

---

(1983), 145 D.L.R. (3d) 610 (B.C.S.C.); *Re T.D.D.*, [1999] S.J. No. 443, 13-year-old suffering from cancer in need of protection when parents planned to treat him only with herbs; as for mentally disabled, see *Fleming v. Reid* (1991), 82 D.L.R. (4th) 298 (Ont. C.A.), statute unconstitutional.

[86] *Raleigh-Fitkin-Paul Morgan Memorial Hospital v. Anderson* (1964), 201 Atl. 2d 537 (N.J.). See *Re D (A Minor)*, [1976] 1 All E.R. 326 (Fam. D.), Court refused to authorize sterilization of retarded girl.

[87] *Winnipeg Child and Family Services (Northwest Area) v. D.F.G.*, [1997] 3 S.C.R. 925, expectant mother who abused drugs could not be forced into protective custody to protect fetus under parens patriae, see Rodgers "Comment", (1998), 36 Alta. L. Rev. 711.

[88] *Villeneuve v. Sisters of St. Joseph*, [1971] 2 O.R. 593; revd in part by [1972] 2 O.R. 119; revd in party by (1974), 47 D.L.R. (3d) 391.

[89] *Burk v. S. et al.* (1951), 4 W.W.R. 520 (B.C.); *cf., Restatement, Torts, Second*, §52.

[90] *Allan v. New Mount Sinai Hospital* (1980), 28 O.R. (2d) 356 (*per* Linden J.); revd on pleading point 33 O.R. (2d) 603*n*.

[91] *Boase v. Paul*, [1931] O.R. 625, at p. 627 (*per* Mulock C.J.O.), dismissed re limitation.

[92] *Parmley v. Parmley*, [1945] S.C.R. 635.

[93] *Schweizer v. Central Hospital* (1974), 6 O.R. (2d) 606.

[94] *Schloendorf v. Society of New York Hospitals* (1914), 211 N.Y. 125, 105 N.E. 92.

[95] *Keane v. Craig* [2000] O.J. No. 2160 (*per* Chilcott J.), doctor also liable in negligence for earlier operation necessitating this latter procedure.

written consent form, so as to limit its scope, by writing in the words "reattach labia" where the nurse had written "vaginal reconstruction", a more extensive procedure. Both the doctor and the nurse, who failed to notify the doctor of the amendment, were held liable.

e) Consent, "Informed Consent" and the Duty of Disclosure

Ever since *Reibl v. Hughes,*[96] the problem that was once described as "informed consent" is no longer to be analyzed with battery theory but rather with negligence theory. Furthermore, the Supreme Court has urged the abandonment of the use of the term "informed consent" which tends to confuse battery and negligence.[97] This does not mean that battery theory is no longer available in actions against medical practitioners; it clearly is, where there has been no consent at all to the treatment, where the treatment given goes beyond the consent given and where the consent is obtained by fraud or misrepresentation and a different surgical procedure is carried out than the one agreed to.[98] So too, where a vaccination was done without consent,[99] or where the wrong disc was operated on,[100] that was battery. Battery, however, is no longer available to patients who have consented to an operation, but who are complaining about the inadequate information given to them about the risks associated with the surgical procedure. Chief Justice Laskin has explained the law in this way:[101]

> In situations where the allegation is that attendant risks which should have been disclosed were not communicated to the patient and yet the surgery or other medical treatment carried out was that to which the plaintiff consented (there being no negligence basis of liability for the recommended surgery or treatment to deal with the patient's condition), I do not understand how it can be said that the consent was vitiated by the failure of disclosure so as to make the surgery or other treatment an unprivileged, unconsented to and intentional invasion of the patient's bodily integrity, I can appreciate the temptation to say that the genuineness of consent to medical treatment depends on proper disclosure of the risks which it entails, but in my view, unless there has been misrepresentation or fraud to secure consent to the treatment, a failure to disclose the attendant risks, however serious, should go to negligence rather than to battery. Although such a failure relates to an informed choice of submitting to or refusing recommended and appropriate treatment, it arises as the breach of an anterior duty of due care, comparable in legal obligation to the duty of due care in carrying out the particular treatment to which the patient has consented. It is not a test of the validity of the consent.

It appears, therefore, that the law of battery survives in the medical context, but it is diminished in scope.

The situations described above[102] would still amount to batteries, since they involve a real absence of consent to the procedure performed. It is also possible,

---

[96]   (1980), 14 C.C.L.T. 1 (S.C.C.). See Rodgers-Magnet, Comment, *ibid.*, at p. 61, 14 C.C.L.T.
[97]   *Ibid.*, at p. 11.
[98]   *Ibid.*, at pp. 13-14.
[99]   *Teows v. Weisner* (2001), 3 C.C.L.T. (3d) 293 (B.C.S.C.).
[100] *Gerula v. Flores* (1995), 126 D.L.R. (4th) 506 (Ont. C.A.).
[101] *Supra,* note 96, at pp. 13-14. *Cf. Ciarlariello v. Schacter, supra,* n. 71.
[102] Section A, 2a) and b).

where a failure to disclose is so major that it could be considered to be a misrepresentation about the basic nature and quality of the medical treatment being furnished, that battery could still be employed. For example, in *Halushka v. University of Saskatchewan*[103] a new, untested anaesthetic agent was used on a student as part of an experiment. He was not told about this when he consented, for a $50 fee, to submit to the test. The researchers had advised him that the test was "safe" and that were was "nothing to worry about". He was not told that a catheter would be inserted into his heart, although they did tell him one would be placed in his vein. The court based its decision for the plaintiff on lack of informed consent amounting to a battery. It may be, however, that, if such a shocking failure to disclose occurred again, a court might still be prepared to utilize battery theory, as permitted by *Reibl v. Hughes,* to impose liability on the ground that because of the gross misrepresentation there really was no consent to this operation in the circumstances.

In the vast majority of cases, however, where there has been a failure to inform patients about the risks of operations they have consented to undergo, the law of negligence will be now employed to resolve the issue.[104]

B. Self-Defence

For centuries the common law has excused intentional interference with the person of another, if one person is threatened with harm by another.[105] Self-preservation is recognized as an inevitable and unavoidable instinct in human beings which must be accepted by the law. Although self-defence is clearly a preventive mechanism, and not an instrument for revenge,[106] the right to repel force with force is not confined to warding off a blow. Tort law does not stay the hand until a battery has actually been committed, for if it did it might "come too late afterwards" to do any good.[107] A person may, therefore, strike the first blow and still claim the privilege of self-defence,[108] as long as the purpose of the blow is to halt future or further aggression and not to punish the attacker for past aggression.[109] In short, "self-defence means defence, not counter-attack".[110]

The privilege of self-defence is available not only where harm is actually threatened by an attacker but also where by a person reasonably believes that an

---

[103] (1965), 53 D.L.R. (2d) 436.
[104] *Infra,* Chapter 5, Section F, 2h), unless the new Health Care Consent Act, 1996, S.O. 1996, c. 2, Schedule A, alters things.
[105] *Chapleyn of Greye's Inn* (1400), Y.B. 2 Hen. IV 8, pl. 40.
[106] *McClelland v. Symons,* [1951] V.L.R. 157, at p. 162.
[107] *Chapleyn of Greye's Inn, supra,* n. 105.
[108] *Bruce v. Dyer,* [1966] O.R. 705; affd [1970] 1 O.R. 482n (C.A.).
[109] *Cachay v. Nemeth* (1972), 28 D.L.R. (3d) 603 (Sask.).
[110] *Harris v. Wong* (1971), 19 D.L.R. (3d) 589 (Sask.) (*per* Disbery J.A.).

attack is imminent.[111] Even though mistaken about whether danger exists, the person will be excused as long as it is a reasonable error.[112]

Force employed by a threatened person for self-defence must be reasonable. Since the right of self-defence is one "which may easily be abused", the courts have condemned measures "out of proportion to the apparent urgency of the occasion".[113] Defensive force is not reasonable if it is either greater than necessary for the purpose of preventing the attack, or disproportionate to the evil being counteracted. In other words, acts of self-defence must be both reasonably necessary as well as reasonably proportionate to the harm being threatened.[114] It has been said that "force must not transgress the reasonable limits of the occasion".[115] Justifiable acts of self-defence, therefore, may be transformed into actionable ones if, in a burst of enthusiasm, the victim viciously attacks the attacker. It is entirely possible for both the original aggressor as well as the victim to be held liable to each other for separate, consecutive acts of assault.

Nevertheless, in appropriate cases it may be permissible to take life, if it is reasonably necessary to defend oneself from death or grievous bodily harm.[116] One may have to retreat first, however, if that is reasonable in the circumstances,[117] but it is not necessary to do so if one is attacked in one's own home.[118]

The matter of reasonableness is a question of fact for the trial judge or jury to decide in the circumstances of each case.[119] The courts seldom encounter any great difficulty distinguishing between reasonable force and force which is excessive. It was as unreasonable two hundred and eighty years ago to bite off someone's finger to prevent a jab in the eye[120] as it is unreasonable today to rebuff a drunk's playful advances to your wife with a vicious karate chop breaking his jaw.[121]

A recent case illustrating the application of these principles is *MacDonald v. Hees*.[122] The defendant, a former cabinet minister in the Diefenbaker government was in Nova Scotia campaigning on behalf of the local Progressive Conservative candidate in the federal election of 1972. The plaintiff, a P.C. worker, together with a friend of his who wished to meet Mr. Hees, went to the motel where he was staying at around midnight. They knocked, and finding the door unlocked, they entered the room. To their surprise they discovered the defendant, who was

---

[111] *Bruce v. Dyer, supra*, n. 108.

[112] *Keep v. Quallman* (1887), 68 Wis. 451, 32 N.W. 233.

[113] *McNeill v. Hill*, [1929] 2 D.L.R. 296, at p. 297 (Sask. C.A.) (*per* Martin J.A.).

[114] *Cottreau v. Rodgerson and Saulnier* (1965), 53 D.L.R. (2d) 549, at p. 544 (N.S.).

[115] *Hartlen v. Chaddock* (1957), 11 D.L.R. (2d) 705, at p. 707 (N.S.) (*per* Ilsley C.J.); *Roundall v. Brodie* (1972), 7 N.B.R. (2d) 489, at p. 489 (*per* Stevenson J.).

[116] *R. v. Smith* (1837), 8 C. & P. 160, 173 E.R. 441.

[117] See Beale, "Retreat from a Murderous Assault" (1903), 16 Harv. L. Rev. 567.

[118] *R. v. Hussey* (1924), 18 Cr. App. Rep. 160.

[119] *Roundall v. Brodie, supra*, n. 115.

[120] *Cockcroft v. Smith* (1705), 11 Mod. Rep. 43, 88 E.R. 872.

[121] *Cachay v. Nemeth, supra*, n. 109.

[122] (1974), 46 D.L.R. (3d) 720 (N.S.).

tired after a hard day of campaigning, already retired for the night. The defendant, who had an early morning appointment, got out of bed, grabbed the plaintiff and threw him towards the door. His head struck the glass and he was injured. In holding the defendant responsible, Chief Justice Cowan rejected the defence of self-defence and explained:

> In my opinion, the defendant in this case was not required to use any force for the protection of himself. I find that at no time did the plaintiff or his associate, Glen Boyd, do anything which could have led the defendant to believe that any force was to be used against the defendant. The defendant's evidence was to the effect that he saw that the plaintiff was smaller than he was; he agreed that the plaintiff did not pose a threat to him; that he was not afraid of the plaintiff or his comrade, and that he was not afraid of any physical violence to his person or property. I find that the defendant was not threatened in any way by the plaintiff or by Glen Boyd, and that the defendant was not under the impression that he was threatened in any way by the use of force. In addition, I find that the force which the defendant used in ejecting the plaintiff from his motel unit was not reasonable, and was far greater than could possibly be considered by any reasonable man to be requisite for the purpose of removing the plaintiff from the motel unit. I also find that the force used by the defendant in ejecting the plaintiff was entirely disproportionate to the evil to be prevented, i.e., the continued presence of the plaintiff in the motel unit.[123]

There are other cases in which people under attack went to extremes defending themselves. When a middle-aged lady strikes a car dealer, suggesting he "try a little honesty", he and another salesperson may have "every right to resist her and to put her out of the premises", but if they drag her across the parking lot after she is physically subdued and threaten to "throw her into the traffic", they use more force than is necessary, and they become liable for assault despite their plea of self-defence.[124] Similarly, although someone disregards repeated warnings and continues to strike golf balls so close to the party ahead as to "justify some alarm on their part", the aggrieved party is still not entitled to strike the offender about the head and face and throw his golf cart through the air.[125] Neither can verbal abuse, a challenge to fight, and the throwing of the first punch combine to justify the infliction of a severe beating upon the challenger, out of all proportion to the threat involved.[126] Courts have wisely observed that "a man of powerful physique would not be justified in exerting his full strength against a puny assailant from whom he had nothing to fear",[127] any more than a skilled fighter would be justified in striking a hard blow against a drunk who was "almost physically helpless".[128]

---

[123] *Ibid.*, at pp. 727-28.

[124] *Cave v. Ritchie Motors Ltd. et al.* (1973), 34 D.L.R. (3d) 141, but no vicarious liability of employer.

[125] *Roundall v. Brodie, supra,* n. 115.

[126] *Hartlen v. Chaddock, supra,* n. 115.

[127] *Johnson v. Erickson,* [1941] 1 W.W.R. 626, at p. 631; affirmed on merit, but reversed as to costs, [1941] 3 D.L.R. 651 (Sask. C.A.).

[128] *Cottreau v. Rodgerson and Saulnier* (1965), 53 D.L.R. (2d) 549, at p. 559 (N.S.).

Recognizing, however, that errors are possible when split-second decisions must be made in response to threatened harm, the courts do not expect people to measure with legal nicety the extent of their blows.[129] There is a distinction drawn by the courts between the amount of force used by a defendant and the actual result of that force. As was explained in *Johnson v. Erickson*:

> If a person has no justification whatever for using any force at all, then, although the force employed had much more serious results than the person using it intended or could reasonably have foreseen, he would still be liable for all the consequences. . . . But if a person employing force to repel an attack uses no more force than was reasonably necessary for the purpose, the mere fact that that force had an effect greater than he intended or expected, would not, in my opinion, make him liable.[130]

Thus, where a blow to the jaw causes severe damage, but is not struck by one possessed of pugilistic skill or great strength, the effect of the blow may be considered purely accidental and not necessarily indicative of an unreasonable use of force.[131] So too, a person with a "glass jaw" who attacks someone cannot complain when a single punch returned in self-defence causes a broken jaw, for the attacker has "invited the treatment he received".[132]

If a person, in self-defence against an attacker, injures an innocent third person, liability will probably be excused as long as negligence is non-existent.[133] It is different, however, if one intentionally injures an innocent person in order to protect oneself from harm threatened by an aggressor. In such a case, liability would probably follow unless the court felt that the defence of necessity was applic-able.[134]

In contrast to the criminal law,[135] the onus of proving self-defence in a civil action rests upon the person invoking the defence. Since it was felt that it would be "both unfair and contrary to experience" to require the plaintiff to disprove the existence of the defence, the onus was placed on the defendant.[136] Not only must the defendant prove that the occasion was one which warranted defensive action, but must also establish that the force used was not excessive.[137] Mr. Justice Spence, speaking for the majority of the Supreme Court of Canada, in *Mann v. Balaban*, summarized the law on this issue as follows:

---

[129] *Wackett v. Calder* (1965), 51 D.L.R. (2d) 598 (B.C.C.A.), one can "reject force with force" and "return blow for blow".

[130] [1941] 1 W.W.R. 626, at p. 630.

[131] *Ibid.*

[132] *Bruce v. Dyer*, [1966] 2 O.R. 705; affd [1970] 1 O.R. 482n (C.A.).

[133] *Prosser and Keeton on the Law of Torts*, 5th ed. (1984), p. 128; *Shaw v. Lord* (1914), 41 Okl. 347, 137 P. 885; *Morris v. Platt* (1864), 32 Conn. 75; *Stanley v. Powell*, [1891] 1 Q.B. 86; Forbes, "Mistake of Fact with Regard to Defences in Tort Law" (1970), 4 Ott. L. Rev. 304.

[134] *Prosser and Keeton, ibid.*, at p. 129; see also Section E.

[135] *R. v. Lobell*, [1957] 1 Q.B. 547 (C.C.A.).

[136] In *Miska v. Sivec*, [1959] O.R. 144, at p. 148 (C.A.).

[137] *Miska v. Sieve, ibid.; O'Tierney v. Concord Tavern Ltd.*, [1960] O.W.N. 533 (C.A.); *contra, McClelland v. Symons*, [1951] V.L.R.157; *Green v. Costello*, [1961] N.Z.L.R. 1010.

> In an action for assault, it has been, in my view, established that it is for the plaintiff to prove that he was assaulted and that he sustained an injury thereby. The onus is upon the plaintiff to establish those facts before the jury. Then it is upon the defendant to establish the defences, first, that the assault was justified and, secondly, that the assault even if justified was not made with any unreasonable force and on those issues the onus is on the defence.[138]

The statement of Ilsley C.J. in *Cottreau v. Rodgerson and Saulnier* is to the same effect:

> I think, therefore, that for the defendants to establish their defence of self-defence, they must show that the force used was no greater than requisite for the purpose or disproportionate to the evil to be prevented.[139]

1. PROVOCATION

Self-defence is a complete defence and should not be confused with provocation, which is not.[140] Provocation is merely a factor to be considered in mitigation of damages. The principle was outlined by Mr. Justice Beck in *Evans v. Bradburn* as follows:

> The instinct of human nature is to resent insult in many cases by physical force; and, according to the circumstances, this is more or less generally approved or even applauded, but the law, probably wisely, does not recognize any provocation, short of an assault or threats creating a case for self-defence, as a justification for an assault, but only takes it into account as a circumstance which may reduce culpable homicide from murder to manslaughter, and in all criminal cases involving an assault as a circumstance going in mitigation of punishment, and in civil cases in mitigation of damages.[141]

In order to amount to provocation, the conduct of the plaintiff must have been "such as to cause the defendant to lose his power of self-control and must have occurred at the time of or shortly before the assault".[142] Prior incidents would have relevance only "if it were asserted that the effect of the immediate provocative acts upon the defendant's mind was enhanced by those previous incidents being recalled to him and thereby inflaming his passion".[143] One cannot coolly and deliberately plan to take revenge on another and expect to rely on provocation as a mitigating factor.

Acts of provocation have included making love to another person's spouse,[144] threatening,[145] swearing,[146] or hitting another person with a hockey stick.[147] Acts

---

[138] (1969), 8 D.L.R. (3d) 548, at p. 558.
[139] *Supra*, n. 128, at p. 554; see also *MacDonald v. Hees, supra*, n. 122.
[140] *Simpson v. Geswein* (1995), 25 C.C.L.T. (2d) 49, at p. 61 (Man. Q.B.) (*per* Krindle J.).
[141] (1915), 25 D.L.R. 611, at p. 612 (Alta.).
[142] *Miska v. Sivec, supra*, n. 136, at p. 149 (per Morden J.A.).
[143] *Ibid.*
[144] *White v. Connolly*, [1927] Q.S.R. 75.
[145] *Bruce v. Dyer, supra*, n. 132.
[146] *Check v. Andrews Hotel Co. Ltd.* (1974), 56 D.L.R. (3d) 364 (Man. C.A.).
[147] *Agar v. Canning* (1965), 54 W.W.R. 302; affd 55 W.W.R. 384 (Man. C.A.).

that do not amount to provocation include legally driving another person's cattle to the pound,[148] or colliding with another person's vehicle.[149]

Despite earlier Canadian authority to the contrary,[150] it now appears that provocation will be taken into account to reduce only the punitive or exemplary damages, but not in mitigation of the compensatory damages.[151] In *Check v. Andrews Hotel Co. Ltd.*[152] a waiter forcefully evicted a patron from a tavern, causing the patron injuries for which he was awarded $2,300 compensatory damages at trial, but no punitive damages. It was argued on appeal (though not at trial) that the plaintiff's conduct in accusing the waiter of prejudice, of practising segregation, and of telling him he was "stupid wrong", constituted provocation and that the compensatory damages that had been awarded should be reduced accordingly. The majority of the Manitoba Court of Appeal dismissed the appeal, holding that compensatory damages should not be reduced by provocation. They felt that provocation should only be permitted to mitigate punitive damages. There is, however, still some uncertainty on the issue,[153] which led MacKinnon A.C.J.O. to say that "the time has come for the Court of final resort in this country to resolve the issue so that there will be unanimity in the way in which the Courts of the various provinces deal with this problem".[154]

C. Defence of Third Persons

One is privileged to defend, not only one's self, but others who are endangered by assailants.[155] Just as tort law recognizes the social value of protecting one's self, it also realizes that citizens will often take steps to save others from danger, and that this should be permitted. For centuries a husband has been privileged to defend his wife,[156] and a wife to protect her husband.[157] A master was allowed to

---

[148] *Fillipowich v. Nahachewsky* (1969), 3 D.L.R. (3d) 554 (Sask.).

[149] *Golnik v. Geissinger* (1967), 64 D.L.R. (2d) 754 (B.C.).

[150] *Griggs v. Southside Hotel Ltd. and German*, [1946] O.W.N. 576; affd [1947] O.R. 674 (C.A.); *Miska v. Sivec*, [1959] O.R. 144; *Bruce v. Dyer*, [1966] 2 O.R. 705; affd [1970] 1 O.R. 482n (C.A.); *Agar v. Canning, supra*, n. 147.

[151] *Lane v. Holloway*, [1968] 1 Q.B. 379, [1967] 3 All E.R. 129 (C.A.); *Simpson v. Geswein, supra*, n. 140, at p. 61.

[152] *Supra*, n. 146; see *Shaw v. Gorter* (1977), 2 C.C.L.T. 111 (Ont. C.A.); *Landry v. Patterson* (1978), 22 O.R. (2d) 335 (C.A.). But *cf.*, *Hurley v. Moore* (1993), 18 C.C.L.T. (2d) 78 (Nfld. C.A.), to the contrary, relying on *Murphy v. Culhane*, [1976] 3 All E.R. 533 (C.A.) See also Klar, *Tort Law*, 2nd ed. (1996), p. 119, favouring *Hurley* and suggesting a contributory fault approach.

[153] *Cachay v. Nemeth* (1972), 28 D.L.R. (3d) 603 (Sask.); *Mason v. Sears* (1979), 31 N.S.R. (2d) 521; *Gambriell v. Caparelli* (1975), 7 O.R. (2d) 205 (C.C.); Atrens, "Intentional Interference with the Person", Linden (ed.), *Studies in Canadian Tort Law* (1968), p. 415, where the traditional Canadian approach is preferred.

[154] *Landry v. Patterson, supra*, n. 152, at p. 339.

[155] *Prosser and Keeton on the Law of Torts*, 5th ed. (1984), p. 129; Fleming, *The Law of Torts*, 9th ed. (1998), p. 94.

[156] *Anon*, (1440), Y.B. 19 Hen.VI. 3 pl. 59; see also *Roundall v. Brodie* (1972), 7 N.B.R. (2d) 486, but privilege exceeded; *Cachay v. Nemeth, supra*, n. 153, privilege exceeded.

[157] *Leeward v. Basilee* (1695), 1 Ld. Raym, 62, 91 E.R. 937.

defend his servant,[158] and a servant could return the favour to his master.[159] A mother may defend her son,[160] and presumably a son his mother. A police officer may defend a citizen,[161] and hopefully *vice versa*. There is no reason to limit this privilege, as the criminal law does, to people who are defending others under their protection,[162] or to prevent the commission of certain offences.[163] The law should allow people to defend themselves, their relatives, employees, friends or even total strangers,[164] equally, as long as they are reasonable in doing so.

As in the defence of self-defence, if one person defends another in the reasonable belief that there is need of protection, the defender will be excused from liability even if mistaken.[165] In *Gambriell v. Caparelli,*[166] a mother, believing her son was being choked by the plaintiff, shouted at him to stop, picked up a three-pronged garden cultivator, struck him three times on the shoulder with it, and finally hit him on the head with considerable force. The mother was relieved of liability on the ground that she really had few options open to her, given her lack of knowledge of English, and her size in relation to the plaintiff's. His Honour Judge Carter, relying on the Compensation for Victims of Crime Act, which he felt implied that the legislature "considered it meritorious to aid one's neighbour", explained:

> Where a person intervening to rescue another holds an honest (though mistaken) belief that the other person is in imminent danger of injury, he is justified in using force, provided that such force is reasonable.[167]

As in self-defence, the person who comes to the assistance of another must not use excessive force, and bears the onus to prove that it has not been so used.[168]

D. Defence of Property

It is permissible to defend one's personal and real property by the use of reasonable force.[169] One may carry or push a trespasser off one's land if the trespasser refuses to leave on request,[170] but it must be done reasonably.[171] Where

---

[158] *Seaman v. Cuppledick* (1615), Owen 150, 74 E.R 966; *cf., Leeward, supra,* n. 157.
[159] *Barfoot v. Reynolds* (1773), 2 Str. 953, 93 E.R. 963.
[160] *Gambriell v. Caparelli, supra,* n. 153.
[161] *Prior v. McNab* (1976), 1 C.C.L.T. 137 (Ont.) (per Reid J.).
[162] Criminal Code, R.S.C. 1985, c. C-46, s. 37.
[163] *Ibid.,* s. 27.
[164] See *Restatement, Torts, Second,* §76; Fleming, *op. cit., supra,* n. 155, at p. 94.
[165] *Prior v. McNab, supra,* n. 151; Fleming, *op. cit., supra,* n. 155, at p. 94.
[166] *Supra,* n. 153.
[167] *Ibid.,* at p. 209.
[168] See *Prior v. McNab, supra,* n. 151.
[169] *Cresswell v. Sirl,* [1948] 1 K.B. 241.
[170] *McDonald v. Hees* (1974), 46 D.L.R. (3d) 720; *Green v. Goddard* (1702), 2 Salk. 641, 91 E.R. 540.
[171] *Cullen v. Rice* (1981), 120 D.L.R. (3d) 641 (Alta. C.A.).

the entry has been a violent one, however, there is no need to make a request prior to reliance upon force.[172] The force used must only be sufficient to expel the intruder and must not include unnecessary beating or wounding.[173] A spring gun is, therefore, not an acceptable method of defending one's property and a landowner will be liable to a trespasser who is shot.[174] There would be no liability, though, if a guard dog bit a trespasser.[175]

The privilege of recapture of property is closely related to the defence of property. It was first recognized where there was a momentary interruption of possession and an immediate repossession. It was then extended to dispossession by fraud or force and where the pursuit was fresh. There are many difficult and confusing decisions in this area, which are beyond the scope of this book.[176]

E. Necessity

A defendant may be excused from intentional tort liability if acting under necessity.[177] The defence of necessity differs from self-defence in that the person whose interest is being sacrificed is innocent of any responsibility for the creation of the danger. In necessity cases, the threat emanates from some external source, whereas in self-defence those whose interests are being infringed are wrongdoers themselves. Nevertheless, the social interest in the preservation of life and property is strong enough to excuse certain invasions of the interests of totally innocent persons. The scope of the privilege, as might be expected, is narrower than self-defence, for the plaintiff's interest deserves greater weight in the scale since the plaintiff has done no wrong.[178]

---

[172] *Supra*, n. 170.

[173] *McDonald v. Hees, supra*, n. 170; *Bigcharles v. Merkel*, [1973] 1 W.W.R. 324, negligence liability for shooting; Posner, "Killing or Wounding to Protect a Property Interest" (1971), 14 J. Law & Econ. 201.

[174] *Bird v. Holbrook* (1828), 4 Bing. 628, 130 E.R. 911; see also *Katko v. Briney* (1971), 183 N.W. 2d 657 (Iowa); *cf., dictum* of Denning M.R. in *Murphy v. Culhane*, [1976] 3 All E.R. 533, at p. 536, if householder shoots burglar, no action for damages on grounds of *volenti* and *ex turpi causa*; Palmer, "The Iowa Spring Gun Case: A Study in American Gothic" (1971), 56 Iowa L. Rev. 1219; Bohlen and Burns, "The Privilege to Protect Property by Dangerous Barriers and Mechanical Devices" (1926), 35 Yale L.J. 527; Hart, "Injuries to Trespassers" (1931), 47 L.Q. Rev. 92.

[175] *Cummings v. Grainger*, [1976] 3 W.L.R. 842 (C.A.). See Dog Owners' Liability Act, R.S.O. 1990, c. D.16, s. 3(2).

[176] See *Devoe v. Long*, [1951] 1 D.L.R. 203 (N.B.C.A.); *Hemmings v. Stokes Poges Golf Club*, [1920] 1 K.B. 720, [1918-19] All E.R. Rep. 798 (C.A.); *Napier v. Ferguson* (1878), 18 N.B.R. 415 (C.A.); *Phillips v. Murray*, [1929] 3 D.L.R. 770 (Sask. C.A.); *Wentzell v. Veinot*, [1940] 1 D.L.R. 536 (N.S.C.A.); see generally Branston, "The Forcible Recaption of Chattels" (1918), 28 L.Q. Rev. 262.

[177] Williams, "Defence of Necessity" (1953), 6 Cur. Leg. Probs. 216.

[178] *Prosser and Keeton, op. cit. supra*, n. 155, at p. 145; Bohlen, "Incomplete Privilege to Inflict Intentional Invasions of Interests of Property and Personality" (1926), 39 Harv. L. Rev. 307.

The defence of necessity is applicable only in situations of imminent peril.[179] It is not available as a justification to the hungry and the homeless who take food or occupy buildings owned by others, for this might lead to disorder and lawlessness.[180] Even if homeless people were permitted to enter a building on a particularly cold evening on the ground of necessity, they would not be allowed to remain therein for an indefinite period of time, and they would be required to leave as soon as the necessitous circumstances subsided.[181]

The plea of necessity is a defence which must be pleaded and proved by the defendant, who bears the onus of proving the facts upon which it is based.[182]

There are two varieties of necessity—public and private. Public necessity involves the interference with private rights in order to preserve the interests of the community at large. In such a case the privilege is complete, that is, the defendant pays nothing and the individual who has suffered loss receives no compensation. The individual's interest has been sacrificed for the public good. A police officer may push someone out the way or trespass on private property to facilitate the arrest of a dangerous criminal.[183] So too, a private house may be destroyed in order to save a town.[184] If a public highway is blocked by snow, the public is permitted to pass by entering neighbouring land as long as they do no unnecessary damage to the property.[185] In the same way, goods may be jettisoned from a ship on a river to save the lives of the passengers.[186] If this occurs on the high seas, however, the law of general average applies and all those who benefit must share the cost of compensation rateably.[187] Similarly, a government cannot destroy private property to advance a war effort without furnishing compensation.[188]

Private necessity transpires when the defendant acts to protect a private interest, rather than that of the public. As one might expect, this privilege is rather circumscribed. As long as no actual damage is caused, it is permissible to intrude on another's property in order to preserve one's own life, health, or property.[189] The defence will not, however, excuse a volunteer with no personal interest to protect from entering another's property in order to protect it from

---

[179] *Southwark London Borough Council v. Williams*, [1971] 2 W.L.R. 467 (C.A.) (*per* Davies L.J.).

[180] *Ibid.* (*per* Denning M.R.).

[181] *Ibid.*

[182] *Sherrin v. Haggerty*, [1953] O.W.N. 962, at p. 963.

[183] *Priestman v. Colangelo and Smythson*, [1959] S.C.R. 615, *dictum* (*per* Locke J.).

[184] *Surocco v. Geary* (1853), 3 Cal. 69; *dictum* in *Saltpetre's Case* (1606), 12 Co. Rep. 12, 77 E.R. 1294.

[185] *Dwyer v. Staunton*, [1947] 4 D.L.R. 393 (Alta.) (Sissons D.C.J.).

[186] *Mouse's Case* (1608), 12 Co. Rep. 63, 77 E.R. 1341.

[187] See *Strang, Steel & Co. v. A. Scott & Co.* (1899), 14 App. Cas. 601.

[188] *Burmah Oil Co. Ltd. v. Lord Advocate*, [1965] A.C. 65, abrogated by the War Damage Act, 1965. *Cf.*, *Saltpetre's Case*, *supra*, n. 184; *U.S. v. Caltex* (1952), 344 U.S. 149; *Note* (1966), 79 Harv. L. Rev. 614.

[189] *Prosser and Keeton, op. cit., supra*, n. 155, at p. 147; *Depue v. Flatau* (1907), 100 Minn. 299, 111 N.W. 1.

damage, when the owner is aware of the danger and does nothing.[190] One may erect an embankment to protect one's land from flooding, even if another's land may be flooded as a result,[191] but after water has collected on one's land, one cannot divert it to one's neighbour's land.[192]

When damage is caused by someone acting under private necessity, there is conflict of authority. On one hand, a line of authority holds that one may inflict property damage in order to preserve human lives or property of greater value.[193] Thus, if a storm threatens a ship, its owner may cause damage to the property of another in order to save it without attracting liability.[194] The owner of property being damaged by an imperilled ship cannot cast it adrift without incurring liability.[195] Necessity is no defence in such a case, however, if the emergency was created by the shipowner's own negligence.[196]

There is another line of authority which recognizes an "incomplete privilege" in these cases. Pursuant to this theory, an intrusion is privileged as long as it is a technical tort only and no damage is inflicted. If loss is caused, however, it must be paid by the person who has received the benefits.[197] Thus, where someone takes food in order to stay alive,[198] where an endangered ship is saved at the expense of a dock owner,[199] or where someone's land is damaged while removing some logs,[200] compensation must be paid. This approach is preferable, for although private interests must yield to the greater public good, there is no reason why they must be sacrificed to other private interests without requiring the beneficiaries to pay for the benefits derived. Similarly, if the steps taken are negligent, damages will have to be paid, despite the necessitous circumstances.[201]

It is not clear whether one may ever take a life on the ground of necessity. For purposes of criminal law, it has been held that starving people adrift in a boat in the sea cannot kill one of their number for food,[202] nor can people in a crowded lifeboat jettison some fellow passengers in order to save themselves

---

[190] *Sherrin v. Haggerty*, [1953] O.W.N. 962.

[191] *Gerrard v. Crowe*, [1921] 1 A.C. 395.

[192] *Whalley v. Lancashire and Yorkshire Ry.* (1884), 13 Q.B.D. 131.

[193] *Esso Petroleum v. Southport Corporation*, [1953] 2 All E.R. 1204, *dictum* (*per* Devlin J.); revd [1954] 2 All E.R. 561; revd [1956] A.C. 218.

[194] *Romney Marsh v. Trinity House Corp.* (1870), L.R. 5 Ex. 204; *cf.*, *Manor & Co. v. The Sir John Crosbie* (1965), 52 D.L.R. (2d) 48; affd [1967] 1 Ex. 94, negligence theory. See Sussman, "The Defence of Private Necessity and the Problem of Compensation" (1967-68), 2 Ott. L. Rev. 184.

[195] *Ploof v. Putnam* (1908), 81 Vt. 47, 71 Atl. 188.

[196] *Bell Canada v. The Ship Mar-Tirenno* (1974), 52 D.L.R. (3d) 702 (F.C.), negligence found.

[197] See *Esso Petroleum v. Southport Corporation, supra*, n. 193.

[198] *Southwark London Borough Council v. Williams*, [1971] 2 W.L.R. 467, *dictum* (*per* Denning M.R.); see also *Vincent v. Lake Erie Transportation, infra*, n. 199.

[199] *Vincent v. Lake Erie Transportation* (1910), 109 Minn. 456, 124 N.W. 221.

[200] *Read v. Smith* (1836), 2 N.B.R. 288.

[201] *Rigby v. Chief Constable of Northamptonshire*, [1985] 2 All E.R. 985 (Q.B.).

[202] *R. v. Dudley and Stephens* (1884), 15 Cox C.C. 624, 14 Q.B.D. 273. See Simpson, *Cannibalism and The Common Law* (1984).

from being swamped,[203] but it may be that if all agreed to such a course of action, and if lots were drawn fairly, it would be acceptable in the direst of emergencies in the absence of any possible alternative.[204] The Supreme Court of Canada has recently redefined necessity for purposes of criminal law, which may have implications for the contours of the defence in tort law.[205]

F. Legal Authority

Legal authority may furnish a defence to intentional tort liability. This is a confusing and complex area, hovering on the borderlands of criminal law, administrative law, constitutional law, and tort law. Legal authority cannot be fully investigated here,[206] but a brief sketch of the general principles is offered.

Although most of the cases deal with the alleged misdeeds of police officers during the course of making arrests[207] this privilege is also available to parents, school teachers,[208] shipmasters,[209] and others who forcibly discipline children or crew members under their control. Minor assaults, batteries, and detentions for disciplinary purposes are excused if they are reasonable,[210] but not if any excessive force is employed.[211]

As for the legal authority to make an arrest at common law, a police officer was permitted to apprehend without warrant anyone reasonably believed to have committed a felony. If the police officer erred about the fact of the commission of the offence or about the individual who committed the offence, the officer was privileged as long as acting reasonably. A private citizen could also make an arrest at common law, but with privilege more restricted. The citizen was excused from liability if reasonably mistaken about the identify of the suspect, but was liable if making a reasonable mistake about the commission of the offence.[212] The principle underscored the value society placed on personal liberty and created a distinction between the professional police, who were given broad protection from their reasonable mistakes, and ordinary citizens, who were encouraged to call the police unless they were absolutely certain of their ground.

---

[203] *U.S. v. Holmes* (1842), 1 Wall Jr. 1.

[204] See Fuller, "The Case of Speluncean Explorers" (1949), 62 Harv. L. Rev. 616.

[205] *Perka v. The Queen*, [1984] 2 S.C.R. 232.

[206] See Wood, "Powers of Arrest in Canada under Federal Law" (1970), 9 West. Ont. L. Rev. 55.

[207] See generally, Weiler, "Control of Police Arrest Practices: Reflections of a Tort Lawyer" in Linden (ed.), *Studies in Canadian Tort Law* (Toronto: Butterworths, 1968), p. 416.

[208] Criminal Code, R.S.C. 1985, c. C-46, s. 43.

[209] *Ibid.*, s. 44.

[210] *Mansell v. Griffin*, [1908] 1 K.B. 947; *Murdock v. Richards,* [1954] 1 D.L.R. 766 (N.S.), no liability.

[211] *Ryan v. Fildes*, [1938] 3 All E.R. 517; *Andrews v. Hopkins*, [1932] 3 D.L.R. 459 (N.S.C.A.).

[212] *Walters v. Smith & Sons Ltd.*, [1914] 1 K.B. 595 (*per* Sir Rufus Isaacs C.J.); *Cronk v. F.W. Woolworth Co.*, [1986] 3 W.W.R. 139 (Sask. Q.B.); *Banyasz v. K-Mart Canada Ltd.* (1986), 57 O.R. (2d) 445 (Div. Ct.); *cf., Sears Canada Inc. v. Smart* (1987), 36 D.L.R. (4th) 756 (Nfld. C.A.), reasonable belief as to person enough to excuse individual if mistaken.

These common law principles were codified in the Criminal Code of Canada prior to 1955, but the new code dropped that approach, replacing it with several detailed provisions. The effect of these new criminal provisions on tort liability remains shrouded in mist to this day, but most judges seem to be incorporating them into tort law, despite the real uncertainty about whether the Parliament of Canada has the constitutional power to interfere with private tort rights, which are generally thought to be within the jurisdiction of the provinces.[213]

The Criminal Code provides a blanket legislative authority for everyone who is required or authorized by law to do anything in the enforcement of the law, if acting on reasonable and probable grounds, to use as much force as is necessary for that purpose.[214] Further, a police officer proceeding lawfully to arrest someone is justified, if that person takes flight, in using as much force as is necessary to prevent the escape, unless the escape can be prevented by reasonable means in a less violent manner.[215] The person so authorized is criminally responsible for any excess of force used.[216] Authority is also given to everyone to use reasonable force to prevent the commission of certain offences that are likely to cause immediate and serious injury to person or property.[217] A person who reasonably arrests the wrong person under a warrant is also relieved of criminal responsibility.[218] Everyone who executes a warrant should carry it and produce it if asked to do so.[219] Whether or not one has a warrant, however, anyone who arrests another must, where it is feasible to do so, give notice of the warrant or the reason for the arrest,[220] but failure to comply with these provisions does not itself deprive the offender of protection from criminal responsibility.[221]

With regard to arrests without warrant, any citizen may arrest a person found committing an indictable offence.[222] A citizen may also arrest a person the citizen believes on reasonable and probable grounds to have committed a criminal offence and who is escaping from and is freshly pursued by persons who have lawful authority to arrest that person.[223] Anyone who is the owner or possessor of property, or anyone authorized by the owner, may arrest without warrant a person found committing a criminal offence in relation to that property.[224] In each of these cases the person arrested must be delivered to a peace officer forthwith.[225]

---

[213] See *infra*, Chapter 7.

[214] Criminal Code, R.S.C. 1985, c. C-46, s. 25(1).

[215] *Ibid.*, s. 25(4); see *infra*, Chapter 5, A.3, for discussion of cases.

[216] *Ibid.*, s. 26.

[217] *Ibid.*, s. 27.

[218] *Ibid.*, s. 28.

[219] *Ibid.*, s. 29(1).

[220] *Ibid.*, s. 29(2).

[221] *Ibid.*, s. 29(3).

[222] *Ibid.*, s. 494(1)(a).

[223] *Ibid.*, s. 494(1)(b).

[224] *Ibid.*, s. 494(2).

[225] *Ibid.*, s. 494(3).

Peace officers have a somewhat broader authority than ordinary persons to apprehend offenders without warrant. Peace officers are permitted to arrest without warrant a person who has committed an indictable offence, or who the officer believes on reasonable and probable grounds has committed or is about to commit an indictable offence.[226] Peace officers are also allowed to arrest anyone they find committing any criminal offence, not only an indictable offence.[227] They may also apprehend someone against whom they reasonably believe a warrant is in force.[228]

These criminal law provisions have been relied upon to a large extent in tort cases where the defence of legislative authority has been raised. Most of the cases have adopted the view that, if there is no criminal responsibility, there should be no civil responsibility, but that should not necessarily follow. One might argue that, even though there is value in consistency, tort law should place less value on the social interest in the apprehension of offenders than the criminal law does. This might lead to a situation where police officers (or citizens), although free of penal responsibility, might be civilly liable for their conduct. This would not necessarily be a bad thing, for there might be conduct that should not be criminal and yet should be regulated by the gentler methods of tort law. This view was recently adopted in *Arnault v. Prince Albert (City) Board of Police Commissioners,*[229] where a police dog was used to capture and subdue a person suspected of breaking and entering. The action was dismissed on the basis that reasonable force was used and that there was no negligence. Mr. Justice Geatros said, however, that an officer's right under subs. 25(4) is "a circumstance apart from any question of negligence on his part. This action is to be determined in the civil, not the criminal, context."

It is clear that the onus is on the defendant to prove the existence of reasonable and probable grounds for an arrest.[230] To excuse themselves the police need not be able to prove a *prima facie* case against an arrested person as long as they have reasonable grounds for suspicion, which may include information not admissible in evidence.[231] Where the facts are clear, the issue of reasonable and probable cause is not for the jury but for the judge. Where there is a dispute

---

[226] *Ibid.*, s. 495(1)(a).

[227] *Ibid.*, s. 495(1)(b); see *R. v. Biron* (1975), 59 D.L.R. (3d) 409 (S.C.C.).

[228] *Ibid.*, s. 495(1)(c).

[229] (1995), 28 C.C.L.T. (2d) 15, at p. 17 (Sask. Q.B.); *cf. C. (T.L.) v. Vancouver* (1995), 28 C.C.L.T. (2d) 35 (B.C.S.C.), in similar circumstances liability was found, but recovery was reduced by 50% because of contributory fault.

[230] *Crowe v. Noon,* [1971] 1 O.R. 530 (*per* Pennell J.); *Frey v. Fedoruk,* [1950] S.C.R. 517, at p. 523 (*per* Cartwright J.); *Sandison v. Rybiak* (1973), 1 O.R. (2d) 74; *Karogiannis v. Poulus,* [1976] 6 W.W.R. 197, at p. 198; *Carpenter v. MacDonald* (1978), 21 O.R. (2d) 165.

[231] *Hussien v. Chong Fook Kam,* [1970] A.C. 942, at p. 948 (P.C.) (*per* Lord Devlin); *Cheese v. Hardy* (1974), 56 D.L.R. (3d) 113 (B.C.).

about the facts. however, the judge should ask the jury for their help in estab-lishing the facts.[232]

A police officer cannot stop a person on the street and ask questions without reasonable grounds for suspicion of a criminal offence. Where the police accosted two teenagers to interrogate them merely because they were "saunter-ing along the street" and one of them was wearing a windbreaker and rubber-soled shoes, it was held that the police could be resisted, and damages for assault and false imprisonment were awarded against them.[233] Nor can an officer arrest a person merely for swearing at the officer.[234] In contrast the police are justified in detaining and searching a person on reasonable suspicion of drug trafficking where the person associates daily with known drug traffickers and is driving around in the early hours of the morning, accompanied by a known drug trafficker, in a purposeless, erratic, and suspicious manner.[235]

Legal authority is frequently raised as a defence in shoplifting cases. Where a storekeeper wrongly believed that a customer had taken a carton of cigarettes and instructed a police officer to arrest him, liability was imposed on the storekeeper, because he had no reasonable basis for his belief, but only an unfounded suspicion. The police officer, who reacted to this request coming from a responsible citizen, was relieved of liability because he had reasonable and probable grounds to believe that an indictable offence had been commit-ted.[236] A distinction must be drawn between the situation where an individual informs the police of certain events and the police decide themselves to make an arrest and the situation where an individual tells the police to stop someone and they do. There is no liability of the informer in the former case, but, in the latter case, the informer is responsible for the arrest, because the police are not acting on their own initiative.[237]

These cases must be contrasted with the case of *Hucul v. Hicks,*[238] where a wallet disappeared from a store window and a suspected customer allowed the storekeeper to search certain pockets but not others before he left the store. The storekeeper was held to be justified in calling a police officer to arrest him.

It should be noted here that "security officers employed to guard against thefts of merchandise have no higher rights of arrest than those conferred on citizens generally".[239] If a mistake is made, liability ensues.[240]

---

[232] See *Kennedy v. Tomlinson* (1959), 20 D.L.R. (2d) 273, at p. 299 (Ont. C.A.) (*per* Schroeder J.A.); *Fletcher v. Collins,* [1968] 2 O.R. 618; *Dallison v. Caffery,* [1965] 1 O.R. 348, [1964] 2 All E.R. 610, at p. 616 (C.A.).

[233] *Koechlin v. Waugh,* [1957] O.W.N. 245 (C.A.).

[234] See *Whitehouse v. Reimer* (1979), 107 D.L.R. (3d) 283 (Alta. Q.B.).

[235] See *Cheese v. Hardy, supra,* n. 231.

[236] *Lebrun v. High-Low Foods Ltd.* (1968), 69 D.L.R. (2d) 433.

[237] *Roberts v. Buster's Auto Towing Service Ltd.* (1976), 70 D.L.R. (3d) 716 (B.C.).

[238] (1965), 55 D.L.R. (2d) 267 (Sask.).

[239] *Dendekker v. F.W. Woolworth Co.,* [1975] 3 W.W.R. 429 (Alta.), liability for detaining suspected brassiere thief.

[240] *Hayward v. F.W. Woolworth Co.* (1979), 8 C.C.L.T. 157 (Nfld.).

Although this problem of shoplifting is a serious one for storekeepers, tort law has chosen to favour the interest in individual freedom over that of protection of property. In the United States a new privilege of temporary detention for investigation is emerging which allows a property owner to detain someone for a short period of time in order to conduct a reasonable search.[241] Such a privilege has much to commend it, but it has not been adopted in Canada.

A creditor is not legally authorized to detain a debtor on the premises until payment of a bill. For example, in *Bahner v. Marwest Hotel Co. Ltd.*,[242] it was held that if there is a disagreement about whether a patron of a restaurant must pay for a bottle of wine ordered but not consumed, this does not justify his detention until he pays, nor does it authorize his subsequent arrest. Both the staff of the restaurant and the police officer called in to assist in this case were unreasonable in their belief that he had committed a crime and that they had the legal authority to arrest him. In the same vein, if the police charge an innkeeper with breaking and entering and possession of stolen goods, when the innkeeper is only exercising legal rights under the Innkeeper's Act in relation to some goods of guests, liability for false imprisonment (an malicious prosecution) may follow, if the officers should have realized that no crime had been committed.[243] Similarly, if a probation officer negligently causes a warrant to be issued against someone the officer wrongly believes has violated the terms of a probation order, the officer may be held liable for false imprisonment (or malicious prosecution).[244]

There is no liability for assault and battery for a search of the rectum of an arrested person reasonably suspected of possession of narcotics, as long as it is done with no more force than is reasonably necessary for the purpose. In *Reynen v. Antonenko et al.*[245] both the police officers and the doctor who was asked to do the examination were relieved of liability on the basis of a common law right to do such a search, and pursuant to s. 25(1) of the Criminal Code, which permitted reasonable force to be employed. It is also permissible for a police officer to grab a suspected trafficker in narcotics by the throat in order to discover whether some narcotics have been swallowed, as long as the officer does not use unreasonable force.[246] Prison guards are authorized to use reasonable force to move a prisoner, but they cannot beat the prisoner while doing so.[247]

---

[241] *Prosser and Keeton, op. cit. supra*, n. 145, at p. 129; "Shoplifting and the Law of Arrest: The Merchant's Dilemma" (1953), 62 Yale L.J. 788.

[242] (1969), 6 D.L.R. (3d) 322; affd (1970), 12 D.L.R. (3d) 646 (B.C.C.A.), punitive damages awarded; see also *Perry v. Fried* (1972), 32 D.L.R. (3d) 589 (N.S.) (*per* Cowan C.J.T.D.N.S.).

[243] *Carpenter v. MacDonald* (1978), 21 O.R. (2d) 165 (Dist. Ct.).

[244] *Willian v. The Queen* (1978), 20 O.R. (2d) 587 (*per* Waisberg C.C.J.).

[245] (1975), 54 D.L.R. (3d) 124, at p. 128 (*per* D.C. McDonald); *cf.*, *Laporte v. The Queen* (1972), 29 D.L.R. (3d) 651 (Que.).

[246] *Scott v. R.* (1975), 61 D.L.R. (3d) 130, at p. 138 (*per* Urie J.).

[247] *Dodge v. Bridge* (1977), 4 C.C.L.T. 83 (*per* Keith J.); vard as to damages (1978), 6 C.C.L.T. 71 (Ont. C.A.).

A police officer who arrests a suspect on a warrant issued for another with an identical name is not liable civilly if making a reasonable mistake as to the identity of the suspect. In *Fletcher v. Collins*,[248] the wrong person was arrested, but because he had the same name as the suspect, and resembled him physically, and because his attitude was uncooperative, it was held that the officer had reasonable and probable grounds for making the arrest. However, if the police arrest the wrong person without reasonable and probable grounds with regard to the circumstances, then liability ensues. For example, if a suspect has been identified as having little or no hair, and the police detain for 30 hours a suspect who possesses a full head of hair, this is not reasonable and the police will be held liable for any losses which may result from the mishap.[249] Once the police discover that they have arrested someone in error, they are obligated to release the person forthwith. Thus, where the wrong person was reasonably arrested, but was then detained for 15-30 additional minutes after the mistake was discovered, he succeeded in false imprisonment.[250]

These cases of mistaken but reasonable arrests can lead to injustice for the innocent victims who may be incarcerated for some time, lose their jobs, and suffer considerable humiliation and deprivation. It might be a sound idea for an *ex gratia* payment to be made in such cases.[251] It would be even better if these innocent victims were fairly compensated under a special scheme created for this purpose.[252]

A person who is arrested must be told the reason for arrest to permit the person to assess whether there is a requirement to submit.[253] The person need not be told the exact charge but rather the facts for which the arrest is being made, for the officer may not even know the charge which will ultimately be laid.[254] The failure to inform a suspect renders the arrest unauthorized for purposes of tort law, and thus civilly actionable. Nor is it acceptable to lay a false charge in order to detain a suspect while the real charge is being investigated further.[255] Whether arrested with or without a warrant, the suspect is entitled to know the true reason for the deprivation of freedom,[256] unless the suspect knows why the arrest is being made, is "caught red-handed and the crime is patent to high heaven",[257] is a violent and dangerous person who must be swiftly subdued, or if

---

[248] [1968] 2 O.R. 618; see also *Crowe v. Noon*, [1971] 1 O.R. 530 (*per* Pennell J.); *Schuck v. Stewart*, [1978] 5 W.W.R. 279 (B.C.).

[249] *Chartier v. Attorney-General (Que.)*, [1979] 2 S.C.R. 474.

[250] *Romilly v. Weatherhead* (1975), 55 D.L.R. (3d) 607 (B.C.) (*per* Hinkson J.).

[251] See *Crowe v. Noon, supra*, n. 248.

[252] Compare with McRuer, *Inquiry into Civil Rights* (1968), Vol. 2, p. 833, where compensation for persons wrongly convicted was suggested.

[253] *Hill v. Chief Constable of the South Yorkshire Police*, [1990] 1 All E.R. 1046 (C.A.).

[254] *Kennedy v. Tomlinson* (1959), 20 D.L.R. (2d) 273, at p. 302.

[255] *Christie v. Leachinsky*, [1947] A.C. 573.

[256] Criminal Code, R.S.C. 1985, c. C-46, s. 29(2).

[257] *Kennedy v. Tomlinson, supra*, n. 243, at p. 302; *Cheese v. Hardy, supra*, n. 231.

there is legislative authority not to inform the suspect.[258] There is nothing wrong with arresting a person on a legitimate charge, while continuing to investigate possible further charges.

This right to know may extend even to a friend of a person being arrested, who may be entitled to be told the reason for the arrest. As Mr. Justice Parker explained in *Sandison v. Rybiak:*

> The prisoner or someone speaking for him or her is entitled to know the reason for the arrest and make a statement in answer to it. The exercise of such a right cannot be converted into obstruction unless it is intemperate, unduly persistent, irrelevant or made in an unreasonable manner. . . .
>
> An accused is not required to submit to a restraint of his freedom until he is told that he is under arrest and the reason for the restraint. . . . .
>
> If an arrest is unlawful then any restriction on the liberty of the subject is false imprisonment.[259]

Persons under arrest should be taken before a judge as soon as practicable,[260] but it may be permissible to wait 24 hours as it is not necessary to place them before the first magistrate available.[261]

The police are authorized to take certain measures in order to prevent the commission of crimes. They may remove an orange lily from someone's clothes in order to prevent violence.[262] They may arrest someone who is reasonably believed to be planning to shoot his wife.[263] Similarly, a police officer may enter premises against the wishes of the occupier, in order to prevent a breach of the peace.[264] The Supreme Court of Canada has indicated that the police are privileged to enter private premises without a warrant to make an arrest, if they believe on reasonable grounds that the person they are seeking is present and if they make a proper announcement to the occupier. Normally, the police should knock at the door, identify themselves and give the reason for their entry, but such an announcement may not be required where it is impracticable.[265]

These tort actions against the police are an important method of supervising police arrest practices, because both the criminal law and the exclusionary rules of evidence furnish insufficient protection to the public.[266] Although a new

---

[258] *Murray v. Ministry of Defence*, [1988] 2 All E.R. 521, at p. 527 (H.L.), army arrest need not explain reason.

[259] (1973), 1 O.R. (2d) 74, at pp. 83-85; see also *R. v. Long*, [1970] 1 C.C.C. 313 (B.C.C.A.), acquittal for obstruction.

[260] *Lewis (John) & Co. Ltd. v. Tims*, [1952] A.C. 676; *Dallison v. Caffery*, [1965] 1 Q.B. 348, [1964] 2 All E.R. 610.

[261] *Scott v. R.* (1975), 61 D.L.R. (3d) 130, at p. 144.

[262] *Humphries v. Connor* (1864), 17 I.C.L.R. 1; see Police Services Act, R.S.O. 1990, c. P-15, s. 42.

[263] *Kennedy v. Tomlinson, supra*, n. 254.

[264] *Thomas v. Sawkins*, [1935] 2 K.B. 249.

[265] See *Eccles v. Bourque* (1974), 41 D.L.R. (3d) 392; affd 27 C.R.N.S. 325 (S.C.C.) (*per* Dickson J.).

[266] *Levitz v. Ryan*, [1972] 3 O.R. 783, at p. 792 (C.A.).

objective method of police self-regulation would be preferable,[267] the tort suit before an independent judge or jury remains a vital, albeit expensive, check on the abuse of police power. Even unsuccessful claims against the police may serve to remind them that although they may escape disciplinary and criminal proceedings for their misdeeds, they may still be required to account for them in a civil suit at the behest of the aggrieved citizen. This cannot help but render the police more sensitive to the individual rights of those they must deal with in their work.

G. Contributory Fault and Apportionment

Traditionally, apportionment of damages was not available in intentional tort cases.[268] Either the defendant was liable or not; the conduct of the plaintiff was relevant only if it amounted to a complete defence, but not otherwise, the theory being that the defendant's wrongful intention so outweighed the plaintiff's contributory fault or negligence as to efface it altogether.[269]

This is no longer the case. It is now possible to apportion damages in cases of intentional torts and trespass actions. The Negligence Act,[270] which permits apportionment, reads as follows:

> 3. In any action for damages that is founded upon the fault or negligence of the defendant if fault or negligence is found on the part of the plaintiff that contributed to the damages, the court shall apportion the damages in proportion to the degree of fault or negligence found against the parties respectively.

This legislation allowed shared responsibility for losses, whereas the common law had cruelly denied compensation to a plaintiff who had been negligent or at fault. The scope of this section has begun to expand, its sensible approach influencing courts to divide responsibility in various new situations. For example, in *Bell Canada v. Cope (Sarnia) Ltd.*[271] Bell sued the defendant both in negligence and trespass for cutting one of its underground service wires. It was established that the plaintiff was contributorily negligent, *inter alia*, in the way it staked its underground wires. The court apportioned damages two-thirds against Bell and one-third against the defendant, explaining that "fault and negligence, as these words are used in the [Negligence Act] are not the same thing. Fault certainly includes negligence, but it is much broader than that. Fault incorporates all intentional wrongdoing, as well as other types of substandard conduct. . . . therefore. . . . a trespass action comes within the opening words of s. 4 of The

---

[267] Grant, "The Control of Police Behaviour" in Tarnopolsky (ed.), *Some Civil Liberties Issues of the Seventies* (1975).

[268] *Hollebone v. Barnard*, [1954] O.R. 236, [1954] 2 D.L.R. 278 (H.C.); *Chernesky v. Armadale Publishers* (1974), 79 D.L.R. (3d) 180 (Sask. C.A.); revd 90 D.L.R. (3d) 321 (S.C.C.).

[269] Williams, *Joint Torts and Contributory Negligence* (1951), p. 197. Alberta Institute of Law Research and Reform, *Contributory Negligence and Concurrent Wrongdoers* (1979).

[270] R.S.O. 1990, c. N.1, s. 3. See *infra*, Chapter 13.

[271] (1980), 11 C.C.L.T. 170, at p. 180; affd 15 C.C.L.T. 190 (Ont. C.A.).

Negligence Act." In another case, *Andersen v. Stevens*,[272] Mr. Justice Macfarlane apportioned damages between defendants whose fraud and defendants whose negligence caused loss to the plaintiff. Mr. Justice Macfarlane astutely declared:

> Resistance to the view that liability should be apportioned between all tortfeasors is based upon the proposition that an intentional tortfeasor ought not to have any right of redress. That concern, in my opinion, can be dealt with by apportioning the blame on the basis of relative or comparative culpability. What is important is that all those persons who have caused the damage or loss should share the liability in accordance with their respective degrees of fault. The legislation would not be sensible or just, and it would fail in its principal purpose if contribution was confined to those found guilty of negligence. In my opinion the Legislature ought not to be understood as having intended that a negligent person, being 10% at fault for the damage should be called upon to pay 100%, and to have no right of recourse against an intentional wrongdoer who had been 90% at fault.
>
> I hold that the word "fault" encompasses both intentional and negligent torts.

In *Long v. Gardner*,[273] Mr. Justice Smith accepted this new order of things but, in the circumstances, declined to apportion because the defendant's act of stabbing the plaintiff was felt to be "markedly or radically different in nature and seriousness from the childish display of emotion" that precipitated the attack, so that it "cannot be said to have played a part in any legal or moralistic sense, in the act of stabbing". Essentially, it could be said that the contribution of the plaintiff to the stabbing was too trivial to be taken into account here. Certain difficulties were raised about the problems of quantifying the shares of responsibility between negligent and intentional wrongdoers, but it seems that these problems are surmountable. A more fascinating notion was alluded to by Mr. Justice Smith, which might lead to provocation being treated as contributory fault, leading to a reduction in damages, something that has not yet been fully explored. Such treatment would likely mean that provocation would lead to a reduction of compensatory as well as punitive damages, unlike the current situation of confusion.[274]

---

[272] (1981), 125 D.L.R. (3d) 736, at pp. 741-42 (B.C.S.C.). Defamation liability split in *Brown v. Cole* (1995), 26 C.C.L.T. (2d) 223 (B.C.C.A.).

[273] (1983), 144 D.L.R. (3d) 73, at pp. 77-78 (Ont. H.C.) (*per* Smith J.). See also Brockenshire J. in *Rabideau v. Maddocks et al.*, unreported, Dec. 23, 1992 (Ont. H.C.J.).

[274] See *supra*, Chapter 2, G. See Klar, *Tort Law*, 2nd ed. (1996), p. 119, advocating this approach; *Hurley*, supra, n. 152; *C. (T.L.) v. Vancouver (City)* (1995), 28 C.C.L.T. (2d) 35 (B.C.S.C.), 50% reduction in thief's recovery against police using excessive force.

Chapter 4

Negligence: The Elements: Damage and Causation

The second basis of liability in tort is negligence. This is certainly the most important field of tort liability today, for it regulates most activities in modern society. Wherever anyone is accidentally injured negligence law may be called in to determine whether there will be compensation. Consequently, negligence law is a vibrant and dynamic instrument.[1] It has to be if it is to survive. As soon as some new type of activity emerges, it is accommodated within the general framework of negligence principles. Because of this, it has been said that "the categories of negligence are never closed".[2] This may be merely the instinct for self-preservation at work, for if negligence law abandoned its fluidity, it would probably wither away. In order to serve the community, the law of negligence, like all law in a free society, must be attuned to the popular will. It may adapt only slowly to new conditions, but it does and must move.

The purposes of negligence law are manifold.[3] One of its prime functions is the provision of compensation for accident victims. But this is not its only goal. If it were, compensation would be furnished to every accident victim, regardless of fault. But negligence law does not aim to compensate everyone — only those whose injuries result from someone else's faulty conduct. One might conclude that the other goals of negligence law would not be adequately served if everyone, the guilty as well as the innocent, were treated equally. The second objective of negligence law — deterrence — seeks to reduce the frequency of accidents. By making only negligent actors liable to pay for the losses they cause, negligence law encourages people to exert themselves to behave carefully in order to avoid liability. Negligence law, like all law, is an educator and a reinforcer of values. Such laudable values as individual responsibility, concern for one's fellow human beings, and respect for the dignity of the individual are embedded in the principles of negligence law. Certain psychological functions

---

[1] See generally Millner, *Negligence in Modern Law* (1967); Smith, *Liability in Negligence* (1984).
[2] See *Donoghue v. Stevenson*, [1932] A.C. 562, at p. 619 (*per* Lord Macmillan).
[3] See *supra*, Chapter 1.

are also served by negligence law, which furnishes a peaceful substitute to those who might indulge in more violent forms of retribution in its absence. In addition, negligence law produces some market deterrence by making accident-prone activities more expensive and therefore less attractive than other safer, less expensive alternatives. Negligence law may also serve society as an ombudsman, focussing attention on abuses of power by industry, the professions, and government agencies.

A. Elements of a Cause of Action for Negligence

The word negligence has two meanings, one restricted and one broad. In its narrow sense, it refers to *conduct* which falls below the standard required by society. In this context, negligence connotes more than a mere state of mind. It refers to an evaluation of a particular course of action, one element of which is the state of mind of the actor. The second and wider meaning of negligence makes reference to a *cause of action for negligence*. Negligence in the first sense is only one fragment of this expanded meaning of negligence.

To establish a cause of action for negligence several elements must be present. There is disagreement, however, over the number of these components. Perhaps the most commonly accepted formulation has been called the "A.B.C. rule".[4] According to this rule, a plaintiff in a negligence action is entitled to succeed by establishing three things to the satisfaction of the court: (A) a duty of care exists; (B) there has been a breach of that duty; and (C) damage has resulted from that breach. This is the traditional English approach to negligence liability, and it has been repeated countless times in the cases.[5] The trouble with the A.B.C. rule is its beguiling simplicity. It blurs together issues which should not be treated under one rubric. Complexities which should be illuminated are disguised. Thus, when the English courts are forced to consider the problem of the extent of liability, none of the three elements seems to cover the issue satisfactorily. Duty, remoteness, and proximate cause may be utilized interchangeably without any explanation.

Another division of the subject of negligence is that advocated by the American scholars.[6] They suggest that there are four elements in a cause of action for negligence: (1) duty; (2) failure to conform to the standard required; (3) a reasonably close causal connection between the conduct and the resulting injury, sometimes termed "proximate cause"; (4) actual loss or damage resulting to the interest of another. This categorization also produces difficulties. A court sometimes handles the proximate cause question in terms of duty or remoteness, which leads to a blending of the first and third elements. Similarly, a court

---

[4]   See Gibson, "A New Alphabet of Negligence", in Linden (ed.), *Studies in Canadian Tort Law* (Toronto: Butterworths, 1968).

[5]   See, for example, *King v. Stolberg* (1968), 78 D.L.R. (2d) 473, at p. 483 (*per* Rae J.); revd in part on the facts, 8 D.L.R. (3d) 362 (B.C.C.A.).

[6]   *Prosser and Keeton on the Law of Torts*, 5th ed. (1984), p. 164; Green, *Judge and Jury* (1930).

sometimes confuses the first and second components. Another deficiency is that this approach neglects the consideration of the conduct of the plaintiff as an element to be assessed in the process.

Professor Fleming, in his masterful text,[7] overcomes this last criticism by adumbrating five elements of a cause of action for negligence. To the four listed above, he adds a fifth component — the absence of any conduct by the injured party which would preclude recovery. Consequently, the defences of contributory negligence, illegality and voluntary assumption of risk are considered as one of the five elements.

This work will utilize a six-part division of negligence in order to facilitate an examination of the subject from all possible angles. A cause of action for negligence arises if the following elements are present: (1) the claimant must suffer some damage; (2) the damage suffered must be caused by the conduct of the defendant; (3) the defendant's conduct must be negligent, that is, in breach of the standard of care set by the law; (4) there must be a duty recognized by the law to avoid this damage; (5) the conduct of the defendant must be a proximate cause of the loss or, stated in another way, the damage should not be too remote a result of the defendant's conduct; (6) the conduct of the plaintiff should not be such as to bar or reduce recovery, that is the plaintiff must not be guilty of contributory negligence and must not voluntarily assume the risk.[8]

The number of elements in a cause of action for negligence does not really matter very much, because they are only artificial divisions scholars construct in order to clarify the different aspects of a negligence case. Sometimes components are substituted for one another. For example, a court may approach a "duty" problem with "proximate cause" language or, depending on your bias, a judge might attack a "proximate cause" question with "duty" vernacular. Judges have frequently intermixed the "causation" and "proximate cause" questions. Although it has been argued that cause-in-fact is purely a factual question and that proximate cause is a legal issue based on policy,[9] not all courts have recognized this. Moreover, it may be well-nigh impossible to eliminate all matters of value from the issue of causation. The whole debate is probably a tempest in a teapot, but if our understanding is at all deepened by it the discussion may be worthwhile.

The treatment of negligence law in this book, pursuant to the suggested six-part division of the subject, will examine each of the elements in turn. The remaining part of this chapter will discuss the first two elements — necessity of damage and causation. Chapter 5 will analyze the standard of care in negligence

---

[7] *The Law of Torts*, 9th ed. (1998). See also Harper, James and Grey, *The Law of Torts*, 2nd ed. (1986).

[8] This structure was adopted by Beaulieu J. in *Ekkebus v. Lauinger* (1994), 22 C.C.L.T. (2d) 148, at p. 158 (Ont. Gen. Div.).

[9] See Green, "The Casual Relation Issue in Negligence Law" (1962), 60 Mich. L. Rev. 547; Malone, "Ruminations on Cause-in-Fact" (1956), 9 Stan. L. Rev. 60; also in Malone, *Essays in Torts* (1986).

law, the third element. Chapters 6 and 7 will continue the analysis of the third element by describing the roles played by custom and legislative violation in negligence law. Chapter 8 will examine proof of negligence, also a part of element three. The concept of duty, the fourth element, will be studied in Chapter 9. The fifth element, remoteness and proximate cause, will be discussed generally in Chapter 10 and more particularly in Chapters 11 and 12. The final chapter in this part of the book, Chapter 13, deals with the sixth element, the conduct of the plaintiff and the defences to a negligence action.

B. Damage

There can be no liability for negligence unless some damage has been suffered by the plaintiff. Although damage is not required in tort actions which developed out of the writ of trespass,[10] some loss is necessary in those tort actions which evolved out of the action on the case. Since negligence is such a cause of action, proof of damage is necessary in order to succeed. Mr. Justice Guy of the Manitoba Court of Appeal has declared:

> In negligence actions . . . . there is no "cause to sue" until the third requirement of the A.B.C. rule — i.e., the damage, has occurred.[11]

Mr. Justice Laskin echoed this view in *Schwebel v. Telekes,*[12] a case that was held to be a contract action, when he stated "where a claim for personal injuries is made, proof of damage would be required to complete the cause of action".

The requirement of damage is not based on history alone; there are policy reasons supporting it. In *Pfiefer v. Morrison,*[13] Wilson J., in dismissing an action, stated:

> In this highly mobile age collisions between motor vehicles occur in great numbers every day. Many of them have grave consequences in injury to persons and damage to property. In other instances, more numerous, slight damage or no damage is caused to the vehicles and there is no injury to person. If, in the latter class of cases, a litigant claiming damages for personal injury is able to establish a cause of action and a right to at least nominal damages merely by proving negligence then, I say, needless lawsuits must proliferate, each one giving damages and costs to persons who have suffered no injury. Such actions would proceed to trial, at no risk to the plaintiff of failure and penalty costs, and with the assurance that he would recover costs. The undesirability of such a state of affairs is self-evident.

---

[10]   *Supra*, Chapter 2 and *infra*, Chapter 8.

[11]   *Long v. Western Propeller Co. Ltd.* (1968), 67 D.L.R. (2d) 345 (Man. C.A.). See generally, McLaren, "The Impact of Limitation Periods on Actionability in Negligence" (1969), 7 Alta. L. Rev. 241; Bowker, "Limitations on Actions in Tort in Alberta" (1962), 2 Alta. L. Rev. 41; Williams, *Limitation of Actions in Canada* (1972); Ontario Law Reform Commission, *Report on Limitation of Actions* (1969).

[12]   [1967] 1 O.R. 541 (C.A.); overruled on another point in *Consumers Glass Co. v. Foundation Co. of Canada* (1985), 33 C.C.L.T. 104 (Ont. C.A.).

[13]   (1973), 42 D.L.R. (3d) 314 (B.C.).

What is meant by the word damage is some "head of loss for which compensation will be awarded".[14] This is to be contrasted with the term damages, which is "generally used to identify the amount of money that is paid by a tortfeasor for inflicting the various items of damage". Thus, the damage caused by negligent conduct may consist of several different items such as medical expenses, hospital bills, loss of income as well as the non-pecuniary heads of loss such as pain and suffering, loss of enjoyment of life, etc. Consequently, negligent conduct can cause several types of damage which may be incurred by various people in more than one place.[15]

Negligence actions have been dismissed, on occasion, despite the clear presence of negligent conduct, on the basis that no loss has been established. For example, in earlier times suits launched by the parents of young children killed in accidents have been dismissed where no damages "either actual or prospective" were incurred.[16]

1. LIMITATION PERIODS

Limitations statutes have created some difficulties in the past. Where statutes clearly specify the particular event from which the time is to run, little difficulty arises. However, most limitation periods stipulate that the time is to run from the date the "cause of action arose".[17] In the past, this was interpreted to mean that the time ran from the date the damage was incurred, because, at that time, all the facts required for liability in negligence were present.[18] Pursuant to this rule, some harsh decisions were rendered, denying plaintiffs the right to sue, even though they had been unaware and unable to become aware of the damage they had suffered prior to the expiry of the limitation period.[19]

All this has now changed, the law having been reshaped to the effect that the time does not usually begin to run until the "date of discoverability of the damage".[20] The shift, like so many others, was begun by Denning M.R. in *Sparham-Souter v. Town & Country Developments (Essex) Ltd.*[21] Alas, it was then snuffed out in England in *Pirelli General Cable Works Ltd. v. Oscar Faber*

---

[14] *Vile v. Von Wendt* (1979), 26 O.R. (2d) 513, at p. 517 (*per* Linden J.).

[15] *Ibid.*, at p. 518.

[16] See *Barnett v. Cohen*, [1921] 2 K.B. 461, four-year-old. See also *Pedlar v. Toronto Power Co.* (1913), 29 O.L.R. 527; affd 30 O.L.R. 581 (C.A.), two-year-old; *Cashin v. Mackenzie*, [1951] 3 D.L.R. 495 (N.S.), five-year-old; *Nickerson v. Forbes* (1955), 1 D.L.R. (2d) 463 (N.S.C.A.), child nearly six; *Alaffe v. Kennedy* (1973), 40 D.L.R. (3d) 429 (N.S.), four-month-old child. *Cf.*, current law, *Thornborrow v. MacKinnon* (1981), 16 C.C.L.T. 198 (*per* Linden J.).

[17] Limitations Act, R.S.O. 1990, c. L. 15, s. 45.

[18] *Roberts v. Read* (1812), 16 East 215, 104 E.R. 1070.

[19] *Archer v. Catton & Co. Ltd.*, [1954] 1 All E.R. 896.

[20] See Wilson J. in *Kamloops v. Nielsen*, [1984] 5 W.W.R. 1, at p. 46 (B.C.C.A.). See also *Peixeiro v. Haberman*, [1997] 3 S.C.R. 549, at p. 564 (S.C.C.) (*per* Major J.).

[21] [1976] 2 All E.R. 65 (C.A.).

& *Partners.*[22] Canada furnished more fertile ground for the idea, which was planted by Mr. Justice La Forest in *N.B. Telephone Co. v. John Maryon Ltd.*[23]

The seedling began to spread roots in the rich terrain of the Supreme Court of Canada in the case of *Kamloops v. Nielsen*,[24] where Madam Justice Wilson condemned the "injustice of a law which statute-bars a claim before the plaintiff is even aware of its existence".[25] She, on behalf of an increasingly independent court, consciously chose to adopt the reasoning of *Sparham-Souter* and to reject that of the House of Lords in *Pirelli*, on the ground that to be required to investigate facts years later was the "lesser of two evils" than to deny compensation altogether.

Mr. Justice Dubin added his voice to those favouring the new rule in *Consumers Glass Co. v. Foundation Co. of Canada*,[26] and extended it equally to cases "sounding in contract or in tort".[27] He explained that

> in cases which are based on a breach of duty to take care, a cause of action does not arise, and time does not begin to run for the purposes of the Limitations Act, until such time as the plaintiff discovers or ought reasonably to have discovered the facts with respect to which the remedy is being sought, whether the issue arises in contract or in tort.[28]

Mr. Justice Dubin recognized that this rule

> may cause wider exposure to some potential defendants than is now current, but it would be a greater injustice to deprive a plaintiff, through no fault of its own, of a cause of action. . . .[29]

The "discoverability rule" is now in full flower. The Supreme Court of Canada in *Central & Eastern Trust Co. v. Rafuse*,[30] through Mr. Justice LeDain, expressed the new principle as follows:

> a cause of action arises for purposes of a limitation period when the material facts on which it is based have been discovered or ought to have been discovered by the plaintiff by the exercise of reasonable diligence. . . .[31]

There has also been legislative reform, as for example, the Ontario Health Disciplines Act, which expressly stipulates a similar principle for negligence in the medical area, that is, no liability unless the action is commenced within one year "from the date when the person commencing the action knew or ought to

---

[22]   [1983] 2 A.C. 1 (H.L.).

[23]   (1982), 24 C.C.L.T. 146 (N.B.C.A.).

[24]   *Supra*, n. 20.

[25]   *Ibid.*, at p. 49.

[26]   *Supra*, n. 12.

[27]   *Ibid.*, at p. 122.

[28]   *Ibid.*

[29]   *Ibid.*, at p. 124.

[30]   (1986), 37 C.C.L.T. 117 (S.C.C.).

[31]   *Ibid.*, at p. 180. See also *Peixeiro*, *supra*, n. 20. All the facts necessary for a cause of action, including identity and acts, need to be known or discoverable; see *Aguonie v. Galion Solid Waste Material* (1998), 38 O.R. (3d) 161 (C.A.) (*per* Borins J. *ad hoc*, as he then was).

have known the fact or facts upon which the person alleges negligence or malpractice".[32] The earlier language in the statute was much narrower, requiring action within one year of the date the "services terminated".[33]

A similar approach has been employed in the language of the Highway Traffic Act which precludes actions being brought after two years "from the time when the damages were sustained".[34]

It seems that, if an action can be based on product liability,[35] wrongful death[36] or negligent tavern-keeper[37] theory, rather than on negligent driving, a longer limitation period will also be available.

Limitation periods set out in the Limitations Act do not run against infants or the mentally disabled.[38] In the past, time did run against children and the mentally disabled when the period within which the action could be brought was enacted in a special statute,[39] but happily this is no longer the case. Thus, children injured in car accidents can sue within two years of attaining majority.[40] In child abuse cases the limitation period is also extended by the discoverability rule.[41]

Some of the shockingly short limitation periods favouring municipal and other governmental organizations have been held to be unconstitutional.[42] We may see other similar decisions in the years ahead, as the discoverability rule has "substantially and permanently changed the landscape of limitation law in Canada.[43]

---

[32] R.S.O. 1990, c. H.4, s. 17. Act not retroactive, see *Martin v. Perrie* (1986), 36 C.C.L.T. 36 (S.C.C.).

[33] In Manitoba this wording excludes the application of the discoverability rule, see *J. (A.) v. Cairnie Estate* (1993), 17 C.C.L.T. (2d) 1 (Man. C.A.); leave to appeal to S.C.C. refused March 3, 1994, B.S.C.C.P. 349. See also *Fehr v. Jacob*, [1993] 5 W.W.R. 1, at p. 6 (Man. C.A.).

[34] R.S.O. 1990, c. H.8, s. 206. See *Peixeiro, supra*, n. 20, wording change is "a distinction without a difference", *per* Major J. at p. 564.

[35] *Clost v. Colautti Construction Ltd.* (1985), 35 C.C.L.T. 259 (Ont. H.C.); *cf., Dufferin Paving & Crushed Stone Ltd. v. Anger*, [1940] S.C.R. 174.

[36] *Burt v. Le Lacheur* (2000), 2 C.C.L.T. (3d) 206 (N.S.C.A.). Time runs from when plaintiff learns death was a wrongful one. See also *Tardif v. Wong* (2000), 2 C.C.L.T. (3d) 135 (Alta. Q.B.) in medical malpractice situation. But *cf. Waschowski v. Hopkinson Estate* (2000), 47 O.R. (3d) 370 (C.A.) where date of death was "pivotal event", *per* Abella J.A.

[37] *Clark v. 449136 Ont. Inc.* (1996), 28 C.C.L.T. (2d) 262, 27 O.R. (3d) 658 (Gen. Div.); affd (1997), 34 O.R. (3d) 742 (C.A.); leave to appeal refused (1998), 227 N.R. 194n.

[38] R.S.O. 1990, c. L.15, s. 47. *Papamonolopoulos v. Board of Education for Toronto* (1986), 38 C.C.L.T. 82 (Ont. C.A.); *Lawson v. Hospital for Sick Children* (1990), 4 C.C.L.T. (2d) 303 (Ont. Div. Ct.); *Toner v. Toner Estate* (1993), 13 O.R. (3d) 617 (Div. Ct.); *Khouri v. Guardsman Equipment Leasing Ltd.* (1992), 34 A.C.W.S. (3d) 847 (Ont. Gen. Div.).

[39] See *Philippon v. Legate*, [1970] 1 O.R. 392 (C.A.), Medical Act.

[40] *Murphy v. Welsh*, [1993] 2 S.C.R. 1069, 18 C.C.L.T. (2d) 101.

[41] *M.(K.) v. M.(H.)*, [1992] 3 S.C.R. 6.

[42] *Streng v. Township of Winchester* (1986), 37 C.C.L.T. 296 (Ont. H.C.) (*per* Smith J.).

[43] *Burt, supra*, n. 36 at p. 219, *per* Chipman J.A.

2. COMBINED ACTION FOR NEGLIGENT CONDUCT NECESSARY

At one time it was possible to bring two separate actions as a result of one negligent act, if two separate injuries were suffered. In *Brunsden v. Humphrey,*[44] for example, the plaintiff was permitted to sue for damages to his cab in one action and for the personal injuries suffered in the same accident in a second action. This is no longer the case, since the Supreme Court of Canada decision in *Cahoon v. Franks.*[45] An action was commenced for damage to the plaintiff's automobile within the time period allotted. After the expiry of the limitation period, the plaintiff was permitted to amend his pleadings to include a claim for personal injuries. The Supreme Court of Canada was of the view that this did not set up a new cause of action. Mr. Justice Hall quoted from the opinion of Porter J.A. of the Albert Court of Appeal as follows:

> . . . "the factual situation" which entitles the plaintiff here to recover damages from the defendant is the tort of negligence, a breach by the defendant of the duty which he owed to the plaintiff at common law which resulted in damage to the plaintiff. The injury to the person and the injury to the goods, and perhaps the injury to the plaintiff's real property and the injury to such modern rights as the right to privacy flowing from the negligence serve only as yardsticks useful in measuring the damage which the breach caused. . . .
>
> To deny this plaintiff the opportunity to have a Court adjudicate on the relief which he claims merely because it lacks ancient form would be to return to those evils of practice which led to judicial amendment and the ultimate legislative abolition of "forms of action" . . . .
>
> The decision in *Brunsden v. Humphrey* may well have persisted in Great Britain largely because the Courts were bound by it. Free as we are to apply reason unhampered by precedent, I am of the opinion that the principle of *Brunsden v. Humphrey* ought not to be adopted.[46]

Mr. Justice Hall concluded that "*Brunsden v. Humphrey* is not now good law in Canada and it ought not to be followed ".

It has been held, however, that a claim by family members for the wrongful death of a relative is not foreclosed by the settlement of an action for personal injuries by the deceased relative before the death since it is "an original statutory cause of action and not a derivative one".[47] Mr. Justice Barry, basing himself squarely on the new discoverability thinking of the Supreme Court of Canada, reopened the issue in *Foley v. Greene*[48] when he said:

> [i]t is possible for there to be two causes of action for personal injury arising from the same breach of duty, where there subsequently arises a physical problem that is significantly different in kind from the problem initially known.

---

[44] (1884), 14 Q.B.D. 141 (C.A.). See also *Sandberg v. Giesbrecht* (1963), 42 D.L.R. (2d) 107 (B.C.S.C.).

[45] [1967] S.C.R. 455.

[46] *Ibid.*, at pp. 459-60.

[47] See Lacourcière J.A. in *Cotic v. Gray* (1981), 33 O.R. (2d) 356 (C.A.).

[48] (1990), 4 C.C.L.T. (2d) 309, at p. 324 (Nfld. S.C.).

There is much to be said for this approach, at least in cases where the personal injuries appear trivial at first, but later much more serious and different symptoms emerge.

C. Causation

The defendant's conduct must cause the plaintiff's loss or else there is no liability.[49] In other words, there must be some connection or link between the wrongful act and the damage. Stated still another way, the accident must result from or be attributed to the act of the wrongdoer. As was declared by Mr. Justice Spence:[50]

> There must be not only negligence but negligence causing the injury before there can be recovery.

This question of cause-in-fact should not be confused with the more complicated issue of proximate cause, which will be dealt with later.[51]

Fortunately, the courts have not been trapped into endless philosophical discourse on the concept of causation. Instead, they have adopted a common sense approach to the problems. Mr. Justice Sopinka has recently reiterated this in *Snell v. Farrell*[52] when he declared that causation need not be proven with "scientific precision". He explained that "Causation is an expression of the relationship that must be found to exist between the tortious act of the wrongdoer and the injury to the victim in order to justify compensation of the latter out of the pocket of the former." Madam Justice Southin[53] has also reminded us that it is not often possible to do a "controlled experiment" to discover the precise cause of an accident.

The most commonly employed technique for determining causation-in-fact is the "but for" test, sometimes called the *sine qua non* test. It works like this: if the accident would not have occurred but for the defendant's negligence, this conduct is a cause of the injury.[54] Put another way, if the accident would have occurred just the same, whether or not the defendant acted, this conduct is not a

---

[49] Hart and Honoré, *Causation in the Law*, 2nd ed. (1985); Fleming, "Probabilistic Causation in Tort Law" (1990), 68 Can. Bar Rev. 661; Malone, "Ruminations on Cause-in-Fact" (1956), 9 Stan. L. Rev. 60; Green, "The Causal Relation Issue in Negligence Law" (1962), 60 Mich. L. Rev. 543; Calabresi, "Concerning Cause and the Law of Torts" (1975), 43 U. Chi. L. Rev. 69; Beverley McLachlin, "Negligence Law — Proving the Connection", in *Torts Tomorrow* (1998), p. 16.

[50] *Joseph Brant Memorial Hospital v. Koziol* (1977), 2 C.C.L.T. 170, at p. 180 (S.C.C.).

[51] See *infra*, Chapter 10.

[52] (1990), 72 D.L.R. (4th) 289, at p. 298 (S.C.C.).

[53] *Lankenau Estate v. Dutton* (1991), 7 C.C.L.T. (2d) 42, at p. 57 (B.C.C.A.); leave to appeal to S.C.C. dismissed Sept. 12, 1992, 91 B.S.C.C. p. 1987, 10 C.C.L.T. (2d) 314.

[54] See *Swanson Estate v. Canada* (1991), 80 D.L.R. (4th) 741, at p. 757 (Fed. C.A.) (*per* Linden J.A.); *Athey v. Leonati*, [1996] 3 S.C.R. 458, 31 C.C.L.T. (2d) 113.

cause of the loss. Thus the act of the defendant must have made a difference.[55] If the conduct had nothing to do with the loss, the actor escapes liability.[56]

The question of causation must be proved to the satisfaction of the court or the jury on the balance of probabilities. It is not enough, for example, to show that a plaintiff's depression was "possibly" caused by the defendant's negligence. Indeed such evidence does not even merit being placed before the jury, at least not without a stern warning about its limitations.[57] Nor is it enough to prove that there was the loss of a chance of avoiding an injury.[58]

It is not necessary, however, for a plaintiff to prove positively that, if it were not for the negligent conduct, the accident would have been prevented; it is enough to show that the negligent act contributed to the accident. Thus, the absence of a crash mat and the lack of supervision during a gymnastics class were held to have contributed to the injury of the plaintiff even though this was not proven conclusively.[59]

Historically, proof of causation has often been difficult, specific evidence of causation being required by the courts. Scientific evidence was often demanded, so that many seemingly meritorious negligence cases foundered on the shoals of causation. For example, when someone suffered a heart attack after falling off a boat into the frigid water of Lake Ontario, the action failed *inter alia* on the basis that it was not established that this result was caused by a negligent rescue effort.[60] Similarly, when someone was injured on an escalator because two scuffling youths caused her to fall, the case was dismissed *in part* because it was not proven that a rubber handrail or the presence of an attendant would have prevented the accident.[61]

In *Davidson v. Connaught Laboratories*[62] a pharmaceutical company was said to have inadequately warned the medical profession about the possible side-effects of an anti-rabies serum, but they were relieved of liability in any event since there was no evidence that it would "have made any difference" to the medical practitioners, who would have recommended the use of the serum even if they had been fully informed of the risk. In other words, the negligent failure to warn the doctors was not a cause of the plaintiff's damage, hence there could be no liability imposed.

---

55   See Hart and Honoré, *op. cit. supra*, n. 49.

56   See Malone, *op. cit. supra*, n. 49. One judge asked, for example, "Would the accident have been prevented by the safety measure?" see *Kauffman v. T.T.C.*, [1959] O.R. 197, at p. 203 (*per* Morden J.A.); affd [1960] S.C.R. 251.

57   *Danjanovich v. Buma*, [1970] 3 O.R. 604, at p. 605 (C.A.). See also *Kramer Service Inc. v. Wilkins* (1939), 184 Miss. 483, 186 So. 625.

58   *Laferriere v. Lawson*, [1991] 1 S.C.R. 541, Quebec law.

59   *Myers v. Peel County* (1981), 17 C.C.L.T. 269 (S.C.C.).

60   *Horsley v. MacLaren, "The Ogopogo"*, [1972] S.C.R. 441.

61   *Kauffman v. T.T.C.*, [1959] O.R. 197 (C.A.); affd [1960] S.C.R. 251; *Stefanyshyn v. Rubin* (1996), 34 C.C.L.T. (2d) 88 (Man. C.A.), failure of doctor to wear his glasses did not contribute to error he made during "blind surgery".

62   (1980), 14 C.C.L.T. 251, at p. 277 (*per* Linden J.).

In dealing with the causation issue courts must often grapple with some complex medical matters. For example, a court may have to decide whether UFFI is harmful,[63] whether drugs cause certain side effects,[64] whether a plaintiff's tuberculosis results from dust and fumes that enter his lungs while on the job,[65] or whether a claimant's lung cancer is caused by smoking.[66] Similarly, where someone fell off a defective wharf into the water and later died, the court had to determine whether the deceased, who had a tubercular condition, would have died when she did irrespective of the accident.[67]

1. INFERRING CAUSATION

Our courts have begun to relax the sometimes rigid application of proof of causation principles, permitting trial judges and even appellate courts to infer causation where they may not have done so before. In 1972, Lord Wilberforce, in *McGhee v. National Coal Board* [68] sought to mollify the rigour of the strict rules of proof of causation. Invoking an ancient common law technique of reform, he proceeded to shift the onus of proof of causation from the plaintiff to the defendant, where the defendant was negligent and where that negligence materially increased the risk of injury.[69] This dramatic innovation was embraced in Canada[70] where a similar notion had been adopted earlier.[71] In the United Kingdom, *McGhee* did not do well, being criticized, explained and finally jettisoned in *Wilsher v. Essex Area Health Authority*,[72] where Lord Bridge suggested that a "robust and pragmatic" approach to causation was preferable to shifting the onus of proof.[73] A similar view had already been expressed by Mr. Justice MacGuigan, who had advocated a "more practical, common-sense approach" to proof of causation.[74]

A significant breakthrough, rejecting the rigidity of the past, was achieved in *Snell v. Farrell*.[75] Worrying about the difficulties surrounding proof of causation,

---

[63] *Berthiaume v. Val Royall Lasalle Ltée*, [1992] R.J.Q. 76 (C.S.).

[64] *Rothwell v. Raes* (1988), 54 D.L.R. (4th) 193 (Ont. H.C.J.) (*per* Osler J.).

[65] *Reed v. Ellis* (1916), 38 O.L.R. 123, 32 D.L.R. 529 (C.A.).

[66] *Pritchard v. Liggett & Myers Tobacco Co.* (1961), 295 F.2d 292.

[67] *York v. Canada Atlantic S.S. Co.* (1893), 22 S.C.R. 167. See also *Barnett v. Chelsea and Kensington Hospital Management Committee*, [1968] 1 All E.R. 1068, person carelessly sent home from hospital died, but the defendant was not the cause of death.

[68] [1972] 3 All E.R. 1008 (H.L.), the majority decided the case using ordinary principles of proof.

[69] See Linden, *Canadian Tort Law*, 4th ed., at p. 101, for details.

[70] *Nowsco Well Service Ltd. v. Canadian Propane Gas* (1981), 16 C.C.L.T. 23, at p. 46 (Sask. C.A.) (*per* Bayda J.A.).

[71] *Cook v. Lewis*, see *infra*, Section 3.

[72] [1988] 2 W.L.R. 557 (H.L.).

[73] *Ibid.*, at p. 569.

[74] *Letnik v. Metro Toronto (Municipality)* (1988), 49 D.L.R. (4th) 707, at p. 721 (Fed. C.A.), "inference overwhelmingly probable" in any event.

[75] *Supra*, n. 52, at p. 300. Fleming, "Comment" (1991), 70 Can. Bar Rev. 136; See also Klar, "Recent Developments in Canadian Law: Tort Law" (1991), 23 Ottawa L. Rev. 177, at p. 229. See also *Laferriere v. Lawson*, *supra*, n. 58, for similar ideas in Quebec law.

especially where the defendants have superior knowledge, Mr. Justice Sopinka reworked the tools. He explained that "the dissatisfaction with the traditional approach to causation stems to a large extent from its too rigid application by the courts in many cases". He opined that causation is a "practical question of fact which can best be answered by ordinary common sense rather than abstract metaphysical theory". Mr. Justice Sopinka declared further:[76]

In many malpractice cases, the facts lie particularly within the knowledge of the defendant. In these circumstances, very little affirmative evidence on the part of the plaintiff will justify the drawing of an inference of causation in the absence of evidence to the contrary. . . .

The legal or ultimate burden remains with the plaintiff, but in the absence of evidence to the contrary adduced by the defendant, an inference of causation may be drawn, although positive or scientific proof of causation has not been adduced.

In other words "it is not essential to have a positive medical opinion to support a finding of causation".[77] Mr. Justice Sopinka indicated that, if necessary, he would open up the causation proof issue even further if he "were convinced that defendants who have a substantial connection to the injury were escaping liability because plaintiffs cannot prove causation under currently applied principles. . .".[78]

Recently, the Supreme Court has done just that when it was held that presumptive evidence of causation is supplied when it is proven that a learned intermediary has been informed of a defect in silicon breast implants, for example.[79] In other words, the plaintiff did not have to prove her doctor would have warned her had he been warned by the manufacturer.[80] Not the same, but in a related development, because of the "unique difficulties in proving causation" in a case of blood donor screening, it is now enough for the plaintiff to show that the defendant's negligence in failing to warn about the tainted blood "materially contributed to the occurrence of the injury." In other words, the conduct was a sufficient condition not a necessary condition.[81]

Hence, it is now open for trial judges to infer causation when there are facts proved that would fairly lead to an inference on the basis of common sense, without the necessity of strict scientific proof, even in medical cases. It will be noted that this type of reasoning is not dissimilar to *res ipsa loquitur* analysis, where courts are permitted to infer negligence, where specific evidence is lacking.[82] If Madam Justice Picard was correct in describing *McGhee* as the

---

[76]   *Ibid.*, at pp. 300-01.
[77]   *Ibid.*, at p. 306.
[78]   *Ibid.*, at p. 299.
[79]   See *infra*, Products Liability, Chapter 16; *Hollis v. Dow Corning Corp.*, [1995] 4 S.C.R. 634.
[80]   See McLachlin, *supra*, n. 49, at p. 24.
[81]   *Walker Estate v. York-Finch General Hospital*, [2001] S.C.J. No. 24, at para. 88.
[82]   See Chapter 8, Proof of Negligence.

"sister" of *res ipsa loquitur*,[83] then it would not be incorrect to call this new inference of causation approach the "twin sister" of *res ipsa*, for its operation is virtually identical.

The new relaxed inference of negligence approach has been followed by Canadian courts[84] and augurs well for a more balanced and humane attitude toward causation in the years ahead. Plaintiff's lawyers, however, would be unwise if they did not continue to seek to establish causation by whatever evidence they can muster. So too, defendants' counsel would be foolhardy if they stopped trying to show absence of causation, as they have done in the past. Let us hope that, with these alterations in our thinking about causation, the courts will be able to do a better job in the future.

2. MULTIPLE CAUSES

There may be more than one cause of an accident. In other words, there may be several factors that contribute to a plaintiff's injury. Defendants who cause losses cannot be excused merely because other causal factors have helped produce the harm. It is sufficient if the defendant's negligence was a cause of the harm. As Mr. Justice Major has explained in *Athey v. Leonati et al.*[85]

> It is not now necessary, nor has it ever been, for the plaintiff to establish that the defendant's negligence was the *sole cause* of the injury. There will frequently be a myriad of other background events which were necessary preconditions to the injury occuring. . . . As long as a defendant is *part* of the cause of an injury, the defendant is liable, even though his [or her] act alone was not enough to create the injury. There is no basis for a reduction of liability because of the existence of other preconditions: defendants remain liable for all injuries caused or contributed to by their negligence.
>
> . . . Apportionment between tortious causes is expressly permitted by provincial negligence statutes and is consistent with the general principles of tort law. The plaintiff is still fully compensated and is placed in the position he or she would have been in but for the negligence of the defendants. Each defendant remains fully liable to the plaintiff for the injury, since each was a cause of the injury. The legislation simply permits defendants to seek contribution and indemnity from one another, according to the degree of responsibility for the injury.

In days gone by, this problem of multiple causes posed problems for some judges, who insisted on searching for the last wrongdoer. This proclivity stemmed in part from their inability to permit contribution and indemnity between wrongdoers at common law. Now that it is allowed by statute, the

---

[83] *Food Giant Markets Ltd. v. Watson Leaseholds Ltd.* (1987), 43 C.C.L.T. 152, at p. 161 (Alta. Q.B.).

[84] *Lankenau Estate v. Dutton, supra,* n. 53, at p. 57 (*per* Southin J.A.); *Swanson Estate v. Canada, supra,* n. 54 (*per* Linden J.A.); *Sigouin v. Wong* (1991), 10 C.C.L.T. (2d) 236 (B.C.); *Cherry v. Borsman* (1992), 12 C.C.L.T. (2d) 137 (B.C.C.A.); *Levitt v. Carr* (1992), 12 C.C.L.T. (2d) 195, at p. 223 (B.C.C.A.); *cf. Logozar v. Golder* (1994), 21 C.C.L.T. (2d) 203 (Alta. C.A.); leave refused (1995), 25 C.C.L.T. (2d) 48; *Doern v. Phillips Estate* (1994), 23 C.C.L.T. (2d) 283 (B.C.), police pursuit was 25% cause of loss.

[85] *Supra,* n. 54.

courts are amenable to holding two or more persons responsible as concurrent tortfeasors.[86]

In such a case, the plaintiff may "elect to recover the full amount of his damage from a tortfeasor only partly to blame",[87] although the plaintiff cannot, of course, recover more than the total damages assessed. Following that, if the tortfeasors pursue each other for indemnity or contribution,[88] they may do so, but this is of little concern to the plaintiff.

The "but for" test ran into stormy sailing where two or more defendants combined to cause loss. If the injury would have transpired if either cause alone had been operating, neither party might be a cause under the "but for" test. Suppose A and B negligently light fires at different places and the fires spread to engulf the plaintiff's house. A and B both might argue that the fire would have resulted without their negligence. Consequently, a blinkered court might hold that neither of the defendants, although both negligent, was the cause of the loss, because it would have occurred in any event.

This just could not be tolerated and, happily, the courts have handled this situation with common sense. They devised the substantial factor test, which holds that if the acts of two people are both substantial factors in bringing about the result, then liability is imposed on both[89] on the theory that both "materially contributed to the occurrence".[90] Consequently, in *Lambton v. Mellish*,[91] two merry-go-round operators were sued for nuisance as a result of the maddening noise made by their organs. Injunctions were granted against them individually, because according to Mr. Justice Chitty:

> If the acts of two persons, each being aware of what the other is doing, amounted in the aggregate to what is an actionable wrong, each is amenable to the remedy against the aggregate cause of complaint. The defendants here are both responsible for the noise as a whole so far as it constitutes a nuisance affecting the Plaintiff, and each must be restrained in respect of his own share in making the noise.

---

[86] See the Negligence Act, R.S.O. 1990, c. N.1, s. 1. For a superb analysis of these problems, see Williams, *Joint Torts and Contributory Negligence* (1951). See also Cooper J.A. in *Goodyear Tire and Rubber Co. of Canada Ltd. v. MacDonald* (1974), 51 D.L.R. (3d) 623 (N.S.C.A.), at pp. 626 *et seq.*; *Ives v. Clare Bros. Ltd.*, [1971] 1 O.R. 417.

[87] See *County of Parkland v. Stetar*, [1975] 2 S.C.R. 884 (*per* Dickson J.); *Economy Foods & Hardware Ltd. v. Klassen* (2001), 5 C.C.L.T. (3d) 12 (Man. C.A.), defendant liable for entire fire though negligent third party could have prevented it.

[88] See generally, Cheifetz, *Apportionment of Fault in Tort* (Canada Law Book, 1981). As to whether a single action or separate actions are required, see *Cohen v. S. McCord & Co.*, [1944] O.R. 568, [1944] 4 D.L.R. 753 (C.A.); *cf.*, *Inglis v. South Shore Sales* (1979), 104 D.L.R. (3d) 507 (N.S.C.A.); *R. v. Thomas Fuller Construction Co. (1958) Ltd.*, [1980] 1 S.C.R. 695, 106 D.L.R. (3d) 193; Klar, *supra*, n. 75, explaining the recent cases.

[89] See *Prosser and Keeton on The Law of Torts*, 5th ed. (1984), p. 354. See also *Anderson v. Minneapolis, etc., R. Co.* (1920), 146 Minn. 430, 179 N.W. 45; *Restatement, Torts, Second*, §432(2); *Pride of Derby & Derbyshire Angling Assoc. Ltd. v. British Celanese*, [1952] 1 All E.R. 1326; affd [1953] 1 All E.R. 179 (C.A.).

[90] *Athey, supra*, n. 54, at p. 120, C.C.L.T. (*per* Major J.).

[91] [1894] 3 Ch. 163, at p. 166 (*per* Chitty J.).

In another case, *Corey v. Havener*,[92] the plaintiff, in a horse and wagon, was passed by two motorists driving at a high rate of speed, one on each side. The horse took fright and the plaintiff was injured. Although the defendants acted independently, judgment was given against both of them for the full amount of the plaintiff's damages because "if each contributed to the injury, that is enough to bind both". A similar case is *Arneil v. Paterson*,[93] where two dogs attacked some sheep, killing several of them. The owners of both dogs were held responsible for the entire damage "because each dog did in the eye of the law occasion the whole of the injury of which the pursuers complain". Thus, if the concurrent negligence of two people combined to kill someone, each would be equally responsible for the death.[94] A group of polluters may be jointly liable though the harm caused by each cannot be determined.[95]

Where a tortious cause has combined with a non-tortious cause to produce an injury, the negligent defendant is responsible for the whole of the damage and no apportionment is allowed, as explained by Major J.:[96]

> If the law permitted apportionment between tortious causes and non-tortious causes, a plaintiff could recover 100 per cent of his or her loss only when the defendant's negligence was the *sole* cause of the injuries. Since most events are the result of a complex set of causes, there will frequently be non-tortious causes contributing to the injury. Defendants could frequently and easily identify non-tortious contributing causes, so plaintiffs would rarely receive full compensation even after proving that the defendant caused the injury. This would be contrary to established principles and the essential purpose of tort law, which is to restore the plaintiff to the position he or she would have enjoyed but for the negligence of the defendant.
>
> . . .
>
> . . . Apportionment between tortious and non-tortious causes is contrary to the principles of tort law, because the defendant would escape full liability even though he or she caused or contributed to the plaintiff's entire injuries. The plaintiff would not be adequately compensated, since the plaintiff would not be placed in the position he or she would have been in absent the defendant's negligence.

If the loss is practically divisible, the court will hold each defendant liable only for the amount of damage that each personally inflicted.[97] Thus, if the court could determine which sheep had been killed by each dog in *Arneil v. Paterson,* each owner would have been required to pay only for the loss caused by the dog each defendant owned. Moreover, if X injures P's leg and Y injures P's arm, each pays only for the damage each inflicted.

A similar division is made when the injuries are not concurrent, but follow one another in time. Thus, if one tortfeasor injures someone's leg, and a second

---

[92] (1920), 182 Mass. 250.

[93] [1931] A.C. 560. See also *Cowan v. Duke of Buccleuch* (1876), 2 App. Cas. 344; *Blair and Sumner v. Deakin* (1887), 57 L.T. 522, 3 T.L.R. 757.

[94] See generally *Prosser and Keeton, op. cit. supra*, n. 89, at p. 313.

[95] *Michie v. Great Lakes Steel* (1974), 495 F. 2d 213 (6th Cir.); cert. denied 419 U.S. 997.

[96] See *Athey, supra*, n. 54, at pp. 121-22, C.C.L.T.

[97] See *Athey, supra*, n. 54.

tortfeasor later injures it further, necessitating amputation of the leg, the first defendant must pay the damages as they would have been assessed on the day before the second injury, and the second defendant would have to compensate only for the *additional* devaluation of the plaintiff caused by the second injury.[98] A more complicated but consistent calculation is undertaken when there are three separate, successive, injuries.[99]

If a non-culpable injury intrudes, a similar result ensues. Thus, where a victim of an accident is off work for 13 months, but three of these months would have been lost in any event because of an unrelated heart condition, recovery can be given only for ten months' lost income, for otherwise the victim would be "overcompensated".[100] So too, if a person is disabled by tortious conduct and it is discovered that a medical condition unconnected to the accident would have caused incapacitation in any event, the damages payable by the tortfeasor must be reduced to the extent that the medical condition caused the loss.[101]

The rationale underlying these successive injury cases has been explained by Major J. in *Athey*[102] as follows:

> . . . the plaintiff is not to be placed in a position *better* than his or her original one. It is therefore necessary not only to determine the plaintiff's position after the tort but also to assess what the "original position" would have been. It is the difference between these positions, the "original position" and the "injured position", which is the plaintiff's loss. In the cases referred to above, the intervening event was unrelated to the tort and therefore affected the plaintiff's "original position". The net loss was therefore not as great as it might have otherwise seemed, so damages were reduced to reflect this.

3. TWO NEGLIGENT DEFENDANTS BUT ONLY ONE CAUSE OF ACCIDENT: ONUS ON DEFENDANTS

Plaintiffs must prove who caused their losses. Pointing to two or more individuals and saying that one of them was the cause is not normally enough.[103] There is, however, an important exception to this principle. It applies where two people are both guilty of negligent conduct in circumstances where the conduct

---

[98] See *Baker v. Willoughby*, [1970] A.C. 483, [1969] 3 All E.R. 1528. For a brief and clear treatment of some of these problems, see Strachan, "The Scope and Application of the 'But For' Causal Test" (1970), 33 Mod. L. Rev. 386. See also Peaslee, "Multiple Causation and Damage" (1934), 47 Harv. L. Rev. 1127; Carpenter, "Concurrent Causation" (1935), 83 U. Pa. L. Rev. 941; Street, "Supervening Events and the Quantum of Damages" (1962), 78 L.Q. Rev. 70; Wagner, "Successive Causes and the Quantum of Damages in Personal Injury Cases" (1972), 10 Osgoode Hall L.J. 369. See also *Stene v. Evans et al.* (1958), 14 D.L.R. (2d) 73 (Alta. C.A.); *Dingle v. Associated Newspapers Ltd.*, [1960] 2 Q.B. 405; affd [1964] A.C. 371; *Long v. Thiessen & Laliberté* (1968), 65 W.W.R. 577 (B.C.C.A.); *Harwood v. Wyken Colliery Co.*, [1913] 2 K.B. 158 (C.A.); *Hicks v. Cooper* (1973), 1 O.R. (2d) 221 (C.A.).

[99] *Berns v. Campbell* (1974), 8 O.R. 680 (Hughes J.).

[100] *Penner v. Mitchell* (1978), 6 C.C.L.T. 132, at p. 141 (Alta. C.A.) (*per* Prowse J.A.).

[101] *Jobling v. Associated Davies Ltd.*, [1980] 3 W.L.R. 704 (C.A.).

[102] *Supra*, n. 54, at p. 124, C.C.L.T.

[103] Compare with Chapter 8, Section E, *infra*.

of only one of them brought about loss to an innocent plaintiff. In such a case, both are considered to be the cause of the plaintiff's loss and both are held responsible, unless they can exculpate themselves. The leading case is *Cook v. Lewis.*[104] While hunting, the plaintiff was shot by one of the two defendants, both of whom had fired at different birds at approximately the same time. Mr. Justice Rand stated:

> . . . if the victim, having brought guilt down to one or both of two persons before the court, can bring home to either of them a further wrong done him in relation to his remedial right of making that proof, then I should say that on accepted principles, the barrier to it can and should be removed.[105]

His Lordship explained that by their conduct the defendants "destroyed the victim's power of proof", by confusing their acts with "environmental conditions". Mr. Justice Rand continued:

> . . . the onus is. . . shifted to the wrongdoer to exculpate himself; it becomes in fact a question of proof between him and the other and innocent member of the alternatives, the burden of which he must bear. The onus attaches to culpability, and if both acts bear that taint, the onus or prima facie transmission of responsibility attaches to both, and the question of the sole responsibility of one is a matter between them.
>
> . . . This is a case where each hunter would know of or expect the shooting by the other and the negligent actor has culpably participated in the proof-destroying fact, the multiple shooting and its consequences. No liability will in any event attach to an innocent act of shooting, but the culpable actor, as against innocence, must bear the burden of exculpation.[106]

Mr. Justice Cartwright agreed that once it was found that the plaintiff was shot by one of two negligent defendants, if it could not be decided which of the two shot him, both defendants should be found liable.

The Supreme Court relied on the similar American case of *Summers v. Tice,* where the court stated:

> When we consider the relative position of the parties and the results that would flow if plaintiff was required to pin the injury on one of the defendants only, a requirement that the burden of proof on that subject be shifted to the defendants becomes manifest. They are both wrongdoers — both negligent towards plaintiff. They brought about a situation where the negligence of one of them injured the plaintiff, hence, it should rest with them each to absolve himself if he can. The injured party has been placed by defendants in the unfair position of pointing to which defendant caused the harm. If one can escape the other may also and plaintiff is remediless. Ordinarily defendants are in a far better position to offer evidence to determine which one caused the injury.[107]

---

[104] [1951] S.C.R. 830. See also *Woodward v. Begbie,* [1962] O.R. 60, two police officers shot at a suspect, but only one hit him; *Saint-Pierre v. McCarthy,* [1957] Que. Q.B. 421 (C.A.). See Hogan, "*Cook v. Lewis* Re-examined" (1961), 24 Mod. L. Rev. 331.

[105] *Ibid.,* at pp. 832-33. See also *Joseph Brant Memorial Hospital v. Koziol* (1977), 2 C.C.L.T. 170, at p. 180 (S.C.C.), explaining the scope of *Cook v. Lewis.*

[106] *Ibid.,* at pp. 833-34.

[107] (1948), 33 Cal. App. 2d 80, 199 P.2d. 1.

This principle has withstood the test of time, but it will not be lightly extended. In *Lange v. Bennett*,[108] the 18-year-old plaintiff was hunting with two 16-year-old friends. He knelt down and then suddenly stood up in the line of fire of the other two boys. A bullet shot by one of them struck him, but it could not be determined which defendant was responsible. Mr. Justice McRuer found that, since the plaintiff was himself contributorily negligent, *Cook v. Lewis* would not apply. He explained:

> Negligence must necessarily be relative to the circumstances in each case and to the ages of the parties in question. The plaintiff at the time of the accident was two years older than the defendant. He kneeled down to shoot and knew that he was in the approximate line of fire of two younger boys, shooting from behind him. He was unquestionably negligent in standing up without warning and putting himself into the line of fire. He must be taken to have known that he might have been struck by a shot fired by either of them and it would be difficult to say in such circumstances which boy fired the shot that struck him. He had himself participated as a "negligent actor" in "the proof destroying fact". To hold on these facts that the one who may have done him no harm should pay damages because he could not clear himself from blame would be grossly unjust. These are not special circumstances. . . .[109]

There is, however, recent authority to the effect that the principle of *Cook v. Lewis* may be available in cases of strict liability and nuisance cases,[110] as well as in other situations.[111]

There has been a related development in the California case of *Sindell v. Abbott Laboratories*[112] which has generated some controversy. It is called "market share" liability. Where liability would otherwise be found against several manufacturers, except for the fact that it cannot be established which of them was the cause of the plaintiff's loss, each of them can be held liable for their "market share" of the loss, unless they can show they did not cause the loss. It is necessary for this device to be used to sue the producers of a substantial share of the market, that is, over 50 per cent. In other words, if it cannot be shown which of several producers caused a loss, rather than dismissing the action, it is felt to be fairer to hold each of them partially to blame in proportion to their share of the market.[113] There has been no indication yet whether this case will be followed in Canada.

---

[108] [1964] 1 O.R. 233.

[109] *Ibid.*, at p. 237.

[110] See *MacDonald v. Desourdy Construction Ltée.* (1972), 27 D.L.R. (3d) 144, at p. 159 (N.S.), *obiter dictum* (Dubinsky J.).

[111] See also *Kolesar v. Jeffries* (1976), 12 O.R. (2d) 142, at p. 161 (C.A.), where onus of proof of cause of death shifted to defendant hospital and nurse, whose negligence deprived plaintiff of ability to prove cause of death. This decision was affirmed by the S.C.C. on another point, but the Court expressly disagreed on this issue (1977), 2 C.C.L.T. 170, at p. 180.

[112] (1980), 607 P. 2d 924 (Calif.).

[113] *Prosser and Keeton, op. cit. supra*, n. 89, pp. 271 and 713.

Chapter 5

Negligence: The Standard of Care

No court in a negligence suit can escape a decision about whether or not the defendant's conduct breached the standard of care fixed by the law. Every single case that comes across a lawyer's desk involves a determination of this issue, that is, whether the conduct was negligent. The bulk of legal talent and judicial resources is expended on this matter. It is therefore necessary to consider this aspect of the law, the third element, in some detail.

The standard of care adopted by negligence law is an objective standard, not a subjective one. The courts utilize the fictional reasonable person to assist them in the task of evaluation. The words "fault" and "blame" are employed, but there is no moral opprobrium attached to this language as there is in the criminal law. These terms have acquired a special meaning in negligence law that varies in accordance with the class of defendant involved. It will be seen that unreasonableness means different things for children, for those with mental disabilities, and for professional people. Although the courts pursue the goal of a common objective standard, it will be seen that subjective elements occasionally intrude.

Every type of conduct imaginable must conform to the guidelines set out by the law of negligence. Not only are motorists and professional people subject to the scrutiny of tort law, but also skiers[1] and racing car drivers.[2] Judges who are immune from negligence liability for their decision-making can be held liable if they swing their office doors open, knocking over a secretary. What is more, the secretary can be held contributory negligent for not using caution against the risk of being hit by the door.[3] An oil company can be held liable for delivering too much oil to a home, causing an overflow that damages the basement, and the householder may be partially to blame for directing the oil company carelessly in that regard.[4] Those who make it necessary for the police to chase them, causing an accident, can be held liable for negligence.[5] One must use reasonable

[1] *Taylor v. The Queen* (1978), 95 D.L.R. (3d) 82; vard 112 D.L.R. (3d) 297 (B.C.C.A.).
[2] *Reese v. Coleman (No. 1)*, [1979] 4 W.W.R. 58.
[3] *O'Connor v. State of South Australia* (1976), 14 S.A.S.R. 187.
[4] *Jasin v. Peoples Co-operative* (1978), 92 D.L.R. (3d) 340 (Man. C.A.).
[5] *A.-G. for Ont. v. Keller* (1978), 19 O.R. (2d) 695.

care to prevent damage caused by third persons, even if caused by criminal acts.[6] An airline can be required to pay damages to its passengers if the latter are negligently misdirected at a terminal causing them to miss their flight. The passengers, also, may be held partially to blame for failing to make proper inquires.[7]

Consequently, the scope of operation of negligence law is very wide indeed. It is plain that there is virtually no activity — new or old, rare or commonplace, dangerous or safe, inside or outside, during the day or the night, in the winter or the summer — which can escape review by negligence standards.

A. Unreasonable Risk

Conduct is negligent if it creates an unreasonable risk of harm.[8] This does not mean that *all* risky conduct attracts liability, for virtually everything that anybody does creates some hazard to somebody. If *every* act involving danger to someone entailed liability, many worthwhile activities of our society might be too costly to conduct. The law of negligence seeks to prevent only those acts which produce an unreasonable risk of harm. In measuring whether the hazard is an unreasonable one, the court balances the danger created by the defendant's conduct, on one hand, and the utility of that conduct, on the other hand. If the hazard outweighs the social value of the activity, liability is imposed; if it does not, the defendant is exonerated.

The two sides of this equation may be broken down further. In assessing the risk, the courts look at two components: (1) the chance or likelihood that the harm will culminate, and (2) the gravity or severity of the potential harm that will ensue if the accident transpires. The other side of the equation also comprises two elements: (1) the purpose or object of the act in question, and (2) the cost or the burden to the actor to eliminate the hazard.

Mr. Justice Learned Hand[9] once attempted to express this notion in algebraic terms. He suggested that liability depended upon whether B is less than PL. P stands for the probability that the risk will eventuate, L represents the gravity of the loss if the injury results and B is the burden of adequate precautions. Professor (now Mr. Justice) Posner has argued that this is an "economic test":

> The burden of precautions is the cost of avoiding the accident. The loss multiplied by the probability of the accident is the cost that the precautions would have averted. If a larger cost could have been avoided by incurring a smaller cost, efficiency requires that the smaller cost be incurred.[10]

---

[6]   *Q. v. Minto Management* (1985), 31 C.C.L.T. 158 (Ont. H.C.).

[7]   *Duemler v. Air Canada* (1980), 109 D.L.R. (3d) 402 (Alta. Q.B.). But not for turbulence, *Quinn v. Canadian Airlines International Ltd.* (1994), 23 C.C.L.T. (2d) 203 (Ont. Gen. Div.).

[8]   Terry, "Negligence" (1915), 29 Harv. L. Rev. 40; Green, "The Negligence Issue" (1928), 37 Yale L.J. 1029; James, "The Nature of Negligence' (1953), 3 Utah L. Rev. 275.

[9]   *United States v. Carroll Towing Co.* (1947), 159 F.2d 169 (2d Cir. Ct. of Appeals).

[10]   *Economic Analysis of Law*, 3rd ed. (1986), p. 147.

This formula is helpful, but a more accurate one would split the burden factor in two — object and cost. The amended equation, therefore, is PL = OC. If the probability multiplied by the loss is greater than the object times the cost, liability ensues; conversely, if the probability times the loss is less than the object times the cost, the conduct is blameless.

This talk of mathematics and economics is somewhat misleading, because evaluation of risk is not an exact science. Rather, like sentencing, it is a very human process.[11] This is necessarily so when each case must be decided by the judge or jury according to its unique circumstances. Rarely can all of the variable facts surrounding an accident be duplicated. Consequently, *stare decisis* is of little avail here. Legal rules are absent. One jury does not bind another, nor does one judge bind the next. The tribunal must make a fresh decision in each case. Values are involved in this determination. What must be judged is whether the conduct of this particular defendant in this singular situation was acceptable or unacceptable to the community. The responsibility rests on the instant judge or jury and authoritative guidance is virtually nonexistent. There is almost no law of negligence — there is merely an approach that each tribunal will utilize.[12]

This has been recently recognized in *McEvay v. Tory*[13] where the court refused to create a specific duty on motorists to stop or slow down when a bus stops, preferring to rely on the flexible standard of reasonableness in the circumstances. It was said "Such an inflexible standard of care would cause traffic to come to a virtual standstill every time 'the man on the Clapham bus' wants to get off."

Let us now look at each of the four factors the courts take into account in passing judgment.

1. PROBABILITY

If there is only a slight chance that an accident will occur, the court may hold that running such a risk is not unreasonable, because "people must guard against reasonable probabilities, but they are not bound to guard against fantastic possibilities".[14] In this context the word "probability" does not mean that an accident must be more likely to happen that not; there need be only a real or substantial risk of harm. One chance of injury in 100 or even 1,000 may suffice.

The leading case in this area is *Bolton v. Stone*,[15] where during a cricket match a batsman hit a ball over the fence into the adjoining highway injuring the plaintiff who was standing there. The cricket ground had been used for some 90 years and no one had ever been injured in this way before although the evidence

---

[11] Hogarth, *Sentencing as a Human Process* (1971).
[12] Green, *Judge and Jury* (1930).
[13] (1990), 4 C.C.L.T. (2d) 141, at p. 147 (B.C.C.A.).
[14] *Fardon v. Harcourt-Rivington* (1932), 146 L.T. 391 (*per* Lord Dunedin). It is not enough that it is "conceivable that some unlucky injury might happen", see *Mullin v. Richards*, [1998] 1 All E.R. 920, at p. 927 (C.A.).
[15] [1951] A.C. 805, [1951] 1 All E.R. 1073 (H.L.).

disclosed that on about six occasions over a period of 30 years a ball had been propelled into the highway. There was further evidence that five or six times during the last few years a ball had been struck into a neighboring house or into its yard, but this property was somewhat closer to the cricket ground than the spot where the plaintiff was injured. The House of Lords found the defendants not liable because "the chance of a person ever being struck even in a long period of years was very small".[16] The test to be applied, according to Lord Reid, was "whether the risk of damage to a person on the road was so small that a reasonable man in the position of the appellants, considering the matter from the point of view of safety, would have thought it right to refrain from taking steps to prevent the danger".[17] As part of this assessment, His Lordship remarked that it should be taken into account not only "how remote is the chance that a person might be struck, but also how serious the consequences are likely to be if a person is struck". Lord Reid contended, however, that it would not be right to take into account "the difficulty of remedial measures", for "if cricket cannot be played on a ground creating a substantial risk, then it should not be played there at all".[18] It is submitted that His Lordship did not intend to forbid consideration of this factor in all cases. He was merely expressing the view that this particular activity, that is playing cricket, was not of sufficient social utility to count for very much on the scale, if it engendered a substantial danger.

Two contrasting Canadian cases illustrate the point. In *Shilson v. Northern Ontario Light and Power Company*[19] the defendants were relieved of responsibility to a 12-year-old boy who was injured by an electric wire as he walked across a ravine on a 12-inch pipe. Mr. Justice Anglin[20] thought that it was most improbable that "even a venturesome and mischievous boy" would try to cross a ravine 17 to 19 feet deep and 300 feet wide on a 12-inch pipe, despite barricades and warning signs. On the other hand, in *Gloster v. Toronto Electric Light Co.*,[21] an eight and one-half-year-old child who was injured when he touched an uninsulated wire 14 to 20 inches away from a bridge was permitted recovery. Mr. Justice Davies indicated that the defendant should have known that a large number of people were crossing the bridge daily and that they were likely to touch this wire, which was within a few inches of the bridge.[22] Thus, in *Shilson*

---

[16] *Ibid.*, at p. 864. One need not weep for Mrs. Stone, who was paid her damages and costs by the defendants following the decision in her favour by the Court of Appeal. After the House of Lords reversed the decision, the defendants, who were supported by the cricketers association in conducting the litigation because they felt an important principle was involved, decided not to pursue Mrs. Stone for repayment of the money they had paid to her. Mrs. Stone had to pay her own costs in the House of Lords, however. See Note (1952), 68 L.Q. Rev. 3.

[17] *Ibid.*, at p. 867.

[18] *Ibid.*

[19] (1919), 59 S.C.R. 443.

[20] *Ibid.*, at p. 446.

[21] (1906), 38 S.C.R. 27.

[22] *Ibid.*, at p. 33.

the chance of injury was so far-fetched that it could be ignored, but in *Gloster* the probability was significant enough to call for safety measures.

Steps must be taken to prevent damage caused by the normal vicissitudes of weather, but it is not necessary to forestall loss resulting from abnormally severe weather conditions, because such events rarely occur. For example, no liability was imposed for loss caused by an unprecedented frost,[23] "an extraordinary fall of rain", or a rain of "exceptional character".[24] Similarly, no blame was attached when a structure blew down as a result of a "sudden and extraordinary wind", described as a "cyclone, tornado, hurricane" which was of a very "unique, severe and exceptional kind, . . . striking. . . with extraordinary force and fury.[25] So too a logging company was relieved of liability for a fire started as a result of its activity, because no one had every heard of a fire being ignited in this way. This was held even though the summer in question was drier than usual, and so more amenable to the outbreak of a fire.[26] On the other hand, damages were awarded for a wall that was blown down by a wind characterized as a "gale" which was "violent, but not of unusual violence".[27] People in San Francisco, for instance, may have to take steps to minimize the risk of an earthquake, since there is a real likelihood that one will occur there, whereas people in Winnipeg do not, since the risk of an earthquake is very remote in that locale.

Extraordinarily sensitive individuals are generally denied special protection because they are seldom encountered.[28] For example, in the case of *Elverson v. Doctors Hospital,*[29] a hospital was relieved of liability for the way in which its nurse tried to elevate the foot of a patient's bed. When the nurse encountered some difficulty, the plaintiff, who was the husband of the patient, tried to help them, but aggravated a pre-existing back condition in so doing. Mr. Justice Evans concluded that this was a "common, everyday occurrence, completely devoid of any inherent danger and the particular susceptibility of the plaintiff was beyond any range of normal expectancy or of reasonable foresight on the part of the nurse".

In *Munshaw Colour Service Limited v. City of Vancouver,*[30] the plaintiff's filter system broke down at a time when the municipality was flushing its sewer. This caused a certain sediment to enter the plaintiff's premises, which spoiled some film. The city was exculpated because it was not expected to foresee that any damage would be caused by some sediment in water which did not render it impure for drinking.[31] Mr. Justice Judson argued that to impose a duty in these

---

[23] *Blyth v. Birmingham Water Works Co.* (1856), 11 Ex. 781, 156 E.R. 1047.

[24] *Judge v. Liverpool* (1916), 28 D.L.R. 617, at p. 622 (*per* Longley J.); affd (1918), 57 S.C.R. 609.

[25] *Valiquette v. Fraser* (1907), 39 S.C.R. 1, at pp. 5-6 (*per* Davies J.).

[26] *Higgins v. Comox Logging Co.*, [1927] S.C.R. 359.

[27] *Nordheimer v. Alexander* (1891), 19 S.C.R. 248, at p. 264 (*per* Patterson J.).

[28] *Nova Mink v. Trans-Canada Airlines*, [1951] 2 D.L.R. 241 (N.S.C.A.).

[29] (1974), 49 D.L.R. (3d) 196, at p. 198; affd (1976), 65 D.L.R. (3d) 382.

[30] [1962] S.C.R. 433.

[31] *Ibid.*, at p. 436 (*per* Cartwright J.).

circumstances would be to "require a standard of perfection".[32] One could not expect a city to think about the effect of its water upon "consumers of peculiar sensitivity". If the city had to consider these "minutiae" in relation to their routine operations, they would not be able to operate a waterworks system. Those with particular requirements above the ordinary must deal with them as part of *their* operation, and cannot expect these extra burdens to be assumed by the municipality.

2. LOSS

When the potential loss is great, the creation of even a slight risk may give rise to liability. Professor Fleming has written that "not only the greater risk of injury, but also the risk of greater injury is a relevant factor".[33] Thus, in *Bolton v. Stone*,[34] for example, if the threatened harm had been a bullet in the heart or a nuclear explosion, rather than just a bump on the head, the defendant might have been liable. Even though it is highly unlikely that lightning will strike at a given place at a given time, one must take precautions against this, because where there is an "extreme hazard", the precautions taken must be "commensurate with the danger".[35]

This concept was recognized in the case of *Paris v. Stepney Borough Council*,[36] where a one-eyed man was blinded when a chip of metal flew into his good eye. The plaintiff alleged that his employer was negligent in failing to provide him with goggles, even though the usual practice in the trade was not to supply them for men engaged in this work, at least if they had sight in both eyes. The House of Lords concluded in a three-two decision that the gravity of the harm likely to be caused would influence a reasonable man and, therefore, even though no duty was owed to a man with sight in both eyes, the duty of care to a one-eyed employee required the supply of goggles. In considering negligence one must look at two factors: the magnitude of risk and the likelihood of injury being caused. The dissenting law lords felt that loss of an eye to a man with sight in both eyes was so serious that there should be liability either to all employees, or to none at all, since it was not a case of trivial as opposed to grave injury.

Dean Prosser summarized the position in this way: "[A]s the gravity of the possible harm increases, the apparent likelihood of its occurrence need be correspondingly less to generate a duty of precaution."[37]

---

[32] *Ibid.*, at p. 442.

[33] *The Law of Torts*, 9th ed. (1998), p. 128. See also Duff J., dissenting, in *Canada & Gulf Terminal Ry. v. Levesque*, [1928] S.C.R. 340, at p. 347.

[34] *Supra*, n. 15.

[35] *Montreal Park & Island Ry. v. McDougall* (1905), 36 S.C.R. 1, at p. 6 (*per* Nesbitt J.).

[36] [1951] A.C. 367, [1951] 1 All E.R. 42.

[37] *Prosser and Keeton on the Law of Torts*, 5th ed. (1984), at p. 171.

3. OBJECT

Even though there is a substantial risk of loss and even though the damage is potentially severe, defendants may be excused from liability if their activities have high social utility. In other words, where the objectives served are laudable enough, risks may be taken.

a) Police Activity Causing Injury to Others

The leading Canadian case is *Priestman v. Colangelo and Smythson*.[38] Smythson, a 17-year-old, stole a car and was driving along Donlands Avenue in East York when he was detected by two police officers who were patrolling in a car. The boy quickly drove off along Mortimer Ave., a side street, and the officers pursued him in an attempt to apprehend him. The police car tried to pass the stolen car on three occasions, but each time Smythson pulled over thwarting their efforts. One of the officers then fired a warning shot into the air. The youth's vehicle only increased its speed. The officer then took aim at the left rear tire and fired. Unfortunately, the police vehicle at that moment hit a bump and the bullet went through the rear window of the vehicle, striking the driver in the neck, causing him to lose consciousness. The car went out of control and fatally injured two young women who were waiting for a bus.

   The Supreme Court of Canada, in a three-two decision, dismissed the claims of the young women's families against the officers,[39] on the ground that the hazard they created was not too great in the light of the social value of capturing a "criminal whose actions . . . constitute a menace to other members of the public".[40] In attempting to stop this fleeing car, the police officers were not obligated to risk their lives again and "no other reasonable or practical means of halting the car[had] been suggested than to slacken its speed by blowing out one of the tires". The court observed that the police could not do anything that came into their mind in order to apprehend a criminal, but certain reasonable risks could be taken for this purpose. For example, it would be permissible to bump into someone while pursuing a pickpocket in a crowd, or to damage private property in order to catch a bank robber who was hiding there, or to shoot at an escaping bank robber who had murdered a bank employee and was firing a revolver at the police officers who were pursuing. A police officer, however, cannot fire into a crowd in the hope of stopping a fleeing criminal who is obscured from view. For the majority, Mr. Justice Locke relied in part on s. 25(4) of the Criminal Code,[41] which "justified" the use of "as much force as is necessary to prevent the escape by flight, unless the escape can be prevented by reasonable means in a less violent manner".

---

[38]   [1959] S.C. R. 615, 19 D.L.R. (2d) 1. See also *Marshall v. Osmond*, [1982] 2 All E.R. 610 (Q.B.), no liability of police to person being pursued, who was hit by car.
[39]   The action was successful against Smythson, but, of course, he was uninsured.
[40]   *Ibid.*, at p. 624 (*per* Locke J.).
[41]   R.S.C. 1970, c. C-34 [now R.S.C. 1985, c. C-46, s. 25(4)].

Mr. Justice Cartwright, dissenting,[42] after balancing the serious risk and the utility of apprehending the offender, concluded that the officer was negligent, and that he was not excused by s. 25(4) of the Criminal Code, which he felt did not apply when "innocent bystanders unconnected with the flight or pursuit" were injured.

A similar decision is *Poupart v. Lafortune*,[43] where some armed robbers opened fire on a police officer when he tried to apprehend them. He fired back and accidentally wounded an innocent bystander. Chief Justice Fauteux excused the police officer for a "police officer incurs no liability for damage caused to another when without negligence he does precisely what the Legislature requires him to do". His Lordship, contrary to Mr. Justice Cartwright's view, indicated that s. 25(4) "relieves the police officer of any civil or criminal liability, not only in respect of the fugitive but also in respect of any person who accidentally becomes an innocent victim of the force used".

One might argue that this was only a *dictum,* because there was a finding in the case of no negligence in the circumstances, hence any consideration of statutory immunity would be superfluous. There is also some question about whether the Federal Parliament is entitled to excuse police officers from civil liability for their conduct, a subject which is usually considered to be within provincial jurisdiction.[44] While it is certainly correct under negligence law to consider the worthy object of apprehending criminals in assessing whether the danger created is unreasonable, the policy of tort law may well impose liability in the circumstances, even though that of the criminal law would not.

There is authority which imposes liability on police officers who injure others by their negligence, notwithstanding s. 25(4). For example, in *Beim v. Goyer,*[45] a police officer accidentally shot a car thief he was chasing over rough ground. The officer was carrying his gun at the time and had previously fired several warning shots. The officer was held liable by the Supreme Court of Canada because an unarmed boy running away on foot posed no danger to the officer or to anyone else. Mr. Justice Ritchie distinguished *Priestman v. Colangelo and Smythson* since in that case it was reasonable for the officer to fire at the time. Mr. Justice Martland dissented and suggested that there was nothing wrong with firing some warning shots into the air while running, because, if the officer had stopped before firing, the chances are that the person would have escaped. He distinguished *Priestman,* where the shot was deliberately fired, from this case where the gun discharged accidentally. According to Mr. Justice Martland, it was not even necessary for the officer to rely upon s. 25(4) of the Criminal Code to excuse his conduct.

---

42 *Supra,* n. 38, at p. 627 (S.C.R.).
43 [1973] S.C.R. 175, 41 D.L.R. (3d) 720, at pp. 725-26.
44 See Hogg, "Comment on *Vapor Canada Ltd.*" (1976), 54 Can. Bar Rev. 361.
45 [1965] S.C.R. 638. See also B.C. MacDonald, "Use of Force By Police to Effect Lawful Arrest" (1966-67), 9 Crim. L.Q. 415; Weiler, "Groping Towards a Canadian Tort Law: The Role of the Supreme Court of Canada" (1971), 21 U. of T.L.J. 267, at p. 314.

A similar decision is *Woodward v. Begbie,*[46] where a prowler was accidentally shot by one of two police officers who fired intending to hit the ground near the fleeing suspect. Mr. Justice McLennan held that s. 25(4) did not immunize the defendant because "more force was used than was necessary and the escape could have been prevented by the more reasonable means of overtaking the plaintiff".[47]

Both *Beim v. Goyer* and *Woodward v. Begbie* indicate that the courts may circumvent the operation of s. 25(4) by holding that the police officers were negligent in the circumstances and could not be immunized by the section. *Priestman v. Colangelo and Smythson* and *Poupart v. Lafortune,* on the other hand, were cases where there was no negligence in the circumstances and the section was not needed to exculpate the officers, who had not fallen below the reasonable standard of care in the circumstances, because their object was valuable enough to the community to offset the risks they had to create. On the whole, however, it would be preferable to minimize the role of s. 25(4) in these tort cases, because it tends to confuse and to place too great a value on the apprehension of criminals at the expense of the innocent people that may be hurt by such activity. The ordinary balancing process of the risk calculus is better suited for these cases.

b) Other Situations

There are other contexts in which risky conduct may be acceptable in the light of the object being served. If a police officer, for example, moves too quickly and slips on ice while chasing a criminal, the officer is not contributorily negligent, since "if there was a risk, the end to be achieved outweighed the risk".[48]

Similarly, it is not contributory negligence to drive an ambulance with unsafe rear-view mirror equipment in war-time, because, as Lord Justice Asquith observed,[49] "the end to be served" overshadowed the risk. His Lordship explained that "if all the trains in this country were restricted to a speed of 5 miles an hour there would be fewer accidents but our national life would be intolerably slowed down". During the war, he suggested, it was necessary to carry on "many highly important operations" with makeshift equipment and it would be demanding too much of the drivers to expect them to behave in an impossible way.

In another case, *Watt v. Hertfordshire County Council,*[50] the defendant's fire station had a heavy jack which stood on wheels and which only one vehicle was properly equipped to carry safely. While that vehicle was out on a service call, an emergency call was received to rescue a woman trapped under a heavy

---

[46] [1962] O.R. 60.
[47] *Ibid.,* at p. 63. See also *Teece v. Honeybourn et al.,* [1974] 5 W.W.R. 592 (B.C.), police 80% at fault for shooting.
[48] *Bittner v. Tait-Gibson Optometrists Co. Ltd.,* [1964] 2 O.R. 52 (C.A.).
[49] *Daborn v. Bath Tramways Motor Co. Ltd.,* [1946] 2 All E.R. 333, at p. 336 (C.A.).
[50] [1954] 2 All E.R. 368 (C.A.).

vehicle. The officer in charge ordered the jack loaded on another lorry, although there was no way of properly securing it. On the way to the scene of the accident, the driver of the lorry had to stop suddenly, causing the jack to roll and injure the plaintiff. The plaintiff's action failed. Lord Justice Denning declared:

> One must balance the risk against the end to be achieved. If this accident had occurred in a commercial enterprise, without any emergency, there could be no doubt that the [plaintiff] would succeed. But the commercial end to make profit is very different from the human end to save life or limb. The saving of life or limb justifies taking considerable risk. . . . I quite agree that fire engines, ambulances and doctors' cars should not shoot past the traffic lights when they show a red light. That is because the risk is too great to warrant the incurring of the danger. It is always a question of balancing the risk against the end.[51]

Where someone takes risks in order to save life in an emergency, allowances are made because of the social value of the end to be achieved.[52] "Reasonable people must be able to handle emergencies reasonably well", but rescuers are not expected to act with textbook perfection in situations of peril.[53] Similarly, those who are injured trying to save themselves from danger are judged rather compassionately.[54]

Nevertheless, one must not stop one's car suddenly to avoid hitting an animal, because regard for "human life and safety must always come first and it is not reasonable that a driver should risk human life or limb in order to preserve the life of an animal".[55]

Where an activity is devoid of social utility, as perhaps a game of cricket,[56] or the illegal release of oil into a bay,[57] a risk is more likely to be judged unreasonable. As Professor Fleming points out, "there is a world of difference between throwing a burning object into the street below just for the fun of it or in order to save a house on fire".[58]

---

[51] *Ibid.*, at p. 371.

[52] *Hogan v. McEwan* (1975), 10 O.R. (2d) 551. See also *Coderre v. Ethier et al.* (1978), 19 O.R. (2d) 503 (*per* Lerner J.), vehicle must make way for emergency vehicle, even if the emergency vehicle is going through red light.

[53] *Cleary v. Hansen* (1981), 18 C.C.L.T. 147, at p. 157 (*per* Linden J.); *Horsley v. MacLaren*, [1970] 2 O.R. 487; affd (1972), 22 D.L.R. (3d) 545 (S.C.C.). *Cf.*, *Vallery v. Po* (1971), 23 D.L.R. (3d) 92 (B.C.), police on way to accident found negligent, despite statute.

[54] *Walls v. Mussens Ltd.* (1969), 11 D.L.R. (3d) 245 (N.B.C.A.); *Zervobeakos v. Zervobeakos* (1970), 8 D.L.R. (3d) 377 (N.S.C.A.); *Neufeld v. Landry* (1975), 55 D.L.R. (3d) 296 (Man. C.A.).

[55] *Molson v. Squamish Transfer Ltd.* (1969), 7 D.L.R. (3d) 553, at p. 557 (B.C.) (*per* Wilson C.J.). *Cf.*, *Hogan v. McEwan, supra*, n. 52.

[56] *Bolton v. Stone, supra*, n. 15.

[57] *The Wagon Mound (No. 2)*, [1967] 1 A.C. 617, at p. 642 (P.C.).

[58] Fleming, *op. cit.*, *supra*, n. 33, at p. 130.

4. COST

The cost of removing the risk must also be thrown onto the scale. Thus, the "ease or difficulty with which the risk can be avoided" must be assessed.[59] Lord Justice Denning has stated that "in measuring due care one must balance the risk against the measures necessary to eliminate that risk".[60] If the cost is minimal, liability is more likely to follow. In *Mercer v. Commissioner for Road Transport and Tramways*,[61] the driver of a vehicle collapsed at the controls and, despite the efforts of the conductors to stop it with the hand brakes, a collision ensued. The plaintiffs alleged that "a dead man's handle" would have prevented this type of accident, although it also would have caused certain problems. The jury's verdict in favour of the plaintiff was upheld. Further, a court may require a taxi company to protect their youthful passengers by either the installation of an inexpensive safety device or by providing a better supervision system.[62] Where there is a high risk of injury to children as a result of street ice-cream vending, however, it may be necessary to supply a second attendant on a truck, even though the company could not carry on its business "profitably" if they did.[63]

If the measures that must be taken are costly, liability is less likely to ensue. Thus, a railroad need not build an over-pass at every level crossing. Nor must it do without a turntable merely because a child may be hurt by it, although it should take less expensive steps to protect children, such as keeping it locked.[64] A doctor, for example, must disclose only the "material" and "unusual or special" risks of an operation being done for the benefit of the health of a patient,[65] but if the purpose is not for the medical welfare of the patient[66] or if it is cosmetic only[67] the doctor must tell more. Presumably, if the goal of the treatment is experimentation only,[68] the doctor may be obligated to tell the patient everything, because the value of saying less is outweighed by the significance of the needless risk being encountered.

---

[59]   *Wang v. Horrod* (1998), 42 C.C.L.T. (2d) 113, at p. 124 (B.C.C.A.) (*per* Rowles J.A.), bus driver case.

[60]   *Watt v. Hertfordshire C.C.*, [1954] 2 All E.R. 368, at p. 371 (C.A.). See also *Latimer v. A.E.C. Ltd.*, [1952] 2 Q.B. 701, at p. 711, [1952] 1 All E.R. 1302 (C.A.), where Denning L.J. stated "in every case of foreseeable risk, it is a matter of balancing the risk against the measures necessary to eliminate it". Affirmed, [1953] A.C. 643, [1953] 2 All E.R. 449.

[61]   (1937), 56 C.L.R. 580.

[62]   *Ware's Taxi Ltd. v. Gilliham*, [1949] S.C.R. 637.

[63]   See *Arnold v. Teno* (1978), 3 C.C.L.T. 272, at p. 286 (S.C.C.).

[64]   *Chicago B. & O. Ry. Co. v. Krayenbuhl* (1902), 65 Neb. 889, 91 N.W. 880. *Cf., Davison v. Snohomish County* (1928), 149 Wash. 109, 270 P. 422, accident-proof bridge need not be built.

[65]   *Reibl v. Hughes* (1980), 14 C.C.L.T. 1 (S.C.C.), see *infra*. Section F.2(h).

[66]   *Videto v. Kennedy* (1980), 27 O.R. (2d) 747, at p. 758 (*per* Grange J.); revd on another point (1981), 33 O.R. (2d) 497 (C.A.).

[67]   *White v. Turner* (1981), 15 C.C.L.T. 81 (*per* Linden J.); *Hankins v. Papillon* (1981), 14 C.C.L.T. 198, at p. 203 (Rothman J.) (Que. S.C.).

[68]   *Halushka v. University of Saskatchewan* (1965), 53 D.L.R. (2d) 436 (Sask. C.A.).

The courts balance each of these factors to determine whether the risk created is an unreasonable one. To assist them in this weighing process they call upon a figure who has become very familiar to the law.

B. The Reasonable Person

The measuring rod used in negligence law to judge an actor's conduct is the reasonable person.[69] In 1850, Baron Alderson furnished the common law world with a definition of negligence that is still appropriate today:

> Negligence is the omission to do something which a reasonable man, guided upon those considerations which ordinarily regulate the conduct of human affairs, would do, or doing something which a prudent and reasonable man would not do. The defendants might have been liable for negligence, if, unintentionally, they omitted to do that which a reasonable person would have done, or did that which a person taking reasonable precautions would not have done.[70]

Other phrases have been used interchangeably to describe the unique individual whose conduct is the model for society to live up to. This creature has also been called the "prudent person".[71] Several other adjectives and combinations of adjectives have been employed, including a person of ordinary prudence",[72] an "ordinarily prudent person",[73] a "prudent and reasonable" person,[74] a "reasonable and prudent" person,[75] a "reasonably careful" person,[76] and a "reasonably prudent and careful" individual.[77] There is even a case which, in another context,

---

[69] *R. v. Coté* (1974), 51 D.L.R. (3d) 244, at p. 252 (*per* Dickson J.); see also generally Seavey, "Negligence — Subjective or Objective?" (1927), 41 Harv. L. Rev. 1; James, "The Qualities of the Reasonable Man in Negligence Cases" (1951), 16 Mo. L. Rev. 1; Parsons, "Negligence, Contributory Negligence and the Man who Does Not Ride the Bus to Clapham" (1958), 1 Melb. U.L. Rev. 163; Green, "The Negligence Issue" (1928), 37 Yale L.J. 1029; Reynolds, "The Reasonable Man of Negligence Law: A Health Report on the 'Odious Creature'" (1970), 23 Okla. L. Rev. 410; Terry, "Negligence" (1915), 29 Harv. L. Rev. 40.

[70] *Blyth v. Birmingham Water Works Co.* (1856), 11 Ex. 781, at p. 784, 156 E.R. 1047; see also *Thompson v. Fraser*, [1955] S.C.R. 419, at p. 425, "Negligence is the failure to use the care a reasonable man would have exercised under the same or similar circumstances . . ." (*per* Estey J.); *Bridges v. North London Ry. Co.* (1874), L.R. 7 H.L. 213, at p. 232. "Negligence consists the doing of some act which a person of ordinary care and skill would not do under the circumstances or in omitting to do some act which a person of ordinary care and skill would do under the circumstances." *Sigerseth v. Pederson*, [1927] S.C.R. 342, at p. 347; *Nova Mink v. Trans-Canada Airlines*, [1951] 2 D.L.R. 241, at p. 254 (N.S.).

[71] *Yachuk v. Oliver Blais Co.*, [1946] S.C.R. 1, at p. 19 (*per* Rand J.); revd [1949] A.C. 386 (P.C.); *J. & R. Weir Ltd. v. Lunham & Moore Shipping Ltd.*, [1958] S.C.R. 46 (*per* Taschereau J.).

[72] *Vaughan v. Menlove* (1837), 3 Bing. N.C. 468, at p. 475, 132 E.R. 490.

[73] *Carnat v. Matthews* (1921), 59 D.L.R. 505, at p. 508 (Alta. C.A.).

[74] *Reid v. Linnell*, [1923] S.C.R. 594, at p. 610.

[75] *Arland v. Taylor*, [1955] O.R. 131, at p. 142 (C.A.); *Ware's Taxi Ltd. v. Gilliham*, [1949] S.C.R. 637, at p. 644 (*per* Rand J.), "reasonable and prudent person".

[76] *Blair v. Grand Trunk Ry.* (1923), 53 O.L.R. 405, at p. 410 (C.A.) (*per* Meredith C.J.C.P.); *Yachuk v. Oliver Blais Co.*, *supra*, n. 70, at p. 12 (*per* Estey J.).

[77] *Village of Kelliher v. Smith*, [1931] S.C.R. 672, at p. 678 (*per* Lamont J.).

imported the concept of a "humane" person.[78] But it is likely that this standard would be considered too hard on defendants to be generally applied at present, although that may change in the coming years.

In England, the reasonable person has been depicted as "the man on the Clapham omnibus".[79] In Canada today it might be more appropriate to portray this creature as "the person on the Yonge Street subway".

This is an objective standard, not a subjective one. An "impersonal" test is employed, which "eliminates the personal equation and is independent of the idiosyncrasies of the particular person whose conduct is in question".[80] If it were otherwise, negligence would be "co-extensive with the judgment of each individual, which would be as variable as the length of the foot of each individual" leaving "so vague a line as to afford no rule at all, the degree of judgment belonging to each individual being infinitely various".[81]

The law has required of everyone a minimum level of performance, whether they are capable of it or not. It is not enough for an actor to plead that he or she did "the best he knew how",[82] for the law "does not attempt to see men as God sees them".[83] This may be hard on the dull and awkward person, but the general welfare of society demands reasonable conduct from everyone.

The reasonable person is not perfect, however, for even "the most excessively careful man will sometimes have an accident".[84] The reasonable individual is "not a seer",[85] nor a "paragon of circumspection",[86] not a "person of infinite-resource-and-sagacity",[87] nor does that individual have the "prophetic vision of a clairvoyant".[88] "Tort law does not require the wisdom of Solomon."[89] Consequently, one may be guilty of an error in judgment, without incurring tort liability, as in the case of "pure misadventure".[90] The reasonable person is not obligated to "exercise the best possible judgment" in an emergency,[91] nor to avoid all possible risks, for as Mr. Justice Taschereau has stated, *"La loi n'exige*

---

[78] *Southern Portland Cement Ltd. v. Cooper*, [1974] A.C. 623 (P.C.) (*per* Lord Reid).

[79] *Hall v. Brooklands Auto-Racing Club*, [1933] 1 K.B. 205, at p. 224 (C.A.) (*per* Green L.J.).

[80] See *Glasgow Corp. v. Muir*, [1943] A.C. 448, at p. 457 (*per* Lord MacMillan).

[81] *Vaughan v. Menlove, supra*, n. 71.

[82] *Ibid.*, at p. 471.

[83] Holmes, *The Common Law* (1881), p. 108.

[84] Harvey C.J. in *Carnat v. Matthews* (1921), 59 D.L.R. 505, at p. 508 (Alta. C.A.). See also Idington J., dissenting, in *Armand v. Carr*, [1926] S.C.R. 575, at p. 588, "the best of mankind make grave mistakes".

[85] *Mt. Isa Mines Ltd. v. Pusey* (1971), 45 A.L.J.R. 88 (*per* Windeyer J.).

[86] *Billings & Sons Ltd. v. Riden*, [1958] A.C. 240, at p. 255 (*per* Lord Reid).

[87] *Mt. Isa Mines v. Pusey, supra*, n. 85, at p. 93.

[88] *Hawkins v. Coulson & Purley U.D.C.*, [1954] 1 Q.B. 319, at p. 341 (C.A.) (*per* Romer L.J.).

[89] *Stewart v. Pettie*, [1995] 1 S.C.R. 131, at p. 150 (*per* Major J.).

[90] *Sigerseth v. Pederson*, [1927] S.C.R. 342, at pp. 346-47.

[91] *Armond v. Carr et al.*, [1926] S.C.R. 575, at p. 581 (*per* Anglin C.J.C.). See also *Moore v. B.C. Electric Ry.* (1917), 35 D.L.R. 771 (B.C.C.A.); *Tatisich and Harding v. Edwards*, [1931] S.C.R. 167.

pas qu'un homme prévoie tous ce qui est possible".[92] What the model human must do is act in accordance with "normality and practicality" rather than "judicial technicality or diversity of view".[93]

A. P. Herbert's delightful caricature of the reasonable person, whose rule of life is "Safety First" and who has all the solid virtues, "save only that peculiar quality by which the affection of other men is won", probably sets too high a standard. According to Herbert, a reasonable individual never

> swears, gambles, or loses his temper, . . . uses nothing except in moderation, and even while he flogs his child is meditating only on the golden mean. Devoid, in short, of any human weakness, with not one signal saving vice, sans prejudice, procrastination, ill-nature, avarice, and absence of mind, as carefully for his own safety as he is for that of others, this excellent but odious creature stands like a monument in our Courts of Justice, vainly appealing to his fellow citizens to order their lives after his own example.[94]

If these words were included in a charge to a jury, it would likely be incorrect. Similarly, the judge who invoked the test of the "ideal man" was probably being too optimistic,[95] and the court, which expected only "common and ordinary caution in the circumstances", may have been too pessimistic.[96]

It is apparent that no such creature as a reasonable person can be found in captivity anywhere on this earth. The being is obviously only a "fictional" or "notional" person.[97] Perhaps the most complete and accurate description of the reasonable individual in the Canadian jurisprudence is that of Mr. Justice Laidlaw in *Arland v. Taylor:*

> [The reasonable person is] a mythical creature of the law whose conduct is the standard by which the Courts measure the conduct of all other persons and find it to be proper or improper in particular circumstances as they may exist from time to time. He is not an extraordinary or unusual creature; he is not superhuman; he is not required to display the highest skill of which anyone is capable; his is not a genius who can perform uncommon feats, nor is he possessed of unusual powers of foresight. He is a person of normal intelligence who makes prudence a guide to his conduct. He does nothing that a prudent man would not do and does not omit to do anything that a prudent man would do. His conduct is guided by considerations which ordinarily regulate the conduct of human affairs. His conduct is the standard "adopted in the community by persons of ordinary intelligence and prudence".[98]

Thus, it is clearly incorrect for a judge or jury to use themselves as the basis for evaluation, instead of the non-existent reasonable person.

Mr. Justice Trueman has observed in this connection that:

---

[92]   *Ouellet v. Cloutier*, [1947] S.C.R. 521, at p. 526.

[93]   *Nova Mink Ltd. v. Trans-Canada Airlines*, [1951] 2 D.L.R. 241, at p. 255 (N.S.) (*per* MacDonald J.).

[94]   *The Uncommon Law*, 7th ed. (1952), pp. 1-6.

[95]   Sedgewick J. in *Prescott v. Connell* (1893), 22 S.C.R. 147, at p. 161.

[96]   *Brown v. Walton*, [1943] 2 D.LR. 437, at p. 444 (C.A.).

[97]   *Nova Mink v. Trans-Canada Airlines*, [1951] 2 D.L.R. 241, at p. 254 (N.S.) (*per* MacDonald J.).

[98]   [1955] O.R. 131, at p. 142 (C.A.).

In determining the standard of duty so defined a judge must not interpose himself, for, the accident having happened, his point of view may be warped by extraneous or subjective considerations, however much he may think he is free from bias. It is for this reason that a jury must not be instructed by the Judge or counsel to put themselves in the place of a defendant in a negligence action when called upon to pronounce upon his conduct.[99]

Trial judges are in error if they ask juries to answer the questions, "Did he do what you would have done?" or "What would I have done?", because the standard is not that of "any individual juryman" but of what a "reasonable and prudent man would do or refrain from doing in the circumstances of the particular case".[100] So too, it is not permissible for trial judges to suggest that jurors put themselves in the driver's seat of a defendant's car and ask "Would I have done that?", for "it is improper for a juryman to judge the conduct of a person in given circumstances by considering, after the event, what he would or would not have done in the circumstances".[101]

The reasonable person test is employed by our courts to evaluate the conduct of the actors that come before them. The exercise is a unique process in which a value judgment based on community standards is reached. In such pursuits it is imperative to control as much as possible the personal biases and whims of the judge and the jury. The reasonable person test is meant to assist in this task. Even though it is doubtful whether this test significantly affects the outcome of many cases,[102] it does inject an aura of objectivity into the deliberations of the tribunal. At the same time it permits a large degree of individualized judgement. It provides us with both certainty and flexibility.

Perhaps the most perceptive explanation of the role of the reasonable person myth was that of Leon Green, who contended that the abstraction of the reasonable individual

is a mere caution, pointing the jury in as dramatic a way as possible in the directions their deliberations should take. The judge through him can indicate to the jury that they are dealing with society's power and not their own; therefore, they should act reasonably and not let their own desires run riot. The formula is as much for controlling the jury's deliberations as for measuring the party's conduct. Its beauty is that it can be used for both purposes without committing the judge to anything and without telling the jury anything that amounts to more than a sobering caution. It does exactly what any good ritual is designed to do; its function is psychological. It serves as a prophylaxis. Nothing more should be expected of it.[103]

---

[99] *Eyers v. Gillis and Warren Ltd.*, [1940] 4 D.L.R. 747, at p. 751 (C.A.).

[100] *Kralj v. Murray*, [1954] O.W.N. 58, at pp. 58-59 (C.A.) (*per* Hope J.A.), no reversal, however.

[101] *Arland v. Taylor*, [1955] O.R. 131, at p. 143 (C.A.) (*per* Laidlaw J.A.), no miscarriage of justice, however.

[102] Edward Green, "The Reasonable Man — Legal Fiction or Psychological Reality?" (1968), 2 Law & Society Rev. 241, at p. 256.

[103] *Judge and Jury* (1930), p. 174.

C. Characteristics of the Reasonable Person

Moral blameworthiness is not a pre-condition to liability for negligence. If the challenged conduct falls below the standard expected of a reasonable person, defendants are considered to be at fault, even in doing their best. It is only in this sense that negligence liability pivots on fault or blame.

1. INTELLIGENCE AND KNOWLEDGE

Everyone is required by tort law to possess a certain modicum of intelligence. Stupid individuals must answer for their foolish ways to their victims, even though they may be forgiven by their Maker.[104] The awkward and the accident-prone must make good any losses they produce.[105] Lord MacMillan has observed, "Some persons are by nature unduly timorous and imagine every path beset with lions. Others, of more robust temperament, fail to foresee or nonchalantly disregard even the most obvious dangers. The reasonable man is presumed to be free both from over-apprehension and from over-confidence".[106]

A reasonable person must know certain common things, for example, that fire burns, knives cut and heavy objects fall when dropped.[107] It should be realized that animals can get into mischief,[108] that defective equipment[109] and open excavations are dangerous,[110] and that snow and ice may fall off a roof.[111] Any prudent person must foresee the hazard of explosives,[112] blowtorches,[113] hot rivets,[114] and poison.[115]

2. CONTROL OF CHILDREN

Another source of danger a reasonable person should guard against is children. It should be known that children may imitate actions they see in the movies, for example, setting fire to bulrushes.[116] One should keep a steam inhalator away from an infant,[117] one should not sell an air gun to a child of 13,[118] and one should

---

[104] *Vaughan v. Menlove* (1837), 3 Bing. N.C. 468, 132 E.R. 490.

[105] James and Dickinson, "Accident Proneness and Accident Law" (1950), 63 Harv. L. Rev. 769.

[106] *Glasgow Corporation v. Muir*, [1943] A.C. 448, at p. 457.

[107] See generally *Prosser and Keeton on the Law of Torts*, 5th ed. (1984), p. 176. See also *Bigras v. Tasse* (1917), 40 O.L.R. 415 (C.A.), fire.

[108] *Kokolsky v. Caine Fur Farms Ltd.* (1961), 31 D.L.R. (2d) 556 (Alta. C.A.); *Fleming v. Atkinson*, [1959] S.C.R. 513, 18 D.L.R. (2d) 81. See generally Williams, *Liability for Animals* (1939).

[109] *Village of Kelliher v. Smith*, [1931] S.C.R. 672, fire extinguisher.

[110] *Reid v. Linnell*, [1923] S.C.R. 594. See also *Dumochel v. Cité de Verdun*, [1959] S.C.R. 668.

[111] *Meredith v. Peer* (1917), 39 O.L.R. 271 (C.A.).

[112] *City of St. John v. Donald*, [1926] S.C.R. 371, at p. 386 (*per* Anglin J.).

[113] *Aga Heat (Canada) Ltd. v. Brockville Hotel Co.*, [1945] S.C.R. 184; *J. & R. Weir Ltd. v. Lunham & Moore Shipping Ltd.*, [1958] S.C.R. 46; *Balfour v. Barty-King*, [1957] 1 All E.R. 156 (C.A.).

[114] *H. & C. Grayson Ltd. v. Ellerman Lines Ltd.*, [1920] A.C. 466.

[115] *Leibel v. South Qu'Appelle*, [1944] 1 D.L.R. 369 (Sask. C.A.), arsenic leaked into well. See also *MacMillan Bloedel (Alberni) Ltd. et al. v. B.C. Hydro* (1971), 22 D.L.R. (3d) 164 (B.C.) (*per* Rae J.), electricity.

[116] *Yachuk v. Oliver Blais Co.*, [1949] A.C. 386 (P.C.).

[117] *Sinclair v. Victoria Hospital ltd.*, [1943] 1 D.L.R. 302 (Man. C.A.).

[118] *Fowell v. Grafton* (1910), 20 O.L.R. 639; affd 22 O.L.R. 550 (C.A.).

take steps to prevent children from falling out of a vehicle,[119] or running on the road.[120] Reasonable people must seek to minimize the danger involved in attracting children to an ice cream vendor's truck parked on the road, for "a pied piper cannot plead his inability to take care of his followers when it was he who played the flute".[121]

Parents, and people who stand in their place, are required to supervise their children reasonably, although, unless made expressly liable by statute,[122] they are not vicariously responsible on the ground of their family relationship alone.[123] Thus, where a 16 year-old "congenital idiot of irresponsible impulses", who was constantly playing with matches, set fire to the plaintiff's property, the father was held liable for negligence in harbouring his "dangerous animal".[124] Similarly, a parent is liable for entrusting an air gun to an 11-year-old without proper training,[125] or for failing to lock up a spring gun, enabling an 11-year-old child to shoot a domestic in the eye.[126] If the parent takes proper precautions, however, no liability will ensue.[127] A parent may be responsible for failing to train a child properly in the use of dangerous objects such as snowmobiles.[128] It is even possible for a parent who permits a child to run on the road to share responsibil-

---

[119] *Ware's Tax Ltd. v. Gilliham*, [1949] S.C.R. 637. *Cf.*, *Boryszko v. Toronto Board of Education*, [1963] 1 O.R. 1, no liability when boy dislodged blocks from pile.

[120] *Mattinson v. Wonnacott* (1975), 8 O.R. (2d) 654.

[121] *Teno v. Arnold* (1975), 7 O.R. 276; affd in part (1976), 11 O.R. 585, at p. 594 (C.A.) (*per* Zuber J.A.); affd but varied (1978), 3 C.C.L.T. 272 (S.C.C.). See also *Gambino v. Dileo*, [1971] 12 O.R. 131.

[122] Parental Responsibility Act, S.O. 2000, c. 4, s. 2, parents liable for property damage caused by their children unless they can prove "reasonable supervision" and "reasonable efforts" to avoid loss.

[123] *Thibodeau v. Cheff* (1911), 24 O.L.R. 214, at p. 218 (C.A.); *Ryan v. Hickson* (1974), 7 O.R. (2d) 352 (*per* Goodman J.). See Alexander, "Tort Responsibility of Parents and Teachers for Damage Caused by Children" (1965), 16 U. of T.L.J. 165; Dunlop, "Torts Relating to Infants" (1966), 5 West L. Rev. 116; Hoyano, "The 'Prudent Parent': The Elusive Standard of Care" (1984), 18 U.B.C.L. Rev. 1.

[124] *Ibid.*, at pp. 216 and 220. See also *School Division of Assiniboine South, No. 3 v. Hoffer and Greater Winnipeg Gas Co.* (1970), 16 D.L.R. (3d) 703; affd [1971] 4 W.W.R. 746; affd [1973] 6 W.W.R. 765.

[125] *Starr and McNulley v. Crone*, [1950] 4 D.L.R. 433 (B.C.).

[126] *Edwards v. Smith*, [1940] 4 D.L.R. 638; affd [1941] 1 D.L.R. 736 (B.C.). See also *Black v. Hunter*, [1925] 4 D.L.R. 285 (C.A.); *Sullivan v. Creed*, [1904] 2 I.R. 317; *Bishop v. Sharrow* (1975), 8 O.R. (2d) 649; *Ingram v. Lowe* (1975), 55 D.L.R. (3d) 292 (Alta. C.A.); *Floyd v. Bowers* (1978), 6 C.C.L.T. 65; affd damages increased (1979), 106 D.L.R. (3d) 702.

[127] *Hatfield v. Pearson* (1956), 6 D.L.R. (2d) 593 (B.C.C.A.). See also *Montesanto v. Di Ubaldo* (1927), 60 O.L.R. 610 (C.A.), where a 15-year-old friend of the defendant's son, of whom he was unaware, injured someone with an air rifle. See generally Wright, "Civil Liability for Fire-Arms" (1968), 11 Can. Bar J. 247.

[128] *Ryan v. Hickson* (1974), 7 O.R. (2d) 352; *School Division of Assiniboine South No. 3 v. Hoffer and Greater Winnipeg Gas* (1970), 16 D.L.R. (3d) 703; affd [1971] 4 W.W.R. 746; affd [1973] 6 W.W.R. 765.

ity for any injury to the child if that parent falls "short of the standard to be expected from a reasonably prudent [parent] under the circumstances".[129]

A fine summary of the principles is contained in *Lelarge v. Blakney*,[130] where Hughes C. J. N. B. declared:

> The parental duty of care is a duty personally imposed upon the parent irrespective of the wrongdoing or the liability of a child. The duty is to supervise and control the activities of the child and, in doing so, to use reasonable care to prevent foreseeable damage to others. The extent of the duty varies with the age of the child. The degree of supervision and control required of a young child may be very different from that required of a child approaching the age of majority. As the age of the child increases and the expectation that he will conform to adult standards of behaviour also increases, the parental duty to supervise and control his activities tends to diminish. . . .
>
> It is apparent, therefore, that some special circumstances must be proven before liability can be imposed upon the parent for the tortious actions of his child.

On the facts of the case, the parent was relieved of liability for an automobile accident in which his 16-year-old son was involved, even though the son had been twice convicted of motor vehicle offences involving the use of lights and had been involved in an earlier accident, the cause of which was not established, for in these circumstances there was no negligence.

Teachers[131] and schools must exercise the "same standard of care over children as would be exercised by a good parent with a large family". In other words, the standard is that of the "reasonably careful parent", who must guard against reasonably foreseeable risks, not remote possibilities.[132]

In *Myers v. Peel County Board of Education*[133] Mr. Justice McIntyre elaborated upon the test, in imposing partial liability for an accident which occurred during a gymnastics class, as follows:

> The standard of care to be exercised by school authorities in providing for the supervision and protection of students for whom they are responsible is that of the careful or prudent parent. . . . It has, no doubt, become somewhat qualified in modern times because of the greater variety of activities conducted in schools, with probably larger groups of students using more complicated and more dangerous equipment than formerly: . . . it remains the appropriate standard for such cases. It is not, however, a standard which can be applied in the same man-

---

[129] *Teno v. Arnold, supra*, n. 121, at p. 596 (*per* Zuber J.A.); revd on the facts of the case (1968), 3 C.C.L.T. 272, at p. 295, mother "entitled to rely on the vendor". See also *Gambino v. Dileo*, [1971] 2 O.R. 131, father 25% to blame.

[130] (1978), 92 D.L.R. (3d) 440, at pp. 446-47 (N.B.C.A.). See also *Nespolon v. Alford* (1998), 40 O.R. (3d) 355 (C.A.), no liability of 15-year-old who dropped off inebriated 14-year-old causing accident.

[131] *Moffat v. Dufferin County Bd. of Education* (1973), 31 D.L.R. (3d) 143 (Ont. C.A.).

[132] *Boese v. Bd. of Education of St. Pauls* (1979), 97 D.L.R. (3d) 643, at p. 648 (*per* Sirois J.), liability for making obese 13-year-old jump from a height of seven feet; *Eaton v. Lasuta et al.* (1977), 2 C.C.L.T. 18, at p. 41 (*per* Murray J.), no liability for accident while plaintiff carrying another student piggy-back; *Piszel v. Bd. of Education for Etobicoke* (1977), 16 O.R. (2d) 22 (C.A.), liability for wrestling accident because system for protective mats inadequate.

[133] (1981), 37 N.R. 227, at p. 235 (S.C.C.). Day care centre must exercise standard of "prudent and careful parent", see *Lapensée v. Ottawa Day Nursery* (1986), 35 C.C.L.T. 129 (Ont. H.C.).

ner and to the same extent in every case. Its application will vary from case to case and will depend upon the number of students being supervised at any given time, the nature of the exercise or activity in progress, the age and the degree of skill and training which the students may have received in connection with such activity, the nature and condition of the equipment in use at the time, the competency and capacity of the students involved, and a host of other matters which may be widely varied but which, in a given case, may affect the application of the prudent parent-standard to the conduct of the school authority in the circumstances.

3. THE NEED TO EXPAND KNOWLEDGE BY CONSULTING

A reasonable person need not be aware of esoteric matters,[134] but as human knowledge expands, the esoteric may become the commonplace. At least one should know when one is ignorant of something and that information or expert advice should be sought. To drive with one's vision obscured[135] or to proceed in the face of an enigma such as a purple traffic light,[136] may well be negligence. There is nothing wrong with doing one's own simple household repairs,[137] but when the task is a complex one, it may be negligent to proceed without expert advice. Thus, those who build bridges without adequate professional counsel about drainage subject themselves to liability even though they may have escaped if they had consulted competent engineers.[138] There are conflicting decisions on the need to consult experts over trees. For example, there is apparently no need for ordinary landowners to confer with specialists to determine if their trees need looping, because they may rely upon their own judgement.[139] On the other hand, if the trees are near a busy highway, if a defect is visible, and if the defendant is a large landowner, there may be a "duty to provide himself with skilled advice about the safety of trees".[140] Here again, it appears that more effort must be expended to avert greater risk. Normally, however, an actor will be relieved of responsibility if following professional advice or if hiring an expert to perform these tasks,[141] because it is eminently reasonable to rely upon others,[142] especially when they are skilled persons.

---

[134] *Nova Mink v. Trans-Canada Airlines*, [1951] 2 D.L.R. 241 (N.S.), presence of mink farm unknown.

[135] *Johnson v. Desharnais*, [1953] 1 S.C.R. 324; *Foster v. Kerr*, [1940] 2 D.L.R. 47 (Alta. C.A.).

[136] *Restatement, Torts, Second*, §289, Comment J.

[137] *Watson v. George* (1953), 89 C.L.R. 409, gas heater; *Wells v. Cooper*, [1958] 2 Q.B. 265 (C.A.), door knob.

[138] *Guelph Worsted Spinning Co. v. City of Guelph et al.* (1914), 30 O.L.R. 466.

[139] *Caminer v. Northern and London Investment Trust Ltd.*, [1951] A.C. 88 (*per* Lord Reid), but *cf.*, Lord Radcliffe, who wanted to make the "standard of the expert the test of liability".

[140] *Quinn v. Scott*, [1965] 1 W.L.R. 1004, at p. 1010 (*per* Glynn-Jones J. Q.B.D.), liability even though defendant hired experts. See also *Ratkevicius v. R.*, [1966] 2 O.R. 774, no liability for tree falling in wind, since inspected three months earlier.

[141] *Earl v. Reid* (1911), 23 O.L.R. 453 (C.A.).

[142] *Canada and Gulf Terminal Ry. Co. v. Levesque*, [1928] S.C.R. 340.

4. PHYSICAL DISABILITY

Negligence law has departed from its objective standard in its treatment of physical disabilities; it has made the standard of care partially subjective in order to take them into account. A person with a hearing disability is not required to hear,[143] a physically disabled person need not be nimble,[144] nor is a person who is blind obliged to see,[145] although they are expected to avoid getting themselves into positions of danger.[146] Where a motorist suffers an unexpected heart attack,[147] an epileptic seizure,[148] or some other sudden attack,[149] there is no liability for any accident that ensues, although if there has been some previous warning about the medical condition the motorist may be negligent in risking a hazardous situation.[150] The defendant seeking to rely on inevitable accident causing a heart attack bears an "onerous" burden, which is as it should be.[151] Special consideration has also been given to women, on the questionable theory that they may not be as strong as men[152] and, of course, to children.[153]

5. SUPERIOR KNOWLEDGE

If people possess superior knowledge, they are obliged to act reasonably as a result. Thus, where the defendant is actually aware of the presence of an inflammable fluid,[154] or of mink that are whelping,[155] or if the defendant is a "skilled

---

[143] *South Australian Ambulance v. Wahlheim* (1948), 77 C.L.R. 215. See also *Dziwenka v. R.*, [1972] S.C.R. 419.

[144] *Goodman v. Norwalk Jewish Centre* (1958), 139 A.2d 812.

[145] *Haley v. London Electricity Bd.*, [1965] A.C. 778. See also ten Broek, "Right to Live: The Disabled in the Law of Torts" (1966), 54 Calif. L. Rev. 841.

[146] *Carroll et al. v. Chicken Palace Ltd.*, [1955] O.R. 798 (C.A.); revd on the facts, [1955] O.R. 23. See also Lowrey, "The Blind and the Law of Tort" (1972), 20 Chitty's L.J. 253.

[147] *Slattery v. Haley* (1922), 52 O.L.R. 95; affd 52 O.L.R. 102 (C.A.); *Ryan v. Youngs*, [1938] 1 All E.R. 522 (C.A.).

[148] *Gootson v. The King*, [1948] 4 D.L.R. 33.

[149] *Buckley v. Smith Transport Ltd.*, [1946] O.R. 798 (C.A.), delusion; *Dessaint v. Carriere*, [1958] O.W.N. 481 (C.A.), dizzy spell; *Boomer v. Penn*, [1966] 1 O.R. 119 (C.A.), diabetic; *Fiala v. Cechmanek* (1999), 45 C.C.L.T. (2d) 198 (Alta. Q.B.), "severe manic episode".

[150] *Turner's Transfer Ltd. v. Anderson* (1962), 37 D.L.R. (2d) 399 (N.S.), deceased knew he was ill. See also *Wright v. Hall* (1930), 38 O.W.N. 260, epileptic; *Hagg v. Bohnet* (1962), 33 D.L.R. (2d) 378 (B.C.C.A.), driver with diabetes had had two blackouts previously and had not gone to doctor; *Gordon v. Wallace* (1973), 2 O.R. (2d) 202, person had heart condition that could cause attack at any time; *Polinski v. Griffin*, [1973] 3 O.R. 353, at p. 355 (C.A.), air crash where pilots knew of heart condition; *Telfer v. Wright* (1978), 23 O.R. (2d) 117 (C.A.), dizzy spells preceded black-out; *Spillane v. Wasserman* (1992), 13 C.C.L.T. (2d) 267 (Ont. Gen. Div.), epileptic, doctor also 40% liable.

[151] *Dobbs v. Mayer* (1985), 32 C.C.L.T. 191 (Ont. Div. Ct.) (*per* Craig J.); see also *Graham v. Hodgkinson* (1983), 40 O.R. (2d) 697, at p. 703 (C.A.), explaining inevitable accident.

[152] *Hassenyer v. Michigan Central R. Co.* (1882), 12 N.W. 155 (Mich.).

[153] See *infra*, Section D.

[154] *J. & R. Weir Ltd. v. Lunham & Moore Shipping Ltd.*, [1958] S.C.R. 46.

[155] *Kokolsky v. Caine Fur Farms Ltd.* (1961), 31 D.L.R. (2d) 556 (Alta. C.A.); affd [1963] S.C.R.

storekeeper",[156] additional demands may be expected. A person who uses a light in a garage must do what "any experienced man would do in the face of the known hazards implicit in the undertaking".[157] Similarly, someone who utilizes an acetylene torch must exercise the care that a "reasonable man, skilled in such things, would exercise in using such a torch in the particular circumstances of time, place and space, and proximity to inflammable objects involved in its use".[158] Someone with actual knowledge of danger has to issue a warning, whereas one who lacks it may not.[159] Of course, those who profess to be experts must live up to the standard of their professional *confrères*.[160] A professional football player, for example, is expected to live up to a higher standard than one who plays for a local team.[161]

There is a special obligation upon drivers of emergency vehicles to be able to handle crises in a more effective way than ordinary drivers because of their training and experience. In *Workers Compensation Board v. Giesbrecht*[162] the defendant ambulance driver, who went the wrong way on a one-way street during weather with poor visibility, was held 75 per cent at fault for the accident and the other driver, who failed to hear the ambulance's siren, was held 25 per cent to blame. The court explained that regular drivers of emergency vehicles are obligated to drive safely under dangerous circumstances for "an ambulance wrecked on the way, or which on its way caused yet another accident, is not entirely useful". Further the court felt that, "while it may be criticized as 'second guessing', one is entitled to question whether agony piled upon agony is a sufficient cause for misjudgment on the part of a professional ambulance driver". Mr. Justice Wilson explained:

> Crises, supposed or real, are often the occasion of a decision which at the time was not the best; hence, the "agony of the moment" doctrine by which sometimes a motorist, faced with an emergency beyond his experience, escapes liability for what would in other circumstances be considered a negligent act. But it is not enough, I think, for the driver of an emergency vehicle, so employed, to rely completely upon the emergency of the moment. In his case, I think, other users of the streets, who may be unaware of any emergency, are entitled to expect the driver of the rescue vehicle to have sufficient experience or training to protect all concerned from rash action. See *Poupart*, . . . where the learned chief justice observed that a

---

315. *Cf.*, *Nova Mink v. Trans-Canada Airline*, [1951] 2 D.L.R. 241, pilot unaware of mink farm below.

[156] *DesBrisay v. Canadian Government Merchant Marine*, [1941] S.C.R. 230, at p. 240.

[157] *Procinsky v. McDermott et al.*, [1955] 4 D.L.R. 606, at p. 609 (Alta. C.A.) (*per* Porter J.A.), no liability.

[158] *Sao Paulo Light S.A. v. Eastern Stevedoring Co. Ltd.* (1961), 30 D.L.R. (2d) 120, at p. 130 (*per* MacDonald J.). The finding of no negligence on the facts was reversed, 40 D.L.R. (2d) 189 (N.S.C.A.).

[159] *Modern Livestock Ltd. v. Elgersma* (1989), 50 C.C.L.T. 5 (Alta. Q.B.).

[160] See *infra*, Section F.

[161] *Condon v. Basi*, [1985] 2 All E.R. 453 (C.A.). As for beekeepers, see *Tutton v. A.D. Walter Ltd.*, [1985] 3 All E.R. 757 (Q.B.).

[162] [1980] 4 W.W.R. 350, at p. 358. See also *Shackleton v. Knittle* (1999), 46 C.C.L.T. (2d) 300 (Alta. Q.B.), no liability when schizophrenic grabbed wheel of ambulance as defendant used care of "competent ambulance driver".

police officer "should, by reason of the training he has received, show more 'sang-froid' and control than another person would": language, to my mind, not inapt to the ambulance man here.

It may be that a similar attitude will be taken toward other people with superior knowledge and experience, such as truck drivers, taxi drivers, racing car drivers and the like.

D. Youth

The standard of the reasonable person has been relaxed in the case of children. "To do otherwise, would be to shut [the law's] eyes, ostrich-like, to the facts of life and to burden unduly the child's growth to majority."[163] After all, a minor's "normal condition is one of recognized incompetency" and, therefore, "indulgence must be shown".[164] But tort law has evinced some ambivalence, vacillating between providing protection for the children, on the one hand, and for their victims, on the other. One of these contradictory sentiments was one uttered by Chief Justice Kenyon who exclaimed that "if an infant commit an assault, or utter slander, God forbid that he should not be answerable for it in a Court of Justice".[165] However, another authority maintained that infants are liable for "actual torts", such as trespass, but are not held liable for deceit, "for if they should [be], all the infants in England might be ruined".[166] Clearly, youth needs a buffer against tort liability for its indiscretions, but the law cannot grant them a licence to injure and maim at will.

The Canadian Criminal Code grants complete immunity from criminal responsibility to children under twelve years of age.[167] The Age of Majority and Accountability Act has sorted out many of the other legal problems related to youth.[168] However, after a study of the cloudy position of young people under tort law, one law reform body decided against making any suggestions for legislative reform.[169] Consequently, the civil courts have been left to wrestle with the question of tort liability of children without any legislative aid. This section will attempt to unravel the tangled skein of the law in this area.

---

[163] Shulman, "The Standard of Care Required of Children" (1927-28), 37 Yale L.J. 618; Bohlen, "Liability in Tort of Infants and Insane Persons" (1924), 23 Mich. L. Rev. 9; Dunlop, "Torts Relating to Infants" (1966), 5 Western L. Rev. 116.

[164] *Charbonneau v. MacRury* (1931), 153 Atl. 457, at p. 462; overruled in *Daniels v. Evans* (1966), 224 A.2d 63.

[165] *Jennings v. Rundall* (1799), 8 Term. Rep. 335, 101 E.R. 1419, at p. 1420.

[166] III *Bacon's Abridgement* (1798), p. 542.

[167] R.S.C. 1985, c. C-46, s. 13.

[168] R.S.O. 1990, c. A.7, "children are minors", not "infants", until they reach age of 18.

[169] Ontario Law Reform Commission, *Report on Family Law, Part I, Torts* (1969).

1. CHILDREN OF TENDER AGE

In the first place, it is clear that children of "tender age" are totally immune from tort liability.[170] Moreover, "the doctrine of contributory negligence does not apply to an infant of tender age".[171] Thus, children of two and one-half years,[172] three years,[173] four years,[174] or five years of age[175] cannot be held guilt of contributory negligence. No definite line has been drawn below which this total immunity operates, but it seems to cut off at a point "where the age is not such as to make a discussion of contributory negligence absurd".[176] The complete exemption probably does not extend beyond five years of age for, according to the Supreme Court of Canada, it was wrong to say that a child of six could not be guilty of contributory negligence.[177]

A typical case dealing with a child of tender years is *Tillander v. Gosselin,*[178] An infant, one week less than three years old, was excused from liability when he injured a baby by dragging her on the ground, because such "an infant is considered to be lacking in sufficient judgment to exercise that reasonable care that is expected of one. His normal condition is one of recognized incompetency and he is devoid of ability to make effective use of such knowledge as he may have at that early age".[179] Therefore, "mere age is not in itself the test, but rather the capacity of the infant to understand and appreciate" danger.[180] Since the action was framed in trespass, the court in *Tillander v. Gosselin* placed the onus of negative intention and negligence upon the defendant, but the burden was discharged by the proof of tender age.

2. CHILDREN BEYOND TENDER AGE

In the matter of children passing beyond tender years, but before reaching full maturity, liability in tort is somewhat befogged. A special standard of care has been developed for this intermediate age group, because "normality is, for

---

[170] *Tillander v. Gosselin,* [1967] 1 O.R. 203, at p. 205 (C.A.) (*per* Grant J.); *Walmsley v. Humenick,* [1954] 2 D.L.R. 232 (B.C.).

[171] *Merritt v. Hepenstal* (1895), 25 S.C.R. 150 (*per* Strong C.J.), quoting Channell B. in *Gardner v. Grace* (1857), 1 F. & F. 359.

[172] *Sangster v. T. Eaton Co. Ltd.* (1895), 24 S.C.R. 708.

[173] *Merritt v. Hepenstal, supra,* n. 169, not stated in decision, but assumed. *Finbow v. Domino* (1957), 11 D.L.R. (2d) 493 (Man.), developmentally disabled child of eight, with mental age of three, not capable of contributory negligence.

[174] *Hudson's Bay Co. v. Wyrzykowski,* [1938] S.C.R. 278, at p. 294 (*per* Hudson J.) and at p. 286 (*per* Davis J.); *Teno v. Arnold, supra,* n. 120, four and one-half years old.

[175] *Ware's Taxi Ltd. v. Gilliham,* [1949] S.C.R.637, at p. 642 (*per* Estey J.). See *Goggin v. Moncton* (1959), 43 M.P.R. 93, at p. 100 (N.B.C.A.), where children four years, six months and five years, nine months not contributorily negligent, but in *Messenger v. Sears* (1960), 23 D.L.R. (2d) 297 (N.S.C.A.), a child of five years, nine months was held 65 per cent at fault when hit by a car.

[176] See Kerwin C.J.C., in *McEllistrum v. Etches,* [1956] S.C.R.787, at p. 793.

[177] *Ibid.,* criticizing Trueman J. in *Eyers v. Gillis & Warren,* [1940] 4 D.L.R. 747 (C.A.).

[178] [1967] 1 O.R. 203 (C.A.).

[179] *Ibid.,* at p. 205.

[180] *Sheasgreen v. Morgan,* [1952] 1 D.L.R. 48, at p. 61-62 (B.C.) (*per* Manson J.).

children, something different from what normality is for adults".[181] The upper age limit which this special standard utilizes is rather rubbery. Mr. Justice Garrow has observed that "there is no hard and fast rule as to what may in civil matters be regarded as the years of discretion. One child at ten years may have more discretion or common sense than his brother at fifteen."[182] Although the age of maturity "cannot be determined with mathematical accuracy",[183] an acceptable age might be 18, which would correspond with the policy embodied in legislation governing the age of majority.[184]

The courts have not altogether abandoned their desire to retain some objectivity in the standard of care required of children between tender age and full maturity. Nor have they been willing to ask whether this particular child has done its best, for that would amount to the adoption of a completely subjective standard for children. "It is not . . . the actual capacity of the child whose conduct is being examined", because, if this were so, the standard would be that of the tribunal itself, with all its "inconvenience and uncertainty".[185] Instead, the courts have employed an "objective criterion",[186] with some subjective elements taken into account.

a) The Test Now Used

The most common formulation of the test is to ask whether the child "exercised the care expected from a child of like age, intelligence and experience".[187] There are three factors involved in this assessment, all of which tend to subjectivize the standard of care. If chronological age only were being considered, one could determine with relative ease the usual caution exercised by children of particular ages. By adding intelligence to the mixture, one must commence an assessment of capacity and knowledge, something that is more subjective and unpredictable. When the experience variable is included, the test becomes even more individualized. Thus, extra precautions may be expected of a 12-year-old child who is possessed of "more than ordinary intelligence" and "shrewdness"[188] and, presumably, from one who is experienced in the injury-producing activity. On the other hand, where children had no *actual* experience with matches or fire, even though they were taught that they were dangerous, they may be relieved of

---

[181] *McHale v. Watson* (1966), 39 A.L.J.R. 459, at p. 464 (*per* Kitto J.).

[182] *Tabb v. Grand Truck Ry.* (1904), 8 O.L.R. 203, at p. 208 (C.A.).

[183] *Charbonneau v. MacRury, supra*, n. 164, at p. 463.

[184] Age of Majority and Accountability Act, R.S.O. 1990, c. A.7, s. 1.

[185] See Rand J., dissenting, in *R. v. Dubeau and Laperrière*, [1946] S.C.R. 415, at p. 446. Because of the "instincts and impulses of the child", the subjective standard would be even more confusing than in the case of adults.

[186] *Ibid.*, at p. 445.

[187] *McEllistrum v. Etches, supra*, n. 176; *Heisler v. Moke*, [1972] 2 O.R. 446, at p. 448 (*per* Addy J.). See also *Restatement, Torts, Second*, §283A.

[188] *Flett v. Coulter* (1903), 5 O.L.R. 375, at p. 378 (*per* Britton J.).

liability for causing a fire, since they did not "appreciate the risk".[189] One commentator has suggested that the test is subjective only for the purpose of determining whether the child was capable of perceiving danger and avoiding the injury, but that thereafter it is an objective standard.[190]

Our courts have not been consistent in utilizing this three-pronged test; some judges have expanded it to four components and others have contracted it to two or only one variable. For example, Mr. Justice Estey once stated that a child's conduct must be measured according to "age, capacity, knowledge and experience".[191] The intelligence factor has here been split into two elements — knowledge and capacity, which may well amount to the same thing. Mr. Justice Moss, on the other hand, once applied a test which had regard only to two factors, the child's "youth and general intelligence".[192] It will be noted that the experience ingredient has been discarded in this criterion, but an astute judge might be able to incorporate it into the phrase "general intelligence".

b) An Alternative Test

There is another standard of care for children which is totally objective and is expressed in terms of age alone, without regard to intelligence or experience at all. For instance, Mr. Justice Rand once compared the actor's conduct with the "normal conduct of average young children".[193] In another case, Mr. Justice Rand has employed the test "prudent child of given years" or "the ordinary child of [particular] years".[194] A similar approach has been taken by Garrow J.A. who asked if a child "displayed . . . such reasonable care as was to have been expected from one of his tender years".[195] This simpler test has also been applied by the Australian High Court in *McHale v. Watson*,[196] where it was contended that the standard to be applied is that which is "normal for a child of relevant age" or a "child of corresponding age". This simplified objective formula has much to commend it. By eliminating the extremely subjective qualities of intelligence and experience, the decisions may be rendered more consistent and, consequently, easier to forecast. However, the cost of such an approach would be that the court would be less able to provide individualized treatment for each child who comes before it, which is also desirable.

---

[189] *Strehlke v. Camenzind*, [1980] 4 W.W.R. 464, six- and eight-year-olds not liable, three alternative tests set out.

[190] Shulman, *supra*, n. 163, at p. 625.

[191] *Yachuk v. Oliver Blais Co.*, [1946] S.C.R. 1, at p. 14; revd on another point, [1949] A.C. 386.

[192] *Potvin v. C.P.R.* (1904), 4 C.R.C. 8, at p. 11 (C.A.). See also Rose J. in *Downing v. Grand Trunk Ry.* (1921), 49 O.L.R. 36, at p. 40.

[193] Dissenting in *Yachuk v. Oliver Blais Co., supra*, n. 191, at p. 19.

[194] *R. v. Dubeau and Laperrière*, [1946] S.C.R. 415, at pp. 445-46, dissenting.

[195] *Tabb v. Grand Trunk Ry., supra*, n. 182, at p. 208.

[196] (1966), 39 A.L.J.R. 459. See also *Heisler v. Moke, supra*, n. 187, where Addy J. commented favourably on the test, but felt bound to apply the more common one.

c) Applications of the Standard

Children have been relieved of tort liability for loss resulting from the use of a bow and arrow,[197] from a dart which ricocheted off a pole,[198] from playing with matches,[199] and from an automobile accident.[200] A 15-year-old girl "swordfighting" with a plastic ruler was not liable for injury to her friend's eye when it broke.[201]

Contributory negligence by children has been held not to have been established where young people were injured while handling gasoline,[202] while playing[203] and while walking on a railroad track.[204] Similarly when a child ran toward a colt and was kicked[205] and when another child's hand was injured when putting it into a cement-mixer,[206] there was no contributory negligence.

Contributory negligence has been found on the part of children who were playing hockey on a slippery street,[207] and who were tampering with explosives left in a field.[208] When a child, who could barely swim, swam away from a boat, contrary to instructions, and drowned,[209] when a child chased a horse and was kicked,[210] and when a child was hit by a train while crossing the track by crawling under cars,[211] contributory negligence was held to be present. So too, if a child pedestrian is struck by a car,[212] or if a child falls off one snowmobile and is hit by another one,[213] contributory negligence may be found.

---

[197] *Walmsley v. Humenick*, [1954] 2 D.L.R. 232 (B.C.), five-year-old.
[198] *McHale v. Watson, supra,* n. 181, 12-year-old.
[199] *Yorkton Agricultural Exhibition Assoc. v. Morley* (1966), 58 D.L.R. (2d) 282 (Sask. C.A.); three boys, six to eight years old.
[200] *Charbonneau v. MacRury* (1931), 153 Atl. 457, 17-year-old, overruled *Daniels v. Evans* (1966), 224 A.2d 63 (N.H.).
[201] *Mullin v. Richards*, [1998] 1 All. E.R. 920 (C.A.).
[202] *Yachuk v. Oliver Blais Co., supra,* n. 191, seven- and nine-year-old.
[203] *Tabb v. Grand Trunk Ry., supra,* n. 182, nine-year-old.
[204] *Acadia Coal Co. Ltd. v. MacNeil*, [1927] S.C.R. 497, seven- and nine-year-olds. See also *Potvin v. C.P.R., supra,* n. 192, eight-year-old.
[205] *Rickard v. Ramsay*, [1936] S.C.R. 302, six-year-old.
[206] *Bouvier v. Fee*, [1932] S.C.R. 118, seven-year-old.
[207] *Holmes and Burke v. Goldenburg*, [1953] 1 D.L.R. 92 (Man. C.A.), eight-year-old.
[208] *R. v. Dubeau & Laperrière, supra,* n. 194, 11- and 12-year-olds.
[209] *Grieco et al. v. L'Externat Classique Ste. Croix*, [1962] S.C.R. 519, 15-year-old.
[210] *Flett v. Coulter* (1903), 5 O.L.R. 375, 12-year-old.
[211] *Downing v. Grand Trunk Ry.* (1921), 49 O.L.R. 36, eight-year-old.
[212] *Mercer v. Gray*, [1941] O.R. 127 (C.A.), six-year-old; *Whitehouse v. Fearnley* (1964), 47 D.L.R. (2d) 472 (B.C.), six-year-old on tricycle rode onto highway. *Dao (Guardian ad litem of) v. Sabatino* (1996), 29 C.C.L.T. (2d) 62 (B.C.C.A.), six-year-old 50 per cent responsible for running on road. But, *cf., Joyal v. Barsby* (1965), 55 D.L.R. (2d) 38 (Man. C.A.), six-year-old not negligent when running onto highway; *Gough v. Thorne*, [1966] 3 All E.R. 398 (C.A.), 13½-year-old not negligent when crossing road after being beckoned to.
[213] *Ryan v. Hickson* (1974), 7 O.R. (2d) 352, nine-year-old.

3. ADULT ACTIVITY

Special rules for children make sense, especially when they are plaintiffs; however, when a young person is engaged in an adult activity which is normally insured, the policy of protecting the child from ruinous liability loses its force. When the rights of adulthood are granted, the responsibilities of maturity should also accompany them. The legitimate expectations of the community are different when a youth is operating a motor vehicle than when playing ball. As one American court suggested,[214] juvenile conduct may be expected from children at play, but "one cannot know whether the operator of an approaching automobile . . . is a minor or adult, and usually cannot protect himself against youthful imprudence even if warned".

There has been a movement toward holding children to the reasonable person standard when they engage in adult activities.[215] A more lenient standard for young people in the operation of motor vehicles, for example, was thought to be "unrealistic" and "inimical to public safety".[216] When a society permits young people of 15 or 16 the privilege of operating a lethal weapon like an automobile on its highways, it should require of them the same caution it demands of all other drivers.[217]

This concept, now embraced by the Ontario Court of Appeal, was initially woven into the fabric of Canadian law by Mr. Justice Goodman (as he then was) in *Ryan v. Hickson*,[218] where a 12-year-old and a 14-year-old were both held partially to blame for the way they operated their snowmobiles, leading to the injury of another child. His Lordship was not content to adopt the three-pronged test usually applied to youngsters. Instead he held that children who engaged in adult activities such as snowmobile driving, which has no statutory restrictions with respect to age, should be given no special privileges but should be required to live up to the standard of the reasonable person.

The Ontario Court of Appeal in *McErlean v. Sarel et al.*[219] has adopted this principle, Mr. Justice Robins declaring the law as follows:

> Where a child engages in what may be classified as an "adult activity", he or she will not be accorded special treatment, and no allowance will be made for his or her immaturity. In those circumstances, the minor will be held to the same standard of care as an adult engaged in the same activity . . . .
>
> Just as the law does not permit a youth engaged in the operation of an automobile to be judged by standards other than those expected of other drivers, it cannot permit youths engaged in the operation of other motorized vehicles (whether there are any statutory restric-

---

[214] *Dellwo v. Pearson* (1911), 107 N.W. 2d 859, at p. 863 (Minn.).

[215] *Daniels v. Evans, supra,* n. 200, 19-year-old motor-cyclist; *Tucker v. Tucker,* [1956] S.A.S.R. 297, 16-year-old driver.

[216] *Ibid.,* at p. 66.

[217] Highway Traffic Act, R.SO. 1990, c. H.8, s. 37, 16 years of age.

[218] (1974), 7 O.R. (2d) 352, nine-year-old found negligent on old basis also.

[219] (1987), 61 O.R. (2d) 396, at p. 412 (C.A.); leave to appeal dismissed Feb. 25, 1988, 28 O.A.C. 399n, but *cf. Nespolon v. Alford, supra,* n. 130, youthful driver dropping someone off in inebriated condition not engaged in adult activity.

tions with respect to age or not) to be judged by standards other than those expected of others engaged in the same or like activity. The critical factor requiring greater care is the motor-powered nature of the vehicle. Automobiles, snowmobiles, power boats, motor cycles, trail bikes, motorized mini-bikes and similar devices are, it is manifest, increasingly available to teenagers, and are equally as lethal in their hands as in the hands of an adult. Machines of this nature, capable as they are of high rates of speed, and demanding as they do the utmost caution and responsibility in conduct, present a grave danger to the teenage operator in particular, and to others in general if the care used in the course of the activity drops below the care which the reasonable and prudent adult would use. The potential risks of harm involved in such activities are apparent, and they must be recognized by parents who permit their teenagers the use of such powerful machines. While teenagers may in other instances be judged by standards commensurate with their age, intelligence and experience, it would be unfair and, indeed, dangerous to the public to permit them in the operation of these power-driven vehicles to observe any lesser standard than that required of all other drivers of such vehicles. The circumstances of contemporary life require a single standard of care with respect to such activities.

E. Mental Illness

Persons suffering from mental illness may not have to comply with the reasonable person standard, the theory being that it is unfair to hold people liable for accidents they are incapable of avoiding.[220] No allowance is made, however, for those who are merely deficient intellectually and therefore cannot live up to the objective standard.[221] Nor is any mercy shown to defendants whose minds are clouded because of drugs or drunkenness.[222] It is only when the inadequacy amounts to a serious mental illness that the excuse is countenanced. The onus is upon the person alleging the mental illness to prove it.[223]

There are good reasons for rejecting the defence of mental illness under the negligence law altogether, and some jurisdictions have done so.[224] Lord Justice Denning has argued in *White v. White* that the civil courts should not excuse a mentally ill person, because they are "concerned not to punish him, but to give redress to the person he has injured".[225] Two early Ontario decisions refused to

---

[220] Robins, "Tort Liability of the Mentally Disabled" in Linden (ed.), *Studies in Canadian Tort Law* (1968), at p. 76. See also Picher, "The Tortious Liability of the Insane in Canada" (1975), 13 Osgoode Hall L.J. 193. The mentally ill may also be excused from intentional tort liability, see *supra*, Chapter 2, A.6.

[221] *Vaughan v. Menlove* (1837), 3 Bing. N.C. 468, 132 E.R. 490.

[222] *Prosser and Keeton on the Law of Torts*, 5th ed. (1984), p. 178. Persons addicted to drugs or alcohol may be denied licences, R.R.O. 1990, Reg. 585, s. 7(b).

[223] *Buckley v. Smith Transport Ltd.*, [1946] O.R. 798 (C.A.) (*per* Roach J.A.); *Baron v. Whalen*, [1938] 1 D.L.R. 787 (B.C.).

[224] *Wenden v. Trikha* (1991), 8 C.C.L.T. (2d) 138 (Alta. Q.B.) (*per* Murray J.); affd on other ground, 14 C.C.L.T. (2d) 225 (Alta. C.A.); leave to appeal refused [1993] 3 S.C.R. ix; *Adamson v. Motor Vehicle Trust* (1959), 58 W.A.L.R. 56; *Sforza v. Green Bus Lines* (1934), 268 N.Y.S. 2d 446; *Restatement, Torts, Second*, §283 B; Dobbs, "The Law of Torts" (2000), p. 284, mentally disabled in U.S. liable for intentional and negligent torts.

[225] [1949] 2 All E.R. 339 (C.A.).

accept the mental illness defence,[226] and advanced three policy reasons to support this conclusion. First, "when one of two innocent persons must bear a loss, he must bear it whose act caused it".[227] Second, if liability is imposed, "the relatives of the lunatic may be under inducement to restrain him". Third, the civil court, by refusing to apply the defence of mental illness, might avoid the vexing problems it has injected into the criminal law and thereby curtail the simulation or pretense of mental illness by tortfeasors. Appealing as these arguments may be, most Canadian courts eventually reversed themselves and granted an exemption from tort liability to the mentally ill.

The criterion to be employed in negligence, however, is still surrounded with uncertainty. The main test used in Canada has been the one enunciated by Mr. Justice Roach in *Buckley v. Smith Transport Ltd.*[228] An employee of the defendant drove its truck through a stop sign into a streetcar. Their defence was that the driver, who had been suffering from syphilis, had been suddenly seized by a delusion that the truck was being electrically guided from head office and that he was unable to control it. On appeal, Roach J.A. dismissed the case, remarking that a mentally ill person might be liable in tort, despite certain delusions. He formulated the test as follows:

> It is always a questions of fact to be determined on the evidence and the burden of proving that a person was without that appreciation and understanding and/or ability is always on those who allege it. Therefore, the question here, to my mind, is not limited to the bare inquiry whether or not [the driver] at the time of the collision was labouring under this particular delusion, but whether or not he understood and appreciated the duty upon him to take care, and whether he was disabled, as a result of any delusion, from discharging that duty.[229]

Since mental illness often relates only to certain perceptions, it is not surprising to learn that the mentally ill are "unquestionably liable in many circumstances",[230] where their mental illness is unrelated to their capacity to engage in the activity being complained of.

This test has been rejected recently in an Alberta case, *Wenden v. Trikha,*[231] where Mr. Justice Murray thoroughly analyzed the cases, the legislation and the policy issues. He noted that tort law's job is not to punish but to compensate, and concluded:

---

[226] *Stanley v. Hayes* (1904), 8 O.L.R. 81, defendant held liable for burning plaintiff's property; *Taggard v. Innes* (1862), 12 U.C.C.P. 77, demurrer to plea of mental illness allowed; see also *Weaver v. Ward* (1616), Hobart 134, 80 E.R. 284.

[227] *Ibid.*, at p. 82, quoting from *Williams v. Hayes* (1894), 143 N.Y. 442. See also Robins, *op. cit.*, *supra*, n. 220, at p. 77, and Picher, *op. cit. supra*, n. 220, at p. 225.

[228] [1946] O.R. 798 (C.A.). Followed but doubted in *Hutchings v. Nevin* (1992), 12 C.C.L.T. (2d) 259 (Ont. Gen. Div.) (Haines J.).

[229] *Ibid.*, at p. 806.

[230] *Slattery v. Haley* (1922), 52 O.L.R. 95, at p. 99; affd 52 O.L.R. 102 (C.A.).

[231] *Supra*, n. 224, at p. 175, mentally ill person held liable but hospital and doctor excused. On appeal, the Court affirmed saying only that even on the "easiest test" the "onus of proof was not satisfied," 14 C.C.L.T. (2d) 225, at p. 231 (Alta. C.A.).

> I see no reason why a person whose mental state is such that he does not appreciate that he owes a duty of care to others while operating his motor vehicle, by reason of which he caused loss or danger to others, should not be subjected to the same criteria for establishing civil liability as anyone else, namely, the objective standard of the reasonable driver.

This sensible development resembles very much the corresponding treatment of youth engaged in adult activities, where full liability is imposed.[232]

If mental illness suddenly renders defendants totally unaware of what they are doing, so that they are moving like sleepwalkers, automatons or someone who has suffered a stroke or seizure,[233] they will be exempted from liability on the ground that there has been no "act" done by the defendant. Mr. Justice Middleton observed in *Slattery v. Haley* that "to create liability for an act which is not wilful and intentional but merely negligent it must be shown to have been the conscious act of the defendant's volition. He must have done that which he ought not to have done or omitted that which he ought to have done, as a conscious being".[234] This is a convenient way of avoiding the issue, but mental illness is rarely of such a nature that it makes a person's mind a total blank.

The puzzle of the liability of the mentally ill in negligence law is not yet satisfactorily resolved. Perhaps the best solution, short of a complete overhaul of the law, would be to treat the mentally ill in the same way as everyone else. Although this might be somewhat hard on them, it is harder still on their victims to excuse them. At least in the automobile cases and other adult activities, they should not be allowed to escape liability,[235] just as young people engaged in adult activities, are held accountable. Moreover, since the highway traffic legislation denies them the privilege of having a licence,[236] they might be precluded from using their own evasion of the law as a defence on a theory akin to estoppel.

There is some evidence that the courts are moving in this direction. In *Roberts v. Ramsbottom*,[237] a defendant, without prior warning, suffered a minor stroke at home, 20 minutes before being involved in a car accident. He had gone out anyway and, along the way, had had two other minor accidents, after which he felt queer. He was not rendered unconscious by the stroke, however, suffering only a "clouding or impairment of his consciousness". Neill J. imposed liability for the collision, saying:

> I am satisfied that in a civil action . . . [a] driver will be able to escape liability if his actions at the relevant time were wholly beyond his control. The most obvious case is sudden unconsciousness. But if he retained some control, albeit imperfect control, and his driving, judged objectively, was below the required standard, he remains liable. His position is the same as the driver who is old or infirm. In my judgment unless the facts establish what the law recog-

---

[232] *McErlean v. Sarel, supra*, n. 219.

[233] See *supra*, Section C.4, for cases of liability because of foresight.

[234] *Ibid.*

[235] This passage was relied on by Murray J. in *Wenden v. Trikha, supra*, n. 224, at p. 175.

[236] O. Reg. 340/94, s. 14(a).

[237] [1980] 1 All E.R. 7 (Q.B.D.).

nizes as automatism the driver cannot avoid liability on the basis that owing to some malfunction of the brain his consciousness was impaired . . . "One cannot accept as exculpation anything less than total loss of consciousness".

It may be that this attitude is a glimpse of things to come. If it is, it would be most welcome.

F. Professional Negligence

The reasonable person standard has not only been diluted for certain types of less capable actors, it has been strengthened for certain individuals of superior capacity. Professional people, for example, cannot escape by performing merely up to the capacity of the ordinarily prudent lay person; more is expected of them and more should be demanded of them. After all, they hold themselves out as being possessed of extra skill and experience. This is why people consult them. That is why they are usually paid for their advice and service. But here too negligence law has striven for an objective standard. Rather than asking whether the performance was to the best of the defendant's ability, the courts assess whether the defendant's conduct was up to the standard of the person of average competence exercising a particular calling.[238] Among the first negligence cases ever prosecuted were actions against persons engaged in public callings such as doctors, and lawyers.[239] As long ago as 1833 Chief Justice Tindal articulated the principle that survives today:

> Every person who enters into a learned profession undertakes to bring to the exercise of it a reasonable degree of care and skill. He does not undertake, if he is an attorney, that at all events you shall gain your cause, nor does a surgeon undertake that he will perform a cure; nor does he undertake to use the highest possible degree of skill. There may be persons who have higher education and greater advantages than he has, but he undertakes to bring a fair, reasonable, and competent degree of skill . . . .[240]

A similar test has issued from Lord Chief Justice Hewart who once stated that "if a person holds himself out as possessing special skill and knowledge . . . [he undertakes] to use diligence, care, knowledge, skill and caution in administering the treatment . . . The law requires a fair and reasonable standard of care and competence.[241] It has also been asserted that "the professional adviser has never been supposed to guarantee the soundness of his advice".[242] An accurate explanation of the standard of care expected of a professional person has been articulated as follows:

---

[238] Dugdale and Stanton, *Professional Negligence*, 2d ed. (1989); Prichard, "Professional Civil Liability and Continuing Competence" in Klar (ed.), *Studies in Canadian Tort Law* (1977).

[239] Arturburn, "The Origin and First Test of Public Callings" (1927), 76 U. Pa. L. Rev. 411.

[240] *Lamphier v. Phipos* (1838), 8 C. & P. 475, at p. 478.

[241] *R. v. Bateman* (1925), 19 Cr. App. Rep. 8, 41 T.L.R. 557, at p. 559.

[242] *Purves v. Landell* (1845), 12 Cl. & Fin. 91, at p. 102, 8 E.R. 1332.

[The] degree of skill consistent with the function discharged, that is, consistent with the measure of skill displayed by others reasonably competent in that professional touching matters of like kind. Perfection is not expected; the world of work, not the ideal of the debating area, is the standard.[243]

In all these cases, the courts are balancing the interests of the clients or patients in receiving skilled service as well as the interests of professional people in a certain degree of autonomy in their dealings with the community. As always, an uneasy compromise has been reached.

Every recognized professional group has its own individual standard — a standard to which all the members of the profession must conform. Surveyors, for an example, must "exercise a reasonable amount of care and a reasonably competent degree of skill and knowledge".[244] A chiropractor's diagnosis, for another example, must be "sufficient by chiropractic standards".[245] A similar obligation, which is said by some to be based on contract,[246] rests on engineers,[247] architects,[248] accountants,[249] and others.[250] A police officer must behave like a "reasonable police officer",[251] an ambulance attendant like a "competent ambulance attendant",[252] and a volunteer firefighter must "perform in a manner

---

[243] *Trident Construction v. W.L. Wardrop & Assoc. Ltd.*, [1979] 6 W.W.R. 481, at p. 533 (Man. Q.B.) (*per* Wilson J.), speaking of an engineer.

[244] *MacLaren-Elgin Corp. v. Gooch*, [1972] 1 O.R. 474 (*per* Lacourcière J.).

[245] *Penner v. Theobald* (1962), 35 D.L.R. (2d) 700, at p. 706 (Man. C.A.). (*per* Schultz J.A.).

[246] Nelson, "The Source of Professional Liability — Tort or Contract?" Law Society of Upper Canada, *Special Lectures on Current Problems in the Law of Contract* (1975), at p. 323. As for accountants, see Dickerson, *Accountants and the Law of Negligence* (1966), p. 3.

[247] *King v. Stolberg* (1968), 70 D.L.R. (2d) 473, at p. 487 (*per* Rae J.); revd in part on the facts, 8 D.L.R. (3d) 362 (B.C.C.A.); *Sutcliffe v. Thackrah*, [1974] 1 All E.R. 859, [1964] A.C. 727; *Carl M. Halvorson Inc. v. Robert McLellan & Co.*, [1973] S.C.R. 65; McLachlin, Wallace and Grant, *The Canadian Law of Architecture & Engineering* 2d ed. (1994), c. 10.

[248] *Clayton v. Woodman & Son Ltd.*, [1962] 2 All E.R. 33 (C.A.). See also *Harries Hall and Kruse v. South Sarnia Properties Ltd.* (1929), 63 O.L.R. 597, at p. 602, and at p. 610 (C.A.) (*per* Masten J.A.), landscape architects; *Bagot v. Stevens Scanlan & Co. Ltd.*, [1966] 1 Q.B. 197, [1964] 3 All E.R. 577; *Nowlan v. Brunswick Const. Ltée* (1973), 34 D.L.R. (3d) 422 (N.B.); affd (1974), 8 N.B.R. (2d) 76; *Dabous v. Zuliani* (1975), 6 O.R. 344, at p. 351 (*per* Morden J.); revd in part (1976), 12 O.R. (2d) 230; *Gordon Shaw Concrete Products Ltd. v. Design Collaborative Ltd.* (1985), 35 C.C.L.T. 100 (N.S.C.A.).

[249] *Haig v. Bamford*, [1976] 3 W.W.R. 331; *Hedley, Byrne Ltd. v. Heller & Partners*, [1964] A.C. 465. Liability for missed time period, *Dyck v. F.M.A. Farm Management Associates Ltd.* (1996), 28 C.C.L.T. (2d) 10 (Sask. Q.B.).

[250] *Babcock v. Servacar Ltd.*, [1970] 1 O.R. 125, garage employee; *Burstein v. Crisp Devine Ltd.*, [1973] 3 O.R. 342, real estate agent; *Cavan v. Wilcox* (1973), 7 N.B.R. (2d) 192, revd [1975] 2 S.C.R. 663, nurse; *Hodgkinson v. Simms*, [1994] 3 S.C.R. 377, 22 C.C.L.T. (2d) 1, financial adviser.

[251] *Doern v. Phillips Estate* (1994), 23 C.C.L.T. (2d) 283 (B.C.S.C.), liability for injury during police pursuit for minor offence.

[252] *Shackleton v. Knittle* (1999), 46 C.C.L.T. (2d) 300 (Alta. Q.B.).

which is reasonable for a volunteer firefighter".[253] Since many of the cases of professional negligence are concerned with lawyers and doctors, perhaps they merit a more detailed treatment.

1. LAWYERS

A lawyer is obliged to act like a "prudent solicitor".[254] In other words, an attorney is liable if it is shown that the "error or ignorance was such that the ordinary competent solicitor would not have made or shown it".[255] The requisite standard of care, therefore, is that of a "reasonably competent solicitor" or that of the "ordinary prudent solicitor".[256] A lawyer must "bring to the exercise of his profession a reasonable amount of knowledge, skill and care in connection with the business of his client".[257]

It may be comforting to some and worrisome to others to learn that it is not necessary for a lawyer to know all the law applicable to the performance of a particular legal service, but there must be a "sufficient knowledge of the fundamental issues or principles of law applicable to the particular work he has undertaken to enable him to perceive the need to ascertain the law on relevant points".[258]

The duty owed by the lawyer to the client was founded on contract, not on tort,[259] for well over a century.[260] Now, however, solicitors may be concurrently liable to their clients either in contract or in tort.[261] Third persons, who may not be clients, may now be able to sue lawyers for negligence in certain circum-

---

[253] *Killips Television Service Ltd. v. Stony Plain (Town)* (2000), 48 C.C.L.T. (3d) 250, at p. 258 (Alta. Q.B.); *cf. Hammond v. Wabana (Town)* (1999), 44 C.C.L.T. (2d) 101 (Nfld. C.A.), enough "to do their best".

[254] *Rowswell v. Pettit et al.*, [1968] 2 O.R. 81, at p. 85 (*per* Moorhouse J.); vard [1969] 1 O.R. 22; affd [1970] S.C.R. 865; *P.A. Wournell Contracting v. Allen* (1979), 100 D.L.R. (3d) 62, at p. 67 (*per* Glube J.); revd on procedural grounds (1980), 108 D.L.R. (3d) 723 (N.S.C.A.). See generally Wade, "The Attorney's Liability for Negligence" (1959), 12 Vand. L. Rev. 755; Bastedo, "A Note on Lawyer's Malpractice' (1970), 7 Osgoode Hall L.J. 311; Mahoney, Note (1985), 63 Can. Bar Rev. 221.

[255] *Aaroe v. Seymour*, [1956] O.R. 736, at p. 737 (C.A.) (*per* LeBel J.).

[256] *Central & Eastern Trust Co. v. Rafuse* (1986), 37 C.C.L.T. 117, at p. 167 (S.C.C.) (*per* LeDain J.).

[257] *Hett v. Pun Pong* (1890), 18 S.C.R. 290, at p. 292 (*per* Ritchie C.J.). See also *Rafuse, supra*, n. 256.

[258] *Rafuse, supra*, n. 256, at p. 167 (*per* LeDain J.).

[259] *Schwebel v. Telekes*, [1967] 1 O.R. 541, at p. 543 (C.A.) (*per* Laskin J.A.), action in contract barred by limitation period running from date to breach. Overruled in *Consumer's Glass Co. v. Foundation Co. of Canada* (1985) 33 C.C.L.T. 104 (Ont. C.A.) (*per* Dubin J.). *Cook v. Swinfen*, [1967] 1 W.L.R. 457 (C.A.); *Rowswell v. Pettit et al., supra*, n. 254; *Banks v. Reid* (1974), 6 O.R. (2d) 404, at p. 411.

[260] *Clark v. Kirby-Smith*, [1964] 3 W.L.R. 239, at p. 241 (Ch.D.). See also *Groom v. Crocker*, [1939] 1 K.B. 194, at p. 205; both doubted in *Midland Bank Trust Co., infra*, n. 264 and now overruled by *Consumer's Glass, supra*, n. 259.

[261] See *Rafuse, supra*, n. 256, at p. 165.

stances.[262] Actions, by disappointed beneficiaries under wills, for example, have succeeded against the lawyers who negligently advised the testators in such a way as to cause them to lose out.[263] It is now clear that " . . . the existence of a contractual duty of care . . . does not preclude a parallel claim in tort . . . ".[264] It has been suggested that a plaintiff can claim either in contract or in tort, basing that claim "on whichever foundation gives him the more favourable position under the [limitation] statute".[265] There is no convincing reason to counteract this rational approach, except the argument that "the court follow blindly previous decisions without considering their rationale and the impact on them of subsequent authority".[266]

A lawyer's duty is not "absolute, ascending into the realm of insurance against loss. It involves only careful, unnegligent advice on matters of law".[267] The creation of an absolute standard for lawyers was wisely resisted so as to insulate the bar from too many crippling law suits. Chief Justice Robinson warned long ago that "the profession of the law would be the most hazardous of all professions, if those who practice it in any of its branches were to be held strictly accountable for the accuracy of their opinions".[268] Indeed, that the judiciary itself felt threatened by a strict liability rule was demonstrated by this *dictum* of Mr. Justice Britton:

> If an attorney or counsel can be held to warrant the correctness of his opinion, honestly formed and honestly given on a question of law, Judges may fear lest an attack be made upon them for difference of opinion.[269]

Consequently, the ordinary care of an average solicitor in good standing suffices.

There is now Canadian authority to the effect that there should be a difference between the standard required of a generalist and that demanded of a

---

[262] *Hedley Byrne Ltd. v. Heller & Partners Ltd.*, [1964] A.C. 465. *Re Fitzpatrick* (1923), 54 O.L.R. 3 (C.A.), is probably no longer good law.

[263] *Whittingham v. Crease & Co.* (1977), 6 C.C.L.T. 1 (B.C.); *Ross v. Caunters*, [1979] 3 W.L.R. 605; *Heath v. Ivens* (1991), 6 C.C.L.T. (2d) 311 (B.C.S.C.); *White v. Jones*, [1995] 2 A.C. 207 (H.L.); *Earl v. Wilhelm* (1997), 40 C.C.L.T. (2d) 117 (Sask. Q.B.); *Makan v. McCawley* (1998), 41 C.C.L.T. (2d) 249 (Ont. Gen. Div.) (*per* Lax J.), but not executors; see *Philp v. Woods* (1985), 34 C.C.L.T. 66 (B.C.S.C.); nor the opposite party, see *Seaway Trust Co. v. Markle* (1991), 7 C.C.L.T. (2d) 83 (Ont. Gen. Div.).

[264] *Midland Bank Trust Co. v. Hett, Stubbs & Kemp*, [1978] 3 All E.R. 571, at p. 609 (Ch. D.) (*per* Oliver J.). See also *Rafuse, supra*, n. 256.

[265] *Jacobson Ford-Mercury Sales v. Sivertz* (1979), 10 C.C.L.T. 274 (*per* Kirke-Smith J.); see also *Power v. Halley* (1978), 88 D.L.R. (3d) 381 (*per* Mifflin C.J.T.D.); affd 17 C.C.L.T. 182 (Nfld. C.A.); *Smith v. McInnis* (1978), 4 C.C.L.T. 145 (S.C.C.) (*per* Pigeon J. dissenting); *cf., Messineo v. Beale* (1978), 5 C.C.L.T. 235, *cf.*, Arnup J.A., at p. 241, contract, with Zuber J.A., at p. 237, contract or tort; *Page v. Dick* (1980), 12 C.C.L.T. 43, contract (*per* R.E. Holland J.). See Irvine, "Contract and Tort: Troubles Along the Border" (1978-79), 10 C.C.L.T. 281.

[266] *Midland Bank Trust Co., supra*, n. 264, at p. 586 (*per* Oliver J.).

[267] *Winrob v. Street and Wollen* (1959), 19 D.L.R. (2d) 172, at p. 176 (B.C.) (*per* Wilson J.).

[268] *Alexander v. Small and Gowan* (1846), 2 U.C.Q.B. 298, at p. 300.

[269] *Howse v. Shaw* (1913), 4 O.W.N. 971, at p. 975.

specialist, as this division is finally being formally recognized in the Canadian legal profession. Mr. Justice Smith, in a *dictum* in *Elcano Acceptance Ltd. v. Richmond, Richmond, Stambler & Mills*[270] stated that a "reasonably competent specialist standard" can be applied in appropriate cases. This makes good sense, as it does in the medical area, because clients expect more and pay more for the advice of specialists, who should bear extra obligations.

Although more is expected of specialists, less is not expected from inexperienced beginners, who are obligated to live up to the standard of the ordinary, reasonable solicitor from the first day after their call to the bar.[271]

The customary practice of solicitors in the same community is the main guide in assessing solicitors' conduct.[272] In *Page v. Dick*,[273] the standard of care required of a lawyer engaged in a "'mixed bag' practice consisting of wills and estates, real estate conveyancing, and some criminal and corporate matters" was that of a "reasonably competent general practitioner in the Toronto area". In a recent case, however, it was said that, unlike in the medical field, the standard of care required of a solicitor was reasonable care and skill, regardless of "geographical location and practising environment". The extent of the duty was "determined by the work undertaken, rather than by his or her particular circumstances."[274] There is much merit in this view, but it is too early to tell whether there will be a change to a homogeneous province-wide standard for all solicitors who undertake particular tasks.

In advising on a commercial lease, it was not negligent for a solicitor to be unaware of the need to make an option in a lease "subject to the Planning Act" for the "state of the art in 1971" did not demand that. Moreover, where it was not apparent to a reasonable solicitor that there would be a severance of the property in question the necessity of this clause would not be apparent. However, a lawyer who knows nothing of company laws should advise a client "to seek other professional assistance" or should "obtain the information himself so that he could properly receive instructions and carry out his duties". If the lawyer proceeds, in spite of this lack of knowledge, and botches up a "routine" incorporation by failing "to follow the ordinary practices of his profession", liability will ensue.[275] Similarly, if a solicitor draws an option to purchase that is unenforceable, in circumstances where a "general practitioner exercising

---

[270] (1985), 31 C.C.L.T. 201, at p. 213 (Ont. H.C.); revd on procedural point 55 O.R. (2d) 56 (C.A.).

[271] *Rowswell v. Pettit*, [1968] 2 O.R. 81, at p. 88; vard [1969] 1 O.R. 22; affd [1970] S.C.R. 865 (*sub nom. Wilson v. Rowswell*).

[272] *Hauck v. Dixon et al.* (1975), 10 O.R. (2d) 605, at p. 611; see also *Grima v. MacMillan*, [1972] 3 O.R. 214, no liability because there was no custom in Windsor, Ontario of searching to see if defendant in action is dead.

[273] (1980), 12 C.C.L.T. 43 (*per* R.E. Holland J.).

[274] See *Marbel Developments Ltd. v. Pirani* (1994), 18 C.C.L.T. (2d) 229, at p. 243 (*per* Newbury J.) (B.C.S.C.), condominium registration problem led to liability.

[275] *P.A. Wournell Contracting v. Allen* (1979), 100 D.L.R. (3d) 62, at p. 67; revd on procedural grounds (1980), 108 D.L.R. (3d) 723 (N.S.C.A.) (*per* Glube J.).

reasonable care and skill" would have handled it as an "ordinary drafting problem", the solicitor is liable for any loss suffered thereby.[276]

There is no liability for a mere "error in judgment", because "a solicitor does not undertake with his client not to make mistakes, but only not to make negligent mistakes".[277] The determination is obviously a "question of degree" and there exists a "borderland" in which it is hard to distinguish between negligence and no negligence.[278]

a) Liability Imposed

Liability is generally imposed when a solicitor fails to take some "routine step" any lawyer would realize is necessary.[279] Thus, when there is doubt about the location of a sewer easement over real property a survey must be sought.[280] Similarly, the omission to inform a mortgagee client that the subject property was owned by the mortgagor's wife, was encumbered and other such matters, amounts to negligence.[281] Neglecting to discover that certain property was "timber land" or subject to an easement[282] or was not wholly owned by the vendor[283] is actionable.[284] A lawyer would be liable also when failing to warn a client about the potential danger of a prior clause in a mortgage,[285] or when neglecting to tell the client that the offer to purchase does not provide for the assumption of a mortgage, when it was expected that it would.[286] So too, a solicitor acting on both sides of a real estate transaction may be negligent for failing to disclose this information to a client.[287]

The failure to register a judgment pursuant to instructions, which enabled other creditors to be preferred over the defendant's client in relation to certain property, was found to be negligence.[288] According to Mr. Justice Strong, the lawyer's retainer extended not only to establish a right and secure a judgment, but also to "get the money".[289] To withdraw from a case without giving notice to

---

[276] See *Jacobson Ford-Mercury Sales v. Sivertz* (1979), 10 C.C.L.T. 274.

[277] *Meakins v. Meakins* (1910), 2 O.W.N. 150, at p. 151 (*per* Riddell J.); see also *Godefroy v. Dalton* (1830), 6 Bing. 460, at p. 467, 130 E.R. 1357.

[278] *Aaroe v. Seymour, supra,* n. 255, at p. 738.

[279] *Ibid.,* at p. 740. See also *Kolan v. Solicitor,* [1970] 1 O.R. 41 (*per* Lacourcière J.), demolition order not discovered; affd [1970] 2 O.R. 686 (C.A.).

[280] *Ibid.*

[281] *Rowswell v. Pettit et al., supra,* n. 254, nominal damages only since no evidence of loss.

[282] *Charette v. Provenzano* (1978), 7 C.C.L.T. 23 (Ont.).

[283] *Messineo v. Beale* (1978), 5 C.C.L.T. 235 (Ont. C.A.).

[284] *Marriott v. Martin* (1915), 7 W.W.R. 1291 (B.C.).

[285] *Palmeri v. Littleton,* [1979] 4 W.W.R. 577.

[286] *McMorran's Cordova Bay v. Harman & Co.,* [1980] 2 W.W.R. 499. Failure to tell of a business associate's criminal record may lead to liability, *Martin v. Goldfarb* (not yet reported) Doc. No. 44653/90, May 7, 1997 (Lederman J.).

[287] *Jacks v. Davis,* [1980] 6 W.W.R. 11.

[288] *Hett v. Pun Pong* (1890), 18 S.C.R. 290.

[289] *Ibid.,* at p. 296.

a client,[290] to allow the limitation period of a meritorious action to expire,[291] or to be so dilatory in prosecuting litigation that an action is dismissed for want of prosecution yields liability.[292] A solicitor who accepts a retainer in a personal injury action is obligated to issue a Writ of Summons before the limitation period expires, even if no specific instructions are obtained from the client to do so because the client cannot be located. The client is not contributorily negligent for failing to contact the solicitor if this does not contribute to the loss.[293]

The giving of erroneous legal advice may also engender responsibility,[294] as for example in relation to the right of a client to inherit land under a fee tail,[295] or in relation to whether an interest rate being charged is illegal[296] or whether a mortgage is invalid because it contravenes the Companies Act.[297]

A lawyer who abuses a confidential fiduciary relationship and seduces the client's wife is liable to pay the nervous shock damage caused to the client.[298]

b) No Liability Imposed

No liability ensues, however, where the lawyer merely makes an error on a complicated issue of law, for if it did, every lawsuit could generate negligence action against the losing lawyer. Thus, where a solicitor incorrectly advised that an action need not be commenced within a certain limitation period,[299] or that litigation should be undertaken,[300] or not undertaken,[301] no liability was imposed.

The lawyer who follows the ordinary practices of the profession will be virtually immune from attack.[302] In *Taylor v. Robertson*[303] a solicitor was relieved of liability since he "followed the usual forms prescribed by the best pleaders" and it was "difficult to see how he could have put in any other defence". Nor was liability visited on a lawyer rushed by a client who refused to investigate

---

[290] *Kern-Hill Co-op Furniture Ltd. v. Schuckett* (1975), 58 D.L.R. (3d) 157 (Man. C.A.).
[291] *Page v. Solicitor* (1971), 20 D.L.R. (3d) 532 (N.B.C.A.); affd (1972), 29 D.L.R. (3d) 386n, lease; *Fyk v. Millar* (1973), 2 O.R. (2d) 39; *Prior v. McNab* (1976), 1 C.C.L.T. 137; *Gouzenko v. Harris* (1976), 72 D.L.R. (3d) 293, at p. 321 (Ont.), no "probability of success" proven, though "nuisance value" shown, $1 damages (*per* Goodman, J.); *Cf., Kitchen v. Royal Airforces Assoc.*, [1958] 2 All E.R. 241. If the claim is groundless, there has been no loss suffered; see *Banks v. Reid* (1974), 6 O.R. (2d) 404, at p. 415.
[292] *Fletcher & Son v. Jubb, Booth & Helliwell*, [1920] 1 K.B. 275 (C.A.).
[293] See *Gray v. Forbes*, [1980] 3 W.W.R. 689.
[294] *Sykes v. Midland Bank*, [1970] 3 W.L.R. 273 (C.A.); see also *Major v. Buchanan* (1975), 9 O.R. 491.
[295] *Otter v. Church, Adams, Tatham & Co.*, [1953] Ch. 280, [1953] 1 All E.R. 168.
[296] *Elcano Acceptance Ltd. v. Richmond, supra*, n. 270.
[297] See *Rafuse, supra*, n. 256.
[298] *Szarfer v. Chodos* (1986), 36 C.C.L.T. 181 (Ont. H.C.).
[299] *Howse Shaw* (1913), 4 O.W.N. 971.
[300] *Meakins v. Meakins* (1910), 2 O.W.N. 150.
[301] *Banks v. Reid* (1974), 6 O.R. (2d) 404, at p. 414, no liability on other grounds.
[302] *Winrob v. Street and Wollen, supra*, n. 267; *Brenner v. Gregory*, [1973] 1 O.R. 252; see also *infra*, Chapter 6.
[303] (1901), 31 S.C.R. 615, at p. 628 (*per* Davies J.).

properly the ownership of certain equipment upon the security of which a loan was advanced.[304] In ascertaining the dimensions of a lot, lawyers must exercise "due care as solicitors, not as surveyors or engineers", for, after all, "a solicitor is not an engineer or a surveyor" and is hired to use "legal skill".[305] Lawyers need not search zoning by-laws if retained after an offer to purchase is executed,[306] nor must they check to see if a proposed defendant has died,[307] nor are they responsible if their clients, without consulting them, fail to do a survey of land being purchased, since there is no reliance in such a case.[308] They may even advise two parties in the same transaction as long as they are not negligent in doing so.[309] A lawyer is not liable for failing to ensure the mental capacity of a testator.[310] So well have lawyers been protected by negligence law that in one case an erroneous opinion on a will did not lead to liability since the undertaking was only to advise on the will, not to advise "truly" on it.[311] Courts have been concerned about the "social costs of defensive litigation" being "higher than the community wishes to pay".[312]

c) Immunity of English Advocates Rejected

Despite this relatively safe position of the legal profession, and despite Canadian authority to the contrary,[313] the House of Lords in *Rondel v. Worsley*[314] clung to the complete immunity from tort liability in England for advocates (including solicitors) in the conduct of litigation. The exemption did not apply to advisory work, drafting or the revision of documents[315] or to exonerate a barrister for failing to sue a particular defendant.[316] Their Lordships relied on three grounds of public policy: first, the proper administration of justice demands that lawyers carry out their duties fearlessly; second, justice would not be served if it were necessary to retry law suits in order to evaluate the conduct of the counsel; and third, it is unfair to make a barrister civilly responsible when unable to refuse to

---

[304] *Millican v. Tiffin Holdings* (1967), 60 D.L.R. (2d) 469.

[305] *Winrob v. Street and Wollen, supra*, n. 267, at pp. 174, 176 (B.C.).

[306] *Hauck v. Dixon* (1975), 10 O.R. (2d) 605.

[307] *Grima v. MacMillan*, [1972] 3 O.R. 214, at least in Windsor, Ontario.

[308] *Brenner v. Gregory*, [1973] 1 O.R. 252.

[309] *Samayoa v. Marks* (1974), 6 O.R. (2d) 419.

[310] *Philp v. Woods, supra*, n. 263.

[311] *Alexander v. Small and Gowan* (1846), 2 U.C.Q.B. 298.

[312] See *Philp v. Woods, supra*, n. 263, at p. 88.

[313] *Leslie v. Ball* (1863), 22 U.C.Q.B. 512 (C.A.). Among the grounds expressed by the Canadian court for the different result was the absence of a split bar and the ability to sue for fees in Ontario; see also *Wade v. Ball* (1870), 20 U.C.C.P. 302.

[314] *Rondel v. Worsley*, [1969] 1 A.C. 191, [1967] 3 All E.R. 993; Catzman, "Comment" (1968), 46 Can. Bar Rev. 505.

[315] *Ibid.*, at p. 232.

[316] *Saif Ali v. Sydney Mitchell & Co.*, [1978] 3 All E.R. 1033 (H.L.); See Catzman, "Comment" (1979), 57 Can. Bar Rev. 339.

accept a brief. Lord Reid was prepared to rely on the duty of barristers to "act honourably in accordance with the recognized standards of their profession".[317]

It has been suggested that *Rondel v. Worsley* might be adopted in Canada,[318] but this should be and has been rightly resisted.[319] Firstly, there is no evidence that the work of our court is hampered by counsel's fear of civil liability. Nor can one point to any alarming increase in the number of legal malpractice suits, although there has been an increase in their number recently. Our courts do not seem overly burdened by whatever retrial of lawsuits is necessitated by the few actions that are launched against lawyers in Canada. Moreover, Canadian barristers are not obligated to accept every client who seeks to retain them. Canadian lawyers do not need such protection, especially since they all must carry liability insurance, and the Canadian public would not be served thereby. Tort law has a role to play in encouraging our bar to live up to at least a minimum level of performance, as lawyers must in the United States.[320] Lastly, if immunity were granted to lawyers, it would be hard to deny it to the medical profession.

The British rule was resoundingly rejected by Krever J. in *Demarco v. Ungaro et al.*[321] The defendants, who were lawyers, brought a motion to strike out a statement of claim alleging negligence against them for losing a case on the ground that they failed to call certain evidence that they should have called. In a learned judgment, dismissing the motion, Mr. Justice Krever held that the immunity afforded a British lawyer has no place in Ontario. He explained:

> I have come to the conclusion that the public interest . . . in Ontario does not require that our Courts recognize an immunity of a lawyer from action for negligence at the suit of his or her former client by reason of the conduct of a civil case in Court. It has not been, is not now, and should not be, public policy in Ontario to confer exclusively on lawyers engaged in court work an immunity possessed by no other professional person. Public policy and the public interest do not exist in vacuum. They must be examined against the background of a host of sociological facts of the society concerned. Nor are they lawyers' values as opposed to the values shared by the rest of the community. In the light of recent developments in the law of professional negligence and the rising incidence of "malpractice" actions against physicians (and especially surgeons who may be thought to be to physicians what barristers are to solicitors). I do not believe that enlightened, non-legally trained members of the community would agree with me if I were to hold that the public interest requires that litigation lawyers be immune from actions for negligence . . . .
>
> Many of the sociological facts that are related to public policy and the public interest may be judicially noticed. The population of Ontario is approximately eight and a quarter million people. In 1978 there were approximately 12,300 lawyers licensed by the Law Society of Upper Canada to practise law in Ontario. All of them have a right of audience in any Court in

---

[317] *Rondel v. Worsley, supra*, n. 314, at p. 231.

[318] Catzman, *supra*, n. 314. See also dictum of Henry J. in *Banks v. Reid* (1974), 6 O.R. (2d) 404, at p. 418.

[319] See Laskin, *The British Tradition in Canadian Law* (1969), p. 26.

[320] Wade, "The Attorney's Liability for Negligence" (1959), 12 Vand. L. Rev. 755.

[321] (1979), 21 O.R. (2d) 673, at pp. 692-93. See Hutchinson, "Comment" (1979), 57 Can. Bar Rev. 346. See *Wernikowski v. Kirkland, Murphy & Ain* (1999), 48 C.C.L.T. (2d) 233 (Ont. C.A.), action by convicted client against barrister may proceed.

Ontario as well as in the Federal Court of Canada and the Supreme Court of Canada. The vast majority of these lawyers are in private practice and, as such, are required to carry liability insurance in respect of negligence in the conduct of their clients' affairs. No distinction is made in this respect between those exclusively engaged in litigation and all other lawyers. The current rate of increase in the size of the profession is approximately 1,000 lawyers annually. It is widely recognized that a graduating class of that size places such an enormous strain on the resources of the profession that the articling experience of students-at-law is extremely variable. Only a small percentage of lawyers newly called to the Bar can be expected to have had the advantage of working with or observing experienced and competent counsel. Yet very many of those recently qualified lawyers will be appearing in Court on behalf of clients. To deprive these clients of recourse if their cases are negligently dealt with will not, to most residents of this Province, appear to be consistent with the public interest.

2. DOCTORS

The standard of care demanded of doctors resembles the one required of lawyers[322] — that is, to act like a reasonably prudent doctor.[323] Their duty, like that of attorneys, once rested exclusively on a contractual foundation, but not any longer; the obligation may now be based either on contract or tort. "A physician, even a specialist, gives no guarantee of success".[324] In undertaking the treatment of a patient, therefore, a doctor gives no implied warranty to effect a cure, and, hence, the doctor is not an insurer, unless there is an *express* agreement to this effect.[325]

Canadian courts have evinced a reluctance to "second-guess" physicians in the practice of their profession.[326] Mr. Justice Gould, for example, has opined, "The less courts try to tell doctors how to practice medicine the better."[327] Our courts have indicated that they know that doctors are human and cannot be expected to perform perfectly all the time. In *White v. Turner*[328] it was said that "Doctors are human, too, and they are entitled to attend conferences and take vacations, as long as appropriate steps are taken to see that a competent substitute is available to their patients during their absence." But this does not mean the courts will shirk their responsibility to impose liability in proper circumstances, for even "highly professional" and "honourable" medical

---

[322] Linden, "The Negligent Doctor" (1973), 11 Osgoode Hall L.J. 31; Picard and Robertson, *Legal Liability of Doctors and Hospitals in Canada*, 3rd ed. (1996); Marshall, *The Physician and Canadian Law*, 2nd ed. (1979).

[323] *ter Neuzen v. Korn*, [1995] 3 S.C.R. 674, at p. 693 (*per* Sopinka J.).

[324] *Johnston v. Wellesley Hospital*, [1971] 2 O.R. 103, at p. 111 (*per* Addy J.).

[325] *Town v. Archer* (1902), 4 O.L.R. 383, at p. 388 (*per* Falconbridge C.J.). See also *Guilmet v. Campbell* (1971), 385 Mich. 57.

[326] *Seyfert v. Burnaby Hospital* (1986), 36 C.C.L.T. 224, at p. 229 (B.C.S.C.) (*per* McEachern C.J.B.C.).

[327] *McLean v. Weir* (1977), 3 C.C.L.T. 801; affd [1980] 4 W.W.R. 330.

[328] (1981), 15 C.C.L.T. 81, at p. 105 (Ont.) (*per* Linden J.); revd on procedural point.

practitioners, "like every other human being does on occasion", may make mistakes that are negligent.[329] In such a case civil liability must follow.

The physician is liable for malpractice when failing to act like a reasonably prudent doctor. This is an objective standard, which takes into account the extra knowledge possessed by the actor. In *Wilson v. Swanson,* Mr. Justice Rand explained that a surgeon undertakes to possess "the skill, knowledge and judgment of the generality or average of the special group or class of technicians to which he belongs and will faithfully exercise them".[330] What the doctor must do is engage in an "honest and intelligent exercise of judgment". If a "substantial opinion" in the profession confirms the doctor's judgment, even though it was wrong, the mishap will be considered only an error of judgment, not "unskilfullness".[331] Another widely-accepted formulation of the standard was expressed by Mr. Justice Schroeder in *Crits v. Sylvester* as follows:

> Every medical practitioner must bring to his task a reasonable degree of skill and knowledge and must exercise a reasonable degree of care. He is bound to exercise that degree of care and skill which could reasonably be expected of a normal prudent practitioner of the same experience and standing. . . .[332]

This *dictum* largely echoes the classic statement of Lord Chief Justice Hewart in *R. v. Bateman,*[333] referred to above. In short, physicians must conform to the "accepted standards of the day".[334] If a physician's conduct complies with the customary practices of the profession the physician is virtually assured of being exonerated when something goes awry,[335] although this defence is not conclusive.[336]

It should be noted that patients must behave in a reasonable fashion too, or else their damages will be reduced or even eliminated altogether. In *Brain v. Mador,*[337] for example, a patient, who failed to take reasonable steps to seek further medical advice following a vasectomy which developed complications, had his damages reduced. His explanation to the effect he did not want to "air dirty laundry" was found to be insufficient.

---

[329] *Moffatt v. Witelson* (1980), 29 O.R. (2d) 7, at p. 12 (*per* Galligan J.).

[330] [1956] S.C.R. 804, at p. 811.

[331] *Ibid.*, at p. 812. See *Maynard v. West Midlands Regional Health Authority*, [1985] 1 All E.R. 635 (H.L.).

[332] [1956] O.R. 132, at p. 143; affd [1956] S.C.R. 991. See also *Gent v. Wilson*, [1956] O.R. 257, at p. 265 (C.A.) (*per* Schroeder J.A.).

[333] (1925), 41 T.L.R. 557, at p. 559.

[334] *Ostrowski v. Lotto*, [1969] 1 O.R. 341, at p. 355 (*per* Keith J.); revd on another point, [1971] 1 O.R. 372 (C.A.); affd [1973] S.C.R. 220.

[335] See, for example, *Johnston v. Wellesley Hospital, supra*, n. 324, at p. 112. See Chapter 6.B.1 Medical Custom, *infra.*

[336] See Linden, "Custom in Negligence Law" (1968), 11 Can. Bar J. 151; Linden, "The Negligent Doctor" (1973), 11 Osgoode Hall L.J. 31, and Chapter 6, *infra*; *cf.*, Weiler, "Groping Towards a Canadian Tort Law" (1971), 21 U. of T.L.J. 267m, at pp. 322 *et seq.*

[337] (1985), 32 C.C.L.T. 157 (Ont. C.A.); see also *Janiak v. Ippolito* (1985), 31 C.C.L.T. 113 (S.C.C.).

a) Specialists

Specialists, as might be expected, must perform at a higher level than general practitioners. They represent themselves as possessing superior skills and additional training. Their fees normally reflect this. Consequently, according to Mr. Justice Abbott in *Wilson v. Swanson,* a specialist must "exercise the degree of skill of an average specialist in his field".[338] Mr. Justice Schroeder has also declared that if a doctor "holds himself out as a specialist, a higher degree of skill is required of him than of one who does not profess to be so qualified by special training and ability".[339]

This principle has been recently reiterated by Mr. Justice Sopinka in *ter Neuzen v. Korn:*[340]

> In the case of a specialist, such as a gynaecologist and obstetrician, the doctor's behaviour must be assessed in light of the conduct of other ordinary specialists, who possess a reasonable level of knowledge, competence and skill expected of professionals in Canada, in that field. A specialist, such as the respondent, who holds himself out as possessing a special degree of skill and knowledge, must exercise the degree of skill of an average specialist in his field. ...

But even a specialist does not have to achieve perfection. If an operation, though unsuccessful, is conducted in a way, "consistent with good orthopedic surgical practice", no liability will ensue.[341] Similarly, a dermatologist escapes responsibility if the procedure adopted is in "accordance with generally accepted good medical practice in the field of dermatology".[342] On the other hand, a dermatologist is liable if burning a patient while treating eczema with a dosage that is too high and administered for too long.[343] A psychologist and psychiatrist will be relieved of liability, when a patient of theirs commits suicide, if they acted "in accord with the accepted practice of psychology and psychiatry at the time".[344] A surgeon, mistakenly believing there was a malignancy, removed more of a patient's insides than was required and was exonerated.[345] A specialist trained in obstetrics and gynecology is not liable if meeting the "standard of proficiency of the average specialist in his field".[346] In the same way a pediatrician was absolved when administering a vaccination which spread infection to

---

[338] [1956] S.C.R. 804, at p. 817; duty to seek specialists, *MacDonald v. York County Hospital* (1974), 1 O.R. (2d) 653, at p. 682 *(per* Dubin J.A.); affd [1976] 2 S.C.R. 825.

[339] *Crits v. Sylvester,* [1956] O.R. 132, at p. 143; affd [1956] S.C.R. 991; *Gent v. Wilson,* [1956] O.R. 257, at p. 265 *(per* Schroeder J.A.). In *McCaffrey v. Hague,* [1949] 2 W.W.R. 539, at p. 542 (Man.), Campbell J. said, "A higher degree of skill is required from one who holds himself out to be a specialist." See also *Rietze v. Bruser (No. 2),* [1979] 1 W.W.R. 31, at p. 45 *(per* Hewak J.).

[340] [1995] 3 S.C.R. 674, at p. 693, sperm infected with H.I.V., new trial ordered.

[341] *Ostrowski v. Lotto, supra,* n. 334, at p. 381 (C.A.).

[342] *Johnston v. Wellesley Hospital, supra,* n. 324, at p. 116.

[343] *McCaffrey v. Hague,* [1949] 2 W.W.R. 539 (Man.).

[344] *Haines v. Bellissimo* (1977), 18 O.R. (2d) 177, 82 D.L.R. (3d) 215 *(per* Griffiths J.), same standard required of both psychologist and psychiatrist here.

[345] *Wilson v. Swanson,* [1956] S.C.R. 804.

[346] *Karderas v. Clow,* [1973] 1 O.R. 730, at p. 738. See *ter Neuzen v. Korn, supra,* n. 340.

other parts of a patient's body.[347] A radiologist, however, must not perform a test (intravenous pyelogram), which he thinks is unjustified, in that the "risks are outweighed by the potential benefits", merely because another doctor asks that it be done. In such circumstances, the radiologist should call the referring doctor to discuss the matter and, if the matter cannot be thus resolved, ought not to do it.[348]

b) Novices and Interns

Although it has toughened its general standard for specialists, tort law has not diluted it for inexperienced doctors. Justice Philp has declared "[t]he same degree of skill is expected of an inexperienced surgeon as of an experienced one."[349] As was explained by Mr. Justice Power in *Wills v. Saunders*,[350] "the standard . . . should not be lower by reason of [a doctor's] inexperience". Hence, a "novice surgeon" who had not performed a particular operation before was made liable when he severed a nerve.[351] Interns who identify themselves as such, however, need only meet the standard of reasonably competent interns.[352] Interns are not given any special dispensation, however, if they present themselves as being fully qualified. In *Vancouver General Hospital v. Fraser*,[353] two interns licensed to practise within the confines of a hospital wrongly read some X-rays of a car accident victim who came to their hospital, talked to his family doctor and then sent him away. The patient later died as a result of complications from a broken neck, which their examination had failed to detect. Their employer, the hospital, was held vicariously liable for their blunder. Mr. Justice Rand based his decision on the fact that the interns' conduct was cloaked with "all the ritual and paraphernalia of medical science." An intern had to be "more than a mere untutored communicant between [the family doctor] and the patient".[354] An intern must exercise the "undertaken degree of skill and that cannot be less than the ordinary skill of a junior doctor". One of the most vital things an intern must have is an "appreciation of his own limitations". By failing to notify a radiologist who was on call at the hospital and by relying on their own imperfect knowledge, they acted negligently. Similarly, a Chinese herbal medicine practitioner needs to abide by the practices of traditional Chinese herbal medicine practitioners, but must also know when to call in a regular doctor.[355]

---

[347] *Gent v. Wilson, supra,* n. 339.

[348] *Leonard v. Knott,* [1980] 1 W.W.R. 673 (B.C.C.A.), 25 per cent liable, referring doctor also 75 per cent liable for death of patient who suffered allergic reaction during unnecessary test.

[349] *Miles v. Judges* (1997), 37 C.C.L.T. (2d) 160, at p. 175 (Ont. Gen. Div.).

[350] (1989), 47 C.C.L.T. 235, at pp. 254-55 (Alta. Q.B.).

[351] *McKeachie v. Alvarez* (1970), 17 D.L.R. (3d) 87, at p. 100 (B.C.) (*per* Wilson J.); see also *Challand v. Bell* (1959), 18 D.L.R. (2d) 150 (Alta.); *Walker v. Bedard,* [1945] O.W.N. 120, at p. 124.

[352] *Aldana v. March* (1999), 44 C.C.L.T. (2d) 164 (B.C.S.C.).

[353] [1952] 2 S.C.R. 36.

[354] *Ibid.,* at p. 46.

[355] *Shakoor v. Situ,* [2000] 4 All E.R. 181, at p. 192 (Q.B.D.), liver failure from herbal treatment of skin problem.

c) Locality Rule

It was once clear that doctors were protected from tort liability if they merely lived up to the standard of the profession in their own community or similar localities.[356] Someone in "country practice" did not have to be as proficient as an urban physician.[357] This idea still has devotees. In the recent case of *McCormick v. Marcotte,* a doctor was held liable when he performed an obsolete type of operation on a patient because he was unable to do the one recommended by a specialist.[358] Mr. Justice Abbott imposed liability and stated that a doctor is required to possess and use, "that reasonable degree of learning and skill ordinarily possessed by practitioners in similar communities in similar cases". He quoted, however, from the trial judge to the effect that this was a "hospital in a well-settled part of the Province [Quebec] within easy reach of the largest centres of population", which makes clear that the statement was an *obiter dictum* only.

The locality rule should be abandoned. This would reflect the improvements in modern communications, medical education and the uniformity of examinations for doctors in Canada.[359] In the case of *Town v. Archer,*[360] Chief Justice Falconbridge criticized the "locality rule" on the ground that "all the men practising in a given locality might be equally ignorant and behind the times, and regard must be had to the present advanced state of the profession and to the easy means of communication with, and access to the large centres of education and science . . . ." In *Town v. Archer* the community in question was Port Perry, which at that time was only two hours travel from Toronto, then a city of a quarter of a million people, with three medical colleges and numerous hospitals. Communications and access to information have improved greatly since then so that there is even less reason to differentiate between localities. Moreover, a principle that permits an inferior brand of medicine for rural Canadians cannot be countenanced. A single standard may promote an upgrading of medical practice across the country. It would also enable plaintiffs to secure medical evidence from a larger pool of experts, a distance advantage.

In practice, however, one cannot expect that all the sophisticated equipment of the Toronto General Hospital will be available in every hospital throughout Canada.[361] Nor can we require the same speed in providing care by a doctor who

---

[356] See Abbott J. in *Wilson v. Swanson,* [1956] S.C.R. 804, at p. 817; *Challand v. Bell, supra,* n. 351. See generally Waltz, "The Rise and Gradual Fall of the Locality Rule in Medical Malpractice Litigation" (1969), 18 De Paul L. Rev. 408.

[357] *Hodgins v. Banting* (1906), 12 O.L.R. 117 (*per* Boyd C.).

[358] [1972] S.C.R. 18, at p. 221. See also *Rodych v. Krasey,* [1971] 4 W.W.R. 358 (Matas. J.); *Tiesmaki v. Wilson,* [1974] 4 W.W.R. 19; affd [1975] 6 W.W.R. 639, at p. 650 (Alta. C.A.).

[359] Uniform exams called "Dominion Councils" are set nationally each year under the Canada Medical Act, see Picard, *op. cit. supra,* n. 322, at p. 177.

[360] (1902), 4 O.L.R. 383, at p. 388. See also *Van Wyk v. Lewis,* [1924] App. Div. 438 (S. Af.).

[361] See *Whiteford v. Hunter* (1950), 94 Sol. Jo. 758 (H.L.).

has to travel longer distances.[362] One attempt to articulate this distinction was made in *Zirkler v. Robertson*:

> It surely cannot be that the skill of a physician attending a patient in a private house [in a rural area] with few conveniences and no assistants, is to be measured by the same standard as the city surgeon, provided with an operation room, nurses and all the aids of a modern hospital.[363]

But this does not mean that there must be a varying standard of care depending on the location. The same disadvantageous conditions exist when a doctor is forced to minister to a patient at the roadside, on the Don Valley Parkway in the heart of Toronto, or in a private home in Vancouver. The difference is not in the *standard of care* demanded of the physician, but in the limited access to the facilities. One cannot expect the same results from treatment in primitive conditions as one can under the best conditions. The rural-urban distinction retains significance in this regard, but it should not be allowed to create a double standard based on geography for Canadian doctors.

d) The Need to Seek Specialist's Advice

A general practitioner should enlist the help of a specialist if a reasonably prudent physician would consider it necessary under the circumstances.[364] For example, a physician must call in a radiologist to read X-rays if the physician is incapable of doing so.[365] A general practitioner need not, however, exhibit the expertise of a radiologist.[366] In one early case, *Jarvis v. International Nickel Ltd.*,[367] a company doctor in the mining town of Copper Cliff, Ontario, failed to call in a specialist, despite the urgings of his patient, because he felt it premature. As a result he failed to diagnose a mastoiditis condition in the ear. Mr. Justice Wright observed that "most medical men would have" called in a specialist and that to do so would have been a "more prudent course".[368] Nevertheless, he dismissed the action since he could not find any authority imposing a legal obligation to seek the advice of a specialist. On the facts, however, it was probably not negligent to refuse to call a specialist in the circumstances, and, in any event, there was a lack of evidence of causal connection in the case.

---

[362] See *Rickley v. Stratton* (1912), 22 O.W.R. 282.

[363] (1897), 30 N.S.R. 61, at p. 70 (C.A.). See also *Rodych v. Krasey, supra*, n. 358, at p. 371.

[364] *MacDonald v. York County Hospital, supra*, n. 338; *Kersey v. Wellesley Hospital* (1988), 46 C.C.L.T. 271 (Ont. H.C.J.), in an urgent situation they must do so quickly. See also *Chow (Litigation Guardian) v. Wellesley Hospital*, [1999] O.J. No. 279, "bad baby" case, should have called in neonatologist.

[365] *Vancouver General Hospital v. Fraser, supra*, n. 353.

[366] *Abel v. Cooke*, [1938] 1 D.L.R. 170 (Alta. C.A.).

[367] (1928), 63 O.L.R. 564.

[368] *Ibid.*, at pp. 570-71.

There is another case, *Kunitz v. Merei*[369] where blindness resulted from a haemorrhage following an operation to remove some polyps from a patient's nose. It was alleged that if an ophthalmologist had been consulted earlier, the blindness might have been avoided. In the circumstances, however, it was held that there was no negligence and, in any event, it was unlikely that an earlier consultation would have averted the danger.[370] Because specialists are more numerous these days, general practitioners tend to rely upon them more than ever. Liability should follow if a doctor fails to call in a specialist, when a prudent practitioner would deem it advisable.[371]

e) Reliance on Other Personnel

A doctor may rely on hospital and other personnel to act reasonably in caring for patients placed under their care. Thus, when a patient suffered brain damage because the nurse in a hospital's recovery room went out for coffee instead of supervising her properly, the hospital was held liable but the doctor was excused from liability.[372] A surgeon who relies on a resident doctor to close up and then leaves the operating room following an operation is not liable for any sponges that may be left behind, although the resident, the nurses, and their employer, the hospital may be.[373]

A doctor may not, however, ignore potential problems that may arise and rely blindly upon others. It is incumbent upon a medical practitioner, for example, either to personally issue a warning to the patient, or to ensure that someone else does so, about the side-effects of any drugs to be administered following an operation. Consequently, where a doctor relinquished the care of his patient to hospital personnel who failed to warn the patient about the danger of haemorrhage from an anti-coagulant drug, Dicumerol, the doctor was made responsible for the additional operation necessitated to correct the situation.[374]

f) Negligence Found

The burden of proof rests on the patient to establish substandard conduct which amounts to negligence.[375] This is not easy for there was once a presumption that licensed and qualified physicians are competent and that their treatments are

---

[369] [1969] 2 O.R. 572 (*per* Stark J.).

[370] *Ibid.*, at p. 587.

[371] McCoid, "The Care Required of Medical Practitioners" (1959), 12 Vand. L. Rev. 549, at pp. 567-68.

[372] *Laidlaw v. Lions Gate Hospital* (1969), 8 D.L.R. (3d) 730 (B.C.). See also *Krujelis v. Esdale* (1972), 25 D.L.R. (3d) 557 (B.C.).

[373] See *Karderas v. Clow*, [1973] 1 O.R. 730 (Cromarty J.), action dismissed because limitation expired. *Cf.*, *Frandle v. MacKenzie* (1988), 47 C.C.L.T. 30; revd (1990), 51 B.C.L.R. (2d) 190 (B.C.C.A.), doctor relying on nurse for sponge count. See also *Shobridge v. Thomas* (1999), 47 C.C.L.T. (2d) 73 (B.C.S.C.), both doctor and nurse liable for gauze left behind after surgery.

[374] *Crichton v. Hastings*, [1972] 3 O.R. 859 (C.A.).

[375] *Walker v. Bedard*, [1945] O.W.N. 120, at p. 122.

correct,[376] but it is doubtful that this is still the case. Malpractice liability is, nonetheless, rarely imposed. A doctor was found liable, however, for wrongly diagnosing as flu a case of meningitis, which caused the death of a patient.[377] So too, a physician who did not warn a patient about the danger involved in the prolonged use of a new drug and failed to notice that the patient was using it when he should not have been can be held responsible.[378] Claimants have been successful when someone was burned during a dermatology treatment,[379] when an explosion occurred during the administration of anaesthetic,[380] when sutures were improperly done[381] and when a sponge was left behind in the patient during a tonsillectomy.[382] Similarly, if a gauze swab chokes someone during dental surgery,[383] if someone's knee cap is broken during exercise treatment,[384] and if the wrong organ is removed,[385] negligence will be found. Liability has also been visited on doctors for misuse of a cautery,[386] for bungling an anaesthetic,[387] for failing to immobilize a patient's neck,[388] for damaging a nerve during the removal of a cyst,[389] for removing the wrong tooth,[390] for some bone chips left behind causing paralysis after a mastoid operation,[391] for delay in diagnosis and treatment[392] and for other negligent forms of treatment.[393]

---

[376] *Ibid.*, at p. 124.

[377] *Dale v. Munthali* (1973), 21 O.R. (2d) 554 (C.A.).

[378] *Crossman v. Stewart* (1977), 5 C.C.L.T. 45 (B.C.), doctor one-third to blame, patient two-thirds.

[379] *McCaffrey v. Hague*, [1949] 2 W.W.R. 539 (Man.). See also *McFadyen v. Harvie*, [1941] O.R. 90; affd [1942] S.C.R. 390.

[380] *Crits v. Sylvester, supra*, n. 339.

[381] *Gallant v. Fialkov* (1989), 50 C.C.L.T. 159 (Ont. H.C.J.).

[382] *Anderson v. Chasney*, [1949] 4 D.L.R. 71 (Man. C.A.); affd [1950] 4 D.L.R. 223. See also *Gloning v. Miller* (1953), 10 W.W.R. 414 (Alta.), forceps; *cf.*, *Jewison v. Hassard* (1916), 28 D.L.R. 584 (C.A.), sponge; *Mahon v. Osborne*, [1939] 1 All E.R. 535 (C.A.).

[383] *Holt v. Nesbitt*, [1951] O.R. 601 (C.A.); affd [1953] 1 S.C.R. 143.

[384] *Guaranty Trust Co. v. Mall Medical Group*, [1969] S.C.R. 541.

[385] *McNamara v. Smith*, [1934] O.R. 249 (C.A.), no liability because no damage suffered by erroneous removal of uvula.

[386] *Crysler v. Pearse*, [1943] O.R. 735, excess of alcohol in high frequency diathermy caused fumes to ignite and burn patient; *Gray v. LaFlèche*, [1950] 1 D.L.R. 337, misuse of cautery during circumcision causing serious injury.

[387] *Jones v. Manchester Corp.*, [1952] 2 All E.R. 125 (C.A.), pentathol administered too quickly; *Villeneuve v. Sisters of St. Joseph*, [1972] 2 O.R. 119 (C.A.); affd on point (1974), 47 D.L.R. (3d) 391, child not immobilized during administration of anaesthesia due to joint negligence of doctor (70%) and nurses (30%). See also *Aynsley v. Toronto General Hospital*, [1972] S.C.R. 435. *Cf.*, *Hughston v. Jost*, [1943] O.W.N. 3, abcess formed; *Webster v. Armstrong*, [1974] 2 W.W.R. 709 (B.C.), no liability when patient disregarded warning and drank coffee prior to operation.

[388] *Morrison v. Hicks* (1990), 4 C.C.L.T. (2d) 148 (B.C.S.C.).

[389] *Fizer v. Keys*, [1974] 2 W.W.R. 14 (Alta.) (Kirby J.).

[390] *Gagnon v. Stortini* (1974), 4 O.R. (2d) 270.

[391] *Eady v. Tenderenda* (1973), 41 D.L.R. (3d) 706; revd (1974), 51 D.L.R. (3d) 79.

[392] *Law Estate v. Simice* (1995), 27 C.C.L.T. (2d) 127 (B.C.C.A.).

[393] *Marshall v. Rogers*, [1943] 4 D.L.R. 68 (B.C.C.A.), diabetic not watched properly during dangerous treatment; *Crichton v. Hastings*, [1972] 3 O.R. 859 (C.A.), failure to inform patient about side-effects of anti-coagulent drug; *Snell v. Farrell* (1990), 4 C.C.L.T. (2d) 229 (S.C.C.);

Doctors may be responsible for mishaps which occur *prior* to treatment or *following* the treatment itself. Thus, for example, if a patient were to fall off an unsafe examining table in a doctor's office, prior to the examination, liability might be imposed if negligence could be proven.[394] Similarly, negligence in postoperative care can yield responsibility, for example, where a cast is applied too tightly and this fact is not discovered by the doctor in sufficient time to prevent the need for amputation.[395]

Doctors may be held responsible for acting unreasonably in related matters other than the actual medical treatment of the patient. A doctor, for example, must carefully inform counsel prosecuting an injury claim about any potential future injury that may arise or be liable for the lesser amount received in the settlement.[396] Similarly, a doctor can be liable for a patient sexually assaulting a fellow patient in a recovery room because there is a duty to protect the "vulnerable".[397] An emergency team that took a drunk person home after a fall was not liable, however, for failing to tell his wife, even though he later suffered a stroke.[398]

g) Errors of Judgment

A mere error of judgment does not yield tort damages. If a doctor "honestly and intelligently" makes a judgment which subsequently turns out to have been wrong, the doctor is protected from liability.[399]

What is meant by the statement "an error of judgment is not negligent" has been explained by Lord Fraser in *Whitehouse v. Jordan*[400] as follows:

> . . . an error of judgment "is not *necessarily* negligent". But, in my respectful opinion, the statement as it stands it not an accurate statement of the law. Merely to describe something as an error of judgment tells us nothing about whether it is negligent or not. The true position is that an error of judgment may, or may not, be negligent; it depends on the nature of the error. If it is one that would not have been made by a reasonably competent professional man professing to have the standard and type of skill that the defendant held himself out as having, and acting with ordinary care, then it is negligent. If, on the other hand, it is an error that a man, acting with ordinary care, might have made, then it is not negligent.

---

cf., *Bolam v. Friern Hospital*, [1957] 2 All E.R. 118, electro-convulsive therapy caused broken bones, but case dismissed.

[394] *Baltzan v. Fidelity Insce.*, [1933] 3 W.W.R. 203 (Sask. C.A.), no liability.

[395] *Badger v. Surkan* (1972), 32 D.L.R. (3d) 216 (Sask. C.A.); *MacDonald v. York County Hospital* (1974), 1 O.R. (2d) 653; see also *Pittman Estate v. Bain* (1994), 19 C.C.L.T. (2d) 1 (Ont. Gen. Div.) (*per* Lang J.), blood case; *Webb v. Motta*, [1998] A.J. No. 1329.

[396] *Kelly v. Lundgard* (1996), 29 C.C.L.T. (2d) 113 (Alta. Q.B.); supp. reasons 32 C.C.L.T. (2d) 191 (Alta. Q.B.).

[397] *H. (M.) v. Bederman* (1995), 27 C.C.L.T. (2d) 152 (Ont. Gen. Div.) (Eberhard J.).

[398] *Davidson v. B.C.* (1995), 28 C.C.L.T. (2d) 124 (B.C.S.C.).

[399] *Badger v. Surkan* (1970), 16 D.L.R. (3d) 146, at p. 162; affd (1972), 32 D.L.R. (3d) 216; see also *Tiesmaki v. Wilson*, [1974] 4 W.W.R. 19; affd [1975] 6 W.W.R. 639 (Alta. C.A.).

[400] [1981] 1 All E.R. 267, at p. 281.

In the case, an attempted forceps delivery failed and had to be stopped. A Caesarean was performed properly, but the baby suffered brain damage from suffocation during the aborted forceps delivery. The action was dismissed on the basis that there was no negligence proven against the doctor.

Consequently, no liability has been imposed where a patient died of shock as a result of a nupercaine anaesthetic injection,[401] where someone's leg became shorter as a result of an operation,[402] where some organs were removed in error,[403] where some unnecessary exploratory surgery was done,[404] and where a vaccination went wrong.[405]

The failure to diagnose a rare condition or disease is not negligence.[406] In *Clark v. Wansborough,* a doctor was sued for failing to discover a dislocated shoulder, after a fractured arm had been X-rayed and treated.[407] No liability was imposed since such a condition was "almost an unheard of thing, it is unique" in that type of fracture. The court indicated that an X-ray examination must always be a question of circumstances depending on the condition of the patient, the character of the injury and the availability of the apparatus.[408]

Doctors were also exonerated when a patient fell,[409] or leaped out of a hospital window,[410] when a patient was not told that deafness might result from the use of a drug,[411] and when a skin treatment caused more pain than was usual.[412] No liability was found where an aorta was ruptured during a disc operation causing the death of a patient,[413] and where hypertension was not treated with drugs because they would not have prevented the stroke.[414] Nor was a doctor held liable when he changed the medication he was giving to an insane person, contributing to an attack on another person.[415]

---

[401] *Walker v. Bedard,* [1945] O.W.N. 120.

[402] *Ostrowski v. Lotto,* [1973] S.C.R. 220; *Hodgins v. Banting* (1906), 12 O.L.R. 117; see also *Town v. Archer, supra,* n. 325.

[403] *Wilson v. Swanson, supra,* n. 356.

[404] *Finlay v. Hess* (1973), 3 O.R. (2d) 91.

[405] *Gent v. Wilson,* [1956] O.R. 257 (C.A.).

[406] *Bell v. R.* (1973), 44 D.L.R. (3d) 549 (Fed. Ct.); *Tiesmaki v. Wilson, supra,* n. 399. See also *Ostash v. Sonnenberg* (1968), 67 D.L.R. (2d) 311 (Alta. C.A.), no liability for failure to detect carbon monoxide poisoning.

[407] [1940] O.W.N. 67, at p. 70.

[408] See also *Moore v. Large,* [1932] 4 D.L.R. 793 (B.C.C.A.); *Sabapathi v. Huntley,* [1938] 1 W.W.R. 817 (P.C.).

[409] *Child v. Vancouver General Hospital,* [1970] S.C.R. 477, hospital liable.

[410] *University Hospital Bd. v. Lepine,* [1966] S.C.R. 561, *cf., Villemure v. L'Hôpital Notre-Dame* (1972), 31 D.L.R. (3d) 454, psychiatric patient, liability.

[411] *Male v. Hopmans,* [1967] 2 O.R. 457. Liability imposed, however, for negligent failure to do tests.

[412] *Johnston v. Wellesley Hospital,* [1971] 2 O.R. 103.

[413] *Chubey v. Ahsan* (1975), 56 D.L.R. (3d) 231; affd [1976] 2 W.W.R. 367 (Man. C.A.).

[414] *Parsons v. Shmok* (1975), 58 D.L.R. (3d) 622 (B.C.).

[415] *Molnar v. Coates* (1991), 5 C.C.L.T. (2d) 236 (B.C.C.A.).

h) Duty of Disclosure

Canadian doctors have a duty to their patients to disclose "the nature of a proposed operation, its gravity, any material risks and any special or unusual risks attendant upon the performance of the operation".[416] Although, in the past, these problems, which were described as issues of "informed consent", could be analyzed with battery law, they must now be handled with negligence principles, according to the decision of *Reibl v. Hughes.*[417] Moreover, the language of "informed consent" should be abandoned in these cases, because it spawns confusion between battery and negligence law. Battery law, however is still available to medical patients, but only where there has been no consent to the operation, where the treatment given goes beyond the consent, or where the consent is obtained by fraud or misrepresentation.[418]

This matter of disclosure of risks by a doctor is not entirely unlike the duty of a manufacturer to warn about the dangerous properties of its products.[419] A patient, about to undergo some medical treatment, is entitled to know something about what is going to be done, the likelihood of its success and the risks involved in the procedure. A patient is also entitled to know about alternative methods of treament or alternative procedures and the risks and advantages relating to these alternative treatments and procedures.[420] The patient needs this information in order to decide whether to go ahead with the treatment or whether to forego it. It is up to the doctor, in the first instance, to determine the content and the amount of the information that should be imparted to the patient, which obviously depends on the individual circumstances of each situation. Herein lies the problem, for, if the doctor errs, the courts may later find the doctor liable for negligence.

The courts do not require doctors to explain to their patients all the details of every procedure and all the things that can possibly go wrong. If that were the case, our doctors would be discussing medicine all day rather than practising it. The courts do not want doctors to confuse or frighten their patients or to burden them with unnecessary data. There is no need, consequently, to tell a patient about the ordinary risks associated with all surgery, since everyone is expected to know about them. Thus, just as one need not warn that a match will burn or that a knife will cut, because that would be redundant, a doctor need not disclose that, if an incision is made, there will normally be some bleeding, some pain and a scar will remain when the cut has healed. So too, it was once thought that

---

[416] *Hopp v. Lepp* (1980), 13 C.C.L.T. 66, at p. 87 (S.C.C.) (*per* Laskin C.J.). The onus is on the defendant, therefore. See *Videto v. Kennedy* (1981), 17 C.C.L.T. 307, at p. 317 (Ont. C.A.).

[417] *Reibl v. Hughes* (1980), 14 C.C.L.T. 1 (S.C.C.) (*per* Laskin C.J.).

[418] *Ibid.*, at pp. 13-14. See also Chapter 3, *supra*. No battery found in *LoKay v. Kilgour* (1984), 31 C.C.L.T. 177 (Ont. H.C.).

[419] *Lambert v. Lastoplex Chemicals Co.*, [1972] S.C.R. 569.

[420] *Van Mol (Guardian ad litem) v. Ashmore* (1999), 44 C.C.L.T. (2d) 228, at p. 261 (B.C.C.A.), liable to child patient; see also statement by La Forest J. in *Hollis v. Dow Corning Corp.,* [1995] 4 S.C.R. 634, at p. 656.

everyone may be expected to know that in any surgical procedure there is a chance of infection, tetanus, gangrene and a possibility of death from the anaesthetic.[421] An opthamologist, moreover, need not warn that eyeglasses may break during a touch-football game, because:

> ... [T]here is no need for a professional person or a manufacturer to warn of dangers that would be as apparent to the consumer as to the manufacturer or which would be as apparent to the patient as to the doctor.[422]

If a patient inquires about a planned procedure, the doctor must respond fully and fairly, so that an inquisitive patient may obtain more information than one who is not so curious.[423] Similarly, if a procedure is for experimental[424] or cosmetic[425] purposes, rather than therapeutic aims, a higher degree of disclosure by the doctor is required, for there is no reason to withhold data. A patient may "well decide that he would prefer to live with a blemish rather than take the risk".[426] In other words, the "frequency of the risk becomes much less material when the operation is unnecessary for [the patient's] medical welfare".[427] On the other hand, there may be "emotional factors" that render a particular patient "unable to cope with facts relevant to recommended surgery" which would justify a doctor "in withholding or generalizing information as to which he would otherwise be required to be more specific".[428] It is incumbent on a doctor to ensure that the patient with a language or other barrier understands what is being communicated.[429] It is obvious that the medical profession is involved in a complex process when it decides what information it must disclose to patients.

i) Reasonable Patient Standard

In the past, the test employed in assessing the acceptability of the decision by doctors was the "professional medical standard",[430] but *Reibl v. Hughes* has transformed the law and decreed that the "reasonable patient standard" must

---

[421] *Kenny v. Lockwood*, [1932] O.R. 141, this decision may no longer be law following *Reibl*. See Picard, *op. cit., supra*, n. 322, at p. 97.

[422] *Moffatt v. Witelson* (1980), 29 O.R. (2d) 7, at p. 14 (*per* Galligan J.), liability for negligent treatment though.

[423] *Smith v. Auckland Hospital*, [1965] N.Z.L.R. 191.

[424] *Halushka v. University of Saskatchewan* (1965), 53 D.L.R. (2d) 436 (Sask. C.A.).

[425] *Dulude v. Gaudette*, [1974] C.S. 618, at p. 621; *White v. Turner* (1981), 15 C.C.L.T. 81; *Drolet v. Parenteau* (1994), 26 C.C.L.T. (2d) 168 (Que. C.A.).

[426] *Hankins v. Papillon* (1980), 14 C.C.L.T. 198, at p. 203 (*per* Rothman J.).

[427] *Videto v. Kennedy* (1980), 27 O.R. (2d) 747, at p. 758 (*per* Grange J.); revd on another issue (1981), 17 C.C.L.T. 307.

[428] *Reibl v. Hughes, supra*, n. 417, at p. 17. See *Hajgato v. London Health Assoc.* (1982), 36 O.R. (2d) 699 (H.C.).

[429] *Adan v. Davis*, [1998] O.J. No. 3030; *Lue v. St. Michael's Hospital*, [1997] O.J. No. 255, if the matter is serious, the obligation may be even higher.

[430] *Male v. Hopmans*, [1966] 1 O.R. 647; affd on this point, [1967] 2 O.R. 457 (C.A.).

now be used by Canadian courts.[431] No longer does the medical profession *alone* collectively determine, by its own practices, the amount of information a patient should have in order to decide whether to undergo an operation as it did under the professional standard. From now on, the court also has a voice in deciding the appropriate level of information that must be conveyed to a patient in the circumstances as a question of fact. The patient's right to know is no longer to be limited by what the medical profession customarily tells them; henceforth, the patient's right to be able to make an intelligent choice about any proposed surgery transcends the interest of the medical profession in setting its own autonomous standards of disclosure.

The essential issue, then, is to determine what reasonable patients in the position of plaintiffs would consider to be "material risks" or "special or unusual risks" about which they would want to receive information.

Before deciding this matter, the court will hear expert medical evidence on the question of what the risks inherent in a particular operation are, how serious these risks are, how frequently these risks may arise and what information medical practitioners usually transmit to their patients in relation to these risks.

The factors that doctors must consider, which were outlined in *Smith v. Auckland Hospital*[432] will probably continue to be relevant to this determination, that is:

> . . . the gravity of the condition to be treated, the importance of the benefits expected to flow from the treatment or procedure, the need to encourage the patient to accept it, the relative significance of its inherent risks, the intellectual and emotional capacity of the patient to accept the information without such distortion as to prevent any rational decision at all, and the extent to which the patient may seem to have placed himself in the doctor's hands . . . .

But that is not *all* the court will have regard to; it will also give due consideration to the evidence of the patient and the family as to the patient's general situation. The court will be interested in the information the individual patient would want to know in the circumstances. The court will then assess what a reasonable patient would like to know in these circumstances.

Weighing all of these factors, the court will decide whether the information given to this patient in these circumstances was sufficient. It is obvious that this is no simple task.

ii) Material Risks and Unusual or Special Risks

The meaning of "material risks" and "unusual or special risks" should now be considered. Madam Justice McLachlin, while on the British Columbia Supreme

---

[431] *Reibl v. Hughes, supra,* n. 417, at p. 16. See also Glass, "Restructuring Informed Consent" (1970), 70 Yale L.J. 1553. *Cf., Sidaway v. Board of Governors of Bethlehem Royal Hospital,* [1985] A.C. 871 (H.L.).

[432] [1964] N.Z.L.R. 241, at p. 250; revd on another point, [1965] N.Z.L.R. 191.

Court, offered some assistance in defining the meaning of 'material', 'special', and 'unusual risks' when she stated in *Rawlings v. Lindsay*:[433]

> a medical person must disclose those risks to which a reasonable patient would be likely to attach significance in deciding whether or not to undergo the proposed treatment. In making this determination, the degree of probability of the risk and its seriousness are relevant factors. Thus an "unusual" or improbable risk should be disclosed if its effects are serious. Conversely, a minor result should be disclosed if it is inherent in or a probable result of the process.

Materials risks are significant risks that pose a real threat to the patient's life, health or comfort. In considering whether a risk is material or immaterial, one must balance the severity of the potential result and the likelihood of its occurring. Even if there is only a small chance of serious injury or death, the risk may be considered material. As explained by Laskin C.J.C., even if a certain risk is a "mere possibility which ordinarily need not be disclosed, yet if its occurrence carries serious consequences, as for example, paralysis or even death, it should be regarded as a material risk requiring disclosure".[434] On the other hand, if there is a significant chance of slight injury this too may be held to be material. As always in negligence law, what is a material risk will have to depend on the specific facts of each case.[435]

As for "unusual or special risks", these are not ordinary, common, everyday matters. These are risks which are somewhat extraordinary, uncommon and not encountered every day, but which are known to occur occasionally. Even though they may be rare occurrences, because of their unusual or special character, the Supreme Court has declared that they should be described to a reasonable patient, even though they may not otherwise be thought to be "material".

There may, of course, be an overlap between "material risks" and "unusual or special risks". If a special or unusual risk is quite dangerous and fairly frequently encountered, it could be classified as a material risk. But even if it is not very dangerous or not frequently met, an unusual or special risk may have to be disclosed.

Pursuant to these principles, it has been held that a neurosurgeon must disclose to a patient a 4 per cent risk of death and a 10 per cent risk of neurological damage which were involved in surgery to remove blockage in one of the arteries in the neck. The operation was not urgent and could have been delayed until after the patient's retirement income was assured, one and one-half years away.[436] If the operation is an experimental one, the duty to disclose is "the most exacting standard of disclosure".[437] Similarly, liability may be imposed against a surgeon who neglects to tell a patient that temporary or permanent stiffness may

---

[433] (1982), 20 C.C.L.T. 301, at p. 306 (B.C.S.C.).

[434] *Reibl v. Hughes, supra,* n. 417, at p. 5.

[435] *Mason v. Forgie* (1984), 31 C.C.L.T. 66; affd 38 C.C.L.T. 171 (N.B.C.A.).

[436] *Ibid. Cf., Dunn v. North York General Hospital* (1989), 48 C.C.L.T. 23 (Ont. H.C.J.) (*per* Austin J.), risk of scarring in removing scar not material.

[437] *Weiss v. Solomon* (1989), 48 C.C.L.T. 280 (Que. S.C.).

result from an osteotomy on an arm.[438] A plastic surgeon must warn that, after sanding of the skin to remove facial spots resulting from birth control pills, the spots may reappear.[439] Similarly, a plastic surgeon must advise a patient that a mammoplasty may result in extensive scarring of the breasts, asymmetry of the nipples and possibly deformed breasts (material risks). Further, the possibility of the scars opening up and requiring corrective surgery should be mentioned (special or unusual risks).[440] The risk of contracting hepatitis from blood is not a "material risk" but an "unusual or special risk", even though it was "extraordinary, uncommon and not encountered every day" because it was "known to occur occasionally".[441] A surgeon may have to tell a patient of the risk of bowel perforation during a sterilization operation, where the surgery is elective and need not be performed then or ever.[442] A country doctor, however, need not warn about the very slight risk of possible paralysis or death from using anti-rabies vaccine, because it might dissuade patients from agreeing to take the vaccine despite the extreme danger of the disease, which is always fatal.[443] Nor must a dentist warn that an injection of local anaesthetic might cause permanent numbness of the mouth where the risk was extremely rare (1 in 800,000) and the patient had had many previous similar injections without incident.[444]

Liability may be imposed for failure to disclose the risk of a stroke from neck manipulation,[445] a heart attack that was not foreseen by a hospital,[446] a wrist being shorter following a procedure,[447] damage to a foetus by an anti-coagulant drug,[448] that a bowel may be perforated during surgery,[449] and that a procedure would be delegated to an assistant resident who performed the procedure incompetently.[450]

It has been suggested that matters concerning a doctor's health or fitness, that is physician-created risks, should be disclosed to patients.[451] For example, a health-

---

[438] *Kelly v. Hazlett* (1976), 15 O.R. (2d) 290, another theory was used, but the case likely would be decided similarly now. See also *Meyer Estate v. Rogers* (1991), 6 C.C.L.T. (2d) 102 (Ont. Gen. Div.), adverse reaction is material risk.

[439] *Hankins v. Pappilon* (1980), 14 C.C.L.T. 198 (Que.).

[440] *White v. Turner* (1981), 15 C.C.L.T. 81 (Ont.).

[441] *Kitchen v.McMullen* (1989), 50 C.C.L.T. 213, at p. 221 (N.B.C.A.) (*per* Stratton C.J.); leave to appeal to S.C.C. dismissed Feb. 22, 1990.

[442] *Videto v. Kennedy* (1980), 27 O.R. (2d) 747; revd (1981), 17 C.C.L.T. 307. See also *Zamparo v. Brisson* (1981), 16 C.C.L.T. 66 (Ont. C.A.).

[443] *Davidson v. Connaught Laboratories* (1980), 14 C.C.L.T. 251 (Ont.), risk between 1 in 600 to 1 in 9,000.

[444] *DeFerrari v. Neville* (1998), 42 C.C.L.T. (2d) 327 (Ont. Gen. Div.).

[445] *Leung v. Campbell* (1995), 24 C.C.L.T. (2d) 63 (Ont. Gen. Div.).

[446] *Briffet v. Gander & District Hospital Board* (1996), 29 C.C.L.T. (2d) 251 (Nfld. C.A.), causation inferred.

[447] *Seney v. Crooks* (1996), 30 C.C.L.T. (2d) 66 (Alta. Q.B.).

[448] *Webster v. Chapman* (1996), 30 C.C.L.T. (2d) 164 (Man. Q.B.); revd in part (1997), 40 C.C.L.T. (2d) 212 (Man. C.A.); leave to appeal refused (1998), 159 D.L.R. (4th) vii (S.C.C.).

[449] *Jaskiewicz v. Humber River Regional Hospital* (2000), 4 C.C.L.T. (3d) 85 (Ont. S.C.J.), no liability, no cause.

[450] *Currie v. Blundell* (1992), 10 C.C.L.T. (2d) 288 (Que. S.C.).

[451] De Ville, "Nothing to Fear but Fear Itself" (1994), 22 Journals of Law, Medicine and Ethics 6.

provider who is an alcoholic, or is addicted to drugs or has AIDS might be held liable for failing to inform patients about this risk.[452] In one recent Canadian case,[453] where the matter was raised, it was held that a surgeon need not reveal that he suffered from epilepsy because he was taking medication to control it and the patient was in no danger. In summary then, this exercise of defining the scope of the duty of disclosure is now a complex one for the courts, requiring much time, effort, thought and evidence. The cooperation and assistance of the medical profession will be vital to the task. One court has described the doctor-patient relationship nowadays as a "joint venture".[454] The courts will, as always, move very cautiously in this area. In most cases, the courts will probably continue to classify as reasonable the customary practices of the profession as to disclosure, since they are, after all, based on experience, common sense and what doctors honestly perceive their patients wish to know. However, it is now open to the courts, if invited, to participate in the process of evaluating the information that has been communicated and to find it wanting in appropriate cases, even if the medical profession disagrees.[455]

iii) Modified Objective Test of Causation

The decision in *Reibl v. Hughes* has also declared that a modified objective test of causation is to be employed in assessing whether the patient would have consented to the operation if properly warned.[456] Unlike the situation in battery, where proof of actual damage is unnecessary, negligence law will only furnish compensation if the substandard conduct being assessed has caused some loss to the plaintiff.

If the patient would still have agreed to the operation, even if supplied with full information about the risks, the failure to inform the patient fully cannot be described as a cause of the damage suffered. Hence, the patient could not succeed in negligence theory. In order to recover in negligence law, therefore, it must be established that the patient would have refused to undergo the surgery if told about all the relevant risks.[457]

There is a danger here, though, that every patient who becomes a plaintiff will insist that they would have foregone the operation if properly warned. Hindsight is always wiser than foresight. The courts have always mistrusted judgments made from hindsight and have sought to minimize the danger of such

---

[452] Furrow, "Must Physicians Reveal Their Wounds?" (1996), 5 Cambridge Quarterly of Health Care Ethics.

[453] *Halkyard v. Mathew* (1998), 43 C.C.L.T. (2d) 171 (Alta. Q.B.); affd [2001] A.J. No. 293, 4 C.C.L.T. (3d) 271 (Alta. C.A.), not cause of injury.

[454] See McIntyre J. in *Seney v. Crooks, supra*, n. 447, at p. 80 (Alta. Q.B.).

[455] It is too early to tell whether the detailed consent provisions in the Health Care Consent Act, 1996, S.O. 1996, c. 2 will affect this jurisprudence.

[456] *Supra*, n. 417.

[457] *Lue v. St. Michael's Hospital* (1999), 46 C.C.L.T. (2d) 153 (Ont. C.A.), reasonable patient would have gone ahead even if told of risk of paralysis.

evidence. Hence the Supreme Court of Canada has adopted a modified objective test here, not a subjective one. It is not enough, therefore, for the court to be satisfied that the patient would have foregone the treatment; it also has to be satisfied that a reasonable patient, in the same situation, would have done so. According to one judge, the question, therefore, is "Would the reasonable patient in the patient's position, knowing of the risks, have consented to the treatment?"[458] Another thought the question was, "Did the plaintiff 'prove on a balance of probabilities that a reasonable person in his position would not have consented to [the procedure] had he been informed of the risk? . . .' "[459] That is the meaning of the test adopted in *Reibl v. Hughes*,[460] and why it has been called the "modified objective test of causation".[461]

The Supreme Court of Canada has recently reaffirmed its commitment to the modified objective test of *Reibl v. Hughes*, but three of the judges indicated a desire to abandon it and to adopt a more subjective test. In *Arndt v. Smith*,[462] a woman sued her doctor for costs incurred in rearing her daughter, who was congenitally injured by chicken pox the woman had contracted during the pregnancy. The claim was based on the ground that the woman would have terminated the pregnancy if the doctor had properly warned her of the risk of injury to the foetus posed by the chicken pox. The action was ultimately dismissed. For the majority, Cory J. explained:

> The [modified objective] test . . . relies on a combination of objective and subjective factors in order to determine whether the failure to disclose *actually* caused the harm of which the plaintiff complains. It requires that the court consider what the reasonable patient *in the circumstances of the plaintiff* would have done if faced with the same situation. The trier of fact must take into consideration any "particular concerns" of the patient and any "special considerations affecting the particular patient" in determining whether the patient would have refused treatment if given all the information about the possible risks . . . . In my view this means that the "reasonable person" who sets the standard for the objective test must be taken to possess the patient's reasonable beliefs, fears, desires and expectations. Further, the patient's expectations and concerns will usually be revealed by the questions posed. Certainly, they will indicate the specific concerns of the particular patient at the time consent was given to a proposed course of treatment. The questions, by revealing the patient's concerns, will provide an indication of the patient's state of mind, which can be relevant in considering and applying the modified objective test.

Thus, it was felt that the modified objective test "serves to eliminate from consideration the honestly held but idiosyncratic and unreasonable or irrational

---

[458] *Haughian v. Paine* (1986), 36 C.C.L.T. 242, at p. 295 (Sask. Q.B.); revd on another point 40 C.C.L.T. 13 (C.A.).

[459] *Kitchen v. McMullen, supra*, n. 441, at pp. 222-23 (*per* Stratton C.J.).

[460] *Supra*, n. 417. See also, for another decision utilizing this objective test, *Petty v. MacKay* (1979), 10 C.C.L.T. 85; affd 31 C.C.L.T. 155 (B.C.C.A.), holding that a reasonable patient, in spite of the plaintiff's evidence to the contrary, would not have forgone the operation if fully informed.

[461] *Mason v. Forgie, supra*, n. 435, at p. 176 (*per* Stratton C.J.N.B.).

[462] (1997), 213 N.R. 243 (S.C.C.); see also *Hollis v. Dow Corning Corp.*, [1995] 4 S.C.R. 634.

beliefs of patients". Three of the judges disagreed, preferring a subjective test,[463] explained by McLachlin J. as follows:

> The approach suggested by the fundamental principles of tort law is subjective, in that it requires consideration of what the plaintiff at bar would have done. However, it incorporates elements of objectivity; the plaintiff's subjective belief at trial that she would have followed a certain course stands to be tested by her circumstances and attitudes at the time the decision would have been made as well as the medical advice she would have received at the time.

Thus, McLachlin J. favoured a test that would ask "what the particular plaintiff would have done in all the circumstances, but accepts that the reasonableness of the one choice over another, as reflected in the medical advice the plaintiff would have received, is an important factor bearing on that decision".

Although there does not seem to be a vast difference between the two approaches, the dissenters' views are clearly more favourable to patients. A careful observer would note that Cory J.'s view is also somewhat more advantageous to patients than the original formulation by Laskin J., which seemed to lack many subjective elements. The subtle difference seems to be one of emphasis mainly and should not lead to different results in many cases. Note, for example, that both Cory and McLachin JJ. agreed on the result in this case.

This modified objective standard governs not only doctors but also dental surgeons,[464] and dentists.[465] It may apply also to "non-surgical" as well as surgical treatment, so that chiropractors are subject to it.[466] It does not, however, cover pharmaceutical manufacturers[467] or producers of breast implant material.[468]

This is a sensible stance which is quite consistent with tort principles in other contexts. For example, the requirement is not unlike the need for proof of reasonable reliance in actions for deceit and negligent misrepresentation. In those types of cases, our courts have avoided assisting gullible fools who rely on every bit of silly advice they receive.[469] Consequently, patients who say they would have foregone life-saving treatment because it might have caused a rash or a headache, cannot recover on the basis of inadequate disclosure, even in the unlikely event that they are believed, because a reasonable patient would have gone ahead in any event.

---

[463] *Arndt, ibid.*, at p. 273. See Osborne, "Causation and the Emerging Canadian Doctrine of Informed Consent to Medical Treatment" (1985), 33 C.C.L.T. 131, at p. 144.

[464] *Diack v. Bardsley* (1984), 31 C.C.L.T. 308 (B.C.C.A.).

[465] *Schinz v. Dickinson* (1984), 31 C.C.L.T. 313, at p. 318 (B.C.C.A.). Duty to warn less because risk "less dramatic".

[466] *Mason v. Forgie, supra,* n. 435.

[467] *Buchan v. Ortho Pharmaceuticals (Canada) Ltd.* (1986), 35 C.C.L.T. 1 (Ont. C.A.).

[468] *Hollis v. Dow Corning Corp., supra,* n. 462, at p. 674 (*per* LaForest J.).

[469] See *Prosser and Keeton on the Law of Torts*, 5th ed. (1984), p. 750.

iv) Summary of Reibl

The New Brunswick Court of Appeal [470] has outlined what it calls the "bipartite test", which is now applied in these cases:

> [W]as the risk one which ought to have been disclosed to the patient and, if so, would a reasonable person . . . after having been fully informed of the risk have consented to the procedure if so informed?

Furthermore, these questions

> must be answered in the proper order so as to preserve the balance of the bipartite test. In this way, the reasonable person in the second half of the analysis can weigh the material risks of proceeding with the treatment against the risks of not proceeding.

In commenting on the objective standard of disclosure and of causation adopted in *Reibl v. Hughes*, Professor Sanda Rodgers-Magnet has written that the approach had the advantage of "logical consistency". She explains as follows:

> The patient is expected, in law, to behave as would a reasonable person in his circumstances. He is to be given the information a reasonable person would expect to receive, and to take the decision a reasonable person would take. Neither physician nor patient may hide behind an amorphous unverifiable experience, whether professional or personal. Each party's behaviour may be measured by the Court against the Court's own experience. Finally, if an objective standard of disclosure increases the burden on the treating physician at the time of risk disclosure to the benefit of the patient, that increase is balanced by an increase of the burden placed on the patient who would allege that a causal element is present. The patient reaps both the benefits and the burdens of being measured by an objective standard.[471]

The modified objective causation theory has played a major role in the cases reported recently, leading to the dismissal of one-half of the decisions.[472] There are, therefore, quite a few decisions denying liability on this basis, perhaps along with other grounds.[473] Some cases still permit recovery, indicating that patients can still meet the modified objective standard.[474] This new idea is controversial and it has been criticized as having provided "little or no improvement".[475] Its future, however, seems secure for the present at least.

---

[470] *Kitchen v. McMullen, supra,* n. 441, at p. 218 (*per* Stratton C.J.), quoting Hoyt J.A. in *Kueper v. McMullin* (1986), 37 C.C.L.T. 318 (N.B.C.A.), no liability here, though risk of hepatitis from blood.

[471] See "Comment" (1980), 14 C.C.L.T. 61, at p. 76.

[472] Picard, *supra,* n. 322, at p. 107.

[473] *Stamos v. Davies* (1985), 33 C.C.L.T. 1 (Ont. H.C.); *Moore v. Bojock* (1986), 36 C.C.L.T. 150 (B.C.C.A.); *Ferguson v. Hamilton Civic Hospital* (1985), 33 C.C.L.T. 56 (Ont. C.A.); *Lokay v. Kilgour, supra,* n. 418; *Petty v. McKay, supra,* n. 460; *Rohde v. Steinhoff* (1995), 25 C.C.L.T. (2d) 62 (B.C.S.C.).

[474] *Sinclaire v. Boulton* (1985), 33 C.C.L.T. 125 (B.C.S.C.); *Graham v. Persyko* (1986), 55 O.R. (2d) 10 (C.A.); *Brain v. Mador, supra,* n. 337; *Mason v. Forgie, supra,* n. 435.

[475] Gochnauer and Fleming, "Case Comment" (1981), 15 U.B.C.L. Rev. 475; Somerville, "Structuring the Issues in Informed Consent" (1981), 26 McGill L.J. 740; Osborne, "Causation

The decision of *Reibl v. Hughes* does not mean that Canadian doctors must now give complicated seminars on medicine to all of their patients. It does mean, though, that more time may have to be spent explaining things to patients than in the past. No doubt, this will render medical practice somewhat less efficient and more costly. Nevertheless, the law, as espoused by the Supreme Court of Canada, requires that patients be treated as intelligent, mature and rational individuals. The ultimate effect of this new approach, hopefully, will be medical practitioners who are even more sensitive, concerned and humane than they now are. Moreover, the doctor-patient relationship should be improved by the better communication in future between doctors and their patients. The high level of trust Canadians now have in their doctors should be even higher. If fewer operations are performed as a result of the expanded information available to patients, that would not necessarily be a bad thing.[476] Another beneficial consequence may be that there will be even fewer malpractice actions started in this country than there now are. "As human relations between doctor and patient atrophy" lawsuits become more commonplace.[477] Hence, if the communications improve, the number of lawsuits should shrink. If these results flow from *Reibl v. Hughes*, it will have rendered our community a most valuable service.

i) Cost Containment Measures

The effect of cost containment measures on the standard of care owed by doctors is generating some litigation and scholarly debate.[478] Can the scarcity of resources and budgetary restraint excuse medical practitioners from providing otherwise reasonable service to their patients? In one such case,[479] Lofchik J. proved unreceptive to this argument, criticizing "production-line medicine", where a day patient complained that he was not advised sufficiently of the risk from anaesthetic nor about alternative forms of anaesthesia available. He stated:

> I must also observe that at times in the course of questioning Dr. Sandler and in cross-examining the plaintiff's expert, it was suggested that the time pressures involved in day surgery require that the most expedient form of anaesthesia be used so as not to upset the routine of those involved in the process. No doubt there are budgetary and time constraints involved

---

and the Emerging Canadian Doctrine of Informed Consent to Medical Treatment" (1985), 33 C.C.L.T. 131; Robertson, "Informed Consent in Canada: An Empirical Study" (1984), 22 Osgoode Hall L.J. 139.

[476] Illich, *The Medical Nemesis* (1976).

[477] Law and Polan, *Pain & Profit: The Politics of Malpractice* (1978).

[478] Irvine, "The Physician's Duty in the Age of Cost Containment" (1994), 22 Man. L.J. 345; Caulfield and Ginn, "The High Price of Full Disclosure" (1994), 22 Man. L.J. 328; Caulfield, "Health Care Reform: Can Tort Law Meet the Challenge?" (1994), 32 Alta.L.Rev. 685; Caulfield and Robertson, "Cost Containment Mechanisms in Health Care" (1999), 27 Man. L.J. 1; Fraser and Avery, "What You Don't Know Can Hurt You" (1994), 3 Health L. Rev. 3.

[479] *De Vos v. Robertson* (2000), 48 C.C.L.T. (2d) 172, at p. 189 (Ont. S.C.J.); see also *Law Estate v. Simice* (1994), 21 C.C.L.T. (2d) 228, at p. 240 (B.C.S.C.) (*per* Spencer J.). See also the California case of *Wickline v. The State*, 228 Cal. Reptr. 661 (1986), where Rowen J. stated: "It's essential that cost limitation programs not be permitted to corrupt medical judgment"; see also *Decock v. Alberta*, [2000] A.J. No. 419.

... but, in my view, this is a case where those constraints worked against the patient's interest by inhibiting the doctors in their judgment of what should be done for him. That is to be deplored ... . I respectfully say it is something to be carefully considered by those who are responsible for the provision of medical care and those who are responsible for financing it. I also say that if it comes to a choice between the physician's responsibility to his or her individual patient and his or her responsibility to the medical care system overall, the former must take precedence in a case such as this. It is difficult in this case to resist the observation that the patient's problems were at least in part related to what might be described as *"production line medicine"*... .

Another issue looming is whether doctors must advise patients about treatment not available in the province involved or in Canada generally, but which can be obtained in the U.S. or elsewhere. While no cases have yet been decided on this issue, it has been pleaded[480] and liability has some support in the literature.[481] An additional problem is whether a hospital committee, a Premier of a Province, or a Minister of Health, whose decisions deny or delay medical care to someone in need of it, may be held liable. There are obvious hurdles in cases such as these, one of them being the difficulty of proving causation, even if one can show that the standard of care has been breached, because all that a patient would often be able to demonstrate is, not that a cure was foregone, but merely that a chance at a slightly better outcome has been lost. A further, perhaps fatal, problem is also the barrier to tort actions against public authorities for what are labelled policy matters.[482] It may be that actions for breach of fiduciary relations in this context may be able to yield more success.[483] Despite these difficulties, efforts of claimants, even unsuccessful ones, well publicized in the press, may contribute to making professionals and politicians more aware of the consequences of their cost-containment policies and encourage them to be more sensitive to the resulting human suffering.

j) Conclusion about Doctors' Liability

The guidelines laid down by negligence law for doctors are sensible; they offer considerable protection to patients without threatening the ordinarily capable physician. Our doctors are aware of the general standard whereby their acts are evaluated, and seem willing to abide by it.[484] Obviously, the law cannot and does not demand too high a standard of medical practitioners, for it would intrude into their professional activities too much.[485] Nevertheless, some doctors feel beleaguered by malpractice actions, even thought they are still relatively rare in

---

[480] *Sallis v. Vancouver Central Hospital* (not yet reported) No. 907316 Vancouver Registry, where a woman died while on a waiting list for cardiac surgery, pre-trial motion at [1996] B.C.J. No. 758. See also action against Premier Klein et al in *Decock v. Alberta*, [2000] A.J. No. 419.

[481] See Fraser and Avery, *supra*, n. 478.

[482] See Chapter 17, Governmental Liability.

[483] *Norberg v. Wynrib*, [1992] 2 S.C.R. 226.

[484] In a survey done at the Osgoode Hall Law School by R.J Gray and G. Sharpe, 96% identified correctly the standard expected of them..

[485] *Roe v. Ministry of Health*, [1954] 2 Q.B. 66 (C.A.) (*per* Denning L.J.).

Canada,[486] in comparison with the United States, where scholars have urged that negligence law in this area be replaced by no-fault accident insurance.[487]

In Canada, even though complaints are heard, there seems little need of this.[488] First, jury trial is generally unavailable here so that doctors are not, as in the United States, left to the mercy of "the twelve", who, according to Falconbridge C. J., may look more favourably upon the patient's case than the doctor's.[489] Second, the controlled use of contingent fees and lower damage awards in Canada prevent an excess of litigation. Consequently, although fees in the C.M.P.A. have risen, they are still modest. Third, the "conspiracy of silence" in the United States has been said to be non-existent in Canada,[490] in spite of evidence frequently emerging to the contrary.[491] Lastly, the potential availability of a malpractice action may serve as a stimulus for ordinary doctors to improve the quality of medicine they practise.[492] Moreover, there are, unfortunately, a small number of doctors who are less competent and less caring than they should be, and who, consequently, generate a large number of malpractice actions.[493] By permitting these actions to continue against these doctors, attention may be focussed on them and, eventually, they may mend their ways or take up alternative work. One author has suggested that it is the "revenge factor" that fuels so much of this type of litigation. He bemoans the "commodification of healing". Patients sue not so much because of the mistakes their doctors make in the treatment; they sue more because they are angry at their doctors who are (or seem to be) unsympathetic, or who fail to apologize, or avoid them when things go wrong.[494] One study showed that, for every six incidents of malpractice, only one lawsuit is commenced.[495] One lesson that medical malpractice litigation teaches, then, is the need for better human relations between doctors and their

---

[486] The *Canadian Medical Protective Association Annual Report* (1999), shows that 100 million dollars was paid out for 31 awards and 396 settlements in 1999; 66 million dollars was paid in legal costs on behalf of 59,000 doctors. There were 1,354 actions started that year.

[487] Ehrenzweig, "Hospital Accident Insurance: A Needed First Step Towards the Displacement of Liability for Medical Malpractice" (1964), 31 U. Chi. L. Rev. 279; O'Connell, *Ending Insult to Injury* (1975); see also Haines, "The Medical Professional and the Adversary Process" (1973), 11 Osgoode Hall L.J. 40.

[488] A voluntary no-fault scheme, retaining tort law, has been suggested by Pritchard, *Liability and Compensation in Health Care* (1990). See Weiler, *Medical Malpractice on Trial* (1991).

[489] *Town v. Archer* (1902), 4 O.L.R. 383, at p. 389.

[490] *Report of the Attorney-General's Committee on Medical Evidence in Court in Civil Cases* (1965).

[491] Gryf-Ostrowski, *The Patient be Damned! A Case of Malpractice* (1976).

[492] Kretzmer, "The Malpractice Suit: Is It Needed?" (1973), 11 Osgoode Hall L.J. 55.

[493] One study showed that in Los Angeles, 46 doctors (.5%) of 8,000 in practice, account for 10% of all the malpractice claims and 30% of the total payments. Each of these 46 was also sued 1½ times per year on the average. See Schwartz and Komesar, *Doctors, Damages and Deterrence: An Economic View* (1978).

[494] Lander, *Defective Medicine* (1978).

[495] Schwartz and Komesar, *op. cit. supra*, n. 493, 24,000 accidents in California yielded 4,000 claims.

patients, a goal that is certainly worth striving for whatever the ultimate destiny of tort law in this area.[496]

G. Aggravated Negligence

There has been much criticism of the idea of drawing distinctions between acts of negligence. Baron Rolfe once said that gross negligence was merely ordinary negligence "with the addition of a vituperative epithet".[497] Some courts have even denied the existence of different types of negligence.[498] Nevertheless, legislation has made this argument largely academic. Some jurisdictions have incorporated an assortment of degrees of care into their statutes which range from wilful and wanton misconduct through recklessness to gross negligence. Despite occasional groans from authors, the courts have been able to manage with these various standards. Perhaps it is not as difficult to understand the differences as some have thought. Judge Macgruder is reputed to have compared the differences among negligence, gross negligence and recklessness to the distinctions among a fool, a damned fool and God-damned fool.

Gross negligence is particularly important in Canada because of two types of legislative provisions. The first type stipulates that a municipality is liable for damages which result from the presence of snow and ice on a sidewalk only in the case of gross negligence.[499] The second type permitted passengers to recover against their host drivers only on the basis of gross negligence or wilful and wanton misconduct, most of which sections have now been repealed.[500]

A work such as this cannot consider the scores of cases defining gross negligence which fill our law reports.[501] It is clear, however, that something more than ordinary negligence is demanded when the prefix "gross" is utilized. It is also obvious that the plaintiff does not have to prove criminal negligence.[502] The Supreme Court of Canada has decided that gross negligence means "very great negligence".[503] Another way gross negligence has been defined in automobile cases is that the conduct must amount to a "marked departure from the standard by which responsible and competent people in charge of motor-cars govern

---

[496] *The Report of the Royal Commission on Civil Liability and Compensation for Personal Injury* (1978) (The Pearson Commision) made no major recommendations for reform in this field, except that strict liability should be imposed in cases of research.

[497] See *Wilson v. Brett* (1843), 11 M. & W. 113, 152 E.R. 737.

[498] *Pentecost v. London District Auditor*, [1951] 2 K.B. 759, at p. 764.

[499] Municipal Act, R.S.O. 1990, c. M.45, s. 284(4).

[500] The Ontario s. 132(3) was repealed by S.O. 1977, c. 54, s. 16.

[501] See Wright, "Gross Negligence" (1983), 33 U. of T.L.J. 184, written in 1927. MacArthur, "Gross Negligence and the Guest Passenger" (1960), 38 Can. Bar Rev. 47; Singleton, "Gross Negligence and the Guest Passenger" (1973), 11 Alta. L. Rev. 165. See, for instance, *Spiller v. Brown*, [1973] 6 W.W.R. 663 (Alta. C.A.); *Doxtator v. Burch*, [1972] 3 O.R. 806 (C.A.); affd (1974), 41 D.L.R. (3d) 768; *Goulais v. Restoule* (1974), 48 D.L.R. (3d) 285.

[502] *Avgeropoulos v. Karanasos*, [1969] 2 O.R. 521, at p. 526 (Dist. Ct.).

[503] See *Kingston v. Drennan* (1897), 27 S.C.R. 46 (*per* Sedgewick J.); *Cowper v. Studer*, [1950] S.C.R. 450 (*per* Locke J.).

themselves".[504] A plaintiff may be required to go even further and show a "very marked departure from the standard of responsible and competent drivers".[505] Gross negligence is a question of fact to be found by the trial judge, or the jury, if there is one.[506]

In deciding whether there has been gross negligence, a court must consider "the cumulative effect of all the factors producing the casualty and not fall into the error, where there are several factors, of considering them individually. Taken alone, in a given set of circumstances, excessive speed, improper lockout, breach of the rules of the road and lack of control, and many others, may or may not amount to gross negligence, but when considered together their totality may be over-whelming."[507] Thus, a defendant who pulls out to pass in dangerous circumstances will be found grossly negligent if also travelling at an excessive rate of speed, with bald tires. Similarly, the consumption of alcohol is a factor that will be considered, along with other acts of negligence, in deciding if the negligence is gross.[508]

It is not necessary, however, for multiple factors to support a finding of gross negligence. Driving around a steep curve at a high rate of speed has itself been held to be gross negligence."[509] Falling asleep at the wheel may also suffice,[510] as would "driving blindly at 50 m.p.h. down the highway in the face of oncoming traffic",[511] allowing one's car to swerve slowly into the left lane,[512] and driving at 20-25 m.p.h. down a steep and icy hill.[513]

The "demarcation line between gross and ordinary negligence is getting more difficult to define or establish in particular cases", according to Mr. Justice MacKinnon, who observed that "the time has come for the Legislature to review the relevant legislation".[514] Mr. Justice Evans, who dissented on the facts, agreed that legislative reform would be preferable to judicial disregard of the distinction between gross and ordinary negligence and suggested that a "return to the common law concept would eliminate the strained and occasionally unnatural interpretation which the Courts have placed upon the legislation".[515] Happily, the

---

[504] *Gordon v. Nutbean; Moehl v. Nutbean*, [1969] 2 O.R. 420, at p. 421 (*per* Haines J.). See also *McCulloch v. Murray*, [1942] S.C.R. 141.

[505] *Roy v. McEwan*, [1969] 2 O.R. 530, at p. 533 (*per* Lacourcière J.); *Halliday v. Essex*, [1971] 3 O.R. 621, at p. 623, *dictum* (*per* Lacourière J.).

[506] *Gordon v. Nutbean, supra*, n. 504, at p. 421.

[507] *Ibid.*

[508] *Roy v. McEwan, supra*, n. 505.

[509] *Avgeropoulos v. Karanasos, supra*, n. 502.

[510] *Girling v. Howden*, [1949] 3 D.L.R. 622 (B.C.C.A.); *Eid v. Dumas*, [1969] S.C.R. 668 (B.C.); *Atkins v. Ulrichsen* (1973), 37 D.L.R. (3d) 368 (B.C.). If no notice, however, not gross negligence, *Ewashko v. Desiatnyk* (1973), 35 D.L.R. (3d) 318 (Man. C.A.).

[511] *Wright v. Burrell* (1973), 32 D.L.R. (3d) 334, at p. 337.

[512] *Goulais v. Restoule* (1974), 48 D.L.R. (3d) 285.

[513] *Engler v. Rossignol* (1975), 10 O.R. (2d) 721 (C.A.).

[514] *Ibid.*, at p. 732. See also Gibson, "Gratuitous Passenger Discrimination" (1968), 6 Alta. L. Rev. 211.

[515] *Ibid.*, at p. 727.

Ontario Legislature responded to this plea, and like British Columbia did before it, abolished the need for a passenger to prove gross negligence against the driver.[516] Other provinces have also done so and those which have not should do the same without delay.

---

[516] S.O. 1977, c. 54, s. 16, repealed s. 132(3) of The Highway Traffic Act, R.S.O. 1970, requiring proof of gross negligence, which existed since 1967. From 1935 to 1967 Ontario barred passengers completely from recovering against their drivers.

Chapter 6

Custom

Human beings are creatures of custom.[1] Sociologists explain that modern societies as well as primitive communities adhere to customs in their manner of worship, mode of dress, way of eating and in many other aspects of their daily lives.[2] "In whatever way a person has done anything once, he has a tendency to do it again: if he has done it several times he has a great tendency so to do it, and what is more, he has a great tendency to make others do it also".[3] The customs followed by a group are its collective habits, analogous to the individual habits of a person, whereby there is a tendency to repeat an act in the same way time after time.[4] This can be advantageous, for efficiency results when energy is channeled; it can also be disadvantageous, because habits are hard to break and not all habits are good. In earlier times, custom was one of the most vital stabilizers in society, its "chief guarantee to order and continuity in the social system".[5] But custom is "a two-edged sword"; it "preserves the useful adjustments of the past, while at the same time it hinders the progress of the future". In other words, custom is the enforcer of what is good in society, but at the same time is a "barrier to all that might be better".[6]

The common law generally and tort law in particular, as might be expected, have been influenced by many of the customary norms of society.[7] In considering whether conduct is negligent, that is, if it departed from the standard of the

---

[1] See Morris, "Custom and Negligence" (1942), 42 Colum. L. Rev. 1147; Fricke, "General Practice in Industry" (1960), 23 Mod. L. Rev. 653; James and Sigerson, "Particularizing Standards of Conduct in Negligence Trials" (1952), 5 Vand. L. Rev. 697; Linden, "Custom in Negligence Law" (1968), 11 Can. Bar J. 151; Weiler, "Groping Towards a Canadian Tort Law: The Role of the Supreme Court of Canada" (1971), 21 U. of T.L.J. 267; see generally Allen, *Law in the Making*, 6th ed. (1958), Chapters I and II.

[2] Sumner and Keller, *The Science of Society* (1972), p. 30.

[3] Bagehot, *Physics and Politics* (1873), p. 41.

[4] Faris, *The Nature of Human Nature* (1973), pp. 307-08; James and Sigerson, *supra*, n. 1, at p. 709.

[5] Bernard, *Social Control in its Sociological Aspects* (1939), p. 554.

[6] *Ibid.*, at p. 555.

[7] Allen, *op. cit, supra*, n. 1.

reasonable person in the circumstances, most courts have agreed that evidence of the customary behavior is, at the very least, relevant.[8] Unfortunately, however, courts have evinced some disagreement over the weight that this evidence should receive; some have declared that custom is conclusive of the standard of care to be applied,[9] others have stated that it is *prima facie* evidence of the appropriate standard,[10] and still others have suggested that it was only some evidence to aid the court or jury in deciding the case.[11] The problem is not dissimilar to the matter of employment of penal statutes in civil litigation,[12] since there is a resemblance between societal norms customarily adhered to and community standards enshrined in criminal legislation. Despite the uncertainty that has surrounded the issue, torts scholars have devoted only scant attention to this aspect of tort law.[13]

A. Policy

The policy reasons for reliance on custom in negligence cases are varied. The desire to foster the stability and security that custom brings to society is one such policy goal. Not only do individuals tend to follow the common practices in their community themselves, but they expect and rely upon others to do likewise. The courts are wise to recognize this as a fact of life,[14] for to attempt to arrest customary practices is to invite resentment, criticism and malaise in society. Furthermore, professional groups should be encouraged to develop a measure of responsible autonomy. By interfering as little as possible in established routines, the courts can spur this development. Sometimes this is rationalized on the ground that a professional person, on being hired, undertakes merely to perform services in the customary way.[15] In their determination of what is acceptable conduct in the circumstances, the courts have relied on general practice because "what is reasonable in a world not wholly composed of wise men and women must depend on what people presumed to be reasonable, constantly do".[16] Professor Wigmore has justified the admissibility of evidence of custom on the ground that it reflects the reaction of many persons to a similar danger indicating a composite judgment about the reasonable precautions to be

---

[8]   Morris, *supra*, n. 1.

[9]   *McDaniel v. Vancouver General Hospital*, [1934] 4 D.L.R. 593, at p. 597 (P.C.) (*per* Lord Alness).

[10] *Cavanagh v. Ulster Weaving Co.*, [1960] A.C. 145.

[11] *Anderson v. Chasney*, [1949] 4 D.L.R. 71, at p. 92 (Man. C.A.) (*per* Dysart J.A.); affd [1950] 4 D.L.R. 223.

[12] See Chapter 7, *infra*.

[13] Fleming, *The Law of Torts*, 9th ed. (1998), p. 133, devotes just over one page to the problem; *Prosser and Keeton on the Law of Torts*, 5th ed. (1984), p. 193, two and one-half pages.

[14] See *Cavanagh v. Ulster Weaving Co.*, *supra*, n. 10, at p. 158 (*per* Lord Simonds).

[15] *Anderson v. Chasney*, *supra*, n. 11, at p. 76, [1949] 4 D.L.R., (dissenting judge).

[16] Maugham; L.J. dissenting in *Marshall v. Lindsey County Council*, [1935] 1 K.B. 516; affd [1937] A.C. 97 (not on this point).

taken.[17] Further, what is customary is often imbued with a moral quality or sense of rightness. When a group adopts a general practice, believing it to be right and proper, it is common for them to demand that others do the same. If they comply, the custom may be viewed as a correct one and deserving of legal absorption.

There are also matters of judicial administration to assess. Firstly, customary practices can provide a fairly precise standard of care to facilitate the courts' task of deciding what is reasonable in the circumstances. Like penal statutes, customs can crystallize the ordinarily vague standard of reasonable care.[18] Understandably, judges and juries welcome this type of direction. Secondly, a court or jury may feel incapable of challenging the practices of a professional group, for example, of which it has little or no knowledge. This professed lack of expertise to assess properly the adequacy of a custom has dampened any eagerness for judicial imposition of superior standards. For example, Lord Justice Scott has asked "How can the ordinary judge have sufficient knowledge of surgical operations to draw such an inference [of negligence] . . . "[19] One judge has asserted that courts are "in no position to say that the expert evidence was wrong in stating that the usual practice among surgeons was followed and reasonable care was exercised",[20] and another had misgivings about a jury that "exceeded its province" in this regard.[21]

The customary practice of a profession or an industry must by definition be feasible; consequently, those who deviate can be held liable without any danger of imposing too onerous an economic burden upon them. There is another side of this coin, however; to demand more of an industry than compliance with the usual practice may be to dictate impossible standards or at least economically infeasible ones,[22] which might have disastrous effects on business. Thus, where a shield on an elevator was considered an "impractical thing",[23] and where a doctor was too busy during an operation to count the sponges,[24] the courts were reluctant to impose liability.[25] Where there would be little or no difficulty encountered in a change of practice, courts have been more willing to impose liability. In *Anderson v. Chasney*,[26] the court, noting that there were too many instances of sponges being left behind after surgery, held that either a sponge

---

[17] Wigmore, *Evidence*, 3rd ed. (1940), Vol. 2, s. 461. See also James and Sigerson, *supra*, n. 1, at p. 711.

[18] James and Sigerson, *supra*, n. 1. See Iacobucci J. in *Waldick v. Malcolm*, [1991] 2 S.C.R. 456, at p. 471, quoting this passage from Linden, "Custom in Negligence Law" (1968), 11 Can. Bar J. 151.

[19] *Mahon v. Osborne*, [1939] 1 All E.R. 535, at p. 541 (C.A.), *res ipsa loquitur* case.

[20] Richards J.A., dissenting in *Anderson v. Chasney*, *supra*, n. 11, at p. 80, [1949] 4 D.L.R.

[21] *Ruch v. Colonial Coach Lines*, [1966] 1 O.R. 621; affd [1969] S.C.R. 106.

[22] Morris, *supra*, n. 1, at p. 1147.

[23] *Morton v. William Dixon Ltd.*, [1908] S.C. 807, at p. 809.

[24] *Jewison v. Hassard* (1916), 28 D.L.R. 584 (Man. C.A.).

[25] *Taylor v. Gray*, [1937] 4 D.L.R. 123, at p. 127 (N.B.C.A.), instrument count.

[26] *Supra*, n. 11, at pp. 87 and 88, [1949] 4 D.L.R., simple facilities.

count or taped sponges should have been used since "neither is impractical". Professor Morris has also contended that to expect more than what is customary from a professional person may be too harsh, for there is no opportunity to learn of any safeguards beyond those employed in the profession.[27]

These are all compelling arguments, but the courts have not abdicated their responsibility to evaluate customs, for negligent conduct cannot be countenanced, even when a large group is continually guilty of it. As explained by Mr. Justice Iacobucci in *Waldick v. Malcolm*, in assessing one's conduct, "it matters little that one's neighbours also act unreasonably".[28] If these common practices were blindly adhered to, warned Mr. Justice Coyne in *Anderson v. Chasney*,[29] the "expert witnesses would, in effect, be the jury to try the question of negligence. That question, however, must continue to be one for the petit jury empanelled to try the case, if it is a jury case, and for the Court, where it is not." The danger of unquestioning obedience was further underscored by Mr. Justice Coyne who cautioned: ". . . there will hardly be a railway, motor or other accident case where the same argument cannot be advanced that it be similarly decided by the railway, motor or other experts." Competition may impede the adoption of safety devices which are available and reasonable. Before the legislation requires their use, an injured individual may approach the court as a "one-man lobby" to challenge the old custom and demand a higher standard.[30] Consequently, no group may exempt itself from civil responsibility by adoption of a negligent practice. "It is the courts and not the particular profession concerned which decide whether negligence is established in a particular case."[31]

Experts may "aid or guide the court in reaching a sound decision. They are never allowed to decide the case. . . . "[32] The courts must not only protect us from experts setting their own absolute rules of conduct, they must also beware of stifling progress. If every deviation from the customary were actionable, even if it were a superior method, industrial progress would be hampered.[33] The courts, recognizing that the heresy of today may become the orthodoxy of tomorrow, have wisely refused to halt all experimentation. It has also been established that what is acceptable in one place and time may be inadequate at another place and time.[34] In deciding what use to make of evidence of custom, the courts must balance the need for social stability as well as the need for progress. In other words, the "law must either grow to fit the custom or it must ignore or suppress it".[35]

---

[27]   See *supra*, n. 1, at p. 1148.
[28]   *Supra*, n. 18, at p. 473.
[29]   *Supra*, n. 11, at p. 81, [1949] 4 D.L.R.
[30]   Weiler, *supra*, n. 1, at p. 319.
[31]   Schultz J.A. in *Penner v. Theobold* (1962), 35 D.L.R. (2d) 700, at p. 712 (Man. C.A.).
[32]   Dysart J.A. in *Anderson v. Chasney*, *supra*, n. 11, at p. 92, [1949] 4 D.L.R.
[33]   *Hunter v. Hanley*, [1955] S.C. 200.
[34]   *London and Lancashire Guarantee and Accident Co. of Canada v. La Cie F.X. Drolet*, [1944] S.C.R. 82.
[35]   Bohannan, *Law and Warfare* (1967), p. 50.

B. Compliance with Custom as Reasonable Care

Those who act in accordance with the general practice of their trade or profession are usually exonerated from civil liability.[36] Indeed, at one time, it was thought that evidence of compliance with general practice was *conclusive* of reasonable care. According to the oft-cited opinion of Lord Alness in *Vancouver General Hospital v. McDaniel*,[37] "a defendant charged with negligence can clear his feet if he shows that he has acted in accord with general and approved practice". Lord Justice Maugham echoed this view in *Marshall v. Lindsey County Council*:

> An act cannot, in my opinion, be held to be due to a want of reasonable care if it is in accordance with the general practice of mankind. What is reasonable in a world not wholly composed of wise men and women must depend on what people presumed to be reasonable, constantly do. Many illustrations might be given and I will take one from the evidence given in this action. A jury could not, in my opinion, properly hold it to be negligent in a doctor or a midwife to perform his or her duties in a confinement without mask and gloves, even though some experts gave evidence that in their opinion that was a wise precaution. Such an omission may become negligent if, and only if, at some future date it becomes the general custom to take such a precaution among skilled practitioners. . . . I do not doubt the general truth of the observation . . . [in *Vancouver General Hospital v. McDaniel*] that a defendant charged with negligence can clear himself if he shows that he has acted in accord with general and approved practice.[38]

As is the case with many such lucid and definitive formulations of principle, these statements, though wrong, strongly influenced later courts. On closer examination, however, one can see that they should not be accepted at face value. *Vancouver General Hospital v. McDaniel* appears to decide that compliance with custom is conclusive evidence of due care, but the holding does not go that far. The decision rests in large measure upon the failure of the plaintiff to adduce convincing evidence that the defendant's system of not segregating smallpox cases "earned the condemnation of medical opinion generally or of any medical man in particular, except for [the plaintiff's witness]".[39] By contrast, the defendant did offer weighty evidence to the effect that the challenged technique "was in accord with general if not with universal practice today in

---

[36] *Dziwenka v. R.*, [1971] 1 W.W.R. 195, at p. 205; revd [1972] S.C.R. 419. Normally, conformity to common practice in any given circumstances is *prima facie* evidence that the proper standard of care is being taken" (*per* Allen J.A.). See also *Baker v. Suzuki Motor Co.* (1993), 17 C.C.L.T. (2d) 241, at p. 259 (Alta. Q.B.) (*per* Bielby J.), product liability case; *Tabrizi v. Whallon Machine Co.* (1996), 29 C.C.L.T. (2d) 176, at p. 188 (B.C.S.C.), "practices should be weighed" but custom can be negligent; *Shakoor v. Situ*, [2000] 4 All E.R. 181 (Q.B.D.), Chinese herbal medicine practitioner and custom.

[37] [1934] 4 D.L.R. 593, at p. 597 (P.C.) No liability for failure to segregate smallpox patients. See also *Karderas v. Clow*, [1973] 1 O.R. 730, at p. 738, no liability for following "standard, approved and widely accepted procedures in allowing a competent resident to do the abdominal closure".

[38] [1935] 1 K.B. 516, at p. 540; affd [1937] A.C. 97.

[39] *Vancouver General Hospital v. McDaniel, supra*, n. 37, at p. 595.

Canada and in the United States," and that this was a reasonable procedure.[40] The influence of Lord Alness must be minimized by his assertion that negligence must be proved "beyond reasonable doubt",[41] a preposterous contention to make in a tort case. In addition, no authority was cited by Lord Alness in support of either of his questionable declarations. Nor does *Marshall v. Lindsey County Council* hold that custom is conclusive. In that case a jury verdict in favour of the plaintiff was affirmed by a majority of the Court of Appeal. Although the practice of mixing patients was unanimously approved, the majority felt that there had been inadequate warnings issued by the hospital about earlier patients suffering from puerperal fever. Lord Justice Maugham dissented on the ground of inadequate warning. He contended that the general practice with regard to both of the alleged acts of negligence was followed and, consequently, the jury verdict of the plaintiff could not be supported on either ground. Paradoxically, as definite as Lord Justice Maugham appears to have been, he thought it necessary to assert that the custom was "founded on good sense",[42] a comment that is totally irrelevant if custom always binds the courts. Finally, the force of these two pronouncements was further diluted by Mr. Justice Coyne, who, in commenting upon them in *Anderson v. Chasney*,[43] suggested that they were "irrelevant to the decision of either court".

Despite the shaky foundation of the principle, there are several older cases in which courts appear to have accepted evidence of conformance with custom as conclusive. In *Savickas v. City of Edmonton*,[44] a child darted in front of the defendant's trolley bus and was injured. The plaintiff alleged as one act of negligence the failure by the defendant to equip its bus with safety bumpers. In response, the defendant's experts testified that they had no knowledge of "any trolley bus with safety devices which is used anywhere". The plaintiff, however, neglected to adduce evidence that the bus lacked "any useful equipment which is used elsewhere".[45] On these facts, it is no wonder that the court invoked Lord Alness's *dictum* and absolved the defendant. A similar case, with an identical result, is *MacLeod v. Roe*.[46] The plaintiff, injured while roller-skating at the defendant's establishment, complained that toe-straps were not supplied to her. Such straps were available to anyone who wished to use them for the price of ten cents. The defendant produced uncontradicted evidence that the provision of "toe-straps [was] not a standard method". The court, after citing Lord Alness, concluded that, "even if they might have been made safer", no liability would follow.[47] Mr. Justice Rand felt that "in the circumstances we must accept the

---

40   *Ibid.*, at pp. 595-96.
41   *Ibid.*, at p. 549.
42   *Marshall v. Lindsey County Council, supra*, n. 38, at p. 542.
43   *Supra*, n. 11, at p. 88, [1949] 4 D.L.R.
44   [1940] 2 W.W.R. 675 (Alta.).
45   *Ibid.*, at p. 678.
46   [1947] S.C.R. 420.
47   *Ibid.*, at p. 423.

standard so established rather than the individual opinion of any judge".[48] In another case, *Cowle v. Filion*,[49] where a child was injured by a car on a residential street, the defendant unsuccessfully alleged that the child's parents were contributorily negligent in the supervision they provided. Accepting "the conduct of other parents or of parents generally . . . as one test of the reasonableness or sufficiency of the actual care in the particular case", the trial judge concluded that there was no suggestion that these parents "took any fewer precautions than those taken by all the other parents in the area".[50] In *Klyne v. Town of Indian Head*,[51] it was held that it was not negligent to fail to provide a glass or plastic shield as a screen on the sides of a hockey rink since it was the custom to furnish these only on rinks in larger centres used by professional players, but not on local rinks used by amateurs alone. Neither was liability imposed in *Ruch v. Colonial Coach Lines*,[52] where an overnight passenger, reclining on the back seat of a bus, was injured when she was bounced around after the bus went over a bump. The jury found that the defendant was negligent in failing to warn the plaintiff of the hazard inherent in using the back seat of the bus in a reclining position. The Ontario Court of Appeal reversed the verdict for the plaintiff and held that the jury had no power to fashion a duty to warn in these circumstances. The Supreme Court of Canada squandered an opportunity to rationalize the law, when Mr. Justice Ritchie,[53] speaking for the majority, declared, "It was proved . . . that the bus seats . . . were up to date and of a type in general use in the industry and I do not think that the mere fact of a passenger being thrown from such a seat through collision or sudden stop necessarily affords proof that the seat itself was unsafe." In his dissenting judgment, Mr. Justice Spence, foreshadowing later clarification, rejected the notion that custom was conclusive.[54] Even though "there was no proof that a precaution such as warning signs or some other means was used customarily in other examples of bus travel", the court must still consider "whether the precaution is one which the reasonable and prudent man would think so obvious that it was folly to omit it as applicable". He felt that the driver should have warned the passengers about reclining in the back seat. A similar view has been taken in cases where the rules of a sport are followed.[55]

These cases, although often quite sweeping in their assertions about the inviolability of custom, do not stand for the proposition that conformance to a general practice can *never* be held negligent; rather, they illustrate that evidence

[48] *Ibid.*, at p. 425.
[49] [1956] O.W.N. 881.
[50] *Ibid.*, at p. 885 (*per* Miller Co. Ct. J.).
[51] (1979), 107 D.L.R. (3d) 692 (Sask. C.A.).
[52] [1966] 1 O.R. 621; affd [1969] S.C.R.
[53] *Ibid.*, at p. 109, S.C.R.
[54] *Ibid.*, at p. 115, See also *Winrob v. Street and Wollen* (1959), 19 D.L.R. (2d) 172, at p. 175 (B.C.), solicitor not liable.
[55] *Hamstra v. B.C. Rugby Union* (1989), 1 C.C.L.T. (2d) 78, at p. 85 (B.C.S.C.).

of an established custom *usually* sways the courts, especially where there is insufficient evidence to contradict their reasonableness.

It is now clear that custom is not *conclusive* of reasonable care. Thus, Mr. Justice Matas has recently reiterated that evidence of compliance with custom "is not conclusive" in a situation where an explosion took place in a school during a chemistry experiment, which was being done in the same way as other schools did it.[56] Following custom then, though influential, is not conclusive of due care.

1. MEDICAL CUSTOM

There is a group of decisions involving doctors and hospitals in which the courts have relieved the defendants of liability on the ground that they acted in accordance with approved methods. Evidence of general practice is rightly accorded more respect in medical matters than it receives in other types of cases because there is greater judicial trust in the reasonableness of the practices of a sister-profession than there is in the methods of business people.[57] As Dean Prichard notes: "in most cases, the court is prepared to rely on institutions within and surrounding the profession to dictate the appropriate standard of competence and to limit itself to assessing whether or not the standard has been breached".[58] Further, in the professional cases the implied contractual undertaking made is merely to employ customary treatment methods.

Typical of the judicial attitude toward medical custom is this statement in *White v. Turner*:[59]

> If the work of a plastic surgeon falls below the accepted practices of his colleagues, he will be held civilly liable for any damage resulting. But if his work complies with the custom of his confrères, he will normally escape civil liability for his conduct, even where the result of the surgery is less than satisfactory.

This principle has been recently reaffirmed by Mr. Justice Sopinka in *ter Neuzen v. Korn*[60] where he stated:

---

[56]   *James v. River East School Division No. 9*, [1976] 2 W.W.R. 557, 64 D.L.R. (3d) 338, at p. 350 (Man. C.A.), Liability. See also *Gaines v. Patio Pools* (1984), 51 B.C.L.R. 121, at p. 127 (C.A.), where Mr. Justice Hutcheon, dissenting on another point, explained that "[e]vidence of common practice in a trade is relevant to the issue of standard of care but such evidence is not conclusive"; see *Waldick, infra*, n. 111.

[57]   Weiler, *supra*, n. 1, at p. 324, says it is conclusive. See *Ostrowski v. Lotto*, [1971] 1 O.R. 372, at p. 382; affd [1973] S.C.R. 220 (*per* Aylesworth J.A.), quoting *Bolam v. Friern Hospital*, [1957] 2 All E.R. 118.

[58]   Prichard, "Professional Civil Liability and Continuing Competence", in Klar (ed.), *Studies in Canadian Tort Law* (1977), p. 377, at p. 382.

[59]   (1981), 15 C.C.L.T. 81, at p. 93 (*per* Linden J.), liability for failure to comply with the "standard practice of plastic surgeons"; *Maynard v. West Midlands Regional Health Authority*, [1985] 1 All E.R. 635 (H.L.); *Quintal v. Datta*, [1988] 6 W.W.R. 481 (Sask. C.A.); Klar, "Recent Developments" (1991), 23 Ott. L. Rev. 177, at p. 216.

[60]   [1995] 3 S.C.R. 674, at pp. 697-98, relying on Fleming, *The Law of Torts*, 7th ed. (1987).

... it is apparent that conformity with standard practice in a profession does not necessarily insulate a doctor from negligence where the standard practice itself is negligent. The question that remains is under what circumstances will a professional standard practice be judged negligent? It seems that only where the practice does not conform with basic care which is easily understood by the ordinary person who has no particular expertise in the practices of the profession.

In most medical cases, therefore, compliance with custom leads to exoneration, even though it is not automatic in every case. For example, in an early case, *Jewison v. Hassard*,[61] a sponge was left in a patient after surgery. The action against the doctor was dismissed on the ground that, since the surgeon was "too busy with his other work to keep count of the sponges", he properly delegated this responsibility to a competent and experienced nurse, which was the usual practice. Mr. Justice Haggart also concluded that the operation was "performed in accordance with up-to-date clinical surgery".[62] In *McFadyen v. Harvie*,[63] a doctor applied a cautery during surgery to an area that had been washed down with iodine and alcohol, burning the patient. No liability was incurred for, according to Robertson C.J.O., the doctor had "followed the recognized practice" in relying upon his assistants in this regard.[64] Mr. Justice Gillanders also agreed to absolve the defendant, who had used the "recognized and approved method".[65] The Supreme Court of Canada, in affirming the Ontario Court of Appeal, merely asserted that it was in accord with the Chief Justice of Ontario.

In *Chubey v. Ahsan*,[66] a doctor was relieved of liability, even though a patient died as a result of a lacerated aorta which occurred during a disc operation, on the ground that he had "followed accepted medical procedures in performing the operation".[67] Nor was he liable for leaving the patient following the surgery because that procedure was "practised by most of the orthopaedic surgeons in this area".[68] His Lordship did remind us in a *dictum*, however, that following custom was not conclusive of due care and that, even if the doctor had "followed the accepted practice of the profession, he could not escape liability if such practice did not meet the legal requirement of care for the patient.[69]

---

[61] (1916), 28 D.L.R. 584, at p. 585 (Man. C.A.) (*per* Richards J.A.). See also *Whiteford v. Hunter*, [1950] W.N. 553 (H.L.).

[62] *Ibid.*, at p. 587.

[63] [1941] 2 D.L.R. 663 (Ont. C.A.); affd [1942] S.C.R. 390.

[64] *Ibid.*, at p. 668 D.L.R; see also *Emmonds v. Makarewicz* (2000), 2 C.C.L.T. (3d) 255 (B.C.C.A.), leaving spilled gall stones behind after laparoscopic surgery is "within general practice" but liable on other grounds.

[65] *Ibid.*, at p. 670.

[66] (1975), 56 D.L.R. (3d) 231; affd [1976] 2 W.W.R. 367 (Man. C.A.).

[67] *Ibid.*, at p. 239 (*per* Solomon J.). See also *Belknap v. Meakes* (1989), 1 C.C.L.T. (2d) 192 (B.C.C.A.).

[68] *Ibid.*, at p. 240.

[69] *Ibid.*

The results of several hospital cases are in harmony. In *Florence v. Les Soeurs de Misericorde*,[70] a hospital that failed to place side rails on a bed was exonerated from liability when a patient, after getting out of bed, fell and injured herself. On the evidence introduced it was clear that it was "not good hospital practice to install guard-rails on a bed occupied by a patient of [her] type," although such rails were customarily employed where patients were unconscious, not mentally alert, or recovering from anaesthesia. With people over 70 years of age, rails might be used during the night at the discretion of the attending nurse. The court concluded that the "defendant acted in accordance with the general and approved hospital practice" and, therefore, it could not be held responsible.[71] Not only did the court in the *Florence* case affirm its respect for the autonomy of the hospital "to run its own affairs" in accordance with its own routines, but it asserted that the "hospital authorities were not in any sense bound by the request of the deceased's son to install guard-rails".[72] If it were otherwise, "conditions would be chaotic, and the routine and ordinary work of a hospital would be seriously interfered with and handicapped. The medical men, administrators of hospitals, and nurses in charge surely are the ones to say what should or should not be done for a patient's welfare, rather than the relatives".[73] In a similar case, *McKay v. Royal Inland Hospital*,[74] where a person suffering from multiple sclerosis fell out of a bed without side-boards while doing therapeutic exercises, the defendant hospital was exculpated. There was "uncontradicted expert evidence that the treatment of the plaintiff in the case accorded with approved practice and that it was given by fully qualified personnel".[75] Consequently, the hospital staff had correctly decided that the presence of side-boards would be psychologically detrimental to the patient and that, if she did her exercises properly, she would not fall out.

The same principles apply to diagnosis as well as to treatment. According to Mr. Justice Schultz in *Penner v. Theobald*,[76] "it is by the methods and practices which characterize his school that [a medical person] must be judged in determining whether or not he was negligent in his diagnosis". Although the court held the defendant chiropractor liable for his negligent *treatment* because "his own testimony is conclusive as to the unwisdom of the practice he followed,"[77] it felt that his *diagnosis* was acceptable because it was "thorough and complete by the standards of that profession".[78] In this decision Mr. Justice

---

[70] (1962), 33 D.L.R. (2d) 587, at p. 590 (Man. C.A.) (*per* Miller C.J.M.).

[71] *Ibid.*, at p. 591.

[72] *Ibid.*, at pp. 593-94.

[73] *Ibid.*, at p. 590. There was doubt about whether there had actually been a *request* to use side-rails, or only a comment to that effect. All of this was *obiter dicta*, in any event, since the absence of guard-rails was not the *cause* of the accident.

[74] (1964), 48 D.L.R. (2d) 665 (B.C.).

[75] *Ibid.*, at p. 670 (*per* Wilson J.).

[76] *Supra*, n. 31, at p. 708.

[77] *Ibid.*, at p. 712.

[78] *Ibid.*, at p. 708.

Schultz recognized the true role of custom in negligence law, when he explained that

> while it is true that in the great majority of alleged malpractice cases a charge of negligence can be met by evidence to the effect that what was done was in accordance with general and approved practice, nevertheless, it is the Courts and not the particular profession concerned which decide whether negligence is established in a particular case.[79]

In spite of several dogmatic judicial statements to the effect that compliance with custom is conclusive evidence of due care, careful analysis of the decisions discloses that the practices in question were either found to have been reasonable or, alternatively, their reasonableness was not challenged by expert evidence. It is wrong, therefore, to contend that a court cannot, even upon expert evidence to that effect, declare negligent certain customary practices to be negligent. In the medical context as well, then, compliance with custom is significant evidence of reasonableness, but it is not conclusive. The case of *Reibl v. Hughes*[80] is consistent with this view.

C. Compliance with Custom as Negligence

Although most of the early cases sanctified custom, there was some authority to the effect that it was possible to be held civilly liable for doing what was generally done in the trade. It was said, however, that only in the case of "faults of omission" was this possible. In *Morton v. William Dixon Ltd.*,[81] a mine-owner failed to employ a safety appliance designed to prevent coal from falling down the mine-shaft into the cage. The plaintiff, an injured miner, recovered at trial, but on appeal a new trial was ordered. Lord President Dunedin stated:

> Where the negligence of the employer consists of what I may call a fault of omission, I think it is absolutely necessary that the proof of that fault of omission should be one of two kinds, either — to show the thing which he did not do was a thing which was commonly done by other persons in like circumstances, or — to show that it was a thing which was so obviously wanted that it would be folly in anyone to neglect to provide it.[82]

In the *Morton* case there was no evidence adduced that such a safety precaution was a "common expedient" nor was there any evidence that it was a "wrong system".[83] Although one witness said that "some pits" had used such an appliance, all the others knew of no such thing and the workmen inspectors looked upon the appliance as an "impractical thing".[84] In the light of this evidence the decision for the plaintiff was held to be in error. As expressed by Lord McLaren, negligence of the plaintiff is only established "if he had ne-

---

[79] *Ibid.*, at p. 712, citing *Anderson v. Chasney.*
[80] (1980), 14 C.C.L.T. 1 (S.C.C.). See also *Brain v. Mador* (1985), 32 C.C.L.T. 157 (Ont. C.A.).
[81] [1908] S.C. 807.
[82] *Ibid.*, at p. 809.
[83] *Ibid.*
[84] *Ibid.*, at p. 810.

glected some precaution that is usual in the trade, or if not proved to be a usual precaution is at least so obvious that he is inexcusable in not having seen the necessity for it".[85]

This approach, although certainly less rigid than that of Lord Alness, is still open to attack on two counts.[86] First, in focussing upon faults of omission, undue emphasis is given to the notion of nonfeasance which for years has needlessly plagued the common law courts.[87] Where a duty to take care exists, it makes no difference that the defendant failed to do something a reasonable person would have done or did something a reasonable person would not have done; the defendant is equally liable in both cases. It is only where there is no relationship between the parties upon which the courts can construct a duty to use reasonable care, that mere inaction cannot yield liability. In approaching the problem this way, perhaps the court was merely giving voice to its "go-slow" policy in fashioning new obligations for industry so as to ensure their practicability. Second, in utilizing the word "folly", Lord Dunedin placed too heavy a burden upon the challenger of an established practice. It is difficult enough to prove that a customary practice is unreasonable; to demonstrate that it is folly is much harder. There is no need to demand such a high degree of proof. By using this term the court was merely reasserting its reluctance to classify the custom of a trade as negligent. Lord McLaren's test, although less stringent than that of Lord Dunedin, was still too strict a requirement, giving unnecessary weight to custom.

Over the years, although lip service was often paid to the word folly,[88] it was gradually recognized that it meant no more than "imprudent" or "unreasonable".[89] On occasion a court has invoked Lord Dunedin's "folly" formula and then slipped imperceptibly into a discussion about whether the practice was "reasonable", without appearing to sense any difference in the two phrases.[90] Lord Keith of Avonholm has rightly pointed out that the "trenchant" formula of Lord Dunedin might have been alternatively worded.[91] Had he wished to do so, he might have said instead that "it would be stupid not to provide it", or "no sensible men would fail to provide it" or "common sense would dictate it should be provided". Each of these phrases expresses the idea of "failure to exercise reasonable care" and all are adequate for the purpose. In other words, declared Lord Keith, "there is no magic in the word 'folly'".

---

[85] *Ibid.*
[86] See Fricke, *supra*, n. 1.
[87] Wright, "Negligent 'Acts of Omission'" (1941), 19 Can. Bar Rev. 465; see also Linden, "Tort Liability for Criminal Nonfeasance" (1966), 44 Can. Bar Rev. 25.
[88] *Morris v. West Hartlepool Steam Navigation Co.*, [1956] A.C. 552; *Kauffman v. Toronto Transit Commission*, [1959] O.R. 197 (*per* Morden J.A.); affd [1960] S.C.R. 251, 2 D.L.R. (2d) 97.
[89] See *Salmond and Heuston on the Law of Torts*, 19th ed. (1987), at p. 264. See also *Cavanagh v. Ulster Weaving Co.*, [1960] A.C. 145, at p. 162; *Ruch v. Colonial Coach Lines, supra*, n. 21 (*per* Spence J. in S.C.R., for example).
[90] *Kauffman v. Toronto Transit Commission, supra*, n. 88 (*per* Morden J.A.).
[91] *Cavanagh v. Ulster Weaving Co., supra*, n. 89, at pp. 165-66.

Other courts have agreed and imposed liability upon persons acting in conformance with the general practice of their callings. *Cavanagh v. Ulster Weaving Co.,*[92] is now the leading House of Lords decision on custom in negligence law. In the course of his employment the plaintiff fell from a roof-ladder while carrying a bucket of cement. There were no hand-rails to assist him but he was given rubber boots to wear since it was wet that morning. Although the plaintiff argued that it was negligent not to have hand-rails, he led no evidence that this was in violation of the custom in the trade. The defendant, however, called an expert who stated that the operation was "perfectly in accord with good practice". Nevertheless, the jury found for the plaintiff. The Court of Appeal in Northern Ireland, relying on Lord Dunedin's formula, reversed on the ground that the jury was not entitled to decide on the evidence adduced that it was folly to follow this practice. In the House of Lords the jury verdict for the plaintiff was restored on the ground that evidence of conformity to custom was not conclusive of reasonable care. Lord Tucker declared that "the practice weighs heavily in the scale on the side of the defendant and the burden of establishing negligence which the plaintiff has to discharge is a heavy one".[93] Nevertheless, explained Viscount Simonds, "such evidence is not so conclusive in the present case as to require the learned trial judge to withdraw the case from the jury".[94] The error of the Court of Appeal, he contended, was that it treated "as conclusive evidence which is not conclusive, however great its weight".[95] Viscount Simonds, however, did favour an important role for general practice for "it would, I think, be unfortunate if an employer who has adopted a practice, system or set-up, call it what you will, which has been widely without complaint, could not rely on it as at least a *prima facie* defence to an action for negligence . . . ".[96] To similar effect is the statement that ". . . the trade custom is *prima facie* proof on a standard of reasonable care and . . . the burden is on the plaintiff to establish that such was not the case.[97]

Another case in which compliance with custom was held negligent was *Fryer v. Salford Corporation.*[98] The plaintiff's skirt caught fire during cooking class at school because there was no guard around the stove where the girl was standing. Despite the uncontradicted evidence of the defendant that such guards were not used by other education authorities, Lord Justice Slesser, affirming the trial judgment for the plaintiff, stated that the danger was "if not self-evident, at any

---

[92] *Ibid.* See also Matas J.A. in *James v. River East School Division et al.,* [1976] 2 W.W.R. 577, at p. 588 (Man. C.A.), liability for accident during chemistry experiment even though customary instructions given.

[93] *Ibid.,* n. 89 at p. 162; see also *General Cleaning Contractors v. Christmas,* [1953] A.C. 180 at p. 192 (*per* Lord Reid).

[94] *Ibid.,* at p. 158.

[95] See [1959] 3 W.L.R. 262, at p. 267.

[96] *Supra,* n. 89, at p. 158.

[97] *Moss v. Ferguson* (1979), 35 N.S.R. (2d) 181, at p. 185 (*per* MacIntosh J.), no liability on the facts of the case.

[98] [1937] 1 All E.R. 617 (C.A.).

rate a danger which ought reasonably to have been anticipated . . . " and by no means "impossible".[99] In *Drewry v. Towns*,[100] there was a similar result. The defendant left his truck on a snowbound highway without lights or other warning in violation of the Highway Traffic Act, but in accordance with the practice of others in the area, and was held guilty of negligence. Mr. Justice Kelly asserted that "[t]he exigencies, occasioned by the depth of snow, did not justify the practice followed by the defendant and others [the farmers living at points off the said highway] of leaving their motor vehicles upon the highway, unattended and unlighted".[101] but this decision is not as disrespectful of custom as might appear. Because penal legislation prohibited this conduct, its policy should take precedence over the customary practices of the community not embodied in legislation. Moreover, the so-called parking "practice" of the farmers in the area was not the type of general practice that earns the acceptance of the courts, that is, the customary way that a business or profession is conducted. It was a mere negligent "habit" of a few farmers and, therefore, does not deserve similar treatment. "Neglect of duty does not cease by repetition to be neglect of duty."[102] Similarly, "no amount of repetition of a careless practice will make it any less careless. The negligent driver is not any less negligent by reason of being ubiquitous."[103]

There are several decisions of the Supreme Court of Canada which touch upon the issue of custom. In *Ware's Taxi Ltd. v. Gilliham*,[104] a taxi company was held liable when a child being transported to school fell out of one of its taxicabs. A majority of the Supreme Court (three-two) was of the view that either better supervision should have been supplied or that a locking device for the rear door, selling for ten dollars, should have been used. The defendants' attempt to establish that they were "acting in accord with the custom among taxi companies" was not accepted. Mr. Justice Estey, for the majority, stated:

> It is true that evidence of established practice or custom may be adduced for the purpose of rebutting an allegation of negligence but in order to establish such it must have been a practice over a long period of years . . . the evidence here does not establish any such custom or practice.[105]

It appears therefore, that the majority decision was taken without proof of a custom either way. Mr. Justice Rand, who dissented, seemed wedded to the

---

[99] *Ibid.*, at p. 621.
[100] (1951), 2 W.W.R. (N.S.) 217 (Man. K.B.).
[101] *Ibid.*, at p. 221.
[102] *Bank of Montreal v. Dominion Gresham Guarantee & Casualty Co.*, [1930] A.C. 659, at p. 666 (P.C.) (*per* Lord Tomlin); *Carpenters Co. v. British Mutual Banking Co.*, [1937] 3 All E.R. 811, at p. 820 (C.A.). See also *J. Nunes Diamonds v. D.E.P. Co.*, [1969] 2 O.R. 473, at p. 481 (*per* Addy J.); affd [1971] 1 O.R. 218 (C.A.; affd [1972] S.C.R. 769.
[103] *King v. Stolberg et al.* (1968), 70 D.L.R. (2d) 473 (B.C. (*per* Rae J.); revd in part on the facts 8 D.L.R. (3d) 362 (B.C.C.A.).
[104] [1949] S.C.R. 637, see Weiler, *supra*, n. 1, for a powerful critique of these cases.
[105] *Ibid.*, at p. 642.

older principle and would have dismissed the action on the ground that the new device was not "feasible" since parents and "the public have not taken them up".[106]

A second Supreme Court of Canada decision is *Kauffman v. Toronto Transit Commission*,[107] where the court upheld the Ontario Court of Appeal's reversal of a jury decision in favour of the plaintiff, a woman who was injured when she was knocked over while ascending an escalator in a subway station in Toronto. One of the arguments she advanced unsuccessfully was that an attendant should have been stationed near the escalator to prevent this type of accident. In the Court of Appeal, Mr. Justice Morden stated that "the defendant followed the usual practice of other carriers in like circumstances" and, reminiscent of Lord Dunedin, that there was no evidence that "the posting of attendants at every operating escalator was such an obvious precaution that it was foolhardy for the defendant to omit to do it".[108] Mr. Justice Morden, abandoning Lord Dunedin unwittingly, then concluded that "it is beyond the province of a jury to find as negligence the failure to take new precautions greater than those commonly in use in similar circumstances *in the absence of evidence that it would be unreasonable and imprudent to omit them*". The Supreme Court affirmed the Court of Appeal's decision without discussing this point at length.[109] Therefore, *Kauffman v. Toronto Transit Commission*, which absolved from tort liability a defendant who complied with the general practice, confirmed that a custom may be declared negligent, but not without evidence to that effect.

The most recent case of the Supreme Court of Canada, *Waldick v. Malcolm*,[110] has clarified Canadian law in a most admirable way. After a careful review of the authorities, Mr. Justice Iacobucci, for a unanimous court, declared that he did not think that a "custom would necessarily be decisive against a determination of negligence. . .".[111] The court held, in an occupier's liability case, that even if it was established that it was customary in a rural community not to salt or sand the ice and snow on one's property, this did not mean that occupiers could not be held negligent for failing to do so. In the words of Mr. Justice Iacobucci:[112]

> In my view, it is far from self-evident that the "practice" of not sanding or salting the driveways in the area should earn the acceptance of the courts.

---

[106] *Ibid.*, at p. 645. Mr. Justice Rand's assimilation of the standard of care owed by parents and by taxicabs was in error because in the latter case there is a greater risk of injury and an economic benefit.

[107] [1959] O.R. 197; affd [1960] S.C.R. 251.

[108] *Ibid.*, at p. 205.

[109] Mr. Justice Kerwin, at p. 255 in [1960] S.C.R., warned against paying too much heed to the word "folly" but rather to concentrate on the reasons underlying it.

[110] [1991] 2 S.C.R. 456. See also *Roberge v. Bolduc*, [1991] 1 S.C.R. 374, at p. 393, following professional practice not decisive of due care in civil law.

[111] *Ibid.*, at p. 473.

[112] *Ibid.*, at p. 474.

[T]he existence of customary practices which are unreasonable in themselves, or which are not otherwise acceptable to courts, in no way ousts the duty of care owed by occupiers. . . .

The Australian courts agree. In *Mercer v. Commissioner for Road Transport and Tramways*,[113] the defendant's train, because its driver collapsed, crashed into another injuring the plaintiff. One of the acts of negligence alleged against the defendant was the absence of a "dead-man's handle", which might have avoided the accident. The jury found for the plaintiff, but this was reversed on appeal, and further overturned by the High Court, which restored the jury verdict for the plaintiff. The majority of the court reasoned as follows: "[a]s has been clearly pointed out, the general practice itself may not conform to the standard of care required for a reasonably prudent man. In such a case it is not a good defence that the defendant acted in accordance with the general practice."[114] The dissenters did not disagree in principle, but felt that there was no evidence demonstrating that the practice was a negligent one. For example, Chief Justice Latham declared: "The mere fact that a defendant follows a common practice does not necessarily show that he is not negligent, though the general practice of prudent men is an important evidentiary fact. A common practice may be shown by evidence to be itself negligent."[115] Mr. Justice Dixon stated that "[i]t cannot be presumed or surmised that a uniformly accepted practice is based upon a disregard or an insufficient regard for human life and safety.[116] Several years later, in *Wise Bros. v. Commissioner for Railways*,[117] the fire precautions taken by a flour mill operator were under attack because a fire on the defendant's property had spread to and damaged the plaintiff's property. The trial judge was reversed on appeal because he had wrongly excluded expert evidence about the usual practice. Mr. Justice McTiernan said:

> [i]t is not enough that they do what is usual if the course ordinarily pursued is imprudent and careless, for no one can claim to be excused for want of care because others are as careless as himself; on the other hand, in considering what is reasonable, it is important to consider what is usually done by persons acting in a similar business.[118]

Neither have our courts left inviolate the practices of the medical profession. If doctors follow procedures shown to be inadequate the courts may adjudge them negligent. Naturally, before they shatter a medical custom, the courts will insist upon clear evidence of its impropriety, since much credence is given to

---

[113] (1937), 56 C.L.R. 580 (Aus. H.C.).

[114] *Ibid.*, at p. 593, citing Salmond.

[115] *Ibid.*, at p. 589.

[116] *Ibid.*, at p. 597.

[117] (1947). 75 C.L.R. 59 (Aus. H.C.).

[118] *Ibid.*, at p. 72. This view has been recently adopted in *Schwab v. Schaloske* (1982), 37 B.C.L.R. 111 (S.C.) (MacKinnon J.), practice re ventilation of silo by farmers followed, but negligent. *Condominium Plan 782-1326 v. Jodoin Developments Ltd.* (1984), 30 Alta. L.R. (2d) 388 (Q.B.) (MacNaughton J.), retaining wall built re custom inadequate; *Murphy v. Atlantic Speedy Propane Ltd.* (1979), 35 N.S.R. (2d) 422, at p. 432 (Hallett J.), practice of not inspecting found negligent.

doctors' reasonableness. In *Anderson v. Chasney*,[119] a sponge was left behind by the defendant during a tonsil and adenoid operation. In the Court of Appeal it was contended that one of two existing security methods, that is, sponge counting or using sponges with tapes, should have been adopted, although it was not proved that it was customary to use either one. "If a practitioner refuses to take an obvious precaution, he cannot exonerate himself by showing that others also neglect to take it," asserted Mr. Justice Coyne in a *dictum*.[120] The Supreme Court of Canada affirmed the result on the ground that a careless search had been conducted. In *Crits v. Sylvester*,[121] the Ontario Court of Appeal held an anaesthetist liable for an explosion which occurred during an operation. The decision rested on the finding that the defendant was not following "his general approved practice in pursuing the course of action outlined by him", but in a *dictum* Mr. Justice Schroeder stated that even if he were following the standard practice, "such evidence is not necessarily to be taken as conclusive on an issue of negligence".[122] Custom, therefore, is influential, but it does not rule.

D. Deviation from Custom

If a plaintiff establishes that a defendant failed to conform with the general practice of the trade or profession, the plaintiff will probably be successful. According to Professor Fleming,[123] "failure to adopt the general practice is often the strongest possible indication of want of care". Dean Prosser, too, asserts that "the failure to comply with customary precaution may, in a particular case, be negligence in itself, especially where it is known that others may rely on it".[124] Thus, failure to sterilize the needle after each inoculation in accordance with the accepted procedure, causes a doctor to be liable to any patient infected as a result.[125] Similarly, failure to do the "customary check" before proceeding to close up after a mammoplasty will cause a plastic surgeon to be held liable.[126] In fields other than medicine, the same principle applies. Thus, when a company that conducts helicopter ski expeditions fails to perform the customary avalanche susceptibility check, and several members of a ski party are then killed, the company will be held liable for their deaths.[127] This is justifiable because evidence of what most of the people in a profession or business do is evidence of what is considered reasonable in the circumstances.[128] Moreover, there is no

---

[119] [1949] 4 D.L.R. 71 (Man. C.A.); affd [1950] 4 D.L.R 223.
[120] *Ibid.*, at pp. 85-86. Weiler, *supra*, n. 1, treats this as a case of non-medical judgment, which he suggests is an exception to a rule of absolute immunity of doctors who conform to custom.
[121] (1956), 1 D.L.R. (2d) 502; affd [1956] S.C.R. 991.
[122] *Ibid.*, at p. 514. See also *Johnston v. Wellesley Hospital*, [1971] 2 O.R. 103, at p. 113 (*per* Addy J.); *Bergen v. Sturgeon General Hospital* (1984), 28 C.C.L.T. 155 (Alta. Q.B.) (Hope J.).
[123] *The Law of Torts*, 9th ed. (1998), p. 133.
[124] *Prosser and Keeton on the Law of Torts*, 5th ed. (1984), p. 195.
[125] *Forsbrey v. Bremner*, Nov. 24, 1967 (Ont.) (Brooke J.), unreported on this point.
[126] *White v. Turner* (1981), 15 C.C.L.T. 81, at p. 96 (*per* Linden J.).
[127] *Lowry v. Canadian Mountain Holidays Ltd.* (1985), 33 C.C.L.T. 261 (B.C.S.C.).
[128] Wigmore, *Evidence*, 3rd ed. (1940), Vol. 2, §461.

problem of infeasibility since, if most are already complying with a custom, it must be economically practicable for those who are not yet conforming thereto. "Super-cautious industrial usages are conceivable, but the self-interest of businessmen checks milquetoastish fears."[129]

Custom is an important factor in activities outside industry and the professions. For example, in sporting activities, custom can guide the courts. In *Gilsenan v. Gunning*[130] Galligan J. employed the customs of skiers in deciding that one skier was liable to another skier for a collision between them which occurred on the slopes. His Lordship explained that "[t]hose customs are helpful in determining what reasonable standard of conduct should be required of skiers".

Nevertheless, subconformity with usage is not conclusive of negligence. The Lord President of the Court of Sessions, Lord Clyde, explained in *Hunter v. Hanley*,[131] that "a deviation from ordinary professional practice is not necessarily evidence of negligence". "It would be disastrous if this were so," he contended, "for all inducement to progress in medical science would then be destroyed." In other words, experimentation with new methods must be permitted if tort law is to avoid thwarting the advancement of science. Thus, it is only where deviation from a customary norm is shown to be "one which no professional man; of ordinary skill would have taken if he had been acting with ordinary care," that negligence is established. Nor is the extent of deviation the test here; it matters not how far or little the defendant departs from the general practice. What is vital, however, is whether the defendant's conduct is negligent. The Lord President declared that *three* matters must be proved by the plaintiff: first, there is a usual and normal practice; second, the defender has not adopted that practice; third, no professional person of ordinary skill would have so acted if behaving with ordinary care.[132] The first two requirements are unassailable, but in the third too heavy a burden is placed on the plaintiff. Once deviation from custom is proved the defendant should be expected to establish reasonable behaviour despite this. In any event, one cannot escape the conclusion that proof of a failure to take the precautions ordinarily taken in the circumstances will be most influential upon the court or jury, even it if is not binding upon them.

The House of Lords, in *Brown v. Rolls Royce Ltd.*,[133] had occasion to consider this matter. A worker who contracted dermatitis from exposure to oil during his work sued the defendant, relying upon its omission to supply barrier cream to its employees, contrary to what was alleged to be the common practice elsewhere. The trial decision for the plaintiff was reversed on two grounds: firstly, there

---

[129] Morris, *supra*, n. 1, at p. 1161.

[130] *Gilsenan v. Gunning* (1982), 22 C.C.L.T. 240, at p. 249 (Ont. H.C.).

[131] [1955] S.C. 200, at p. 206. New trial ordered where jury found for defendant after being told departure from custom was "gross negligence". Two judges relied on the gross negligence point alone.

[132] *Ibid.*

[133] [1960] 1 All E.R. 577 (H.L.).

was no proof that the barrier cream would have prevented dermatitis, that is, evidence of causation was lacking; secondly, since evidence of non-compliance with custom was not conclusive and since the defendant relied on competent medical evidence in not supplying this cream, it could be exonerated. Lord Denning stated that "if the defenders do not follow the usual precautions, it raises a *prima facie* case against them in this sense, that it is evidence from which negligence may be inferred, but not in the sense that it 'must' be inferred unless the contrary is proved. At the end of the day, the court has to ask itself whether the defenders were negligent or not."[134] Lord Keith of Avonholm contended that "a common practice in like circumstances not followed by an employer may no doubt be a weighty circumstance to be considered by judge or jury in deciding whether failure to comply with this practice, taken along with all the other material circumstances in the case, yields an inference of negligence on the part of the employers".[135] In the last analysis, however, "the ultimate test is lack of reasonable care for the safety of the workman in all the circumstances of the case".

It is submitted that some of the language in these cases minimizes the importance of evidence of failure to conform with custom.[136] To be sure, courts cannot and should not be bound by the general practice of a trade; however, to hold that violation of custom is merely *some* evidence of negligence gives this significant fact insufficient weight and is tantamount to treating this evidence like any other type of proof. Violation of custom is worthy of greater respect. Deviation from the usual practice should provide a presumption or at least *prima facie* evidence of negligence, so that evidence of non-compliance alone, without any rebuttal or explanation by the defendant, would normally lead to a finding of negligence. In other words, a deviant defendant should be required to justify departure from the normal routines of the profession. This the defendant may do by establishing that conduct was just as safe or safer than the general practice or by demonstrating that the customary method was unsafe. This would afford greater respect to the customs of industry, without making them conclusive. It would also provide more predictability. This approach should not preclude the court from holding, in particular situations, that a departure from custom is either binding or merely some evidence of negligence; there is no reason why deviation from custom cannot whisper negligence as well as shout it aloud as in the past was the case with *res ipsa loquitur*.[137] Normally, however, it should be treated as *prima facie* evidence of negligence or as presumptive evidence of negligence.

Though not evidence of a reasonable standard of care *per se*, failing to abide by one's own custom or habit may influence the court, just as breaching a custom of industry does. Prosser and Keeton explain that evidence of this is

---

[134] *Ibid.*, at p. 582.
[135] *Ibid.*, at p. 581.
[136] Fricke, *supra*, n. 1, at p. 656.
[137] Fleming, 7th ed. (1987), at p. 300, dropped in later editions.

relevant because it shows knowledge of the risk involved.[138] Thus, in *Lowry v. Canadian Mountain Holidays Ltd.*,[139] where a company departed from safety procedures set out in the industry's operating handbook, the odds were very much against their being absolved. When it was discovered that the booklet was written and produced by the company's president, there was even less chance that the company would escape liability. Gould J. felt that no better source of information existed.[140] Likewise, in *Heeny v. Best*,[141] it was held that even though there was no established custom among chicken farmers to install alarms to warn of oxygen deficiency, a farmer who did possess one, but neglected to operate it, could be partly liable for losses suffered when his chicks died from lack of oxygen. He had recognized the risk to his chicks, yet failed to take reasonable care to protect them.

E. Proof of Custom

Several problems of proof arise in these custom cases. Parties who rely on either their own compliance with custom or the other person's departure from general practice bear the onus of proof that the custom is in effect.[142] For example, if, in the defence of their conduct, surgeons assert that they conformed to general practice, "the onus is on the surgeon to prove it by evidence".[143] This is normally done by introducing experts in the field to inform the court about their customary procedures.

Where the existence of a custom is obvious to all, a court may assume that there is a general practice in effect. However, "Only in the rarest and most patently obvious cases will the courts take judicial notice of a custom".[144] In *Ruch v. Colonial Coach Lines*,[145] it was so evident that bus companies followed the practice of not warning passengers who reclined their seats, that evidence to that effect was unnecessary. This is a dangerous practice. It would be preferable for courts to demand evidence of the general practice or not to rely on custom at all. "Counsel who wish to rely on custom would be most unwise to attempt to do so without adducing expert evidence of general practice."[146]

To offer evidence of the custom at one hospital is insufficient; proof of a more widely practised procedure is required.[147] The general practice that governs is the one followed in the country where the defendant resides. A doctor in the

---

[138] *Prosser and Keeton, op. cit. supra*, n. 124, at pp. 195-96.

[139] *Supra*, n. 127. See also *M. (M.) v. K. (K.)* (1989), 50 C.C.L.T. 190, at p. 207 (B.C.C.A.), policy of government department relevant evidence of standard of care.

[140] *Ibid.*, at p. 277.

[141] (1979), 11 C.C.L.T. 66 (Ont. C.A.).

[142] Quoted by Iacobucci J. in *Waldick v. Malcolm, supra*, n. 110, at p. 472.

[143] *Anderson v. Chasney, supra*, n. 119, at p. 82, [1949] 4 D.L.R.

[144] See *Waldick, supra*, n. 110, at p. 472 (*per* Iacobucci J.).

[145] [1966] 1 O.R. 621; affd [1969] S.C.R. 106.

[146] See *Waldick, supra*, n. 110, at p. 472.

[147] *Anderson v. Chasney, supra*, n. 119, at p. 85. See also *Florence v. Les Soeurs de Misericorde, supra*, n. 70, at p. 593 (*per* Miller C.J.M.).

United Kingdom, therefore, was not negligent for failing to use a cystoscope for an examination, as his British colleagues agreed that it was "against approved practice in England", despite evidence that in the United States such an instrument was commonly used.[148] Because this equipment was comparatively new in the United Kingdom, the defendant did not own one, whereas in the United States there was a more abundant supply. Since the defendant complied with the custom in his own country, he "cleared his feet".

There is Canadian jurisprudence that it is the custom in the community or region that is relevant, at least in professional liability cases. For example, in *Grima v. MacMillan*,[149] where a lawyer issued a writ against a defendant without first checking whether he was alive, Parker J. employed the custom which prevailed in that specific community, absolving the defendant solicitors because their behaviour was "no different that that of any reasonable competent and diligent solicitor in the City of Windsor".[150] Likewise, in *Hauck v. Dixon*,[151] a case involving an Ottawa lawyer who failed to search by-laws in a real estate deal, the appropriate standard of care utilized was that of the "standard practice of solicitors in the City of Ottawa" at the relevant time,[152] which led to his being absolved of liability.

One need only follow the custom in vogue *at the time* one acts. For example, using cast iron to construct an elevator in 1925, in accordance with the practice at the time, was reasonable and no liability could be visited upon the defendant for an accident that transpired in 1938, even though newer, less brittle materials were then available.[153] Mr. Justice Davis declared that building "according to the rules of the art and with the material which at the time was generally accepted in Canada as sufficient" met the test of reasonableness.[154]

Conduct which conforms with custom will not normally be held to be negligent without proof that it is.[155] The burden of convincing the court that the common practice is a negligent one rests on the party challenging it, since the custom is usually viewed as *prima facie* evidence of reasonableness.[156] Merely to allege that it is negligent will not suffice,[157] nor will it be enough to show that the practice "might have been made safer",[158] or that certain safety devices were available.[159] The usual way to do this is to lead expert evidence to the effect that

---

[148] *Whiteford v. Hunter* (1950), 94 Sol. Jo. 758 (H.L.).

[149] [1972] 3 O.R. 214.

[150] *Ibid.*, at p. 223.

[151] (1976), 10 O.R. (2d) 605 (H.C.).

[152] *Ibid.*, at p. 611.

[153] *London and Lancashire Guarantee and Accident Co. of Canada v. La Cie F. X. Drolet*, [1944] S.C.R. 82.

[154] *Ibid.*, at p. 91.

[155] *Morton v. William Dixon Ltd., supra*, n. 81, at p. 809.

[156] See *Moss v. Ferguson, supra*, n. 97, at p. 185 (*per* MacIntosh J.).

[157] *Savickas v. City of Edmonton, supra*, n. 44.

[158] *MacLeod v. Roe*, [1974] S.C.R. 420, at p. 424 (*per* Kerwin J.).

[159] *Ware's Taxi Ltd. v. Gilliham*, [1949] S.C.R. 637.

the practice followed is a negligent or unreasonable one. Occasionally, courts have held that compliance with custom is negligent without the aid of expert evidence. This will never be done, however, where the issues are "complicated", but only where the "ordinary experience of jurymen or a court is sufficient to enable them to pass upon the question whether such conduct constituted negligence".[160] In other words, "expert testimony is not necessary for proof of negligence in non-technical matters or matters of which an ordinary person may be expected to have knowledge.[161] A trial judge may hold that a common practice is negligent if it can be done "without the necessity of judging matters requiring diagnostic or clinical expertise"; otherwise evidence is required.[162] For example, where sponges or instruments are left behind in surgical patients, "the opinion of one [person] is about as good as that of another".[163] Similarly, when a doctor fails to rule out a potentially fatal but easily operable condition during diagnosis, ordinary common sense tells us that it is not acceptable.[164] Nevertheless, counsel would in most cases commit a tactical error of the gravest sort by attempting to discredit a customary procedure without expert evidence of its unreasonableness.

The customary conduct may not be applicable in the circumstances of the particular case and thus may afford no comfort to the person invoking it. In *Paris v. Stepney Borough Council*,[165] for instance, a one-eyed worker received an injury to his good eye. Although it was customary not to provide safety goggles to ordinary workers, it was negligence not to provide them to the plaintiff because of the likelihood of "grave injury". Lord McDermott stated "whatever may be said of the respondents' duty to their two-eyed employees, there was ample evidence to sustain the view that they failed in their duty to the appellant".[166] Thus, customary precautions may be insufficient in situations that are unusual. Procedures that are normal for the protection of ordinary epileptics in hospitals may not be adequate for persons suffering from automatism epilepsy.[167] The usual practice of bumping railway cars together may not be reasonable on a day when workers must stand on the top of icy cars.[168] In certain circumstances, it cannot be said that there is a customary practice, as when electric shocks are

---

[160] *Anderson v. Chasney, supra,* n. 119, at p. 82, [1949] 4 D.L.R. (*per* Coyne J.) and at p. 73, [1949] 4 D.L.R. (*per* McPherson C.J.M.). See also *Crits v. Sylvester, supra,* n. 121. See *ter Neuzen v. Korn, supra,* n. 60, at p. 695 (*per* Sopinka J.).

[161] *Mehigan v. Sheehan* (1947), 51 A. 2d 632, sponge.

[162] *Emmonds v. Makarewicz* (2000), 2 C.C.L.T. (3d) 255, at p. 263 (B.C.C.A.), gall stone spillage not "so fraught with obvious risk, such that anyone is capable of finding it negligent".

[163] *Taylor v. Gray,* [1937] 4 D.L.R. 123, at p. 127 (N.B.C.A.) (*per* Baxter C.J.), instrument.

[164] *Bergen v. Sturgeon General Hospital, supra,* n. 122.

[165] [1951] A.C. 367.

[166] *Ibid.,* at pp. 390-91.

[167] *University Hospital Board v. Lepine* (1964), 50 W.W.R. 709; revd on other grounds [1966] S.C.R. 561, not foreseeable that automatist would leap out of fourth floor unbarred window of the hospital.

[168] *Texas & Pacific Ry,. Co. v. Behymer* (1963), 189 U.S. 468; *Cavanagh v. Ulster Weaving Co., supra,* n. 91, wet boots *cf.* dry ones.

emitted from a bus.[169] Lastly, when there is a request for something out of the ordinary from a hospital, their regular procedures need not necessarily be changed.[170]

F. Causation

The conduct which deviates from custom must be the cause of the injury. If there is no connection between the offending act and the accident, no civil liability can be imposed. In the *Kauffman v. Toronto Transit Commission* case,[171] for example, there was no evidence that the presence of an attendant would have prevented the accident. So too, the absence of hand-rails on a hospital bed was not the cause of a patient's fall, because, even if the hand-rails had been there, the plaintiff could have climbed over them and fallen while out of bed.[172] Similarly, lack of a causal relation will defeat a plaintiff where there is no evidence that skate straps, if supplied, would be used,[173] or that barrier cream, if furnished, would prevent dermatitis.[174]

In conclusion, judges, like other human beings, recognize the merit of stability. Custom has strongly influenced negligence law, but the courts have retained the power to control these practices if they do not measure up to the standard of reasonableness, which is as it should be.

---

[169] *Gray v. City of Edmonton*, [1940] 2 W.W.R. 669 (Alta.).

[170] *Florence v. Les Soeurs de Misericorde, supra*, n. 70.

[171] *Supra*, n. 88, alternate holding.

[172] *Florence v. Les Soeurs de Misericorde, supra*, n. 70, at p. 590.

[173] *MacLeod v. Roe, supra*, n. 46.

[174] *Brown v. Rolls Royce Ltd., supra*, n. 133.

Chapter 7

Statutory Violations and the Standard of Care in Negligence

The common law treatment of legislation has never been satisfactory. The way in which criminal statutes have been used in determining the incidence of tort liability is no exception.[1] Sometimes judges have stretched the scope of penal enactments, yet, on other occasions, they ignored them altogether. For one example of this paradoxical situation, evidence that *conduct* violated a penal statute was admissible, whereas proof of a criminal *conviction* for its violation was inadmissible in a later civil case.[2] This has now changed; evidence of both a guilty plea[3] and a conviction[4] are now admissible. In this era of increasing legislative regulation of human activity, the way negligence law handles legislative prohibitions is becoming increasingly important, and confusion

---

[1] Alexander, "Legislation and the Standard of Care in Negligence" (1964), 42 Can. Bar Rev. 243; Linden, "Tort Liability for Criminal Nonfeasance" (1966), 44 Can. Bar Rev. 25; Williams, "The Effect of Penal Legislation in the Law of Tort" (1960), 23 Mod. L. Rev. 233; V.C. MacDonald, "The Negligence Action and the Legislature" (1935), 13 Can. Bar Rev. 535; Fricke, "The Juridical Nature of the Action Upon the Statute" (1960), 76 L.Q. Rev. 240, " Thayer, "Public Wrong and Private Action" (1914), 27 Harv. L. Rev. 317; Morris, "The Relation of Criminal Statutes to Tort Liability" (1938), 46 Harv. L. Rev. 453; Morris, "The Role of Criminal Statutes in Negligence Actions" (1949), 49 Colum. L. Rev. 21; James, "Statutory Standards and Negligence in Accident Cases" (1951), 11 La. L. Rev. 95; Lowndes, "Civil Liability Created by Criminal Legislation" (1932), 16 Minn. L. Rev. 361; Gregory, "Breach of Criminal Licencing Statutes in Civil Litigation" (1951), 36 Cornell L.Q. 622; Cronkite, "Effect of Violation of Statute by the Plaintiff in a Tort Action" (1929), 7 Can. Bar Rev. 67; Stanton, *Breach of Statutory Duty in Tort* (1985).

[2] *Hollington v. Hewthorn & Co. Ltd.*, [1943] 1 K.B. 587, [1943] 2 All E.R. 35 (C.A.), careless driving conviction was inadmissible in negligence case, see comment by C.A. Wright (1943), 21 Can. Bar Rev. 653; *Jalakas v. Thompson*, [1959] O.W.N. 324 (Master S.C.O.), assault case. The U.K. by statute now permits such evidence to be introduced. See Civil Evidence Act, 1968; *Wauchope v. Mordecai*, (1970) 1 All E.R. 417 (C.A.). But *quaere* the effect of *McIlkenny v. Chief Constable of West Midlands*, [1980] 2 All E.R. 227 (C.A.), one cannot relitigate same issue in civil case that was decided in criminal case.

[3] *Re Charlton*, [1969] 1 O.R. 706 (C.A.); *Ferris v. Monahan* (1956), 4 D.L.R. (2d) 539 (N.B.C.A.).

[4] *Simpson v. Geswein* (1995), 25 C.C.L.T. (2d) 49 (Man. Q.B.).

serves no one. Happily, the Supreme Court of Canada has evinced some bold leadership recently in an effort to dissipate the fog that has enveloped this area of the law.[5]

On the rare occasion that the legislature expressly declares its will on the matter of civil liability, no difficulty arises. Anyone who contravened a provision of the Railway Act of Canada, for example, was made civilly responsible "to any person injured by any such act or omission for the full amount of damages sustained thereby".[6] Civil liability was expressly imposed on persons who tampered with gates or fences or who permitted people or cattle to stray on a railway.[7] Another statute is the Liquor Licence Act of Ontario,[8] which confers rights of action where persons commit suicide or are killed accidentally as a result of liquor sold to them while they are intoxicated by persons to whom their intoxication is apparent. It has been suggested that s. 24(1) of the Canadian Charter of Rights and Freedoms has created a new "constitutional tort", giving individuals who have been damaged by a violation of the Charter the right to sue for damages.[9] There are other statutes of this type.[10]

Most legislators, however, have not been so considerate. In the more common situation, legislatures have merely proscribed certain conduct, specified a penalty and said nothing about tort liability — something which judges and authors have rightly bemoaned.[11] It is here that bewilderment has reigned.

A. Background

The main reason for this was that judges usually insisted that they were enforcing the intention of the legislature.[12] The trouble with this theory was that there was no such intention apparent in the vast majority of these enactments.[13] As a result, civil courts were searching vainly for something that was not there — "the will o' the wisp of a non-existent intention".[14] Because of this, the

---

[5]   *R. in right of Canada v. Saskatchewan Wheat Pool*, [1983] 1 S.C.R. 205.

[6]   R.S.C. 1985, c. R-3 [repealed S.C. 1996, c. 10, s. 185], see *Colonial Coach Lines v. Bennett and C.P.R.*, [1968] 1 O.R. 333 (C.A.), fencing regulation case.

[7]   *Ibid.*, s. 360.

[8]   R.S.O. 1990, c. L.19, s. 39. See also *Menow v. Honsberger and Jordan House Ltd.*, [1970] 1 O.R. 54; affd [1974] S.C.R. 239.

[9]   See Pilkington, "Damages as a Remedy for Infringement of the Canadian Charter of Rights and Freedoms" (1984), 62 Can. Bar Rev. 517; Gibson, *The Law of the Charter — General Principles* (1986), Chapter III; *Crossman v. R.* (1984), 9 D.L.R. (4th) 588 (F.C.T.D.); *Bertram S. Miller Ltd. v. R.* (1985), 18 D.L.R. (4th) 600 (F.C.T.D.); Cooper-Stephenson, *Charter Damage Claims* (1990). See also *Bourgoin SA v. Ministry of Agriculture, Fisheries and Food*, [1985] 3 All E.R. 585 (C.A.), E.E.C. Treaty breach. See *infra*, Chapter 9 for discussion.

[10] For example, Municipal Act, R.S.O. 1990, c. M.45, s. 284; Victorian Mines Act (1958), s. 411(1).

[11] Fricke, *supra*, n. 1. Lord du Parcq in *Cutler v. Wandsworth Stadium*, [1949] A.C. 398, at p. 410.

[12] For example, see *Cunningham v. Moore*, [1973] 1 O.R. 357, at p. 359 (*per* R. Holland J.); *Re McIssac and Beretanos et al.* (1971), 25 D.L.R. (3d) 610 (B.C.).

[13] Wright, "The English Law of Torts: A Criticism" (1955), 11 U. of T.L.J. 84, at p. 94.

[14] Fleming, *The Law of Torts*, 7th ed. (1987), pp. 115 *et seq.*

imposition of civil liability became rather capricious and impossible to predict "on any rational basis".[15] Lord Denning M.R. once described the laws in this area as a "guess-work puzzle" and opined that one "might as well toss a coin to decide it".[16]

This fruitless exercise has a long and complicated history which need no longer be recounted here[17] because the Supreme Court of Canada has saved us from the need to engage in that frustrating effort, which, however, must still be endured by courts elsewhere.[18]

Needless to say, the courts had fashioned various devices to assist them in their imaginary quest for the intention of the legislation, such as looking at the type of penalty imposed, its severity, whether it created a public duty or a private obligation[19] and other similar techniques.[20] It was all a most hypocritical and unsatisfactory activity, reflecting no credit on our jurisprudence.[21]

Various other reasons for relying on legislative standards had also been advanced. One of the most fashionable rationales, articulated by Professor Thayer, was that, since the legislature forbids certain conduct as "dangerous" and "unreasonable" it would be an "unjust reproach to the ordinary prudent man to suppose he would do such a thing in the teeth of the ordinance".[22] In other words, reasonable people obey the criminal law, so that if a statute is violated, the offender cannot have acted reasonably. "The statute has defined what is reasonable".[23]

Another less well-known theory proposed by Professor Thayer was "statutory nuisance".[24] Drawing an analogy to the private action for public nuisance, he suggested that a violator of a statute is guilty of a "public wrong" and, consequently, "acts at his peril". Reminiscent of the Massachusetts "outlaw rule",[25] this approach was not without its analogs elsewhere in tort law, as where a trespasser causes extra harm without additional fault,[26] or where someone creates

---

[15] See Williams, *supra*, n. 1, at p. 233.
[16] See *Ex p. Island Records Ltd.*, [1978] Ch. 122, at 134.
[17] See Linden, *Canadian Tort Law*, 3rd ed. (1982), p. 181.
[18] See *Lonrho Ltd. v. Shell Petroleum Co. Ltd.*, [1982] A.C. 173, at p. 183 (H.L.); see also Frankel, "Implied Rights of Action" (1981), 67 Va. L. Rev. 553.
[19] See *Pugliese v. National Capital Comm.* (1977), 3 C.C.L.T. 18, at p. 54; vard [1979] 2 S.C.R. 104.
[20] See Linden, *op. cit. supra*, n. 17, at p. 183.
[21] Williams, *supra*, n. 1.
[22] Thayer, *supra*, n. 1, at p. 526.
[23] *Pugliese v. National Capital Comm., supra*, n. 19, at p. 115 (*per* Pigeon J.); see also Schroeder J. in *Horne v. Fortalsky*, [1952] O.W.N. 121, at p. 122 (H.C.); *Prosser and Keeton on the Law of Torts*, 5th ed. (1985), p. 221. This is essentially the situation in Quebec, see Civil Code of Quebec, S.Q. 1991, c. 64, s. 1457.
[24] See *supra*, n. 1, at p. 327. See also *Siemers v. Eisen* (1880), 43 Cal. App. 418.
[25] See *Prosser and Keeton, op. cit. supra*, n. 23. This rule has now been largely abrogated by statute, see Mass. Laws, 1959, c. 250.
[26] *Turner v. Throne*, [1960] O.W.N. 20; *Wyant v. Crouse* (1961), 127 Mich. 158, 86 N.W. 527.

a public nuisance without fault.[27] Thus, since the defendant is a "wrong-doer", the defendant, rather than the completely innocent plaintiff, should shoulder any losses which result from the transgression. This theory had infiltrated the Canadian jurisprudence,[28] but it, like the other theories, was totally incapable of explaining all the cases.[29]

Not only was the real reason underlying the use of penal statutes impossible to discern, but the way these statutes could be used, that is, the legal effect given to them when relied upon, was also unpredictable. On some occasions, the legislation was employed in deciding whether a duty was owed. Whether the statutory tort theory was adopted or whether the statute was merely considered a "fortifying element" in the creation of a duty was difficult to forecast. That issue will not be considered in this chapter, although it will be dealt with elsewhere.[30] On other, more frequent occasions, violation of statute was used in the standard of care issue. This issue is the concern of this chapter. It was a very complex matter which sometimes led to a finding of negligence *per se, prima facie* or presumptive evidence of negligence, or merely some evidence of negligence.[31]

Little guidance was available as to which effect should be accorded a statutory violation and why. There was no rhyme or reason to it. A judge was required to perform very much like an orchestra conductor — calling on one instrument or another, a flute or a trumpet — depending on the force the judge felt the statute should be accorded. Seldom, however, did the result achieved resemble music; more frequently discordant sounds rent the air (and filled the law reports). Some scholars surrendered and offered gloomy forecasts to the effect that "the courts are unlikely to discard their traditional approach to statutes".[32]

B. *R. in Right of Canada v. Saskatchewan Wheat Pool*

It became imperative to sort out the mess. In the case of *R. in right of Canada v. Saskatchewan Wheat Pool*[33] the Supreme Court of Canada, in a learned, bold, unanimous decision, simplified the Canadian law and rendered it more intellectually defensible. The court decisively buried the intention theory and the nominate tort of statutory breach which was based on that theory. It located tort liability for breach of statute squarely within negligence law. It also rejected the view that unexcused breach constitutes negligence *per se* giving rise to absolute

---

[27] See, generally, Prosser, "Private Action for Public Nuisance" (1966), 52 Va. L. Rev. 997.

[28] *Kerr v. Townsend* (1917), 12 O.W.N. 166, at p. 167; *Menow v. Honsberger and Jordan House Hotel, supra*, n. 6.

[29] See Fricke, *supra*, n. 1, at p. 241.

[30] *Infra*, Chapter 9.

[31] For a description of the varying uses see *Johnston v. A.G. of Can.* (1981), 34 O.R. (2d) 208 (H.C.); affd Div. Ct. (*per* Reid J.), endorsement.

[32] Alexander, *supra*, n. 1, at p. 276. Linden, *op. cit. supra*, n. 17, at p. 204.

[33] *Supra*, n. 5. See Forell, "Statutes and Torts" (2000), 36 Willamette L. Rev. 865, praising this decision.

liability, and the position that it furnished *prima facie* evidence of negligence, preferring instead the approach that proof of statutory breach be admissible as evidence of negligence. In other words, the court held that a statutory formulation of a duty of care in a penal statute *may* provide a specific, useful standard of reasonable conduct, upon which a civil court (or jury) *may* rely, if it chooses to do so.

In the case, the plaintiff had incurred expenses as a result of receiving from the defendant wheat which was infested with rusty grain beetle larvae. The defendant was in breach of the Canadian Grain Act which forbade the "discharge . . . from an elevator any grain . . . that is infested or contaminated", but its conduct, according to all the evidence, was completely free of any negligence. On the basis of the new analysis, the plaintiff's action was dismissed, reversing the trial judge's decision in the plaintiff's favour.

Mr. Justice Dickson, as he then was, explored the historical roots of the problem, analyzed the English and American law, considered extensively the views of the scholars and text writers, observed that there were two different views contending for acceptance, and concluded that it was "now imperative for this Court to choose".[34] His Lordship went on to reject the intention theory as "capricious and arbitrary", and as a "'bare-faced fiction' at odds with accepted canons of statutory interpretation".[35] Instead, he associated himself with the views of Winfield and Jolowicz, who wrote that the use of legislation in tort cases was "in truth a question to be decided by the court", and Prosser, who had written:

> . . . the courts are seeking . . . to further the ultimate policy for the protection of individuals which they find underlying the statute, and which they believe the legislation must have had in mind. The statutory standard of conduct is simply adopted, out of deference and respect for the legislature.

In addition, he quoted a statement of Lord Macnaghten to the effect that "considerations of policy and convenience" were to be taken into account.[36] Finally, he relied on a passage in Professor Fleming's textbook which stated:

> Any recovery of damages for injury due to [a] violation [of statute] must . . . rest on common law principles. But though the penal statute does not create civil liability the court may think it proper to *adopt* the legislative formulation of a specific standard in place of the unformulated standard of reasonable conduct. . . .

Thus, the Supreme Court of Canada unequivocally recognized that it is not the intention of the legislature that governs the impact of criminal violations on tort liability; it is the judiciary that decides whether a penal infraction will be

---

[34] *Ibid.*, p. 212.
[35] *Ibid.*, p. 216.
[36] *Pasmore v. Oswaldtwistle Urban Council* [1898] A.C. 387, at p. 397.

relied upon.[37] When it is said that civil liability hinges on the meaning of the statute, this effect is usually "*given*" to the legislation by the court and not "*found*" therein as claimed.[38]

A few astute and candid members of the judiciary had expressed similar views earlier. Chief Justice Owen Dixon was probably the most ingenuous when he pointed out, in *O'Connor v. Bray*,[39] that this exercise was probably more a matter "governing the policy of the provision rather than the meaning of the instrument". Mr. Justice Grange has advised that the best way to decide whether a breach of statute gives rise to tort liability is to "consider the statute, balance the policy objectives and decide whether or not to give effect to it in a particular case as a ground for civil liability".[40] Mr. Justice LeDain has also explained that "in the final analysis, [it is] a question of policy".[41] The Supreme Court has now definitively established that civil liability for breach of statute is a "creature of the court", not of the legislature.[42] This is a welcome development because it is both accurate and honest.

Having articulated a sound theoretical basis for relying on penal statutes in tort cases, Mr. Justice Dickson went on the furnish clear directions on *how* they should be employed. Henceforth, "proof of statutory breach, causative of damages, may be evidence of negligence".[43] This means, of course, that the judge or jury may take into account the fact of a statutory breach in their deliberations, but they are not controlled by this evidence. Hence, although there is no *obligation* on a defendant, who has contravened a statute, to prove use of reasonable care (as had been the case since *Sterling Trusts*[44]) if the defendant chooses to remain silent, negligence may be found on that evidence alone.

In arriving at this conclusion, affording less weight to statutory violation than heretofore, Mr. Justice Dickson offered several reasons. First, because it avoids the "fictitious hunt for legislative intent", it is more "intellectually acceptable".[45] Second, it avoids the "inflexible application of the legislature's criminal standard of conduct to a civil case".[46] Third, nowadays legislation frequently deals expressly with the matter of "individual compensation", which has become an "active concern of the legislator".[47] This leads to the sensible inference that, if no express provision for compensation is included, there is no legislative

---

[37] Wright, "The English Law of Torts: A Criticism", *supra*, n. 13, at p. 94. Lord Denning M.R. in *Scott v. Green & Sons*, [1969] 1 W.L.R. 301, at p. 204 (C.A.): "The statute does not *by itself* give rise to a civil action, but it forms the foundation on which the common law can build a cause of action." See generally *Johnston v. A.G. Can.*, *supra*, n. 31 (*per* Linden J.).

[38] Lowndes, *supra*, n. 1, at p. 362.

[39] (1937), 56 C.L.R. 464, at p. 486.

[40] *Unsworth v. Mogk* (1979), 27 O.R. (2d) 645, at p. 648.

[41] *C.P. Air Lines v. The Queen* (1978), 87 D.L.R. (3d) 511, at p. 517.

[42] Morris, *supra*, n. 1, at p. 47 (Colum. L. Rev.).

[43] *Supra*, n. 5, at p. 227, subject to the exception re industrial safety statutes.

[44] *Sterling Trusts Corp. v. Postma*, [1965] S.C.R. 325.

[45] *Supra*, n. 5, at p. 222.

[46] *Ibid.*, at p. 223, industrial safety statutes are to remain an exception, leading to absolute liability.

[47] *Ibid.*, at p. 224.

intention to this effect. Fourth, the need for compensation through tort law has diminished as non-tort compensation schemes have been erected.[48] Fifth, tort law is moving away from absolute liability toward a purer fault regime. Negligence and fault provide a good reason for shifting a loss to a defendant because the defendant has "done some act which should be discouraged". However, there is "little in the way of defensible policy for holding a defendant who breached a statutory duty unwittingly to be negligent and obligated to pay even though not at fault". Further, he explains that "[m]inimum fault may subject the defendant to heavy liability".[49] "Inconsequential violations should not subject the violator to any civil liability at all but should be left to the criminal courts for enforcement of a fine". He concludes by explaining that "[t]he tendency of the law of recent times is to ameliorate the rigors of absolute rules and absolute duty . . . as contrary to natural justice". The "imposition of heavy financial burden . . . without fault . . . does not incline one to interfere"; thus, "[i]t is better that the loss lies where it falls".[50]

a) The Aftermath

The decision in *Saskatchewan Wheat Pool* has been embraced enthusiastically by the judiciary in Canada. In a later case,[51] the Supreme Court has reiterated that the fact of a violation "alone does not ground liability." Mr. Justice LeDain, in *Baird v. R. in right of Canada*[52] has declared that civil liability is no longer to be determined "by conjectures as to legislative intention but by the application, in a public law context, of the common law principles governing liability for negligence. The liability is not to be regarded as created by the statute, where there is no express provision for it." Mr. Justice Krever has also adopted and explained the decision in *James St. Hardware & Furniture Co. v. Spizziri*:[53]

> . . . mere breach of a statute does not itself give rise to liability. The civil consequences of a breach of statute are to be subsumed in the law of negligence although the statute may be examined to see whether it contains a useful standard of reasonable conduct. . . .

The courts are now prepared to consider violations of municipal by-laws in the same way as statutes, to be evidence of negligence, whereas in the past they evinced some distrust of subordinate legislative provisions.[54] Mr. Justice Henry, for example, treated as "an element of negligence" a breach of a by-law

---

[48] *Ibid.*
[49] *Ibid.*
[50] *Ibid.*, at p. 225.
[51] *Stewart v. Pettie*, [1995] 1 S.C.R. 131, 23 C.C.L.T. (2d) 89, at p. 101 (*per* Major J.); see also *Ryan v. Victoria (City)* (1999), 44 C.C.L.T. (2d) 1, at p. 16 (S.C.C) (*per* Major J.).
[52] (1983), 148 D.L.R. (3d) 1, at p. 9.
[53] (1985), 51 O.R. (2d) 641, at pp. 651-52; see also *Palmer v. N.S. Forest Industries* (1983), 2 D.L.R. (4th) 397, at p. 491 (N.S.S.C.).
[54] Fleming, *op. cit. supra*, n. 14, at pp. 128-29; *Porter v. Joe* (1979), 106 D.L.R. (3d) 206; *Martin v. Lowe* (1980), 109 D.L.R. (3d) 133.

requiring cab owners to keep their vehicles in good repair in a case where a passenger was injured when a door fell off the cab.[55] Furthermore, the failure to conform to a police policy manual[56] or some policy of the government[57] may be considered as evidence of negligence as well. Mr. Justice Cory has said[58] that the violation of a statute is a "public indicator" of negligence and a "factor" to be weighed.

Governmental conduct that breached a statute dealing with fishing licensing and the revocation of such licences was held to amount to evidence of negligence, where fishers, who relied on receiving a licence which they did not get, spent money to refit a boat.[59] The failure to inspect a gas furnace prior to activating it, in violation of a statute, was also negligent.[60]

Some courts have indicated that evidence of a breach of statute may be admissible in tort actions other than those based on negligence. Mr. Justice Strayer suggested that it may be of use in the intentional tort area.[61] Mr. Justice Kroft suggested, in *B.G. Ranches Ltd. v. Manitoba Agricultural Lands Protection Board*[62] that the evidence may be relevant if the conduct (in breach of the statute) is "an integral part of some specific tort". Someone who violates a press ban on the publication of the name of a sexual assault victim may be liable in tort, for, although the *Criminal Code* provision cannot *per se* found an action in tort, its existence "provides evidence of a private law duty".[63] A doctor who failed to report to the Registrar of Motor Vehicles the epilepsy of a patient was held partially liable for it was a "serious breach of statutory duty to the general public and the plaintiffs are members of the general public".[64] So, too, the breach of the *Broadcast Act* may lead to civil liability.[65] Such decisions are certainly consistent with *Saskatchewan Wheat Pool's* philosophy and may lead to a wider judicial use of evidence of legislative breach than in the past, even though the

---

[55] See *Fraser v. U-Need-A-Cab Ltd.* (1983), 1 D.L.R. (4th) 268, at p. 278 (H.C.), alternate holding.

[56] *Fortey (Guardian ad litem of) v. Canada (Attorney General)* (1999), 46 C.C.L.T. (2d) 271, at p. 280 (B.C.C.A.), failure to provide prisoner with medical attention which violated policy manual was evidence of negligence.

[57] *M. (M.) v. K. (K.)* (1987), 11 B.C.L.R. 90, at p. 96 (S.C.); revd on other grounds (1989), 50 C.C.L.T. 190, at p. 206 (B.C.C.A.).

[58] *Galaske v. O'Donnell*, [1994] 1 S.C.R. 670, 21 C.C.L.T. (2d) 1, at p. 15, violation of seat belt law.

[59] *Comeau's Sea Foods Ltd. v. Canada (Minister of Fisheries & Oceans)* (1995), 24 C.C.L.T. (2d) 1, at p. 47 (F.C.A.), revd on ground that no violation occurred, see [1997] 1 S.C.R. 12.

[60] *Aiello v. Centra Gas Ontario Inc.* (1999), 47 C.C.L.T. (2d) 39, at p. 68 (Ont. S.C.J.).

[61] *Evans v. Canada* (1986), 4 F.T.R. 247, at p. 248 (F.C.T.D.).

[62] (1983), 21 Man R. (2d) 285, at p. 294 (Q.B.). See also *Murray v. Canada (Government of)* (1983), 47 N.R. 299 (Fed. C.A.), no liability for breach of statute without proof of negligence or "intention" (*per* Heald J.A.).

[63] *C. (P.R.) v. Canadian Newspaper Co.* (1983), 16 C.C.L.T. (2d) 275 (B.C.S.C.) (*per* Melvin J.); see also *R. (L.) v. Nyp* (1993), 16 C.C.L.T. (2d) 281 (Ont. Gen Div.).

[64] *Spillane v. Wasserman* (1992), 13 C.C.L.T. (2d) 267 (Ont. Gen. Div.) (*per* Boland J.), physician 40% responsible for accident.

[65] *Whistler Cable T.V. v. I.P.E.C. Canada Inc.* (1992), 17 C.C.L.T. (2d) 16, at p. 23 (B.C.S.C.) (*per* Braidwood J.), there is a "tort of statutory breach distinct from negligence liability".

force of the evidence, once introduced, may be more limited. Another dramatic use of a penal statute has been in a contract action for breach of the implied warranties of fitness and merchantability, something said to be entirely apart from *Saskatchewan Wheat Pool.*[66]

C. Analysis of *R. in right of Canada v. Saskatchewan Wheat Pool*

This decision has been welcomed by Professor Brudner because of the clarification of the law it has achieved and because the "search for a fictitious legislative intention" need no longer be conducted.[67] Professor Fridman has written that it is a decision of "utmost importance . . . which . . . exemplifies the independence of the Canadian judiciary".[68] It is both "convincing and justifiable",[69] "freeing the Canadian tort law from the disfiguring barnacles that have clung to the hull of English tort law".[70] He concludes that the "heyday of civil liability based on breach of criminal statute has passed".[71] One English commentator has described the decision as "remarkable"[72] and another agreed that the "evidence of negligence approach is to be preferred" to the English treatment.[73]

The decision has attracted some criticism as well. Professor Brudner, for example, wrote that the decision was "lamentable" for two reasons. First, he suggests, that the court has "disarmed itself of a means by which to extend common-law duties in the face of obsolete precedents without subjecting defendants to unfair surprise". Second, he argues, that "by opting for the evidence-of-negligence rule it has not only surrendered the advantages of precise and uniform standards of care; it has also adopted a principle antithetical to the sovereignty of law".[74]

To an extent, both of these complaints are well founded, but they are exaggerated. First, civil courts are still free to extend tort duties by relying on penal legislation, just as they did in the past. Defendants would be most unwise to ignore penal statutes regulating them. The difference will be that, in utilizing statutes in the future, our courts will not be able to hide behind the disguise of the intention of the legislature in doing so. Henceforth, courts will be required to operate more openly (which is not necessarily a bad thing, even if it inhibits them to some extent). Second, the existence of some discretion does not make

---

[66] *Wild Rose Mills Ltd. v. Ellison Milling Co.* (1985), 32 B.L.R. 125, at p. 134 (B.C.S.C.). See also finding civil liability for breach of Charter, *Patenaude v. Roy* (1988), 46 C.C.L.T. 173 (Que. S.C.).
[67] Brudner, "Comment" (1984), 62 Can. Bar Rev. 668, at p. 669.
[68] "Civil Liability for Criminal Conduct" (1984), 16 Ott. L. Rev. 34, at p. 61.
[69] *Ibid.*, at p. 62.
[70] *Ibid.*, at p. 65.
[71] *Ibid.*, at p. 52.
[72] Rogers, "Rusty Beetles in the Elevator" (1984), 43 Cambridge L.J. 23, at p. 24.
[73] Matthews, "Negligence and Breach of Statutory Duty" (1984), 4 Oxford J.L.S. 429, at p. 433.
[74] *Supra*, n. 67, at p. 669.

the system lawless, nor does it violate the goal of sovereignty of law. Although there may be more discretion at play in the system, there was considerable discretion at play before, under the *prima facie* evidence principle and even under the negligence *per se* approach. That is what made this area of the law so unsatisfactory in the first place. Civil courts in the future will behave responsibly in utilizing breach of statute in civil cases, explaining their treatment more fully and honestly than in the past. There may appear to be less certainty, but, in reality, by employing the new reasoning, we may even get more predictability in the future, rather than less, as Professor Brudner fears.

Treating breach of statute as evidence of negligence is not a novel notion. Professor Glanville Williams has reminded us that, over 100 years ago, breach of statute had been treated as evidence of negligence.[75] Professor Wigmore had also countenanced the use of violation of legislation as evidence of "custom or usage having orthodox status".[76]

The advantages and disadvantages of using breach of statute as evidence of negligence had been discussed in the law journals long before *Saskatchewan Wheat Pool*. For example, Professor Lowndes, in support of the evidence of negligence approach, had argued that creating tort liability on the basis of a penal statute was a "perilous speculation", even though it was certainly legitimate to say that a breach of statute is an "element of a tort resting on negligence", which "colours" the conduct.[77] Professor Morris had also supported the evidence of negligence rule as "more elegant"[78] and more "flexible", because it "warns the jury about the legislative standard", and suggests that they be "cautious in substituting their own" for it.[79]

On the other side, Professor Glanville Williams opined that the evidence of negligence rule was "too weak" if the jury can ignore the statutory breach.[80] Professor Thayer felt that that approach was "perplexing and difficult of comprehension", because it allowed the jury to "stamp with approval, as reasonable conduct, the action of one who has assumed to place his own foresight above that of the legislature".[81]

It may be said that the evidence of negligence rule is only superficially simpler. The really difficult issues may be avoided by handing everything to the jury to resolve, but this denies us reasoned conclusions to guide us in the future. This illusion of simplicity may also mean that cases are less likely to be settled because the counsel will find it harder to forecast what the judge or jury is likely to do with evidence of statutory violation than in the past.

---

[75] (1960), 23 Mod. L. Rev. 233; *Blamires v. Lancashire and Yorkshire Ry.* (1873), L.R. 8 Ex. 283.
[76] *Evidence in Trials at Common Law* (1979), §461(6), at p. 606.
[77] See *supra*, n. 1, at pp. 365 and 375.
[78] *Supra*, n. 1, at p. 34 (Colum. L. Rev.).
[79] *Supra*, n. 1, at p. 461 (Harv. L. Rev.).
[80] See *supra*, n. 1, at p. 252 (Mod. L. Rev.).
[81] *Supra*, n. 1, at p. 322 (Harv. L. Rev.).

The ultimate result of all this is that Canadian plaintiffs may be less likely to recover, either by settlement or after trial, because their strategic position has been weakened by the shift from the *prima facie* evidence of negligence rule, which had been the operative principle prior to *Saskatchewan Wheat Pool*, to the evidence of negligence rule. No longer does the defendant violator bear the onus of proving care; it is now up to the plaintiff to prove that the defendant, in breach of statute, was negligent. Even though the plaintiff can rely on the statutory breach as one piece of evidence, additional evidence of wrongdoing against the violator may be required in order to succeed.

These concerns may be unfounded. The evidence of negligence rule appears to accord less weight to the statutory violation, but the "two rules are capable of being so administered that their results approach each other in practice".[82] This is so because the American negligence *per se* approach is only utilized for *unexcused* violations of statutes. The main difference now is who decides the issue of excuse. Under the negligence *per se* approach, this issue was dealt with by the judge, but, under the evidence of negligence treatment, the issue is handled by the jury. This may lead to more unpredictability, because there may be a tendency now to submit more "lame excuses" to the jury to consider, rather than having the court reject them outright, without any need of using the jury. In all probability, however, the actual results should "differ little".[83] This is especially so in Canada, where judges alone try most of these cases, and, where they do not, they may, in their charge to the jury, comment on the evidence, guiding the jury so that it will not be misled by flimsy excuses. If the judicial attitude evinced in the past is any guide to the future, courts will remain skeptical of excuses advanced by statutory violators.[84]

Using statutory violations as evidence of negligence is so attractive that some jurisdictions have — by legislation — expressly directed their courts to use them in this way. In the United Kingdom, for example, the Road Traffic Act stipulates that evidence of a violation of the Highway Code may be "relied upon by any party to the proceedings as tending to establish or negative any liability which is in question in those proceedings".[85] Despite the dangers of juries being swayed by flimsy excuses, the tide seems to be moving in this direction in the United States[86] both by statute,[87] and by court decisions.[88]

---

[82]   Harper, James and Gray, *The Law of Torts*, 2nd ed. (1986), Vol. 3, p. 642.
[83]   See Morris, *supra*, n. 1, at p. 35 (Colum. L. Rev.).
[84]   See Cartwright J. in *Rintoul v. X-Ray & Radium Industries*, [1956] S.C.R. 674; Schroeder J.A. in *Carvalho v. Baldwin*, [1962] O.R. 545, at p. 547 (C.A.).
[85]   1960, s. 74(5) (U.K.); *Powell v. Phillips*, [1972] 3 All E.R. 864, at p. 867 (C.A.).
[86]   Harper, James and Gray, *op. cit. supra*, n. 82, at p. 626.
[87]   Mass. Ann. Laws (1959), c. 90, s. 9, evidence; see also California Evidence Code (1967), s. 669; negligence presumed but rebutted if acted reasonably; *Atkins v. Bisigier* (1971), 94 Cal. Reptr. 99; Minnesota Stats. Ann. (1960), s. 196.96, *prima facie* evidence.
[88]   See *Duplechain v. Turner* (1984), 444 So. 2d 1322, at 1326 (La.), "guidelines to consider"; also in Ark., Ill., D.C.; see Harper, James and Gray, *op. cit. supra*, n. 82, Vol. 3, at p. 617.

Adopting this technique of treating legislation in these cases is certainly a promising reform of the law, which happens to be consistent with the Supreme Court's efforts in other areas to eliminate *res ipsa loquitur,* various presumptions and reverse onuses of proof, which are confusing in their day-to-day operation. Let us hope that the courts will utilize the new approach with sensitivity, clarity and honesty.

D. Why Civil Courts Rely on Penal Statutes

It is wise for courts not to ignore relevant penal legislation in their deliberations over civil liability. Now, as before, there are sound policy grounds for judicial reliance on criminal legislation in civil cases, even though it does not expressly seek to control them. These policies will lead to continuing widespread use of statutes in tort cases.

a) Respect for the Legislature

The primary motivating force behind judicial reliance on penal statutes is the desire to be appropriately respectful to the legislature by giving full effect to its wishes. There are both philosophical and pragmatic reasons for this. Professor Thayer has based his thesis on the philosophical view that, where a "state has spoken through a legislative body having authority", approval of a violation "is not consistent with proper respect for another branch of government".[89] He urged the courts to study the statutes in question "to extract . . . declared legislative policy" and to further it.[90] Another distinguished American jurist has also criticized the courts' failure to rely upon policies enacted into legislation "by the supreme law-making body . . . as a social datum or as a point of departure for the process of judicial reasoning . . .".[91] He urged that statutes be treated as "a judicial precedent, as both a declaration and a source of law, and as a premise of legal reasoning". In other words, since the general will of the people in democratic countries is expressed in legislation, the judiciary should promote the aims contained therein.

b) Expertise

One of the pragmatic reasons why common law should follow the dictates of statutes is that the legislatures have much larger facilities than courts for investigation, research, hearings, debates and the like.[92] Consequently, their

---

[89]   Thayer, *supra,* n. 1, at p. 324.
[90]   *Ibid.,* at p. 343.
[91]   Stone, "The Common Law in the United States" (1936), 50 Harv L. Rev. 4, at p. 13. See also Landis, "Statutes and the Sources of Law" in *Harvard Legal Essays* (1934), at p. 213, and Pound, "Common Law and Legislation" (1908), 21 Harv. L. Rev. 383, at pp. 406-07.
[92]   See Fricke, *supra,* n. 1, at p. 225; Morris, *supra,* n. 1, at p. 23 (Colum. L. Rev.). See also *Rudes v. Gottschalk* (1959), 159 Tex. 552, 324 S.W. 2d 201 "by reason of its organization and investi-

product is deserving of judicial respect, for the "judgment of amateurs" would be thereby replaced by "that of experts and professionals".[93] It is wise to bring the expert judgment of people intimately acquainted with construction, industrial operations, and accident prevention into the judicial deliberations on these matters in civil cases. Moreover, the courts need not worry about relying upon the standards created by legislatures, for they are unlikely to be "impractical", as the standards set by judge or jury may sometimes be.[94]

c) Strengthening Criminal Law

Another practical policy consideration is that the criminal legislation will be rendered "more effective" if tort law adopts it.[95] According to one commentator, "liability based on fault is a desirable complement to the criminal law if conduct which is unduly risky is to be discouraged".[96] Professor Glanville Williams has argued that "judges have created the tort of breach of statutory duty partly because they have thought the criminal sanction provided by the statute to be insufficient".[97] In other words, an award of tort damages may serve as an additional deterrent to offenders. On a few rare occasions judicial pronouncements have disclosed this, as when Mr. Justice Idington declared that to permit a breach of statute to go unrecompensed makes a "hollow mockery" of the legislation,[98] and when Mr. Justice Rand protested that if an infringement did "not call down accountability, the regulation might almost as well be abolished".[99] Mr. Justice Adamson envisioned a kind of partnership between penal sanctions and tort liability in the enforcement of automobile regulations, when he stated in *Voth v. Friesen* that,

> Unless judges and juries in both criminal and civil cases lay more stress on the duty of the motorists and the danger to themselves and others by the breach of those regulations, and strictly enforce their observance in the interest of public safety, serious accidents and loss of life will continue.[100]

Thus, civil courts are, to some extent at least, reasoning by analogy to legislation and are applying the "indirect pressure of civil liability . . . to compel conformance to the legislative rule".[101] Moreover, improved enforcement of penal legislation may be encouraged by dangling the carrot of a tort judgment

---

gating processes, [the Legislature] is generally in a better position to establish . . . tests than are judicial tribunals".

[93] Fleming, *The Law of Torts,* 9th ed. (1998), at p. 137 *et ff.*

[94] Morris, *supra,* n. 1 at p. 23 (Colum. L. Rev.).

[95] Fricke, *supra,* n. 1, at p. 255.

[96] Morris, *supra,* n. 1, at p. 458 (Colum. L. Rev.).

[97] Williams, "Aims of the Law of Tort" (1951), 4 Current Legal Problems 137, at p. 150.

[98] *Fralick v. Grand Trunk Railway* (1910), 43 S.C.R. 494, at p. 510.

[99] *Brooks v. Ward and R.,* [1956] S.C.R. 683, at p. 687, Mr. Justice Rand dissented in part in the decision. See also *Bruce v. McIntyre,* [1955] S.C.R. 251, at p. 254.

[100] *Voth v. Friesen* (1955), 15 W.W.R. 625, at p. 628 (Man. C.A.).

[101] Landis, "Statutes and the Sources of Law" (1965), 2 Harv. J. Leg. 7, at p. 14 reprinted from *Harvard Legal Essays* (1934).

before would-be informers.[102] The profit motive may operate here, as it does elsewhere in society, to spur conduct that might not otherwise be undertaken. Perhaps an even more important consideration is the fact that penal statutes are woefully deficient in providing compensation for those victimized by their violation. This lacuna might be partially filled by tort law.

d) Administrative Efficiency: Particularizing the Standard of Care

Administrative efficiency also influences the courts' use of penal statutes, because the application of the precise standards enacted in legislation "smooths up civil procedure".[103] In Professor Fleming's words, this "promotes fixed and predictable standards of negligence" in place of the "featureless generality of the jury verdict".[104] Rather than relying upon the jury groping toward the vague reasonable person criterion *via* the "untutored social judgment of twelve traveling salesmen, or bricklayers, or plumbers, or shopkeepers . . . ",[105] the court welcomes the aid of detailed statutory commands in deciding what is reasonable. The determination of reasonableness, therefore, need no longer be left to the chance opinion of the jury.[106] In this context, the legislation is said to "concretize," or "crystallize" or "formulate" the standard to be followed,[107] which has led one author to term this process "a case-solving device".[108] This commentator has actually gone so far as to contend that civil courts follow statutes *only* because of increased "facility in solving cases rather than because of reasons of social or legal policy".

Following *Saskatchewan Wheat Pool*, the value of this effect may be diminished somewhat, but the specific terms of the statute will continue to be relied on in most cases, unless there is good reason not to. The statute may no longer be definitive, but it will still offer help as a likely indicator of reasonableness.

e) Control of the Jury

Reliance upon legislative provisions may also assist the judiciary in controlling the jury,[109] a goal that appears to be gaining favour these days. By instructing the jury to find for the plaintiff if there has been a breach of statute, as is done with negligence *per se* theory, the judge is able to guide them more effectively than if merely telling them to do so if there has been "unreasonable conduct". Even

---

[102] Fricke, *supra*, n. 1, at p. 251.

[103] Morris, *supra*, n. 1, at p. 47 (Colum. L. Rev.).

[104] Fleming, *op. cit. supra*, n. 93.

[105] Lowndes, *supra*, n. 1, at p. 368.

[106] Fletcher Moulton L.J. in *Britannic Merthyr Coal Co. v. David*, [1909] 2 K.B. 164 (*sub nom. David v. Britannic Merthyr Coal Co.*); affd [1910] A.C. 74, [1908-10] All E.R. Rep. 436.

[107] Williams, *supra*, n. 1, at p. 234.

[108] Foust, "The Use of Criminal Law as a Standard of Civil Responsibility in Indiana" (1959), 35 Ind. L.J. 45, at pp. 59 and 68. See also Gregory, *supra*, n. 1.

[109] Fleming, *op. cit. supra*, n. 93.

though the judiciary may be abdicating some of its own authority in this process, the legislative branch of government — the democratic one — expands its influence accordingly, which is desirable.[110] The negligence *per se* device may have been used, in part, to prevent soft-hearted American juries from refusing to employ the defence of contributory negligence against plaintiffs who violated legislation. In Canada, where comparative negligence legislation permits a reduction rather than a total deprivation of damages where plaintiffs contribute to their own injury, this problem was less pronounced, so that negligence *per se*, which furnished more control was less needed.

In the new era of *Saskatchewan Wheat Pool*, this ability to control juries will be diminished to a degree, but it will still be of considerable effect. Instead of telling the jury that statutory breach amounts to negligence *per se* or *prima facie* evidence, the court will explain that it is only some evidence of negligence. Hopefully, however, juries will continue to pay serious attention to the fact of violation of statute, unless there is good reason to do otherwise.

f) Stricter Liability

The final reason why civil courts utilize penal violations is that they can thereby move closer to a regime of stricter liability. Since most courts are wary of "simon-pure judicial law making", reliance upon criminal legislation may serve as a technique for accomplishing this indirectly.[111] One scholar has argued that this device "transforms liability-only-for fault into liability without fault",[112] but perhaps this latter contention, in view of the various limitations on the use of statutes in civil cases, is exaggerated somewhat. Professor Fleming was probably closer to the mark when he wrote that there was a "tendency to promote, if not strict, at any rate stricter liability".[113]

In the past, legislation supplied an additional arrow for the plaintiff's bow and thereby improved the chance of success. Not only was the plaintiff able to plead common law negligence, but also could contend that a breach of statute, which might or might not be negligent, caused the injury. This did not normally weaken the plaintiff's case since the ordinary negligence theory could be turned to if the plaintiff failed to prove the violation.

In addition, the adoption of penal standards in negligence cases may have encouraged speedier settlements of claims. Uncertainty surrounding law or fact impedes negotiation and generates litigation, with its attendant delays. The diminution of this uncertainty, through the establishment of more precise standards, facilitated the settlement process, which normally operated in the claimant's favour.[114]

---

[110] Malone, "Contrasting Images of Torts — The Judicial Personality of Justice Traynor" (1961), 13 Stan. L. Rev. 771, at p. 783.

[111] Morris, *supra*, n. 1, at p. 24 (Colum. L. Rev.).

[112] *Ibid.*, at p. 28.

[113] Fleming, *op. cit. supra*, n. 93.

[114] See generally, Ross, *Settled Out of Court* (1970).

Although *Saskatchewan Wheat Pool* may have weakened this tendency, it has certainly not eliminated it. Plaintiffs can still plead a violation of statute as an additional ground of negligence, so that there is still more chance of success than when there is no statutory contravention. Plaintiffs, therefore, are still better off, but perhaps less so than heretofore.

g) Opposing Policy Considerations

There are, of course, contrary viewpoints about whether the civil courts should follow the criminal law. It may be said that it is equally disrespectful to the legislature for a court to do what the elected body is perfectly at liberty to do, yet refrains from doing. The courts should give a statute full effect, but they should not go beyond its declared intention,[115] for to do so is to "usurp the function of the legislature".[116] In fact, one author has suggested that if a penal violation had "no bearing" upon civil liability, this would not be "entirely unappealing".[117] Further, in buttressing the criminal law with civil damage awards, one runs the risk of imposing potentially ruinous civil liability, which may be inappropriate for a minor infraction of a petty regulation.[118] In the same way, the professionalism of the legislature may be overestimated. Some criminal regulations may be hurriedly passed, ill-considered, badly outdated, overly harsh, or politically motivated.[119] This argument is particularly apt when one considers the dozens of inferior legislative and quasi-legislative bodies disgorging regulations, orders-in-council, ordinances, by-laws, rulings and the like by the thousands. The purity of the common law might well be protected from pollution by these frequently uncommon enactments. The argument, however, assumes that once a court decides to rely upon a penal provision in some case, it will therefore be compelled to follow willy-nilly every relevant criminal statute in every tort case. This just is not so, for the court is free to choose when it will accept a statutory standard and when it will refuse to do so.[120] If it is invoked, the court has the power to accord it either modest or significant weight as it chooses. Another policy reason fettering judicial acceptance of legislative provisions is the desire to restrain the undue spread of tort liability.[121] At the root of this judicial attitude is the idea of "no liability without fault", that is, unless defendants are to blame for accidents, they should not have to respond in damages, whether or not their conduct has violated a statute. Moreover, defenders of the civil jury would also argue that it should be kept free of judicial control.

---

[115] Thayer, *supra*, n. 1.

[116] Lowndes, *supra*, n. 1.

[117] *Ibid.*

[118] Morris, *supra*, n. 1, at p. 23 (Colum. L. Rev.). See also *Saskatchewan Wheat Pool, supra*, n. 5.

[119] *Ibid.*

[120] *Ibid. Saskatchewan Wheat Pool, supra*, n. 5.

[121] *Makarsky v. C.P.R.* (1904), 15 Man. R. 53, at p. 80 (C.A.); *Maitland v. Raisbeck and Hewitt*, [1944] 1 K.B. 689, [1944] 2 All E.R. 272 (C.A.), where the court expressed a reluctance to make the driver into an insurer of defects in a motor vehicle.

As has always been the case, all of these policy objectives must be balanced by the courts in deciding whether they will rely on a statutory breach in a particular case. *Saskatchewan Wheat Pool* has brought this exercise more into the open, and has furnished the court with more flexibility, which should make for more honest reasoning and better judicial craftsmanship.

E. The Limitations

Prior to *Saskatchewan Wheat Pool*, the civil courts fashioned certain restraints upon their use of penal legislation in tort suits. These limitations delineated certain boundaries beyond which the courts did not generally travel in furthering the legislative policy embodied in the criminal statutes being evaluated. Thus, civil courts did not generally admit any evidence of a breach unless the provision of the legislative proscription was violated, unless some loss was caused to the plaintiff thereby, unless the accident was of a kind the statute was aimed at preventing, and unless the plaintiff was within the class of persons protected by the enactment.[122] These rules did not tell us when the civil courts would rely on penal violations; they merely provided an indication of when they would *not* do so. They were principles of exclusion, not of inclusion. If these pre-conditions were not met, the statute was not normally considered relevant to the case.

Following *Saskatchewan Wheat Pool*, it appears that these limiting principles will continue to be used by Canadian courts, even though they were largely based on the intention theory and even though scholars have argued that they were not appropriate in an evidence of negligence regime.[123] The fact that there has been a breach of a penal statute dealing with safety should, by itself, lead a civil court to consider this evidence, without regard to the various limitations that had been used before to restrict the scope of the statutory tort approach, they suggested. Nevertheless, despite the discarding of the intention theory, courts are still loath to push the policy of the legislature enshrined in criminal legislation too far beyond the scope of the statutory language. They are, after all, enlarging the impact of the legislation by considering these penal violations in civil cases at all. To allow individuals never contemplated recovery for accidents never envisioned, it is felt, would be going too far. Consequently, the common law courts stopped short of doing this, although no such squeamishness is evinced in Quebec.[124]

---

[122] See Fleming, *op. cit. supra*, n. 14, at p. 131.

[123] Lowndes, *supra*, n. 1, at p. 375; Morris, *supra*, n. 1, at p. 477 (Harv. L. Rev.).

[124] Apparently violation of a specific statute is considered wrongful and anyone injured thereby may recover, the only limitation being causation and, perhaps, Act of God. See Newman, "Breach of Statute as the Basis of Responsibility in the Civil Law" (1949), 27 Can. Bar Rev. 782. See also Civil Code of Quebec, S.Q. 1991, c. 64, s. 1457.

1. NEED FOR STATUTORY BREACH

There will be no reliance on a criminal violation if the terms of the legislation
have not been departed from. The onus rests upon the person alleging a breach
to prove one.[125] Hence, where the evidence disclosed that certain automobile
lights were built as prescribed in the statute,[126] were illuminated,[127] and were
visible from the required distance,[128] no civil liability was imposed. In *Adam v.
Campbell*,[129] although the defendant was held liable on other grounds, no
responsibility was founded upon the violation, because the evidence proved that
the emergency brake equipment complied with the regulations. No tort responsibility was found in one case because the reduced speed limit section was not
applicable when there was a "clear view" of the intersection.[130] Nor was the
widow of a man who drank some wood alcohol that was not labeled poison
entitled to recovery, since the statute in question was not construed to apply to
this product.[131] Similarly, no statutory breach was found where a disease
affecting animals was not infectious or communicable.[132]

When the legislation is nearly, but not actually, contravened, the courts have
resisted widening the operation of the statute by analogy. Lord Justice Denning
explained that "undue complications will be brought into these cases if,
whenever the courts were considering common law obligations, they had to
consider all the statutory regulations which nearly apply but which do not in fact
apply".[133] Consequently, where a scaffold 34 inches wide was prescribed for
workers toiling more that six feet six inches above ground, no liability was
imposed when a worker fell from a scaffold nine inches wide but only six feet
from the ground.

It is another matter when the statutory terms are violated, but by reason of
some technicality a criminal prosecution would have been disallowed. Thus,
where a resolution which authorized a certain stop sign never became effective
because of defects in its publication, civil liability was still imposed upon
someone who disobeyed this stop sign. Mr. Justice Traynor in *Clinkscales v.*

---

[125] *Kuhnle v. Ottawa Electric Ry.*, [1946] 3 D.L.R. 681 (Ont. C.A.).

[126] *Bolton v. Charkie* (1953), 8 W.W.R. 412 (Alta.).

[127] *MacLeod v. Dockendorf* (1955), 36 M.P.R. 284 (P.E.I.); *Dawson v. Oberton* (1952), 6 W.W.R. (N.S.) 465 (Alta. C.A.).

[128] *Gillies v. Lye* (1926), 58 O.L.R. 560.

[129] [1950] 3 D.L.R. 449, negligence *after* brakes failed.

[130] *Davis v. Alles* (1926), 29 O.W.N. 466 (C.A.), held for 33 1/3%, however, on common-law negligence. See also *Luck v. Toronto Railway* (1920), 48 O.L.R. 581, 58 D.L.R. 145 (C.A.).

[131] *Antoine v. Duncombe* (1906), 8 O.W.R. 719.

[132] *Modern Livestock Ltd. v. Elgersma* (1990), 50 C.C.L.T. 5, at p. 38 (Alta. Q.B.) (*per* Andrekson J.). See also *Lake v. Callison Outfitters Ltd.* (1991), 7 C.C.L.T. (2d) 274 (B.C.S.C.), government not liable for failing to ensure, before granting guide licence, under Wildlife Act, that compulsory insurance provision in that Act complied with.

[133] *Chipchase v. British Titan Products Co. Ltd.*, [1956] 1 Q.B. 545, [1956] 1 All E.R. 613, at p. 614 (C.A.). See also *Moore v. Dering Coal Co.* (1909), 89 N.E. 674 (Ill.). Coal mine not in operation, therefore, requirements not applicable.

Carver suggested that "[e]ven if the conduct cannot be punished criminally because of irregularities in the adoption of the prohibitory provisions, the legislative standard may nevertheless apply if it is an appropriate measure for the defendant's conduct".[134] In other words, "[f]ailure to observe a stop-sign is unreasonably dangerous conduct whether or not the driver is immune from criminal prosecution because of some irregularity in the erection of the stop-sign". Similarly, the breach of an order of a provincial body which lacked the constitutional power to regulate a railway might be relied upon as "evidence . . . presenting a standard of reasonableness upon which a jury might act".[135]

a) Compliance with Legislation

It should be pointed out, however, that compliance with legislation does not immunize defendants from liability under ordinary negligence principles. The Supreme Court of Canada has recently adopted this principle in *Ryan v. Victoria (City)*[136] where Mr. Justice Major declared:

> [M]ere compliance with a statute does not, in and of itself, preclude a finding of civil liability.

Further, he asserted, ". . . one cannot avoid the underlying obligation of reasonable care simply by discharging statutory duties." Those principles were henceforth to apply as well to railways, which heretofore had been granted a special status to the effect that, unless there were special or exceptional circumstances, they were immune from tort liability if they discharged their statutory obligations.[137] Mr. Justice Major explained that, since this rule was "no longer . . . justified" and had "lost its relevance", the "time has come for that rule to be set aside".[138]

There are other cases consistent with this principle. In one case, a person was held contributorily negligent for failure to wear a seat belt, even though there was no technical violation of the compulsory seat belt law, which governed only while a person was driving on a highway. Mr. Justice Vancise explained that the fact that there was no statutory standard of behaviour is "not determinative of civil liability". He stated: "Positive legislative action or legislative inaction by exempting the requirement to wear a seat belt off the highway is not determinative of liability."[139] Hence, neither compliance nor non-compliance with statutory standards is controlling.

---

[134] (1943), 22 Cal. App. 2d 72, 136 P. 2d 777, at p. 778.

[135] *Littley v. Brooks and C.N.R.*, [1930] S.C.R. 416, [1930] 4 D.L.R. 1.

[136] (1999), 44 C.C.L.T. (2d) 1, at p. 16, relying in part on this text and the Quebec law. Motorcyclist injured when his tire was caught in flangeway of authorized rail track.

[137] *Paskivski v. Canadian Pacific Ltd.* (1975), 57 D.L.R. (3d) 280, at p. 285 (S.C.C.).

[138] *Ryan, supra,* n. 136, at p. 17.

[139] See *Rinas v. City of Regina* (1983), 26 Sask. R. 132, at p. 139 (Q.B.).

Another case on this point is *Bux v. Slough Metals Ltd.*,[140] where the plaintiff injured his eye when he was splashed by some molten metal which he was removing from a furnace. The evidence indicated that if he had been wearing the safety goggles which the employer was required by regulation to supply, he would not have been injured. The goggles had been provided to the workers but to the employer's knowledge they were not used because the lenses tended to mist up very quickly. The employer did not enforce the wearing of the goggles. The court found that there was no breach of statutory duty but, nevertheless, held the employer negligent at common law for not forcing the employees to use the goggles or for not providing better ones. The employer argued that compliance with the statutory duty absolved him from any breach of his common law duty. In response to this, Stephenson L.J. said:

> There is, in my judgment, no presumption that a statutory obligation abrogates or supersedes the employer's common law duty or that it defines or measures his common law duty either by clarifying it or by cutting it down — or indeed by extending it. It is not necessarily exhaustive of that duty or co-extensive with it and I do not, with all due respect to counsel for the defendants' argument, think it is possible to lay down conditions in which it is exhaustive or to conclude that it is so in this case. The statutory obligation may exceed the duty at common law or it may fall short of it or it may equal it. The court has always to construe the statute or statutory instrument which imposes the obligation, consider the facts of the particular case and the allegations of negligence in fact made by the particular workman and then decide whether, if the statutory obligation has been performed, any negligence has been proved. In some cases such proof will be difficult or impossible; in others it may be easy.

Where the non-statutory rules or policies of an activity are followed, this is normally determinative of due care. For example, when a "scrum" collapsed during a rugby game, injuring the plaintiff, no liability was imposed because the defendant had obeyed the *Laws of the Game*, which were said to reflect the appropriate standard of care.[141]

2. OFFENDING CONDUCT MUST CAUSE LOSS

Even if there is a statutory infraction, this will not be relevant if the offending conduct has not caused the injury complained of.[142] The onus of establishing causation between the criminal act and the harm resulting is upon the plaintiff.[143] The plaintiff must show that, "but for" the criminal conduct of the defendant, this accident would not have transpired. The courts have shrunk from permitting people to sue wrongdoers who contravene the criminal law if they have suffered no harm as a result of that wrongdoing, for just as negligence in the air will not do, neither will crime in the air. Thus, where someone in violation of a lighting

---

[140] [1974] 1 All E.R. 262 (C.A.).

[141] See *Hamstra v. B.C. Rugby Union* (1989), 1 C.C.L.T. (2d) 78, at p. 85 (B.C.S.C.).

[142] See *Daniels v. Vaux*, [1938] 2 K.B. 203, [1938] 2 All E.R. 271; *Belair v. Thiessen* (1984), 29 Sask. R. 224 (Q.B.); *Red River Construction (1972) Ltd. v. MacKenzie & Feimann Ltd.* (1983), 22 Man. R. (2d) 57, at p. 61 (Q.B.) (*per* Scollin J.).

[143] *Fuller v. Nickel*, [1949] S.C.R. 601, at p. 606; *Underwood v. Rayner Construction Co.* (1953), 34 M.P.R. 229 (N.B.C.A.).

statute is involved in a collision at a well-lighted intersection,[144] or street,[145] or where the motorist's vehicle was actually seen[146] or should have been seen,[147] civil liability will not ensue, although sometimes it may be appropriate to apportion liability between the offender and the other person.[148] Similarly, if effective brakes could not have prevented a collision with two women who darted out,[149] or with a vehicle that turned left into the driver's path,[150] a motorist with criminally defective brakes will be exonerated. An identical result will follow where a speeding violation does not contribute to the collision.[151] So too, if a failure to obey a hit-and-run statute does not contribute to the death or further injury of the victim, a defendant will not be held liable,[152] as where the victim died instantly or was taken immediately to the hospital.[153] Nor will liability be imposed where the neglect to insure, in violation of a statute, did not contribute to the inability of a victim to recover.[154] If the lack of prior approval[155] or of a building permit,[156] in violation of the law, did not cause a loss by fire, no liability will ensue. This is only an application of the fundamental tort principle which demands that offending conduct culminate in harm to the plaintiff for an action to lie.

3. ACCIDENT MUST BE OF A TYPE STATUTE SOUGHT TO PREVENT

Even after the violation and causation hurdles are overcome, a civil court may still refuse to rely on the breach on the ground that the accident was not of a kind that the legislation was aimed at preventing. This concept originated in the case of *Gorris v. Scott*,[157] where shipowners failed to provide the type of animal pens required by statute. If the defendant had supplied these pens, the plaintiff's sheep would not have been swept overboard and lost. No civil liability was imposed for the penal infraction, however, since "the damage was of such a

---

[144] *Collins v. General Service Transport Ltd.* (1927), 38 B.C.R. 512, [1927] 2 D.L.R. 353 (C.A.)

[145] *Peacock v. Stephens*, [1927] 3 W.W.R. 570 (Sask. C.A.).

[146] *Morrison v. Ferguson* (1930), 1 M.P.R. 81 (N.S.C.A.).

[147] *Holgate v. Canadian Tumbler Co.* (1931), 40 O.W.N. 565 (C.A.); *Antoine v. Larocque*, [1954] O.W.N. 641; affd [1955] O.W.N. 134 (C.A.).

[148] As in *Underwood v. Rayner Construction, supra*, n. 143.

[149] *Johnson v. Sorochuk*, [1941] 1 W.W.R. 445 (Alta.).

[150] *Payne v. Lane*, [1949] O.W.N. 284.

[151] *Odlum and Sylvester v. Walsh*, [1939] 2 D.L.R. 545; *McKenzie v. Robar*, [1953] 1 D.L.R. 449.

[152] See generally, *Boyer v. Gulf, C. & S.F.R. Co.* (1957), 306 S.W. 2d 215 (Tex. Civ. App.); *Hallman v. Cushman* (1941), 196 S.C. 402, 13 S.E. 2d 498; *Brooks v. Willig Transport Co.* (1953), 40 Cal. App. 2d 669, 255 P. 2d 802. But *cf.* language in *Battle v. Kilcrease* (1936), 54 Ga. App. 808, 189 S.E. 573.

[153] *People v. Scofield* (1928), 203 Cal. App. 703, 265 P. 914; *People v. Martin* (1931), 114 Cal. App. 337, 300 P. 108.

[154] *Daniels v. Vaux, supra*, n. 138.

[155] *Belmont Hotel v. Atlantic Speedy Propane Ltd.* (1985), 64 N.B.R. (2d) 271, at p. 279 (C.A.).

[156] *James St. Hardware & Furniture Co. v. Spizziri, supra*, n. 53, at p. 642.

[157] (1874), L.R. 9 Exch. 125.

nature as was not contemplated at all by the statute."[158] According to the court, the statute in question, which was called the Contagious Diseases (Animals) Act, was aimed at preventing the spread of disease among cattle rather than protecting them from being washed overboard. Consequently, before relying on statutes, courts must now ask, "Was the object of the statutory provision to prevent damage of the nature which occurred?"[159]

Pursuant to this theory, where someone violated a wartime speed limit of 35 m.p.h. and collided with the plaintiff, no damages were awarded on the ground that the purpose of the statute was to conserve gasoline rather than safety.[160] Where a particle of wire was thrown out of a machine that was unfenced, contrary to a statute to this effect, liability was not based on the infraction, although common law negligence was found.[161] Similarly, the fact that the defendant violated some licensing statute will not be used in an action based on negligent driving,[162] nor can it be pleaded.[163] Although the courts usually justify these decisions on the grounds of causation,[164] or proximate cause,[165] a better reason for this would be that the main purpose of licensing legislation is not to prevent negligent driving, but rather to collect revenue and to ensure that drivers are properly qualified.[166] There is some disagreement over whether evidence of the breach of a penal drunk driving law is admissible.[167]

In another case,[168] a boy was injured by a pointed hood ornament on a parked car. Although the defendant had violated a statute forbidding any ornament, "which extends or protrudes to the front of the face of the radiator grill of such motor vehicle", liability was denied. The court was of the view that the danger which the statute was designed to combat was injury produced by a "pointed ornament when the car was in movement", not when the car was stationary.[169] There are numerous cases of this sort.[170]

---

[158] *Ibid.*, at p. 128, *per* Kelly C.B.

[159] *Pugliese v. National Capital Comm., supra*, n. 19, at p. 53.

[160] *Cooper v. Hoeglund* (1946), 221 Minn. 446, 22 N.W. 2d 450.

[161] *Kilgollan v. Wm. Cooke Co. Ltd.*, [1956] 2 All E.R. 294 (C.A.). See also *Keating v. Elvan Reinforced Concrete Co. Ltd.*, [1968] 1 W.L.R. 722 (C.A.); *Thordarson v. Zastre* (1968), 70 D.L.R. (2d) 91 (Alta. C.A.).

[162] *Godfrey v. Cooper* (1920), 46 O.L.R. 565, 51 D.L.R. 455 (C.A.). See also *City of Vancouver v. Burchill*, [1932] S.C.R. 620, [1932] 4 D.L.R. 200.

[163] *Field v. Supertest Petroleum Corp.*, [1943] O.W.N. 482.

[164] *Paulsen v. C.P.R.* (1963), 40 D.L.R. (2d) 761 (Man. C.A.).

[165] *Godfrey v. Cooper, supra*, n. 162.

[166] *Cf., Brown v. Shyne* (1926), 242 N.Y.S. 476. 151 N.E. 197, doctor practising without a licence not liable on this ground alone.

[167] *Contra, Watt v. Bretag* (1981), 27 S.A.S.R. 301; *cf.* Traynor dissenting in *Stickel v. San Diego Electric Ry. Co.* (1948), 195 P. 2d 416 (Calif.).

[168] *Hatch v. Ford Motor Co.* (1958), 163 Cal. App. 2d 293, 329 P. 2d 605.

[169] *Ibid.*, at p. 299 in Cal. App., and p. 608 in P.

[170] See also *Beauchamp v. Ayotte*, [1971] 3 O.R. 22, statute not used where drunk person fell down steps which were in violation of fire regulations laws. *Wolfe v. Dayton* (1975), 55 D.L.R. (3d) 552 (B.C.), horse allowed to run at large in violation of statute, no liability for damage; *Fullowka v. Royal Oak Mines Inc.* (1996), 30 C.C.L.T. (2d) 21, at p. 39 (N.W.T.S.C.), mining safety

Sometimes the courts were more liberal in their use of legislation.[171] In *Paulsen v. C.P.R.*,[172] a section of the Railway Act required railways to erect and maintain four foot six inch fences on each side of the railway. "Such fences shall be suitable and sufficient to prevent cattle and other animals from getting on the railway." A child of 27 months was struck by a train operated by the defendant railway. The Manitoba Court of Appeal held that the absence of a fence was a cause of the child's injuries and the defendant was, accordingly, liable in damages. The defendant's argument that the section was passed "for the safe passage of trains" was not adopted, nor was the argument that infant trespassers were not intended to be protected by the statute.

One decision indicating how far courts will go in relying on legislation is *Stavast v. Ludwar*,[173] where the defendant's son left his automobile unlocked, with the engine running in the parking lot of a beer parlour while he went inside to talk to his parents. The car was stolen by an unknown person who, while driving it, collided with the plaintiff's vehicle, causing damage. Judge Gansner imposed liability upon the defendant for the damage so caused. He relied in part upon s. 182 of the Motor-vehicle Act of British Columbia which made it an offence for any person to leave a motor vehicle standing or parked without having stopped the engine, locked the ignition, removed the key and braked the vehicle. In his reasons for judgment the learned trial judge concluded:

> Obviously s. 182 was enacted with a view to reducing the opportunities for the theft of motor vehicles. An unattended vehicle left temporarily on a little-traveled country road with its motor running is unlikely to provide many opportunities for theft. A vehicle so left unattended on a city street is, of course, in graver danger of being stolen. It is rather difficult to conceive of a riskier place to leave a motor vehicle with its engine running than at night on the street 10 feet away from the door of a beer parlour.

His Honour felt that the violation of this statute was an "effective cause" of the loss and, therefore, imposed responsibility.

Where regulations under a wildlife act required a barrier to be built in order to protect the public from coming into contact with wild animals, liability was found in favour of a child who climbed over the barrier at a zoo and was bitten by a wolf. McKay J. stated that the barrier did not comply with the regulations which set a "minimum standard", although he felt that this would not "*ipso facto* create liability".[174]

Following *Saskatchewan Wheat Pool*, the use of penal statutes will probably be more frequent, even though their force will be less. Maybe there will be

---

statute not relevant to injury from explosion caused criminally during strike; revd in part (1996), 36 C.C.L.T. (2d) 58 (N.W.T. C.A.); leave to appeal refused [1997] 2 S.C.R. xvi.

[171] See *Ross v. Hartman* (1943), 139 F. 2d 14, liability for violation of ordinance requiring that car be locked. But *cf.*, *Anderson v. Thiesen* (1950), 231 Minn. 369, 43 N.W. 2d 272. See also *Dooley v. Cammell Laird & Co. Ltd.*, [1953] 1 Lloyd's Rep. 271 (Liverpool Assizes).

[172] (1963), 40 D.L.R. (2d) 761 (Man. C.A.).

[173] [1974] 5 W.W.R. 380 (B.C.) (Gansner Co. Ct. J.). See also *Hewson v. City of Red Deer* (1975), 63 D.L.R. (3d) 168 (Alta), liability without statute.

[174] *Maynes v. Galicz* (1975), 62 D.L.R. (3d) 385, at p. 393 (B.C.).

fewer examples of judicial narrow-sightedness in the application of the *Gorris v. Scott* rule. Since these principles are similar to the ordinary remoteness rules of negligence law, the courts should be willing to look at the legislation as long as the risks are reasonably anticipated as likely to follow from a violation.[175]

4. PLAINTIFF MUST BE AMONG GROUP STATUTE AIMS TO PROTECT

The plaintiff must be under the protective legislative umbrella. If the plaintiff is not one of those whom the criminal statute attempted to protect, the civil court will be loath to rely on the breach. Some courts have declared that they could not rely on a statute in a tort case unless it was designed to protect a particular class of people and not the general public.[176] Sometimes they posed the issue in terms of whether the legislature intended to create a public duty alone or a duty to individuals as well.[177] This has been criticized by Lord Justice Atkin, who commented in *Phillips v. Britannia Hygienic Laundry Co.*,[178] that "it would be strange if a less important duty which is owed to a section of the public may be enforced by action, while a more important duty owed to the public cannot". Therefore, bringing "himself within the benefit of the act", allows the plaintiff to rely on its breach. In other words, the plaintiff may do so if the plaintiff is someone whom the legislature sought to protect.[179]

Before *Saskatchewan Wheat Pool* there were cases in which the claimant was foreclosed from recovery on this basis. Industrial safety statutes have been held to protect workers only and not firefighters,[180] police officers,[181] or other visitors to the premises. Similarly, the rules of the road were not meant to protect people on the sidewalk,[182] pure food statutes were not supposed to aid customers other than the purchaser,[183] and safe building laws were to be of no avail to trespass-ers.[184] Because of this limitation, the courts have refused to allow a servant to recover damages from an uninsured owner, because the legislation was designed to protect third persons and not the employees of the owner.[185]

---

[175] See *Prosser and Keeton, op. cit. supra.*, n. 23, at p. 227.

[176] *Henzel v. Brussels Motors Ltd.*, [1973] 1 O.R. 339 (Co. Ct.).

[177] See *Prosser and Keeton, op. cit. supra*, n. 23, at p. 220.

[178] [1923] 2 K.B. 832, at pp. 841-42 (C.A.).

[179] See *Commerford v. Halifax School Commrs.*, [1950] 2 D.L.R. 207, at p. 212 (N.S.). See also *Monk v. Warbey*, [1935] 1 K.B. 75 (C.A.); *Ostash v. Sonnenberg* (1968), 67 D.L.R. (2d) 311 (Alta. C.A.).

[180] *Kelly v. Henry Muhs Co.* (1904), 71 N.J.L. 358, 59 Atl. 23; *Goodman v. New Plymouth Fire Board*, [1958] N.Z.L.R. 767.

[181] *Davy v. Greenlaw* (1975), 101 N.H. 134, 135 A. 2d 900, also different type of risk; *cf.*, *Parker v. Bernard* (1883), 135 Mass. 116, where wording of statute broader.

[182] *Westlund v. Iverson* (1922), 154 Minn. 52, 191 N.W. 253.

[183] *Square v. Model Farm Dairies*, [1939] 2 K.B. 365. See also *Read v. Croyden Corp.*, [1938] 4 All E.R. 631, only ratepayer could complain of bad water.

[184] *Flanagan v. Sanders* (1904), 138 Mich. 253, 101 N.W. 581.

[185] *Semtex Ltd. v. Gladstone*, [1954] 1 W.L.R. 945; *Gregory v. Ford*, [1951] 1 All E.R. 121.

Occasionally, the civil courts were generous in extending the scope of penal statutes to include any member of the public who may be injured by the prohibited conduct. This might be done where pure food laws,[186] or enactments which require labels on poison,[187] or forbid the sale of firearms to children are involved.[188] Similarly, construction safety legislation has been held to cover not only professional "constructors", who hire workers, but also amateurs who use their friends to do construction work.[189]

Following *Saskatchewan Wheat Pool* one might have hoped for a more liberal use of these statutes, since their effect now is only as some evidence of negligence, and not conclusive or even presumptive of negligence. The early indications, however, are to the contrary. In one case, the lack of a fire extinguisher contrary to a by-law was held not to be relevant to assist the owner of a vehicle which burned, rather than the owner of the premises which were meant to be protected.[190] In another, it was held that an Occupational Health and Safety Act was concerned only with the "protection of persons" not property, and, hence, irrelevant.[191]

F. Unresolved Issues

1. ARE OTHER PROCEDURAL EFFECTS POSSIBLE?

Although *Saskatchewan Wheat Pool* holds that violations of statute are to be evidence of negligence, it recognizes that "industrial legislation historically has enjoyed special consideration", leading to "absolute liability".[192] The court has clearly permitted that treatment to continue as an exception, even though it is hard to see how it will be of much use in the light of our extensive workers' compensation legislation in Canada.[193]

The court did not mention the other types of legislation which have been accorded significant weight by Canadian civil courts in the past. For example, breach of pure food legislation has led to negligence *per se* in the past.[194] Similarly, legislation dealing with dangerous activities has been afforded greater effect than ordinary legislation. For example, breach of laws regulating the

---

[186] *Meshbesher v. Channellene Oil* (1909), 107 Minn. 104, 119 N.W. 428.
[187] *Osborne v. McMasters* (1889), 40 Minn. 203, 41 N.W. 543.
[188] *Henningsen v. Markowitz* (1928), 230 N.Y.S. 313.
[189] *Unsworth v. Mogk* (1979), 27 O.R. (2d) 645.
[190] *Russel v. Mugford* (1985), 54 Nfld. & P.E.I.R. 26 (Nfld. S.C.) (Goodridge J.).
[191] See *James St. Hardware & Furniture Co. v. Spizziri, supra*, n. 53, at p. 651 (Krever J.); see also *Carleton Condo Corp. No. 11 v. Shenkman Corp.* (1985), 14 D.L.R. (4th) 571 (H.C.), unit owners or occupiers only get the benefit of statute, not defendant.
[192] *Supra*, n. 5, at p. 223.
[193] *Ryan v. Workmen's Compensation Bd. (Ont.), PPG Industries Canada Inc. and Tyaack* (1984), 6 O.A.C. 33 (Div. Ct.), no civil action allowed in worker's compensation situation.
[194] See *Curll v. Robin Hood Multifoods Ltd.* (1974), 56 D.L.R. (3d) 129 (N.S.); *Heimler v. Calvert Caterers Ltd.* (1975), 4 O.R. (2d) 667; affd 8 O.R. (2d) 1 (C.A.); see also in the U.S., *Doherty v. S.S. Kresge* (1938), 278 N.W. 437.

handling of gas[195] and aircraft traffic[196] have led to negligence *per se*. While there is much to be said for the continuation of this treatment for these kinds of statutes, it is unlikely that it will continue. It is more probable that, in theory, they will be used as evidence of negligence only, but that, in practice, courts and juries will find liability for their breach more frequently than they will for violations of other statutes, because the activities they regulate are more hazardous.

2. WHEN WILL A VIOLATION BE EXCUSED?

Although there is no longer any onus on a defendant who breaches a statute to furnish evidence of use of reasonable care, the defendant would be tactically unwise to remain mute when it is established there was a statutory violation. The mere fact of a legislative breach *may* be enough evidence for a court to hold a violator liable, even though it is at liberty to dismiss the case in such a situation. In *Saskatchewan Wheat Pool*, the defendant offered copious evidence of the great care it took in handling the grain, which influenced the court's decision. Similarly, violators in the future would be wise to offer whatever exculpatory evidence they have at their disposal. In all likelihood, if the breach was caused by an Act of God[197] or by some other unforeseeable event, there will be no liability. If, in breaching the statute, the violator substituted equally or more effective safety measures, for example, liability will probably be avoided.[198] Swerving to avoid a baby carriage when someone's brakes fail will probably continue to excuse a driver, in spite of a statutory violation.[199] It may not be enough, however, for violators merely to testify that they were unaware of the fact that they breached the statute, but if they reasonably believed they complied with the statute and have taken all reasonable steps to do so, they may be exonerated.[200]

In conclusion, although there are still come loose ends left, the law governing the use of statutes in the standard of care cases in negligence law has been reshaped rather well. The fictional hunt for legislative intention will no longer embarrass the Canadian courts. The formula — evidence of negligence — is sensible and workable, even if it does leave more discretion to the courts and even though it offers less protection for plaintiffs. All in all, the state of the Canadian law in this area is more satisfactory now than it has ever been.

---

[195] See *Ostash v. Sonnenberg* (1968), 67 D.L.R. (2d) 311 (Alta. C.A.); *Lemesurier v. Union Gas Co. of Canada Ltd.* (1975), 57 D.L.R. (3d) 344, at p. 350 (*per* Zuber J.).

[196] *Northern Helicopters Ltd. v. Vancouver Soaring Assn.* (1972), 31 D.L.R. (3d) 321 (B.C.).

[197] *Hall v. Toronto-Guelph Express*, [1929] 1 D.L.R. 375 (S.C.C.).

[198] *McCallum v. Tetroe* (1958), 25 W.W.R. 49 (Man. C.A.); *Tinling v. Bauch and Kutzy* (1951), 59 Man. R. 310.

[199] *Avalon Telephone Co. v. Vardy* (1961), 47 M.P.R. 126 (Nfld.).

[200] *Ibid.*, p. 215.

Chapter 8

Proof of Negligence

The segment of a negligence trial concerned with issues of law is usually less important and less time-consuming than the portion that deals with matters of fact. Every trial lawyer knows that, most frequently, law suits will flower or founder on the factual evidence assembled.

In Canada the issues of fact may be tried by a jury or by a judge alone. In Ontario and British Columbia civil jury trials are still relatively common, but in other provinces and throughout the Commonwealth they are become increasingly rare. A Canadian jury may be composed of six, seven, eight, nine or 12 members.[1] The judge presides over a jury trial, rules on the admissibility of the evidence, decides if there is enough evidence to be submitted to the jury, comments upon its strengths and weaknesses and, finally, instructs the jury on the law. Special verdict procedure is normally employed, whereby the jury answers a series of specific questions directed to it. Attacks have been made upon the civil jury system, but its survival, at least in the short run, seems assured.[2]

A. The Burden of Proof Generally

While a work such as this cannot deal at length with the law of evidence, some attention must be paid to the question of burden of proof, because there are times when a negligence case stands or falls on the simple question of who bears the onus of proof.[3] Ordinarily, the plaintiff must plead and prove negligence in order to succeed[4] and must convince the court or the jury on the balance of probabilities. If, at the end of the trial, the evidence is "evenly balanced", the

---

[1] See Laskin, *The British Tradition in Canadian Law* (1969), p. 45.

[2] Haines, "The Future of the Civil Jury" in *Studies in Canadian Tort Law* (1968). See also Joiner, *Civil Justice and the Jury* (1962); Devlin, *Trial by Jury* (1956).

[3] For example, *National Trust Co. v. Wong Aviation Ltd.*, [1969] S.C.R. 481.

[4] See *Prosser and Keeton on the Law of Torts*, 5th ed. (1984), pp. 235 *et seq.* Fleming, *The Law of Torts*, 9th ed. (1998), pp. 45 *et seq.* Morris, "Proof of Negligence" (1953), 47 N.W.L. Rev. 817. Proof of causation is also required, see *supra*, Chapter 4, and see *Snell v. Farrell*, [1990] 2 S.C.R. 311.

plaintiff will lose the case.[5] In other words, in contrast to the reasonable doubt standard in criminal cases, the plaintiff must establish by relevant evidence that it is more likely than not that the defendant was to blame for the plaintiff's injury. If the evidence shows only that the defendant *may* have been at fault, the plaintiff will fail. It is not enough, for example, to prove that a child was run over by a train,[6] or that a pedestrian was stuck by a car.[7] More than that is required, at least in the absence of a statutory provision to the contrary.[8]

Sometimes the burden of proof is shifted to the defendant. When this is done courts may elicit evidence from a person who would not normally testify. Liability may also be expanded without the necessity of dramatic breaks with the past. Thus, a bailee must ordinarily explain what became of goods if unable to return them.[9] By statute, a motor vehicle driver must disprove negligence if the driver collides with a pedestrian or other non-vehicular object.[10] Similarly, where there is evidence that one or other or both of two motorists are responsible for a car crash, liability will be split between them equally unless they exonerate themselves.[11] There are also some historical holdovers which have evinced amazing vitality. For example, a person who injures someone as a result of a direct invasion,[12] or a dangerous product,[13] is required to disprove negligence. And lastly, there was, until recently, the occult doctrine of *res ipsa loquitur*, which occasionally shifted the burden of proof from the plaintiff's shoulders.[14] These exceptions are becoming so numerous that one might conclude that a new principle is emerging to the effect that the defendant, not the plaintiff, now usually bears the burden of proof, save for exceptional situations. Such a development would not be inconsistent with the forces at work within modern negligence law.

B. Inferring Negligence: The "Expired" Maxim of *Res Ipsa Loquitur*

Assisting plaintiffs in proving negligence for more than a century was once the mysterious doctrine of *res ipsa loquitur*,[15] erected upon a chance remark in Latin by

---

5   *Saillant v. Smith* (1973), 33 D.L.R. (3d) 61, at p. 63 (*per* Jessup J.A.).
6   *Richardson v. C.N.R.* (1926), 60 O.L.R. 296 (C.A.); *Wakelin v. The London and South Western Ry. Co.* (1886), 12 App. Cas. 41 (H.L.).
7   *Luxton v. Vines* (1952), 85 C.L.R. 352.
8   Highway Traffic Act, R.S.O. 1990, c. H-8, s. 193.
9   *Pratt v. Waddington* (1911), 23 O.L.R. 178 (C.A.), but, *cf.*, *Wong Aviation, supra*, n. 3.
10   *Supra*, n. 8. See also Phelan, "Onus Under the Highway Traffic Act", *Special Lectures of the Law Society of Upper Canada* (1955), at p. 215.
11   See Section E, *infra*.
12   See Section G, *infra*.
13   *Ives v. Clare Brothers Ltd.*, [1971] 1 O.R. 417.
14   Section D.1.c, *infra*.
15   Wright, "*Res Ipsa Loquitur*" in Linden (ed.), *Studies in Canadian Tort Law* (1968) p. 41; Prosser, "*Res Ipsa Loquitur* in California" (1949), 37 Calif. L. Rev. 183, 223; Fridman, "The Myth of *Res Ipsa Loquitur*" (1954), 10 U. of T.L.J. 233; Jaffe, "*Res Ipsa Loquitur* Vindicated"

a Judge during the argument of the case of *Byrne v. Boadle*.[16] Now "expired" in Canada, this "doctrine" or "maxim" or "principle", as it was sometimes described, allowed the plaintiffs to overcome, at least initially, the burden of proof that rested upon them, where there was little or no specific proof of negligence. The courts, using *res ipsa*, accepted, at least as some circumstantial evidence of negligence, proof that the accident would not occur in the absence of negligence and that the negligence was likely attributed to the defendant. There was a great deal of confusion surrounding *res ipsa,* especially about its procedural effect. Critics urged that it be relegated to the ash heap and recently the Supreme Court of Canada responded by doing just that in *Fontaine v. British Columbia (Official Administrator)*.[17] Basing himself squarely on Dean Wright,[18] his former professor, and recognizing the criticisms of the authors, Mr. Justice Major unequivocally declared:

> [T]he law would be better served if the maxim was treated as expired and no longer used as a separate component in negligence actions. After all, it was nothing more than an attempt to deal with circumstantial evidence. That evidence is more sensibly dealt with by the trier of fact, who should weigh the circumstantial evidence with the direct evidence, if any, to determine whether the plaintiff has established on a balance of probabilities a *prima facie* case of negligence against the defendant. Once the plaintiff has done so, the defendant must present evidence negating that of the plaintiff or necessarily the plaintiff will succeed."[19]

As for the disposition of the case before the Court, a highway accident in which a truck ran off the road without any apparent explanation killing its two occupants, the trial judge's decision to dismiss the case was affirmed, as the evidence produced at the trial was "neutral", that is, not enough "circumstantial evidence from which it could be inferred that the accident was caused by negligence attributable to [the defendant]."[20] This result was no different than many earlier decisions which employed *res ipsa* theory. The position, therefore, now is precisely as Dean Wright had proposed in his great article:[21]

> What is required is a situation where the happening of the accident itself will afford the basis from which an inference can be drawn as a matter of ordinary experience that there was negligence and that the defendant was the person who was negligent.

It should also be mentioned that long ago, Justice Idington, in *Canadian Northern Railway Co. v. Horner*,[22] had opined that *res ipsa loquitur* was "nothing but a concise expression of common sense applied to circumstantial evidence", but it took nearly eight decades for his view to finally prevail.

(1951), 1 Buffalo L. Rev. 1; Paton, *"Res Ipsa Loquitur"* (1936), 14 Can. Bar Rev. 480; Schiff, "A *Res Ipsa Loquitur* Nutshell" (1976), 26 U.T.L.J. 451.

[16] (1863), 2 H. & C. 722, 159 E.R. 299 (Ex.).

[17] [1998] 1 S.C.R. 424, 156 D.L.R. (4th) 577, [1998] 7 W.W.R. 25, 223 N.R. 161.

[18] Wright, *supra*, n. 15.

[19] *Fontaine, supra,* n. 17, at p. 435 S.C.R.

[20] *Ibid.*, at p. 435 S.C.R.

[21] *Supra*, n. 15, at p. 46.

[22] (1921), 61 S.C.R. 547, at p. 553, 58 D.L.R. 154, [1921] 1 W.W.R. 969.

C. When Negligence May Be Inferred

1. ACCIDENTS GIVING RISE TO AN INFERENCE OF NEGLIGENCE

While the language of *res ipsa* is no longer to be used, the fact situations that gave rise to *res ipsa* in the past may offer some aid to courts about when negligence may be inferred.[23]

If, in the ordinary course of events, an accident would not occur in the absence of negligence, a court might infer negligence. It is not always apparent, however, what the ordinary experience of mankind is. It was because of lack of popular appreciation of what is abnormal, that *res ipsa loquitur* was for a time held to be inapplicable to medical malpractice.[24] However, it is now clear that evidence may be introduced to enlarge the court's understanding of what is normal or abnormal in various situations. In *Interlake Tissue Mills v. Salmon and Beckett*,[25] for example, it was held to be permissible to lead expert evidence to the effect that with reasonable care the roller in question could have been moved without damaging the copper screen.

a) Falling Objects

Following *Byrne v. Boadle*, a number of cases dealing with falling objects led to findings of negligence. A lump of coal falling off a railway locomotive,[26] or off a derrick being unloaded,[27] a tractor part falling while being transported by truck,[28] a roof blowing off and hitting a parked car,[29] and bags of sugar dropping on a plaintiff,[30] were all incidents in which negligence was indicated. Similarly, where some Christmas decorations fell on a pedestrian,[31] where a mirror

---

[23]   Irvine, *The Law of Torts* (2000) at p. 50, "many of the old res ipsa loquitur cases will continue to be a reliable guide in the use of circumstantial evidence."

[24]   *Clark v. Wansborough*, [1940] O.W.N. 67, at p. 72, overruled in *Nesbitt v. Holt*, [1953] S.C.R. 143; affg [1951] O.R. 601 (C.A.).

[25]   [1948] O.R. 950, [1949] 1 D.L.R. 207 (C.A.). Not to lead such evidence may be fatal, as in *Hobson v. Munkley* (1976), 1 C.C.L.T. 163, where medical negligence not inferred on evidence of damaged ureter (*per* Krever J.). See annotation by Ellen Jacobs.

[26]   *O'Brien v. Michigan Central Ry.* (1909), 19 O.L.R. 345 (C.A.).

[27]   *Bisnaw v. Shields* (1904), 7 O.L.R. 210 (C.A.). See also *Smith v. Baker & Sons*, [1891] A.C. 325, stone fell from crane.

[28]   *Proctor & Gamble Co. v. Cooper's Crane Rental*, [1973] 2 O.R. 124 (C.A.).

[29]   *Legacy v. Chaleur Country Club Ltd.* (1974), 53 D.L.R. (3d) 725 (N.B.C.A.), no liability, though, because independent contractor.

[30]   *Scott v. London Dock Co.* (1865), 3 H. & C. 596, 159 E.R. 665.

[31]   *Saccardo v. Hamilton*, [1971] 2 O.R. 479, at p. 490 (*per* Osler J.). "Things properly secured do not simply fall of their own weight in the absence of negligence or intervention by some third person."

standing against a wall in a department store fell on a child,[32] and where some baskets and tinned goods dropped on a customer in a supermarket,[33] negligence was inferred. If an elevator,[34] or scaffolding,[35] descends unexpectedly, negligence may be implied. When water leaked through the plaintiff's ceiling from the defendant's premises damaging some goods,[36] when some acid used to clean windows seeped into the plaintiff's show window,[37] and when some plaster fell on a plaintiff,[38] negligence was inferred. A pattern which flew out of a lathe,[39] a piece of wood which was thrown off a power saw,[40] some yoghurt which fell on the floor of a supermarket,[41] and a park bench which broke,[42] were also found to support an inference of lack of due care.

b) Explosions

Explosions of various kinds may bespeak negligence. In *Corsini v. City of Hamilton*,[43] a child was injured when an underground explosion blew a heavy metal cover into the air and exposed him to flames from an underground chamber, in addition to the injuries from the original force of the explosion. Mr. Justice Middleton imposed liability and rejected the evidence of proper construction of the chamber. A similar result was obtained when an explosion occurred in a sewer.[44] In *Kirk v. McLaughlin Coal & Supplies Ltd.*,[45] an oil furnace exploded causing damage to the home of the plaintiffs, who could not establish its cause. Mr. Justice Evans asserted simply that "it is common knowledge that oil furnaces do not normally explode". Contrasting with this case is *Clayton v. J.N.Z. Investments, Ltd.*,[46] where a pipe leading to a radiator in the plaintiff's apartment burst. Chief Justice Gale refused to infer negligence

---

[32] *Sangster v. T. Eaton Co.* (1894), 25 O.R. 78; affd (1895), 24 S.C.R. 708, new trial ordered. *Scott* cited, but *res ipsa* not mentioned by name; *Bennett v. Chemical Construction (G.B.) Ltd.*, [1971] 3 All E.R. 822 (C.A.), panels stacked against wall toppled over.

[33] *Anderson v. Great Atlantic and Pacific Tea Co.*, [1952] O.W.N. 323 (C.A.).

[34] *Neal v. T. Eaton Co.*, [1933] O.R. 573 (C.A.). See also *Westenfelder v. Hobbs Mfg. Co.* (1925), 57 O.L.R. 31 (C.A.), crate falling over treated as *res ipsa* case, but jury exonerated defendant.

[35] *Michaud v. Edwards*, [1920] 3 W.W.R. 186 (Sask. C.A.), court did not mention *res ipsa*.

[36] *Kullberg's Furniture Ltd. v. Flin Flon Hotel Co.* (1958), 26 W.W.R. 721 (Man. C.A.).

[37] *Capital Building Cleaners v. Slater-Sherwood* (1930), 65 O.L.R. 364 (C.A.).

[38] *Sereduik v. Posner*, [1928] 1 W.W.R. 258 (Man. C.A.). See also *Roberts v. Mitchell* (1894), 21 O.A.R. 433 (C.A.), overhanging cornice fell.

[39] *McDonnell v. Alexander Fleck Ltd.* (1908), 12 O.W.R. 84, defendant met onus.

[40] *Serota v. Belway*, [1919] 2 W.W.R. 267; affd [1919] 2 W.W.R. 904 (Sask. C.A.).

[41] *Ward v. Tesco Stores Ltd.*, [1976] 1 All E.R. 219 (C.A.).

[42] *McPhee v. City of Toronto* (1915), 9 O.W.N. 150 (C.A.), *res ipsa* not mentioned.

[43] [1931] O.R. 598 (C.A.).

[44] *Rideau Lawn Tennis Club v. Ottawa*, [1936] O.W.N. 347 (C.A.). See also *R. v. Consumers' Gas Co.*, [1926] Ex. C.R. 137; affd [1926] S.C.R. 709; *Toronto Ry. Co. v. Fleming* (1913), 47 S.C.R. 612, controller of electric car exploded. *Cf.*, *Collier v. City of Hamilton* (1914), 32 O.L.R. 214 (C.A.); *Wright v. Mitchell* (1919), 17 O.W.N. 290, acetylene gas explosion not *res ipsa loquitur*.

[45] (1967), 66 D.L.R. (2d) 321, at p. 322 (Ont. C.A.).

[46] (1968), 1 D.L.R. (3d) 440, at p. 441 (C.A.).

because the court could not bring itself "to agree that the mere statement of the plaintiff to the effect that the pipe had burst constitutes evidence of negligence on the part of the defendants. Any number of causes might have been the underlying reason for the failure of the pipe . . . ."

In the same vein, a tire which explodes while being changed,[47] and a glass door which shatters inexplicably,[48] are cases where an inference may be drawn.

c) Traffic and Ground Transportation

Transportation accidents sometimes allow an inference of negligence to be made. If a strap on a streetcar breaks while being held by the plaintiff,[49] and if a pedestrian is run over in broad daylight by a streetcar,[50] or a bicycle,[51] the circumstances "call rather loudly . . . for justification or excuse" by the defendant. A horse running away and overturning the sleigh it is pulling,[52] and an automobile skidding,[53] turning over as a result of sudden braking,[54] or moving forward unexpectedly while the defendant is in the driver's seat,[55] are all incidents in which negligence may be inferred.

However, the mere fact that the door of a truck,[56] or a taxi,[57] opens unexpectedly causing the plaintiff to fall out, does not speak of negligence. Nor can one infer negligence when a child is found beside a railway track with a severed leg,[58] when someone suffering from arteriosclerosis falls out of a berth on a train,[59] or when a child who puts his head out a train window is killed when hit by a pole.[60]

While most ordinary highway accidents do not permit an inference of negligence, some of the following might: where a car inexplicably leaves the road,[61] or

---

[47] *Westlake v. Smith Transport Ltd.* (1973), 2 O.R. (2d) 258; *cf., Lappa v. Firestone Tire & Rubber Co. of Canada Ltd.* (1964), 46 D.L.R. (2d) 506 (Sask. C.A.).

[48] *Pearson v. Fairview Corp.* (1975), 55 D.L.R. (3d) 522 (Man.).

[49] *Brawley v. Toronto Railway Co.* (1919), 46 O.L.R. 31, 49 D.L.R. 452.

[50] *Forwood v. City of Toronto* (1892), 22 O.R. 351 (C.A.).

[51] *Woolman v. Cummer* (1912), 4 O.W.N. 371, at p. 372 (C.A.).

[52] *Crawford v. Upper* (1889), 16 O.A.R. 440 (C.A.).

[53] *Gauthier & Co. v. R.*, [1945] S.C.R. 143, statutory violation and *res ipsa* jumbled up, but explanation accepted.

[54] *Andanoff v. Smith and Nadeff*, [1935] O.W.N. 415 (C.A.).

[55] *Lawson v. Watts* (1957), 7 D.L.R. (2d) 758 (B.C.); *C & S Tire Service v. R.* (1972), 29 D.L.R. (3d) 492 (Fed. Ct.), runaway car.

[56] *Gallagher v. Green*, [1958] O.W.N. 442; affd (1959), 19 D.L.R. (2d) 490.

[57] *Petrie v. Speers Taxi Co.*, [1952] O.R. 731 (C.A.).

[58] *Richardson v. C.N.R.* (1926), 60 O.L.R. 296 (C.A.).

[59] *Weisbrod v. C.N.R.* (1932), 41 O.W.N. 143.

[60] *Hadden v. Canadian National Electric Rys.* (1930), 39 O.W.N. 245, 37 C.R.C. 410. See also *Johnson v. Toronto Transit Commission*, [1936] O.W.N. 192, allegation that arm resting on sill of streetcar window found to be pure conjecture.

[61] *Wedley v. Hunchak* (1967), 62 W.W.R. 360 (B.C.); *Hayduk v. Pidoborozny* (1971), 19 D.L.R. (3d) 160; revd on other grounds, [1972] S.C.R. 879.

runs into a bridge abutment,[62] or suddenly begins to gyrate wildly,[63] or where a horse runs into a motor vehicle,[64] or a streetcar is derailed,[65] or where a train runs into a standing car.[66] In *Canadian Northern Railway Co. v. Horner*,[67] for example, a worker was killed when a train was derailed because of an open switch. The attempt of the defendant to place the blame on a third person angered Mr. Justice Idington because, in his view, no one had searched for the criminal nor did anyone really believe that there was one. His Lordship commented sarcastically that it was "only looked on as fit to ask judges and juries to accept it".[68] Mr. Justice Anglin merely asserted that the switch would not be unlocked unless a servant of the railway had neglected a duty.[69]

d) Air Crashes

An inference of negligence is often made in air crash cases. In *Malone v. Trans-Canada Airlines*,[70] an aeroplane, inexplicably, crashed after a precipitous descent from 800-1,000 feet altitude. Robertson C.J.O. observed that air travel was a "common means of transport" and therefore, "with experienced and careful pilots and proper equipment, a passenger has the right to expect that he will be carried safely to his destination".[71] There was no indication of bad weather (though it was wintry and windy), the motor was normal, and there was no evidence of ice on the wings.[72] The possible explanations of latent defect, metal fatigue, physical collapse of the pilot and atmospheric conditions were rejected, but the jury did think the accident could have been caused by flying too low. When a propeller broke after take-off because of internal weakness, and the plaintiff was injured in the crash, negligence was inferred.[73] Similarly, when a plane crash results from a pilot's heart attack, where the pilot was aware of the heart problem,[74] an inference was drawn.

There are conflicting cases. In *National Trust Co. Ltd. v. Wong Aviation Ltd.*,[75] the defendant rented an aeroplane, flew it off and was never seen again.

---

62 *Doxtator v. Burch*, [1972] 1 O.R. 321; affd [1972] 3 O.R. 806 (C.A.); affd (1973), 41 D.L.R. (3d) 768.
63 *Jackson v. Millar*, [1976] 1 S.C.R. 225.
64 *Johnson v. Schmon*, [1943] O.W.N. 673.
65 *Alliance Insurance Co. v. Winnipeg Electric Ry.*, [1921] 2 W.W.R. 816 (Man. C.A.).
66 *Meenie v. Tillsonburg, Lake Erie & Pacific Ry.* (1905), 6 O.W.R. 955 (C.A.).
67 (1921), 61 S.C.R. 547.
68 *Ibid.*, at p. 551.
69 *Ibid.*, at p. 558. See also *Pyne v. C.P.R.*, [1919] 3 W.W.R. 125 (P.C.); *Comber v. Toronto Ry.* (1922), 22 O.W.N. 591 (C.A.).
70 [1942] O.R. 453 (C.A.). See "Comment" (1942), 20 Can. Bar Rev. 705.
71 *Ibid.*, at p. 458.
72 *Ibid.*, at p. 459.
73 *Nystedt v. Wings Ltd.*, [1942] 3 W.W.R. 39 (Man.). See also *Galer v.Wings Ltd.*, [1939] 1 D.L.R. 13; *Fosbroke-Hobbes v. Airwork Ltd.*, [1937] 1 All E.R. 108; *Zerka v. Lau-Goma Airways Ltd.*, [1960] O.W.N. 166 (C.A.).
74 *Polinski v. Griffin*, [1973] 3 O.R. 353 (C.A.).
75 [1969] S.C.R. 481, case turns primarily on bailment law.

An action against his estate was dismissed on the ground, *inter alia*, that "weather conditions . . . were such as to support an inference that air turbulence, carburetor icing or loss of vision with reference to the ground might well have caused the loss of the aircraft without any negligence on [the defendant's] part".[76] In contrast with the *Malone* case, the claimant in this case failed to eliminate these other potential causes of the accident. In *McDonald Aviation Co. Ltd. v. Queen Charlotte Airlines Ltd.*,[77] a rented plane was destroyed in a crash as a result of some unknown cause. An action for part of the value of the plane, *inter alia*, was dismissed by the court. Robertson J.A., for the majority, concluded that the cause of the crash was unknown.[78] The dissent of Mr. Justice O'Halloran is much preferred.[79] He asserted that planes are not normally destroyed in ordinary flight. Air crashes are no longer caused by a "mysterious, unfathomable or improbable agency. . . . If planes are properly serviced and properly flown then in the absence of evidence of the cause of the accident there is no reason why an accident should occur if negligence is not present."

e) Fires

Unexplained fires can give rise to an inference, as in cases where a truck,[80] a television set,[81] a juke box,[82] or a furnace,[83] inexplicably burst into flame. In *United Motors Service Inc. v. Hutson*,[84] an inference was drawn when a fire broke out as the defendant cleaned a concrete garage floor with gasoline. In *Shell Oil Co. v. White Motor Co.*,[85] the owner of a service station recovered for damages to its building as a result of a fire started by a mechanic using an oxyacetylene torch. Although negligence was clearly proven, the court relied on *res ipsa loquitur* as an alternative rationale. Where someone removed a three-quarters full gas tank from a car and started a fire,[86] where a fire broke out as a

---

[76] *Ibid.*, at p. 490 (*per* Ritchie J.).

[77] (1951), 3 W.W.R. (N.S.) 385, [1952] 1 D.L.R. 291 (B.C.C.A.). See also *Tataryn v. Cooperative Trust Co.* (1974), 54 D.L.R. (3d) 154 (Sask.), where passengers may have been responsible for crash.

[78] *Ibid.*, at p. 402.

[79] *Ibid.*, at p. 393.

[80] *Chabot v. Ford Motor Co.* (1982), 22 C.C.L.T. 185 (Ont. H.C.).

[81] *Wylie v. R.C.A. et al.* (1973), 5 Nfld. & P.E.I.R. 147; *contra, MacLachlin and Mitchell Homes v. Frank's Rentals* (1979), 106 D.L.R. (3d) 245 (Alta. C.A.); *Gladney v. Simpson-Sears* (1975), 10 Nfld. & P.E.I.R. 424 (P.E.I.), not clear fire originated in T.V. set.

[82] *Tsakiris v. Universal Music Manitoba (1971) Ltd.*, [1974] 3 W.W.R. 3 (Man.) (*per* Wright J.).

[83] *Carter v. Steelgas Utilities Ltd.* (1974), 52 D.L.R. (3d) 377 (Man. C.A.); *cf., Katterback v. Setrakov*, [1971] 2 W.W.R. 308 (Sask. C.A.), fire in house not *res ipsa* case.

[84] [1937] S.C.R. 294. But *cf., Katterback v. Setrakov, supra,* n. 83, *res ipsa* not applied where an unexplained fire occurred in a dwelling which was left unattended.

[85] [1957] O.W.N. 229, 8 D.L.R. (2d) 753.

[86] *Canadian Imperial Bank of Commerce v. Whiteside* (1968), 70 D.L.R. (2d) 229; affd 2 D.L.R. (3d) 611 (Man. C.A.). *Cf., Johnson v. Conrow and Preuss* (1951), 2 W.W.R. (N.S.) 230 (Alta.), truck destroyed by fire in garage, explanation accepted.

result of welding activity,[87] and where a child was burned by a propane gas stove which emitted a flame when he turned it on,[88] negligence was inferred. In *Hutterly v. Imperial Oil Co. Ltd. and Calder*,[89] a car caught fire while being repaired in the defendant's service station. The court imposed liability on the ground that automobiles do not catch fire while being repaired or while having their gas drained unless somebody is negligent. It is not enough for the defendant to point out other *possible* explanations. For example, it is not enough to say that it might have been caused by lightning.

Where, however, a fire started in the gas tank of a motorcycle six years after it was purchased, no negligence was inferred because the "damage could have arisen by factors equally consistent with no negligence as with negligence on the part of the defendants".[90]

f) Defective Products

Defects in products may lead to inferences of negligence as where broken glass is found in bread,[91] or in a Coke bottle,[92] where chlorine is discovered in a beer bottle,[93] or a stone in a bun.[94] If underwear contains a chemical that causes dermatitis,[95] or someone is injured when a ladder gives way,[96] or if someone is burned during a permanent wave hair treatment,[97] it speaks of negligence. Where, on the other hand, an old engine,[98] or a set of power brakes,[99] are repaired by the defendant and break down after a few months, an inference was not permissible.

---

[87] *Erison v. Higgins* (1974), 4 O.R. (2d) 631 (C.A.).

[88] *Greschuk v. Kolodychuk* (1959), 27 W.W.R. 157 (Alta. C.A.).

[89] [1956] O.W.N. 681 (*per* Ferguson J.); *contra, Pleasant Valley Motel (1972) Ltd. v. Lepage* (1978), 94 D.L.R. (3d) 73, no liability for unexplained fire which started in truck and burned motel. *Paquette v. Labelle* (1981), 33 O.R. (2d) 425 (C.A.), fire not started in a "thing", therefore, not *res ipsa*.

[90] See *Baker v. Suzuki Motor Co.* (1993), 17 C.C.L.T. (2d) 241, at p. 265 (Alta. Q.B.) (*per* Bielby J.).

[91] *Arendale v. Canada Bread Co.*, [1941] O.W.N. 69 (C.A.). See *infra*, Section D. 3.

[92] *Zeppa v. Coca-Cola Ltd.*, [1955] O.R. 855, [1955] 5 D.L.R. 187 (C.A.).

[93] *Varga v. John Labatt Ltd.*, [1956] O.R. 1007.

[94] *Chaproniere v. Mason* (1905), 21 T.L.R. 633 (C.A.).

[95] *Grant v. Australian Knitting Mills*, [1936] A.C. 85.

[96] *McHugh v. Reynolds Extrusion Co.* (1974), 7 O.R. (2d) 336, but no liability because of explanation.

[97] *David Spencer Ltd. v. Field*, [1939] S.C.R. 36.

[98] *Scott-D'Amboisie Construction Co. v. Reo Motors*, [1958] O.R. 711 (C.A.).

[99] *Phillips v. Ford Motor Co.*, [1971] 2 O.R. 637 (C.A.), manufacturers not liable either, because of "too great a lapse of time".

g) Medical Cases

Medical mishaps occasionally permit inferences of negligence. When a sponge
was left behind in a patient's windpipe by a dental surgeon,[100] when a mishap
occurred during anaesthesia,[101] and when a three-year-old was burned by steam
which escaped from an inhalator in a hospital,[102] negligence was inferred. So too,
an inference is allowed where a patient is hospitalized for one condition and
ends up suffering from an entirely different one[103] or where a new anaesthetic
procedure goes wrong in circumstances where "in the ordinary course of things
it would probably not have occurred" if the anaesthetist had exercised due
care.[104]

In the past, Canadian courts used caution, however, in their application of *res
ipsa* in medical mishap situations, in order to avoid placing too heavy a burden
on the medical profession.[105] Thus, where a spinal anaesthetic caused some
paralysis of the patient's legs, Andrews J. refused to invoke *res ipsa* and
explained:[106]

> The human body is not a container filled with a material whose performance can be predicta-
> bly charted and analysed. It cannot be equated with a box of chewing tobacco or a soft drink.
> Thus, while permissible inferences may be drawn as to the normal behaviour of these types
> of commodities the same kind of reasoning does not necessarily apply to a human being. Be-
> cause of this medical science has not yet reached the stage where the law ought to presume
> that a patient must come out of an operation as well or better than he went into it. From my
> interpretation of the medical evidence the kind of injury suffered by the plaintiff could have
> occurred without negligence on anyone's part. Since I cannot infer there was negligence on
> the part of the defendant doctors the maxim of *res ipsa loquitur* does not apply.

Similarly, where the patient's ureter was damaged during an operation to
remove an ovary, Mr. Justice Krever refused to infer negligence since it could
not be said "as a matter of common experience" that this demonstrated the
failure to use reasonable care.[107] Further, a sodium pentathol injection that leaked
into surrounding tissue,[108] a broken jaw suffered during a wisdom tooth

---

[100] *Holt v. Nesbitt*, [1951] O.R. 601 (C.A.); affd [1953] 1 S.C.R. 143. See also *Mahon v Osborne*,
       [1939] 2 K.B. 14 (C.A.), swab in abdomen; *Taylor v. Gray*, [1937] 4 D.L.R. 123 (N.B.C.A.),
       forceps left in abdomen. *Cf.*, *Hutchinson et al. v. Robert*, [1935] O.W.N. 315 (C.A.).

[101] *Martel v. Hotel-Dieu St. Vallier*, [1969] S.C.R. 745; *Villeneuve v. Sisters of St. Joseph*, [1971] 2
       O.R. 593; revd in part by [1972] 2 O.R. 119, which was revd in part by (1974), 47 D.L.R. (3d)
       391; *cf.*, *Hughston v. Jost*, [1943] 1 D.L.R. 402.

[102] *Harkies v. Lord Dufferin Hospital* (1931), 66 O.L.R. 572 (*per* Raney J.).

[103] *Rietze v. Bruser (No. 2)*, [1979] 1 W.W.R. 31 (*per* Hewak J.), Paget's disease treatment, patient
       gets Volkmann's contracture; *Eady v. Tenderenda*, [1975] 2 S.C.R. 599, facial paralysis.

[104] *Holmes v. London Hospital Trustee Bd.* (1977), 5 C.C.L.T. 1, at p. 18 (*per* Robins J.).

[105] *Wilcox v. Cavan* (1975), 50 D.L.R. (3d) 687 (S.C.C.) (*per* Ritchie J).

[106] *Girard v. Royal Columbian Hospital* (1976), 66 D.L.R. (3d) 676, at p. 691.

[107] *Hobson v. Munkley* (1976), 1 C.C.L.T. 163, at p. 175, criticized by Teplitsky and Weisstub
       (1978), 56 Can. Bar Rev. 122. See generally Picard, *Legal Liability of Doctors and Hospitals in
       Canada*, 2nd ed. (1984), p. 260.

[108] *Hughston v. Jost*, [1943] 1 D.L.R. 402. *Cf.*, *Villeneuve v. Sisters of St. Joseph*, [1971] 2 O.R.
       593; vard [1972] 2 O.R. 119 (C.A.); which was revd in part by (1974), 47 D.L.R. (3d) 391,

extraction,[109] and disc surgery that caused arterial damage and death[110] did not trigger an inference.

h) Other Situations

Other assorted situations can give rise to an inference. An eight-year-old boy who slipped on the sidewalk and fell on an exposed electric wire which had come loose in a storm got the advantage of an inference.[111] This was so even though the wire fell at approximately 6:20 p.m. and the boy was injured at 7:00 p.m. A power shovel which digs under a road and cuts a telephone wire can speak of negligence.[112] Where some workers damaged a screen on a machine as they were moving a roller, an inference was found.[113] Since a stirrup on a riding horse should not come loose, if properly attached, this "calls for an explanation" if this occurs.[114]

i) Inference Not Drawn

Many accidents offer no hint of negligence. For example, if a three-year-old child cuts her leg while descending an escalator, this does not signal negligence.[115] Mr. Justice McGillivray stated: "Little girls, like others, can hurt their legs on stairs that do not move as well as on stairs that do." Similarly, if an airplane disappears, explanations other than negligence are possible.[116] A chain that breaks,[117] and a derrick that falls,[118] do not necessarily speak of negligence.

j) Inference of Gross Negligence

Res ipsa loquitur was employed to permit an inference of gross negligence, and there is no reason to think that such an inference would not continue to be drawn without the use of *res ipsa*. In *Walker v. Coates*,[119] a Volkswagen in which the plaintiff was a guest passenger veered across the centre of the road at a high rate of speed and collided with a road sign, killing the driver and injuring the plaintiff. Mr. Justice Ritchie declared:

---

liability where pentathol injection caused loss of arm. See also *Martel v. Hotel-Dieu St. Vallier*, [1969] S.C.R. 745, liability of anaesthetist.

[109] *Fish v. Kapur*, [1948] 2 All E.R. 176.

[110] *Kapur v. Marshall* (1978), 4 C.C.L.T. 204 (Ont. C.A.).

[111] *Ottawa Electric Co. v. Crepin*, [1931] S.C.R. 407 (*per* Newcombe J.); affg (1930), 66 O.L.R. 409 (C.A.).

[112] *Bell Telephone Co. v. I. B. Purcell Ltd.*, [1962] O.W.N. 184 (Co. Ct.).

[113] *Interlake Tissue Mills Co. v. Salmon and Beckett*, [1948] O.R. 950, [1949] 1 D.L.R. 207 (C.A.).

[114] *M. v. Sinclair* (1980), 15 C.C.L.T. 57 (*per* Lerner J.).

[115] *Richer v. A.J. Freiman Ltd.*, [1965] 2 O.R. 750, at p. 753 (C.A.). Evidence of reasonable care in any event.

[116] *National Trust Co. Ltd. v. Wong Aviation Ltd.*, *supra*, n. 75.

[117] *Haywood v. Hamilton Bridge Works Co.* (1914), 7 O.W.N. 231.

[118] *Brotherson v. Corry* (1902), 1 O.W.R. 34 (C.A.).

[119] [1968] S.C.R. 599.

If the rule of *res ipsa loquitur* is accepted in cases where proof of "negligence" is in issue, I can see no logical reason why it should not apply with equal force when the issue is whether or not there was "very great negligence" provided, of course, that the facts of themselves afford "reasonable evidence, in the absence of explanation by the defendant, that the accident arose" as a result of "a very marked departure from the standards" [of the reasonable person].

This case has been followed consistently by Canadian courts which have inferred gross negligence where vehicles have inexplicably left the road,[120] run into a bridge abutment,[121] or begun to gyrate wildly.[122]

k) Inference of Contributory Negligence

Res ipsa was held to provide evidence of negligence, even where there was proof of contributory negligence by the plaintiff. In *Westlake v. Smith Transport Ltd.*,[123] a tire on a truck exploded while an attempt was being made to remove it for repairs. Evidence that the plaintiff was negligent in failing to protect himself was held not to have constituted an explanation consistent with no negligence on the part of the defendant, but only to have demonstrated contributory negligence by the plaintiff. Mr. Justice Lieff held the defendant 65 per cent at fault, and the plaintiff 35 per cent. This type of conclusion would be permissible without reliance on *res ipsa*.

2. NEGLIGENCE ATTRIBUTED TO DEFENDANT

Before an inference can be drawn, the accident must not only speak of negligence, but the negligence must be attributed to the defendant. In other words, the plaintiff must prove that the defendant was responsible for the accident. Hopefully the language of "control", used in *res ipsa* cases, will be abandoned in the years ahead. If the plaintiff's evidence points the finger at two or more possible culprits, instead of one alone, the plaintiff will usually fail.[124] If it is shown that a cigarette of one of two hotel guests caused a fire, there can be no liability.[125] Similarly, if the negligence could be equally the plaintiff's or the defendant's, any inference of responsibility is inappropriate.[126] The ordinary two-car collision

---

[120] *Tucker v. Latt*, [1972] 2 O.R. 409 (*per* Keith J.), motorcycle leaves road.

[121] *Doxtator v. Burch*, [1972] 1 O.R. 321; affd [1972] 3 O.R. 806 (C.A.); affd (1973), 41 D.L.R. (3d) 768.

[122] *Jackson v. Millar*, [1976] 2 S.C.R. 225. See also *Van der Zouwen v. Koziak* (1971), 25 D.L.R. (3d) 354 (Alta. C.A.); *Mabey v. Robertson* (1969), 8 D.L.R. (3d) 84 (Alta.).

[123] (1973), 2 O.R. 258 (*per* Lieff J.).

[124] But see, *infra*, Section E. Particular Exceptions to the Need to Isolate the Defendant.

[125] *Valleyview Hotel Ltd. v. Montreal Trust Co.* (1985), 33 C.C.L.T. 282 (Sask. C.A.) (*per* Tallis J.A.).

[126] *Renner v. Joyce*, [1944] 3 W.W.R. 657 (Sask. C.A.), whitewash in sprayer escaped, injuring operator. See also *Hollis v. Birch* (1993), 16 C.C.L.T. (2d) 140, at p. 154; affd [1995] 4 S.C.R. 634, 129 D.L.R. (4th) 609, 27 C.C.L.T. (2d) 1.

does not implicate a defendant, since more than one actor is usually involved.[127] Similarly, where several people may have been responsible for an electrical fire in a house under construction, no negligence by the defendant can be inferred, since "too many possibilities of tampering and damage to the electrical work were open and available".[128]

a) Medical Situations

When something goes wrong during the course of medical treatment in a hospital it does not necessarily implicate the doctor, who may not have had control over all the assistants. Consequently, a plaintiff who was burned by a flash of flame during a cautery procedure could not recover against the doctor who performed it, because others were involved in preparing the patient.[129] Similarly, in *Morris v. Winsbury White*,[130] a doctor performed an operation on the plaintiff. The post-operative treatment involved the insertion of tubes into the plaintiff's body and their frequent replacement. The tubes were originally inserted by the defendant during the operation, but the replacements were made subsequently by resident doctors and nurses. Sometime after the plaintiff's discharge from hospital a portion of a tube was found in his bladder. In an action for negligence against the doctor, Tucker J. exonerated the defendant doctor because, while at the hospital, the plaintiff was treated by several doctors and nurses, so that the doctor was not in control of the defendant for the whole period.[131]

b) Defendant Not Responsible

In *Scrimgeour v. Board of Management of the Canadian District of the American Lutheran Church*,[132] a student resident of the defendant's college suffered a severe shock from a defective lamp connected to a dormitory bed in an unusual way. Since the lamp had been issued to another student, it was not under the control of the school at the time of the accident. The court felt that the college could not be expected to check these lamps "day by day or even week by week," since that would place an "insuperable burden" upon them. *Norton-Palmer Hotel Ltd. v. Windsor Utilities Commission* was concerned with an explosion of an electric transformer in a locked room in the basement of a hotel.[133] The court

---

[127] *Wing v. London General Omnibus Co.*, [1909] 2 K.B. 652, at p. 664; *Petrie v. Speers Taxi Co.*, [1952] O.R. 731, at p. 738 (C.A.) (*per* Roach J.A.); *Moore v. Toronto Transit Commn.*, [1944] O.W.N. 183.

[128] *Everatt v. Elgin Elecrric Ltd.*, [1973] 3 O.R. 691, at p. 711 (*per* Lerner J.). See also *Nichols v. R.A. Gill Ltd.* (1974), 51 D.L.R. (3d) 493.

[129] *McFadyen v. Harvie*, [1941] O.R. 90 (C.A.); affd [1942] S.C.R. 390.

[130] [1937] 4 All E.R. 494.

[131] See, generally, on this question, Linden, "Changing Patterns of Hospital Liability in Canada" (1967), 5 Alta. L. Rev. 212.

[132] [1947] 1 W.W.R. 120 (Sask. C.A.) (*per* Gordon J.A.).

[133] [1942] O.R. 170 (*per* Hogg J.).

decided that even though the utilities commission had a key to the padlock that held the door, this did not point to their negligence. The equipment was the property of the plaintiff, had been installed by employees of the plaintiff, and the room had been entered for inspection by electrical contractors and an engineer of the hotel. Consequently, there was not sufficient "control" by the defendant to allow an inference.[134] Similarly, if a student pilot, flying an airplane with dual controls, is injured in a crash, it cannot be said that the plane was in the sole control of the defendant's employee, who accompanied the pilot.[135] In addition, where a brick fell on the plaintiff from a wall of an old building on a golf course, liability was denied against the golf club because it was not "chargeable with the management or mismanagement of the thing causing [the injury]".[136] Also were a rider fell off a galloping horse when the saddle turned, *res ipsa* was held inapplicable because the horse was not under the "sole management and control of the defendant or someone for whom he was responsible".[137]

c) Confusion Over Word "Control"

Some needless confusion arose in the *res ipsa* cases by the insistence upon a literal interpretation of the words "control" or "management". These words were not holy; they were merely meant to express the idea of responsibility being brought home to the defendant.[138]

Happily, our courts abandoned their literal reliance on the notion of "control" or "management". Justice Evans (as he then was) expressed the proper approach in *Kirk v. McLaughlin Coal and Supplies Ltd.*,[139] where an oil furnace exploded causing damage to the plaintiffs' residence. The defendant supplied oil, serviced and cleaned the plaintiffs' furnace. The plaintiffs established that they did not touch the furnace at all and that no one else had serviced it. Although the trial judge had refused to invoke *res ipsa loquitur*, Justice Evans disagreed:

> Having ruled out intervention on the part of the plaintiffs and having accepted the evidence that the defendant alone serviced the furnace, the trial judge in my opinion was forced to conclude that effective "control" was in the hands of the defendant. I do not consider "control" to mean physical custody or possession. It is sufficient to establish "control" if it is demonstrated that the servicing and repairing of the furnace was the exclusive province of the defendant and that no other agency intervened.

---

[134] *Cf., Corsini v. City of Hamilton*, [1931] O.R. 598 (C.A.), liability when gas vapour in an underground chamber explodes.

[135] *McWilliam v. Thunder Bay Flying Club*, [1950] O.W.N. 696. See also *Tataryn v. Co-Operative Trust* (1974), 54 D.L.R. (3d) 154 (Sask.), passengers may have been cause.

[136] *Summers v. Niagara Parks Comm. and Niagara-on-the-Lake Golf Club*, [1945] O.R. 326; affd [1945] O.R. 802, at p. 809 (C.A.) (*per* Laidlaw J.A.).

[137] *Saillant v. Smith*, [1973] 2 O.R. 105, at p. 107 (C.A.) (*per* Jessup J.A.), explanation also acceptable.

[138] Wright, *supra*, n. 15, at p. 47.

[139] [1968] 1 O.R. 311 (C.A.). See also *Saccardo v. Hamilton*, [1971] 2 O.R. 479, at p. 490 (*per* Osler J.); *Westlake v. Smith Transport Ltd.* (1973), 2 O.R. (2d) 258, at p. 269 (*per* Lieff J.).

It is, therefore, permissible for the claimant to establish the "control" of the defendant by adducing evidence that other potential intruders were not likely responsible for the accident.[140] Another case where this was done is *Interlake Tissue Mills Co. Ltd. v. Salmon and Beckett*.[141] A copper screen on the plaintiff's machine was damaged while some other work was being done in the plaintiff's plant. Mr. Justice Roach, in ordering a new trial, stated that *res ipsa loquitur* would apply if the plaintiff showed that none of his maintenance crew had been in the immediate neighbourhood of the screen. If this were so, the damage could not have been caused by them. Consequently, this would point the finger at the defendants as the culprits.

It is possible for two defendants to have "control" of something at the same time, permitting an inference to be drawn against both of them on the basis that both are "linked" to the accident. Thus, where a T.V. set, manufactured by one defendant and rented by a second defendant, caught fire both may be held liable. Clement J.A. explained that the evidence must be assessed in relation to each alleged tortfeasor to see whether it supports an inference of negligence and whether the alleged tortfeasor has met it acceptably. Thus, "if on a reasonable view of the evidence the application of the maxim is warranted against two or more alleged tortfeasors, one or more may repel the inference of negligence raised against him or them and so be absolved. If neither or none can, I do not see any strain on justice to hold both culpable, presumably in such proportion as may be determined under the Contributory Negligence Act."[142]

D. Procedural Effect

Now that *res ipsa* is dead, there is no need to discuss at length its procedural effect, a topic that filled ten pages in previous editions.[143] It will now be up to the judges and juries to weigh the circumstantial evidence of negligence and of the defendant's role in the accident and decide whether liability will be imposed or not.

1. ONUS SHIFT IN SPECIFIC SITUATIONS

In the past, *res ipsa loquitur* did more than demand an explanation from the defendant in certain situations; it placed on the defendant the burden of disproof, as is the case with the onus sections of the highway traffic acts in most provinces.[144] This was the dominant English usage.[145] It is not easy to forecast whether

---

[140] See also *Lloyde v. West Midlands Gas Bd.*, [1971] 1 All E.R. 1240, at p. 1277 (C.A.).

[141] [1948] O.R. 950 (C.A.). See also *Chabot v. Ford Motor Co.*, *supra*, n. 80, at p. 226.

[142] *MacLachlin and Mitchell Homes Ltd. v. Frank's Rentals* (1979), 106 D.L.R. (3d) 245 (Alta. C.A.), neither liable, however, on the facts of one and a half years having passed and of eight different lessees having used the T.V.

[143] See Linden, *Canadian Tort Law*, 6th ed. (1997), at p. 247 *et ff.*

[144] See *Winnipeg Electric Co. v. Geel*, [1932] A.C. 690.

[145] *Ibid.* See also *Moore v. R. Fox & Sons*, [1956] 1 Q.B. 596, [1956] All E.R. 182 (C.A.). *Colvilles Ltd. v. Devine*, [1969] 1 W.L.R. 475 (H.L.), explosion.

these situations will still give rise to an onus shift or whether they will merely permit an inference. It is, therefore, necessary to discuss these special cases.

a) Food Products

In the food products liability area it was clearly established in Canada that the doctrine of *res ipsa loquitur* did considerably more than just get a claimant past a non-suit. It undoubtedly shifted the onus of disproof of negligence to the manufacturer. In other words, a producer of a food product in which some foreign object is found had to satisfy the court that there was no negligence.[146] Although the language of *res ipsa* was not always used, its aims of flushing out evidence, expanding liability, and supervising entrepreneurs were being served.

The special function of *res ipsa* survived the scrutiny of Mr. Justice Schroeder in *Phillips v. Ford Motor Co.*[147] During the course of an *obiter dictum*, Mr. Justice Schroeder alluded to "the earlier cases involving the manufacture of food and drink, [where] the presence of a snail in a bottle of ginger beer, of a mouse in a bottle of Coca-Cola or of glass in a bun, afforded evidence of a defect in the product which clearly shifted the onus to the defendant". He did not comment on whether or not he thought they were correctly decided. It also emerged intact from *Hellenius v. Lees*,[148] where Mr. Justice Laskin, dissenting, cited the classic Wright article and stated that *res ipsa loquitur* "means only that there is circumstantial evidence from which an inference of negligence is warranted". Following this he stated enigmatically, "I leave to another occasion consideration of the extent or trend to reliance on *res ipsa loquitur* as a means of shifting the burden of proof or of imposing strict liability for defectively manufactured products."

It is pretty obvious that *res ipsa* was being used in these cases as a technique to forge stricter liability for defective products in Canada. Cautious courts, worried about openly changing the law utilized it as an instrument of policy. Whether this impetus will continue in the post-*res ipsa* era remains to be seen.

b) Fires and Air Crashes

There have been some other situations, such as fire cases, where an onus has been placed on the defendant to explain that the cause of the accident was not his negligence.[149] In *Interprovincial Pipe Line Co. v. Sellers Oil Field Service*

---

[146] *Zeppa v. Coca-Cola Ltd.*, [1955] O.R. 855 (C.A.); *Varga v. John Labatt Ltd.*, [1956] O.R 1007. See Chapter 16. Products Liability, for a thorough examination of the cases. See *Brunski v. Dominion Stores Ltd.* (1981), 20 C.C.L.T. 14 (Ont. H.C.) (*per* Linden J.), applying it to bottler and producer of bottle.

[147] [1971] 2 O.R. 637, at p. 656 (C.A.).

[148] [1971] 1 O.R. 273, at p. 288 (C.A.); affd [1972] S.C.R. 165.

[149] *Shell Oil Co. v. White Motor Co.*, [1957] O.W.N. 229, 8 D.L.R. (2d) 753, at p. 758; *Greschuk v. Kolodychuk* (1959), 27 W.W.R. 157 (Alta. C.A.).

Ltd.,[150] Justice Wilson of Manitoba observed in a fire case that a defendant had to demonstrate "not only the probability that the mechanism or agent to which he points could have caused the loss, but the probability of the presence of that mechanism or agent". His Lordship felt that it was not sufficient to raise a "conjectural possibility", for this was no substitute for the balance of probabilities.

There is authority in an air crash case to the same effect. Mr. Justice Laidlaw in *Zerka v. Lau-Goma Airways Ltd.*,[151] in an *obiter dictum*, stated that it is "not sufficient to show that there were several hypothetical causes of an accident consistent with an absence of negligence. A defendant must go further and show either that there was no negligence or must give an explanation of the cause of the accident which did not connote negligence".

Another case in which a heavy burden was placed on a defendant was *Nystedt v. Wings Ltd.*,[152] where Mr. Justice Dysart asserted that if the defendant wants to "neutralize or overcome" the inference, the defendant has a "duty of going forward", but that if the rebuttal succeeds the plaintiff still bears the onus of proof. He suggested that there is a "blanket negligence" which spreads over the whole case and requires the defendant to stop every gap through which the inference arises. His Lordship said that this applies where the evidence is peculiarly within the defendant's knowledge and "operates in the interests of justice as between the parties".[153]

It may well be that in these types of cases the courts are unwilling to relieve defendants of responsibility unless the defendants satisfy the courts that they are not negligent, which they might not be able to do without proving the actual cause of the loss. In this way the courts are indirectly enlarging liability for these risky activities.

c) Dangerous Things and Latent Defects

Another disguised attempt at judicial law-making not based on *res ipsa* was made by Justice Wright in *Ives v. Clare Bros. Ltd.*[154] The category of things dangerous in themselves was resurrected to the extent that the onus of disproof of negligence was placed upon the defendant in such a case.

In England the concept of latent defect also furnishes a cloak for judicial legislation. In *Pearce v. Round Oak Steelworks*,[155] the plaintiff was working with a machine when a bolt broke, causing the machine to fall on him. The court imposed liability, but did not rely on *res ipsa loquitur*. Nevertheless, it held that there was a burden on the defendant to rebut the evidence of want of reasonable

---

[150] (1975), 58 D.L.R. (3d) 719, at p. 723 (Man.).
[151] [1960] O.W.N. 166, at p. 167 (C.A.).
[152] [1942] 3 W.W.R. 39 (Man.).
[153] *Ibid.*, at p. 50.
[154] [1971] 1 O.R. 417. *Cf.*, *Dahlberg v. Naydiuk* (1969), 10 D.L.R. (3d) 319 (Man. C.A.).
[155] [1969] 3 All E.R. 680 (C.A.).

care,[156] which it failed to do, because it refused to give evidence. The court confessed its "pleasure at being able to arrive at such a conclusion in conformity with the decided cases in circumstances where a workman is injured . . . and the defendants furnish no explanation at all of why that accident occurred".[157] So too, in *Henderson v. Henry E. Jenkins & Sons*,[158] the brakes on a truck failed when the pipe carrying the brake fluid corroded. Liability was imposed on the theory of latent defect, because the defendant failed to rebut the onus upon it to disprove negligence. It had to adduce evidence of the entire history of the vehicle, which it failed to do.

E. Particular Exceptions to the Need to Isolate the Defendant

There has been some loosening up of the requirement that an inference must implicate the defendant alone. This has occurred where it was extremely difficult to obtain reliable evidence of what had transpired, as in accidents occurring in the operating room and in certain types of automobile collisions. Let us explore these two situations in turn.

1. MULTIPLE DEFENDANTS IN THE OPERATING ROOM: *YBARRA V. SPANGARD*

The Supreme Court of California, in the well-known case of *Ybarra v. Spangard*,[159] in an attempt to counteract the so-called "conspiracy of silence" in medical malpractice cases, indicated a willingness to hold liable a whole surgical team — the innocent together with the guilty — for the negligence of one person. During the course of surgery for appendicitis, the plaintiff suffered an injury to his shoulder which developed into paralysis of the muscles. He brought an action against all of the people that could be implicated; the diagnostician, the surgeon, the anaesthetist, the owners of the hospital, and two nurses. At the trial, the plaintiff was non-suited. On appeal, however, the non-suit was set aside and the case was sent back for a new trial in accordance with the doctrine of *res ipsa loquitur*. The court declared: "Without the aid of the doctrine a patient who received permanent injuries of a serious character, obviously the result of someone's negligence, would be entirely unable to recover unless the doctors and nurses in attendance voluntarily chose to disclose the identity of the negligent person and the facts establishing liability." In the trial which was held later, the court found the defendants all liable even though each of them testified that they "saw nothing occur which could have produced the injury". This was so, even though "all of them were not present at all times".[160]

---

[156] *Ibid.*, at p. 681.
[157] *Ibid.*, at p. 682 (*per* Davies L.J.).
[158] [1970] A.C. 282, [1969] 3 All E.R. 756.
[159] (1944), 154 P. 2d 687.
[160] See (1949), 208 P. 2d 445, (2nd D.C.A.) (*per* Dooling J.).

Dean Wright has described this result as "guilt by association with a vengeance".[161] He criticized the case because a policy decision was made under the guise of *res ipsa loquitur*. Nevertheless, it was a salutary method of securing evidence where it could not be flushed out by more traditional means. Although perhaps not laudable, it is not at all novel for courts to use fictions to reform the law. It would be preferable if courts had the courage to do so openly but stealth may be better that stagnation.

Ybarra v. Spangard has been followed in *Anderson v. Somberg*[162] where a forceps broke during surgery, injuring the plaintiff. When the jury dismissed an action against the manufacturer, the hospital, the doctor and the distributor, the appeal court sent the case back for a new trial on the ground that at least one defendant should have been held responsible. The court held that the burden of proof shifts to the defendants and explained:

> All those in custody of that patient who owed him a duty, as here, the manufacturer and the distributor, should be called forward and should be made to prove their freedom from liability.
>
> The rule would have no application except in those instances where the injury lay outside the ambit of the surgical procedure in question; for example, an injury to an organ, when that organ was itself the object of medical attention, would not by itself make out a *prima facie* case for malpractice or shift the burden of proof to the defendants.

There was a strong dissent contending that such a holding would "visit liability, in a wholly irrational way, upon parties that are more probably than not totally free of blame". At the new trial, the jury found against the manufacturer and distributor.[163]

This extension of *res ipsa* has not won wide support. For example, one court refused to apply *Ybarra* against the four occupants of a hotel room in which a fire was started by a cigarette.[164] The only support for this principle in the Commonwealth is an *obiter dictum* by Lord Justice Denning in *Roe v. Ministry of Health*.[165] "If an injured person shows that one or other of two persons injured him, but cannot say which of them it is, he is not defeated altogether. He can call on each of them for an explanation." Even Lord Justice Denning, however, later disavowed this rule,[166] which has been described as "somewhat alarming".[167] In a world without *res ipsa* no one can foretell the destiny of this principle.

There has been one controversial decision, enlarging upon the *Ybarra* concept. In *Sindell v. Abbott Labs*,[168] the California Supreme Court refused to

---

[161] Wright, *"Res Ipsa Loquitur"* in *Studies in Canadian Tort Law* (1968), at p. 54. See also Seavey, *"Res Ipsa Loquitur: Tabula in Naufragio"* (1950), 63 Harv. L. Rev. 643. *Cf.*, Prosser, *"Res Ipsa Loquitur* in California" (1948), 37 Calif. L. Rev. 183, at p. 223.

[162] (1975), 338 A. 2d 1 (N.J.).

[163] (1978), 386 A. 2d 413.

[164] *Firemen's Fund v. Knobbe* (1977), 562 P. 2d 825 (Nev.).

[165] [1954] 2 Q.B. 66 (C.A.).

[166] *Baker v. Market Harborough Industrial Co-operative Society*, [1953] 1 W.L.R. 1472 (C.A.).

[167] Wright, *supra*, n. 161.

[168] (1980), 163 Cal. Reptr. 132. See Delgado, "Beyond *Sindell*: Relaxation of Cause-In-Fact Rules for Indeterminate Plaintiffs" (1980), 70 Calif. L. Rev. 881; Rosenberg, "The Causal Connection

dismiss an action against five pharmaceutical companies which produced the cancer-causing drug D.E.S., even though there was no way to prove which individual defendant actually supplied the particular D.E.S. which damaged the plaintiff. The court felt that if a substantial percentage of the drug makers were joined, each could be held for the portion of the judgment represented by its share of the market during the time in question. It is too early to tell whether this market share principle will be limited to the area of products liability, whether it will mushroom into other areas, or whether, as many devoutly wish, it will die.

2. CERTAIN UNEXPLAINED COLLISIONS ON THE ROAD: JOINT LIABILITY UNLESS NEGLIGENCE DISPROVED

There is another group of situations where, by analogy, the philosophy embedded in *res ipsa*, along with the aid of contributory negligence legislation, has been employed to dramatically limber up the treatment of proof problems in certain auto accident cases. Although this development was described by Dean C.A. Wright as startling,[169] it has firmly established itself in our law.

The leading case is *Baker v. Market Harborough Industrial Co-operative Society*,[170] where two automobiles, travelling in opposite directions, crashed in the centre of the road. Both drivers were killed. In holding both drivers equally to blame, Lord Justice Denning stated:

> On proof of the collision in the centre of the road the natural inference would be that one or other were to blame. . . . Every day, proof of the collision is held to be sufficient to call on the two defendants for an answer. Never do they both escape liability. One or the other is held to blame, and sometimes both. If each of the drivers were alive and neither chose to give evidence, the court would unhesitatingly hold that both were to blame. They would not escape simply because the court had nothing by which to draw any distinction between them. So, also, if they are both dead and cannot give evidence, the result must be the same. In the absence of any evidence enabling the court to draw a distinction between them, they must be held both to blame, and equally to blame.[171]

Lord Justice Denning warned that not every motor vehicle collision can be handled in this way:

> It is very different from a case *where one or other only* is to blame but clearly not both. Then the judge ought to make up his mind between them. . . . But when both may be to blame, the judge is under no such compulsion and can cast the blame equally on each.
> [Italics mine.]

---

in Mass Exposure Cases: A 'Public Law' Vision of the Tort System" (1984), 97 Harv. L. Rev. 851; Twerski, "Market Share" (1989), 55 Brooklyn L. Rev. 869; Keeton (ed.), *Prosser and Keeton on the Law of Tort*, 5th ed. (Minnesota: West Publishing Co., 1984), p. 713.

[169] *Supra*, n. 161, at p. 55.

[170] [1953] 1 W.L.R. 1472 (C.A.).

[171] *Ibid.*, at p. 1476.

This principle was reaffirmed in *France v. Parkinson*,[172] where Lord Justice Somervell stated that "in a case of a collision at cross-roads where both roads were of equal status, in the absence of special circumstances, the balance of probabilities were in favour of both drivers having been negligent." The great Prosser has supported this view and has asserted: "There is room for a conclusion of the jury that when two vehicles collide and injure a third person the great probability is that *both* drivers were at fault. Certainly that is the experience of liability insurance companies. . . ."[173] There is no reason why this statement should not apply equally when no third party is involved.[174]

This theory has been adopted in Canada in *Leaman v. Rea*.[175] Two cars, travelling in opposite directions, collided very close to the centre of the highway. Both drivers testified that they had remained on their own side of the road. The trial judge dismissed the case because he could not decide which one to believe. The Appeal Division reversed the decision and entered a judgment for the plaintiff for 50 per cent of his loss against the defendant and a judgment for the defendant for 50 per cent of his loss against the plaintiff. Mr. Justice Bridges stated:

> where there has been a collision between two motor vehicles under such circumstances that there must have been negligence on the part of one or both drivers, and the Court is unable to distinguish between such drivers as to liability, both drivers should be found equally at fault.[176]

Mr. Justice Harrison concurred and declared that "in the absence of any evidence enabling the Court to draw a distinction between the parties, they must be held both to blame and equally to blame". He felt that, where there was "clearly fault, since we have a collision in broad daylight between two cars travelling in opposite directions on a road the travelled portion of which is 26 feet wide, both parties must be held liable and in equal degree".

In reaching this conclusion, however, His Lordship observed that since the damages assessed did not differ substantially in amount "the result of holding both parties to blame may not be greatly different from dismissing both claims. . . ." But such a result follows only if one assumes that neither party is insured and that there must be a set-off. If, on the other hand, both parties are insured, as is normally the case, and if there is no set-off,[177] it makes all the difference in the

---

[172] [1954] 1 All E.R. 739 (C.A.). See also *W.M. Wood (Haulage) Ltd. v. Redpath*, [1966] 3 All E.R. 556 (Q.B.D.), where the parties *agreed* that both were to blame, but argued that the other was more to blame. Liability was split equally.

[173] Prosser, *supra*, n. 161, at p. 207.

[174] Although problems would arise if there were no contributory negligence legislation, as is the case in many American states.

[175] [1954] 4 D.L.R. 423 (N.B.C.A.).

[176] *Ibid.*, at p. 426.

[177] *Wells v. Russell*, [1952] O.W.N. 521 (C.A.); *Lewenza v. Ruszczak*, [1960] O.W.N. 40 (C.A.). *Cf.*, *Schellenberg v. Cooke* (1960), 25 D.L.R. (2d) 607 (Sask. C.A.); *Johnny's Taxi v. Ostoforoff* (1962), 33 D.L.R. (2d) 85 (Sask. C.A.).

world. In other words, where the damages suffered by both parties are equal, the insurance company of the defendant would pay one-half of the plaintiff's loss and the insurance company of the plaintiff would pay one-half of the defendant's loss. Both parties would recover one-half of their losses, instead of nothing. Even if an uninsured driver is involved, the uninsured motorist regime would step in and the result would be the same. Consequently, this device broadens the incidence of the compensation for Canadians injured on the road.

A similar result was reached in *Wood v. Thompson and Tomko*,[178] where the plaintiff's husband was a passenger in Thompson's car when it collided with a car driven by Tomko. The plaintiff's husband, Thompson and Tomko, were all killed in the accident and there were no witnesses to the collision. The plaintiff brought action for damages accruing from her husband's death against the personal representatives of Thompson and Tomko. The trial judge, Campbell J., found that both cars were in good operating condition. There were no skidmarks to show the course of the cars. The only evidence was some glass near the centre of the roadway and the ultimate position of both cars some 48-50 feet from this spot. Campbell J., after citing *Baker* and *Leaman*, concluded simply: "I find the defendants equally to blame."[179]

The most recent application of this principle was in *Davison v. Leggett*,[180] where the trial judge dismissed a head-on collision case because he could not tell who was at fault and it was feasible that neither party was negligent. On appeal, Lord Justice Denning said that counsel wrongly tried to revive the "fallacy" that the "plaintiff must prove that the defendant was negligent". His Lordship declared: "Prima facie one or other or both are to blame. If the judge cannot say which it was, he should find that they are both to blame and equally to blame." Lord Justice Sacks agreed that this was a "salutary rule within which the law would be in a sad condition in relation to passengers in cars as well as drivers."

a) Requirement of Some Evidence That Both Parties Negligent

It should be emphasized that there must be some evidence that *both* parties are negligent; if the proof merely shows that *one or other* of the parties was to blame, but not both, the action must be dismissed. This was made clear by Lord Justice Denning in *Baker* and was underscored by the Supreme Court of Canada in *Wotta v. Haliburton Oil Well Cementing Co. Ltd.*[181] Two large motor vehicles, proceeding in opposite directions, collided. The only witnesses to the accident were the two drivers and their evidence was conflicting. It appeared that the forward part of each vehicle passed the other and contact occurred between the

---

[178] (1957), 11 D.L.R. (2d) 452 (Man.).

[179] His Lordship also referred to the section of the Act permitting split liability where there was doubt about the proportion of blame.

[180] (1969), 133 J.P. 552, at p. 553 (C.A.); *Nettleship v. Weston*, [1971] 3 All E.R. 581 (C.A.) (*per* Denning M.R.).

[181] [1955] S.C.R. 377, [1955] 2 D.L.R. 785.

rear parts of both trucks. There were no marks on the road to assist in determining the respective position of the trucks. The trial judge was unable to make any finding of negligence and dismissed the action and the counterclaim. This judgment was upheld by the Saskatchewan Court of Appeal and by the Supreme Court of Canada. Taschereau J. stated that, if *Leaman v. Rea* meant that where the evidence shows that *one of two* drivers was negligent and the court is unable to distinguish between them, then both should be found equally at fault, it should be overruled. There is no principle on which a person may be held liable unless negligence is proved. There was no evidence here, as in the other cases, from which an inference could be drawn that *both* parties were negligent. Locke J. indicated that in *Leaman v. Rea*, the evidence disclosed a collision in the centre of the road, from which it could be inferred there was negligence by *both* drivers. In this case there was no evidence to justify an inference that *both* drivers were negligent, and liability cannot be imposed on the basis that *one or other* of the drivers was negligent.

A trial judge must consider not only the guilty of *each* of the parties but also the possibility that *both* parties were negligent. In *Fogel v. Satnik*,[182] the trial judge dismissed a motor vehicle action saving, "if [plaintiff's witness] A's version is correct, the defendant is entirely to blame; and conversely, if the defendant is to be believed, the plaintiff's negligence was the sole cause of action. . . . I am completely unable to make a finding as to credibility." The Court of Appeal found this procedure wanting and ordered a new trial on the ground that the trial judge "did not consider the possibility of *both* drivers of the vehicles being at fault",[183] and it was "quite open to the learned trial judge to find that both the plaintiff and the defendant were negligent".[184]

b) Multiple Defendants But No Liability

One should not be deluded into thinking that all automobile collision claims will now be successful. In *Haswell v. Enman*,[185] one party died, the other party had amnesia and other evidence was almost non-existent. The court dismissed both actions. Davey J.A. stated that "the cause of the collision is surrounded by so much speculation and conjecture that it is impossible to find that either party discharged the burden of proving negligence resting upon him".[186] This was a case of "absence of evidence" rather than one of "the probabilities being evenly divided". A similar result was obtained in *Binda v. Waters Construction Co.*,[187] where the plaintiff motorist, proceeding north, collided with a tractor travelling south. The accident occurred in a dense cloud of smoke or steam blown across the highway by a nearby railway locomotive. There being ample room for both

---

[182] (1960), 23 D.L.R. (2d) 630 (Ont. C.A.).
[183] *Ibid.*, at p. 632. See also *Bray v. Palmer*, [1953] 2 All E.R. 1449 (C.A.).
[184] *Ibid.*, at p. 634.
[185] (1961), 28 D.L.R. (2d) 537 (B.C.C.A.).
[186] *Ibid.*, at p. 539.
[187] (1960), 24 D.L.R. (2d) 431 (Man. C.A.).

vehicles to pass on the highway, the crucial fact issue at the trial was on which side of the highway the accident occurred. The trial judge, after stating that there was "no evidence," found that both parties were equally responsible, purportedly in accordance with the contributory negligence legislation. The Manitoba Court of Appeal said that this was improper and sent the case back for a new trial.[188] The court did not cite any of the cases referred to here, not even the *Wood v. Thompson and Tomko* case decided in the same province. Mr. Justice Freedman stated:

> The statutory provision is not a substitute for a judicial finding of negligence, nor does its existence obviate the need of the tribunal making such a judicial finding. Admittedly the learned trial judge faced a difficult problem. But the resolution of that problem called for a judicial decision on the issue of negligence. Only then could the statutory provision be called into play. Instead the learned trial judge resorted to the section and found equal responsibility on the basis thereof. His use of the section in these circumstances involved him — altogether innocently of course — in an abdication of the judicial task which he was required to perform.[189]

The High Court of Australia has reached the same position. In *Nesterczuk v. Mortimore*,[190] two vehicles headed in opposite directions struck one another a glancing blow. Each party claimed that the other had crossed the centre line. The trial judge decided that neither party had established that the other was to blame and this was affirmed. Mr. Justice Windeyer explained that "very seldom would the proper inference from the mere fact of a collision in the centre of a road be that the drivers were equally to blame".[191] Many other circumstances are involved. The trial judge did not have to be persuaded by either party, nor did he have to hold both parties to blame, if he could not decide which one was at fault. "Doubtless the facts spoke for themselves, and eloquently, of negligence: but of whose negligence they had nothing to say. And when the parties themselves spoke, what they said left the learned trial judge still in doubt."[192] Mr. Justice Owen cast some doubt upon the statements of Lord Justice Denning. He agreed that an unexplained collision in the centre of the road leads to a reasonable inference of negligence, but he would not accept the "view that there is some principle of law which insists that both parties must be held to be blameworthy when that hypothesis is not a more probable one than that one or the other was wholly responsible". He added that "no court is entitled to make a finding which is not justified by the evidence".[193] The dissenting judge, McTiernan A.C.J., thought that the "probabilities are that neither of the parties was keeping a

---

[188] Relying on *Waring v. Jarvis*, [1956] O.W.N. 661 (C.A.), where a trial judge was criticized for dismissing a claim and counterclaim because he did not believe either party's story. The Court of Appeal sent it back for a new trial with instructions to consider *all* the evidence, not just that of the two parties.

[189] *Supra*, n. 187, at p. 434.

[190] (1965-66), 39 A.L.J.R. 288.

[191] *Ibid.*, at p. 291.

[192] *Ibid.*, at p. 293.

[193] *Ibid.*, at p. 295. See also *Salt v. Imperial Chemical Industries, The Times*, Feb. 11, 1955.

proper look out, and that each was driving in dangerous proximity to the other vehicle."[194]

This new development is a welcome one for it yields a result more in accord with the balance of probabilities, it helps to extract evidence that might otherwise be withheld, and it spreads more broadly the inevitable losses generated by vehicular traffic.

F. Statutory Onus Shift

Most highway traffic legislation shifts the onus of disproof of negligence to the driver. For example, section 193 of the Highway Traffic Act of Ontario reads as follows:

> (1) When loss or damage is sustained by any person by reason of a motor vehicle on a highway, the onus of proof that the loss or damage did not arise through the negligence or improper conduct of the owner or driver of the motor vehicle is upon the owner or driver.
> (2) This section does not apply in cases of a collision between motor vehicles or to an action brought by a passenger in a motor vehicle in respect of any injuries sustained while a passenger.[195]

The effect of this section, which assists pedestrians primarily, was explained by Lord Wright in *Winnipeg Electric Co. v. Geel*, as follows:

> The statute creates, as against the owners and drivers of motor vehicles, in the conditions therein laid down, a rebuttable presumption of negligence. The onus of disproving negligence remains through the proceedings. If, at conclusion of the evidence, it is too meagre or too evenly balanced to enable the tribunal to determine this issue as a question of fact, then, by force of the statute, the plaintiff is entitled to succeed.[196]

Consequently, all a plaintiff pedestrian has to do is to prove the fact of being struck by a motor vehicle on a highway and the plaintiff will succeed, unless the court is convinced, on the balance of probabilities, that the defendant was not negligent. If the scales are evenly balanced at the end of the trial, the onus section comes into play and the plaintiff succeeds. If, of course, the court is unable to find, on the evidence, that there was no negligence, the defendant is entitled to succeed.[197]

The purpose of the onus section has been well articulated in *MacDonald v. Woodard* in these terms:

> This section was enacted in order to overcome difficulties experienced by plaintiffs in obtaining and presenting sufficient evidence of a motorist's negligence to avoid a non-suit at the close of their case. Knowledge of relevant acts and circumstances leading up to an accident might be in the possession only of the defendant and injustice might result if a plaintiff was unable to overcome the initial obstacle of a *prima facie* case and to avoid having his case

---

[194] *Ibid.*, at p. 290.
[195] R.S.O. 1990, c. H.8.
[196] [1932] A.C. 690.
[197] *Gordon v. Trottier*, [1974] S.C.R. 158.

determined before all the evidence was before the Court. Hence the introduction of a type of statutory *res ipsa loquitur* doctrine under which the owner or driver is *prima facie* liable for damage caused by his motor vehicle unless he satisfied the Court on a preponderance of evidence that he was not in fact negligent.[198]

Since a work such as this cannot describe all of the detailed law in connection with the onus section, the specialized works should be consulted.[199]

1. CARRIER CASES

Carriers of people and goods have always been expected to deliver them safely.[200] Passengers who are injured on public transportation, for example, "enjoy the benefit of a burden that shifts to the defendant to prove that the carrier was being operated in a skilled and prudent manner".[201] It is a "very high degree of care" that is demanded of a carrier. This shift of onus is justified on several bases:[202]

> First, passengers on a public carrier are entitled to expect that they will be carried to their destinations in safety and thus, the standard of care for public carriers is high....

> Secondly, the driver of the carrier is the person who knows whether the vehicle was being driven in a safe, proper and prudent manner. The passenger cannot be expected to know what happened. For example, in this case, the passenger was still proceeding down the aisle and could have no knowledge of why the bus, having left the stop, suddenly jerked to a stop.

> Thirdly, a shifting burden will encourage public carriers to adopt proper reporting procedures so that facts are ascertainable after an incident occurs. If the party with the knowledge were not called on to answer, the incentive to keep proper records from which the truth can be ascertained disappears. Even worse, there might be an incentive not to keep records.

> Finally, drivers of all vehicles have a high duty of care and responsibility. While we are not prepared to entertain the argument made for the first time on appeal that s. 180 of the *Highway Traffic Act* applies to public carriers, we note the heavy onus placed on ordinary drivers by s. 180(1) of the *Highway Traffic Act*. That section provides:

> > If a person sustains loss or damage by reason of a motor vehicle in motion, the onus of proof in any civil proceeding that the loss or damage did not entirely or solely arise through the negligence or improper conduct of the owner or driver of the motor vehicle is on that owner or driver.

---

[198] (1973), 2 O.R. 438, at p. 440 (*per* Matheson C.C.J.).

[199] Phelan, *Highway Traffic Law*, 3rd ed. (1969), Segal, *Manual of Motor Vehicle Law*, 3rd ed. (1982); Phelan, "Onus Under the Highway Traffic Act" in *Special Lectures on Evidence* (1955); *Hartman v. Fisette* (1976), 66 D.L.R. (3d) 516, at p. 522 (S.C.C.), proof by defendant that plaintiff partially to blame did not constitute a complete excuse.

[200] *Day v. Toronto Transportation Commission*, [1940] S.C.R. 433, [1940] 4 D.L.R. 484.

[201] *Nice v. Calgary (City)* (2000), 190 D.L.R. (4th) 402, 83 Alta. L.R. (3d) 1, 2 C.C.L.T. (3d) 86 (C.A.); leave to appeal to S.C.C. refused (2001), 196 D.L.R. (4th) vii (S.C.C.).

[202] *Ibid.*, at p. 96 C.C.L.T.

Section 180 of the *Highway Traffic Act* shifts the onus to all operators of *any motor vehicle* in motion where damage occurs as a result of that motor vehicle. The party with the knowledge is called upon to answer. Considering that a public carrier is paid to carry its passengers and considering the high standard of care imposed by *Day*, justification of a lesser burden than that facing ordinary drivers is difficult.

G. Trespass, Case, and Inevitable Accident

1. TRESPASS OR CASE

a) History

The historical roots of tort law are still influential in the field of burden of proof.[203] Despite attacks by scholars,[204] and judges,[205] "the shades of trespass as a form of action still flit uneasily among the cases."[206] The writ of trespass was available from the thirteenth century as a remedy for directly inflicted injury.[207] In the early fourteenth century the writ of trespass on the case was developed for situations of indirect injury.[208] An illustration of the distinction between these two forms of action might be helpful. If someone threw a log at, and struck, the plaintiff, trespass was the appropriate writ. If the log was left on the road, however, and the plaintiff tripped over it, case was the proper action.[209]

One important distinction between these two actions concerned the burden of proof. In trespass, the harm was *prima facie* wrongful and the defendant was obliged to prove justification or excuse. In case, on the other hand, the plaintiff bore the burden of proving either wrongful intent or negligence.[210] The causal relationship gradually became less important and the focus was shifted to whether the conduct was intentional or negligent, with trespass used most frequently for the former and case for the latter. It was possible, however, to use alternative remedies; both trespass and case could be launched for direct but unintentional invasions. The procedural advantages of case and the problems associated with proving directness gradually led to the more frequent use of case in negligence actions.[211] With the passage of the Judicature Acts of 1873 and

---

[203] See Winfield and Goodhart, "Trespass and Negligence" (1933), 49 L.Q. Rev. 359; Fridman, "Trespass or Negligence" (1971), 9 Alta. L. Rev. 250; Trindade, "Comment" (1971), 49 Can. Bar Rev. 612.

[204] Wright, "*Res Ipsa Loquitur*" in Linden (ed.), *Studies in Canadian Tort Law* (1968) p. 41, Fleming, *The Law of Torts*, 9th ed. (1998) pp. 24 *et seq.*

[205] Denning M.R. in *Letang v. Cooper*, [1965] 1 Q.B. 232, [1964] 2 All E.R. 929 (C.A.); Diplock L.J. in *Fowler v. Lanning*, [1959] 1 Q.B. 426, [1959] 1 All E.R. 290.

[206] Burns, "Comment" (1970), 48 Can. Bar Rev. 728, at p. 730.

[207] Pollock and Maitland, II *History of English Law* (1895), p. 525. See also Malone, "Ruminations on the Role of Fault in the History of Torts" (1970), 31 La. L. Rev. 1.

[208] Kiralfy, *The Action on the Case* (1951), p. 7.

[209] See Fleming, *op. cit. supra*, n. 204, at p. 16.

[210] *Ibid.*, at p. 20.

[211] Winfield and Goodhart, *supra*, n. 203, at p. 366.

1875, it was thought that these quaint distinctions would be buried forever. But this was not to be. The alternative bases of action lingered on.

b) *Cook v. Lewis*

In *Cook v. Lewis*,[212] the Supreme Court of Canada stated that "where a plaintiff is injured by force applied directly to him by the defendant his case is made by proving this fact and the onus falls upon the defendant to prove that such trespass was utterly without his fault" and "the defendant is entitled to judgment if he satisfies the onus of establishing the absence of both intention and negligence on his part."[213] This principle has been religiously followed in Canada ever since that time, despite considerable criticism.

c) Modernization in England

In 1959, Mr. Justice Diplock (as he then was) in *Fowler v. Lanning* tried to lay the trespass action to rest.[214] The plaintiff had pleaded merely that the defendant shot him and that he sustained damages thereby. The defendant attacked the pleading and succeeded. After an extremely learned discourse on the history of the old forms of action, Mr. Justice Diplock concluded that the "onus of proving negligence, where the trespass is not intentional, lies upon the plaintiff, whether the action be framed in trespass or negligence". This was consistent with the rule as to highway accidents,[215] and with the position reached by the American courts in 1850 in *Brown v. Kendall*.[216] It was also in harmony with the scholarly judgment of Mr. Justice Clyne in *Walmsley v. Humenick*,[217] a case where a five-year-old child shot another child in the eye with a bow and arrow. His Lordship opined that it was "curious that since the passing of the Judicature Acts a situation should arise where on the same facts the plaintiff's action must fail if it is framed in negligence, but might succeed if it is brought in trespass."[218] His Lordship later indicated, however, that Mr. Justice Cartwright had placed the "seal of authority" on this view in *Cook v. Lewis*.[219] He concluded that the defendant must succeed because the "plaintiffs have been unable to prove that the infant defendant was negligent in view of his age". In the alternative, if *Cook v. Lewis* were to be applied, His Lordship held that "the same result would ensue

---

[212] [1951] S.C.R. 830, [1951] 1 D.L.R. 1, relying on *Stanley v. Powell*, [1891] 1 Q.B. 86. See also *Woodward v. Begbie*, [1962] O.R. 60.

[213] *Ibid.* (*per* Cartwright J.); see also *Scalera v. Non-Marine Underwriters, Lloyd's of London*, [2000] 1 S.C.R. 551, 185 D.L.R. (4th) 1, 253 N.R. 1, [2000] 5 W.W.R. 465 (*per* McLachlin J.); see also Sullivan, "The Trespass to the Person in Canada" (1987), 19 Ottawa L. Rev. 533.

[214] *Supra*, n. 205.

[215] There is considerable doubt as to this, see *Walmsley v. Humenick*, [1954] 2 D.L.R. 232, at p. 242 (B.C.).

[216] (1850), 60 Mass. 292.

[217] *Supra*, n. 215.

[218] *Ibid.*, at p. 244.

[219] *Ibid.*, at p. 251.

because it has been demonstrated that the infant defendant because of his tender years was incapable of negligence". There was no proof of intention.

A few years later, Lord Justice Denning applied what most people felt was the *coup de grâce* in *Letang v. Cooper*,[220] when he asserted:

> . . . the distinction between trespass and case is obsolete. We have a different sub-division altogether. Instead of dividing actions for personal injuries into *trespass* (direct damage) or *case* (consequential damage), we divide the causes of action now according as the defendant did the injury intentionally or unintentionally. If one man intentionally applies force directly to another, the plaintiff has a cause of action in assault and battery, or, if you so please to describe it, in trespass to the person. . . . If he does not inflict injury intentionally, but only unintentionally, the plaintiff has no cause of action today in trespass. His only cause of action is in negligence, and then only on proof of want of reasonable care. If the plaintiff cannot prove want of reasonable care, he may have no cause of action at all. Thus, it is not enough nowadays for the plaintiff to plead that the "defendant shot the plaintiff". . . . He must also allege that he did it intentionally or negligently. If intentional, it is the tort of assault and battery. If negligent and causing damage, it is the tort of negligence.
>
> The modern law on this subject was well expounded by my brother Diplock J., in *Fowler v. Lanning* with which I fully agree. But I would go this one step further: when the injury is not inflicted intentionally, but negligently, I would say that the only cause of action is negligence and not trespass. If it were trespass, it would be actionable without proof of damage; and that is not the law of today.

d) Canadian Resistance to Change

But the Canadian courts did not give up. The action of trespass for negligent conduct, with its attendant onus shift, has demonstrated an incredible resilience. In *Tillander v. Gosselin*,[221] Justice Grant was confronted with a claim involving a three-year-old defendant who had dragged a baby out of her carriage and injured her. His Lordship surveyed the cases and concluded that,

> in an action for damages in trespass where the plaintiff proves that he has been injured by the direct act of the defendant, the onus falls on the defendant to prove that his act was both unintentional and without negligence on his part. If he fails to do so, the plaintiff must succeed; but if he succeeds, he is entitled to judgment dismissing the claim.

He dismissed the case, however, on the ground that he was satisfied that the infant defendant was neither negligent nor acting deliberately. A similar conclusion was reached by Justice Brooke in *Ellison v. Rogers*,[222] a case where the plaintiff was hit in the eye by a golf ball hit by the defendant. His Lordship agreed with the plaintiff's contention that in a trespass action "the onus is on the defendant to disprove that the striking was either negligent or intentional. . . ." . His

---

[220] [1965] 1 Q.B. 232, [1964] 1 All E.R. 929 (C.A.). See also *Kruber v. Grzesiak*, [1963] V.R. 621; *Beals v. Haywood*, [1960] N.Z.L.R. 131.

[221] [1967] 1 Q.R. 203; affd 61 D.L.R. (2d) 192n (C.A.). See also *Tsouvalla v. Bini*, [1966] S.A.S.R. 157.

[222] (1967), 67 D.L.R. (2d) 21.

Lordship, however, felt that this onus had been satisfied by the defendant and dismissed the action.

The health of this principle was also demonstrated in *Dahlberg v. Naydiuk*.[223] The action, framed in both negligence and trespass, arose when a farmer was accidentally shot by a hunter who fired over the farmer's land. Justice Dickson referred to the onus shift as "one of those strange anomalies of the law" and quoted Dean Wright's critique of the rule as "irrational and unnecessary".[224] Nevertheless, he held that "[i]f such a change is to be made in the law it must be made by a court higher than this".[225] An insight into the policy rationale behind the stubborn longevity of this principle is provided by this statement of Justice Dickson:

> Hunters must recognize that firing over land without permission of the owner constitutes a trespass to land and if injury to person results, trespass to person. A hunter who fires in the direction in which he knows or ought to know farm buildings are located must accept full responsibility for resultant damage to person or property. It is no answer to say he thought the buildings were unoccupied. There are vast areas of western Canada in which deer abound and where no farming activities are carried on. Even in farming areas there are often hills from which one can fire at game in the valley below without risk of injury to others. If a hunter chooses to hunt in a farming area he must do so in full awareness of the paramount right of the farmer to carry on his lawful occupation without risk of injury from stray bullets.[226]

There is ample evidence in the recent Canadian cases that the principle of *Cook v. Lewis* retains its original vitality. In *Goshen v. Larin*,[227] for example, the plaintiff was injured by a referee at a wrestling match, who knocked the plaintiff over while fleeing from irate fans. An action framed in trespass for direct injury was held to be appropriate, but the Court of Appeal was convinced by the defendant that he was not negligent in the difficult circumstances.

MacDonald J.A., even though he described the "English judicial view . . . as being a fair and just one . . .", felt bound by the Supreme Court of Canada and outlined the law in the following clear terms:

> The law in Canada at present is this: In an action for damages in trespass where the plaintiff proves that he has been injured by the direct act of the defendant, the onus falls upon the defendant to prove that his act was both *unintentional* and *without negligence* on his part, in order for him to be entitled to a dismissal of the actions.[228]

A defence of the trespass action has been advanced in *Bell Canada v. Cope (Sarnia) Ltd.*[229] in these terms:

---

[223] (1969), 10 D.L.R. (3d) 319 (Man. C.A.).

[224] *Ibid.*, at p. 328.

[225] *Ibid.*, at pp. 328-29.

[226] *Ibid.*, at p. 330.

[227] (1975), 56 D.L.R. (3d) 719 (N.S.C.A.); revg (1974), 46 D.L.R. (3d) 137; leave to appeal to S.C.C. refused Dec. 16, 1974. See also *Teece v. Honeybourn*, [1974] 5 W.W.R. 592, 54 D.L.R. (3d) 549; *Bell Canada v. Bannermount Ltd.*, [1973] 2 O.R. 811 (C.A.), wire cut by drilling.

[228] *Ibid.*, at p. 722.

[229] (1980), 11 C.C.L.T. 170, at p. 180 (*per* Linden J.).

Despite many attacks by Judges and scholars, the trespass action has survived in Canada, even though it has long been eclipsed both in the United Kingdom and in the United States. The trespass action still performs several functions, one of its most important being a mechanism for shifting the onus of proof of whether there has been intentional or negligent wrongdoing to the defendant, rather than requiring the plaintiff to prove fault. The trespass action, though perhaps somewhat anomalous, may thus help to smoke out evidence possessed by defendants, who cause direct injuries to plaintiffs, which should assist Courts to obtain a fuller picture of the facts, a most worthwhile objective.

2. INEVITABLE ACCIDENT

Another quaint holdover from days gone by is the defence of inevitable accident.[230] Although once useful as a defence to the action for trespass, it seems to have no place in modern negligence law. Today, defendants in negligence cases normally do not need to avail themselves of the plea of inevitable accident; all they have to do is deny that they were negligent.[231] Thus, if a defendant shows that an accident was caused by a bee[232] or a partridge[233] flying in the open window of a car, no liability will be imposed as long as there was no negligence on the part of the driver.

This does not seem to have stopped our courts from invoking this ancient defence occasionally. The onus is clearly on the defendant to establish inevitable accident.[234] The theory of the defence is that the defendant can escape liability if showing one of two things: (1) "the cause of the accident, and . . . the result of that cause was inevitable", or (2) "all the possible causes, one or other of which produced the effect, and . . . with regard to every one of these possible causes that the result could not have been avoided"[235]

This standard, though certainly a high one, is not a "test of perfection". It is, therefore, wrong for a trial judge to charge a jury that the defendant must show that the "accident could not possibly be prevented" by the exercise of reasonable care and that the test was a "severe test".[236]

It is not easy to escape liability by relying on inevitable accident. In *Telfer v. Wright*,[237] the defendant blacked out while driving a car. The car crossed over the centre line and collided with the plaintiff's vehicle. The Court of Appeal,

---

[230] See Ryan J.A. dissenting in *Boutcher v. Stewart et al.* (1989), 50 C.C.L.T. 77, at p. 82 (N.B.C.A.).

[231] *Sinclair v. Maillett*, [1951] 3 D.L.R. 216 (N.B.) (*per* Harrison J.). See also *Hogan v. McEwan* (1975), 64 D.L.R. (3d) 37, at p. 54 (Ont.) (*per* Henry J.), defendant swerved to avoid dog.

[232] *Sinclair v. Nyehold*, [1972] 5 W.W.R. 461 (B.C.C.A.).

[233] *Boutcher v. Stewart, supra*, n. 230.

[234] *United Motors Service Inc. v. Hutson*, [1937] S.C.R. 294 (*per* Duff C.J.). See also *Aubrey v. Harris*, [1957] O.W.N. 133, 7 D.L.R. (2d) 545.

[235] See *The Merchant Prince*, [1892] P. 179 (C.A.) (*per* Fry L.J.). See also *Rintoul v. X-Ray & Radium Industries*, [1956] S.C.R. 674, at p. 678; *Blackman v. Andrews*, [1971] 2 W.W.R. 744 (Sask.).

[236] See *Goveia v. Lalonde* (1977), 1 C.C.L.T. 273 (Ont. C.A.).

[237] (1978), 23 O.R. 117, at pp. 118-19 (C.A.). See also *Perry v. Banno* (1993), 15 C.C.L.T. (2d) 199 (B.C.S.C.), onus on defendant not met.

reversing the trial judge, rejected the defence of unavoidable accident, since the defendant had suffered a dizzy spell several minutes before the accident, had stopped the car, but then started it up again. Six months earlier he had suffered similar symptoms.

Justice Maurice Lacourcière explained:

> The defendant, being on the wrong side of the road, had to meet the onus of explaining how the accident could have occurred without his negligence . . . .
>
> We are all of the view that the learned trial Judge erred in applying the defence of unavoidable accident when the evidence disclosed that the defendant had, on at least two previous occasions, experienced symptoms similar to those he suffered immediately before the collision. . . .
>
> While an unconscious person obviously cannot be guilty of negligence it is also clear that his unconsciousness will not be a defence if he had reasonable grounds to anticipate that it would occur. . . . In circumstances such as the present, it is up to the defendant to rebut the inference of breach of duty and lack of reasonable care, and in most cases this is done by showing that there was no evidence of knowledge of prior disability, or foresight of probable harm. A motorist has the duty of making sure that he is in a proper state of health to operate a motor vehicle. He must not expose other persons to the risk or the possibility that he may suffer an attack of a kind that would impair his ability to control his motor vehicle as he proceeds on the highway. A motorist who is aware he suffers from a disability is under a heavy duty to take the necessary precautions to avoid the possibility of this disability implicating him as the cause of an accident.

It has been suggested that the defence of inevitable accident be abolished,[238] but this advice has been ignored.

3. HISTORICAL ANOMALIES OR TOOLS FOR JUSTICE?

One cannot help but conclude that these historical anomalies may have social utility in the modern world. In addition to being relics of the past, they may turn out to be harbingers of the future. Because they aid the injured plaintiffs with their problems of proof, these ideas tend to broaden liability for those accidents where the injury happens to be directly caused. Professor Atrens,[239] after arguing that this is an unconvincing reason for shifting the onus of proof, observed: "If it is desired to facilitate recovery for personal injuries the reverse onus should apply to indirect injuries as well."

Our courts are moving in this direction. The onus of disproof of negligence now rests on defendants in cases of dangerous articles, some breaches of statute, pedestrian accidents, certain collision cases, carrier cases and where the injury is directly caused if the trespass action is used. This is a welcome trend if it helps to place all the evidence before the courts. Cat and mouse games are not tolerable in modern trials. Discovery proceedings facilitate full disclosure, but the parties are usually less than cooperative. By shifting the onus to the defendants to explain what occurred, the court may obtain more complete evidence

---

[238] Legislative Assembly of Ontario, Select Committee on Automobile Insurance, *Final Report* (1963).

[239] *Studies in Canadian Tort Law* (1968), p. 396. See also Burns, *supra*, n. 206, at p. 733.

than if the plaintiffs shoulder the onus of proof. The civil liberties interests of criminal law, which demand *prima facie* proof of wrongdoing before calling upon an accused to answer, are not as compelling in civil cases. Disclosure serves society more than secrecy if dangerous conduct is brought to light thereby.

In *Fowler v. Lanning*, Lord Justice Diplock expressed his concern over forcing a "defendant to come to trial blindfold", and his joy over "stripping the bandage . . . from the defendant's eyes".[240] However, in removing the bandage from the defendant's eyes, it may be placed on the plaintiff's eyes and on the eyes of the court. The ancient ways fostered openness. Those who cling to the anomalies, rather than being reactionaries, may turn out to be more progressive than they realized. Those who seek the overthrow of trespass and inevitable accident in the interest of clarity and modernity may be rendering a disservice to the goal of loss distribution they so avidly espouse.[241] Fictions and historical anomalies may be preferable to injustice.

---

[240] *Supra*, n. 205, at p. 441.

[241] Fleming, *op. cit. supra*, n. 204, at p. 23, urging abandonment of "cabalistic learning about trespass and care".

Chapter 9

Duty

However negligent defendants are they will not be held liable unless they owe a duty to be careful.[1] In other words, if the law does not recognize any obligation to exercise caution, actors are not responsible civilly for their carelessness. "A man is entitled to be as negligent as he pleases towards the whole world if he owes no duty to them."[2]

The duty concept is a control device that enables courts to check the propensity of juries to award damages in situations where matters of legal policy would dictate otherwise.[3] The existence of a duty is a question of law for the court to decide.[4] Consequently, defendants may raise the duty issue in an attack on the pleadings,[5] thereby halting a law suit against them before it reaches the jury. Moreover, courts of appeal are able to reverse jury verdicts and trial judges' decisions with the duty technique. But the trouble with the duty notion in the past was said to be that, basically, "it is a shorthand statement of a conclusion, rather than an aid to analysis in itself".[6] More recently the duty issue has been recognized as largely a matter of policy. The concept of duty is not known in the civil law.[7]

---

[1] Fleming, "Remoteness and Duty: The Control Devices in Liability for Negligence" (1953), 31 Can. Bar Rev. 471; Prosser, "Palsgraf Revisited" (1953), 52 Mich. L. Rev. 1; Green, "The Duty Problem in Negligence Cases" (1928), 28 Colum. L. Rev. 1014; Heuston, "*Donoghue v. Stevenson* in Retrospect" (1957), 20 Mod. L. Rev. 1; J.C. Smith, "The Mystery of Duty" in Klar (ed.), *Studies in Canadian Tort Law* (1977), p. 1; J.C. Smith, *Liability in Negligence* (1984).

[2] *Le Lievre v. Gould*, [1893] 1 Q.B. 491, at p. 497 (C.A.) (*per* Esher M.R.).

[3] Fleming, *The Law of Torts*, 8th ed. (1998), p. 149. See also *Nova Mink v. Trans-Canada Airlines*, [1951] 2 D.L.R. 241 (N.S.C.A.).

[4] Fleming, *ibid.*

[5] For example, *Donoghue v. Stevenson*, [1932] A.C. 562; *Home Office v. Dorset Yacht Co. Ltd.*, [1970] 2 All E.R. 294; *Rondel v. Worsley*, [1969] 1 A.C. 191.

[6] *Prosser and Keeton on the Law of Torts*, 5th ed. (1984), p. 358. See J.C. Smith, *Liability in Negligence, op. cit. supra*, n. 1, "it is easier for the judge to sneak in his conclusion in the disguise of a premise about the existence of a duty, than to attempt to articulate some of the policy premises which were the actual bases of his decision".

[7] See Lord Goff in *Smith v. Littlewoods Organization Ltd.*, [1987] 1 All E.R. 710, at p. 736 (H.L.).

After a rather late appearance in the mid-nineteenth century,[8] the duty concept was employed to prevent the undue curtailment of freedom of action during that period of industrial expansion. By means of the duty notion, certain types of negligent conduct were exempted from judicial scrutiny altogether. For a long time, manufacturers of products were shielded from tort actions by third persons with whom they had no contractual relations.[9] Negligent statements were not fully supervised by the civil courts.[10] No civil liability arose from nonfeasance, because there was said to be no duty to act.[11] Duty was also utilized to keep the extent of liability within acceptable limits by withholding compensation for certain interests not deemed worthy of protection. Hence, there was no duty to prevent negligent interference with mental tranquillity or with economic relations.[12]

In the past few decades, however, these restrictions have been jettisoned or severely circumscribed. The no-privity rule was exploded, negligent statements came under the purview of the law, and some nonfeasance situations began to attract liability. Gradually the courts began to compensate for certain invasions of mental and economic security.

A. The Neighbour Principle

The impetus came from the prophetic *dictum* of Lord Atkin when he sought, in the case of *Donoghue v. Stevenson*,[13] to outline a "general conception of relations giving rise to a duty of care, of which the particular cases found in the books are but instances". He declared:

> The rule that you are to love your neighbour becomes in law you must not injure your neighbour; and the lawyer's question, Who is my neighbour? receives a restricted reply. You must take reasonable care to avoid acts or omissions which you can reasonably foresee would be likely to injure your neighbour. Who, then, in law, is my neighbour? The answer seems to be — persons who are so closely and directly affected by my act that I ought reasonably to have them in contemplation as being so affected when I am directing my mind to the acts or omissions which are called in question.

---

[8] *Vaughan v. Menlove* (1837), 3 Bing N.C. 468, 132 E.R. 490; *Langridge v. Levy* (1837), 2 M. & W. 519, 150 E.R. 863; affd *Levy v. Langridge* (1838), 4 M. & W. 337, 150 E.R. 1458; *Winterbottom v. Wright* (1842), 10 M. & W. 109, 152 E.R. 402. See Winfield, "Duty in Tortious Negligence" (1934), 34 Colum. L. Rev. 41.

[9] See *infra*, Chapter 16.

[10] See *infra*, Chapter 12.

[11] *Infra*, Section C.

[12] See *infra*, Chapter 11.

[13] *Supra*, n. 5, at p. 580. This echoed the earlier statement of Brett M.R. in *Heaven v. Pender* (1883), 11 Q.B.D. 503 (C.A.), as follows: "Whenever one person is by circumstances placed in such a position with regard to another that everyone of ordinary sense who did think could at once recognize that if he did not use ordinary care and skill in his own conduct with regard to those circumstances he would cause danger of injury to the person or property of the other, a duty arises to use ordinary care and skill to avoid such danger." See articles written for 50th anniversary of case: Linden, "The Good Neighbour on Trial" (1983), 17 U.B.C.L. Rev. 59 *et seq.*; Smith and Burns, "The Good Neighbour on Trial: Good Neighbours Make Bad Law" (1983), 17 U.B.C.L. Rev. 93. See also "'Viva *Donoghue v. Stevenson!*' in *Donoghue v. Stevenson* and the Modern Law of Negligence" (1991), *The Paisley Papers*, at p. 227.

This statement of the neighbour principle has served as a springboard for later courts to make inroads into the various no-duty rules established earlier, but it was not totally triumphant. It operated as a "general road sign",[14] not as a binding rule. According to Lord Reid, the neighbour principle "ought to apply unless there is some justification or valid explanation for its exclusion".[15] In other words, the court held that a duty arises wherever some harm is reasonably foreseeable, unless good policy reasons exist for denying such a duty.

One attempt at explaining the situation is that of Lord Wilberforce in *Anns v. Merton London Borough Council*[16] who said

> . . .the position has now been reached that in order to establish that a duty of care arises in a particular situation, it is not necessary to bring the facts of that situation within those of previous situations in which a duty of care has been held to exist. Rather the question has to be approached in two stages. First one has to ask whether, as between the alleged wrongdoer and the person who has suffered damage there is a sufficient relationship of proximity of neighbourhood such that, in the reasonable contemplation of the former, carelessness on his part may be likely to cause damage to the latter — in which case a prima facie duty of care arises. Secondly, if the first question is answered affirmatively, it is necessary to consider whether there are any considerations which ought to negative, or to reduce or limit the scope of the duty or the class of person to whom it is owed or the damages to which a breach of it may give rise: . . .

This "two-step approach" to the test of duty was adopted by the Supreme Court of Canada in *Kamloops v. Nielsen*[17] where Madam Justice Wilson particularized it to a degree:

> (1) is there a sufficiently close relationship between the parties . . . so that, in the reasonable contemplation of the [defendant], carelessness on its part might cause damage to that person? If so,

> (2) are there any considerations which ought to negative or limit (a) the scope of the duty and (b) the class of persons to whom it is owed or (c) the damages to which a breach of it may give rise?

This test was consistently followed in other Supreme Court of Canada cases.[18] Following the retreat from *Anns* in the United Kingdom,[19] the Supreme Court of

---

[14] Fleming, *op. cit. supra*, n. 3, at p. 137.

[15] *Home Office v. Dorset Yacht Co. Ltd.*, [1970] 2 All E.R. 294 (H.L.).

[16] [1977] 2 W.L.R. 1024 (H.L.); See also *Batty v. Metropolitan Property Realisations*, [1978] 2 W.L.R. 500 (C.A.).

[17] [1984] 2 S.C.R. 2, at p. 10. See Major J. in *Ryan v. Victoria (City)*, [1999] 1 S.C.R. 201, 168 D.L.R. (4th) 513, [1999] 6 W.W.R. 61, 44 C.C.L.T. (2d) 1, at p. 14.

[18] *B.D.C. Ltd. v. Hofstrand Farms Ltd.*, [1986] 1 S.C.R. 228, at p. 243 (*per* Estey J.); *Just v. British Columbia* (1989), 64 D.L.R. (4th) 689 (S.C.C.); *Rothfield v. Manolakos* (1989), 63 D.L.R. (4th) 449 (S.C.C.) (*per* Cory J.), *Anns* is "sound".

[19] See *Murphy v. Brentwood District Council*, [1990] 2 All E.R. 908 (H.L.), economic loss cases limited by proximity requirement as well as foresight and fairness; see also *Sutherland Shire Council v. Heyman* (1985), 157 C.L.R. 424 (H.C. Aust.). The House of Lords continues to complicate the duty issue, extending the new limits into losses that are not purely economic, but physical, over the objection of Lord Lloyd who charged, in dissent, that the "retreat" is turning

Canada, in *Canadian National Railway Co. v. Norsk Pacific Steamship Co.*,[20] unanimously and resoundingly refused to alter its course and reiterated its faith in *Anns*. Madam Justice McLachlin[21] explained that the approach still required that two questions be asked: "(1) is there a duty relationship sufficient to support recovery? and, (2) is the extension desirable from a practical point of view, *i.e.*, does it serve useful purposes or, on the other hand, open the floodgates to unlimited liability". The *Anns* two-stage approach has been gradually refined and elaborated by the Supreme Court, now superbly and concisely summarized in *Edwards v. Law Society of Upper Canada*[22] by McLachlin C.J. and Major J. as follows:

> 9 At the first stage of the *Anns* test, the question is whether the circumstances disclose reasonably foreseeable harm and proximity sufficient to establish a *prima facie* duty of care. The focus at this stage is on factors arising from the relationship between the plaintiff and the defendant, including broad considerations of policy. The starting point for this analysis is to determine whether there are analogous categories of cases in which proximity has previously been recognized. If no such cases exist, the question then becomes whether a new duty of care should be recognized in the circumstances. Mere foreseeability is not enough to establish a *prima facie* duty of care. The plaintiff must also show proximity - that the defendant was in a close and direct relationship to him or her such that it is just to impose a duty of care in the circumstances. Factors giving rise to proximity must be grounded in the governing statute when there is one, as in the present case.
>
> 10 If the plaintiff is successful at the first stage of *Anns* such that a *prima facie* duty of care has been established (despite the fact that the proposed duty does not fall within an already recognized category of recovery), the second stage of the *Anns* test must be addressed. That question is whether there exist residual policy considerations which justify denying liability. Residual policy considerations include, among other things, the effect of recognizing that duty of care on other legal obligations, its impact on the legal system and, in a less precise but important consideration, the effect of imposing liability on society in general.

The *Anns* case is, therefore, alive and well in Canada even though it has been buried in the land of its birth. This is encouraging because it was merely a "gloss"[23] on the neighbour principle espoused in *Donoghue v. Stevenson* which is and should remain the bedrock principle of negligence law.

Foresight of risk remains important, therefore, but policy factors must also be taken into account in assessing whether or not to establish a duty of care. The fact is that some foreseeable risks are not within the scope of the duty owed,

---

"into a rout", see *Marc Rich & Co. AG v. Bishop Rock Marine Co. Ltd.* (The "Nicholas H"), [1995] 3 All E.R. 307 (H.L.). This retrogressive and overly complicated development has been wisely ignored by the Supreme Court of Canada and, hence, is given little attention in this book.

20 (1992), 91 D.L.R. (4th) 289 (S.C.C.). See also *Hercules Management Ltd. v. Ernst & Young* (1997), 146 D.L.R. (4th) 577 (S.C.C.).

21 *Ibid.*, at p. 364.

22 2001 SCC 80, 2001 Can. Sup. Ct. LEXIS 8, [2001] S.C.J. No. 77, at para. 9 and 10. See the complete analysis of this issue in *Cooper v. Hobart*, 2001 SCC 79 , 2001 Can. Sup. Ct. LEXIS 81, [2001] S.C.J. No. 76, at para. 20-39. See also *Ryan v. Victoria (City)*, *supra*, n. 17, at pp. 14-15, C.C.L.T.

23 *Cooper v. Hobart*, *ibid.*, at para. 21.

while some unforeseeable risks are considered within the duty.[24] Nevertheless, Lord Atkin's neighbour principle, as revised by *Anns*, unleashed a force that can be used to expand the reach of negligence law, even though some courts will continue to resist its allure. It can also be used to contract the scope of negligence law.[25] For, after all, as was explained by President Robin Cooke of the New Zealand Court of Appeal, "the decision on a duty of care issue depends on a judgment, not a formula".[26]

1. POLICY FACTORS INFLUENCING DUTY ISSUE

Debates over whether a duty will be established or denied in particular circumstances will exercise the courts increasingly in the years ahead as new claims for protection are advanced. It has now been officially recognized that this is a question of public policy which the courts in each jurisdiction will have to decide for themselves in the novel circumstances of the cases that come before them. As Denning M.R. once declared prophetically in *Dorset Yacht Co. Ltd. v. Home Office*:

> It is, at bottom a matter of public policy which we, as judges, . . . must resolve. This talk of "duty" or "no duty" is simply a way of limiting the range of liability for negligence.[27]

On another occasion, Denning M.R. put it this way:

> It is a question of policy, which we, as Judges, have to decide. The time has come when, in cases of new import, we should decide them according to the reason of the thing.[28]

Another frank acceptance of judicial responsibility issued from Lord Pearce, who asserted that the scope of the duty of care in negligence "depends ultimately on the courts' assessment of the demands of society [for protection] from the carelessness of others".[29]

Many policy matters must be taken into account by the courts in determining whether or not they will impose a duty.[30] One matter courts will consider is the administrative factors, such as the possibility of opening the floodgates of litigation.[31] This factor is rarely conclusive; "[d]enial of the existence of a cause of

---

[24]   Green, "*The Wagon Mound (No. 2)* — Foreseeability Revised", [1967] Utah L. Rev. 197.

[25]   See *Hercules Management Ltd., supra,* n. 20, for example.

[26]   See *South Pacific Mfg. v. N.Z. Consultants* (1992), 2 N.Z.L.R. 282, at p. 295 (C.A.).

[27]   [1969] 2 All E.R. 564, at p. 567; affd [1970] 2 All E.R. 294 (H.L.). See generally Weinrib, "*Dorset Yacht* Case: Causation, Care and Criminals" (1971), 4 Ott. L. Rev. 389.

[28]   *Dutton v. Bognor Regis United Building Co.*, [1972] 1 All E.R. 462, at p. 475 (C.A.). See also *Collins v. Haliburton, Kawartha, Pine Ridge District Health Unit*, [1972] 2 O.R. 508.

[29]   *Hedley Byrne Ltd. v. Heller & Partners Ltd.*, [1963] 2 All E.R. 575, at p. 615. See also Lord Diplock's judgment in *Home Office v. Dorset Yacht Co. Ltd., supra,* n. 15.

[30]   Symmons, "The Duty of Care in Negligence: Recently Expressed Policy Elements" (1971), 34 Mod. L. Rev. 394 and 528.

[31]   *Ibid.*, at p. 402.

action is seldom, if ever, the appropriate response to fear of its abuse".[32] Nevertheless, this was one of the reasons for refusing liability in the economic sphere and in the mental suffering cases. As better mechanisms for controlling the scope of liability for these interests emerged, a limited duty was held to exist.[33] The type of harm is relevant, therefore, as physical loss will receive greater protection than financial losses.

Another factor courts assess is the desirability of leaving certain activities free of control by tort action. An immunity may be created in order to spare some specified actors the need to be constantly looking over their shoulders.[34] For example, judges[35] and other quasi-judicial officers[36] are immune from civil suits for their errors, as long as they act in good faith. A law society, for example, may not be liable for losses caused by fraudulent solicitors because it failed to supervise or investigate them properly, unless there was malice or bad faith,[37] since it acts in a quasi-judicial capacity. A professional association of accountants was also cleared of liability for theft by one of its members when it failed to notify clients that he had been disciplined.[38] The professional associations of dentists and hygienists are not liable for errors made by the people they supervise.[39] Nor is the military or an individual soldier under a tort duty to use care to protect another soldier under battle conditions.[40] In the United Kingdom, there is a reluctance to create civil duties on police to prevent crime,[41] on fire

---

[32] See *Phelps v. Hillingdon London Borough Council*, [2000] 4 All E.R. 504 (H.L.), at p. 530 (*per* Lord Nicholls), educational malpractice case.

[33] See *infra*, Chapters 11 and 12.

[34] Symmons, *supra*, n. 30, at p. 528.

[35] *Sirros v. Moore*, [1974] 3 All E.R. 776; *Re Clendenning and Bd. of Police Commrs. for City of Belleville* (1976), 15 O.R. (2d) 97, at p. 101 (Div. Ct.); *Unterreiner v. Wilson* (1983), 40 O.R. (2d) 197; affd 41 O.R. (2d) 472 (C.A.). See also D. Thompson, "Judicial Immunity and the Protection of Justices" (1958), 21 Mod. L. Rev. 517; A. Rubinstein, "Liability in Tort of Judicial Officers" (1964), 15 U. of T.L.J. 317; Feldthusen, "Judicial Immunity: In Search of an Appropriate Limiting Formula" (1980), 29 U.N.B.L.J. 73.

[36] *Sutcliffe v. Thackrah*, [1974] A.C. 727 (H.L.), arbitration; *Everett v. Griffiths*, [1921] 1 A.C. 631 (H.L.), chairman of Board of Guardians of mental institution; *Toews v. MacKenzie*, [1977] 6 W.W.R. 738, 81 D.L.R. (3d) 302 (B.C.), warden of prison releasing inmate on temporary pass. *Cf.*, *Johnson v. California* (1968), 447 P. 2d 353 (S.C. Cal.), no immunity of parole officers; *Arenson v. Casson, Beckman, Rutley & Co.*, [1975] 3 All E.R. 901, valuer liable unless judicial function performed.

[37] *Voratovic v. Law Society of Upper Canada* (1978), 20 O.R. (2d) 214; *Calvert v. Law Society of Upper Canada* (1981), 32 O.R. (2d) 176 (*per* Steele J.); *Edwards v. Law Society of Upper Canada*, *supra*, n. 22, "plaintiffs not clients", Law Society Act s. 9 immunity also.

[38] *Schilling v. Certified General Accountants Ass'n of B.C.* (1996), 29 C.C.L.T. (2d) 44 (B.C.C.A.); leave to appeal to S.C.C. refused (1997), 141 D.L.R. (4th) vii (S.C.C.); see also *Kripps v. Touche Ross & Co.* (1992), 94 D.L.R. (4th) 284 (B.C.C.A.).

[39] *Rogers v. Faught* (2001), 5 C.C.L.T. (3d) 109 (Ont. S.C.J.) (*per* Cameron J.).

[40] *Mulcahy v. Ministry of Defence*, [1996] 2 All E.R. 758 (C.A.), no liability to soldier knocked down by Howitzer fire during Gulf War.

[41] *Alexandrou v. Oxford*, [1993] 4 All E.R. 328 (C.A.); *Hill v. Chief Constable of West Yorkshire*, [1988] 2 All E.R. 238 (H.L.); *cf. Swinney v. Chief Constable of Northumbria Police Force*, [1996] 3 All E.R. 449 (C.A.).

departments for failing to put out fires,[42] on non-profit classification societies who give careless advice about the safety of ships,[43] and on municipal authorities which fail to move buildings which block the view of motorists.[44] English barristers are immune from civil liability for the careless conduct of a trial in part on this basis.[45] In Canada this immunity has been resoundingly rejected in *Demarco v. Ungaro*,[46] where Mr. Justice Krever held that it was contrary to the public policy of Ontario to confer on a lawyer engaged in court work an immunity enjoyed by no other professional person.

In conflict with these goals is the need to deter negligent conduct and to furnish incentives to caution. Thus, the courts have brought the business of giving advice under the umbrella of negligence law.[47] The product of the legislatures may also be used as ammunition in this task of strengthening tort law.[48] The necessity for compensation is another strong influence on the courts to enlarge the area of their supervision. In short, most of the policy ends of tort law enter the deliberations on the duty question.

The duty concept has generated problems. One reason for this is that the courts have blurred the duty of care with the remoteness and standard of care issues.[49] Instead of merely deciding that there is or is not a duty owed for certain types of conduct or to protect specified interests and then permitting trial courts and juries to mould that duty, appeal courts have retained a very close check on its evolution. This certainly makes the job of appeal court judge more interesting, but it also increases the incidence of cases that must go to the highest court of the land for decisions on questions of law. One would have thought that the English courts would have learned from their disastrous experience in the occupiers' liability cases, where they so over-burdened the field with specific rules for each different class of entrant onto private property, that legislation was necessitated to abolish the distinctions and to replace them with a common duty of care.[50] It would be preferable if the courts refrained from

---

[42] *John Munroe (Acrylics) Ltd. v. London Fire and Civil Defence Authority*, [1996] 4 All E.R. 318 (Q.B.); *cf. Capital & Counties p.l.c. v. Hampshire County Council*, [1996] 4 All E.R. 336 (Q.B.), misfeasance.

[43] *Marc Rich & Co. A.G. v. Bishop Rock Marine Co. Ltd.*, [1995] 3 All E.R. 307 (The "Nicholas H").

[44] See *Stovin v. Wise*, [1996] 3 All E.R. 801 (H.L.).

[45] *Rondel v. Worsley*, *supra*, n. 5. No immunity for failing to sue necessary party, however, see *Saif Ali v. Sydney Mitchell*, [1978] 3 All E.R. 1033 (H.L.).

[46] (1979), 21 O.R. (2d) 673 (H.C.); *Wechsel v. Stutz* (1980), 15 C.C.L.T. 132 (Ont. Co. Ct.), no liability for cross-examination alleged negligent. See Bogart, "Immunity of Advocates from Suit: The Unresolved Issue" (1980), 29 U.N.B. L.J. 27.

[47] *Hedley Byrne Ltd. v. Heller & Partners Ltd.*, *supra*, n. 29.

[48] Symmons, *supra*, n. 30, at p. 536. See generally Linden, "Tort Liability for Criminal Nonfeasance" (1966), 44 Can. Bar Rev. 250.

[49] *Prosser and Keeton on the Law of Torts*, 5th ed. (1984), at p. 275. See, for example, Lord Diplock in *Mutual Life v. Evatt*, *infra*, Chapter 12, c. 1, and *Home Office v. Dorset Yacht*, *supra*, n. 15.

[50] See generally, Fleming, *op. cit. supra*, n. 3, at p. 499.

using the duty concept to set detailed standards of care, as urged by Justice Major in *Ryan* where he warned:[51]

> However, the *Anns/Kamloops* test is not concerned with legislative or judicial policies which, as in this case, define the conduct required to meet an existing duty. Such policies relate to the standard of care. As a practical matter, the distinction between limiting the "scope" of a legal duty under the *Anns/Kamloops* test or limiting the requisite standard of care to discharge that duty is an elusive one. Both formulations go to reducing a defendant's exposure to liability, and in most cases the outcome will be the same under either approach. As a matter of analytical coherence, however, the distinction is important. . . . Without it, the entire analysis of duty and standard would be collapsed together into the *Anns/Kamloops* framework, a purpose for which that test was not designed.

In considering duty, appeal courts should limit themselves to the broad policy issues, that is, matters of "extension or the limits to the law of negligence".[52] They should not engage in second-guessing trial decisions on essentially factual matters. Similarly, courts should avoid overloading the duty issue with considerations better left to be dealt with under the proximate cause, remoteness or voluntary assumption of risk issues. This may not make the decisions easier, but they may be rendered more understandable. Perhaps then the mystery of duty will be banished.[53]

This chapter, which treats the fourth element of a negligence action, will now consider the problem of the unforseeable plaintiff and will then examine the failure to act in negligence law. The next chapter will discuss proximate cause and remoteness, the fifth element. The following chapter will concentrate on the judicial treatment of certain imperfectly protected interests, an aspect of the fifth element. All of these matters may be properly viewed as duty problems, but some may also be analyzed as remoteness issues or in other ways.

B. The Unforeseeable Plaintiff

Plaintiffs may not recover damages unless defendants owe them a duty of care. Unlike the position at criminal law, a tort duty is not owed to the world. Only certain individuals may claim the protection of tort law. This determination of duty is a conclusion of law that permits courts to prohibit litigation by some people. Here, too, the courts have invoked the concept of risk and foreseeability to help them decide which plaintiffs are covered by the duty of care.

The leading case is *Palsgraf v. Long Island Railroad Co.*[54] The defendant's guard, in trying to assist a man who was rushing for a departing train, pushed him, thereby knocking from his arms a package of fireworks. Somehow an explosion ensued, which knocked over a scale, which in turn hit the woman

---

[51] See *supra*, n. 17, at p. 15 (C.C.L.T.).

[52] See J.C. Smith, "Clarification of Duty-Remoteness Problems Through a New Physiology of Negligence: Economic Loss, A Test Case" (1974), 9 U.B.C.L. Rev. 213, at p. 220; see also Smith, *Liability in Negligence* (1984).

[53] See J.C. Smith, *supra*, n. 1.

[54] (1928), 162 N.E. 99. See Prosser, "Palsgraf Revisited" (1952), 52 Mich. L. Rev. 1.

plaintiff who was standing some distance away. She was denied recovery on the ground that she was beyond the range of foreseeable danger. Mr. Justice Cardozo rationalized the position as follows:

> The conduct of the defendant's guard, if a wrong in its relation to the holder of the package, was not a wrong in its relation to the plaintiff standing far away. Relatively to her it was not negligence at all. . . . If no hazard was apparent to the eye of ordinary vigilance, an act innocent and harmless, at least to outward seeming, with reference toward her, did not take to itself the quality of a tort because it happened to be a wrong, though apparently not one involving the risk of bodily insecurity, with reference to someone else. "In every instance before negligence can be predicated of a given act, back of the act must be sought and found a duty to the individual complaining.". . . The plaintiff sues in her own right for a wrong personal to her, and not as the vicarious beneficiary of a breach of duty to another. . . .[55]

Mr. Justice Andrews, who spoke for the dissenting minority, rejected this view and argued:

> Every one owes to the world at large a duty of refraining from those acts which unreasonably threaten the safety of others. Such an act occurs. Not only is he wronged to whom harm might reasonably be expected to result, but he also who is in fact injured, even if he be outside . . . the danger zone. There needs to be duty due the one complaining but this is not a duty to a particular individual because as to him harm might be expected.[56]

The approach of Mr. Justice Cardozo won the day not only in the United States but also in England with the decision of *Bourhill v. Young*.[57] The plaintiff, a pregnant fishwife, was just getting off a tram when the defendant motorcyclist crashed into a car behind the tram and out of sight of the plaintiff. She heard the impact and later saw the blood at the scene of the accident. This caused her to suffer a miscarriage. Her negligence action was dismissed on the ground, *inter alia*, that she was an unforseeable plaintiff. Lord Wright decided that she could not rely on the defendant's breach of duty to the motorist and declared:

> If the appellant has a cause of action it is because of a wrong to herself. She cannot build on a wrong to someone else. Her interest, which was in her bodily security, was of a different order from the interest of the owner of the car.[58]

The courts have not been unduly strict with regard to the persons who are entitled to claim for negligence. For example, as will be seen below, rescuers are considered to be foreseeable plaintiffs, despite the fact that they are often not really within the realm of prevision.[59] Someone who was running behind a truck preparing to steal a ride on it was allowed to recover when hit by a container which fell off the truck, because a duty is owed to anyone "who happened to be

---

[55] *Ibid.*

[56] *Ibid.*, at p. 103.

[57] [1943] A.C. 92.

[58] *Ibid.*, at p. 108.

[59] *Infra*, Chapter 10, I.

at the crucial moment in the neighbourhood of this dangerous thing".[60] Protection may be afforded to especially sensitive plaintiffs such as blind people,[61] and mink farmers, whose animals may devour their young if frightened during the whelping season.[62]

1. BORN-ALIVE CHILDREN AND PRENATAL ACCIDENTS

Born-alive children are now considered foreseeable plaintiffs and are owed a duty of care by tortfeasors in relation to pre-natal events,[63] although this was not always so.[64] The child must be born alive, however, in order to be able to sue.[65] This was explained by Major J. in *Dobson (Litigation Guardian of) v. Dobson*,[66] as follows:

> The law of tort views a born alive child as a person capable of suing third parties for damages resulting from injuries inflicted on her as a foetus. Absent the born alive child, however, foetal injuries are legally irrelevant. Thus, while there is no liability for prenatal injuries, there is liability for *post*-natal injuries resulting from prenatal events caused by a third party's negligence.

This development was slow in coming. The Supreme Court of Canada in *Montreal Tramways Co. v. Léveillé*,[67] upheld a judgment from a Quebec court in favour of a plaintiff for prenatal injuries sustained by him when his mother, seven months pregnant, was injured by the negligent operation of the defendant's tram car. The plaintiff claimed that he had been born with club feet as a consequence. The Supreme Court upheld the judgment on the ground that under the civil and Roman law, unborn children subsequently born alive are deemed to be living and to possess all rights, including the rights of action they would have

---

60   *Farrugia v. Great Western Ry. Co.*, [1947] 2 All E.R. 565 (C.A.). See also *Law v. Visser*, [1961] Queensland R. 46, liability when "bundle" on road, run over by defendant at night, turned out to be a person.

61   *Haley v. London Electricity Bd.*, [1965] A.C. 778; *Carroll v. Chicken Palace Ltd.*, [1955] O.R. 23; but revd on the facts, [1955] O.R. 798, [1955] 3 D.L.R. 681; ten Broek, "Right to Live: The Disabled in the Law of Torts" (1966), 54 Calif. L. Rev. 841.

62   See, for example, *Nova Mink v. Trans-Canada Airlines*, [1951] 2 D.L.R. 241; *Sullivan v. Hydro Electric Power Commn. of Ontario* (1960), 23 D.L.R. (2d) 756; *MacGibbon v. Robinson*, [1953] 2 D.L.R. 689 (B.C.C.A.); *Grandel v. Mason*, [1953] 1 S.C.R. 459.

63   See *Duval v. Seguin*, [1972] 2 O.R. 686, at p. 701 (*per* Fraser J.); affd (1974), 1 O.R. (2d) 482; *Pinchin v. Santam Insurance Co.*, [1963] 2 S.A. 254; *Watt v. Rama*, [1972] V.R. 353. See generally, Samuels, "Injuries to Unborn Children" (1974), 12 Alta. L. Rev. 266; Gordon, "The Unborn Plaintiff" (1965), 63 Mich. L. Rev. 579; Winfield, "The Unborn Child" (1942), 4 U. of T.L.J. 278, 8 Camb. L.J. 76; Bennett, "Liability of Manufacturers of Thalidomide" (1965), 39 A.L.J. 256; Lovell and Griffith-Jones, "The Sins of the Fathers' — Tort Liability for Pre-Natal Injuries" (1974), 90 L.Q. Rev. 531.

64   *Walker v. Great Northern Ry. Co. of Ireland* (1891), 28 L.R. Ir. 69.

65   *Davey v. Victoria General Hospital* (1995), 27 C.C.L.T. (2d) 303 (Man. Q.B.); see also *Gibbons v. Port Hope & District Hospital* (1999), 124 O.A.C. 149 46 C.C.L.T. (2d) 266 and 268 (C.A.), point conceded.

66   [1999] 2 S.C.R. 753, 174 D.L.R. (4th) 1, 45 C.C.L.T. (2d) 217, at p. 255.

67   [1933] S.C.R. 456, [1933] 4 D.L.R. 337.

had, if actually born at the date of the accident. By a majority, the court held that the evidence of causal connection between the defendant's conduct and the resulting harm furnished more than a mere conjectural basis.

It was not entirely clear that this civil law decision would be followed by the common law courts. *Duval v. Seguin*[68] clarified the position. The injured plaintiff, Ann Duval, had been *en ventre sa mère* at the time of an auto accident, which took place some 31 weeks after the date of conception. She was born prematurely, some two or three weeks after the accident, physically disabled and mentally retarded as a result. Mr. Justice Fraser, at trial, held that a duty was owed to an unborn child if it was subsequently born alive. Explaining this conclusion, His Lordship declared:

> Procreation is normal and necessary for the preservation of the race. If a driver drives on a highway without due care for other users it is foreseeable that some of the other users of the highway will be pregnant women and that a child *en ventre sa mère* may be injured. Such a child therefore falls well within the area of potential danger which the driver is required to foresee and take reasonable care to avoid. . . .
>
> [A]n unborn child is within the foreseeable risk incurred by a negligent motorist. When the unborn child becomes a living person and suffers damages as a result of pre-natal injuries caused by the fault of the negligent motorist the cause of action is completed. A tortfeasor is as liable to the child who has suffered prenatal injury as to the victim with a thin skull or other physical defect. In the instant case the plaintiff sues, as a living person, for damages suffered by her since her birth as a result of prenatal injury caused by the fault of the defendant. In my opinion she is entitled to recover such damages.[69]

His Lordship observed that the older cases denying liability for prenatal injuries were based on difficulties of proof of causation and the fear of perjury. He felt that scientific advances improved the chances of establishing causation. He also thought that to refuse to recognize such a right would be "manifestly unjust and unreasonable".

The holding in this case has now been enshrined in legislation which reads:

> No person is disentitled from recovering damages in respect of injuries for the reason only that the injuries were incurred before his or her birth.[70]

This makes good sense, since pregnancy is not an altogether unexpected event in our society. Ever since the thalidomide tragedy it has become apparent that the foetus is a fragile being which can be damaged prior to birth, and which needs protection from negligent conduct.

This duty to a born-alive child for negligent conduct prior to its birth is not owed to it by its own mother. In *Dobson v. Dobson*[71] the majority of the Supreme Court of Canada, led by Justice Cory, held that a mother, who drives negligently, owes no duty to her foetus or subsequently born child because such a duty would interfere

---

[68] *Supra*, n. 63.
[69] *Ibid.*, at pp. 701-02.
[70] The Family Law Act, R.S.O. 1990, c. F.3, s. 66.
[71] *Supra*, n. 60.

with the privacy and autonomy rights of women in that it might lead to the judicial regulation of life-style decisions of pregnant women. It was also thought that it would be difficult to articulate satisfactory standards of conduct for pregnant women. Such a duty, if one were to be created, must be established by the legislature, as was done in the U.K., but only with regard to automobile accidents.[72] The dissenting Justices, led by Justice Major, thought there would be no intrusion on the driving conduct of pregnant women, since they already owed a general duty to the public and even to their passengers, including their other children as well as the unborn children of their pregnant passengers. They felt the life-style issues should be dealt with later in cases, as they may arise, and not in this case.

Following *Dobson*, it is now obvious that no duty would be owed to a born-alive child for the negligent "lifestyle" choices of a pregnant mother.[73]

The duty of care owed to born-alive children in the U.S. is highly complex and controversial.[74] Some American courts have recognized actions on behalf of children whose injury could be attributed to a pre-conception event,[75] but others have refused to do so.[76]

2. WRONGFUL BIRTH, WRONGFUL LIFE, WRONGFUL PREGNANCY

A cause of action now exists for negligence which results in "wrongful birth", "wrongful life" or "wrongful pregnancy".[77] According to Lax J.,[78] a "wrongful birth" action is usually brought by the parents of a child born with birth defects who allege that their entitlement to make an informed choice regarding whether or not to proceed with a pregnancy was denied by the negligent conduct of a doctor. In Canada, "wrongful birth" claims arising from the birth of an injured

---

[72]   Congenital Disabilities Act, 1976 (U.K), s. 1(1).

[73]   *Winnipeg Child and Family Services (Northwest Area) v. G. (D.F.),* [1997] 3 S.C.R. 925, 152 D.L.R. (4th) 193, not a tort case.

[74]   See Dobbs, *The Law of Torts,* (2000) for a complete summary of the American development.

[75]   *Renslow v. Mennonite Hospital* (1977), 367 N.E. 2d 1250 (Ill.), birth defect because of Rh factor sensitization; see also *Jorgensen v. Meade Johnson Lab, Inc.* (1973), 483 F. 2d 237 (10th Cir.), claim for twins born with mental deficiencies as result of oral contraceptive taken by mother prior to conception.

[76]   See *Albala v. City of New York* (1981), 445 N.Y.S. 2d 108, preconception tort arising from negligently performed abortion denied; *Enright by Enright v. Eli Lilly & Co.* (1991), 570 N.E. 2d 198 (N.Y.), no cause of action in negligence for child born with birth defects as a result of damage to mother's reproductive system caused by her *in utero* exposure to DES; and *Hegyes v. Unjian Enterprises, Inc.* (1991), 286 Cal. Rptr. 85 (Cal. App. 2 Dist.), no duty extended to a child who alleged preconception negligence against driver involved in car accident with her mother two years prior to the child's conception.

[77]   See Fleming, *supra,* n. 3, at p. 184 ". . . the defendant has not caused the infant's injury but merely failed to prevent its birth". See Morrissey, "Wrongful Life Actions in the 1990's; The Continuing Need to Define and Measure a Plaintiff's Injury" (1991), 23 Univ. of Toledo Law Rev. 157; Rodgers-Magnet, "Action for Wrongful Life" (1979), 7 C.C.L.T. 242; Tedeschi, "On Tort Liability for Wrongful Life" (1979), 7 C.C.L.T. 242; Tedeschi, "On Tort Liability for Wrongful Life", [1966] Israel L. Rev. 513.

[78]   *Kealey v. Berezowski* (1996), 30 O.R. (3d) 37 (Ont. Gen. Div.).

child have yielded damages for both pain and suffering by the parents and damages for the cost of raising the child, as in *Cherry (Guardian) v. Borsman*,[79] where, following a failed abortion, the parents of a severely handicapped child and the child recovered.[80] It is unlikely that an action by a biological father, who is not married to the mother, seeking the cost of raising the child would succeed.[81]

"Wrongful life" actions arise from similar situations, but are usually brought on behalf of the child. Generally, courts have been reluctant to recognize such actions because of the difficulty in quantifying the difference between a healthy life, a life with birth defects and non-existence. It is also "repugnant to our cultural ethos to complain about the circumstances of one's conception".[82] An independent "wrongful life" action by an injured child has yet to succeed in a Canada,[83] although the court in *Cherry* awarded damages to the injured child in conjunction with the "wrongful birth" claims of its parents. In *Arndt v. Smith*,[84] the British Columbia Supreme Court stated that the abandonment of a wrongful life claim brought by an injured child following her mother's infection with chicken pox during pregnancy was a proper acceptance of ". . . the inevitable finding of the Court that no such action lies".[85]

Finally, "wrongful pregnancy" is a third and related action which is brought by parents who allege that a particular act of negligence has resulted in an unplanned pregnancy which may produce a healthy or an injured child. It differs from "wrongful birth" to the extent that it deals with pre-conception rather than post-conception negligence. In such cases, where the child is born healthy, Canadian courts have been willing to award damages related to the pregnancy

---

[79] (1992), 94 D.L.R. (4th) 487 (B.C.C.A.); leave to appeal to S.C.C. refused April 15, 1993, B.C.S.C. at 798.

[80] See also *H. (R.) v. Hunter* (1996), 32 C.C.L.T. (2d) 44 (Ont. Gen. Div.), [1966] O.J. No. 4477, in which McLean J. of the Ontario Court General Division awarded almost 3 million dollars to the parents of two boys suffering from a severe form of muscular dystrophy which was inherited by them through their mother. The damages reflect the past and future lost income of the mother and the cost of caring for the children until their deaths. See also *Krangle (Guardian Ad Litem Of) v. Brisco* (2000), 2 C.C.L.T. (3d) 13 (B.C.C.A.); leave to appeal allowed (2000), 193 D.L.R. (4th) vi.

[81] *Kovacvich v. Ortho Pharmaceutical (Canada) Ltd.* (1995), 25 C.C.L.T. (2d) 295 (B.C.S.C.). But see *Freeman v. Sutter* (1995), 26 C.C.L.T. (2d) 99 (Man. Q.B.) (Master Harrison); affd 29 C.C.L.T. (2d) 220 (Man. Q.B.); revd 29 C.C.L.T. (2d) 215 (Man. C.A.).

[82] Fleming, *supra*, n. 3, at p. 184. See also *Jones (Guaradian Ad Litem Of) v. Rostvig* (1999), 44 C.C.L.T. (2d) 313 (B.C.S.C.).

[83] *Kealey, supra*, n. 78, at p. 54.

[84] [1994] 8 W.W.R. 568 (B.C.S.C.); revd on other grounds, [1995] 7 W.W.R. 378 (B.C.C.A.), decision of the trial judge restored, (1997), 213 N.R. 243 (S.C.C.). Cory J. held for the majority that a doctor's failure to warn a pregnant mother of the risks to the foetus by the mother's chicken pox did not affect her decision to continue the pregnancy and so did not cause the loss suffered by the birth of an injured child.

[85] In the U.K., "wrongful life" actions are also unavailable for children, see *McKay v. Essex Area Health Authority*, [1982] 2 All E.R. 771 (C.A.).

and birth itself, but not for the cost of raising the child.[86] In *Cryderman v. Ringrose*,[87] the Alberta Court of Appeal awarded $5,000 for pain and suffering as a result of an abortion necessitated by a failed sterilization. In *Doiron v. Orr*,[88] although no negligence was found when a child was born following an unsuccessful sterilization procedure, Garett J. would have awarded $1,000 in pain and suffering. He refused to assess damages for the cost of raising the child, labelling the claim as "grotesque". In *Suite v. Cooke*,[89] the Quebec Court of Appeal insisted on considering not simply the cost of maintaining the child, but also the emotional benefit and financial support which a healthy child would eventually bring to the family.

More recently, in *Kealey v. Berezowski*,[90] Lax J. adopted a different approach to the assessment of damages for the unplanned birth of a healthy child following a negligently performed sterilization procedure. An award of $30,000 in general damages was given to the mother for having to undergo the pregnancy, labour, delivery and a second tubal ligation. The mother and the father were also awarded special damages for lost income. No damages were awarded, however, for the cost of rearing a child whom the plaintiffs loved and were able to provide for financially. Rather than basing this decision on public policy arguments or on a corresponding benefits and burdens analysis, Lax J. found that such damages did not ". . . fall within the scope of the wrongdoing", because the existence of the healthy child did not in itself constitute a harm. Referring to the court's reasons in *Doiron, supra,* Lax J. commented that "[t]he time has long passed when a court is free (if indeed, there ever was such a time) to dismiss a claim such as this as 'grotesque'. . .".[91]

C. Failure to Act

The common law has treated the Good Samaritan with uncommon harshness over the years, while the priest and the Levite have been treated with uncommon generosity.[92] Those who attempt in good faith to assist someone in peril expose

---

[86] See, however, *Troppi v. Scarf* (1971), 18 N.W. 2d 511 (Mich.) where damages were allowed for the cost of rearing a child.

[87] (1978), 89 D.L.R. (3d) 32 (Alta. C.A.). See also *McFarlane v. Tayside Health Board*, [1999] 4 All E.R. 961 (H.L.).

[88] (1978), 20 O.R. (2d) 71 (H.C.J.).

[89] [1955] A.Q. No. 696. See also *Cataford v. Moreau* (1978), 114 D.L.R. (3d) 585 (Que. S.C.).

[90] *Supra*, n. 75. See also *Thake v. Maurice*, [1986] 1 All E.R. 497 (C.A.), a doctor liable for pain and suffering of birth because negligently performed sterilization operation. Loss not set-off by the joy of caring for a healthy baby. The lower court had also awarded damages for the cost of providing for the child's birth and upkeep, which award was not disputed before the Court of Appeal. Now, however, these latter damages would not be covered, see *McFarlane*, n. 87.

[91] *Kealy, supra*, n. 78, at p. 61.

[92] See Ames, "Laws and Morals" (1908), 22 Harv. L. Rev. 97, reprinted in *Selected Essays on the Law of Torts*, p. 13; Bohlen, "The Moral Duty to Aid Others as a Basis of Tort Liability" (1908), 56 U. Pa. L. Rev. 217, 316; Linden, "Tort Liability for Criminal Nonfeasance" (1966), 44 Can. Bar Rev. 25; Linden, "Rescuers and Good Samaritans" (1971), 34 Mod. L. Rev. 241, reprinted in

themselves to potential civil liability if they bungle the attempt, but those who stand idly by without lifting a finger incur no liability, although the latter conduct is probably more reprehensible and more deserving of a civil sanction. It is certainly no credit to the common law that there is no duty to rescue a drowning person,[93] to warn a blind person who is stepping in front of a moving automobile,[94] or to prevent someone from walking into the mouth of a dangerous machine.[95] Doctors, who faithfully subscribe to the Hippocratic Oath, are not subject to civil liability if they hypocritically refuse to attend a dying patient.[96] Nor does the common law require one to feed the starving, to bind up the wounds of those who are bleeding to death,[97] or to prevent a child from engaging in dangerous conduct.[98] A neighbour need not warn anyone when he smells gas from a leak that later causes an explosion.[99]

The common law has acknowledged on occasion that "the impulsive desire to save human life when in peril is one of the most beneficial instincts of humanity",[100] and that "to protect those who are not able to protect themselves is a duty which everyone owes to society".[101] Nevertheless, on the question of civil liability, it has adopted a hands-off policy. The regulation of this type of conduct has been assigned to the "higher law" and to the "voice of conscience" both of which would appear "singularly ineffective either to prevent the harm or to compensate the victim".[102]

The situation has been well described by Mr. Justice Sopinka of the Supreme Court of Canada when he explained:[103]

> The good Samaritan deserves the world's accolades because he had no legal duty to act and would not have been civilly liable if he, too, had crossed over to the other side as did the Levite and the priest.

(1972), 10 Alta. L. Rev. 89; Weinrib, "The Case for a Duty to Rescue" (1980), 90 Yale L.J. 247; Law Reform Commission of Canada, *Omissions, Negligence and Endangering*, Working Paper 46 (1985).

[93] *Osterlind v. Hill* (1928), 263 Mass. 73, 160 N.E. 301; *contra*, if passenger or employee. See *Horsley v. MacLaren*, [1969] 2 O.R. 137; revd [1970] 2 O.R. 487; affd (1972), 22 D.L.R. (3d) 545 (S.C.C.), overruling *Vanvalkenberg v. Northern Navigation Co.* (1913), 30 O.L.R. 142, 19 D.L.R. 649 (C.A.).

[94] *Restatement, Torts, Second*, §314, Illustration 1.

[95] *Buch v. Amory Manufacturing Co.* (1896), 69 N.H. 257, 44 Atl. 809; *Gautret v. Egerton* (1867), L.R. 2 C.P. 371

[96] *Hurley v. Eddingfield* (1901), 156 Ind. 416, 59 N.E. 1058; *Smith v. Rae* (1919), 46 O.L.R. 518 (C.A.). See Gray and Sharpe, "Doctors, Samaritans and the Accident Victim" (1975), 11 Osgoode Hall L.J. 1.

[97] *Allen v. Hixson* (1900), 111 Ga. 460, 36 S.E. 810.

[98] *Sidwell v. McVay* (1955), 282 P. 2d 756 (Okla.).

[99] *Aiello v. Centra Gas Ontario Inc.* (1999), 47 C.C.L.T. (2d) 39 (Ont. S.C.J.), gas company and others held liable, but not neighbour or neighbour's expert workers.

[100] *Scaramanga v. Stamp* (1880), 5 C.P.D. 295, at p. 304 (C.A.); Cockburn C.J., cited in *Love v. New Fairview Corp.* (1904), 10 B.C.R. 330 (C.A.).

[101] *Jenoure v. Delmege*, [1891] A.C. 73, at p. 77 (P.C.).

[102] *Prosser and Keeton on the Law of Torts*, 5th ed. (1984), at p. 375.

[103] See *Hall v. Hebert*, [1993] 2 S.C.R. 159, 15 C.C.L.T. (2d) 93, at p. 137, dissenting.

In short, our courts have established no general civil duty to render assistance to individuals in danger. The examples are all instances of mere nonfeasance, and there is generally no liability for nonfeasance, although Quebec,[104] several U.S. states and most European countries recognize such an obligation.[105] Professor Bohlen has written that "There is no distinction more deeply rooted in the common law than that between misfeasance and nonfeasance, between active misconduct working positive injury to others and passive inaction. . . ."[106] Indeed, he insisted that requirements of positive action are "exceptional" and "abnormal". This distinction, admittedly a difficult one to draw in practice, is supported by some[107] and attacked by others.[108] In any event, courts do apply different concepts to cases of inaction than they do to cases of positive action.

This is not merely cruelty for its own sake. An historical explanation is that the early courts did not wish to concern themselves with the supervision of acts and omissions because they encountered sufficient difficulties in their regulation of the more flagrant positive aggressions.[109] Only when one person voluntarily undertook an obligation by entering into a special relationship with another, as in the case of gratuitous bailment for example, did the courts impose a duty of care upon the bailee in favour of the bailor.[110]

1. POLICY UNDERLYING NONFEASANCE RULE

But no legal doctrine can long survive for historical reasons alone. There are also various policy reasons that may explain the longevity of the nonfeasance principle. Firstly, through this doctrine the common law in manifesting its concern for rugged individualism, self-sufficiency, and the independence of human kind.[111] However, a call for help in time of emergency is a natural reaction of even the most individualistic people. Indeed it is not a virtue to stubbornly resist help in time of danger and it may be a vice of the common law

---

[104] *Gaudreault v. Drapeau* (1987), 45 C.C.L.T. 202 (Que. S.C.), based on Quebec Charter of Rights which creates a duty to rescue. Vermont, Minnesota and Rhode Island also require rescue; see Shapo, *The Law of Torts* (2000), p. 300.

[105] Dawson, "*Negotiorum Gestio:* The Altruistic Intermeddler" (1961), 74 Harv. L. Rev. 1073; Rudzinski, "The Duty of Rescue: A Comparative Analysis" printed in Radcliffe (ed.), *The Good Samaritan and The Law* (1966); "Failure to Rescue: A Comparative Study" (1952), 52 Colum. L. Rev. 631.

[106] Bohlen, *supra*, n. 92, at pp. 219 and 221.

[107] Wright, "Negligent 'Acts or Omissions'" (1941), 19 Can. Bar Rev. 465, at p. 473; Thayer, "Public Wrong and Private Action" (1914), 27 Harv. L. Rev. 317. See also, *Wasney v. Jurazsky* (1933), 41 Man. R. 46, [1933] 1 W.W.R. 155 (C.A.), relying on Thayer: *East Suffolk Rivers Catchment Bd. v. Kent*, [1941] A.C. 74.

[108] Morris, *Studies in the Law of Torts* (1952), p. 141. See *Vancouver v. McPhalen* (1911), 45 S.C.R. 194, where Mr. Justice Idington said ". . . the sooner the distinction between nonfeasance and misfeasance . . . is discarded, the better."

[109] *Prosser and Keeton, op. cit. supra*, n. 102, at p. 373.

[110] Bohlen, *supra*, n. 92, at p. 316; *Coggs v. Bernard* (1703), 2 Ld. Raym. 909, 91 E.R. 25.

[111] McNiece and Thornton, "Affirmative Duties in Tort" (1949), 58 Yale L.J. 1272, at p. 1288; Hale, "Prima Facie Torts, Combination and Nonfeasance" (1946), 46 Colum. L. Rev. 198, at p. 213.

to expect such conduct.[112] Moreover, the *laissez-faire* philosophy of earlier times is being gradually eclipsed by legislation requiring positive conduct. Statutes have been passed which require individuals, under threat of criminal prosecution, to serve their country in time of war and peace, to pay income taxes and to file tax returns, to disclose certain political affiliations and certain financial dealings, and to insure themselves against disability, penury in old age, and the inability to pay for medical services.[113] The common law courts should reflect these changing attitudes and conditions.

Secondly, it is argued that the law should not try to enforce unselfishness by making one serve one's fellows, because this would be an undue infringement of personal liberty;[114] a type of "compulsory altruism".[115] In addition, it is often much more burdensome to demand positive conduct of people than to regulate the way they engage in positive conduct. It has been suggested that the enforcement of morality should be left to the individual conscience.[116] Let those who refuse to offer assistance be branded a "moral monster" by their peers or by their church,[117] but let us not transmit tort law into "an instrument to enforce general unselfishness".[118] Underlying all of this is the notion that the proper function of the common law is to prevent people from harming one another rather than to force them to confer benefits upon one another merely because they are human beings.[119]

Thirdly, courts have hesitated to compel people to expose themselves to danger in order to assist someone else.[120] Few, if any, would criticize those who, for fear of their own safety, fail to leap upon the armed attacker of a complete stranger. Most people are not made that way, and the common law wisely recognizes this. But this contention is largely illusory because, if a general duty to assist were created, no court would expect rescuers to hurl themselves upon the assailant of a third person and engage in mortal combat. This duty need only be a "duty of easy rescue",[121] which would require taking reasonable steps, such as shouting or calling the police. This judicial reticence may also be attributed in part to the fact that injured rescuers used to be denied damages on the ground of voluntary assumption of risk or because they were the "cause of [their] own misfortune".[122] This impediment to recovery has now been obliterated and rescuers are entitled to recover in tort from anyone who negligently places

---

[112] Hale, *supra*, n. 111, at p. 213.
[113] Snyder, "Liability for Negative Conduct" (1949), 35 Va. L. Rev. 446.
[114] See Minor, "Moral Obligation as a Basis of Liability" (1923), 9 Va. L. Rev. 421, at p. 422.
[115] *Stovin v. Wise*, [1996] 3 All E.R. 801, at p. 806, *per* Lord Nicholls.
[116] Ames, *supra*, n. 92.
[117] See *Buch v. Amory*, *supra*, n. 95.
[118] Hale, *supra*, n. 111, at p. 215.
[119] Ames, *supra*, n. 92, at p. 16 (in *Selected Essays*).
[120] McNiece and Thornton, *supra*, n. 107, at p. 1288; Hale, *supra*, n. 111, at p. 215.
[121] See Weinrib, *supra*, n. 92, at p. 268. See also Law Reform Commission of Canada, *supra*, n. 92.
[122] See, for example, *Kimball v. Butler Bros.* (1910), 15 O.W.R. 221 (C.A.); *Anderson v. Northern Ry. Co.* (1875), 25 U.C.C.P. 301 (C.A.).

another in a position of danger which invites rescue,[123] from individuals who place *themselves* in such a predicament,[124] and even where rescuers are injured by the supervening negligence of a third party.[125]

Some of the reasons given against the creation of a general duty to render assistance to one in danger are administrative in nature.[126] Firstly, there is the problem of selecting the individual to be sued. It is a difficult matter to single out the person on the crowded beach who is to bear the responsibility for the failure to rescue the drowning person. Whoever is chosen might well point to the others and say, "Why me?" This is not, however, an insurmountable obstacle. All of the individuals who were aware of the situation and were capable of assisting *should* be held responsible. It should not be a valid defence for one culprit to point to another who has escaped that obligation; it does not render one any less culpable.

Secondly, it has been suggested that if we decree that one person must assist another person in peril, hordes of rescuers might impede each other in the rush to comply with the law and the person in trouble might end up worse off, rather than better. This fear is completely unfounded because usually several people can better effect a rescue than one person alone.[127]

A third problem is that the scope of the duty defies precise delineation. It is no easy task to decide the degree of danger to which one should be required to expose oneself, the type of aid that must be offered, and the length of time for which the obligation will extend. But these problems can be solved, as are many others in tort law, by requiring reasonable steps to be taken by all rescuers after their initial intervention. The common law has long been accustomed to drawing lines and making distinctions. There is no reason why feasible rules cannot be fashioned on a case to case basis.

It is time for the common law to establish a duty of rescue since it would give "expression to the law's understanding of liberty", it would reveal the law's "attitude of benevolence" and it would "render concrete the notion of ethical dealing between persons".[128] To that end, the courts should adopt the test propounded by Dean Prosser, which is as good a start on a guideline as common lawyers are accustomed to: "knowledge of serious peril, threatening death or great bodily harm to another, which an identified defendant might avoid with

---

[123] *Wagner v. International Railway* (1921), 232 N.Y. 176, 133 N.E. 437; *Haynes v. Harwood*, [1935] 1 K.B. 146 (C.A.); *Morgan v. Aylen*, [1942] 1 All E.R. 489; *Seymour v. Winnipeg Electric Railway Co.* (1910), 13 W.L.R. 566, 19 Man. R. 412 (C.A.). If conduct is rash, no recovery, however, *McDonald v. Burr*, [1919] 3 W.W.R. 825, 49 D.L.R. 396 (Sask. C.A.). See generally, Linden, "Down with Foreseeability: Of Thin Skulls and Rescuers" (1969), 47 Can. Bar Rev. 545; see generally, Chapter 10.1.

[124] *Baker v. Hopkins*; *Ward v. Hopkins*, [1959] 1 W.L.R. 966, [1959] 3 All E.R. 225 (C.A.); *Horsley v. McLaren*, *supra*, n. 90; *Carney v. Buyea*, 271 App. Div. 338, 651 N.Y.S. 2d 902.

[125] *Chapman v. Hearse* (1961), S.A.S.R. 51; affd 106 C.L.R. 112.

[126] See McNiece and Thornton, *supra*, n. 107, at p. 1288.

[127] Hale, *supra*, n. 111, at p. 215.

[128] Weinrib, *supra*, n. 92, at p. 293.

little inconvenience, creates a sufficient relation to impose a duty of action".[129] No court, however, has yet adopted this humane rule, although Quebec, Europe and several U.S. legislatures have.[130]

2. DUTY TO RESCUE: SPECIAL SITUATIONS

Despite the many policy reasons militating against the creation of a duty to help others, the courts, in response to the dictates of humanitarianism, have fashioned obligations to assist in specific situations. For instance, where one *negligently* places another in a position of danger, one is under an obligation to render assistance.[131] Thus, if one negligently injured another, one is obliged to secure medical assistance in order to minimize the injury. This duty is also imposed in some jurisdictions where the injury is caused, albeit innocently, by some instrumentality under the actor's control.[132]

There is a growing group of special relations which import an obligation to engage in positive conduct for the benefit of another. Normally, there is some element of control or some economic benefit inuring to the person as a result of the relation, which justifies the creation of the duty.[133] For example, if there is a contract of a bailment,[134] a failure to act may be actionable. It is not enough, however, if the contract is with a third person, as where a doctor agreed with a husband to attend his wife at childbirth.[135] Carriers, innkeepers, warehousepeople and public utilities, who hold themselves out to the public as being prepared to give service, are subject to this responsibility.[136] So too, an employer may be obliged to provide aid to a servant in peril,[137] or an employee who gets drunk at an office party,[138] a shopkeeper to an invitee,[139] a school to a pupil,[140] a ship's captain

---

[129] *Prosser and Keeton, op. cit. supra*, n. 102, at p. 377. See also Rudolph, "The Duty to Act: A Proposed Rule" (1965), 44 Neb. L. Rev. 499.

[130] Franklin, "Vermont Requires Rescue" (1972), 25 Stan. L. Rev. 51. See *supra*, n. 104.

[131] *Northern Central Ry. Co. v. State* (1868), 29 Md. 420.

[132] *Restatement, Second, Torts*, §322. See also *Ayres & Co. v. Hicks* (1942), 220 Ind. 86, 40 N.E. 2d 334; 41 N.E. 2d 356, invitee also.

[133] Bohlen, *supra*, n. 92; McNiece and Thornton, *supra*, n. 111.

[134] *Turner v. Stallibrass*, [1898] 1 Q.B. 56 (C.A.); *Kelly v. Metropolitan Railway Co.*, [1895] 1 Q.B. 944 (C.A.); *Lee Cooper Ltd. v. C.H. Jeakins & Sons Ltd.*, [1965] 1 All E.R. 280, [1967] 2 Q.B. 1.

[135] *Smith v. Rae* (1919), 46 O.L.R. 518 (C.A.), *dictum*.

[136] Arturbun, "The Origins and First Test of Public Callings" (1927), 75 U. Pa. L. Rev. 217; *Restatement, Second, Torts*, §314A.

[137] *Harris v. Pennsylvania R. Co.* (1931), 50 F. 2d 866; *Szabo v. Pennsylvania R. Co.* (1945), 123 N.J.L. 331, 40 A. 2d 562.

[138] *Hunt (Litigation Guardian of) v. Sutton Group Incentive Realty Inc.* (2001), 4 C.C.L.T. (3d) 277 (Ont. S.C.J.), 25% liable to drunk employee hurt while driving home, not social host situation, see p. 292 (*per* Marchand J.); *cf.*, *John v. Flynn*, [2001] O.J. No. 2578, 54 O.R. (3d) 774 (C.A.).

[139] *Ayres and Co. v. Hicks* (1942), 220 Ind. 86, 40 N.E. 2d 334; 41 N.E. 2d 356, instrumentality also.

[140] *Pirkle v. Oakdale Union Grammar School* (1953), 40 Cal. App. 2d 207, 253 P. 2d 1; see also *Hamstra v. B.C. Rugby Union* (1989), 1 C.C.L.T. (2d) 78 (B.C.S.C.); *Moddejonge v. Huron County Bd. of Education*, [1972] 2 O.R. 437 (H.C.J.); *Dziwenka v. R.*, [1972] S.C.R. 419; *Bain v. Calgary Board of Education* (1993), 18 C.C.L.T. (2d) 249 (Alta. Q.B.), "close legal proximity". For other relations importing liability, see McNiece and Thornton, *supra*, n. 111.

to a passenger,[141] and a driver to a child passenger.[142] Obligations to take positive action are also imposed upon occupiers of premises to make their property safe for the reception of certain entrants and for passersby on the highway.[143] A parent may be required to protect a child from abuse by another parent.[144] A police officer may owe a civil duty to report dangerous road conditions.[145] So too, it is possible for the police to be held liable to a rape victim, who was a prime target of a serial rapist in her neighbourhood, for failing to warn her about the danger. Mr. Justice Moldaver explained that "the police have a duty to warn citizens of foreseeable harm".[146] Institutions which have custody over people, such as hospitals,[147] jails,[148] and the like,[149] may be obliged to take reasonable steps to protect those under their care. There will undoubtedly be additions to this list of special situations in the years ahead, because "the categories are no more closed than other categories of negligence".[150]

---

[141] *Horsley v. MacLaren*, [1970] 2 O.R. 487; affd (1972), 22 D.L.R. (3d) 545 (S.C.C.).

[142] *Galaske v. O'Donnell*, [1994] 1 S.C.R. 670, failure to apply seat belt.

[143] See Fleming, *The Law of Torts*, 9th ed. (1998), Chapter 22; *Prosser and Keeton, op. cit. supra*, n. 102, Chapter 11. See also *Sturdy v. R.* (1974), 47 D.L.R. (3d) 7 (Fed. Ct. T.D.), no liability for bear attack in national park.

[144] *H. (D.L.) v. F. (G.A.)* (1987), 43 C.C.L.T. 110 (Ont. H.C.J.).

[145] *Schacht v. R.*, [1973] 1 O.R. 221, 30 D.L.R. (3d) 641 (*per* Schroeder J.A.); vard 55 D.L.R. (3d) 96 (*sub nom. O'Rourle v. Schacht*), excavation; see also *Millette v. Cote*, [1971] 2 O.R. 155 (*per* Galligan J.); revd on this point because of lack of causation, [1972] 3 O.R. 224; revd in part (1974), 51 D.L.R. (3d) 244, ice. *Cf., Lafleur v. Maryniuk* (1990), 4 C.C.L.T. (2d) 78 (B.C.S.C.), police not required to prevent impaired drivers from continuing to drive; *Edgar v. Richmond Twp.* (1991), 6 C.C.L.T. (2d) 241 (B.C.S.C.), person jumped out window during police "rescue".

[146] *Doe v. Metropolitan Toronto (Municipality) Commrs. of Police* (1990), 5 C.C.L.T. (2d) 77, at p. 84 (Ont. Div. Ct.).

[147] *Lawson v. Wellesley Hospital* (1975), 9 O.R. (2d) 677 (C.A.); affd on other grounds, [1978] 1 S.C.R. 893; *cf., Wenden v. Trikha* (1991), 8 C.C.L.T. (2d) 138 (Alta. Q.B.), affd 14 C.C.L.T. (2d) 225 (Alta. C.A.), leave to appeal to S.C.C. refused, [1993] 3 S.C.R. ix, not liable for insane person's motoring negligence.

[148] *Williams v. New Brunswick* (1985), 34 C.C.L.T. 299 (N.B.C.A.); *MacLean v. R.*, [1973] S.C.R. 2, at pp. 6-7, 27 D.L.R. (3d) 365, at p. 368 (*per* Hall J.), liability when bale of straw knocked prisoner over and disabled him; *Timm v. R.*, [1965] 1 Ex. C.R. 174, at p. 178, duty to take care, but no liability when prisoner knocked off truck by another prisoner; *Ellis v. Home Office*, [1953] 2 All E.R. 149, at p. 154 (C.A.) (*per* Singleton L.J.), duty but no liability for injury of one prisoner by another; *Howley v. R.*, [1973] F.C. 184, no liability for stabbing; *Reeves v. Commissioner of Police of the Metropolis*, [1999] 3 All E.R. 897 (H.L.), liability for suicide based on "complete control" of deceased, who was held equally responsible. See also *Funk Estate v. Clapp* (1988), 54 D.L.R. (4th) 512 (B.C.C.A.), no liability for suicide, though duty.

[149] *Home Office v. Dorset Yacht Co. Ltd.*, [1970] 2 All E.R. 294 (H.L.), liable for Borstal boys who damaged yacht during an escape attempted due to negligence of guards; *MacAlpine v. H. (T.)* (1991), 7 C.C.L.T. (2d) 113 (B.C.C.A.), duty but no liability re statute; *R. (G.B.) v. Hollett* (1996), 30 C.C.L.T. (2d) 215 (N.S.C.A.); leave to appeal to S.C.C. refused May 15, 1997, B.S.C.C. at 922, reform school liable for sexual assault by employee; *Barrett v. Enfield London Borough Council*, [1999] 3 All E.R. 193 (H.L.), children in government's care can sue for mental damage; *cf., P. Perl Exporters Ltd. v. Camden London Borough Council*, [1983] 3 All E.R. 161, no liability for vandals who entered from defendant's property.

[150] *Stovin v. Wise*, [1996] 3 All E.R. 801, at p. 806 (*per* Lord Nicholls).

3. MISFEASANCE: CREATION OF RISK

Courts have categorized conduct which superficially resembles nonfeasance as misfeasance in order to impose civil liability.[151] Thus, the failure of a driver to apply the brakes of a speeding automobile, the omission of a proper signal for a proposed left turn, and neglecting to shut off the steam of a train in order to avoid an accident,[152] are considered properly to be negligent, positive conduct rather than failure to act.

Akin to this is the situation where the defendants themselves *create a risk* of injury to some third person,[153] for which an obligation to aid may spring up even where the defendants are innocent of any negligence. For example, in the case of *Oke v. Wiede Transport Ltd.*,[154] the defendant, without negligence, collided with a metal traffic signpost on the gravel strip dividing two lanes of a highway. He left it, bent over and projecting at right angles, without reporting to the authorities. The plaintiff motorist, illegally using the median strip to pass another vehicle, was fatally injured when he was impaled by this post. Although the majority of the Manitoba Court of Appeal dismissed the action on the ground of lack of foresight, Freedman J.A. dissented and argued that the defendant was not in the same position as any other motorist with regard to the dangerous signpost. Firstly, he had collided with the post, albeit without negligence. Secondly, he had collided with the sign and had had an opportunity to observe the hazard it created, while a passing motorist could do so only fleetingly. Thirdly, he had "participated in the creation of the "hazard", recognized his obligation to do something, and even took some steps in that direction. This dissent may well be a premonition of things to come.

Another significant case is *Menow v. Honsberger and Jordan House Ltd.*,[155] where an intoxicated patron of a bar was turned out of a hotel that was situated near a busy highway. As he walked along the road in a drunken state, after having been given a lift by a passing motorist and let off again, the plaintiff was run over by an automobile which was negligently driven. Mr. Justice Haines, at trial, held Menow, the plaintiff, the motorist who struck him, and the hotel, equally responsible for the accident. He felt that the innkeeper was partially at fault on the ground, *inter alia*, that his employees "owed the plaintiff a common

---

[151] *Prosser and Keeton, op. cit. supra*, n. 102, at p. 374.

[152] *Southern Ry. Co. v. Grizzle* (1960), 124 Ga. App. 735, 53 S.E. 2d 244; *cf., Kelly v. Metropolitan Railway Co.*, [1985] 1 Q.B. 944 (C.A.).

[153] See *Hardy v. Brooks* (1961), 103 Ga. App. 124, 118 S.E. 2d 492, cow left on road; *Simonsen v. Thorin* (1931), 120 Neb. 684, 234 N.W. 638, pole left on street.

[154] (1963), 41 D.L.R. (2d) 53 (Man. C.A.).

[155] [1970] 1 O.R. 54, at p. 62; affd [1971] 1 O.R. 129 (C.A.); affd [1974] S.C.R. 239. See Binchy, "Drink Now — Sue Later' (1975), 53 Can. Bar Rev. 344; *Schmidt v. Sharpe* (1983), 27 C.C.L.T. 1 (Ont. H.C.) (*per* Gray J.). See Kligman, "Innkeepers' Liability: Of the Alcoholic Excesses of Patrons" (1984), 27 C.C.L.T. 49, for an excellent summary of the cases. *Cf.*, where social host did not contribute to guest's drinking and did attempt to stop it, *Baumeister v. Drake* (1986), 38 C.C.L.T. 1 (B.C.S.C.), and where negligent, *Kelly v. Gwinnell* (1984), 476 A. 2d 1219 (N.J.).

law duty of care not to eject him if they knew or ought to have known that he would thereby be placed in a position of danger to his personal safety".

In affirming the decision, Mr. Justice Laskin (Martland and Spence JJ., concurring) of the Supreme Court of Canada relied on several factors and observed:

> If the hotel's only involvement was the supplying of beer consumed by Menow, it would be difficult to support the imposition of common law liability upon it for injuries suffered by Menow after being shown the door of the hotel and after leaving the hotel. Other persons on the highway, seeing Menow in an intoxicated condition, would not, by reason of that fact alone, come under any legal duty to steer him to safety, although it might be expected that good Samaritan impulses would move them to offer help. They would, however, be under a legal duty, as motorists for example, to take reasonable care to avoid hitting him, a duty in which Honsberger failed in this case. The hotel, however, was not in the position of persons in general who see an intoxicated person who appears to be unable to control his steps. It was in an invitor-invitee relationship with Menow as one of its patrons, and it was aware, through its employees, of his intoxicated condition, a condition which, on the findings of the trial judge, it fed in violation of applicable liquor licence and liquor control legislation. There was a probable risk of personal injury to Menow if he was turned out of the hotel to proceed on foot on a much-travelled highway passing in front of the hotel.
>
> There is, in my opinion, nothing unreasonable in calling upon the hotel in such circumstances to take care to see that Menow is not exposed to injury because of this intoxication. No inordinate burden would be placed upon it in obliging it to respond to Menow's need for protection. A call to the police or a call to his employer immediately come to mind as easily available preventative measures; . . . .
>
> The result to which I would come here does not mean (to use the words of the trial judge) that I would impose "a duty on every tavern-owner to act as a watch dog for all patrons who enter his place of business and drink to excess". A great deal turns on the knowledge of the operator (or his employees) of the patron and his condition where the issue is liability in negligence for injuries suffered by the patron.[156]

Mr. Justice Ritchie, (Judson J. concurring), based his decision on somewhat narrower grounds:

> For my part, however, the circumstances giving rise to the appellant's liability were that the innkeeper and his staff, who were well aware of the respondent's propensity for irresponsible behaviour under the influence of drink, assisted or at least permitted him to consume a quantity of beer which they should have known might well result in his being incapable of taking care of himself when exposed to the hazards of traffic. Their knowledge of the respondent's somewhat limited capacity for consuming alcoholic stimulants without becoming befuddled and sometime obstreperous, seized them with a duty to be careful not the serve him with repeated drinks after the effects of what he had already consumed should have been obvious.
>
> In my view, it was a breach of this duty which gave rise to liability in the present case.[157]

This obligation of taverns has been reaffirmed by the Supreme Court of Canada recently in *Stewart v. Pettie*,[158] where Mr. Justice Major declared that there was:

---

[156] [1974] S.C.R. 239, at p. 247.

[157] *Ibid.*, at p. 251.

[158] [1995] 1 S.C.R. 131, 23 C.C.L.T. (2d) 89, at p. 101, but no liability re no negligence and no proof of causation; see also *Hague v. Billings* (1989), 48 C.C.L.T. 192 (Ont. H.C.J.); revd in part

. . . no question that commercial vendors of alcohol owe a general duty of care to persons who can be expected to use the highways.

It is also an obligation placed on those who organize competitive events for profit to see that drunk people do not participate.[159] Social hosts have not yet been held liable.[160]

Courts have held liable owners of vehicles who have permitted,[161] or instructed,[162] impaired persons to drive their cars, on the theory that a duty is owed not to "put [someone] in the position where foreseeably he could suffer injury". A similar result follows if an owner of a motorcycle lends it to a young, unlicensed driver, who is hurt.[163] The negligent storing of a rifle can also lead to liability when someone gets shot as a result.[164]

Common carriers have been held liable for ejecting intoxicated passengers into situations of peril.[165] Similarly, where an occupier sent an ill visitor out of the house into a wintery night, the occupier was made to pay damages for the additional injuries suffered.[166] These situations are not ones of simple failure to act or nonfeasance; rather, the defendant is held liable for the positive creation of danger to the plaintiff.

4. UNDERTAKINGS AND RELIANCE

A mere gratuitous promise to render aid has long been held insufficient to create a duty to act in the absence of consideration.[167] Where the promised performance is undertaken and is negligently performed, however, liability may be imposed.[168] The law of contracts has been a willing accomplice in this endeavour,

---

(1993), 15 C.C.L.T. (2d) 264 (Ont. C.A.) on appeal percentage of hotel liability lowered to 15 per cent, where drivers drank and smoked marijuana causing accident; *Gouge v. Three Top Investment Holdings Inc.* (1994), 22 C.C.L.T. (2d) 281 (Ont. H.C.), hotel liable for over-serving motorcyclist who caused accident.

[159] *Crocker v. Sundance Northwest Resorts Ltd.* (1988), 44 C.C.L.T. 225 (S.C.C.), tube race.

[160] *Baumeister v. Drake* (1986), 38 C.C.L.T. 1 (B.C.S.C.), no negligence; *Haggarty v. Desmarais* (2000), 5 C.C.L.T. (3d) 38 (B.C.S.C.). Liability in the U.S. has been found, *Kelly v. Gwinnell*, 476 A.2d 1219 (N.J. 1984); see Olah, "Toward Social Host Liability in Alcohol Induced Torts" (1987), 8 Adv. Q. 36.

[161] *Hempler v. Todd* (1970), 14 D.L.R. (3d) 637 (Man.). *Cf., Pizzolon v. Pedrosa* (1988), 46 C.C.L.T. 243 (B.C.S.C.), no knowlege of drunkenness.

[162] *Ontario Hospital Services Commn v. Borsoski* (1973), 7 O.R. (2d) 83, 54 D.L.R. (3d) 339, at p. 351 (*per* Lerner J.), 75 per cent liability owner, 25 per cent driver.

[163] *Stermer v. Lawson* (1977), 79 D.L.R. (3d) 366 (B.C.), contributory negligence, percentage varied (1979), 11 C.C.L.T. 76 (B.C.C.A.).

[164] *Anderson v. Williams* (1997), 36 C.C.L.T. (2d) 1 (N.B.C.A.), dangerous boyfriend of owner shot third person.

[165] *Dunn v. Dominion Atlantic Ry. Co.* (1920), 60 S.C.R. 310, [1920] 2 W.W.R. 705; *Howe v. Niagara, St. Catharines & Toronto Ry. Co.* (1925), 56 O.L.R. 202, [1925] 2 D.L.R. 115 (C.A.).

[166] *Depue v. Flatau* (1907), 100 Minn. 299, 111 N.W. 1.

[167] *Thorne v. Deas* (1809), 4 Johns N.Y. 84.

[168] See, for example, *Baxter & Co. v. Jones* (1903), 6 O.L.R. 360, 2 O.W.N. 573; *Braun v. Riel* (1931), 40 S.W. 2d 621 (Mo.), *Restatement, Torts, Second*, §324A.

stretching the doctrine of consideration and promissory estoppel.[169] The theory underlying this is that there has been an aggravation of the plight of the victim, rather than a mere failure to confer a benefit.[170] One might call such conduct misfeasance, rather than nonfeasance.

One such case is *Baxter & Co. v. Jones*,[171] in which the defendant insurance agent was asked to obtain some fire insurance for the plaintiff. As the plaintiff's manager was signing the application and paying the premium, he asked the defendant to notify their other insurance companies that they had obtained this additional insurance. The defendant agreed to do this, but neglected to transmit the notice. When a fire occured, the other companies raised as a defence the lack of notice, but finally settled with the plaintiff for $1,000 less than they would otherwise have had to pay. The plaintiff successfully sued the agent for reimbursement of this loss. Mr. Justice Maclennan appeared to base his decision on a type of contract theory and stated that "as part of his undertaking to procure the new insurance . . . he undertook and agreed that it should not be done injuriously to the plaintiff. His omission to give notices has that effect."[172] Mr. Justice Osler, rather than basing his decision on contrary theory, stressed the fact that the defendant undertook to give the notice.[173] If he had refused, which he might have done, the plaintiffs would "have known that they must look after it themselves . . . . But the whole business having been ultimately entrusted to and assumed by the defendant before any part of it had been completed, the plaintiffs have a right to complain that the defendant negligently proceeded with it only so far as to be detrimental to them." His Lordship then concluded that the transaction was one of "mandate so that if the defendant had not entered upon the execution of the business entrusted to him he would have incurred no liability".

Although it might be argued that *Baxter & Co. v. Jones* can be described as a contract case, a similar result may follow without a contract.[174] Indeed, a promise may not even be necessary, as long as detriment to the plaintiff is induced by the defendant's conduct. For example, in *Morash v. Lockhart & Ritchie Ltd.*,[175] an insurance agent was held partially at fault (25 per cent) for failing to notify his client that his insurance was about to expire because "where such a practice has been adopted clients expect the service and rely upon it for protection against the lapse of their policies".[176] By its "past conduct" the defendant "created for

---

[169] See generally, Seavey, "Reliance Upon Gratuitous Promises or other Conduct" (1951), 64 Harv. L. Rev. 913.

[170] *Prosser and Keeton, op. cit. supra*, n. 102, at p. 381.

[171] *Supra*, n. 168. See also *Milroy v. Toronto-Dominion Bank* (1997), 35 C.C.L.T. (2d) 37 (Ont. Gen. Div.), insurance agent liable for failing to tell about renewal..

[172] (1903), 6 O.L.R. 360, at p. 368.

[173] *Ibid.*, at pp. 363-64.

[174] *Myers v. Thompson*, [1967] 2 O.R. 335 (C.A.); *Siegal v. Spear & Co.* (1925), 138 N.E. 414 (N.Y.).

[175] (1978), 95 D.L.R. (3d) 647 (N.B.C.A.).

[176] *Ibid.*, (*per* C.J. Hughes); *Twardy v. Humboldt Credit Union Ltd.* (1985), 34 C.C.L.T. 140 (Sask. Q.B.).

itself a self-imposed duty in law to renew the plaintiff's policy, or at least to have advised the plaintiff that it had expired".[177] Similarly, someone, who undertook to give advice to a purchaser of a used car and negligently failed to inform that it had been involved in an accident, was held liable on the basis of a voluntary assumption of duty and reliance upon it.[178]

In the same way, in *Zelenko v. Gimbel Bros.*,[179] the deceased was taken ill in the defendant's store. The defendant undertook to render medical aid and placed her in its infirmary, where she received no medical care for six hours. The segregation of the plaintiff made it difficult for any bystander to summon an ambulance. Mr. Justice Lauer, of the Supreme Court of New York, stated that "if a defendant undertakes a task, even if under no duty to undertake it, the defendant must not omit to do what an ordinary man would do in performing the task".

There is a conflicting Ontario case which seems to hold that an undertaking and reliance are not sufficient to generate a duty. In *Soulsby v. City of Toronto*,[180] the defendant gratuitously erected a gate at a railway crossing and stationed a guard there. During the summer, the guard closed the gate when a train approached and opened it when it was safe for traffic. The plaintiff, relying on the defendant's practice, came along on October 30, found the gate open and crossed the tracks, whereupon he was hit by a passing train. Mr. Justice Britton dismissed the case on the ground that there was no duty to keep the gate closed when trains passed. His Lordship distinguished *Baxter v. Jones* as a case of mandate, which did not exist here. He contended that liability may be imposed for the improper performance of a voluntary undertaking, but not for merely neglecting to act. The watchman was not at the gate at all, which was similar to the situation at night or during the winter season.

This case was wrongly decided. All of the elements necessary for the creation of a duty were present: an undertaking, reliance, and resulting loss to the plaintiff, factors which should take a case out of the realm of mere nonfeasance. It is possible to explain the case in two ways. The first is causation. The accident would still have happened had the guard been on duty. Lending support to this view is the fact that the plaintiff failed to notice the danger, even though he

---

[177] *Ibid.*, (*per* Ryan J.A.). See also *Trident Construction v. Wardrop*, [1979] 6 W.W.R. 481, at p. 532, engineer and builder; *cf.*, *Mason v. Morrow's Moving & Storage Ltd.* (1978), 5 C.C.L.T. 59 (B.C.C.A.), no duty on bailor to warn of lack of insurance; see Litman (1978), 16 Alta. L. Rev. 20; *Vienneau Assur. Ltée v. Roy* (1986), 35 C.C.L.T. 249 (N.B.C.A.), no custom or undertaking to renew policy.

[178] *Chaudhry v. Prabhaker*, [1988] 3 All E.R. 718 (C.A.). *Cf.*, *Maxey v. Canada Permanent Trust Co.* (1984), 9 D.L.R. (4th) 380 (Man. C.A.), no liability on mortgage company for not insuring house.

[179] (1935), 287 N.Y.S. 134. See also *De Long v. Erie County* (1982), 455 N.Y.S. 2d 887, 911 number undertook to respond to call for help from burglar, liable for injuries to caller; *Barrett v. Ministry of Defense*, [1995] 3 All E.R. 87 (C.A.), liability to drunken sailor who choked on vomit after taken back to cabin re undertaking in "assumed responsibility".

[180] (1907), 15 O.L.R. 13.

knew as much as the gatekeeper would have known and had the same opportunity to observe the situation. Secondly, since the defendant was a municipality, the court might have been loath to saddle it with onerous duties.

A preferable decision, with the opposite conclusion on similar facts, is *Mercer v. South Eastern and Chatham Railway Co.*,[181] where the defendants had made a practice of keeping a wicket gate locked to pedestrians when a train was passing. This practice was known to the plaintiff who was injured by a passing train when, owing to carelessness of the defendant's servant, the gate was left unlocked. The defendants were held liable. Lush J. felt that:

> to those who knew of the practice that was a "tacit invitation" to cross the line. . . . It may seem a hardship on a railway company to hold them responsible for the omission to do something which they were under no legal obligation to do, and which they only did for the protection of the public. They ought, however, to have contemplated that if a self-imposed duty is ordinarily performed, those who know of it will draw an inference if on a given occasion it is not performed. If they wish to protect themselves against the inference being drawn they should do so by giving notice, and they did not do so in this case.[182]

The point is further illustrated by *Barnett v. Chelsea and Kensington Hospital Management Committee*.[183] A person started to vomit after drinking some "tea" and went to a hospital for help. He told the nurse his problem, she in turn told the medical casualty officer, who sent a message back through her to the effect that the patient should go home and see his own doctor. The plaintiff died some hours later of arsenical poisoning. Although Mr. Justice Nield found that the defendant's negligence did not cause the death, he indicated, in a *dictum*,[184] that because there was a "close and direct relationship between the hospital and the [plaintiff] . . . there was imposed on the hospital a duty of care". Mr Justice Nield distinguished the case of the hospital that "closes its doors and says that no patients can be received".[185] Similarly, a doctor who accepts a charity patient can be held liable.[186] In the same way, responding to a 911 call means that the ambulance operator assumes a duty of care. Thus, if there is a delay of 40 minutes before the ambulance arrives, when the caller could have been driven more quickly to the hospital if told of the potential delay, liability may follow, at least, where there is no good reason for the delay. Lord Woolf M.R. explained that "[t]the acceptance of the call in this case established the duty of care."[187]

The Supreme Court of Canada has indicated that an undertaking and reliance thereon may lead to the establishment of a legal duty to take care, at least in the

---

[181] [1922] 2 K.B. 549.

[182] *Ibid.*, at p. 554.

[183] [1968] 1 All E.R. 1068 (Q.B.D.).

[184] *Ibid.*, at p. 1072.

[185] In the U.S., since 1986, the Emergency Medical Treatment and Active Labor Act (EMTALA) requires medicare hospitals to provide screening and emergency treatment to anyone, not just medicare covered, see Dobbs, *supra*, n. 74 at p. 671.

[186] *Prosser and Keeton, op. cit. supra*, n. 102, at p. 378; *Smith v. Rae, supra*, n. 135 (*dictum*).

[187] *Kent v. Griffiths*, [2000] 2 All E.R. 474, at p. 487 (C.A.).

case of some government safety activity. In *R. v. Nord-Deutsche et al.*[188] employees of the Crown negligently permitted a set of range lights upon which pilots relied to become displaced, and thereby contributed to a collision between two ships. At trial, Mr. Justice Noël based liability on the ground that the Crown had "engendered reliance on the guidance afforded by [the lights],"[189] and was therefore required to keep them in good working order or, failing that, to warn about the danger. In the Supreme Court of Canada, Mr. Justice Ritchie divided liability among the Crown and the two ship owners and explained that there was a "breach of duty on the part of the servants of the Crown responsible for the care and maintenance of the range light . . . upon which lights mariners were entitled to place reliance".[190]

Similarly, in *Grossman and Sun v. R.*,[191] the Crown was held liable when a maintenance foreman at an airfield negligently failed to place warning flags around a ditch on the runway, causing damage to an aeroplane and injury to a passenger. Mr. Justice Kellock indicated that a duty was owed by the employee not only to his employer, but also to pilots, who were "entitled to rely" on its proper discharge.[192]

Another case in which liability was imposed on the Crown in *Hendricks v. R.*,[193] where the applicant's wife was drowned in a boating accident. The Crown employees negligently omitted to replace signs warning boaters "Danger—Falls Ahead", which had been knocked over. Because of this, as well as the contributory negligence of the suppliant and his wife, the falls were not noticed until too late, the boat went over the falls and capsized. An additional reason for imposing liability on the Crown was that it had actually created the danger to navigation by building the obstruction below the water level. In the same way, by undertaking to erect a barrier as a median on a highway, the government department may be held liable for "misfeasance", when the barrier is only 18" high, instead of 30" high as required by the policy of the department.[194]

These cases raise the prospect of government liability for the acts of safety personnel who inspect and approve machinery, buildings and the like, and upon whose assurance the public relies.[195]

---

[188] [1971] S.C.R. 849. *Cf., Cleveland-Cliffs S.S. v. R.*, [1957] S.C.R. 810. See also *infra*, Chapter 17.

[189] [1969] 1 Ex. C.R. 117, at p. 196.

[190] *Supra*, n. 188, at p. 863.

[191] [1952] 1 S.C.R. 571.

[192] *Ibid.*, at p. 614. Mr. Justice Estey felt that there was a negligent "performance" of the duty, rather than a mere failure to act. See *ibid.*, at p. 619. Compare with *R. v. Anthony*, [1946] S.C.R. 569, no liability for military activity of firing tracer bullets, which caused fire, since no private duty owed but only military duty.

[193] [1970] S.C.R. 237. See also *County of Parkland v. Stetar*, [1975] 2 S.C.R. 884; *Berezowski v. City of Edmonton* (1986), 38 C.C.L.T. 96 (Alta. C.A.).

[194] *Malat v. The Queen* (1980), 14 C.C.L.T. 206, at p. 215 (B.C.C.A.) (*per* Hinkson J.A.).

[195] See Chapter 17.

5. DUTY OF THE RESCUER: EAST SUFFOLK RIVERS CATCHMENT BOARD V. KENT

A mystifying case that needlessly continues to plague the courts is *East Suffolk Rivers Catchment Board v. Kent.*[196] A public authority began to fix a damaged sea wall, which had permitted the plaintiff's land to be flooded. The authority delayed the work and the plaintiff's land was submerged for a much longer period than it would have been if the work had been done properly. The defendant agency was, nevertheless, relieved of liability, because the plaintiff's position was not worsened by its actions. Viscount Simon L.C. indicated that, if they had "inflicted fresh injury",[197] such as flooding more land or prolonging the period of flooding beyond what it would have been if they had never interfered, they would be held liable. The court explained that they did not "cause the loss; it was caused by the operations of nature, which the appellants were endeavouring, not very successfully, to counteract".[198] The court resisted placing any more stringent obligations upon the public authority for fear that this would deter it from doing its duty, or place an undue strain on its resources.

Since most of these cases involved public authorities and municipalities, it was thought that the *Kent* rule would be limited to such bodies.[199] Moreover, it might be argued that the House of Lords was merely restating the trite law that there must be some loss caused by negligent conduct for liability to be imposed. Since no loss was caused by the defendant, there could be no liability for the mere failure to confer a benefit.[200] The *Kent* case has been criticized by Lord Salmon as "not very satisfactory", a conclusion that most would readily adopt.[201]

Unfortunately, the Ontario Court of Appeal decision in *Horsley v. MacLaren*,[202] resurrected the *Kent* doctrine. In the *Horsley* case, Matthews fell overboard and the defendant yacht-owner, MacLaren, began a rescue attempt by backing towards him. Expert evidence was adduced to the effect that this was the wrong procedure. Horsley then jumped overboard in an attempt to rescue Matthews but died before he was rescued himself. At trial, Mr. Justice Lacourcière exacted the standard of reasonable care usually demanded from a rescuer and asked, "What could the reasonable boat operator do in the circumstances . . .?"[203] Because the defendant used the "wrong procedure" in backing the boat

---

[196] [1941] A.C. 74, [1940] 4 All E.R. 527. See also *Neabel v. Town of Ingersoll*, [1967] 2 O.R. 343; *Sheppard v. Glossop Corp.*, [1921] 3 K.B. 132 (C.A.); *Stevens-Willson v. City of Chatham* [1933] O.R. 305; affd [1934] S.C.R. 353; *Wing v. Moncton*, [1940] 2 D.L.R. 740 (N.B.C.A.); *Moch v. Rensselaer Water Co.* (1928), 247 N.Y. 160, 159 N.E. 896.

[197] *Ibid.*, at p. 84.

[198] *Ibid.*, at p. 88.

[199] Fleming, *op. cit. supra*, n. 143, at p. 157.

[200] See *McCrea v. White Rock* (1975), 56 D.L.R. (3d) 525, at p. 551 (B.C.C.A.).

[201] *Anns v. Merton*, [1977] 2 W.L.R. 1024, at p. 1043.

[202] [1970] 2 O.R. 487; revg [1969] 2 O.R. 137; affd on other grounds, [1972] S.C.R. 441, 22 D.L.R. (3d) 545.

[203] [1969] 2 O.R. 137, at pp. 145-46 (C.A.).

up and because of his "excessive consumption of alcohol", Mr. Justice Lacour-cière held that he was negligent.

The Court of Appeal, however, reversed the decision of the trial judge and decided that the defendant was guilty only of an error in judgment, which did not amount to negligence. Mr. Justice Jessup relied upon the *Kent* case and adopted its test for these rescue cases. He contended that "where a person gratuitously and without any duty to do so undertakes to confer a benefit upon or go to the aid of another, he incurs no liability unless what he does worsens the condition of the other".[204] Mr. Justice Jessup rejected the rationale used by the trial judge and argued: "I think it is an unfortunate development in the law which leaves the Good Samaritan liable to be mulcted in damages, and apparently in the United States, it is one that has produced marked reluctance of doctors to aid victims." Mr. Justice Schroeder echoed this view and argued:

> if a person embarks upon a rescue, and does not carry it through, he is not under any liability to the person to whose aid he has come so long as discontinuance of his efforts did not leave the other in a worse condition than when he took charge.[205]

Since MacLaren's rescue effort had not worsened either Matthew's or Horsley's position, even though it may not have complied with the standard of "textbook perfection", he was relieved of responsibility.

In the Supreme Court of Canada, the majority did not deal with this point, and Mr. Justice Laskin, dissenting, left it to be decided on another occasion:

> Whether a case involving the exercise of statutory powers (but not duties) by a public authority should govern the issue of liability or non-liability to an injured rescuer is a question that need not be answered here.[206]

Further doubt has been cast on *Kent* by Madam Justice Wilson, who distinguished it in *City of Kamloops v. Nielsen*, and by Lord Wilberforce, in *Anns*, who suggested that today the municipality might held liable.[207]

The purpose of using the *Kent* rule here is to encourage potential rescuers by reducing the risk of liability to them if their effort is unsuccessful. This is a wise policy, as long as it does not foster careless rescue operations. It is possible, however, to mismanage a rescue attempt horribly, and yet not worsen the position of an already doomed person. On the other hand, it is possible for a careful rescuer to worsen the position of the person being saved. This is therefore, a poor test by which to affix or deny liability.

---

[204] [1970] 2 O.R. 487, at pp. 500 and 502.

[205] *Ibid.*, at p. 495.

[206] [1972] S.C.R. 441, 22 D.L.R (3d) 545, at p. 561. See Alexander, "One Rescuer's Obligation to Another: The Ogopogo Lands in the Supreme Court of Canada" (1972), 22 U. of T.L.J. 98.

[207] [1984] 2 S.C.R. 2, at p. 15.

6. GOOD SAMARITAN LEGISLATION

It became obvious that legislation was needed to establish a rule that would not inhibit would-be rescuers and that, at the same time, was not too inviting to bunglers. An approach pioneered in the United States, where legislation was enacted relieving doctors and nurses and sometimes ordinary citizens from liability for their conduct at the scene of an accident, unless guilty of gross negligence, has been adopted. The Alberta Emergency Medical Aid Act, for example, states:

> If, in respect of a person who is ill, injured or unconscious as the result of an accident or other emergency,
>
> a) a physician, registered health discipline member, or registered nurse voluntarily and without expectation of compensation or reward renders emergency medical services or first aid assistance and the services or assistance are not rendered at a hospital or other place having adequate medical facilities and equipment, or
>
> b) a person other than a person mentioned in class (*a*) voluntarily renders emergency first aid assistance and that assistance is rendered at the immediate scene of the accident or emergency,
>
> the physician, registered health discipline member, registered nurse or other person is not liable for damages for injuries to or the death of that person alleged to have been caused by an act or omission on his part in rendering the medical services or first aid assistance, unless it is established that the injuries or death were caused by gross negligence on his part.[208]

Such an approach retains some control over the conduct of rescuers, while at the same time it does not frighten them away. Although one might quarrel with some of the conditions in the statue such as the necessity to rescue "without expectation of compensation," its general thrust is welcome. It is hard to tell whether it will really increase the frequency of rescue effort, but at least the excuse of fear of liability will be unavailable in the future to those who do not offer assistance.

Perhaps the time has arrived for the courts to proclaim that everyone who is aware of another in peril and is able to assist without risk to themselves has a duty to do so.[209] Indeed, there are so many exceptions to the nonfeasance rule that one might argue that we are almost there already. This solution would redress the paradox of the Good Samaritan, not by relieving Good Samaritans, of liability, but by holding them responsible for their negligence, along with those who fail to act. The adoption of such a rule might be expedited if the crime

---

[208] R.S.A. 1980, c. E-9, s. 2 [am. R.S.A. 1980, c. H-5.1 (Supp.), s. 34; S.A. 1984, c. 53, s. 27]. Five other provinces and the two territories have now enacted similar legislation. See Good Samaritan Act, R.S.B.C. 1996, c. 172; Emergency Medical Aid Act, R.S.S. 1978, c. E-8; Volunteer Services Act, R.S.N.S. 1989, c. 497; Emergency Medical Aid Act, R.S.N. 1990, c. E-9; Medical Act, R.S.P.E.I. 1988, c. M-5, s. 50, ordinary negligence standard; Emergency Medical Aid Act, R.S.N.W.T. 1988, c. E-4; Emergency Medical Aid Act, R.S.Y. 1986, c. 52.

[209] Such a duty has been suggested in criminal law, see Law Reform Commission of Canada, Working Paper 46 (1985), *supra*, n. 92. It is established in Quebec, see *Gaudreault v. Drapeau* (1987), 45 C.C.L.T. 202 (Que. S.C.).

victim compensation schemes[210] were amended to provide reparation for rescuers, whether or not they are hurt by a criminal act.

D. Legislation and Nonfeasance

Our legislatures, more than the courts, have been influenced by the ethical and religious precepts of Western civilization in this area. They have occasionally demanded affirmative conduct by making nonfeasance a crime. For example, where drivers of motor vehicles are involved in collisions, they are required to stop, to give their names and addresses, and "to render all possible assistance", whether they were at fault in the accident or not.[211] Another relatively common statute penalizes owners of motor vehicles who fail to insure against their liability to a third person. There are enactments which require individuals to assist a police officer in the apprehension of a criminal if so required, to rescue someone found at sea, and to supply food, clothing and medical assistance to near relatives. Municipal ordinances frequently order abutting owners to keep the public sidewalk bordering their property free and clear of ice and snow. Thus, failure to act may amount to a crime.

Some writers have denounced as "notorious"[212] and "improper"[213] any judicial use of these penal statutes as a basis for the creation of new tort duties, while others have defended such action.[214] Since creating a new tort duty is more serious than merely clarifying the standard of care to be used where a duty already exists, the courts might be expected to be more reluctant to do the former.[215] By advocating a limited use of statutes and by explaining such use as a "mere procedural change", Professor Thayer may have been attempting to win,[216] in an atmosphere of judicial hostility, at least some recognition for criminal legislation in tort cases. Perhaps if he had urged reliance on legislation to create new duties as well as to set standards, the courts would have resisted both.

Nevertheless, the civil courts have created new tort duties by analogy to these penal statues. As they did when they invoked criminal legislation to set specific standards of care where a duty already existed, the courts claimed to base their

---

[210] Compensation for Victims of Crime Act, R.S.O. 1990, c. C.24.

[211] For statutory references, see n. 238, *infra*.

[212] Fleming, 7th ed. (1987), at p. 118, footnote 82, phrase dropped in later editions.

[213] Williams, "The Effect of Penal Legislation in the Law of Torts" (1960), 23 Mod. L. Rev. 233. See also Gregory, "Breach of Criminal Licensing Statutes in Civil Litigation", 36 Cornell L.Q. 622; Thayer, "Public Wrong and Private Action" (1914), 27 Harv. L. Rev. 317.

[214] Morris, "The Role of Criminal Statutes in Negligence Actions" (1949), 49 Colum. L. Rev. 21; see also Morris, *Studies in the Law of Torts* (1952), p. 141; Alexander, "Legislation and the Standard of Care in Negligence" (1964), 42 Can. Bar Rev. 243.

[215] See Alexander, *ibid.*, at pp. 255-56. See also *Seneca College v. Bhadauria* (1981), 17 C.C.L.T. 106 (S.C.C.) (*per* Laskin C.J.C.).

[216] Thayer, *supra*, n. 213.

decisions on the intention of the statute.[217] The real reason, however, is that the contravention of a penal decree is one of the factors, a significant one, courts will consider when faced with a tort action based on the offending conduct. Where they are sympathetic to the legislative goal, the courts advance the policy by providing a civil remedy. Where, on the other hand, they are apathetic or antipathetic to the statutory aim, they refuse to impose civil liability for criminal nonfeasance. This is their prerogative, but it would be better if the real reasons for their decisions were articulated, which may well be done now in the post-*Saskatchewan Wheat Pool* era. An analysis of several groups of cases will now be made to discover when the courts created new tort duties based on penal legislation.

1. COMPULSORY INSURANCE

Some jurisdictions have made it a crime to drive an uninsured automobile.[218] The primary object of these laws was to ensure the existence of a fund out of which the injured plaintiff could satisfy any potential judgment, at least to the dollar limits required. They benefit the solvent defendant who might be mulcted in damages only incidentally, though it was inevitable that they should do so. Prior to the passage of these statutes, there was no civil duty to insure oneself against public liability. Following their enactment, the English courts in the celebrated and much impugned case of *Monk v. Warbey*,[219] imposed upon violators a new civil obligation toward persons injured by the uninsured vehicle. The defendant Warbey permitted his motor vehicle to be used by Knowles, who allowed a third person, May, to use it. Although the owner himself was insured against third party risks, neither Knowles nor May was, which was a breach of the statute.[220] May negligently caused injury to the plaintiff Monk who sued Knowles, May and Warbey. Interlocutory judgments were obtained against Knowles and May, but they could not satisfy them. The matter proceeded against Warbey on the theory that his violation of the penal statute gave rise to tort liability on his part. The trial judge accepted this view and he was affirmed by the Court of Appeal.

Lord Justice Greer, applying *Groves v. Wimborne*,[221] stated that, unless a contrary viewer was expressed in the statute, a civil obligation was conferred by the contravention of criminal legislation. He formulated the principle as follows: "*prima facie* a person who has been injured by a breach of a statute has a right to recover damages from the person committing it unless it can be established by considering the whole of the Act that no such right was intended to be given. So

---

[217] See Chapter 5, *supra*. No longer since *R. in right of Canada v. Saskatchewan Wheat Pool*, [1983] 1 S.C.R. 205; see also LeDain J. in *Baird v. R. in right of Canada* (1983), 148 D.L.R. (3d) 1, at p. 8 (Fed. C.A.).

[218] For example, Compulsory Automobile Insurance Act, R.S.O. 1990, c. C.25, s. 2; Mass. Ann. Laws, c. 90; N.Y. Vehicle and Traffic Law, §310; N.C. Sess. Laws of 1957, c. 1939.

[219] [1935] 1 K.B. 75 (C.A.).

[220] 20 and 21 Geo. V, c. 43.

[221] [1898] 2 Q.B. 402, [1885-9] All E.R. Rep. 147 (C.A.).

far as that being shown in this case, the contrary is establish."[222] Two of the judges purported to rely on a section of the Act, which permitted money deposits in lieu of insurance, as evidence of a legislative intention to confer civil rights.[223]

The real reason for the decision was not the interpretation exercise engaged in by the court; rather it was the desire to advance the legislative policy of supplying auto accident victims with an insurance fund to pay any tort judgment they might secure. Supplementary to this was the feeling that the criminal sanction alone was inadequate to effectuate this purpose. Lord Justice Greer maintained that the Act "would indeed be no protection to a person injured by the negligence of an uninsured to whom a car had been lent by the insured owner, if no civil remedy were available for a breach of the section".[224] His Lordship further stated that "to prosecute for a penalty is no sufficient protection and is poor consolation to the injured person though it affords a reason why persons should not commit a breach of the statute". This reasoning was echoed by Lord Justice Maugham when he said:

> [The section] was passed for the purpose of giving a remedy to third persons who might suffer injury by the negligence of an impecunious driver of a car. . . .[W]hen the Act was passed it was within the knowledge of the Legislature that negligence in the driving of cars was so common an occurrence with the likelihood of injury to third persons that it was necessary in the public interest to provide machinery whereby those third persons might recover damages.[225]

Moreover, no administrative problems of selection and the like intruded to thwart this aim. Thus, because the court was sympathetic to the legislative policy of protecting the financial interests of persons injured by uninsured drivers, it added to the regular criminal sanction a new tort duty to provide insurance coverage. The language of legislative interpretation was a cloak which shielded only imperfectly the judicial desire to buttress this worthwhile policy of the statute.

a) Critique

This decision has been assailed by Glanville Williams[226] as "an improper type of judicial invention". Professor Fleming once described it as "a most blatant arrogation of legislative authority," being "difficult to justify on any account,[227] and as an example of judicial discretion being stretched "beyond . . . legitimate bounds".[228] At the same time Fleming argued, without seeing the inconsistency in his position, that it is easy and proper to infer a legislative intention to create

---

[222] *Monk v. Warbey, supra*, n. 219, at p. 81.
[223] See *ibid.*, Roche L.J. at p. 86, Maugham L.J., at p. 86.
[224] *Ibid.*, at pp. 80 and 81.
[225] *Ibid.*, at pp. 85 and 86.
[226] *Supra*, n. 213, at p. 259.
[227] *The Law of Torts*, 2nd ed. (1961), p. 134, footnote 12.
[228] *Ibid.*, at p. 127, "a notorious lapse".

private rights from statutes which set specific safety standards.[229] However, if it is proper to conjure up a fictional legislative intention to fix the standard of care, it can be no less proper to do likewise to create a new duty of care. Both are disingenuous tactics invoked by courts to reach certain desired conclusions. The true reason for Fleming drawing this distinction is probably that he, like Thayer before him, does not want to seek too much, in order to avoid judicial opposition to *all* use of criminal statutes in tort cases. Professor Fleming once contended[230] that legislation should not be used to establish new tort duties because "the jump from ordinary negligence to strict liability is one thing, that from no duty to strict liability is quite another". It is not necessary, however, to go all the way from no duty to strict liability; the court on the basis of a statute, may create a duty to use only reasonable care.[231] While both of these reasons may have been valid grounds for advising caution, they should no longer prevent courts from creating new civil duties by analogy to penal statutes in proper cases.

Despite these criticisms, *Monk v. Warbey* appears to be well entrenched in English law, having received the imprimatur of the House of Lords in *McLeod (or Houston) v. Buchanan*.[232] Lord Wright has said that "the provision is an important element in the policy of the legislature to secure the benefit of insurance for sufferers of road accidents".[233] There are some limits on the scope of *Monk v. Warbey*. Only owners of automobiles can be held civilly liable and not auctioneers,[234] or anyone else who merely assisted someone in violating the section, since owners alone have enough control over motor vehicles to forbid their unlawful use.[235] It has been held that this provision has not been passed for the benefit of servants of uninsured owners, but for the benefit of third parties.[236] Moreover, there will be no recovery against offending owners if the cause of their losses was not the lack of insurance, but the delays of the plaintiffs in the prosecution of their claims.[237]

2. HIT-AND-RUN STATUTES

In recent years many jurisdictions have enacted criminal statutes forcing motorists involved in accidents to stop, give their names and addresses and

---

[229] *Ibid.*

[230] *Op. cit. supra*, n. 227, at p. 133. This sentence does not appear in the later editions.

[231] See *Read v. Croydon Corp.*, [1938] 4 All E.R. 631.

[232] [1940] 2 All E.R. 179 (H.L.).

[233] *Ibid.*, at p. 186. Counsel did not even question *Monk v. Warbey*. His Lordship spoke of the section being "imperative" and "precise" and of the "wrongdoing motor vehicle".

[234] *Walkins v. O'Shaughnessy*, [1939] 1 All E.R. 385 (C.A.).

[235] *Goodbarne v. Buck*, [1940] 1 K.B. 771, [1940] 1 All E.R. 613 (C.A.).

[236] *Semtex Ltd. v. Gladstone*, [1954] 1 W.L.R. 945, [1954] 2 All E.R. 206; *Gregory v. Ford*, [1951] 1 All E.R. 121.

[237] *Daniels v. Vaux*, [1938] 2 K.B. 203, [1938] 2 All E.R. 271. *Cf., Martin v. Dean*, [1971] 3 All E.R. 279 (Q.B.D.).

render assistance.[238] The purposes of this legislation are to encourage Good Samaritanism and to prevent the evasion of criminal and civil responsibility. Prior to the passage of this legislation, no duty to render aid was recognized where the driver *innocently* caused the original peril,[239] but there was such an obligation where the injury was *tortiously* inflicted.[240] After the hit-and-run statutes, a new civil duty to offer assistance was established, even where the initial injury was innocently caused by the driver.

In the first case on this, *Langenstein v. Reynaud*,[241] judgment went against a defendant who failed to stop after colliding with a pedestrian, in violation of a hit-and-run statute. The death of the victim was either caused or hastened when a second automobile collided with him while he lay helpless on the road. The court stated that, if the defendant had stopped and removed the victim to a place of safety as the law directed, the second accident would not have occurred. The only reason given for the decision was: "He certainly knew in his conscience that he was doing wrong in fleeing from the scene of the accident, leaving his victim prostrate in the street. . . ."[242] Unfortunately, the authority of the case is weakened because the facts of the case would indicate that the defendant was at fault in causing the accident initially. Shortly thereafter, in *Battle v. Kilcrease*,[243] the Georgia Court of Appeals expressed the view that no error was committed when the jury was charged to the effect that it could find negligence as a matter of law where someone failed to stop, contrary to a statutory provision. A verdict for the plaintiff was upheld, but the court failed to cite one case or to give any reason for its decision. Again, the facts appear to manifest some earmarks of negligence by the defendant.[244] In *Summers v. Dominguez*,[245] the California court

---

[238] See, for example, Canadian Criminal Code, R.S.C. 1985, c. C-46, s. 252, "offer assistance"; Highway Traffic Act, R.S.O. 1990, c. H.8, s. 200(1)(b), "render all possible assistance"; Calif. Vehicle Code, §20003, "render to any person injured in the accident reasonable assistance".

[239] *Prosser and Keeton, op. cit. supra*, n. 102, at p. 377; *Union Pacific v. Cappier* (1903), 66 Kan. 649, 72 P. 281; *Turbeville v. Mobile Light and R. Co.* (1930), 121 Ala. App. 91, 127 So. 519. There is some authority to indicate that if peril is caused innocently by the defendant there may be a duty to minimize ensuing damage. *Ayres & Co. v. Hicks* (1942), 220 Ind. App. 86, 40 N.E. 2d 334; *Prosser and Keeton, ibid.*, at p. 377; *Restatement, Torts, Second*, §322, has adopted this position.

[240] *Ibid., Racine v. C.N.R.*, [1923] 1 W.W.R. 1439, [1923] 2 D.L.R. 572, 19 Alta. R. 529 (C.A.); *Trombley v. Kolts* (1938), 29 Cal. App. 2d 699; *North Central R.R. Co. v. Price* (1868), 29 Md. 420, 96 Am. Dec. 545.

[241] (1930), 13 La. App. 272, 127 So. 764 (C.A.).

[242] *Ibid.*, at p. 766. So.

[243] (1936), 54 Ga. App. 808, 189 S.E. 573.

[244] The case seems to declare that there is no necessity for proof of additional harm resulting from the failure to render aid, but the case really turned on the punitive damages point and the issue of whether breach of this statute could be evidence of original negligence. *Cf.*, *Petroleum Carrier Corp. v. Snyder*, 161 F. 2d 323 (5th Cir.), where no liability, because no evidence of additional damage.

[245] (1938), 29 Cal. App. 2d 308, 84 P. 2d 237 (D.C.A.). The plaintiff ultimately did not have to rely on this proposition and removed it from his pleading, allowing his case to rest solely on the negligence which caused the original accident.

declared in a *dictum* that a separate civil action could be maintained for the wilful breach of a statutory duty to render aid, regardless of any negligence of the plaintiff which may have contributed to the initial injury. The court again did not articulate any reasons for the decision. In *Hallman v. Cushman*,[246] the Supreme Court of South Carolina indicated that it would allow a jury to consider evidence of a failure to stop in order to assess additional damages for pain and suffering caused thereby. The case turned largely on other matter, however.

Probably the leading case is *Brooks v. E. J. Willig Transport Co.*[247] The court upheld a jury instruction to the effect that knowingly refusing to stop after an accident, which proximately caused the death of the plaintiff, was a breach of a civil duty that did not depend on the negligence of the driver or on the lack of contributory negligence by the victim. Chief Justice Gibson stated the principle as follows:

> One who *negligently* injures another and renders him helpless is bound to use reasonable care to prevent any further harm which the actor realizes or should realize threatens the injured person. This duty existed at common law although the accident was caused in part by the negligence of the person who was injured. . . [T]he Vehicle Code require[s] an automobile driver who injures another to stop and render aid. *This duty is imposed upon the driver whether or not he is responsible for the accident, and a violation gives rise to civil liability if it is a proximate cause of further injury or death.* [Italics mine.][248]

The court did not favour posterity with any reasons for its decision, nor did it cite the earlier case of *Summers v. Dominguez*, decided in the same state. Dean Prosser has asserted that the *Brooks* case suggests that the duty to render assistance may have existed at common law in California, even in the absence of the fault of the driver.[249] It is submitted that he is in error. A careful scrutiny of the reasons will demonstrate that the Supreme Court of California recognized the duty to render aid at common law only where one person *negligently* injured another. However, since the statute did not differentiate between the case where there was negligence and one where there was no negligence, the court was now prompted to fix civil liability on the driver for failure to render aid *"whether or not he is responsible for the accident"*.[250] The word "responsible" here means "legally responsible," which the defendant would not be, unless at fault. Thus, the Supreme Court of California was prepared to utilize the hit-and-run statute to fashion a new tort duty to render aid, even in the absence of any initial negligence causing the injury. In the *Brooks* case also, however, there was a strong likelihood that the defendant driver had been negligent originally. This new duty was said to exist in *Boyer v. Gulf, C. & S. F. R. Co.*[251] where the plaintiff's wife

---

[246] (1941), 196 S.C. 402, 13 S.E. 2d 498.

[247] (1953), 40 Cal. App. 2d 669, 255 P. 2d 802.

[248] *Ibid.*, at pp. 808-09, P. 2d.

[249] *Op.cit.*, *supra*, n. 102, at p. 377. *Restatement, Torts, Second*, §322 has now accepted this concept.

[250] *Brooks v. Willig Transport & Co.*, *supra*, n. 247, at p. 808, P. 2d.

[251] (1957), 306 S.W. 2d 215 (Tex. Civ. App.). See also *Brumfield v. Wofford* (1958), 143 W. Va. 332, 102 S.E. 2d 103.

was killed at a crossing. This was, however, *obiter dictum*, because there was no evidence that the failure to help proximately caused the death. Again, no policy reasons were offered by the court.

a) Policy

The reasons for the establishment of the new duty to aid in hit-and-run cases, although unarticulated by the courts, are fairly obvious. The civil courts are buttressing the legislative policy of promoting Good Samaritanism on the highways. By imposing the further burden of civil liability upon offending motorists, the judiciary hopes to deter some hit-and-run violations, save a few lives, and diminish some suffering. The courts may be inflicting an additional tort sanction to express the moral repugnance they feel toward these offenders.[252] The facts that American courts admit evidence of the violation of hit-and-run legislation in order to prove that the *original* accident was negligently caused,[253] and that they permit punitive damages to be awarded in these circumstances,[254] lend some credence to this view. A hit-and-run statute provides the courts with a convenient mechanism through which to impose liability on these offenders. This development has been facilitated by widespread auto insurance coverage. It may have been easier for the courts to act because of the similarity to the cases where injuries are caused by defendants' negligence or by their instrumentality. So too, the absence of any administrative problems in the selection of persons to be held may have helped the courts to overcome any latent misgivings. In any event, it is now clear that those who hit-and-run, even if they are originally innocent, owe a civil duty to their victims.

3. OTHER LEGISLATION RELIED ON IN CREATING NEW TORT DUTIES

There are a good number of other penal enactments which have prompted courts to fashion new tort duties.

a) Canada Shipping Act

The Canada Shipping Act,[255] for example, levies a fine against a master of a vessel who fails to "render assistance to every person. . .who is found at sea and in danger of being lost. . .". This statute had an important bearing on the lower court's decision in *Horsley v. MacLaren*[256] to establish a new civil obligation on the part of a ship-master to aid a passenger who falls overboard. Numerous

---

[252] The statute carries with it a "moral odium", see *Greyhound Co. v. Ault* (1956), 328 F. 2d 198, 202 (5th Cir.).

[253] *Battle v. Kilcrease, supra,* n. 243; *Hallman v. Cushman, supra,* n. 237; *Brooks v. Willig Transport, supra,* n. 247.

[254] *Battle v. Kilcrease* and *Hallman v. Cushman,* both *ibid.*

[255] R.S.C. 1985, c. S-9, s. 451(1).

[256] (1972), 22 D.L.R. (3d) 545; affg [1970] 2 O.R. 487; revg [1969] 2 O.R. 137.

issues are raised in the *Horsley* case, but only the duty question is considered
here. Mr. Justice Lacourcière, the trial judge, although he held the defendant not
liable on the ground of causation, expanded the "quasi-contractual" duty of the
carrier to the passenger, so that it would apply to the masters of a pleasure boat
and an invited guest. His Lordship, relying in part upon the Canada Shipping
Act, declared:

> Parliament reflecting the conscience of the community has seen fit to impose on the master a
> duty to render assistance to any stranger, including an enemy alien "found at sea and in dan-
> ger of being lost". . .; the common law can be no less solicitous for the safety of an invited
> guest and must impose upon the master the duty to attempt a rescue, when this can be done
> without imperilling the safety of the vessel, her crew and passengers. The common law must
> keep pace with the demands and expectations of a civilized community, the sense of social
> obligation, and brand as tortious negligence the failure to help a man overboard in accor-
> dance with the universal custom of the sea.[257]

The Court of Appeal, while reversing part of the decision of the trial judge, did
not interfere with his reasoning on this point. Mr. Justice Jessup argued that the
Canada Shipping Act covered not only strangers "found at sea" but also
passengers.[258] He declared that he was unable to "adopt . . . an interpretation
which would ascribe to Parliament a solicitude for the lives of alien enemies at
the same time denied by it to passengers and crew of Canadian ships". His
Lordship also agreed with Mr. Justice Lacourcière's imposition of a duty of care
upon a master of a ship to a passenger who falls overboard, in the following
words:

> A passenger on a ship is in the position of total dependence on the master and I think that pe-
> culiar relationship must now be recognized as invoking a duty of the master, incident to the
> duty to use due care in the carriage by sea of a passenger, of aid against the perils of the sea.
> Falling overboard is such a peril and in that situation I do not think the common law can do
> otherwise than to adopt the statutory duty to render assistance.

Mr. Justice Schroeder (MacGillivray J. A. concurring), was slightly more
cautious in articulating his reasons for decision.[259] He denied that the breach of a
statute could "create" a legal duty to rescue and asserted that the learned trial
judge rightly declined to treat it thus. Nevertheless, he observed:

> Parliament, in enacting the section, gave expression to humanitarian principles which
> should guide the consciences of civilized men in their relations even to an enemy who was
> found in peril at sea and this must have an important bearing on the question as to whether a
> moral or social duty . . . can be ripened into a legal duty not only to come to his passenger's
> aid, but also to exercise reasonable care in the rescue procedure.

---

[257] [1969] 2 O.R. 137, at p. 143. See also *Scott v. Green*, [1969] 1 W.L.R. 301, at p. 304 (*per*
Denning M.R.).
[258] [1970] 2 O.R. 487, at pp. 500 and 501.
[259] *Ibid.*, at p. 492.

The Supreme Court of Canada agreed that a duty rested upon a host and owner of a pleasure boat "to do the best he could to effect the rescue of one of his guests who had accidentally fallen overboard,"[260] but Mr. Justice Ritchie made it clear that the existence of this duty was "in no way dependent upon the provisions [of the Canada Shipping Act]".[261] Mr. Justice Laskin, dissenting on another point, concurred and, though he did not base his decision solely on the statute, suggested that "the legislative declaration of policy in [the section] is a fortifying element in the recognition of the [common law] duty, being in harmony with it . . . ."[262]

The courts, therefore, do not believe that criminal statutes by themselves create tort duties, but they do recognize that new tort obligations may be established by analogy to these penal provisions.

b) Railway Act [now Canada Transportation Act]

Another case that is consistent with this view is *Colonial Coach Lines v. Bennett and C.P.R.*[263] The plaintiff's bus was damaged when it collided with a cow that had escaped from a farmer's land onto the highway through a defective fence along the railway's right of way. In holding the railway partially responsible to the plaintiff, Mr. Justice Laskin relied to some extent on two sections of the Railway Act of Canada. Section 277 created an obligation to erect fences "suitable to prevent cattle . . . from getting on the railway lands" and s. 392 imposed a civil liability for failing to do so, if the loss occurred on "railway lands". Mr. Justice Laskin reasoned as follows:

> [Although] the railway's strict liability under s. 392 extends generally to injury on the railway right of way arising from a failure to fence, it may incur liability beyond this scope for injury off the right of way which, by reason of what it knew or ought to have known, could reasonably be foreseen as likely to occur if it failed to keep in repair a fence known to it to be defective. This liability for negligence is not founded merely on breach of a statutory duty to prevent the escape, from the adjoining land, of cattle which, if not contained, might stray on to a highway open from the right of way and expose oncoming traffic to the risk of injury. The triggering elements of liability are the railway's awareness of the defective condition of the fence and failure to take remedial measures to avert injury which could be reasonably foreseen. Existence of a statutory obligation to fence and actual assumption thereof by the railway were simply facts in the raising of a duty of care to the plaintiff by the railway when it knew that the obligation had not been met.[264]

Here too, the statute helps, but it does not necessarily rule.

---

[260] (1972), 22 D.L.R. (3d) 545, at p. 546.

[261] *Ibid.*, at p. 552.

[262] *Ibid.*, at p. 560.

[263] (1967), 66 D.L.R. (2d) 396 (Ont. C.A.).

[264] *Ibid.*, at p. 403.

c) Criminal Code: Duty to Provide Necessaries

The Canadian Criminal Code[265] provides that,

215. (1) Every one is under a legal duty
(a)   as a parent, foster parent, guardian or head of a family, to provide necessaries of life for a child under the age of sixteen years;
(b)   to provide necessaries of life to their spouse or common-law partner; and
(c)   to provide necessaries of life to a person under his charge if that person
    (i)   is unable, by reason of detention, age, illness, mental disorder or other cause, to withdraw himself from that charge, and
    (ii) is unable to provide himself with necessaries of life.

An offence is committed if any of the above individuals fails, without lawful excuse, to perform that duty if the person to whom it is owed is destitute or if the failure to perform the duty endangers the life or the permanent health of that person. The statutory purpose is to ensure that dependent members of a family are taken care of by the other members of that family who are able to do so. Governments are also seeking to minimize the size of their welfare budgets by using the criminal law to force wayward parents, spouses and children to exercise a degree of familial responsibility that may not otherwise be forthcoming.

Dean Prosser has suggested that civil liability may be imposed if any of the beneficiaries of this legislation becomes ill or dies as a result of a refusal by his or her relatives to supply food, shelter or medical help, since such a duty resembles the obligation already imposed upon a jailer to a prisoner and upon a school to its pupils.[266] Authority for this is, at best, only scant.

One case recognizes the possibility that a civil duty may be founded on statutes requiring the provision of necessaries or requiring parents to protect their children. A mother was sued for failing to protect her daughter from child abuse by the father. The court refused to strike out the claim, saying that, although "novel", there might exist either a common law duty or one based on the statute.[267] Broad statements may be found to support the view that "the provision of these necessaries is equally a civil obligation . . . (as a criminal one),"[268] and

---

[265]   R.S.C. 1985, c. C-46, s. 215(1). See also the Child and Family Services Act, R.S.O. 1990, c. C.11, s. 79(2), which prohibits a person from inflicting abuse upon a child, or permitting a child to suffer abuse. Further, s. 79(3) forbids leaving a child without "making provision for his or her supervision and care that is reasonable in the circumstances". Section 81(2) grants the Official Guardian the right to sue for damages on behalf of a child "because the child has suffered abuse".

[266]   *Op. cit., supra*, n. 102, at p. 377.

[267]   See *H. (D.L.) v. F. (G.A.)* (1987), 43 C.C.L.T. 110 (Ont. H.C.J.) (McDermid L.J.S.C.); see also under criminal law, *R. v. Popen* (1981), 60 C.C.C. (2d) 232 (Ont. C.A.).

[268]   *Algiers v. Tracy* (1916), 30 D.L.R. 427, at p. 429, *dictum*, where a conviction was upheld for the failure to provide for a wife whose parents were looking after her.

there are some to the opposite effect,[269] but the courts do not appear to have squarely faced the issue of tort liability arising out of the breach of one of these statutes. One reason for the lack of decisions was the marital immunity, which prohibited a wife from suing her husband and which has finally been abolished by statute.[270] No such immunity from suit exists between parent and child in English law or Canadian law, where "a wrongdoer [is not] . . . relieved of responsibility for the consequences of his negligence merely because the injured party happens to be his own child".[271] For some strange reason the American courts adopted one, which is, at last, beginning to give way.[272]

There are a few cases where parents have sued third persons for expenses incurred in the exercise of their statutory duty as parents. Thus, parents were entitled to recover the costs expended for the care of their children, who were injured by the defective wiring of the defendant,[273] and by being run over by the defendant's dray.[274] So too, a mother was allowed to recover from her husband amounts required to support her children on the basis of this legislation.[275] In one old case, however, a plaintiff father was denied recovery for expenses incurred when the defendant made the plaintiff's daughter pregnant,[276] and at least one Canadian judge has suggested that no civil rights can flow from a breach of the section in the Canadian Criminal Code.[277]

There is another group of cases where third persons, relying on these provisions, have sued parents for services or goods supplied to their children. There has been a tendency to deny recovery here on the ground of a civil statutory duty, but the courts have found implied promises to pay on the part of these parents.[278]

As the family immunities disappear, as the social problems attendant on broken homes expand, as government welfare costs increase, we can expect the

---

[269] *Childs v. Forfar* (1921), 51 O.L.R. 210, at p. 216 (C.A.); *St. Catharines Hospital v. Sviergula*, [1961] O.R. 164, at p. 167 (*per* Aylen J.). See also *Young v. Gravenhurst* (1911), 24 O.L.R. 467, at p. 480 (C.A.), criminal duty owed at common law, but not civil duty.

[270] See Family Law Act, R.S.O. 1990, c. F.3, s. 64(2): "A married person . . . has the same right of action in tort against his or her spouse as if they were not married".

[271] See Lord Fleming in *Young v. Rankin*, [1934] S.C. 499, at p. 520 (Scotland); followed in *Deziel v. Deziel*, [1953] 1 D.L.R. 651 (Ont.), child recovers from parent; see also *dictum* of Anglin J. in *Fidelity & Casualty Co. v. Marchand*, [1924] S.C.R. 86, at p. 93. Now in Family Law Act, R.S.O. 1990, c. F.3, s. 65.

[272] See the New Hampshire case permitting child to sue father for negligence in driving an automobile, *Briere v. Briere* (1966), 224 A. 2d 588.

[273] *Young v. Gravenhurst* (1911), 24 O.L.R. 467 (C.A.).

[274] *Banks v. Shedden Forwarding Co.* (1906), 11 O.L.R. 483 (C.A.).

[275] *Feasey v. Feasey*, [1946] O.W.N. 145 (Master).

[276] *Grinnell v. Wells* (1844), 7 Man. & G. 1033, 135 E.R. 419.

[277] Meredith J., dissenting, in *Banks v. Shedden Forwarding, supra*, n. 274, at p. 492, and in *Childs v. Forfar, supra*, n. 269, at p. 212. See also, Aylen J. in *St. Catharines Hospital v. Sviergula, supra*, n. 269.

[278] See *Vernon Jubilee Hospital v. Pound*, [1932] 2 D.L.R. 813 (B.C.); *St. Catharines Hospital v. Sviergula, supra*, n. 260; *Childs v. Forfar, supra*, n. 260. See also *Baseley v. Forder* (1868), L.R. 3 Q.B. 559.

courts to begin to create tort duties for failure to comply with this legislation. Since the problem of selection is minimal, since the lack of action here is so morally reprehensible to virtually everyone, and since financial support can be provided without any physical danger to the offender, the eventual imposition of a tort duty appears inevitable. The presence of the penal provisions should facilitate and hasten that development.

d) Police

Courts have rendered the police subject to affirmative duties of actions, often relying at least in part, on legislation. For example, in *O'Rourke v. Schacht*,[279] a well-lighted barrier which marked a detour around some highway construction was knocked over by a car at night, so that it was no longer visible to other motorists on the highway. The Ontario Provincial Police investigated the accident, but failed to take steps to warn oncoming traffic about the danger on the road. The plaintiff was injured when he drove his automobile into the unmarked excavation. The Police Act of Ontario requires, *inter alia*, that the Ontario Provincial Police "shall maintain a traffic patrol" and the Highway Traffic Act empowered the police officers to "direct traffic" in order to "ensure orderly movement" and "to prevent injury or damage to persons or property".

Mr. Justice Schroeder, of the Ontario Court of Appeal, allowed the plaintiff to recover 50 per cent of his damages against the police administration and relied for his decision in part upon the Police Act. His Lordship said that the police officers were "under a statutory duty to maintain a traffic patrol of the highway in question", and "were under a duty by virtue of their office to take appropriate measures in the face of a hazardous condition such as they encountered here to warn approaching traffic of its presence". He explained that "the duties which I would lay upon them stem not only from the relevant statutes to which reference has been made, but from the common law, which recognises the existence of a broad conventional or customary duty in the established constabulary as an arm of the State to protect the life, limb and property of the subject."

The Supreme Court of Canada affirmed this decision, even though it did excuse one of the several police officers involved. Mr. Justice Spence quoted at length from Mr. Justice Schroeder's opinion, which he described as "forthright and enlightened", and concluded:

> I have the same view as to the duty of a police officer under the provisions of the said s. 3(3) of the Police Act in carrying out police traffic patrol. In my opinion, it is of the essence of that patrol that the officer attempt to make the road safe for traffic. Certainly, therefore, there should be included in that duty the proper notification of possible road users of a danger arising from a previous accident and creating an unreasonable risk of harm.[280]

---

[279] (1973), 30 D.L.R. (3d) 641; vard (1975), 55 D.L.R. (3d) 96 (S.C.C.).
[280] *Ibid.*, at p. 120, 55 D.L.R.

In a dissenting opinion, Martland J. (Judson and Pigeon JJ. concurring) stated that he found nothing in the legislation that would "indicate an intention on the part of the Legislature to impose a liability upon a member of that Force who fails to carry out a duty assigned to him under the statute".

Another similar case is *R. v. Coté; Millette v. Kalogeropoulos.*[281] Mr. Justice Galligan, at trial, held both the Ontario Department of Highways and the Ontario Provincial Police partly to blame for a car accident caused in part by the icy condition of a highway. The Department was liable on the basis of s. 30 of the Highway Improvement Act,[282] and the police were held liable for failing to notify the Department of Highways about the dangerous icy conditions on the highway. His Lordship explained:

[T]here is a basic and fundamental duty on the part of the police officer to observe and report dangerous conditions seen by him on his patrol. . . .

On appeal, the Court of Appeal held the Department 75 per cent and the driver 25 percent at fault, and reversed the decision against the police on the ground that there was no evidence of a causal connection between their failure to notify and the collision.

The Supreme Court of Canada did not deal with the duty of the police, but it altered the division of responsibility among the other parties, 25 per cent to the Department and 75 per cent to the motorist. Mr. Justice Dickson indicated that the imposition of liability on the Department did "not import recognition of any general duty to sand or salt highways, failure in the discharge of which would expose the Minister to civil claims",[283] but rested on the "highly special dangerous situation at a certain location in the highway which otherwise, to persons reasonably using the same, was quite passable and usable to traffic." (The trial judge had called it a "killer strip".)[284]

When the actor or the one who fails to act is a governmental institution, things are more complicated. Not only must the courts grapple with the difficult

---

[281] [1971] 2 O.R. 155; revd in part [1972] 3 O.R. 224; revd in part (1974), 51 D.L.R. (3d) 244. See also *Simms v. Metro Toronto* (1978), 4 C.C.L.T. 214 (Ont. C.A.), criticizing *Landriault v. Pinard* (1976), 1 C.C.L.T. 216 (Ont. C.A.); see also *McAlpine v. Mahovlich* (1979), 9 C.C.L.T. 241 (Ont. C.A.); *Wuerch v. Hamilton* (1980), 15 C.C.L.T. 280; *cf.*, *Barratt v. North Vancouver* (1980), 14 C.C.L.T. 169 (S.C.C.), no liability on municipality for pothole contributing to accident.
[282] R.S.O. 1970, c. 201 [now Public Transportation and Highway Improvement Act, R.S.O. 1990, c. P.50, s. 33.]
[283] *Supra*, n. 281, at p. 252, 51 D.L.R. (3d).
[284] *Ibid.*, at p. 167, [1971] 2 O.R. Other cases regarding dangerous road conditions are *Levine v. Morris*, [1970] 1 All E.R. 114 (C.A.), liability for negligent design of highway; *Millar & Brown Ltd. v. Vancouver* (1965), 59 D.L.R. (2d) 640 (B.C.C.A.); revg 56 D.L.R. (2d) 190, no liability for overhanging tree; *Cox v. Sydney Mines* (1969), 4 D.L.R. (3d) 241 (N.S.C.A.), no liability for condition of road at railway crossing. See generally, Fitzpatrick *et al.*, *The Law and Roadside Hazards* (1974).

duty issues, but they must also struggle with the matter of judicial regulation of governmental activity. This subject is considered below.[285]

e) Charter Damage Claims

Violations of the Canadian Charter of Rights and Freedoms may give rise to civil actions for damages.[286] For example, damages have been awarded for the ". . . cruel and unusual treatment" suffered by a plaintiff at the hands of federal customs officers,[287] and for the conduct of police officers who refused to allow a lawyer access to his client once an interview with police had begun, contrary to paragraph 10(b) of the Charter.[288] Although the basis on which such actions may succeed has yet to be firmly established, tort law is likely to play a central role in its development.[289] At least one Canadian Court has referred to a Charter damage claim as a "constitutional tort".[290]

Subsection 24(1) provides that:

> 24(1) Anyone whose rights or freedoms, as guaranteed by this Charter, have been in-fringed or denied may apply to a court of competent jurisdiction to obtain such remedy as the court considers appropriate and just in the circumstances.

Where damages are claimed under this subsection, what is "appropriate and just in the circumstances" will be determined not only by reference to the nature of

---

[285] See *infra*, Chapter 17 for fuller discussion of problem.

[286] See *Doe v. Metropolitan Toronto (Municipality) Commissioners of Police* (1998), 39 O.R. (3d) 487, 126 C.C.C. (3d) 12 (Gen. Div.), liability of policy for rape of plaintiff, *inter alia*, because s. 7 violated. In *Chrispen v. Kalinowski* (1997), 35 C.C.L.T. (2d) 214, 117 C.C.C. (3d) 176 (Sask. Q.B.), liability for illegal search and seizure was imposed for breach of s. 8, as it was reckless and not in good faith. Although the Supreme Court of Canada has yet to rule specifically on this issue, in *R. v. Mills*, [1986] 1 S.C.R. 863, at p. 965, McIntyre J. affirmed the existence of broad powers for courts in fashioning remedies for breach of the Charter. Commenting on subsection 24(1), he wrote that "[i]t is difficult to imagine language which could give the Court a wider and less fettered direction".

[287] See *Rollinson v. Canada* (1994), 20 C.C.L.T. (2d) 92, in which Muldoon J. of the Federal Court Trial Division awarded $8,000 in general damages in addition to special, general and punitive damages for liability in tort, to a plaintiff whose sections 7, 8, 12 and 15 Charter rights had been violated by federal customs officers. See also *Lord v. Allison* (1986), 3 B.C.L.R. (2d) 300 (S.C.), also section 10 violation.

[288] *Crossman v. R.*, [1984] 1 F.C. 681, 9 D.L.R. (4th) 588 (T.D.).

[289] In his book, *Charter Damage Claims* (Toronto: Carswell, 1990), K. Cooper-Stephenson writes at page 68 ". . . that tort law's blend of corrective and distributive justice can provide a rational principled core to the Charter damages remedy, and that tort law might thus be a source which can be used to inform and structure the Charter damages remedy in a significant way". See also Roach, *Constitutional Remedies in Canada* (Aurora: Canada Law Book Co., 2000) at c. 11.

[290] In *R. v. McGillivray* (1990), 56 C.C.C. (3d) 304, at p. 309, Ryan J.A. of the New Brunswick Court of Appeal referred to a costs and damages claim against the Crown for violation of the claimant's section 7 right to "life, liberty and security of the person" as a "constitutional tort". Ryan J.A. found in that case that a claim for damages against the Crown could not be made in the context of a criminal law case but would instead require commencement of a civil proceeding in order to allow a proper assessment of the issue. See also *Crossman, supra*, n. 288.

the Charter right itself but also, where helpful, by reference to basic tort principles. Sometimes the Charter may be superfluous because tort law by itself covers the conduct in question.[291] In other situations, it may not be clear whether the constitutional tort claim will be treated in the same way as a simple tort claim. As Rice J. A. wrote, in concurring reasons in *R. v. McGillivray*:[292]

> [d]amages to be awarded for a breach of the Charter may be similar to damages usually awarded in tort cases but owing to the nature of the right that was infringed the remedy to be awarded under s. 24(1) would not necessarily be tantamount or restricted to the same kind and measure of compensation as in a tort action.[293]

According to one analysis, "the extent and significance of this 'constitutionalizing' of tort law will depend on two factors: first, the range of interests protected by constitutional guarantees; and, second, the range of actors to whom the constitution applies".[294] The first factor is an issue for Charter jurisprudence generally. The second factor has, however, been a particularly important issue in cases dealing with Charter damage claims. Subsection 32(1) provides that the Charter applies "to the Parliament and government of Canada in respect of all matters within the authority of Parliament. . ." and "to the legislature and government of each province in respect of all matters within the authority of the legislature of each province". The Ontario Court of Appeal has held in *Prete v. Ontario*[295] that the Crown is not protected from a finding of liability for malicious prosecution under section 7 of the Charter by either the immunity clause in the Proceedings Against the Crown Act[296] or the time limit imposed by the Public Authorities Protection Act.[297] Carthy J. A. reasoned that "[t]he remedy section of the *Charter* would be emasculated if the provincial government, as one of the very powers the *Charter* seeks to control, could declare itself immune".[298] This decision may encourage the utilization of Charter claims for actions involving agents of the Crown as compared to straight common law actions, very few of which have so far been undertaken, presumably because ordinary tort law suffices in many Charter breach cases. Courts have been unwilling, however, to disturb the long-held view that a judge cannot be held personally liable for an unconstitutional order.[299]

---

[291] *Bauder v. Wilson* (1988), 43 C.R.R. 149 (B.C.S.C.), tort damages for assault caused during arrest.

[292] *Supra*, n. 290, at p. 306.

[293] See also *R. v. Hamill* (1984), 14 C.C.C. (3d) 338 (B.C.C.A.), appeal dismissed [1987] 1 S.C.R. 301 for a discussion of the difference between damages at common law and damages for breach of the Charter.

[294] Pilkington, "Damages as a Remedy for Infringement of the Canadian Charter of Rights and Freedoms" (1984), 62 Can. Bar Rev. 517, at p. 544.

[295] (1993), 18 C.C.L.T. (2d) 54 (Ont. C.A.); leave to appeal to S.C.C. refused 175 N.R. 322n.

[296] R.S.O. 1980, c. 393 (now R.S.O. 1990, c. P.27).

[297] R.S.O. 1980, c. 406 (now R.S.O. 1990, c. P.38).

[298] *Prete, supra*, n. 295, at pp. 60-61.

[299] In *R. v. Germain* (1984), 53 A.R. 264, at p. 274 (Q.B.), McDonald J. held that "[t]here can be no suggestion that an order of compensation could be made against the judge personally".

A further issue arises with respect to the level at which liability is assigned as both governments and individual government officials may be held liable for constitutional wrongs.[300] Whether a government is held directly or vicariously liable for the actions of its employees or whether a government official is held personally liable for a Charter breach will likely depend upon the nature of the wrong and what the claimant hopes to achieve by virtue of the claim. While personal liability may help to foster accountability within government, ". . . individual liability alone may be ineffective, both as a means of compensating the plaintiff and as a means of deterring infringements of constitutional rights", particularly where the wrong is part of a large systemic problem.[301] Furthermore, personal liability of individual government officials may be protected by the principle of qualified immunity if it is established that the official acted in good faith on the basis of existing constitutional law.[302] In *Persaud v. Donaldson*,[303] the Ontario Court held that, absent evidence of reckless conduct, "[t]he mere failure to disclose sufficient written information in obtaining a search warrant, or the enforcing of a warrant later held to be invalid, will not of itself attract personal liability, at least as here where good faith is established".[304]

Finally, damages for breach of the Charter may be awarded in order to compensate the plaintiff, to deter future conduct or to punish the wrongdoer. Canadian courts have taken very different positions on this issue, with some finding that a damage award for a Charter violation ought only to serve punitive and deterrence functions,[305] while another has adopted a strictly compensatory approach, refusing to award damages following an unreasonable search and seizure because there was ". . . no solid evidence that the appellants really

---

[300] Pilkington, *supra*, n. 294, at pp. 555-557; 561-567.

[301] *Ibid.*, at p. 562.

[302] Pilkington, *supra*, n. 294, observes at p. 558 that ". . . since a primary purpose of imposing liability in damages is to deter unconstitutional acts, it makes sense to limit liability to those acts which are clearly unconstitutional, particularly in light of the evolutionary character of constitutional rights".

[303] (1997), 32 O.R. (3d) 349, at p. 355 (Ont. Div. Ct.), *per* O'Leary, Doubliere and Bell JJ.; revg (1995), 25 O.R. (3d) 270 (Ont. Gen. Div.).

[304] See also *Lagiorgia v. R.*, [1985] 1 F.C. 438, 18 C.R.R. 438, 18 C.R.R. 348 (T.C.); revd on other grounds by [1987] 3 F.C. 28, 87 D.T.C. 5245 (C.A.), in which no damages were awarded where a raid pursuant to subsection 231(4) of the Income Tax Act was undertaken in good faith and in accordance with the law at the time.

[305] See *Scorpio Rising Software Inc and Pederson v. Saskatchewan (Attorney-General)* (1986), 46 Sask. R. 230 at 235, in which McLellan J. of the Saskatchewan Court of Queen's Bench found that an award of damages for violation of section 8 of the Charter would require evidence of ". . . malice, bad faith, gross negligence or wilful disregard of the applicant's rights by the police officer". See also *Crossman*, *supra*, n. 288, in which the court stated at p. 600 that damages ". . . should be sufficiently punitive to act as a deterrent." Punitive damages are available in the United States for constitutional torts: see *Smith v. Wade*, 103 S.Ct. 1625, at pp. 1631-1637 (1983), in which the Supreme Court affirmed the availability of punitive damages where "gross negligence" is established.

suffered damage as a consequence of the illegal seizures".[306] In her analysis of Charter damage claims, Professor Pilkington has suggested that substantial damages should be awarded on the basis of "interference with the right alone" and should not be based on proof of consequential injuries.[307] She argues that: "[l]imiting damages to consequential injuries not only detracts from the vindication of constitutional rights but also undermines their deterrence value".[308] Although the Court in *Crossman v. R.* invoked punitive and deterrence rationales in favour of a damage award for violation of the paragraph 10(b) right to counsel, it ultimately awarded damages because ". . . the failure to impose some sanction would be to condone the unfair, and . . . illegal conduct of the police officer in question".[309] This is tantamount to an award of damages on the basis of interference with the right alone, as Professor Pilkington advocates. As with other aspects of this emerging area of the law, the basis upon which Charter damages ought to be assessed has yet to be resolved.[310]

f) *Lawson v. Wellesley Hospital*

Not only do courts rely on criminal statues to create novel civil duties, but they resist legislative attempts to exempt tortious conduct from civil liability. In *Lawson v. Wellesley Hospital*,[311] a plaintiff was attacked by a patient in a mental hospital. The defendant argued on a preliminary question of law, that it was exempt from liability by virtue of s. 59 of the Mental Health Act,[312] which stipulates: "No action lies against any psychiatric facility or any officer, employee or servant thereof for a tort of any patient." Mr. Justice Dubin, for the

---

[306] *Vespoli v. R.* (1984), 84 D.T.C. 6489 at 6491 (F.C.A.). Similarly, in *Germain, supra*, n. 299, at p. 275, the court referred to damage awards generally as providing monetary "compensation", although it did not award damages in that case. In the context of section 10 of the *Charter of Human Rights and Freedoms*, R.S.Q. c. C-12, a Quebec court awarded damages as compensation for a patient's humiliation, trauma and inconvenience when a dentist refused to treat him because he was HIV positive: *Hamel v. Malaxos* (1993), 20 C.C.L.T. (2d) 272 (Que. Ct.).

[307] *Supra*, n. 294, at p. 569. Professor Pilkington relies on *Ashby v. White* (1703), 2 Ld. Raym. 938, 92 E.R. 126 (K.B.; H.L.), a case in which the House of Lords awarded damages to a plaintiff who was denied the right to vote in order to vindicate the right *per se* and to prevent such conduct in the future. In *Carey v. Piphus*, 435 U.S. 247 (1978), however, the United States Supreme Court held that damages awarded under section 1983 serve a compensatory purpose only. It rejected the argument made in the context of a due process claim that damages should be used to deter future constitutional violations even where no harm, other than the violation of due process itself, was suffered.

[308] Pilkington, *supra*, n. 294, at p. 570. See also Pilkington, "Monetary Redress for Charter Infringement" in Sharpe (ed.), *Charter Litigation* (Toronto: Butterworths, 1987), at p. 307.

[309] *Crossman, supra*, n. 288, at p. 598.

[310] For a comprehensive and recent treatment of the Canadian case law, see Oonagh E. Fitzgerald, *Understanding Charter Remedies: A Practitioner's Guide* (Scarborough, Ont.: Carswell, 1994).

[311] (1975), 9 O.R. (2d) 677 (C.A.); affd on other grounds (1977), 76 D.L.R. (3d) 688 (S.C.C.). See also *Stewart v. Extendicare Ltd.* (1986), 38 C.C.L.T. 67 (Sask. Q.B.), hospital liable for one patient injuring another.

[312] R.S.O. 1970, c. 296 [now R.S.O. 1990, c. M.7, s. 79].

majority of the Court of Appeal, rejected this argument and sent the case on for trial. He explained that if a person "by reason of mental illness, is incapable of appreciating the nature or quality of his acts, such person has committed no tort since the intention, which is an essential element of the cause of action, is missing."[313] Consequently, since no "tort" had been committed, the statute was inapplicable to excuse the defendant hospital of its liability. Mr. Justice Dubin went on the explain, however, that if the patient committed a "tort", according the "legal meaning" of the word, the hospital would be excused, but the patient would be personally responsible. This case has been affirmed by the Supreme Court of Canada on other grounds; that is, the action was for the tort of the hospital, not for the tort of a patient. Chief Justice Laskin said it would be "incongruous" if "a hospital's liability for breach of duty of control and supervision of its mentally ill patients should depend on their degree of mental illness".

g) Other Situations

There are many other assorted instances where courts have used criminal legislation to advance into new areas of tort liability. Cases may be found where liability was imposed for criminally failing to supply fire escapes on a build-ing,[314] or neg-lecting to convey children to school,[315] and for omitting to remove a trolley pole from a highway in violation of legislation.[316] Where a public official failed to submit a petition of right contrary to the statutory provisions,[317] and where the defendant refused the deliver a ballot to a person with voting rights,[318] civil responsibility was imposed. If someone leaves a car running in front of a beer parlour in breach of a penal statute, and someone steals it and it collides with another vehicle, liability ensues.[319]

4. LEGISLATION NOT RELIED ON TO FASHION NEW DUTY

There are cases where the courts have refused to rely on penal statutes to create novel civil duties. The reason most commonly given in these situations is that the legislation evinced no intention of creating tort liability. It is suggested,

---

[313] *Supra*, n. 311, at p. 684.

[314] *Solomons v. R. Gertzenstein Ltd.*, [1954] 2 Q.B. 243; *Love v. New Fairview Corp.* (1904), 10 B.C.R. 330 (C.A.).

[315] *Ridings v. Elmhurst School Trustees*, [1927] 2 W.W.R. 159, [1927] 3 D.L.R. 173 (Sask. C.A.).

[316] *Simonsen v. Thorin* (1931), 120 Neb. 684, 234 N.W. 638.

[317] *Norton v. Fulton* (1907), 39 S.C.R. 202; affd [1908] A.C. 451 (P.C.).

[318] *Anderson v. Hicks* (1902), 35 N.S.R. 161 (C.A.).

[319] *Stavast v. Ludwar*, [1974] 5 W.W.R. 380 (B.C.) (Gansner Co. Ct. J.); *Ross v. Hartman*, 78 App. D.C. 217, 139 F. 2d 14 (C.A.D.C.), liability when plaintiff run over by thief who drove truck away, as result of defendant's breach of car-locking ordinance. See also *Hewson v. Red Deer* (1975), 63 D.L.R. (3d) 168 (Alta.), same result without statute. *Cf.*, *Moore v. Fanning* (1987), 41 C.C.L.T. 67 (Ont. H.C.J.), no liability in circumstances for fatal accident.

however, that there is no more and no less legislative intention visible here than in the other cases. The true rationale is policy.

a) Snow-Clearing By-Laws

In municipalities, by-laws frequently require abutting property owners to clear ice and snow from the public sidewalks adjacent to their property. These enactments normally impose a small fine for failure to comply and often provide that, upon notice to the owner, the work may be done by the municipality at the expense of the owner. The violation of this legislation has not given rise to a new tort duty of positive action in the absence of express language to the contrary,[320] anywhere except in West Virginia.[321] Abutting property owners, therefore, are not made civilly liable for criminal *failure* to clear snow or ice from the public sidewalk in front of their property, whereas they may be if they have injured someone by a positive act.[322] In so holding, most courts have maintained that the primary purpose of these ordinances is to reduce the cost to the municipality of keeping their streets in repair, and that the protection of the pedestrian is only a by-product of these enactments.[323]

The leading Canadian case is *Commerford v. Halifax School Commissioners*,[324] where a by-law of the City of Halifax requiring abutters to clear ice and snow from the adjoining sidewalks was breached. In deciding that there would be no tort liability imposed as a result of this breach, the court remarked that there was no evidence of any intention to confer civil liability in the by-law. The court pointed out that since the by-law contained a provision which did expressly create civil liability for the breach of certain sections, none would be imposed for the violation of any other sections without a clear statutory direction to that effect. Furthermore, the municipality had not been empowered to fashion a new tort liability and the inadequacy of the penalty demonstrated a legislative benevolence toward homeowners rather than an intention to impose an additional civil sanction. Relying on the Thayer article, therefore, the Nova Scotia court in *Commerford* refused to create a civil duty toward pedestrians on the basis of the by-law. This decision has remained unchallenged, although in *Hagen v. Goldfarb*,[325] a Nova Scotia court later held a defendant owner liable on the basis of negligence and nuisance, for injuries caused by ice formed on the sidewalk from water running off a broken moulding on the roof. The court relieved the tenant from liability, however, because of *Commerford*.

---

[320] *Willis v. Parker*, 225 N.Y. Supp. 159, 121 N.E. 810; *Texas Co. v. Grant* (1944), 143 Tex. 145, 182 S.W. 2d 996.

[321] *Rich v. Rosenshine* (1947), 131 W. Va. 30, 45 S.E. 2d 499; *Barniak v. Grossman* (1956), 141 W. Va. 760, 93 S.E. 2d 49.

[322] Morris, *supra*, n. 214, at p. 147 (in *Studies*).

[323] *King v. Crosbie Inc.* (1942), 91 Okla. 525, 131 P. 2d 105.

[324] [1950] 2 D.L.R. 207 (N.S.).

[325] (1961), 28 D.L.R. (2d) 746, at p. 756 (N.S.).

A similar approach has been taken by the American courts. They normally invoke rather strict rules of statutory interpretation and say something like, "If it had been the intention of the Legislature to cast upon property owners . . . the primary duty of keeping the streets reasonably safe . . . it doubtless would have found apt words to create such a duty",[326] or they may proclaim that, "The court is to go no faster and no farther than the Legislature has gone."[327] Another favourite device of the court is to conclude that the statute created a "public duty" only and did not create any private duty to individual pedestrians.[328] Sometimes, courts declare that the statute was meant only as an aid to the city in performing its primary duty of snow removal,[329] or that the owner was no more the cause of the injury than the pedestrian.[330]

i) Policy

These statements are, of course, specious; they merely disguise the true reasons for decision, although several valid ones do exist. One reason for the refusal to expand tort liability here is that these criminal duties are imposed by inferior legislative bodies, whose wisdom is distrusted by the courts.[331] It is for this reason that some American courts treat municipal ordinance violations as mere evidence of negligence, whereas statutory breaches may, in the United States, amount to negligence *per se*.[332] In one case, although a statute imposed civil liability on a person who caused injury to another while in breach of *any* statute, the court held that this provision would not be applied to a breach of an ordinance rather than a statute.[333] Courts may also resist the loss of uniformity in the common law from one town to the next, which would follow from their adoption of all by-laws. Most importantly, the courts probably do not sympathize with the policy of these ordinances. Insofar as they diminish the cost and expense of municipal government alone, it is hard to object to the passage of these ordinances,[334] but it is another matter where there is a wholesale transference of the primary burden of street maintenance from the municipalities to thousands of individuals who may or may not exercise the responsibility

---

[326] *Stevens v. Neligon* (1933), 116 Conn. 307, at p. 312, 164 Atl. 661, at p. 663.

[327] *Howard v. Howard* (1921), 120 Me. 479, at p. 480, 115 Atl. 259, at p. 260, in another context; *Willoughby v. City of New Haven* (1935), 123 Conn. Supp. 446, 197 Atl. 85.

[328] *Clark v. Stoudt* (1944), 73 N.D. 165, 12 N.W. 2d 708; *King v. Crosbie, supra*, n. 323, at p. 108, P. 2d, "protect public at large"; *Rees v. Cobb & Mitchell Co.* (1930), 131 Ore. 665, 283 P. 1115, at p. 1116, "duty to city".

[329] *Western Auto Supply v. Phelan* (1939), 104 F. 2d 85 (9th Cir.); *King v. Crosbie, supra*, n. 323, at p. 108, P. 2d.

[330] *Clark v. Stoudt, supra*, n. 328, at p. 710, N.W. 2d.

[331] See Alexander, *supra*, n. 214, at p. 258.

[332] See *Prosser and Keeton, op. cit. supra*, n. 102, at p. 230; *Sellers v. Cline* (1946), 160 Pa. Super. 85, at p. 86, 49 Atl. 2d 873, at p. 874.

[333] *Equitable Life v. McLellan* (1941), 286 Ky. 17, 149 S.W. 2d 730.

[334] *Ouelette v. Miller* (1936), 134 Me. 162, 183 Atl. 341; *Kirby v. Boylston Market*, 80 Mass. 249, 74 Am. Dec. 682; *Willoughby v. City of New Haven, supra*, n. 327.

adequately. "Responsibility would be divided to the detriment of the public service. . . . " and the "Municipality would relax its care and supervision," if this were permitted.[335] As long as the city is enlisting property owners as deputy street commissioners to assist it in its primary responsibility, the court will not object,[336] but when the municipality attempts to relieve itself completely of its obligation, the court refrains from encouraging this. There is also the feeling of unfairness toward the abutter, who is not only made to tend the public sidewalk on behalf of the municipality, but to bear a civil obligation to anyone injured by the omission to do so.[337] In addition, there is general judicial opposition to new tort obligations and to drastic departures from time-worn practices. Since at common law abutters were not obligated to care for the sidewalk, a penal municipal ordinance should not alter that without clearly so stating, for that would be to effect too "radical a change",[338] which "would add greatly to common law liabilities"[339] and might lead to civil obligations that would be formidable.[340] Lastly, there is seldom any urgency to impose liability here in order to compensate the injured, because the cases are frequently contests to resolve which of two defendants, the landowner or the municipality, will bear the costs of these accidents on the sidewalk, rather than to decide whether they will be borne by anyone.[341]

In conclusion, the abutter decisions do not support the general principle Thayer derives from them to the effect that civil courts should never follow the criminal law by inventing new tort duties;[342] there just is no strong policy reason for them to do so in the abutter cases,[343] as there is in the other cases.

b) Human Rights Legislation

For a time it appeared that a victim of discrimination could sue civilly, but that is no longer the case. In *Bhadauria v. Seneca College*,[344] Madam Justice Bertha Wilson created a new tort of discrimination. Her approach was bold and simple. Basing her reasoning on the preamble to the Ontario Human Rights Code, which she said evidenced the "public policy" of the province respecting fundamental human rights, she stated:

---

[335] *Equitable Life v. McLellan, supra*, n. 333, at p. 753, S.W. 2d.

[336] See *Clark v. Stoudt, supra*, n. 328.

[337] *Grooms v. Union Guardian Trust Co.* (1944), 309 Mich. 437, 15 N.W. 2d 698; *Taggart v. Bouldin* (1933), 111 N.J.L. 464, 168 Atl. 570.

[338] *Willoughby v. City of New Haven, supra*, n. 327, at p. 89, Alt.

[339] *Grooms v. Union Guardian Trust Co., supra*, n. 337, at p. 729, N.W. 2d.

[340] *Willoughby v. City of New Haven, supra*, n. 327, at p. 89, Alt.

[341] In the *Willoughby* case, *ibid.*, for example, the defendant bank was relieved of responsibility on the basis of the abutter ordinance, but the city was held liable. Sometimes municipalities are relieved of civil liability on the basis of the immunity, but often a statutory liability is expressly created.

[342] Thayer, *supra*, n. 213, at p. 329.

[343] Morris, *supra*, n. 214, at p. 148 (in *Studies*).

[344] (1979), 11 C.C.L.T. 121 (Ont. C.A.).

> If we accept that "every person is free and equal in dignity and rights without regard to race, creed, colour, sex, marital status, nationality, ancestry or place of origin", as we do, then it is appropriate that these rights receive the full protection of the common law.

Invoking the case of *Ashby v. White* to the effect that if a plaintiff "has a right, he must of necessity have a means to vindicate and maintain it, and a remedy if he is injured in the exercise of enjoyment of it", Her Ladyship concluded that the common law affords a remedy. The court did not deal with the issue of whether the Code itself gave rise to a civil cause of action.

This decision, which was described as "eminently sensible", was quickly followed in *Aziz v. Adamson*[345] where it was said that "the Courts of Ontario should cooperate with the Legislature . . . in promoting the public policy enshrined in The Ontario Human Rights Code" and should, "support a cause of action in tort for discrimination". Professor Gibson hailed the *Seneca College* decision as a "blessed event" for the law of torts[346] and hoped that the "infant tort of discrimination can grow to productive adulthood".

This was not to be. The Supreme Court of Canada, some 18 months later, ended the life of the new tort of discrimination.[347] Chief Justice Laskin, speaking for a unanimous court, praised Madam Justice Wilson's view as a "bold one" which "may be commended as an attempt to advance the common law", but held that the Code foreclosed a "civil action based directly on the breach thereof" as well as any "common law action based on an invocation of the public policy expressed in the Code". The Chief Justice stated that the Code "laid out the procedures for vindication of that public policy". The civil courts are not an alternative route to recovery, he decided, but are a "part of the enforcement machinery under the Code" to be involved only through the appeal procedure[348] or perhaps through judicial review.

The Supreme Court, thus, has held that a cause of action in tort for discrimination was not available either under the common law nor for breach of the provisions of the statute. It was thought that the legislature meant to grant *exclusive* jurisdiction to the Commission in the field of human rights, the courts' role being limited to a supervisory one and not as an additional path to tort compensation. The fact that the Commission has the power to award damages undoubtedly influenced that view.[349]

---

[345] (1979), 11 C.C.L.T. 134 (Ont.) (*per* Linden J.).

[346] "The New Tort of Discrimination: A Blessed Event for the Great-Grandmother of Torts" (1980), 11 C.C.L.T. 141, at p. 150.

[347] (1981), 17 C.C.L.T. 106, 37 N.R. 455 (S.C.C.). See also *Tenning v. Govt. of Manitoba* (1984), 4 D.L.R. (4th) 418 (Man. C.A.); *Chapman v. 3M Canada* (1995), 24 C.C.L.T. (2d) 304 (Ont. Gen. Div.); affd (1997), 37 C.C.L.T. (2d) 319 (Ont. C.A.); *Allen v. C.F.P.L. Broadcasting Ltd.* (1995), 24 C.C.L.T. (2d) 297 (Ont. Gen. Div.); but *cf.*, *Lehman v. Davis* (1993), 16 O.R. (3d) 338 (Ont. Gen. Div.), *dictum* to the contrary.

[348] Section 14d(4), now s. 42(3).

[349] Section 14c, now s. 42(1). See generally Hunter, "Civil Actions for Discrimination" (1977), 55 Can. Bar Rev. 106. A similar approach was taken in *Frame v. Smith*, [1987] 2 S.C.R. 99, in the

It may be, however, that violation of the Canadian Charter of Rights and Freedoms now may permit a civil action for damages in these circumstances.[350]

c) Other Legislation

There are other cases where the courts have abstained from imposing tort liability for criminal nonfeasance. Perhaps, the best known of these is *Cutler v. Wandsworth Stadium*,[351] where a bookmaker was denied recovery against the defendant which failed to provide him with adequate space for his endeavours at a dog-racing track in England, as required by the Betting and Lotteries Act. The House of Lords barely veiled its disapproval of the policy of the statute, at least insofar as it aided the bookmakers to increase their profits, when Lord Simonds said that the statute is not "the charter of the bookmakers".[352] The House of Lords distinguished this statute from those which were passed to better the lot of workers by placing new duties upon employers for the benefit of their employees. It then concluded that the penalties provided in the Act were "effective sanctions" and stood "in no need of aid from civil proceedings".[353]

In another case, *C. P. Air Lines Ltd. v. The Queen*,[354] the plaintiff sued the Crown for failing to keep the runways of the airports free of snow, which caused the cancellation of some of its flights, resulting in economic loss. The plaintiff relied on s. 3(c) of the Aeronautics Act,[355] which placed a duty on the Minister to "maintain all government aerodromes", as a basis for a civil duty owed to it. There was a strike on progress and the Crown did not hire outside personnel to do the work but relied only on certain of its employees that were prohibited from striking. The action was dismissed on the basis that the conduct of the Crown had been reasonable in the circumstances, so that there had been no negligence and no breach of duty, if one existed. Despite a concession that there was a duty to keep the aerodromes "operational at all reasonable times", Kerr J. felt that the Act did not "create Crown liability for the kind of loss in respect of which the claim in the present case is made." LeDain J. agreed that the statute did not give the airlines a "right of action for the economic loss that may result to them from a failure to perform the duty to maintain government aerodromes". His Lordship, in a *dictum*, pointed out that the question was one of "policy", which depended mainly on statutory construction. He did not think that "reliance on a public service is sufficient to create a private right of action". The Act created only a "public duty". He concluded:

---

family law context; but compare *Phillips v. Harrison* (2000), 4 C.C.L.T. (3d) 248 (Man. C.A.), where Steel J.A. allowed defamation action despite availability of grievance procedure.

[350] Pilkington, *supra*, n. 294. See also Cooper-Stephenson, *supra*, n. 289.

[351] [1949] A.C. 398. See also *Coote v. Stone*, [1971] 1 All E.R. 657 (C.A.).

[352] *Ibid.*, at p. 404.

[353] *Ibid.*, at p. 414. See also *Green v. Portsmouth Stadium Ltd.*, [1953] 2 All E.R. 102 (C.A.).

[354] (1978), 87 D.L.R. (3d) 511 (Fed. C.A.); *cf.*, *The Queen in right of Canada v. The Queen in right of P.E.I.* (1977), 83 D.L.R. (3d) 492 (Fed. C.A.).

[355] R.S.C. 1970, c. A-3, now only discretionary power, see R.S.C. 1985, c. 33 (1st Supp.), s. 4.2(b).

To ascribe to Parliament an intention to give the commercial airlines a right of action for
economic loss resulting from a failure to keep an airport open would be to ascribe to it an intention to create a category of Crown liability extending in nature and scope far beyond that
for injury to person or property then existing under federal legislation. There would have to
be a clear indication of an intention to transfer loss of this kind from the airlines to the public
treasury.[356]

This reasoning, though couched in the language of intention, shows that the
court was sensitive to the practical problem of creating tort liability for economic loss caused by labour strife. It did not feel it was advisable to stretch the
responsibility of the Crown, as set out in the statute, to cover such losses as
these, even though a statutory obligation may have been breached. It would be
too onerous a responsibility. Moreover, the difficulty courts have with compensation for economic losses generally played a role here; the courts might well come
to a different conclusion if someone was injured[357] or an airplace was damaged
as a result of a breach of the statute. There will undoubtedly be more cases such
as these in the years ahead.

Similarly, no tort action will lie for a breach of anti-combines legislation in
Canada,[358] wages cannot be recovered on the basis of a penal violation,[359] nor
will compensation be awarded to a criminal whose name is wrongfully published contrary to an Identification of Criminals Act.[360]

In *Edmonton Mint Ltd. v. The Queen*,[361] it was held that the Customs Tariff,[362]
and the Marking of Imported Goods Order enacted pursuant to it, if violated by
certain importers, do not create a civil cause of action in their competitors.
Primrose J. relying on *Cutler* stated:

I cannot find that the scheme of the legislation intended to create for the benefit of individuals any rights enforceable by action, and that the remedies provided by the order are the only
remedies available to the public for the observance of the statutory duty.[363]

In all of these cases, the courts are unwilling to use the breach of criminal
statutes to create tort liability, since the policies of the legislation did not appear
to the judiciary to be worthy of further advancement.

The fate of s. 129(b) of the Criminal Code of Canada,[364] which penalizes
anyone who "omits, without reasonable excuse, to assist a public officer or
peace officer in the execution of his duty in arresting a person or in preserving

---

[356] *Supra*, n. 354, at p. 520.
[357] *Johnston v. A.-G. Can.* (1981), 18 C.C.L.T. 245 (*per* Linden J.); affd Div. Ct. (Reid J.),
endorsement.
[358] *Transport Oil Co. v. Imperial Oil Co. and Cities Service Co.*, [1935] O.R. 111; affd at p. 215
(C.A.). But *cf.*, Duff C.J., in *Philco Products v. Thermionics Ltd.*, [1940] 4 D.L.R. 1, at p. 3.
[359] *Outen v. Stewart*, [1932] 3 W.W.R. 193, 40 Man. R. 557.
[360] *Pullan v. McLellan*, [1946] 2 D.L.R. 606 (B.C.).
[361] (1978), 94 D.L.R. (3d) 312.
[362] R.S.C. 1970, c. C-41 [now R.S.C. 1985, c. 41 (3rd Supp.)].
[363] *Supra*, n. 361, at p. 318.
[364] R.S.C. 1985, c. C-46. Also Criminal Code, s. 217, which requires one to complete an act
undertaken, if omission to do so endangers life.

the peace, after having reasonable notice that he is required to do so," is still undecided with regard to a civil duty. The fact that the Compensation for Victims of Crime Act[365] provides benefits to anyone injured while assisting a police officer points toward the creation of a new tort duty to help, at least in those jurisdictions which compensate crime victims. The usual reluctance of the law of torts to force individuals to engage in dangerous rescue operations is somewhat overcome if that person is entitled to financial benefits for any injury incurred while so doing.

5. LIMITING PRINCIPLES

The same limiting principles developed to prevent promiscuous use of criminal legislation in setting standards of care, are used in these nonfeasance cases. Causation must be proved,[366] and the harm caused must be of the kind the legislation is aimed at preventing, and plaintiffs must bring themselves within the protective legislative umbrella.

That the court will not rely as readily on criminal legislation to create a new duty as it will to fix the standard of care where a duty already exists cannot be denied, since the former is a more drastic step for a court to take. However, courts have fashioned new tort duties by analogy to criminal legislation. Such creativity, it is submitted, is proper and justified if done with discretion and candour.[367]

---

[365] *Supra*, n. 210.

[366] See *Daniels v. Vaux*, [1938] 2 K.B. 203, [1938] 2 All E.R. 271.

[367] Wright, "Note" (1941), 19 Can. Bar Rev. 51, at p. 52; Alexander, *supra*, n. 214, at p. 276; Morris, *supra*, n. 214.

Chapter 10

Remoteness of Damage and Proximate Cause: Extent of Liability

Negligent defendants who owe a general duty are not liable unless their conduct is the "proximate cause" of the plaintiffs' losses. Causation alone is not enough; it must be demonstrated that the conduct is the *proximate* cause of the damage. Put another way, the losses or injuries incurred by plaintiffs must not be "too remote" a consequence of the act.

This topic of remoteness, or proximate cause, the fifth element, will be discussed in this chapter. It has provided much exercise for courts and legal scholars, who have been unable to resist its allure and have been enticed into many a lengthy treatise on the issue. As a result, the law reports and the law reviews[1] are flooded with material[2] on this problem, none of which, alas, has authoritatively settled the matter.

A. The Problem of Remoteness Defined

Most of the difficulty in this area stems from an unfortunate blurring of two issues that should not be intermingled: (1) cause-in-fact, and (2) proximate cause or remoteness. If the cause-in-fact issue were kept separate from the proximate

---

[1] Fleming, "The Passing of Polemis" (1961), 39 Can. Bar Rev. 489; J.C. Smith, "Requiem for Polemis" (1965), 2 U.B.C.L. Rev. 159; J.C. Smith, "The Limits of Tort Liability in Canada: Remoteness, Foreseeability and Proximate Cause", in Linden (ed.) *Studies in Canadian Tort Law* (1968) p. 88; MacLaren, "Negligence and Remoteness — The Aftermath of Wagon Mound" (1967), 1 Sask. L. Rev. 45; Linden, "Down with Foreseeability" (1969), 47 Can. Bar Rev. 545; Williams, "The Risk Principle" (1961), 77 L.Q. Rev. 179; Green, "Foreseeability in Negligence Law" (1961), 61 Colum. L. Rev. 1401; Prosser, "Palsgraf Revisited" in *Selected Topics on The Law of Torts* (1953), at 191. Fridman and Williams, "The Atomic Theory of Negligence" (1971), 45 A.L.J. 117.

[2] Hart and Honoré, *Causation in The Law*, 2nd ed. (1985); Green, *Rationale of Proximate Cause* (1927); Keeton, *Legal Cause in The Law of Torts* (1963); Smith, *Liability in Negligence* (1984), Chapter 7 *et seq*; Stapleton, "Legal Case" (2001), 54 Vanderbilt L. Rev. 941, legal cause controls the "voraciousness of negligence".

cause or remoteness issue, much of the confusion would vanish. In this book an attempt has been made to keep them distinct.[3] Although one cannot totally and completely divorce the two issues, it can be said that cause-in-fact is fundamentally a question of fact, which can be treated relatively expeditiously in most tort litigation. Proximate cause or remoteness, on the other hand, cannot be handled so simply, because it deals with the limits of liability for negligent conduct, which involve more complicated legal analysis. This process of determining the *extent* of liability (not its *basis*) demands delicate value judgments and the drawing of fine lines. It is more a question of law and policy than fact.

The matter under consideration here is the extent to which an actor, who admittedly owes a duty, will be held liable for substandard conduct. In other words, "We are only concerned with the limits or the extent of liability for conduct which was admittedly negligent."[4] Will someone, negligently dropping a lighted match into a waste basket, be held liable for damages for the building if it burns down, for the entire block if it goes, for the whole city if it is destroyed? Must that person compensate someone who is burned in the neighboring building? What if the victim receives only a slight burn, but later develops cancer? What if the victim becomes mentally deranged because of disfigurement? What about economic losses that result? What if a rescuer is hurt trying to extricate the victim? What if the doctor treating the victim bungles the operation? What if the victim commits suicide? Such tantalizing problems are the concern of this chapter.

This has become one of the most complex areas of tort law. Many verbal formulae, such as proximate cause, remoteness, natural and probable consequences, risk, duty, and foresight, have been advanced at various times to assist the court to distinguish between the consequences which will produce liability and those which will not. The elements of duty and remoteness are sometimes confused.

Some of the difficulty may well result from the rivalry between the courts and juries, who are sometimes felt to be too sympathetic to plaintiffs. With certain of these limitation devices, such as duty, courts can exert some control over jury decisions by treating these problems as questions of law. On the other hand, there is authority to the effect that a "remoteness" question must be submitted to the jury. For example, Mr. Justice Master, in *Barnard v. Carnegie* said: "The question of remoteness of damage is a question of fact upon the circumstances of each case . . . and the question must be submitted to the jury."[5] Similarly, the proximate cause technique has been handled as a question of fact and within the province of the jury by Mr. Justice Garrow, who remarked in

---

[3]   *Supra*, Chapter 4. Each is considered as a separate element.
[4]   *Cotic v. Gray* (1981), 17 C.C.L.T. 138 (Ont. C.A.) (*per* Lacourcière J.A.); affd (1984), 26 C.C.L.T. 163 (S.C.C.).
[5]   (1924), 26 O.W.N. 264, at p. 265 (C.A.); *McKelvin v. London* (1892), 22 O.R. 70, at p. 77 (C.A.).

Fraser v. Algoma Central & Hudson Bay Railway: "Proximate cause is a question of fact, and therefore for the jury . . . subject of course to this, that the Court must first say whether there is any evidence from which the jury acting reasonable could draw the necessary inference . . . ".[6] It seems that there is a good deal of flexibility in the use of these various word formulae, which is good, but this begets confusion, which is bad.

B. Early Techniques for Limiting Liability

At one time the courts flirted with the notion of holding actors liable for all of the consequences of their negligent conduct, whether or not they were foreseeable or direct.[7] This prospect was described as unthinkable[8] and startling, and before very long the idea of unlimited liability was abandoned. The courts could not, in conscience, impose liability on negligent tortfeasors for everything that flowed from their conduct. Liability had to be confined in some way.

Once it was agreed that limits had to be placed upon liability for negligent acts, a test had to be devised to do the job. This was easier said than done. It was concluded that no liability would attach for consequences that were "too remote". Alternatively stated, for liability to ensue, the offending conduct must be the "proximate cause" of the damage. These phrases were primarily restatements of the problem, except that they did point out the need for a reasonably close connection between the acts of defendants and the resulting losses to plaintiffs before liability would be imposed.

One test utilized for a time, and now out of use, was that of directness. It was best articulated in the case of *Re Polemis and Furness, Withy & Co. Ltd.*[9] A plank was negligently dropped into the hold of a ship. This caused a spark, igniting some gas vapour which had leaked into the hold, completely destroying the ship. The charterers were held liable for the ship, even though they could not anticipate that the plank would cause a spark. It was, apparently, enough that they could foresee *some* damage to the ship. Lord Justice Scrutton stated that foresight was relevant only to determine whether the act was negligent. Once that is decided, the actor is liable for all damage "directly traceable to the negligent act, and not due to the operation of independent causes having no connection with the negligent act . . . . Once the act is negligent, the fact that its exact operation was not foreseen is immaterial."[10] Lord Justice Warrington expressed it thus:

> The presence or absence of reasonable anticipation of damage determines the legal quality of the act as negligent or innocent. If it be thus determined to the negligent, then the question

6   (1904), 3 O.W.R. 104, at p. 105 (C.A.).
7   *Smith v. London and South Western Ry.* (1870), L.R. 6 C.P. 14.
8   Fleming, *supra*, n. 1, at p. 491.
9   [1921] 3 K.B. 560.
10 *Ibid.*, at p. 577.

whether particular damages are recoverable depends only on the answer to the question whether they are the direct consequence of the Act . . . .[11]

It all seemed delightfully simply, and logical, but it proved unsatisfactory. To be sure, some expressed their "faith in the capacity of our judges to answer these questions",[12] and others praised *Polemis* for its flexibility and its "appeal to common sense" which "allows scope for the intuitive judgment".[13] For, after all, it was contended, "the correct solution to a remoteness problem is felt rather than deduced from formulated principles".[14] Moreover, "it would not occur to the ordinary man to question the justice" of the rule that "the defendant must take the plaintiff and the consequences as he finds them".[15] Despite these accolades, the directness formula led to a "long period of baffling and sterile discourse amidst a labyrinth of pseudo-logical and metaphysical controversy".[16] The pages of the law reports were filled with colourful metaphors like chains, links, gears and nets. Terms such as immediate cause, precipitating cause, condition, *causa causans* and *causa sine que non* were borrowed from philosophy and Latin, but they obscured rather than explained the reasons for the decisions.[17] Moreover, the issue of factual cause was mixed up with the value choices of proximate case. *Polemis* did not deserve to survive. It was rightly jettisoned in *The Wagon Mound (No. 1)*[18] and supplanted by the foresight test.

C. The Rise of Foresight: *The Wagon Mound (No. 1)*

The influential proponents of the foresight test had attacked *Polemis* viciously and argued, that in order to be consistent and logical, the concept of foresight had to limit liability for negligence as well as create it.[19] They asserted that the foresight doctrine was a "comparatively simple rule"[20] which permitted an "empirical determination"[21] of the scope of liability. They assured us that the principle was a just and fair one.[22]

---

[11]   *Ibid.*, at p. 574.

[12]   Lord Wright, "*Re Polemis*" (1951), 14 Mod. L. Rev. 395, at p. 405.

[13]   Payne, "Foresight and Remoteness of Damage in Negligence" (1962), 25 Mod. L. Rev. 1, at p. 9.

[14]   *Ibid.*, at p. 22.

[15]   *Ibid.*, at p. 11.

[16]   Fleming, *supra*, n. 1, at p. 491.

[17]   C.A. Wright, "The Law of Torts: 1923-1947" (1948), 25 Can. Bar Rev. 46, at pp. 57 *et seq.*

[18]   *Overseas Tankship (U.K.) Ltd. v. Mort's Dock and Engineering Co., The Wagon Mound (No. 1)*, [1961] A.C. 388 (P.C.).

[19]   Seavey, "Mr. Justice Cardozo and The Law of Torts" (1939), 52 Harv. L. Rev. 372, 48 Yale L.J. 309, 39 Colum. L. Rev. 20.

[20]   Goodhart, "The Imaginary Necktie and The Rule in Re Polemis" (1952), 68 L.Q. Rev. 514, at p. 533.

[21]   Williams, *supra*, n. 1, at p. 190.

[22]   Seavey, *supra*, n. 19.

In 1961 the Privy Council finally succumbed and, in the case of *Overseas Tankship (U.K.) Ltd. v. Mort's Dock and Engineering Co.*,[23] usually called *The Wagon Mound (No. 1)*, it trumpeted the triumph of simplicity, logic and justice throughout the Commonwealth,[24] when Lord Simonds declared that, "it is the foresight of the reasonable man which alone can determine responsibility".[25]

The facts of *The Wagon Mound (No. 1)* were that careless employees of the charterer of the ship "Wagon Mound" spilled some oil into Sydney Harbour. The oil floated over to the plaintiff's dock where some repair work was going on. Although the work was initially stopped, it was resumed when the plaintiff's manager was informed that there was no danger. Two days later the oil on the water ignited, damaging the dock and two ships moored there. According to the trial judge, the fire was caused by some drops of molten metal from the welding or cutting operations that fell on some floating cotton waste, which acted as a wick to ignite the oil. He also held that it was not reasonably foreseeable that oil could burn on water.

The trial judge, following *Polemis*, imposed liability since the negligent spilling of the oil was the direct cause of the fire. He was affirmed on appeal. The defendants then by-passed the High Court of Australia and appealed directly to the Privy Council, which overruled *Polemis* and dismissed the action based on negligence. Viscount Simonds expressed the policy basis of the decision in this way:

> It is not probable that many cases will . . . have a different result, though it is hoped that the law will be . . . simplified, and that in some cases, at least, palpable injustice will be avoided. For it does not seem consonant with current ideas of justice or morality that for an act of negligence, however slight or venial, which results in some trivial foreseeable damage the actor should be liable for all consequences however unforseeable and however grave, so long as they can be said to be "direct". It is a principle of civil liability, subject only to qualifications which have no present relevance, that a man must be considered to be responsible for the probable consequences of his act. To demand more of him is too harsh a rule, to demand less is to ignore that civilised order requires the observance of a minimum standard of behaviour.[26]

Over the years it has become apparent that the great expectations of Viscount Simonds and those who viewed *The Wagon Mound (No. 1)* as a panacea were never realized. The idea of foresight helped to improve things, but confusion, illogic and injustice have not been banished; they still reign. It is somewhat disheartening to see, despite the supposed victory of clarity, that some of the most bizarre events imaginable have been held perfectly expectable and, at the same time, some of the most commonplace consequences have been said to be

---

[23] *Supra*, n. 18.
[24] See generally Fleming, *supra*, n. 1.
[25] *Supra*, n. 18, at p. 424.
[26] *Supra*, n. 18, at p. 422.

totally unforseeable. Moreover, the courts have visibly retreated from the initial purity of the foresight test in at least two significant ways.

D. Retreat: *Hughes v. Lord Advocate*: Type of Damage

The foresight principle was diluted in *Hughes v. Lord Advocate*,[27] where the House of Lords explained that, under *The Wagon Mound (No. 1)*, one need not foresee the exact way in which an accident occurs, as long as one anticipates the general type of consequence that transpires. This did much to mollify the potential harshness of the foresight principle.

In the *Hughes* case, the employees of the defendant left some paraffin lamps burning beside a manhole, in Edinburgh, Scotland, when they went for afternoon tea. A curious eight-year-old boy appeared, with a friend, picked up one of the lamps, entered the shelter and descended into the manhole. On his way out, the boy tripped over the lamp, which fell into the manhole, causing an explosion with flames reaching a height of 30 feet. This caused the boy to fall into the hole, where he sustained severe burns.

Both lower courts dismissed the case on the basis of *The Wagon Mound (No. 1)*. The House of Lords, however, reversed the decision and held the defendants liable. Lord Pearce felt that it would be unfair to demand too much precision in the test of foreseeability, since "the facets of misadventure are innumerable".[28] Although there was an "unexpected manifestation of the apprehended physical danger", one should not hold that those "who create the risk of fire are excused from the liability for the damage of fire, because it came by way of explosive combustion". He concluded that "the resulting damage, though severe, was not greater than or different in kind from that which might have been produced had the lamp spilled and produced a more normal conflagration".[29] Lord Guest reasoned:

> explosion is only one way in which burning can be caused. Burning can also be caused by the contact between liquid paraffin and a naked flame. In the one case paraffin vapour and in the other case liquid paraffin is ignited by fire. I cannot see that these are two different types of accident. They are both burning accidents and in both cases the injuries would be burning injuries.

Lord Reid concluded that it is no defence that an "accident was caused by a known source of danger, but caused in a way which could not have been foreseen".[30]

Mr. Justice Dickson, of the Supreme Court of Canada, has recently articulated the test as follows:

---

[27]   [1963] A.C. 837, [1963] 1 All E.R. 705.
[28]   *Ibid.*, at p. 857.
[29]   *Ibid.*, at p. 856.
[30]   *Ibid.*, at p. 847.

It is not necessary that one foresee the "precise concatenation of events"; it is enough to fix liability if one can foresee in a general way the class or character of injury which occurred.[31]

Chief Justice Scott wisely employed the test recently when a child's eye was injured while bending a coat hanger in art class at school, saying that the risk to the eye was "not of a kind vastly different" than any other physical injury that must be guarded against.[32]

The House of Lords has recently expressed its fealty to *Hughes v. Lord Advocate* in the case of *Jolley v. Sutton London Borough Council*,[33] where a 14-year-old boy was severely injured when an abandoned cabin cruiser on the Council's land fell on him as he lay underneath it trying to repair it. While the Council admitted that it may have been negligent with regard to an accident involving the rotten planking giving way when children climbed on it, they urged that the accident was taken out of the realm of foreseeability because the boy, in order to work on the boat, had propped it up, rendering it unstable. Lord Steyn rejected this argument, reminding us that these cases were "very fact-sensitive"[34] and hence, the finding of the trial judge that this accident was not "very different" than what might occur during the "normal" play[35] of children was unassailable. Lord Hoffman agreed that "what must have been foreseen is not the precise injury which occurred but injury of a given description. The foreseeability is not as to the particulars but the genus".[36] He agreed with the trial judge, taking into account the "rich fantasy life of children", who described the risk as being that children would "meddle with the boat at the risk of some physical injury."[37]

The *Hughes v. Lord Advocate* qualification has made the foresight formula more flexible, but it has also created a source of confusion. It is no easy matter to determine when a consequence is of the same kind as the one foreseen, but occurs in an unforeseeable way, and when the accident is of a different type altogether.

---

[31] *R. v. Coté* (1974), 51 D.L.R. (3d) 244, at p. 252. See also *Abbott et al. v. Kasza*, [1975] 3 W.W.R. 163, at p. 172; vard [1976] 4 W.W.R. 20 (Alta. C.A.), where D.C. MacDonald J. explained that "the manner in which the damage did occur must be foreseeable in the sense that although the precise manner in which it occurred was not foreseeable, nevertheless the kind of damage which did occur was foreseeable and the precise manner in which the damage occurred was a variant of the foreseeable or within the risk created by the negligence or not fantastic or highly improbable".

[32] *Michaluk (Litigation Guardian of) v. Rolling River School Division No. 39* (2001), 5 C.C.L.T. (3d) 1, at p. 10 (Man. C.A.).

[33] [2000] 3 All E.R. 409 (H.L.).

[34] *Ibid.*, at p. 416.

[35] *Ibid.*, at p. 415.

[36] *Ibid.*, at p. 418.

[37] *Ibid.*

1. CASES IMPOSING LIABILITY

A number of liberal decisions demonstrate that the courts can stretch their description of the "class or character" of an accident. In *Lauritzen v. Barstead*,[38] liability was ascribed in rather strange circumstances. The plaintiff asked the defendant for a ride in his car to a nearby town. While in the town the defendant did considerable drinking and eventually became intoxicated. He asked the plaintiff to drive the car back. On the way back the defendant decided he wanted more beer and ordered the plaintiff to take a turn-off into the first town. The plaintiff refused and continued on the highway. The defendant grabbed at the steering wheel putting the car out of control and off the road. While the plaintiff was out of the car investigating the situation, the defendant made an attempt to drive back on the road, but this merely resulted in the car becoming more precariously situated on the bank of a ditch some 30 feet in depth. The plaintiff tried to walk down for help, but was forced to turn back because of the cold. The plaintiff and the defendant agreed to stay in the car overnight. While the plaintiff was sleeping, the defendant drove the car across the prairie toward a river intending to drive to town on the frozen surface, but the car went into a hole and became hopelessly stuck. The plaintiff made several other efforts to go for help, but was turned back by the wind and the cold. About 36 hours after they left the road, the plaintiff walked several miles down river where he was found by a farmer. Frostbite necessitated the amputation of parts of both feet. In an action by the plaintiff for damages, it was argued that *The Wagon Mound (No. 1)* prevented recovery for the plaintiff's injuries. Kirby J. held the defendant liable. He ought to have foreseen "the dangerous consequences likely to flow from his negligent act in grabbing the steering wheel. It does not seem to me that . . . the *Wagon Mound* case implies that recovery of damages should be conditional upon foreseeablility of the particular harm and the precise manner or sequence of events in which it occurred."[39] The loss of consortium which occurred when the plaintiff's wife left him because she did not want to live with a disabled person was, however, held to be "too remote". In another case, *Bradford v. Robinson Rentals Ltd.*,[40] it was held that a frostbite injury, suffered by the driver of an unheated vehicle, was the same type of injury as an illness due to exposure to cold.

There are numerous other cases where somewhat odd results have yielded liability. In *Weiner v. Zoratti*[41] a motorist who ran into a fire hydrant was held liable for damage caused when water ran into an open window of the plaintiff's

---

[38] (1965), 53 W.W.R. 207 (Alta.). See also *Stewart v. West African Terminals*, [1964] 2 Lloyd's Rep. 371, having one's finger crushed by a cable in a pulley is the same type of accident as tripping over the cable or straining oneself lifting it out of the way.

[39] *Ibid.*, at pp. 216-17.

[40] [1967] 1 All E.R. 267 (*per* Rees J.).

[41] (1970), 11 D.L.R. (3d) 598 (Man.); *Kennedy v. Hughes Drug (1969) Inc.* (1974), 47 D.L.R. (3d) 277 (P.E.I.).

basement. Mr. Justice Matas declared that one need not look at the "specific foreseeability of each specific event" nor "embark on an exercise in metaphysical subtleties". He concluded that the loss was "direct, probable and foreseeable", in the same way it would be if a piece of the hydrant hit someone. In *McKenzie v. Hyde*,[42] liability was imposed upon someone who, during digging operations, broke a gas line, permitting gas to seep into a nearby basement window, ignite and explode. Mr. Justice Dickson felt that there was "nothing peculiar" about the consequences which were of a "class or character foreseeable as a possible result of the negligence". His Lordship explained that he could not say that the damage or the explosion was "freakish" or "one in a million".[43]

In *Hoffer v. School Division of Assiniboine South*,[44] a 14-year-old boy started his father's snowmobile in a negligent manner, cause it to escape from his control. It collided with a defected and unprotected gas-riser pipe. This caused some gas to escape and enter a window of a nearby school building where it exploded. The school sued the 14-year-old, his father and the gas company which had improperly installed the gas-riser pipe. All three defendants were found liable to the plaintiff for the damage, and among themselves, responsibility was apportioned 50 per cent to the gas company, 25 per cent to the son, and 25 per cent to the father.

In discussing the liability of the boy, Dickson J.A. (as he then was) stated:

> It is enough to fix liability if one could foresee in a general way the sort of thing that happened. The extent of the damage and its manner of incidence need not be forseeable if physical damage of the kind which in fact ensues is foreseeable. In the case at bar, I would hold that the damage was of the *type* or *kind* which any reasonable person might foresee. Gas-riser pipes on the outside of . . . buildings are common. Damage to such a pipe is not of a kind that no one could anticipate. When one permits a power toboggan to run at large, or when one fires a rifle blindly down a city street, one must not define narrowly the outer limits of reasonable provision. The ambit of foreseeable damage is indeed broad.[45]

Another strange case is *Prasad v. Prasad*,[46] where a father allowed his son to play with a knife which had apparently been left on a sofa. The plaintiff came to visit the father, sat down on the sofa and leaned back, and was pierced in the back by the knife. The father was held responsible for this rather bizarre accident on the ground that he was negligent in failing to supervise his child properly in the handling of the knife. Mr. Justice Rae stated, "the harm occasioned the plaintiff here, it seems to me, was of such a class or general character as to be within the scope of foreseeable risk. What occurred was but a variant of the foreseeable . . . . It was not necessary that the precise manner of its occurrence should have been envisioned."

---

[42] (1967), 64 D.L.R. (2d) 362; affd 66 D.L.R. (2d) 655 (Man.).
[43] *Ibid.*, at pp. 375-76.
[44] [1971] 4 W.W.R. 746; affd [1973] 6 W.W.R. 765 (S.C.C.); both affg (1970), 16 D.L.R. (3d) 703.
[45] *Ibid.*, at p. 752.
[46] (1974), 54 D.L.R. (3d) 451 (B.C.).

Falkenham v. Zwicker[47] is another odd case. The defendant motorist negligently crashed into a wire fence while trying to avoid hitting a cat. As a result some metal fence staples that held the fence were thrown into an empty field. In the spring when the plaintiff farmer was fixing his fences, he noticed some staples were missing. He spent some time looking for them and found a few, but not all of them. Later, when cows were released into the field, several of them fell ill with "hardware disease" from having ingested metal staples. Mr. Justice MacIntosh held the defendant liable, stating that the

> damage was of the type or kind which a reasonable person might foresee. Damage to the plaintiff's wire fence under the circumstances is what a reasonable person could anticipate. It is common knowledge that wire on a pasture fence is usually held by means of staples. Breaking of the fence, as was done in this instance, indicates a reasonable foreseeability of staples being ejected and eventually damaging the cattle that use this pasture.[48]

The court went on to reduce the plaintiff's damage because he failed to "mitigate his loss" rather than because of contributory negligence. Since the plaintiff took only 15 minutes to search for the staples this was not "reasonable steps to take in mitigation of damages". The plaintiff was awarded 60 per cent of his loss.

There are similar cases. For example, it has been held to be forseeable that if a bull escaped from the defendant's pasture it might impregnate six heifers, in heat, who were too young to breed, the result of which would require that the heifers be replaced.[49] So too, if one can foresee that a dog may jump on someone, one can also foresee that the dog may bite that person, because if one is aware that a dog would "cause harm", one cannot "escape liability by submitting that the extent of that harm was not foreseeable".[50] It has also been held to be forseeable that one might burn to death after mistakenly pouring a pail of cleaning fluid over oneself while trying to put out a negligently started fire.[51]

2. CASES DENYING LIABILITY

The courts are not always so anxious to assist claimants. At times they insist that accidents are different in kind than those foreseen. In *Doughty v. Turner Manufacturing Co. Ltd.*,[52] a worker was injured by some molten cyanide which escaped from a heating cauldron in the defendant's plant. The cauldron's asbestos cover had been negligently knocked into the cyanide by another employee. It did not splash, but it caused an eruption because a chemical change took place. Although the trial judge was convinced that *Hughes v. Lord Advocate* applied, the Court of Appeal distinguished it and dismissed the case.

---

[47] (1978), 93 D.L.R. (3d) 289 (N.S.).
[48] *Ibid.*, at p. 292.
[49] *Weeks v. Weeks* (1977), 18 Nfld. & P.E.I.R. 1 (P.E.I.).
[50] *Kirk v. Trerise* (1979), 103 D.L.R. (3d) 78, at p. 85 (*per* Andrews J.).
[51] *Workers Compensation Bd. v. Schmidt* (1977), 80 D.L.R. (3d) 696 (Man. Q.B.).
[52] [1964] 1 All E.R. 98 (C.A.).

The risk of being splashed, according to the court, was of a different kind than the danger of being burned by an explosion caused by a chemical reaction. It is difficult to understand why the court did not take the more obvious course and hold that, although the burning occurred in an unforeseeable manner, still the same type of risk was created. Perhaps this consequence was a somewhat more abnormal occurrence than the one in *Hughes*. Perhaps the availability of an alternative remedy under workers' compensation legislation made it easier for the court to deny liability. Perhaps it was a negative reaction to the direction in which the law was moving as a result of *Hughes*. Nevertheless, *Doughty* demonstrated that there were boundaries beyond which the scope of foresight would not be extended.

Another such case is *Tremain v. Pike*,[53] where a farmhand contracted Weil's disease as a result of contact with rat's urine. The court held that there was no evidence of negligence by the employer in controlling the rats and that too great an effort would be necessitated to check all disease from rats. In an *obiter dictum*, Lord Justice Payne indicated that this rare disease was not the usual type of sickness one could expect from a rat bite or from food contaminated by rats.[54] The "damage . . . [was] . . . unforeseeable and too remote" since the "risk of initial infection was not reasonably foreseeable". His Lordship distinguished *Bradford v. Robinson Rentals Ltd.*,[55] where a frostbite injury suffered by a driver of an unheated vehicle was held to be of the same kind as an illness due to exposure to cold.

In *Oke v. Weide Transport Ltd.*,[56] the defendant motorist, who had knocked over a metal post on a strip of gravel between two highway lanes, left the post bent over and the deceased, improperly using the strip for the purpose of passing another car, was killed when the post came up through the floor boards of his car and impaled him. The majority of the Manitoba Court of Appeal held the defendant not liable, purporting to following *The Wagon Mound (No. 1)*. The majority reasoned that the defendant could not have anticipated that someone would endeavor to pass a car at a point where it was wrong to do so, or that the damaged post would come up through the floor of the car and cause a fatal accident. It was a "freak accident" and the defendant could not reasonably have foreseen such an unusual occurrence. Freedman J.A., dissenting, said it was not necessary to foresee "either the precise manner in which the accident would occur or that its consequences would be so tragic . . . . It is enough that he ought to have foreseen that with the sign-post left in the state it was, it could be a source of danger to any motorist entering upon the highway strip . . . and become the cause of an automobile accident . . . of some kind."

---

[53] [1969] 3 All E.R. 1303. See also *Yorkton Agricultural Exhibition Assoc. v. Morley* (1966), 58 D.L.R. (2d) 282; affd (1967), 66 D.L.R. (2d) 37, children started unforeseeable fire.

[54] *Ibid.*, at pp. 1307 and 1309.

[55] [1967] 1 All E.R. 267, discussed *supra*, n. 40.

[56] (1963), 41 D.L.R. (2d) 53 (Man. C.A.).

In the case of *Harsim Construction Limited v. Olsen*,[57] an electrician negligently caused a short circuit while replacing a subsidiary circuit breaker. The main circuit breaker, which should have "blown" or "kicked out" and cut off the power, failed to do so. The power continued to flow and a fire resulted. Mac-Donald J. of the Alberta Supreme Court held that the plaintiff's damages should be limited to the costs of replacing the main circuit breaker, and not for the entire damages caused by the fire because the latter were "too remote". His Lordship explained:

> There was no reason for the defendant to foresee that the circuit breaker would not work or might not work, although that proved possible. However, the fact that the circuit breaker did not work would be considered as improbable. The responsibility of the defendant was for damage that would not be improbable or that would not be unpredictable to a reasonable man under the same circumstances.[58]

In *Wade v. C.N.R.*,[59] it was held, despite a jury verdict in the boy's favour, that "no reasonable occupier could have reasonably foreseen that a child playing on a pile of sand some 50 feet from the track when the engine went by, would leave this place of safety, run towards the track and attempt to jump on the ladder of a boxcar". A requirement for such detailed provision as this is rarely found in our courts, but, on occasion, it is open to a court, if it chooses, to deny compensation in this way to a dull-witted 8-year-old child who loses a leg trying to steal a ride on a train.[60]

In *Trevison v. Springman*,[61] where the defendant's son, who had been known to steal, set fire to a neighbour's house, the court dismissed the case explaining:

> The manner of causing damage to the plaintiffs by arson was entirely different in type from what [the defendant] ought to have considered a possibility. Theft and break-in were her son's propensities. That had already occurred the night before the arson when the son stole property from the house. His return the following night and his sudden decision to burn the house to try to cover his tracks was not a foreseeable consequence of any theft from it. There has never been a suggestion in his previous conduct that he might commit arson . . . the setting afire of the plaintiff's house was completely beyond the realm of possibilities that should have been within . . . contemplation.

The law of Quebec has incorporated this idea of reasonable foresight as well. For example, where a teacher bangs a pointer on the table to get the attention of students, thereby damaging the hearing of a student, there is no liability because

---

[57]   (1972), 29 D.L.R. (3d) 121 (Alta.).
[58]   *Ibid.*, at p. 125.
[59]   (1978), 80 D.L.R. (3d) 214 (S.C.C.) (*per* de Grandpré J.).
[60]   For a severe critique of this case see Gibson, "Comment" (1978), 56 Can Bar. Rev. 693.
[61]   (1995), 28 C.C.L.T. (2d) 292 at pp. 299-300 (B.C.S.C.) (*per* Spencer J.); affd (1997), 75 A.C.W.S. (3d) 391 (B.C.C.A.).

such a consequence is unforseeable. As was explained by Vallerand J.A.: [The accident was] exceptionelles . . . imprévisibles pour le *bon père de famille.*"[62]

One can expect many more bewildering cases as the courts continue their efforts to describe and categorize the incredible variety of accidents that happen in this unpredictable world.[63] After studying these decisions, one cannot avoid the conclusion that there is little logic in this process. The verbal dexterity of counsel in classifying the accident seems to be all-important.[64] The ability to forecast results, one of the prime goals of foresight, remains largely unachieved.

E. Further Retreat: *The Wagon Mound (No. 2)*: Possibility of Damage

Another qualification to *The Wagon Mound (No. 1)* was established by the Privy Council in *The Wagon Mound (No. 2)*.[65] This decision holds that liability may be imposed, even though a loss is not reasonably foreseeable, if there is a "possibility" or a "real risk" of damage.

The Wagon Mound (No. 2) arose out of the same conflagration that produced *The Wagon Mound (No. 1)*. In this case, however, the plaintiffs were the owners of the ships moored at the wharf, instead of the dock owners. Consequently, these plaintiffs could strenuously press their claim on the basis of foreseeability, whereas the dock owners could not without risking a finding of contributory negligence against them for negligent welding. At that time contributory negligence was still a complete bar to recovery in New South Wales. Freed of this tactical disadvantage, the plaintiffs adduced additional evidence which enabled the court to arrive at a slightly different finding of fact. Both trial courts agreed that a fire was not reasonably foreseeable. However, Mr. Justice Walsh in *The Wagon Mound (No. 2)* found that the risk of fire from the spillage could be regarded as a "possibility, but one that would become an actuality only in very exceptional circumstances",[66] while in *The Wagon Mound (No. 1)*, Mr. Justice Kinsella had held that the oil was not "capable of being set on fire". Mr. Justice Walsh felt bound to dismiss the case, nevertheless, on the negligence theory, but he did impose liability in nuisance.

---

[62]   *Lamoureux c. Estrie (Commn. scolaire régionale)* (1988), 45 C.C.L.T. 285, at p. 289 (Que. C.A.).

[63]   See J.C. Smith and MacLaren, both *supra*, n. 1 for additional cases.

[64]   Fridman and Williams, "The Atomic Theory of Negligence" (1971), 45 A.L.J. 117.

[65]   *The Wagon Mound (No. 2)*, [1967] 1 A.C. 617, [1966] 2 All E.R. 709. See J.C. Smith "The Limits of Tort Liability in Canada: Remoteness, Foreseeability and Proximate Cause" in Linden (ed.), *Studies in Canadian Tort Law* (1968); Glasbeek, "*Wagon Mound II* — Re Polemis Revived; Nuisance Revised" (1967), 6 Weston L. Rev. 192; Dias, "Trouble on Oiled Waters: Problems of The Wagon Mound (No. 2)", [1967] Camb. L.J. 62; Green, "The Wagon Mound No. 2 — Foreseeability Revised", [1967] Utah L. Rev. 197; Smith, *Liability in Negligence* (1984).

[66]   [1963] 1 Lloyd's Rep. 402, at p. 426.

When the case came before the Privy Council, it was decided that the limits of liability in nuisance were the same as in negligence. The Privy Council went on to evaluate the nature of the conduct of the defendant in the light of the risk. Because there was "no justification whatever for discharging the oil", because it was "an offence to do so" and because "it involved considerable loss financially", there was "no question of balancing the advantages and disadvantages".[67] The only issue "is whether a reasonable man . . . would have known there was real risk of the oil on the water catching fire in some way: if it did, serious damage to ships or other property was not only foreseeable but very likely". The Privy Council then rejected the idea that just because a "real risk" is "remote" it cannot be reasonably foreseeable. Instead it asserted:

> If a real risk is one which would occur to the mind of a reasonable man in the position of the defendant's servant and which he would not brush aside as far-fetched, and if the criterion is to be what that reasonable man would have done in the circumstances, then surely he would neglect such a risk if action to eliminate it presented no difficulty, involved no disadvantage, and required no expense.[68]

The case of *Bolton v. Stone* was distinguished by Lord Reid since the conduct there was not unlawful. It was, therefore, "justifiable not to take steps to eliminate a real risk if it is small and if the circumstances are such that a reasonable man . . . would think it right to neglect it".

It is difficult to tell what effect *The Wagon Mound (No. 2)* had on *The Wagon Mound (No. 1)*. One might minimize its importance by contending that the facts found in the second trial were different to those found in the first trial and therefore the cases are clearly distinguishable. It might also be said, in disparagement of *The Wagon Mound (No. 2)* that it was concerned with the negligence issue only and it did not have to deal with the remoteness problem at all.[69] This, of course, would render the language of the court *obiter dicta*. Further, one could suggest that the only conduct that falls within the principle is unlawful and unjustifiable conduct which lacks any social utility. Since the bulk of human activity is not of that type, its sphere of operation would be quite limited. On the other hand, the idea of strict liability for unlawful conduct is not entirely novel, for trespassers have long been held liable for the unforeseeable consequences of their conduct[70] and violators of certain statutes have also been held similarly liable.[71] Consequently, there are analogs in tort law for such a position.

Professor Leon Green has criticized *The Wagon Mound (No. 2)* because it overloads the foreseeability concept.[72] While he describes it as a "delightful and useful fiction", which along with the reasonable person fiction enables a jury to

---

67   [1967] 1 A.C. 617, at p. 642.
68   [1966] 3 W.L.R. 498, at p. 512.
69   Green, *supra*, n. 65, at p. 202; Glasbeek, *supra*, n. 65, at p. 200.
70   *Turner v. Thorne*, [1960] O.W.N. 20.
71   *Menow v. Honsberger*, [1970] 1 O.R. 54; affd [1971] O.R. 129; affd [1974] S.C.R. 239.
72   Green, *supra*, n. 65, at p. 206.

make a "fresh judgment" in each case, he opposes it as a judge's formula. As such, it is "too glaringly fictitious unless given substantive additives so as to convert it into a meaningful concept for the assessment of policy factors". He agrees that courts should consider the risks a defendant "should have taken into account when engaged in conduct hurtful to the plaintiff," but he does not believe it "adequate" for the determination of the extent of liability. For that purpose "policy factors that give rationality to the law" are more important than foreseeability.

Nevertheless, some writers have attached considerable significance to *The Wagon Mound (No. 2)*. Professor J.C. Smith believes that *The Wagon Mound (No. 2)* "makes a substantial change in *The Wagon Mound* rule in that it extends the application of the test of foreseeability of damage to possibility rather than probability".[73] He asserts that the law is now "little different than it was under *In re Polemis*, since almost any kind of damage can be foreseeable as possible". Another scholar has written that "for all practical purposes" the *Polemis* test has been restored, for "surely all direct consequences must be regarded as possible if the ordinary man is not required to foresee how they are to eventuate".[74]

Although *The Wagon Mound (No. 2)* has certainly swung the pendulum back in the direction of *Polemis*, it is premature to sing a dirge for *The Wagon Mound (No. 1)*, which is still being cited frequently.[75] More and more, however, courts have been relying the "possibility test" of *Wagon Mound (No. 2)*. For example, Mr. Justice Dickson once explained *The Wagon Mound (No. 2)* as follows:[76]

> These words would suggest that recovery may be had, provided the event giving rise to the damage is not regarded as "impossible", and even though it "very rarely happened", "only in very exceptional circumstances". The test of foreseeability of damage becomes a question of what is possible rather than what is probable.[77]

Mr. Justice Ruttan also cited *The Wagon Mound (No. 2)* in holding the British Columbia government liable for building an 18" median on a highway instead of a 30" median and stated:[78]

> So here there was a real risk, however remote, and it was very simple to remove the risk with no great expense or inconvenience.[79]

Another case in which the possibility test was employed is *Price v. Milawski*,[80] where Mr. Justice Arnup wrote:

---

[73] J.C. Smith, *supra*, n. 65, at p. 102; Smith, *op. cit. supra*, n. 65, at p. 109.

[74] Glasbeek, *supra*, n. 65, at p. 200.

[75] But see *McKenzie v. Hyde* (1967), 64 D.L.R. (2d) 362, at p. 365; "The injury complained of was of a class or character foreseeable as a possible result of the negligence."

[76] *Hoffer v. School District of Assiniboine South* (1971), 21 D.L.R. (3d) 608; affd [1973] 6 W.W.R. 765 (S.C.C.).

[77] *Ibid.*, at p. 613.

[78] *Malat v. The Queen* (1978), 6 C.C.L.T. 142; affd (1980), 14 C.C.L.T. 206 (B.C.C.A.).

[79] *Ibid.*, at p. 152.

A person doing a negligent act may, in circumstances lending themselves to that conclusion, be held liable for future damages arising in part from the subsequent negligent act of another, and in part from his own negligence, where such subsequent negligence and consequent damage were reasonably foreseeable as a possible result of his own negligence.[81]

In *Leonard v. Knott*,[82] it was said that, although the risk of fatality from a particular medical treatment was only one in 50,000 or less, this was nevertheless a "real risk" notwithstanding the fact that it was a "relatively remote risk" and hence was within the range of foreseeability required. Chief Justice Scott of Manitoba cast some light on this issue when he explained that there "may be possibilities that are not so remote or fantastic as to be unforeseeable."[83]

It should be noted that none of these cases seems to place any stress on the need for the conduct of the defendant to be devoid of any social utility, which was once thought to be a precondition for reliance on the "possibility test". It now seems that any type of conduct can be subject to *The Wagon Mound (No. 2)*.

This possibility test is attractive in many ways. It does reflect more accurately the actual decisions of the courts, even though they have purported to be using the foresight formula in arriving at those conclusions. The courts have been rather liberal in decided which consequences are foreseeable and have resisted denying liability on the basis of foresight, except in the most freakish cases. The possibility test would ensure that very few remoteness cases would be decided against plaintiffs, which is probably a wise policy. It would also be more honest. Although it is still to early to tell whether *The Wagon Mound (No. 2)* will ultimately supplant *The Wagon Mound (No. 1)*, it is not entirely unlikely that it will.

F. The Failure of Foresight

The naïve hopes expressed by Lord Simonds in *The Wagon Mound (No. 1)* have not been met. Firstly, simplicity has certainly eluded us. Rational analysis, instead of being obscured by the language of causation, is now hidden behind the verbiage of foreseeability. Dean C.A. Wright, a stout defender of the risk-duty approach — a generalized version of the foresight test, realized that the duty concept was every bit as fictional as proximate cause.[84] Talk of risk

---

[80]   (1977), 82 D.L.R. (3d) 130. See also *Cotic v. Gray* (1981), 17 C.C.L.T. 138, at p. 147 (Ont. C.A.) (*per* Lacourcière J.A.), p. 47; affd (1984), 26 C.C.L.T. 163 (S.C.C.).

[81]   *Ibid.*, at p. 141. See also *Gallant v. Beitz: Nissan Automobile Co. (Canada) Ltd. v. Third Party* (1983), 42 O.R. (2d) 86, at p. 91 (H.C.); "The test for determining remoteness now is foreseeability of the possibility of the type of harm that transpires." (*per* Linden J.).

[82]   [1980] 1 W.W.R. 763, at p. 696 (B.C.C.A.). At trial it was found "possible" and not "far-fetched", see [1978] 5 W.W.R. 511. See also *Shirt v. Wyong Shire Council*, [1978] 1 N.S.W.L.R. 631.

[83]   *Michaluk (Litigation Guardian of) v. Rolling River School Division No. 39* (2001), 5 C.C.L.T. (3d) 1, at p. 7, child's eye hurt by coat hanger at school.

[84]   *Supra*, n. 17, at p. 60.

furnishes no solution, he argued, since value choices must still be made by the courts. He was hopeful, however, that the fundamental issue for solution would be clarified. Unhappily, this did not happen in the decade following *The Wagon Mound (No. 1)*. Some judges are misled as much by foresight as by directness. In fact, the settled rules governing common remoteness situations have occasionally been threatened by the new foresight analysis,[85] something that should be avoided if we want to prevent every single remoteness case from being dealt with as a matter of first impression.

Secondly, the foresight test is not any more logical than the directness test.[86] It is no more illogical to make careless people who put the whole thing in motion responsible for all the consequences, however unforeseeable, than it is to relieve them from unanticipated results. Despite the fact that the results are worse than expected, the defendant did, after all, create the initial risk. Had the defendant acted in accordance with the community standard, there would have been no accident and no loss at all. This analysis only points out that the choice of the test to be applied in remoteness cases is not based on logic, but on values.

Thirdly, the foresight test is no more just than the directness test; indeed it is less so.[87] The defendant who risks only trivial harm and then is burdened with the enormous cost of unanticipated consequences surely deserves our sympathy. Nevertheless, the injustice is more marked if the totally innocent plaintiff is forced to bear the burden of the unexpected results of someone else's negligence. The position of the Privy Council becomes even less tenable when one realizes that most defendants are insured for the consequences of their negligence. Rather than personally paying the damages awarded against them, they are spread throughout their industry by way of the insurance premiums collected. The latter result is probably more in harmony with community notions of justice in a modern welfare state than the rather anachronistic view of Lord Simonds.

G. A New Approach to Remoteness

It must now be apparent to everyone that there are no easy answers to the remoteness and proximate cause issues. *Polemis* has been discarded. *The Wagon Mound (No. 1)* has been undermined. Similarly, all future attempts to resolve this issue with an automatic formula are doomed. No one magic phrase can furnish answers to all of the freakish and bizarre situations which arise in

---

[85] For example, *Horsley v. MacLaren*, [1970] 2 O.R. 487; affd on other grounds, [1972] S.C.R. 441; *Ostrowski v. Lotto*, [1969] 1 O.R. 341; revd on another point [1971] 1 O.R. 372; affd [1973] S.C.R. 220.

[86] Fleming, *supra*, n. 1, at p. 501.

[87] *Ibid.*, at pp. 502 *et seq.*

negligence cases. These "flukes",[88] by their very nature, cannot be tamed by legal rules.

Not every accident, however, is unique. Certain events tend to recur from time to time. For such recurring situations, we can and should develop stable legal rules. It should be easy to forecast the outcome of a thin-skull case, for example, or a rescuer case, because these cases recur and the rules are settled. The law regarding some of these recurring events will be discussed later.

Understandably, the courts have encountered most difficulty in handling uncommon results that do not recur. In these rare situations, courts have occasionally been bewitched by the word foresight and, as a result, have arrived at unsatisfactory decisions. They must resist the allure of foreseeability, because its power is largely illusory. It can be as broad or as narrow as the beholder wishes. It can disguise value choices a much as directness did. As Mr. Justice Haines has opined, the "foreseeability concept is a strained mode of analysis, a fiction at best justifiable as a jury formula, but one too transparent for meaningful use by Judges".[89] If we must use the term foreseeability, we must not allow it to blind us. Foresight does not excuse courts from the onerous responsibility of making difficult decisions.

Simply stated, the issue here is whether the defendant, whose conduct has fallen below the accepted standard of the community, should be relieved from paying for damage his conduct helped to bring about.[90] By formulating the question in this way, we spotlight the value choice which must be made in disposing of the case. There is no need to disguise the fact that some intuition and feeling are involved in this determination,[91] but we must also insert as much rationality as we can into the process. A new approach to remoteness would recognize this basic truth.

It would also be helpful if the courts would approach these remoteness cases with the attitude that a person found to have been negligent should only be relieved of liability if the result of the negligence was truly "freakish", "one in a million",[92] "fantastic or highly improbable".[93] In other words, there should be an assumption of liability unless the court is convinced that it would be too harsh a result in the circumstances.

---

[88]   I would like to thank my former colleague Paul C. Weiler for supplying this word which, though somewhat inelegant, perfectly describes the type of case under consideration.

[89]   *A.G. Ont. v. Crompton* (1976), 74 D.L.R. (3d) 345, at p. 349 (Ont.).

[90]   See *Gallant v. Beitz: Nissan Automobile Co.*, *supra*, n. 81 (*per* Linden J.).

[91]   MacLaren, *supra*, n. 1, at p. 75: "In the final analysis the answer one comes up with depends more on one's feelings about the scope of liability and the equities of the case than anything else." Two cases have used the phrase "instinctive feeling", *Lamb v. Camden London Borough Council*, [1981] 2 All E.R. 408 (C.A.); *Crossley v. Rawlinson*, [1981] 3 All E.R. 674 (Q.B.).

[92]   See Dickson J.A. in *McKenzie v. Hyde*, *supra*, n. 75, at pp. 375-76.

[93]   *Abbott, et al. v. Kasza*, [1975] 3 W.W.R. 163, at p. 172 (*per* D.C. MacDonald J.); varied [1976] 4 W.W.R. 20 (Alta. C.A.). Stratton C.J.N.B. adopted this approach in *Williams v. New Brunswick* (1985), 34 C.C.L.T. 299, at p. 316 (N.B.C.A.).

In these one-in-a-lifetime-situations, we might have to recognize that the best we can do is to return to the much-maligned approach of Mr. Justice Andrews, the dissenting judge in *Palsgraf v. Long Island Railroad*.[94] In analyzing the proximate cause technique of limiting liability, Mr. Justice Andrews uttered what seemed at that time to be heresy:

> What we . . . mean by the word "proximate" is that, because of convenience, of public policy, of a rough sense of justice, the law arbitrarily declines to trace a series of events beyond a certain point. This is not logic. It is practical politics.

Although Mr. Justice Andrews believed that foresight should have "some bearing" on the question, he was skeptical that any one consideration could solve all the problems. He declared: "It is all a question of expediency. There are no fixed rules to govern our judgment."

Mr. Justice Andrews suggested that the courts must consider a variety of matters: (a) was there a "natural and continuous sequence between the cause and effect"? (b) was the conduct a "substantial factor" in producing the result? (c) was there a "direct connection"? and (d) was the result "too remote . . . in time and space"? He concluded by stating:

> [W]e draw an uncertain and wavering line, but draw it we must as best we can . . . . It is all a question of fair judgment, always keeping in mind the fact that we endeavor to make a rule in each case that will be practical and in keeping with the general understanding of mankind.

The analysis of Mr. Justice Andrews was adopted by the United States Court of Appeals, Second Circuit in *"Kinsman No. 1"*,[95] where a ship negligently moored in the Buffalo River, near Buffalo, N.Y., broke loose and drifted downstream toward a drawbridge. Despite frantic telephone calls the bridge was not raised in time to prevent the ship from colliding with it and bringing it down. As a result the river flooded, causing damage to various people. The plaintiffs in *"Kinsman No. 1"* suffered property damage as a result of the flooding. Their action was successful and an appeal was dismissed. Friendly C.J. explained:

> We see no reason why an actor engaging in conduct which entails a large risk of small damage and a small risk of other and greater damage, of the same general sort, from the same forces, and to the same class of person, should be relieved of responsibility for the latter simply because the chance of its occurrence, if viewed alone, may not have been large enough to require the exercise of care. By hypothesis the risk of the lesser harm was sufficient to render his disregard of it actionable; the existence of a less likely additional risk that the very forces against whose action he was required to guard would produce other and greater damage than could have been reasonably anticipated should inculpate him further rather than limit his liability. This does not mean that the careless actor will always be held for all damages for which the forces that he risked were a cause in fact. Somewhere a point will be reached when courts will agree that the link has become too tenuous — that what is claimed to be conse-

---

[94] (1928), 248 N.Y. Supp. 339, 162 N.E. 99, at p. 104.
[95] (1964), 338 F. 2d 708.

quence is only fortuity. Thus, if the destruction of the Michigan Avenue Bridge had delayed the arrival of a doctor, with consequent loss of a patient's life, few judges would impose liability on any of the parties here, although the agreement in result might not be paralleled by similar unanimity in reasoning. . . .

Where the line will be drawn will vary from age to age; as society has come to rely increasingly on insurance and other methods of loss-sharing, the point may lie further off than a century ago. Here it is surely more equitable that the losses from the operators' negligent failure to raise the Michigan Avenue Bridge should be ratably borne by Buffalo's taxpayers than left with the innocent victims of the flooding; yet the mind is also repelled by a solution that would impose liability solely on the City and exonerate the persons whose negligent acts of commission and omission were the precipitating force of the collision with the bridge and its sequelae. We go only so far as to hold that where, as here, the damages resulted from the same physical forces whose existence required the exercise of greater care than was displayed and were of the same general sort that was expectable, unforseeability of the exact developments and of the extent of the loss will not limit liability. Other fact situations can be dealt with when they arise.

The same reasoning was employed in a second action arising out of the same ship and bridge collision, "*Kinsman No. 2*."[96] This claim was made by the owners of some wheat stored aboard another ship berthed in the harbour below the bridge. The plaintiff's wheat was not damaged, but as a result of the accident, it could not be unloaded because the ship could not be moved to the grain elevator which was located above the bridge. This entailed additional costs for extra transportation and storage, as well for the purchase of replacement wheat. Kaufman C.J., in "*Kinsman No. 2*" observed:

On the previous appeal we stated aptly: "somewhere a point will be reached when courts will agree that the result has become too tenuous — that what is claimed to be consequence is only fortuity." [Citation omitted.] We believe that this point has been reached with [these] claims. . . . The instant claims occurred only because the downed bridge made it impossible to move traffic along the river. Under all the circumstances of this case, we hold that the connection between the defendants' negligence and the claimants' damages is too tenuous and remote to permit recovery. "The law does not spread its protection so far."

The necessity of such a pragmatic approach has been acknowledged by Mr. Justice Clement of the Alberta Court of Appeal, who reasoned as follows:

The common law has always recognized that causation is a concept that in the end result must be limited in its reach by a pragmatic consideration of consequences: the chain of cause and effect can be followed only to the point where the consequences of an act will be fairly accepted as attributable to that act in the context of social and economic conditions then prevailing and the reasonable expectations of members of the society in the conduct of each other.[97]

---

[96]   (1968), 388 F. 2d 281.
[97]   *Abbott et al. v. Kasza*, [1976] 4 W.W.R. 20, at p. 28 (Alta. C.A.).

Some courts have openly admitted that they are utilizing a hindsight test in these cases. In other words, looking back, the court must find that the accident was extraordinary in order to relieve a defendant of liability.[98]

In deciding remoteness questions, therefore, the courts should approach them with an open mind, without the blinkers of directness or foresight. All the tests enumerated above should be exploited. The ideas of risk and foresight are a helpful beginning. In addition, however, certain policy factors should be assessed. If the case deals with a personal injury rather than a property loss, this should be considered. If the defendant is an industrial enterprise rather than a private citizen, this should be evaluated. The probability of insurance coverage for the type of activity in general (although not for the specific defendant) cannot be ignored. The potential for deterrence and education must be examined. If any prophylactic power remains in tort law, it would be strengthened by forcing entrepreneurs to pay for all the costs of their negligent activities, including some marginally foreseeable results, so that they will be stimulated to exercise greater care. In addition, perhaps an occasional award for a bizarre event will publicly dramatize the importance of safety measures. Lastly, general or market deterrence may be accomplished by transferring the entire cost of mishaps to the activity which produces them. It is only after full consideration of all of these policy matters and after employing each of the available tests that a court should try to decide a case. Even then it might occasionally be wise to put the matter before a jury for a decision.[99]

Professor Joseph C. Smith has explained that what the courts are searching for here is a "just balance or relationship of proportion between the degree of fault in comparison with the magnitude of damage".[100] He suggests that the person at fault "should bear the loss, except where the fault is insignificant or the damage is so extensive that it is out of all proportion in comparison with the fault". This is a helpful addition to the factors the courts must consider, but it will not solve all the cases either, as Professor Smith readily admits.

In sum, it is hard to escape the conclusion that the best we can ever do in novel situations is to rely on the common sense of the judge and jury.[101] It is not conceding defeat to admit that these judgments lie "in the realm of values and

---

[98] *Leposki v. Ry. Express Agency, Inc.* (1962), 297 F. 2d 849 (U.S.C.A., 3rd Cir.); *Dellwo v. Pearson* (1961), 107 N.W. 2d 859 (Minn.). See also *McLoughlin v. O'Brian*, [1982] 2 All E.R. 298, at p. 303 (H.L.) (*per* Lord Wilberforce).

[99] *Marshall v. Nugent* (1955), 222 F. 2d 604 (*per* Magruder J.).

[100] *Supra*, n. 65, at p. 112. For a more detailed treatment, see Smith, *Liability in Negligence, op. cit., supra*, n. 2, at pp. 138 *et seq.*

[101] Fitzpatrick C.J. in *Canadian Northern Ry. v. Diplock* (1916), 53 S.C.R. 376, who argued that these tests are "only a guide in the exercise of common sense".

what you choose depends on what you want".[102] It is merely being realistic. Mr. Justice Morden recognized this when he said in *Duwyn v. Kaprielian*:[103]

> . . . there is a significant element of experience and value judgment in the ultimate application of the foresight requirement.[104]

We should not despair, however. Guidelines can and have been developed for many of the *recurring* situations which arise in the proximate cause cases. Fortunately, not all accidents have weird results; the consequences of many of them are quite common and predictable. For these, the courts over the years have fashioned consistent responses. We will now turn to some of these situations, and will discuss in turn the thin-skull cases, rescuers, and intervening forces.

H. Recurring Situations: The Thin-Skull Problem

The most common recurring situation is the thin-skull problem. It is, therefore, the easiest to handle because the rules are most settled.

Since the turn of the century, it has been accepted that negligent defendants must take their victims as they find them. The thin-skull rule was enunciated before *Polemis*, by Lord Justice Kennedy in *Dulieu v. White and Sons*,[105] in these words:

> If a man is negligently run over or otherwise negligently injured in his body, it is no answer to the sufferer's claim for damage that he would have suffered less injury, or no injury at all, if he had not had an unusually thin skull or an unusually weak heart.

This view was reiterated by Lord Justice MacKinnon in *Owens v. Liverpool*,[106] as follows:

> One who is guilty of negligence to another must put up with idiosyncrasies of his victim that increase the likelihood or extent of damage to him — it is no answer to a claim for a fractured skull that its owner had an unusually fragile one.

The court did not cite *Polemis*, which had been decided in the interim, nor did it give any reasons for its decision. It merely asserted that if the defendant's negligence "in fact caused" the damage, the defendant should have to pay.

Following *The Wagon Mound (No. 1)*, some feared that the thin-skull rule would have to be jettisoned on the ground that unusual susceptibility is not

---

[102] Gregory, "Proximate Cause in Negligence — A Retreat from Rationalization" (1938), 6 U. Chi. L. Rev. 36, at p. 47. See also J.C. Smith, *supra*, n. 65, at p. 114.

[103] (1978), 7 C.C.L.T. 121.

[104] *Ibid.*, at p. 136. See also Zuber J.A. in *Spagnolo v. Margesson's Sports Ltd.* (1983), 41 O.R. (2d) 65 at p. 66 (C.A.), "the term 'reasonably foreseeable' contains more policy than fact".

[105] [1901] 2 K.B. 669, at p. 679, plaintiff pregnant and driver did not anticipate that she was in this condition.

[106] [1939] 1 K.B. 394, at p. 400 (C.A.), funeral case of doubtful application.

reasonably foreseeable. This was not to be, however. In *Smith v. Leech Brain & Co. Ltd.*,[107] a worker's lip was burned by the spattering of some molten metal, which triggered the development of cancer at a spot where he had premalignant cancerous tissues. When, three years later, he died as a result of this, his widow sued the employer. Instead of invoking *The Wagon Mound (No. 1)* and discarding the thin-skull rule, as he might well have done, Lord Chief Justice Parker chose to preserve it. His Lordship stated that *The Wagon Mound* "did not have . . . the thin-skull cases in mind. It has always been the law of this country that the tortfeasor takes his victim as he finds him". He declared that "not a day . . . goes by where some trial judge does not adopt that principle . . ." and "if the Judicial Committee had any intention of making an inroad in that doctrine, I am quite satisfied that they would have said so".[108] He reasoned also that one need not foresee the *extent* of the injury, but only the *type* of injury. Parker C.J. stated:

> The test is not whether these employers could reasonably have foreseen that a burn would cause cancer and that he would die. The question is whether these employers could reasonably foresee the type of injury he suffered, namely the burn. What, in this particular case, is the amount of damage which he suffers as a result of the burn depends on the characteristics and constitution of the victim

His Lordship pointed out that he was following *The Wagon Mound (No. 1)* or the other cases prior to *Polemis*, but not the *Polemis* case, in reaching his decision.[109]

The principles have been concisely explained by Mr. Justice Major in *Athey v. Leonati*[110] as follows:

> The respondent argued that the plaintiff was pre-disposed to disc herniation and that this is therefore a case where the "crumbling skull" rule applies. The "crumbling skull" doctrine is an awkward label for a fairly simple idea. It is named after the well-known "thin-skull" rule, which makes the tortfeasor liable for the plaintiff's injuries even if the injuries are unexpectedly severe owing to a pre-existing condition. The tortfeasor must take his or her victim as the tortfeasor finds the victim, and is therefore liable even though the plaintiff's losses are more dramatic than they would be for the average person.
>
> The so-called "crumbling skull" rule simply recognizes that the pre-existing condition was inherent in the plaintiff's "original position". The defendant need not put the plaintiff in a position *better* than his or her original position. The defendant is liable for the injuries caused, even if they are extreme, but need not compensate the plaintiff for any debilitating effects of the pre-existing condition which the plaintiff would have experienced anyway. The defendant is liable for the additional damage but not the pre-existing damage . . . Likewise, if there is a measurable risk that the pre-existing condition would have detrimentally affected the plaintiff in the future, regardless of the defendant's negligence, then this can be taken into

---

[107] [1962] 2 Q.B. 405. See also *Corrie v. Gilbert*, [1965] S.C.R. 457, liability for phlebitis, without citing *Wagon Mound (No. 1)*, *Hughes* or *Smith v. Leech Brain*. Relied on *Marcroft v. Scruttons Ltd.*, [1954] 1 Lloyd's Rep. 395 (C.A.).

[108] [1962] 2 Q.B. 405, at p. 414.

[109] *Ibid.*, at p. 415.

[110] [1996] 3 S.C.R. 458, at pp. 473-74.

account in reducing the overall award . . . . This is consistent with the general rule that the plaintiff must be returned to the position he would have been in, with all of its attendant risks and shortcomings, and not a better position.

It seems, therefore, that the courts view with favour those with thin skulls, whatever test is in vogue. The reason why this is so, however, has not yet been explained satisfactorily. An examination of the numerous thin-skull cases will now be undertaken in a search for the answer.

1. PRE-EXISTING CONDITIONS

There are dozens of cases consistently employing the thin-skull rule. Strangely, however, there are few cases actually involving thin skulls rather than other pre-existing weaknesses. One such case is *Hole v. Hocking*,[111] where an apparently minor bump on the head contributed to a sub-arachnoid haemorrhage that damaged the brain permanently. Despite the judge's complaint that he disliked trying to "calculate the incalculable" the defendant was held responsible. Another is *Wilson v. Birt Ltd.*,[112] where the victim was hit on the head or neck by a pole that fell from a scaffolding. As a result of the blow and a pre-existing condition, the plaintiff contracted epilepsy and serious damage to the tissues under the brain in the sub-arachnoid space. He recovered for these losses on the reasoning that if the "variety of damage . . . [is] reasonably foreseeable the fact that the plaintiff is peculiarly prone to more excessive injury is not relevant to the defendant's liability".[113]

The principle is applied to other pre-existing susceptibilities as well. One who has a weak heart, for example, will be recompensed for all damages, because, according to one judge, one can anticipate that some people might have unsound hearts.[114] In *Peacock v. Mills and the City of Calgary*,[115] the plaintiff had a precondition of disc degeneration which was aggravated in an accident. The Alberta Court of Appeal increased the damages awarded at the trial, but felt that the fact of predisposition is "an element to be taken into account in assessing damages". Similarly, one is liable for the full amount of the damages incurred by someone with a weak or "rotten" disc, if one's negligence "aggravates or brings into activity a dormant or diseased condition or one to which a person is predisposed".[116] In *Feldstein v. Alloy Metal Sales*,[117] the court was prepared to

---

[111] [1962] S.A.S.R. 128.

[112] [1963] 2 S.A. 508.

[113] *Ibid.*, at p. 519 (*per* Mr. Justice Harcourt).

[114] *Williams v. B.A.L.M. Ltd.*, [1951] N.Z.L.R. 893. See also *Love v. Port of London Authority*, [1959] 2 Lloyd's Rep. 541.

[115] (1964), 50 W.W.R. 626 (Alta. C.A.). The trial judge and the dissenter believed that the defendant only speeded up what would have occurred anyway, see p. 629.

[116] *Owen v. Dix* (1946), 210 Ark. 562, 196 S.W. 2d 913, at p. 915; *Pesonen v. Melnyk* (1993), 17 C.C.L.T. (2d) 66 (B.C.C.A.).

[117] [1962] O.R. 476, case dismissed. See also *La Brosse v. Saskatoon* (1968), 65 W.W.R. 168 (Sask.), arthritis.

allow compensation for injury to a woman's neck, shoulder and arm which arose because she had suffered from a malignancy and had undergone radiation treatment 19 years earlier. The court relied on the *Polemis* rule in doing so, after stating that this was damage "a reasonable man could not foresee". Despite this reasoning, the result would not differ by one iota today. So too, when a person with polio virus received an electric shock which produced poliomyelitis, compensation was allowed.[118] In *Watts v. Rake*,[119] the plaintiff's leg was broken. Because of the accident, the quiescent spondylitis from which he suffered developed into arthritis 13 years earlier than it ordinarily would have. Mr. Justice Dixon of the Australian High Court concluded simply that, "if the injury proves more serious in its incidents and its consequences because of the injured man's condition, that does nothing but increase the damages the defendant must pay". To sever the remaining leg of a one-legged person or to put out the eye of a one-eyed person, contended Mr. Justice Dixon, "is to do a far more serious injury" than if the person had two legs or two eyes.[120] In fixing damages, however, the court warned that the circumstances of the case, including the peculiar susceptibility, must be taken into account.

One of the best known cases in this area is *Warren v. Scruttons Ltd.*[121] The plaintiff, who had an ulcer on his left eye, cut his finger on a wire in the defendant's equipment. Because this wire had some kind of "poison" on it, the plaintiff contracted fever and virus, one of which caused further ulcers to appear on his eye. The negligent defendant was held liable for the aggravated injury, since "any consequence which results because the particular individual has some peculiarity is a consequence for which the tortfeasor is liable".[122] No other reason was offered. It was flatly asserted that "that is the right principle". In assessing damages, however, the court took into account the fact that the injured eye was somewhat inferior and was subject to other injuries as well.

In *Smith v. Maximovitch*,[123] the plaintiff lost eight teeth in a collision. Because his remaining teeth were in poor condition, as a result of pyorrhea, they were unsuitable to anchor bridgework and, therefore, all the teeth had to be extracted and dentures put in. The claimant received damages for all the teeth, except that they were evaluated in accordance with their worth at the time of loss. Mr. Justice Disbery stated that the duty to use care on the highway extends not only to the healthy but also to "persons afflicted with disease or a weakness . . . . The plaintiff was entitled to keep his natural teeth no matter how neglected and loose they might be, and to refrain from seeking the pleasures of the dentist's chair. So

---

[118] *Sayers v. Perrin*, [1966] Q.L.R. 89 (Full Ct.).
[119] (1960), 108 C.L.R. 158 (H.C. Aus.).
[120] *Ibid.*, at p. 160.
[121] [1962] 1 Lloyd's Rep. 497 (Q.B.D.).
[122] *Ibid.*, at p. 502.
[123] (1968), 68 D.L.R. (2d) 244 (Sask.).

also he was entitled to continue to keep and 'enjoy', if that word may be used, his pyorrhea, even though such was detrimental to his health."[124]

An attempt was made to distinguish between the legal treatment of a "thin skull" and a "crumbling skull", where maladies were merely exacerbated or accelerated, but this has been nipped in the bud.[125] Whereas the factual situation differs slightly, there is no difference between these two situations in terms of tort liability for the consequences; the only difference is in the assessment of damages, they being less in cases of pre-existing frailty and deteriorating conditions[126] than with completely healthy persons. Thus, when an accidental injury caused a relapse of multiple sclerosis dormant for 16 years, the defendant was held responsible, but for an appropriately reduced amount.[127]

Where death ensues as a result of a pre-existing susceptibility, liability also follows. When a person suffering from high blood pressure and a heart condition died three days after being injured by a thrown wheel, the tortfeasor was held liable for the death.[128] In one case, a train brakeman struck his head, an abscess developed, a dormant cancerous condition was activated, and death from cancer of the brain resulted.[129] A jury decision for the plaintiff was affirmed.

If someone is rendered incapable of pursuing a rare leisure activity, as a result of an injury, compensation may be forthcoming for this loss.[130]

Women are fully compensated, even though they may receive injuries that would not be suffered by men. For example, a pregnant woman who miscarries or has a stillborn child,[131] or a woman with ovaries weakened by an operation, who was injured as a result of a sudden stoppage of a train, can recover on the ground that "the weak will suffer more than the strong".[132] It is unlikely that modern views about equality would alter this outcome.

The thin-skull principle has even been extended to accord protection to obese people who, because of their large size, may suffer more and take longer to heal than people of average size. When a "large and somewhat fleshy" woman (to use Mr. Justice Thompson's diplomatic terms) slipped on a toy on the floor of the defendant's department store and sprained her ankle, she was entitled to recover for her

---

[124] *Ibid.*, at pp. 246-47. See also *Graham v. Rourke* (1988), 43 C.C.L.T. 119 (Ont. H.C.J.), life of vulnerable person ruined.

[125] *Price v. Garcha* (1989), 2 C.C.L.T. (2d) 265 (B.C.C.A.) (*per* Wallace J.A.); affg (1988), 44 C.C.L.T. 1 (*per* Gow J.). See *Athey, supra, n.* 110.

[126] *Pryor v. Bains and Johal* (1986), 69 B.C.L.R. 395, at p. 397 (C.A.); *Athey, ibid.*

[127] *York v. Johnston* (1997), 37 C.C.L.T. (2d) 299 (B.C.C.A.).

[128] *Barnaby v. O'Leary* (1956), 5 D.L.R. (2d) 41, at p. 44 (N.S.) (*per* Doull J.).

[129] *Heppner v. Atchison T. & S.F.R.R. Co.* (1956), 297 S.W. 2d 497 (Mo.).

[130] *Watson v. Grant* (1970), 72 W.W.R. 665 (B.C.) (*per* Aikins J.), inability to build sailboat compensable.

[131] *Malone v. Monongahela Valley Traction* (1927), 104 Va. 417.

[132] *Linklater v. Minister of Railways* (1900), 18 N.Z.L.R. 536, at p. 540 (*per* Williams J.).

aggravated injuries.[133] A similar view prevailed where a negligent waitress spilled hot coffee on an obese woman, for the defendants "took her as they found her".[134]

The thin-skull rule has even been applied to a "thin-skinned" automobile.[135] The driver of a Volkswagen car was speared and killed by a highway sign-post that ripped through the floorboards. The court rejected the defendant's contention that the plaintiff would have been injured less seriously, if his automobile had not had an unusually thin skin. Where injury to a person is foreseeable, suggested the court, recovery is not limited to injuries that are "usual and commonplace".

One problem that is sometimes wrongly considered as a remoteness question is that of the "shabby millionaire".[136] The negligent wrongdoer must pay the full income loss of the victim, even if the victim earns a million dollars a year. Similarly, if a wrongdoer breaks or loses an antique vase or other valuable property, the owner must be compensated for its full value. In *Thiele and Wesmar v. Rod Service (Ottawa) Ltd.*,[137] it was held that it was "foreseeable" that some stolen business records would cost $1,200 to replace, an amount far in excess of the insurance policy limits. Although resembling them, these cases differ from the thin-skull cases in that they are concerned "with responsibility not for unexpected consequences, but for the unexpectable cost of expected consequences".[138] If, however, extra loss is incurred because of the impecuniosity of the plaintiff,[139] this is not compensable, for a thin pocket book is less worthy of protection than a thin skull. Mr. Justice Muldoon has criticised this as "un-Canadian."[140]

Finally, it should be noted that, in assessing the amount that is to be paid to a thin-skull person as a compensation for loss, the value of that thin skull is less than that of a normal skull. In other words, although the wrongdoer must pay for the consequences of injuring vulnerable people, the actual cost of doing so is less than it would be for injuring in the same way a person who was not overly susceptible to the injury.[141]

---

[133] *Diederichs v. Metropolitan Stores Ltd.* (1956), 6 D.L.R. (2d) 751, at p. 756 (Sask.).

[134] *Thompson v. Lupone* (1948), 135 Conn. Supp. 236, 62 A. 2d 861.

[135] *Oke v. Carra* (1963), 38 D.L.R. (2d) 188, at p. 195; revd on another point 41 D.L.R. (2d) 53 (Man. C.A.). See also *Oke v. Wiede Transport Ltd.* (1963), 41 D.L.R. (2d) 53 (Man. C.A.).

[136] See Lord Justice Scruttin in *The Arpad*, [1934] All E.R. Rep. 326, [1934] P. 189, at p. 202 (C.A.). See also *Shulhan v. Peterson et al.* (1966), 57 D.L.R. (2d) 491 (Sask.), substitute vehicle kept for longer than normal period because of strike.

[137] [1964] 2 O.R. 347 (C.A.).

[138] Fleming, *The Law of Torts*, 9th ed. (1998), p. 236.

[139] *Dredger Liesbosch v. S.S. Edison (Owners)*, [1933] A.C. 449. *Cf.*, under contract principles, *Groves-Raffin Construction Ltd. v. Bank of Nova Scotia* (1975), 51 D.L.R. (3d) 380, at p. 413 (B.C.); *Freedhoff v. Pomalift Industries Ltd.*, [1970] 3 O.R. 571; varied [1971] 2 O.R. 773 (C.A.). *Contra*, Wexler, "The Impecunious Plaintiff" (1987), 66 Can. Bar Rev. 129.

[140] *Rollinson v. R.* (1994), 20 C.C.L.T. (2d) 92 (F.C.T.D.), at p. 108.

[141] See *Athey v. Leonati, supra*, n. 110, at p. 458.

2. PERSONS RENDERED MORE SUSCEPTIBLE

If the negligence of the defendant *renders* the skull of the plaintiff thin, making the plaintiff more susceptible to additional injury or sickness, the defendant is responsible for the further complications.[142] In *Oman v. MacIntyre*,[143] for instance, the plaintiff's leg was fractured as he worked in a ditch. A fat embolism and bronchopneumonia developed. A lung tracheotomy was performed, but the plaintiff died as a result. Lord Milligan held that one need not foresee the "full effects of the injury", because if liability follows for "unforeseen complications", it should also follow for death.[144] In *Winteringham v. Rae*,[145] the claimant was bitten by a dog. When given a tetanus injection, he suffered a reaction, called serum neuritis, which partially paralyzed his arm. Liability was affixed for the increased injury because of the increased susceptibility. Mr. Justice Parker indicated that these susceptibility cases may be an exception to the foreseeability rule. Similarly, where "poison" enters the plaintiff's system through a finger cut on the defendant's milk bottle top and causes death, the defendant is responsible, whether this is anticipated or not.[146] Also, where a boy is hit by a pipe, rendering his spine and hip joint more prone to tuberculosis, he can recover for this consequence as well as the original injury.[147]

3. MENTAL REPERCUSSIONS

If a physical injury triggers mental suffering or nervous disorders, the defendant must pay for these results, even if they are more serious than one might expect.[148] As early as 1911, in *Toronto Railway Co. v. Toms*,[149] the Supreme Court of Canada recognized that the "nervous system is as much a part of a man's physical being as muscular or other parts". The Supreme Court expressed its concern about the "danger of simulation" and "self-deception", but it felt that trial courts could distinguish the phony claims from the real ones. Consequently, recovery was granted to the plaintiffs for mental suffering incurred as a result of being thrown against a seat of a streetcar when it hit a train. In *Canning v. McFarland and Gray*,[150] the injured plaintiff recovered for a "traumatic neuro-

---

[142] This sentence was quoted with approval by Morse J. in *Holian v. United Grain Growers* (1980), 11 C.C.L.T. 184, at p. 199 and by O'Sullivan J.A. in *Powell v. Guttman (No. 2)* (1978), 6 C.C.L.T. 183, at p. 194 (Man. C.A.). See also Harradence J.A. in *Logozar v. Golder* (1994), 21 C.C.L.T. (2d) 203, at p. 213.

[143] [1962] S.L.T. 168, [1962] S.L.T. (N) 15.

[144] *Ibid.*, at p. 171.

[145] [1966] 1 O.R. 727. See also *Robinson v. Post Office*, [1974] 1 W.L.R. 1176 (C.A.).

[146] *Koehler v. Waukesha Milk Co.* (1928), 190 Wis. 52, 208 N.W. 901.

[147] *Champlin Refining Co. v. Thomas* (1939), 93 F. 2d 133 (10th cir.).

[148] This sentence of the text was adopted by Cowan C.J.T.D. in *Sullivan v. Riverside Rentals Ltd.* (1973), 36 D.L.R. (3d) 538, at p. 559; affd 47 D.L.R. (3d) 293 (C.A.).

[149] (1911), 44 S.C.R. 268, at p. 276 (*per* Davies C.J.).

[150] [1954] O.W.N. 467, at p. 471. See also *Dvorkin v. Stuart*, [1971] 2 W.W.R. 70 (Alta.); *Blowes v. Hamilton*, [1970] 1 O.R. 310, at p. 315.

sis" that developed. Mr. Justice Schroeder clearly articulated the prevailing view that "medicine today recognizes traumatic neurosis as a real injury for which compensation must be given". A similar case was *Varga v. John Labatt Ltd.*,[151] where a plaintiff was made ill when he drank a bottle of beer with chlorine in it. Mr. Justice Wells awarded damages for mental suffering incurred as a result of an hysteria condition and stated, "if you injure a person who suffers from hysteria, you must take him as you find him, and if the injury is out of all proportion to the event, if it is genuine, then the one who suffers is entitled to damages".[152] So it is where the plaintiff has a "vulnerable personality" that flares up into an "hysterical neurosis".[153] In *Enge v. Trerise*,[154] a young girl was left with a scar after an accident. As a result of latent schizophrenic tendencies, she became schizoid, withdrawn, depressed, heard voices and worried about the scar. The court ordered a new trial and made it quite clear that these mental repercussions were compensable. The dissenting judge remonstrated in vain that wrongdoers should not be held for these "irrational" and "morbid" reactions that were "unforeseeable", not "direct", and not "caused by" the injury.[155] In *Regush v. Inglis*,[156] the plaintiff received damages for deep depression following an accident which made it impossible to carry on her business.

In *Negretto v. Sayers*,[157] a woman whose pelvis was fractured had a post-concussional psychosis as a result of a "pre-existing tendency to mental disorder". In applying the thin-skull rule, the court tried to explain that the principle is not inconsistent with foresight for the "consequences of even the simplest accident are unpredictable".[158] One must foresee any consequences "between a negligible abrasion and permanent incapacity or death". Mr. Justice Chamberlain admitted that the defendant did not expect to run down anyone, let alone someone with a personality defect, yet one should foresee that a pedestrian might be hit "with quite possible disastrous consequences of one sort or another". In *Leonard v. B.C. Hydro*,[159] a woman on a bus fell and injured her buttocks slightly. This led to a psychotic condition. Although the judge refused to compensate her because it was found that she was not suffering at all but was only simulating pain, he stated in an *obiter dictum* that the defendants must

---

[151] [1956] O.R. 1007. See also *Smith v. Christie, Brown & Co. Ltd.*, [1955] O.R. 301; affd [1955] O.W.N. 570 (C.A.).
[152] *Ibid.*, at p. 1022.
[153] *Love v. Port of London Authority*, [1959] 2 Lloyd's Rep. 541. See also *Beiscak v. National Coal Bd.*, [1965] 1 All E.R. 895.
[154] (1960), 26 D.L.R. (2d) 529. See also *Elloway v. Boomars* (1968), 69 D.L.R. (2d) 605 (B.C.), schizophrenia; *Alexander v. Knights* (1962), 197 Pa. Super. 799, 177 A. 2d 142.
[155] *Ibid.*, at pp. 530 *et seq.*
[156] (1962), 36 W.W.R. 611 (B.C.). *Cf.*, *Ostrowski v. Lotto*, [1969] 1 O.R. 341; revd on another point, [1971] 1 O.R. 372; affd [1973] S.C.R. 220.
[157] [1963] S.A.S.R. 313, at p. 317.
[158] *Ibid.*, at pp. 318 and 319.
[159] (1965), 50 W.W.R. 546, at p. 553.

accept the risk of a "frail skull or a weak heart . . .", as well as the risk of "aggravating the condition of a psychotic".

One rather weird case is *Bates v. Fraser*.[160] For many years the woman plaintiff had suffered from Parkinson's disease. Some time later she was hit on the head, got amnesia, and the symptoms of Parkinson's disease disappeared. When she was later injured by the defendant she was dazed, began to cry and shake, suffered mental shock, and numerous other symptoms which led to the return of Parkinsonism with muscular rigidity. The court found that she was an "hysterical personality with hysterical susceptibility" and the defendant was liable to the extent that his conduct was the cause of the aggravation of her mental or physical disability. Mr. Justice Grant, in concluding his reasons,[161] felt that, although a defendant might be expected to anticipate emotional stress and hysteria from an accident but not Parkinsonism, "they are nevertheless liable", if there is a "positive relationship". A rather similar case is *Richards v. Baker*,[162] where a mother suffering from a small adenoma of the thyroid developed a toxicosis and sub-acute neurasthenia as a result of shock suffered on the death of her child.

Another fascinating case is *Malcolm v. Broadhurst*,[163] where a wife and husband were injured in an auto accident. Both suffered physical injuries and both had mental and nervous repercussions. The wife, because of her vulnerable personality, had additional nervous symptoms as a result of the effect on her of a change in her husband's behaviour. Compensation was awarded for all of these items by Geoffrey Lane J., who said:

> . . . there is no difference in principle between an eggshell skull and an eggshell personality. . . . Exacerbation of her nervous depression was a readily foreseeable consequence of injuring her. . . . Once damage of a particular kind, in this case psychological, can be foreseen, . . . the fact that it arises in or is continued by reason of an unusual complex of events does not avail the defendant . . . .[164]

There are more cases, all consistent. In *Duwyn v. Kapielian*,[165] a child injured in an accident was treated in such a way by a parent who had guilt feelings about the accident that the child was caused additional mental suffering. Recovery for this additional loss was allowed as "within the limits of foreseeability", by analogizing the ineffective parental care with improper medical treatment. In

---

[160] [1963] 1 O.R. 539, 38 D.L.R. (2d) 30.

[161] *Ibid.*, at p. 38, D.L.R.

[162] [1943] 5 S.A.S.R. 245.

[163] [1970] 3 All E.R. 508. See also *Sullivan v. Riverside Rentals Ltd.* (1973), 36 D.L.R. (3d) 538 (C.A.) (*per* Cowan C.J.T.D.); *Marconato v. Franklin*, [1974] 6 W.W.R. 676, at p. 689 (B.C.) (Aikins J.), liability for personality change of person more susceptible to suffering than average person; but *cf.*, *Dietelback v. Public Trustee* (1973), 37 D.L.R. (3d) 621 (B.C.), where no physical injury to wife, no liability.

[164] *Ibid.*, at p. 511.

[165] (1978) 7 C.C.L.T. 121 (*per* Morden J.A.).

Holian v. United Grain Growers[166] the court held that the plaintiff's chronic depression, which resulted from exposure to a poisonous chemical substance, was reasonably foreseeable and within the thin-skull principle, even though it was due to his "particular susceptibility to emotional injury". Mr. Justice Morse explained:

> The fact that the plaintiff reacted in an unexpected way does not render the injury unforesee-able or free the defendant from liability, provided that, as in this case, there is a direct link between the cause of the injury and the damage sustained.[167]

This principle has been reiterated recently by Griffiths J.A. who declared:[168]

> the law of damages draws no distinction between the eggshell skull and the eggshell personality. In each case, the tortfeasor takes the victim as found.

A person was even permitted to collect damages from a defendant who injured him causing a personality change that led him to commit rapes, for which he was imprisoned for life.[169]

4. EVIDENCE OF CAUSATION

One recurrent problem is the thin-skull cases is that of causation. Unless it is established that the defendant's conduct actually *caused* the aggravated harm, no liability will be imposed. Thus, where it was alleged that a death ensued from an occlusion of an artery, which had been caused by an earlier occlusion that resulted from an injury negligently inflicted by the defendant, the case was not even allowed to proceed to the jury on the ground that there was no evidence of causation.[170] In *Enge v. Trerise*,[171] although the majority permitted recovery, a dissenting judge contended that there was no evidence that the defendant's negligence caused the mental disorder alleged to have resulted from a scar. He felt that the only proof before the court was that this mental disorder was "precipitated" by the scar, which was not the same as "causing" it. The dissenter was too particular about the language used by medical experts who rarely invoke the language of causation. In *Hawley v. Ottawa Gas Co.*,[172] a plaintiff caught pneumonia after his injury had healed and as he was about to leave the hospital. The court held that there was no evidence of causal connection between the injury and the pneumonia and dismissed his case.

---

[166] (1980), 11 C.C.L.T. 184.

[167] *Ibid.*, at p. 200.

[168] *Bechard v. Haliburton Estate* (1991), 10 C.C.L.T. (2d) 156, at p. 172 (Ont. C.A.). See also 156, at p. 172 (Ont. C.A.). See also *Yoshikawa v. Yu* (1996), 28 C.C.L.T. (2d) 217 (B.C.C.A.).

[169] *Meah v. McCreamer*, [1985] 1 All E.R. 367 (Q.B.) (Woolf J.).

[170] *Von Hartman v. Kirk*, [1961] V.R. 554.

[171] (1960), 26 D.L.R. (2d) 529.

[172] (1919), 15 O.W.N. 454; affd 16 O.W.N. 106 (C.A.). See also *Oakes v. Spencer*, [1964] 1 O.R. 537 (C.A.), spinal disability not caused by operation; *Leonard v. B.C. Hydro* (1965), 50 W.W.R. 546, psychotic condition simulated as "avenue of escape" from unhappy life.

5. POLICY

These cases demonstrate that those with thin skulls collect whatever test is used, because judges believe that it is unjust to deny recovery for the aggravated injuries. It may be contended that the thin-skull rule is within the foresight doctrine because it is foreseeable that anything can happen to a fragile human being who is hurt in an accident.[173] But the rule has been supported in the absence of a foreseeability basis by Madam Justice Wilson who opined:[174]

> The concept that the wrongdoer takes his victim as he finds him has little to do with foresee-ability. It has a great deal to do with who, as a policy matter, should bear the loss when for reasons of peculiar vulnerability the victim of the defendant's negligence suffers greater injury or a different type of injury than the average victim would have suffered. It premises, as it were, a norm of vulnerability of the average person and makes the wrongdoer rather than the victim bear the damage suffered by those falling short of the norm.

It seems, then, that it does not matter whether the thin-skull consequences are said to be foreseeable or whether they are treated as an exception to the foreseeability requirement — in either case, as a matter of policy, the wrongdoer must bear the cost.

The policy reasons supporting this view are not hard to discern. It is difficult to distinguish between injuries that are foreseeable and those that are not from an administrative point of view. To avoid this complex job, the courts may have decided to reimburse the plaintiff for all the physical and menial consequences of the injury.[175] The thin-skull rule is also demonstrative of the respect that tort law holds for an individual, even if frail. In other words, every human being is entitled to receive reparation for all that is lost from the person who caused the loss. Other factors to be considered are the loss distribution and social welfare goals of tort law and deterrence, both specific and general. Actors might exercise more care in the conduct of their activities, if they knew that they were responsible not only for foreseeable injuries, but also for unforeseeable ones. Better social cost accounting will result if we make the activity that triggers these results bear the entire cost of the accidents it produces. It is plain that the thin-skull rule is alive and well and is here to stay.

I. Another Recurring Situation: The Rescuer

A negligent wrongdoer is liable to reimburse a rescuer for losses incurred during a rescue attempt.[176] It is said that this is so because such a deliverer is foresee-

---

[173] *Negretto v. Sayers, supra*, n. 149. See Rowe, "The Demise of the Thin Skull Rule?" (1977), 40 Mod. L. Rev. 1.

[174] *Cotic v. Gray* (1981), 17 C.C.L.T. 138, at p. 178; affd (1984), 26 C.C.L.T. 163 (S.C.C.).

[175] *Toronto Ry. Co. v. Toms, supra*, n. 149.

[176] See generally Linden, "Rescuers and Good Samaritans" (1971), 34 Mod L. Rev. 241; Linden, "Down with Foreseeability: Of Thin Skulls and Rescuers" (1969), 47 Can. Bar Rev. 545; Low, "Volenti, Duty and The Rescuer" (1959), 17 Fac. L. Rev. 118; Tiley, "The Rescue Principle"

able, but other verbal formulae have been used over the years to achieve the same results. The tests used do not matter very much, as long as the courts are not led astray by them. Unfortunately, because of its alluring simplicity, the foresight test has done just that on occasion.

There was a time when rescuers fared badly in the courts. Both causation[177] and voluntary assumption of risk[178] were invoked to deny them compensation. The earliest instance of reparation to a rescuer was the Manitoba case of *Seymour v. Winnipeg Electric Ry.*,[179] decided in 1910. Foreshadowing what was to emerge later in the United States and England, the court refused to follow earlier contrary authority and declared, on demurrer, that a rescuer could recover from a negligent wrongdoer. Mr. Justice Richards, after recognizing that "the promptings of humanity towards the saving of life are amongst the noblest instincts of mankind", asserted that "the trend of modern legal thought is toward holding that those who risk their safety in attempting to rescue others who are put in peril by the negligence of third persons are entitled to claim such compensation from such third persons for injuries they may receive in such attempts".[180] This is particularly the case if "those whom it sought to rescue are infirm or helpless". As an afterthought, Mr. Justice Richards added that the company had "notice" that "some brave man is likely to risk his own life to save the helpless", which indicated that the idea of notice or knowledge (or foresight if you will) was a relevant consideration even in those days.

Twenty-three years after the Canadian courts had pretty well sorted out the problem of the rescuer, the English courts, oblivious to our pioneering effort, were still floundering around with the concepts of causation and *volenti*. For example, in *Cutler v. United Dairies (London) Ltd.*,[181] the plaintiff was injured when he tried to hold the head of a runaway horse in response to the driver's shout for help. The jury's verdict for the plaintiff was overturned and the action dismissed on the ground that "the damage must be on his own head" because of "*volenti*" and because "a new cause has intervened".[182] Lord Justice Slesser drew a distinction between a case where someone dashes out to save a child in danger, because "there is no *novus actus interveniens*. . . . However heroic and laudable may have been this act, it cannot properly be said that it was not in the legal sense the cause of the accident."[183] The opposite result was arrive at in *Brandon v. Osborne Garrett Co.*[184] where Mr. Justice Swift submerged the impediment of

---

(1967), 30 Mod. L. Rev. 25; Goodhart, "Rescue and Voluntary Assumption of Risk" (1934), 5 Camb. L.J. 192; Maxwell, "Rescuer and Victim Tort Law" in Law Society of Upper Canada, *Special Lectures on New Developments in the Law of Torts* (1973).

[177] *Anderson v. Northern Ry. Co.* (1875), 25 U.C.C.P. 301 (C.A.).

[178] *Kimball v. Butler Bros.* (1910), 15 O.W.R. 221 (C.A.).

[179] (1910), 13 W.L.R. 566 (Man. C.A.).

[180] *Ibid.*, at pp. 568 and 588.

[181] [1933] 2 K.B. 297 (C.A.).

[182] *Ibid.*, at p. 303 (*per* Scrutton L.J.).

[183] *Ibid.*, at p. 306.

[184] [1924] 1 K.B. 548.

Cutler by categorizing as "instinctive" the rescue act of a wife, who tried to pull her husband away from glass falling from a skylight. This sorry state of affairs could not continue for long.

The breakthrough came in the United States eleven years after the *Seymour* case, when Mr. Justice Cardozo, in *Wagner v. International Railroad Co.*,[185] eloquently articulated the principle that was destined to be adopted throughout the common-law world:

> Danger invites rescue. The cry of distress is the summons to relief. The law does not ignore these reactions of the mind in tracing conduct to its consequences. It recognizes them as normal. It places their effects within the range of the natural and probable. The wrong that imperils life is a wrong to the imperiled victim; it is a wrong also to his rescuer. The risk of rescue, if only it be not wanton, is born of the occasion. The emergency begets the man. The wrongdoer may not have foreseen the coming of a deliverer. He is accountable as if he had.

In 1935 the English courts finally succumbed to the Canadian and American lead and recognized the claim of the rescuer. In *Haynes v. Harwood*,[186] a police constable tried to push a woman out of the way of a runaway horse and was injured in the attempt. Distinguishing the *Cutler* case on the grounds that "nobody was in any danger" there,[187] and that a police officer was "expected to" aid those in danger "in pursuance of a duty",[188] the trial judge found for the officer. The Court of Appeal affirmed the decision, declaring that "it would be a little surprising if a rational system of law . . . denied any remedy to a brave man".[189] Lord Justice Maugham articulated very clearly the appropriate process of decision-making in this area. The question is whether the act is "so exceptional" that it should be treated as a *novus actus*.[190] "The law has to measure the interests which he sought to protect and the other interests involved",[191] he explained. One must take into account the "energy and courage" of the reasonable person, the degree of danger involved and the response of the rescuer. If the problem is approached in this way, a more rational and understandable determination can be made. The Australians also recognized the duty to the deliverer of the grounds that "a reasonable person would have foreseen the possibility of rescue".[192]

The English courts, after their initial reluctance, have showered attention on the rescuer. In *Videan v. British Transport Commission*,[193] compensation was awarded to the rescuer of a child trespasser who was denied recompense. The

---

[185] (1921), 232 N.Y. Supp. 176, 133 N.E. 437. See also *Moddejonge v. Huron County Bd. of Education*, [1972] 2 O.R. 437, at p. 444 (*per* Pennell J.).

[186] [1934] 2 K.B. 240; affd, [1935] 1 K.B. 146 (C.A.).

[187] *Ibid.*, at p. 249.

[188] *Ibid.*, at p. 250.

[189] [1935] 1 K.B. 146, at p. 152 (C.A.).

[190] *Ibid.*, at p. 161.

[191] *Ibid.*, at p. 162.

[192] *Chester v. Waverley Municipal Council* (1939), 62 C.L.R. 1, at p. 38 (*per* Evatt J.), dissenting.

[193] [1963] 2 All E.R. 860 (C.A.).

majority based its decision on the special duty of an employer to his station-master and reserved judgment on whether an ordinary member of the public would be equally protected. The mental gymnastics engaged in by Lord Justice Denning, concurring, were wondrous to behold.[194] He found that, although the child trespasser was himself not reasonable foreseeable, his rescuer was! He reasoned that one need not foresee the particular emergency, only that a stationmaster might attempt a rescue of someone, in this case his child. Perhaps a more revealing rationale, however, was Lord Justice Denning's statement to the effect that "Whoever comes to the rescue, the law should see that he does not suffer for it." So favoured are rescuers today that they have been allowed reparation for mental suffering where ordinary bystanders would be denied it. In *Chadwick v. British Transport Commission*,[195] someone who suffered anxiety neurosis when he help rescue operations after a train wreck, was awarded damages. "The very fact of rescue must . . . involve unexpected things happening" and one need not foresee "every step".

This liability to the rescuer stems from an independent duty owed by negligent persons directly to all potential rescuers; it is not based on a derivative duty founded on a primary duty to persons endangered.[196] Consequently, a rescuer may recover, even though there is no liability to the original person on the ground of no causation, contributory negligence or similar defences.

1. DUTY OF PERSONS BEING RESCUED TO THEIR OWN RESCUERS

Negligent actors are liable not only for those injured while helping third persons they endanger, but if they get themselves into trouble, they owe a duty to their own rescuers.[197] Although there was some earlier authority to the contrary,[198] the courts later heeded the eloquent plea of the late Dean C.A. Wright to extend "their humanitarian doctrine of rescue this far".[199] Foresight, he suggested, was not the only basis for deciding these cases; instead, he contended that "as between a careless man and the heroic rescuer the policy of the law favours shifting the loss from the latter to the former". Although fault to a third person is the usual situation, "fault with respect to oneself should also suffice".[200]

---

[194] *Ibid.*, at p. 868.

[195] [1967] 2 All E.R. 945 (K.B.D.).

[196] *Horsley v. MacLaren* (1972), 22 D.L.R. (3d) 545, at p. 558 (*per* Laskin J.); *Corothers v. Slobodian* (1975), 51 D.L.R. (3d) 1, at p. 5 (S.C.C.) (*per* Ritchie J.).

[197] *Ibid.*, at p. 558.

[198] *Dupuis v. New Regina Trading Co. Ltd.*, [1943] 4 D.L.R. 275 (Sask. C.A.).

[199] "Case and Comment" (1943), 21 Can. Bar Rev. 758, at p. 763. See *Horsley v. MacLaren* (1972), 22 D.L.R. (3d) 545, at p. 558 (*per* Laskin J.).

[200] *Ibid.*, at p. 764 and 765.

This theory was first adopted judicially in *Baker v. Hopkins*.[201] The case concerned a doctor who was overcome by gas fumes while attempting to rescue a worker trapped in a mine. The action against the mine operators succeeded, and because the worker being aided was found to be 10 per cent at fault, the court considered the duty of the rescued to his rescuer. In a *dictum*, Mr. Justice Barry disapproved of *Dupuis* and stated that, although one does not owe a duty to preserve one's own safety, "if by his own carelessness a man puts himself into a position of peril of a kind that invites rescue, he would in law be liable for an injury caused to someone who he ought to have foreseen would attempt to come to his aid."[202] On appeal, the trial judge's decision was upheld, but the judges did not comment on this point.[203]

In *C.N.R. v. Bakty*[204] an action was brought on behalf of a railway conductor, who injured his back while trying to rescue the defendant, who was hurt when he negligently collided with the train. Praising the "courage and humanity" of the conductor, the court allowed recovery and explained that "it should be reasonably foreseeable to the driver of a car who carelessly runs into a train that someone will come to his aid".

In Australia rescued persons are responsible to their rescuers. In *Chapman v. Hearse*,[205] Dr. Cherry was killed when a negligent motorist, Hearse, collided with him while he was helping Chapman, who had been injured on the highway because of his own negligence. When Dr. Cherry's family sued the motorist, Hearse, they added the careless person being helped, Chapman, as a third party. The court was, therefore, faced with the question of whether a rescued person owed a duty to his rescuer. Without mentioning the *Dupuis* and *Baker* cases, the court found Chapman, the person being rescued, 25 per cent at fault, and stated that, if support were necessary, "ample can be found in the analogous rescue cases". The Australian High Court, therefore, assumed that individuals bear an obligation to potential rescuers to keep themselves out of positions of peril.

This point has now been placed beyond dispute in Canada by the dictum of Mr. Justice Laskin, in *Horsley v. MacLaren, The Ogopogo*, to this effect:

> . . . a person who imperils himself by his carelessness may be as fully liable to a rescuer as a third person would be who imperils another.[206]

This principle has been stretched to the extent that one rescuer owes a duty to another potential rescuer to exercise reasonable care during the course of the first rescue.[207]

---

[201] [1958] 3 All E.R. 147 (Q.B.D.); affd [1959] 1 W.L.R. 966, [1959] 3 All E.R. 225 (C.A.). See also *Carney v. Buyea* (1946), 651 N.Y.S. 2d 902.

[202] *Ibid.*, at p. 153.

[203] Lord Justice Morris specifically avoids the question in [1959] 3 All E.R., at p. 234.

[204] (1977), 18 O.R. (2d) 481, at p. 485 (*per* Leach C.C.J.).

[205] [1961] S.A.S.R. 51; affd 106 C.L.R. 112.

[206] *Horsley v. MacLaren* (1972), 22 D.L.R. (3d) 545, at p. 558 (S.C.C.).

[207] *Ibid.* See also Alexander, "One Rescuer's Obligation to Another: 'The Ogopogo' Lands in the Supreme Court of Canada" (1972), 22 U. of T.L.J. 98.

2. RESCUE OF PROPERTY

As one might expect, the law's concern over rescuers of property was not as intense as it was when people were being saved.[208] By 1892, however, the Supreme Court of Canada in *Prescott v. Connell*[209] recognized that someone hurt attempting to protect endangered property could recover from the negligent wrongdoer.

This duty is owed even to people injured while protecting their own property. In *Hutterly v. Imperial Oil Co. Ltd. and Calder*,[210] the plaintiff tried to drive his own car out of a burning garage and was injured in the attempt. The negligent defendant was held liable for the loss to the car and the injury to the plaintiff on the ground that the plaintiff's attempt to save his property was not unreasonable. This was so even though he could have escaped himself without being injured. People injured while helping to put out fires caused by negligence are also recompensed, whether the building belongs to a third person,[211] or even to the defendant.[212] As a general principle, it has been declared that "persons injured in seeking to avoid damage to property may be entitled to recover form the original wrongdoer, even though they voluntarily assumed the risk of injury".[213]

Not only is compensation for personal injuries allowed, but if property is damaged during the course of rescue, it too is covered. In *Thorn v. James*,[214] a servant tried to protect his employer's separator from a fire by hooking some horses to it and pulling it free. He failed; both the separator and the horses were burned. The original negligent defendant had to pay for the horses in addition to the separator, because the rescue effort was reasonable in the circumstances. Similarly, the cost of a rescue effort may be recovered, as where expenses were incurred putting out a fire caused by a negligent driver.[215]

3. THE CONDUCT OF THE RESCUER

a) Reasonably Perceived Danger

A rescuer will not be protected in every instance; there must be some reasonably perceived danger to person or goods and the conduct of the rescuer must not be foolhardy. This does not mean that there has to be actual danger, nor does it mean that perfection is demanded in the actor's conduct.

---

[208] *Eckert v. Long Island Ry.* (1871), 43 N.Y. 502. See also *Wilkinson v. Kinneil Cannel & Coking Coal Co.* (1897), 34 S.L.R. 533 (*per* Lord Young; *Love v. New Fairview Corp.* (1904), 10 B.C.R. 330 (C.A.) (*per* Martin J.).

[209] (1893), 22 S.C.R. 147; affg 220 O.A.R. 49, horses endangered.

[210] (1956), 3 D.L.R. (2d) 719.

[211] *Russell v. McCabe*, [1962] N.Z.L.R. 392.

[212] *Hyett v. Great Western Ry. Co.*, [1948] 1 K.B. 345 (C.A.).

[213] *Toy v. Argenti*, [1980] 3 W.W.R. 276 (B.C.) (*per* Esson J.), plaintiff 30% to blame.

[214] (1903), 14 Man. R. 373.

[215] *Attorney General for Ontario v. Crompton* (1976), 1 C.C.L.T. 81 (Ont.) (*per* Haines J.).

The early cases seemed to require *actual* danger to someone before a duty to the rescuer would be created,[216] but this served to impede rather than to encourage rescue attempts. All that is required now is a reasonable belief that someone is in peril. A rescuer will now be compensated even if the rescue attempt could not have been successful, as where the person being rescued was already dead.[217] In *Ould v. Butler's Wharf*,[218] a rescuer, wrongly believing that a fellow worker was in danger of being hit by the hook of a crane, tried to push him out of the way. When he did this, the supposedly endangered man dropped the case of rubber he was carrying on the rescuer's foot. Although the rescuer may have been wrong in his assessment of the danger, Mr. Justice Gorman permitted him to recover, because he felt there was an "imminent serious accident".[219] In other words, a futile rescue attempt may be compensated by tort law as long as it is a reasonable one. This is understandable because it is often difficult to know in advance whether the rescue operation will succeed. If there is a reasonable chance of saving some children lost in the woods or some miners buried in a mine, the common law should encourage these efforts.

On the other hand, if a situation is "completely devoid of any inherent danger",[220] no liability will be imposed, as where a patient's husband was injured while assisting a nurse in a hospital when an orderly was readily available. The reasoning in the judgment relied upon notions of foreseeability and the particular susceptibility of the plaintiff's back.

b) The Foolhardy Rescuer

Not only must there be a situation of reasonably perceived danger, but the response of the rescuer must not be a rash one. If a would-be rescuer standing on the Peace Tower jumps off to save a child in the road and is killed, the rescuer's spouse will not be compensated. This result is normally justified on the ground that the rescuer was "foolhardy",[221] "rash",[222] "needlessly reckless"[223] or that the rescuer conducted the rescue with "gross rashness and recklessness".[224] The currently popular explanation of these cases is that such a foolhardy rescue attempt is not foreseeable and, hence, no duty is owed. This is no more satisfactory than the other theories, such as *volenti* and causation, that were advanced

---

[216] *McDonald v. Burr*, [1919] 3 W.W.R. 825 (Sask. C.A.); *Brine v. Dubbin*, [1933] 2 W.W.R. 25 (Alta.); *Haynes v. Harwood*, [1935] 1 K.B. 146 (C.A.).

[217] *Wagner v. International Railway* (1921), 232 N.Y. Supp. 176, 133 N.E. 437.

[218] [1953] 2 Lloyd's Rep. 44.

[219] *Ibid.*, at p. 46.

[220] *Elverson v. Doctor's Hospital* (1974), 49 D.L.R. (3d) 196, at p. 198 (*per* Evans J.A.), nurse not negligent; affd (1976), 65 D.L.R. (3d) 382. See also *Papin v. Ethier* (1995), 26 C.C.L.T. (2d) 290 (Que. S.C.), no chance to save person.

[221] *Baker v. Hopkins*, *supra*, n. 201, at p. 153 (*per* Barry J.).

[222] *Haigh v. Grand Trunk Pacific Ry. Co.* (1914), 7 W.W.R. (N.S.) 806 (Alta.).

[223] *Seymour v. Winnipeg Electric Railway Co.* (1910), 13 W.L.R. 566, at p. 571 (Man. C.A.).

[224] *Woods v. Caledonian Ry.* (1886), 23 S.L.R. 798.

in the past for reaching this same conclusion. They all disguise rather than illuminate the true reasons for the decisions.

The courts rightly feel that it is unfair to make the original wrongdoer pay for the additional losses of a foolish rescuer. It is true that such losses are rather unexpected consequences and thus might be termed unforeseeable, but there is more to it than that. Tort law seeks to encourage people to aid one another, but not to do so stupidly. By denying compensation to the foolhardy rescuer, tort law is trying to reduce the frequency of reckless rescue efforts.

The courts have not been overly stringent in their assessment of the humane conduct of would-be rescuers. They almost never conclude that a rescuer has been foolhardy. In *Moddejonge v. Huron County Board of Education*,[225] an employee of the defendant school board took some students for a swim. Due to negligent supervision, two female students were carried out into deep water by a surface current caused by a fresh breeze that developed suddenly. Geraldine Moddejonge, a fellow student, swam to their assistance, successfully rescued one of them, but drowned while trying to save the second girl. The parents of both drowned girls recovered from the school board. In discussing the conduct of the rescuer, Mr. Justice Pennell observed:

> It was delicately argued that the efforts of Geraldine Moddejonge constituted a rash and futile gesture; that reasonableness did not attach to her response. Upon this, the rescue of Sandra Thompson is sufficient answer. One must not approach the problem with the wisdom that comes after the event. Justice is not to be measured in such scales. To Geraldine Moddejonge duty did not hug the shore of safety. Duty did not give her a choice. She accepted it. She discharged it. More need not be said. The law will give her actions a sanctuary.

In another case, *Corothers v. Slobodian*,[226] the Supreme Court of Canada had occasion to consider the conduct of a plaintiff rescuer. The plaintiff Bonnie Corothers, was driving along the highway when the vehicle in front of her, driven by Anton Hammerschmid, collided with a vehicle being driven negligently by one Neil Poupard, who was killed in the accident. The plaintiff stopped her car and went over to assist. Seeing that several people had been severely injured, she decided that she should try to get help. She ran along the highway, waving her arms at the oncoming traffic, intending to enlist their help. At a point about 50 feet down the road, she was injured when struck by a semi-trailer truck, driven by Slobodian, who slammed on his brakes when he saw her, causing the truck to jackknife. The plaintiff sued Slobodian and the estate of Poupard.

The Supreme Court exonerated the truck-driver, Slobodian, on the ground that his conduct was only an "error of judgment" because, when "faced with a gesticulating woman on the side of the highway . . . he was acting in a moment of imminent emergency".[227] The plaintiff succeeded, however, against Poupard,

---

[225] [1972] 2 O.R. 437, at p. 444.

[226] (1975), 51 D.L.R. (3d) 1 (S.C.C.).

[227] *Ibid.*, at p. 10 (*per* Ritchie J.).

the original negligent driver, because her acts "in attempting to flag down the approaching traffic were . . . perfectly normal reactions to the cry of distress" and could not be described as wanton.[228]

Another fascinating case, stretching the rescue doctrine to its limits, is *Urbanski v. Patel*,[229] where a father, who donated a kidney to his daughter, sued the doctor whose negligence precipitated the event. He was successful, the court holding that it was "entirely foreseeable that one of her family would be invited, and would agree, to donate a kidney for transplant, an act with accords, too, with the principle developed in many 'rescue cases' ". Consequently, this was not a "foolish" act by a rescuer, which should lead the court to deny recovery; on the contrary, such a selfless and heroic act deserved compensation.

c) The Contributorily Negligent Rescuer

Even though it has been employed sensibly, the foolhardiness test is an unsatisfactory tool for distinguishing between careless rescuers, because it is too blunt. It leads to only two alternative solutions: (a) total victory for the non-foolhardy rescuer, or (b) total defeat for the foolhardy one. These two choices, however, are not sufficiently flexible. The courts are wise to promote cautious rescue efforts and to discourage foolish ones, but they need a more sensitive technique to accomplish this. Comparative negligence is such a device.

There is now some evidence that the courts are ready to utilize comparative negligence in those cases where it is appropriate.[230] There has been some unfortunate loose talk to the effect that contributorily negligent rescuers cannot recover at all. Foolhardiness and recklessness have been blurred with mere carelessness. For example, an English court once stated that if a rescuer "did something a reasonable person ought not to have done",[231] recovery will be denied, but this was prior to the enactment of the negligence act in the United Kingdom. Such a result may have been tolerable at that time because both foolhardy rescue attempts and negligent ones yielded precisely the same result, but not longer.

Today, several solutions are possible under the legislation. For example, an utterly hopeless and ridiculous rescue effort might still go uncompensated because it is "unforeseeable" and outside the scope of the duty. Some rescue attempts, however, may not be carefully executed and yet may not be utterly devoid of merit. There is no reason why a reduced award cannot be given in such a case to reward the rescuer for heroism, without ignoring the fact that the rescuer was careless.

---

[228] *Ibid.*, at p. 5.
[229] (1978), 84 D.L.R. (3d) 650, at p. 671 (Man. Q.B.) (*per* Wilson J.). See Robertson, "Comment" (1980), 96 L.Q.R. 19.
[230] *Horsley v. MacLaren* (1972), 22 D.L.R. (3d) 545, at p. 565 (*per* Laskin J.), no contributory negligence found.
[231] *Brandon v. Osborne Garrett & Co.*, [1924] 1 K.B. 548, at p. 552.

The ordinary principles of contributory negligence should obtain here. The case of *Sayers v. Harlow Urban District Council*,[232] lends some support to this view. A woman was trapped in a public lavatory through the negligence of the defendant. She was injured while trying to climb out. In order to avoid coming to the conclusion that there was no duty owed the plaintiff, who was a kind of "self-rescuer," the court found that she was not guilty of conduct that was "unwise or imprudent or rash or stupid". Nevertheless, it held that the plaintiff "cannot entirely be absolved from some measure of fault," and deprived her of one quarter of her damages.

Comparative negligence was also employed in *Holomis v. Dubuc*.[233] The deceased passenger was involved in a seaplane collision which occurred as the plane landed on an unmarked lake in a fog. The deceased, who might also be term a self-rescuer, jumped out of the sinking plane and into the water without one of the life jackets which were readily available. He was drowned and his family sued. Their recovery was reduced by 50 per cent on the basis of the deceased's negligence in failing to take a life jacket with him. The carrier was also liable because the "probability that a surprised and frightened passenger would leap from a sinking aircraft is entirely within the foresight of the reasonable man".[234]

A case along these lines is *Toy v. Argenti*,[235] where the plaintiff was injured trying to protect his car from damage by the defendant's car, which was moving toward it with no one at the controls. Treating him as a rescuer of property, Esson J. allowed him to recover part of his damages. The hopelessness of the endeavour did not count against the plaintiff, but by persisting in the dangerous rescue attempt in order to avoid trivial damage, he was found to have been contributorily negligent, and his recovery was reduced by 30 per cent. Mr. Justice Esson explained:

> In persisting to the point he did in attempting to avoid insignificant damage, the plaintiff acted unreasonable, even on the relaxed definition of "reasonable" which has been applied in the rescue cases . . . I consider [his conduct] to have been a failure to exercise reasonable care for his own safety in all the circumstances and thus to be contributory negligence.

A similar principle was enunciated in *Cleary v. Hansen*[236] where it was said,

> even during an attempt to assist someone in an emergency, the law expects reasonable care to be exercised, even though the standard is relaxed to a certain extent. The court does not expect perfection, but rescuers must be sensible. They, like anyone else, must weigh the ad-

---

[232] [1958] 2 All E.R. 342 (C.A.). See also Brown, "A Study of Negligence" (1932), 10 Can. Bar Rev. 557, at pp. 573-74. See also judgment of Laskin J. in *Horsley v. MacLaren, supra*, n. 199, at p. 565.

[233] (1974), 56 D.L.R. (3d) 351 (B.C.).

[234] *Ibid.*, at p. 363.

[235] [1980] 3 W.W.R. 276, at p. 284 (B.C.).

[236] (1981), 18 C.C.L.T. 147, at p. 156 (*per* Linden J.), 10% fault.

vantages and risks of their conduct. Their conduct too, however laudable, must measure up to the standard of the reasonable person in similar circumstances.

There is no reason why this approach should not be utilized in dealing with all rescue cases when the injured rescuer is negligent but not quite foolhardy. It would permit a wider range of potential outcomes to these cases, whose facts are always so incredibly varied. It would, therefore, enable the courts to influence the conduct of rescuers and would-be rescuers with a more sensitive set of tools than they now possess.

d) *"The Ogopogo"* Case

"The Ogopogo" case dealt with some of these issues concerning a careless rescuer.[237] At the trial Mr. Justice Lacourcière clearly expressed the rules governing rescuers. He felt that the conduct of Horsley, who leaped off a yacht into the lake to help a passenger who had fallen overboard, was not "futile, reckless, rash, wanton or foolhardy". Nor was Horsley guilty of contributory negligence. His Lordship did not think it mattered that the person being rescued could not have been helped. *Volenti* was rejected because it was not pleaded and because there was no free and voluntary assumption of risk. Mr. Justice Lacourcière concluded that the rescuer should succeed because he was "within the risk created by the defendant's negligent conduct".

The Court of Appeal reversed the decision, withholding compensation to Horsley. Mr. Justice Jessup did agree that a rescue attempt by a passenger is generally foreseeable in a situation of a mishandled rescue attempt. Nevertheless, he held that this *particular* rescue could not reasonably have been anticipated because the rescuer had been warned to remain in the cabin due to his inexperience with boating.[238] Mr. Justice Schroeder circumscribed even further the protection afforded to rescuers by listing a series of factual circumstances which he thought made the rescue attempt unforeseeable.[239] According to Mr. Justice Schroeder, since the need for the rescue attempt was doubtful and since the conduct of it was substandard, Horsley should have been refused compensation altogether on the basis of lack of foresight and absence of duty. It was a sad day for the Canadian rescuer.

The majority of the Supreme Court of Canada, although it affirmed the dismissal of Horsley's claim, rested its decision on the absence of negligence by MacLaren. It disassociated itself from the Court of Appeal's conclusion that Horsley's rescue effort was unforeseeable.[240] This was a most welcome redemption from a misuse of foresight theory.

---

[237] *Horsley v. MacLaren*, [1969] 2 O.R. 137; revd [1970] 2 O.R. 487; affd (1972), 22 D.L.R. (3d) 545. See *supra*, Chapter 10.

[238] [1970] 2 O.R. 487, at p. 502.

[239] *Ibid.*, at p. 496.

[240] See *supra*, n. 199, at p. 552 (*per* Ritchie J.) and at p. 564 (*per* Laskin J.).

It would have been preferable if the Supreme Court had accepted the trial judge's finding of negligence by MacLaren and imposed liability. At the same time the court should have held that the plaintiff was contributorily negligent. His award might have been reduced by 25 or even 50 percent. If this technique had been utilized the court may have been able, not only to reward the rescuer, but also to penalize him by cutting his award. Of course, if the plaintiff could not swim or if it was obvious to everybody that the person in the water was already dead, the court would have been justified in denying recovery altogether.

e) Onus of Proof

It has been wisely held that the onus of showing that a rescuer was foolhardy rests on the defendant,[241] which is consistent with the ordinary principle concerning contributory negligence. Moreover, where there is a jury it must decide as a matter of fact whether the rescuer was needlessly reckless[242] and, presumably, contributorily negligent. The courts have wisely refrained from demanding too much from deliverers; for instance, where a rescuer was injured trying to save a child in circumstances where it may have been necessary, he was permitted recovery.[243]

4. POLICY

Somehow similar decisions are reached in rescue cases whatever formula is used. This is because the courts have wisely decided to use tort law to encourage rescuers by rewarding them if they are injured.[244] Our sense of the moral correctness of helping one's neighbour is thus reinforced. In addition, the courts are hopeful that they will deter, both specifically and generally, individuals, institutions and industries from causing accidents. If people know that they will be liable not only to those they injure but to their rescuers as well, they may take greater pains for safety. An activity should pay its way, which includes not only the expenses of those hurt by the activity directly, but also those of the rescuers of the injured. Furthermore, the loss distribution and social welfare goals of tort law are served by spreading liability in these circumstances.

J. Intervening Forces

There was once a time when negligent actors could be insulated from liability for consequences brought about by an intervening force which came into

---

[241] *Baker v. Hopkins, supra*, n. 201, at p. 224, [1959] 3 All E.R. (*per* Willmer L.J.).

[242] *Anderson v. Northern Ry. Co.* (1875), 25 U.C.C.P. 301, at p. 323 (C.A.) (*per* Strong J.), 2-2 decision for defendant. *Seymour v. Winnipeg Electric Railway Co., supra*, n. 223, at p. 571.

[243] *Morgan v. Aylen*, [1942] 1 All E.R. 489.

[244] If there is any indication that someone is an avenger rather than a rescuer, he or she may be denied compensation, see *Jones v. Wabigwan*, [1968] 2 O.R. 827; revd [1970] 1 O.R. 366 (C.A.).

operation after their act was complete.[245] The true nature of the problem was clouded by phrases such as *actus novus interveniens*, the "last wrongdoer" and the everpresent discussion of causation. Today, however, it is clear that wrong-doers are not immune from responsibility in these circumstances. This was so before *The Wagon Mound (No. 1)* and even before *Polemis*. Again, the language used by the courts is of little help; the issue is simply whether it is fair to hold negligent actors liable when the conduct of others is also involved in bringing about the accident. Judicial decisions in the recurring situations offer some guidance in sorting out these problems, but the process "is something like having to draw a line between night and day; there is a great duration of twilight".[246]

There are some factual situations that might be categorized alternatively as duty, standard of care, or remoteness problems. Although dealt with here, they might fit equally in the standard of care chapter.[247] For example, loss caused by ice,[248] flooding,[249] or other bad weather,[250] can be attributed to someone who fails to take reasonable steps to avoid its effect. No liability would be imposed, however, if an earthquake or an extremely severe and unprecedented frost caused the damage.[251] The harmful acts of animals may produce liability for their owners,[252] as long as the results are not too unexpected.[253]

The mischievous acts of children can be ascribed to those who negligently create the opportunities for their dangerous conduct, as where stones were thrown at a horse causing it to bolt,[254] where gasoline was ignited,[255] where a snowmobile was mishandled,[256] and where a gun was fired accidentally.[257] In

---

[245] See generally *Prosser and Keeton on the Law of Torts*, 5th ed. (1984), p. 301; Fleming, *The Law of Torts*, 9th ed. (1998), p. 246.

[246] See Blackburn J. in *Hobbs v. London and South Western Ry. Co.* (1875), 10 L.R. Q.B. 111, at p. 121.

[247] See Chapter 5.

[248] *R. v. Coté* (1974), 51 D.L.R. (3d) 244; *Abbott et al. v. Kasza*, [1975] 3 W.W.R. 163; vard [1976] 4 W.W.R. 20 (Alta. C.A.).

[249] *C.P.R. v. Calgary*, [1971] 4 W.W.R. 241 (Alta.).

[250] *Bowman v. Columbia Telephone Co.* (1962), 406 Pa. 455, 179 A. 2d 197.

[251] *Blyth v. Birmingham Waterworks Co.* (1856), 11 Ex. 781.

[252] *Aldham v. United Dairies (London) Ltd.*, [1940] 1 K.B. 507 (C.A.); *Fleming v. Atkinson*, [1959] S.C.R. 513; *Kirk v. Trerise* (1979), 103 D.L.R. (3d) 78, dog bite; *Weeks v. Weeks* (1977), 18 Nfld. & P.E.I.R. 1, bull impregnating young heifers prematurely; Williams, *Liability for Animals* (1939).

[253] *Lathall v. Joyce & Son*, [1939] 3 All E.R. 854.

[254] *Haynes v. Harwood*, [1935] 1 K.B. 146 (C.A.); *Lynch v. Nurdin* (1841), 1 Q.B. 20, 113 E.R. 1041; *cf.*, *Donovan v. Union Cartage Co. Ltd.*, [1933] 2 K.B. 71; *Scott v. Philp* (1922), 52 O.L.R. 513 (C.A.).

[255] *Yachuk v. Oliver Blais Co.*, [1949] A.C. 386. See also *Bowman v. Rankin* (1963), 41 W.W.R. 700 (Sask.).

[256] *Ryan v. Hickson* (1975), 7 O.R. (2d) 352; *Hoffer v. School Division of Assiniboine South*, [1973] 6 W.W.R. 765.

[257] *Edwards v. Smith*, [1941] 1 D.L.R. 736; *Sullivan v. Creed*, [1904] 21 R. 317; *Bishop v. Sharrow* (1975), 8 O.R. (2d) 649; *Ingram v. Lowe* (1975), 55 D.L.R. (3d) 292 (Alta. C.A.); *cf.*, *Hatfield v.*

Harris v. Toronto Transit Commission, a child's arm, which was sticking out of the window of a bus, was fractured when the bus collided with a pole. In imposing partial liability, the Supreme Court of Canada[258] stated that the driver "should have foreseen the likelihood of child passengers extending their arms through the window, notwithstanding the warning". Similarly, where ice cream is sold to children under conditions which endanger their safety, liability may be imposed.[259] Parents must also take steps to protect their children from themselves.[260]

The inmates of institutions such as schools,[261] hospitals and prisons may render their "keepers" liable for injuries to themselves and the third persons. For example, where a child ran out of a school yard and caused the death of a motorist who swerved to avoid him, the school was held responsible.[262] A school and a bus company were held partially to blame when a 5-year-old child was allowed to get off a bus at the wrong place and ran into the path of a car.[263] A hospital and a psychiatrist were held liable for the suicide of a patient,[264] and a hospital has been held responsible for an attack by a mental patient on another person.[265] When an escapee of a mental hospital with a history of sexual crime committed another sexual assault, the hospital was held liable.[266] Prison authorities may be held liable if they permit one prisoner to injure another,[267] but only if they are negligent.[268] Some Borstal boys who were working on an island in the custody of police officers damaged a yacht which they set it motion during an

---

[258] *Pearson* (1956), 6 D.L.R. (2d) 593 (B.C.C.A.). See generally, Alexander, "Tort Responsibility of Parents and Teachers for Damage Caused by Children" (1965), 16 U. of T.L.J. 165; Dunlop, "Torts Relating to Infants" (1966), 5 West. L. Rev. 116; Wilson, "Parental Responsibility for the Acts of Children" (2000), 79 Can. Bar Rev. 369.

[258] [1967] S.C.R. 460, at p. 465 (*per* Ritchie J.). See also *Bohlen v. Perdue and City of Edmonton*, [1976] 1 W.W.R. 364 (Alta.), adult recovers for injury, arm sticking out bus window hit pole.

[259] *Teno v. Arnold* (1975), 7 O.R. (2d) 276; affd (1976), 11 O.R. (2d) 585 (C.A.); vard (1978), 3 C.C.L.T. 272 (S.C.C.).

[260] *Ibid.*; *Gambino v. Dileo*, [1971] 2 O.R. 131.

[261] School partly liable to nursing student who hurt back while lifting, *Zaba v. Saskatchewan Institute of Applied Science & Technology* (1995), 28 C.C.L.T. (2d) 96 (Sask. Q.B.); revd (1997), 38 C.C.L.T. (2d) 312, [1997] 8 W.W.R. 414 (Sask. C.A.), no causation.

[262] *Carmarthenshire County Council v. Lewis*, [1955] A.C. 549, [1955] 1 All E.R. 565.

[263] *Mattinson v. Wonnacott* (1975), 8 O.R. (2d) 654 (Cory J.); see also *Dziwenka v. R.*, [1972] S.C.R. 419.

[264] *Villemure v. L'Hôpital Notre-Dame* (1972), 31 D.L.R. (3d) 454; *cf.*, *Stadel v. Albertson*, [1954] 2 D.L.R. 328 (Sask. C.A.); *University Hospital Bd. v. Lepine*, [1966] S.C.R. 561; Note, (1967), 5 Osgoode Hall L.J. 105.

[265] *Lawson v. Wellesley Hospital* (1975), 9 O.R. (2d) 677 (C.A.); affd [1978] 1 S.C.R. 893. See also *Stewart v. Extendicare Ltd.* (1986), 38 C.C.L.T. 67 (Sask. Q.B.).

[266] *Holgate v. Lancashire Mental Hospitals Bd.*, [1937] 4 All E.R. 19.

[267] *MacLean v. R.*, [1973] S.C.R. 2, at p. 6, prisoner disabled by bale of straw knocking him to ground.

[268] *Ellis v. Home Office*, [1953] 2 All E.R. 149 (C.A.), no liability; *Timm v. R.*, [1965] 1 Ex. C.R. 174, at p. 178, no liability for fall after push; *Howley v. R.*, [1973] F.C. 184, 36 D.L.R. (3d) 261, no liability for stabbing.

escape attempt.[269] The Home Office was held liable because it ought to have foreseen that this was likely to occur if the supervision was careless. On the other hand, if a prisoner is let out on a day pass and injures someone by driving negligently, the prison authorities are not liable if they acted reasonably.[270]

One individual may be occasionally liable for negligence in failing to control the wrongful conduct of another who is mentally disabled, for example. But, if there is no negligence by the caregiver, there can be no liability, as when there was no reason to foresee that a mentally disabled person would attack another shopper at a Costco store.[271] It was a "mere possibility" that the caregiver might have foreseen, which is not enough. There must be "reasonable foresight of a likely risk of harm". Other assorted intervening conduct may produce additional burdens for negligent actors. Where somebody is hurt trying to escape from danger,[272] or during a rescue attempt,[273] the one who created the hazard must pay. If someone steps on the accelerator instead of the brake in an emergency created by another person,[274] or if someone is kicked by a jostled passenger on a streetcar,[275] the original actors bear the cost. In *McKelvin v. London*,[276] the plaintiff recovered for a fractured leg he received as he was helping his horse up after it had tripped over a stone negligently left on the road. Mr. Justice Falconbridge stated that, "if the intervening person's act is innocent, the intervention is no defence". In *Winnipeg Electric Railway Co. v. Canadian Northern Railway Co. and Bartlett*,[277] the deceased either jumped or fell off the back of a streetcar when it was negligently driven in front of an approaching train. The Supreme Court of Canada, before both *Polemis* and *The Wagon Mound (No. 1)*, held that:

> Where there is a duty to take precautions to obviate a given risk the wrongdoer who fails in this duty cannot avoid responsibility for the very consequences it was his duty to provide against by suggesting that the damages are too remote, because the particular manner in which those consequences came to pass was unusual and not reasonably foreseeable.

In *Gilchrist v. A. & R. Farms Ltd.*,[278] the plaintiff, a hired man on the defendant's farm, injured his back when he tried to lift a broken door. The majority of the

---

[269] *Home Office v. Dorset Yacht Co. Ltd.*, [1970] 2 All E.R. 294 (H.L.).

[270] *Toews v. MacKenzie* (1977), 81 D.L.R. (3d) 302 (*per* Hutcheon J.); affd [1980] 4 W.W.R. 108 (B.C.C.A.). See also *Wenden v. Trikha* (1991), 8 C.C.L.T. (2d) 138 (Alta. Q.B.), doctor and hospital not liable for insane driver's negligence. No liability for suicide, though duty exists, *Funk Estate v. Clapp* (1988), 54 D.L.R. (4th) 512 (B.C.C.A.); *cf., Knight Home Office*, [1990] 3 All E.R. 237 (Q.B.D.), prison standard of care less than hospital, no liability.

[271] *Robertson v. A.(A.)* (2000), 2 C.C.L.T. (3d) 120, at p. 130 (B.C.S.C.).

[272] *Sayers v. Harlow Urban District Council*, [1958] 2 All E.R. 342 (C.A.).

[273] See *supra*, Section I.

[274] *Fujiwara v. Osawa*, [1973] 1 W.W.R. 364; affd [1937] 3 W.W.R. 670; affd [1938] S.C.R. 170.

[275] *Reinhart v. Regina City*, [1944] 2 W.W.R. 313; affd [1944] 3 W.W.R. 333 (Sask. C.A.).

[276] (1892), 22 O.R. 70, at p. 77 (C.A.).

[277] (1920), 59 S.C.R. 352, at p. 367 (*per* Duff J.).

[278] [1966] S.C.R. 122, 54 D.L.R. (2d) 707. See also *Saccardo v. Hamilton*, [1971] 2 O.R. 479, at p. 498, plaintiff's effort to work aggravated back condition, originally negligent defendant liable.

Supreme Court of Canada held the defendants liable on the ground, not of reasonable foresight, but because they had *actually foreseen* the danger. The minority judges felt that there should be no duty to take care in the case and voiced their concern about burdening financially oppressed Canadian farmers with the obligation of repairing everything on their premise in order to protect their hired help.

1. FALLS DURING CONVALESCENCE

The original tortfeasor is liable for certain ulterior consequences, as where the plaintiff falls during convalescence. In *Wieland v. Cyril Lord Carpets Ltd.*,[279] the plaintiff, who had been negligently injured on a bus, was unable to see through her bi-focals properly because of a collar she had to wear. When she fell while descending some stairs and aggravated her injury, Mr. Justice Eveleigh held the original tortfeasor responsible for the additional damages. He asserted that one need not foresee the "precise mechanics" or the way the injury occurs. The second fall was "attributable to the original negligence". His Lordship contended that it was "foreseeable that one injury may affect a person's ability to cope with the vicissitudes of life and thereby be a cause of another injury and if foreseeability is required . . . foreseeability of the general nature will . . . suffice". In the Canadian case of *Block v. Martin*,[280] someone who had been negligently injured fell while fishing and fractured his leg. Mr. Justice Mac-Donald of Alberta felt that the fracture would not have occurred unless the earlier injury was unhealed. In other words, it was a "definite, contributing, predisposing case".

On the other hand, in *McKew v. Holland et al.*,[281] the House of Lords purported to fashion a rather incongruous boundary for this type of liability. The plaintiff's leg had been weakened in an accident so that it gave way beneath him occasionally. As he commenced to descend some steep stairs, unassisted and without holding on, his leg collapsed and he began to fall. He pushed his daughter out of the way and tried to jump so as to land in a standing position, but he broke his ankle, a much more serious injury than the original one. Lord Reid agreed that, if the plaintiff had acted reasonably he could recover because the second injury would be "caused" by the first.[282] But, argued His Lordship, if he "acts unreasonably he cannot hold the defender liable for injury caused by his own unreasonable conduct," which was "*novus actus interveniens*". What

---

[279] [1969] 3 All E.R. 1006, at p. 1010. See also *Jacques v. Mathews*, [1961] S.A.S.R. 205; *Fishlock v. Plummer*, [1950] S.A.S.R. 176 (Aus.); *Squires v. Reynolds* (1939), 125 Conn. Supp. 366, 5 A. 2d 877.

[280] [1951] 4 D.L.R. 121, at p. 126 (Alta.). See also *Boss v. Robert Simpson (Eastern) Ltd.* (1968), 2 D.L.R. (3d) 114, at p. 126 (*per* Coffin J.), liability for later falls, not result of plaintiff being "careless or negligent".

[281] [1969] 3 All E.R. 1621 (H.L.). *Cf.*, *Goldhawke v. Harder* (1976), 74 D.L.R. (3d) 721 (B.C.S.C.), liable since reasonable conduct on crutches.

[282] *Ibid.*, at p. 1623.

followed was "caused by his own conduct and not by the defender's fault or the disability caused by it". The court reverted incomprehensibly to the discredited causation language, as in days of old, and asserted that unforeseeability does not come into it. Although no liability is imposed for unforeseeable consequences, "it does not follow that he is liable for every consequence which a reasonable man could foresee". Lord Reid thought that "it is not at all unlikely or unforeseeable that an active man who has suffered such a disability will take some quite unreasonable risk. But if he does, he cannot hold the defender liable for the consequence."

There is also an Ontario case, *Priestley v. Gilbert*,[283] in which the plaintiff's leg was seriously injured as the result of an accident in which the defendant driver was found to have been grossly negligent. At a Christmas party, after becoming quite intoxicated, the plaintiff began dancing, and as his leg was still weak from the injury, he fell and broke it again. In refusing the claim for damages arising from this second break, Osler J. stated:

> . . . there is an onus upon a person who knows or should know of a physical weakness to act reasonably and carefully and to protect himself from harm . . . [T]o get up and dance on this occasion was not a reasonable action in his condition . . . and the principle of *novus actus interveniens* protects the defendant from responsibility for that injury.

This approach is lacking in sophistication. The damage from a fall is brought about by two concurrent causes: (1) the original injury, *and* (2) the conduct of the plaintiff. If injured plaintiffs act negligently and fall, they cannot expect to be treated in the same was as if they were careful. But neither should they always be absolutely precluded from compensation for the extra loss. The proper solution is to apportion liability and to reduce their awards to the extent that their negligence contributed to their additional loss. If they are totally foolhardy, of course, the courts may choose to deny them all compensation, but this should not occur if they are merely negligent. There are, after all, many situations where intervening negligence does not immunize original wrong-doers. Consistency *is* a virtue.

2. INTERVENING NEGLIGENCE

Negligent intervening forces may render defendants liable as well. Once the last wrong-doer doctrine created an immunity in such situations, but this is no longer the case. Contribution and indemnity statutes have empowered the courts to allocate losses between wrong-doers, whereas at common law this was not possible. Moreover, the mystery of causation theory is being gradually dissipated. Thus, when someone negligently allows a cow to escape onto a highway where it is hit by a negligent motorist, the original actor cannot escape liabil-

---

[283] [1972] 3 O.R. 501, at p. 508; affd (1973), 1 O.R. (2d) 365 (C.A.); *Armstrong v. Stewart* (1978), 7 C.C.L.T. 164 (Ont. H.C.).

ity.[284] If a defendant company negligently fails to construct a walkway around one of its construction hoardings, forcing a pedestrian onto the roadway, there to be struck by a car driven by a negligent motorist, the company is responsible.[285] If an intoxicated person is ejected from a beverage room onto a busy highway and is struck by a car driven by a negligent motorist, the hotel must share the blame.[286] It appears, therefore, that motorists as well as others may be required to foresee the negligence of other motorists, such as going through a red light, and take defensive steps to avoid accidents.[287] So too, when a guest negligently knocked over a light pillar at a New Year's eve dance, the hotel was held liable because such a fixture was unsuited for a crowded dance floor, and because it had permitted overcrowding.[288] The court concluded that it was a "normal incident of the hotel's negligence".[289]

Representative of this liberal view is *Goodyear Tire and Rubber Co. of Canada Ltd. v. MacDonald*,[290] where a sign fell off the defendant's truck causing a collision in which the plaintiff's vehicle was damaged. The plaintiff's driver was unable to stop his vehicle in time because the road had been made slippery by a patch of fresh tar 15 feet long. The defendant argued that he should be absolved of responsibility because this amounted to a *novus actus interveniens*. Mr. Justice Cooper, of the Nova Scotia Court of Appeal, rejected this contention and declared that a *novus actus interveniens* is a "conscious act of human origin intervening between a negligent act or omission of a defendant and the occurrence by which the plaintiff suffers damages. . . . There was no such intervening act here. . . ."[291]

There are times when courts have held that intervening negligence is not foreseeable. In *Hollett v. Coca-Cola Ltd.*,[292] the defendant was exonerated for an accident caused when a drunk, unlicensed, 15-year-old broke into its yard, took a truck which had been left unlocked with its keys in the ignition, and negligently injured the plaintiff. Cowan C.J.T.D. felt that it was not foreseeable that

---

[284] *Martin v. McNamara Construction Co.*, [1955] O.R. 523.

[285] *M'Kenna v. Stephens and Hall*, [1923] 2 I.R. 112.

[286] *Menow v. Honsberger and Jordan House Ltd.*, [1970] 1 O.R. 54; affd [1971] 1 O.R. 129; affd [1974] S.C.R. 239. Also if third party hurt, *Hague v. Billings* (1989), 48 C.C.L.T. 192 (Ont. H.C.J.).

[287] *Smith v. Sambuco* (1978), 5 C.C.L.T. 215, at p. 219 (*per* Sullivan C.C.J.). See also *Gellie v. Naylor* (1986), 55 O.R. (2d) 400, at p. 402 (C.A.), pedestrian.

[288] *Fetherston v. Neilson and King Edward Hotel*, [1944] O.R. 470; revd in part, [1944] O.R. 621 (C.A.).

[289] Wright, "Case and Comment" (1944), 22 Can. Bar Rev. 725, at p. 727.

[290] (1974), 51 D.L.R. (3d) 623 (C.A.).

[291] *Ibid.*, at p. 626.

[292] (1980), 11 C.C.L.T. 281. See also *Toews v. MacKenzie*, [1980] 4 W.W.R. 108 (B.C.C.A.); *Spagnolo v. Margesson's Sports Ltd.*, *supra*, n. 97, not foreseeable that stolen car would be negligently driven six days later; perhaps different if accident during flight from theft. See Peck, [1969] Wisc. L. Rev. 909, showing stolen cars involved in collisions 200 times more often than normal accident rate and that 18% of stolen cars are involved in accidents.

the "vehicle would be moved", nor that "the person who moved it would be negligent in its operation at a place and time separated by some distance and by some hours from the taking of the vehicle . . .".

Akin to this is the problem of whether intervening inspection will relieve negligent actors of their responsibility. At one time, the possibility of intermediate inspection excused negligent actors;[293] but more and more modern courts are refusing to grant salvation on the "gospel of redemption" by inspection.[294] In *Grant v. Sun Shipping Co.*,[295] repairers neglected to close the hatch covers on a ship where they had been working. The plaintiff stevedore, believing the hatches to be closed, fell into the hold and was injured. Although shipowners might have discovered the danger by conducting a proper inspection, the repairers were not excused by this fact. Both defendants "directly contributed to cause injury and damage to another" and "the person injured may recover damages from any one of the wrongdoers, or from all of them". In *Ostash v. Sonnenberg*,[296] the Alberta Court of Appeal refused to relieve one negligent defendant from liability on the ground that another defendant could have discovered the defect. Chief Justice Smith, relying on *Grant v. Sun Shipping Co. Ltd.*, stated: "my view is that there were separate acts of negligence on the part of two persons which directly contributed to cause injury and damage to the plaintiffs and that therefore they are entitled to recover from both of them".[297] Where someone actually discovers the danger, but does nothing to minimize it, however, that person may be made exclusively responsible.[298]

These developments, made possible by legislation, should encourage wider compensation, for example, where one defendant is insolvent, uninsured or out of the jurisdiction. Moreover, the dominant participants in these various activities should exert more pressure for safety on their weaker collaborators, rather than employing the ingenuity to find a way of wriggling out of responsibility.

3. INTERVENING INTENTIONAL AND CRIMINAL CONDUCT

Negligent actors may be liable for damage caused by intervening intentional and criminal conduct if their acts created an unreasonable risk of such loss. In

---

[293] *Donoghue v. Stevenson*, [1932] A.C. 562. See *infra*, Chapter 16.

[294] *Ives v. Clare Bros. Ltd.*, [1971] 1 O.R. 417, at pp. 421-22 (*per* Wright J.).

[295] [1948] A.C. 549, [1948] 2 All E.R. 238.

[296] (1968), 67 D.L.R. (2d) 311 (Alta. C.A.).

[297] *Ibid.*, at p. 328.

[298] *Stultz v. Benson Lumber* (1936), 6 Cal. App. 2d 688, 59 P. 2d 100. See also cases of intervention by parents in dangerous conduct by children; *Pittsburgh v. Horton* (1908), 87 Ark. 576, 113 S.W. 647; *Henningsen v. Markowitz* (1928), 230 N.Y. Supp. 313. See *J.B. Hand & Co. v. Best Motor Accessories Ltd.* (1962), 34 D.L.R. (2d) 282 (Nfld. C.A.); *Great Eastern Oil Co. v. Best Motor Accessories Ltd.*, [1962] S.C.R. 118. But *cf., Good-Wear Treaders v. D. & B. Holdings* (1979), 8 C.C.L.T. 87 (N.S.C.A.).

Stansbie v. Troman,[299] a decorator left in charge of a dwelling departed for nearly two hours without locking the door. When some articles were stolen while the decorator was gone, he was made liable because he failed to take care to "guard against the very thing that happened". Similarly, in *Walker v. DeLuxe Cab Ltd.*,[300] the defendant was held liable when the plaintiff's baggage was stolen along with the taxi cab which had been left at the curb with the ignition key in it. The same result followed when certain records were stolen out of an unattended and unlocked van.[301] These cases may not be dealing with remoteness problems at all, but rather standard of care questions.

Where goods are stolen from someone left unconscious on the road as a result of negligent driving, the driver may be liable for the theft and other consequences. These cases are properly treated as remoteness questions, because there has been a determination of liability for negligent conduct, and the extent of that liability is in issue. In *Patten v. Silberschein*,[302] the defendant negligently struck the plaintiff, rending him unconscious. While he was unconscious the plaintiff lost $80 from his pocket. Liability was imposed on the *Polemis* theory, although the court felt that the damage was not in the "natural and probable consequence of the defendant's negligence". In *Duce v. Rourke*,[303] on the other hand, the court disagreed with *Patten v. Silberschein* and exonerated the negligent defendant from liability for some tools stolen from the injured plaintiff's car after he was taken to the hospital. The court stated that *Polemis* did not apply to the theft which was a "consequence of some conscious intervening independent act, for which the defendant was in no way responsible". After an exhaustive review of the cases, Mr. Justice Egbert concluded that the proximate cause of an injury is to be arrived at "not by a consideration of the philosophical or metaphysical aspects of the theory of causation, but . . . selected on practical considerations of justice and expedience".[304] He further proclaimed that "an intervening act or omission *may* relieve the wrongdoer from liability but will not, generally speaking, relieve him of liability if such intervening act or omission is the natural and probable result of the initial wrongful act or omission, and was, or should have bee, foreseen and guarded against by the original wrongdoer". In the United States liability was imposed for some barrels stolen when the driver of a wagon was stunned in an accident.[305] This was considered a "natural and

---

[299] [1948] 2 K.B. 48, [1948] 1 All E.R. 599 (C.A.). *Cf.*, *P. Perl (Exporters) Ltd. v. Camden London Borough Council*, [1983] 3 All E.R. 161 (Q.B.), in circumstances no liability.

[300] [1944] 3 D.L.R. 175 (Ont.); C.A. Wright, "Case and Comment" (1944), 22 Can. Bar Rev. 725.

[301] *Thiele and Wesmar v. Rod Service (Ottawa) Ltd.*, [1964] 2 O.R. 347 (C.A.).

[302] [1936] 3 W.W.R. 169 (B.C.).

[303] (1951), 1 W.W.R. (N.S.) 305, at p. 339 (Alta.). See also *Abbott et al. v. Kasza*, [1975] 3 W.W.R. 163, at p. 175; varied [1976] 9 W.W.R. 20 (Alta. C.A.) (*per* D.C. MacDonald J.), no recovery for tools and personal effects assumed stolen from overturned truck.

[304] *Ibid.*, at pp. 305 and 306.

[305] *Brower v. N.Y. Central Ry.* (1918), 103 Alta. 166 (N.J.).

probably" result of depriving the plaintiff of his driver's protection of the property in the street of a large city.

Although the conflict in the cases is disconcerting, there is no need to get overly excited about these property losses. The amounts involved are seldom large. The interest being protected is not very important. Our prime concern should be to assure that accident victims are properly looked after, that they are taken to hospital if injured. The courts must not inhibit negligent defendants from aiding their victims to get to the hospital by keeping them in the vicinity of the accident to guard against theft of loose property. Perhaps the best that can be done is to let the jury or trial judge decide whether the defendant acted reasonably following the accident in the light of the circumstances of each case.

A case demonstrating the extent to which the principle of *novus actus interveniens* has been restricted is *Canphoto Ltd. v. Aetna Roofing (1965) Ltd.*,[306] where the employees of the defendant company left three propane gas tanks in a public laneway over a weekend. In doing so, they breached a provincial regulation concerning the storage of such tanks with respect to the required distances which they should be kept from buildings and fences. They were also found to be negligent in failing to chain the tanks closed and in an upright position. During the night someone apparently meddled with the tanks, causing a serious fire which damaged the plaintiff's premises.

Wilson J. gave judgment for the plaintiff, rejecting the contention of the defendants that the meddling with the tanks constituted an intervening act which broke the chain of causation. Citing Greer L.J. in *Haynes v. Harwood*,[307] he stated: "If what is relied upon as *novus actus interveniens* is the very kind of thing which is likely to happen if the want of care which is alleged takes place, the principle embodied in the maxim is no defence . . . ." Referring to Lush J., in another case, Mr. Justice Wilson found that the intervention was not a "fresh, independent cause" of the damage and that ". . . the person guilty of the original negligence will still be the effective cause if he ought reasonably to have anticipated such interventions . . .".

A similar case is *Holian v. United Grain Growers*,[308] where some mischievous boys took some fumigant tablets used to kill insects from the defendant's shed and placed them in the plaintiff's car as a "stink bomb" causing illness to the plaintiff. Morse J. imposed liability since this theft and injury was "within the risk created by the negligence of the defendant in leaving the shed unlocked and unattended". The defendant "need not have been able to foresee the precise way in which the plaintiff in this case came to be injured. It is sufficient if the

---

[306] [1971] 3 W.W.R. 116 (Man.). See also *Hewson v. City of Red Deer* (1975), 63 D.L.R. (3d) 168 (Alta.), liability for unknown third person who set tractor in motion; *Stavast v. Ludwar*, [1974] 5 W.W.R. 380 (B.C.).

[307] [1935] 1 K.B. 146 (C.A.).

[308] (1980), 11 C.C.L.T. 184, at p. 191 (Man. Q.B.).

type of accident was reasonably foreseeable." Apparently, intervening vandal-ism may be foreseen.[309]

It has been held that arson is a reasonably foreseeable event, which may render liable a negligent wrongdoer. In *Williams v. New Brunswick*,[310] a prisoner set fire to a lockup causing the death of 21 inmates. An action by the families of some of them succeeded against the city for negligence allowing the prisoner to obtain matches. In a thorough and thoughtful opinion, Chief Justice Stratton indicated how far the law, in this area, had advanced, concluding that the consequence of the negligence may "fairly be regarded as within the ambit of the risk created by that negligence". The result, he felt, was neither "freakish, fantastic or highly improbable but rather was foreseeable and proximate and constituted a substantial factor in the loss that occurred".

Similarly, the courts have decided that rape is something to be foreseen and guarded against. As Mr. Justice Gray stated, in *Q. v. Minto Management*,[311] in holding an apartment manager liable to a tenant who was raped by the janitor: "If the landlord fails to provide proper locks, the likelihood of criminal activity increases." A doctor was found liable for a sexual assault to a vulnerable patient by another patient.[312]

There is American authority to the effect that one person may be liable for the act of murder by another. When someone creates an unreasonable risk of homicide by issuing a large life insurance policy in favour of a person who has no insurable interest in the life of the person insured, liability may ensue if the beneficiary murders the person insured to collect the insurance money.[313] Similarly, a city was held liable when an informer was murdered because he had not been adequately protected by the police.[314] So too, a psychotherapist may in the right circumstances be held liable if one of his patients murders someone,[315]

---

[309] *Ward v. Cannock Chase District Council*, [1985] 3 All E.R. 537 (Ch.). *Cf., King v. Liverpool City Council*, [1986] 3 All E.R. 544 (C.A.).

[310] (1985), 34 C.C.L.T. 299 (N.B.C.A.), at p. 319. The city recovered 50% from the builder also. *Cf., Smith v. Littlewoods Organization Ltd.*, [1987] 1 All E.R. 710 (H.L.), no liability for fire which was started by vandals in cinema under construction and which spread to neighbour's property; see also *P. Perl (Exporters) Ltd. v. Camden London B.C.*, [1983] 3 All E.R. 161.

[311] (1985), 31 C.C.L.T. 158, at p. 172 (Ont. H.C.). *Allison v. Rank City Wall Can. Ltd.* (1984), 45 O.R. (2d) 141 (H.C.) (Smith J.), assault, liability under Occupier's Liability Act, R.S.O. 1980, c. 322 [now R.S.O. 1990, c. O.2].

[312] *H.(M.) v. Bederman* (1995), 27 C.C.L.T. (2d) 152 (Ont. Gen. Div.).

[313] *Liberty National Life Ins. v. Weldon* (1958), 267 Ala. 171, 100 So. 2d 696; *Ramey v. Carolina Life Ins. Co.* (1964), 244 S.C. 16, 135 S.E. 2d 362 *Cf., Galanis v. Mercury International Ins.* (1967), 247 Cal. App. 2d 690, 55 Cal. Reptr. 890, airport insurance vendor not liable for suicide-murder.

[314] *Schuster v. City of New York* (1958), 5 N.Y. 2d 75, 180 N.Y. Supp. 2d 265, 154 N.E. 2d 534.

[315] *Tarasoff v. Regents of U.C.* (1976), 131 Cal. Reptr. 14; Stone, "The Tarasoff Decision: Suing Psychotherapists to Safeguard Society" (1976), 90 Harv. L. Rev. 358, (1978), 31 Stan. L Rev. 165; Fleming and Maximov, "The Patient or His Victim: The Therapist's Dilemma" (1974), 62 Calif. L. Rev. 1025. But no liability for unforeseeable stabbing, *Molnar v. Coates* (1989), 49 C.C.L.T. 134 (S.C.); affd (1991), 5 C.C.L.T. (2d) 236 (B.C. C.A.).

or if a patient commits suicide as a result of his negligence, but not otherwise.[316] *Soldier of Fortune Magazine* has been held liable for a shooting that was arranged through an advertisement offering a "gun for hire".[317] In the past, criminal conduct was rarely anticipated, but nowadays, it has become more commonplace, resulting in broader liability.

4. INTERVENING CONDUCT THAT EXONERATES

Not all intervening intentional, criminal or negligent conduct produces liability; the decision seems to turn primarily on the degree of risk of the wrongful act. In *Oke v. Weide Transport Ltd.*,[318] for example, the defendant knocked over a metal post on a strip of gravel between two highway lanes and left it bent over. The deceased, who was improperly using the strip for passing, was killed when the post came up through the floor boards of his car and impaled him. The majority of the Manitoba Court of Appeal dismissed the action against the defendant on the ground that he could not anticipate that someone would try to pass a car at a point where it was wrong to do so. This is a strange result, considering that the defendant himself had earlier been in the very same position. The dissent of Mr. Justice Freedman is to be preferred. According to him, one need not foresee the precise manner in which an accident occurs. The post was a "source of danger to a motorist" and could be cause of an accident of some kind, including one where the highway traffic law is violated, a not infrequent occurrence.

In *Philco Radio and Television Corp. v. Spurling Ltd.*,[319] some highly in-flammable celluloid film scrap, carelessly left on the premises of a factory, exploded after a typist carelessly approached it with a cigarette. Liability was imposed, but the court warned that the result would have been otherwise if the evidence had shown that the material was deliberately ignited "for the purpose of seeing what kind of fire it would make", unless done so by a child or pyromaniac known to be in the neighbourhood.

Thus, if an arsonist or murderer had entered the house left unattended by the decorator in *Stansbie v. Troman* and had burned or killed, no liability would have been imposed, because such consequences are just too uncommon and too disproportionate to the negligence of the defendant. It might be otherwise, however, if a distinct risk of fire or murder existed, as where an arsonist or a murderer was known to be in the vicinity.[320]

---

[316] *Haines v. Bellissimo* (1977), 82 D.L.R. (3d) 215 (Ont.), no liability; *Bellah v. Greenson* (1978), 146 Cal. Reptr. 535, no liability.

[317] See *Braun v. Soldier of Fortune Magazine* (1992), 968 F. 2d 1110; cert. denied (1993), 113 S.Ct. 1028. *Cf., Eimann v. Soldier of Fortune Magazine* (1989), 880 F. 2d 830; cert. denied (1990), 493 U.S. 1024, no liability. The magazine no longer takes such ads.

[318] (1963), 41 D.L.R. (2d) 53 (Man. C.A.).

[319] [1949] 2 All E.R. 882 (C.A.).

[320] *Cf., Hines v. Garrett* (1921), 131 Va. 125, 180 S.E. 690, railway liable for rape of woman by hoboes after railway let her off in their vicinity. See also *Connie Francis v. Howard Johnson* (N.J.), 1976, hotel held liable for rape, $2,500,000 damages.

In *Bradford v. Kanellos*,[321] a flash fire was negligently caused in a restaurant. An employee activated a fire extinguisher system which released some gas creating a hissing sound. A patron shouted that gas was escaping and that there was danger of an explosion. In the stampede that followed, the plaintiff was injured, even though the fire was quickly extinguished. The original wrong-doer was relieved of responsibility by the majority of the Supreme Court of Canada (Martland J., Judson and Ritchie JJ. concurring) on the ground that the injury resulted from a hysterical conduct of the patron" and that it was not a "consequence fairly to be regarded as within the risk created by the respondent's negligence in permitting an undue quantity of grease to accumulate on the grill".[322]

The dissenting viewpoint is more in harmony with the decisions and is to be preferred. Mr. Justice Spence (Laskin J. concurring) asserted:

> I am not of the opinion that the persons who shouted the warning of what they were certain was an impending explosion were negligent. I am, on the other hand, of the opinion that they acted in a very human and usual way and that their actions . . . were utterly foreseeable and were a part of the natural consequences of events leading inevitably to the plaintiff's injury . . . . Even if the actions of those who called out "gas" and "it is going to explode" were negligent . . . then I am of the opinion that the plaintiffs would still have a right of action against the defendants . . . .

When people unreasonably refuse medical care their tort damages will be reduced because of their failure to mitigate their loss, but they will not be denied compensation.[323] A similar result could be achieved by applying the Negligence Act as well.

These are difficult cases to fathom. There is little precision in the decisions, which seem to fall on either side of the line, depending on how expectable or unexpectable the courts feel the consequences to be.

5. INTERVENING MEDICAL ERROR

Errors in medical treatment pose some fascinating problems. *Mercer v. Gray*[324] has been the leading Canadian case for years. A child's broken leg became worse when her doctors mistakenly failed to cut her cast soon enough after a cyanosed condition became evident. At the trial, the damages suffered as a result

---

[321] [1971] 2 O.R. 393; affd (1973), 40 D.L.R. (3d) 576. See also *Wright v. McCrae*, [1965] 1 O.R. 300 (C.A.). No liability when stranger started defendant's bulldozer and damaged house; *Ratich v. Hourston* (1986), 35 C.C.L.T. 267 (B.C.S.C.), unforeseeable person could not escape fire.

[322] *Ibid.*, at pp. 578 and 582, D.L.R. See also *Schlink v. Blackburn* (1993), 18 C.C.L.T. (2d) 173 (B.C.C.A.), "panic" and reckless.

[323] *Ippolito v. Janiak* (1981), 18 C.C.L.T. 39 (Ont. C.A.); *Brain v. Mador* (1985), 32 C.C.L.T. 157 (Ont. C.A.); leave to appeal to S.C.C. refused 13 O.A.C. 79n; *Gray v. Gill* (1993), 18 C.C.L.T. (2d) 120, at p. 133 (B.C.S.C.) (*per* Selbie J.); but *cf.*, where reasonable refusal to mitigate, *Engel v. Kam-Ppelle Holdings Ltd.* (1993), 15 C.C.L.T. (2d) 245 (S.C.C.).

[324] [1941] O.R. 127, [1941] 3 D.L.R. 564 (C.A.). See also *Fillion v. Rystau* (1966), 56 W.W.R. 425 (Man.); *David v. Toronto Transit Commn.* (1977), 77 D.L.R. (3d) 717 (Ont.) (*per* Parker J.).

of the lack of skill in treatment were not taken into account. The Ontario Court of Appeal sent the case back for a new trial on the ground that, "if reasonable care is used to employ a competent physician or surgeon to treat personal injuries wrongfully inflicted, the results of the treatment, even though by an error of treatment the treatment is unsuccessful, will be a proper head of damages". Mr. Justice McTague indicated, however, that, if the treatment "is so negligent as to be actionable", it would be *"novus actus interveniens* and the plaintiff would have his remedy against the physician or surgeon".[325] Such a principle distinguishes between innocent errors of judgment and actionable mistakes.

It has been made clear that the onus rests on defendants to prove that the intervening medical error was a negligent one, if they are to escape liability for it. In *Papp v. Leclerc*[326] Lacourcière J.A. stated:

> Every tortfeasor causing injury to a person placing him in the position of seeking medical or hospital help, must assume the inherent risks of complications, *bona fide* medical error or misadventure, and they are reasonable and not too remote. . . . It is for the defendant to prove that some new act rendering another person liable has broken the chain of causation.[327]

A decision accepting this dichotomy and imposing liability on an original wrongdoer for the consequences of improper medical treatment is *Watson v. Grant*,[328] where two unnecessary operations were performed on an injured plaintiff. In awarding damages for the extra loss, Mr. Justice Aikens explained:

> I commence with the proposition that if A. injures B., it is reasonably foreseeable that B. will seek advice and treatment for his injuries. It seems to me equally obvious that it is foreseeable that B. will seek advice and treatment from a person who is qualified and authorized to diagnose and treat injuries, namely a qualified doctor. The reasonable man, in my opinion, would be aware that a doctor may err in diagnosis or in treatment, or both, without the patient, who has done all he can reasonably be expected to do in going to a qualified person for help, having any reason to suppose he is being badly advised or treated. Returning to my example, if A. injures B. thereby putting B. in the position where he has to have medical help, there is inherent risk that B. may suffer further loss or injury because of *bona fide* error on the part of the doctor. I may, I think, properly assume that the great majority of people who are injured or are ill are well aware that the doctor chosen may make some mistake or diagnosis or treatment, but are driven by necessity to accept the risk. It seems to me plain that it is reasonably foreseeable that a person injured to the extent that medical help is required, is driven to accept the risk of medical error.
>
> In my opinion, it is reasonable that an injured person who seeks medical help may, not will, suffer further loss or damage because of error in medical treatment.
>
> I wish to make it clear that I am not expressing an opinion on the position as to remoteness or foreseeability if it had been established that Dr. Jain had been negligent in respect of the last two operations. In conclusion on this branch of this case, I hold that the defendants are liable in respect to the last two operations.

---

[325] *Ibid.*, at p. 131.
[326] (1977), 77 D.L.R. (3d) 536 (Ont. C.A.).
[327] *Ibid.*, at p. 539.
[328] (1970), 72 W.W.R. 665, at p. 272 (B.C.).

A similar case is *Thompson v. Toorenburgh*,[329] where a woman with a minor heart condition received injuries in an accident which resulted from the defendant's negligence. She was treated for lacerations at the hospital then released. She returned to the hospital later the same evening and died of a pulmonary edema precipitated by the accident. It was clear from the evidence that proper medical treatment at the time of the readmission could have saved her life. Kirke Smith J. held that the defendant was liable for the death: "That there was such error [of medical treatment] here is not open to question: but I think . . . there was no break, in the circumstances of this case, in the chain of causation." There was no specific finding, however, indicating whether medical error was a negligent or a non-negligent one.[330]

Although these cases are generally decided satisfactorily, it is confusing to make liability for the medical error turn on whether or not there is actionable negligence. It is true that if doctors are in fact negligent, there will rarely be any difficulty in collecting from them or their insurers as there is with impecunious intervening actors. Many tactical difficulties arise in medical malpractice actions, though, such as problems of evidence, lack of a jury, and a standard of care that is hardly stringent. It seems rather harsh to require injured plaintiffs to undertake two actions to recover their full damages, when the original defendants set the whole thing in motion. It would be preferable, except in the extreme cases, to hold liable the initial defendants who could then sue the negligent physicians for contribution. The wrong-doer instead of the innocent injured persons would thus bear the procedural burdens.

Such is the law in the United States. In *Thompson v. Fox* it was put as follows:

> Doctors, being human, are apt occasionally to lapse from prescribed standards, and the likelihood of carelessness, lack of judgment or of skill, on the part of one employed to effect a cure for a condition caused by another's act, is therefore considered in law as an incident of the original injury, and, if the injured party has used ordinary care in the selection of a physician or surgeon, any additional harm resulting from the latter's mistake or negligence is considered as one of the elements of the damages for which the original wrongdoer is liable.[331]

The Canadian law is moving in the same sensible direction. In *Kolesar v. Jeffries*,[332] Mr. Justice Haines indicated that an original defendant may be responsible for the later negligence of a doctor or hospital which aggravates a plaintiff's injuries "unless it is completely outside the range of normal experi-

---

[329] (1972), 29 D.L.R. (3d) 608 (B.C.); affd (1975), 50 D.L.R. (3d) 717.

[330] See also *Winteringham v. Rae*, [1966] 1 O.R. 727, reaction to an injection held compensable, no allegation of malpractice, case treated as one of abnormal susceptibility, an "exception" to *The Wagon Mound (No. 1)*. And see also *Robinson v. Post Office*, [1974] 1 W.L.R. 1176 (C.A.), encephalitis reaction compensable.

[331] (1937), 192 Alt. 107, at p. 108 (Pa.).

[332] (1974), 9 O.R. (2d) 41; varied (1976), 12 O.R. (2d) 142; affd on other grounds, without mentioning this point (1977), 77 D.L.R. (3d) 161 (S.C.C.). *Cf.*, *David v. Toronto Transit Commn.*, *supra*, n. 324.

ence". This test implies that certain acts of medical malpractice might well be within the realm of reasonable foresight and, therefore, compensable, whereas other, presumably gross and shocking acts of malpractice, would be beyond the scope of foresight and not compensable.

A more far-reaching decision is *Price v. Milawski*[333] where Arnup J.A. held that one negligent doctor could be liable for the additional loss caused by another doctor's negligence. He explained:

> . . . a person doing a negligent act may, in circumstances lending themselves to that conclusion, be held liable for future damage arising in part from the subsequent negligent act of another, and in part from his own negligence, where such subsequent negligence and consequent damage were reasonably foreseeable as a possible result of his own negligence.
>
> It was reasonably foreseeable by Dr. Murray that once the information generated by his negligent error got into the hospital records, other doctors subsequently treating the plaintiff might well rely on the accuracy of that information, *i.e.*, that the X-ray showed no fracture of the ankle. It was also foreseeable that some doctor might do so without checking, even though to do so in the circumstances might itself be a negligent act. The history is always one factor in a subsequent diagnosis and the consequent treatment. Such a possibility was not a risk which a reasonable man (in the position of Dr. Murray) would brush aside as far-fetched — see *"Wagon Mound" (No. 2)*.
>
> The later negligence of Dr. Carbin compounded the effects of the earlier negligence of Dr. Murray. It did not put a halt to the consequences of the fist act and attract liability for all damage from that point forward. In my view the trial Judge was correct in holding that each of the appellants was liable to the plaintiff and that it was not possible to try to apportion the extent to which each was responsible for the plaintiff's subsequent operation and his permanent disability.[334]

This case appears to be in conflict with *Mercer v. Gray*, but Mr. Justice Arnup referred to it without adverse comment and purported to follow it. There is a real likelihood, however, that future courts will consider *Mercer v. Gray* to have been overruled and, consequently, will permit recovery in all of these cases. Such a solution would be more in accord with the general principles of remoteness as well as with the American rule. It would still allow contribution in appropriate cases, but would ensure that plaintiffs are initially covered, whether doctors are negligent or not. Following that, steps could be taken by wrongdoers to get reimbursement from doctors without impeding plaintiffs' recovery.

6. SUICIDE

A negligent wrong-doer may be held liable for the death of the victim if that victim commits suicide. Where suicidal tendencies are absent,[335] hospitals will

---

[333] (1977), 82 D.L.R. (3d) 130 (Ont. C.A.). See also *Powell v. Guttman (No. 2)* (1978), 6 C.C.L.T. 183 (Man. C.A.) (*per* O'Sullivan J.A.); *Katzman v. Yaeck* (1982), 37 O.R. (2d) 500 (C.A.).

[334] *Ibid.*, at p. 141. See also *Cabral v. Gupta* (1992), 13 C.C.L.T. (2d) 323 (Man. C.A.), doctor failed to find metal particle in eye leading to blindness, no deduction from defendant's liability.

[335] *Stadel v. Albertson*, [1954] 2 D.L.R. 328 (Sask. C.A.). See also *University Hospital Bd. v. Lepine*, [1966] S.C.R. 561, jump out of window by epileptic not fatal, no liability. See Roth, "Note" (1967), 5 Osgoode Hall L.J. 105.

not be held liable, but, if these tendencies are foreseeable, liability may be imposed.[336] Psychologists will be relieved from liability for patient's suicides if they are not negligent in preventing them,[337] but they will be held responsible if they are. Prisons may also be liable in suicide cases.[338]

Whether a tortfeasor who injures someone will be liable to the victim if the victim later commits suicide is an unsettled question. In *Pigney v. Pointer Transport Services Ltd.*,[339] an accident victim suffering from anxiety neurosis hanged himself. He was not insane; he knew what he was doing and that it was wrong. Relying on *Polemis*, the court imposed liability because the death was "directly traceable" to the physical injury.[340] In its reasons, however, the court found that it was "clearly a matter which could not reasonably have been foreseen".[341] This latter statement may embarrass future judges in the new era of foresight, but there is every reason to believe that suicide will remain a consequence for which a tortfeasor may be held.

In another case, *Cotic v. Gray*,[342] a jury verdict imposing liability on a wrong-doer when his victim committed suicide was upheld. The deceased hanged himself, while psychotic, because of grief he suffered due to being involved in an accident, caused by the negligence of the defendant, in which he was injured and two people were killed. He blamed himself for the deaths, though he was not responsible for them. In a learned decision Lacourcière J.A. concluded that the deceased:

> by reason of history of emotional problems, was exceptionally vulnerable to a psychotic reaction following a motor vehicle accident. Because of the so-called "egg-shell" or "thin skull" principle, the appellant has to take his victim as he finds him, a psychologically vulnerable individual. It must also be assumed that the jury were satisfied, on the preponderance of the evidence, that the accident, while not necessarily the sole cause, was a direct and substantial cause without which the suicide would not likely have happened.[343]

His Lordship felt that it was "unnecessary to decide . . . whether the deceased's suicide was foreseeable in the general sense as a consequence 'of a kind which human experience indicates may result from an injury' . . . or whether the suicide was unforeseeable but treated as an exception to the foreseeability requirement". Madam Justice Wilson agreed, but based her reasons squarely on

---

[336] *Villemure v. L'Hôpital Notre-Dame* (1972), 31 D.L.R. (3d) 454.

[337] *Haines v. Bellissimo* (1977), 82 D.L.R. (3d) 215.

[338] *Reeves v. Commissioner of Police of the Metropolis,* [1999] 3 All E.R. 897 (H.L.), police liable when person in custody hung self with shirt, deceased 50 per cent responsible. *Funk Estate v. Clapp* (1988), 54 D.L.R. (4th) 512 (B.C.C.A.), duty but no liability; *Knight v. Home Office,* [1990] 3 All E.R. 237 (Q.B.D.), no liability in circumstances.

[339] [1957] 1 W.L.R. 1121, [1957] 2 All E.R. 807.

[340] *Ibid.,* at p. 810, All E.R.

[341] *Ibid.,* at p. 809.

[342] (1981), 17 C.C.L.T. 138; affd (1984), 26 C.C.L.T. 163 (S.C.C.), issue treated as a factual one, decided by the jury.

[343] *Ibid.,* at p. 175.

the thin-skull rule to the effect that "a wrongdoer rather than the victim, bears the damage suffered by those falling short of the norm", and she felt, foreseeability had little to do with this.

Another suicide decision is *Swami v. Lo (No. 3)*,[344] where the plaintiff's husband took his own life after being injured by the negligence of the defendant. The injury had caused severe pain which led to a state of depression, resulting in the suicide. The deceased was sane when he took his life. Gould J. denied liability. Refusing to follow *Pigney v. Pointers* which was decided before *The Wagon Mound (No. 1)*, His Lordship said that the suicide "was not an injury of the type nor of the extent which could have been foreseen". He indicated, though, that if there had been an "injury to the head, which then led to mental disturbance, that culminated in suicide, the plaintiff's argument may be been more persuasive". Gould J. concluded that the death:

> resulted from something which was not a reasonably foreseeable consequence of the motor vehicle accident, but rather resulted from suicide, which may be characterized as a *novus actus interveniens*. Death was brought about by an act of the plaintiff himself, for which the defendant cannot be held liable.[345]

On different facts, courts have held that suicide was foreseeable and, hence, compensable. In *Hayes Estate and Hayes v. Green and Green*,[346] for example, Justice Maurice imposed liability for suicide, explaining:

> Because human beings are by nature very fragile creatures, it is foreseeable . . . that anything might happen to a person injured in an accident.

A different approach was taken by Galligan J. in *Robson v. Ashworth*,[347] who denied compensation to the family of a medical patient who committed suicide while sane, explaining that it is a "well-recognized rule of public policy that survivors of a person who commits suicide are not entitled to benefit from the suicide". He indicated that it would be different if the person committed suicide while insane as in *Cotic v. Gray*.

These cases are reflective of an emerging view, like the one the Americans have adopted, which is a compromise position whereby liability is imposed if suicides occur while the victims are insane, but not if sane persons wilfully

---

[344] (1979), 11 C.C.L.T. 210 (B.C.). See also *Richters v. Motor Tyre*, [1972] Q.L.R. 9.

[345] *Ibid.*, at p. 216. See also *Wright Estate v. Davidson* (1992), 88 D.L.R. (4th) 698, at p. 705 (B.C.C.A.), "Not Reasonably Foreseeable".

[346] (1983), 30 Sask. R. 166, at p. 168 (Q.B.); *cf.*, *Wright Estate v. Davidson* (1989), 49 C.C.L.T. 116, at p. 132 reversed by B.C.C.A., *supra*, n. 345. Leave to appeal to S.C.C. dismissed Dec. 10, 1992, 92 B.S.C.C., p. 2730, McKenzie J. quoting *Hayes Estate v. Green*.

[347] (1985), 33 C.C.L.T. 229, at p. 250 (Ont. H.C.) affd (1987), 40 C.C.L.T. 164 (Ont. C.A.); *Funk v. Clapp* (1983), 12 D.L.R. (4th) 62 (B.C.S.C.); *Hyde v. Thameside Area Health Authority, The Times*, April 16, 1981 (Lord Denning, M.R.).

destroy themselves.[348] That is certainly a tenable view. Another related solution is to hold that if the deceased understood what they were doing, but failed to appreciate that it was wrong, the original tortfeasors should be held,[349] but not otherwise. A third way to treat these suicide cases is to handle them all in the same way. We might recognize that accident victims are rendered susceptible to depression, one potential result of which is suicide. Rarely does one take one's own life except where one's mental stability is affected. Therefore, despite its rarity, suicide might be held not too remote, foreseeable, if you will, and negligent defendants might be required to compensate for it whether the victims are insane or not. Evidence of this would be required, of course.

Perhaps another approach that might be considered is that of contributory fault. There is obviously much sympathy for the suicide victims in these cases. There is also, however, reason to be concerned for the wrongdoers, who may be burdened with the responsibility for the deaths of their victims, even though it is by their own hands. The wording of our Negligence Act[350] may be broad enough to permit a reduced recovery to the families of suicide victims, on the basis that their contributory "fault" contributed to the damages suffered. This would give the courts a flexible tool for handling these cases in future. Where the victims were so insane that they could not be held responsible for the suicide, the families may recover in full. Where the victims are lucid, and commit suicide without sufficient cause, the courts may attribute part, or even all, of the loss to what they might hold to be the contributory fault of the victims. If this method were adopted, a wider range of alternatives would be placed in the hands of the courts to assist them to resolve these very complex issues with more sensitivity than at the present time.[351]

---

[348] *Daniels v. New York, N.H. & H.R. Co.* (1903), 183 Mass. 393, 67 N.E. 424, insane; *McMahon v. New York* (1955), 141 N.Y.S. 2d 190, sane.

[349] *Haber v. Walker*, [1963] V.R. 339; *Murdoch v. British Israel Federation*, [1942] N.Z.L.R. 600.

[350] R.S.O. 1990, c. N.1, s. 3.

[351] Some support is found for this approach in the *dictum* of Galligan J. in *Robson v. Ashworth*, *supra*, n. 338, no liability, but if so, only 10% by defendant, 90% by deceased. See also *Reeves*, *supra*, n. 338, where House of Lords split liability for suicide between police and deceased.

Chapter 11

Negligent Infliction of
Psychiatric Damage

Although foreseeability is still the major criterion for determining the limits of
tort responsibility, the courts have not extended it into all areas. Certain interests
are still imperfectly protected, even though damage to them can be expected.
The reason for this time lag is that bodily security must be assured before courts
can turn their attention to more ephemeral and less immediate interests. Initially,
therefore, the judicial reaction was to completely deny any compensation for
mental suffering, for damage to economic interests, or for negligent misstatements. The notion of duty was frequently utilized to explain these immunities,
but on occasion remoteness and causation language were also invoked. These
anachronisms began to collapse under the onslaught of the "neighbour principle"
of *Donoghue v. Stevenson*. The courts did not, however, sweep away all vestiges
of their earlier reticence. Instead, they chipped away at these blanket immunities, moving from the duty rationale, which lends itself to a complete denial of
liability, over to remoteness and proximate cause reasoning, which can be
controlled more sensitively. Foreseeability has played an important role in all
this, but it has not solved everything. Doubts have been expressed about its
ability to solve all the problems, and additional tests (like proximity) have been
resurrected. There are still difficult value choices to be made in this area.

In this chapter, which continues the discussion of element five, we shall
examine the problem of negligent infliction of psychiatric damage. In the
following chapter we shall consider injuries to economic interests including
liability for negligent misstatements.

A. Introduction

Tort law was slow to grant protection to the interest in mental tranquillity. The
phrase "nervous shock",[1] which was used to describe this type of damage, is no

---

[1] See Mullany and Handford, *Tort Liability for Psychiatric Damage: The Law of "Nervous Shock"*
(London: Sweet & Maxwell, 1993), a superb treatment of the subject. This section will not

longer in favour; it is now preferable to refer to this kind of loss as "psychiatric damage", which includes "all relevant forms of mental illness, neurosis and personality change".[2] The law of assault and defamation protected the mind to a degree but these were isolated and special instances. In general, it was contended in the past that, "Mental pain or anxiety the law cannot value, and does not pretend to redress, when the unlawful act complained of causes that alone."[3] A similar view was expressed by the Privy Council in *Victorian Railway Commissioners v. Coultas,*[4] where a woman fainted and suffered severe "nervous shock" when she was almost hit by a train at a railway crossing. Sir Richard Couch asserted that, "Damages arising from mere sudden terror unaccompanied by any actual physical injury, but occasioning a nervous or mental shock, cannot under such circumstances, . . . be considered a consequence which, in the ordinary course of things, would flow from the negligence. . . ."[5]

1. POLICY

His Lordship offered two policy reasons for this decision. Firstly, he contended that, "it would be extending the liability for negligence much beyond what that liability has hitherto been held to be". He feared that, "in every case where an accident caused by negligence had given a person a serious nervous shock, there might be a claim for damages on account of mental injury". This is, of course, the "floodgates" argument that is dredged up to counteract any new claim that cries out for protection. This concern was recently repeated by Chief Justice McEachen who worried about "a flood of both valid and invalid claims," that needed to instill a "healthy measure of judicial scepticism if there is to be a fair adjudication".[6] In response, one can only assert that "it is the business of the courts to make precedent where a wrong calls for redress, even if lawsuits must be multiplied".[7]

The second policy rationale for denying recovery was the "difficulty which now often exists in cases of alleged physical injuries of determining whether they were caused by the negligent act would be greatly increased and a wide field opened for imaginary claims".[8] This argument not only heaps distrust on the capacity of the legal system to discover the truth, but it refuses "redress in meritorious cases" in order to "prevent the possible success of unrighteous or

---

address intentional infliction of mental suffering, which is dealt with in Chapter 2, E, *supra*.

[2]   See *Attia v. British Gas*, [1987] 3 All E.R. 455, at p. 462 (C.A.) (*per* Bingham L.J.), leave to appeal refused, [1988] 1 All E.R. xvi; see also *Alcock v. Chief Constable of S. Yorkshire Police*, [1991] 3 W.L.R. 1057 (H.L.), where this phrase is employed frequently.

[3]   Lord Wensleydale in *Lynch v. Knight* (1861), 9 H.L. Cas. 577, at p. 598, 11 E.R. 854.

[4]   (1888), 13 App. Cas. 222. See also *Penman v. Winnipeg Electric Ry.*, [1925] 1 D.L.R. 497 (Man.).

[5]   *Ibid.*, at p. 225.

[6]   *Devji v. Burnaby (District)* (1999), 47 C.C.L.T. (2d) 111, at p. 127 (B.C.C.A.).

[7]   *Prosser and Keeton on the Law of Torts*, 5th ed. (1984), p. 360.

[8]   *Victorian Railway Commrs., supra*, n. 4, at p. 226.

groundless actions".[9] If our courts are "so naive . . . so gullible, . . . so devoid of worldly knowledge, . . . so childlike in their approach to realities that they can be deceived and hoodwinked by claims that have no factual, medical or legalistic basis . . . then all our proud boasts of the worthiness of our judicial system are empty and vapid indeed".[10] The remedy for fraud is to be found in a vigorous search for the truth, not in the abdication of judicial responsibility.

There are other policy considerations to be assessed before recognizing tort liability for psychiatric damage. The law should not provide compensation for trivial matters such as a mere fright. Instead, it should foster the growth of tough hides not easily pierced by emotional responses.[11] Moreover, human activity should not be unduly burdened by being required to pay for all the unpleasant feelings engendered by its negligent activities in addition to physical injuries.[12] Psychiatric damage cases create administrative problems for judges who will be forced to measure the immeasurable and distinguish what may be the indistinguishable. But such matters are the staple diet of the law. Mr. Justice McQuarrie has responded to this as follows: "The ease with which in the one case the damages are capable of being ascertained, and the difficulty which in the other case may frequently arise, cannot be made the test of liability."[13] One can readily understand the desire of the judiciary to conserve energy and to avoid embarrassment, but this attitude could not be permitted to retard forever the development of protection for a deserving claim.[14]

2. IMPACT RULE

For a time, however, the courts awarded damages for nervous shock only where there was also some physical injury inflicted or at least where there was an "impact".[15] In other words, recovery was parasitic. Damages were awarded for mental suffering when someone was thrown against a seat in a streetcar,[16] and

---

9   Kennedy L.J. in *Dulieu v. White & Sons*, [1901] 2 K.B. 669, at p. 681.
10 Musmanno J. dissenting in *Bosley v. Andrews* (1958), 393 Pa. 161, 142 A. 2d 263, overruled in *Neiderman v. Brodsky* (1970), 436 Pa. 401, 261 A. 2d 84.
11 Perhaps this policy was pressed too far when an Australian court, in *Chester v. Waverley Municipal Council* (1939), 62 C.L.R. 1, denied recovery to a mother who suffered "nervous shock" on seeing the drowned body of her child. This decision has been weakened, if not overruled, in *Mount Isa Mines Ltd. v. Pusey* (1971), 45 A.L.J.R. 88.
12 Fleming, *The Law of Torts*, 9th ed. (1998), p. 173.
13 *Horne v. New Glasgow*, [1954] 1 D.L.R. 832, at p. 844 (N.S.), noted by Lederman (1954), 32 Can. Bar Rev. 325. See also *McLoughlin v. O'Brian*, [1982] 2 All E.R. 298, at p. 303 (H.L.), for a good policy discussion.
14 Mullany, "Fear For the Future: Liability for Infliction of Psychiatric Disorder," in Mullany (ed.), *Torts in the Nineties* (New Zealand: The Law Book Company, 1997).
15 See, generally, on mental repercussions of physical injuries, Chapter 10, Section H.3, *supra*. See also Linden, "Down with Foreseeability: Of Thin Skulls and Rescuers" (1969), 47 Can. Bar Rev. 545.
16 *Toronto Railway Co. v. Toms* (1911), 44 S.C.R. 268.

when someone's throat was scratched by some broken glass found in bread.[17] In *Pollard v. Makarchuk*,[18] a mother, who was slightly injured in a car accident, won damages for shock suffered when she saw her daughter, who had been injured in the same accident, lying on the pavement and believed her to be dead. In fact, her daughter had been only slightly injured. The court relied on directness theory, but there is little doubt that the decision is equally defensible on foresight reasoning.

The impact requirement was eventually debased to such an extent that it was found to have occurred when dust got in someone's eye,[19] when smoke was inhaled,[20] and incredibly, when a horse at a circus "evacuated his bowels" on someone.[21] It soon became apparent that this rule could not survive.

3. BREAKTHROUGH AND TEMPORARY BOUNDARIES

The initial breakthrough was *Dulieu v. White & Sons*[22] where, despite the absence of any impact, damages were awarded for "nervous shock". The plaintiff, who was pregnant, was standing behind the bar in her husband's public house when the defendant's horse-van was negligently driven into the room. She suffered a severe shock which led to illness and a miscarriage. Mr. Justice Kennedy, in finally opening the door to nervous shock claims, was careful not to open it too far. He suggested that "the shock, where it operates through the mind, must be a shock which arises from a reasonable fear of immediate personal injury to oneself".[23] Someone who suffers shock from fear of imminent injury to her- or himself is still allowed to succeed, as where a plaintiff is shocked on discovering a mouse in a bag of flour,[24] or metal and blue mold in bread.[25] It is still the case that, where physical injury is foreseen by the conduct of the defendant, it is not necessary to foresee psychiatric damage, so if psychiatric damage results to one who is physically in foreseeable danger that will suffice, for that person is a "primary victim". It is different for "secondary victims", who must establish foresight of psychiatric damage in order to collect.[26]

Having smashed the impact theory, therefore, the courts began to search for other ways to limit "nervous shock" liability to prevent it from getting out of control. The Kennedy limitation was only the first of several guidelines, which have been described as "empirical" and "pragmatical" rather than "logical

---

[17] *Negro v. Pietro's Bread Co.*, [1933] O.R. 112 (C.A.).

[18] (1958), 16 D.L.R. (2d) 225, at p. 230 (Alta.).

[19] *Porter v. Delaware L. & W.R. Co.* (1906), 63 Atl. 860 (N.J.).

[20] *Morton v. Stack* (1930), 170 N.E. 869 (Ohio).

[21] *Christie Bros. Circus v. Turnage* (1928), 144 S.E. 680 (Ga.).

[22] [1901] 2 K.B. 669. See also *Austin v. Mascarin*, [1942] O.R. 165.

[23] *Ibid.*, at p. 681.

[24] *Curll v. Robin Hood Multifoods Ltd.* (1974), 56 D.L.R. (3d) 129 (N.S.) (*per* Cowan C.J.T.D.).

[25] *Taylor v. Weston Bakeries* (1976), 1 C.C.L.T. 158 (Sask. D.C.).

[26] *Page v. Smith*, [1995] 2 All E.R. 736, at p. 761 (H.L.) (*per* Lord Lloyd).

application[s] of principles".[27] It was soon overthrown by *Hambrook v. Stokes Brothers*,[28] where a runaway truck injured a child and inflicted such a shock on the mother that she became ill and eventually died. The mother had not actually witnessed the accident itself, but she had rushed in a panic to the scene when she saw the unattended truck crash into a wall near her, after it came around the corner from the street where she had earlier left her children. The Kennedy limitation was jettisoned because it would permit recovery for a mother, "timid and lacking in the motherly instinct", who feared only for herself, while withholding damages from another mother situated beside her, "courageous and devoted to her child", who worried only about her child and not at all for herself. Lord Justice Bankes fashioned another formula that would permit the mother to win compensation, if she "either saw or realized by her own unaided senses, and not from something which someone told her, and . . . the shock was due to a reasonable fear of immediate personal injury either to herself or to her children". A similar Canadian case was *Horne v. New Glasgow*,[29] where a runaway truck crashed into the plaintiff's living room. Although she suffered no injury by impact, the plaintiff complained of "nervous shock". Mr. Justice MacQuarrie granted recovery on the ground that her mental suffering flowed from a combination of a belief that her home was destroyed and fear for her parents and her own safety.[30]

Another limitation was based on a doubtful interpretation of *Hambrook*, which emphasized the need for the plaintiff to be "within the area of physical risk" before recovery would be permitted.[31] It achieved some popularity,[32] and attracted some criticism,[33] prior to its eventual demise.

B. The Present Law

Today, there are two requirements that must be met before liability will be imposed for negligent infliction of psychiatric damage. We shall deal with each one in turn. The first requirement has to do with the type of damage that must be suffered, while the second is related to foreseeability.

---

[27] Windeyer J. in *Mount Isa Mines Ltd. v. Pusey* (1971), 45 A.L.J.R. 88, at p. 97.

[28] [1925] 1 K.B. 141 (C.A.).

[29] [1954] 1 D.L.R. 832 (N.S.).

[30] *Ibid.*, at p. 840.

[31] *Waube v. Warrington* (1935), 216 Wis. 603, 258 N.W. 497; *Amaya v. Home Ice* (1963), 59 Cal. App. 2d 295, 379 P. 2d 513. See also *Restatement, Torts, Second*, §§313 and 436.

[32] Magruder, "Mental and Emotional Disturbances in the Law of Torts" (1936), 49 Harv. L. Rev. 1033; Wright, *infra*, n. 37.

[33] Rendall, "Nervous Shock and Tortious Liability" (1962), 2 Osgoode Hall L.J. 291; Goodhart, "The Shock Cases and the Area of Risk" (1953), 16 Mod. L. Rev. 14.

1. TYPE OF DAMAGE

To this day the courts steadfastly refuse to allow tort damages for every emotional upset and insist upon some physical symptoms like a heart attack or a miscarriage,[34] or some "recognizable psychiatric illness",[35] like schizophrenia or morbid depression.[36] Mere emotional upsets, no matter how distressing, are not alone sufficient to found a cause of action."[37] The temporary emotion of fright, for example, is so trivial and so easily faked that it cannot be permitted to support an action.[38] Grief alone will not yield damages.[39] Nor will liability be imposed because of a few tears or a sleepless night.

As Mr. Justice Morden has explained in *Duwyn v. Kaprielian*,[40] the "kind of 'nervous shock' for which recovery may be had involves something more than general emotional upset". Consequently, a mother, whose child was injured in a minor accident, was denied compensation because, being hypersensitive, she became emotionally upset as a result of having to cope with the child during its period of recuperation, for this was not a "foreseeable response".

In *Hinz v. Berry*,[41] the distinction between compensable and non-compensable damage was dramatized. It was held that the damage resulting form the shock of witnessing the accident was recoverable, but damages were denied for depression resulting from grief and sorrow for a lost husband, anxiety about the welfare of children injured in the accident, financial stress because of the loss of a breadwinner, and the need for adjusting to a new life. The position was accurately summed up by Mr. Justice Windeyer in *Mount Isa Mines Ltd. v. Pusey*,[42] in these words:

---

34   *Dulieu v. White & Sons, supra*, n. 22.
35   *Hinz v. Berry*, [1970] 1 All E.R. 1074, at pp. 1075, 1077, 1078 (C.A.). *Page v. Smith,* [1995] 2 All E.R. 736, at p. 760 (H.L.) (*per* Lord Lloyd). See also *Beaulieu v. Sutherland* (1986), 35 C.C.L.T. 237, at p. 247 (B.C.S.C.), no "recognized mental illness" suffered (*per* Leff J.); *Heighington v. Ontario* (1987), 60 O.R. (2d) 641; affd. 69 O.R. (2d) 484 (C.A.). *Cf.*, *McDermott v. Ramadanovic Estate* (1988), 44 C.C.L.T. 249, at p. 259 (B.C.S.C.) (*per* Southin J.), "scar on the mind" or "emotional scar" sufficient; *Cox v. Fleming* (1993), 13 C.C.L.T. (2d) 305 (B.C.S.C.); affd (1995) 15 B.C.L.R. (3d) 201 (C.A.).
36   *Mount Isa Mines Ltd., supra*, n. 27.
37   Wright, "Comment on *Owens v. Liverpool*" (1939), 17 Can. Bar Rev. 56, at p. 58. See also *Miner v. C.P.R.* (1911), 3 Alta. L.R. 408, 18 W.L.R. 476 (C.A.). But *cf.*, *Owens v. Liverpool*, [1939] 1 K.B. 394 (C.A.), coffin overturned in accident.
38   Prosser, *op. cit., supra*, n. 7, at p. 329.
39   *Alaffe v. Kennedy* (1973), 40 D.L.R. (3d) 429, at p. 432 (N.S.) (*per* Gillis J.). But, in Alberta, by statute, "damages for bereavement" of $43,000 may be awarded to family members, the Fatal Accidents Act, R.S.A. 1980, c. F-5, s. 8(2). "Loss of companionship" is compensable in Ontario, see Family Law Act, R.S.O. 1990, c. F.3, s. 61(2)(e), but a parent cannot sue for nervous shock under s. 61(1) of the Family Law Act, see *Macartney v. Islic* (2000), 48 C.C.L.T. (2d) 19 (Ont. C.A.).
40   (1978), 7 C.C.L.T. 121, at p. 142. See also *Peters-Brown v. Regina District Health Board* (1996), 31 C.C.L.T. (2d) 302 (Sask. C.A.).
41   *Supra*, n. 35.
42   *Supra*, n. 27, at p. 92.

Sorrow does not sound in damages. A plaintiff in an action of negligence cannot recover damages for a "shock", however grievous, which was no more than an immediate emotional response to a distressing experience, sudden, sever and saddening. It is, however, today a known medical fact that severe emotional distress can be the starting point of a lasting disorder of mind or body, some form of psycho-neurosis or a psychosomatic illness. For that . . . damages may be had. It is in that consequential sense that the term "nervous shock" has come into the law.

Where a "reactive depression" was not caused by the shock of the accident but by the sorrow resulting from the injury to his wife, a husband was denied recovery.[43]

This view has been challenged recently by Madame Justice Molloy who has argued that, if the damages are trivial, there should be only "trivial damages" awarded, but "emotional pain was real, foreseeable and . . . compensable".[44]

It must be noted that the civil law of Quebec never had any difficulty compensating for psychiatric damage, including compensation for grief, caused by the fault of a tort feasor. As Justice L'Heureux-Dubé recently declared:[45]

[C]ompensation for the grief and distress felt when someone close to us dies — the prejudice commonly referred to as *solatium doloris* or injury to feelings — is clearly consistent with the civil law's full recognition of damages . . . . It is not hard to understand that the death of one's own child is in all respects an extremely distressing, indeed even traumatizing event. The suffering that accompanies this unnatural event has no equivalent in intensity aside from the immeasurable joy that can result from the birth of a child.

2. REASONABLE FORESIGHT OF PSYCHIATRIC DAMAGE

It must also be demonstrated that the "psychiatric damage" suffered was a foreseeable consequence of the negligent conduct.[46] In *Bourhill v. Young*,[47] a pregnant woman, descending from a bus, heard a motorcyclist passing on the other side of the vehicle and then the loud noise of a collision 40-50 feet ahead of the bus. As a result, she just "got in a pack of nerves". Later, after the cyclist's dead body had been removed, she saw blood on the road. When her child was stillborn a month later, the plaintiff attributed it to the shock she had suffered. Lord Porter, invoking the duty method of limiting liability, observed that "to establish a duty towards herself, the appellant must still show that the cyclist should reasonably have foreseen emotional injury to her as a result of his

---

[43] See *Beecham v. Hughes* (1988), 45 C.C.L.T. 1 (B.C.C.A.).

[44] *Mason v. Westside Cemeteries Ltd.* (1996), 29 C.C.L.T. (2d) 125, at pp. 146 and 147 (Ont. Gen. Div.); ashes of deceased lost; see also Robertson, "Liability for Nervous Shock" (1994), 57 Mod. L. Rev. 649, arguing that nervous shock should be treated like any other injury.

[45] *Augustus v. Gosset* (1996), 34 C.C.L.T. (2d) 111, at pp. 155 and 161, para. 27 and 47 (S.C.C.), parent suing for loss of child shot by the police. See also Fatal Accidents Act, R.S.N.B. 1973, c. F-7, s. 3(4) allowing damages for "grief suffered by the parents as a result of the death."

[46] The U.K. courts have added a requirement for proximity as well as for foresight. See *Alcock*, *infra*, n. 56; *McLoughlin v. O'Brian*, *infra*, n. 55.

[47] [1943] A.C. 92. See Wright, "Comment" (1943), 21 Can. Bar Rev. 65.

negligent driving and . . . I don't think she has done so".[48] Thus, foresight of shock became the touchstone of liability.

The apparent simplicity of this solution has proved illusory. In *King v. Phillips*,[49] for example, a taxicab driver negligently backed his cab over a little boy on a tricycle. The mother, who was in her home about 70-80 yards away, heard screams, looked out the window and saw her child's tricycle under the car but could not see the boy. She rushed out to the roadway where she saw the lad running toward her only slightly injured. She became ill as a result of the shock. In denying recovery, Lord Justice Denning founded his decision on foresight, but he employed remoteness analysis rather than the duty language used in *Bourhill v. Young*. His Lordship observed that "the test of liability for shock is foreseeability of injury by shock". He then came to the startling conclusion that shock to the mother was unforeseeable because "the slow backing of the taxicab was very different from the terrifying descent of the runaway lorry"[50] in *Hambrook v. Stokes*. To say that slowly running over a child is less likely to cause shock to the mother than doing so quickly is unrealistic. Indeed, Professor Goodhart has suggested that the opposite would be true,[51] although a more serious injury might be contemplated at higher rates of speed.[52]

In a Canadian decision, *Marshall v. Lionel Enterprises Inc.*,[53] Mr. Justice Haines chose to frame the current law in terms of foreseeability as follows:

> It would seem both logical and necessary that the test be foreseeability of nervous shock rather than just foreseeability of injury. While nervous shock may result in physical damage and while physical injury may often result in nervous shock, the two cannot be so closely liked as to be inseparable. Foreseeability of nervous shock may result from the same facts as does the foreseeability of physical injury or it may result from entirely different facts. For the present at least, I am convinced that foreseeability of the one type of injury cannot be automatically assumed from the foreseeability of the other. For this reason, the test must be the foreseeability of nervous shock itself.

This principle was accepted by the Ontario Court of Appeal when Griffiths J.A. declared unequivocally, ". . . reasonable foresight of nervous shock to the plaintiff is the touchstone of liability".[54]

The House of Lords belatedly almost came around to this view in *McLoughlin v. O'Brian*,[55] where it was held that foresight was the dominant test of

---

[48] *Ibid.*, at p. 119.
[49] [1953] 1 Q.B. 429, [1953] 1 All E.R. 617 (C.A.). Doubted by Lord Oliver in *Alcock*, *supra*, n. 2, at p. 1114.
[50] *Ibid.*, at p. 442.
[51] "Emotional Shock and the Unimaginative Taxicab Driver" (1953), 69 L.Q. Rev. 347, at p. 352.
[52] Rendall, *supra*, n. 33, at p. 306.
[53] [1972] 2 O.R. 177, at p. 185.
[54] *Bechard v. Haliburton Estate* (1991), 10 C.C.L.T. (2d) 156, at p. 164, rescuer-like bystander recovered. See also *Nespolon v. Alford* (1998), 40 O.R. (3d) 355 (C.A.), not foreseeable to teenaged boys that driver of vehicle non-negligently killing one of them would suffer post-traumatic stress disorder, *per* Abella J.A.

liability but not the exclusive one; matters of policy and factual proximity had to be weighed by the courts in addition to foreseeability of "nervous shock". More recently the House of Lords in *Alcock v. Chief Constable of South Yorkshire Police*[56] divided about whether foresight was enough in these psychiatric damage cases. Lord Keith thought "it was sufficient that reasonable foreseeability should be the guide".[57] Lord Ackner, however, felt that "reasonable foreseeability would be too wide unless it were 'limited by the notion of proximity' ".[58] Lord Jauncey also felt that "proximity in the relation of the parties also constitutes an important control on the test of reasonable foreseeability".[59] Lord Oliver stated that there were twin questions involved here: reasonable foresight as well as "degree of directness or proximity".[60] It is hard to see that the words "proximity" or "directness" add very much to the exercise of determining which cases of psychiatric damage will be covered and which will be excluded. If something is reasonably foreseeable it is likely that it is also proximate or direct; if something is proximate or direct, it is likely that it is also foreseeable. In all these cases, like in other remoteness situations, the judiciary must exercise caution in drawing lines, ensuring that liability is imposed only in appropriate circumstances.

It is obvious that the reasonable foresight test does not magically solve all the problems; it is too general by itself. Various fact situations recur, however, and lead to solutions in the circumstances of each case. In the last few years, with foresight being used as an umbrella theory, the contours of liability for psychiatric damage are coming into focus as the recurring cases are sorted out. Let us examine the factual patterns that have been addressed.

a) Witnessing Accident

It has now been established that someone who witnesses an accident may recover for psychiatric damage suffered as a result. In *Hinz v. Berry*,[61] a pregnant woman witnessed an accident in which a runaway car killed her husband and injured several of her children. The court, in granting her damages for "nervous shock", appeared to rest liability on the simple fact that she had actually witnessed the accident.[62] One judge noted the fact that she was "a close relative",[63] while another remarked that this was an "exceptionally tragic accident",[64] but neither seemed to think these facts were controlling. A mother who suffered

---

[55] [1982] 2 All E.R. 298 (H.L.).

[56] [1991] 3 W.L.R. 1057 (H.L.)

[57] *Ibid.*, at p. 1100.

[58] *Ibid.*, at p. 1105.

[59] *Ibid.*, at p. 1121.

[60] *Ibid.*, at p. 1109.

[61] [1970] 1 All E.R. 1074 (C.A.). See also *Dillon v. Legg* (1968), 441 P. 2d 912.

[62] *Ibid.*, at p. 1078 (*per* Willmer L.J.).

[63] *Ibid.*, at p. 1075 (*per* Denning M.R.).

[64] *Ibid.*, at p. 1077 (*per* Pearson L.J.).

"nervous shock" on seeing her baby born deformed was also entitled to tort compensation.[65] Someone who witnesses their house burning down, if they can prove that "psychiatric damage" occurred and was reasonably foreseeable, may recover damages.[66]

The issue of whether witnessing an accident on television can be equated to seeing and hearing it first hand has arisen. In *Alcock v. Chief Constable*[67] 16 relatives of some of the 95 individuals killed and 400 injured in the Hillsborough football stadium disaster sued for psychiatric damaged suffered on seeing the events on television. The defendant admitted negligence in controlling the crowd and liability for the physical injuries, but denied any duty to these plaintiffs. The House of Lords dismissed all the claims. Lord Keith stated: "The viewing of the television scenes did not create the necessary degree of proximity".[68] In part, this was because it did not depict the suffering of any recognizable individuals, since the broadcasting code of ethics prohibited this. The possibility of liability to T.V. viewers, however, was not ruled out. Lord Justice Nolan, in the Court of Appeal, offered a hypothetical situation in which there might be liability, as where a "publicity seeking organisation made arrangements for a party of children to go up in a balloon, and for the event to be televised so that their parents could watch, it would be hard to deny that the organizers were under a duty to avoid mental injury to the parents . . . [and] there would be a breach of duty if . . . the balloon crashed"[69] or burst suddenly "into flames".[70] In such a case, said Lord Ackner, the "impact of the simultaneous television pictures would be as great, if not greater, than the actual sight of the accident".[71] No court would deny compensation for psychiatric damage to family members of the crew of the Challenger spacecraft who witnessed the televised coverage of the explosion on takeoff, while allowing it to those who witnessed the tragic event in person. No judge could say, in those circumstances, that the loss was not foreseeable, nor proximate.

It is not even necessary that an accident actually occur, as long as there is a reasonable belief that one is threatened. In *Dooley v. Cammell Laird & Co. Ltd.*[72] a crane-operator suffered "nervous shock" when, because of a defective rope, he accidentally dropped something into the hold of a ship causing him to fear that he would injure a fellow worker. As long as his fear was not "baseless or

---

[65] *S. v. Distillers Co. (Biochemicals) Ltd.*, [1969] 3 All E.R. 1412.

[66] *Attia v. British Gas plc.*, [1987] 3 All E.R. 455 (C.A.), leave to appeal refused, [1988] 1 All E.R. xvi.

[67] *Supra*, n. 56.

[68] *Ibid.*, at p. 1102. Lord Jauncey, at p. 1125, stated it was "not equivalent to actual sight or hearing".

[69] *Ibid.*, at p. 1094.

[70] *Ibid.*, at p. 1108 (*per* Lord Ackner).

[71] *Ibid.*, at p. 1108.

[72] [1953] 1 Lloyd's Rep. 271.

extravagant", it was a "consequence reasonably to have been foreseen that he may himself suffer a nervous shock".[73]

b) Seeing Aftermath of Accident

Plaintiffs do not have to witness the accident, as long as they arrive upon the scene soon afterward and see its aftermath with their own unaided senses.[74] In *Boardman v. Sanderson*,[75] a father who did not see an accident in a garage, which involved his son, ran immediately to the scene in response the infant's screams. Lord Justice Ormerod declared that the defendant owed a duty "not only to the infant but also to the near relatives of the infant who were, as he knew, on the premises, within earshot, and likely to come upon the scene if any injury or ill befell the infant".[76]

Similarly, in *Marshall v. Lionel Enterprises Inc.*,[77] a wife who alleged that she had seen the aftermath of an accident in which her husband was seriously injured by a defective snowmobile, was said to have stated a cause of action for "nervous shock" in her pleadings.

In *Benson v. Lee*,[78] a mother went to the scene of an accident in which her child had been injured, accompanied the child to the hospital in an ambulance and was told later that the child had died. The court indicated that her shock was foreseeable if it was experienced by "direct perception" of the accident itself or its "immediate aftermath".

Recovery will also be allowed to relatives who do not attend "at or near the scene of the accident at the time or shortly afterwards", but who go to the hospital immediately after the accident and witness the suffering. In *McLoughlin v. O'Brien*,[79] the plaintiff's husband and three children were injured in a car accident while she was at home two miles away. She was told about the accident, went immediately to the hospital, saw the injured members of her family suffering and was told that one of her children had died from injuries. She suffered "nervous shock" as a result. The House of Lords imposed liability because such a consequence was foreseeable and because reasons of policy did not militate against allowing recovery in these circumstances. Lord Wilberforce

---

[73] *Ibid.*, at p. 277 (*per* Donovan J.).

[74] *Hambrook v. Stokes Brothers*, *supra*, n. 28.

[75] [1964] 1 W.L.R. 1317 (C.A.). See also *Archibald v. Braverman* (1969), 275 Cal. App. 2d 290, 79 Cal. Rptr. 273.

[76] *Ibid.*, at p. 1322.

[77] *Supra*, n. 53. See also *Fenn v. Peterborough et al.* (1976), 1 C.C.L.T. 90, at p. 129; affd but damages varied (1979), 25 O.R. (2d) 399 (C.A.), annotated by L. Klar in 1 C.C.L.T., at p. 92.

[78] [1972] V.R. 878. See also *Dziokonski v. Babineau* (1978), 389 N.E. 2d 1295. But *cf. Brown v. Hubar* (1974), 3 O.R. (2d) 448 (H.C.J.); *McMullin v. F.W. Woolworth* (1974), 9 N.B.R. (2d) 214, at p. 216; *Dube (Litigation Guard of) v. Penlon Ltd.* (1994), 21 C.C.L.T. (2d) 268, at p. 302 (Ont. Gen. Div.), malpractice injury to child not "immediate and direct", not "assault on the mind [leading] directly to ... psychiatric illness" (*per* Zuber J.).

[79] *Supra*, n. 13. *Cox v. Fleming* (1993), 13 C.C.L.T. (2d) 305, saw suffering in hospital.

felt that the courts had to consider the class of persons whose claims should be covered, the proximity of such persons to the accident and the means by which the shock was caused.[80]

If someone arrives at the hospital or mortuary eight or nine hours after the accident, however, this may not qualify.[81] Although this could be described as part of the "aftermath" it would not be part of the "*immediate* aftermath".[82] Lord Jauncey indicated that one should be at the scene soon after the accident occurs in order "to rescue or comfort a victim", but this may be drawing the line too narrowly.[83] In *Devji v. Burnaby (District)*,[84] informed of the death of one of their family members at about 11 p.m., some of the family went to the hospital to identify the body, which they viewed at about 12.30 p.m. the next day. Their claim was dismissed, as a matter of policy, apparently as being insufficiently close or proximate although admittedly foreseeable and undoubtedly most painful to them. Moreover, the circumstances did not cause "fright, terror or horror".

c) Relationship

It is not necessary for shocked persons to be relatives of the injured individuals, though this would, undoubtedly, assist their cases. It is now "settled law that the rescuer who witnesses a horrible accident to the victim is entitled to recover", as is someone "performing a role similar to that of the rescuer".[85]

Workers are allowed to recover for nervous shock they suffer when they witness accidents to their fellow workers.[86] In the Australian case of *Mount Isa Mines Ltd. v. Pusey*[87] the plaintiff worker heard a loud noise which resulted from a short circuit. He hurried to the floor above and helped one of two electricians who had been horribly burned in the accident. The electrician he assisted died nine days later. The plaintiff developed symptoms of schizophrenia as a consequence of his involvement. Mr. Justice Windeyer, in a penetrating analysis of what he termed the "blessed, and sometimes overworked, word 'foreseeability' ",[88] concluded that the question was "not whether shock would be likely to produce this particular illness, but whether there was a real risk that a foreseeable accident such as occurred would cause a man in the power-house to suffer a

---

[80]   *Ibid.*, at p. 304.
[81]   *Alcock, supra*, n. 56, at p. 1107. See also *Talibi v. Seabrook* (1995), 28 C.C.L.T. (2d) 254 (Alta. Q.B.), son saw mother's body at hospital.
[82]   *Ibid.* (*per* Lord Ackner).
[83]   *Ibid.*, at p. 1125.
[84]   (1999), 47 C.C.L.T. (2d) 111, at p. 133 (B.C.C.A.).
[85]   See *Bechard v. Haliburton Estate* (1991), 10 C.C.L.T. (2d) 156, at p. 171 (Ont. C.A.) (*per* Griffiths J.A.); see also *Chadwick v. British Transport Commission*, [1967] 2 All E.R. 945, rescuer at "gruesome" railway disaster.
[86]   *Dooley v. Cammell Laird & Co. Ltd.*, [1953] 1 Lloyd's Rep. 271; *Carlin v. Helical Bar* (1970), 9 K.I.R. 954.
[87]   (1971), 45 A.L.J.R. 88.
[88]   *Ibid.*, at p. 93.

nervous shock having lasting mental consequences".[89] He pointed out that the plaintiff was not a relative nor even a friend of the injured person. "He did not know him, except perhaps as a fellow in the power-house." Mr. Justice Windeyer explained that judicial reliance upon relationship was "originally a humane and ameliorating exception to the general denial that damages could be had for nervous shock," but it should not be used to restrict liability to relatives alone. The prime consideration is whether claimants were "neighbours", which category would include both relatives and rescuers, but not "curious strangers" or "mere bystanders". His Lordship felt that the relationship of employer and servant between the plaintiff and the defendant could also support the duty.[90] Mr. Justice Walsh agreed that, "there is no rule of law which made it a condition of the respondent's right to recover that he should have been a close relative", although he did feel that "a family relationship" may be "a relevant and important fact in deciding the question whether or not injury of that kind to the plaintiff was reasonably foreseeable".[91]

The House of Lords recently affirmed this view. In *Alcock*,[92] it was said that even a bystander, who is not a rescuer and who is not involved as a fellow employee, may be able to recover if a "reasonably strong-nerved person" would have been shocked, as in a case of a "petrol tanker careening out of control into a school in session and bursting into flames".[93] Close relatives and friends are more likely to suffer shock than more remote relatives and strangers. The evidence will not normally show psychiatric damage unless there is closeness in the relationship, but a close family relationship is not always enough. As Lord Ackner has reminded us, "[t]he quality of brotherly love is well known to differ widely — from Cain and Abel to David and Jonathan".[94] Lord Keith has also remarked that[95]

[c]lose ties of love and affection are numerous . . . [and] [t]hey . . . may be stronger in the case of engaged couples than in that of persons who have been married to each other for many years.

Lord Jauncey outlined a sensible approach as follows:[96]

. . . The underlying logic of allowing claims of parents and spouses is that it can readily be foreseen by the tortfeasor that if they saw or were involved in the immediate aftermath of a serious accident or disaster they would, because of their close relationship of love and affection with the victim be likely to suffer nervous shock. There may, however, be others whose ties of relationship are as strong. I do not consider that it would be profitable to try and define

---

[89] *Ibid.*, at p. 95.
[90] *Ibid.*, at p. 96.
[91] *Ibid.*, at p. 101. See also *McLoughlin v. O'Brian, supra*, n. 13, at p. 311.
[92] See *supra*, n. 56.
[93] *Ibid.*, at p. 1106 (*per* Lord Ackner).
[94] *Ibid.*, at p. 1108.
[95] *Ibid.*, at p. 1100.
[96] *Ibid.*, at p. 1124.

who such others might be or to draw any dividing line between one degree of relationship and another. To draw such a line would necessarily be arbitrary and lacking in logic. In my view the proper approach is to examine each case on its own facts in order to see whether the claimant has established so close a relationship of love and affection to the victims as might reasonably be expected in the case of spouses or parents and children. If the claimant has so established and all other requirements of the claim are satisfied he or she will succeed since the shock to him or her will be within the reasonable contemplation of the tortfeasor. If such relationship is not established the claim will fail.

Lord Oliver expressed a similar attitude:[97]

> . . . I see no logic and no virtue in seeking to lay down as a matter of "policy" categories of relationship within which claims may succeed and without which they are doomed to failure in limine. So rigid an approach would, I think, work great injustice and cannot be rationally justified. Obviously a claim for damages for psychiatric injury by a remote relative of the primary victim will factually require most cautious scrutiny and faces considerable evidentiary difficulties. Equally obviously, the foreseeability of such injury to such a person will be more difficult to establish than similar injury to a spouse or parent of the primary victim. But these are factual difficulties and I can see no logic and no policy reason for excluding claims by more remote relatives. Suppose, for instance, that the primary victim has lived with the plaintiff for 40 years, both being under the belief that they are lawfully married. Does she suffer less shock or grief because it is subsequently discovered that their marriage was invalid? The source of the shock and distress in all these cases is the affectionate relationship which existed between the plaintiff and the victim and the traumatic effect of the negligence is equally foreseeable, given that relationship, however the relationship arises. Equally, I would not exclude the possibility envisaged by my noble and learned friend, Lord Ackner, of a successful claim, given circumstances of such horror as would be likely to traumatize even the most phlegmatic spectator, by a mere bystander. That is not, of course, to say that the closeness of the relationship between plaintiff and primary victim is irrelevant, for the likelihood or unlikelihood of a person in that relationship suffering shock of the degree claimed from the event must be a most material factor to be taken into account in determining whether that consequence was reasonably foreseeable. In general, for instance, it might be supposed that the likelihood of trauma of such a degree as to cause psychiatric illness would be less in the case of a friend or a brother-in-law than in that of a parent or fiancé.

These views as to the relationship of the parties are most helpful in their rationality and their flexibility.

There have been further recent developments in the United Kingdom. In *McFarlane v. E.E. Caledonia Ltd.*,[98] the right of a bystander has been restricted, so that the duty is owed to a witness, even of "horrific events", only if "a sufficient degree of proximity" is present, that is, there must be "both nearness in time and place and a close relationship of love and affection between the plaintiff and the victim". Whether Canadian courts will be as tough as this is doubtful, given our different, more generalized and more generous approach to these matters.

---

[97] *Ibid.*, at pp. 1117-18 (*per* Lord Oliver).
[98] [1994] 2 All E.R. 1, at p. 14 (C.A.), leave to appeal refused (*per* Stuart-Smith L.J.), witness to oil rig explosion 100 meters away cannot sue.

The House of Lords has tried, in *Page v. Smith*,[99] to distinguish between primary victims, who are endangered, and secondary victims, who are not at risk in the accident. For the primary victims, only foresight of physical harm is needed. For the secondary victims, "certain control mechanisms" were established to "limit the number of potential claimants". For the secondary victims, foresight of psychiatric injury to a "person of normal fortitude" is required, but not for primary victims. The question in all cases is whether the defendant can reasonably foresee ". . . risk of personal injury, whether physical or psychiatric".[100] If the answer is yes, the duty is established even if no physical injury occurs. There is "no justification for regarding physical and psychiatric injury as different 'kinds of damage' ". It makes no difference that the victim is "predisposed to psychiatric illness" or "that the illness takes a rare form or is of unusual severity".[101] This is a complex structure, but there is little merit in it, except for the slightly improved position of so-called primary victims.

The suggestion that people who negligently endanger themselves cannot be liable for psychiatric damage caused to others is suspect because people can be liable to their own rescuers.[102] There should be no difference between people negligently injuring themselves who thereby cause shock to others and people negligently injuring themselves who thereby cause others to rescue them. Both are equally foreseeable consequences of the negligence and both should be equally compensable, if lawsuits are started and the other elements are proven.

d) Person Informed of Accident

Liability has not yet been imposed for psychiatric damage suffered by someone who is merely told about an accident.[103] Hearing distressing news does not sound in damages in the same way as does nervous shock from witnessing distressing events. . . . No action lies against either the bearer of the bad tidings or the person who caused the event of which they tell. There is no duty in law to break bad news gently or not to create bad news."[104]

One Canadian trial judge in *Abramzik v. Brenner*,[105] awarded damages to a mother for "nervous shock" suffered when she was informed that two of her

---

[99] [1995] 2 All E.R. 736, at p. 767 (*per* Lord Lloyd), person physically at risk recovered for psychiatric illness caused when an old condition flared up unforeseeably after the person was involved in a minor accident.

[100] *Ibid.*, at p. 768.

[101] *Ibid.*

[102] See *supra*, Chapter 10. But see *Greatorex v. Greatorex*, [2000] 4 All E.R. 769 (Q.B.D.), father could not sue son for shock suffered from seeing aftermath of self-inflicted injury.

[103] Fleming, "Distant Shock in Germany (And Elsewhere)" (1972), 20 Am. J. Comp. L. 485; *Kelley v. Kokua Sales* (1975), 532 P. 2d 673 (Hawaii); *Strong v. Moon* (1992), 13 C.C.L.T. (2d) 296 (B.C.S.C.), 11-year-old child was told his mother was "road pizza" by schoolmates who saw accident, no liability.

[104] See *Mount Isa Mines Ltd. v. Pusey, supra*, n. 27, at p. 97 (*per* Windeyer J.).

[105] Siris J., in (1965), 54 D.L.R. (2d) 639.

children had been killed through the defendant's negligence, but he was reversed on appeal.[106] Chief Justice Culliton concluded that the plaintiff did "not prove that the shock which she experienced . . . was one which the defendant . . . ought, as a reasonable person, to have foreseen as a result of her conduct".[107]

This principle of non-liability has been invariably followed since. In *Dietelbach v. Public Trustee*,[108] for instance, a wife who suffered grief after being told of her husband's injury and later seeing his personality change, was denied recovery. Mr. Justice Kirke Smith explained:

> Foreseeability of injury by nervous shock is the test; were it otherwise, the ripples caused by the throwing of a stone into the pond would run too wide.[109]

This principle has been clearly reiterated recently in *Rhodes v. C.N.R. Co.*[110] by Mr. Justice Martin Taylor, in denying recovery to a mother who was informed of her son's death in a railway accident that had occurred far away. He stated:

> . . . someone who suffers psychological injury as a result of being informed of the death of a relative, or of ruminating on the circumstances of the relative's death, or of visiting the scene some days later cannot, in the absence of any unexpected alarming or horrifying experience caused by the circumstances of the accident, be said to have been closely and directly affected by the negligence which caused it.

There were several other sets of reasons, which, although agreeing in the result, revealed the differences of view of the British Columbia Court of Appeal concerning the tests of foresight, proximity and directness to be employed here, particularly whether there has to be causal proximity, temporal proximity, geographical proximity and emotional proximity, as well as directness. A recent attempt in England to alter this rule was quickly halted by the House of Lords,[111] indicating that the law has stabilized on this issue at least.

---

[106] (1967), 65 D.L.R. (2d) 651 (Sask. C.A.). See Glasbeek, "Comment" (1969), 47 Can. Bar Rev. 96. There is no longer any support for "a substantive tort" here, see *Turton v. Buttler* (1987), 42 C.C.L.T. 74 (Alta. H.C.); *Anderson v. St. Pierre* (1987), 46 D.L.R. (4th) 754 (Man. Q.B.).

[107] *Ibid.*, at p. 658 (Sask. C.A.).

[108] (1973), 37 D.L.R. (3d) 621 (B.C.); see also *Babineau v. MacDonald* (1975), 59 D.L.R. (3d) 671, at p. 678 (N.B.C.A.).

[109] *Ibid.*, at p. 624.

[110] (1990), 5 C.C.L.T. (2d) 118, at p. 132 (B.C.C.A.). Leave to appeal to S.C.C. dismissed, 136 N.R. 80. See also *Beecham v. Hughes* (1988), 45 C.C.L.T. 1 (B.C.C.A.), for a lengthy and confusing discussion of the issues by a court not in total agreement. See also *Jaensch v. Coffey* (1984), 58 A.L.J.R. 426, for a thorough but inconclusive discussion.

[111] *Alcock v. Chief Constable of South Yorkshire Police*, [1991] 3 All E.R. 1057, at p. 1101 (*per* Lord Keith), at p. 1104 (*per* Lord Ackner), at p. 1120 (*per* Lord Oliver), "doubting"; *Hevican v. Ruane*, [1991] 3 All E.R. 65 (Q.B.) and *Ravenscroft v. Rederiaktiebølaget Transatlantic*, [1991] 3 All E.R. 73 (Q.B.); revd [1992] 2 All E.R. 470 (C.A.).

e) Person Injured in Same Accident Later Told About Tragedy

There is one situation in which those who have suffered psychiatric damage as a result of being told about a tragedy can recover — if they have themselves also been physically injured in the same accident. In *Schneider v. Eisovitch*,[112] the plaintiff and her husband were being driven in the defendant's motor car when the defendant negligently caused the car to leave the highway and crash into a tree. As a result, the plaintiff's husband was killed and the plaintiff rendered unconscious. While in the hospital, the plaintiff was informed of her husband's death, and this shock, in addition to the shock she suffered in the accident itself, had serious consequences. In an action for damages for personal injuries brought by the plaintiff, the trial judge indicated that the "nervous shock" to the plaintiff resulted in recurrent attacks of neurodermatitis. This was due to three factors: (a) the shock of the accident; (b) the shock on hearing in the hospital that her husband had been killed; (c) the continued strain of adjusting her life after her husband's death. Mr. Justice Paull allowed damages for (a) and (b), but refused to grant any for (c). His Lordship reasoned as follows:

> It cannot be doubted and is not challenged by counsel for the defendant that if the plaintiff had not herself been injured but had seen her husband killed the resultant shock would have been actionable. It would be a direct consequence of the defendant's negligent act. If the plaintiff had been conscious after the accident but had gained the first knowledge of her husband's death by someone screaming "Raphael is dead" and then seen that fact for herself, would liability depend on whether the hearing or the sight produced the shock? Would not each equally have been a direct and natural consequence of the negligent act? Approached in this way, it seems to me to follow that once a breach of duty is established the difference between seeing and hearing is immaterial. Hearing can be just as direct a consequence as seeing. The fact that owing to unconsciousness in this case a period of time elapsed before the news was heard makes no difference provided the news was a consequence which flowed directly from the breach of duty towards the plaintiff, any more than it makes any difference that an operation take place after an interval of time. The fact that the defendant by his negligence caused the death of the plaintiff's husband does not give the plaintiff a cause of action for the shock caused to her, but the plaintiff having a cause of action for the negligence of the defendant may add the consequence of shock caused by hearing of her husband's death when estimating the amount recoverable on her cause of action.[113]

It will be noted that this case if founded upon the directness test of *Polemis*, which has been overruled, but it is now clear that the new foresight approach would yield the same result in these circumstances. In *Andrews v. Williams*,[114] a person injured in an accident was later told that his mother was killed in the same accident. The depression suffered as a result of this information was held to be compensable as "reasonably foreseeable consequence".[115]

---

[112] [1960] 1 All E.R. 169. See Burnett, "Comment" (1960), 38 Can. Bar Rev. 615.

[113] *Ibid.*, at p. 175.

[114] [1967] V.R. 831.

[115] *Ibid.*, at p. 832 (*per* Winneke J.). See also *Vana v. Tosta*, [1968] S.C.R. 71, at pp. 80-82 (*per* Ritchie J.).

f) Hypersensitive Individuals

Where individuals suffer psychiatric damage because of their "particular hypersensitivity",[116] there is no liability to them. In other words, where an ordinary person of reasonable mental fortitude would not normally suffer psychiatric damage, someone who does so because of their unique vulnerability cannot recover. In *White v. Chief Constable of South Yorkshire*,[117] some police officers were denied compensation for mental suffering while helping victims of a soccer disaster because they were required to evince "reasonable fortitude and robustness." Relying in part on this case, Justice MacPherson in a learned decision[118] denied tort recovery to the parents of an 11-year-old child, who drank some contaminated Beatrice Grape Nectar at school. The parents were called and took her to the hospital where no alarming symptoms were observed. There was nausea and regurgitation, but no vomiting nor loss of consciousness. She returned to school the next day. The parents, however, became extremely concerned, even obsessed, about the health of the child, receiving information about possible after-effects which did not transpire. The father was even hospitalized much later. MacPherson J. held that there could be no liability here for the results were not foreseeable, the event was not witnessed by the parents and the recovery of the child was completely normal. In becoming obsessed by the event, the parents demonstrated they lacked the "reasonable robustness and fortitude" expected of Canadians.

g) Negligent Communication

Where someone receives negligent communication to the effect that they may be infected with Hepatitis B when they are not, and this causes psychiatric damage, liability may be found.[119] In another case, *Lew v. Mount Saint Joseph Hospital Society*,[120] a case for nervous shock was allowed to proceed when a hospital was alleged to have negligently failed to warn the plaintiff about the terrible condition of his wife who had suffered a brain injury in that she was attached to numerous tubes. Thus, it may be that the negligent communication of bad news might give rise to liability.[121]

h) Conclusion

Foresight, therefore, is still the current catchword, but it has always been too general to decide cases by itself. Proximity is of little aid except to restrain our judges from being too generous. No particular case dealing with specific fact

---

[116] See *Duwyn v. Kaprelian* (1978), 7 C.C.L.T. 121 (Ont. C.A.).

[117] [1998] 3 W.L.R. 1509, at p. 1512 (H.L.) (*per* Lord Griffiths).

[118] *Vanek v. Great Atlantic and Pacific Co. of Canada Ltd.* (1999), 48 O.R. (3d) 228 (C.A.).

[119] See *Anderson v. Wilson* (1999), 44 O.R. (3d) 673 (C.A.), class action can proceed. See also Mullany, "Careless Communication" in *Torts Tomorrow* (1998), at p. 195.

[120] (1992), 36 C.C.L.T. (2d) 35, [1998] B.C.J. No. 2461; affd [1998] B.C.J. No. 1264.

[121] See *Guay v. Sun Publishing*, [1953] 2 S.C.R. 216, negligent story that wife killed in accident, no liability.

situation can freeze for all time the scope of liability. Fact finders, including juries, must be allowed some scope to decide cases on their individual facts. Indeed, Mr. Justice Haines has wisely suggested that "the law imposes no predetermined limitations on the position the plaintiff must occupy in order to be compensated for nervous shock".[122]

In determining whether psychiatric damage is reasonably foreseeable, the courts can do no better than to examine a series of factors and make an assessment based upon them.[123] They must consider the temporal and geographical proximity of the plaintiff to the accident, whether the plaintiff actually saw the mishap or came upon the scene shortly thereafter, whether the plaintiff and the victim were related in some way and whether the accident was a serious one.[124] The recurring cases will be gradually sorted out, but much will always depend upon the good sense of the judge or jury.[125]

One wonders whether the time has yet arrived when we might consider adopting Madam Justice Southin's suggestion:[126]

> [T]he question of policy is better answered not by saying that scars on the flesh are compensable but scars on the mind are not but by making all awards for scars on the mind . . . conventional . . . as damages for pain and suffering have been. . . .

Or, even better, dare we dream of a legislative solution along the lines of the one in Australia?[127] Will we ever recognize that the grief suffered on losing a loved one is real and no less worth of compensation than the hurt of a scratched arm? Indeed, there are many who would say that a broken heart is much harder to endure than a broken leg. Lord Oliver has admitted[128] that there is

> . . . no readily discernible logical reason why he who carelessly inflicts an injury upon another should not be held responsible for its inevitable consequences not only to him who may conveniently be termed "the primary victim" but to others who suffer as a result. It cannot, I think be accounted for by saying that such consequences cannot reasonably be foreseen. It is readily foreseeable that very real and easily ascertainable injury is likely to result to those dependent upon the primary victim or those upon whom, as a result of negligently inflicted injury, the primary victim himself becomes a dependent.

He explained simply that there is a need to avoid "the impracticability or unreasonableness of entertaining claims to the ultimate limits of the consequences of human activity". Perhaps our legislators will take up this issue in the years ahead.

---

[122] *Marshall v. Lionel Enterprises Inc.*, *supra*, n. 53, at p. 187.

[123] Lord Scarman in *McLoughlin v. O'Brian*, *supra*, n. 13, at p. 34. See also *Fenn, supra*, n. 77.

[124] This may be the real explanation for *King v. Phillips*.

[125] *Marshall v. Lionel Enterprises Inc.*, *supra*, n. 53, at p. 187 (*per* Haines J.); *Bourhill v. Young*, *supra*, n. 47, at p. 110. See excellent statistical analysis in Smith, *Liability in Negligence* (1984), p. 155.

[126] See *Rhodes v. C.N.R. Co.*, *supra*, n. 110, at p. 182.

[127] See Lord Oliver in *Alcock, supra*, n. 56, at p. 1120.

[128] *Ibid.*, at pp. 1112 and 1113.

Chapter 12

Negligent Infliction of
Pure Economic Loss

Negligently inflicted pure economic losses were always treated differently. Prior to the House of Lords' 1963 decision in *Hedley Byrne & Co. v. Heller & Partners Ltd.*,[1] recovery for pure economic loss in negligence was virtually unknown. Since then, recovery in various and different circumstances has proliferated, transforming not only negligence law but also general commercial law.[2]

At the outset it is necessary to distinguish pure economic loss from consequential economic loss. Consequential economic loss is financial loss causally connected to physical damage to the plaintiff's own person or property. An injured employee, for example, may suffer consequential economic loss in the form of medical expenses or loss of earnings. Consequential loss is usually governed by the same principles of recovery that apply to the physical damage itself. On the other hand, a *pure* economic loss is a financial loss which is not causally connected to physical injury to the plaintiff's own person or property. Pure economic loss is governed by the special or restrictive duties of care discussed in this chapter.

---

[1]   [1964] A.C. 465, [1963] 2 All E.R. 575 (H.L.).

[2]   See generally Feldthusen, *Economic Negligence*, 4th ed. (2000); Cane, *Tort Law and Economic Interests*, 2d ed. (1996); Bernstein, *Economic Loss* (1993); Banakas, *Tortious Liability for Pure Economic Loss: A Comparative Study* (1989); Feldthusen, "Liability for Pure Economic Loss: Yes, But Why?" (1998), 28 U. W. Aus. L. Rev. 84; Feldthusen and Palmer, "Economic Analysis in the Supreme Court of Canada" (1995), 74 Can. Bar Rev. 427; Stapleton, "Duty of Care and Economic Loss: A Wider Agenda" (1991), 107 L.Q. Rev. 249; Blom, "Economic Loss: Curbs on the Way Ahead?" (1987–88), 12 Can. Bus. L.J. 275; Schwartz, "Economic Loss in American Tort Law: The Examples of J'Aire and of Products Liability" (1986), 23 San Diego L. Rev. 37; Smillie, "Negligence and Economic Loss" (1982), 32 U.T.L.J. 231; Smith, "Clarification of Duty-Remoteness Problems Through a New Physiology of Negligence: Economic Loss, A Test Case" (1974), 9 U.B.C.L. Rev. 213; Stevens, "Negligent Acts Causing Pure Financial Loss: Policy Factors at Work" (1973), 23 U.T.L.J. 431; Harvey, "Economic Losses and Negligence" (1972), 50 Can. Bar Rev. 580; Atiyah, "Negligence and Economic Loss" (1967), 83 L.Q. Rev. 248.

The Supreme Court of Canada, based on the work of Bruce Feldthusen,[3] has recognized five different categories of negligence claims for pure economic loss, each governed by its own special duty of care.[4] The Supreme Court left open the possibility that new categories might emerge, but indicated that lower courts should exercise caution and not strain to create new categories.[5] The five categories of pure economic loss are illustrated by the following examples:

1. *Negligent Misrepresentation*: An investor relies on negligently pre-pared corporate financial accounts to invest in a company which subse-quently goes bankrupt. Had the accounts been properly prepared, the bankruptcy would have been predictable. The investor sues the ac-countant.

2. *Negligent Performance of a Service*: A lawyer negligently draws a will in violation of the *Wills Act*, and in consequence the intended benefici-ary is deprived of an inheritance. The frustrated beneficiary sues to re-cover the lost gift, even though the beneficiary had not been aware of the intended gift, and had not otherwise relied on it.

3. *Defective Products or Buildings*: A builder negligently constructs a home with faulty foundations. The home poses a risk of collapsing. The non-privity owner sues the builder for the cost of remedying the dan-gerous defect.

4. *Relational Economic Loss* (consequent on physical damage to a third party): A negligent ship captain allows his vessel to damage a railway bridge. The bridge is owned by the government, who recovers routinely in negligence for the physical damage to the bridge. A railway com-pany sues to recover extra shipping expenses it incurred because it had to reroute its trains while the government bridge was being repaired.

5. *Independent Liability of Statutory Public Authorities*: A statutory pub-lic authority is given discretion to inspect a building construction. It either fails altogether to inspect, or inspects in a manner which the court finds unreasonable. As a result, a latent defect goes undiscovered.

---

[3] Feldthusen, *Economic Negligence, ibid.*

[4] These categories were cited with approval by La Forest J. in dissent in *Canadian National Railway Co. v. Norsk Pacific Steamship Co.* (1992), 91 D.L.R. (4th) 289, 11 C.C.L.T. (2d) 1 (S.C.C.), and adopted by the full court in *Winnipeg Condominium Corp. No. 36 v. Bird Con-struction Co.*, [1995] 1 S.C.R. 85, 121 D.L.R. (4th) 193; *D'Amato v. Badger*, [1996] 2 S.C.R. 1071, 137 D.L.R. (4th) 129; and *Bow Valley Husky (Bermuda) Ltd v. Saint John Shipbuilding Ltd.*, [1997] 3 S.C.R. 1210, 153 D.L.R. (4th) 385. See also Klar, "Recent Developments in Canadian Law: Tort Law" (1991), 23 Ottawa L. Rev. 177; Bernstein, *supra*, n. 2; and Schwartz, *supra*, n. 2.

[5] Subsequently, in *Martel Building Ltd. v. Canada*, [2000] 2 S.C.R. 860, 193 D.L.R. (4th) 1, the Court declined to recognize a new category. The plaintiff bidder sought to impose upon a tender-calling authority, a duty in drafting tender specifications. Another attempt at creating a new category failed in *Status Electrical Corp. v. University of British Columbia* (2000), 6 C.L.R. (3d) 85 (B.C.S.C.).

When the defect is discovered, the owner sues the authority to recover the cost of remedying the defect.[6]

The first four categories will be discussed in this chapter, whereas the fifth one will be examined in Chapter 17.

At one time it was common to speak of an "exclusionary rule" governing all claims for pure economic loss in negligence, and later of an exclusionary rule subject to exceptions. In fact, there is not now, nor was there ever, any such comprehensive exclusionary rule. There did exist a well-recognized rule precluding recovery for the fourth category, relational economic loss, a rule which persists subject to a few narrow exceptions today. Claims of the other sort were rarely litigated in negligence until the 1960s. Until then, it was assumed that such claims were actionable in contract, if at all. Today, recovery for pure economic loss in negligence is possible in each of misrepresentation, services, product defect and public authority cases provided the special category-specific conditions for a duty of care are met. Recovery for relational loss is possible in exceptional circumstances only.

It is apparent that the first two categories, misrepresentation and services, are quite similar to one another. Typically, defendants in misrepresentation actions are those like accountants who provide professional services in the form of representations. This makes the plaintiff's reliance on the representation a key element in the action. Typical defendants in the services category provide professional services in the form of acts, not words. Sometimes the economic injury occurs without any reliance by the plaintiff. The other three categories of economic loss are quite different from misrepresentation and services, and quite different from one another. This explains why the Supreme Court has allowed the jurisprudence within each category to develop separately.

Despite these differences, all types of pure economic loss share certain features that distinguish them from personal injury and property damage. These basic distinctions account for the courts' modifying the *prima facie* proximity test for duty of care. They include the possibility of indeterminate liability; the difference between social loss and transfer of wealth; and the relevance of existing and potential contractual allocation of loss.

Ordinarily in a physical damage case the defendant owes a duty to foreseeable plaintiffs for foreseeable harm. In economic loss cases, duty defined in foreseeability terms alone may create the potential for indeterminate liability — indeterminate in amount, time, and class. Concern about potentially indeterminate liability has dominated the economic loss case law. Unless the foreseeability approach to duty is modified, the potential for indeterminate liability is greatest in cases of misrepresentation and relational loss. This potential for

---

[6] In the fourth edition of his book, Feldthusen re-defined this category as *"Public Authority's Failure to Confer an Economic Benefit"*. This has not been adopted or considered by the Supreme Court.

indeterminate liability has therefore influenced the courts to adopt restrictive duties of care in misrepresentation and relational loss. In contrast, there is no obvious reason to think that indeterminate liability is more likely in the services, defective product, or public benefits cases than it is in ordinary physical damage cases. Other factors account for the special duties in these categories.

A purely financial loss is qualitatively different from a serious personal injury. That alone could justify the law drawing a distinction between personal injury and economic loss. However, that will not explain a distinction between property damage and economic loss. What distinguishes both personal injury and damage to property on the one hand and most pure economic loss on the other is that physical damage inevitably constitutes a social loss. When persons or property are injured or damaged, something of value is destroyed permanently. The law can compensate the victim by transferring resources from the defendant to the plaintiff, but at the end of the transfer process the deficit to society remains. Accordingly, a *prima facie* duty of care based on foreseeability of harm makes good sense.

In contrast, many pure economic losses involve not social loss, but mere transfers of wealth. One person's gain becomes another's loss, but nothing is destroyed. Such transfers, however foreseeable, are not necessarily objectionable. Unsuccessful investments, for example, are foreseeable, but not, without more, socially objectionable. Indeed, ordinary commerce would grind to a halt were the law to seek to deter transfers of wealth to the same extent it seeks to deter destruction. The court must know much more about the circumstances than foreseeability before determining whether the conduct producing a transfer of wealth should be deterred, or encouraged.

One important circumstance is whether the loss in question has already been allocated to the plaintiff by contract. If so, the court must discover a legitimate reason to change the contractual allocation. The case against tort liability is strongest when the risk of economic loss had previously been allocated by contract from the defendant to the plaintiff. It may also be relevant whether the plaintiff had an opportunity to protect itself by contract from the risk of economic loss and declined to do so.[7] Few victims of accident-caused physical damage have an opportunity to arrange their potential losses by contract with the defendant. Many plaintiffs in pure economic loss cases have had such an opportunity, and some have actually done so.

The Supreme Court's refusal to recognize a new category of economic loss claim in *Martel Building Ltd. v. Canada*[8] illustrates how some of the above factors are taken into account. A commercial tenant brought an action against a government landlord, complaining about the landlord's unfair behaviour during the lease negotiation process. The Supreme Court used the two-step *Anns* approach to determine whether a new category of economic loss claim should be

---

7   See the reference to "channeling", below, at p. 442.

8   *Supra*, n. 5.

established. Proximity was readily established, but the claim failed for policy reasons at step two.[9] The court noted that the loss was a mere transfer of wealth, not an actual social loss. It also expressed reluctance to have the courts assume a commercial regulatory function, and indicated a desire to discourage unnecessary litigation. Perhaps the key reason for disallowing the claim was expressed by Iacobucci and Major JJ. for the court as follows:

> It would defeat the essence of negotiation and hobble the marketplace to extend a duty of care to the conduct of negotiations, and to label a party's failure to disclose its bottom line, its motives or its final position as negligent. Such a conclusion would of necessity force the disclosure of privately acquired information and the dissipation of any competitive advantage derived from it, all of which is incompatible with the activity of negotiating and bargaining.[10]

A. Negligent Misrepresentation

Until the 1960s there was no liability for economic loss caused by negligent misrepresentation. Negligent misrepresentations that caused physical harm posed little difficulty.[11] However, unless there was a contractual or fiduciary relationship between the parties[12] or unless the plaintiff could prove fraud,[13] misrepresentations leading to economic loss were not actionable. In 1963, in the now-famous decision in *Hedley Byrne v. Heller*,[14] the House of Lords recognized that an action for misrepresentation could support a claim for pure economic loss. This decision has proven to be one of the most influential

---

[9]   The *Anns* approach is discussed in more detail *infra*, n. 41.

[10]   *Supra*, n. 5, at p. 886, S.C.R.

[11]   *Clay v. A.J. Crump & Sons Ltd.*, [1964] 1 Q.B. 533 (C.A.); *Clayton v. Woodman & Son (Builders) Ltd.*, [1962] 2 All E.R. 33, [1962] 2 Q.B. 546 (C.A.). See also *Kripps v. Touche Ross & Co.* (1992), 94 D.L.R. (4th) 284, at p. 291 (B.C.C.A.) (*per* Taylor J.A.); *Robson v. Chrysler Corp. (Canada)* (1962), 32 D.L.R. (2d) 49 (Alta. C.A.); *Kubach v. Hollands*, [1937] 3 All E.R. 907 (K.B.); *Watson v. Buckley, Osborne, Garrett & Co.*, [1940] 1 All E.R. 174 (K.B.); *Pease v. Sinclair Refining Co.* (1939), 104 F.2d 183; *Lambert v. Lastoplex Chemicals Co.*, [1972] S.C.R. 569; *Grange Motors (Cymbran) Ltd. v. Spencer*, [1969] 1 W.L.R. 53 (C.A.); *Sharp v. Avery and Kerwood*, [1938] 4 All E.R. 85 (C.A.); *The Apollo*, [1891] A.C. 499 (H.L.); *Hawke v. Waterloo-Wellington Flying Club Ltd.*, [1972] 1 O.R. 78 (Co. Ct.); *Gertsen v. Metropolitan Toronto (Mun.)* (1973), 2 O.R. (2d) 1, at p. 28 (H.C.J.); *Manitoba Sausage Mfg. Co. v. Winnipeg (City)* (1976), 1 C.C.L.T. 221 (Man. C.A.); *Hendrick v. DeMarsh* (1984), 45 O.R. (2d) 463 (H.C.J.).

[12]   See generally Feldthusen, *Economic Negligence*, *supra*, n. 2, chapter 2; Cane, "The Metes and Bounds of Hedley Byrne" (1981), 55 Aust. L.J. 862, at p. 864; Bishop, "Negligent Misrepresentation Through Economists' Eyes" (1980), 96 L.Q. Rev. 360; Fridman, "Negligent Misrepresentations" (1976), 22 McGill L.J. 1; Symmons, "The Problem of the Applicability of Tort Liability to Negligent Misstatements in Contractual Situations: A Critique of the Nunes Diamonds and Sealand Cases" (1975), 21 McGill L.J. 79; Goodhart, "Liability for Innocent but Negligent Misrepresentations" (1964), 74 Yale L.J.; Craig, "Negligent Statements, Negligent Acts and Economic Loss" (1976), 92 L.Q. Rev. 213.

[13]   *Derry v. Peek* (1889), 14 App. Cas. 337; *Pasley v. Freeman* (1789), 3 Term Rep. 51, 100 E.R. 450; *Goad v. Canadian Imperial Bank of Commerce*, [1968] 1 O.R. 579 (H.C.J.).

[14]   *Hedley Byrne & Co. v. Heller & Partners Ltd.*, [1963] 2 All E.R. 575, [1964] A.C. 465 (H.L.).

decisions ever rendered in private law generally and in negligence law in particular.

The initial reluctance to recognize the action was based on a number of factors that distinguish misrepresentation actions for economic loss from standard negligence actions for physical damage governed by *Donoghue v. Stevenson.*[15] The dominant concern remains that a duty in speech based on foreseeability alone could expose the defendant to "liability in an indeterminate amount for an indeterminate time to an indeterminate class".[16] Because "[w]ords are more volatile than deeds", and "travel fast and far afield", and "are used without being expended", the size and width of the range of possible claims are so enormous that the courts resisted entering the field.[17] Physical damage itself is a rough-and-ready limiting factor, whereas the number of economic losses that might arise in reliance on a single negligent statement, especially with modern information technology, is indeterminate, and frighteningly large. Although the concern about indeterminate liability appears to have provided the courts with sufficient justification for adopting a restricted duty of care,[18] other concerns are also important. Taken together, these factors have led the courts to adopt a limited duty of care in negligence.

First, any physical damage constitutes a social loss; that is, there exist fewer social resources after the negligent act than before. In contrast, losses suffered in reliance on negligent advice are almost invariably transfers of wealth, not true social losses. One party's loss is another's gain. As explained earlier, there is no justification for a presumption that all foreseeable transfers of wealth are objectionable, as there is for physical damage.[19] The justification for duty must be richer than foreseeability alone.[20]

Second, freedom of speech is an important social value in a constitutional democracy. A requirement to exercise reasonable care in speech restricts free speech. Such an inhibition must be imposed thoughtfully, and only in circumstances that justify infringing the defendant's right of expression.

Third, professional advice is the subject of the typical misrepresentation action. Accountants' financial statements are a common example. These financial statements, like other forms of professional advice, are bought and sold in commercial markets pursuant to contractual arrangements. It is often foreseeable that the information will be seen by non-contracting parties, and that these parties might reasonably assume the information to be accurate and rely on it to their financial detriment. However, this sort of foreseeability alone cannot justify allowing non-contracting parties to appropriate the benefit of the

---

[15]   [1932] A.C. 562 (H.L.).

[16]   *Ultramares Corp. v. Touche Niven & Co.*, 255 N.Y. 170, at p. 179, 174 N.E. 441 (1931).

[17]   *Supra*, n. 14, at p. 534, A.C. (*per* Lord Pearce).

[18]   See *Hercules Managements Ltd. v. Ernst & Young, infra*, n. 35.

[19]   Above, at p. 4 (text prior to n. 7).

[20]   On the question of justification generally, see Feldthusen, "Liability for Pure Economic Loss: Yes, But Why?", *supra*, n. 2.

financial service for free. Some narrower definition of the relationship than that of foreseeable plaintiff and some more circumscribed definition of the case for duty than that of foreseeable harm are required to justify liability, quite independent of the concern over indeterminate loss. Moreover, given the predominantly commercial nature of most misrepresentation actions, the courts must also be sensitive to the general concerns of commercial law. It makes little sense, for example, to develop a clear and certain law of contract to govern commerce and to allow it to be circumvented by an uncertain law of negligence.[21]

Finally, misrepresentations do not injure anyone directly. The plaintiff must take some action in reliance on the statement before any harm occurs. This gives the plaintiff opportunities for self-protection not available in most physical injury situations. The reasonableness of the plaintiff's reliance is central to the duty-of-care analysis; critical to the issue of causation in fact; and also relevant on the question of contributory negligence.

Perhaps the breakthrough in *Hedley Byrne* would not have occurred had it not been for the powerful dissenting judgment by Lord Denning in the earlier Court of Appeal case, *Candler v. Crane, Christmas & Co.*[22] The plaintiff had subscribed to shares in a company on the strength of certain negligently prepared accounting documents. The majority of the Court of Appeal denied liability on the traditional ground that different rules apply to negligent misstatements than to the negligent circulation of chattels. In dissent, however, Lord Justice Denning assailed the majority as "timorous souls who were fearful of allowing a new cause of action" and who tried to inhibit the "bold spirits" from creating one. Lord Justice Asquith, writing for the majority, stated that he was not "concerned with defending the existing state of the law or contending that it is strictly logical. It clearly is not — but I am merely recording what I think it is. If this relegates me to the company of 'timorous souls', I must face that consequence with such fortitude as I can command".[23]

The majority decision in *Candler* was not received enthusiastically,[24] and cracks in the no-liability rule eventually began to appear. In *Boyd v. Ackley*,[25] an accountant who negligently prepared financial statements for company shareholders was held liable to the shareholders in contract. In an *obiter dictum*, the court indicated a willingness to hold him liable, even in the absence of a contract, because of the close relationship between the accountant and the shareholders. In an Australian case, an accountant appointed under a statute was held liable for a careless statement to a municipality with whom he had no

---

[21] See *Canadian Pacific Hotels Ltd. v. Bank of Montreal*, [1987] 1 S.C.R. 711, 40 D.L.R. (4th) 385.

[22] [1951] 1 All E.R. 426, [1951] 2 K.B. 164 (C.A.).

[23] *Ibid.*, at p. 195, K.B.

[24] See Fridman, *supra*, n. 12; Goodhart, *supra*, n. 12; Seavey, "*Candler v. Crane, Christmas & Co*: Negligent Misrepresentations by Accountants" (1951), 67 L.Q. Rev. 466.

[25] (1962), 32 D.L.R. (2d) 77 (B.C.S.C.).

contact.[26] With these cases, and others like them, the stage was set for a dramatic reversal.

The "bold spirits" finally conquered, and the "timorous souls" were vanquished in *Hedley Byrne*.[27] The plaintiff, a firm of advertising agents, placed several orders for television time and advertising space in newspapers on behalf of a client, Easipower Ltd., on terms under which the plaintiff became personally liable. The plaintiff caused its bank, the National Provincial Bank Ltd., to make inquiries concerning the financial position of Easipower. The National Bank telephoned the defendants, who were bankers for Easipower, and asked in confidence and without responsibility on behalf of the defendants about the respectability and standing of Easipower, and whether the latter would be good for an advertising contract. Some months later, the National Bank wrote to the defendants again asking them, in confidence, whether they would consider Easipower trustworthy to the extent of £100,000 per annum in advertising contracts. The defendants replied to both inquiries that Easipower was a respectably constituted company and considered good for its normal business requirements. The defendants' letter in reply to the second inquiry read, "For your private use and without responsibility on the part of the bank or its officials". The defendants' replies to the National Provincial Bank's inquiries were communicated to the plaintiff, who, relying on these replies, placed orders for advertising time and space on behalf of Easipower Ltd. Soon after, the latter went into liquidation, and the plaintiff lost over £17,000 on the advertising contracts.

The House of Lords dismissed the case on the basis of the words "without responsibility" in the defendant's letter. However, it went out of its way in a lengthy *dictum* to overthrow *Candler v. Crane, Christmas & Co.*, and to establish a new liability principle for negligent statements that cause economic loss. All five Law Lords agreed that a duty could be imposed in certain circumstances for negligent words in the absence of contract and without fiduciary relations. Several of the Lords borrowed from the language of business and contract. Lord Pearce, for example, observed that to impart a duty, the representation must normally concern "a business or professional transaction".[28] Lord Devlin declared that a duty to take care in word includes relationships "equivalent to contract" where there is an "assumption of responsibility", or an "implied"

---

[26] *Shire of Frankston and Hastings v. Cohen*, [1960] A.L.R. 249 (H.C.).

[27] *Supra*, n. 14; see Goodhart, *supra*, n. 12; Glasbeek, "Limited Liability for Negligent Misstatement" in Linden (ed.), *Studies in Canadian Tort Law* (Toronto: Butterworths, Law Review 1968), at p. 115; Gordon, "*Hedley, Byrne & Co. Ltd. v. Heller & Partners Ltd.* in the House of Lords" (1964–65), 2 U.B.C. 113; Walker, "The Bold Spirits Have Conquered: *Hedley, Byrne & Co. Ltd. v. Heller & Partners Ltd.*" (1964), 3 Osgoode Hall L.J. 89; Stevens, "*Hedley, Byrne & Co. Ltd. v. Heller & Partners Ltd.*: Judicial Creativity and Doctrinal Possibility" (1964), 27 Mod. L. Rev. 121.

[28] *Supra*, n. 14, at p. 617, All E.R.

undertaking.[29] Others, however, offered a more liberal foundation for the limit. Lord Reid, for example, emphasized reasonable reliance.[30] Similarly, Lord Morris of Borth-y-Gest opined that, where a defendant "quite irrespective of contract" knows that another will reasonably rely on the defendant's judgment or skill, a duty will arise.[31]

Today, the assumption-of-responsibility approach favoured by many academics[32] appears to have been adopted by the House of Lords.[33] In contrast, most Canadian cases subsequent to *Hedley Byrne* favoured the broader views endorsed in earlier editions of this book and did not insist upon an "undertaking" or something "equivalent to contract", as proposed by Lord Devlin. In *Fletcher v. Manitoba Public Insurance Co.*,[34] for instance, Madam Justice Wilson explained that a duty of care would be owed if someone (i) relies on information, (ii) the reliance is reasonable, and (iii) the defendant knew, or ought to have known, that he or she could rely on the information. Madam Justice Wilson concluded in the case that the plaintiff was a "neighbour", that the reliance was expected, and that compensation should therefore be awarded. Essentially, this is the approach endorsed by the Supreme Court in its most recent decision on point, *Hercules Managements Ltd. v. Ernst & Young.*[35] As we shall see, as a fuller understanding of the purposes of the special duty enquiry has developed over the years, there probably remains little difference in practice between the two approaches.[36]

In a recent case, *Queen v. Cognos Inc.*,[37] the Supreme Court of Canada reviewed the law relating to negligent misrepresentation. Mr. Justice Iacobucci

---

[29] *Ibid.*, at p. 610.

[30] *Ibid.*, at p. 583.

[31] *Ibid.*, at p. 594.

[32] Professor Blom, for example, argues that there should be no liability unless a "reasonably sceptical and prudent person" would think he or she had an "assurance, equivalent in weight to a promise". Blom, "Economic Loss: Curbs on the Way Ahead" (1987), 12 Can. Bus. L.J. 275, at p. 292; see also *"Donoghue v. Stevenson* and The Modern Law of Negligence", in *The Paisley Papers* (1991), at p. 175. Others call for an "undertaking" or an "assumption of responsibility" by a defendant for liability to be imposed. See Smith, *Liability in Negligence* (1984); Feldthusen, *Economic Negligence, supra*, Blom, *ibid.*, at p. 291; Smillie, "Negligence and Economic Loss", *supra*, n. 2. Still others feel that there should be an intention to be bound by the statement. See *Shirlyn Fishing Co. v. Pumps & Power Ltd.* (1990), 3 C.C.L.T. (2d) 304 (B.C.C.A.).

[33] The strongest support comes from *Hedley Byrne* itself. See *supra*, n. 14, at pp. 483-93 (A.C.) (*per* Lord Reid); at pp. 502-3 (*per* Lord Morris); at p. 505 (*per* Lord Hodson); at pp. 528-30 (*per* Lord Devlin); and at pp. 539-40 (*per* Lord Pearce). More recently, see *Henderson v. Merrett Syndicates Ltd.*, [1995] 2 A.C. 165 (H.L.(E.)); *Williams v. Natural Life Health Foods Ltd.*, [1998] 2 All E.R. 577 (H.L.(E.)); *White v. Jones*, [1995] 2 W.L.R. 187 (H.L.); *Dean v. Allin & Watts*, [2001] E.W.C.A. Civ. 758 (C.A.); *Merrett v. Babb*, [2001] 3 W.L.R. 1 (C.A.).

[34] [1990] 3 S.C.R. 191, at p. 212, 74 D.L.R. (4th) 636. This has now been adjusted in *Queen v. Cognos Inc.*, [1993] 1 S.C.R. 87, 99 D.L.R. (4th) 626.

[35] [1997] 2 S.C.R. 165, 146 D.L.R. (4th) 577.

[36] *Infra*, n. 90.

[37] *Supra*, n. 34.

definitively summarized the jurisprudence and outlined five general requirements for imposing liability for negligent representations:

> ... (1) there must be a duty of care based on a "special relationship" between the representor
> and the representee; (2) the representation in question must be untrue, inaccurate, or mis-
> leading; (3) the representor must have acted negligently in making said representation; (4)
> the representee must have relied, in a reasonable manner, on said negligent misrepresenta-
> tion; and (5) the reliance must have been detrimental to the representee in the sense that dam-
> ages resulted.[38]

The first requirement has subsequently been elaborated on by the Supreme
Court in *Hercules*[39] to require a duty based generally on "foreseeable reasonable
reliance". Otherwise, the five requirements advanced in *Cognos* provide a useful
framework in approaching a case involving negligent misrepresentation.

1. DUTY OF CARE

The first requirement in *Cognos* is that there must be a duty of care based on a
"special relationship" between the representor and the representee. In *Hercules*,[40]
the Supreme Court outlined the methodology to be employed in considering
whether a duty of care exists. The defendants were accountants who were hired
to prepare audited financial statements as required by statute. The plaintiffs,
shareholders, claimed that the audits were negligently prepared. They claimed to
have suffered two different types of loss in reliance: loss on additional investments they were induced to make on the basis of the accounts; and devaluation
of their existing shareholdings. Their claim ultimately failed because of a
concern with potentially indeterminate liability.

In particular, the court indicated that the same two-stage *Anns* approach to
duty of care was to be employed for negligent misrepresentation as for any other
negligence case.[41] In *Kamloops City v. Neilsen*,[42] the Supreme Court itself had
earlier reformulated the *Anns* test as follows:

(1)   is there a sufficiently close relationship between the parties (the [defendant] and the
       person who has suffered the damage) so that, in the reasonable contemplation of the
       [defendant], carelessness on its part might cause damage to that person? If so,
(2)   are there any considerations which ought to negative or limit (a) the scope of the duty
       and (b) the class of persons to whom it is owed or (c) the damages to which a breach of
       it may give rise?

---

[38]   *Ibid.*, at p. 110, S.C.R.
[39]   *Supra*, n. 35.
[40]   *Ibid.*
[41]   *Anns v. Merton London Borough Council*, [1978] A.C. 728 (H.L.), at pp. 751-52 (*per* Lord
        Wilberforce).
[42]   [1984] 2 S.C.R. 2, at pp. 10-11, 10 D.L.R. (4th) 641.

a)   Step One – Proximity

The first branch of the *Anns/Kamloops* test looks for a degree of proximity sufficient to justify the imposition of a *prima facie* duty of care. La Forest J. spoke for the full court in *Hercules*.[43] He observed that:

> . . . the term "proximity" itself is nothing more than a label expressing a result, judgment or conclusion; it does not, in and of itself, provide a principled basis on which to make a legal determination.

He continued:

> . . . if "proximity" is meant to distinguish the cases where the defendant has a responsibility to take reasonable care of the plaintiff from those where he or she has no such responsibility, then in negligent misrepresentation cases, it must pertain to some aspect of the relationship of reliance. To my mind, proximity can be seen to inhere between a defendant-representor and a plaintiff-representee when two criteria relating to reliance may be said to exist on the facts: (a) the defendant ought reasonably to foresee that the plaintiff will rely on his or her representation; and (b) reliance by the plaintiff would, in the particular circumstances of the case, be reasonable. To use the term employed by my colleague, Iacobucci J., in *Cognos* . . . , the plaintiff and the defendant can be said to be in a "special relationship" whenever these two factors inhere.[44]

The court recognized explicitly that the standard "foreseeable harm to a foreseeable plaintiff" approach that governs physical damage negligence is an inadequate foundation for *prima facie* duty with misrepresentations that lead to financial loss.[45] For this reason foreseeable reasonable reliance was introduced at the proximity stage. However, foreseeable reasonable reliance *simpliciter* will not do the job. As La Forest J. himself acknowledged, foreseeable reasonable reliance is virtually inevitable whenever a professional person circulates professional advice to the public.[46] The foreseeable reasonable reliance test taken literally would mean that any professional advisor who publishes information would have to exculpate itself from a duty to anyone who foreseeably and reasonably relies upon it. True, the concern about indeterminate liability led the court in *Hercules* to negative the duty at stage two of the analysis. However, quite apart from indeterminate liability, there is no apparent justification for casting the net of *prima facie* duty so widely.

The court in *Hercules* identified five general *indicia* of reasonable reliance. It is apparent that these factors require a great deal more than simple reasonable reliance based on the plaintiff's assumption that advice provided by a professional was prepared with due care. The *indicia* are:

---

[43]   *Supra*, n. 35.
[44]   *Ibid.*, at pp. 187-88, S.C.R.
[45]   *Ibid.*, at pp. 188-89.
[46]   *Ibid.*, at pp. 200-01.

(1) The defendant had a direct or indirect financial interest in the transaction in respect of which the representation was made.

(2) The defendant was a professional or someone who possessed special skill, judgment or knowledge.

(3) The advice or information was provided in the course of the defendant's business.

(4) The information or advice was given deliberately, and not on a social occasion.

(5) The information or advice was given in response to a specific enquiry or request.

In *Keith Plumbing & Heating Co. v. Newport City Club Ltd.*,[47] Mr. Justice Esson of the British Columbia Court of Appeal examined in depth the question of what constitutes reasonable reliance for the purpose of duty of care in misrepresentation. He said:

> It is not enough, as a basis for imposing liability, to find that it was reasonable from the point of view of the plaintiff to rely on the defendant's representations. . . .
>
> . . . I would suggest, in light of the law laid down in *Hercules*, that the more relevant question is whether the reliance was reasonable having regard to all of the circumstances known to and affecting both parties. In this case, while it may be said that the contractors took a gamble, it was not a matter of choosing to rely upon the Bank as a matter of business efficacy. Rather, it was a matter of taking the gamble because there was no alternative course and because, as appears from the evidence in this case, it is a common practice for banks to provide such information to contractors. It is, of course, also significant that the five *indicia* identified by Professor Feldthusen in the passage adopted in *Hercules* were all present in this case.
>
> The confusion inherent in the term "reasonable reliance" might be reduced if the term "justifiable reliance" was employed to state the test for imposing liability. That is a term which Professor Blom has employed in this context. . . .
>
> > In a case of negligent misstatement causing pure economic loss on a contract or other financial transaction, it is not enough that the average person would foreseeably rely on the defendant's statements. The defendant owes the plaintiff no duty of care unless a reasonably prudent and sceptical person, in the plaintiff's position, would have been led by the defendant's words or conduct to believe that he had an assurance of the defendant's taking reasonable care, equivalent in weight to the defendant's promise.
> >
> > Only in such a case can the plaintiff truly be said to have placed justifiable reliance on the defendant. This distinction between the plaintiff who foreseeably relies, and the plaintiff who is justified in relying, also mitigates the risk of liability to an indeterminately large group. The relationship between the defendant and such a large group will seldom justify the inference of an assurance like the one suggested here.

---

[47] (2000), 184 D.L.R. (4th) 75, at pp. 113-14, [2000] 6 W.W.R. 65 (B.C.C.A.), leave to appeal to S.C.C. refused, S.C.C. Bulletin, 2000, 1875. This case presents the most extensive judicial discussion of the difference between the several duty approaches.

Although foreseeable reasonable reliance was brought to the forefront in *Hercules*, the concept has always been important in Canadian misrepresentation law. It seems reasonable to assume that earlier decisions regarding reasonable reliance may still prove helpful after *Hercules*. For example, in *J. Nunes Diamonds Ltd. v. Dominion Electric Protection Co.*,[48] an unidentified worker was sent by the defendant company to check over a "burglar alarm service". In response to an inquiry about its effectiveness, the worker responded that even the company's engineers could not enter the building without the alarm going off. The premises were later broken into and valuable jewellery was stolen. Mr. Justice Schroeder refused to base any corporate responsibility upon these statements, which were unauthorized and unrelated to the worker's job. Although this stand is somewhat harsh, it may be explained on the ground that the plaintiff's reliance was totally unreasonable in the circumstances. Similarly, reliance cannot be placed on a gas-truck driver's assurance that there was no danger of leaking gas, when, in fact, there was, because the driver was not a skilled service person.[49] Nor should one place reliance on an adversary, such as someone else's agent,[50] the insurance adjuster of someone who has negligently damaged one's car,[51] or the vendor of a hotel who gives a statement about its profitability.[52]

Statements of opinion, likewise, cannot reasonably be relied on. As Mr. Justice Bouck explained, "[n]ot every wrong statement by a defendant should automatically attract liability".[53] Thus, where statements of opinion about a future event are so extravagant or suspicious that an ordinary person would not believe them, no liability will ensue. Nor can what is usually regarded as mere puffery form the basis of a *Hedley Byrne* action.[54]

The courts have also correctly denied recovery for negligent advice given in a casual way; otherwise, "it would be extremely hazardous for an attorney to give an opinion on any point of law in the course of a journey".[55] If the negligent advice were given in the confines of an office in a business connection, however, a lawyer may well be held liable, because then the reliance would be reasonable. The law is well illustrated by the case of *John Bosworth Ltd. v.*

---

[48] [1971] 1 O.R. 218, at p. 227 (C.A.); affd [1972] S.C.R. 769, 26 D.L.R. (3d) 699, other grounds as well. Compare *Agopsowicz v. Honeywell Ltd. – Honeywell Ltée*, [1997] 7 W.W.R. 299, 156 Sask. R. 5 (Q.B.).

[49] *Klein v. Canadian Propane Ltd.* (1967), 64 D.L.R. (2d) 338 (B.C.S.C.).

[50] *Adams-Eden Furniture Ltd. v. Kansa General Insurance Inc.* (1996), 141 D.L.R. (4th) 288, [1997] 2 W.W.R. 65 (Man. C.A.).

[51] *Sulzinger v. C.K. Alexander Ltd.*, [1972] 1 O.R. 720 (C.A.); see also *Kamahap Enterprises Ltd. v. Chu's Central Market Ltd.* (1989), 64 D.L.R. (4th) 167, 1 C.C.L.T. (2d) 55 (B.C.C.A.).

[52] *Kingu v. Walmar Ventures Ltd.* (1986), 10 B.C.L.R. (2d) 15, 38 C.C.L.T. 51 (C.A.).

[53] *Williams v. Bd. of School Trustees of School Dist. No. 63 (Saanich)* (1986), 37 C.C.L.T. 203, at p. 210 (B.C.S.C.); affd 14 B.C.L.R. (2d) 141 (C.A.), opinion about outcome of union grievance being no problem proved wrong.

[54] *Andronyk v. Williams* (1985), 21 D.L.R. (4th) 557 (Man. C.A.).

[55] *Fish v. Kelly* (1864), 17 C.B.N.S. 194, 144 E.R. 78, at p. 83.

Professional Syndicated Developments Ltd.,[56] where a developer was held to have unreasonably relied on informal statements about zoning regulations. The statements were made by a mayor, who was not responsible for zoning matters, at a social luncheon and during an unsolicited telephone conversation. In denying liability, Mr. Justice Robins explained that:

> . . . to recover on the rationale of *Hedley Byrne*, the plaintiff must do some act to his economic detriment in reliance on the representation, and he must have had reasonable grounds for relying on the representation. It is one thing, for instance, to rely on serious statements made in the context of business or professional relationships and quite another to rely on those made on informal or social occasions.[57]

Another decision along these lines is *Shirlyn Fishing Co. v. Pumps & Power Ltd.,*[58] where negligent advice about the capacity of a pump on a fishing boat was given over the telephone by a dealer in pumps to an unidentified caller who did not say how the information would be used. The court held that no duty was owed in these circumstances because no reasonable person would suppose that the "gratuitous information" carried legal weight, having been given in an "informal" context and without any "intention to be bound". This was not a situation in which the inquirer was reasonable in relying on the information, nor would the defendant have foreseen reliance.

Finally, in *Sharadan Builders Inc. v. Mahler,*[59] town officials were excused from liability when they did not inform the plaintiff's solicitor about the restrictions of a conservation authority in regard to the issuance of building permits. The court explained that the officials did not hold themselves out as being "engaged in the business of or otherwise expert in advising upon requirements for building permits other than those imposed by the municipality itself".[60] In other words, the plaintiff was not reasonable in relying upon the advice of the officials in the circumstances.

Similarly, there is no "representation" that would subject anyone to liability if there is merely a "forecast of the future", for example, where the head of a racing commission predicts that there will continue to be a racing track, despite certain financial difficulties.[61] In the same way, a public announcement concerning a proposed downtown development, which was never undertaken, could not be relied on.[62] In these circumstances, reliance is simply not reasonable, and recovery is rightfully withheld.

---

[56]   (1979), 97 D.L.R. (3d) 112 (Ont. S.C.).

[57]   *Ibid.*, at p. 122.

[58]   *Supra*, n. 32, at p. 316.

[59]   (1978), 22 O.R. (2d) 122 (C.A.) (*per* Jessup J.A.).

[60]   *Ibid.*, at p. 123.

[61]   *Andronyk, supra*, n. 54.

[62]   *Executive Holdings Ltd. v. Swift Current (City of)* (1984), 36 Sask. R. 15 (Q.B.); *Dorsch v. Weyburn* (1985), 23 D.L.R. (4th) 379 (Sask. C.A.).

It is not necessary for that information or advice to be requested for one to foresee that it will be reasonably relied upon, but this may be a factor courts will consider in determining whether a defendant would realize that someone would rely on the advice or information.[63]

It is furthermore clear that if defendants warn plaintiffs that they are not assuming any obligation with regard to the information given, there will be no liability.[64] This is understandable, for those who base a business decision on unfounded information are unworthy of tort law's protection, either because they have voluntarily assumed the risk or because they have not reasonably relied on the statement. Many Canadian banks are now disclaiming responsibility in these situations as a matter of course.[65] It is odd that auditors and others do not follow suit. If more reliable information is needed, the inquirer should be prepared to pay for it.

Employing this rigorous approach to reliance also resolves other important policy considerations. By requiring reasonable reliance, the court takes into account the fact that no harm would come from information or advice alone unless and until action is taken by the plaintiff in reliance. The considered application of the five *indicia* from *Hercules* should effectively preclude the possibility of a plaintiff appropriating the defendant's professional services without the defendant's knowledge or against the defendant's will. The justifiable reliance inquiry also addresses the concern about inhibiting unduly the defendant's right of free speech. The *indicia* above would suggest that the information or advice was offered in a considered fashion, and that a reasonable defendant would have expected there to be legal consequences to follow if the advice was not prepared with due care.

In fact, where the information or advice is tendered in the first instance pursuant to contract (as it was tendered by contract between the defendants and the corporation in *Hercules*), the court need not be concerned about liability inhibiting speech. Rather, the concern becomes, as it did in *Hercules*, to whom and for what beyond the contractual obligations ought the defendant to be held liable. It is in a case like *Hedley Byrne*,[66] where there was no contractual obligation to supply information or advice to anyone, that care must be taken to protect the defendant's right to speak freely without unexpected legal obligations attaching. This is accomplished by the search for justifiable reliance at the proximity stage.

---

[63] See Klar, *supra*, n. 4, at p. 185; *392980 Ontario Ltd. v. Welland (City)* (1984), 45 O.R. (2d) 165, 6 D.L.R. (4th) 151 (H.C.J.); *Foster Advertising v. Keenberg* (1987), 35 D.L.R. (4th) 521 (Man. C.A.); leave to appeal to S.C.C. refused (1987), 80 N.R. 314*n*. Twaddle J.A. relied on lack of inquiry as a factor in holding no expected reliance.

[64] See *supra*, n. 14.

[65] See Walker, *supra*, n. 27. But see *supra*, n. 47.

[66] *Supra*, n. 14.

b) Step Two – Reasons to Limit or Negative

Of all the concerns about liability in misrepresentation, none has dominated the case law more than the concern about potentially indeterminate liability. The plaintiff's claim failed in *Hercules* despite a finding of proximity. The outcome was determined at branch two of the duty analysis, where the question of potentially indeterminate liability emerged as a reason to negative liability.

The plaintiffs relied on an earlier decision of the Supreme Court of Canada, *Haig v. Bamford*,[67] which had held that liability would extend to members of a known limited class, which the shareholders in *Hercules* certainly were. The Supreme Court distinguished *Haig* as a case in which the defendants had known the precise amount at risk when they provided the negligent statements.[68] The court imposed an additional criterion in *Hercules*, that the defendant not only know the identity of the plaintiff (or the class of plaintiffs) who would rely on the statement, but also that the statement itself would be:

> . . . used by the plaintiff for precisely the purpose or transaction for which it was prepared. The crucial importance of this additional criterion can clearly be seen when one considers that even if the specific identity or class of potential plaintiffs is known to a defendant, use of the defendant's statement for a purpose or transaction other than that for which it was prepared could still lead to indeterminate liability.[69]

This additional requirement is conveniently known as the "end and aim" rule, a term derived from the seminal decision of the New York Supreme Court in *Glanzer v. Shepard*.[70] Although the paths taken by the courts to their conclusions have differed, the leading decisions of the House of Lords[71] and the High Court of Australia,[72] like *Hercules*, have all consistently limited liability to losses suffered in the very transaction that the information or advice was intended to influence.[73] Another way of expressing this is to say that liability has been confined by the responsibility the defendant assumed and by the scope of the plaintiff's justifiable reliance.

The presence of a relevant contractual relationship between the parties is a second consideration that may lead the courts to limit or negative a *prima facie* duty established by foreseeable reasonable reliance. It is clear that a pre- or existing contractual relationship is very helpful to a plaintiff seeking to establish a relationship of sufficient proximity to justify the recognition of a duty of care in negligence.[74] The controversial issue has been whether the presence of the

---

[67]   [1977] 1 S.C.R. 466, 72 D.L.R. (3d) 68.

[68]   *Supra*, n. 35, at p. 199, S.C.R.

[69]   *Ibid.*, at p. 203. See also *Lakefield (Village) v. Black* (1998), 166 D.L.R. (4th) 96 (Ont. C.A.).

[70]   233 N.Y. 236, 135 N.E. 275 (1922).

[71]   *Caparo Industries plc v. Dickman*, [1990] 1 All E.R. 568.

[72]   *Esanda Finance Corp. v. Peat Marwick Hungerfords (Reg)* (1997), 142 A.L.R. 750.

[73]   See also *Price Waterhouse v. Kwan*, [2000] 3 N.Z.L.R. 39 (C.A.).

[74]   The presence of a contractual relationship may be less relevant today now that the Supreme Court has switched emphasis from the "special relationship" in *Cognos* to foreseeable reasonable

contractual relationship should limit or eliminate the duty that would otherwise exist. The question has arisen in three different situations: pre-contractual representations; post-contractual representations; and concurrent liability when the same statement is relied upon as both a negligent misrepresentation and as a term of a contract. A single general principle has emerged from these three lines of authorities. Unless there is something in the contract that specifically negates liability for negligent misrepresentation, the mere existence of the contract, albeit that it deals with the same subject matter as the alleged negligent misrepresentation, does not limit or negative the duty.

The first important Canadian case was *J. Nunes Diamonds Ltd. v. Dominion Electric Protection.*[75] It dealt with an alleged post-contractual representation that a burglar alarm system could not be circumvented in an action by a jeweller who had been robbed after the alarm had been bypassed. The claim failed because the majority believed that to allow the claim would be to override an exclusion clause in the contract. Speaking for the majority, Mr. Justice Pigeon observed:

> [T]he basis of tort liability considered in *Hedley Byrne* is inapplicable to any case where the relationship between the parties is governed by a contract unless the negligence relied on can properly be considered as "an independent tort" unconnected with the performance of that contract.[76]

Mr. Justice Spence dissented. He was less worried about tort law's interference with the purity of contract law. On the contrary, His Lordship relied on the existence of the contractual relation in deciding that a *Hedley Byrne* duty was owed, because this meant that a "relationship" existed between the plaintiff and the defendant.[77] The case was not as helpful a precedent as it might have been because the majority's analysis of "independent tort" was incomplete, and because the plaintiff's claim could justifiably have been dismissed on several other grounds.[78]

The next important decision of the Supreme Court was *Central Trust Co. v. Rafuse.*[79] This case dealt with the possibility of concurrent liability. Mr. Justice Le Dain, in a learned and comprehensive opinion, explained that the existence of a contract "should [not] preclude reliance on a concurrent or alternative liability in tort" and that the plaintiff has the right "to assert the cause of action that appears to be most advantageous to him".[80] Mr. Justice Le Dain warned, however, that "concurrent . . . liability in tort will not be admitted if its effect would

---

reliance in *Hercules*. But see *R.M. Turton v. Kerslake and Partners*, [2000] 3 N.Z.L.R. 406 (C.A.).

[75] [1972] S.C.R. 769, 26 D.L.R. (3d) 699.

[76] *Ibid.*, at p. 777, S.C.R.

[77] *Ibid.*, at p. 810.

[78] See Feldthusen, *Economic Negligence, supra*, n. 2, at pp. 81-82.

[79] [1986] 2 S.C.R. 147, 37 C.C.L.T. 117; rehearing [1988] 1 S.C.R. 1026.

[80] *Ibid.*, at pp. 205-06, S.C.R.

be to permit the plaintiff to circumvent or escape a contractual exclusion or limitation of liability".[81]

In *BG Checo International Ltd. v. British Columbia Hydro & Power Authority*,[82] the Supreme Court reinforced and clarified this point. Madam Justice McLachlin and Mr. Justice La Forest explained:

[A] plaintiff may sue either in contract or in tort, subject to the limit the parties themselves have placed on that right by their contract. . . .

The rule is that one cannot sue concurrently in contract and tort where the contract limits or contradicts the tort duty. It is rather that the tort duty, a general duty imputed by the law in all relevant circumstances, must yield to the parties' superior right to arrange their duties in a different way. In so far as the tort duty is not contradicted by the contract, it remains intact and may be sued upon.[83]

As regards negligent misstatements made during pre-contractual negotiations, courts were historically less hesitant to impose liability. In the classic case *Esso Petroleum Co. v. Mardon*,[84] a petroleum company negligently overstated the sales capacity of a service station to a prospective tenant who, relying on this misstatement, subsequently entered the lease. Business proved poor for the tenant, but he eventually recovered his losses through a negligence claim. In affirming the trial decision, Lord Denning M.R. stated:

[I]f a man, who has or professes to have special knowledge or skill, makes a representation by virtue thereof to another — be it advice, information or opinion — with the intention of inducing him to enter a contract with him, he is under a duty to use reasonable care to see that the representation is correct, and that the advice, information or opinion is reliable. If he negligently gives unsound advice or misleading information or expresses an erroneous opinion, and thereby induces the other side to enter into a contract with him, he is liable in damages.

This approach was adopted in *Sodd Corp. v. Tessis*.[85] A trustee in bankruptcy negligently advised a purchaser of certain of the bankrupt company's wares, and the court imposed liability on the basis that there was a "pre-contractual negligent misrepresentation" that led to "a special relationship creating a duty of care to the plaintiff".[86] The Manitoba Court of Appeal adopted a similar attitude in *Andronyk v. Williams*,[87] where the court held that a duty of care will arise during pre-contract negotiations where one party makes statements that are reasonably foreseen to cause economic loss.

---

[81] *Ibid.*, at p. 206.

[82] [1993] 1 S.C.R. 12, 99 D.L.R. (4th) 577.

[83] *Ibid.*, at p. 27, S.C.R.

[84] [1976] 2 All E.R. 5, at p. 16, [1976] 2 W.L.R. 583 (C.A.). See also *Rainbow Industrial Caterers Ltd. v. Canadian National Railway* (1988), 54 D.L.R. (4th) 43, [1989] 1 W.W.R. 673 (B.C.C.A.).

[85] (1997), 17 O.R. (2d) 158, 79 D.L.R. (3d) 632 (C.A.).

[86] *Ibid.*, at p. 160, O.R. See also *Herrington v. Kenco Mortgage & Invts. Ltd.* (1981), 125 D.L.R. (3d) 377 (B.C.S.C.) (*per* Paris J.).

[87] *Supra*, n. 54. See also *Rainbow Caterers*, *supra*, n. 84.

Finally, in *Cognos*, this issue was treated as follows:

[T]he fact that the alleged negligent representations are made in a pre-contractual setting, such as during negotiations or in the course of an employment hiring interview, and the fact that a contract is subsequently entered into by the parties do not, in themselves, bar an action in tort for damages caused by said misrepresentations.[88]

Following the *BG Checo* case, the contract will affect the tort duty only if the parties restrict or waive the duty respecting representations.[89] This attitude demonstrates that negligence law protects negotiating parties in the same way as it assists others in the community in other situations, which is as it should be. Negligent statements are no more defensible in a pre-contractual context than elsewhere. The courts should combat it in that situation in the same way as they do in other contexts. The defendant enjoys the opportunity to eliminate the duty by the express words of the contract if that is the wish of the parties.

It would also appear that *Hercules* has resolved which of three competing approaches to duty of care commonly found in the case law — special relationship, foreseeable reasonable reliance or voluntary assumption of responsibility — will now govern the law of misrepresentation in Canada. Foreseeable reasonable reliance appears to have won the day. However, the difference between and among these tests may be less than first appears. Regardless of which nominal test the courts employ, they have typically considered precisely the same factors to determine whether the test has been satisfied.[90]

The disadvantage of the "special relationship" approach is that the term, like proximity, is merely a conclusory label; " . . . it does not, in and of itself, provide a principled basis on which to make a legal determination".[91] However, as a label it is useful to signal that negligent misrepresentation is a tort where liability is based on some form of antecedent relationship between the parties more closely defined than by foreseeability alone.

Voluntary assumption of responsibility is the approach most consistent with the decision in *Hedley Byrne* itself,[92] and it enjoys the most support among recent appellate judgments in England.[93] With this approach, one considers the *indicia* listed above for the purpose of determining whether one can infer that the speaker assumed responsibility to the plaintiff. This approach resembles

---

[88] *Supra*, n. 34, at p. 112, S.C.R. See also *Beer v. Townsgate* (1997), 36 O.R. (3d) 136 (C.A.); leave to appeal to S.C.C. refused (1998), 228 N.R. 92*n* (S.C.C.).

[89] *Supra*, n. 82.

[90] Interestingly, the factors cited in *Hercules* were taken from Feldthusen, *Economic Negligence*, *supra*, n. 2, at p. 65, which the Court quoted. Feldthusen used these factors to infer assumption of responsibility, not reasonable reliance. This suggests that the two approaches are essentially the same and that the court saw them as such. See also *Fashion Brokers v. Clarke Hayes*, [2000] Lloyd's Rep. P.N. 398, [2000] P.N.L.R. 473 (C.A.).

[91] *Supra*, n. 35, at p. 187.

[92] Recall the claim failed because the defendant indicated expressly that it provided its advice "without responsibility".

[93] *Supra*, n. 33.

most closely the law of contract, albeit without privity and consideration. It emphasizes that information is property that ought only to be surrendered voluntarily. Where the court goes beyond reliance *simpliciter* and employs the same *indicia* to determine whether reliance was justified, this should lead to the same end.[94]

Perhaps the only situation in which the choice between justifiable reliance and voluntary assumption of responsibility might make a difference is where disclamatory language is used. This was the opinion of the majority in the British Columbia Court of Appeal which in a 2-1 judgment recognized a duty of care based on justifiable reliance by the plaintiff in the face of clear disclamatory language.[95]

c) What Defendants?

One of the shortcomings of the "special relationship" approach to duty is that it suggests that duty in misrepresentation might be confined to certain professionals. The leading case was at one time *Mutual Life & Citizens' Assurance Co. v. Evatt*,[96] where an insurance company negligently advised a potential investor about a subsidiary company. When the investor lost money invested in reliance upon this advice, the investor launched an action against the insurance company. The majority of the Privy Council, led by Lord Diplock, overturned the Australian High Court and held that no action would lie unless it was alleged that the defendants were in the "business of giving advice upon investments or in some other way had let it be known to him that they claimed to possess the necessary diligence to give reliable advice to him upon the subject-matter of his inquiry".[97]

The limitation espoused by Lord Diplock did not survive the test of time. The limitation made sense on the facts in *Mutual Life*, but was unnecessarily general. Canadian courts, in particular, were quick to adopt a broader view imposing liability in a far wider array of circumstances than that permitted by *Mutual Life*.[98] It was in *Queen v. Cognos* where *Mutual Life* was unequivocally cast aside. Indicating his "support for a more flexible approach on this question", Mr. Justice Iacobucci of the Supreme Court of Canada stated:

---

[94] Fleming, *The Law of Torts*, 9th ed. (1998), at p. 200, speaks of a voluntary assumption of responsibility to a plaintiff known to be reliant.

[95] *Keith Plumbing & Heating Co. v. Newport City Club Ltd.*, *supra*, n. 47, at p. 108 (D.L.R.).

[96] [1971] 2 W.L.R. 23 (P.C. Aus.). See also *Bank für Handel and Effekten v. Davidson & Co.* (1975), 55 D.L.R. (3d) 303 (B.C.C.A.) (*per* Bull J.A.); Goodhart, "Comment" (1971), 87 L.Q. Rev. 147; Pickford, "A Mirage in the Wilderness: *Hedley, Byrne* Considered" (1971), 34 Mod. L. Rev. 328; Glasbeek, "Comment" (1972), 49 Can. Bar Rev. 128.

[97] *Mutual Life v. Evatt, ibid.*, at p. 35.

[98] *Patrick L. Roberts Ltd. v. Sollinger Industries Ltd.* (1978), 19 O.R. (2d) 44 (C.A.); *Blair v. Canada Trust Co.* (1986), 32 D.L.R. (4th) 515, 9 B.C.L.R. (2d) 43 (S.C.); *Farish v. National Trust Co.*, [1975] 3 W.W.R. 499 (B.C.S.C.); *Nelson Lumber Co. v. Koch* (1980), 111 D.L.R. (3d) 140, [1980] 4 W.W.R. 715 (Sask. C.A.).

... I reject the so-called restrictive approach as to who can owe a *Hedley Byrne* duty of care, often associated with the majority judgment in *Mutual Life & Citizens' Assur. Co. Ltd. v. Evatt* [1971] A.C. 793 (P.C.). In my opinion, confining this duty of care to "professionals" who are in the business of providing information and advice such as doctors, lawyers, bankers, architects, and engineers, reflects an overly simplistic view of the analysis required in cases such as the present one. The question of whether a duty of care with respect to representations exists depends on a number of considerations including, but not limited to, the representor's profession. While this factor may provide a good indication as to whether a "special relationship" exists between the parties, it should not be treated in all cases as a threshold requirement. There may be situations where the surrounding circumstances provide sufficient indicia of a duty of care, notwithstanding the representor's profession.[99]

Mutual Life is now dead, and the law in this area consequently makes more sense. The class of potential defendants includes virtually all professional people whose function it is to advise others in all manner of things. The courts have applied *Hedley Byrne* to doctors,[100] lawyers,[101] accountants,[102] architects,[103] engineers,[104] bankers,[105] stock appraisers,[106] real estate appraisers,[107] public weighers,[108] abstractors,[109] real estate agents,[110] insurance agents,[111] stock brokers,[112] financial

---

[99] *Supra*, n. 34, at pp. 117-18 S.C.R.

[100] *Smith v. Auckland Hospital Bd.*, [1965] N.Z.L.R. 191.

[101] *34/6/1 B.C. Ltd. v. Blaikie* (2000), 83 B.C.L.R. (3d) 120, 2 C.C.L.T. (3d) 290 (S.C.); *Burman's Beauty Supplies Ltd. v. Kempster* (1974), 4 O.R. (2d) 626 (Co. Ct.).

[102] *Law Society v. KPMG Peat Marwick*, [2000] 1 All E.R. 515 (Ch.D.); *Haig v. Bamford, supra*, n. 67; *Toromont Industrial Holdings Ltd. v. Thorne, Gunn, Helliwell and Christenson* (1975), 10 O.R. (2d) 65 (H.C.); affd and vard (1976), 14 O.R. (2d) 87 (C.A.). See also *West Coast Finance Ltd. v. Gunderson, Stokes, Walton & Co.*, [1975] 4 W.W.R. 501 (B.C.C.A.).

[103] *Sutcliffe v. Thackrah*, [1974] A.C. 727, [1974] 1 All E.R. 859 (H.L.); *Saxby v. Fowler* (1977), 3 Alta. L.R. (2d) 47, 2 C.C.L.T. 195 (C.A.).

[104] *Burnett v. Took Engineering*, [2000] B.C.J. No. 2302 (S.C.); *Carl M. Halvorson Inc. v. Robert McLellan & Co.*, [1973] S.C.R. 65; *University of Regina v. Pettick* (1991), 77 D.L.R. (4th) 615, 90 Sask. R. 241 (C.A.).

[105] *Advanced Glazing Systems v. Frydenlund* (2000), 2 C.L.R. (3d) 241, 32 R.P.R. (3d) 162 (B.C.S.C.); *supra*, n. 47; *Goad v. Canadian Imperial Bank of Commerce, supra*, n. 13; *Zahara v. Hood*, [1977] 1 W.W.R. 359 (Alta. Dist. Ct.); *NBD Bank, Canada v. Dofasco Inc.* (1999), 181 D.L.R. (4th) 37, 47 C.C.L.T. (3d) 213 (Ont. C.A.).

[106] *Arenson v. Casson, Beckman, Rutley & Co.*, [1975] 3 All E.R. 901 (H.L.).

[107] *Cai-Van Hotel Ltd. v. Globe Estates Ltd.*, [1974] 6 W.W.R. 707 (B.C.S.C.).

[108] *Glanzer v. Shepard, supra*, n. 70.

[109] *Dickle v. Abstracted Co.* (1890), 89 Tenn. 431. See also *York v. Alderney Consultants* (2000), 187 N.S.R. (2d) 383 (S.C.).

[110] *Dodds v. Millman* (1964), 45 D.L.R. (2d) 472 (B.C.S.C.); *Hopkins v. Butts* (1967), 65 D.L.R. (2d) 711 (B.C.S.C.); *Bango v. Holt* (1972), 21 D.L.R. (3d) 66 (B.C.S.C.); *Avery v. Salie*, [1972] 3 W.W.R. 759 (Sask. Q.B.); *Hauck v. Dixon* (1975), 10 O.R. (2d) 605 (H.C.J.).

[111] *Myers v. Thompson*, [1967] 2 O.R. 335 (H.C.J.); affd [1961] 2 O.R. 335n (C.A.); *Fletcher v. Manitoba Public Insurance Co., supra*, n. 34; *Fine's Flowers Ltd. v. General Accident Assurance Co.* (1974), 5 O.R. (2d) 137 (H.C.J.); affd 17 O.R. (2d) 529 (C.A.); but see *Sulzinger v. C.K. Alexander Ltd., supra*, n. 51, at p. 722 (C.A.).

[112] *Central B.C. Planers Ltd. v. Hocker* (1970), 10 D.L.R. (3d) 699 (B.C.C.A.), affd (1971), 16 D.L.R. (3d) 368n (S.C.C.); *Culling v. Sansai Securities Ltd.* (1974), 45 D.L.R. (3d) 456 (B.C.S.C.).

advisers,[113] trust companies,[114] car sales people,[115] automobile repairers,[116] municipal officials,[117] and other government employees.[118] A duty will also be imposed upon any defendant who clearly assumes responsibility for the accuracy of the information, gives an undertaking or an assurance "equivalent to contract," or otherwise communicates an intention to be bound. Thus, in *W.B. Anderson & Sons Ltd. v. Rhodes (Liverpool) Ltd.*,[119] a commission agent negligently advised several fruit sellers that his client, a proposed purchaser, was creditworthy. The sellers delivered stock relying on this advice, and the purchaser promptly went bankrupt. The sellers' action against the commission agent succeeded, the court explained, because the information he gave was "not casual or perfunctory",[120] but was sought and given "in a business connection" and there was a "relation equivalent to contract".[121]

d) What Plaintiffs?

One must also examine the status of the plaintiff when seeking to establish a duty of care. Being a foreseeable neighbour is not enough in this context. For many years, this difficulty was a point of controversy over which the courts polarized. One view held that, for liability to be affixed, a defendant had to pass information *directly* to the plaintiff, or to someone the defendant knew would transmit it to the plaintiff for a defined purpose, or that a plaintiff had to be an "identified person".[122] Thus, where an accountant furnished his client with numerous copies of erroneous statements, unaware to whom and for what purpose they would be shown, he was not held liable.[123] On the other hand, a public weigher, paid by a seller, who falsely informed a purchaser about the weight of goods delivered;[124] a valuer, hired by a property owner, who gave a

---

[113] *Farish, supra*, n. 98.

[114] *Ibid.*

[115] *Fan v. Garrett*, [2000] O.J. No. 4235 (S.C.); *Reid v. Traders General Insurance Co.* (1963), 41 D.L.R. (2d) 148 (N.S.T.D.).

[116] *Babcock v. Servacar Ltd.*, [1970] 1 O.R. 125 (Co. Ct.).

[117] *Windsor Motors Ltd. v. Powell River (Dist.)* (1969), 4 D.L.R. (3d) 155 (B.C.C.A.); *Ministry of Housing & Local Gov't v. Sharp*, [1970] 2 Q.B. 223 (C.A.); *Gadutsis v. Milne*, [1973] 2 O.R. 503 (H.C.J.); *The Pas (Town) v. Porky Packers Ltd.* (1974), 46 D.L.R. (3d) 83 (Man. C.A.); revd on other grounds, [1977] 1 S.C.R. 51, [1976] 3 W.W.R. 138.

[118] *Patrick L. Roberts Ltd. v. Sollinger Industries Ltd.* (1978), 19 O.R. (2d) 44 (C.A.); *Dubnick v. Winnipegosis*, [1985] 2 W.W.R. 437 (Man. Q.B.); affd [1985] 5 W.W.R. 758 (Man. C.A.); *Bell v. Sarnia (City)* (1987), 59 O.R. (2d) 123 (H.C.J.); *Spinks v. Canada*, [1996] 2 F.C. 563, 134 D.L.R. (4th) 223 (C.A.). See Chapter 17, for details.

[119] [1967] 2 All E.R. 850 (Cairns J.). See also *Beaver Lumber Co. v. McLenaghan* (1982), 143 D.L.R. (3d) 139, [1983] 2 W.W.R. 171 (Sask. C.A.).

[120] *Ibid.*, at p. 862.

[121] *Ibid.*

[122] *Ministry of Housing & Local Gov't v. Sharp, supra*, n. 117, at p. 290.

[123] *Ultramares Corp. v. Touche Niven & Co., supra*, n. 16.

[124] *Glanzer v. Shepard, supra*, n. 70.

careless report to a mortgagee's lawyer;[125] and an auditor who furnished an investor with a balance sheet prepared for another use,[126] were all found liable.

The competing view looked to foreseeable reliance as the determining factor. Thus, Lord Justice Salmon once declared that "a man may owe a duty of care in what he writes or says just as much as in what he does".[127] Mr. Justice Ruttan once observed in a *dictum* that liability would be imposed for loss suffered by "another person who [the defendant] knows or should know will place reliance on his advice".[128] Hence it was said that a real estate appraiser would be liable to anyone who suffered injury in connection with "any transactions relating to the land" such as a "mortgage, credit rating, or sale".[129] In the same vein, it was held that where circumstances brought certain corporate shareholders "within the contemplation of the [defendant] accountants", a duty is owed to the shareholders.[130] Lastly, Lord Denning declared that the

> . . . duty to use due care in a statement arises . . . from the fact that the person making it knows, or ought to know, that others, being his neighbours in this regard, would act on the faith of the statement being accurate. That is enough to bring the duty into being. It is owed . . . to the person to whom the certificate is issued and whom he knows is going to act on it . . . . But it is also owed to any person whom he knows, or ought to know, will be injuriously affected by a mistake. . . .[131]

A half-way house between these competing positions has now emerged in the Canadian jurisprudence, as in most other jurisdictions.[132] As noted earlier, based on *Haig v. Bamford*,[133] the plaintiff need not receive the information directly but must be a member of a known limited class. In addition, based on *Hercules*,[134] the defendant must also know that the statement itself would be " . . . used by the plaintiff for precisely the purpose or transaction for which it was prepared".[135]

---

[125] *Cann v. Willson* (1888), 39 Ch. D. 39; *Smith v. Eric S. Bush*, [1989] 2 All E.R. 514 (H.L.).

[126] *Diamond Manufacturing Co. v. Hamilton*, [1969] N.Z.L.R. 609 (C.A.).

[127] *Ministry of Housing & Local Gov't v. Sharp*, *supra*, n. 117, at p. 278.

[128] *Cari-Van Hotel Ltd. v. Globe Estates Ltd.*, *supra*, n. 107, at p. 715.

[129] *Ibid.*, at pp. 716-17. See also *Beebe v. Robb* (1977), 81 D.L.R. (3d) 349 (B.C.S.C.).

[130] See *Toromont Industrial Holdings Ltd. v. Thorne, Gunn, Helliwell and Christenson*, *supra*, n. 102 (*per* Holland J.); but see *Caparo Industries plc v. Dickman*, *supra*, n. 71; *Esanda Finance Corp. v. Peat Marwick Hungerfords (Reg)*, *supra*, n. 72.

[131] *Ministry of Housing & Local Gov't v. Sharp*, *supra*, n. 117, at p. 268.

[132] See *Caparo Industries plc v. Dickman*, *supra*, n. 71; *Esanda Finance Corp. v. Peat Marwick Hungerfords (Reg)*, *supra*, n. 72.

[133] *Supra*, n. 67. See also *Edgeworth Construction Ltd. v. N.D. Lea & Associates Ltd.*, [1993] 3 S.C.R. 206; *Royal Bank of Canada v. Burgoyne* (1995), 147 N.S.R. (2d) 5, 28 C.C.L.T. (2d) 191 (S.C.); revd 152 N.S.R. (2d) 150 (C.A.); *cf. Auto Concrete Curb Ltd. v. South Nation River Conservation Authority*, [1993] 3 S.C.R. 201, 17 C.C.L.T. (2d) 123; *supra*, n. 102.

[134] *Supra*, n. 35.

[135] *Ibid.*, at p. 203, S.C.R.

2. UNTRUE, INACCURATE OR MISLEADING STATEMENT

The second *Cognos* criterion is that the defendant must have made an untrue, inaccurate, or misleading statement. Although for the majority of cases this criteria poses little difficulty,[136] its application is not entirely without controversy. While a literal falsity clearly qualifies as an untrue or inaccurate statement, the courts have decided that one may mislead by implication and even by things that have been left unsaid. In *Cognos*, for example, Iacobucci J. stated that there is "considerable authority for the more flexible view that in *appropriate circumstances*, implied misrepresentations can, and often do, give rise to actionable negligence. . . . In my opinion, a flexible approach to this issue is preferable".[137] This approach was taken in *Doherty v. Allen*, where the court held that the failure to warn of impending danger was "by implication from the circumstances" to be a misrepresentation of safety.[138]

So, too, can omissions give rise to actionable negligence. In *Spinks v. Canada*,[139] the Federal Court of Appeal held a defendant liable for not fully disclosing information pertinent to the plaintiff's pension rights. The plaintiff was an employee of the Australian public service who emigrated to Canada to work for the Atomic Energy Commission Limited. Upon his sign-up, the employer failed to inform the plaintiff that his Australian pension rights could be "bought back" and thereby rolled into a Canadian public service pension. The court stated simply that "[a] person may be 'misled' by a failure to divulge as much as by advice that is inaccurate or untrue" and that "[m]issing information can be just as harmful as mistaken information".[140] Similarly, the failure to inform on insurance matters may also give rise to liability. In *Fletcher v. Manitoba Public Insurance Co.*,[141] the failure of the agent for the government insurer to inform the plaintiff properly about the availability of underinsured motorist coverage led to economic losses. Liability was imposed. Insurance agents have also been held liable to their clients for failing to advise them to take out sufficient insurance to cover their property.[142] A real estate agent who acted on the sale of a dairy farm

---

[136] See *Biggerstaff v. 934169 Ontario*, [2000] O.J. No. 300 (Ont. S.C.); affd [2000] O.J. No. 4761 (Ont. C.A.), for an example of failing to meet this threshold.

[137] *Supra*, n. 34, at p. 131, S.C.R.

[138] (1988), 55 D.L.R. (4th) 746 at p. 752 (N.B.C.A.). See also *392980 Ontario Ltd. v. Welland (City)*, *supra*, n. 63.

[139] *Supra*, n. 118 (*per* Linden J.A.).

[140] *Ibid.*, at pp. 236 and 230 D.L.R.

[141] *Supra*, n. 34; see Streusser, "Comment" (1990), 5 C.C.L.T. (2d) 64, criticizing the case on various grounds.

[142] *McCann v. Western Farmers Mutual Ins. Co.* (1978), 20 O.R. (2d) 210 (H.C.). See also *Mason v. Morrow's Moving & Storage Ltd.*, [1977] 2 W.W.R. 738, 2 C.C.L.T. 118 (B.C.S.C.); revd [1978] 4 W.W.R. 534, 5 C.C.L.T. 59 (B.C.C.A.).

was held liable for failing to inform the purchaser that the milk quota was to be reduced on the farm's sale because of the rules of the Milk Marketing Board.[143]

Obligations to inform may likewise arise upon the happening of future contingencies. Thus, where a statement is true at the time it is made, but later becomes untrue in circumstances of which the defendant is aware, the defendant may be obliged to disclose the change in circumstance to the plaintiff. Thus, in *De Groot v. St. Boniface General Hospital*,[144] the defendant was held liable for failing to advise the plaintiff of a significant change in his job prospects. The plaintiff was a surgeon who had recently completed his residency requirements at the defendant hospital. Before leaving to complete his education overseas, the plaintiff applied to the hospital for general and specialized surgical privileges upon his return. He was told that both would be granted. Relying on this, he eventually returned to take up a position. Upon returning, however, he was told that his general privileges had been reconsidered. The court found both the senior surgeon and the hospital liable for failing to inform the plaintiff of the hospital's change of attitude at the time the change occurred. Likewise, in *Gallant v. Central Credit Union Ltd.*,[145] the plaintiff was advised by the defendant to change his mortgage over from the defendant credit union to a mortgage company. The plaintiff followed the advice, and the defendant aided in the preparation of documents. As an incident of the changeover, the plaintiff was required to cancel the life and disability insurance he held on the previous mortgage and take out a new policy. The new policy he acquired, however, lacked disability coverage, and he was not informed of this by the defendant. The plaintiff subsequently became disabled and sued the defendant for the "negligent non-statement". The Court held that the defendant had a duty to inform the plaintiff of the change in circumstances, saying that "it almost goes without saying that a failure to provide essential information can give rise to liability".

Beyond instances where a plaintiff is misled through implication or omission are cases, replete in number, where straight untruth has formed the basis for a negligence action. A real estate agent who erroneously informed a purchaser that a piece of land was an "apartment site" was held responsible for not checking this fact, even where the owner had fraudulently misled him.[146] An insurance broker who recommended that insurance be purchased from a financially shaky company was required to reimburse the client for both the civil damages and criminal penalties that the client was forced to pay as a result of not being

---

[143] *Olsen v. Poirier* (1978), 21 O.R. (2d) 642 (H.C.) (*per* Steele J.); affd (1980), 28 O.R. (2d) 744 (C.A.); but see *Saul v. Himel* (1994), 120 D.L.R. (4th) 432, 22 C.C.L.T. (2d) 292, at p. 299 (Ont. Gen. Div.).

[144] [1993] 6 W.W.R. 707, 87 Man. R. (2d) 57 (Q.B.).

[145] (1994), 125 Nfld. & P.E.I.R. 66, 22 C.C.L.T. (2d) 251, at p. 259 (P.E.I.T.D.). See also *Banque de la Cité S.A. v. Westgate Insurance*, [1989] 2 All E.R. 952 (C.A.).

[146] *Hopkins v. Butts, supra*, n. 110.

insured.[147] Where an architect mistakenly estimated the cost of a building beyond a reasonable range of error,[148] and where a garage person made a negligent diagnosis of a car,[149] liability may be rendered. Similarly, where the value of a pension plan was negligently estimated, causing certain employees to leave their employment prematurely, liability also followed.[150]

3. STANDARD OF CARE

The third *Cognos* requirement simply requires that the defendant must have acted negligently in making the misrepresentation. Stated otherwise, the defendant must have breached the standard of care. The standard of care applicable to negligent misrepresentation cases was discussed by Iacobucci J. where he stated:

> The applicable standard of care should be the one used in every negligence case, namely the universally accepted, albeit hypothetical, "reasonable person". The standard of care required by persons making representations is an objective one.[151]

The objective nature of the test was stated by the court as follows:

> Although the representor's subjective belief in the accuracy of the representations and his moral blameworthiness, or lack thereof, are highly relevant when considering whether or not a misrepresentation was fraudulently made, they serve little, if any, purpose into an inquiry into negligence. As noted above, the applicable standard of care is that of the objective reasonable person. The representor's belief in the truth of his or her representations is irrelevant to that standard of care.[152]

The court also noted that the standard of care requires something greater than common honesty, but does not reach the heights of a warranty. Neither does it require full disclosure in every instance where a defendant is called upon to advise.[153] Rather, "it is a duty to exercise such reasonable care as the circumstances require to ensure that representations made are accurate and not misleading".[154] The standard must be assessed by reference to all circumstances relevant to whether the plaintiff was reasonably misled. In addressing the standard of disclosure required of a government staffing officer, the court stated in *Spinks*:

> I might emphasize that the standard of care here is that which is reasonably expected of a staffing officer in the circumstances. I am not suggesting that the failure to divulge every bit of irrelevant and arcane information will breach the standard of care. An advisor's responsi-

---

[147] *Osman v. J. Ralph Moss Ltd.*, [1970] 1 Lloyd's Rep. 313 (C.A.).
[148] *Saxby v. Fowler, supra*, n. 103.
[149] *Babcock v. Servacar Ltd., supra*, n. 116.
[150] *Manuge v. Prudential Assurance Co.* (1977), 81 D.L.R. (3d) 360 (N.S.T.D.).
[151] *Supra*, n. 34, at p. 121, S.C.R.
[152] *Ibid.*, at p. 125, S.C.R.
[153] *Ibid.*, at pp. 120-21, S.C.R.
[154] *Ibid.*, at p. 121, S.C.R.

bility is not one of complete or perfect disclosure. Trivia need not be mentioned. The duty, rather, is one of reasonable disclosure, and what is reasonable varies according to circumstances. The failure to divulge is but one factor among others to be considered when deciding whether there has been negligence.[155]

Similarly, Mr. Justice Strayer, as he then was, stated that the standard of disclosure to be observed concerns that which is "within the competence of the defendant".[156]

If the defendant is a professional person, however, the standard of the reasonable professional person must be observed. Where auditors are involved, for example, they must perform as reasonable auditors. Moreover, they cannot merely comply with the custom of the profession. As Finch J.A. has explained:

> A professional body cannot bind the rest of the community by the standard it sets for its members. Otherwise, all professions could immunize their members from claims for negligence.[157]

In other words, the regular standard of care in negligence law applies to misrepresentation.

4. REASONABLE RELIANCE

The fourth requirement in *Cognos*[158] is that the plaintiff must have reasonably relied upon the representation. Following the decision in *Cognos*, in *Hercules*[159] reliance became the foundation for duty of care. However, reliance is relevant for an additional reason. It states a factual test of causation. Causation is a universal requirement that must be proved in all negligence cases. In this context, causation is normally proven by showing that the plaintiff relied on the statement. Thus, where a plaintiff in a negligence statement action fails to prove that he *in fact* relied on the statement, the action will fail (even if it would have been reasonable to do so). As McGillivray J.A. explained in *Farmer v. H.H. Chambers Ltd.*:

> To recover under the rationale of the *Hedley Byrne* case, representation must not only be made but it has to be such as to cause the plaintiff, as a result, to do some act to his detriment.[160]

Similarly, when a purchaser did not rely exclusively on a real estate agent to fill out a document, but also showed it to his lawyer, liability was denied.[161] Nor was

---

[155] *Supra*, n. 118, at p. 586 (*per* Linden J.A.).
[156] *Rothwell v. R.* (1985), 2 F.T.R. 6, 10 C.C.E.L. 276, at p. 282.
[157] *Kripps v. Touche Ross & Co.*, [1997] 6. W.W.R. 421, at p. 441, 89 B.C.A.C. 288.
[158] *Supra*, n. 34.
[159] *Supra*, n. 35.
[160] [1973] 1 O.R. 355, at p. 357 (C.A.).
[161] *Burstein v. Crisp Devine Ltd.*, [1973] 3 O.R. 342 (H.C.J.) (*per* Grant J.). See also *Kamahap Enterprises Ltd. v. Chu's Central Market Ltd.*, *supra*, n. 51; *Al-Kandari v. J.R. Brown & Co.*, [1988] 1 All E.R. 833 (C.A.).

liability affixed against a repairer when car brakes failed. The vehicle's owner was aware of the defect and was unaware that they were being inspected by the defendant. There was no reliance to the owner's detriment.[162] Also, where the plaintiff knows as much as the employees of the defendant municipality about the effect of certain municipal by-laws, the plaintiff cannot be said to have relied on a misrepresentation when spending money to build an abattoir where such was prohibited. Mr. Justice Spence has observed that the representations must be:

> ... made to a person who has no expert knowledge himself by a person whom the representee believes has a particular skill or judgment in the matter, and that the representations were relied upon to the detriment of the representee.[163]

5. RESULTING DAMAGE

The final requirement from *Cognos* is that damage must have ensued. As in all negligence actions, there can be no liability unless the plaintiff has suffered some loss as a result.

6. CONTRIBUTORY NEGLIGENCE

It appears that contributory negligence and apportionment may now be utilized in negligent statement cases.[164] In *Grand Restaurants of Canada Ltd. v. Toronto (City)*, for example, Mr. Justice Trainor, in imposing liability against the city for giving a restaurateur false information about the existence of a "current file", held that the plaintiff should bear 50 per cent of the responsibility for not checking the data. He explained: "In the case of fault that contributes to the damage suffered, reliance that is 'unreasonable' simply goes to reducing damages otherwise recoverable by the plaintiff; it does not go to cancelling the *prima facie* liability of the defendant."[165]

---

[162] *Algee v. Surette* (1972), 9 N.S.R. (2d) 60, at p. 73 (C.A.).

[163] *The Pas (Town) v. Porky Packers*, [1977] 1 S.C.R. 51, [1976] 3 W.W.R. 138, at p. 155. See also *Gorham v. British Telecommunications plc*, [2000] 1 W.L.R. 2129, [2000] 4 All E.R. 867 (C.A.).

[164] See *Bloor Italian Gifts v. Dixon* (2000), 48 O.R. (3d) 760, 187 D.L.R. (4th) 64 (C.A.); *Sirois v. Federation des Enseignants du Nouveau Brunswick* (1994), 8 D.L.R. (4th) 279 (N.B.Q.B.).; *245229 B.C. Ltd. v. O'Hara*, [1993] B.C.J. No. 511 (S.C.); *Hongkong Bank of Canada v. Touche Ross & Co.* (1989), 36 B.C.L.R. (2d) 381 (C.A.); *Maritime Life Assurance Co. v. Royal Trust Corp. of Canada*, [1989] O.J. 1034 (H.C.); *Spiewak v. 251268 Ontario Ltd.* (1987), 61 O.R. (2d) 655 (H.C.J.); *H.B. Nickerson & Sons Ltd. v. Wooldridge* (1980), 115 D.L.R. (3d) 97 (N.S.C.A.); *Brown & Huston Ltd. v. York (City)* (1983), 5 C.L.R. 240 (Ont. H.C.); vard (1985), 17 C.L.R. 192 (Ont. C.A.); *Sirois v. L'association des Enseignants Francophones du Nouveau- Brunswick* (1984), 8 D.L.R. (4th) 279 (N.B.Q.B.); *Grand Restaurants of Can. Ltd. v. Toronto (City); Chuzar Restaurants Ltd. v. Grand Restaurants of Can. Ltd.* (1981), 32 O.R. (2d) 757 (H.C.J.); affd (1982), 39 O.R. (2d) 752 (C.A.).

[165] *Ibid.*, at p. 775.

A similar approach was taken by Mr. Justice Hart in *H.B. Nickerson & Sons Ltd. v. Wooldridge*,[166] where a plaintiff in a negligent misrepresentation case recovered for losses when a job was lost, but his damages were cut by 40 per cent because of his contributory negligence in failing to make inquiries. Previous editions of this book have taken the position that if both parties cause the loss, both should share the cost of it, just as they do in other negligence cases. Other authors have questioned whether contributory negligence is appropriate in misrepresentation, particularly where reasonable reliance is the very foundation of the duty.[167] It is not easy to reconcile foreseeable reasonable reliance as the very basis of the duty as held in *Hercules* with the remarks of Trainor J. quoted above. It is less controversial to recognize a duty, but reduce liability for contributory negligence when the contributory negligence goes not to the fact of loss, but only to the extent of the loss.[168]

B. Negligent Performance of a Service

The second category of economic loss case recognized by the Supreme Court of Canada is the negligent performance of a service.[169] Cases in this category closely resemble the misrepresentation cases except that the service does not consist of providing information or advice. Instead, the negligently performed professional service manifests itself in an act, not by a representation. It follows that there will usually be less concern over potentially indeterminate loss. The basis of liability in these service cases may also exhibit a close relationship to liability in contract, and concurrent liability is not unlikely.

The most straightforward variation, and the one most closely related to misrepresentation, consists of the defendant's voluntary undertaking to perform a service, the plaintiff's reliance upon the undertaking, the defendant's failure to perform the undertaking carefully, and the resultant economic loss. In *Olsen v. Poirier*,[170] the plaintiff, a recent immigrant, was defrauded by the vendor into believing that he would obtain a certain milk quota when he purchased a farm. In fact, the government's policy was to reduce the quota on sale, rendering the property useless for the plaintiff's purposes. This the plaintiff discovered after purchasing the farm. He brought an action against the vendor in contract, and was successful in having the contract of sale rescinded. There was no consideration to support an action in contract against the real estate agent, so it was

---

[166] *Supra,* n. 164. See also *Royal Bank of Canada v. Burgoyne* (1995), 147 N.S.R. (2d) 5, 28 C.C.L.T. (2d) 191 (S.C.); revd 152 N.S.R. (2d) 150 (C.A.); and *Gallant v. Central Credit Union Ltd., supra,* n. 145.

[167] Klar, *supra,* n. 4, at p. 200; Feldthusen, *Economic Negligence, supra,* n. 2, at pp. 113-15.

[168] *Revelstoke Credit Union v. Miller* (1984), 24 B.L.R. 271, 28 C.C.L.T. 17 (B.C.S.C.). See also *Morash v. Lockhart & Ritchie Ltd.* (1978), 95 D.L.R. (3d) 647 (N.B.C.A.)

[169] See also the discussion in Chapter 16.

[170] *Supra,* n. 143. See also *Chand v. Sabo Brothers Realty Ltd.* (1979), 96 D.L.R. (3d) 445 (Alta. C.A.).

crucial that the plaintiff be permitted to proceed against her in tort. The agent had held herself out as an expert in milk quotas and otherwise behaved in a manner which would justify the inference that she had undertaken to act on the plaintiff's behalf in securing the quota, and the court justifiably held her liable in negligence. There are similar decisions in which insurance agents have been held liable for failing to honour undertakings to secure cover for the plaintiff.[171]

Another series of cases deals with actions brought by the disappointed beneficiaries of wills against the solicitor who drew the will. One of the earliest such decisions was rendered in British Columbia in *Whittingham v. Crease & Co.*,[172] where the potential beneficiary was allowed to recover against the solicitor who carelessly allowed the will to be executed invalidly. The court decided that the solicitor could "reasonably foresee that if he, in the performance of his duty, failed to see that the will was properly witnessed, then that neglect would cause the very loss the plaintiff has suffered". Interestingly, the court based its decision on the principles of *Hedley Byrne*[173] and emphasized that the plaintiffs had been aware of the terms of the will and hence reliant. Shortly thereafter, in *Ross v. Caunters*,[174] the English Court of Chancery permitted a frustrated beneficiary who had been unaware of the will to recover when deprived of the gift by the solicitor's negligence, thus emphasizing that reliance was not the foundation for duty. Today, liability in cases of this sort has been imposed in most jurisdictions,[175] including Canada.[176] There are also a few applications of the same principles outside the wills context.[177]

Yet another sort of negligent service case was considered by the Supreme Court of Canada in *B.D.C. Ltd. v. Hofstrand Farms Ltd.*[178] The reasons why the action failed are instructive. An employee of the Crown Land Grant Office arranged to assist the plaintiff by forwarding a grant to another title office by courier. The courier promised next day delivery, but negligently mis-sorted the

---

[171] *Fletcher v. Manitoba Public Insurance Co., supra,* n. 34; *Morash v. Lockhart & Ritchie Ltd., supra,* n. 168. See also *Midland Bank Trust Co. v. Hett, Stubbs & Kemp,* [1979] Ch. 384, [1978] 3 All E.R. 571, at p. 595; *Tracy v. Atkins* (1979), 105 D.L.R. (3d) 632, at p. 638 (B.C.C.A.); *McNeil v. Village Locksmith Ltd.* (1981), 129 D.L.R. (3d) 543, at p. 547 (Ont. H.C.J.).

[172] (1978), 88 D.L.R. (3d) 353, at p. 373, [1978] 5 W.W.R. 45 (B.C.S.C.). See also Klar, "A Comment on *Whittingham v. Crease*" (1979), 6 C.C.L.T. 311.

[173] *Supra,* n. 14.

[174] [1980] Ch. 297, [1979] 3 All E.R. 580. See also *White v. Jones,* [1995] 2 A.C. 207, [1995] 1 All E.R. 691 (H.L.) (*per* Lord Browne-Wilkinson); and *Hill v. Van Erp* (1997), 142 A.L.R. 687 (H.C.).

[175] See *Biakanja v. Irving,* 157 Cal. Rptr. 407, 598 P.2d 60 (S.C. 1979).

[176] The law is discussed thoroughly in *Earl v. Wilhelm* (2000), 183 D.L.R. (4th) 45, [2000] 4 W.W.R. 363 (Sask. C.A.), where the court overturned a lower court finding of contributory negligence against the testator.

[177] See *Bailey v. HSS Alarms,* [2000] WL 675447 (C.A.); *Gorham v. British Telecommunications plc, supra,* n. 163. But see *Briscoe v. Lubrizol Ltd.,* [2000] I.C.R. 694, [2000] P.I.Q.R. P39 (C.A.).

[178] [1986] 1 S.C.R. 228, 36 C.C.L.T. 87, at p. 94 (*per* Estey J.). See also Blom, "Slow Courier in the Supreme Court" (1986-87), 12 Can. Bus. L.J. 43.

envelope so that delivery took several days. The late delivery caused the plaintiff to default on his contract to sell the lands to another party, and resulted in his suffering a $77,000 loss. The Supreme Court dismissed the action on grounds quite similar to those it would develop much later in *Hercules*.[179] It held that there was no sufficient relationship of proximity such as to satisfy the first branch of the *Anns* test.[180] The defendant had no knowledge of the existence of the plaintiff nor any "actual or constructive knowledge . . . that the rights of a third party could in any way be affected".[181] The court was also concerned with the problem of potentially indeterminate liability. It held that the plaintiff could not be regarded as a member of a class reasonably within the defendant's contemplation, "so as to put a reasonable practical limitation" on liability.[182]

Finally, consider the decision of the Manitoba Court of Appeal in dismissing a claim by the father who was compelled to pay child support after the defendant doctor failed to perform a successful abortion. In the accompanying annotation, Professor Irvine refers to this as a negligent performance of a service case leading to economic loss, and distinguishes the case from the frustrated beneficiary cases on the basis of the "end and aim" rule.[183] The English courts have considered a number of similar claims and resolved the issue more directly by holding that the ordinary costs of rearing a child are not recoverable in negligence on policy grounds, whether categorized as consequential or pure economic loss.[184]

C. Defective Products and Structures

The third category of pure economic loss cases recognized by the Supreme Court of Canada deals with claims to recover the cost of repairing or replacing defective products or structures.[185] The law does not distinguish between products and structures in this area, and the term "product" will be used in this chapter to describe products or structures. Typically, these product quality claims are brought by the owner of the defective product against the remote manufacturer or builder with whom the plaintiff is not in privity of contract. Nevertheless, it remains central to understanding this area that products are invariably exchanged in

---

[179] *Supra*, n. 35.
[180] *Supra*, n. 178.
[181] *Ibid.*, at p. 241, S.C.R.
[182] *Ibid.*
[183] *Freeman v. Sutter*, [1996] 4 W.W.R. 748, 110 Man. R. (2d) 23 (C.A.). But see *Goodwill v. British Pregnancy Advisory Service*, [1996] 2 All E.R. 161 (C.A.).
[184] *McFarlane v. Tayside Health Board*, [2000] 2 A.C. 59, [1999] 3 W.L.R. 1301 (H.L.); *Greenfield v. Irwin*, [2001] 1 W.L.R. 1279 (C.A.); *Parkinson v. St. James and Seacroft University Hospital NHS Trust*, [2001] 3 W.L.R. 376, [2001] 3 All E.R. 97 (C.A.).
[185] *Supra*, n. 4.

commercial markets where the transactions are governed by express or implied contractual terms as to product quality.[186]

"Pure economic loss" has a specific meaning in the product liability context. The term refers to any damage to the product itself except damage caused by an external calamitous accident.[187] Accordingly, a claim for damage to a house that stands on faulty foundations with cracks in the walls and ceilings is a claim for pure economic loss. If the walls and ceilings had suffered the same cracks because of a falling tree, this would be ordinary property damage.[188] If the sag in the foundations causes cracks to appear in other parts of the house such as the walls, one cannot treat the problem with the foundations as economic loss and the problem with the walls as property damage.[189]

There is no category of economic loss claim where there exists greater diversity between and among the various common law jurisdictions as to whether economic loss may be recovered in negligence. The rule in Canada is that one may recover economic loss related to correcting dangerous defects in the product or structure.[190] The question of recovery for non-dangerous defects was left open by the Supreme Court.[191] The overwhelming majority of jurisdictions in the United States do not permit recovery in tort for either dangerous or non-dangerous defects. The plaintiff must rely on contractual and statutory sales law remedies, if any.[192] Similarly, the House of Lords has ruled that no product defect economic loss is recoverable in negligence.[193] Australia[194] and New

---

[186] See generally Harris, "Murphy Makes It Eight — Overruling Comes to Negligence" (1991), 11 Ox. J. Leg. Stud. 416; Fleming, "Negligent Economic Loss in America" in *Negligence after Murphy v. Brentwood DC* (1991), Legal Research Foundation, Auckland, 26, at p. 33; Cohen, "Bleeding Hearts and Peeling Floors: Compensation for Economic Loss at the House of Lords" (1984), 18 U.B.C. L. Rev. 289; Cane, "Physical Loss, Economic Loss and Products Liability" (1979), 95 L.Q.Rev. 117; Waddams, "Products Liability — Duty to Warn — Economic Loss" (1974), 52 Can. Bar Rev. 96; Harvey, "Negligence — Products Liability — Economic Loss — *Rivtow Marine Ltd. v. Washington Iron Works and Walkem Machinery & Equipment Ltd.*" (1974), 9 U.B.C. L. Rev. 170; Franklin, "When Worlds Collide: Liability Theories and Disclaimers in Defective-Product Cases" (1966), 18 Stan. L. Rev. 974.

[187] Indeed, Canada may adopt explicitly the emerging view elsewhere that accident-caused damage would be regarded as "property damage" only in an action against a stranger to the commercial chain. See *Murphy v. Brentwood District Council*, [1990] 2 All E.R. 908, [1990] 3 W.L.R. 414, at p. 440 (*per* Lord Bridge), at p. 456 (*per* Lord Jauncey) (H.L.); *Aloe Coal Co. v. Clark Equipment Co.*, 816 F.2d 110 (3d Cir.), cert. denied, 484 U.S. 853 (1987); and *King v. Hilton-Davis*, 855 F.2d 1047 (3d Cir. 1988), cert. denied, 488 U.S. 1030 (1989).

[188] The seeming illogic of the distinction has bothered many courts. However, as explained below, the distinction rests on the ability of the parties to allocate the risk amongst themselves by contract.

[189] Attempts to separate items of damage in this manner were once known as the "complex structure theory". This has been rejected. See *Winnipeg Condominium Corp. No. 36 v. Bird Construction*, *supra*, n. 4 ; *Murphy v. Brentwood District Council*, *supra*, n. 187.

[190] *Winnipeg Condominium Corp. No. 36 v. Bird Construction*, *ibid.*

[191] *Ibid.*

[192] See *East River Steamship Corp. v. Transamerica Delaval*, 476 U.S. 858, 106 S. Ct. 260 (1986).

[193] *Murphy v. Brentwood District Council*, *supra*, n. 187.

[194] *Bryan v. Maloney* (1995), 128 A.L.R. 163.

Zealand[195] both allow recovery for economic loss in respect of defects in residential housing construction, whether or not the defect was dangerous. It is not clear whether the courts there will extend these holdings to the commercial building or product markets. Finally, a small and declining number of U.S. states allow tort recovery for both dangerous and merely shoddy product defects.[196]

The reasons behind the no-recovery position adopted in most United States jurisdictions and England were explained best by the United States Supreme Court in *East River Steamship.*[197] The Court said that the traditional tort law concern with personal safety is reduced when the only injury is to the product itself. Economic losses can be easily insured. Contract law, and the law of warranty in particular, is well suited to commercial controversies because the parties may set the terms of their own agreements. The manufacturer can restrict its liability, within limits, by disclaiming warranties or limiting remedies, and in exchange, the purchaser pays less for the product. Since a commercial situation generally does not involve large disparities in bargaining power, there is no reason to intrude into the parties' allocation of the risk.[198] As Justice Posner put it in *Miller v. United States Steel Corp.*:

> Tort law is a superfluous and inapt tool for resolving purely commercial disputes. We have a body of law designed for such disputes. It is called contract law. Products liability law has evolved into a specialized branch of tort law for use in cases in which a defective product caused, not the usual commercial loss, but a personal injury to a consumer or bystander.[199]

The Canadian "dangerous defect" exception can be traced to a powerful dissenting judgment of Justice Laskin in *Rivtow Marine Ltd. v. Washington Iron Works.*[200] The plaintiff chartered a crane for use in its seasonal logging business. The crane developed a serious structural defect that posed an imminent risk of personal injury. The manufacturer admitted the defect was due to its negligent design. The defect in the plaintiff's crane was then discovered during the subsequent investigation ordered by the Workers' Compensation Board. The plaintiff was forced to remove the crane from service for repairs during its peak business period. The plaintiff sued the manufacturer in negligence for the cost of repairing the crane and for the consequential loss of profits during the down time.

The full court in *Rivtow* held that as soon as the manufacturer became aware of the dangerous defect, it came under a duty to warn the plaintiff of the

---

195 *Invercargill City Council v. Hamlin*, [1996] 1 N.Z.L.R. 513 (P.C.); *Riddell v. Porteous*, [1999] 1 N.Z.L.R. 1 (C.A.).

196 See *Santor v. A & M Karagheusian, Inc.*, 44 N.J. 52, 207 A.2d 305 (1965).

197 *Supra*, n. 192.

198 The Australian and New Zealand rule, *supra*, n. 194 and n. 195, might not be inconsistent with this reasoning if it could be explained with a consumer protection rationale outside the commercial market.

199 902 F.2d 573, at p. 574 (7th Cir. 1990).

200 [1974] S.C.R. 1189.

potential danger.[201] The plaintiff successfully recovered the difference between what the loss of profits would have been had the manufacturer given a timely warning and what they were during the peak season, that difference being directly caused by the failure to warn. The failure to warn did not cause the plaintiff to incur the cost of repair nor the ordinary consequential loss of profit, and this claim was denied by the majority of the court. Laskin J. dissented. He would have allowed recovery for the ordinary cost of repairs. He believed that such liability would promote safety, and he saw the plaintiff's incurring the cost of repair as analogous to mitigating damages for property damage that would occur if the crane was left to collapse.[202] This dissent was expressly adopted in the House of Lords in *Anns v. Merton London Borough Council,*[203] where it remained the law of England until *Anns* was overruled in *Murphy v. Brentwood District Council.*[204]

Laskin J.'s dissent was embraced by the Supreme Court of Canada in *Winnipeg Condominium v. Bird Construction Co.,*[205] and it is the law today in Canada. In *Winnipeg Condominium*, La Forest J. spoke for a unanimous court in holding that a general contractor responsible for the construction of a building could be held liable for negligence to a subsequent purchaser of the building who is not in contractual privity with the contractor for the cost of repairing dangerous defects in the building arising out of negligence in its construction.[206] Critics have suggested that the risk of defect in this and similar cases has already been allocated by the parties in the contractual chain, presumably to the party able to deal most efficiently with the risk.[207] If the builder did not assume this risk,

---

[201] Arguably, duty to warn cases constitute another category of recoverable pure economic loss yet to be considered by the Supreme Court. For examples of cases considering the duty to warn, see *Bow Valley Husky (Bermuda) Ltd. v. Saint John Shipbuilding Ltd.*, *supra*, n. 4, at p. 1242 S.C.R.; *McGauley v. British Columbia* (1990), 44 B.C.L.R. (2d) 217 (S.C.); revd (1991), 56 B.C.L.R. (2d) 1 (C.A.); *Modern Livestock Ltd. v. Elgersma* (1989), 74 Alta. L.R. (2d) 392 (Q.B.); *British Columbia Ferry Corp. v. T & N plc.* (1994), 95 B.C.L.R. (2d) 87 (S.C.); affd [1996] 4 W.W.R. 161 (B.C.C.A.); *Agopsowicz v. Honeywell Ltd.*, *supra*, n. 48.

[202] He seems to have assumed that the plaintiff could have recovered the cost of repairing the crane if it had collapsed. This may not be so. See *Murphy v. Brentwood District Council*, *supra*, n. 187.

[203] *Supra*, n. 41.

[204] *Supra*, n. 187.

[205] See Rafferty, "Recovery of Purely Economic Loss in the Tort of Negligence: Liability of Builders to Subsequent Purchasers for Construction Defects" (1996), 34 Alta. L. Rev. 472; Moran, "Rethinking *Winnipeg Condominium*: Restitution, Economic Loss, and Anticipatory Repairs" (1997), 47 U.T.L.J. 115; Siebrasse, "The Choice Between Implied Warranty and Tort Liability for Recovery of Pure Economic Loss in 'Contract-Torts': A Comparison of Judicial and Private Ordering in the Real Property Market" (1996), 19 Dalhousie L. J. 247; Feldthusen, "*Winnipeg Condominium Corporation No. 36 v. Bird Construction Co. Ltd.*: Who Needs Contract Anymore?" (1995), 25 Can. Bus. L.J. 143-55; Palmer, "Bird: A Confusion Between Property Rules and Liability Rules" (1995), 3 Tort L. Rev. 240.

[206] *Supra*, n. 4, at p. 90, S.C.R.

[207] Feldthusen and Palmer, *supra*, n. 2.

presumably the purchase price was lower than if it had.[208] The possibility of the parties allocating the risk amongst themselves in advance of the loss arising is precisely what distinguishes product defect economic loss from external accident-caused physical damage. If the critics are correct, the liability rule will not promote additional safety, but merely complicate commercial transactions. On the other hand, if there is reason to expect systemic inequality in bargaining power or other shortcomings to contractual risk allocation, something the Court did not discuss in *Winnipeg Condominium*, the tort remedy may be justified.[209] There is no reason to expect that the Supreme Court will change its mind and adopt the total exclusionary approach favoured in England and the United States in the near future. It should be noted that, if the parties wish to do so, they can always reallocate by contract the risk of liability for dangerous defects under the rule in *Winnipeg Condominium*.

It is, however, more of an open question whether the Canadian courts will extend recovery in negligence to non-dangerous defects. The English courts do not permit tort recovery for any defects, dangerous or not. Gradually most American states that once allowed tort recovery for non-dangerous defects are abandoning that position, opting instead to deal with merely shoddy products by commercial and consumer law statutes and the common law of contract. The Canadian decisions following *Winnipeg Condominium* dealing with non-dangerous defects seem to fall into three categories. Some refuse to strike a claim for non-dangerous defects on a preliminary motion, and hold that this is a viable issue to be determined at trial.[210] Others seem to misinterpret *Winnipeg Condominium*, and allow recovery.[211] Finally, there are those where recovery has been denied either because the loss has been allocated by a contract between the parties[212] or because the loss is held to be unrecoverable for other reasons.[213] If the Canadian courts do decide to extend negligence law to non-dangerous

---

[208] Certainly, the defendant in *Winnipeg Condominium Corp. No. 36 v. Bird Construction Co.* was not paid to assume this risk, and someone who was paid to assume it is now in the fortunate position of having the court reallocate its responsibility.

[209] As may be the case in the New Zealand and Australian decisions discussed *supra*, n. 194 and n. 195.

[210] *Condominium Plan No. 9421710 v. Christenson* (2001), 5 C.C.L.T. (3d) 135 (Alta. Q.B.); *Campbell v. Flexwatt Corp.*, [1996] B.C.J. No. 1487 (S.C.); *Harder v. Denny Andrews Ford Sales Inc.*, [1995] 9 W.W.R. 439 (Alta. Master).

[211] *Pacific Lumber & Shipping Co. v. Western Stevedoring Co.*, [1995] B.C.J. No. 866 (S.C.); *Chaytor v. Walsh*, [1997] B.C.J. No. 733 (S.C.); *Marshall v. North Okanagan (Regional District)*, [1996] B.C.J. No. 2028 (S.C.).

[212] *Town Concrete Pumping Ltd. v. Gegra Equipment Ltd.*, [1995] B.C.J. No. 1859 (S.C.); *University of Manitoba v. Smith Carter Architects & Engineers Inc.*, [1996] M.J. No. 72 (Q.B.).

[213] *Spouler v. Coast Canada Construction*, [1997] B.C.J. No. 3123 (S.C.); *TransCanada Pipelines Ltd. v. Solar Turbines Inc.*, [1998] O.J. No. 3594 (Gen. Div.); *Gorski v. General Motors of Canada Ltd.*, [1998] B.C.J. No. 3106 (Prov. Ct.); *Privest Properties Ltd. v. Foundation Co. of Canada* (1997), 143 D.L.R. (4th) 635 (B.C.C.A.).

defects, it is most likely they will do so for defective residential housing as has happened in Australia and New Zealand.

D. Relational Economic Loss

The fourth category of economic loss case recognized by the Supreme Court of Canada is known as relational economic loss.[214] In these cases, the defendant negligently causes personal injury or property damage to a third party. The plaintiff suffers pure economic loss by virtue of some relationship, usually contractual, it enjoys with the injured third party or the damaged property. For an example of relational loss, consider the facts in the well-known Canadian case *Canadian National Railway Co. v. Norsk Pacific Steamship Co.*[215] A barge being towed by the defendant negligently struck and damaged a rail bridge owned by the government. The defendant was liable to the owner without controversy for the physical damage to the bridge. The plaintiff was a railroad company that used the bridge under contract with the owner. It sued to recover relational loss — the cost of rerouting its trains during the repair period. As discussed below, the claim succeeded, but in most unusual circumstances.[216] The Supreme Court appeared to reverse itself several years later, and it is unlikely that the claim in *Norsk* would succeed today.[217]

For more than a century, the common law has entertained, and for the most part rejected, claims for relational economic loss.[218] A firm exclusionary rule existed to preclude recovery for negligent interference with contractual relations until the 1960s.[219] The courts then began to reconsider the rule after the decision in *Hedley Byrne*.[220] Consensus remained that negligence claims for relational loss should generally fail. The courts were well aware that recognizing claims for foreseeable relational loss would expose the defendants to potentially indeterminate and crippling liability. This was evident from a series of high-profile claims in England by businesses that had suffered relational loss

---

[214] *Supra*, n. 4.

[215] *Supra*, n. 4.

[216] The decision was 4-3 for recovery. However, the reasoning was 3-3-1, Justice Stevenson gave the single judgment siding with Justice McLachlin and two others in the result. However, all six of the other justices who heard the case rejected the reasoning of Mr. Justice Stevenson.

[217] The issue was revisited in *Bow Valley Husky (Bermuda) Ltd. v. Saint John Shipbuilding Ltd.*, *supra*, n. 4.

[218] See generally Stapleton, "Duty of Care and Economic Loss: A Wider Agenda" (1991), 107 L.Q. Rev. 249; Siebrasse, "Economic Analysis of Economic Loss in the Supreme Court of Canada: Fault, Deterrence, and Channelling of Losses in *CNR v. Norsk Pacific Steamship Co.*" (1994), 20 Queen's L.J. 1; Atiyah, *supra*, n. 2; Smith, *supra*, n. 2; Smillie, *supra*, n. 2; Feldthusen and Palmer, *supra*, n. 2; Feldthusen, *Economic Negligence*, *supra*, n. 2.

[219] *Anthony v. Slaid*, 52 Mass. 290 (1846); *Cattle v. Stockton Waterworks Co.* (1875), L.R. 10 Q.B. 453, [1874-80] All E.R. Rep. 220; *Simpson v. Thomson* (1877), 3 App. Cas. 279 (H.L.); and *Robins Dry Dock & Repair Co. v. Flint*, 272 U.S. 303, 48 S. Ct. 134 (1927).

[220] *Supra*, n. 14.

consequent on damage to the electricity supply.[221] The number of potential claimants who might be dependent on a single electrical cable was staggering. At the same time, many courts were uncomfortable with what they perceived as an artificial distinction between economic loss and physical damage, and were emboldened by developments in cases like *Hedley Byrne*. A tendency developed to recognize a general exclusionary rule, but to craft an exception in the particular relational loss case where the problem of indeterminate liability could be avoided.[222]

The Supreme Court of Canada did not deal directly with a relational loss claim until its 1992 decision in *Canadian National Railway Co. v. Norsk Pacific Steamship Co.*[223] As explained above, unfortunately the Court split 3-3-1. However, the reasons for judgment of McLachlin J. on behalf of three of the four majority judges, and of La Forest J. for the three dissenting judges, constitute an exhaustive and impressive judicial treatment of the topic of relational loss. It is not possible to do either justice in the few paragraphs that follow.

The differences between McLachlin J. and La Forest J. reflected a philosophical debate that had been latent in the case law for years. McLachlan J.'s judgment was a strong statement of what might be called the "case-by-case" approach to economic loss generally, of which relational loss is but a variation. She adopted, as had MacGuigan J.A. in the court below, proximity — physical, circumstantial, causal, and assumed proximity — as the appropriate "test" for duty. She stressed the relevance of the defendant's fault in causing the loss, and was sceptical about whether the defendant's ability to insure was relevant either in law or on the particular facts.

La Forest J., in contrast, was interested in certainty. He criticized the proximity formulations as too vague to offer any assistance to a presiding judge. He employed a range of policy arguments to support a general exclusionary rule

---

[221] *Spartan Steel & Alloys Ltd. v. Martin & Co. (Contractors) Ltd.*, [1973] 1 Q.B. 27, [1972] 3 All E.R. 557 (C.A.); *S.C.M. (U.K.) Ltd. v. W.J. Whittall & Son Ltd.*, [1971] 1 Q.B. 337, [1970] 3 All E.R. 245 (C.A.); *Electrochrome Ltd. v. Welsh Plastics Ltd.*, [1968] 2 All E.R. 205 (Glamorgan Assizes); *Celanese Ltd. v. A.H. Hunt (Capacitors) Ltd.*, [1969] 1 W.L.R. 959, [1969] 2 All E.R. 1252 (Q.B.).

[222] *Seaway Hotels Ltd. v. Cragg (Canada) Ltd. and Consumers Gas Co.* (1960), 21 D.L.R. (2d) 264 (Ont. C.A.); *Dominion Tape of Canada Ltd. v. L.R. McDonald & Sons Ltd.* (1971), 21 D.L.R. (3d) 299 (Ont. Co. Ct.); *Gypsum Carrier Inc. v. R.* (1977), 78 D.L.R. (3d) 175 (F.C.T.D.); *Canadian National Railway v. The Harry Lundeberg* (1977), 78 D.L.R. (3d) 175 (F.C.T.D.); *Weller & Co. v. Foot & Mouth Disease Research Institute*, [1966] 1 Q.B. 569, [1965] 3 All E.R. 560;*Caltex Oil (Aust.) Pty. Ltd. v. Dredge Willemstad* (1976), 11 A.L.R. 227 (H.C.) (*per* Gibbs J.). A "known plaintiff" approach was favoured by Stevenson J. in *Canadian National Railway Co. v. Norsk Pacific Steamship Co.*, supra, n. 4, but rejected by all six other judges. For other approaches leading to recovery in particular cases see *Canadian National Railway Co. v. Norsk Pacific Steamship Co.*, supra, n. 4 (*per* McLachlin J.) and *Perre v. Apand Pty. Ltd.*, [1999] 73 A.L.R. 1190.

[223] *Supra*, n. 4.

subject to some specific exceptions. These included the fact that many of the traditional aims of tort law such as deterrence could and would be accomplished in the plaintiff's action against the victim of physical damage. Increasing the deterrence measure by recognizing additional claims for relational loss might lead to over-deterrence, especially given that many relational losses do not constitute true social losses at all. Additional liability for relational loss increases the transaction costs associated with a single accident and also creates the problem of potentially indeterminate liability. La Forest J. surmised that the typical plaintiff, aware of the risks inherent in the relationship, was a more efficient insurer than the typical defendant. Moreover, the potential plaintiff in a relational case enjoys the opportunity to protect itself by "channeling" the risk to the other party in the relation by contract.

La Forest J. would have allowed recovery for relational loss only in exceptional categories of cases that could be defined clearly and in advance of the accident. He identified the recognized exceptions as (1) cases where the claimant has a possessory or proprietary interest in the damaged property;[224] (2) general average cases;[225] and (3) cases where the relationship between the claimant and property owner constitutes a joint venture. McLachlin J. indicated that the plaintiff in *Norsk* fell within the joint venture exception, whereas La Forest J. could see no meaningful distinguishing feature of the relationship between the plaintiff and the bridge owner to support a clear principled exception.

Academics seemed to prefer La Forest J.'s judgment over that of McLachlin J.[226] The English courts declined to follow the decision in *Norsk*.[227] The Supreme Court itself moved quickly towards the La Forest J. approach in two subsequent decisions, *D'Amato v. Badger*,[228] and, with McLachlin J. herself graciously leading the Court, in *Bow Valley Husky (Bermuda) Ltd. v. Saint John Shipbuilding Ltd.*[229]

---

[224] The main authorities deal with chartered ships and the distinction between charter by demise and time charters. See for example *Candlewood Navigation Corp. v. Mitsui O.S.K. Lines Ltd.*, [1986] A.C. 1, [1985] 2 All E.R. 935 (P.C.); *Chargeurs Réunis Compagnie Française v. English & American Shipping Co.* (1921), 9 Lloyd's List L.R. 464 (Ad.); *Elliott Steam Tug Co. v. Shipping Controller*, [1922] 1 K.B. 127 (C.A.); *Warner Quinlan Asphalt Co. v. R.*, [1924] S.C.R. 236, 2 D.L.R. 853; and *Robins Dry Dock & Repair Co. v. Flint, supra*, n. 219.

[225] This is a principle by which the carrier and cargo owners share *pro rata* the risk of damage to the ship. See *Morrison S.S. Co. v. Greystoke Castle (Cargo Owners)*, [1947] A.C. 265, [1946] 2 All E.R. 696, at p. 703 (H.L.).

[226] See Feldthusen, *Economic Negligence, supra*, n. 2, chapter 5; Tilbury, "Purely Economic Loss in the Supreme Court of Canada" (1994), 2 Torts L.J. 1; Fleming, "Economic Loss in Canada" (1993), 1 Tort L. Rev. 68; Markesinis, "Compensation for Negligently Inflicted Pure Economic Loss: Some Canadian Views" (1993), 109 L. Q. Rev. 5; Bernstein, *supra*, n. 2, at pp. 166-72.

[227] *Landcatch Ltd v. International Oil Pollution Compensation Fund*, [1998] 2 Lloyd's Rep. 552 (Court of Session); *Londonwaste Ltd. v. Amec Civil Engineering Ltd.* (1997), 53 Con. L.R. 66, 83 Build. L.R. 136 (Q.B.D.).

[228] *Supra*, n. 4.

[229] *Supra*, n. 4. See also *Dempsey v. Dempsey* (1999), 224 N.B.R. (2d) 224 (Q.B.).

In *D'Amato*, the corporate plaintiff was jointly owned by two persons who personally performed the corporate business. As a result of the defendant's negligence, one of the owners was disabled, causing corporate loss over and beyond that suffered by the injured co-owner, who was the key employee. The Court unanimously denied the corporate plaintiff's claim for relational loss, holding that the claim failed on either the McLachlin J. or La Forest J. approach. However, it is difficult to see why the plaintiff failed the "joint venture" exception that McLachlin J. had recognized in *Norsk*.

The *Bow Valley* case arose from a fire aboard an offshore oil rig that put the rig out of service for several months. The rig owner claimed for damage to property, and consequential losses. The two relational loss claimants were oil exploration companies using the rig pursuant to contractual arrangements. They were also the majority shareholders, directly or indirectly through subsidiary companies, of the rig owner. Their claims failed. The following principles, summarized by McLachlin J., were adopted by the full Supreme Court:[230]

> (1) relational economic loss is recoverable only in special circumstances where the appropriate conditions are met;[231] (2) these circumstances can be defined by reference to categories, which will make the law generally predictable; (3) the categories are not closed. La Forest J. identified the categories of recovery of relational economic loss defined to date as: (1) cases where the claimant has a possessory or proprietary interest in the damaged property; (2) general average cases; and (3) cases where the relationship between the claimant and property owner constitutes a joint venture.

But the Court was sensitive to the number of exceptions overwhelming the rule itself. "(C)ourts should not assiduously seek new categories; what is required is a clear rule predicting when recovery is available."[232]

In summary, the exceptions to the exclusionary rule for relational loss are few and narrowly drawn. Two apply almost exclusively in maritime law. Unfortunately, the third, the "joint venture" exception, was not clearly defined. Even so, this will be a difficult threshold to cross. The plaintiffs in both *D'Amato* and *Bow Valley* appear closer to being in a joint venture with the property owner than did the plaintiff in *Norsk*. It is likely that a true sharing of both the same risks and the spoils of the enterprise will be required.

---

[230] *Supra*, n. 4, at p. 406, D.L.R.

[231] *Ibid.*, at p. 428 D.L.R. Iacobucci J. for the majority referred to this as the "general exclusionary rule".

[232] *Ibid.*, at p. 407.

Chapter 13

Defences to Negligence: The Conduct of the Plaintiff

Despite the presence of a duty, a breach of duty and resulting damage, a plaintiff's claim may still be defeated on the basis of certain defences grounded on the plaintiff's own conduct. This is a legacy of the individualism of the common law. The rationale behind these defences is that the law should assist only those persons who are deemed worthy of its protection. Thus, individuals who are negligent with regard to their own safety are denied the protection of the law in whole or in part. Similarly, anyone who consents to assume the risk of injury is undeserving of the law's attention. So, too, violators of the law may place themselves beyond tort law's protective umbrella. This chapter examines the defences of contributory negligence, voluntary assumption of risk, and the re-emerging defence of illegality. This is the sixth and last element.

A. Contributory Negligence

If a plaintiff's own negligence contributes to a loss, the right to tort recovery is affected.[1] Today, the amount is merely reduced in proportion to the fault, but previously such a plaintiff was denied recovery altogether.

Contributory negligence, as a complete defence, first reared its ugly head in *Butterfield v. Forrester*.[2] The defendant obstructed a street by placing a pole across it. The plaintiff, who was riding a horse "violently" down the road, failed to see the pole, rode against it and fell with his horse. The jury found for the defendant, which decision was affirmed on appeal. Bayley J. thought that if the

---

[1] James, "Contributory Negligence" (1953), 63 Yale L.J. 691; Bohlen, "Contributory Negligence" (1908), 21 Harv. L. Rev. 233; Malone, "The Formative Era of Contributory Negligence" (1946), 41 Ill. L. Rev. 151, reprinted in Malone, *Essays in Torts* (1986); Klar, "Contributory Negligence and Contribution Between Tortfeasors" in Klar (ed.), *Studies in Canadian Tort Law* (1977), p. 145. See generally Williams, *Joint Torts and Contributory Negligence* (1951); Gregory, *Legislative Loss Distribution in Negligence Actions* (1936); Schwartz, *Comparative Negligence* (1974); Chiefetz, *Apportionment of Fault in Tort* (1981).

[2] (1809), 11 East 60, 103 E.R. 926.

plaintiff had used care and had not been riding "as fast as his horse could go", he could have avoided the accident. He concluded that "the accident appeared to happen entirely from his own fault". Lord Ellenborough added:

> One person being in fault will not dispense with another's using ordinary care for himself. Two things must concur to support this action, an obstruction in the road by the fault of the defendant and no want of ordinary care to avoid it on the part of the plaintiff.

It should be noted that the phrase "contributory negligence" was nowhere mentioned by the court, but this case is, nevertheless, thought to be the origin of the so-called "stalemate rule". The court did not even consider as a possible solution the division of responsibility, which was the usual treatment of these cases under the civil law and in admiralty at the time.

The reasons underlying this harsh rule are difficult to support. First, the early common law sought to isolate *the cause* of an accident rather than consider the possibility of there being *several causes*. Thus, plaintiffs were viewed as the sole cause of their own misfortunes, even though they may have been only *one* of several causes. Second, careless individuals were thought to be unworthy of judicial protection. Frequently, the courts asserted simply that, where both parties were guilty of negligence contributing to the disaster, "neither could recover against the other".[3] Lord Blackburn declared, "if there is blame causing the accident on both sides, however small that blame may be on one side, the loss lies where it falls".[4] The theory, according to Viscount Simon, was that "where a man is part author of his own injury, he cannot call on the other party to compensate him in full".[5] A third rationale of the stalemate rule was to provide a subsidy to enterprises in meeting the enormous costs of accidents produced by their burgeoning activities.[6] This was a high social price to pay for economic progress.

Fourth, a central aim of contributory negligence was deterrence. If individuals did not take care of themselves, they could not recover in tort, even if the other party was also negligent. Consequently, it was hoped, future plaintiffs would take greater care for their own safety if they wanted to be able to recover. The deficiency of this reasoning was that, while contributory negligence may have deterred negligent plaintiffs, it shielded negligent defendants from liability at the same time. The deterrent force of tort law was, therefore, weakened against them. Moreover, the denial of *all* recovery to the negligent plaintiffs was too stiff a penalty to exact. It could not last, for the result was too cruel even for the absolutism of nineteenth-century morality.[7]

---

[3] *Pickworth v. Keifer* (1924), 26 O.W.N. 159, at p. 161 (C.A.) (*per* Masten J.A.); see also *Fewings v. Grand Trunk Railway* (1909), 1 O.W.N. 1, at p. 3 (C.A.).

[4] *Cayzer, Irvine & Co. v. Carron Co.* (1884), 9 App. Cas. 873, at p. 881.

[5] *Nance v. B.C. Electric Ry. Co. Ltd.*, [1951] A.C. 601, at p. 611, [1951] 2 All E.R. 448 (P.C.).

[6] See Malone, *supra*, n. 1.

[7] See Green, *Judge and Jury*, p. 122; McLachlin J. in *Bow Valley Husky (Bermuda) Ltd. v. Saint John Shipbuilding Ltd.*, [1997] 3 S.C.R. 1210, 153 D.L.R. (4th) 385, at p. 1263 (S.C.R.), para. 94; the ban,

1. THE MEANING OF CONTRIBUTORY NEGLIGENCE

a) Standard of Care

The standard of care required of a plaintiff is generally no different than that demanded of a defendant. In other words, one must act as a reasonable person for one's own safety, as well as for the protection of others.[8] The obligation was expressed by Viscount Simon in *Nance v. B.C. Electric Railway*[9] as follows:

> . . . a defendant must prove to the satisfaction of the jury that the injured party did not in his own interest take reasonable care of himself and contributed, by this want of care, to his own injury.

Glanville Williams, however, has suggested that the actual standard of care required of a plaintiff, as compared to a defendant, has often been lower in practice than in theory. He has suggested that "the reasonable defendant is not allowed to have lapses, but the reasonable plaintiff is".[10] Such a principle has never been officially recognized, but judges and juries may well have acted under it, at least prior to the time of apportionment legislation. For example, a manger of a premises was held negligent when a mink coat was stolen from the unattended cloak room, whereas the coat's owner was held not contributorily negligent for making use of the unattended cloak room.[11]

There are many cases dealing with the acts of plaintiffs who contributed to the accidents that befell them. For example, boaters were held contributorily negligent for drownings which resulted from failure to wear life jackets,[12] and for failure to keep a proper lookout for a waterfall.[13] Similarly, a pedestrian may be held partially at fault for walking in the middle of the road and for not facing the traffic.[14] Contributory negligence has been found against someone for petting a dangerous dog after being warned not to,[15] for getting drunk and participating in a tube race,[16] for failure to warn a golfer of presence,[17] and for failing to follow instructions in the post-operative phase of surgery.[18] Moreover, a snowmobile passenger who is not safely seated is contributorily negligent for

---

in relation to Maritime law, "no longer comport[s] with the modern view of fairness and justice . . . [nor] the goal of modern tort law of encouraging care and vigilance."

[8] Williams *op.. cit. supra*, n. 1, at p. 353. See Chapter 5, *supra*, for a detailed treatment of the standard of care.

[9] *Supra*, n. 5, at p. 611.

[10] Williams, *op. cit. supra*, n. 1, at p. 353.

[11] *Hansen v. "Y" Motor Hotel Ltd.*, [1971] 2 W.W.R. 705 (Alta. C.A.). See also *Logan v. Asphodel*, [1938] O.W.N. 215, at p. 218 (*per* MacKay J.).

[12] *Chamberland v. Fleming* (1984), 29 C.C.L.T. 213 (Alta. Q.B.), 25% maximum deductible.

[13] *Hendricks v. R.*, [1970] S.C.R. 237.

[14] See *Lepine v. De Meule* (1973), 30 D.L.R. (3d) 49; affd with modification of damages (1973), 36 D.L.R. (3d) 388 (N.W.T.C.A.); *Luckner v. Neath* (1966), 58 D.L.R. (2d) 662 (Sask. C.A.).

[15] *Witman v. Johnson* (1990), 5 C.C.L.T. (2d) 102 (Man. Q.B.).

[16] *Re Crocker and Sundance Northwest Resorts Ltd.*, [1988] 1 S.C.R. 1186.

[17] *Finnie v. Ropponen* (1987), 40 C.C.L.T. 155 (B.C.S.C.).

[18] *Brushett v. Cowan* (1987), 42 C.C.L.T. 64; revd in part (1990), 69 D.L.R. (4th) 743 (Nfld. C.A.).

failing to warn the driver of that fact.[19] Also one must take reasonable steps to protect one's property.[20]

There are also cases in which there has been no contributory negligence proven,[21] as where a police officer drove over the speed limit during a chase when it was "reasonably necessary to carry out his statutory duty".[22]

The plaintiff's responsibility depends in no way upon any duty owed by the injured party to the person sued.[23] It is possible, however, for negligent conduct to be dangerous not only to the actor, but also in relation to other persons. To the extent that one must avoid endangering others by one's own conduct, a contributorily negligent plaintiff may owe a duty to someone else. Hence, if two motorists negligently collide with one another, their conduct may render them *both* liable to each other, as well as contributorily negligent with regard to their own safety. Similarly, one who steps off a curb into the path of a moving car endangers not only himself but also the motorist and other traffic on the road.

The defence of contributory negligence is available even if the defendant is in violation of a statute.[24] In the United States, some courts have forbidden the use of contributory negligence where the defendant has contravened certain statutes for the protection of children, workers and the like.[25] There is no evidence that this idea has infiltrated Canadian law, except perhaps in an indirect way. In *Adams v. Dias*[26] for example, the Supreme Court of Canada reversed a finding of contributory negligence because the defendant was guilty of an "unusual and unexpected violation" of the law.

b) Emergencies

In emergency situations, people who are injured while taking steps to protect themselves are judged compassionately. Although "reasonable people must be able to handle emergencies reasonably well", they are not expected to live up to

---

[19] *Ainge v. Siemon*, [1971] 3 O.R. 119.

[20] *Heeney v. Best* (1979), 108 D.L.R. (3d) 367 (Ont. C.A.).

[21] For example, *Rogers v. Hill* (1973), 37 D.L.R. (3d) 468 (B.C.), hunting accident; *Law v. Upton Lathing Ltd.* (1971), 22 D.L.R. (3d) 407 (Ont. C.A.), no warning about reading label.

[22] *A.G. Ont. v. Keller* (1978), 23 O.R. (2d) 143 (C.A.).

[23] Williams, *op. cit. supra*, n. 1, at p. 611; See *Froom v. Butcher*, [1975] 3 W.L.R. 379, at p. 333 (C.A.) (*per* Lord Denning M.R.); *Bell Canada v. Cope (Sarnia) Ltd.* (1980), 11 C.C.L.T. 170, at p. 179 (*per* Linden J.); Klar, "Developments in Tort Law: The 1979-80 Term" (1981), 2 Supreme Court L. Rev. 325, at p. 346.

[24] *Grand Trunk Pacific Ry. v. Earl*, [1923] S.C.R. 397; *Graham v. R.* (1978), 90 D.L.R. (3d) 223 (Sask. Q.B.), defendant in breach of highway maintenance statute.

[25] See *Dart v. Pure Oil Co.* (1947), 223 Minn. 526, 27 N.W. 2d 555, for example, Prosser, "Contributory Negligence as a Defense to Violation of Statute" (1948), 32 Minn. L. Rev. 105.

[26] [1968] S.C.R. 931 (*per* Ritchie J.). See *Ball v. Richard Thomas and Baldwins Ltd.*, [1968] 1 All E.R. 389 (C.A.), where Davies L.J. stated "when a breach of a statutory duty has been found on the part of the employers, it would be wrong to attribute to the injured workman too large a share of the responsibility for his own injury".

a "standard of perfection".[27] In *Walls v. Mussens Ltd.*,[28] the defendant had negligently caused a fire in the plaintiff's garage. Arriving on the scene, the plaintiff joined with the defendant and other in throwing snow on the fire. The plaintiff failed to use an available fire extinguisher, which might have been able to put out the fire. The court ruled that the plaintiff was not contributorily negligent. Hughes J.A. wrote that "the test to be employed is not whether the plaintiff exercised a careful and prudent judgment in doing what he did, but whether what he did was something an ordinarily prudent person might reasonably have done under the stress of the emergency. . . . The plaintiff's reaction to the emergency was merely to do what the others were doing and I cannot say that it was something an ordinarily prudent man might not reasonably have done in the circumstances."

A similar case is *Zervobeakos v. Zervobeakos*,[29] where the plaintiff was a lodger on the second storey of a house who wakened to find himself imperilled by a fire caused by the negligence of the owner of the house. Exiting through a window he slipped from a sloping ledge and fell to the ground, sustaining injuries. The plaintiff would probably have been rescued, without injury, if he had remained at the window and had not ventured outside. The Nova Scotia Court of Appeal held that the plaintiff was not contributorily negligent. McKinnon C.J.N.S. stated that a person placed in a "perilous position" cannot be required to "exercise as much judgment and self-control in attempting to avoid danger as would reasonably be expected of him under ordinary circumstances".

Police officers injured during the course of their duties have been exonerated of contributory negligence. In one case while chasing a suspect an officer drove his cruiser 85 miles per hour on an icy road and struck a pole, but this was said to have been "no more than was reasonably necessary to carry out his statutory duty".[30]

Chief Justice Freedman of Manitoba has best expressed the attitude of the courts in these cases in *Neufeld v. Landry*,[31] as follows:

> The conduct of the plaintiff driver must be assessed in the light of the crisis that was looming up before her. If in the "agony of the moment" the evasive action she took may not have been as good as some other action she might have taken — a doubtful matter at best — we would not characterize her conduct as amounting to contributory negligence. It was the defendant who created the emergency which led to the accident. It does not lie in his mouth to be minutely critical of the reactive conduct of the plaintiff whose safety he had imperiled. . . .

---

[27] See Linden J. in *Cleary v. Hansen* (1981), 18 C.C.L.T. 147, at p. 157; *Holomis v. Dubuc* (1974), 56 D.L.R. (3d) 351 (B.C.) (*per* Verchere J.).

[28] (1969), 11 D.L.R. (3d) 245 (N.B.C.A.). See also *Molson v. Squamish Transfer Ltd. et al.* (1969), 7 D.L.R. (3d) 553 (B.C.).

[29] (1970), 8 D.L.R. (3d) 377 (N.S.C.A.).

[30] *A.G. Ont. v. Keller* (1978), 94 D.L.R. (3d) 632, at p. 635 (Ont. C.A.); see also *Lewis v. Todd* (1980), 115 D.L.R. (3d) 257 (S.C.C.).

[31] (1974), 55 D.L.R. (3d) 296, at p. 298 (Man. C.A.).

c) Causation and Proximate Cause

The contributory negligence of plaintiffs must be a cause of the loss to count against them.[32] The "but for" test has often been employed here to determine causation. As one court stated, "contributory negligence involves not only a finding of negligence but of such negligence as but for it the accident would not have happened".[33] Latin phrases have also been invoked. Mr. Justice Riddell has explained that contributory negligence must be a "real *causa causans*" and not a "mere *causa sine qua non*".[34] Sometimes, the court asserts merely that the negligence must be an "effective cause of the damage".[35]

Not only must the contributory negligence be a cause of the loss, it must be a proximate cause. In other words, the loss must result from the type of risk to which plaintiffs expose themselves, not from a totally different hazard. Thus, a plaintiff who drives without a license is not precluded from recovery if this act is not a proximate cause of the accident.[36] In *Long v. McLaughlin*,[37] a ten-year-old boy was standing on the running board of the defendant's bakery truck when it ran into a tree. The trial judge, with the aid of a jury, found the bakery 75 per cent responsible and the boy 25 per cent contributorily negligent. The finding against the bakery was affirmed, but the Supreme Court of Canada allowed a cross-appeal by the boy, holding that there was no evidence of contributory negligence on his part to submit to the jury. Anglin C.J.C., declared:

> In order to constitute contributory negligence it does not suffice that there should be some fault on the part of the plaintiff without which the injury that he complains of would not have been suffered; a cause which is merely *sine qua non* is not adequate. As in the case of primary negligence charged against the defendant, there must be proof, or at least evidence from which it can reasonably be inferred, that the negligence charged was a proximate, in the sense of an effective, cause of such injury. . . .[38]

The accident, in other words, did not culminate from the risk created by the plaintiff. The boy, however, would certainly have been held contributorily negligent if he had fallen off the truck, since that was the danger he had exposed himself to by standing on the running board.

---

[32] *Koeppel v. Colonial Coach Lines Ltd.*, [1933] S.C.R. 529; *Long v. McLaughlin*, [1927] S.C.R. 303, at p. 311; *F.W. Argue v. Howe*, [1969] S.C.R. 354; *Lillos v. Tilden Rent-A-Car* (1987), 80 A.R. 32 (Q.B.).

[33] *Luck v. Toronto Ry.* (1920), 48 O.L.R. 581, at p. 586 (C.A.).

[34] *Ottawa Civic Hospital v. Gibson* (1929), 36 O.W.N. 200, at p. 201 (C.A.).

[35] MacDonald J.A. in *Rose v. Sargent*, [1949] 3 D.L.R. 688 (Alta. C.A.).

[36] *Godfrey v. Cooper* (1920), 46 O.L.R. 565 (C.A.).

[37] [1927] S.C.R. 303, [1927] 2 D.L.R. 186. See the discussion in Williams, *op. cit. supra*, n. 1, at p. 263.

[38] *Ibid.*, at p. 310.

A contrasting case is *Jones v. Livox Quarries Ltd.*,[39] where a worker riding on the back of a vehicle, contrary to instructions, was injured when another vehicle ran into the back of his vehicle. The court cut the worker's award by 20 per cent because it felt that there was a risk, not only of his falling off, but also of his being injured in a collision. Another illustrative case is *Smithwick v. Hall & Upson Co.*,[40] where a worker was warned against going on a slippery platform which had no railing. Notwithstanding this, he walked onto the platform and was injured when a brick wall of the defendant's building gave way, fell on the plaintiff and threw him off the platform. His failure to heed the warning was not held to be contributory negligence because he had exposed himself only to the hazard of falling off the platform by slipping on the ice, not to the risk of being hit by a falling wall. The court stated that the negligent act must operate as a "proximate cause or one of the proximate causes, and not merely as a condition".

d) Onus on Defendant and Pleading Points

Contributory negligence is a defence, proof of which must be adduced by the defendant. Mr. Justice Duff once stated that "the onus of proving contributory negligence in the first instance lies on the defendant and it would be the duty of the jury to find the issue in favour of the plaintiff, unless satisfied that the defence had been affirmatively proved".[41]

The defendant should plead the defence,[42] although this may not be absolutely necessary,[43] because amendments are often permitted.[44] It is sufficient to allege that the accident arose out of the plaintiff's own fault in order to raise the contributory negligence defence,[45] but the defence cannot be raised for the first time on appeal.[46]

2. UNDERMINING THE STALEMATE RULE

The complete bar was not popular with the courts for very long. Various techniques were devised to mollify the harshness of the stalemate rule. For example, some courts shut their eyes when juries apportioned damages, in

---

[39] [1952] 2 Q.B. 608, [1952] 1 T.L.R. 1377 (C.A.). See also *Meyer v. Hall* (1972), 26 D.L.R. (3d) 309 (Alta. C.A.), no need to guard against "unusual" conduct of driver, in parking without brake on.

[40] (1890), 59 Conn. 261, 21 Atl. 924.

[41] *B.C. Electric Ry. v. Dunphy* (1919), 59 S.C.R. 263, at p. 268. See also *Arkell v. T.H. & B. Ry.* (1922), 53 O.L.R. 1, at p. 5, [1923] 3 D.L.R. 828 (C.A.), where Masten J. stated, "The onus of proving affirmatively that there was contributory negligence on the part of the plaintiffs rests on the defendants."

[42] Williston and Rolls, *The Law of Civil Procedure* (1970), p. 705.

[43] *Campbell v. Dickison* (1958), 41 M.P.R. 75 (N.B.).

[44] *Foster v. Morton* (1956), 38 M.P.R. 316, at p. 328, 4 D.L.R. (2d) 269 (N.S.C.A.).

[45] *Comer v. Kowaluk*, [1938] O.R. 655 (C.A.).

[46] *S.S. Pleiades and Page v. Page and S.S. Jane and Lesser*, [1891] A.C. 259 (C.A.); *cf.*, *Katz v. Taylor*, [1939] O.W.N. 482 (C.A.), new trial ordered.

apparent contravention of the law.[47] This subterfuge did not, however, become formalized in the common law.

a) "Last Clear Chance"

Soon a more sturdy doctrine was fashioned to undermine the stalemate rule. It was called "last clear chance", "last opportunity" or "ultimate negligence". The seminal case was *Davies v. Mann*[48] where the plaintiff negligently left his donkey on the highway with its legs tied. The defendant negligently drove his wagon and horses into the animal and killed it. Liability was imposed on the defendant, despite the contributory negligence of the plaintiff, because according to Lord Abinger the defendant might have avoided the animal with proper care. The case was later explained on the ground that the defendant was held totally responsible because he had the "last opportunity of avoiding the accident".[49] Another rationale of the case rested on causation theory; where the defendant could have avoided the accident, he, and not the plaintiff, was the sole cause of it.[50] This explanation was unsatisfactory because, when two co-defendants caused damage to a third person in similar circumstances, the last opportunity rule was of no aid to either of them.[51]

The best explanation of the last clear chance theory was that it was a technique for imposing liability on the defendant, when the defendant's negligence was relatively greater than the plaintiff's.[52] That this was so is evident from two extensions of the last opportunity rule. First, if the last opportunity was last due to negligent inattention, the defendant would still be treated as though able to avoid the accident.[53] Second, if unable to avoid the accident by some earlier act of negligence, last clear chance would still be applied against the defendant.[54]

---

[47] *Raisin v. Mitchell* (1839), 9 C. & P. 613; *Smith v. Dobson* (1841), 3 Man. & G. 59, 133 E.R. 1057. See MacIntyre, "The Rationale of Last Clear Chance" (1940), 18 Can. Bar Rev. 665, reprinted in Linden (ed.), *Studies in Canadian Tort Law* (1968), p. 160.

[48] (1842), 10 M. & W. 546, 152 E.R. 588. Approved in *Radley v. London and North Western Ry. Co.* (1876), 1 App. Cas. 754. See MacIntyre, *supra*, n. 47, for a brilliant analysis of the doctrine. See also MacIntyre, "Last Clear Chance after Thirty Years Under the Apportionment Statutes" (1955), 33 Can. Bar Rev. 257; Bowker, "Ten More Years Under the Contributory Negligence Acts" (1968), 2 U.B.C.L. Rev. 198.

[49] Salmond, *The Law of Torts*, 3rd ed. (1912), p. 39, now in its 21st edition (1996).

[50] See, for example, Schroeder, "Courts and Comparative Negligence", [1950] Ins. L.J. 791, at p. 794.

[51] *Topping v. Oshawa St. Ry.* (1931), 66 O.L.R. 618, [1931] 2 D.L.R. 263 (C.A.). See also MacIntyre, *supra*, n. 47, at p. 674.

[52] MacIntyre, *supra*, n. 47, at p. 665.

[53] *Radley v. London and North Western Ry. Co.* (1876), 1 App. Cas. 754.

[54] *B.C. Electric Ry. v. Loach*, [1916] 1 A.C. 719, defective brakes kept defendant from exercising last opportunity. See also *Alford v. Magee* (1952), 85 C.L.R. 437, [1952] A.L.J. 101.

b) Agitation for Reform

Despite extensions like these which stretched the doctrine almost to the breaking point, injured people were still being denied compensation because of their contributory negligence. Reform of the "monstrously unjust" situation was overdue.[55] Agitation commenced in the law reviews,[56] bar association meetings and even in judicial opinions. Several Justices of the Supreme Court of Canada in *Grand Truck Pacific Ry. v. Earl*[57] turned a "wistful eye" to the more "equitable" Quebec principle of "common fault". In one of those unfortunately rare occasions in Canadian history when common lawyers were wisely influenced by the civil law, Ontario enacted the first apportionment statute a year later in 1924.[58] In the next few years all the other common law provinces followed suit.[59] It took somewhat longer for the legislation to spread to the United Kingdom[60] and Australia.[61] After a slow start, apportionment has now invaded the United States.[62] These comparative negligence provisions have had an enormous impact in expanding the incidence of recovery in negligence cases.

3. APPORTIONMENT LEGISLATION

The apportionment legislation was meant to assist injured plaintiffs, who had been denied compensation altogether, to recover some part of their losses where they were contributorily negligent. It merely eliminated the defendants' right to rely on contributory negligence as a complete defence.[63] The Negligence Act of Ontario[64] states:

> In any action for damages that is founded upon the fault or negligence of the defendant if fault or negligence is found on the part of the plaintiff that contributed to the damages, the court shall apportion the damages in proportion to the degree of fault or negligence found against the parties respectively.

---

[55] Schroeder, *supra*, n. 50, at p. 793.

[56] See Bowker, *supra*, n. 48, at p. 201, for a fine history of the debate. See also McMurchy, "Contributory Negligence — Should the Rule in Admiralty and Civil Law be Adopted?" (1923), 1 Can. Bar Rev. 844; Anglin, "Law of Quebec and Other Provinces" (1923), 1 Can. Bar Rev. 33, at p. 49.

[57] [1923] S.C.R. 397, at p. 398 (*per* Duff J.), at p. 406 (*per* Anglin J.) and at p. 408 (*per* Mignault J.).

[58] S.O. 1924, c. 32. Williams, *Joint Torts and Contributory Negligence* (1951), p. 257, thought that it was significant that Ontario was a neighbouring province of Quebec.

[59] The uniform act was adopted by all of them, except Ontario and Manitoba, see Bowker, *supra*, n. 48, at p. 202.

[60] Law Reform (Contributory Negligence) Act, 1945.

[61] See Fleming, *The Law of Torts*, 9th ed. (1998), p. 306.

[62] Over 40 states now permit some form of apportionment, see *Prosser and Keeton on the Law of Torts*, 5th ed. (1984), p. 471. Eight of these did so by judicial decision, including California, Florida, Michigan and Illinois. See Fleming, "Comparative Negligence at Last — By Judicial Choice" (1976), 64 Calif. L. Rev. 239; see generally Schwartz, *Comparative Negligence* (1974).

[63] *Stark v. Batchelor* (1928), 63 O.L.R. 135, at p. 141, [1928] 4 D.L.R. 815 (C.A.).

[64] R.S.O. 1990, c. N.1, s. 3.

It further stipulates that "if it is not practicable to determine the respective degree of fault or negligence as between any parties to an action, such parties shall be deemed to be equally at fault or negligent".[65] If the action is tried by a jury, it is for them to determine the degree of fault or negligence as a question of act.[66] If it is a trial by judge alone, "[a]pportionment of fault is primarily and properly a matter within the discretion of the trial Judge. . . ." [and] "except in a strong and exceptional case, an appellate Court will not feel free to substitute its apportionment of fault for that made by the trial Judge, unless there has been palpable and demonstrable error in appreciation of the legal principles to be applied or misapprehension of the facts by the trial Judge".[67]

Contributory negligence legislation has been held to be applicable not only in negligence actions, but also in trespass cases,[68] battery,[69] fraud actions,[70] negligent statement,[71] defamation,[72] and even lawsuits founded on contract.[73]

a) Survival of Last Clear Chance

In the first few cases decided under the new statute in Ontario, Mr. Justice Riddell set a pattern for the future treatment of apportionment in Canada. He asserted that the legislation was passed not for "academic or statistical purposes, but as a practical remedy for some existing evil".[74] He also declared:

> The statute was intended simply for the relief of a plaintiff who would have failed in obtaining any damages at all under the existing law, it being proven that he was guilty of contributory negligence. That that was the whole object of the statute I have no doubt, and it should not be extended.[75]

Consequently, according to Mr. Justice Riddell, if the doctrine of ultimate negligence had been available prior to the passage of the act, it would survive

---

[65]   *Ibid.*, s. 4.

[66]   *Ibid.*, s. 6.

[67]   *Taylor v. Asody* (1974), 49 D.L.R. (3d) 724, at p. 728 (S.C.C.) (*per* Dickson J.), dissenting.

[68]   *Bell Canada v. Cope (Sarnia) Ltd.* (1980), 11 C.C.L.T. 170; affd (1980), 15 C.C.L.T. 190 (Ont. C.A.); *Long v. Gardner* (1983), 144 D.L.R. (3d) 73 (Ont. H.C.).

[69]   *Brushett v. Cowan, supra,* n. 18.

[70]   *Andersen v. Stevens* (1981), 125 D.L.R. (3d) 736 (B.C.S.C.). *Cf., United Services Funds (Trustees of) v. Richardson Greenshields of Can. Ltd.* (1988), 48 D.L.R. (4th) 98 (B.C.S.C.) (*per* Southin J.).

[71]   *Grand Restaurants of Canada Ltd. v. Toronto (City)* (1981), 32 O.R. (2d) 757, at p. 775 (H.C.J.); affd (1982), 39 O.R. (2d) 752, (C.A.).

[72]   *Browne v. Cole* (1995), 26 C.C.L.T. (2d) 223, at p. 229 (B.C.C.A.) (*per* Hollindrake J.A.).

[73]   *Speed & Speed Ltd. v. Finance America Realty Ltd.* (1979), 12 C.C.L.T. 4 (N.S.C.A.); *Tompkins Hardware v. Northwestern Flying Services* (1982), 22 C.C.L.T. 1 (Ont. H.C.); *Canadian Western Natural Gas v. Pathfinder Surveys* (1980), 12 C.C.L.T. 211 (Alta. C.A.); *Fuerst v. St. Adolphe Co-op Parc Inc.*, [1990] 3 W.W.R. 446 (Man. C.A.), contractual entrant.

[74]   *Walker v. Forbes* (1925), 56 O.L.R. 532, at p. 535, [1925] 2 D.L.R. 725.

[75]   *Farber v. Toronto Transit Commn.* (1925), 56 O.L.R. 537, at p. 540, [1925] 2 D.L.R. 729, plaintiff's negligence not *causa causans,* therefore no apportionment.

afterwards.[76] This was a dreadful error on his part, for the doctrine of last clear chance retained no *raison d'être* after the advent of apportionment legislation. It was a device that enabled courts to award damages to a plaintiff in those cases where the defendant's negligence was subsequent in time to the plaintiff's. It also provided a disguise whereby the courts could compare negligence and saddle the more negligent party, if a defendant, with sole responsibility. Once apportionment legislation permitted a comparison of fault in the open, there was no need to do it in stealth. Yet accepted ways die slowly.

The doctrine of ultimate negligence has lived long past its indicated demise. It has been attacked repeatedly by scholars and judges, but stubbornly refuses to die. Professor MacIntyre has urged that "every vestige of last clear chance must be swept away in favour of apportionment".[77] He has described its justification on the theory of causation as "semantically indefensible and therefore deplorable because productive of muddled thinking". He proclaimed that the "retention of the 'last chance', 'ultimate negligence' or 'proximate cause' doctrine in contributory negligence cases after the apportionment statues becomes absurd".[78] Similarly, Mr. Justice Henderson once confided that he was "unable to appreciate that the doctrine of ultimate negligence has survived the provisions of the Negligence Act".[79] More recently Mr. Justice Macfarlane of the British Columbia Court of Appeal wisely declared that the "doctrine of last clear chance . . . has been overtaken by the provisions of the *Negligence Act* [of British Columbia]".[80]

Even though some courts recognize that last clear chance is still in existence, they are most reluctant to apply it, preferring instead to apportion liability wherever possible. Where stationary vehicles are struck by moving vehicles on highways, for example, judges tend to apportion liability between the moving and the stationary vehicle, unless it can be said that "clearly . . . the second negligent act was the sole cause of a resulting collision".[81] Moreover, the jury is rarely asked questions requiring a consideration of last clear chance.[82]

There are still cases, however, where last clear chance is invoked; although in practice, the issue is now rarely placed before the jury,[83] this will be done "where a

---

[76] *Mondor v. Luchini* (1925), 56 O.L.R. 576, [1925] 2 D.L.R. 746, 50-50 split in pedestrian case.

[77] *Supra*, n. 47, at p. 690.

[78] *Supra*, n. 48, at p. 283.

[79] *Gives v. C.N.R.*, [1941] O.R. 341, at pp. 344-45 (C.A.). See also Laskin J. in *R.A. Beamish Stores Co. Ltd. v. F.W. Argue Ltd.*, [1966] 2 O.R. 615, at p. 623; revd [1969] S.C.R. 354 (*sub nom. F.W. Argue v. Howe*). Dickson J. also harbours the "gravest doubts" about its survival, see *Hartman v. Fisette* (1976), 66 D.L.R. (3d) 516.

[80] *Frandle v. MacKenzie* (1990), 5 C.C.L.T. (2d) 113, at p. 116 (B.C.C.A.).

[81] *Bruce v. McIntyre*, [1954] O.R. 265, at p. 273 (*per* Pickup C.J.O.); affd [1955] S.C.R. 251; *Irvine v. Metropolitan Transport Co. Ltd.*, [1933] O.R. 823, at p. 836 (C.A.) (*per* Masten J.A.).

[82] Schroeder, *supra*, n. 50, at p. 797.

[83] *Davies v. Swan Motor Co. (Swansea) Ltd.*, [1949] 1 All E.R. 620 (C.A.); *Proctor v. Dyck*, [1952] Q.R. 95, at p. 106; revd on other grounds, [1953] 2 D.L.R. 257 (S.C.C.); *Watson and Rayson v. Toronto Transit Commn and Lunau*, [1949] O.W.N. 431 (C.A.). See Schroeder, *supra*, n. 50, at p. 797.

clear line can be drawn between the negligence of the plaintiff and the defendant".[84]

In *Brooks v. Ward and R.*[85] last clear chance was employed where someone saw a car in his path in plenty of time to avoid it. Mr. Justice Taschereau stated:

> Where a clear line can be drawn between the negligence of the plaintiff and the defendant, it is not a case of contributory negligence at all. When a driver sees a car in his path, and has plenty of opportunity to avoid it but fails to do so there is no contributory negligence and he must bear the full responsibility.[86]

In another Ontario case,[87] the plaintiff was standing on a ladder, painting, in an alley near his home when the defendant motorist negligently ran into him, knocking him to the ground. The defendant motorist negligently ran into him, knocking him to the ground. The defendant was held solely responsible, since he could have become aware of the plaintiff's negligence and could have avoided causing the damage. Chief Justice Porter concluded that the defendant was the "effective cause" of the accident.

b) The Plaintiff and Last Clear Chance

The doctrine of last clear chance has even been utilized against *plaintiffs*. Such an employment of the doctrine is somewhat bizarre. At common law contributorily negligent plaintiffs could recover nothing, whether or not they had the last clear chance. Hence, this doctrine was only relevant when it could be used against a defendant to assist a plaintiff. A defendant had no use for it whatsoever. After the arrival of apportionment legislation, however, last clear chance was used to deny all recovery to plaintiffs, who might otherwise be entitled to receive some part of their loss. In *Milligan v. MacDougall*,[88] for example, the plaintiff was barred from recovery on the ground that he had the last opportunity to avoid the accident. The plaintiff observed that the defendant was driving on the wrong side of the road, but took no steps to avoid him. The court decided that there was a "clearly visible dividing line" between the defendant's negligence and the plaintiff's ultimate negligence. The dissenting judge, while admitting that "the doctrine of last clear chance undoubtedly survives", thought

---

[84] *McKee and Taylor v. Malenfant*, [1954] S.C.R. 641, at p. 655 (*per* Kellock J.); *Admiralty Commrs v. The Volute (Owners)*, [1922] 1 A.C. 129, [1921] All E.R. Rep. 193; *Sigurdson v. B.C. Electric Ry.*, [1953] A.C. 291, at p. 299; *Dugas v. LeClaire* (1962), 32 D.L.R. (2d) 459 (N.B.C.A.). Newfoundland, Alberta and Saskatchewan have legislation dealing with the issue.

[85] [1956] S.C.R. 683.

[86] *Ibid.*, at p. 686. *Cf., Bruce v. McIntyre*, [1954] O.R. 265; affd [1955] S.C.R. 251, at p. 252.

[87] *Pritiko v. Hamilton*, [1960] O.W.N. 360 (C.A.). For other last clear chance cases, see *Fairweather v. Renton* (1963), 39 D.L.R. (2d) 249 (N.B.C.A.); *Great Eastern Oil Co. v. Best Motor Accessories Ltd.*, [1962] S.C.R. 118; *Boreham v. St. Pierre* (1964), 50 W.W.R. 621 (B.C.S.C.); *Seniunas v. Lou's Transport*, [1972] 2 O.R. 241, "ultimate negligence": *Cetinski v. Forman*, [1972] 2 O.R. 484.

[88] (1962), 32 D.L.R. (2d) 57 (P.E.I.C.A.). See also *Boulay v. Rousselle* (1984), 30 C.C.L.T. 149 (N.B.Q.B.).

that its invocation should be discouraged and that the plaintiff did not have to "outguess" a negligent driver.[89] A similar case is *Hunter v. Briere*.[90] A plaintiff motorcyclist collided with a stalled car and was denied compensation completely despite the negligence of the car's owner in running out of gas. According to the court, there was a "clear line of demarcation" between both acts of negligence, so that the plaintiff's negligence "can be separated from the defendant's negligence". The plaintiff's negligence was the "ultimate negligence". Such results demonstrate the utter bankruptcy of the last clear chance doctrine. It should be laid to rest forever.[91]

c) The Operation of Apportionment Legislation

The operation of apportionment legislation is relatively straightforward in most cases, although it may become rather complex when multiple parties are involved. Apportionment will be employed when the fault of two persons combine to cause a loss, that is, when there is concurrent negligence of two individuals.[92] There is no apportionment between a negligent and a non-negligent cause.[93] The Canadian practice is to look at the "causative conduct in terms of relative or comparative blameworthiness or culpability".[94] It has recently been repeated that the job of the court in apportioning damages is to "assess the respective blameworthiness", not the "extent to which the loss may be said to have been caused by the conduct of each." In other words, one considers whether there was "extreme carelessness" or merely a "minor lapse". In the decision involving the burning of a wharf,[95] it was held that the defendant and the owner should share the blame equally since their fault was "different in kind", but not "in degree".

The court takes a "common sense approach", free of "definitions and refinements".[96] The degree of fault of each party is a question of fact. If the trier of fact is unable to decide upon the degree of fault, it should split responsibility into two equal parts, as directed by the statute, but this provision "should not be relied on too heavily, however, lest the tribunal abdicate its proper function".[97]

---

[89] *Ibid.*, at p. 63. See also *Cousins v. Nesbitt and Weeks* (1964), 44 D.L.R. (2d) 316 (P.E.I.C.A.).

[90] (1989), 49 C.C.L.T. 93, at p. 100 (Man. Q.B.) (*per* Wright J.).

[91] See Bowker, *supra*, n. 48, at p. 204, for a description of the abortive attempts to abolish the rule by legislation. Mr. Justice Dickson (as he then was) expressed his "gravest doubt" that the doctrine survives, see *Hartman v. Fisette* (1976), 66 D.L.R. (3d) 516 (S.C.C.). See also *Frandle* case, *supra*, n. 80.

[92] *Clyke v. Blenkhorn* (1958), 13 D.L.R. (2d) 293, at p. 303 (N.S.C.A.) (*per* MacDonald J.). See generally Chiefetz, *Apportionment of Fault in Tort* (1981), for a thorough analysis of the problems.

[93] *Athey v. Leonati*, [1996] 3 S.C.R. 458, 31 C.C.L.T. (2d) 113.

[94] *Supra*, n. 92, at p. 304. The "degrees of culpability" are assessed, see Klar, "Recent Developments", *infra*, n. 300; *Ottosen v. Kasper* (1986), 37 C.C.L.T. 270 (B.C.C.A.).

[95] See Finch J.A. in *Alberta Wheat Pool v. Northwest Pile Driving Ltd.* (2000), 2 C.C.L.T. (3d) 53, at p. 66 and p. 67 (B.C.C.A.).

[96] *Ibid.*, at pp. 295 and 299.

[97] *Ibid.*, at p. 305.

The main purpose of this section is merely to "discourage too meticulous scrutiny". Courts of Appeal are discouraged from interfering with apportionments done by Trial Judges, unless there is a demonstrable error in the appreciation of the facts or relevant legal principles.[98]

A simple illustration may explain the way the scheme functions. Assume for a plaintiff's injury that the plaintiff is found to be 25 per cent at fault and the defendant 75 per cent at fault. The plaintiff is entitled to a judgment for 75 per cent of losses suffered, whereas at common law nothing would have been awarded.

Let us assume further that the plaintiff and the defendant were both motorists, that the plaintiff's damages were assessed at $1,000 and that the defendant also suffered losses in the amount of $2,000. If both claim against each other, the plaintiff will recover 75 per cent of $1,000 or $750, and the defendant in a counterclaim will receive 25 per cent of $2,000 or $500. According to the more desirable practice,[99] there will be no set-off. The plaintiff will obtain a judgment for $750 against the defendant and the defendant will get a judgment for $500 against the plaintiff. Both of these judgments will be paid by the respective insurers.[100] Consequently, partial compensation is received by both parties.

d) Multiple Parties

When more than two parties are involved things get more complicated. In *Menow v. Honsberger and Jordan House Ltd.*,[101] the plaintiff and each of the two defendants were held equally at fault, so that the plaintiff was entitled to recover two-thirds of his loss from either of the two defendants, who were jointly and severally liable to him.[102] They, in turn, would be entitled to contribution from one another.[103]

Justice Bastarache has recently explained how apportionment works in multiple party situations in *Ingles v. Tutkaluk Construction Ltd.*[104] as follows:

> When there are two or more tortfeasors, and a plaintiff has also been found negligent, the proper approach to apportionment is to first reduce the extent of the recoverable damages in

[98] *Ingles v. Tutkaluk Construction Ltd.*, [2000] 1 S.C.R. 298, 183 D.L.R. (4th) 193 (*per* Bastarache J.).

[99] Wright, "The Adequacy of the Law of Torts", [1961] Camb. L.J. 44, reprinted in Linden (ed.), *Studies in Canadian Tort Law* (1968), p. 579.

[100] See *Wells v. Russell*, [1952] O.W.N. 521 (C.A.); *Lewenza v. Ruszczak*, [1960] O.W.N. 40 (C.A.); *cf.*, Saskatchewan where a set-off is made so that the plaintiff would recover only $750 - $500 = $250. See *Schellenberg v. Cooke* (1960), 25 D.L.R. (2d) 607 (Sask. C.A.); *Johnny's Taxi v. Ostoforoff* (1962), 33 D.L.R. (2d) 85, at p. 89 (Sask. C.A.).

[101] [1970] 1 O.R. 54; affd [1971] 1 O.R. 129; affd [1974] S.C.R. 239.

[102] The result is the same when the plaintiff is not contributorily negligent. See *County of Parkland No. 31 v. Stetar*, [1975] 2 S.C.R. 884, 50 D.L.R. (3d) 376, at p. 386, where Mr. Justice Dickson explained that the plaintiff may "elect to recover the full amount of his damage from a tortfeasor only partly to blame".

[103] See generally, Klar, "Contribution Between Tortfeasors" (1975), 13 Alta. L. Rev. 359; Weinrib, "Contribution in a Contractual Setting" (1976), 54 Can. Bar Rev. 338.

[104] [2000] 1 S.C.R. 298, 183 D.L.R. (4th) 193, at p. 338 (S.C.R.), para. 57.

proportion with the plaintiff's negligence, and then to apportion the remaining damages between the defendants, in accordance with their fault.

There is a recent case in which four different people were held equally to blame for an accident.[105] There are limitless possibilities here to test the skill of the mathematician.[106]

When a plaintiff is found negligent to a certain degree in an action against two or more other parties, the plaintiff, after the deduction of his portion, is entitled to recover the entire remaining portion of loss from each of the others, even if one defendant is later relieved of responsibility. In *Colonial Coach Lines v. Bennett and C.P.R.*,[107] the defendant Bennett's cow escaped through a defective fence along the defendant C.P.R.'s land onto a highway, where it was hit by the plaintiff's bus. The cow was killed and the bus damaged. At trial, the jury found the plaintiff 35 per cent at fault, Bennett 5 percent at fault and the railway 60 percent at fault. The trial judge, however, dismissed the case against the railway and proceeded to split the 60 per cent attributed to it between the other two parties, according to the ratio of the fault of each to their total fault. The plaintiff was therefore held 87 1/2 per cent to blame and Bennett 12 1/2 per cent. The Court of Appeal reversed the trial judge on the negligence point and entered judgment in the proportions found by the jury. In an *obiter dictum*, however, Mr. Justice Laskin stated:

> It is appropriate to add as well that as against the plaintiff the defendant Bennett could not limit his ability to 5 per cent of the damages suffered by the plaintiff. The Negligence Act, R.S.O. 1960, c. 261, declares, by s. 2(1), the *joint and several* liability of two or more negligent defendants; and if Bennett was the only defendant at fault, he would be liable for all of the plaintiff's damages subject only to diminution to the extent of the latter's contributory fault.[108]

It is apparently possible, however, for a jury to apportion negligence 10 per cent to the defendant, 15 per cent to the plaintiff and 75 per cent to no one.[109]

Mr. Justice Schroeder exhibited his overall satisfaction with our comparative negligence legislation with these words:

> . . . the change effected by our statute was more consonant with the modern needs and concepts of society in a changing world, and better adapted to the requirements and habits of the age in which we live; . . . the doctrines established long before the days of the steam engine, the incandescent lamp, the modern automobile and the jet-propelled aeroplane, no longer served to promote the welfare of the members of our modern society and needed to be

---

[105] *Teno v. Arnold* (1976), 11 O.R. (2d) 585 (C.A.); vard (1978), 3 C.C.L.T. 272 (S.C.C.).
[106] See *Lecomte v. Bell Telephone Co. Ltd. and Ottawa*, [1932] 3 D.L.R. 220 (Ont.); *Nesbitt v. Beattie*, [1955] O.R. 111 (C.A.). *Cf.*, *Catt v. Coveyduck and Matheson*, [1950] O.W.N. 176.
[107] [1968] 1 O.R. 333, 66 D.L.R. (2d) 396.
[108] *Ibid.*, at pp. 403-04, O.R. See also *County of Parkland No. 31 v. Stetar, supra*, n. 102.
[109] See *Houle v. B.C. Hydro and Power Authority* (1972), 29 D.L.R. (3d) 510 (*per* Ruttan J.) (B.C.).

replaced by a law which was better adjusted to the increasing complexities of the daily routine and the greater tempo of life in our day and generation.[110]

He concluded that there is not "a progressive and socially conscious member of the judiciary or of the bar of our province who would wish to repeal the legislation . . . and return to the discarded common law doctrine of contributory negligence".[111]

4. THE SEAT BELT DEFENCE

Seat belts worn properly minimize the injuries incurred in accidents. One Canadian study concluded that "lap seat belts reduce the risk of major or fatal injury by 60%".[112] The author further declared that they "have never been shown to worsen injury, and while themselves producing injuries, they have prevented more serious ones". Surprisingly, despite this overwhelming statistical evidence, Canadian courts were originally ambivalent about the seat belt defence,[113] but now there is a clear trend in the cases to apportion damages where a passenger fails to buckle up.

Mr. Justice Cory of the Supreme Court of Canada has clearly summarized the law in *Galaske v. O'Donnell*,[114] for the majority:

> It has long been recognized that all occupants of a motor vehicle have a duty to wear their seat belts . . . Canadian Courts have recognized that passengers and drivers have a duty to ensure their own safety in a car by wearing seat belts. A failure to do so will result in an assessment of contributory negligence against that person. . . .
>
> The Courts in this country have consistently deducted from five to 25 percent from claims for damages for personal injury on the grounds that the victims were contributorily negligent for not wearing seat belts. This has been done whenever it has been demonstrated that the injuries would have been reduced if the belts had in fact been worn.

---

[110] *Supra*, n. 50, at p. 792.

[111] *Ibid.*, at p. 801. There was one lone dissenter who wrote a book condemning the reform, see David, *Common Law and Statutory Amendment in Relation to Contributory Negligence in Canada* (1936), reviewed by MacDonald (1936), 14 Can. Bar Rev. 368.

[112] Hodson-Walker, "The Value of Safety Belts: A Review" (1970), 102 Can. Med. Assoc. J. 391, citing the major medical studies in the field.

[113] See generally Linden, "Seat Belts and Contributory Negligence" (1971), 49 Can. Bar Rev. 475; Williams, "Comment" (1975), 53 Can. Bar Rev. 113. The American case law is divided. Comparative negligence states are more likely to permit it. A list of three dozen cases appears at (1970), 53 Marq. L. Rev. 226. Some U.S. legislatures have forbidden their courts to rely on the seat belt defence. See Kircher, "The Seat Belt Defence — State of The Law" (1970), 53 Marq. L. Rev. 172, at p. 176. The periodical literature in the U.S. has mushroomed. See especially, Roethe, "Seat Belt Negligence in Automobile Accidents", [1967] Wisc. L. Rev. 288; Levy, "The Seat Belt Defense — The Sophist's Escape" (1967), 41 Temp. L.Q. 126; West, "Should Failure to Wear Seat Belts Constitute a Defense" (1968), 10 Ariz. L. Rev. 523; "The Seat Belt Defense: A New Approach" (1969-70), 38 Fordham L. Rev. 94. See also the fine bibliography in (1970), 53 Marq. L. Rev. 227.

[114] [1994] 1 S.C.R. 670, 21 C.C.L.T. (2d) 1, at pp. 10-11, majority expressly relying on the fifth edition of this textbook. Driver partially liable for failing to see that child was strapped in seat.

a) Seat Belt Defence Applied

The first Canadian decision on the seat belt defence was *Yuan v. Farstad*.[115] Mr. Justice Monroe of the British Columbia Supreme Court found the defendant motorist entirely to blame for causing an auto accident which injured the plaintiff, Mrs. Yuan, and killed her husband, Dr. Yuan. Because Dr. Yuan, the driver of the blameless automobile, was not wearing an available seat belt at the time of the collision, he was ejected and fatally injured. Mrs. Yuan, who was a passenger in her husband's car had no seat belt available to her. At the time she was seated in the front seat, between her husband, who was the driver, and another passenger, and the vehicle was fitted with only two belts, one on each side of the front seat. Mrs. Yuan was allowed to recover 100 per cent of her damages for her own personal injuries, but the award for the death of her husband was reduced by 25 per cent, because of his contributory negligence in failing to buckle up.

The defendant introduced expert advice, through a retired police force captain and a doctor, to prove that Dr. Yuan's failure to wear the seat belt permitted him to be ejected, causing his death.[116] The police captain testified that seat belts "lessen the severity of the injuries in most automobile accidents". The doctor stated that seat belts "prevent ejection from a vehicle and lessen the severity of any steering wheel injury because it prevents body displacement". He admitted that belts cause abdominal injuries on occasion, but this was "so rare as to be improbable and, in any case, is correctable by surgery". The doctor concluded that the "fatal injuries would not have happened if the deceased had been wearing a seat belt at the time of the collision". This expert evidence was uncontroverted. Mr. Justice Monroe, basing his decision on this evidence and "upon the general knowledge of mankind", found that "lap seat belts are effective in reducing fatalities and minimizing injuries. . .".[117] He adopted the view of Mr. Justice Frankfurter who once said "there comes a point where this court should not be ignorant as judges of what we know as men". If the deceased had been wearing a seat belt, according to the judge, he would have suffered injury to his chest, but he would have been neither ejected nor killed.

Mr. Justice Munroe asserted that an automobile collision is reasonable foreseeable to a person driving a car in the city, and therefore, "a person must use reasonable care and take proper precautions for his own safety, and such precautions include the use of an available seat belt".[118] He admitted that he was proceeding in this way, "despite the apparent absence of any Canadian precedents upon the matter". Acknowledging that the deceased "was committing neither a crime nor a breach of a statute" in driving without his seat belt done

---

[115] (1967), 66 D.L.R. (2d) 295 (B.C.). See also *Earl v. Bourdon* (1975), 65 D.L.R. (3d) 646, at p. 655 (B.C.) (*per* Rae J.); *Ohlheiser et al. v. Cummings*, [1979] 6 W.W.R. 282 (Sask. Q.B.), 25% reduction.

[116] *Ibid.*, at p. 301.

[117] *Ibid.*

[118] *Ibid.*, at p. 302.

up, His Lordship stated that this was not determinative of the issue. The defendants, he contended, were entitled to be relieved of some degree of responsibility for the resulting injuries. His Lordship concluded by stating that "where a motorist fails to use an available seat belt and where it is shown that injuries sustained by him would probably have been avoided or of less severity had he been wearing a seat belt, then the provisions of . . . the Contributory Negligence Act are applicable".

Mr. Justice Munroe was somewhat influenced by the existence of legislation in British Columbia which required the installation of two seat belts in the front seat of each vehicle. Although such an enactment, he stated, did not make the use of belts mandatory, it does "give some legislative sanction to the wearing of same". His Lordship also relied upon two American decisions, which reached the same conclusion, the latter one in the total absence of any seat belt legislation.[119]

The court apportioned 25 per cent of the blame to Dr. Yuan and 75 per cent to the defendant driver, because the deceased would be "uninjured and alive were it not for the negligence of the defendant driver in causing the collision".[120] No contributory negligence was found against Mrs. Yuan for two reasons. First, there was no evidence of causal relation between her injury and her failure to wear seat belts. Second, no belt was available to Mrs. Yuan where she was seated in the front seat, making it "impractical if not impossible" for her to use a seat belt.

Another case in which the seat belt defence as *Jackson v. Millar*,[121] where a 16-year-old unbuckled passenger was ejected from a vehicle while it was making some violent gyrations cause by the gross negligence of the driver, another youth of 16. Mr. Justice Osler found that there was a seat belt in working order available to the plaintiff in the front passenger seat and that he was aware of this. Nevertheless, he did not choose to avail himself of it. Moreover, at the time of the accident he was slouched against the right-hand front door. The court concluded that "if Jackson had remained within the car he would not have suffered the injuries he received", which injuries were caused "principally, if not entirely by coming into contact with the ground after separating from the automobile".[122] Despite the absence of expert evidence concerning the efficacy of seat belts, His Lordship felt that the fact proven entitled him to find contributory negligence. He explained:

> As a matter of law, therefore, I find that his injuries were contributed to by his own negligence which consisted of failure to make use of a readily available seat belt at a time when he deliberately chose to rest a portion of his weight upon the car door. In the event that the

---

[119] *Bentzler v. Braun* (1967), 34 Wis. 2d 362, 149 N.W. 2d 626; *Mortenson v. South Pacific Co.* (1966), 53 Cal. Rptr. 851.

[120] *Yuan v. Farstad, supra,* n. 111, at p. 303.

[121] [1972] 2 O.R. 197; revd on another point [1973] 1 O.R. 399; revd [1976] 1 S.C.R. 225, 59 D.L.R. (3d) 246, at p. 256.

[122] *Ibid.*, at pp. 204-05.

automobile should be subjected to any sort of violent force, these acts and omissions on Jackson's part were such as to ensure the probability of this ejection from the car, the very event that occurred.[123]

Mr. Justice Osler allocated 10 per cent of the blame to the plaintiff and 90 per cent to the defendant. Although the Court of Appeal reversed the decision on another point, Mr. Justice Evans stated that he was "prepared to accept the conclusion of the trial judge with respect to the finding of contributory negligence on the part of the infant plaintiff". The Supreme Court of Canada restored the trial judge's decision but this point was not dealt with on the appeal at all.

The English courts have now unequivocally accepted the seat belt defence in *Froom v. Butcher*,[124] where Lord Denning M.R. declared that the reasonable person "should always, if he is wise, wear a seat belt". It should be worn: "Not only on long trips, but also on short ones. Not only in the town, but also in the country. Not only when there is fog, but also when it is clear. Not only by fast drivers, but also by slow ones. Not only on motorways, but also on sideroads".[125]

Reflecting the dominant position in Canada is the pronouncement of Mr. Justice MacPherson in *Ohlheiser v. Cummings*:[126]

> The wearing of seat belts was a nuisance to all of us initially. In time, they became a habit, like driving on the right or the myriad of other things we do, willingly or unwillingly, in our complicated society to make it work better. Bad things can be said about seat belts, but, on balance, they are good. They keep many people form being injured and occupying beds in hospitals that might well be occupied by others whose need is great but who are not in the emergency category. When we all pay for one another's hospital and medical care and other losses, through taxes or insurance, we each have a right to say to a driver and to a passenger: "Fasten your seat belts, in my interest if not in your own. If you don't fasten them, then you may have to pay part of your loss if you are hurt." What we have here is not a new interference with private rights, but the creation of a new public duty in the automobile age.[127]

It is also negligent to fail to fasten the shoulder harness as well as the lap belt,[128] except perhaps when one removes an "irritating" shoulder harness which is rubbing one's neck and places it under an arm.[129] It is not an excuse to be unaware that there are seat belts in the vehicle if one reasonably should know

---

[123] *Ibid.*, at p. 205.

[124] [1975] 3 All E.R. 520, at p. 527 (C.A.). See also *Pasternack v. Poulton*, [1973] 2 All E.R. 74; *Geier v. Kujawa, Weston and Warne Bros. Transport Ltd.*, [1970] 1 Lloyd's Rep. 364.

[125] *Ibid.*, at p. 525.

[126] [1979] 6 W.W.R. 282. See also Fulton J. in *Gagnon v. Beaulieu*, [1977] 1 W.W.R. 702 (B.C.S.C.), for a good summary of the current law. A 15-year-old was held 15% liable for not buckling up, though not legally required, see *Gray v. Macklin* (2000), 4 C.C.L.T. (3d) 13, 7 M.V.R. (4th) 264 (Ont. S.C.J.).

[127] *Ibid.*, at p. 286. See also *Shaw v. Roemer* (1982), 22 C.C.L.T. 43 (N.S.C.A.) (*per* Hart J.A.); see also *Bulmer v. Horsman* (1987), 42 C.C.L.T. 220 (N.B.C.A.).

[128] *Ulveland v. Marini* (1970), 4 C.C.L.T. 102 (B.C.), 15% deduction.

[129] *Anderson v. Davis* (1979), 10 C.C.L.T. 120 (B.C.).

that there are.[130] It is not negligent to fail to advise a passenger to wear his belt,[131] except perhaps if a child is involved.

In jurisdictions where the legislatures have mandated seat belt use,[132] the failure to wear them, when "required by law" to do so, was said to be both "illegal and negligent".[133] Where, however, a legislature has refused to enact such a legislation, or where it exempts children,[134] a court may refuse to invoke the seat belt defence.[135] It is not necessary, however, for there to be mandatory seat belt legislation in order for a court to hold that failure to buckle up constitutes negligence.[136] It is wise for the court to examine all the facts of the accident in detail in order to determine whether it was negligent to fail to strap in the specific circumstances.[137]

It is clear that the onus is on the defendant to prove that there was a failure to wear belts, that this amounted to negligence and that the injuries would have been prevented or lessened if the belts had been worn.[138] On the other hand, the onus is on the plaintiff to prove that it was not unreasonable to fail to buckle up. Thus, an asthmatic may convince a court of the absence of negligence due to the fact that the seat belt may cause the asthma to become worse.[139]

b) Seat Belt Defence Not Applied

Several reported Canadian decision have refused to invoke the seat belt defence in mitigation of damages. One early case was *MacDonnell v. Kaiser*,[140] where Mr. Justice Dubinsky of the Nova Scotia Supreme Court refused to adopt the seat belt defence (a) because it was not pleaded, and (b) because he had doubts about the evidence concerning the general effectiveness of seat belts. Mr. Justice Dubinsky's comments on the latter point are, therefore, purely *obiter*. Nevertheless, after referring to a rather undistinguished and incomplete article by an

---

[130] *Haley v. Richardson* (1975), 10 N.B.R. (2d) 653, at p. 667 (C.A.) (*per* Hughes C.J.).

[131] *Beaver v. Crowe* (1975), 49 D.L.R. (3d) 114 (N.S.). *Cf.*, *Ducharme v. Davies* (1981), 12 Sask. R. 137; revd in part [1984] 1 W.W.R. 699 (C.A.), infant not contributorily negligent. See *Galaske, supra*, n. 114.

[132] Highway Traffic Act, R.S.O. 1990, c. H.8, s. 106(3). All Canadian provinces now require passengers to strap in.

[133] *Quinlin v. Steffans* (1980), 12 C.C.L.T. 162, at p. 169 (*dictum per* Cromarty J.), 15% deduction, but no liability. Perhaps only evidence of negligence in the light of *R. in right of Canada v. Saskatchewan Wheat Pool*, [1983] 1 S.C.R. 205. See also *Galaske v. O'Donnell, supra*, n. 114, at p. 15, C.C.L.T. (*per* Cory J.).

[134] *Pelletier v. Olson* (1987), 42 C.C.L.T. 129 (Sask. Q.B.).

[135] *Genik v. Ewanylo* (1980), 12 C.C.L.T. 121 (Man. C.A.) (*per* Monnin J.A.).

[136] *Wallace v. Berrigan* (1988), 47 D.L.R. (4th) 752 (N.S.C.A.).

[137] *Supra*, n. 135 (*per* Hubbard J.A.).

[138] *Gagnon v. Beaulieu*, [1977] 1 W.W.R. 702 (B.C.) (*per* Fulton J.), 25% deduction where plaintiff ejected from vehicle. See also *Beaver v. Crowe, supra*, n. 131.

[139] *Reekie v. Messervey* (1986), 4 B.C.L.R. (2d) 194; supplementary reasons 10 B.C.L.R. (2d) 231.

[140] (1968), 68 D.L.R. (2d) 104 (N.S.), *cf.*, *Beaver v. Crowe, supra*, n. 131, defence available, but no proof of cause by defendant. The Nova Scotia Court of Appeal has probably overruled this decision in *Shaw v. Roemer, supra*, n. 127.

American negligence lawyer,[141] His Lordship concluded that "the effectiveness of seat belts is still in the realm of speculation and controversy". He did not foreclose "revised thinking" in the light of future expert testimony, but for the time being "there is too much indecision about the matter even among the experts". Mr. Justice Dubinsky rightly rejected the argument that the failure to wear a seat belt constituted negligence *per se*.[142] That could not have been the case without at least the violation of a statute requiring seat belt use, which had not yet been enacted at that time. His Lordship refused to hold that "a motorist who drives carefully and lawfully should be stamped with the mark of careless-ness. that he has not discharged his duty as a reasonable man, simply because he has not fastened to his person a seat belt. Most people know the true reasons for the slaughter on the highways".[143] Mr. Justice Dubinsky expressed his concern that a logical extension of the seat belt defence would lead to motorists being made to wear should harnesses, crash helmets, and, perhaps, drive armoured cars.[144] The court concluded by expressing its reticence about judicial creativity in areas where the legislatures have not spoken.

One eloquent refusal to succumb was voiced by Mr. Justice Sirois in *Reineke v. Weisgerber*:[145]

> The seat belt, harness and head rest age is still in its infancy. While . . . [those] involved in automobile safety have learned a great deal during the past few years, . . . they still have a long row to hoe before the dust has settled and the public are apprised of what is best in this regard. There have been terrible accidents from which, amazingly enough, unrestrained peo-ple were fortunate enough to walk away unscathed. And that at the opposite end of the spec-trum a fatality may result from a relatively minor collision. I have no doubt that with the number of motor vehicle accidents constantly increasing, with the tempo of research on the upswing, and with ever solicitous legislators always on their guard to do more things "gra-tuitously" for an ever increasing number of people who cannot think for themselves anymore, legislation will soon come to pass making the wearing of safety gear in vehicles compulsory. However, perhaps the remedy lies not *after* something has happened but before it has been initiated — such as being more careful in the issues of operator's licenses for one thing. The old saying that an ounce of prevention is worth a pound of cure still makes sense in this area as well as in others. Having said earlier that no final consensus has yet been reached by the research people in the field of automobile safety, the proposition that a person driving down the highway on his proper side of the road is entitled to assume that other persons using the highway will obey the laws of the road still appeals to me and it is not negligence not to strap oneself in a seat like a dummy, a robot or an astronaut.[146]

Most of the other Canadian cases rejecting the seat belt defence are founded on the lack of convincing evidence in the particular case that the failure to wear the belts caused or aggravated the injury suffered.[147] For example, in the Quebec

---

[141] Kleist, "Seat Belt Defense — An Exercise in Sophistry" (1967), 18 Hastings L.J. 613.

[142] *MacDonnell v. Kaiser, supra,* n. 140, at p. 107.

[143] *Ibid.*, at p. 108.

[144] See also *Hunt v. Schwanke*, [1972] 2 W.W.R. 541, at p. 543 (Alta.).

[145] [1974] 3 W.W.R. 97 (Sask.). See also *O'Brien v. Covin* (1974), 19 N.S.R. (2d) 659 (*per* Hart J.).

[146] *Ibid.*, at p. 112.

[147] This passage was relied on by Cory J. in *Galaske v. O'Donnell, supra,* n. 114, at p. 10, C.C.L.T.

decision of *Dame Lynch v. Grant*,[148] Mr. Justice Challies disposed of the matter on the ground of no causation; in other words, there was no evidence to indicate that the plaintiff's injuries would have been any less serious had she been wearing a seat belt at the time of the accident. Mr. Justice Challies stated: *"il n'y a aucune preuve, par expertise ou autrement, que les dommages subis par la demanderesse auraient été moindres si elle avait porté une ceinture de sécurité lors de l'accident"*.[149] Similarly, in *Anders v. Sim*,[150] Mr. Justice Riley, of the Alberta Supreme Court, concluded that the "failure to wear a seat belt does not *per se* constitute contributory negligence".[151] His Lordship disagreed with *Yuan* and quoted at length from *MacDonnell v. Kaiser* with approval. His comment about the quality of the evidence offered by the defence, however, probably offered a more solid basis for refusing to apply the seat belt defence: "[The evidence of the witness] produced as an expert (if he be one), is so inaccurate and so incomplete and really so unreliable that I find the defendant was wholly and solely to blame for the accident in question."

So too, in *Van Spronsen v. Gawor*,[152] His Honour, Judge Colter of Middlesex County, refused to reduce the damages of the plaintiff who neglected to buckle up. His Honour thought that it "may well be that . . . the defence might be open" where there was expert evidence that the deceased could have avoided death by wearing a belt.[153] Judge Colter did not, however, have sufficient evidence adduced before him to permit him to apportion the damages on any basis other than "pure speculation".[154]

On the basis of these cases, it is apparent that the language of our legislation permits apportionment whenever a plaintiff's failure to buckle up contributes to the plaintiff's *loss or damage*. To exploit the defence, however, the defendant must not only convince the court that seat belts are effective in general, but also that a belt would have helped *this plaintiff* in *this particular accident*. Usually expert evidence is required for this, although the court does not always insist upon it.[155]

---

[148] [1996] Que. S.C. 479.

[149] *Ibid.*, at p. 480.

[150] (1970), 11 D.L.R. (3d) 366 (Alta.).

[151] *Ibid.*, at p. 368.

[152] [1971] 2 O.R. 729.

[153] *Ibid.*, at p. 730.

[154] *Ibid.*, at p. 731. See also *Hunt v. Schwanke*, [1972] 2 W.W.R. 541 (Alta.); *Rigler v. Miller* (1972), 26 D.L.R. (3d) 366 (B.C.); *Dover v. Gooddy* (1972), 29 D.L.R. (3d) 639 (P.E.I.); *Heppell v. Irving Oil Co. Ltd.* (1973), 40 D.L.R. (3d) 476 (N.B.C.A.), defence not pleaded and evidence not showing that injuries would have been less: *Bown v. Rafuse* (1969), 8 D.L.R. (3d) 649 (N.S.).

[155] For some helpful ideas, see Bowman, "Practical Defense Problems — The Trial Lawyer's View" (1970), 53 Marq. L. Rev. 191; Huelke, "Practical Defense Problems — The Expert's View" (1970), 53 Marq. L. Rev. 203.

c) Problems of Calculation

Apportionment in the seat belt area is replete with complexities. For example, certain losses are not affected in the least by the failure to buckle up. The portion of the loss consisting of damage to the vehicle, for instance, must be borne completely by a negligent defendant and not at all by the plaintiff.[156] Further, let us suppose that an unbuckled passenger suffers a broken leg with damages evaluated at $3,000. Let us also assume that, if strapped in, the passenger would have suffered only some serious bruising that by itself would yield an assessment of $1,000. The plaintiff's contributory negligence in not wearing the belt should not reduce the damages for the loss which would have occurred in any event, that is the first $1,000.

It may be argued in such a case that the defendant is responsible *only* for the first $1,000 because the defendant was in no way the cause of the additional $2,000 loss. It might be said that the plaintiff's failure to use the belt was *the sole cause* of this additional loss. Consequently, it might be contended that the defendant should pay nothing toward the extra $2,000 damages on the theory that they are "avoidable consequences" or because the plaintiff "failed to mitigate damages".[157] Although such an approach is a possible compromise in jurisdictions where contributory negligence is still a complete defence, the Canadian courts can be more flexible. They should divide the $2,000 addition loss resulting from the absence of the belt "in proportion to the degree of negligence found against the parties" in relation to that loss. Thus, if the court finds that the plaintiff was 25 per cent to blame for neglecting to buckle up, the plaintiff should lose 25 per cent of the loss attributable to this act. Consequently, the plaintiff should be awarded $1,000, plus 75 per cent of $2,000, for a total of $2,500.

In *Pelletier v. Olson*,[158] the trial judge deducted 50 per cent of the damages in a fatal accident of the plaintiff because "death would not have occurred if the seat belt had been used". Therefore, the plaintiff and defendant were "equally responsible for the fatality".

The calculations become more complicated if the plaintiff is also partly to blame for the accident itself. Suppose the plaintiff is found to be 50 per cent to blame for the accident itself, and 25 per cent for the additional injury. The plaintiff should, therefore, collect one-half of $1,000 = $500, plus-half of 75 percent of $2,000 = $750, for a total of $1,250. Mathematical dexterity may be needed in the years ahead, but so far the courts have not been drawn into these pitfalls.

---

[156] West, *supra*, n. 113, at p. 528.

[157] *Prosser and Keeton on the Law of Torts*, 5th ed. (1984), p. 458. See Levy, *supra*, n. 113. See old cases where plaintiff denied damages for failure to seek competent medical advice. *Vinet v. R.* (1905), 9 Ex. C.R. 352; *McKervey v. Butler Bros.* (1910), 15 O.W.R. 175 (C.A.). More recently, on duty to mitigate, see *Janiak v. Ippolito* (1985), 31 C.C.L.T. 113 (S.C.C.).

[158] (1987), 42 C.C.L.T. 129, at p. 136 (Sask. Q.B.) (Malone J.).

One intelligent approach to the potential calculation problems was suggested by Lord Denning M.R. whereby there would be a standard reduction of 25 per cent, if all of the injury would have been avoided by the belts, and 15 per cent, if the injury would only have been belts, and 15 per cent, if the injury would only have been partially prevented.[159]

d) In Defence of the Seat Belt Defence

At the heart of the seat belt defence controversy is the standard of care to be expected of reasonable motorists in connection with their own safety. There is no longer any doubt that seat belts reduce the frequency and severity of car crash injuries. One study showed that the cost of medical treatment for belted victims was about one half that for unbelted victims.[160] The opponents of seat belts who express the fear that belted passengers will be trapped in burning, submerged or overturned cars are worrying about are exceedingly rare accidents.[161] If such accidents do occur, belted occupants may well be better off, because they may remain conscious and be able to escape. When injuries are caused by belts,[162] they are usually less severe than those that would have occurred without them. Moreover, some of these injuries are due to the improper use of the belts. To those who complain that seat belts are inconvenient, uncomfortable, and that they crease clothing, the response is that this is a small price to pay for greater safety.

Years ago the financial cost and trouble of installing belts might have inhibited a judicial finding of contributory negligence, but today all Canadian automobiles are automatically equipped with belts, making this a non-issue. The problem is that, despite their almost universal availability in Canadian cars, too few motorists wear belts consistently.[163] One study has shown that only 35 per cent of occupants wear belts, 42 per cent where they are required and 8 per cent where they are not.[164] The compulsory seat belt legislation has, therefore, increased the frequency of their use and contributed to a reduction in injuries and death on the roads of Ontario,[165] but even penal legislation of this sort cannot make seat belt use universal. All the provinces of Canada have enacted compulsory seat belt laws which will certainly encourage their use, but this will not

---

[159] *Froom v. Butcher, supra,* n. 124, at p. 528.

[160] $228 versus $419, Monitoring System Committee, "Changes in the Number and Cost of Motor Vehicle Injury Victims in Ontario", M.O.T.C. (1978).

[161] See Roethe, *supra,* n. 113, at p. 292. Fire occurs in 2% of injury-producing accidents, and submersion in 3%. Rollover occurred in 20% of injury-producing accidents in 1961, but it is less frequent today, see Snyder, "The Seat Belt as a Cause of Injury" (1970), 53 Marq. L. Rev. 21. See also Denning M.R. in *Froom* case, *supra,* n. 124.

[162] Snyder, *supra,* n. 161.

[163] See Auto Industries Highway Safety Committee, *National Survey of Seat Belt Installation and Use* (1967).

[164] Campbell, "Transport Canada's Policy on Occupant Restraint", in *International Symposium on Occupant Restraint* (1981), p. 136.

[165] *The Globe and Mail,* June 23, 1976, p. 5.

ensure that all vehicle passengers will wear them. Eventually the air bag, which is now being built into many cars, will be included in all automobiles, at which time auto crash injuries will be dramatically cut.

Until that time, however, tort law should lend its weight to legislative efforts to encourage motorists to buckle up. Although the deterrent force of tort law has been diminished by the advent of liability insurance, it may still have some effect in this context. Tort law should inform unbuckled plaintiffs that they will not be able merely to shrug their shoulders in the case of an accident and point to their insurance companies. Rather, they should be told that if they fail to strap in and are injured in the accident, it will cost them money in that their tort recovery will be cut down. Our courts have encouraged safety measures in the past by holding that it is contributory negligence to fail to use safety rope,[166] or to wear a life jacket,[167] or safety goggles.[168] Similarly, a motorcyclist neglecting to wear a safety helmet in violation of legislation requiring this,[169] will be held contributorily negligent. The same result should flow from the failure to strap in, especially when legislation requires it.

B. Voluntary Assumption of Risk

A plaintiff otherwise entitled to tort recovery may be denied it on the ground of voluntary assumption of risk.[170] In other words, if *volenti non fit injuria* or consent is present, an action for negligence will fail, just as it does in the intentional tort area. This is so because "no act is actionable as a tort at the suit of any person who has expressly or impliedly assented to it".[171]

The policies underlying this principle reflect the stout individualism of the early common law. According to that philosophy, one was free to work out one's own destiny.[172] Consequently, anyone could agree to encounter risks without judicial interference. The price paid for this freedom was that, if things went wrong, one had to bear the loss bravely without succour from the law. This

---

[166] *Carter v. Christ* (1933), 148 So. 714 (La.).

[167] *Chamberland v. Fleming, supra*, n. 12, 25% maximum reduction.

[168] *Nashville C. & St. L. Ry. v. Coleman* (1924), 151 Tenn. 443, 269 S.W. 919. In Wisconsin under the workers' compensation legislation, workers who fail to use safety devices have their awards cut by 15%, see Roethe, *supra*, n. 113, at p. 297.

[169] Higway Traffic Act, R.S.O. 1990, c. H.8, s. 104(1); *O'Connell v. Jackson*, [1971] 3 All E.R. 129 (C.A.), 15% reduction for not wearing crash helmet; *cf.*, *Hilder v. Associated Portland Cement Manufacturing Ltd.*, [1961] 3 All E.R. 709, where failure to wear helmet not contributory negligence, but helmet not required by law and no proof of cause.

[170] James, "Assumption of Risk" (1952), 61 Yale L.J. 141; Bohlen, "Voluntary Assumption of Risk" (1906), 20 Harv. L. Rev. 14; Green "Assumed Risk as a Defense" (1961), 22 La. L. Rev. 77; Wade, "The Place of Assumption of Risk in the Law of Negligence" (1961), 22 La. L. Rev. 5; Payne, "Assumption of Risk and Negligence" (1957), 35 Can. Bar Rev. 950; Hertz, "Volenti Non Fit Injuria: A Guide" in Klar (ed.), *Studies in Canadian Tort Law* (1977), p. 101; Jaffey, "Volenti non Fit Injuria" (1985), 44 Camb. L.J. 87.

[171] *Carnegie v. Trynchy* (1966), 57 W.W.R. 305 (Alta.) (*per* Dechene J.).

[172] Bohlen, *supra*, n. 170, at p. 14.

promoted rugged independence, something that was prized in those days. Another rationale behind the *volenti* principle contains an element of the fault principle. If people consent to run the risk of injury, they do not "deserve" the protection of the common law, because they are "co-authors" of the harm inflicted upon themselves.[173] A third justification for this doctrine is that if someone manifests a willingness to assume the risk of an accident, a defendant who relies on this should be shielded from responsibility. If rendered accountable in such circumstances, the defendant would refuse to co-operate with consenting plaintiffs in the future, and their freedom of choice would be diminished.[174]

1. *VOLENTI* IS A DEFENCE

Voluntary assumption of risk is a defence.[175] It must be pleaded and proved by the defendant.[176] For example, Mr. Justice Spence has declared that "it is for the defendants to establish the defence of *volenti non fit injuria*".[177]

There have been attempts to subsume voluntary assumption of risk within the duty issue. In other words, it has been argued that no duty of care is owed to one who consents to a risk.[178] Canadian courts have been attracted toward this approach occasionally,[179] but they should not adopt it.[180] It is preferable to treat *volenti* as a defence for several reasons. First, the duty concept is already overloaded, being used to decide disparate issues like the extent of liability, the unforeseeable plaintiff, the standard of care, and other matters. More clarity would be possible if we kept the duty notion uncluttered by *volenti*. Second, tort

---

[173] Keeton, "Assumption of Risk in Products Liability Cases" (1961), 22 La. L. Rev. 122, at p. 151. See also *Tomlinson v. Harrison*, [1972] 1 O.R. 670, at p. 677, *ex turpi causa* theory used by Addy J.

[174] Mansfield, "Informed Choice in the Law of Torts" (1961), 22 La. L. Rev. 17, at p. 25. For an economic analysis of *volenti*, see Posner, *Economic Analysis of Law*, 3rd ed. (1986).

[175] See Lord Oaksey in *London Graving Dock Co. Ltd. v. Horton*, [1951] A.C. 737, at p. 758, where he stated "the maxim *volenti non fit injuria* is a maxim which affords a defence to a person who has committed a breach of duty".

[176] *McWilliam v. Thunder Bay Flying Club*, [1950] O.W.N. 697, at p. 697, defendant not allowed to rely on defence, but discussed anyway.

[177] *Aldridge and O'Brien v. Van Patter, Martin and Western Fair Assoc.*, [1952] O.R. 595, at p. 602. See also *Lehnert v. Stein*, [1963] S.C.R. 38, at p. 43 (*per* Cartwright J.) and at p. 39 (*per* Kerwin C.J.); *Car and General Insurance Corp. v. Seymour*, [1956] S.C.R. 322, at p. 324 (*per* Rand J.) and at p. 331 (*per* Kellock J.); *Thompson v. Sbranchella*, [1956] O.W.N. 349, at p. 350 (C.A.) (*per* McRuer J.); *Osborne v. London & North Western Ry. Co.* (1888), 21 Q.B.D. 220, at p. 223; *Tobin v. Fennell* (1962), 35 D.L.R. (2d) 513, at p. 522 (N.S.) (*per* Currie J.).

[178] See *Dann v. Hamilton*, [1939] 1 K.B. 509, at p. 512, where Mr. Justice Asquith declared "the plea of *volenti* is a denial of any duty at all". See also Payne, *supra*, n. 170; Bohlen, *supra*, n. 170; Fleming, *The Law of Torts*, 9th ed. (1998), Chapter 13.

[179] *Halliday v. Essex*, [1971] 3 O.R. 621, at p. 623; *Atwell v. Gertridge* (1958), 12 D.L.R. (2d) 669, at p. 677 (N.S.); *Hagerman v. Niagara Falls* (1980), 114 D.L.R. (3d) 184 (Ont.); *Dolby v. McWhirter* (1979), 99 D.L.R. (3d) 727 (Ont.).

[180] See n. 177 for cases. See also *Fink v. Greeniaus* (1973), 2 O.R. (2d) 541, at p. 552 (*per* Van Camp J.).

obligations should be constant so that actors will understand what is expected of them. To say that a driver owes a duty to drive carefully to one passenger but not to another is anomalous. A driver should owe the same duty of care to all passengers. However, the driver should not be liable when one of the passengers agrees to accept the risk, but this is because of the plaintiff's own conduct, not because of lack of duty. Even though legal liability may vary, the duty owed should not. Third, to incorporate *volenti* into duty would be to eliminate a distinct procedural advantage presently enjoyed by an injured plaintiff. It is the defendant, not the plaintiff, who must now lead evidence of consent. To insist that the plaintiff prove absence of consent may lead to the denial of recovery in cases where proof is lacking. Fourth, *volenti* is a question of fact normally decided by the jury, something that may broaden the incidence of compensation. By transforming it into a duty matter, it becomes the task of the court to decide it, which may reduce the frequency of recovery.[181]

2. THE MEANING OF *VOLENTI*

The defence of *volenti* may arise either by express agreement or it may be implied from the conduct of the parties.[182] The situations where consent is expressly given are not difficult to deal with.[183] The court must decide, of course, whether there was actual or manifested agreement to the terms of the contract, which may be included on tickets, signs, or standard form contracts.[184] When these provisions are given effect, they are strictly construed against the party relying on them.[185]

One case demonstrating the effectiveness of an express agreement is *Birch v. Thomas*,[186] where the defendant, the driver of an uninsured motor vehicle, had a notice on his car windshield stating that all passengers rode at their own risk. He informed the plaintiff of the presence of the notice and its message when the

---

[181] *Prosser and Keeton on the Law of Tort*, 5th ed. (1984), p. 481. See also Bastarache J. in *Ingles*, *supra*, n. 98.

[182] *Dokuchia v. Domansch*, [1944] O.W.N. 461, at p. 464 (C.A.). See also *Regal Oil & Refining Co. and Regal Distribution Ltd. v. Campbell*, [1936] S.C.R. 309, at p. 320.

[183] See *A.E. Farr Ltd. v. The Admiralty*, [1953] 2 All E.R. 512; *Dyck v. Manitoba Snowmobile Assn. Inc.* (1981), 21 C.C.L.T. 38 (Man. C.A.), every form protected defendant; Cootes, *Exception Clauses* (1964); Seddon, "Fault Without Liability" (1981), 55 Aust. L.J. 22.

[184] See *Olley v. Marlborough Court Ltd.*, [1949] 1 K.B. 532, [1949] 1 All E.R. 127 (C.A.); *Alderslade v. Hendon Laundry Ltd.*, [1945] 1 K.B. 189 (C.A.); *Karroll v. Silver Star Mountain Resorts Ltd.* (1988), 47 C.C.L.T. 269 (B.C.S.C.) (*per* McLachlin J.), skier's signed release waived liability; see also *London Drugs Ltd. v. Kuehne & Nagel International Ltd.*, [1993] 1 W.W.R. 1 (S.C.C.), concerning protection for third parties by such waivers: Fleming, *op. cit. supra*, n. 178, p. 330. See also *Greeven v. Blackcomb Skiing Enterprise Ltd.* (1994), 22 C.C.L.T. (2d) 265 (B.C.S.C.), terms on ticket not shown to plaintiff.

[185] *White v. John Warwick & Co. Ltd.*, [1953] 2 All E.R. 1021, [1953] 1 W.L.R. 1285, at p. 1292 (C.A.); *Alderslade v. Hendon Laundry Ltd.*, [1945] 1 K.B. 189 (C.A.). See generally Cumming, "Judicial Treatment of Disclaimer Clauses in Sale of Goods Transactions in Canada" (1972), 10 Osgoode Hall L.J. 281.

[186] [1972] 1 All E.R. 905 (C.A.).

plaintiff entered the automobile. The Court of Appeal unanimously held that the maxim *volenti non fit injuria* applied and the plaintiff could not recover for personal injuries suffered through the defendant's negligent driving. The courts are, however, tending to require proof that the small print on a ticket, for example, has actually been brought to the attention of the plaintiff.[187]

The cases where the consent is implied from the acts of the plaintiff are more complicated. It is clear that mere knowledge of the danger is not enough for the *volenti* defence to be applied. "*Volenti non fit injuria* is not the equivalent of *scienti non fit injuria*."[188] Thus, driving instructors who are undoubtedly aware of the danger involved in their work, are not held *volenti*, even though they may be held partially to blame.[189]

a) Traditional Definition

The traditional requirements to establish the defence of voluntary assumption of risk were: "(1) that the plaintiff clearly knew and appreciated the nature and character of the risk he ran, and (2) that he voluntarily incurred it".[190] In other words, it had to be demonstrated that the plaintiff not only "perceived the existence of the danger, but also fully appreciated it and voluntarily assumed the risk, and that is a question of fact".[191]

Consequently, if there is no knowledge of the danger, there can be no assumption of the risk. For example, when three people died as a result of carbon monoxide poisoning because of a defective muffler, there was no *volenti* since they were unaware that the muffler was broken.[192] In addition, the risk must be freely encountered. When there is no free choice, as in the rescue cases,[193] in the case of heli-skiers following their leader[194] and in the employment situation,[195] there is no *volenti*. Similarly, if a police officer takes a risk by setting up a

---

[187] *Wilson v. Blue Mountain Resorts Ltd.* (1974), 4 O.R. (2d) 713, at p. 718 (*per* R. Holland J.).

[188] *Sarnia v. Shepley*, [1969] 2 O.R. 42, 4 D.L.R. (3d) 315.

[189] *Nettleship v. Weston*, [1971] 3 All E.R. 581 (C.A.); *Lovelace v. Fossum*, [1972] 2 W.W.R. 161 (B.C.).

[190] Lamont J. in *Village of Kelliher v. Smith*, [1931] S.C.R. 672, at p. 679, quoting Lord Atkinson in *C.P.R. v. Fréchette*, [1915] A.C. 871, at p. 880 (P.C.).

[191] Gillanders J.A. in *Harrison v. Toronto Motor Car Ltd. and Krug*, [1945] O.R. 1, at p. 9 (C.A.); *Young v. Younger*, [1945] O.R. 97; affd [1945] O.R. 467 (C.A.).

[192] *Kowton v. Public Trustee of Alberta* (1966), 57 W.W.R. 370 (Alta.).

[193] *Haynes v. Harwood*, [1935] 1 K.B. 146, at p. 157 (C.A.); *Baker v. Hopkins*, [1959] 3 All E.R. 225, at p. 237 (C.A.).

[194] *Lowry v. Canadian Mountain Holdings Ltd.* (1985), 33 C.C.L.T. 261 (B.C.S.C.); see also *Delaney v. Cascade River Holdings Ltd.* (1983), 44 B.C.L.R. 24 (C.A.).

[195] *Bowater v. Rowley Regis Corp.*, [1944] 1 K.B. 476, at p. 479 (C.A.) (*per* Scott L.J.) ". . . a man cannot be said to be truly 'willing' unless he is in a position to choose freely. . . ." See also *Smith v. Baker & Sons*, [1891] A.C. 325; *Dann v. Hamilton*, [1939] 1 K.B. 509; *Burnett v. British Waterways Bd.*, [1972] 1 W.L.R. 1329, [1973] 2 All E.R. 631 (C.A.). But *cf.*, *Imperial Chemical Industries Ltd. v. Sharwell*, [1964] 2 All E.R. 999 (H.L.). See also Workplace Safety and Insurance Act, 1997, S.O. 1997, c. 16, Sched. A, ss. 115, 116.

roadblock in the line of duty,[196] or if someone "impelled by a call of nature" traverses a dangerous floor to get to a privy,[197] they will not be denied recovery.

b) Definition Narrowed

More recently the Supreme Court of Canada has reshaped the doctrine of *volenti non fit injuria* so as to restrict its application to instances where the court finds an agreement, express or implied, to exempt the defendant from liability.[198] Demonstrative of the rather hostile judicial attitude toward the defence of *volenti* is *Lagasse v. Rural Municipality of Richot*,[199] where the plaintiff's late husband, a tractor operator, agreed to plow some snow on a lake at the request of the defendant municipality. While he was plowing the snow, the ice gave way, the tractor sank into the lake and the plaintiff's husband was drowned. In deciding if *volenti non fit injuria* applied, Matas J. quoted the statement of Denning M.R. in *Nettleship v. Weston*:

> This brings me to the defence of volenti non fit injuria. . . . In former times this defence was used almost as an alternative defence to contributory negligence. Either defence defeated the action. Now that contributory negligence is not a complete defence, but only a ground for reducing the damages, the defence of volenti non fit injuria has been closely considered, and, in consequence, it has been severely limited. Knowledge of the risk of injury is not enough. Nor is a willingness to take the risk of injury. Nothing will suffice short of an agreement to waive any claim for negligence. This plaintiff must agree, expressly or impliedly, to waive any claim for injury that may befall him due to the lack of reasonable care by the defendant: or more accurately, due to the failure of the defendant to measure up to the standard of care that the law requires of him. . . .[200]

Matas J. concluded:

> Nothing in [the deceased's] words or conduct, either by express or by necessary implication, showed that he gave a real consent to the assumption of risk without compensation or that he absolved the defendants from duty to take care.[201]

His Lordship went on, however, to reduce the widow's recovery by 25 per cent because of her husband's contributory negligence. This restrictive view of *volenti* means that courts rarely invoke the defence nowadays.

Chief Justice MacKeigan has underscored the view that the voluntary assumption of risk defence should be avoided where possible, especially in actions by passengers of automobiles, when he stated in *Crossan v. Gillis*:[202]

---

[196] *Hambley v. Shepley* (1967), 63 D.L.R. (2d) 94 (C.A.).

[197] *Rush v. Commercial Realty Co.* (1929), 145 Atl. 476.

[198] See *infra*, Section 4, for discussion of cases. See also *Hagerman, supra*, n. 179, at p. 191 (*per* Labrosse J.).

[199] [1973] 4 W.W.R. 181 (Man.). See also *Crocker v. Sundance Northwest Resort Ltd.* (1988), 44 C.C.L.T. 225 (S.C.C.).

[200] *Ibid.*, at p. 189.

[201] *Ibid.*, at p. 190.

[202] (1979), 7 C.C.L.T. 269, at p. 277 (N.S.C.A.); *Ferris v. Stubbs* (1978), 89 D.L.R. (3d) 364 (N.B.C.A.); *Schmidt v. Sharpe* (1983), 27 C.C.L.T. 1, at p. 16 (Ont. H.C.) (*per* Gray J.); *cf.*, *Henderson v. Pearson Forest Products Ltd.* (1979), 10 C.C.L.T. 209 (Ont.).

... for the *volenti* defence to succeed, the Canadian law now requires proof that a bilateral bargain was actually made, expressly or by necessary implication from the facts, with the onus on the defendant to advance such proof, a burden especially difficult to discharge in passenger gross negligence cases.

Volenti has not disappeared altogether, however. In *Benjamin v. Boutilier*,[203] the defendant was using a bulldozer to backfill around the plaintiff's house. The conditions were wet and the defendant warned the plaintiff that it was dangerous to fill closer than seven feet to the house. The plaintiff instructed the defendant to proceed, regardless of the conditions. Damage resulted to the foundation of the house when a rock rolled off a mound and collided with the wall. The court found that the operator-defendant was negligent in proceeding with the work when his common sense told him it was dangerous. The court dismissed the action, however, because the plaintiff had voluntarily consented to take the risk.

c) Effect of Defendant's Violation of Statute on Defence of *Volenti*

The defence of *volenti* is sometimes unavailable to defendants who are themselves in violation of a statute. Where a defendant breaches legislation requiring that a highway be kept in good repair, the offender cannot rely on voluntary assumption of risk.[204] Similarly, if the plaintiff is injured at work because of a violation of the Factories Act, *volenti* cannot be invoked by the employer so as to thwart the policy of protecting workers from injury.[205] On the other hand, the fact that the Criminal Code or a speeding statute is contravened by a defendant does not render inapplicable the *volenti* defence, because these statutes are not aimed at the highly desirable social goal of worker safety with which consent cannot interfere.[206] Recently, it has been established that an employer may rely on *volenti* where the statute is violated, not by the employer, but by one of the workers.[207]

3. SPORTS

Those who are injured during sporting events are often met by the defence of voluntary assumption of risk.[208] In denying recovery it is often said that specta-

---

[203] (1970), 17 D.L.R. (3d) 611 (N.S.).

[204] *Greer v. Mulmur* (1926), 59 O.L.R. 259, at p. 265 (C.A.) (*per* Masten J.A.) and at p. 267 (*per* Riddell J.A.), dissenting. See also *Jessen v. Livingstone*, [1929] 2 D.L.R. 474, at p. 479 (Sask. C.A.) (*per* McKay J.A.); *Baddeley v. Granville* (1887), 19 Q.B.D. 423.

[205] *McClemont v. Kilgour Mfg Co.* (1912), 27 O.L.R. 305, at p. 312 (C.A.) (*per* Teetzel J.). See also *Rodgers v. Hamilton Cotton Co.* (1892), 23 O.R. 425, at p. 435.

[206] See *Miller v. Decker*, [1957] S.C.R. 624, at p. 634 (*per* Kellock J.).

[207] See *Imperial Chemical Industries v. Sharwell*, [1964] 2 All E.R. 999 (H.L.). See Atiyah, "Causation, Contributory Negligence and *Volenti Non Fit Injuria*" (1965), 43 Can. Bar Rev. 609.

[208] See generally Barnes, *Sports and the Law in Canada*, 2nd ed. (Toronto: Butterworths, 1988); Siskind, "Liability for Injuries to Spectators" (1968), 6 Osgoode Hall L.J. 305.

tors and participants accept the risks "inherent to" or "incidental to" the game.[209] It would be preferable, however, to say that "conduct of the participants that present obvious or necessary risks normal to the sport in question is not negligence".[210] For example, where a golf ball strays from the fairway, as is so often the case, there is no negligence, but where a snowmobile collides with another snowmobile from the rear there is negligence.[211]

a) Spectators

In *Elliott v. Amphitheatre Ltd.*,[212] the defendant was excused from liability when a puck flow over the boards of its hockey rink and hit an 18-year-old spectator in the eye. MacDonald C.J.K.B.[213] observed that the proprietor was not an insurer and that the "spectators assume the risk peculiar to that form of entertainment". The plaintiff, who was a hockey player himself, chose to sit in the front row, outside the protection of the screens that had been installed at both ends of the rink in accordance with the customary method of building hockey arenas. In addition, no special precautions must be taken by a participant in a sport for the safety of a spectator.[214]

In contrast with the *Elliot* case is *Payne and Payne v. Maple Leaf Gardens, Stewart and Marucci*.[215] A Toronto Maple Leaf player named Gaye Stewart, during a game with the Chicago Black Hawks, got into a fight over a hockey stick he mistakenly believed to be his own. During the scuffle which took place near the boards and away from the play, the female plaintiff was struck by Stewart's stick. Stewart received a minor penalty for his violation and, in the law suit that followed, he was held liable to the plaintiff and her husband for their loss. Mr. Justice Laidlaw explained that no liability would flow from an ordinary escape of a puck or stick during play, because the spectators are taken to "have assumed the risk of injuries resulting from them". However, although the plaintiffs were season's ticket holders, they could not be held to have "assumed the risk of injuries resulting directly from negligence or improper conduct on the part of the player. Such a player could not properly say that they

---

[209] Parlee J. in *MacLeod v. Roe*, [1947] 1 D.L.R. 135, at p. 148; revd on another ground [1947] S.C.R. 420.

[210] *Dolby v. McWhirter* (1979), 99 D.L.R. (3d) 727, at p. 728 (*per* Reid J.). See also *Hagerman*, *supra*, n. 179.

[211] *Ibid.*

[212] [1934] 3 W.W.R. 225 (Man.). See also *Murray v. Harringay Arena Ltd.*, [1951] 2 K.B. 529, [1951] 2 All E.R. 320 (C.A.), six-year-old child denied recovery when puck went over boards.

[213] *Ibid.*, p. 228; see also *Klyne v. Town of Indian Head* (1979), 107 D.L.R. (3d) 692 (Sask. C.A.), no liability since no violation of custom by not having shields on sides of rink. See also *Hagerman*, *supra*, n. 179.

[214] *Wooldridge v. Sumner*, [1962] 2 All E.R. 978 (C.A.), horse ran over photographer. See *Wilks v. Cheltenham Home Guard Motor Cycle and Light Car Club*, [1971] 2 All E.R. 369 (C.A.), no liability to spectators at motorcycle scramble.

[215] [1949] O.R. 26, [1949] 1 D.L.R. 369 (C.A.).

assumed a risk created by his own wrongdoing."[216] The owners of the arena were excused from liability because they could not expect such unusual behaviour from a player, and, therefore, were in no way negligent.

b) Participants

Participants in sports are also denied recovery for injuries incurred during the ordinary course of play. A hockey player consents to being body-checked by another player and is properly denied compensation for such contact. However, a player may be permitted to recover against another player in certain circumstances. In *Agar v. Canning*,[217] for example, the defendant struck the plaintiff across the face with his stick after he had been hooked on the back of the neck by the plaintiff. Despite this provocation, liability was imposed by Mr. Justice Bastin on the ground that there was a "definite resolve to cause serious injury to another" which does "not fall within the scope of the implied consent" and goes "beyond the limit marking exemption from liability".[218] His Lordship articulate the bounds of the consent as follows:

> . . . Hockey necessarily involves violent bodily contact and blows from the puck and hockey sticks. A person who engages in this sport must be assumed to accept the risk of accidental harm and to waive any claim he would have apart from the game for trespass to his person in return for enjoying a corresponding immunity with respect to other players. It would be inconsistent with this implied consent to impose a duty on a player to take care for the safety of other players corresponding to the duty which, in a normal situation, gives rise to a claim for negligence. Similarly, the leave and licence will include an unintentional injury resulting from one of the frequent infractions of the rules of the game.
>
> The conduct of a player in the heat of the game is instinctive and unpremeditated and should not be judged by standards suited to polite social intercourse.
>
> But a little reflection will establish that some limit must be placed on a player's immunity from liability. Each case must be decided on its own facts so it is difficult, if not impossible, to decide how the line is to be drawn in every circumstance. But injuries inflicted in circumstances which show a definite resolve to cause serious injury to another, even where there is provocation and in the heat of the game, should not fall within the scope of the implied consent.[219]

Golfers are denied tort reparation when they are struck by golf balls that accidentally veer off the fairway in the normal course of play. In *Ellison v. Rogers*,[220] the defendant golfer hooked a ball instead of slicing it, as he usually did, and accidentally injured the plaintiff, another golfer. Neither the defendant

---

[216] *Ibid.*, at p. 373, D.L.R. See also *Reese v. Coleman et al.*, [1976] 3 W.W.R. 739, at p. 741 (Sask.) (*per* MacPherson J.), no assumption of risk where violation of rules at snowmobile race, owners liable.

[217] (1965), 54 W.W.R. 302; affd 55 W.W.R. 384 (Man. C.A.).

[218] *Ibid.*, at p. 304. See also *Wooldridge v. Sumner, supra*, n. 214.

[219] *Ibid.* See also *Zapf v. Muckalt* (1995), 26 C.C.L.T. (2d) 61 (B.C.S.C.); affd (1996), 31 C.C.L.T. (2d) 201 (B.C.C.A.), violation of rule led to liability; *Unruh v. Webber*, [1994] 5 W.W.R. 27 (B.C.C.A.).

[220] [1968] 1 O.R. 501 (*per* Brooke J.).

nor the operators of the golf course were held liable. Mr. Justice Brooke equated the position of the spectator and the golf player and declared that "the normal risk assumed . . . is the danger usually found" on the golf course.[221] His Lordship remarked that "the action of other golfers is not a risk for which the proprietor of a golf course is liable if it is the normal risk of the game".

If dangerous activities were permitted on the course, however, the proprietors might well be held liable, in addition to the perpetrator. In *Ratcliffe v. Whitehead*,[222] for example, the defendant hit a golf ball directly at a group of golfers from a distance of only 40-80 yards. Mr. Justice Adamson felt that this risk was not assumed. "If it were to be found that it is a risk incidental to the game to have balls driven almost directly at one, it would, to say the least, interfere with the alleged pleasure and healthfulness of the game."[223] He further stated that "every one knows that a golf ball does not always go in exactly the direction intended, in fact for most people it rarely does."[224] Someone who accepts a ride on a snowmobile is said to voluntarily assume the risk of falling off, but is "entitled to expect that his driver will not be negligent in the sense that he will act within the standard of care to be expected from a reasonably prudent driver engaged in that particular sport".[225] Nor does a snowmobile passenger accept the risk of being negligently struck[226] or run over by another snowmobile following behind, although contributory negligence may be found.[227]

Similarly, although a skier may not consent to the risk of being run into by another negligent skier, he may be found contributorily negligent for not keeping a proper lookout.[228] In another skiing case,[229] a skier was entitled to recover 75 per cent of his damages from the operator of a ski resort, when he fell into a gully about which he was not given adequate warning. The skier was also held 25 per cent to blame. Mr. Justice Richard Holland observed:

> Skiing is well recognized as a dangerous sport and anyone taking part in such a sport must, I would think, accept certain dangers which are inherent in such sport in so far as such dangers are obvious or necessary.

The skier, however, did not accept this risk, which was not obvious, or necessary, or known to him. So too, a water skier may assume the risk of hitting an obstruction, but not the risk of a boat driver's negligent failure to warn about such an obstruction.[230]

---

[221] *Ibid.*, at p. 513.
[222] [1933] 3 W.W.R. 447 (Man.). See also *MacLeod v. Roe, supra*, n. 209, at p. 139 (*per* O'Connor J.), plaintiff did not accept risk of negligence, where there was no strap on a rented roller skate.
[223] *Ibid.*, at p. 448.
[224] *Ibid.*, at p. 450.
[225] *Ainge v. Siemon*, [1971] 3 O.R. 119, at p. 122 (*per* Addy J.).
[226] See *Dolby v. McWhirter, supra*, n. 210, 100% liability.
[227] *Ainge, supra*, n. 225, plaintiff 25% at fault, defendant 75%.
[228] *Fink v. Greeniaus* (1973), 2 O.R. (2d) 541.
[229] *Wilson v. Blue Mountain Resorts Ltd.* (1974), 4 O.R. (2d) 713, at p. 718.
[230] *Rootes v. Shelton*, [1968] A.L.R. 33, 116 Com. L.R. 383.

It has recently been held that an intoxicated person who agreed to engage in a dangerous tube race at a ski resort did not voluntarily assume the risk of his injury, although he was found contributorily negligent. In *Crocker v. Sundance North-west Resorts Ltd.*[231] the Supreme Court of Canada again utilized the narrow definition of the defence and reversed the majority of the Ontario Court of Appeal, which had erroneously, over Dubin J.A.'s dissent, held that drunks who engage in risk activity "cannot have their cake and eat it".[232]

Volenti is being misused when it is invoked in sports cases, except where a plaintiff expressly contracts out of liability. When the courts say that the risk of being hit by a puck or a golf ball is assumed by the plaintiff, that is not what they mean, they should explain instead that there is no negligence in such a case.[233] Hence, it is wrong to say that there has been *consent* to negligence.[234] Any talk of voluntary assumption of risk, therefore, is superfluous. *Volenti* should not be invoked unless someone is negligent and wants to avoid liability on the basis of the consent of the victim. In most of these cases, fortunately, when the courts do find that there is negligence, they usually do not apply the *volenti* defence.

4. WILLING PASSENGERS

Most of the problems associated with voluntary assumption of risk involve passengers in motor vehicles who accept rides with drivers who are intoxicated or who engage in extremely dangerous activities, such as racing. There is a series of four significant decisions of the Supreme Court of Canada that deal with the problem of *volenti* and the willing passenger.

In the leading case, *Car & General Insurance Corp. v. Seymour*,[235] a 19-year-old waitress, whose "sophistication was not of the deepest sort",[236] was injured when the car in which she was a passenger went off the road due to the gross negligence of her host. The defendant driver, who was a "dominating and agressive" person,[237] had been drinking heavily, and when his passenger urged him to let his brother drive, he refused, insisting that he knew what he was

---

[231] (1988), 44 C.C.L.T. 225 (S.C.C.).

[232] (1985), 33 C.C.L.T. 73, at p. 87 (Ont. C.A.) (*per* Finlayson J.A.).

[233] See *Vander Linden v. Kellett* (1972), 21 D.L.R. (3d) 256 (B.C.), no negligence when horse-riding plaintiff injured. See also *Fink v. Greeniaus* (1973), 2 O.R. (2d) 541, at p. 552 (*per* Van Camp J.); *Gillmore v. London County Council*, [1938] 4 All E.R. 331 (K.B.D.) (*per* du Parcqu L.J.); *Hagerman, supra*, n. 175; *Dolby, supra*, n. 206.

[234] *White v. Blackmore*, [1972] 3 All E.R. 158 (C.A.) (*per* Lord Denning M.R.); see also *Reese v. Coleman*, [1976] 3 W.W.R. 739; *King v. Redlich*, [1984] 6 W.W.R. 705 (B.C.S.C.); affd 35 C.C.L.T. 201 (B.C.C.A.).

[235] [1956] S.C.R. 322. See also *Imperial Chemical Industries Ltd., supra*, n. 207. See also *Owens v. Brimmell*, [1976] 3 All E.R. 765 (Q.B.D.). 20% contributory negligence for driving with drunk driver.

[236] *Ibid.*, at p. 327 (*per* Rand J.).

[237] *Ibid.*

doing. The plaintiff was in an unfamiliar part of the country and in surroundings where she was likely to be intimidated.

Mr. Justice Rand, after redefining the voluntary assumption of risk doctrine, refused to apply it. He observed that "the unilateral formula, adequate to the early situations, is both inadequate and inappropriate to a bilateral relation in which two persons are co-operating in complementary action".[238] His Lordship declared that the defendant had not established that the plaintiff had "accepted the continuing journey or gave him any reason to infer that she did, on the terms that she released him from responsibility for care". Further, Mr. Justice Rand asserted that the defendant could not say that the "risk of injury from his own misconduct was required by him to be and was accepted by the complainant as . . . a term [of the undertaking]".[239] His Lordship insisted that the basic understanding must be reduced to an actual or constructive "exchange of terms".[240]

Mr. Justice Kellock agreed, stating simply that the onus was on the defendant to demonstrate that the plaintiff agreed expressly or by implication to exempt him from liability, which he had failed to do.[241] Nevertheless, the court felt that the plaintiff had been contributorily negligent by maintaining herself in a situation fraught with danger and affirmed a 25 per cent reduction of her award.

The second case in the series was *Miller v. Decker*,[242] where some teenage boys set out together to "go beering" and then to a dance. They became intoxicated and ended up in an automobile collision in which the plaintiff was injured as a result of the gross negligence of the driver. In a three-two decision, the Supreme Court of Canada dismissed the action on the basis of *volenti*. Mr. Justice Rand distinguished the *Seymour* case in that here the three boys were acting together in a "common purpose", the drinking each of each of them being an "encouragement" to the others.[243] Each of the boys was fully aware of what was going on and each voluntarily committed himself to the special dangers entered upon.[244] If one of the boys had suggested to the driver that he would be held legally responsible for his negligent driving, he would have been told to go in another car. The defendant would have required the boys to assume the risks they all could foresee, and, if sober, the plaintiff would probably have agreed to this. Consequently, "those who deliberately commit themselves to the vortex of such risks can claim no greater indulgence".[245] Mr. Justice Abbott dissented because he did not believe that there was evidence of an agreement, express or implied, to exempt the defendant from liability.[246]

---

[238] *Ibid.*, at p. 328.

[239] *Ibid.*, at p. 324.

[240] *Ibid.*, at p. 326.

[241] *Ibid.*, at p. 332.

[242] [1957] S.C.R. 624.

[243] *Ibid.*, at p. 630. Mr. Justice Kellock thought that the drinking was all part of the plan.

[244] *Ibid.*

[245] *Ibid.*, at p. 631.

[246] *Ibid.*, at p. 636.

The third case was *Lehnert v. Stein*.[247] The defendant, who had been drinking, met the plaintiff at a restaurant and invited her to accompany him to a nightclub, which she did. At this nightclub, the defendant imbibed four drinks, totalling ten ounces of liquor, in less than two hours. The plaintiff, who had consumed only one drink, was aware of the defendant's condition. She considered calling a taxi, but when he urged her to let him take her home, she "lacked the resolution to refuse".[248] On the way home, the defendant drove at a high rate of speed, lost control of the car and collided with two power poles, injuring the plaintiff. In a four-one decision, the Supreme Court of Canada refused to bar her recovery on the basis of *volenti*, although it did reduce it by 25 percent on account of contributory negligence. Mr. Justice Cartwright, for the majority, declared in an oft-quoted passage that, "the burden lies upon the defendant of proving that the plaintiff, expressly or by necessary implication, agreed to exempt the defendant from liability".[249] His Lordship concluded that, although she had incurred the "physical risk", she had not assumed the "legal risk", nor had she waived her rights, nor had she communicated this to the defendant.[250] He distinguished this case from *Miller v. Decker*, where an agreement was implied because there was "active encouragement" by the plaintiff of the defendant's acts.

The fourth Supreme Court of Canada decision is *Eid v. Dumas*,[251] where the plaintiff got the defendant to drive him somewhere after work. The plaintiff, over the defendant's objections, kept him awake until 4 a.m., when he finallly fell asleep at the wheel and ran into a culvert, injuring the plaintiff. The majority of the court decided that the plaintiff was not *volens* since there was no "waiver of the right of action".[252] Mr. Justice Ritchie, speaking for the majority, thought that he had not taken upon himself the whole risk of being injured, nor did the defendant accept him into his automobile on any such footing. There was no reason to expect that there was any risk of his going to sleep at the wheel, since he was sober, the trip was only 30 miles and he could have stopped if he was too tired to continue. Mr. Justice Ritchie did not even feel that he was guilty of any contributory negligence. Martland J., although agreeing that the plaintiff was not *volens*, dissented on the issue of contributory negligence.

Professor Weiler has written that this decision has tacitly overruled *Miller v. Decker*,[253] but this is not the case. *Eid v. Dumas* merely demonstrates that the Supreme Court of Canada, just like other courts,[254] is rightly reluctant to invoke *volenti*, and views the facts in the most favourable light for the plaintiff.

---

[247] [1963] S.C.R. 38.

[248] *Ibid.*, at p. 43.

[249] *Ibid.*

[250] *Ibid.*, at p. 44, relying on Williams, *Joint Torts and Contributory Negligence*.

[251] [1969] S.C.R. 668, 5 D.L.R. (3d) 561.

[252] *Ibid.*, at p. 566, D.L.R.

[253] Weiler, "Groping Towards a Canadian Tort Law" (1971), 21 U. of T.L.J. 267, at p. 287.

[254] *Crossan v. Gillis, supra*, n. 198 (*per* MacKeigan C.J.). See also *Schmidt v. Sharpe, supra*, n. 202, at p. 16 (*per* Gray J.).

Mr. Justice Estey has recently reiterated these principles in *Dubé v. Labar*,[255] where he stated:

> Thus volenti will arise only where the circumstances are such that it is clear that the plaintiff, knowing of the virtually certain risk of harm, in essence bargained away his right to sue for injuries incurred as a result of any negligence on the defendant's part. The acceptance of the risk may be express or may arise by implication from the conduct of the parties, but it will arise . . . only where there can truly be said to be an understanding on the part of both parties that the defendant assumed no responsibility to take due care for the safety of the plaintiff, and that the plaintiff did not expect him to.
>
> Common sense dictates that only rarely will a plaintiff genuinely consent to accept the risk of the defendant's negligence. . . .
>
> The defence of volenti will . . . necessarily be inapplicable in the great majority of drunken driver-willing passenger cases. It requires an awareness of the circumstances and the consequences of action that are rarely present on the facts of such cases at the relevant time.

The operation of *volenti*, therefore, has thus been limited to those situations in which there is an express or implied agreement by the plaintiff to exempt the defendant. The Supreme Court, however, did not establish any firm guidelines beyond this new verbal formula. Willing passengers, therefore, can still be barred from recovery on the ground of voluntary assumption of risk on occasion, but it is difficult to discern when.

a) *Volenti* Applied

The cases dealing with willing passengers fall into two main categories: (a) decisions denying liability on the ground of *volenti*, which are usually rather "extreme" cases,[256] involving "special circumstances" like "active encouragement"[257] or "common purpose" on the part of the plaintiff; (b) cases permitting recovery in whole or in part which reject the *volenti* defence, a good number of which involve plaintiffs who are women,[258] young people or other individuals considered to be in a position of inequality with the driver.

Volenti was utilized to refuse recovery in a number of earlier cases involving alcohol. For example, where both the plaintiff and the defendant had become intoxicated together, and the plaintiff persuaded the defendant to drive somewhere as a "joint venture", *volenti* was present.[259] Similarly, in *Deauville v. Reid*,[260] where a passenger and driver, acting in a "common purpose", formed a "common intention of making a night of drinking", *volenti* was applied. Chief

---

[255] (1986), 36 C.C.L.T. 105, at pp. 114 *et seq.* (S.C.C.), jury award dismissing case upheld. See also Cory J. in *Hall v. Hebert*, [1993] 2 S.C.R. 159, 15 C.C.L.T. (2d) 93, at p. 124, using similar language.

[256] *Skinner v. Shawara* (1959), 67 Man. R. 90, at p. 104.

[257] See Matas J. in *Cherrey v. Steinke* (1980), 13 C.C.L.T. 50, at p. 63, see annotation by Irvine, 13 C.C.L.T., at p. 51. See also O'Sullivan J.A., describing *volenti* as a way for courts to "express their disapproval of plaintiff's conduct by dismissing [their] claims".

[258] See, for example, *Stevens v. Hoeberg*, [1972] 3 O.R. 840 (*per* Lerner J.).

[259] *Supra*, n. 256. See *Quinlin v. Steffans* (1980), 12 C.C.L.T. 162.

[260] (1966), 52 M.P.R. 218, at p. 223 (N.B.C.A.).

Justice Bridges of New Brunswick indicated that, if the defendant had asked the plaintiff whether he would hold him responsible for his driving, the plaintiff would have answered that he would not. His Lordship remarked that the parties were soldiers who "belonged to a class which is more ready to take a risk than the average person" and there was "active encouragement".[261]

In *Champagne v. Champagne*,[262] two brothers drank together from 10 a.m. to 2 p.m. and they continued to imbibe as they were driving along in an automobile. Mr. Justice Brown, commenting on the apparent conflict in the cases, suggested that it arose from "our frailty in perception rather than in the inherent inconsistencies".[263] The "fraternal mutuality of this brief but intense debauch" was significant to His Lordship, for it signalled a "double-minded dedication to the achievement of drunkenness". He concluded that there was "*Volens*, old-fashioned and absolute".[264]

Similarly, in *Conrad v. Crawford*,[265] the plaintiff, the defendant and a friend went on a beer-drinking joy-ride in the defendant's car. All three became intoxicated. When the defendant's driving attracted the attention of the police, he attempted to elude them. He lost control of his car and crashed into a telephone pole, injuring the plaintiff. Although the defendant was judged to be guilty of gross negligence, Mr. Justice Hughes denied recovery to the plaintiff because the defendant had shown that he "not only assumed the physical, but the legal risk". "The inference to be drawn from the circumstances of the whole transaction is that the plaintiff . . . agreed, by necessary implication of his conduct and the evidence he gave, to exempt the defendant . . . from liability for any damage suffered by him or as a result of the latter's negligence." It was a "pre-concerted expedition" and "encouragement" to continue drinking.

Another case employing *volenti* is *Priestley v. Gilbert*,[266] where the plaintiff was severely injured when the car which the defendant was driving, and in which he was a passenger, went out of control and collided head-on with an approaching vehicle. Both young men had drunk to excess. In determining whether the maxim applied, Schroeder J.A., for the court, stated: "On the facts and circumstances disclosed by the record it appears to us that the plaintiff must be taken by implication to have consented to the physical and legal risk of injury involved. This may be inferred from the joint venture undertaken by these friends of long standing, involving, as it did, the consumption by them of copious quantities of spirits and beer and the driving of his motor vehicle by the

---

[261] *Ibid.* See also *Tobin v. Fennell* (1962), 35 D.L.R. (2d) 513 (N.S.), plaintiff suggested getting more liquor, sober driver available.

[262] (1969), 67 W.W.R. 764 (B.C.). See also *Allen v. Lucas* (1972), 25 D.L.R. (3d) 218 (Sask. C.A.); *Morris v. Murray*, [1990] 3 All E.R. 801 (C.A.), *volenti* to fly with extremely drunk pilot.

[263] *Ibid.*, at p. 766.

[264] *Ibid.*, at p. 768. See also *Dubois v. Canada Permanent Trust* (1970), 75 W.W.R. 107 (Man.) (*per* Matas J.), large quantity of liquor purchased, amounted to "active encouragement". *Cf.*, *Hoplock v. Zaporzan* (1970), 74 W.W.R. 594 (Man.) (*per* Matas J.), 50-50 split.

[265] [1972] 1 O.R. 134.

[266] (1973), 1 O.R. (2d) 365 (C.A.).

respondent Gilbert when he might, as he did, become hopelessly intoxicated and grossly impaired." The court dismissed the contention that the plaintiff's intoxicated state precluded the implication that he had consented to take the legal risk. There are other drinking cases involving *volenti* as well.[267]

One helpful attempt at distinguishing between the cases employing the *volenti* defence and those that do not was made by Mr. Justice Lieff in *McDonald v. Dalgleish*:[268]

> Where drinking had been involved, the distinguishing factor between those cases where *volens* had been found and those where it has not, appears to be whether the parties set out the commencement of the evening, or whenever the events occurred, with the common intention and for the common purpose of drinking together until the end of the evening. One can distinguish between the cases which might be determined "the common enterprise" type of situation . . . and those cases which may be referred to as the "drive home" cases. . . .[269]

There are cases involving conduct other than drinking which invoke the *volenti* defence. In *Schwindt v. Giesbrecht*,[270] a vehicle was stopped by the R.C.M.P. The plaintiff, a passenger, then urged the driver, "let's give them a run for it" and the driver took off. The plaintiff also obtained the agreement of the other passengers to chip in and share the fine, if the R.C.M.P. should eventually catch them. An accident ensued and the plaintiff sought to recover. Mr. Justice Egbert dismissed the claim, observing that there was a difference between mere "passive acceptance" of a risk and the situation in this case, where there was "incitement" or "instigation" by the plaintiff.[271] Similarly, in *Frehlick v. Anderson*,[272] a 17-year-old boy was denied compensation because of *volenti*. He had climed onto the fender of the defendant's vehicle when it was stopped at a service station and refused to get off. The defendant started off down the highway, his vision blocked by the plaintiff, and collided with another vehicle, injuring the plaintiff. Chief Justice Lett of British Columbia held that he had given an "effective consent", the whole venture being a "common enterprise upon which both parties were engaged".[273] A man who sat on a box in the back of a pick-up truck was held to have assumed the risk of being thrown off when the driver swerved to avoid a bump.[274]

One vivid case exhibiting the continuing willingness to invoke *volenti* in outrageous cases is *Deskau v. Dziama; Brooks v. Dziama*,[275] where the defendant and a number of friends drove to a gravel road on which there was a series of

---

[267] *Boulay v. Wild*, [1972] 2 W.W.R. 234 (Alta. C.A.); *Allen v. Lucas* (1972), 25 D.L.R. (3d) 218 (Sask. C.A.), "common purpose" to avoid apprehension by police: *Tomlinson v. Harrison*, [1972] 1 O.R. 670, *ex turpi causa* also used.

[268] [1973] 2 O.R. 826.

[269] *Ibid.*, at p. 837.

[270] (1958), 13 D.L.R. (2d) 770 (Alta.).

[271] *Ibid.*, at p. 775.

[272] (1961), 27 D.L.R. (2d) 46 (B.C.).

[273] *Ibid.*, at p. 53.

[274] *Ruest v. Desjardins* (1972), 7 N.B.R. (2d) 91.

[275] [1973] 3 O.R. 101, 36 D.L.R. (3d) 36.

steep hills. The group divided into two for the purposes of taking turns riding with the defendant who negotiated the hills at very high speed in an attempt to cause the vehicle to leave the ground as he crested each hill. On the second turn the car went out of control and crashed. Both passengers were seriously injured and sued the defendant alleging gross negligence. In dismissing their action, Keith J. stated that the plaintiffs had voluntarily assumed the inherent risks:

> The nature of the risk that these plaintiffs voluntarily assumed was unlimited in the circumstances. Any one of many things could and was likely to bring about disaster. For example, as happened in this case, the defendant was apparently momentarily stunned when his head hit the steering wheel on the return of the vehicle from its free flight on the third crest, immediately interfering with his power to control the vehicle, even if nothing broke when the car being subjected to such abuse, hit the ground. There was the distinct possibility of striking a stone or a rut in the gravel road, which would throw the car out of control. . . . One need not further elaborate on the possibilities inherent in this venture that would mean nothing but disaster and serious injury, if not death. . . .
>
> In my view, this is one of those cases in which the doctrine is applicable, and therefore I do not propose to discuss the alternative defence raised in this case of contributory negligence, since that defence can only arise in cases where the circumstances do not justify the application of the doctrine of *volenti*.[276]

b) *Volenti* Defence Rejected

Voluntary assumption of risk was not applied in the larger group of cases. For example, a 17-year-old backseat passenger was found to be neither *volens* nor contributorily negligent, even though he did not object to the high speed at which the driver was travelling.[277] He was not under any obligation to jump out of the car or to turn off the key. Two plaintiffs, 16 and 17, who accepted a lift from an unlicensed driver, 14 years old, did not waive their rights, but they were found 50 per cent responsible for their loss.[278] Nor was a 16-year-old girl denied recovery for failing to remonstrate when her driver participated in a race, although she was held 25 per cent to blame.[279] When a 14-year-old was injured in a stolen car being driven at great speed by a 15-year-old who had driven just once before, he was not *volens*, but he was contributorily negligent to the extent of 50 per cent.[280]

There are a number of decisions where the courts might well have employed *volenti* doctrine, but they have exhibited a distaste for its harshness, preferring instead to apportion damages. In *Lackner v. Neath*,[281] for example, the plaintiff

---

[276] *Ibid.*, at pp. 105-06, O.R.

[277] *Simpson v. Parry* (1968), 65 W.W.R. 606 (B.C.).

[278] *Dorn v. Stevens* (1963), 39 D.L.R. (2d) 761 (Alta.).

[279] *Prior v. Kyle* (1965), 55 W.W.R. 1 (B.C.C.A.). See also the dissenting opinion of Davey J.A.

[280] *Rondos v. Wawrin* (1969), 62 W.W.R. 369. Reversed on the ground that the defence of *ex turpi causa non oritur actio* applied (1968), 64 W.W.R. 690, 68 D.L.R. (2d) 658 (Man. C.A.).

[281] (1966), 57 W.W.R. 496, 58 D.L.R. (2d) 662 (Sask. C.A.). See also *Nettleship v. Weston*, [1971] 3 All E.R. 581 (C.A.), driving instructor not *volenti* though contributorily negligent. See also *Lovelace v. Fossum*, [1972] 2 W.W.R. 161 (B.C.).

stood on the bumpers of two cars while one was pushing the other, in order to keep them level. When he fell off and was injured, the court refused to invoke *volenti non fit injuria* against him. Culliton C.J.S. observed that *volenti* would not be applied unless the plaintiff "(a) voluntarily assumed the physical risk; and (b) [a]greed to give up his right for negligence, or, to put it more briefly, that the plaintiff accepted both the physical and legal risk".[282] He concluded that, although the plaintiff clearly accepted the physical risk, there was no "agreement, express or implied, by which the plaintiff gave up his right of action". Nevertheless, the court cut his award by 60 per cent on the basis of contributory negligence. It would not have been difficult to find a waiver of legal rights in this case, yet the court balked at dismissing the claim altogether.

In *Carnegie v. Trynchy*,[283] two girls in one car engaged in some drag racing and speed-clocking with two boys in another car, as they drove along a highway at 85-100 m.p.h. The plaintiff passenger had encouraged the race and had given signals, yet *volenti* was not used against her. Despite the fact that she undertook a "great physical risk", Mr. Justice Dechene decided that there was no agreement exempting the driver from legal liability.[284] His Lordship frankly observed that the defence of *volenti* was being "applied with diminishing frequency".[285] He did reduce her recovery by 50 per cent, however, since she had disregarded her own safety by her conduct. Occasionally, a plaintiff who drinks along with the driver,[286] and even one who buys some of the spirits being consumed,[287] may be held not to have assumed the risk.

Exemplary of the more liberal approach to these cases is *Halliday v. Essex*,[288] where the plaintiff and a group of friends decided to spend a "drinking weekend" at a cottage. Late one night, the group, all of whom were intoxicated, went for a drive. An accident ensued. Lacourcière J. ruled that the plaintiff did not impliedly agree to "release the defendant from his responsibility for care" because he was drunk and "was in no position to appreciate the nature and extent of the risk and to freely release the defendant of his obligation to drive safely". The plaintiff was found to be 40 per cent contributorily negligent.

More recently, it has been held that there was not even any contributory negligence by an automobile passenger who was killed in an accident when his

---

[282] *Ibid.*, at pp. 499-500, W.W.R.

[283] (1966), 57 W.W.R. 305 (Alta.). See also *McDonald v. Dalgleish*, [1973] 2 O.R. 826, drag race, plaintiff 25% to blame.

[284] *Ibid.*, at p. 308.

[285] *Ibid.*, at p. 307, citing Cartwright J. in *Lehnert v. Stein*, [1963] S.C.R. 38, who suggested that the scope of the defence was being "progressively curtailed".

[286] *Marasek v. Condie* (1958), 12 D.L.R. (2d) 252 (Alta.), 15% negligent; *Pitre v. Comeau* (1972), 7 N.B.R. (2d) 116, 25% reduction.

[287] *Arwell v. Getridge* (1958), 12 D.L.R. (2d) 669 (N.S.) (*per* Ilsley C.J.N.S.), 45% reduction; *Halliday v. Essex*, [1971] 3 O.R. 621 (*per* Lacourcière J.), group of youths purchased quantity of spirits for snowmobile weekend, no agreement to release, 40% negligent.

[288] *Halliday v. Essex, supra*, n. 287. See also *Mongovius v. Marchand* (1988), 44 C.C.L.T. 18 (B.C.S.C.), *ex turpi* used.

driver feel asleep at the wheel. This accident was not foreseeable because the driver could easily have stopped to rest if tired.[289]

In summary, our courts occasionally still deny recovery altogether on the basis of *volenti*, where the circumstances are extreme enough to warrant such a course, but they are properly reluctant to do so, unless there is a "pre-release".[290] To be sure, the process has been rightly described as a bit fanciful.[291] It is often hard to discern any real difference in the facts of many of the cases involving *volenti* and those which do not. Although the courts insist that they are searching for an express or implied waiver of legal rights, they seem rather to be assessing the degree of involvement by plaintiffs in the drinking or wrong-doing. Where the plaintiffs' conduct is really outrageous, therefore, or where they have encouraged or fully become part of the dangerous activity, they may be said to have been *volens*. Otherwise, the courts use contributory negligence analysis and merely reduce the damage award. There is little doubt that the courts prefer to avoid the defence of *volenti*, which denies injured plaintiffs all financial help. Instead a much more supple tool, contributory negligence, is preferred. In this way compensation will be more widespread and, it is hoped, both plaintiffs and defendants will be deterred from future wrongful conduct.

C. Illegality

A plaintiff who is harmed while acting illegally or immorally may be denied tort recovery. This defence of illegality "skulks furtively behind the Latin maxim *ex turpi causa non oritur actio*".[292] Although much criticized by scholars,[293] it has "stubbornly and somewhat irrationally survived".[294] Used primarily in the contract context, it spilled over into the tort domain and had some currency for a time.[295] It has now been dealt an almost mortal blow by the Supreme Court of Canada. Writing for the majority in *Hall v. Hebert*, McLachlin J. explained the current status of the defence as follows:[296]

> There is a need in the law of tort for a principle which permits judges to deny recovery to a plaintiff on the ground that to do so would undermine the integrity of the justice system. The power is a limited one. Its use is justified where allowing the plaintiff's claim would introduce inconsistency into the fabric of the law, either by permitting the plaintiff to profit from

---

[289] *Bresch (Guardian ad litem of) v. Mallis Estate* (1996), 29 C.C.L.T. (2d) 160 (B.C.S.C.).

[290] O'Sullivan J.A. dissenting in *Cherrey v. Steinke* (1980), 13 C.C.L.T. 50, at p. 66, arguing that contract rules relating to implied terms be employed.

[291] See Gordon, "Drunken Drivers and Willing Passengers" (1966), 82 L.Q. Rev. 62, also at (1966), 14 Chitty's L.J. 203.

[292] Cory J., dissenting, in *Hall v. Hebert*, [1993] 2 S.C.R. 159, 15 C.C.L.T. (2d) 93, at p. 124.

[293] Gibson, "Illegality of Plaintiff's Conduct as a Defence" (1969), 47 Can. Bar Rev. 89; see also Fridman, "The Wrongdoing Plaintiff" (1972), 18 McGill L.J. 275; Weinrib, "Illegality as a Tort Defence" (1976), 26 U. of T.L.J. 28.

[294] Cory J. in *Hall*, *supra*, n. 292, at p. 131.

[295] *Tomlinson v. Harrison*, [1972] 1 O.R. 670 (H.C.J.); *Tallow v. Tailfeathers*, [1973] 6 W.W.R. 732 (Alta. C.A.).

[296] *Supra*, n. 292, at p. 110.

an illegal or wrongful act, or to evade a penalty prescribed by criminal law. Its use is not justified where the plaintiff's claim is merely for compensation for personal injuries sustained as a consequence of the negligence of the defendant.

Thus, the defence is no longer available at all in personal injury cases, for there is no profit in receiving compensation for injury. It can be used only in limited situations otherwise. Mr. Justice Cory, concurring, would have abolished it altogether, leaving as a remnant only the power of the court to deny recovery in some of the more flagrant situations on public policy grounds.

The majority in *Hall v. Hebert* specified clearly that the plaintiff's illegal conduct must be raised as a defence, not as a factor going to the existence of a duty of care.[297] Consequently, the onus is on a defendant to plead and prove illegal conduct which would amount to such an affront to the integrity of the legal system that the court must deny recovery in a situation where the claim would be otherwise valid. This is no easy task.

Fortunately, there never was much judicial enthusiasm for this defence. Indeed, "cases where a tort action has been defeated by the *ex turpi causa* maxim [were] exceedingly rare".[298] In the vast majority of cases where the defence might have been employed, the claimant would have lost in any event on the basis of *volenti*.[299] Moreover, if one were to re-examine the *volenti* cases carefully, one would discern a flavour to some of them, indicating that the courts are really relying on the defence of "illegality", while insisting that they are denying reparation because of *volenti*.[300] Courts have wisely manifested a decided preference to deal with these problems under contributory negligence rather than *volenti* or *ex turpi causa*.[301]

For a time it did not seem that proof of causation was required, but ever since the case of *Canada Cement Lafarge v. B.C. Lightweight Aggregate Ltd.*,[302] it is clear that, in those few cases where the defence might be used, the illegal conduct must cause the loss of the plaintiff before the defence will be invoked.

In the United Kingdom., the defence has been applied[303] to deny a motorcycle passenger recovery from the estate of his driver because the passenger had engaged in unlawful conduct by encouraging the driver to drive recklessly, intending to frighten members of the public. This was permitted despite a legislative provision that precluded agreements negating or restricting liability in this context because this was an "illegal agreement" to carry out an "illegal

---

[297] *Ibid.*, at p. 112.

[298] Estey J. in *Canada Cement, infra,* n. 302, at p. 476.

[299] See, for example, *Tomlinson, supra,* n. 295, and *Tallow, supra,* n. 295.

[300] See Klar, "Recent Developments" (1991), 23 Ott. L. Rev. 177, at p. 235, for a useful explanation of the recent cases.

[301] See *Teece v. Honeybourn,* [1974] 5 W.W.R. 592 (B.C.S.C.), person shot while escaping arrest held contributorily negligent, but not *volenti* or *ex turpi causa;* see also *Bigcharles v. Merkel,* [1973] 1 W.W.R. 324 (B.C.S.C.), person shot while escaping after burglary held 75% to blame.

[302] [1983] 1 S.C.R. 452 (*per* Estey J.). See also *Norberg v. Wynrib,* [1992] 2 S.C.R. 226, at p. 262 (*per* LaForest J.).

[303] *Pitts v. Hunt,* [1990] 3 All E.R. 344 (C.A.), discussing s. 148(3) of Road Traffic Act 1972.

purpose" and, hence, was not covered by the word "agreement". The defence of *ex turpi* was held not to apply, however, where someone committed suicide in prison, because it did not "affront the public conscience" or "shock the ordinary citizen" considering the "change in public attitute to suicide generally" since the Suicide Act of 1961.[304]

The tantalizing possibility of invoking the Negligence Act in cases of illegality was posited in *Lewis v. Sayers*.[305] The intoxicated owner of a vehicle allowed an intoxicated friend to drive them both on a short trip during which the driver negligently collided with a parked car. The defence of *volenti* was held not to apply because there was no bargain, express or implied, to give up the right of action. Gould D.C.J., nevertheless, apportioned liability 50-50 on the ground that the Ontario Negligence Act covered such conduct. He explained:

> The defendant relied mainly upon the maxim *ex turpi causa non oritur actio* and this matter was argued at length and requires serious consideration. If the defendant should succeed in establishing either of these special defences, my previous findings as to negligence and respective degrees of fault would be of no importance, as the plaintiff would be absolutely debarred from recovering against the defendant. I was referred to the article on this subject by Mr. Dale Gibson printed in 47 *Can. Bar Rev.* 89 (1969), and to a long list of cases, many of which are referred to in the article . . . these cases, of course, make it very clear that the maxim *ex turpi causa non oritur actio* under proper circumstances applies and is frequently used in our Courts.
>
> The two Manitoba cases of *Ridgeway v. Hilhorst* and *Rondos v. Wawrin*, although different in their facts from the present case, both suggest that the *ex turpi causa* doctrine might apply here. An important consideration, however, is that the Manitoba statute which corresponds to s. 4 of the Ontario *Negligence Act* is worded differently, in that it refers only to negligence rather than to fault or negligence. The result would appear to be that the Ontario statute applies to a considerably wider range of situations than the Manitoba Act. Section 4 of the Ontario *Negligence Act* reads as follows:
>
> > 4. In any action for damages that is founded upon the fault or negligence of the defendant if fault or negligence is found on the part of the plaintiff that contributed to the damages, the court shall apportion the damages in proportion to the degree of fault or negligence found against the parties respectively.
>
> It appears to me that in a case to which, by reason of its facts, s. 4 of the *Negligence Act* applies, the Ontario Legislature has quite deliberately substituted for the *ex turpi causa* rule a positive direction that the Court shall make a finding as to the degree of fault or negligence to be attributed to each party and shall apportion the damages accordingly. I realize of course that s. 4 was enacted primarily to do away with the absolute defence formerly available in cases of contributory negligence, but the wording is equally apt in relation to the defence now under discussion, to which the added words "fault or" seem to apply with particular force. The defence *ex turpi causa non oritur actio* seems necessarily to involve a situation where both parties are alleged to be at fault, and so long as it is remembered that s. 4 applies

---

[304] *Kirkham v. Chief Constable of the Greater Manchester Police*, [1990] 3 All E.R. 246, at p. 251 (C.A.) (*per* Lloyd L.J.), no liability on other grounds; *cf.*, *Hyde v. Thameside Area Health Authority* (1981), The Times, 16 April, [1981] C.A. Transcript 130.

[305] [1970] 3 O.R. 591, 13 D.L.R. (3d) 543 (Dist. Ct.). See Chiefetz, *Apportionment of Fault in Tort* (1980), p. 193. See also *Funk v. Clapp* (1986), 68 D.L.R. (4th) 229 (B.C.C.A.), but *cf.*, *Hall v. Hebert, supra*, n. 292.

only where the fault of each has contributed to the damages, in my opinion, the section leaves no room for the application of the maxim.[306]

Such an approach to the treatment of illegal conduct was employed not in the reasoning but in the disposition of *Hall v. Hebert* where the plaintiff, a drunk driver, was held equally liable with the drunk owner of the vehicle who had allowed him to drive his car. McLachlin J. explained:[307]

> The doctrine of ex turpi causa non oritur actio properly applies in tort where it will be necessary to invoke the doctrine in order to maintain the internal consistency of the law. Most commonly, this concern will arise where a given plaintiff genuinely seeks to profit from his or her illegal conduct, or where the claimed compensation would amount to an evasion of a criminal sanction. This appellant need not be denied recovery since these grounds are not relevant to his claim. The compensation sought by this appellant is for injuries received. This compensation can be reduced to the extent of the appellant's contributory negligence, but cannot be wholly denied by reason of his disreputable or criminal conduct.

A similar view was enunciated by Cory J., concurring, who stated that:

> In a situation in which the plaintiff's conduct is relevant to the issue of damages, it will be best considered in the context of contributory negligence or in the admittedly rare case of voluntary assumption of the risk of injury from engaging in the dangerous activity.[308]

Further, if a plaintiff's conduct is "in contravention of the law", he may well be found "guilty of contributory negligence or indeed of being the author of his own misfortune. Yet simply because the plaintiff was a wrongdoer does not necessarily mean that he can have no remedy at law. . . ."[309]

In conclusion, the elimination of *ex turpi causa* in injury cases, and its near elimination in other tort cases, is most welcome. It makes much more sense to treat a plaintiff's illegal conduct as contributory negligence and reduce the recovery accordingly rather than to deny recovery altogether. This technique makes tort law a much more humane and flexible instrument, something that is to be encouraged.

---

[306] *Ibid.*, at pp. 597-98, O.R.
[307] *Supra*, n. 292, at p. 114, C.C.L.T.
[308] *Ibid.*, at p. 130.
[309] *Ibid.*, at p. 135.

Chapter 14

Strict Liability

The third basis of responsibility in tort is strict liability. One person may be required to compensate another for injury or damages, even though the loss was neither intentionally nor negligently inflicted. This type of tort liability is still relatively rare in Canada where the fault theory continues to thrive.

Although one could point to many developments in Canadian social welfare legislation that furnish compensation to injured people on a no-fault basis, they do not really have anything to do with strict or *tort* liability. These legislative compensation schemes render superfluous any consideration of tort theory in the areas where they operate. They were enacted, fundamentally, to replace or to supplement the segments of the tort compensation system that provided inadequate reparation, such as workers' compensation, victims of crime, no-fault auto insurance and so forth.

There have also been common law developments moving tort law away from fault and closer to a regime of strict liability. For example, the objective theory of the reasonable person, the use of statutes in negligence litigation, the now expired doctrine of *res ipsa loquitur*, contributory negligence legislation, and other developments have indirectly edged negligence law toward a stricter form of liability.[1]

This chapter is devoted to a study of the situations where the courts have openly admitted that there can be tort liability for unintended and non-negligent harm — the principle of *Rylands v. Fletcher*.[2]

It is generally agreed that *Rylands v. Fletcher* expounds a doctrine of strict liability,[3] although some persist in describing the theory as one of "absolute

---

[1] Ehrenzweig, *Negligence Without Fault* (1951), also at (1966), 54 Calif. L. Rev. 1422; Fleming, *The Law of Torts*, 9th ed. (1998), Chapter 15.

[2] (1868), L.R. 3 H.L. 330; affg (1866), L.R. 1 Ex. 265. See Prosser, "The Principle of *Rylands v. Fletcher*, in *Selected Topics on the Law of Torts* (1953), at p. 153; Bohlen, "The Rule in *Rylands v. Fletcher*" (1911), 59 U. Pa. L. Rev. 298, 373, 423; Stallybrass, "Dangerous Things and Non-Natural User of Land" (1929), 3 Camb. L.J. 376; Thayer, "Liability Without Fault" (1916), 29 Harv. L. Rev. 801.

[3] *Northwestern Utilities Ltd. v. London Guarantee and Accident Co.*, [1936] A.C. 108, [1935] 4 D.L.R. 737, at p. 742 (*per* Lord Wright); *Benning v. Wong* (1969), 43 A.L.J.R. 467, at p. 485.

liability".[4] It has been suggested that "when stated without the exceptions it is a rule of absolute liability but there are so many exceptions to it that it is doubtful whether there is much of the rule left".[5]

Strict liability works to advance the various goals of tort law. The victims of these activities are awarded compensation even in the absence of fault, because it is believed that it is appropriate to do so. Deterrence is achieved because those subjected to strict liability should exercise "supercare" in order to avoid being made to pay for the damages they cause. The educational aims of tort law are achieved by teaching society that certain types of activities labour under special responsibilities. By holding such enterprises strictly liable the psychological needs of their victims and of people in general may be met. Market deterrence is achieved by making these enterprises pay for all the costs of accidents generated by them, whether or not they are negligent. Lastly, the ombudsman role of tort law is served by focusing attention on the kinds of things that may go wrong with these unique activities, fostering re-assessment of the value of these pursuits and the way they are regulated.

Although more than a century has elapsed since *Rylands v. Fletcher* was decided, it remains an unsolved mystery. Agreement cannot even be reached about whether *Rylands v. Fletcher* was an important decision. Some authors have suggested that it was "epochal in its consequences",[6] and a "great advance in the rationalization of the common law,"[7] while others have contended that it was "unnecessary", because the same results could be achieved under negligence law combined with *res ipsa loquitur*.[8] There is no doubt that there is much overlap between strict liability and negligence. Most cases decided with the *Rylands v. Fletcher* theory could be resolved in the same way on negligence principles. There are some cases, however, which would have been dismissed were it not for the strict liability theory.[9] Therefore it is not irrelevant. It can make a difference to the outcome of litigation. At the very least its potential use can affect settlement negotiations.

Rylands v. Fletcher has disturbed scholars and judges over the years. One author argued that it was "irrational", "out-of-date" and an "impediment to the

---

[4]   See *Gertsen v. Metropolitan Toronto* (1973), 2 O.R. (2d) 1, at p. 19 (*per* Lerner J.).
[5]   Scrutton L.J. in *St. Anne's Well Brewery Co. v. Roberts* (1928), 140 L.T. 1, at p. 6 (C.A.).
[6]   Wigmore, "Responsibility for Tortious Acts: Its History" (1894), 7 Harv. L. Rev. 315, 383, 441, at p. 454.
[7]   Bohlen, "The Rule in *Rylands v. Fletcher*" (1910-11), 59 U. Pa. L. Rev. 298, 373, 423, at p. 433; see also Gregory, "Trespass to Negligence to Absolute Liability" (1951), 37 Va. L. Rev. 359, at p. 377.
[8]   J. Smith, "Tort and Absolute Liability" (1917), 30 Harv. L. Rev. 241, 319, 409, at p. 414; Blackburn, "The Rule in *Rylands v. Fletcher*" (1961), 4 Can. Bar J. 39.
[9]   See, for example, *MacDonald v. Desourdy Construction Ltée* (1972), 27 D.L.R. (3d) 144 (N.S.), blasting; *Mortimer v. B.A. Oil Co.*, [1949] 2 W.W.R. 107; affd [1950] 1 W.W.R. 49 (Alta. C.A.); *Powell v. Fall* (1880), 5 Q.B.D. 597 (C.A.); *Morwick v. Provincial Contracting Co.* (1923), 55 O.L.R. 71 (C.A.), engine.

development of a logical and symmetrical doctrine of responsibility for torts".[10] Another author called the principle "intolerable" and praised those courts that rejected it.[11] Still others criticized it as a snare that lured "prolific plaintiffs" into groundless law suits in the hope of winning, only to disappoint them by ultimate defeat.[12]

Rylands v. Fletcher has had its ups and downs. Its role has been enlarged[13] and reduced on several occasions. Our courts cannot decide whether they like or dislike *Rylands v. Fletcher*.[14] Their attitude is schizoid — shifting from hostility to hospitality and then back again. Professor Fridman has described the rise and fall of *Rylands v. Fletcher*,[15] but it has not fallen at all. It may not have risen as some hoped it would. It may have been wounded in the United Kingdom[16] and largely ignored in the United States. It has certainly been misunderstood everywhere. Nevertheless, it is not dead, but alive and well in Canada.

A. The Origin of Strict Liability

The facts of *Rylands v. Fletcher* are too familiar to be repeated in detail. The plaintiff, Fletcher, was mining coal with the permission of the landowner. Rylands and Horrocks owned a mill near the land under which Fletcher was working. They obtained the same owner's permission to build a reservoir to supply water to their mill on this land. They employed competent contractors to construct it. Although neither Rylands or Horrocks knew that coal had been worked under the site of reservoir, it was in fact situated over some old coal mines which communicated with the workings of Fletcher. After the reservoir was completed and filled with water, one of the old shafts gave way and water flooded Fletcher's workings. Because the contractors had encountered some old shafts when building the reservoir, they were found negligent in failing to support the reservoir adequately, but no negligence was attributed to Rylands and Horrocks.

An action was brought against Rylands and Horrocks. Under the law as it was at that time, trespass, nuisance, and vicarious liability were unavailable, but his did not stop Mr. Justice Blackburn from imposing liability on the defendants. His rationalization was as follows:

> We think that the true role of law is, that the person who for his own purposes brings on his lands and collects and keeps there anything likely to do mischief if it escapes, must keep it in

---

[10]   V.C. MacDonald, "The Rule in *Rylands v. Fletcher* and its Limitations" (1923), 1 Can. Bar Rev. 140, at p. 157.

[11]   Thayer, "Liability Without Fault" (1916), 29 Harv. L. Rev. 801, at p. 814.

[12]   See *Benning v. Wong* (1969), 43 A.L.J.R. 467 (*per* Windeyer J.); see also Blackburn, "The Rule in *Rylands v. Fletcher*" (1961), 4 Can. Bar J. 39.

[13]   *Skubiniuk v. Hartmann* (1914), 24 Man. R. 836, at p. 843 (C.A.).

[14]   Goodhart, "*Rylands v. Fletcher* Today" (1956), 72 L.Q. Rev. 184, at p. 186.

[15]   See (1956), 34 Can. Bar Rev. 810.

[16]   *Cambridge Water Co. v. Eastern Counties Leather*, [1994] 2 A.C. 264, [1994] 1 All E.R. 53 (H.L.), a branch of nuisance requiring foresight.

at his peril, and, if he does not do so, is *prima facie* answerable for all the damage which is the natural consequence of its escape. He can excuse himself by shewing that the escape was owing to the plaintiff's default; or perhaps that the escape was the consequence of *vis major*, or the act of God; but as nothing of this sort exists here, it is unnecessary to inquire what excuse would be sufficient. The general rule, as above stated, seems on principle just. The person whose grass or corn is eaten down by the escaping cattle of his neighbour, or whose mine is flooded by the water from his neighbour's reservoir, or whose cellar is invaded by the filth of his neighbour's privy, or whose habitation is made unhealthy by the fumes and noisome vapours of his neighbour's alkali works, is damnified without any fault of his own; and it seems but reasonable and just that the neighbour, who has brought something on his own property which was not naturally there, harmless to others so long as it is confined to his own property, but which he knows to be mischievous if it gets on his neighbour's, should be obliged to make good the damage which ensues if he does not succeed in confining it to his own property. But for his act in bringing it there no mischief could have accrued, and it seems but just that he should at his peril keep it there so that no mischief may accrue, or answer for the natural and anticipated consequences. And upon authority, this we think is established to be the law whether the things so brought be beasts, or water, or filth, or stenches.[17]

On appeal to the House of Lords, Lord Cranworth merely repeated what Justice Blackburn had said:

> If a person brings, or accumulates, on his land anything which, if it should escape, may cause damage to his neighbour, he does so at his peril. If it does escape and cause damage, he is responsible, however careful he may have been, and whatever precautions he may have taken to prevent the damage.[18]

If this had been the end of the matter, the ensuing confusion surrounding *Rylands v. Fletcher* might have been contained with manageable bounds. However, Lord Cairns, during the course of his concurring reasons, chose to use a particularly rubbery phrase — "non-natural" — which has bedeviled courts and scholars ever since:

> ... if the Defendants, not stopping at the natural use of their close, had desired to use it for any purpose which I may term a non-natural use, for the purpose of introducing into the close that which in its natural condition was not in or upon it, for the purpose of introducing water wither above or below ground in quantities and in a manner not the result of any work or operation on or under the land, and if in consequence of their doing so, or in consequence of any imperfection in the mode of their doing so, the water came to escape and pass off into the close of the Plaintiff, then it appears to me that that which the Defendants were doing they were doing at their own peril; and if in the course of their doing it, the evil arose to which I have referred, the evil, namely, of the escape of the water and its passing away to the close of the Plaintiff and injuring the Plaintiff, then for the consequence of that, in my opinion, the Defendants would be liable .... [19]

Mr. Justice Blackburn had employed similar language — "not naturally there" — but his words have been largely ignored, whereas scores of later cases sought

---

[17] (1866), L.R. 1 Ex. 265, at p. 279.
[18] (1868), L.R. 3 H.L. 330, at p. 340.
[19] *Ibid.*, at p. 339.

to cast light on the phrase used by Lord Cairns. There is no inkling in the reasons of any of the judges that there was any disagreement among them. Nor was there any indication that they were creating new law. They all seem to be merely reiterating law that had already been settled. Nevertheless, the permutations and combinations of the three simple ideas incorporated in these statements — non-natural use, mischief, and escape — have exercised judges and scholars for over a century now. The words are so flexible that courts which are hostile to strict liability may restrict their operation, whereas courts which are friendly to strict liability may stretch them to embrace a great many activities of modern living.

So muddled has the subsequent treatment of the principle become that it has been contended that there may be "not one rule in *Rylands v. Fletcher* but two," and the courts may choose to invoke "Lord Blackburn's version or Lord Cairns' more flexible one . . . according to the circumstances of the case in hand".[20]

We shall now examine the scope of *Rylands v. Fletcher*.

B. The Scope of Strict Liability

Under the traditional view of *Rylands v. Fletcher*, a strict liability will be imposed if two elements are present: (a) a non-natural use of land, and (b) an escape.[21] Let us consider these two concepts and how they have been interpreted in the cases.

1. NON-NATURAL USE

The judges who first used the term "non-natural" would probably be surprised by the way it has been explained by later judges.[22] Although the phrase was originally meant only to underscore the notion that land, in its natural state, could not be the subject of tort liability, this was soon altered. The judges who opposed the idea of strict liability fastened on to the phrase "non-natural" and employed it, whenever possible, to exempt certain common, ordinary activities from the operation of the rule, despite the mischief they might cause upon escape. The judges who were attracted to strict liability sought to preserve as much as possible of the underlying philosophy of *Rylands v. Fletcher* by reducing the impact of the non-natural use limitation.

In *Rickards v. Lothian*,[23] where some water escaped from a lavatory, Lord Moulton restricted the scope of *Rylands v. Fletcher* in these words:

It is not every use to which land is put that brings into play that principle. It must be some special use bringing with it increased danger to others, and must not merely be the ordinary use of the land or such a use as is proper for the general benefit of the community . . . .

---

[20] *J.P. Porter Co. Ltd. v. Bell*, [1955] 1 D.L.R. 62, at p. 66 (N.S.C.A.) (*per* MacDonald J.).

[21] *Read v. Lyons & Co. Ltd.*, [1947] A.C. 156; *Storms v. M.G. Henninger Ltd.*, [1953] O.R. 717, at p. 727 (C.A.) (*per* Laidlaw J.A.).

[22] Newark, "Non-Natural User and *Rylands v. Fletcher*" (1961), 24 Mod. L. Rev. 557.

[23] [1913] A.C. 263, at p. 280 (P.C.), act of third party.

As a result of this case, "non-natural" came to mean special, exceptional, unusual, or out of the ordinary. In the same way, the word "natural" took on the meaning normal, common, everyday, or ordinary, rather than primitive or in a state of nature. In addition, the notion of increased danger was introduced as a consideration, rather than the mere possibility of mischief or harm being caused in the case of an escape.

Mr. Justice LaForest in *Tock v. St. John's Metropolitan Area Bd.*[24] has added another ingredient to the mix, "damage occurring from a user inappropriate to the place where it is maintained . . . [such as a] pig in the parlour". He explained that non-natural use is a "flexible concept that is capable of adjustment to the changing patterns of social existence". Now let us examine the cases to see which activities have been subject to strict liability and which have not.

a) Water

Rylands v. Fletcher has not been applied to an overflow from a domestic hot water heater,[25] or other home plumbing system,[26] or to a sprinkler system.[27] The rule does not cover legislatively authorized sewers and storm drains built by municipal governments for they are "ordinary and proper for the general benefit of the community".[28]

If water is carried in large quantities in water mains under the street,[29] however, or if it is pumped into a boiler and through a circulating apparatus to wash photographic film in a laboratory,[30] or other commercial use[31] liability follows. If it is used in a creamery,[32] or if it is collected at a dam,[33] or a dyke,[34] strict liability ensues. The escape of filth and sewage from a drainpipe always seems to attract liability, whether it is carried in larger quantities,[35] or for domestic use only.[36]

---

[24] [1989] 2 S.C.R. 1181, at pp. 1190 and 1189.

[25] *Imperial Tobacco v. Hart* (1917), 51 N.S.R. 370; affd 51 N.S.R. 387, 36 D.L.R. 63 (C.A.).

[26] *Carstairs v. Taylor* (1871), L.R. 6 Ex. 217; *Ross v. Fedden* (1872), L.R. 7 Q.B. 661; *Blake v. Woolf*, [1898] 2 Q.B. 426.

[27] *Peters v. Prince of Wales Theatre*, [1943] 1 K.B. 73, [1942] 2 All E.R. 533 (C.A.).

[28] *Tock v. St. John's, supra*, n. 24, at pp. 1190; *cf., Lawrysyn v. Town of Kipling* (1964), 50 W.W.R. 430; affd (1965), 55 W.W.R. 108 (Sask. C.A.).

[29] *Charing Cross, West End & City Electricity Supply Co. v. London Hydraulic Power Co.*, [1914] 3 K.B. 772 (C.A.).

[30] *Western Engraving Co. v. Film Laboratories Ltd.*, [1936] 1 All E.R. 106 (C.A.).

[31] *Wei's Western Wear Ltd. v. Yui Holdings* (1983), 5 D.L.R. (4th) 681 (Alta. Q.B.).

[32] *Crown Diamond Paint Co. v. Acadia Holding Realty Ltd.*, [1952] 2 S.C.R. 161 (*per* Rand and Rinfrett JJ.).

[33] *Kelley v. C.N.R.*, [1950] 1 W.W.R. 744 (B.C.C.A.).

[34] *Latta v. Kelly*, [1925] 1 D.L.R. 116 (N.S.).

[35] *Smeaton v. Ilford Corp.*, [1954] 1 Ch. 450, [1954] 2 All E.R. 923.

[36] *Humphries v. Cousins* (1877), 2 C.P.D. 239; *Ballard v. Tomlinson* (1885), 29 Ch. D. 3, 115 (C.A.).

b) Fire

The use of fire for domestic purposes is usually considered natural and, consequently, no strict liability is imposed for fires in fireplaces,[37] or where a piece of pipe is lit to see if a chimney is clear.[38] If fire is used for purposes of husbandry, there is usually no strict liability.[39]

Fire will give rise to strict liability, however, when used for industrial or transportation purposes, as where a locomotive,[40] or a traction engine gave off sparks.[41] Fire used in unusual ways will also attract *Rylands v. Fletcher* liability, as where a blow torch was used to thaw some frozen pipes,[42] or where fire was employed to fumigate a hen house,[43] or to smoke out a rat.[44] Similarly, where an unextinguished match was thrown away and caused a fire,[45] or where a fire built on the cornice of the building to smoke out a sparrow's nest got out of hand,[46] strict liability ensued. Some decisions hold liable a landowner for any escape of fire from the premises caused by "anyone other than a stranger".[47]

c) Electricity, Gas and Explosives

Rylands v. Fletcher does not cover ordinary amounts of household electricity,[48] or gas,[49] nor does it apply to the use of propane gas for cooking,[50] or to a domestic gas heater.[51] On the other hand, strict liability encompasses those who use or transport large quantities of gas,[52] or electricity.[53]

---

[37] *Sochacki v. Sas*, [1947] 1 All E.R. 344.

[38] *J. Doltis Ltd. v. Isaac Braithwaite & Sons Ltd.*, [1957] 1 Lloyd's Rep. 522.

[39] *Curtis v. Lutes*, [1953] O.R. 747 (C.A.); *cf.*, *Gogo v. Eureka Sawmill*, [1944] 3 W.W.R. 268; vard [1945] 3 W.W.R. 446 (C.A.); *Smith v. Widdicombe* (1987), 39 C.C.L.T. 98; affd [1987] 6 W.W.R. 687 (Man. C.A.).

[40] *Jones v. Festiniog Ry. Co.* (1868), L.R. 3 Q.B. 733.

[41] *Morwick v. Provincial Contracting Co.* (1923), 55 O.L.R. 71 (C.A.); *Powell v. Fall* (1880), 5 Q.B.D. 597 (C.A.).

[42] *Balfour v. Barty-King*, [1956] 1 All E.R. 555; affd on other grounds [1957] 1 Q.B. 496, [1957] 1 All E.R. 156 (C.A.).

[43] *Creaser v. Creaser* (1907), 41 N.S.R. 480 (C.A.).

[44] *Mulholland v. Tedd Ltd. v. Baker*, [1939] 3 All E.R. 253.

[45] *Furlong v. Carroll* (1882), 7 O.A.R. 145.

[46] *Sturge v. Hacket*, [1962] 3 All E.R. 166, [1962] 1 W.L.R. 1257 (C.A.).

[47] *Wager v. Molyneaux* (1988), 47 C.C.L.T. 73, at p. 77 (Alta. Q.B.); *Franks v. Sanderson* (1988), 44 C.C.L.T. 208 (B.C.C.A.); *H. & N. Emanuel Ltd. v. Greater London Council*, [1971] 2 All E.R. 835 (C.A.).

[48] *Collingwood v. Home & Colonial Stores*, [1936] 1 All E.R. 74; affd [1936] 3 All E.R. 200 (C.A.).

[49] *Miller v. Robert Addie & Sons, Collieries*, [1934] S.C. 150.

[50] *O'Neill v. Esquire Hotels Ltd.* (1972), 30 D.L.R. (3d) 589 (N.B.C.A.).

[51] *Bloom v. Creed and Consumers' Gas Co.*, [1937] O.R. 626 (C.A.).

[52] *Northwestern Utilities Ltd. v. London Guarantee and Accident Co.*, [1936] A.C. 108; *Hanson v. Wearmouth Coal Ltd. and Sunderland Gas Co.*, [1939] 3 All E.R. 47 (C.A.); *Lohndorf et al. v. B.A. Oil Co. Ltd.* (1956), 24 W.W.R. 193 (Alta.).

[53] *Eastern and Southern African Telephone Co. v. Cape Town Tramways Cos.*, [1902] A.C. 381, at p. 392 (P.C.); *Toronto Power Co. v. Raynor* (1914), 32 O.L.R. 612; revd on another ground (1915), 51 S.C.R. 490.

There are some strict liability cases involving highly inflammable material.[54] Gasoline stored indoors in drums,[55] or in the gas tanks of automobiles,[56] has given rise to strict liability for fire caused by its escape. Similarly, where an engine which was still hot was washed with gasoline,[57] where a person riding on a truck fender poured gasoline into the carburetor and caused an explosion,[58] and where some gas which was taken out of a truck's gas tank combined with an electric trouble lamp to cause an explosion,[59] strict liability was employed. The manufacture[60] and use of explosives usually attract strict liability,[61] as where a plaintiff was hit on the head by a stone thrown up from a blast at the defendant's quarry.[62] There are, however, contrary decisions, primarily in Western Canada.[63]

d) Other Strict Liability Activities

Rylands v. Fletcher has been employed in cases involving poisonous fumes from a fumigation operation,[64] gas vapour from a factory,[65] the death of a cow caused by arsenic from a smelter,[66] and to the herbicide 2-4D, which was sprayed by aeroplane, damaging neighbour's crops, since this was an "unusual operation" involving "increased danger".[67] Strict liability has also been applied to such

---

54   *Attorney General of Canada v. Diamond Waterproofing* (1974), 4 O.R. (2d) 489 (C.A.), naptha vapour; see also *Mason v. Levy Auto Parts of England Ltd.*, [1967] 2 Q.B. 530, [1967] 2 All E.R. 62.

55   *Chamberlin v. Sperry*, [1934] 1 D.L.R. 189 (Man.); *Jefferson v. Derbyshire Farmers Ltd.*, [1921] 2 K.B. 281, [1920] All E.R. Rep. 129 (C.A.).

56   *Musgrove v. Pandelis*, [1919] 2 K.B. 43 (C.A.); *Perry v. Kendricks Transport*, [1956] 1 All E.R. 154, [1956] 1 W.L.R. 85 (C.A.).

57   *Brody's Ltd. v. C.N.R.*, [1929] 2 D.L.R. 549; affd [1929] 4 D.L.R. 347 (Alta. C.A.).

58   *Dokuchia v. Domansch*, [1945] O.R. 141 (C.A.).

59   *Ekstrom v. Deagon and Montgomery*, [1946] 1 D.L.R. 208 (Alta.); *Ira-Berg Ltd. v. Skrow's Produce* (1990), 76 D.L.R. (4th) 431 (Ont. Gen. Div.), propane gas leaked out of truck causing damage.

60   *Rainham Chemical Works Ltd. v. Belvedere Fish Guano Co.*, [1921] A.C. 465; *cf.*, *Read v. Lyons & Co. Ltd.*, [1947] A.C. 156.

61   *J.P. Porter Co. Ltd. v. Bell*, [1955] 1 D.L.R. 62 (N.S.C.A.).

62   *Miles v. Forest Rock Granite Co. Ltd.* (1918), 34 T.L.R. 500 (C.A.); see also *MacDonald v. Desourdy Construction Ltée* (1972), 27 D.L.R. (3d) 144 (N.S.); *Lindsay v. R.* (1956), 5 D.L.R. (2d) 349; *Aikman v. George Mills & Co.*, [1934] O.R. 597; *Pilliterri v. Northern Construction Co.* (1930), 66 O.L.R. 129, [1930] 4 D.L.R. 731.

63   *Clarkson v. Hamilton Powder Co.* (1909), 10 W.L.R. 102 (Can.); *Strapazon v. Oliphant Munson Collieries Ltd.*, [1920] 2 W.W.R. 793 (Alta. C.A.); *Pietrzak v. Rocheleau*, [1928] 1 W.W.R. 428 (Alta. C.A.), axe struck dynamite.

64   *Schubert v. Sterling Trusts Corp.*, [1943] O.R. 438; *Skubiniuk v. Hartmann* (1914), 20 D.L.R. 323; affd 7 W.W.R. 392 (Man. C.A.).

65   *Heard v. Woodward* (1954), 12 W.W.R. (N.S.) 312 (B.C.).

66   *Cairns v. Canada Refining Co.* (1914), 6 O.W.N. 562.

67   *Mihalchuk v. Ratke* (1966), 57 D.L.R. (2d) 269 (Sask.); *cf.*, *Cruise v. Niessen*, [1977] 2 W.W.R. 481; revd [1978] 1 W.W.R. 688 (Man. C.A.); *Bridges Brothers v. Forest Protection* (1976), 72 D.L.R. (3d) 335 (N.B.Q.B.), nuisance theory used, not *Rylands*.

diverse things as a flagpole,[68] a band of gypsies,[69] stock car racing,[70] a chair-o-plane at a fairground,[71] and pile driving which causes vibrations.[72] So too, flecks of paint falling from a bridge being painted,[73] Christmas decorations that fell from above a street injuring someone,[74] and the overloading of an upper storey of a building,[75] were held to be subject to strict liability. Wild animals and domestic animals with known vicious propensities have also attracted strict liability.[76]

One revealing case is *Gertsen v. Metropolitan Toronto*,[77] where the defendants used organic matter as land fill in a residential area. As it decomposed, it generated methane gas which escape onto adjoining lands and into the plaintiff's garage. One day when the plaintiff turned on the ignition of his car, an explosion occurred destroying the garage, damaging the car and injuring the plaintiff. Mr. Justice Lerner imposed liability on negligence, nuisance and strict liability theories. He explained that the gas was a "dangerous substance" which "escaped onto the plaintiffs' land and caused them damage". Therefore, *prima facie*, liability should follow without proof of negligence. He went on to explain that if the:

> potential source of mischief is an accepted incident of some ordinary purpose to which the land is reasonably applied by the occupier, the *prima facie* rule of absolute responsibility for the consequences of its escape must give way. In applying this qualification, the courts have looked not only to the thing or activity in isolation, but also to the place and manner in which it is maintained and its relation to its surroundings. Time, place and circumstance, not excluding purpose, are most material. The distinction between natural and non-natural use is both relative and capable of adjustment to the changing patterns of social existence.[78]

---

[68] *Shiffman v. Order of St. John of Jerusalem*, [1936] 1 All E.R. 557; *cf.*, *Booth v. St. Catherines*, [1946] O.R. 628 (C.A.), liability for negligence; revd [1947] O.W.N. 165; restored, [1948] S.C.R. 564.

[69] *Attorney General v. Corke*, [1933] Ch. 89.

[70] *Aldridge and O'Brien v. Van Patter, Martin, and Western Fair Assoc.*, [1952] O.R. 595; *cf.*, where no escape, *Deyo v. Kingston Speedway Ltd.*, [1954] O.R. 223; affd [1955] 1 D.L.R. 718 (S.C.C.).

[71] *Hale v. Jennings Brothers*, [1938] 1 All E.R. 579 (C.A.).

[72] *Hoare & Co. v. McAlpine*, [1923] 1 Ch. 167.

[73] *Vaughn v. Halifax-Dartmouth Bridge Commn.* (1961), 29 D.L.R. (2d) 523 (N.S.C.A.).

[74] *Saccardo v. Hamilton*, [1971] 2 O.R. 479, at p. 492.

[75] *Madder v. A.E. MacKenzie & Co.*, [1931] 1 W.W.R. 344, negligence also; affd [1931] 3 W.W.R. 540 (Man. C.A.).

[76] See *May v. Burdett* (1846), 9 Q.B. 101, 115 E.R. 1213; *Behrens v. Bertram Mills Circus Ltd.*, [1957] 2 Q.B. 1, [1957] 1 All E.R. 583; *Bacon v. Ryan* (1995), 27 C.C.L.T. (2d) 308 (Sask. Q.B.), controller of dangerous dog liable; *Sgro v. Verbeek* (1980), 28 O.R. (2d) 712 (*per* Craig J.), no liability since no knowledge of vicious propensity of dog; *Kirk v. Trerise* (1979), 103 D.L.R. (3d) 78 (B.C.); revd (1981), 122 D.L.R. (3d) 642 (B.C.C.A.), no liability where dog bit visitor because heretofore it only licked people, decision under B.C. legislation; Fleming, *The Law of Torts*, 9th ed. (1998), p. 395; see generally North, *Modern Law of Animals* (1972).

[77] (1973), 2 O.R. (2d) 1.

[78] *Ibid.*, at pp. 19-20.

In deciding whether the garbage fill was a natural or non-natural use of land, Mr. Justice Lerner stressed that the purpose was "selfish and self-serving" and not justifiable on any "overriding public welfare theory" which was to the "general benefit of the community". In the light of the time, place, circumstances, and purpose, he held that the activity was a "non-natural use of the land".

e) Cases Where Strict Liability Not Applied

Rylands v. Fletcher does not regulate many assorted ordinary activities that cause accidents; it will not apply to automobiles,[79] to a branch of a tree that falls,[80] to ice that forms out of water discharged from an eavestrough,[81] to a fire extinguisher that explodes,[82] nor to deer hunting.[83] Similarly, raising hogs, even diseased ones, is an "ordinary use", not a "non-natural" one.[84] Where a brick wall collapses,[85] where there is an explosion in a munitions plant in wartime,[86] and where a child is hurt as a result of a defective railing,[87] *Rylands v. Fletcher* is inapplicable, for these are not "unusual" activities that are "essentially dangerous" in themselves. The erection of inanimate things, like guy wires, is not controlled by strict liability.[88]

2. ESCAPE

In addition to a non-natural user, there must normally be an escape before *Rylands v. Fletcher* can by employed. In *Read v. Lyons*,[89] Lord Chancellor Viscount Simon explained that there had to be an "escape from a place which the defendant has occupation of, or control over, to a place which is outside his occupation or control . . .". Consequently, where an explosion occurred in a munitions plant, injuring the plaintiff who was an employee in the plant, strict liability was held inapplicable.

---

[79] *Wing v. London General Omnibus Co.*, [1909] 2 K.B. 652 (C.A.).

[80] *Noble v. Harrison*, [1962] 2 K.B. 332 (D.C.); *Bottoni v. Henderson* (1978), 21 O.R. (2d) 369 (*per* Steele J.), tree "naturally there" when land acquired and not "brought there".

[81] *Mussett v. Reitman's (Ont.) Ltd.*, [1955] O.W.N. 855, [1953] 3 D.L.R. 780. Nor is salt placed on a road in winter subject to strict liability, see *Schenck v. R. in right of Ontario* (1981), 23 C.C.L.T. 14; affd [1987] 2 S.C.R. 289, however liable in nuisance.

[82] *Village of Kelliher v. Smith*, [1931] S.C.R. 672.

[83] *Dahlberg v. Naydiuk* (1969), 10 D.L.R. (3d) 319 (Man. C.A.).

[84] *Modern Livestock Ltd. v. Elgersma* (1989), 50 C.C.L.T. 5, at p. 51 (Alta. Q.B.).

[85] *St. Anne's Well Brewery Co. v. Roberts* (1928), 140 L.T. 1 (C.A.); *Ilford Urban Council v. Beal*, [1925] 1 K.B. 671, retaining wall cracked sewer; *Wilkins v. Leighton*, [1932] 2 Ch. 106; *cf.*, damaged wall, *McNerney v. Forrester* (1912), 22 Man. R. 220, 2 D.L.R. 178 (C.A.).

[86] *Read v. Lyons & Co. Ltd.*, [1947] A.C. 156, [1946] 2 All E.R. 471.

[87] *Barker v. Herbert*, [1911] 2 K.B. 633, at p. 642 (C.A.) (*per* Fletcher Moulton L.J.), nuisance case.

[88] *Salt v. Cardston* (1919), 49 D.L.R. 229, at p. 231 (Alta. C.A.); revd on another point (1920), 60 S.C.R. 612.

[89] [1947] A.C. 156; [1946] 2 All E.R. 471.

As a result of this requirement of escape, a number of cases in which a non-natural use of land was involved have been dismissed. For example, in *Deyo v. Kingston*,[90] two spectators at a stock car race were injured (one fatally) when a racing car went out of control and collided with them. Mr. Justice Roach dismissed the action because *inter alia*, there was "no escape from the lands occupied by and under the control of the respondent corporation".[91] A contrasting case is *Aldridge and O'Brien v. Van Patter, Martin, and Western Fair Assoc.*,[92] where liability was imposed for a similar incident when a stock car escaped, crashed through a fence and injured the plaintiff, who was in an adjoining park.

This requirement of escape makes little sense.[93] Where two people are injured by the same type of conduct, their tort recovery should not depend on whether they were on the land or off the land upon which the activity was conducted. Such distinctions are ludicrous. Indeed, it might be argued that a preferable differentiation, if one were required, would allow the person on the land to recover but deny compensation to the person off the land. A more rational treatment, however, would be to ignore the escape limitation, as the Americans have done.[94]

The courts have, fortunately, been rather liberal in their interpretation of when an escape has occurred. Thus, where damages were caused as a result of "escapes" from hydraulic mains,[95] electric cables,[96] or water mains[97] under highways that were not owned by the defendants, strict liability has been imposed. A steam engine that travels along the road shooting out sparks,[98] and a steam roller that crushes pipes under the highway,[99] were found to involve escapes. Similarly, a pile driver that caused vibrations which damaged the plaintiff's home attracted strict liability for the "escape", because someone who "causes vibrations to escape is in much the same position as a person who brings water on to his own premises an allows it to escape".[100] Canadian courts have sometimes ignored the escape concept completely, as where someone in an upper storey of premises suffered damages as a result of a fire caused by a spark from a motor car below.[101] Eventually, perhaps, this requirement of escape will

---

[90] [1954] O.R. 223; affd [1955] 1 D.L.R. 718 (S.C.C.).

[91] *Ibid.*, at p. 233.

[92] [1952] O.R. 595, [1952] 4 D.L.R. 93.

[93] Lord Goff in *Cambridge Water, supra,* n. 16, notwithstanding.

[94] Wright, "The Law of Torts: 1923-1947" (1948), 26 Can. Bar Rev. 46, at p. 77.

[95] *Charing Cross, West End & City Electricity Supply Co. v. London Hydraulic Power Co.,* [1914] 3 K.B. 772 (C.A.).

[96] *Midwood & Co. v. Manchester Corp.,* [1905] 2 K.B. 597 (C.A.).

[97] *National Telephone Co. v. Baker,* [1893] 2 Ch. 186.

[98] *Powell v. Fall* (1880), 5 Q.B.D. 597 (C.A.).

[99] *Gas Light and Coke Co. v. St. Mary Abbott's Kensington, Vestry* (1885), 15 Q.B.D. 1 (C.A.).

[100] *Bower v. Richardson Construction Co.,* [1938] O.R. 180, at p. 184 (C.A.) (*per* Fisher J.A.); *cf., Barrett v. Franki Compressed Pile Co.,* [1955] O.R. 413 (Schroeder J.).

[101] *Brody's Ltd. v. C.N.R.,* [1929] 2 D.L.R. 549; affd other grounds, [1929] 4 D.L.R. 347 (Alta. C.A.); see also *Chamberlin v. Sperry,* [1934] 1 D.L.R. 189 (Man.), gasoline caused fire and damaged leased premises. See Wright, *supra,* n. 94, at p. 77. *Cf.,* cases strangely holding "inten-

be so diluted that it will cease to exist altogether, for it serves no purpose at all today.

3. PERSONAL INJURY AND ADJOINING LANDOWNERS

Rylands v. Fletcher applies to cases involving personal injuries and is not limited to actions between adjoining landowners. Although there is some authority to the effect that the principle is restricted to disputes between adjoining landowners, and is not available in personal injury cases,[102] that "alarming retrogressive tendency"[103] has now been totally discredited.[104] Lord Goddard remarked that if a fire spreads, the person responsible may be liable "not merely to an adjoining owner who suffers damage, but to any other person who suffers damage. If I happen to be on somebody else's land at a time when a fire spreads to that land and my motor car or property is destroyed, I have just as much right against the person who improperly allows the fire to escape from his land as the owner of the land on which I happen to be."[105] Mr. Justice Laidlaw also felt that *Rylands v. Fletcher* was not confined to landowners but made the owner of a dangerous thing liable "for any mischief thereby occasioned", both "on or off the premises of the owner".[106] Lord Justice Taylor has opined: "I can see no difference in principle between allowing a man-eating tiger to escape from your land onto that of another and allowing it to escape from the back of your wagon parked on the highway."[107]

There are numerous cases both before and after *Read v. Lyons*, which have permitted recovery for personal injuries on the basis of *Rylands v. Fletcher*. In *Hale v. Jennings Brothers*,[108] for example, the personal injury caused by the chair-o-plane was held to be compensable. So too, individuals injured by an electric wire hanging in the street,[109] by a rock thrown up by blasting,[110] and by a

---

tional" release of something not an escape, *Rigby v. Chief Constable of Northamptonshire*, [1985] 2 All E.R. 985 (Q.B.); *North York v. Kert Chemical Industries Inc.* (1985), 33 C.C.L.T. 184 (Ont. H.C.J.).

[102] See Lord Macmillan in *Read v. Lyons & Co. Ltd.*, [1947] A.C. 156.

[103] Harper, James and Gray, *The Law of Torts*, 2nd ed. (1986), p. 802.

[104] See *Perry v. Kendricks Transport*, [1956] 1 All E.R. 154, [1956] 1 W.L.R. 85, at p. 92 (C.A.) (*per* Parker L.J.); *Charing Cross, West End & City Electricity Supply Co. v. London Hydraulic Power Co.*, [1914] 3 K.B. 772, at p. 779 (C.A.) (*per* Lord Sumner); see also Tylor, "Restriction of Strict Liability" (1947), 10 Mod. L. Rev. 396; Goodhart, "Rule in *Rylands v. Fletcher*" (1947), 63 L.Q. Rev. 160.

[105] See *Sochacki v. Sas*, [1947] 1 All E.R. 344; see also *Vaughan v. Halifax-Dartmouth Bridge Commn.* (1961), 29 D.L.R. (2d) 523 (N.S.C.A.).

[106] *Dokuchia v. Domansch*, [1945] O.R. 141, at p. 146 (C.A.); see also *Ekstrom v. Deagon and Montgomery*, [1946] 1 D.L.R. 208 (Alta..); *Crown Diamond Paint Co. v. Acadia Holding Realty Ltd.*, [1952] 2 S.C.R. 161.

[107] *Rigby v. Chief Constable, supra*, n. 101, at p. 996.

[108] [1938] 1 All E.R. 579 (C.A.).

[109] *Bell Telephone v. Ottawa Electric Co.* (1920), 19 O.W.N. 71; affd but directing new assessment (1920), 19 O.W.N. 580.

[110] *Miles v. Forest Rock Granite Co. Ltd.* (1918), 34 T.L.R. 500 (C.A.); *Lindsay v. R.* (1956), 5 D.L.R. (2d) 349.

falling flagpole,[111] succeeded on strict liability theory. When people were killed by the gas fumes of a fumigation exercise liability ensued.[112] Similarly, after *Read v. Lyons*, damages for personal injuries sustained as a result of an escaping stock car were held to be recoverable "by anyone to whom the probability of such damage would naturally be foreseen".[113] Courts in both England,[114] and Australia,[115] have continued to permit recovery for personal injuries.

This makes eminent good sense. It is unthinkable that our courts could possibly value property interests over human safety. If non-natural use of land is subject to strict liability to adjoining landowners, it must, *a fortiori*, be similarly dealt with where personal injuries are caused.

From these cases one can distinguish a distinct line drawn between those ordinary activities in which people generally engage, on one hand, for which liability will be imposed only for negligence, and the more unusual activities involving additional risks undertaken by business and government, on the other hand, for which it is felt that a stricter form of liability is more appropriate.

4. EMERGING THEORY OF STRICT LIABILITY FOR ABNORMALLY DANGEROUS ACTIVITIES

There is an alternative theory of strict liability lurking among the decisions, which is only dimly perceived by Canadian judges. Occasionally, language appears in a *Rylands v. Fletcher* decision that furnishes a slimpse of a new basis of strict liability, free of the historic restraints of non-natural use, escape and mischief. This emerging theory can be termed strict liability for abnormally dangerous activities.[116] Pursuant to this principle, there are a limited number of activities so fraught with abnormal risk for the community that the negligence standard is felt to provide insufficient protection against them. Consequently, these extra-hazardous activities should be governed by a stricter form of liability that insists on compensation for all the losses they generate, even when they are conducted with reasonable care.

The late Dean C. A. Wright perceived the enormous significance and potential of strict liability when he rationalized it in this way: "[A]nyone, who in any community pursues his own advantage by activities which are 'extraordinary' in that community, is liable for damage caused to interests of others who are held

---

[111] *Shiffman v. Order of St. John of Jerusalem*, [1936] 1 All E.R. 557.

[112] *Schubert v. Sterling Trusts Corp.*, [1943] O.R. 438.

[113] *Aldridge and O'Brien v. Van Patter, Martin, and Western Fair Assoc.*, [1952] O.R. 595 (*per* Spence J.), alternative ground; *cf.*, *dictum* in *McDonald v. Associated Fuels Ltd.*, [1954] 3 D.L.R. 775, at p. 781 (B.C.).

[114] *Perry v. Kendricks Transport*, [1956] 1 All E.R. 154, [1956] 1 W.L.R. 85 (C.A.); but see *Dunne v. North Western Gas Bd.*, [1964] 2 Q.B. 806, at p. 838, [1963] 3 All E.R. 916 (C.A.), indicating the question may still be open.

[115] *Benning v. Wong* (1969), 43 A.L.J.R. 467, at p. 475, subject to *Cambridge Water, supra*, n. 16.

[116] *Restatement, Torts, Second*, §520.

to consent only to normal risks."[117] Dean Wright distinguished the role of *Rylands v. Fletcher* from that of negligence:

> Any person in the exercise of an independent right is entitled to expect that other persons in the exercise of like rights will not cause injury to interests deemed worthy of protection either by failure to exercise care in the conduct of rights which are deemed "standard", "normal" or "natural" in the community, or by failure, whether careless or not, so to control conduct that is not "natural", "normal" or standard" that results in harm to such interests.[118]

In other words, there are two general types of activities which are regulated by two different theories of tort liability. Firstly, there are ordinary pursuits that create normal risks, which are controlled by negligence law. Secondly, there are other "types of conduct which, although they cannot be styled wrongful, are either so fraught with danger, or so unusual in a given community, that it is felt that the risk of loss should be shifted from the person injured to the person who, merely by engaging in such conduct, created the risk which resulted in harm".[119]

This is a rational dichotomy that is being advanced by other scholars, who distinguish activities which create normal risks from those of "an 'unusual' nature creating risks not treated as part of the give-and-take of 'normal' social living".[120] Professor Bohlen viewed the rule in *Rylands v. Fletcher* as a compromise between negligence liability and the outright prohibition of certain dangerous conduct, under which it was "possible to allow the individual freedom to enjoy his property, or to exercise his activity as he may conceive that his interests demand and at the same time to see to it, that he shall do so at his own cost and not at the cost of others who are not interested in his individual successes". The principle of strict liability, he observed, "recognizes that there are certain dangerous activities, which, while the dangers incident thereto are not so great as to require their prohibition, should be carried on only at the risk of him who profits by them".[121] A similar rationale called "conditional fault" was offered by Professor (now Justice) Robert Keeton, who linked it to negligence theory and individual responsibility. He contended that "one should not engage in this type of conduct, because of risk or certainty of losses to others, without making reasonable provision for compensation of losses".[122] More recently, in a most penetrating article, Professor Fletcher supported the concept of strict liability on a basis of "non-reciprocal" risks. He argued that a "victim has a right to recover for injuries caused by a risk greater in degree and different in order form those created by the victim and imposed on the defendant".[123] One example of non-reciprocal risk is that posed by aircraft to landowners on the ground, as

---

[117] "The Law of Torts: 1923-1947" (1948), 26 Can. Bar Rev. 46, at p. 78.

[118] *Ibid.*, at p. 79.

[119] Wright, *Cases on the Law of Torts*, 4th ed. (1967), p. 772.

[120] Dunlop, "Liability for Damage Caused by Things" (1962), 40 Can. Bar Rev. 240, at p. 241.

[121] See, "The Rule in *Rylands v. Fletcher*" (1910-11), 59 U. Pa. L. Rev. 298, 373, 423, at p. 433.

[122] "Conditional Fault in the Law of Torts" (1959), 72 Harv. L. Rev. 401, at p. 427.

[123] "Fairness and Utility in Tort Theory" (1972), 85 Harv. L. Rev. 537, at p. 542; *cf.*, Coleman, "Justice and Reciprocity in Tort Theory" (1975), 14 U.W.O.L. Rev. 105.

contrasted with the reciprocal risk that one plane in the air creates for another plane. Professor Ehrenzweig called the theory "negligence without fault",[124] and explained that "anticipation of harm at the time of the start of the activity rather than at the time of the injurious conduct determines the scope of liability". He felt that non-fault liability was "the price which must be paid to society for the permission of a hazardous activity". It is a matter of simple justice.

Judicial recognition of this new theory is not as open nor as prevalent. One must examine the cases with a microscope to glimpse what is transpiring. Normally, these clues are buried within the discussion of *Rylands v. Fletcher*, but if one searches carefully, one may occasionally see evidence of the emerging view. In *Rickards v. Lothian* (itself a case which did much to restrict the operation of *Rylands v. Fletcher*), the phrase "increased danger" was employed in defining what was a non-natural use of land.[125] Mr. Justice Rand, of the Supreme Court of Canada, once based a decision on the "enhanced risk" involved in bringing water onto premises.[126] In one of the Canadian cases imposing strict liability for fumigating activity, Mr. Justice Hogg utilized the term "increased danger",[127] and in another, Mr. Justice Galt referred to the "extreme danger" of the material being used.[128] Lord Justice Scott spoke of the "inherently dangerous" activity in describing the chair-o-plane in *Hale v. Jennings Brothers*[129] and Lord Wright has used the phrase "extraordinary danger" to categorize the work of carrying gas in mains.[130] In imposing strict liability for stock car racing, the term "dangerous thing" was employed;[131] for gasoline, the phrases "dangerous substance"[132] and "inherently dangerous substance"[133] were used; for setting off explosives, the words "extraordinary danger" were used;[134] and blasting was called "extra-hazardous" or "inherently dangerous".[135]

[124] (1966), 54 Calif. L. Rev. 1422.

[125] *Supra*, n. 23. See also *Wei's Western Wear Ltd. v. Yui Holdings Ltd.* (1983), 27 C.C.L.T. 292, at p. 296 (Alta. Q.B.).

[126] *Crown Diamond Paint Co. v. Acadian Holding Realty Ltd.*, [1952] 2 S.C.R. 161, one judge agreed, two others held negligence, and one judge dissented.

[127] *Schubert v. Sterling Trusts Corp.*, [1943] O.R. 438, at p. 445.

[128] *Skubiniuk v. Hartmann* (1914), 24 Man. R. 836, at p. 839 (C.A.); see also "dangerous substance", at p. 846 and "dangerous work", at p. 871.

[129] [1938] 1 All E.R. 579 (C.A.).

[130] *Northwestern Utilities Ltd. v. London Guarantee & Accident Co.*, [1936] A.C. 108, [1935] 4 D.L.R. 737, at p. 741.

[131] *Aldridge and O'Brien v. Van Patter, Martin, and Western Fair Assoc.*, [1952] O.R. 595, [1952] 4 D.L.R. 93, at p. 741.

[132] *Ekstrom v. Deagon and Montgomery*, [1946] 1 D.L.R. 209 (Alta.) (*per* Parlee J.); *Dokuchia v. Domansch*, [1944] O.W.N. 461, "dangerous thing"; affd [1945] O.R. 141 (C.A.).

[133] *Ira-Berg v. Skrow's Produce*, *supra*, n. 59, at p. 436.

[134] *Lindsay v. R.* (1956), 5 D.L.R. (2d) 349, at p. 366 (Ex. Ct.) (*per* Cameron J.); see also *Benning v. Wong*, *supra*, n. 115, at p. 469 (*per* Barwick C.J.), gas.

[135] *MacDonald v. Desourdy Construction Ltée* (1972), 27 D.L.R. (3d) 144 (N.S.) (*per* Dubinsky J.).

One factor that seems to be taken into account in these cases is whether the conduct is motivated by the pursuit of profit. If it is felt that the defendant created the increased danger for the "purpose of profit",[136] or for "selfish and self-serving" reasons,[137] it is more likely that strict liability will be invoked. Similarly, if defendants undertake pursuits, "for their own purposes",[138] they should expect less sympathy than when they do so for the "public welfare".[139]

Enough has been said to demonstrate that Canadian courts, in these strict liability cases, are concerned with more than non-natural use, mischief and escape as outlined in *Rylands v. Fletcher*. Although these phrases are still frequently employed in the cases, there are also references to increased dangers or extra-hazardous activities, concepts that resemble the notions of abnormal danger[140] and ultra-hazardous activities,[141] employed in the American jurisprudence. The latter concepts are a more appropriate foundation for strict liability today than the archaic language of *Rylands v. Fletcher*. They provide a better reason for adopting a different standard of care to regulate a particular group of activities.

The House of Lords is of a different mindset pursuing its general retreat from modern tort law theory. In *Cambridge Water Co. v. Eastern Counties Leather*,[142] the defendant contaminated the plaintiff's water supply by allowing a leather-tanning solvent to leak onto the concrete floor of its tannery. The solvent then found its way into the ground from where the plaintiff's water came. The defendant was excused from liability, even though it was held that the defendant's use was a non-natural use, because it was not reasonably foreseeable that the water could be contaminated in this way. All that could be reasonably foreseen was a person being overcome by the fumes. Lord Goff sought to confine *Rylands v. Fletcher* to a mere species of nuisance where there was an isolated escape from land, opposing the development of a principle of strict liability for ultrahazardous operations. Happily, the Canadian courts have refused to follow the House of Lords on this path of retreat, much like they have refused to retreat along with the English in other areas of tort law.[143]

In conclusion therefore, those who create extraordinary peril to society should be treated in an extraordinary way. Rather than being subject to negli-

---

[136] *Hale v. Jennings Brothers*, [1938] 1 All E.R. 579, at p. 585 (C.A.); *Wei's Western Wear, supra*, n. 125, at p. 297.

[137] *Gertsen v. Metropolitan Toronto* (1973), 2 O.R. (2d) 1, at p. 21.

[138] *Northwestern Utilities Ltd., supra*, n. 130, at p. 741, D.L.R.

[139] *Gertsen v. Metropolitan Toronto, supra*, n. 137.

[140] *Restatement, Torts, Second* §520.

[141] *Ibid.*, §§519, 520.

[142] [1994] 2 A.C. 264; [1994] 1 All E.R. 53 (H.L.). See also the Australian case of *Burnie Port Authority v. General Jones Pty Ltd.* (1994), 68 Aust. L.J.R. 331 (H.C.), *Rylands v. Fletcher* "absorbed' by negligence; see Fleming, "The Fall of a Crippled Giant" (1995), 3 Tort L. Rev. 56.

[143] See Cusinato J. in *Smith Bros. Excavating Windsor Ltd. v. Camion Equipment Leasing Inc.* (1994), 21 C.C.L.T. (2d) 113, at p. 141 (Ont. Gen. Div.), methanol escape subject to *Rylands* but foresight required, no loss proved.

gence law, which applies to the ordinary risks of society, they should be subject to strict liability, which applies to risks that are not ordinary. When it also appears that the activity is pursued for profit or for the purpose of the actor, it is hard to avoid the conclusion that liability should be strict.[144] Further, when one realizes that such activities are usually, though not always, conducted by business enterprises or by governments who can usually afford to furnish compensation for the victims of their actions, the case for strict liability becomes unanswerable.

Mr. Justice Windeyer of Australia once recognized what had become of *Rylands v. Fletcher*, and had suggested that, although strict liability was not "called into existence in 1866 for the purpose of ensuring that industrial enterprises make good the harm they do", that was the "socially beneficial result" of the doctrine. His Lordship explained further:

> Actions for negligence dominate the work of common law courts today, mainly because railway trains, motor-cars and industrial machinery have so large a place in men's lives. But to regard negligence as the normal requirement of responsibility in tort, and to look upon strict liability as anomalous and unjust, seems to me to mistake present values as well as past history. In an age when insurance against all forms of liability is commonplace, it is surely not surprising or unjust if law makes persons who carry on some kinds of hazardous undertakings liable for the harm they do, unless they can excuse or justify it on some recognized ground. That is, I think the position today in the countries of the common law. In England, and in those countries which have the common law as it is in England, this comes about through the principle of *Rylands v. Fletcher*.[145]

This version of *Rylands v. Fletcher* is full of potential for the future. It furnishes a third base of tort liability — strict liability — which can regulate certain types of activities for which negligence law provides insufficient protection. The concept lies hidden in the cases, waiting to be discovered. If it is reoriented in the way suggested, one could forecast that the future of *Rylands v. Fletcher* will be one of steady growth and service to society, and not one of decay and ultimate eclipse.

C. Defences to Strict Liability

There are five major defences open to defendants who are *prima facie* subject to the rule in *Rylands v. Fletcher*. Two of these, act of God and default of the plaintiff, were recognized in the original formulation of the rule and the others developed in subsequent cases. It is clear that the onus of proof of each of these

---

[144] See *Danku v. Town of Fort Frances* (1976), 73 D.L.R. (3d) 377 (*per* Fitzgerald C.C.J.), it is just that loss falls on person conducting enterprise "for the purpose of profit", rather than on an innocent neighbour. See also *Wei's Western Wear Ltd. v. Yui Holdings* (1983), 27 C.C.L.T. 292 (Alta. Q.B.) (*per* Medhurst J.).

[145] *Benning v. Wong, supra,* n. 115, at p. 487. See also *Report of the Royal Commission on Civil Liability and Compensation for Personal Injury* (1978), recommending preparation of a statutory list of "unusually hazardous things", or things that threaten "serious and extensive casualties". But *cf., Cambridge Water Co., supra,* n. 16.

defences rests on the defendants, who must bring themselves within one of them to be excused.[146] There is no question that the existence of these defences, have diluted the power of *Rylands v. Fletcher* and have brought it closer to negligence theory. This does not mean, however, that strict liability has been rendered meaningless, although its impact has certainly been reduced by them.

1. CONSENT OF THE PLAINTIFF

The consent of the plaintiff is a defence to strict liability in the same way as it is in cases of intentional torts and negligence. When the consent is expressly given there is rarely any problem with it. Implied consent, however, is more difficult to handle. A tenant, for example, consents to non-negligently produced damage caused by an escape of water from the part of the premises occupied by the landlord, if it was collected for the tenant's benefit.[147] Someone renting premises near a quarry consents to any damage arising from its normal operation, in the absence of negligence.[148] So too, a tenant impliedly consents to the presence of a sprinkler system, if knowing about it, and cannot recover damages for the escape of water, unless negligence is proved for the tenant takes "the place as he found it for better or worse".[149] Some of these cases have been disposed of on the ground of natural use,[150] or on the theory of common benefit,[151] but this reasoning is now largely discredited.[152]

Where there is no benefit to the plaintiff, however, the court is less likely to imply consent, as where water was collected to wash the defendant's films, but was of no use at all to the plaintiff.[153] Even where there is some benefit the plaintiff is entitled to the protection of strict liability if the plaintiff does not consent to the installation, as where gas pipes under the road exploded and did damage to a gas consumer's home nearby.[154]

There has been no movement toward the restriction of the consent defence in this context as there has been in the negligence area. It may well be that courts have found it convenient to restrict the scope of strict liability in this way. It would be preferable, however, if some consistency were to be achieved between consent in this context and voluntary assumption of risk in the negligence context. The person conducting non-natural activities should bear the losses

---

[146] *Ibid.*, at p. 489.
[147] *Carstairs v. Taylor* (1871), L.R. 6 Ex. 217.
[148] *Thomas v. Lewis*, [1937] 1 All E.R. 137.
[149] *Peters v. Prince of Wales Theatre*, [1943] 1 K.B. 73, [1942] 2 All E.R. 533 (C.A.) (*per* Goddard L.J.). See also *Pattison v. Prince Edward Region Conservation Authority* (1984), 53 O.R. (2d) 23, at p. 29 (H.C.); affd 27 O.A.C. 174 (C.A.).
[150] *Anderson v. Oppenheimer* (1880), 5 Q.B.D. 602 (C.A.).
[151] *Hess v. Greenaway* (1919), 45 O.L.R. 650 (C.A.).
[152] *Peters v. Prince of Wales Theatre, supra,* n. 149. But see *contra, Danku v. Town of Fort Frances, supra,* n. 144, principle does not apply to person carrying on undertaking for the "general benefit of the community at large" (*per* Fitzgerald D.C.J.).
[153] *Western Engraving Co. v. Film Laboratories Ltd.*, [1936] 1 All E.R. 106 (C.A.).
[154] *Supra,* n. 130.

caused, unless there has been a clear waiver of legal rights. Mere knowledge should not be equivalent to consent here, for that is an artificial result where there is no real choice by the plaintiff.[155]

2. DEFAULT OF THE PLAINTIFF

The default of the plaintiff was recognized as a defence in *Rylands v. Fletcher* itself.[156] It is akin to the defence of contributory negligence and supportable on the same grounds, although some courts have been reluctant to use contributory negligence as a defence in strict liability cases.[157] Thus, in *Dunn v. Birmingham Canal*,[158] a mine-owner was denied compensation when he carelessly worked his mine under the defendant's canal, causing himself damage by flooding. Similarly, when a horse died after it reached over into the defendant's property and ate from a poisonous tree, the owner was refused reparation.[159]

It is unclear whether a plaintiff who engages in a sensitive activity is denied access to *Rylands v. Fletcher*. In one case, where sensitive telegraphic communications were interfered with by the escape of electricity, the court stated that a person could not "increase liabilities of his neighbour by applying his own property to special uses, whether for business or pleasure".[160] On the other hand, where pile-driving caused damage to a hotel, it was not a defence to plead that the building was vulnerable to collapse, for the plaintiff was not putting it to any supersensitive use.[161]

Whether contributory negligence legislation could be applied and damages apportioned in cases such as these is not yet clear. At least one author believes that the English legislation, which uses the language of "fault", would be employed.[162] The Ontario Negligence Act, which allows for apportionment in actions founded upon the "fault or negligence of the defendant," might be applied, if the court were willing to stretch the meaning of the words to incorporate this type of conduct, which would be in harmony with the growing feeling that there should be apportionment in strict liability cases.[163]

3. ACT OF GOD

The defence of act of God was also recognized in *Rylands v. Fletcher*, but it has been only rarely applied. This term is meant to encompass not every storm or rainfall but only the extraordinary phenomena of nature which cannot be

---

[155] See Chapter 13, *supra*.
[156] (1866), L.R. 1 Ex. 265, at p. 179; affd (1868), L.R. 3 H.L. 330.
[157] Prosser, *supra*, n. 2, at p. 522.
[158] (1872), L.R. 7 Q.B. 244; affd L.R. 8 Q.B. 42 (Ex. Ch.).
[159] *Ponting v. Nokes*, [1894] 2 Q.B. 281, also no escape.
[160] *Eastern and South African Telephone Co. v. Cape Town Tramways Cos.*, [1902] A.C. 381, at p. 393 (P.C.).
[161] *Hoare & Co. v. McAlpine*, [1923] 1 Ch. 167.
[162] *Winfield and Jolowicz On Tort*, 15th ed. (1998), at p. 378.
[163] See Cheifetz, *Apportionment Fault in Tort* (1981), p. 179. *Supra*, Chapter 3.

foreseen. The leading case is *Nichols v. Marsland*,[164] where an unprecedented rainstorm caused flooding from certain dams of the defendant which swept away some bridges on the plaintiff's property. The jury found that there was no negligence and that the flooding could not have been reasonably anticipated. Mellish L.J., in denying liability, explained that a defendant cannot be "said to have caused or allowed the water to escape, if the act of God or the Queen's enemies was the real cause of its escaping without any fault on the part of the defendant".[165] In the same way, when flooding is caused by the gnawing of rats on a wooden conduit pipe, the defence may be applicable,[166] as it would be if lightning,[167] or a hurricane was the cause of a loss.

The courts have not been hospitable to this defence which, if broadly interpreted, could threaten the influence of strict liability. Consequently its scope has been limited to those circumstances which "no human foresight can provide against and of which human prudence is not bound to recognize the possibility".[168] Where there is a severe rainstorm causing a flood which damages property, strict liability will be utilized.[169] A high wind is not an Act of God unless it is of "such exceptional strength that no one could be reasonably expected to anticipate or provide against it".[170]

The courts have been wise to limit this defence, for one of the risks involved in the conduct of non-natural activities is that forces of nature may cause them to go awry. In such a situation it is appropriate that the person who creates the abnormal risk should bear the loss, rather than the innocent victim.[171] Since "[t]here is nothing so certain as that which is unexpected", the scope of this defence should be narrowed.[172]

4. DELIBERATE ACT OF THIRD PERSON

If a defendant can prove that the escape in question was caused by a third person's "conscious act of volition",[173] the defendant will be exempted from strict liability. The onus is clearly on the defendant to establish this.[174] It is not

---

[164] (1876), 2 Ex. D.1 (C.A.); *cf.*, *Greenock Corp. v. Caledonian Ry. Co.*, [1917] A.C. 556.

[165] *Ibid.*, at p. 5.

[166] *Carstairs v. Taylor* (1871), L.R. 6 Ex. 217 (*per* Kelly C.B.).

[167] *Hargrave v. Goldman*, [1965] A.L.R. 377, at p. 386.

[168] *Greenock Corp. v. Caledonian Ry. Co.*, [1917] A.C. 556, quoting Lord Westbury in *Tennent v. Earl of Glasgow* (1864), 2 Macph. (Ct. of Sess.) (H.L.) 22.

[169] See MacDonald, "The Rule in *Rylands v. Fletcher* and its Limitations" (1923), 1 Can. Bar Rev. 140, at p. 145.

[170] *Cushing v. Walker & Son*, [1941] 2 All E.R. 693, at p. 695 (*per* Hallett J.). See also *Greenwood Tileries Ltd. v. Clapson*, [1937] 1 All E.R. 765, at p. 722, high tide; *Slater v. Worthington's Cash Stores (1930) Ltd.*, [1941] 1 K.B. 488, at p. 492 (C.A.), snow storm.

[171] See Goodhart, "The Third Man" (1951), 4 Cont. Leg. Prob. 177, at p. 178.

[172] *Ruck v. Williams* (1858), 3 H. & N. 308, at p. 318 (*per* Bramwell B.), 157 E.R. 488.

[173] *Dominion Natural Gas Co. Ltd. v. Collins and Perkins*, [1909] A.C. 640, at p. 647. See generally, Martland, "The Act of a Stranger as a Limitation of the Rule in *Rylands v. Fletcher*" (1934-35), 1 Alta. L.Q. 239.

[174] *A. Prosser & Son Ltd. v. Levy*, [1955] 3 All E.R. 577, [1955] 1 W.L.R. 1224 (C.A.).

enough that a third person unleash the force that causes the damage; it must be done deliberately.[175] If it is foreseeable that a third person may interfere, even negligently, strict liability is still available.[176]

The defence has been employed where a third person maliciously plugged a pipe in a lavatory causing a flood,[177] where some children threw a lighted match into a vehicle's gas tank,[178] and where someone emptied a reservoir into the defendant's reservoir causing a flood, because the loss was "caused by a stranger over whom and at the spot where they had no control".[179]

The courts are rather unwilling to utilize this defence except in very clear cases, for to do so would impair the efficacy of strict liability. Thus, where conduct of a third person brings about the loss, strict liability will be imposed where that act is foreseeable or if it could have been prevented by the defendant. In *Hale v. Jennings Brothers*,[180] for example, a chair-o-plane at a fairground came loose and struck the plaintiff as a result of a passenger tampering with it. Liability was imposed because this was

> just the kind of behaviour which ought to have been anticipated as being a likely act with a percentage of users of the apparatus. People go there in a spirit of fun. Many of them are ignorant, and many of them are wholly unaware of the dangers incidental to playing with the chairs in that sort of way, and they cause a danger that they do not in the least realize. That kind of accident does not come within the exceptions to the rule at all.[181]

In other words, the accident which occurred was the very type of thing that has to be prevented by actors at their peril. Similarly, in *North Western Utilities Ltd. v. London Guarantee & Accident Co.*,[182] strict liability was imposed against a gas company for an escape of gas due to a leak in its pipes caused by the construction operations of a third party, because such operations were foreseeable and could have been guarded against.[183] Employees (unless they enter where they are forbidden to do so),[184] and independent contractors,[185] over whom the defendant exercises control are not considered strangers for purposes of this defence.

---

[175] *Rickards v. Lothian*, [1913] A.C. 263 (P.C.); *Box v. Jubb* (1879), 4 Ex. D 76; *Raffan v. Canada Western Natural Gas Co.* (1915), 8 W.W.R. 676 (S.C.C.) (*per* Anglin J.).

[176] *Hale v. Jennings Brothers*, [1938] 1 All E.R. 579 (C.A.).

[177] *Rickards v. Lothian*, [1913] A.C. 263 (P.C.).

[178] *Perry v. Kendricks Transport*, [1956] 1 All E.R. 154, [1956] 1 W.L.R. 85 (C.A.).

[179] *Box v. Jubb* (1879), 4 Ex. D. 76.

[180] *Supra*, n. 176, at p. 585.

[181] [1938] 1 All E.R. 579 (C.A.) (*per* Scott L.J.).

[182] [1936] A.C. 108.

[183] See Martland, *supra*, n. 173; *Shell-Mex and B.P. Ltd. v. Belfast Corp.*, [1952] N.I. 72; *Weisler v. North Vancouver* (1959), 17 D.L.R. (2d) 319 (B.C.); *Lewis v. North Vancouver* (1963), 40 D.L.R. (2d) 182 (B.C.), reservoir.

[184] *Stevens v. Woodward* (1881), 6 Q.B.D. 318 (D.C.).

[185] *Balfour v. Barty-King*, [1957] 1 Q.B. 496, at p. 506, [1957] 1 All E.R. 156 (C.A.).

It has been argued that this exception merges *Rylands v. Fletcher* with negligence, but this is not so.[186] The courts are less likely to invoke this defence in a strict liability case than they are in a negligence case, since it is more narrowly defined here. Further, the onus is on defendants to bring themselves within the defence under strict liability, whereas, in the negligence suit, it is for the plaintiffs to prove negligence.

5. LEGISLATIVE AUTHORITY

Where an activity is authorized by legislation, no strict liability is imposed unless the defendant is found to have been "negligent". This partial immunity was first enunciated in 1860 in the case of *Vaughan v. Taff Vale Railway Co.*,[187] where it was said that when the legislation has "sanctioned the use of particular means . . . the parties are not liable for any injury . . . unless they have contributed to it by some negligence".[188] Consequently, courts have distinguished between one group of activities which may subject an enterprise to strict liability, and another group of legislatively authorized pursuits, which do not import liability, except where some fault is proven.[189] The main rationale for this partial immunity (in addition to history) is the old standby of the intention of the legislature. It is pretty obvious, however, that no intention with regard to civil liability is usually articulated in the statute. It is, therefore, up to the courts to determine the best way to treat these legislatively authorized activities.[190]

As might be expected, the common law courts have sought to preserve the protection afforded individuals by its principle of strict liability, and have stoutly resisted the invasion of the defence of legislative authority. Various legal devices have been employed in this endeavour. For example, the courts strictly construe the legislation authorizing the activity in question.[191] One court has proclaimed that grants of legislative authority are not "charters to commit torts".[192] Nor do they grant a "carte blanche" to create nuisances.[193] Consequently, unless the legislation clearly authorizes the particular activity in question, the civil courts will impose strict liability as they normally do. The courts have held that there was no legislative intention to grant any immunity where some locomotive sparks set fire to a haystack,[194] where sewage was

---

[186] Fleming, *op. cit. supra*, n. 1, at p. 388.

[187] (1860), 5 H. & N. 679, 157 E.T.R. 1351. See also *Partridge v. Etobicoke*, [1956] O.R. 121, at p. 129 (C.A.), no liability because no negligence re electric wires.

[188] *Ibid.*, at p. 1354, E.R. (*per* Cockburn J.).

[189] See Linden, "Strict Liability, Nuisance and Legislative Authorization", [1966] 4 Osgoode Hall L.J. 196.

[190] See, *infra*, Chapter 15, the discussion on legislative authority as a defence to nuisance.

[191] *Gertsen v. Metropolitan Toronto* (1973), 2 O.R. (2d) 1, at p. 23 (*per* Lerner J.).

[192] *Quebec Railway Co. v. Vandry*, [1920] A.C. 662, at p. 679 (P.C.).

[193] *Midwood & Co. v. Manchester Corp.*, [1905] 2 K.B. 597, at p. 606 (C.A.).

[194] *Jones v. Festiniog Railway Co.* (1868), L.R. 3 Q.B. 733; *cf.*, *C.P.R. v. Roy*, [1902] A.C. 220 (P.C.).

emitted from an authorized building,[195] where a nuisance was caused by a sewer,[196] a smallpox hospital,[197] or a horse stable[198] and other similar situations.

Another technique used by the courts to limit the impact of legislative authorization has been the restriction of the notion of implied authority. The courts will imply a legislative intention to authorize certain harm only where the damage is a necessary or inevitable result of the authorized act.[199] An intention to excuse the defendant from liability is rarely implied, but it once was where vibrations were caused by a locomotive on an authorized railway, because this could not possibly be avoided.[200]

A similar method of interpretation adopted by certain courts in the past infers that the authorizing legislation was not intended to legalize damage because it was "permissive" only and not "imperative".[201]

Civil courts have placed the onus of proof in these cases on the defendants to demonstrate that their otherwise tortious conduct was authorized by the legislation and that the damage caused was inevitable.[202] This rule was recently reasserted by Justice Major in *Ryan v. Victoria (City)*,[203] when, in a public nuisance context, he confirmed that the defence was "at best, a narrow defence." He stated:

> The traditional rule is that liability will not be imposed if an activity is authorized by statute and the defendant proves that the nuisance is the "inevitable result" or consequence of exercising that authority.

In the light of the inability of the Supreme Court to achieve a majority in its effort to limit or eliminate the defence in *Tock*, he restated the "traditional view" which remains the most "predictable" and "simplest to apply", as described by Justice Sopinka in *Tock*:[204]

> The defendant must negative that there are alternate methods of carrying out the work. The mere fact that one is considerably less expensive will not avail. If only one method is practically feasible, it must be established that it was practically impossible to avoid the nuisance. It is insufficient for the defendant to negative negligence. The standard is a higher one. While the defence gives rise to some factual difficulties, in view of the allocation of the burden of proof they will be resolved against the defendant.

---

195 *Attorney General v. Colney Hatch Lunatic Asylum* (1868), 4 Ch. App. 146, 19 L.T. 708; *Burgess v. Woodstock*, [1955] O.R. 814.

196 *Attorney General v. Leeds Corp.* (1870), 5 Ch. App. 583, 22 L.T. 320, at p. 321.

197 *Metropolitan Asylum District v. Hill* (1881), 6 App. Cas. 193.

198 *Rapier v. London Tramways Co.*, [1893] 2 Ch. 588 (C.A.).

199 *Manchester Corp. v. Farnworth*, [1930] A.C. 171, [1929] All E.R. Rep. 90; *Whitehouse v. Fellowes*, 10 C.B.N.S. 765, at p. 870. See also *Schenck v. Regina, supra*, n. 81.

200 *Hammersmith & City Railways Co. v. Brand* (1869), L.R. 4 H.L. 171.

201 See *Burniston v. Corp. of Bangor*, [1932] N.I. 178; *J.P. Porter Co. Ltd. v. Bell*, [1955] 1 D.L.R. 62, at p. 71 (N.S.C.A.).

202 *Vaughan v. Halifax-Dartmouth Bridge Commn.* (1961), 46 M.P.R. 14, at p.19, 29 D.L.R. (2d) 523 (N.S.C.A.); *Bower v. Richardson Construction Co.*, [1938] O.R. 180, at p. 185 (C.A.); *Schenck v. Regina, supra*, n. 81; *Vergamini v. Hamilton-Wentworth* (1986), 54 O.R. (2d) 494 (Dist. Ct.).

203 [1999] 1 S.C.R. 201, 168 D.L.R. (4th) 513, at p. 238 (S.C.R.), para. 54.

204 [1989] 2 S.C.R. 1181, at p. 1226, 64 D.L.R. (4th) 620.

The courts have also manifested their antipathy toward the immunity by fashioning a specialized definition of the word "negligence", as used in the context of the partial immunity. Ordinarily negligence is the absence of reasonable care in the circumstances, having regard to the gravity of the harm, the likelihood of its occurrence, and the utility of the defendant's conduct. Rather than adopt this familiar meaning in this context, the courts have narrowed it by holding that "if the damages could be prevented it is, within the rule, 'negligence' not to make such reasonable exercise of powers".[205] Similarly, it has been suggested that "it is negligence to carry out work in a manner which results in damage unless it can be shown that that, and that only, was the way in which the duty could be performed".[206] Defendants who wish to rely on legislative authority as a defence, therefore, bear the onus of convincing the court that the activity was carried on in the only way possible;[207] if they fail, they will be held to be "negligent" and consequently outside the protection of the partial immunity.

In deciding whether a court will restrict the operation of these legislatively authorized activities, various policy factors are taken into account, which is as it should be. Immunity will tend to be invoked and recovery denied where a plaintiff is seeking to gain increased compensation by avoiding a statutory compensation scheme, where the defendant is a non-profit-making operation,[208] where the authority is by statute rather than by an inferior legislative enactment, and where a particularly important industry is involved. On the other hand, courts will tend to avoid the immunity and impose strict liability where the defendant is a profit-making organization,[209] where the legislative authority is a by-law or government contract, where the defendant's conduct was particularly reprehensible and where the loss could easily have been avoided.[210]

The courts have struggled to circumscribe the impact of authorizing legislation and have preserved, as best they could, the pre-existing strict liability rights. The philosophy that emerges from the cases is that if legislatures wish to immunize certain activities for the public good, they should do so expressly and provide for alternative compensation to the victims of this exercise of public power. If they do not do so expressly, the duty of tort law is to protect the private rights of the individuals as long as this can be achieved without doing violence to the legislation.

---

[205] *Geddis v. Bann Reservoir Proprietors* (1878), 3 App. Cas. 430, at p. 455.

[206] *Provender Millers Ltd. v. Southampton County Council*, [1940] 1 Ch. 131, at p. 140, [1939] 4 All E.R. 157.

[207] *Manchester Corp. v. Farnworth*, [1930] A.C. 171; *Lawrysyn v. Town of Kipling* (1966), 55 D.L.R. (2d) 471 (Sask. C.A.); *cf.*, *Benning v. Wong* (1969), 43 A.L.J.R. 467.

[208] *Dunne v. North Western Gas Bd.*, [1964] 2 Q.B. 806 (C.A.); *Benning v. Wong, supra*, n. 207; *Boxes Ltd. v. British Waterways Bd.*, [1971] 2 Lloyd's Rep. 183 (C.A.).

[209] Compare treatment of two defendants in *Danku, supra*, n. 152.

[210] See Linden, *supra*, n. 189, at p. 206.

D. Vicarious Liability

Another form of strict liability is called vicarious liability. An employer may be liable for the torts of employees, vicariously, regardless of whether that employer was personally at fault. One policy reason for this was to ensure that a victim of wrongdoing had a solvent defendant from whom to collect. Moreover, it was fair to require the employer to stand behind the employee because, in most cases, that employer controlled the employee and benefitted from that employee's conduct. It might also encourage care in the selection of employees so as to reduce their tortious conduct.[211] The tort for which the employer is held liable vicariously must normally occur during the course and scope of the employment.[212] This vicarious liability must be distinguished from the negligence liability of employers, who carelessly select, train and supervise their employees. Such liability is based on fault, not vicarious liability, which is a "species of strict liability".[213]

In the past, the test of whether an employee rendered the employer liable vicariously depended on whether he could be considered a "servant", that is, the employer or "master" exercised detailed control over the manner in which the servant did his work. Nowadays the courts more commonly use the language of employer and employee in this area.[214] They have developed other tests including one called the "organization test", whereby it would be decided whether an employer could be fairly held vicariously liable.[215] There is, however, no universal test. The court must consider the "total relationship of the parties" in order to determine whether there is an employer-employee relationship. As Justice Major explained:

> The central question is whether the person who has been engaged to perform the services is performing them as a person in business on his own account. In making this determination, the level of control the employer has over the worker's activities will always be a factor. However, other factors to consider include whether the worker provides his or her own equipment, whether the worker hires his or her own helpers, the degree of financial risk taken by the worker, the degree of responsibility for investment and management held by the worker, and the worker's opportunity for profit in the performance of his or her tasks.

> It bears repeating that the above factors constitute a non-exhaustive list, and there is no set formula as to their application. The relative weight of each will depend on the particular facts and circumstances of the case.[216]

Vicarious liability can extend to intentional torts perpetrated by employees, such as "bouncers" who eject patrons with more force than is indicated by the

---

[211] *671122 Ontario Ltd. v. Sagaz Industries Canada Inc.*, 2001 S.C.C. 59, at para. 29 *et ff.* See also *Bazley v. Curry*, [1999] 2 S.C.R. 534, at para. 26-36.

[212] See *T.G. Bright & Co. Ltd. v. Kerr*, [1939] S.C.R. 63, [1939] 1 D.L.R. 193. See generally Fleming, *The Law of Torts*, 9th ed. (1998), at p. 409.

[213] *671122 Ontario Ltd. v. Sagaz Industries Canada Inc., supra*, n. 211, at para. 26.

[214] *671122 Ontario Ltd. v. Sagaz Industries Canada Inc., supra*, n. 211, at para. 25.

[215] *Co-operators Insurance Association v. Kearney*, [1965] S.C.R. 106, 48 D.L.R. (2d) 1. See Fleming, *supra*, n. 212, at p. 416.

[216] *671122 Ontario Ltd., supra*, n. 211, at para. 47 and 48. See also *Wiebe Door Services v. M.N.R.*, [1986] 3 F.C. 533 (C.A.) (*per* MacGuigan J.A.).

situation.[217] It may be used in cases of theft and fraud by employees.[218] Lately, it has been employed in cases of sexual wrongdoing by employees, where there was a significant connection between the wrong and the creation of the risk of such a wrong by an employer while engaging in the enterprise. In other words, where the "employer's enterprise created or materially enhanced the risk of the tortious act", vicarious liability is justified. Liability in these cases is also thought to deter such acts by fostering closer supervision and better selection of employees.[219]

An employer may be held not vicariously liable where the employee is transferred or loaned to another employer, as in the case of an operating room, where the nurses and the other medical staff of the hospital are transferred to and under the control of the surgeon, who is said to be the "captain of the ship."[220] Similarly, if an independent contractor is given the responsibility of doing a job, and causes a fault-based accident, that independent contractor may be vicariously liable for any injury caused his employees, but not the person who hired him to do the job.[221] As Justice Major has explained:[222]

> [I]t does not make sense to anchor liability on an employer for acts of an independent contractor, someone who was in business on his or her own account. In addition, the employer does not have the same control over an independent contractor as an employee to reduce accidents and intentional wrongs by efficient organizations and supervision.

Some duties are, however, "non-delegable" and, if so, the original employer cannot escape liability by delegating the responsibility to an independent contractor. Where a statutory duty to maintain the highway is placed upon a governmental authority, for example, that duty cannot be delegated to an independent contractor; the defendant remains personally liable for any negligence of the independent contractor or its employees.[223]

---

[217] *Griggs v. Southside Hotel Ltd.*, [1947] O.R. 674 (C.A.).

[218] *Lloyd v. Grace, Smith & Co.*, [1912] A.C. 716 (H.L.); *R. v. Levy Brothers Co.*, [1961] S.C.R. 189, 26 D.L.R. (2d) 760.

[219] *Bazley v. Curry*, [1999] 2 S.C.R. 534, 174 D.L.R. (4th) 45 ("Childrens Foundation"), at para. 39, *cf.*, *Jacobi v. Griffiths*, [1999] 2 S.C.R. 570, 174 D.L.R. (4th) 71. See also *Lister v. Hesley Hall Ltd.*, [2001] U.K.H.L. 22, [2001] 2 All E.R. 769, at para. 28 (*per* Lord Steyn), "The question is whether the warden's torts were so closely connected with his employment that it would be fair and just to hold the employers vicariously liable."; see also *G.(E.D.) v. Hammer* (2001), 4 C.C.L.T. (3d) 204 (B.C.C.A.), school not liable for janitor's sex abuse.

[220] *Toronto General Hospital v. Matthews*, [1972] S.C.R. 435, 25 D.L.R. (3d) 241.

[221] See Fleming, *supra*, n. 212, p. 419.

[222] *671122 Ontario Ltd. v. Sagaz Industries Canada Inc.*, *supra*, n. 212, at para. 35.

[223] *Lewis (Guardian ad litem of) v. British Columbia*, [1997] 3 S.C.R. 1145, 153 D.L.R. (4th) 594; *Mochinski v. Trendline Industries Ltd.*, [1997] 3 S.C.R. 1176, 154 D.L.R. (4th) 212; see Fleming, *op.cit.*, n. 212, at p. 434; *B.(M.) v. British Columbia* (2001), 4 C.C.L.T. (3d) 163 (B.C.C.A.), Crown owes non-delegable duty to foster children.

Chapter 15

Nuisance

The tort of nuisance, though largely misunderstood in the past and though largely supplanted by legislation in recent years, is still very much alive in Canada today. Part of the problem is that nuisance has often been confused with trespass, *Rylands v. Fletcher*, and negligence. Moreover, courts have employed the nuisance concept to regulate "a group of disparate sins ranging . . . from unwitting and indirect interference with proprietary interests in land on the one hand, to the negligent causation of personal injury to users of the highway on the other, with no obvious touchstones for contrasting or comparing situations".[1] It is not really as bad as all that. As in every area of the law, there are some basic principles that can be discerned from the case law that furnish a central core or rationality to the law of nuisance, despite some instances of lingering irrationality.

Nuisance is a field of liability. It describes a type of harm that is suffered, rather than a kind of conduct that is forbidden.[2] In general, a nuisance is an unreasonable interference with the use and enjoyment of land by its occupier or with the use and enjoyment of a public right to use and enjoy public rights of way. For the most part, whether the intrusion resulted from intentional, negligent or non-faulty conduct is of no consequence, as long as the harm can be categorized as a nuisance. This is understandable if one considers that the French word *nuisance*, derived from the Latin *nocumentum*, which means annoyance, inconvenience, or hurt, was imported unchanged into English law.[3]

Underlying the present law of nuisance is the Latin maxim *sic utere tuo ut alienum non laedas* (use your own property so as not to injure that of your neighbours). This basic principle gives some coherence to the otherwise confusing case law in this area. Basically, what the courts are doing here is

---

[1] McLaren, "Nuisance in Canada", in Linden (ed.), *Studies in Canadian Tort Law* (Toronto: Butterworths, 1968), pp. 325, 321. See generally Bilson, *The Canadian Law of Nuisance* (1991).

[2] Fleming, *The Law of Torts*, 9th ed. (1998), p. 457; *Pugliese v. National Capital Commn.* (1977), 3 C.C.L.T. 18; affd but vard, 8 C.C.L.T. 69 (S.C.C.).

[3] See *Prosser and Keeton on the Law of Torts*, 5th ed. (1984), p. 624. See Spencer, "Public Nuisance — a Critical Examination", [1989] Camb. L.J. 55, for some interesting history.

furnishing compensation to those whose use and enjoyment of private land or public rights is being interfered with by the unreasonable use of another's land.

The source of the confusion is largely historical, as is so often the case. There are, through accidents of history, two different kinds of nuisance — public nuisance and private nuisance. Public nuisance began its career as a crime, and still is punishable as such in Canada today.[4] The gravamen of the offence was the blocking of public highways or encroachments on the royal domain. These public or common nuisances, as they were sometimes called, were expanded to include smoke from factories and pollution of rivers which inconvenienced the public generally.[5] It was not until the sixteenth century that a private right to sue for public nuisance was first recognized.[6] Private nuisance, on the other hand, developed separately from the old assize of nuisance in the thirteenth century, which was also a criminal writ, but one which permitted damages to be awarded to private individuals for invasions of their land because of things being done on nearby land. This remedy was supplanted eventually by the action on the case for nuisance, the parent of today's private nuisance action. It is, therefore, not difficult to understand why this is still a hazy area.

Nuisance law — in its public and private forms — now covers a wide range of objectionable activities, such as noise,[7] vibrations, noxious odours, air and water pollution.[8] Its scope has been extended to regulate obstruction of streets and highways, dangerous structures, and interference with riparian rights.[9] Using more modern terminology, nuisance law has become a citizen's weapon in the battle for a better environment.[10] The primary struggle is now a legislative and administrative one, for many statutes, both federal and provincial, have been enacted supplying public officials with wide powers to control all forms of pollution.[11] Some doubts have been expressed about the efficacy of the new anti-

---

[4]   Criminal Code, R.S.C. 1985, c. C-46, s. 180.

[5]   Winfield, "Nuisance as a Tort" (1931), 4 Camb. L.J. 189; Newark, "The Boundaries of Nuisance" (1949), 65 L.Q. Rev. 480.

[6]   Prosser, *op. cit. supra*, n. 3, at p. 618.

[7]   See Silverman and Evans, "Aeronautical Noise in Canada" (1972), 10 Osgoode Hall L.J. 607; Fitzgerald, "Aircraft Noise in the Vicinity of Aerodromes and Sonic Boom" (1971), 21 U. of T.L.J. 226.

[8]   Van Vliet *et al.*, "Geophysical Damage to Property and Related Problems" (1966), 5 Alta. L.R. 29; Elder (ed.), *Environmental Management and Public Participation* (1976); Anisman, "Water Pollution Control in Ontario" (1972), 5 Ott. L. Rev. 342; Landis, "Legal Controls of Pollution in the Great Lakes" (1970), 48 Can. Bar Rev. 66.

[9]   LaForest, "Riparian Rights in New Brunswick" (1960), 3 Can. Bar J. 135.

[10] McLaren, "The Common Law Nuisance Actions and the Environmental Battle" (1972), 10 Osgoode Hall L.J. 505; McLaren, "The Law of Torts and Pollution" in Law Society of Upper Canada, Special Lectures on *New Developments in the Law of Torts* (1973). Ironically, the remedy can be used against protesters like those opposing logging, see *International Forest Products Ltd. v. Kern* (2000), 78 B.C.L.R. (3d) 168 (S.C.).

[11] Environmental Protection Act, R.S.O. 1990, c. E.19. See also *Friends of Oldman River Society v. Canada (Minister of Transport)*, [1992] 1 S.C.R. 3; see also Law Reform Commission of Canada, *Pollution Control in Canada* (Working Paper 44, 1985).

pollution legislation,[12] and calls for greater public participation have been issued.[13] Consequently, the legislative system remains imperfect, leaving a complementary role for the private nuisance action, despite its many deficiencies as a technique for improving the environment.[14] Tort law, then, is available to fill in the gaps left by the statutory scheme in this sphere of regulation, as elsewhere. Despite all the legislative activity, therefore, the law of nuisance is far from irrelevant today.

A. Public Nuisance

It is possible to bring a private tort suit for a public nuisance if the claimant has suffered special damage as a result of it.[15] Most of the litigation about public nuisance, however, is conducted in criminal courts or by public officials, such as the attorneys-general, as representative of the common good.

Usually, the phrase "public nuisance" describes a criminal or quasi-criminal offence which involves actual or potential interference with public convenience or welfare.[16] In other words, it is an attack on the rights of the public generally to live their lives unaffected by inconvenience, discomfort and other forms of interference.[17] A public nuisance must materially affect the reasonable comfort and convenience of life of a class of Her Majesty's subjects.[18] It is not necessary to establish that *every* member of the public has been affected, as long as a substantial number is. Whether the number of persons affected is sufficient to be described as a class is a question of fact.[19] One test is to ask whether the nuisance is "so widespread in its range or indiscriminate in its effect that it is not reasonable to expect one person to take proceedings on his own responsibility to put a stop to it, but that it should be taken on the responsibility to the community at large".[20]

The term "public rights" has been given a broad interpretation and encompasses a wide range of interests including the right to fish in public waters,[21] the

---

[12] Good, "Anti-Pollution Legislation and its Enforcement: An Empirical Study" (1971), 6 U.B.C.L. Rev. 271; Law Reform Commission of Canada, *Crimes Against the Environment* (Working Paper 44, 1985).

[13] Emonds, "Participation and the Environment: A Strategy for Democratizing Canada's Environmental Protection Laws" (1975), 13 Osgoode Hall L.J. 783.

[14] Elder, "Environmental Protection through the Common Law" (1973), 12 U.W.O.L. Rev. 107.

[15] Prosser, "Private Action for Public Nuisance" (1966), 52 Va. L. Rev. 997; Spencer, "Public Nuisance — A Critical Examination", [1989] Camb. L.J. 55.

[16] McLaren, *supra*, n. 1.

[17] See Major J. in *Ryan v. Victoria (City)*, [1999] 1 S.C.R. 201.

[18] *Salmond and Heuston on The Law of Torts*, 19th ed. (1987), p. 60.

[19] *Ibid.* See also *Attorney-General v. P.Y.A. Quarries Ltd.*, [1957] 1 All E.R. 894 (C.A.).

[20] *Attorney-General v. P.Y.A. Quarries Ltd.*, *supra*, n. 18, at p. 908 (*per* Denning L.J.). Three people insufficient, *R. v. Lloyd* (1802), 4 Esp. 200, 170 E.R. 691; seven families are enough. *A.G.B.C. ex rel. Eaton v. Haney Speedways Ltd.* (1963), 39 D.L.R. (2d) 48 (B.C.S.C.).

[21] *Attorney-General of British Columbia v. Attorney-General of Canada* (1913), 15 D.L.R. 308, at p. 315 (P.C.) (*per* Lord Haldane); *Attorney-General of Canada v. Attorney-General of Quebec* (1921), 56 D.L.R. 358, at p. 361 (P.C.) (*per* Lord Haldane).

right to navigate public waters free from obstruction,[22] and the right to travel a highway unimpeded.[23] Less well-defined are interests such as interference with public health, public morals,[24] public comfort[25] or the breach of a public right created by statute.[26] Public nuisance may be caused by such disparate things as an oil spill,[27] a railway track on a city street endangering motorcyclists,[28] a backed up sewer,[29] or by noise from light aircraft.[30] Thus, although the entire population need not be affected, a public nuisance must relate to an interest common to all.[31]

A proceeding in respect of a public nuisance, whether civil or criminal, is normally commenced by the official representative of that public interest. Thus, a criminal prosecution may lie for "common nuisance", an indictable offence under the Criminal Code for which a penalty of up to two years may be imposed.[32] The prosecution is generally conducted by the Attorney-General,[33] since private prosecutions are strictly circumscribed.[34] Even so, a private

---

22 *Wood v. Esson* (1884), 9 S.C.R. 239, at p. 243 (*per* Strong J.).
23 *Iverson v. Moore* (1699), 91 E.R. 1224.
24 Prostitution on streets is public nuisance, *A.G.B.C. v. Couillard* (1985), 31 C.C.L.T. 26 (B.C.S.C.).
25 *Attorney-General of Ontario v. Orange Productions* (1971), 21 D.L.R. (3d) 257 (Ont.), application for interim injunction to restrain the defendants from holding an outdoor music or rock festival.
26 *Attorney-General v. Bastow*, [1957] 1 All E.R. 497, at p. 500 (Q.B.) (*per* Devlin J.), prohibited use of land for habitation. The authority of the Attorney-General to seek injunctive relief, even though the statute prescribes a remedy, is canvassed in *Attorney-General v. Chaudry*, [1971] 1 W.L.R. 1614, 1623 (C.A.).
27 *R. v. The Ship "Sun Diamond"* (1983), 25 C.C.L.T. 19 (F.C.T.D.).
28 See *Ryan, supra*, n. 17.
29 *Clemmens v. Kenora (Town)* (1999), 6 M.P.L.R. (3d) 59 (Ont. S.C.J.).
30 *A.G. Man. v. Adventure Flight Centres* (1983), 25 C.C.L.T. 295 (Man. Q.B.).
31 Estey, "Public Nuisance and Standing to Sue" (1972), 10 Osgoode Hall L.J. 563, at p. 564.
32 Section 180 of the Criminal Code, R.S.C. 1985, c. C-46 reads:
    (1) Every one who commits a common nuisance and thereby
        (a) endangers the lives, safety or health of the public, or
        (b) causes physical injury to any person,
            is guilty of an indictable offence and liable to imprisonment for a term not exceeding two years.
    (2) For the purposes of this section, every one commits a common nuisance who does an unlawful act or fails to discharge a legal duty and thereby
        (a) endangers the lives, safety, health, property or comfort of the public; or
        (b) obstructs the public in the exercise or enjoyment of any right that is common to all the subjects of Her Majesty in Canada.
33 This jurisdiction apparently derives from the historical right of the sovereign to intervene to protect public rights and to prevent public injuries in the capacity of *parens patriae*. The sovereign's proper legal representative in the courts is the Attorney-General who appears on behalf of the Crown: see Robertson, *The Law and Practice of Civil Proceedings By and Against the Crown* (1908).
34 Barton and Peel, *Criminal Procedure in Practice* (1979), pp. 58-60. As to the circumstances and the extent to which "private prosecutions" can be conducted, see *R. v. Schwerdt* (1957), 23 W.W.R. 374 (B.C.); *R. v. Powell*, [1938] 1 W.W.R. 347 (Alta. C.A.); *R. v. Unwin*, [1938] 1

prosecutor can only proceed with the knowledge and under the control of the Crown.[35]

In the case of civil proceedings, the Attorney-General also has the responsibility for commencing an action to enjoin the continuance of a public nuisance.[36] As long as the suffering or inconvenience is general and uniformly injurious, there is no place for an independent action by private citizens, either as individuals or in a group.[37] The role of ordinary individuals is merely to urge the government to act, and it is in this sense that public nuisance is "within the ambit of administrative discretion".[38]

Private citizens are entitled to sue for public nuisance by way of civil action in tort, only if it causes "special damage" to them, over and above the general suffering or inconvenience to the public.[39] In other words, individual tort claimants must demonstrate that the injury or damage suffered has placed them in a different position than other members of the public. The rationale for this is, apparently, that a wrongdoer should not be punished "one hundred times for the same cause".[40] Another concern may have been to reduce claims for trivial losses.

The phrase "special damage" is not used in the traditional sense of calculable pecuniary loss; rather, what is meant is "particular" damage, that is, a special

---

W.W.R. 339 (Alta. C.A.); *R. ex rel. McLeod v. Boulding*, [1920] 3 W.W.R. 52 (Sask. C.A.); Law Reform Commission of Canada, *Private Prosecutions* (Working Paper 52, 1986).

[35] Estey, *supra*, n. 31, at p. 566.

[36] *Ibid.*; McLaren, "Nuisance in Canada", *supra*, n. 1, at pp. 325-26. The provincial Attorney-General is the proper authority to commence civil proceedings: *Cairns v. Canadian Refining Co.* (1913), 25 O.W.R. 384; revd 26 O.W.R. 490 (C.A.); *Ontario (Attorney General) v. Dieleman* (1994), 117 D.L.R. (4th) 449 (Ont. Gen. Div.); *Oak Bay v. Gardner* (1914), 17 D.L.R. 802 (B.C.C.A.); *St. Lawrence Rendering Co. v. Cornwall*, [1951] 4 D.L.R. 790 (Ont.); *Grant v. St. Lawrence Seaway Authority*, [1960] O.R. 298 (C.A.). The Attorney-General for Canada is the proper authority where the matter lies within federal jurisdiction. *Attorney-General of Canada v. Brister*, [1943] 3 D.L.R. 50 (N.S.).

[37] *Turtle v. Toronto* (1924), 56 O.L.R. 252 (C.A.). However, a private citizen may join with the Attorney-General in a "relator" capacity, see *Oak Bay v. Gardner*, *supra*, n. 36; *Grant v. St. Lawrence Seaway Authority*, *supra*, n. 36.

[38] McLaren, *supra*, n. 1, at p. 326; Estey, *supra*, n. 31, at p. 567. The Attorney-General's ability to act is, therefore, not contingent upon the existence of a relator and, indeed, the common practice appears to be for the Attorney-General to act on own initiative. The exercise of this discretion is not subject to judicial review, *Grant v. St. Lawrence Seaway Authority*, *supra*, n. 36; *McLeod v. White* (1955), 37 M.P.R. 341 (N.B.); *Attorney-General v. Brister*, *supra*, n. 36.

[39] Fleming, *The Law of Torts*, 9th ed. (1998), p. 460; *Canada Paper Co. v. Brown* (1922), 63 S.C.R. 243; *Turtle v. Toronto*, *supra*, n. 34; *Whaley v. Kelsey*, [1928] 2 D.L.R. 268 (Ont. C.A.); *Filion v. New Brunswick International Paper Co.*, [1934] 3 D.L.R. 22 (N.B.C.A.). Stated another way, the action shall be brought by the Attorney-General unless a private individual can prove that (1) the interference with the public right is concomitantly an interference with a private right of the individual, or (2) a statute has given the individual a special protection or benefit which has been invaded, or (3) the individual can show some particular direct damage over and above that incurred by the rest of the community, *McLeod v. White*, *supra*, n. 38, at p. 358 citing *Halsbury's Laws of England*, 2nd ed., at pp. 13-15. See also Estey, *supra*, n. 31, at p. 568; *Stein et al. v. Gonzales et al.*, [1984] 6 W.W.R. 428, 14 D.L.R. (4th) 263, 31 C.C.L.T. 19 (B.C.S.C.).

[40] *Walsh v. Ervin*, [1952] V.L.R. 361.

loss suffered by an individual which is not shared by the rest of the community. It was once said that the loss must be different in kind and degree, but the more modern view is that recovery is permitted in either case, as long as the damage to the plaintiff is "more than mere infringement of a theoretical right which the plaintiff shares with everyone else".[41] Thus, where there is personal injury or damage to a chattel or loss of profits from a commercial operation as a result of the public nuisance, this is actionable as special damage.[42]

The distinction presents problems. In *Hickey v. Electric Reduction Co. of Canada Ltd.*,[43] relief was denied to fishermen who lost business income as the result of the discharge of poisonous waste from the defendant's phosphorous plant into Placenta Bay, Newfoundland. The court held that, since the right to fish in the sea and public navigable waters was free and open to all, the plaintiffs could not show any "peculiar damage". Their right, said the court, was "a right in common with all Her Majesty's subjects", and, consequently, not particular, and, hence, actionable only at the suit of the Attorney-General.[44] Much to be preferred is the reasoning in an American decision,[45] which permitted commercial fishermen and clam diggers to recover since they had a "special interest" worthy of protection from the action of the defendant in discharging oil into the bay. This special interest emanated from the fact that the pecuniary loss they suffered was different in kind, because the plaintiffs had an "established business making a commercial use of the public right" with which the defendant interfered. Perhaps the *Hickey* case could be distinguished on the ground that the fishermen were the community, to all intents and purposes, so that there was no special group suffering any different loss than they did.[46]

The private action for public nuisance is frequently encountered where the plaintiff is injured or where the plaintiff's chattel is damaged by reason of a dangerous condition of property near a highway. Thus, for example, where a wall adjoining a highway collapses and injures a boy, he will be allowed to recover for public nuisance.[47] This would be the case even if the plaintiff had not actually been on the defendant's property when hurt but near the highway.[48] If a long way from the road, however, the plaintiff could not recover for public nuisance,[49] but would have to rely on negligence law.

---

[41] Fleming, *op. cit. supra*, n. 39, at p. 462.

[42] McLaren, *supra*, n. 1, at p. 331. *Cf.*, Estey, *supra*, n. 31, at p. 568.

[43] (1971), 21 D.L.R. (3d) 368 (Nfld.). See also *Stein v. Gonzales, supra*, n. 39, prostitution on street not cause of special damage to shop owner; *cf.*, *Tate and Lyle Industries Ltd. v. Greater London Council*, [1983] 1 All E.R. 1159 (H.L.), river obstruction affecting business is special damage.

[44] *Filion v. N.B. International Paper*, [1934] 3 D.L.R. 22. See also *Re Exxon Valdez* (1997), 104 F.3d 1196 (9th Cir.), no special harm suffered by native Alaskans compared to other Alaskans.

[45] *Burgess v. M/V Tamano* (1973), 370 F. Supp. 247 (U.S.D.C.), but note that local business people were denied compensation because their loss of customers was only indirect and, consequently, the loss was only one that was greater in degree.

[46] McLaren, "The Law of Torts and Pollution", *supra*, n. 10, at p. 314.

[47] *Mint v. Good*, [1951] 1 K.B. 517.

[48] *Harrold v. Watney*, [1898] 2 Q.B. 320 (C.A.).

[49] *Hardcastle v. S. Yorkshire Ry.* (1859), 157 E.R. 761.

Another situation where civil liability for public nuisance is often imposed is where a highway is obstructed and an accident ensues as a result. In *Ware v. Garston Haulage Co.*,[50] the plaintiff motorcyclist collided with a truck, which was unlighted and unattended on a highway at night. In the action which followed, liability was imposed on the ground that "If any thing is placed on a highway being an obstruction to those who are using the highway on lawful occasions . . . and an accident results, there is an actionable nuisance." This decision has been criticized,[51] but it has not been overruled.

The principle will not protect a snowmobiler, traveling on a frozen river, who collides with a wharf because, although the "importance of highways as a mode of transportation has merited recognition from earliest time" . . . , "rights of passage on water are not as rigidly protected".[52]

Later cases have limited the application of the principle. In *Maitland v. Raisbeck*,[53] a slow-moving truck whose rear-light was out, without any fault on the part of its driver, was hit by a bus. It was explained that such an obstruction does not by itself create a nuisance. The court declared that a nuisance is established only if someone "allows the obstruction to continue for an unreasonable time or in unreasonable circumstances, but the mere fact that an obstruction has come into existence cannot turn it into a nuisance. It must depend on the facts of each case whether or not a nuisance is created."[54] Consequently, long-term obstructions of the highway may amount to public nuisances but short-term ones, especially if there is no negligence involved, will not.[55]

The tendency in Canada has been to handle these public nuisance cases as if the obligation of the landowner was to use reasonable care. Thus negligence should be demonstrated where something falls from a building,[56] where a fence falls,[57] where water escapes and freezes on the sidewalk,[58] or where smoke from burning straw obstructs the view of a motorist on the adjoining highway.[59]

Apart from the question of duration, the nature of the delay or inconvenience must be of a "substantial character, direct and not merely consequential"[60] so as

---

[50] [1944] 1 K.B. 30.
[51] Laskin, Comment (1944), 22 Can. Bar Rev. 468.
[52] *Chessie v. J.D. Irving Ltd.* (1982), 22 C.C.L.T. 89, at p. 95 (N.B.C.A.) (*per* La Forest J.A.).
[53] [1944] K.B. 689 (C.A.).
[54] *Ibid.*, at p. 692.
[55] *Arm River Enterprises v. McIvor* (1978), 85 D.L.R. (3d) 758; *Assie v. Saskatchewan Telecommunications* (1979), 90 D.L.R. (3d) 410, 7 C.C.L.T. 39.
[56] *Marchyshyn v. Fane Auto Works*, [1932] 1 W.W.R. 689. See also *Ross et al. v. Wall et al.* (1980), 14 C.C.L.T. 243 (B.C.C.A.), awning falling on sidewalk; *Assie v. Saskatchewan Telecommunications, supra*, n. 55, electric guy wires over highway.
[57] *Cowan v. Harrington*, [1938] 3 D.L.R. 271.
[58] *Hagen v. Goldfarb* (1961), 28 D.L.R. (2d) 746; *Mussett v. Reitmans (Ontario) Ltd.*, [1955] 3 D.L.R. 780.
[59] *Zaruk v. Schroderus* (1976), 71 D.L.R. (3d) 216.
[60] *Walsh v. Ervin, supra*, n. 40, at p. 369 (*per* Sholl J.); *Vanderpant v. Mayfair Hotel Co. Ltd.*, [1930] 1 Ch. 138, at p. 154.

to be in keeping with the notion of special damage.[61] Further, every obstruction will not constitute a public nuisance because the law must hold an even balance between the conflicting claims of those who have an interest in the use of the highway.[62] It has been said that the law relating to the user of the highway is, in truth, the law of give and take, since the user must expect to be exposed to some inevitable risk of inconvenience and discomfort.[63] Thus, a person has the right to obstruct a highway with scaffolding and hoarding for the purpose of repairing a house[64] so long as the inconvenience to the public is reasonably necessary.[65] Similarly, a person may temporarily obstruct the highway by parking to let off passengers, by laying a horsepipe across it,[66] or by digging a temporary trench[67] for the purpose of obtaining water.

Public nuisance has been used to prevent prostitution on the streets of Vancouver, for instance, when Chief Justice McEachern granted an injunction forbidding it in a particular area of the city, proclaiming proudly that "if the legislative branch of the government has failed in this regard (that is, combating prostitution on the streets of Vancouver), the common law will not be found wanting".[68] A similar effort by a group of business people from the area to which the prostitutes had moved following the injunction order was unsuccessful, however, as they could not prove that they had suffered special damage.[69] The courts of Nova Scotia, on the other hand, refused to exercise their discretion in this way, in part because it was "an attempt to control prostitution rather than for the purposes of abating a public nuisance".[70]

It appears that the categories of public nuisance remain open. Residents living near a new runway at an airport tried to launch a class action alleging noise pollution.[71] Other residents tried to combat a land-fill site.[72] In the U.S. street gangs have been sued by cities in an effort to clean up the streets and make them safer.[73]

---

[61] Fleming, *op. cit. supra*, n. 39, at p. 412.

[62] *Harper v. G.N. Haden & Sons Ltd.*, [1933] Ch. 298, at p. 320 (*per* Romer L.J.).

[63] *Ibid.*, at p. 316.

[64] *Ibid.*

[65] *Almeroth v. Chivers Ltd.*, [1948] 1 All E.R. 53, pile of slates left at side of curb for collection held to be a nuisance in the absence of any evidence that this was a necessary means of carrying out work.

[66] *Trevett v. Lee*, [1955] 1 W.L.R. 113 (C.A.).

[67] *Wall v. Morrissey*, [1969] I.R. 10.

[68] *A.G.B.C. v. Couillard, supra*, n. 24, at p. 34.

[69] *Stein v. Gonzales* (1985), 31 C.C.L.T. 19 (B.C.S.C.).

[70] *A.G.N.S. v. Beaver* (1985), 32 C.C.L.T. 170 (N.S.C.A.); see also Cassels, "Prostitution and Public Nuisance: Desperate Measures and the Limits of Civil Adjudication" (1985), 63 Can. Bar Rev. 764; Klar, "Recent Developments in Canadian Law: Tort Law" (1985), 17 Ott. L. Rev. 325; MacLauchlan, "Criminal Law Meets the Civil Law" (1985), 42 C.R. (3d) 284.

[71] *Sutherland v. Canada (Attorney General)* (1997), 15 C.P.C. (4th) 329 (B.C.S.C.), but class not certified because of individual issues.

[72] *Hollick v. Toronto (City)* (1999), 46 O.R. (3d) 257 (C.A.), no common issue, but leave to appeal to S.C.C. granted.

[73] *People ex. rel. Gallo v. Acuna*, 929 P.2d 596 (1997 Cal.).

Protesters have been sued when they blocked access to an abortion clinic[74] and to logging operations[75] and when, as a self-proclaimed "poop patrol", they sought to impede the use of the roads near a hog farm to transport malodorous manure.[76]

B. Private Nuisance

Private nuisance may be defined as an unreasonable interference with the use and enjoyment of land. This may come about by physical damage to the land, interference with the exercise of an easement, or with mineral rights[77] *profit à prendre* or other similar right, or injury to the health, comfort or convenience of the occupier.[78] In short, it is an environmental tort.[79] The use of the term "unreasonable" indicates that the interference must be such as would not be tolerated by the ordinary occupier. The court need not, therefore, be concerned with the effect of the defendant's conduct on any other members of the community, other than the occupier.[80] Mr. Justice LaForest has recently explained that actionable nuisances include "only those inconveniences that materially interfere with ordinary comfort as defined according to the standards held by those of plain and sober tastes", that is, it shields only against "interferences to their enjoyment of property that were unreasonable in the light of all the circumstances".[81]

The harm in nuisance cases is normally caused indirectly, in contrast to trespass which arises from the direct, physical invasion by the defendant or some tangible object. The injury in nuisance, then, is often termed "consequential". In nuisance, actual damage is an essential element to be proved, whereas trespass is actionable without proof of damage.[82]

Responsibility for private nuisance is not restricted to the occupiers of adjoining lands. Anyone who actively creates a nuisance, whether or not in occupation of the land from which it emanates, can be liable and this "liability continues so long as the offensive condition remains regardless of his ability to abate it and stop the harm".[83]

The onus of proof that the defendant caused an unreasonable interference with the use and enjoyment of the plaintiff's land rests on the plaintiff, but once

---

[74] *Ontario (Attorney General) v. Dieleman* (1994), 117 D.L.R. (4th) 449 (Ont. Gen. Div.).

[75] See *International Forest Products, supra*, n. 10.

[76] *Metz Farms v. Committee Against Hog Factories* (2001), N.B.J. No. 62 (C.A.).

[77] *Falkoski v. Osoyoos (Town)* (1998), 46 M.P.L.R. (2d) 215 (B.C.S.C.), new residential development approved by town hindered plaintiff's access to his mineral rights.

[78] See *Salmond and Heuston on The Law of Torts*, 19th ed. (1989), p. 59; Fleming, *The Law of Torts*, 9th ed. (1998), p. 464.

[79] Gearty, "The Place of Private Nuisance in a Modern Law of Torts," [1989] Cambridge L.J. 214, at p. 215, advocating the use of nuisance merely to protect property from non-physical damage.

[80] *Cairns v. Canadian Refining Co.* (1914), 6 O.W.N. 562 (C.A.).

[81] See *Tock v. St. John's Metropolitan Area Bd.*, [1989] 2 S.C.R. 1181, at p. 1191.

[82] McLaren, *supra*, n. 1, at p. 338.

[83] Fleming, *op. cit. supra*, n. 78, at p. 476.

that is shown, the onus is on the defendant to establish that the use of the land was reasonable.[84]

1. UNREASONABLE INTERFERENCE

In determining whether there has been an unreasonable interference with the use and enjoyment of the plaintiff's land, the court balances the gravity of the harm caused against the utility of the defendant's conduct in all the circumstances. As for the harm element, the court examines the type and severity of the interference, its duration, the character of the neighborhood and the sensitivity of the plaintiff's use. As for the conduct of the defendant, the court looks at the object of the activity undertaken and the attitude of the actor towards the neighbours.[85]

a) Type and Severity of Harm

The interference caused to the plaintiff's use of the land must be substantial. No compensation will be awarded for trivial annoyances. If tangible damage is caused by the defendant, the court is more likely to brand it as a nuisance, as where chemicals emitted from the defendant's foundry damaged the paint on vehicles in the plaintiff's yard,[86] where salt on roads contaminated well water causing the loss of nursery stock,[87] or where the defendant's driving of trucks on a dirt road damaged a house and made it impossible to cultivate land.[88]

Damages for injury to health may be recovered in an action for nuisance if there is also interference with the use and enjoyment of land,[89] but it is still unclear whether, standing alone, personal injury is actionable under nuisance theory.

If the defendant's conduct causes only an inconvenience or a minor discomfort to the plaintiff, it is unlikely that the court will hold it to be a private nuisance as the *Restatement of Torts* explains:

> Life in organized society and especially in populous communities involves an unavoidable clash of individual interests. Practically all human activities, unless carried on in a wilderness, interfere to some extent with others or involve some risk of interference, and these interferences range from trifling annoyances to serious harms. It is an obvious truth that each individual in a community must put up with a certain amount of annoyance, inconvenience,

---

[84] *Radstock Co-Op & Industrial Society v. Norton Radstock Urban District Council*, [1968] Ch. 605 (C.A.).

[85] McLaren, *supra*, n. 1, p. 346.

[86] *Russell Transport v. Ontario Malleable Iron*, [1952] O.R. 621; see also *St. Helen's Smelting v. Tipping* (1865), 11 H.L.C. 642, 11 E.R. 1483; *Scarborough Golf & Country Club v. City of Scarborough* (1986), 55 O.R. (2d) 193, at p. 232 (*per* Cromarty J.), water damaged golf club.

[87] *Phillips v. Brockville (City)* (1999), 5 M.P.L.R. (3d) 173 (Ont. S.C.J.).

[88] *Kent v. Dominion Steel & Coal Co.* (1965), 49 D.L.R. (2d) 241; *Schenck v. Ontario* (1981), 20 C.C.L.T. 128; additional reasons 23 C.C.L.T. 14; affd 15 D.L.R. (4th) 320 (C.A.); affd [1987] 2 S.C.R. 289, salt on winter roads damaging fruit trees.

[89] *Bottom v. Ontario Leaf Tobacco Co.*, [1935] O.R. 205 (C.A.). See also *Morris v. Dominion Foundries & Steel*, [1947] O.W.N. 413; *Muirhead v. Timber Bros. Sand & Gravel* (1977), 3 C.C.L.T. 1 (Ont.).

and interference, and must take a certain amount of risk in order that all may get on together. The very existence of organized society depends on the principle of "give and take, live and let live", so that the law of torts does not attempt to impose liability or shift the loss in every case where one person's conduct has some detrimental effect on another. Liability is imposed only in those cases where the harm or risk to one is greater than he ought to be required to bear under the circumstances.[90]

Whether an annoyance is trifling and must be put up with or whether it is serious and actionable is not always easy to determine. It is clear that "not all amenities . . . commonly associated with beneficial use of land are vindicated by the law of private nuisance".[91] Thus, just because a person's peace of mind may be affected, an action in nuisance does not necessarily lie. For example, the use of land for an isolation hospital, however unpopular and disconcerting that may be, rarely amounts to a nuisance.[92] To interfere with a person's view or privacy by building a highway next to their land is no nuisance.[93] Neither is a nuisance caused if the defendant fails to preserve the aesthetic appearance of a land for the neighbour's benefit.[94] Nor is it a nuisance to spy on someone from a distance.[95] The ordinary use of poorly-constructed residential property, even if it is noisy, is not a nuisance.[96]

On the other hand, it has been held that a bawdy house could be a nuisance,[97] as could be an offensive odour from a piggery,[98] or a mushroom farm,[99] dust from a sawmill,[100] and noise from a go-kart club[101] or a corporate recreation area in a rural location.[102] So, too, some American courts have branded funeral parlours as potential nuisances.[103]

---

[90] See 4 *Restatement of Torts, Second,* Comment "G", p. 112. Copyright 1965 by The American Law Institute. Reprinted with the permission of the American Law Institute. See also *Bamford v. Turnley* (1862), 3 B. & S. 66, 122 E.R. 27 (Ex.).

[91] Fleming, *op. cit. supra,* n. 78, p. 467.

[92] See *Shuttleworth v. Vancouver General Hospital,* [1927] 2 D.L.R. 573; *Cf., Metropolitan Asylum District v. Hill* (1881), 6 App. Cas. 193, smallpox hospital held to be nuisance.

[93] *St. Pierre v. Ontario,* [1987] 1 S.C.R. 906, 39 D.L.R. (4th) 10, 40 C.C.L.T. 200. See also *Jagtoo v. 407 E.T.R. Concession Co.,* [1999] O.J. No. 4944, unsuccessful effort to have Highway 407 declared a nuisance.

[94] *Walker v. Pioneer Construction Co. (1967) Ltd.* (1975), 8 O.R. (2d) 35; *Muirhead v. Timber Bros. Sand & Gravel, supra,* n. 78. See also Silverstone, "Visual Pollution: Unaesthetic Use of Land as Nuisance" (1974), 12 Alta. L. Rev. 542, for an argument in opposition to this view.

[95] *Victoria Park Racing & Recreation Grounds Co. v. Taylor* (1937), 58 C.L.R. 479, but *cf., Poole v. Ragen,* [1958] O.W.N. 77, police enjoined from shadowing plaintiff's boat as it travelled across harbour.

[96] *Southwark London Borough Council v. Mills,* [1999] 4 All E.R. 449 (H.L.) (*per* Lord Hoffman).

[97] *Thompson-Schwab v. Costaki,* [1956] 1 W.L.R. 335.

[98] *Sullivan v. Desrosiers* (1986), 40 C.C.L.T. 66 (N.B.C.A.); *Fogarty v. Daurie* (1986), 40 C.C.L.T. 48 (N.S.C.A.).

[99] *Pike v. Tri Gro Enterprises Ltd.,* [1999] O.J. No. 3217 (S.C.).

[100] *MacNeill v. Devon Lumber Co.* (1987), 42 C.C.L.T. 192 (N.B.C.A.).

[101] *Tetley v. Chitty,* [1986] 1 All E.R. 663.

[102] *Ward v. Magna International Inc.* (1994), 21 C.C.L.T. (2d) 178 (Ont. Gen. Div.).

[103] *Kundinger v. Bagnas Co.* (1941), 298 N.W. 386 (Mich.).

It has been proclaimed by Mr. Justice Robins in *Nor-Video Services Ltd. v. Ontario Hydro*,[104] that the "category of interests covered by the tort of nuisance ought not to be and need not be closed . . . to new or changing developments associated from time to time with normal usage and enjoyment of land". Consequently, although once thought to be insignificant,[105] the right to receive television signals was held to be within the legitimate scope of protection of nuisance law. In the *Nor-Video* case, the plaintiff cable television company sued the defendant authority for locating one of its electrical power installations where it would interfere with the plaintiff's transmission and reception of television broadcast signals. Although only minimal damages were awarded, because there was no proof of any large losses, Robins J. rejected the contention that interference of this nature was not important enough to constitute a legal nuisance:

> . . . it is argued that since the interference in this case is to a "recreational facility" it cannot constitute a sufficient interference with ordinary beneficial enjoyment as to amount to a legal nuisance. With deference I cannot agree. Whatever may have been the situation in England at the time of *Bridlington*, in my opinion it is manifest that in Canada today television viewing is an important incident of ordinary enjoyment of property and should be protected as such. It is clearly a principle source of information, education and entertainment for a large part of the country's population; an inability to receive it or an unreasonable interference with its reception would to my mind undoubtedly detract from the beneficial use and ownership of property even applying the test of "plain, sober and simple notions" referred to in the above passage . . . .
> The notion of nuisance is a broad and comprehensive one which has been held to encompass a wide variety of interferences considered harmful and actionable because of their infringement upon or diminution of an occupier's interest in the undisturbed enjoyment of his property; its social value and utility to a community, perhaps even more so to a remote community such as the one in this case, cannot be doubted.[106]

In the result, the court held that the interests of Hydro in conducting its undertaking did not, in the circumstances, outweigh those of the plaintiff in having its enterprise protected from invasion. Perhaps the use of solar energy for heating purposes will be similarly protected by nuisance law.[107]

Nuisance is usually thought to be a continuing wrong, that is, the establishment or maintenance of some state of affairs which continuously or repeatedly causes the escape of noxious material onto the plaintiff's land.[108] Consequently, the escape of something on a single occasion would not normally be considered

---

[104] (1978), 4 C.C.L.T. 244, at p. 256. See also McIntyre J. in *St. Pierre v. Ontario* (1987), 75 N.R. 291, at p. 301 (S.C.C.) "I do not suggest that the categories of nuisance are or ought to be closed."

[105] *Bridlington Relay Ltd. v. Yorkshire Electricity Bd.*, [1965] Ch. 436.

[106] *Supra*, n. 104, at pp. 255-56. Compare *Hunter v. Canary Wharf Ltd.* [1997] A.C. 655 (H.L.), reaching opposite conclusion.

[107] See Bowden, "Protecting Solar Access in Canada: The Common Law Approach" (1985), 9 Dal. L.J. 261, discussing *Prah v. Moretti*.

[108] *Salmond and Heuston, op. cit. supra*, n. 78, at p. 59.

a nuisance.[109] However, it might be otherwise if this was considered to be evidence of the existence of a potentially dangerous or harmful situation, as where golf balls frequently entered the plaintiff's premises from an adjoining golf club.[110] Thus, a plaintiff has often succeeded in nuisance where there has been only a single escape of a dangerous thing such as sewage,[111] water,[112] gas,[113] metal foil,[114] or fire.[115] In the language of Salmond:

> The truth is that all wrongful escapes of deleterious things, whether continuous, intermittent, or isolated, are equally capable of being classed as nuisances. The type of harm caused by the escape, the gravity of that harm, and the frequency of its occurrence are each relevant (but not conclusive) factors in determining whether the defendant has maintained on his premises a state of affairs which is a potential nuisance.[116]

Thus, a "tolerable balance" must be struck between the competing interests of landowners "each invoking the privilege to exploit the resources and enjoy the amenities of his property without undue subordination to the reciprocal interests of the other".[117] The ultimate question to be asked is whether the defendant is using the property reasonably having regard to the fact that the defendant has a neighbour.

It seems that the courts are less sympathetic where the damage alleged is merely inconvenience or discomfort. It must be shown that there was material interference with "the ordinary comfort physically of human existence, not merely according to elegant or dainty modes and habits of living, but according to plain and sober and simple notions among . . . people".[118]

---

[109] *Bolton v. Stone*, [1950] 1 K.B. 201 (C.A.), where a cricket ball hit out of the playing field struck the plaintiff standing on the highway. The fact that balls only occasionally reached the highway was evidence that no dangerous state of affairs existed. The claim in nuisance was not pursued in the House of Lords; [1951] A.C. 850. But see *Castle v. St. Augustine's Links Ltd.* (1922), 38 T.L.R. 615, golf balls frequently sliced onto highway from adjoining tee a nuisance.

[110] *Segal v. Derrick Golf & Winter Club* (1977), 2 C.C.L.T. 222 (Alta.); *Lester-Travers v. City of Frankston*, [1970] V.R. 2; *Transcona Country Club v. Transcona Golf Club (1982) Inc.*, [2000] 8 W.W.R. 259 (Man. Q.B.).

[111] *Buysse v. Shelburne* (1984), 28 C.C.L.T. 1 (Ont. Div. Ct.).

[112] *Canada (A.G.) v. Ottawa-Carleton (Regional Municipality)* (1991), 5 O.R. (3d) 11 (C.A.); *Scarborough Golf & Country Club v. Scarborough*, supra, n. 86 (*per* Cromarty J.).

[113] *Midwood & Co. Ltd. v. Manchester Corp.*, [1905] 2 K.B. 597; *Northwestern Utilities Ltd. v. London Guarantee & Accident Co. Ltd.*, [1936] A.C. 108.

[114] *British Celanese Ltd. v. A.H. Hunt Ltd.*, [1969] 1 W.L.R. 959.

[115] *Spicer v. Smee*, [1946] 1 All E.R. 498.

[116] *Salmond and Heuston, op. cit. supra*, n. 78, at p. 49. See, for example, *Atwell et al. v. Knights*, [1967] 1 O.R. 419, escape of obnoxious smell from house, frequent but not continuous, held to be private nuisance.

[117] Fleming, *op. cit. supra*, n. 78, p. 467.

[118] *Walter v. Selfe* (1851), 4 De G. & Sm. 315, at p. 322, 64 E.R. 849, at p. 852 (*per* Knight Bruce V.C.), burning of bricks.

b) Character of Locale

The court will also consider the "physical milieu" in which the alleged nuisance exists in order to determine the appropriate standard of tolerance against which to measure the interference. In this regard, reference to relevant zoning legislation is only of limited assistance.[119] The standard to be expected in a predominantly residential area will obviously differ from that in an industrial or commercial one. This idea was well-explained by Thesiger L.J. in *Sturges v. Bridgman.*[120]

> . . . whether anything is a nuisance or not is a question to be determined, not merely by an abstract consideration of the thing itself, but in reference to its circumstances; what would be a nuisance in *Belgrave Square* would not necessarily be so in *Bermondsey*; and where a locality is devoted to a particular trade or manufacture carried on by the traders or manufacturers in a particular and established manner not constituting a public nuisance. Judges and juries would be justified in finding, and may be trusted to find, that the trade or manufacture so carried on in that locality is not a private or actionable wrong.

Thus, while an injunction will be granted to a plaintiff, whose home is in a good residential area, against the use by the defendant of an adjoining house for prostitution,[121] or to people in a quiet rural area against a noisy airport,[122] the court will not enjoin the noise emanating from a stone-cutting operation in a commercial railway area[123] nor from a biscuit factory in a manufacturing section of the city.[124] A miniature racing car ride in downtown Niagara Falls attracted liability because it changed the "character of the neighbourhood noise from noise that is generally not intrusive or irritating to noise that is irritating and intrusive".[125]

The process of determining the proper standard becomes more difficult when the area is one of mixed or changing use, and the tendency of the courts has

---

[119] McLaren, *supra*, n. 1, p. 349. But the fact that the defendant is conducting business in conformance with the use designated by the by-law will not necessarily protect the defendant from an action in nuisance. See *Beamish v. Glenn* (1916), 28 D.L.R. 702 (Ont. C.A.), blacksmith's shop; *Savage v. MacKenzie* (1961), 25 D.L.R. (2d) 175 (N.B.C.A.), junkyard. The converse is, of course, also true, that the breach of a by-law is not *ipso facto* a nuisance. See, *Miller v. Krawitz*, [1931] 2 D.L.R. 784 (Man. K.B.), fox farm in subdivision planned for residential development.

[120] (1879), 11 Ch. D. 852, at p. 865.

[121] *Thompson-Schwab v. Costaki, supra*, n. 97.

[122] *A.G. Man. v. Adventure Flight Centres, supra*, n. 30. On an island without a fire department debris causing a risk of fire is a nuisance, *Turner et al. v. Delta Shelf Co.* (1995), 24 C.C.L.T. (2d) 107 (B.C.S.C.).

[123] *Oakley v. Webb* (1916), 38 O.L.R. 151.

[124] *Hourston v. Brown-Holder Biscuits Ltd.* (1936), 10 M.P.R. 544; affd [1937] 2 D.L.R. 53 (N.B.C.A.); *Osler Developments v. British Columbia*, [2001] B.C.J. No. 111, hotel could not prevent noise from bridge traffic because in industrial area.

[125] *Banfai v. Formula Fun Centre Inc.* (1984), 34 C.C.L.T. 171, at p. 177 (*per* O'Leary J.).

been to attempt to isolate a small area around the properties in question and determine its peculiar character.[126]

Further, although in general the character of the area dictates the expected tolerance level, limits are placed on how far this protection will extend. Thus, in *Appleby v. Erie Tobacco Co.*,[127] the defendant was enjoined from emitting noxious odours from its tobacco factory. It was explained that, although a local standard in a particular district may be higher than in another, "yet the question in each case ultimately reduces itself to the fact of nuisance or no nuisance having regard to all the surrounding circumstances".[128] As it was once expressed by Cozens Hardy L.J.:[129]

> A resident in such a neighbourhood must put up with a certain amount of noise. The standard of comfort differs according to the situation of the property, and the class of people who inhabit it. . . . But whatever the standard of comfort in a particular district may be, I think the addition of a fresh noise caused by the defendant's works may be so substantial as to create a legal nuisance. It does not follow that because I live, say, in the manufacturing part of Sheffield I cannot complain if a steam-hammer is introduced next door, and so worked as to render sleep at night almost impossible, although previously to its introduction my house was a reasonably comfortable abode, having regard to the local standard; and it would be no answer to say that the steam-hammer is of the most modern approved pattern and is reasonably worked. In short . . . it is no answer to say that the neighbourhood is noisy, and that the defendant's machinery is of first-class character.

The severity of damage makes a difference, even in a poor locale. The "class authority" in these cases is to this effect:[130]

> My Lords, in matters of this description it appears to me that it is a very desirable thing to make the difference between an action brought for a nuisance upon the ground that the alleged nuisance produces injury to the property, and an action brought for a nuisance on the ground that the thing alleged to be a nuisance is productive of sensible personal discomfort. With regard to the latter, namely, the personal inconvenience and interference with one's enjoyment, one's quiet, one's personal freedom, anything that discomposes or injuriously affects the senses or the nerves, whether that may or may not be denominated a nuisance, must undoubtedly depend greatly on the circumstances of the place where the thing complained of actually occurs. If a man lives in a town, it is necessary that he should subject himself to the consequences of those operations of trade which may be carried on in his immediate locality, which are actually necessary for trade and commerce, and also for the enjoyment of property, and for the benefit of the inhabitants of the town and of the public at large. If a man lives in a street where there are numerous shops, and a shop is opened next door to him, which is carried on in a fair and reasonable way, he has no ground for complaint, because to himself individually there may arise much discomfort from the trade carried on in that shop. But when an occupation is carried on by one person in the

---

[126] McLaren, *supra*, n. 1, at p. 350.

[127] (1910), 22 O.L.R. 533.

[128] *Ibid.*, at p. 536 (*per* Middleton J.). But see, *Muirhead v. Timber Bros. Sand & Gravel Ltd. et al.*, *supra*, n. 89; *Andreae v. Selfridge & Co. Ltd.*, [1938] Ch. 1, [1937] 3 All E.R. 255 (C.A.).

[129] *Rushmer v. Polsue & Alfieri Ltd.*, [1906] 1 Ch. 234, at p. 250 (C.A.); affd [1907] A.C. 121, cited with approval in *Appleby, supra*, n. 127.

[130] *St. Helen's Smelting Co. v. Tipping* (1865), 11 H.L. Cas. 642, at p. 650, 11 E.R. 1483, as it was described by McRuer C.J.H.C. in *Russell Transport, supra*, n. 86, at p. 628.

neighbourhood of another and a result of that trade, or occupation, or business, *is a material injury to property*, then there unquestionably arises a very different consideration. I think, my Lords, that in a case of that description, the submission which is required from persons living in society to that amount of discomfort which may be necessary for the legitimate and free exercise of the trade of their neighbours, would not apply to circumstances *the immediate result of which is sensible injury to the value of the property.*

Certain interferences may be acceptable during the day, when the city is busy, but not at night, when the city is asleep. In *Walker et al. v. Pioneer Construction Co. (1967) Ltd.*[131] it was held that, while the noise emitted from the defendant's asphalt plant, which was located in a mixed use area, was not a nuisance during normal working hours, the night-time and early-morning operations were quite a different matter, amounting to an actionable nuisance. With regard to this aspect, Morden J. stated:

> . . . In complaining of the noise at night and, with greater relevance on the evidence with re-spect to recent operations, in the early morning, I do not think that "the law of give and take" obliges them to absorb this interference without some form of redress. The character of the neighbourhood is not such that the defendant can reasonably expect to indulge itself during normal sleeping hours as it does during the balance of the day. Apart from the intermittent noises of a traffic flow, of reduced proportions, during the night and the odd train, the evi-dence does not indicate any other significant sources of sound or noise in the area during the night and early morning. This comparative stillness is substantially interrupted by the start-up of the asphalt plant, for the most part at 6 a.m. While it may well be important to the defen-dant, if its interests alone are looked at, to get an early start, it is unreasonable to expect the plaintiffs to put up with the noise at that time or earlier. In this regard, to refer to the lan-guage of Fleming quoted earlier, the defendant is not using its property reasonably having regard to the fact that it has a neighbour.[132]

It is no defence to the plaintiff's claim that the plaintiff came to the nuisance. As McRuer C.J.H.C. stated in *Russell Transport Ltd. v. Ontario Malleable Iron Co. Ltd.*:[133]

> Any argument based on the fact that the nuisance may have existed before the plaintiffs pur-chased their property is completely answered by the statement of Lord Halsbury in *Fleming et al. v. Hislop et al.* (1886), 11 App. Cas. 686, where he said at p. 696: "If the Lord Justice Clerk means to convey that there was anything in the law which diminished the right of a man to complain of a nuisance because the nuisance existed before he went to it, I venture to think that neither in the law of England nor in that of Scotland, is there any foundation for any such contention. It is clear that whether the man went to the nuisance or the nuisance to the man, the rights are the same, and I think that the law in England has been settled, cer-tainly for more than 200 years. . . ."

---

[131] (1975), 8 O.R. (2d) 35.
[132] *Ibid.*, at pp. 49-50.
[133] *Supra*, n. 86, at p. 627. See also Goodearle J. in *Ward v. Magna International Inc.* (1994), 21 C.C.L.T. (2d) 178, at p. 191 (Ont. Gen. Div.), citing this textbook; *Osler Developments, supra*, n. 124, may be a factor though.

c) Abnormal Sensitivity

If the plaintiff's use of property or the plaintiff's own physical or mental make-up is abnormally sensitive, recovery for nuisance may be denied.[134] This follows because the standard employed in determining whether the defendant's activity is an unreasonable interference is an objective one. Thus the defendant's conduct need only be governed with reference to the reactions of normal persons in the particular locality and not with reference to the idiosyncrasies of any particular plaintiff.[135] Where a plaintiff had a large signboard on one building illuminated with advertising material from a "projecto-scope" on another building, and the defendant, which had premises across the street, illuminated its building in such a way that the reflection of its light made it difficult to read the plaintiff's signboard, the plaintiff was denied an injunction because the use of its premises was of an "exceptional and delicate nature", and not in the "class of ordinary or usual business entitled to protection from interference by a neighbouring owner in the exercise of his reasonable rights on his own property".[136] Similarly, there was no nuisance found where the defendant, who manufactured paper boxes requiring hot, dry air, damaged the plaintiff's special quality paper which the defendant warehoused. The latter activity was held to be an "exceptionally delicate trade".[137] Neither can a mink ranch, which is a business of a "delicate and sensitive nature", expect to be protected from activity which would not be considered unreasonable by the ordinary person.[138] Nor can retirees recover for noise from a nearby dog pound, when other neighbours, even closer than they, were not disturbed.[139]

Where the real reason for injury to the plaintiff is the plaintiff's own peculiar physiology and not unreasonable conduct by the defendant, liability in nuisance will be denied since "this branch of the law pays no regard to the special needs of invalids".[140] Thus, a plaintiff, who had an asthmatic condition which was brought on because of contact with the defendant's horses, was not entitled to protection since the condition was one of "abnormal sensitiveness".[141] Damage due to allergies are not compensable.[142]

However, abnormal sensitivity loses its character as a defence where the extent of interference would have been excessive even in normal circum-

---

[134] McLaren, *supra*, n. 1, p. 352.

[135] Fleming, *op. cit. supra*, n. 78, at p. 421.

[136] *Noyes v. Huron & Erie Mortgage Corp.*, [1932] O.R. 426, at p. 431 (*per* Wright J.). For a similar American case, see, *Amphitheatres Inc. v. Portland Meadows et al.* (1948), 198 P.2d 847 (Ore.).

[137] *Robinson v. Kilvert* (1889), 41 Ch.D. 88 (C.A.).

[138] *Rattray v. Daniels* (1959), 17 D.L.R. (2d) 134 (Alta. C.A.).

[139] *Woodman v. Capital (Regional District)*, [1999] B.C.J. No. 2262 (S.C.).

[140] *Bloodworth v. Cormack*, [1949] N.Z.L.R. 1058, at p. 1064.

[141] *O'Regan v. Bresson* (1977), 3 C.C.L.T. 214; *cf.*, *Maker v. Davanne Holdings*, [1955] 1 D.L.R. 728, plaintiff with heart ailment granted injunction to prevent continuous movement of goods of defendant.

[142] *MacNeill v. Devon Lumber Co.*, *supra*, n. 100.

stances,[143] or where the defendant could easily have suspended operations or carried them on in another manner without exposing the plaintiff to the risk of harm.[144]

d) Utility of Defendant's Conduct

In deciding whether there has been unreasonable interference, the court also examines the utility of the defendant's conduct. In general, it is not a requirement of nuisance law to prove that the conduct of the defendant was negligent or intentional. In other words, fault is not a necessary element of nuisance liability. "Put another way, nuisance is not a branch of the law of negligence."[145]

When the courts examine whether there has been an unreasonable interference, they are using the word "reasonable" in a particular way, not in the usual way it is employed in negligence cases. The concept of "unreasonable risk" involves the notion of foreseeable harm to which a reasonable person would not expose others, while unreasonableness in nuisance relates primarily to the character and extent of the harm actually caused. In addition, the "duty" not to expose one's neighbours to a nuisance is not necessarily discharged by exercising reasonable care or even all possible care. In that sense, therefore, nuisance liability is strict.[146] However, the question of whether the defendant took all reasonable precautions is relevant as to whether the plaintiff was subjected to unreasonable interference.[147] These principles were explained by McRuer C.J.H.C. in *Russel Transport*:[148]

> . . . "Reasonable" as used in the law of nuisance must be distinguished from its use elsewhere in the law of tort and especially as it is used in negligence actions. "In negligence, assuming that the duty to take care has been established, the vital question is, 'Did the defendant take reasonable care?' It is true that the result of a long chain of decisions is that unreasonableness is a main ingredient of liability for nuisance. But here 'reasonable' means something more than merely 'taking proper care'. It signifies what is legally right between the parties, taking into account all the circumstances of the case, and some of these circumstances are often such as a man on the Clapham omnibus could not fully appreciate".

Thus, in nuisance, the defendant may make "reasonable" use of property in such a way that a neighbour may be adversely affected, whereas, in negligence, if the defendant has a duty to protect persons such as the plaintiff from the risk

---

[143] *McKinnon Industries Ltd. v. Walker*, [1951] 3 D.L.R. 577, at p. 581 (P.C.) (*per* Lord Simonds), orchids damaged by sulphur dioxide gas.

[144] *MacGibbon v. Robinson*, [1953] 2 D.L.R. 689 (B.C.C.A.), stump blasting near mink farm; *Grandel v. Mason*, [1953] 1 S.C.R. 459, highway construction near mink farm.

[145] Osborne J.A. in *Canada (A.G.) v. Ottawa-Carleton, supra*, n. 112, at p. 20 (C.A.).

[146] *Farrell v. John Mowlem & Co. Ltd.*, [1954] 1 Ll. Rep. 437, at p. 440 (Q.B.); *B.C. Pea Growers Ltd. v. Portage La Prairie* (1964), 49 D.L.R. (2d) 91, at p. 94 (Man. C.A.), affd [1966] S.C.R. 150, 54 D.L.R. (2d) 503; *Atwell v. Knights* (1967), 61 D.L.R. (2d) 108, at p. 110 (Ont.); *Bottom v. Ontario Leaf Tobacco, supra*, n. 89.

[147] See Fleming, *op. cit. supra*, n. 78, p. 471.

[148] *Supra*, n. 86, at p. 629.

of injury of a particular type, liability will attach where the defendant ought to have foreseen such injury resulting as a consequence of conduct. Further, in nuisance, once the interference is shown, the onus rests on the defendant to establish reasonable user.[149]

Perhaps a distinction lies between those nuisances, both continuing and past, of which the parties are aware, and those of which there is no knowledge or perception on the part of the defendant of actual or potential interference with the plaintiff's interests.[150] Thus, it may be, with regard to the latter type of case, that the application of the concept of reasonable use becomes more appropriate. Indeed, it has been suggested that "it is only when negligence has not been or is not likely to be found, that the need to determine the character of the defendant's undertaking becomes crucial to the question of whether liability can be imposed, for it is here that the issue of how far the court can go beyond the fault doctrine becomes a dominant factor in the decision-making process".[151]

The character of the defendant's conduct can be most relevant if it is malicious. Thus, if acts otherwise acceptable are done wantonly and maliciously, the basis of the defence of reasonable user may disappear.[152] For example, an injunction was granted to prevent hammering and beating trays against a party wall, although the noise would not have been sufficient to warrant an injunction had it been made for legitimate purpose, because it was maliciously intended to disrupt a neighbour whose occupation was music teacher.[153] Similarly, damages and an injunction were awarded against a man who directed his son to fire guns on his own land as near as possible to his neighbour's breeding pens in order to frighten silver fox vixen and cause them to refuse to breed and miscarry, although he would have been entitled to shoot on his own land to keep rabbits down or for pleasure[154] So too, a person might be liable in nuisance for persistent telephone calls of a harassing nature, [155] or other acts intended to annoy or harass

---

[149] Fleming, *op. cit. supra*, n. 78, p. 473.

[150] McLaren, *supra*, n. 1, at p. 362.

[151] *Ibid.*, p. 365; McLaren, "The Common Law Nuisance Action & The Environmental Battle" (1972), 10 Osgoode Hall L.J. 505, at pp. 521-28. See *Humphries v. Cousins* (1877), 2 C.P.D. 239; *Esco v. Fort Henry Hotel Co. Ltd.*, [1962] O.R. 1057; *Chandler Electric Co. v. H.H. Fuller & Co.* (1892), 21 S.C.R. 337. McLaren points out that it would be hard for a defendant to plead ignorance with regard to most continuing nuisances as, by the time the matter reaches the courts, the defendant, no doubt, has been fully apprised of the problem. In this context, given the defendant's knowledge, continuation of the nuisance can be characterized as an intentional tort.

[152] Fleming, *op. cit. supra*, n. 78, at p. 472. See *A.G. Man. v. Campbell* (1983), 26 C.C.L.T. 168; affd but vard (1985), 32 C.C.L.T. 57 (Man. C.A.), farmer built tower to obstruct aircraft, held malicious.

[153] *Christie v. Davey*, [1893] 1 Ch. 316.

[154] *Hollywood Silver Fox Farm v. Emmett*, [1936] 1 All E.R. 825.

[155] *Motherwell v. Motherwell* (1977), 73 D.L.R. (3d) 62, [1976] 6 W.W.R. 550 (Alta. C.A.); *Stoakes v. Brydges*, [1958] O.W.N. 5; *Alma v. Nakir*, [1966] 2 N.S.W.R. 396.

a neighbour.[156] It is now clear that the language to the contrary in *Mayor of Bradford v. Pickles*[157] does not apply to nuisance cases.

Another factor courts consider in determining if the conduct is unreasonable is the importance of the defendant's enterprise and its value to the community. Thus, a defendant may be treated less harshly if the defendant's activity is of considerable public value or essential and unavoidable in the particular locality.[158] Hence, to build a highway adjacent to someone's farm is not a nuisance, in spite of the disruption it causes, because highways are needed. "In the balance process inherent in the law of nuisance" explained Mr. Justice McIntyre in the *St. Pierre v. Ontario* case,[159] "their utility for the public good far outweighs the disruption and injury which is visited on some adjoining lands." To hold the government liable for building a road would place an "intolerable burden on the public purse". However, this factor is not given undue weight. Indeed, where tangible damage or injury is suffered, or a significant degree of inconvenience or discomfort is occasioned by a plaintiff, the courts will not shrink from imposing liability[160] however valuable the defendant's enterprise may be.

The main effect of evidence of value to the community is to produce a more lenient attitude toward the remedy given, so that injunctions are less likely to be granted in such circumstances.[161]

In sum, whether there has been an unreasonable interference with the use and enjoyment of the plaintiff's land is a question of judgment based on all the facts in the circumstances. As is so often the case in tort law, much is left to the good sense of the judge to arrive at an appropriate decision after weighing the various factors, such as extent of harm, the nature of the locality, the type of use by the plaintiff and the quality of the defendant's conduct. As a result there are no definitive guidelines for the courts here, which certainly breeds uncertainty, but there is considerable flexibility built into the process, which should foster just decisions in the circumstances of each case.

---

[156] *Foster v. McCoy* (1998), 203 N.B.R. (2d) 252 (Q.B.).

[157] [1895] A.C. 587.

[158] Some measure of forbearance is to be expected from adjacent occupiers where they are merely inconvenienced and all reasonable precautions are taken to minimize the disturbance. See *Andreae v. Selfridge & Co. Ltd.*, *supra*, n. 128; *Grandel v. Mason*, *supra*, n. 144. See Fleming, *op. cit. supra*, n. 78, at p. 422.

[159] *Supra*, n. 104, at p. 303 (S.C.C.). See also *Jagtoo v. 407 E.T.R. Concession Co.*, *supra*, no. 93, claim dismissed.

[160] *Shelfer v. London Electric Co.*, [1895] 1 Ch. 287, at p. 316; *Walker v. McKinnon Industries Ltd.* [1949] 4 D.L.R. 739, at pp. 764-65 (Ont.).

[161] *Black v. Canadian Copper* (1917), 12 O.W.N. 243; affd (1920), 17 O.W.N. 399 (C.A.) (*sub nom. Taillifer v. Canadian Nickel Co.*); see Nedelsky, "Judicial Conservatism in an age of Innovation: Comparative Perspectives on Canadian Nuisance Law 1880-1930", in Flaherty, *Essays in the History of Canadian Law*, vol. 1 (1981). See also Tromans, "Nuisance — Prevention or Payment?" (1982), 41 Camb. L.J. 87.

2. PARTIES

a) Who May Sue?

The action for private nuisance is normally maintainable by the owner or possessor of the land affected. Thus, a tenant is entitled to sue but not a mere licensee.[162] Those with easements and mineral rights may also sue.[163] Although members of the possessors' family were once denied compensation, it now appears that they may recover for damage resulting from private nuisance.[164] A reversioner is not normally allowed to sue unless there is likely to be permanent damage to the property, such as structural damage to a house by vibrations.[165]

b) Who May be Sued? The Problem of Nonfeasance

Actions for nuisance lie not only against the people who actually caused it, but also against those who have inherited the situation from the primary culprit. If people permit a nuisance, which they did not create, to continue, they may be required to answer for it because they have "adopted" it as their own.[166]

This was so where the new occupier was unaware of the nuisance,[167] but this is now in doubt.[168] People may be held liable in nuisance for the acts of others even when they do not take place on their land,[169] as where they attract a crowd which misbehaves "if the experience of mankind must lead anyone to expect the result".[170] Where a number of people come to watch at a rifle range,[171] use a lane next to a dance hall,[172] skate at a roller-skating rink in a residential area[173] or

---

[162] *Salmond and Heuston, op. cit. supra*, n. 78, p. 70.

[163] *Falkoski v. Osoyoos (Town)* (1998), 46 M.P.L.R. (2d) 215 (B.C.S.C.).

[164] *Muirhead v. Timber Bros. Sand & Gravel Ltd., supra*, n. 89. See also *MacNeill v. Devon Lumber Co., supra*, n. 100, at p. 197 (N.B.C.A.) (*per* Stratton C.J.), "right of occupation . . . of the family residence" by children supports action. But *cf., Hunter v. Canary Wharf Ltd., supra*, n. 106, family members cannot sue; only those with proprietary interest can.

[165] *Colwell v. St. Pancras B.C.*, [1904] 1 Ch. 707.

[166] See *Sedleigh-Denfield v. O'Callaghan*, [1940] A.C. 880, at p. 897; *Sampson v. Hodson-Pressinger*, [1981] 3 All E.R. 710 (C.A); *Turner v. Delta Shelf Co.* (1995), 24 C.C.L.T. (2d) 107 (B.C.S.C.). But *cf., Kraps v. Paradise Canyon Holdings Ltd.*, [1998] B.C.J. No. 709, new owners had no time to fix nuisance.

[167] *Wringe v. Cohen*, [1940] 1 K.B. 229.

[168] Fleming, *op. cit. supra*, n. 78, p. 477; Klar, *Tort Law* 2d. ed. (1996), at p. 539, "Liability is predicated on actual or constructive knowledge of the hazardous condition, and the occupier's lack of reasonable care in responding to it."

[169] *A.G. v. Corke*, [1933] Ch. 89; *A.-G. v. Stone* (1895), 12 T.L.R. 76; see also *Lippiatt v. S. Gloucestershire Council,* [1999] 4 All E.R. 149 (C.A.), travellers occupying defendant's land made mess on plaintiff's land. Compare with *Hussain v. Lancaster City Council, ibid.*, at p. 125, no liability for harassment.

[170] *R. v. Moore* (1832), 3 B. & Ad. 184, at p. 188, 110 E.R. 68.

[171] *Ibid.*

[172] *Johnson v. Clinton*, [1943] 4 D.L.R. 572.

[173] *Newell v. Izzard*, [1944] 3 D.L.R. 118 (N.B.).

where students at a secondary school[174] or people in a restaurant[175] cause a nuisance, liability may also follow.

In the context of the relationship of landlord and tenant, the general rule was that the responsibility for disrepair rested with the tenant as occupier, subject to certain exceptions.[176] For example, landlords would not escape responsibility for premises in a ruinous condition merely by the letting or by taking a covenant to repair if they were aware of the defect or could have ascertained it by the exercise of reasonable care.[177] The modern trend has been to develop the notion of "control" exercised by landlords and to impute knowledge to them in order to establish a duty to protect against dangerous conditions arising from a state of disrepair.[178] Tenants will be liable to third parties for nuisances of which they are aware even though the landlord has given a covenant to repair,[179] and despite the fact that such covenant may allocate as between the two the burden of repair or of abating the nuisance.[180]

Owners are not responsible for any nuisance created by tenants unless the premises were let for a purpose calculated to cause a nuisance.[181] The nuisance must have been either expressly authorized or a necessary consequence of the purpose for which the property was let.[182] Such will not be implied merely

---

174 *Matheson v. Northcote College*, [1975] 2 N.Z.L.R. 106.

175 *Horse & Carriage Inn v. Baron* (1975), 53 D.L.R. (3d) 426.

176 Fleming, *op. cit. supra*, n. 78, at p. 481.

177 *Spicer v. Smee*, *supra*, n. 115, electrical fire; *St. Anne's Well Brewery Co. v. Roberts et al.* (1928), 44 T.L.R. 703, at pp. 706-08 (C.A.), wall collapsing; *Nikka Overseas Agency v. Canada Trust Co. et al.* (1961), 31 D.L.R. (2d) 368, oil fire; *Aldridge v. Van Patter et al.*, [1952] O.W.N. 516, stock car leaving track.

178 Fleming, *op. cit. supra*, n. 78, p. 482. This matter may now be settled in Ontario with regard to residential premises by virtue of s. 94(1) of the Landlord and Tenant Act, R.S.O. 1990, c. L.7 [now Tenant Protection Act, 1997, S.O. 1997, c. 24, s. 24], which imposes the obligation to repair on the landlord. There is, therefore, a right in the landlord to regain control over the property sufficient to make him liable in nuisance. See *Brewer et al. v. Kayes et al.*, [1973] 2 O.R. 284.

179 *St. Anne's Well Brewery*, *supra*, n. 161. The landlord will also be liable if the nuisance existed at the commencement of the tenancy, and it was known or ought to have been known by the landlord to exist.

180 In the absence of a controlling covenant, there may be contribution for nuisance: *Brew Bros. Ltd. v. Snax (Ross) Ltd.*, [1970] 1 Q.B. 612 (C.A.). Apportionment legislation would be applicable to nuisance cases. See, for example, ss. 2, 3, Negligence Act, R.S.O. 1990, c. N.1.

181 *Rich v. Basterfield* (1847), 136 E.R. 715, no liability for smoke from chimney as tenant could have used alternate fuel which did not produce such smoke; *Harris v. James* (1876), 45 L.J.Q.B. 545, blasting operations and burning of lime; *Winter v. Baker* (1887), 3 T.L.R. 569, running a fair; *Jenkins v. Jackson* (1888), 40 Ch.D. 71, dancing and entertainment in premises above plaintiff; *Breathour v. Bolster* (1864), 23 U.C.Q.B. 317 (C.A.), flood of water, from dam leased together with mill; *Banfai v. Formula Fun Centre*, *supra*, n. 125, owner, Hydro, liable for car race course run by tenant because this was planned purpose of lease.

182 *Smith v. Scott et al.*, [1972] 3 W.L.R. 783. That a nuisance will result must be a "virtual certainty" as opposed to a possibility or even a probability. Thus, a landlord will not be liable for a use made by the tenant which is not contemplated by the lease; see *Rich v. Basterfield*, *supra*, n. 181; *O'Leary v. Smith*, [1925] 2 D.L.R. 1022 (Man. C.A.), stove fire kindled by tenant.

because landlords, although having knowledge of the nuisance, did not terminate the tenancy[183] or intercede.[184]

As has been noted, the essential element in the duty imposed upon individuals to guard against the creation or continuation of dangerous conditions is knowledge. Apparently excepted from the general principle stated in *Sedleigh-Denfield* was the duty in relation to the natural condition of land[185] or its "natural" use for "time-honoured" purposes such as farming and mining.[186] However, this "bastion of immunity" may also be showing "signs of cracking", particularly with the recognition of liability for negligence in failing to abate dangerous natural growths such as encroaching or decaying trees.[187] Indeed, it now may be the law in England, at least, that there is a duty imposed upon occupiers to safeguard their neighbours against hazards arising on the occupier's land, whether by human agency or natural causes.[188]

---

[183] *Bowen v. Anderson*, [1894] 1 Q.B. 164; *Gandy v. Jubber* (1864), 122 E.R. 762, at p. 911. These cases held that a landlord was not to have been deemed to have relet the premises and thereby continued a nuisance simply by permitting the tenant to overhold at the end of the term. Thus, the proposition would be differently stated if there was, in fact, a reletting.

[184] *British Office Supplies (Auckland) Ltd. v. Auckland Masonic Institute*, [1957] N.Z.L.R. 512, at p. 517, quoting from *Salmond on Torts*, 11th ed., p. 264. It appears that the law in Canada with regard to landlords and tenants is the same as heretofore stated. See *Williams' Canadian Law of Landlord and Tenant*, 4th ed., pp. 406-08, at p. 466.

[185] See, for example, *Bottoni v. Henderson* (1979), 21 O.R. (2d) 369, tree not nuisance; *Reed v. Smith* (1914), 17 D.L.R. 92 (B.C.C.A.); *Patterson v. Canadian Robert Dollar Co. Ltd.*, [1929] 3 D.L.R. 38 (B.C.C.A.), both dealt with falling branches from decayed trees. But see *contra*, *Smith v. Giddy*, [1904] 2 K.B. 448, plaintiff's horse died from eating leaves of tree overhanging from defendant's property. See also *Giles v. Walker*, [1890], 240 Q.B.D. 656, no liability for dispersal of thistle seeds; *Sparkle v. Osborne* (1908), 7 C.L.R. 51, no liability for spread of prickly pear.

[186] The concept of "natural user" is undoubtedly tied with the notion of "reasonable user" which will be dealt with further on. The problem of the extent of the right of a landowner to excavate on own property and thereby cause damage to neighbour's property has been extremely nettlesome. See: *Storms v. M.G. Henninger Ltd.*, [1953] O.R. 717 (C.A.); *Rade et al. v. K. & E. Sand & Gravel (Sarnia) Ltd.*, [1970] 2 O.R. 188. See also *Pugliese v. National Capital Commn.* (1979), 8 C.C.L.T. 69 (S.C.C.), wherein it was held that the right of the landowner to obstruct gravel and sand as a reasonable user of property was, in Ontario, subject to the limitation provided in s. 37 of the Ontario Water Resources Commission Act [now Ontario Water Resources Act, R.S.O. 1990, c. O.40, s. 34]. This, in effect, prescribed what was a reasonable user.

[187] The courts have injected the element of knowledge of the danger as a necessary ingredient to the cause of action. This trend has been said to be far more apparent in England than in Canada. See McLaren, *supra*, n. 1, at p. 336, citing as examples: *Noble v. Harrison*, [1926] 2 K.B. 332; *Caminer v. Northern & London Investment Trust*, [1951] A.C. 88; *Davey v. Harrow Corp.*, [1958] 1 Q.B. 60; *Quinn v. Scott*, [1965] 2 All E.R. 588. See also: Goodhart, "Liability for Things Naturally on Land" (1930), 4 Camb. L.J. 13; Noel, "Nuisances from Land in its Natural Condition" (1942), 56 Harv. L. Rev. 772.

[188] *Goldman v. Hargrave*, [1967] 1 A.C. 645, at pp. 657-62 (P.C.) (*per* Lord Wilberforce). The scope of the duty was said to depend on what was "reasonable" in the circumstances, and this, in turn, devolved from the knowledge of the hazard, the foreseeability of the danger in not checking or removing it, and the ability to abate it: see pp. 663-64. See also *Leakey et al. v. National Trust for Places of Historic Interest or Natural Beauty*, [1980] 1 All E.R. 17, [1980] 2 W.L.R. 65 (C.A.). It may be that an exception still exists with regard to water. It still appears to be a gener-

C. Defences

There are several defences that may be raised in nuisance cases which may excuse a defendant from liability for conduct which would otherwise be actionable.

1. LEGISLATIVE AUTHORITY

If a nuisance has been legislatively authorized, no liability is imposed. Such authority may be express or implied, but rarely in specific words. The immunity is normally implied, based on the intention of the legislature, but it is narrowly defined. If the legislative mandate can be fulfilled without interfering with private rights, no immunity is permitted. In other words, if the damage inevitably flows from the exercise of legislative power, there is no liability, but not otherwise. This is sensible for tortious conduct should not be lightly excused on the basis of legislative enactments which do not specifically deal with the issue.[189]

The onus of proving inevitability rests on the defendants.[190] It was once said that it could be satisfied by showing that all reasonable care was exercised in the light of current scientific knowledge and practical feasibility. This principle was expressed as follows in *Manchester v. Farnworth*.[191]

> When Parliament has authorized a certain thing to be made or done in a certain place, there can be no action for nuisance caused by the making or doing of that thing if the nuisance is the inevitable result of the making or doing so authorized. The onus of proving that the result is inevitable is on those who wish to escape liability for nuisance, but the criterion of inevitability is not what is theoretically possible but what is possible according to the state of scien-

---

ally-accepted principle that there is an immunity from damage caused by water, naturally on the land, whose flow is not interfered with. See *Neath Rural District Council v. Williams*, [1951] 1 K.B. 115; *Loring v. Brightwood Golf & Country Club Ltd.* (1974), 44 D.L.R. (3d) 161 (N.S.C.A.); *270233 Ont. Ltd. v. Weall and Cullen Nurseries Ltd.* (1993), 17 C.C.L.T. (2d) 176 (Ont. Gen. Div.) (*per* Spence J.). However, it is otherwise when the occupier impedes the natural absorption or drainage by artifical structures. See *Hurdman v. N.E. Rwy. Co.* (1878), 3 C.P.D. 168 (C.A.); *Berry v. Trinidad Leaseholds*, [1953] 4 D.L.R. 504 (Ont. C.A.); *Trans Mountain Pipeline Co. Ltd. v. Nicola Valley Sawmills Ltd.* (1976), 62 D.L.R. (3d) 279 (B.C.). Perhaps these cases can be viewed as instances of misfeasance. This doctrine has often been invoked in cases dealing with the accumulation of ice or snow. A negligence standard is superimposed with regard to whether the occupier had knowledge or means of knowledge of the danger and made reasonable efforts to prevent the risk of injury. See *Taylor et al. v. Robinson*, [1933] O.R. 535; *Hagen v. Goldfarb*, *supra*, n. 58; *O'Leary v. Melitides* (1959), 20 D.L.R. (2d) 258 (N.S.); *Van Zeeland v. Campbelltown* (1978), 23 N.B.R. (2d) 656 (Q.B.).

189 *Vaughan v. Taff Vale Railway* (1860), 5 H. & N. 679, 157 E.R. 1351; *Hammersmith and City Railway Co. v. Brand* (1869), L.R. 4 H.L. 171; Linden, "Strict Liability, Nuisance and Legislative Authorization" (1966), 4 Osgoode Hall L.J. 196.

190 *Oosthoek v. Thunder Bay (City)* (1997), 139 D.L.R. (4th) 611 (Ont. C.A.).

191 [1930] A.C. 171 (H.L.). *Allen v. Gulf Oil*, *infra*, n. 195, liable unless "impossible" to operate refinery without nuisance; *Schenck v. R. in right of Ontario* (1981), 23 C.C.L.T. 147 (Ont. H.C.).

tific knowledge at the time, having also in view a certain common sense appreciation which cannot be rigidly defined, of practical feasibility in view of situation and of expense.[192]

The legislative authority is usually interpreted rather strictly. It has been held that a nuisance may be excused only if the legislation authorized a particular use in a particular area.[193] Similarly, if defendants exceed the bounds of the permit they have been issued, they will not escape liability.[194] The damage must be practically impossible to avoid for the immunity to be invoked.

Sometimes the courts have gone to extreme lengths to avoid legalizing what would otherwise be nuisances, as where it was held that authorizing the defendant to acquire land "for the construction of refinery" did not necessarily include the power to *use* the land as a refinery, if to do so would amount to nuisance.[195] This decision, however, has been reversed by the House of Lords which, calling this interpretation "artificial", held that the authority "to construct must in this case carry authority to use".[196]

The traditional approach to this issue has recently been considered by the Supreme Court of Canada in two cases. In the first, the traditional defence was employed and defended by Mr. Justice Sopinka in *Tock v. St. John's Metropolitan Area Bd.*,[197] a municipal flooding case, where he indicated that the current law is workable and that courts "strain against a conclusion that private rights are intended to be sacrificed for the common good". In determining whether or not a consequence was inevitable, he stated that:

> The defendant must negative that there are alternate methods of carrying out the work. The mere fact that one is considerably less expensive will not avail. If only one method is practically feasible, it must be established that it was practically impossible to avoid the nuisance. It is insufficient for the defendant to negative negligence. The standard is a higher one.[198]

The other members of the Supreme Court, although agreeing with most of the general principles, sought to restrict the scope of the already narrow immunity even more, but no clear majority view emerged. Madam Justice Wilson (Lamer, L'Heureux-Dubé concurring), while conceding that this type of legislation has not been significant in the past, suggested, in a powerful and well-reasoned judgment, that statutory powers framed in discretionary or permissive terms should attract liability for any tortious conduct done pursuant to them. In other words, when a choice about the place and manner of doing something existed,

---

[192] *Ibid.*, at p. 183 (*per* Viscount Dunedin). See also *Dufferin Paving & Crushed Stone v. Anger*, [1940] S.C.R. 174; *Portage La Prairie v. B.C. Pea Growers*, [1966] S.C.R. 150.

[193] *Metropolitan Asylum v. Hill* (1881), 6 App. Cas. 193, smallpox hospital; *Rapier v. London Tramways Co.*, [1893] 2 Ch. 588 (C.A.), stable; *Madge v. Penge Urban Council* (1917), 86 L.J. Ch. 126, public urinal.

[194] *Solloway v. Okanagan Builders* (1976), 71 D.L.R. (3d) 102 (B.C.). See also *National Capital Commn. v. Pugliese* (1980), 97 D.L.R. (3d) 631, at p. 639 (S.C.C.) (*per* Pigeon J.).

[195] *Allen v. Gulf Oil*, [1979] 3 All E.R. 1008 (C.A.).

[196] [1981] 1 All E.R. 353, at p. 357 (*per* Lord Wilberforce).

[197] [1989] 2 S.C.R. 1181, at p. 1226, 64 D.L.R. (4th) 620.

[198] *Ibid.*, at p. 1226, D.L.R.

the actor must act in "strict conformity with private rights" and must choose a plan and manner of acting that does not cause tortious damage. The inevitable result doctrine, according to Madam Justice Wilson, should be offered only to those cases where there was "no choice as to the way in which or the place where it engages in the nuisance-causing activity".[199]

In a learned and elegant judgment, Mr. Justice La Forest (Dickson C.J. concurring), viewing the defence as a "legacy of the Victorian age", advocated the most radical departure from the current law. For Mr. Justice La Forest, the preferred approach is to treat cases involving a public body in the same way as claims in a nuisance between two private individuals, unless there is an express exception from liability.[200] Mr. Justice La Forest refused to don the "cloak of a soothsayer to plumb the intent of the legislature".[201] He opined that the costs of inevitable damage in providing "services that benefit the public at large should be borne equally by all those who profit from the service".[202] The only question for the courts to address, according to his approach, is "whether, given all the circumstances, it is reasonable to refuse to compensate the aggrieved party for the damage he has suffered".[203]

Both the novel approaches suggested by Madam Justice Wilson and Mr. Justice La Forest have been criticized by Professor Hogg[204] for throwing well settled law into confusion for reasons he felt were "unpersuasive". The truth is that the differences among the three approaches were of little practical significance in that the result of very few cases, if any, would turn on which one is employed.[205] In the second case, *Ryan v. Victoria (City)*,[206] the temporary confusion was ended when the court unanimously returned to the traditional approach which had been voiced by Justice Sopinka. That case involved a motorcyclist who was seriously injured when one of his tires lodged in a gap of a railway track, which ran down a city street. The plaintiff sued the railways which owned and leased the tracks and the city in public nuisance, and on other grounds. The railways argued, *inter alia,* that they were protected by the defence of statutory authority, that they had statutory authority to operate trains and construct tracks and that they abided by all the regulations governing these activities.

Justice Major confirmed that this was "at best, a narrow defence," opined that the traditional view was the most "predictable" and the "simplest to apply" and, in a unanimous decision, adopted Justice Sopinka's view of the defence, to this effect:

---

[199] *Ibid.*, at p. 1222.

[200] As in *Arif v. Fredericton (City)* (1986), 77 N.B.R. (2d) 34 (Q.B.); *North Vancouver (Municipality) v. McKenzie Barge & Marine Ways Ltd.*, [1965] S.C.R. 377.

[201] *Supra*, n. 197, at p. 1201, S.C.R.

[202] *Ibid.*

[203] *Ibid.*

[204] "Defence of Statutory Authority: Comment on *Tock*" (1990), 69 Can. Bar Rev. 589, at p. 596.

[205] For example, see *Canada (A.G.) v. Ottawa-Carleton, supra*, n. 111, at p. 19, a municipal flooding case, where it was stated that liability would be imposed whichever approach was used.

[206] [1999] 1 S.C.R. 201, at p. 238; see also discussion in Chapter 14.

Statutory authority provides, at best, a narrow defence to nuisance. The traditional rule is that liability will not be imposed if an activity is authorized by statute and the defendant proves that the nuisance is the "inevitable result" or consequence of exercising that authority.

Applying that approach, Justice Major found nothing "inevitable" about the hazards created on the street in Victoria. The regulations the railways referred to prescribed a minimum width for the flangeways. The railways' decision to exceed that minimum was a matter of discretion, as was their decision not to employ flange fillers when such products became available; neither were the "inevitable result" of complying with regulations.

In cases before *Tock* and *Ryan* it was said that where the statute is merely permissive, and the grantee has a discretion as to where to locate, such discretion must be exercised in strict conformity with private rights.[207] Similarly, where a statute empowered a municipality to build a sewer, it did not condone the escape of raw sewage.[208] So too, legislation permitting sewer lagoons did not allow for the creation of a nuisance, unless expressly so stated.[209]

Private rights may be preserved, apart from any statutory remedy, if the project can be shown to be capricious or unreasonable or "so fraught with manifest danger to others that [nobody] acting *bona fide* and rationally, not recklessly, would ever have undertaken it".[210] Further, the authority will not be protected if the injury is collateral to the exercise of the statutory power, and the damage results not from the carrying out of the operation planned but through some unintended negligent act.[211]

It is to be emphasized that the defence is available only in the limited circumstances of legislative authorization. It is no defence for an individual to claim that a nuisance, although injurious, is beneficial to the public at large. Neither, in this context, could a defendant successfully plead the "place from which the nuisance proceeds is a suitable one for the purpose of carrying on the operation complained of, and that no other place is available from which less mischief would result".[212] If no place can be found where such an operation will not cause a nuisance, then it cannot be carried on at all, except with consent or by legislative authority.[213]

The principles outlined above are, of course, equally applicable to subcontractors as well as to the authorized party.[214]

---

[207] *Metropolitan Asylum, supra*, n. 193, at p. 213. See also *Tock v. St. John's, supra*, n. 197, at pp. 629-30, 635, D.L.R. (*per* Wilson J.).

[208] *Buysse v. Shelburne, supra*, n. 111.

[209] *Von Thurn Und Taxis v. Edmonton*, [1982] 4 W.W.R. 457 (Alta. Q.B.).

[210] *Marriage v. East Norfolk Catchment Bd.*, [1950] 1 K.B. 284, at p. 309 (C.A.).

[211] *Ibid.* See also *Diversified Holdings v. R. in right of B.C.* (1982), 23 C.C.L.T. 156 (B.C.C.A.), negligent and unreasonable behaviour not protected.

[212] *Salmond and Heuston, op. cit. supra*, n. 78, p. 79. See also *Buysse v. Shelburne, supra*, n. 111.

[213] *Ibid.*

[214] See, for example, *Pilliterri v. Northern Construction Co.* (1930), 66 O.L.R. 128, [1930] 4 D.L.R. 731.

2. STATUTORY IMMUNITY

Statutory immunity should not be confused with the defence of legislative or statutory authority. A statutory immunity is expressly provided for by the legislature, whereas the defence of legislative authority depends upon implication. As the defence of legislative or statutory authority lost its teeth, municipalities and other government agencies sought legislative protection against nuisance claims with some success. Self-serving legislation which explicitly relieves municipalities and others of liability for nuisance has been enacted, for example, in Ontario's Municipal Act[215] as follows:

> **331.2** (1) No proceedings based on nuisance, in connection with the escape of water or sewage from sewer works or water works, shall be commenced against,
>
> (a) a municipality or local board;
>
> (b) a member of a municipal council or of a local board;
>
> (c) an officer, employee or agent of a municipality or local board.

Similar provisions can be found in other provinces as well.[216] So far, these provisions are being carefully scrutinized by the courts, which, understandably, will only invoke the defence when the language clearly covers the situation being complained of.[217]

The agricultural community also sought protection from nuisance claims when their new suburban neighbours began to complain about the stench, flies, and pesticide which are commonplace and necessary in farming. A right to farm movement was born in the United States and succeeded in obtaining protective legislation there. The movement spread to Canada, where legislation has been enacted as well in all the provinces except Newfoundland, which generally ensures that "well-managed farms, that operate according to generally accepted agricultural practices, and that do not pollute or otherwise threaten public health and safety, are granted immunity from common-law nuisance liability. As well, in several provinces this immunity is extended against restrictive local by-laws."[218]

Some provinces have gone still further, protecting all businesses, not just agricultural ones, from liability for odours, unless the business breached a provincial land-use control statute or regulation.[219] Early indications are that these provisions, like those dealing with municipalities, will be narrowly

---

[215] R.S.O. 1990, c. M.45, as amended by S.O. 1996, c. 32, s. 55; see Osborne, *The Law of Torts* (2000), Chapter 6.

[216] See, for example, Local Government Act, R.S.B.C. 1996, c. 323, s. 288; City of St. John's Act, R.S.N. 1990, c. C-17, s. 179. Governmental or quasi-governmental bodies other than municipalities may have similar statutory immunity. See, for example, Hydro and Power Authority Act, R.S.B.C. 1996, c. 212, s. 31.

[217] See, for example, *Jansen Contracting Ltd. v. North Cowichan (District)* (1999), 69 B.C.L.R. (3d) 60 (C.A.); *Form-Rite Contracting Ltd. v. Prince George (City)* (1999), 69 B.C.L.R. (3d) 372 (B.C.S.C.).

[218] See Kalmakoff, "The Right to Farm" (1999), 62 Sask. L.R. 225.

[219] See, for example, Manitoba's Nuisance Act, R.S.M. 1987, c. N.120.

construed so as not to restrict common-law rights without explicit wording to that effect.[220]

3. PRESCRIPTION

A prescriptive right may be acquired to continue to commit certain nuisances, if they are done continuously for 20 years.[221] The theory is that the conduct of the defendant may be validated retrospectively, thereby giving the defendant a right in the nature of an easement appurtenant to the land.[222]

Recognition of these prescriptive rights has occurred where rain or snow was discharged from an overhanging eave[223] or where smoke was emitted through a party wall.[224] However, where the invasion involves the "general spreading of an intangible agency such as smell, noise or smoke", the result is less certain[225] because in such circumstances, there can be no definite means of measuring the user by which the extent of the right is ascertained.[226]

A prescriptive right cannot be claimed where the nuisance was not actionable or preventable by the plaintiff for any part of the period of user. Thus, if the defendant's activity was secret,[227] or it did not become a nuisance until the occurrence of some other event,[228] or the deleterious consequences resulting from the use only became apparent at a subsequent date,[229] or the land affected was vacant for part of the 20-year period,[230] no prescriptive right exists. In other words, the conduct in question must have constituted an actionable nuisance for the full 20 years of the prescription period.

---

[220] See, for example, *Pyke v. Tri Gro Enterprises Ltd.*, [1999] O.J. No. 3217, a case involving a nuisance claim by neighbours of a mushroom farm in Whitby, east of Toronto, which considers Ontario's Farming and Food Production Protection Act, 1998, S.O. 1998, c. 1 and its predecessor legislation applying it rather restrictively.

[221] The Limitations Act, R.S.O. 1990, c. L.15, s. 31. But note that pursuant to s. 51 of The Land Titles Act, R.S.O. 1990, c. L.5, notwithstanding anything in The Limitations Act, The Land Titles Act or any other Act, no title is acquired or deemed to be acquired by possession or prescription with regard to land registered under The Land Titles Act.

[222] McLaren, *supra*, n. 1, at p. 373.

[223] *Wood v. Gibson* (1897), 30 N.S.R. 15 (C.A.); *Hall v. Alexander* (1902), 3 O.L.R. 482 (C.A.); *De Vault v. Robinson* (1920), 54 D.L.R. 591 (Ont. C.A.); *Harvey v. Walters* (1873), L.R. 8 C.P. 162.

[224] *Lane v. George* (1904), 4 O.W.R. 539; see also *Jones v. Pritchard*, [1908] 1 Ch. 630.

[225] McLaren, *supra*, n. 1, p. 374.

[226] Fleming, *op. cit. supra*, n. 78, p. 490. McLaren suggests that the law may be otherwise in Canada citing *Danforth Glebe Estates Ltd. v. W. Harris & Co.* (1919), 16 O.W.N. 41, at p. 42 (C.A.) (*per* Riddell J.); *Duchman v. Oakland Dairy Co.*, [1929] 1 D.L.R. 9, at p. 28 (Ont. C.A.) (*per* Masten J.A.).

[227] *Liverpool Corp. v. H. Coghill & Son Ltd.*, [1918] 1 Ch. 307, borox discharged into sewers.

[228] *Sturges v. Bridgman* (1879), 11 Ch. D. 852 (C.A.), operation of heavy machinery did not cause a problem until the plaintiff, a doctor, built a consulting room at the bottom of his garden.

[229] *Russell Transport Co. Ltd. v. Ontario Malleable Iron Co. Ltd.*, [1952] 4 D.L.R. 719, discharge of corrosive substances into the air.

[230] *Danforth Glebe Estates*, *supra*, n. 226.

No prescriptive right can be acquired in respect of a public nuisance since, as a criminal offence both by statute and at common law, it can never have a lawful beginning. Nor can it be in the public interest to give it legitimacy.[231]

4. ACQUIESCENCE OR CONSENT

For acquiescence to be invoked there must be overt consent to or active encouragement of the defendant's activity.[232] Merely standing idly by is not enough. Thus, acquiescence is distinguishable from the doctrine of *laches*.[233] A plaintiff, therefore, who agrees to the construction of a dam in order to get the benefit of a higher water level, forgoes the right to compensation for flooding because of prior consent.[234]

If the basis of the defendant's claim is unreasonable delay or *laches*, this is more likely to go to the question of substituting damages for an injunction rather than denying a remedy altogether.[235] The view has also been expressed that the court will give credence to such an allegation only if there was something in the nature of fraud or unconscionable conduct on the part of the plaintiff.[236]

5. CONTRIBUTORY NEGLIGENCE AND *VOLENTI NON FIT INJURIA*

It is not clear whether the defence of contributory negligence is available in a nuisance action. Perhaps the most intelligent analysis is that of Fleming, who asserts that it may be available only in some cases. Where the law of private nuisance seeks to adjust competing uses of land, contributory negligence does not play a significant part.[237] However, where it is used to secure damages for public nuisance on a highway, the negligence of the plaintiff may be most relevant for "a careless plaintiff cannot improve his position by claiming for nuisance rather than negligence".[238] Thus, where a nuisance by flooding is caused in part as a result of the negligent failure of the plaintiff to warn the defendant about the danger, the plaintiff's compensation will be reduced because of contributory negligence.[239]

---

[231] Fleming, *op. cit. supra*, n. 78, p. 490; McLaren, *supra*, n. 1, p. 373.

[232] See *Heenan v. Dewar* (1870), 17 Gr. 638 (Ch.); affd 18 Gr. 438. See also *Sanson v. Northern Rwy. Co.* (1881), 29 Gr. 459 (Ch.); *McCallum v. District of Kent*, [1943] 3 W.W.R. 489 (B.C.C.A.).

[233] McLaren, "The Common Law Nuisance Actions and the Environmental Battle" (1972), 10 Osgoode Hall L.J. 505, at p. 544.

[234] *Pattison v. Prince Edward Region Conservation Authority* (1984), 53 O.R. (2d) 23 (H.C.) (*per* Walsh J.); affd (1988), 45 C.C.L.T. 166 (C.A.).

[235] *Kerr on Injunctions*, 6th ed. (1927); see *Nestor v. Hayes Wheel Co.* (1924), 26 O.W.N. 129.

[236] *Radenhurst v. Coate* (1857), 6 Gr. 139 (C.A.); *Kerr on Injunctions, op. cit. supra*, n. 235, p. 35 and cases cited.

[237] Fleming, *op. cit. supra*, n. 78, p. 491.

[238] *Ibid.*, p. 411.

[239] *Koch Industries v. Vancouver*, [1982] 4 W.W.R. 92 (B.C.S.C.), 50%. See also *Bell Canada v. Cope (Sarnia) Ltd.* (1980), 11 C.C.L.T. 170; affd 15 C.C.L.T. 190 (Ont. C.A.), trespass action.

Volenti is not available as a defence where the plaintiff "comes to the nuisance". It was once thought that a person could not complain of a nuisance if, with full knowledge of it, that person chose to become the owner or occupier of the land affected by it. However, this is no longer the law — the maxim *volenti non fit injuria* has no application here.[240] The modern view is that, in the absence of a prescriptive right, the newcomer to the land is entitled to the reasonable and enjoyable use of the property, subject to the proviso that the newcomer has to accept the existing character of the neighbourhood. Further, an activity does not necessarily become a nuisance merely because a novel use is being made of newly-acquired property.[241]

6. ACT OF THIRD PERSON

The intervening act of a third party may be a defence if it is unforeseeable, but not if it is the kind of act which should have been foreseen by the defendant.[242] A contractor can be held responsible for the conduct of a subcontractor whose blasting caused damage by vibrations to the plaintiff's house.[243] This is so if there is knowledge of the conduct of the independent contractor or if the work is found to be inherently dangerous.[244]

It is possible for two defendants to be jointly responsible for a nuisance.[245] It is not a defence to argue that the defendant's action alone, without the conduct of another person doing the same thing at the same time, would not have amounted to a nuisance.[246] In other words, if one person's conduct helps to bring about a nuisance, no exoneration will be given to that person even though the conduct of others was also required to create the nuisance. The apportionment legislation, however, applies to permit contribution over among these joint tortfeasors.

---

[240] *Sturges v. Bridgman, supra*, n. 228.

[241] Fleming, *op. cit. supra*, n. 78, p. 491.

[242] *Cunningham v. McGrath Bros.*, [1964] I.R. 209, ladder, causing partial obstruction to footpath, moved by unknown person and then causing injury to plaintiff when it fell. But see *Tidy v. Cunningham* (1915), 22 D.L.R. 151 (B.C.S.C.), unknown person cutting gas pipe under street. It is not necessary to show that the particular accident and damage resulting therefrom were probable. It is sufficient if the accident was of a class that might well be anticipated as one of the reasonable and probable results of the wrongful act; *Haynes v. Harwood*, [1935] 1 K.B. 146 (C.A.), action in negligence. See also *Clark v. Chambers* (1878), 3 Q.B.D. 327; *Northwestern Utilities Ltd. v. London Guarantee & Accident Co.*, [1936] A.C. 108 (P.C.); *Gertsen v. Metro Toronto* (1973), 2 O.R. (2d) 1.

[243] *Aikman v. George Mills & Co. et al.*, [1934] O.R. 597, [1934] D.L.R. 264. See also *Hounsome v. Vancouver Power Co.* (1913), 3 W.W.R. 953, 9 D.L.R. 823 (B.C.C.A.); affd 49 S.C.R. 430; *Bower v. Peate* (1876), 1 Q.B.D. 321.

[244] *Schoeni v. R.*, [1943] O.R. 478; affd [1944] O.R. 38.

[245] *Brew Bros. Ltd. v. Snax (Ross) Ltd.*, [1970] 1 Q.B. 612 (C.A.).

[246] *Lambton v. Mellish*, [1894] 3 Ch. 163.

D. Remedies

1. INJUNCTION

Nuisance is one of the few areas the law of torts where courts may issue injunctions. It must be recalled that an injunction, whether it is interlocutory or permanent, is an equitable remedy and is, therefore, granted on the basis of a discretion which resided in the court. The court may grant a prohibitory injunction, which orders a nuisance-maker to refrain from a certain activity, or a mandatory injunction which directs someone to do something, like moving an offending structure.[247]

Not infrequently in these cases, the injunction will not come into force immediately, so as to permit the defendant some time to abate the nuisance.[248] A limited injunction may be granted, possibly along with damages.[249]

The court will be guided by the same principles in nuisance cases as apply ordinarily to the granting of injunctions.[250] Thus it must be shown that damages would not afford the plaintiff an adequate remedy. This is generally not difficult where it is likely that the nuisance activity will recur. But an injunction will lie only on proof of substantial injury[251] and if the defendant claims the right to continue with the conduct. In addition, since the granting of an injunction is discretionary, the conduct of both parties may be taken into consideration in deciding whether an injunction should issue.[252]

The economic benefit derived from the defendant's enterprise is of some concern to the courts, but it does not control. The prevailing attitude is that individual property rights are to be subordinated to the "public good" only by statutory authorization.[253] As was stated by Lindley L.J. in *Shelfer v. London Electric Lighting Co.*:[254]

---

[247] The principles under which a mandatory order will issue were reviewed in *Morris v. Redland Bricks Ltd.*, [1970] A.C. 652, at pp. 665-67 (H.L.) (*per* Lord Upjohn). These included the probability that grave damage would accrue to the plaintiff in future, the cost to the defendant, and whether damages would be a sufficient remedy.

[248] *Beamish v. Glenn* (1916), 36 O.L.R. 10, 28 D.L.R. 702 (C.A.); *Taylor v. Mullen Coal Co.* (1915), 7 O.W.N. 764; affd 8 O.W.N. 445 (C.A.); *McMaster v. Bell Bros.* (1931), 40 O.W.N. 536; *Joyce v. Yorkton Gun Club Inc.* (1990), 84 Sask. R. 289 (Q.B.); affd (1992), 97 Sask. R. 243 (C.A.).

[249] *Kennaway v. Thompson*, [1981] Q.B. 88, [1980] 3 All E.R. 329 (C.A.), waterskiing not stopped but controlled. See also *Romburgh v. Crestbrook Timber Ltd.* (1966), 55 W.W.R. 557, partial injunction and damages awarded for smoke and ashes from sawmill.

[250] Fleming, *op. cit. supra*, n. 78, p. 445.

[251] *Ibid.*

[252] Thus, acquiescence or delay on the part of the plaintiff will be a factor as will a high-handed attitude displayed by the defendant toward the rights of the plaintiff. Evidence of reasonable efforts to prevent or minimize the offending activity may also militate against the granting of an injunction.

[253] The traditional English approach was severe in outlook reflecting "very clearly a nineteenth century socio-economic philosophy which stressed the sanctity of individual rights": McLaren, "The Common Law Nuisance Actions and the Environmental Battle" (1972), 10 Osgoode Hall L.J. 505, at p. 548. For an economic analysis, see Calabresi and Melamed, "Property Rules, Liability Rules, and Inalienability: One View of the Cathedral" (1972), 85 Harv. L. Rev. 1089; for a discussion of the protection of agriculture, see *supra*.

[254] [1895] 1 Ch. 287, at p. 316.

... [T]he circumstance that the wrongdoer is in some sense a public benefactor (*e.g.* a gas or water company or a sewer authority) ever been considered a sufficient reason for refusing to protect by injunction an individual whose rights are being persistently infringed. Expropriation, even for a money consideration, is only justifiable when Parliament has sanctioned it. Courts of Justice are not like Parliament, which considers whether proposed works will be so beneficial to the public as to justify exceptional legislation, and the deprivation of people of their rights with or without compensation.

As a corollary, little credence is given to the argument advanced by some defendants that an injunction would cause economic hardship to them.[255] This stern view is undoubtedly explicable in part to the fact that the only remedy which a court of equity was able to grant here was an injunction, until legislative reform permitted damages in lieu of an injunction or in addition to an injunction.[256]

The criteria which govern whether an injunction should issue were not altered by the statutory change in the law, so that damages are to be awarded and an injunction denied only in "special cases."[257]

The jurisdiction of the court also extends to grant a *quia timet* injunction, even though no actual damage has yet been suffered, if there is a strong probability that the nuisance will in fact arise[258] or that the damage, if it does occur, will be irreparable.[259]

2. DAMAGES

Damages may be sought in addition to, or as an alternative to, an injunction. Generally speaking, damages will be granted instead of an injunction where the latter would be oppressive to the defendant or where the plaintiff's injury is adequately compensable in money. The accepted criteria as to when damages

---

[255] See *Imperial Gas, Light & Coke Co. v. Broadbent* (1895), 7 H.L.C. 600, 11 E.R. 239. Most Canadian authorities appear to follow the English principle with regard to the exercise of the power to grant injunctive relief. See *Canada Paper Co. v. Brown* (1922), 63 S.C.R. 243, 66 D.L.R. 287; *Groat v. Edmonton*, [1928] S.C.R. 522, [1928] 3 D.L.R. 725; *Stephens v. Richmond Hill*, [1955] O.R. 806, [1955] 4 D.L.R. 572; affd but vard as to damages [1956] O.R. 88, 1 D.L.R. (2d) 569; *K.V.P. Co. v. McKie*, [1949] S.C.R. 698, [1949] 4 D.L.R. 497; *Gauthier v. Naneff*, [1971] 1 O.R. 97, 14 D.L.R. (3d) 513.

[256] Lord Cairns' Act of 1858 has been carried over into s. 99 of the Courts of Justice Act, R.S.O. 1990, c. C.43, which provides:

A court that has jurisdiction to grant an injunction or order specific performance may award damages in addition to, or in substitution for, the injunction or specific performance.

[257] *Shelfer v. London Electric Lighting, supra,* n. 254.

[258] *Earl of Ripon v. Hobart* (1834), 3 M. & K. 169, at p. 176, 40 E.R. 65, at p. 68; *A.G. v. Manchester Corp.*, [1893] 2 Ch. 87; *Hooper v. Rogers*, [1975] Ch. 43 (C.A.); *Guardian Assce. Co. Ltd. v. Matthew* (1919), 58 S.C.R. 47.

[259] *Fletcher v. Bealy* (1885), 28 Ch. D. 688. See also Fleming, *op. cit. supra,* n. 78, p. 493; McLaren, *supra,* n. 1, p. 551; *Mendez v. Palazzi* (1976), 68 D.L.R. (3d) 582; see *Caddy Lake Cottagers Assn. v. Florence-Nora Access Road. Inc.* (1998), 126 Man. R. (2d) 230 (C.A.), interim injunction granted to stop road being built in quiet, forested area.

would be substituted for an injunction were set out by A.L. Smith L.J. in *Shelfer v. London Electric Lighting Co.*: [260]

(1)   If the injury to the plaintiff's legal rights is small.
(2)   And is one which is capable of being estimated in money.
(3)   And is one which can be adequately compensated by a small money payment.
(4)   And the case is one in which it would be oppressive to the defendant to grant an injunction. . . .[261]

Damages for a continuing nuisance are recoverable for loss suffered right up to the date of judgment,[262] which avoids the necessity of successive actions. The amount awarded, as in a negligence action, includes compensation for damages which are a reasonably foreseeable consequence of the nuisance,[263] such as diminution in the value of the land.[264] In addition, where the court exercises its jurisdiction to award damages in lieu of an injunction, such award may also include compensation for any prospective loss which the injunction, had it been granted, would have prevented.[265]

As has been noted, compensation in nuisance is not dependent upon proof of physical injury. Damages will be awarded for substantial interference with the profits.[266] Compensation, of course, may include damages for loss of or injury to chattels.[267] Although "damage is the gist of nuisance", this is not rigidly insisted upon where to do so would risk a prescriptive right "ripening" against the plaintiff by continued user.[268]

3. ABATEMENT

Abatement, a "self-help" remedy, is available to an individual victim of nuisance where speed is required to end the offending conduct. It is permitted in

---

[260] *Shelfer v. London Electric Lighting, supra*, n. 254, at pp. 322-23.
[261] This test was adopted by the Supreme Court of Canada in *Canada Paper Co. v. Brown, supra*, n. 255, at p. 252, S.C.R. (*per* Duff J.). See also *Duchman v. Oakland Dairy Co. Ltd.* (1929), 63 O.L.R. 111 (C.A.).
[262] *Hole v. Chard Union*, [1984] 1 Ch. 293. This avoids the necessity of the plaintiff bringing successive separate actions.
[263] "*The Wagon Mound (No. 2)*", [1967] 1 A.C. 617.
[264] *Butt v. Oshawa*, [1926] 4 D.L.R. 1138, 59 O.L.R. 520; *Godfrey v. Good Rich Refining Co.*, [1939] O.R. 106; affd [1940] O.R. 190 (C.A.); *Culp and Hart v. East York*, [1956] O.R. 983; affd [1957] O.W.N. 515 (C.A.).
[265] In effect, then, s. 99 of the Courts of Justice Act, R.S.O. 1990, c. C.43 permits an award of damages to be made in lieu of a *quia timet* injunction, see *Leeds Industrial Co-operative Society Ltd. v. Slack*, [1924] A.C. 851, at p. 857 (*per* Viscount Finlay).
[266] Fleming, *op. cit. supra*, n. 78, p. 496.
[267] *British Celanese v. Hunt*, [1969] 1 W.L.R. 959; *Heintzman & Co. Ltd. v. Hashman Construction Ltd.*, [1973] 1 W.W.R. 202 (Alta.).
[268] Fleming, *op. cit. supra*, n. 68, p. 496.

situations of emergency[269] only and has been discouraged by the courts for obvious reasons.[270]

Abatement is not confined to cases where the offending condition can be removed from the land of the party aggrieved (such as encroaching tree branches or roots), but also justifies entry upon the land of another and the use of reasonable force to accomplish the purpose.[271] Since it is looked upon by the courts as a privilege, it must be taken not to inflict unnecessary damage,[272] and the least detrimental of possible alternative methods of abating must be adopted.[273]

It has been suggested that an abatement cannot be justified unless a mandatory injunction would have issued. Thus, the privilege will not lie where the damage caused by abating is wholly disproportionate to the harm threatened.[274] Sometimes, however, abatement is permissible where there would be no remedy in damages, such as in a case of a threat of imminent danger, where no harm has yet occurred.[275]

Notice to the offender is not necessarily required prior to invoking the remedy, although it is certainly advisable. None may be necessary where there is no need to enter upon someone else's land,[276] where there is an emergency,[277] and probably where the land belongs to the original creator of the nuisance.[278] However, notice is required where the nuisance was created, not by the present occupier, but by a predecessor in title, where the nuisance arose from an omission, and where the abatement would necessitate the demolition of an inhabited house.[279]

Only persons who would be successful in a cause of action are entitled to abate. Thus, a private individual cannot abate a public nuisance unless suffering some particular injury over and above that suffered by the rest of the public. Similarly, removing an obstruction from the road does not justify damage, if a person can pass by without doing anything.[280]

---

[269] See Fleming, *op. cit. supra*, n. 78, p. 496; Estey, *supra*, n. 31, p. 581.

[270] *Lagan Navigation Co. v. Lamberg Bleaching, Dyeing & Finishing Co.*, [1927] A.C. 226, at pp. 244-45 (*per* Lord Atkinson).

[271] *Jones v. Williams* (1843), 11 M. & W. 176, 152 E.R. 764.

[272] *Roberts v. Rose* (1865), 3 H. & C. 162, 159 E.R. 490; *Lorrain et al. v. Norrie* (1912), 6 D.L.R. 122, 46 N.S.R. 177 (C.A.).

[273] *Lagan Navigation*, *supra*, n. 270, at p. 245.

[274] Fleming, *op cit. supra*, n. 78, p. 496.

[275] In *Lemmon v. Webb*, [1894] 3 Ch. 1, [1895] A.C. 1 (H.L.), the defendant was held to have been justified in cutting down some branches of the plaintiff's tree that were overhanging onto the defendant's property even though no actual harm had yet been suffered.

[276] *Lemmon v. Webb, ibid.*; *Phoenix v. Quagliotti* (1909), 11 W.L.R. 659, at p. 661 (B.C.).

[277] *Jones v. Williams, supra*, n. 271; *Suttles v. Cantin* (1915), 24 D.L.R. 1, 8 W.W.R. 1293 (B.C.C.A.).

[278] *Ibid.*

[279] Fleming, *op. cit. supra*, n. 78, p. 496.

[280] *Ibid.*

The decision to abate must be carefully made since it is an alternative remedy to damages. Once a nuisance has been abated, no right of action for compensation for past injury will lie.[281]

---

[281]　*Lagan Navigation, supra*, n. 270, at p. 244.

Chapter 16

Products Liability

This is an age of consumption. The manufacture of products has become one of our most important economic activities. Billions of dollars worth of goods are being fabricated annually in Canada to satisfy the apparently insatiable appetites of our consumers. But consumption is not always pleasurable; danger lurks in defective products. People may be hurt when things go wrong with the articles they use. Food products may contain some surprises. Mr. Justice Middleton has joked[1] about the "extended list of cases based on the fondness of mice and snails to seek a last resting place in ginger beer bottles where they remain undiscovered until they reveal themselves in ripened condition to a dissatisfied customer . . . ". Such incidents are all too common.

To curtail the number of mishaps resulting from imperfect products, governments now regulate the manufacture of some goods. For example, the Federal Government now supervises food, drug, and cosmetic production and sales in Canada.[2] The automobile producers have finally been brought under some control.[3] Hazardous products are being especially regulated.[4] New departments of government, both federal and provincial, are asserting the interests of consumers at last. These are significant improvements, even though there is still a long way to go before product safety becomes foolproof.

Despite these developments, accidents will still occur. Injured consumers will still have need of legal recourse to recover damages for their losses. The law has woven a rather complicated pattern in this area.[5] There are two main routes to recovery, depending on the relationship between the consumer and the person from whom the article was acquired. If the relationship of buyer and seller exists between the claimant and defendant, the consumer may be able to rely on

---

[1] *Negro v. Pietro's Bread Co.*, [1933] O.R. 112, at p. 115 (C.A.).

[2] Food and Drugs Act, R.S.C. 1985, c. F-27.

[3] Motor Vehicle Safety Act, S.C. 1993, c. 16.

[4] Hazardous Products Act, R.S.C. 1985, c. H-3.

[5] See generally Waddams, *Products Liability*, 3rd ed. (Toronto: The Carswell Co., 1993); Stapleton, *Product Liability* (1994). Edgell, *Product Liability in Canada* (Toronto: Butterworths Canada Ltd., 2000); Dobbs, *The Law of Torts* (2000) Chapter 24. For procedural and jurisdictional complications, see Sharpe, *Interprovincial Product Liability Litigation* (1982).

contract theory, which is a form of strict liability based on the law of warranties.[6] If there is no contractual dealing between the parties, tort theory, which is fundamentally founded on negligence law, is the only avenue of recovery.[7] A consumer may have a series of potential defendants to pursue, or may end up with no one to whom loss can be shifted. In either event, it can be a complex and costly undertaking.

This chapter will examine the law of sales to the extent that it is available to an injured consumer. It will then consider the role of negligence law in supplying reparation to persons hurt by defective products.

A. Contract Theory

Contract or warranty theory, which renders a seller strictly liable for defective products, may be available to the injured consumer.[8] As the earlier rule of *caveat emptor* began to crumble in the nineteenth century,[9] it was gradually replaced by the implied warranties of reasonable fitness and of merchantable quality. These warranties were established as a matter of policy, independent of any showing of factual consent, because reputable merchandisers stood behind their products already and because they could pass these expenses on as a cost of doing business.[10] These warranties, once tortious in nature, assumed the attributes of contractual provisions,[11] and were embodied in the English Sale of Goods Act of 1893, which legislation has been adopted throughout the Commonwealth.[12]

Pursuant to s. 14 of this statute, the following obligations exist: (1) "where the buyer, expressly or by implication, makes known to the seller the particular purpose for which the goods are required so as to show that the buyer relies on the seller's skill or judgment, and the goods are of a description that it is in the course of the seller's business to supply (whether he is the manufacturer or not),

---

[6] Ziegel, "The Seller's Liability for Defective Goods at Common Law" (1966), 12 McGill L.J. 183; Prosser, "The Implied Warranty of Merchantable Quality" (1943), 21 Can. Bar Rev. 446; Thompson, "Manufacturer's Liability" (1970), 8 Alta. L. Rev. 305; Waddams, "Implied Warranties and Products Liability", in Law Society of Upper Canada, *Special Lectures on New Developments in the Law of Torts* (1973); Waddams, "The Strict Liability of Suppliers of Goods" (1974), 37 Mod: L Rev. 154.

[7] Linden, "Products Liability in Canada" in Linden (ed.), *Studies in Canadian Tort Law* (Toronto: Butterworths, 1968), p. 216; Prosser, "The Fall of the Citadel (Strict Liability to the Consumer)" (1966), 50 Minn. L. Rev. 791; Stradiotto, "Products Liability in Tort" in *Special Lectures on New Developments in the Law of Torts* (1973); Mueller, "Product Liability in Tort", Law Society of Upper Canada, Special Lectures, *Torts in the 80s* (1983).

[8] *Moore v. Cooper Canada Ltd.* (1990), 2 C.C.L.T. (2d) 57 (Ont. H.C.). Under strict liability proof of reasonable care will not shelter a defendant from liability as it would in negligence. Unlike absolute liability, however, strict liability does require a plaintiff to establish that the product was defective.

[9] The history is outlined in Prosser, *supra*, n. 6, at pp. 447 *et seq.*

[10] See Prosser, *ibid.*, at p. 450.

[11] See *The Canadian Indemnity Co. v. Andrews & George Co.*, [1935] 1 S.C.R. 19, at p. 26.

[12] For example, Sale of Goods Act, R.S.O. 1990, c. S.1, s. 15, which was originally enacted in 1920, Stats. Ont., c. 40.

there is an implied condition that the goods will be reasonably fit for such purpose, but in the case of a contract for the sale of a specified article under its patent or other name there is no implied condition as to its fitness for any particular purpose," and (2) "where goods are bought by description from a seller who deals in goods of that description (whether he is the manufacturer or not), there is an implied condition that the goods will be of merchantable quality, but if the buyer has examined the goods, there is no implied condition as regards defects that such examination ought to have revealed". Unsound goods will frequently violate both of these warranties,[13] but they do not cover exactly the same territory. Certain articles may be of merchantable quality and yet not be reasonably fit for the buyer's purpose and vice versa.

It has been decided that the sale of a food product which violates the provisions of the Food and Drugs Act is automatically in breach of both the warranties of fitness and merchantability because such a sale is prohibited. Mr. Justice Mackoff, in *Wild Rose Mills Ltd. v. Ellison Milling Co.*[14] explained this new principle in this way:

> By the Food and Drugs Act and Reg. B. 15,002, Parliament has set standards which must be adhered to by manufacturers and vendors of food products. The purpose of the legislation is to ensure that food products do not contain toxic substances in an amount which is deemed to be hazardous to the health of consumers. Food products which do not meet those standards are considered to be unfit for human consumption and their sale is forbidden. It is difficult to imagine a food product which can be regarded as being less reasonably fit for its intended purpose or of lesser merchantable quality than one which by law is deemed to be hazardous to the health of the consumer and the sale of which is prohibited by law. In selling such a product to the plaintiff the defendant was in breach of the implied terms of the contract of sale.

It has been held that semen that was supplied during artificial insemination, and that was contaminated by H.I.V. is not subject to implied warranties under the Sale of Goods Act. The supply of semen in these circumstances was held by Sopinka J. in *ter Neuzen v. Korn*[15] not to be primarily a contract for the sale of semen but, rather, a contract for medical services, even though the provision of semen was an important component of the service. Further, the court refused to imply any common-law warranties. Because there was no way for the doctor to trace back the liability to the manufacturer in this case, an important reason for the creation of implied warranties is absent. "Biological products are not manufactured goods in the same sense as commercial goods."[16] Moreover, some biological products carry certain inherent risks and are, hence, "inherently dangerous" so physicians "cannot control the safety of these products beyond

---

[13] *Farmer v. Canada Packers Ltd.*, [1956] O.R. 657; *Buckley v. Lever Brothers Ltd.*, [1953] O.R. 704, [1953] 4 D.L.R. 16.

[14] (1985), 32 B.L.R. 125, at pp. 134-35 (B.C.S.C), negligence also found. See also *Gee v. White Spot Ltd.* (1986), 32 D.L.R. (4th) 238 (B.C.S.C.)

[15] [1995] 3 S.C.R. 674.

[16] *Ibid.*, at p. 717.

exhibiting the reasonable care expected of a professional". A new trial was ordered on the other issues of negligence and damages.

In *Pittman Estate v. Bain*,[17] it was held that H.I.V. tainted blood supplied during cardiac surgery, because it was "not a manufactured product", would not be subject to either a statutory or a common-law implied warranty by the hospital that the blood would be free from disease. Madame Justice Susan Lang explained that blood is "biologic" and as such "may be unavoidably unsafe". Donors give it without charge to the Red Cross. There is no way to pass the loss up the ladder to a manufacturer. To hold a hospital strictly liable for blood would "discourage those responsible for our health care from exercising their professional judgment, because they are concerned about their own liability".[18] Liability was imposed, nevertheless, on the hospital, the doctor and the Red Cross, not for negligence in the original transfusion, but for failing to promptly warn the Pittman family once the defendants learned of the possibility of the blood being contaminated with H.I.V.

Neither of the warranties is available against a private person, since it was felt that expectations are raised only where the seller is a dealer in goods. Let us now look at each of the warranties in turn.[19]

1. REASONABLE FITNESS FOR THE PURPOSE

In order to claim the benefit of the warranty of reasonable fitness, it must be established that the buyer expressly or impliedly made known to the seller the particular purpose for which the goods were bought so as to show that the buyer relied on the seller's skill or judgment. There need not be total reliance on the seller, as long as there is substantial reliance.[20] Thus, if the buyer has some knowledge of the goods or has obtained expert advice, the buyer may still be protected by the warranty.[21] These requirements have been liberally applied so that if someone purchases from a retailer "the reliance will be in general inferred from the fact that the buyer goes to the shop in the confidence that the tradesman has selected his stock with skill and judgment".[22] Hence, where one buys a hot-

---

[17] (1994), 19 C.C.L.T. (2d) 1 (Lang J.). See also *Robb v. Canadian Red Cross*, [2000] O.J. No. 2396, blood clotting factor concentrate made from whole blood for hemopheliacs also biological product.

[18] *Ibid*., at p. 99.

[19] See generally Atiyah, *The Sale of Goods*, 8th ed. (1990); Fridman, *Sale of Goods in Canada*, 4th ed. (1995); Chalmers, *The Sale of Goods Act. 1893*, 18th ed. (1981).

[20] See Schroeder J.A. (dissenting) in *Weller v. Fyfe*, [1965] 1 O.R. 15, at pp. 27-28, 46 D.L.R. (2d) 531 (C.A.). See *Ashington Piggeries v. Chrisopher Hill*, [1972] A.C. 441, seller included toxic ingredient into animal feed formula specified by buyer. See Waddams, *op. cit. supra*, n. 5, at p. 75, "partial reliance is enough".

[21] See Lacourcière J. in *Canada Building Materials v. W.R. Meadows of Canada Ltd.*, [1968] 1 O.R. 469; *Hayes v. Regina*, [1959] S.C.R. 801.

[22] *Grant v. Australian Knitting Mills*, [1936] A.C. 85, at p. 99. See also *Farmer v. Canada Packers Ltd.*, *supra*, n. 13.

water bottle,[23] or underwear from a store,[24] milk from a dairy,[25] or bread from a baker,[26] reliance is assumed to the extent that the buyer's use is a normal one. Where a buyer orders "black Italian cloth," which usually serves as a coat lining, without any special notice, the warranty is available if the fabric is unsuitable as a lining.[27] It is primarily when the purchaser's purpose is a special one, that it must be brought to the seller's attention. For example, if doors are required for a stadium which is pressurized, the company constructing them must be informed of this peculiarity.[28] If the seller's judgment is not relied upon at all, the warranty is inapplicable.[29] In *Smith Sheet Metal Works Ltd. v. Bingham and Hobbs Equipment Ltd.*,[30] for example, the warranty was not enforced because the buyer, alone, selected some cables for a glasswashing machine without any reliance upon the seller. The buyer had made the purpose known to the seller, but did not ask for an opinion. In fact, the purchaser had ignored a warning by the vendor about uncertainty as to the performance capacity of the cables. Similarly, a vendor selling nitrate pellets as fertilizer cannot be held responsible if they fail to detonate when used as explosives.[31] Further, if the buyer relies on the expertise of government inspectors, and not the sellers, as to the quality of fitness, the warranty does not apply.[32]

The content of the warranty is as varied as the types of goods and purposes available on the market. In *Canada Building Materials v. W.R. Meadows of Canada Ltd.*,[33] the buyer bought some anti-corrosive material called Galvafroid to protect its transfer cars on racks during the production of cement blocks. The special conditions were made known to the seller who was relied on substantially. When the material failed to prevent corrosion, under admittedly difficult conditions, liability was imposed. Likewise, in *R.W. Heron Paving Ltd. v. Dilworth Equipment Ltd.*[34] where asphalt plants could produce only 3,600 lbs. of asphalt, instead of 4,000 lbs. as they were supposed to, they were held "not reasonably fit in that they did not produce the required tonnage of asphalt". If a

---

[23] *Preist v. Last*, [1903] 2 K.B. 148 (C.A.). See also *Gorman v. Ear Hearing Services Ltd.* (1969), 8 D.L.R. (3d) 765 (P.E.I.), hearing aid.

[24] *Grant v. Australian Knitting Mills*, *supra*, n. 22.

[25] *Frost v. Aylesbury Dairy Co.*, [1905] 1 K.B. 608 (C.A.).

[26] *Negro v. Pietro's Bread Co.*, *supra*, n. 1. With regard to the purchase of a car, see *Marshall v. Ryan Motors Ltd.* (1922), 65 D.L.R. 742, at p. 747 (Sask. C.A.); *Freeman v. Consolidated Motors Ltd.* (1968), 65 W.W.R. 234, at p. 238 (Man.).

[27] *John MacDonald & Co. v. Princess Manufacturing Co.*, [1926] S.C.R. 472, [1926] 1 D.L.R. 718.

[28] *Industrial Door Co. Ltd. v. Shanahan's Ltd.* (1985), 14 C.L.R. 303 (B.C.S.C.).

[29] *Tregunno v. Aldershop Distributing Co-op. Co.*, [1943] O.R. 795 (C.A.).

[30] [1949] 4 D.L.R. 363 (B.C.).

[31] *Corbett Construction v. Simplot Chemical*, [1971] 2 W.W.R. 332 (Man.). See also *C.C.H. v. Mollenhauer Contracting* (1974), 51 D.L.R. (3d) 638 (S.C.C.); *Baker v. Suzuki Motor Co.* (1993), 17 C.C.L.T. (2d) 241, at p. 268 (Alta. Q.B.), no negligence re motorcycle purchase.

[32] *Claude and Conrad Toner Ltd. v. Hettema Inc.*, [1999] N.B.J. No. 54; affd [1999] N.B.J. No. 571 (C.A.); leave to appeal denied [2000] S.C.C.A. No. 74, regarding merchantability of potatoes.

[33] [1968] 1 O.R. 469.

[34] [1963] 1 O.R. 201, at p. 209 (Wells J.).

truck is unsuitable for the heavy work for which it is acquired,[35] if a stallion bought for breeding cannot perform this task,[36] if certain boxes for sending clothing across the country are inadequate,[37] if wireless technology bought to integrate a computer system does not work,[38] if a heat pump that was supposed to heat a home fails to do so because of low water pressure,[39] if roofing material cannot be exposed to sunlight,[40] or if a cow bought for milking is no good for that purpose,[41] the warranty is breached. A Bugatti car has been held not to be a comfortable car for touring purposes, as required by the buyer.[42] When it is explained that coal must be suitable for burning in a particular ship, it must conform to this specification.[43] When white aluminum siding is requested, mauve, pink or lilac-tinted siding will not do.[44] Similarly, milk infected with typhoid fever,[45] a bun with a stone in it,[46] a hot-water bottle that burst,[47] and a motor home that bursts into flames shortly after purchase,[48] are not reasonably fit. Also unfit are a muskrat fur coat that keeps coming apart,[49] a plastic clothes pin that shatters injuring the plaintiff in the eye,[50] and Antarctic whalemeat infected with botulinus toxin that kills the mink to which it is fed.[51] Further, a cement foundation may be unfit because it did not meet the minimum building code or C.S.A. Standards.[52]

Not only does this warranty apply to the goods proper, but it also covers the container or package in which the product comes, since both are "goods supplied" under a contract of sale.[53] In *Marleau v. People's Gas Supply Co. Ltd.*,[54] the plaintiff was injured when a container of acetylene gas exploded in a

---

[35]   *Randall v. Sawyer-Massey Co. Ltd.* (1918), 43 O.L.R. 602; *Evanchuk Transport v. Canadian Trailmobile*, [1971] 5 W.W.R. 317 (Alta. C.A.).

[36]   *Wood v. Anderson* (1915), 33 O.L.R. 143 (C.A.).

[37]   *Dominion Paper Box Co. v. Crown Tailoring Co.* (1918), 42 O.L.R. 249 (C.A.).

[38]   *T.K.M. Communications v. A.T. Schindler Communications Inc.*, [1998] O.J. No. 1745.

[39]   *Johnson v. Maritime Water Treatment Ltd.* [1999] N.B.J. No. 593.

[40]   *Newberry Energy Ltd. c.o.b. Mohawk Distributors Ltd. v. Parthenon Building Systems Ltd.* (1985), 14 C.L.R. 165 (Sask. Q.B.).

[41]   *Gagnon v. Geneau* (1951), 27 M.P.R. 305, [1951] 1 D.L.R. 516 (N.B.C.A.).

[42]   *Baldry v. Marshall*, [1925] 1 K.B. 260, [1924] All E.R. Rep. 155 (C.A.).

[43]   *Manchester Liners Ltd. v. Rea Ltd.*, [1922] 2 A.C. 74, [1922] All E.R. Rep. 605.

[44]   *Associated Siding Applicators Ltd. v. Jonesson (E.C.) Contractors Ltd.* (1985), 57 A.R. 136 (Q.B.).

[45]   *Frost v. Aylesbury Dairy Co.*, *supra*, n. 25.

[46]   *Chaproniere v. Mason* (1905), 21 T.L.R. 633 (C.A.).

[47]   *Preist v. Last*, *supra*, n. 23.

[48]   *Miller v. Cobra Industries Inc.*, [1998] O.J. No. 381; affd [2000] O.J. No. 4609.

[49]   *Chomyn v. American Fur Co.*, [1948] 2 W.W.R. 110 (Sask.).

[50]   *Buckley v. Lever Brothers Ltd.*, [1953] O.R. 704, [1953] 4 D.L.R. 16.

[51]   *Farmer v. Canada Packers Ltd.*, [1956] O.R. 657.

[52]   *Alie v. Bertrand & Frère Construction*, [2000] O.J. No. 1360, vard on another point [2001] O.J. No. 2014, the "Infamous Cement Case".

[53]   *Geddling v. Marsh*, [1920] 1 K.B. 668, [1920] All E.R. Rep. 631, mineral water bottle burst; *Morelli v. Fitch and Gibbons*, [1928] 2 K.B. 636, [1928] All E.R. Rep. 610.

[54]   [1940] S.C.R. 708, [1940] 4 D.L.R. 433. See also *Bradshaw v. Boothe's Marine Ltd. et al.*, [1973] 2 O.R. 646, where a defective propane gas tank on cabin cruiser caused fire.

garage due to some unknown cause. Although the gas was purchased from the defendant, the container was not. It was supplied on a rental basis and had to be returned after the gas was used up. There was evidence that the explosion was not caused by anything external, but by something internal. The Supreme Court of Canada held that this warranty (as well as the warranty of merchantable quality) had been violated. Samples or free goods are also subject to implied warranties, even though it is sometimes difficult to classify the transaction as a sale.[55] Another important case along these lines is *Hart v. Bell Telephone*,[56] where someone who received an electric shock, while using a pay telephone, recovered on the basis of an implied warranty that the "equipment was reasonably safe for use", despite the absence of negligence.

Sometimes, the implied warranty of fitness does not protect the buyer. For example, it was said[57] that the failure of a breast implant, which ruptured, did not necessarily establish that it was unfit; that would be mere "speculation". Allergies create problems. In *Griffiths v. Peter Conway Ltd.*,[58] a plaintiff who had unusually sensitive skin contracted dermatitis from a Harris tweed coat. The Court of Appeal held that there was no violation of the warranty because the buyer did not inform the seller about her abnormality or idiosyncrasy to enable him to exercise his skill or judgment. Another similar case is *Yachetti v. John Duff & Sons*.[59] The plaintiff bought a pound of pork sausage from a meat pedlar, Paolini, who had bought the pork from the meat packer, had ground it up and had made sausage out of it. The plaintiff tasted some of the pork as it was cooking and contracted trichinosis. Her action against the seller *inter alia* was dismissed, because the normal way to eat pork is after cooking it. This use was abnormal. If the seller had been told that it would be eaten raw, liability might have ensued, but he had not been so notified. Similarly where goods are misused by the purchaser,[60] or where bread is made "ropy" by conditions in the bakery rather than by the flour supplied,[61] the warranty is not breached.

2. MERCHANTABLE QUALITY

The implied warranty of merchantable quality covers much of the territory dealt with by the warranty of reasonable fitness, but it is somewhat wider in scope.

---

[55] *Buckley v. Lever Bros.*, *supra*, n. 50; *Hartman v. R.* (1973), 2 O.R. (2d) 244, 42 D.L.R. (3d) 488 (C.A.); Waddams, *op. cit. supra*, n. 5, at p. 101.

[56] (1979), 10 C.C.L.T. 335 (Ont. C.A.); *cf. Frie v. Saskatchewan Telecommunications*, [1979] 6 W.W.R. 60, equipment reasonably safe, though plaintiff killed while talking on telephone when lightning hit wire.

[57] See Prowse J.A. in *Hollis v. Birch* (1993), 16 C.C.L.T. (2d) 140, at p. 161 (B.C.C.A.); affd on other grounds [1995] 4 S.C.R. 634.

[58] [1939] 1 All E.R. 685 (C.A.). See also *Ingham v. Emes*, [1955] 2 Q.B. 366, [1955] 2 All E.R. 740, hair dye.

[59] [1942] O.R. 682. See also *Heil v. Hedges*, [1951] 1 T.L.R. 512.

[60] *Ontario Sewer Pipe Co. v. MacDonald* (1910), 2 O.W.N. 483 (C.A.), culvert pipes misused.

[61] *Alder v. Maple Leaf Milling Co.* (1926), 30 O.W.N. 411 (Lennox J.), not necessary to consider warranty.

There must be a "sale by description" for the warranty to be invoked. Whenever the buyer has not seen the goods, the sale is obviously one by description.[62] But there can also be a sale by description where the goods are seen.[63] The phrase probably applies to sales where no words are spoken, as in a self-service store, for example, as long as there is a label or some other description of the goods.[64] A sale is not by description, however, where it is made clear that the buyer is purchasing a particular thing because of its unique qualities and that no other will do.[65] A similar result would occur where the buyer points to some goods and says, "I want these goods", without describing them. If the buyer examines the goods, the warranty is not available as the examination should reveal any defects. There is no obligation upon the buyer to inspect the goods prior to purchase, nor to retain an expert for the purpose.[66] However, this obligation may exist in the civil law.[67] If undertaking to check the goods, the buyer need not do so with a microscope or take them apart.[68] Upon examination the buyer waives the right only to those defects a typical inspection would reveal. Thus, the warranty was not excluded where a reasonable inspection would not have revealed the presence of arsenic in beer,[69] and where a child's catapult toy broke during ordinary use.[70]

The meaning of merchantable quality has evolved through many cases. The matter of merchantability is a question of fact.[71] It is not necessary to show that a thing is "valueless" to hold it "defective".[72] The most frequently quoted definition is that of Lord Justice Farwell, in *Bristol Tramways Co. Ltd. v. Fiat Motors Ltd.*,[73] who interpreted the phrase to mean that "the article is of such quality and in such condition that a reasonable man acting reasonably would after a full examination accept it under the circumstances of the case in performance of his offer to buy that article, whether he buys it for his own use or in order to sell again". Lord Wright, in *Grant v. Australian Knitting Mills*,[74] has asserted that "merchantable does not mean that the thing is saleable in the market simply because it looks all right; it is not merchantable in that event if it has defects unfitting it for its only proper use but not apparent on ordinary examination". In other words, not only must the article be saleable in the market,

---

[62]	*Varley v. Whipp*, [1900] 1 Q.B. 513, at p. 516 (per Channell J.).

[63]	*Grant v. Australian Knitting Mills*, [1936] A.C. 85.

[64]	See Ziegel, *supra*, n. 6, at p. 187.

[65]	*Ibid.*

[66]	*Ibid.*, at p. 190.

[67]	Durnford, "What is an Apparent Defect in the Contract of Sale" (1963-64), 10 McGill L.J. 60.

[68]	Ziegel, *supra*, n. 6, at p. 190.

[69]	*Wren v. Holt*, [1903] 1 K.B. 610.

[70]	*Godley v. Perry*, [1960] 1 W.L.R. 9, [1960] 1 All E.R. 36. See also *Buckley v. Lever Bros. Ltd.*, [1953] O.R. 704.

[71]	*F.E. Hookway Co. Ltd. v. Alfred Issac & Sons*, [1954] 1 Lloyd's Rep. 491, at p. 512.

[72]	*Chomyn v. American Fur Co., supra*, n. 49.

[73]	[1910] 2 K.B. 831, at p. 841 (C.A.).

[74]	[1936] A.C. 85, at pp. 99-100. See also *B.S. Brown & Son v. Craiks Ltd.*, [1970] 1 All E.R. 823 (H.L.), price relevant consideration.

but it must also be reasonably fit for the general purposes such goods serve. It should be realised, however, that "a short formula of words cannot provide a safe definition of 'merchantable' which can be used in all circumstances".[75]

The courts have placed stringent demands upon sellers under this warranty. If the goods are unmerchantable, the seller is accountable even if honest or incapable of discovering the defect.[76] Often insignificant faults render goods unmerchantable. For example, *International Business Machines Co. Ltd. v. Shcherban*,[77] a buyer was allowed to reject a scale which cost $294, because the glass in its dial was broken, even though the glass could be replaced for a mere 30 cents. Similarly, in *Jackson v. Rotax Motor & Cycle Co.*,[78] 364 of the 609 motor horns supplied to the buyer were scratched and dented because of poor packing. The warranty of merchantability was held to have been breached, even though the horns worked and could have been patched up cheaply. Thus, even though the damaged goods may be serviceable, they are not acceptable as new goods.

A number of cases demonstrate the parameters of protection provided by the warranty. In *Marleau v. People's Gas Supply Co. Ltd.*,[79] liability was imposed on the basis of this warranty (as well as that of reasonable fitness) where a container of acetylene gas exploded from an unknown cause, which was internal to the container. A muskrat fur coat that keeps tearing,[80] a plastic clothespin that shatters, injuring someone,[81] and a bottle of chocolate milk containing broken glass,[82] are unmerchantable. Antarctic whalemeat infected with botulinus toxin that killed mink to which it was fed,[83] a tree stump cutting machine that failed to reach specification,[84] a farm combine subject to dangerous electrical malfunctions,[85] and anti-freeze that was not permanent or "good like Prestone",[86] were also held to be unsatisfactory. A truck that bursts into flames is clearly not merchantable,[87] nor is a motor home that combusts within three months of purchase,[88] nor is computer equipment which needs repairs from the start in

---

[75] *Strandquist v. Coneco Equipment* (1999), 48 C.C.L.T. (2d) 209, at p. 215 (Alta. C.A.).

[76] *Chomyn v. American Fur Co., supra*, n. 49.

[77] [1925] 1 D.L.R. 864 (Sask. C.A.). *Cf.*, complicated custom-made goods. *Casden v. Caper Enterprises Ltd.*, F.C.A. February 8, 1993, yacht.

[78] [1910] 2 K.B. 937 (C.A.).

[79] [1940] S.C.R. 708. See also *Bradshaw v. Boothe's Marine Ltd. et al.*, [1973] 2 O.R. 646.

[80] *Chomyn v. American Fur Co., supra*, n. 49.

[81] *Buckley v. Lever Brothers Ltd., supra*, n. 50.

[82] *Shandloff v. City Dairy Ltd.*, [1936] O.R. 579, [1936] 4 D.L.R. 712 (C.A.).

[83] *Farmer v. Canada Packers Ltd.*, [1956] O.R. 657.

[84] *Weller v. Fyfe*, [1965] 1 O.R. 15, 46 D.L.R. (2d) 531 (C.A.).

[85] *Olshaski Farms Ltd. v. Skene Farm Equipment Ltd.* (1987), 49 Alta. L.R. (2d) 249 (Q.B.).

[86] *Thorncrest Motors Ltd. v. Freedman*, [1953] O.W.N. 632. See also *Stephenson v. Sanitaris Ltd.* (1913), 30 O.L.R. 60 (C.A.), non-intoxicating hop ale; *Parkhill & Co. v. McCabe* (1922), 53 O.L.R. 117 (C.A.), car of good onions.

[87] Nor is it reasonably fit for the purpose, see *Chabot v. Ford Motor Co.* (1982), 22 C.C.L.T. 185 (Ont. H.C.) (*per* Eberle J.).

[88] *Miller v. Cobra, supra*, n. 48.

order to be usable.[89] In *Algoma Truck & Tractor Sales Ltd. v. Bert's Auto Supply Ltd.*,[90] the defendant sold to the plaintiff a reconditioned cylinder head which it had bought from a manufacturer without looking at the crate. When it turned out that the machinery could not be used, it was held that there was a breach of both warranties which had been incorporated in the deal by an oral guarantee. The court felt that there was no need to prove the exact cause of the defect if it was in the article when it was received.

A container must also comply with the standard of merchantability. In *Morelli v. Fitch and Gibbons*,[91] the plaintiff was injured when the bottle of Stone's ginger wine, which had been bought from the defendant, broke as the plaintiff uncorked it. In *Wilson v. Rickett Cockerell & Co. Ltd.*,[92] some coal merchants were held liable when an explosion resulted because the Coalite they delivered contained an explosive among the pieces of coal. Not merely the pieces of coal, but *all* the goods delivered, were considered "goods supplied". In the same way, instructions that accompany a product are also "goods" that are covered by the warranty of merchantability.[93]

There are a few situations where the seller escaped liability. In *Henry Kendall & Sons v. Wm. Lillico & Sons*,[94] some turkey feed was held to be merchantable, even though it killed some of the buyer's turkeys. Lord Reid said that "merchantable can only mean commercially saleable". However, the powerful dissent by Lord Pearce, to the effect that "seconds" are not necessarily merchantable, is to be preferred. Where certain yarn was not suitable for the plaintiff's specific purpose, although otherwise acceptable, there was said to be no violation of this warranty.[95]

The article must be of merchantable quality not only at the time of the sale, but also for a reasonable time thereafter.[96] Thus, where a $400,000 tree feller caught fire after a short period of use it was not merchantable, because if a vendor had told his buyers that "these machines were liable to self-destruct by fire after a few months' use ... we doubt that any reasonable person would have bought one."[97] There are limits to the durability required of goods, however. Where an electric

---

[89] *Villeseche v. Total North Communication Ltd.*, [1997] Y.J. No. 51 (C.A.).

[90] [1968] 2 O.R. 153.

[91] [1928] 2 K.B. 636, [1928] All E.R. Rep. 610.

[92] [1954] 1 Q.B. 598 (C.A.).

[93] *Wormell v. R.H.M. Agriculture (East) Ltd.*, [1986] 1 All E.R. 769 (Q.B.).

[94] [1969] 2 A.C. 31, [1968] 2 All E.R. 444.

[95] *J. & C.B. Clay Ltd. v. Henry Davis & Co. Ltd.* (1931), 40 O.W.N. 459; approved (1932), 41 O.W.N. 132. See also *Yachetti v. John Duff & Sons Ltd.*, *supra*, n. 54; *Massey-Harris Co. Ltd. v. Skelding*, [1934] 3 D.L.R. 193 (S.C.C.), tractor; *Cotter v. Luckie*, [1918] N.Z.L.R. 811, sterile bull.

[96] *Mash & Murrell Ltd. v. Joseph Emanuel Ltd.*, [1961] 1 All E.R. 485; revd on the facts, [1962] 1 All E.R. 77; *Beer v. Walker* (1877), 46 L.J.Q.B. 677. Some provinces enacted durability warranties, see Consumer Protection Act, S.S. 1996, c. C-30.1, s. 48(g); Consumer Protection Act, R.S.N.S. 1989, c. 92, s. 26; Consumer Product Warranty and Liability Act, S.N.B. 1978, c. C-18.1, s. 12.

[97] *Strandquist v. Caneco Equipment*, *supra*, n. 75, at p. 217.

blanket caused a fire 10 - 15 years after its purchase, there was no liability, as the plaintiffs could not prove that a defect existed at the time of sale.[98] Further, peaches, however, need not be of such a quality that they can withstand being shipped over long distances under poor conditions.[99]

a) Used Goods

The warranty of merchantable quality applies to second-hand goods. This does not mean, however, that someone who buys used goods should expect to receive new ones. In *Bartlett v. Sidney Marcus Ltd.*[100] Lord Justice Denning stated that a used car should be "in a roadworthy condition, fit to be driven along the road in safety, even though not as perfect as a new car".

There are Canadian *obiter dicta* to the contrary, but they are unworthy of support. For example, in *Presley v. MacDonald*,[101] a County Court Judge stated that "it is well-established, that if a prospective purchaser chooses an article such as a second-hand car from a second-hand dealer, and in the exercise of his own judgment buys the car without any warranty or misrepresentation by the seller, the purchaser in such cases would have no cause of action against the seller for any defect in the car". No authority was cited by the court in support of this proposition.

A new theory was used when damages were awarded to the purchaser of a used Oldsmobile when the car's transmission broke down causing an accident a few days after purchase. The court based its decision on a warranty contained in a "certificate of mechanical fitness", given pursuant to the Highway Traffic Act that read: "We hereby certify that the . . . vehicle is in a safe condition to be operated on a highway."[102]

As these certificates become more widely used across Canada, this rationale may supplant the implied warranties as far as used cars are concerned. This is a welcome development since buyers of used goods should receive sound goods that are in a decent state of repair, although they certainly cannot expect new goods. "'Used' goods and 'defective' goods are not interchangeable terms."[103]

---

[98] *McCann v. Sears Canada Ltd.* (1998), 43 B.L.R. (2d) 217 (Ont. Gen. Div.); affd (1999), 122 O.A.C. 91 (Div. Ct.).

[99] *Tregunno v. Aldershop Distributing Co-operative Co. Ltd.*, [1943] O.R. 795 (C.A.).

[100] [1965] 1 W.L.R. 1013, at p. 1016, [1965] 2 All E.R. 753 (C.A.). See also *Freeman v. Consolidated Motors Ltd.* (1968), 65 W.W.R. 234, 69 D.L.R. (2d) 581 (Man.); *Peters v. Parkway Mercury Sales Ltd.* (1975), 58 D.L.R. (3d) 128 (N.B.C.A.), no liability for defective transmission in six-year-old car; *Green v. Holiday Chevrolet-Oldsmobile.*, [1975] 4 W.W.R. 445, 55 D.L.R. (3d) 637; see Waddams, *op. cit. supra*, n. 5, at p. 89.

[101] [1963] 1 O.R. 619, 38 D.L.R. (2d) 237, at p. 238. See also *Godsoe v. Beatty* (1958), 19 D.L.R. (2d) 265 (N.B.C.A.).

[102] See also *Henzl v. Brussels Motors Ltd.* (1972), 31 D.L.R. (3d) 131 (Fogarty C.C.J.). *Cf., Schmidt v. International Harvester Co.* [1962], 38 W.W.R. 180, at p. 183 (Man.), certificate did not affect contract because aimed at roadworthiness only.

[103] Ziegel, *supra*, n. 6, at p. 190.

b) Critique: Privity Rule, Disclaimer Clauses and Other Limitations

The protection afforded consumers by sales law is inadequate.[104] Firstly, persons who are not in contractual relations with the seller are unable to secure reparation on the basis of the implied warranties because of an absence of privity. This is unfortunate for a great many consumers and users injured by a defective article, who have not purchased it from a seller. Moreover, it is the innocent retailer who must bear this warranty burden, rather than the manufacturer of the article who is usually the real culprit.

Because of this some legislatures have extended the responsibility beyond the immediate parties to the contract.[105] The courts have also used some ingenuity to stretch the operation of these warranties to third persons. For example, in *Lockett v. A. & M. Charles Ltd.*,[106] the implied warranty of fitness was extended to cover a woman at a hotel who ordered and ate some fish that was not fit for human consumption, even though her husband, who accompanied her, had paid for it. Mr. Justice Tucker was of the view that a "person who orders and consumes food is liable to pay for it as between himself and the proprietor of the restaurant", regardless of the arrangements made for payment between the guests themselves. Sometimes courts use agency theory to hold the seller liable in warranty to third persons, as where a father buys food for members of his family.[107]

A significant breakthrough has also come in *Murray v. Sperry Rand*,[108] where a farm implement manufacturer was held liable to a farmer, with whom he was not in a buyer-seller relationship, because the machine did not live up to the claims made about it in the sales brochure, on the ground that the manufacturer's case is presented to the customer in this way "just as directly as he would if they were sitting down together to discuss the matter". So too, in *Leitz v. Saskatoon Drug & Stationery Co.*,[109] a distributor (as well as a vendor) of sunglasses was held liable for some defective sunglasses, which shattered when hit by a baseball, on contract theory (as well as negligence) because it made an affirmation on a tag to the effect that the glasses were "first in safety", which enticed the consumer to purchase the glasses, and in which there was expressed an intention to induce contractual relations.[110] There had been an earlier case

---

[104] See Waddams, *op. cit, supra*, n. 5, for a more thorough examination of the present system's shortcomings and also the Ontario Law Reform Commission's *Report on Products Liability* (1979).

[105] See, for example, Uniform Commercial Code S. 2-318; Consumer Protection Act, S.S. 1996, c. C-30.1; Consumer Product Warranty and Liability Act, S.N.B. 1978, c. C-18.1.

[106] [1938] 4 All E.R. 170.

[107] *Greenberg v. Lorenz* (1961), 173 N.E. 2d 773 (N.Y.C.A.).

[108] (1979), 23 O.R. (2d) 456 (*per* Reid J.).

[109] [1980] 5 W.W.R. 673 (*per* Sirois J.).

[110] The vendor was allowed reimbursement against the distributor for the entire judgment as well as costs, see also *McMorran v. Dominion Stores* (1977), 1 C.C.L.T. 259 (*per* Lerner J.); *Lambert v. Lewis*, [1980] 2 W.L.R. 299 (C.A.); revd [1982] A.C. 225 (H.L.); *cf.*, *Willis v. F.M.C. Machinery & Chemicals Ltd.* (1976), 68 D.L.R. (3d) 127 (P.E.I.).

where a manufacturer of trucks was held responsible in warranty when the vehicles broke down, even though it was not a party to the actual contract of sale.[111] The buyer had dealt with the manufacturer, told it of his purpose and had relied upon its advice, but the actual sale was made through an intermediary. One can expect this trend to continue particularly in the aftermath of the spectacular decision of *General Motors v. Kravitz*,[112] even though it was based on the civil law of Quebec.

Secondly, disclaimer clauses are being used by sellers to rob these warranties of their efficacy.[113] Most sale of goods statutes permit the parties to contract out of the warranties. For example, the Ontario Act provides that "where any right, duty or liability would arise under a contract of sale by implication of law, it may be negatived or varied by express agreement or by the course of dealing between the parties, or by usage, if the usage is such as to bind both parties to the contract".[114] This right has been taken up with a vengeance by most sellers, particulary those who deal in larger appliances and vehicles. Sweeping terms in fine print often deprive buyers of the protection afforded by the implied warranties.[115]

Some legislatures have prohibited these disclaimer clauses in certain situations.[116] In Manitoba, for example, the Consumer Protection Act declares that the seller's warranties and conditions are included in every sale and hire-purchase, "notwithstanding any agreement to the contrary".[117] Ontario has also enacted a more limited provision in an amendment to its Consumer Protection Act in these terms:

> The implied conditions and warranties applying to the sale of goods by virtue of the *Sale of Goods Act* apply to goods sold by a consumer sale and any written term or acknowledgment, whether part of the contract of sale or not, that purports to negative or vary any of such implied conditions and warranties is void and, if a term of a contract, is severable therefrom, and such term or acknowledgment shall not be evidence of circumstances showing an intent that any of the implied conditions and warranties are not to apply.[118]

A "consumer sale" is defined as a "contract for the sale of goods made in the ordinary course of business to a purchaser for the purchaser's consumption or use . . . ".[119] There are other such statutory provisions.[120]

---

[111] *Ford Motor Co. of Canada Ltd. v. Haley* (1967), 62 D.L.R. (2d) 329 (S.C.C.); affg. 57 D.L.R. (2d) 15 (Alta. C.A.).

[112] [1979] 1 S.C.R. 790. See Bridge, (1980), 25 McGill L.J. 335. See also *Algoma Truck & Tractor Sales Ltd. v. Bert's Auto Supply Ltd.*, [1968] 2 O.R. 153.

[113] See generally, Coote, *Exception Clauses* (1964); Waddams, *op. cit. supra*, n. 5, chapter 7.

[114] Sale of Goods Act, R.S.O. 1990, c. S.1, s. 53.

[115] *Air Nova v. Messier-Dowty Ltd.*, [2000] O.J. No. 39 (C.A.), exclusionary clause prevented carrier from recovering for crash caused by collapse of landing gear.

[116] Cumming, "The Judicial Treatment of Disclaimer Clauses in Sale of Goods Transactions in Canada" (1972), 10 Osgoode Hall L.J. 281.

[117] R.S.M. 1987, c. C200, s. 58.

[118] Consumer Protection Act, R.S.O. 1990, c. C.31, s. 34(2).

[119] *Ibid.*, s. 34(1).

[120] See Waddams, *op. cit. supra*, n. 5, at p. 74.

There has been judicial as well as legislative reaction to disclaimer clauses. The doctrine of fundamental term, which has been said to be a matter of construction only,[121] was developed in England and, whatever its basis, is a "phenomenon" that is "alive and prospering" in Canada.[122] It inhibits sellers from contracting out of the very root of their contract. For example, in *Karsales [Harrow] Ltd. v. Wallis*,[123] the defendant bought a second-hand Buick. When it was delivered it would not run and had to be towed to the defendant's place of business. Although an exculpatory clause expressly provided that there was no condition or warranty that the vehicle was roadworthy, the Court of Appeal denied the right of the seller to enforce the contract against the defendants after their fundamental breach of the contract. It was their duty to supply a car, but a car that will not go is "not a car at all".[124] Lord Justice Parker stated that where a vehicle is "incapable of self-propulsion except after a complete overhaul . . . there was a breach of fun-damental term".[125]

The Canadian courts have followed suit, applying the doctrine against sellers who supplied insulating material that did not function,[126] a boat engine that was not workable,[127] and a car that did not run.[128] Some United States courts have held these exclusionary clauses void as they work against public policy,[129] but such courage has not yet been shown in Commonwealth courts (except under the Quebec civil law).[130] They have been content instead to fight a rear guard action by using a variety of techniques to combat these disclaimers, including strict

---

[121] *Suisse Atlantique etc. v. N.V. Rotterdamsche Kolen Centrale*, [1967] 1 A.C. 361, [1966] 2 All E.R. 61. See *Photo Production v. Securicor Transport*, [1980] 1 All E.R. 556; Ziegel, "The House of Lords Overrules *Harbutt's Plasticine*" (1980), 30 U. of T.L.J. 421, giving a thorough picture of the present situation.

[122] *Heffron v. Imperial Parking Co.* (1974), 3 O.R. (2d) 722, at p. 731 (C.A.) (*per* Estey J.A.); *Chomedy Aluminum v. Belcourt Construction* (1979), 97 D.L.R. (3d) 170; affd [1980] 2 S.C.R. 718. See also *Lightburn v. Belmont Sales Ltd.* (1969), 6 D.L.R. (3d) 692 (B.C.); *R.G. McLean Ltd. v. Canadian Vickers Ltd.*, [1971] 1 O.R. 207 (C.A.); *Knowles v. Anchorage Holdings Co. Ltd.* (1964), 46 W.W.R. 173, 43 D.L.R. (2d) 300 (B.C.); *Western Tractor Ltd. v. Dyck* (1969), 7 D.L.R. (3d) 535 (Sask. C.A.); *Western Processing & Cold Storage Ltd. v. Hamilton Construction Co. Ltd.* (1965), 51 W.W.R. 354 (Man. C.A.); *Allan v. Bushnell T.V. Co. Ltd.*, [1969] 1 O.R. 107, at p. 117 (*per* Leiff J.); *Pippy v. R.C.A. Victor Co. Ltd.* (1964), 49 D.L.R. (2d) 523 (N.S.); *Chabot v. Ford Motor Co., supra*, n. 81.

[123] [1956] 1 W.L.R. 936, [1956] 2 All E.R. 866 (C.A.).

[124] *Ibid.*, at p. 942, W.L.R. (*per* Birkett L.J.).

[125] *Ibid.*, at p. 943.

[126] *Western Processing & Cold Storage Ltd. v. Hamilton Construction Co. Ltd., supra*, n. 122.

[127] *Knowles v. Anchorage Holdings Co. Ltd., supra*, n. 122.

[128] *Lightburn v. Belmont Sales Ltd., supra*, n. 122. See also *Gibbons v. Trapp Motors Ltd.* (1970), 9 D.L.R. (3d) 742 (B.C.).

[129] *Henningsen v. Bloomfield Motors, Inc.* (1960), 32 N.J. 358, 161 A. 2d 69; *Western Tractor Ltd. v. Dyck, supra*, n. 122.

[130] *G.M. v. Kravitz*, [1979] 1 S.C.R. 790.

construction of the terms,[131] use of the *contra proferentem* rule,[132] and the refusal to include a clause as part of the contract if it appears in a brochure.[133]

The third shortcoming of sales law is that these warranties are not available if the conditions are not met. Thus, where a purchase is by trade name,[134] where there is an inspection, where there is no reliance, or where the seller is not a dealer in goods, the warranties do not avail an injured consumer.

These are substantial inadequacies, which have led to some legislative reform as well as calls for legislative reform.[135] Nevertheless, if a consumer's claim is defeated by any of these impediments all is not lost because tort law is waiting in the wings to fill the gap.

B. Tort Theory

Tort theory was of little help to the injured consumer, even where negligence in manufacture was established, until the early part of this century. To win recovery from a producer of defective goods privity of contract was generally necessary. Indeed, Lord Abinger, in *Winterbottom v. Wright*,[136] foresaw "the most absurd and outrageous consequences, to which I can see no limit . . . unless we confine the operation of such contracts as this to the parties who entered into them". This decision, however, did not foreclose actions for indemnity. An injured purchaser could, under the Sale of Goods Act, sue the seller, who could sue the supplier, who could, in turn, sue the manufacturer.[137] This was a circuitous and wasteful game of musical chairs. Moreover, if one party along the line was insolvent and uninsured, some innocent distributor might be denied reimbursement while the fabricator, the real villain, escaped civil liability. Thus, for a time, it was possible for a manufacturer to snap its fingers at third party victims of its negligently produced articles, an intolerable sacrifice on the altar of *laissez-faire*.

Understandably, the courts rebelled and began to invent exceptions to the no-privity rule of *Winterbottom v. Wright*. If having any *knowledge* of the defect and failing to inform the consumer of it, or, if misrepresenting the article as safe, the producer would be held liable on a theory of "something like fraud".[138]

---

[131] *Cork v. Greavette Boats Ltd.*, [1940] O.R. 352, [1940] 4 D.L.R. 202 (C.A.). See Waddams, *op. cit. supra*, n. 5, at p. 166, indicating other devices available, including unconscionability.

[132] *Eggen Seed Farms Ltd. v. Alberta Wheat Pool* (1997), 205 A.R. 77 (Q.B.), clause concerning unmerchantable fertilizer held ambiguous and construed against the drafter.

[133] *Canada Building Materials v. W.R. Meadows of Canada Ltd.*, [1968] 1 O.R. 469, 66 D.L.R. (2d) 674.

[134] *O'Fallon v. Inecto Rapid (Canada) Ltd.*, [1940] 4 D.L.R. 276 (B.C.C.A.).

[135] Ontario Law Reform Commission, *Report on Products Liability* (1979); See Linden, "Commentary" (1980), 5 Can. Bus. L.J. 92.

[136] (1842), 10 M. & W. 109, at p. 114, 152 E.R. 402, at p. 405.

[137] See for example, *Bradshaw v. Boothe's Marine Ltd. et al.*, [1973] 2 O.R. 646, 35 D.L.R. (3d) 43.

[138] *Prosser and Keeton on The Law of Torts*, 5th ed. (1984), p. 682. See also *Ross v. Dunstall* (1921), 62 S.C.R. 393, 63 D.L.R. 63, at p. 68; *Nokes v. Kent Co.*(1913), 23 O.W.R. 771, 9 D.L.R.

Similarly, liability could be imposed for articles that were inherently dangerous to human safety or dangerous *per se*, such as guns, explosives and poisons.[139] But these inadequate safeguards could not serve a burgeoning industrial society and, in 1916, the New York Court of Appeals expanded the inherently dangerous exception so as to engulf the original rule. Mr. Justice Benjamin Cardozo, in *MacPherson v. Buick Motor Co.*,[140] declared simply that the category of inherently dangerous things would henceforth include "anything which would be dangerous if negligently made". The back of the no-privity defence was thus broken and the first "assault upon the citadel" was victorious.[141]

It is commonly, although wrongly, believed that this development worked its way into the law of the Commonwealth 16 years later through the decision of *Donoghue v. Stevenson*.[142] This is erroneous, however, for on two occasions prior to 1932, Canadian courts demonstrated that they were prepared to follow the principle of *McPherson v. Buick*. One of these cases is *Ross v. Dunstall*,[143] where Justice Duff, on the Supreme Court of Canada, cited the *McPherson* decision in imposing liability for a defective gun. Even though Mr. Justice Cardozo's expanded version of the dangerous product exception was not necessary for its decision, since a gun is clearly an inherently dangerous thing, the Supreme Court of Canada at least signalled that it was aware of the developments in the United States and approved of them.

Far more important, however, was the decision of *Buckley v. Mott*.[144] This was not a case involving a "dangerous product", but one in which the new negligence principle of *McPherson* had to be invoked if liability was to be imposed. The plaintiff was injured by some powdered glass which found its way into a chocolate cream bar that he had purchased from a retailer. In the suit, the manufacturer contended that it owed no duty to the plaintiff, since he had no contract with the manufacturer, but only with the retailer. Mr. Justice Drysdale who, like Justice Cardozo, treated a chocolate bar as a dangerous article, rejected this argument and remarked:

> In the American Courts it is held that where defendants manufacture and put a dangerously faulty article in its stock for sale, they are therein negligent and liable to an action for such negligence, it being the proximate cause of injury to plaintiff without any reference to contract relation existing between him and the plaintiff. . . . [T]here was a duty to the public not

---

772, liabililty for defective bridge; *Levy v. Langridge* (1837), 2 M. & N. 519, 150 E.R. 863; affd 4 M. & W. 337, 150 E.R. 1458.

[139] Stalleybrass, Dangerous Things and Non-Natural User" (1929), 3 Camb. L.J. 376. See also *Thomas v. Winchester* (1852), 6 N.Y. 397; *Dominion Natural Gas Co. v. Collins*, [1909] A.C. 640; *Ives v. Clare Brothers Ltd.*, [1971] 1 O.R. 417.

[140] (1916), 217 N.Y. Supp. 382, 111 N.E. 1050.

[141] At least as to negligence liability. For a more detailed description see Prosser, "The Assault Upon the Citadel (Strict Liability to the Consumer)" (1960), 69 Yale L.J. 1099.

[142] [1932] A.C. 562. See Linden, "Viva *Donoghue v. Stevenson*", in *The Paisley Papers* (1991).

[143] (1921), 62 S.C.R. 393, 63 D.L.R. 63, at p. 69 (*per* Mr. Justice Duff).

[144] (1920), 50 D.L.R. 408 (N.S.).

to put on sale such a dangerous article as the chocolate bar in question; that defendants were
guilty of negligence in this respect, which was the proximate cause of plaintiff's injuries.[145]

Thus, the Canadian courts applied negligence principles in product liability
cases more than a decade before the English courts did. Because of its absence
of penetrating analysis and modesty of prose, however, *Buckley v. Mott* has been
largely ignored.[146] Ironically, the acclaim for transforming our products liability
law was won by *Donoghue v. Stevenson*, on the basis of its superior reasoning
and memorable language, even though the Canadian courts arrived there first.

There is no Canadian lawyer who cannot recall the facts of *Donoghue v.
Stevenson*, and the principles that were established in that case. It was alleged that
someone bought a bottle of ginger beer for a friend, who drank the contents of the
bottle, discovered the remains of a decomposed snail in it, and suffered damages
as a result. The friend sued the manufacturer, even though there was no contract
between her and the defendant. The case was never actually tried, but on a
demurrer the House of Lords ultimately held that a manufacturer owed a duty to
third persons who could reasonably be foreseen as being affected by negligent
conduct, despite the fact that there was no privity of contract between them. Lord
Atkin wove what had been termed "absurd and outrageous" by Lord Abinger into
the fabric of English and Canadian law. The new principle, which dominates the
Canadian law of products liability to this day, was formulated as follows:

> a manufacturer of products, which he sells in such a form as to show that he intends them to
> reach the ultimate consumer in the form in which they left him with no reasonable possibility
> of intermediate examination, and with the knowledge that the absence of reasonable care in
> the preparation or putting up of the products will result in an injury to the consumer's life or
> property, owes a duty to the consumer to take that reasonable care. . . .[147]

Upon this foundation an entirely new structure of products liability has been
erected and is still being built.[148] This growth has been somewhat abortive in
Canada, for in the United States products liability law underwent another
metamorphosis to a regime of strict liability.[149] Strangely, this doctrine has not so
much as tiptoed across the Canadian border, despite the fact that more of the
manufactured goods sold in Canada are produced in the United States or by
Canadian corporations owned by American interests.[150] Although the processing
methods are the same, the articles are the same, and the advertising is the same,
the protection afforded a Canadian consumer by Canadian courts is less than that
accorded to an American consumer by United States civil courts. More startling

---

[145] *Ibid.*, at p. 409.

[146] Until recently rediscovered by MacKeigan C.J.N.S. in *Smith v. Inglis* (1978), 6 C.C.L.T. 41, at p.
48. See also articles by Linden, *supra*, n. 7.

[147] *Supra*, n. 142, at p. 599. See Heuston, "*Donoghue v. Stevenson* in Retrospect" (1957), 20 Mod.
L. Rev. 1; V.C. MacDonald, "Comment" (1932), 7 Can. Bar Rev. 478.

[148] See 17 U.B.C. L. Rev. for a series of essays on this landmark decision, written on the occasion of
the case's 50th birthday.

[149] See generally, Prosser, "The Fall of the Citadel (Strict Liability to the Consumer)" (1966), 50
Minn. L. Rev. 791.

[150] See on this problem generally, Gordon, *A Choice for Canada* (1966).

is the fact that American corporations are more prone to civil liability in their homeland than they are in Canada. Whether strict liability in tort will be kept out of Canada forever, or whether it will eventually be adopted in the aftermath of N.A.F.T.A., is a tantalizing but unanswered question at this time.[151]

1. WHAT PRODUCTS?

Virtually every type of product under the sun may now give rise to tort liability. Although some of the original statements in the House of Lords seemed to limit the duty to manufacturers of "articles of food and drink" or "articles of common household use",[152] others applied it more generally to any "manufactured products".[153] Indeed, Lord Buckmaster, in dissenting, contended that the principle could not be limited to food alone, and that ". . . it must cover the construction of every article" including "the construction of a house". "If one step, why not fifty?" he warned.[154] Without any doubt whatsoever, the 50 steps have been taken over the intervening years. Defective food products like chocolate milk,[155] bread,[156] flour,[157] cherries jubilee,[158] prepared foods,[159] soda pop,[160] beer,[161] pork,[162] and substandard food containers,[163] may attract liability. The protection spread to articles that might be subject to intimate bodily contact such as hair dye,[164] underwear,[165] other clothing,[166] bath salts,[167] perfume,[168] combs,[169] cigarettes,[170] oral contraceptives,[171] drugs,[172] surgical equipment,[173] and

---

[151] See Section 5(e).
[152] *Supra*, n. 142, at p. 583 (*per* Lord Atkin).
[153] *Ibid.*, at p. 599.
[154] *Ibid.*, at p. 577.
[155] *Shandloff v. City Dairy Ltd.*, [1936] O.R. 579, [1936] 4 D.L.R. 712 (C.A.).
[156] *Arendale v. Canada Bread Co.*, [1941] O.W.N. 69, [1941] 2 D.L.R. 41 (C.A.).
[157] *Curll v. Robin Hood Multifoods Ltd.* (1974), 56 D.L.R. (3d) 129 (Cowan C.J.T.D.N.S.).
[158] *Schwartz v. Hotel Corp. of America (Man.) Ltd.*, [1971] 3 W.W.R. 320 (Man. C.A.), "Great care must be taken in the preparation of food using open flame and inflammable materials" (*per* Hunt J.).
[159] *Heimler v. Calvert Caterers Ltd.* (1974), 4 O.R. (2d) 67; affd (1975), 8 O.R. (2d) 1 (C.A.).
[160] *Zeppa v. Coca-Cola Ltd.*, [1955] O.R. 855, [1955] 5 D.L.R. 187 (C.A.).
[161] *Varga v. John Labatt Ltd.*, [1956] O.R. 1007, 6 D.L.R. (2d) 336.
[162] *Yachetti v. John Duff & Sons Ltd.*, [1942] O.R. 682, [1943] 1 D.L.R. 194, no liability on other grounds.
[163] *Swan v. Riedle Brewery Ltd.*, [1942] 2 D.L.R. 446, [1942] 1 W.W.R. 577 (Man.); *Chapman v. Seven-Up Sussex Ltd.* (1970), 2 N.B.R. (2d) 909; *Cohen v. Coca-Cola*, [1967] S.C.R. 469, 62 D.L.R. (2d) 285.
[164] *Watson v. Buckley*, [1940] 1 All E.R. 174.
[165] *Grant v. Australian Knitting Mills*, [1936] A.C. 85.
[166] *La Frumento v. Kotex Co.* (1928), 226 N.Y. Supp. 750.
[167] *Levi v. Colgate-Palmolive Proprietary Ltd.* (1941), 41 S.R. (N.S.W.) 48.
[168] *Carter v. Yardley* (1946), 319 Mass. 92, 64 N.E. 2d 693.
[169] *Smith v. S.S. Kresge Co.* (1935), 79 F. 2d 361.
[170] *Meditz v. Liggett & Meyers Tobacco Co.* (1938), 3 N.Y. Supp. 2d 357.
[171] *Buchan v. Ortho Pharmaceuticals (Canada) Ltd.* (1986), 25 D.L.R. (4th) 658 (Ont. C.A.). See also *Hollis v. Dow Corning Corp.*, [1995] 4 S.C.R. 634, silicone breast implant.
[172] *Davidson v. Connaught Laboratories* (1980), 14 C.C.L.T. 251 (Ont.).
[173] *Murphy v. St. Catherines General Hospital*, [1964] 1 O.R. 239, 41 D.L.R. (2d) 697.

even a pet turtle.[174] When tort responsibility was imposed for a glue can that opened unexpectedly,[175] a defective oil pump,[176] fertilizer,[177] weed spray,[178] fireworks,[179] an automobile,[180] a tire,[181] an elevator,[182] a radiator,[183] a ladder,[184] a stove,[185] a ceiling fan,[186] a television set,[187] a water heater,[188] a truck,[189] a helicopter,[190] and an overhead trolley,[191] it became apparent that all other manufactured products would also be controlled by tort law's requirement of reasonable care.

Indeed, the only "products" that were able to withstand the inexorable spread of *Donoghue v. Stevenson* were houses and the fixtures they contained. By distinguishing *Donoghue v. Stevenson* as dealing with chattels only the English courts clung to *Malone v. Laskey*,[192] and refused, at first, to apply the duty of care to the builder, repairer or vendor of real property. There they dug in, and only in the last several decades have they surrendered to the inevitable, by holding a repairer,[193] and a builder,[194] of real property liable for their negligence like anybody else. As early as 1939, Mr. Justice Adamson of Manitoba, in a strong *dictum*,[195] indicated the foolishness of distinguishing for this purpose between chattels and realty when he declared: "I can see no reason why the legal liability for negligently erecting a heavy fixture in a cottage should be different from negligently erecting a similar fixture in a railway coach or large motor bus." Refusing to follow the earlier real property cases, Mr. Justice Adamson asserted that he was bound by the Privy Council's decision in *Grant v. Australian Knitting Mills* which he felt was indistinguishable. Nevertheless, the

---

[174] *McMullin v. F.W. Woolworth* (1974), 9 N.B.R. (2d) 214.

[175] *Stewart v. Lepage's Inc.*, [1955] O.R. 937.

[176] *Castle v. Davenport-Campbell Co.*, [1952] 3 D.L.R. 540 (Ont.C.A.).

[177] *Majorcsak v. Na-Churs Plant Food Co.*, [1964] 2 O.R. 38; revd on other grounds, [1969] 1 O.R. 299.

[178] *Ruegger v. Shell Oil Co.*, [1964] 1 O.R. 88, 41 D.L.R. (2d) 183.

[179] *Martin v. T.W. Hand Fireworks Co.*, [1963] O.R. 443, 37 D.L.R. (2d) 455.

[180] *Marschler v. G. Masser's Garage*, [1956] O.R. 328, 2 D.L.R. (2d) 484.

[181] *Good-Wear Treaders v. D. & B. Holdings* (1979), 8 C.C.L.T. 87 (N.S.C.A.).

[182] *Haseldine v. Daw & Son Ltd.*, [1941] 2 K.B. 343, [1941] 3 All E.R. 156 (C.A.).

[183] *Johnson v. Summers*, [1939] 2 D.L.R. 665, [1939] 1 W.W.R. 362 (Man.).

[184] *Kalash v. L.A. Ladder Co.*(1934), 1 Cal. App. 2d 229, 34 P. 2d 481; *cf.*, *McHugh v. Reynolds Extrusion* (1974), 7 O.R. (2d) 336, no liability.

[185] *Coakley v. Prentiss-Wabers Stove Co.* (1923), 182 Wis. 92, 195 N.W. 388; *Lemesurier v. Union Gas Co. of Canada Ltd.* (1975), 8 O.R. (2d) 152, 57 D.L.R. (3d) 344.

[186] *Farro v. Nutone Electrical Ltd.* (1990), 68 D.L.R. (4th) 268 (Ont. C.A.).

[187] *Wylie v. R.C.A. et al.* (1973), 5 Nfld. & P.E.I.R. 147 (Nfld.).

[188] *Ostash v. Sonnenberg* (1968), 67 D.L.R. (2d) 311 (Alta. C.A.).

[189] *Chabot v. Ford Motor Co.*, *supra*, n. 87.

[190] *Can-Arc Helicopters Ltd. v. Textron Inc.* (1991), 86 D.L.R. (4th) 404 (B.C.S.C.).

[191] *Dransfield v. British Insulated Cables Ltd.*, [1937] 4 All E.R. 382.

[192] [1907] 2 K.B. 141 (C.A.); *Otto v. Bolton and Norris*, [1936] 2 K.B. 46, [1936] 1 All E.R. 960; *Bottomley v. Bannister*, [1932] 1 K.B. 458 (C.A.).

[193] *Billings & Sons Ltd. v. Riden*, [1958] A.C. 240, [1957] 3 All E.R. 1, hoarding.

[194] *Sharpe v. E.T. Sweeting & Son Ltd.*, [1963] 2 All E.R. 455, canopy; see also *Alie v. Bertrand & Frère Construction*, *supra*, n. 52, defective cement.

[195] *Johnson v. Summers*, *supra*, n. 183, at p. 667, D.L.R.

action involving a hot water radiator which fell on the plaintiff was dismissed on other grounds, and this opinion does not appear to have been followed in later cases. It was not until *Lock v. Stibor*,[196] in which both the vendor and the builder of a home were found liable to a third person injured by a defective cupboard, that *Malone v. Laskey* was finally finished in Canada.

2. WHAT DEFENDANTS?

The case of *Donoghue v. Stevenson* dealt with the imposition of liability upon manufacturers. Consequently, the producers of such varied articles as under-wear,[197] and weed spray,[198] must observe reasonable care. Liability has been imposed upon a dairy,[199] and upon a bakery,[200] for glass particles discovered in their products, upon soft drink producers for such items as a mouse,[201] a chain,[202] glass,[203] caustic soda,[204] and chlorine,[205] and upon other preparers of food.[206] The reconditioner of a cylinder has been treated like a manufacturer.[207] In one old case,[208] however, there was an indication that a meat packer might not be considered a "manufacturer", but this statement is of doubtful authority today.

The duty extends beyond manufacturers. The bottlers of soft drinks normally must pay damages for the various intruders that emerge from their handiwork, even where the bottles are purchased from a third party.[209] The maker of the soft drink syrup is not usually responsible when a bottle, over which it never had any control, explodes.[210] A glue producer was held liable when the top of a glue can flew off unexpectedly, whereas the maker of the container was not, since the

---

[196] [1962] O.R. 963, 34 D.L.R. (2d) 704. See also *Dutton v. Bognor Regis United Building Co.*, [1972] 1 All E.R. 462, at p. 471 (C.A.) (*per* Denning, M.R.), *obiter dictum*; *Anns v. Merton London Borough Council*, [1978] A.C. 728. See Waddams, *op. cit, supra*, n. 5, at p. 27.

[197] *Grant v. Australian Knitting Mills, supra*, n. 165.

[198] *Ruegger v. Shell Oil Co., supra*, n. 178.

[199] *Shandloff v. City Dairy Ltd.*, [1936] O.R. 579 (C.A.).

[200] *Arendale v. Canada Bread Co., supra*, n. 156.

[201] *Saddlemire v. Coca-Cola Co.*, [1941] 4 D.L.R. 614 (Ont. C.A.); *Mathews v. Coca-Cola Co.*, [1944] 2 D.L.R. 355 (Ont. C.A.).

[202] *Corona Soft Drinks Co. v. Champagne* (1938), 64 Que. K.B. 353.

[203] *Ferstenfeld v. Kik Cola Co.* (1939), 77 Que. S.C. 165, no liability on other grounds.

[204] *Willis v. Coca-Cola Co.*, [1934] 1 W.W.R. 145 (B.C.C.A.), no liability on other grounds.

[205] *Varga v. John Labatt Ltd.*, [1956] O.R. 1007, 6 D.L.R. (2d) 336.

[206] *Heimler v. Calvert Caterers Ltd.* (1974), 4 O.R. (2d) 667; affd (1975), 8 O.R. (2d) 1 (C.A.).

[207] *Algoma Truck and Tractor Sales Ltd. v. Bert's Auto Supply Ltd.*, [1968] 2 O.R. 153, 68 D.L.R. (2d) 363.

[208] *Yachetti v. John Duff & Sons Ltd., supra*, n. 162, no liability on other grounds. *Cf., Janatovic v. Mitic*, April 21, 1976 (*per* Estey C.J.H.C.).

[209] *Swan v. Riedle Brewery Ltd.*, [1942] 2 D.L.R. 446, [1942] 1 W.W.R. 577 (Man.), no liability on other grounds. See also *Chapman v. Seven-up Sussex Ltd.* (1970), 2 N.B.R. (2d) 909, bottler owes duty re container.

[210] *Yelland v. National Cafe*, [1955] 5 D.L.R. 560 (Sask. C.A.). But *cf., Brunski v. Dominion Stores Ltd.* (1981), 20 C.C.L.T. 14 (Ont. H.C.) (*per* Linden J.), bottler and bottle manufacturer both held liable.

negligence consisted of the former's failure to warn.[211] In the same way, because the public relies on their advertising, because they have the opportunity to inspect each part for safety, and because of the difficulty in discovering which one of the many components is to blame for an accident, the assemblers of products such as automobiles,[212] buildings,[213] and composite surgical instruments,[214] labour under this duty. Of course, if the producer of a specific component part could be proved negligent, it would undoubtedly also be held liable to the consumer or would be required to indemnify the assembler for any damages the latter had to pay as a result of the former's fault.[215]

The courts have not stopped there, but have placed repairers as well as producers and assemblers under the obligation to use care. In his dissent in *Donoghue v. Stevenson*,[216] Lord Buckmaster pointed out the inevability of this development if the majority view prevailed, and later courts, ironically, have utilized his *dictum* in visiting liability upon repairers.[217] For example, in *Marschler v. G. Masser's Garage*,[218] a negligent repairer of automobile brakes was held liable to indemnify the car owner for an amount paid in settlement to a third person whom the owner had injured. Mr. Justice LeBel stated:

> ... the repairer of chattels ... may be, and sometimes is, held liable to persons who are complete strangers to him. His responsibility may extend to an indefinite number of persons for indefinite amounts of money over indefinite periods of time for the person who repairs the brakes of a motor vehicle must be assumed to know that if his work is done carelessly that vehicle may cause injury and damage not only to the person with whom he made his contract to repair, but also to others who may be passengers in the vehicle or lawfully upon the highway.[219]

Similarly, repairers of a truck wheel,[220] and of an elevator,[221] were held responsible. A repairer's duty may extend to include a duty to warn of design or manufacturing defects of which the repairer is, or should be, aware.[222] This duty

---

[211] *Stewart v. Lepage's Inc., supra*, n. 175.

[212] *MacPherson v. Buick Motor Co.* (1916), 111 N.E. 1050; *Ford Motor Co. v. Mathis* (1963), 322 F.2d 267.

[213] *Kenlee Lands Inc. v. Northumberland Construction Ltd.* (1973), 36 D.L.R. (3d) 270 (P.E.I.).

[214] *Murphy v. St. Catherines General Hospital, supra*, n. 173, at p. 707; *Farro v. Electrical Ltd.* (1990), 68 D.L.R. (4th) 268 (Ont. C.A.), liability of fan maker for defect in motor component causing fire.

[215] *Evans v. Triplex Safety Glass Co. Ltd.*, [1936] 1 All E.R. 283, defective windshield. But *cf.*, *Goldberg v. Kollman Instruments* (1963), 191 N.E. 2d 81, where the maker of a defective altimeter was absolved, although the aeroplane manufacturer was held liable.

[216] [1932] A.C. 562, at p. 577.

[217] *Haseldine v. Daw & Son Ltd.*, [1941] 2 K.B. 343, [1941] 3 All E.R. 156 (C.A.) (*per* Scott L.J.).

[218] [1956] O.R. 328, 2 D.L.R. (2d) 484.

[219] *Ibid.*, at p. 491, D.L.R.

[220] *Stennett v. Hancock and Peters*, [1939] 2 All E.R. 578.

[221] *Haseldine v. Daw & Son Ltd., supra*, n. 205. See also *Maindonald v. Marlborough Aero Club*, [1935] N.Z.L.R. 371.

[222] *Trans-Canada Forest Products Ltd. v. Heaps, Waterous Ltd.*, [1954] 2 D.L.R. 545 (S.C.C.); *Nicholson v. John Deere Ltd.* (1986), 34 D.L.R. (4th) 542 (H.C.); affd (1989), 57 D.L.R. (4th)

does not compel repairers to fix the defect; they are only required to properly advise the owner about the problem.[223]

The duty has been broadened still further. A person who installs or erects a product at its place of use is neither a manufacturer nor a repairer, yet that person, too, must exercise reasonable care. Thus, where a steam valve was negligently installed in a ship,[224] where an elevator was improperly set up in a building,[225] where a negligently installed gas furnace exploded,[226] and where a radiator was negligently placed in a home,[227] civil liability ensued. In this way, a wholesaler,[228] or a distributor of a product,[229] may be responsible, even though not participating in its actual production. Someone who merely inspects,[230] or recommends,[231] the use of a product without giving adequate warning may be caught. Government inspectors can be held liable as well.[232] So too, liability may be imposed on one who applies or administers a product, as where dangerous spray was applied to cattle,[233] where fertilizer was mixed with a dangerous substance,[234] where liquid flooring caught fire while being applied[235] and where harmful hair dye was used on a plaintiff.[236] One court went as far as to indicate that a customer in a store, injured by an exploding jar on a shelf, might be able to recover from the storekeeper merely on the basis of the latter's "control" of the product,[237] but another court stopped short of placing responsibility on a waiter who served a bottle of beer containing chlorine where he had no

---

639 (Ont.C.A.). But see *Can-Arc Helicopters Ltd. v. Textron, supra,* n. 190, where the court determined that, had a warning been issued by the repairer, it would have been disregarded by the owner. The court did not hold the repairer liable since, under the circumstances, the lack of warning could not be a cause of the accident.

[223] *Can-Arc Helicopters Ltd. v. Textron Inc., supra,* n. 190.

[224] *Howard v. Furness Houlder Argentine Lines Ltd.,* [1936] 2 All E.R. 781; *Malfroot v. Noxal Ltd.* (1935), 51 T.L.R. 551, motorcycle sidecar installer; *Lemesurier v. Union Gas Co. of Canada Ltd.* (1975), 8 O.R. (2d) 152, gas stove installer.

[225] *London & Lancashire Guaranty & Accident Co. v. La Cie F.X. Drolet,* [1944] S.C.R. 82, [1944] 1 D.L.R. 561.

[226] *Aiello v. Centra Gas Ontario* (1999), 47 C.C.L.T. (2d) 39 (Ont. S.C.J.).

[227] *Johnson v. Summers,* [1939] 2 D.L.R. 665, [1939] 1 W.W.R. 362.

[228] *O'Fallon v. Inecto Rapid Canada Ltd.,* [1940] 4 D.L.R. 276 (B.C.C.A.).

[229] *Watson v. Buckley, supra,* n. 164. See also *Pack v. Warner County* (1964), 44 D.L.R. (2d) 215, at p. 227 (Alta. C.A.); *Kubach v. Hollands,* [1937] 3 All E.R. 907; *Phillips v. Ford Motor Co.,* [1970] 2 O.R. 714; revd on other grounds [1971] 2 O.R. 637 (C.A.).

[230] See *Ostash, supra,* n. 188, *Dutton v. Bognor Regis United Building Co.,* [1972] 1 All E.R. 462 (C.A.); *Anns v. Merton London Borough Council, supra,* n. 196.

[231] *Pack v. Warner County* (1964), 44 D.L.R. (2d) 215 (Alta. C.A.), spray dangerous to animals, *Hanberry v. Hearst Corp.* (1969), 81 Cal. Reptr. 519.

[232] *Ingles v. Tutkaluk Construction Ltd.,* [2000] 1 S.C.R. 298; *Cook v. Bowen Island Realty Ltd.,* [1997] B.C.J. No. 2319; affd [2000] B.C.J. No. 1635, inspector approved inadequate sewage disposal system, others also liable. See Chapter 17.

[233] *Ibid.*

[234] *Majorcsak v. Na-Churs Plant Food Co., supra,* n. 177.

[235] *Atlantic Building Contractors v. Wright* (1970), 2 N.B.R. (2d) 926.

[236] *Watson v. Buckley, supra,* n. 164.

[237] *Nernberg v. Shop Easy Stores Ltd.* (1966), 57 D.L.R. (2d) 741 (Sask. C.A.), alternative holding on occupier's liability. *Cf., Hart v. Dominion Stores Ltd.,* [1968] 1 O.R. 775, 67 D.L.R. (2d) 675.

knowledge of the defect.[238] Liability may be incurred also by negligent sellers,[239] renters,[240] users,[241] and even donors of chattels.[242]

3. WHAT PLAINTIFFS?

In describing the range of claimants to whom the manufacturers owed the new privity-less duty of care, Lord Atkin used the term "consumers" or "ultimate consumers".[243] During the intervening years, as might have been prophesied, this vague term has been stretched to cover a wide assortment of potential claimants. Obviously, any actual "purchasers" of a product would enjoy the protection. Thus, one who buys a bottle of soda pop in a restaurant,[244] drugstore,[245] a cigar store,[246] or from some other retailer,[247] may launch an action, not only against the seller, but against the manufacturer of that product. It appears to make no difference that the person is a gratuitous recipient of the product,[248] or a subsequent purchaser from the original buyer.[249] Similarly, where the product was purchased indirectly through an "agent" of the claimant, the duty is still owed, as in the case of a daughter who sent her father to a cafe to buy her a soft drink,[250] a mother who sent her small son to the drug store for some hair dye,[251] and a plaintiff whose friend purchased a bottle of beer for him in a hotel.[252] The duty extends to any member of the purchaser's family, such as a young child injured by a defective product bought by an older sister,[253] or by his parents,[254]

---

[238] *Varga v. John Labatt Ltd.*, [1956] O.R. 1007, 6 D.L.R. (2d) 336.

[239] *Good-Wear Treaders, supra,* n. 181, seller of retreaded tires; *Andrews v. Hopkinson,* [1957] 1 Q.B. 229, [1956] 3 All E.R. 422, brakes on secondhand car defective; *Nernberg v. Shop-Easy Stores Ltd.* (1966), 57 D.L.R. (2d) 741 (Sask. C.A.). *Cf., Rae v. T. Eaton Co. (Maritimes) Ltd.* (1961), 28 D.L.R. (2d) 522 (N.S.).

[240] *White v. John Warwick & Co. Ltd.,* [1953] 1 W.L.R. 1285, [1953] 2 All E.R. 1021 (C.A.); *Chapman v. Sadler,* [1929] A.C. 584.

[241] *Westlake v. Smith Transport* (1973), 2 O.R. (2d) 258, truck owner liable for defective tire exploding; *Good-Wear Treaders, supra,* n. 181; *Pearson v. Fairview Corp.* (1975), 55 D.L.R. (3d) 522 (Man. Q.B.), occupier liable for defective glass door; see Waddams, *op. cit. supra,* n. 5, at p. 24.

[242] *Hawkins v. Coulsdon and Purley, U.D.C.,* [1954] 1 Q.B. 319, at p. 333, [1954] 1 All E.R. 97 (C.A.).

[243] *Donoghue v. Stevenson,* [1932] A.C. 562, at p. 599.

[244] *Mathews v. Coca-Cola Co.,* [1944] 2 D.L.R. 355 (Ont. C.A.); *Corona Soft Drinks Co. v. Champagne* (1938), 64 Que. K.B. 353.

[245] *Zeppa v. Coca-Cola Ltd.,* [1955] O.R. 855, [1955] 5 D.L.R. 187 (C.A.).

[246] *Saddlemire v. Coca-Cola Co.,* [1941] 4 D.L.R. 614 (Ont. C.A.).

[247] *Willis v. Coca-Cola Co.,* [1934] 1 W.W.R. 145 (B.C.C.A.); *Shandloff v. City Dairy Ltd.,* [1936] O.R. 579 (C.A.), chocolate milk.

[248] *Pack v. Warner County* (1964), 44 D.L.R. (2d) 215 (Alta. C.A.).

[249] *Power v. Bedford Motor Co.,* [1959] I.R. 391; *Nicholson v. John Deere Ltd., supra,* n. 222.

[250] *Yelland v. National Cafe,* [1955] 5 D.L.R. 560 (Sask. C.A.).

[251] *O'Fallon v. Inecto Rapid (Canada) Ltd.,* [1940] 4 D.L.R. 276 (C.A.).

[252] *Varga v. John Labatt Ltd.,* [1956] O.R. 1007, 6 D.L.R. (2d) 336; *cf., Lockett v. A. & M. Charles Ltd.,* [1938] 4 All E.R. 170.

[253] *Arendale v. Canada Bread Co.,* [1941] 2 D.L.R. 41 (Ont. C.A.).

[254] *Rae v. T. Eaton Co. (Maritimes) Ltd.* (1961), 28 D.L.R. (2d) 522 (N.S.), no liability on other grounds.

and a wife injured by an exploding beer bottle purchased by her husband.[255] Other members of the household such as cleaning staff,[256] and a social guest,[257] are also protected.

Occasionally, a court does not show any concern at all about whether the claimant is a purchaser, a relative, or a member of the buyer's household,[258] which indicates that the scope of the duty is even broader than this. Anyone who is contemplated as a user or handler of the product,[259] or who "takes control of it" is considered to be in the "same relationship as a consumer",[260] as is anyone who would reasonably "come in contact with" the article.[261] The Alberta Court of Appeal stated that the duty extended to all "potential users" of the item in question.[262] Consequently, any reasonably foreseeable bystander, including anyone lawfully on the road like a pedestrian,[263] a passenger,[264] or a spectator at a fireworks display,[265] can now sue. The loss suffered is not limited to physical injury, but can include property damage and certain economic losses.[266] Moreover, plaintiffs by subrogation, including a city that paid worker's compensation benefits to an injured employee,[267] an insurance company that reimbursed someone injured in the elevator of its insured,[268] a new home warranty programme that reimbursed homeowners for a faulty heating system,[269] and a hospital required to compensate anyone injured by its defective equipment,[270] are countenanced as legitimate claimants. The late Chief Justice Porter, of the Ontario Court of Appeal, accurately summed up the law when he

---

[255] *Swan v. Riedle Brewery Ltd.*, [1942] 2 D.L.R. 446, [1942 1 W.W.R. 577 (Man.), no liability on other grounds.

[256] *Johnson v. Summers*, [1930] 2 D.L.R. 665, [1939] 1 W.W.R. 362 (Man.).

[257] *Lock v. Stibor*, [1962] O.R. 963, 34 D.L.R. (2d) 704.

[258] *Stewart v. Lepage's Inc.*, [1955] O.R. 937.

[259] *Barnett v. Packer & Co.*, [1940] 3 All E.R. 575, confectioner handling candy was cut by steel.

[260] *Shields v. Hobbs Manufacturing Co.*, [1962] O.R. 355, at p. 359 (*per* Porter C.J.O.); affd [1962] S.C.R. 716.

[261] *Rae v. T. Eaton Co. (Maritimes) Ltd.*, *supra*, n. 254, at p. 530.

[262] *Ostash*, *supra*, n. 188.

[263] *Stennett v. Hancock and Peters*, [1939] 2 All E.R. 578; *Good-Wear Treaders v. D. & B. Holdings* (1979), 8 C.C.L.T. 87 (N.S.C.A.), highway user.

[264] *Ibid.*, (*dictum*). See also *Malfroot v. Noxal Ltd.* (1935), 51 T.L.R. 551; *Phillips*, n. 229.

[265] *Martin v. T.W. Hand Fireworks Co.*, [1963] O.R. 443, 37 D.L.R. (2d) 455.

[266] *Pack v. Warner County* (1964), 44 D.L.R. (2d) 215; *Grant v. Cooper*, [1940] N.Z.L.R. 947.

[267] *Christie v. Putherbough Construction* (1959), 18 D.L.R. (2d) 250 (Ont.), no liability on other grounds.

[268] *London & Lancashire Guarantee & Accident Co. of Canada v. La Cie F.X. Drolet*, [1943] Que. K.B. 511, no recovery on other grounds; affd [1944] S.C.R. 82.

[269] *Ontario New Home Warranty Program v. Chevron Chemical Co.* (1999), 46 O.R. (3d) 130 (S.C.J.).

[270] *Murphy v. St. Catherines General Hospital*, [1964] 1 O.R. 239, 41 D.L.R. (2d) 697, at p. 707 (*dictum*).

declared that the term "consumer" now applies to anyone who could be considered one's "neighbour" in the broadest sense.[271]

4. INTERMEDIATE INSPECTION

Lord Atkin's formulation of the principle of *Donoghue v. Stevenson*[272] contained two requirements which have been largely misunderstood: the duty was to be owed only where (a) the products were "intended to reach the ultimate consumer in the form in which they left him", and (b) there was "no reasonable possibility of intermediate examination". Over the intervening years these words have been automatically and persistently followed as if they had been embodied in a statute,[273] despite the fact that Lord Atkin was merely alluding to the traditional tort problems of proof of causation and intervening cause.[274]

a) Proof of Causation

In demanding proof that the product was in the same condition when it left the manufacturer's plant as it was when it did the damage complained of, the courts are merely reiterating the sensible view that a producer will not be held liable for damage it did not cause. Earlier the courts had flirted with a requirement that the product be in a sealed container, but this was soon abandoned.[275] Nevertheless, some courts have gone overboard in the strength of the evidence of causation that they require. In *Ferstenfeld v. Kik Cola Co.*,[276] for instance, one reason why the court refused to impose liability was that the bottle of soda pop in question had been opened in the store where it had been purchased by a third person, and had then been transported across a crowded street to the plaintiff, who drank it. Although the court admitted that it was "unlikely" that the deleterious substance got into the soda pop at that time, it felt that the "possibility" of this eventuality could not be excluded. The Quebec Superior Court, purporting to follow the gospel according to *Donoghue v. Stevenson*, once stated that "the article should reach the consumer in precisely the same condition as it left his [the defendant's] hands and control".[277]

Happily, that extreme view has not dominated the more recent cases. To be sure, the courts still insist upon proof that the contents of an offending bottle of soda pop were the same when they left the defendant as when they caused the damage,[278] but the obligation to show subsequent interference now appears to

---

[271] *Shields v. Hobbs Manufacturing, supra*, n. 260, at p. 359.

[272] [1932] A.C. 562, at p. 599.

[273] See protestation to the contrary in *Salmond and Heuston on The Law of Torts*, 19th ed. (1987), p. 349, especially at footnote 69. This mode of exposition has been adopted for clarity.

[274] See Fleming, *The Law of Torts*, 9th ed. (1998), p. 542, for the best treatment of this problem. Mr. Justice Gillanders seemed to recognize this in *Mathews v. Coca-Cola Co.*, [1944] 2 D.L.R. 355, at p. 372 (Ont. C.A.).

[275] *Grant v. Australian Knitting Mills*, [1936] A.C. 85, at p. 104.

[276] (1939), 77 Que. S.C. 165.

[277] *Ibid.*, at p. 167.

[278] *Mathews v. Coca-Cola Co., supra*, n. 274, at p. 356 (*per* Robertson C.J.O.).

rest on the manufacturer or repairer.[279] The determination of whether the consumer used the article "exactly as it left the maker" now centres around whether "the maker may be said to control the thing until it is used".[280] Consequently, the producer will be held liable if retaining the effective (but not necessarily physical) control over the product.[281] Recovery may still be denied, however, when there is a long time between the purchase and the accident because this diminishes the likelihood of the manufacturer being the cause of the defect.[282]

b) Intervening Cause: Probability of Intermediate Examination

It must also be demonstrated that there has been no "intervening cause": that is, no tampering with the product by third persons so as to insulate the original manufacturer from responsibility. This is the true meaning of Lord Atkin's phrase "reasonable possibility of intermediate examination".[283] That this five-word statement was not meant to be oracular is evidenced by the other synony-mous phrases appearing in the judgment. Where "a party who has the means and opportunity of examining the manufacturer's product before he re-issues it to the actual user is interposed"[284] there is no duty. In other words, if "there can be no inspection by the consumer"[285] there would be a duty owed. This was so because when a product "has passed into other hands it may well be exposed to vicissi-tudes which may render it defective or noxious and for which the manufacturer could not in any view be held to be to blame".[286]

Gradually Lord Atkin's standard was relaxed so that a mere "possibility" of examination would not suffice to obliterate the duty; for this result there must have been a "reasonable *probability* of intermediate examination".[287] In other words, according to Lord Justice Goddard,[288] there should be "no reason to contemplate an examination by the retailer or ultimate user," because Lord Atkin really meant "possibility in a commercial sense". The late Chief Justice Porter of the Ontario Court of Appeal echoed the newer view when he stated that a duty would exist if it were "apparent on the balance of probabilities that there would be no intermediate inspection . . .".[289] "[T]he kind of inspection

---

[279] *Marschler v. G. Masser's Garage, supra*, n. 218, no interference found.

[280] *Grant v. Australian Knitting Mills*, n. 275, at p. 104.

[281] See Gillanders J.A., in *Mathews v. Coca-Cola Co., supra*, n. 274, at p. 372.

[282] *Phillips v. Chrysler Corp.*, [1962] O.R. 375, 32 D.L.R. (2d) 347, no liability on other grounds as well. See also Schroeder J.A. in *Phillips v. Ford Motor Co.*, [1971] 2 O.R. 637, at p. 654 (C.A.); see *McCann v. Sears Canada Ltd., supra*, n. 98, electric blanket caused fire 10-15 years after purchase.

[283] *Donoghue v. Stevenson*, [1932] A.C. 562, at p. 599.

[284] *Ibid.*, at p. 622 (*per* Lord MacMillan).

[285] *Ibid.*, at p. 582 (*per* Lord Atkin). See also *Quinton v. Robert & Robert (1978) Ltee* (1988), 235 A.P.R. 64 (Nfld. S.C.), no expectation of inspection by distributor.

[286] *Ibid.*, at p. 622 (*per* Lord MacMillan).

[287] *Paine v. Colne Valley Electricity Supply Co.*, [1938] 4 All E.R. 803 (per Lord Goddard).

[288] *Haseldine v. Daw & Son Ltd.*, [1941] 2 K.B. 343, [1941] 3 All E.R. 156 (C.A.).

[289] *Shields v. Hobbs Manufacturing*, [1941] O.R. 355, at p. 359; affd [1962] S.C.R. 716.

intended is one that is practicable or is contemplated by the parties. A mere opportunity to inspect is not enough".[290] Nor will a producer be relieved of liability if he proves that an inspection was "capable of being made".[291] Mr. Justice Robertson once held that there was no reasonable possibility of an intermediate examination even though he felt that it was "not impossible that a suspicious person making a careful examination in a strong light would have discovered [the mouse in the bottle]".[292] Perhaps the *dictum* most accurately reflecting the Canadian view is that the manufacturer would be liable if ". . . in the ordinary course of business and in the manner in which the goods are distributed, there is no reasonable probability that there will be intermediate examination".[293]

The trouble with all this verbalizing is that we are still using the blunt instruments of the stone age to do sophisticated surgery. No longer must the court place liability upon *one* defendant, the "last wrong-doer". It is, since the passage of the negligence acts, at liberty to split the responsibility between two or more defendants and it may order contribution and indemnity among them. Because of this, the issue of intermediate inspection can be approached from the opposite direction. We should not ask whether the negligent producer could have foreseen the probability of an examination; rather, we should question whether it is proper to relieve him *completely* of liability because of some third person's intervention. This might help us to focus on the alternative of holding both the maker and the inspector jointly responsible and ordering indemnity or contribution between them. Recent cases have shown an acceptance of this new approach and an abandonment of the older, more rigid treatment of these issues.[294]

c) Actual Knowledge of Defect

In some situations the original producer may well be excused from responsibility, as where a defect is *actually discovered* by some intermediary, who then proceeds nonetheless to use the product. In *Taylor v. Rover Co. Ltd.*,[295] the plaintiff was injured when a splinter of steel flew from the top of a chisel he was using during the course of his employment with the first defendant. The chisel was manufactured by the second defendant. Because the defect in the chisel had actually been discovered by the first defendant when another employee had been injured earlier in the same way, the manufacturer was relieved of liability. The court distinguished the situation where there was a mere failure to discover the defect and held that "it was the keeping of the chisel in circulation with the knowledge that it was dangerous that caused the accident". To relieve the

---

[290] Mr. Justice LeBel in *Marschler v. G. Masser's Garage, supra*, n. 218, at p. 493.
[291] See Mr. Justice Gillanders in *Mathews v. Coca-Cola Co., supra*, n. 274, at p. 372.
[292] *Mathews v. Coca-Cola Co., supra*, n. 274, at p. 360.
[293] *Stewart v. Lepage's Inc., supra*, n. 258, at p. 939.
[294] *Smith v. Inglis Ltd.* (1978), 6 C.C.L.T. 41 (N.S.C.A.).
[295] [1966] 2 All E.R. 181.

original wrong-doer where there is actual knowledge of a defect by an intervening agency is consistent with ordinary negligence principles, since such a *deliberate* act of a third person is probably not a foreseeable consequence of negligent production.[296] This treatment does not differ from that accorded to intentional acts such a murder and arson which are usually considered to be "superseding causes" that insulate the original tortfeasors.[297] In the United States, liability may also be shifted from the manufacturer in these circumstances, but their courts have not found it necessary to use the bewildering and misleading incantation of Lord Atkin.[298] This result follows merely because it seems sensible to relieve the original negligent wrong-doer completely where there is a flagrant intervention by a third person. As will be seen, where such intervention is foreseeable, however, liability can be imposed.[299]

There are some dreadful cases where courts have wrongly relieved manufacturers, as for example, where a defect is not actually discovered by the intermediary. In *Buckner v. Ashby and Horner, Ltd.*,[300] the defendant *knew* that its defectively built entrance to an air raid shelter would be inspected by a third party. It was checked, but the defect was not discovered. Mr. Justice Atkinson denied liability on the ground, *inter alia*, that there had been an intervention of a "conscious agency which might and should have averted the mischief".[301] Likewise an installer was insulated from tort liability where the terms of a contract provided for an intermediate inspection, which was not carried out.[302] In the same vein, producers of certain products have been allowed to protect themselves by warning their intermediaries to take precautions for the safety of their ultimate purchasers.[303]

It has also been held that a supplier of Christmas decorations, which fell and injured someone, may be insulated from liability where a negligent installer had complete control of their erection.[304] There is older authority that permits manufacturers to rely on normal inspection procedures by public authorities,[305] but it is of doubtful validity today.[306] The problem is that such results no longer correspond with the treatment of intervening negligence in other situations.[307]

---

[296] See generally, Fleming, "The Passing of Polemis" (1961), 39 Can. Bar Rev. 489. See also Smith, "Requiem for Polemis" (1965), 2 U.B.C.L. Rev. 159.

[297] *Restatement, Torts, Second*, p. 440.

[298] See *Prosser and Keeton on the Law of Torts*, 5th ed. (1984), pp. 301 *et seq.*

[299] See *Smith v. Inglis, infra*, n. 329.

[300] [1941] 1 K.B. 321; affd [1941] 1 K.B. 337 (C.A.).

[301] *Ibid.*, at p. 335.

[302] *Christie v. Putherbough* (1959), 18 D.L.R. (2d) 250 (Ont.), defective hoist, plaintiff was also aware of danger.

[303] *Holmes v. Ashford*, [1950] 2 All E.R. 76 (C.A.); *Kubach v. Hollands*, [1937] 3 All E.R. 907.

[304] *Saccardo v. Hamilton*, [1971] 2 O.R. 479.

[305] *Maindonald v. Marlborough Aero Club*, [1935] N.Z.L.R. 371.

[306] *Ostash v. Sonnenberg* (1968), 67 D.L.R. (2d) 311 (Alta. C.A.); *Dutton v. Bognor Regis United Building Co., supra*, n. 196.

[307] *Menow v. Honsberger and Jordan House Ltd.*, [1971] 1 O.R. 54; affd [1971] 1 O.R. 129; affd [1974] S.C.R. 239; *McKenna v. Stephens and Hall*, [1923] 2 I.R. 112.

The consumer has not been sufficiently protected thereby and manufacturers have not been encouraged enough to supervise their dealers and service people.

d) Modern View of Shared Responsibility

The trend in the more recent cases, happily, is against exonerating the original wrongdoer. Often, it is simply held that there was no reasonable opportunity to inspect in the case at hand. Thus, in cases involving soft drinks,[308] or chocolate milk,[309] in containers, it is generally asserted that no such chance existed. Occasionally the meaning of this phrase is stretched, as in *Castle v. Davenport-Campbell*[310] where the manufacturer of an oil furnace was held liable, even though it had been installed by a third person, since no one "could reasonably be expected to have taken the pump apart or to have examined its interior".[311]

Both the negligent manufacturer and the negligent intervenor are now usually held jointly liable. In *Grant v. Sun Shipping*,[312] the negligent omission of an intermediary to inspect the defendant's work did not dissolve the latter's duty to the plaintiff; rather, both were held responsible as concurrent tortfeasors. Similarly, in *Pack v. Warner County*,[313] the maker of a product printed on its bottle a caution warning against breathing its spray and permitting contact with skin. It was held liable, nevertheless, since this was an insufficient notice to the distributor to make an inspection. In addition, the person who applied the spray was held jointly responsible to the plaintiff for failure to read the label and to make proper inquiries. In *Ives v. Clare Brothers Ltd.*,[314] the negligent producer of a defective gas furnace was held jointly liable with the corporation that supplied gas and service when, as a result of some screws coming loose, injury was caused to the plaintiffs. The service people were in a position to warn the plaintiff of the danger from these loose screws or to repair them, having been called to the house on three occasions, but they failed to appreciate their duty and did nothing. Mr. Justice Wright rejected the argument of defence counsel which he termed "a doctrine of forgiveness of sin by inspection". Nor would he accede to the view that the negligence of the repairer was the "proximate cause" of the loss. His Lordship contended that,

> where there are duties on two or more parties and negligence by each causing or contributing to the cause of damage, it is the *Negligence Act* and not the doctrine of proximate cause which is applied. If this is so, then inspection may cease to be the gospel of redemption it

---

[308] *Zeppa v. Coca-Cola Ltd.*, [1955] O.R. 855, [1955] 5 D.L.R. 187 (C.A.).
[309] *Shandloff v. City Dairy Ltd.*, [1936] O.R. 579 (C.A.).
[310] [1952] O.R. 565, [1952] 3 D.L.R. 540 (C.A.).
[311] *Ibid.*, at p. 546, D.L.R. (*per* Hogg J.A.). See also *Ruegger v. Shell Oil Co.*, [1964] 1 O.R. 88, where a similar result was obtained and the court did not even discuss intermediate examination.
[312] [1948] A.C. 549, [1948] 2 All E.R. 238; see also *Dutton v. Bognor Regis United Building Co.*, *supra*, n. 196; *Ostash v. Sonnenberg*, *supra*, n. 306.
[313] (1964), 44 D.L.R. (2d) 215 (Alta C.A.).
[314] [1971] 1 O.R. 417. *Cf.*, *Dahlberg v. Naydiuk* (1969), 10 D.L.R. (3d) 319 (Man. C.A.).

sometimes appears to be, but will continue to be, as it should be, a significant element of fact in considering liability.[315]

The *Ives* decision makes it clear that intervening negligence by failure to inspect or failure to warn does not exculpate a negligent manufacturer. Instead of losing the original defendant, the plaintiff gains an additional defendant. Such a development is welcome for it broadens compensation and acts as a stimulant to care. It should also foster settlement and curtail the wasteful battles between defendants that delay litigation and increase costs.

e) Negligent Plaintiff as Intermediate Inspector

A similar evolution has occurred where the *plaintiff* is the one who is supposed to make the intermediate examination.[316] Under Lord Atkin's test there was an absence of duty alike if the inspection was to be made by a third person or by the consumer himself. Now, *before* the passage of the comparative negligence acts, it made no difference whether the plaintiff was denied compensation because of no duty or because of contributory negligence, but, *after* this legislation was enacted, it made a great deal of difference. If the duty rationale were used, the plaintiff could recover nothing, while if the contributory negligence approach were employed, the plaintiff might receive a portion of the loss. The shortcomings of the "all-or-nothing-at-all" duty approach are illustrated by the decisions of *Saddlemire v. Coca-Cola Co.*,[317] and *Mathews v. Coca-Cola Co.*,[318] whose facts are almost identical in that the plaintiff became ill from drinking a bottle of soda pop containing a mouse. In *Saddlemire* the plaintiff was denied reparation because he failed to make a proper inspection; in *Mathews*, the plaintiff recovered after the court held that there was "no reasonable possibility of intermediate examination". Inexplicably, the second court did not cite *Saddlemire* which was decided three years earlier in the same province. Also surprising is the fact that in neither case did the court even consider the possibility of apportionment of damages pursuant to the contributory negligence legislation that had been in effect in Ontario at that time for nearly two decades.[319]

Much superior is the new contributory negligence technique stumbled upon by the Supreme Court of Canada in *Shields v. Hobbs Manufacturing Co.*[320] In that case a manufacturer sold negligently constructed electrical equipment to the

---

[315] *Ibid.*, at pp. 421 and 422.
[316] See *Tompkins Hardware Ltd. v. North Western Flying Services Ltd.* (1982), 22 C.C.L.T. 1 (Ont. H.C.), where a pilot who became aware of a defect in his plane but continued to fly it, resulting in a crash, had his award reduced by 20% because of his careless behaviour.
[317] [1941] 4 D.L.R. 614 (Ont. C.A.).
[318] [1944] 2 D.L.R. 355 (Ont. C.A.).
[319] Stats. Ont. 1924, c. 32. Now the Negligence Act, R.S.O. 1990, c. N.1.
[320] [1962] S.C.R. 716; affg [1962] O.R. 355 (Ont. C.A.). *Cf.*, *Meilleur v. U.N.I.-Crete Canada Ltd.* (1985), 32 C.C.L.T. 126 (Ont. H.C.), in which a contributorily negligent worker recovered 25% of his damages against defendants who did not adequately fulfil duty to warn re product.

deceased's employer. The deceased was electrocuted when he negligently began to install the machine without a prior test by grounding, as required by statute. The majority of the court permitted the widow to recover,[321] but reduced her damages by 50 per cent on account of the contributory negligence of her husband in failing to ground the machine in violation of the statute. Although Chief Justice Kerwin, speaking for the majority, reached the proper conclusion, he did not seem to perceive the issue in its proper context. He merely stated that "[t]here was no apparent reason for any person . . . to open and examine the box".[322] Mr. Justice Ritchie, on the other hand, who presented the minority view, came to the wrong result, but he did see the issue more clearly. He, relying upon Lord Atkin's phrase, argued that no duty arose where there was a chance of an intermediate examination. It did not matter, he reasoned, whether this inspection was done by opening up the box or whether there was another simpler method of testing the product. Since the grounding of the machine was ordained by law, it was an examination that was reasonably contemplated. There was no "direct relation" and, hence, no duty was owed to the deceased.[323]

Despite the absence of an expressed rationale, the majority holding of *Shields v. Hobbs Manufacturing Co.* augurs a significant departure from the earlier manner of deciding these cases. From now on, it is suggested, the problem of a plaintiff's failure to inspect will be handled not as one of duty, but as a question of contributory negligence.[324] This does not mean that where *actually discovering* a defect and continuing to use the product a consumer will always recover part of the damages, since the defence of voluntary assumption of risk is still available and permits a court to dismiss the action in a proper case.[325] Mere knowledge, however will not suffice for this defence to apply.[326] Although cases like *Farr v. Butters Brothers and Co.*,[327] might well be decided similarly, the rationale used may now be *volenti* rather than "no duty".[328] The employment of contributory negligence and voluntary assumption of risk theories in these cases is to be preferred over duty analysis because they are simpler, they point out the policy conflicts more clearly, they are more consistent with general negligence principles, they result in wider liability and they encourage safety.

---

[321] *Ibid.*, Kerwin C.J., Martland J., and Judson J.

[322] *Ibid.*, at p. 360, O.R.

[323] *Ibid.*

[324] See Fleming, *op. cit. supra*, n. 274, at p. 542; *McCain Foods Ltd. v. Grand Falls Industries Ltd.* (1991), 80 D.L.R. (4th) 252 (N.B.C.A.).

[325] See generally *Lehnert v. Stein*, [1963] S.C.R. 38; *Miller v. Decker*, [1957] S.C.R. 624, 9 D.L.R. (2d) 1, *supra*, Chapter 13.

[326] *Billings & Sons Ltd. v. Riden*, [1958] A.C. 240, [1957] 3 All E.R. 1, division of liability where defect discovered.

[327] [1932] 2 K.B. 606 (C.A.).

[328] *Cf., Denny v. Supplies Transport Co. Ltd.*, [1950] 2 K.B. 374 (C.A.), knowledge of plaintiff does not exonerate defendant where no alternative way to load barge.

f) New Approach to Intervening Deliberate Conduct

This dramatic trend toward shared responsibility has been applied in cases where there has been a deliberate, but foreseeable, interference with or use of a product. In *Smith v. Inglis Ltd.*,[329] the plaintiff touched his oven while touching his used refrigerator which had been manufactured by the defendant. The shock he received resulted from: (1) an electrical defect in the refrigerator caused by the negligence of the manufacturer; and (2) the absence of a safety prong on the plug of the refrigerator, the prong having been deliberately removed by someone some time earlier. Instead of relieving the manufacturer of liability on the basis of *novus actus interveniens*, as might well have been the result in earlier times, Chief Justice MacKeigan adopted a fresh approach and refused to exonerate the manufacturer. His Lordship explained that since "everyone in the business knew or should have known that [these] prongs are often cut off", the manufacturer should have "foreseen that this might happen". The plaintiff, however, was also held partially to blame since he should have checked the plug when he bought the used refrigerator because, having some knowledge of electrical hazards, he "must have been aware of the danger of using a two-prong plug in a three-holed outlet and did not reasonably guard against the danger".

A similar result occurred in *Good-Wear Traders v. D & B Holdings*,[330] where a retreaded tire was sold with a warning that it should not be used on the front end of a loaded gravel truck. This caution was disregarded by the buyer, and the seller knew it would be. When an accident ensued, Chief Justice MacKeigan held the seller 20 per cent responsible on the ground that by "supplying the tires . . . and knowing the danger [the buyer] proposed to create, [the seller] became a participant in so creating and letting loose the danger". Thus, this was categorized as a case of a "dangerous product being supplied to a person whom the supplier knew or should have known would use it dangerously". There was a duty not to sell the tires, he explained, when the buyer "made clear its intention to use them on the . . . truck on the highway", which "duty was breached by selling the tires with knowledge of the intended use", since that "ought to have been anticipated as being a probable result of the sale of the tires. . .".

These cases manifest a shift away from the older decisions, placing them in considerable jeopardy. This new, flexible approach to this issue is in harmony with the currents of development in modern negligence law.[331] Further activity in this area can be expected for it has much to commend it.

---

[329] (1978), 6 C.C.L.T. 41 (N.S.C.A.).

[330] (1979), 8 C.C.L.T. 87 (N.S.C.A.), trucker 80% liable.

[331] *Williams v. New Brunswick* (1985), 34 C.C.L.T. 299 (N.B.C.A.), arson foreseeable; *Ward v. Cannock Chase District Council*, [1985] 3 All E.R. 537 (Ch.), vandalism foreseeable.

5. THE STANDARD OF CARE

a) Negligence

The standard of care demanded by tort law of these Canadian manufacturers, distributors, repairers and others is to "use reasonable care in the circumstances and nothing more".[332] If the possibility of injury is very remote, for example, no liability will be imposed.[333] Professor Fleming,[334] however, has suggested that the standard has "assumed some characteristics of strict liability . . ." and Professor Alexander[335] has said that, although negligence is relied upon "in theory", "our courts, in these products liability cases are in fact imposing virtually strict liability". It is true that, by employing devices like *res ipsa loquitur* in the past, our courts have leaned somewhat in this direction,[336] but proof of fault in the design, testing,[337] processing, packaging, and distribution of goods is still necessary.

By and large liability will be found where someone blunders, but not otherwise. If a test is not "commercially feasible",[338] or if government inspectors authorize the sale of a particular product,[339] no liability will be incurred. Naturally, the custom of the industry will be given substantial weight in determining this standard, but it will not be conclusive.[340] As in other situations, evidence of the violation of a penal statute will be relied upon by civil courts in establishing the appropriate standard of care.[341]

In defective food cases, our courts now insist that food handlers exhibit an extremely high standard of care. Although they have not yet openly embraced a regime of strict liability, the standard they have set "approximates to and almost becomes an absolute liability. . . . The degree of care is extremely high."[342]

Canadian courts have scrutinized the processing methods of those in the food business rather stringently. In the case of *Smith v. Pepsi-Cola*,[343] for example, the inspecting method of the Pepsi-Cola people was assessed and found wanting because it was "far from a foolproof process". Because the court was not convinced that it was a "dependable process", it held them liable in negligence

---

[332] *Phillips v. Ford Motor Co.*, [1971] 2 O.R. 637, at p. 653 (C.A.) (*per* Schroeder J.A.); *Donoghue v. Stevenson*, [1932] A.C. 562.

[333] *Allard v. Manahan*, [1974] 3 W.W.R. 588 (B.C.).

[334] Fleming, *op. cit. supra*, n. 274, at p. 539.

[335] "Recent Developments in the Law of Torts", in *Special Lectures of the Law Society of Upper Canada* (1966), at p. 42.

[336] Dunlop, "The Law of Torts" in McWhinney (ed.), *Canadian Jurisprudence* (1958), at p. 159.

[337] *Western Processing & Cold Storage Ltd. v. Hamilton Construction Co. Ltd.* (1965), 51 D.L.R. (2d) 245 (Man. C.A.), insulating material not tested.

[338] *Yachetti v. John Duff & Sons Ltd.*, [1942] O.R. 682, [1943] 1 D.L.R. 194, at p. 197.

[339] *Ibid.*, at p. 201, D.L.R., pork.

[340] *Supra*, Chapter 6.

[341] See generally, *supra*, Chapter 7.

[342] *Heimler v. Calvert Caterers Ltd.*, *supra*, n. 206, at p. 2, 8 O.R. (*per* Evans J.A.), liability for food contaminated with typhoid germs.

[343] (1967), C.C.H. Can. Sales & Credit Law Guide, §21-014, at p. 4142.

(as well as under the Sale of Goods Act) for glass particles in a bottle. Similarly, in *Hart v. Dominion Stores Ltd.*,[344] the inspection methods of Coca-Cola Ltd. were found to be "perfunctory" and "totally inadequate" to prevent explosions of their bottles. The court relied on the Quebec case of *Cohen v. Coca-Cola Ltd.*,[345] where Mr. Justice Abbott asserted that "the bottler of carbonated beverages owes a duty to furnish containers of sufficient strength to withstand normal distribution and consumer handling". This is a tough standard, and so it should be, but it is still open to the bottler to convince the court that it acted carefully and in accordance with a reasonable custom of the trade.

b) Negligent Design

Our courts have imposed liability for negligent design as well as careless production. Mr. Justice Edson L. Haines, in *Phillips v. Ford Motor Co.*,[346] held the auto producer liable for negligently designing car brakes with a defective fail-safe system. When the power brakes operated properly, they needed only 25 pounds of force to stop the vehicle, but when they did not, 250 pounds of force were needed. This was found to be inadequate design. It was suggested, moreover, that the defendants had a duty to warn the consumer about the danger of this design. The Supreme Court of Canada,[347] has expressed a similar view and the British[348] cases are in accord. More than this, manufacturers must design their products so as to minimize the losses that may result from mishaps involving them. The design must be reasonably safe for the environment in which it is to be used.[349] Thus, an automobile manufacturer must take "reasonable care to design its products in a reasonably crashworthy manner".[350]

---

[344] [1968] 1 O.R. 775, at p. 779, 67 D.L.R. (2d) 675. See also *Brunski v. Dominion Stores Ltd.* (1981), 20 C.C.L.T. 14 (Ont. C.A.).

[345] [1967] S.C.R. 469, at p. 473. For an examination of the Quebec law see Heller, "Manufacturers' Liability for Defective Products" (1969), 15 McGill L.J. 142.

[346] [1970] 2 O.R. 714; revd on other grounds [1971] 2 O.R. 637 (C.A.); *Gallant v. Beitz: Nissan Automobile Co. (Canada) Ltd. Third Party* (1983), 42 O.R. (2d) 86, at p. 90 (H.C.); *Nicholson v. John Deere Ltd.* (1986), 58 O.R. (2d) 53; *Baker v. Suzuki Motor Co.* (1993), 17 C.C.L.T. (2d) 241 (Alta. Q.B.), no liability when fire caused after motorcycle collision.

[347] *Rivtow Marine Ltd. v. Washington Iron Works* (1973), 40 D.L.R. (3d) 530 (S.C.C.) (*per* Laskin J.), defectively designed crane.

[348] *Davie v. New Merton Bd. Mills Ltd.*, [1959] A.C. 604, at p. 626 (*per* Viscount Simonds), [1959] 1 All E.R. 346; *Hinduston S.S. Co. v. Siemens Brothers & Co. Ltd.*, [1955] 1 Lloyd's Rep. 167, at p. 177 (*per* Willmer J.).

[349] *Rentway Canada Ltd./Ltee v. Laidlaw Transport Ltd.* (1989), 49 C.C.L.T. 150, at p. 163 (Ont. H.C.) (*per* Granger J.).

[350] Zarnett, "Tort Liability for Defective Automobile Design" (1975), 13 Osgoode Hall L.J. 483; Lemer, "Strict Products Liability: The Problem of Improperly Designed Products" (1982), 20 Osgoode Hall L.J. 250. In the U.S., see *Larsen v. G.M.* (1968), 391 F. 2d 495, defective steering mechanism; *Dyson v. G.M.* (1969), 298 F. Supp. 1064, roof collapse, can go to jury: *Mickle v. Blackman* (1969), 252 S.C. 202, 166 S.E. 2d 173; *Grundmanis v. B.M.C.* (1970), 308 F. Supp. 303, gas tank rupture caused fire; see also Katz, "Liability of Automobile Manufacturers for Unsafe Design of Passenger Cars" (1956), 69 Harv. L. Rev. 863; Katz, "Negligence in Design: A

It has also been contended that cigarette manufacturers must make "fire safe cigarettes" because cost-effective ways to do it are known.[351]

c) Warning

Manufacturers are subject to a duty to warn customers and others who may reasonably be affected[352] about any dangerous properties of their product,[353] whether they are "inherent dangers" or "dangers attendant on the use".[354] However, no amount of warning will exonerate a manufacturer who produces an inherently dangerous article when a method exists for manufacturing the same article without risk of harm.[355] Even where a product is dangerous to only a few people, they must be warned so that they may test the product before using it,[356] but a caution is unnecessary if the danger is "a mere possibility".[357] Naturally, a product is not considered dangerous merely because it does not safeguard against unrelated dangers not caused by the product or its use. Where a hockey helmet was designed to protect a player's head but not the neck, the helmet was not judged dangerous for failing to safeguard against neck injuries.[358]

A consumer is under a corresponding duty to read and heed warnings and instructions, or bear the entire consequences of injury,[359] or have the recovery reduced.[360] In other words, if the consumer did not read the warning, or if upon reading it, did not heed it, it cannot be said that the failure to warn caused the accident and, hence, the action must fail on this basis.[361] The absence of the warning must be a cause of the accident.

Current Look", [1965] Ins. L.J. 5; Nader and Page, "Automobile Design and the Judicial Process" (1967), 55 Calif. L. Rev. 645; Goodman, *Automobile Design Liability* (1970).

[351] *Ragoonanan Estate v. Imperial Tobacco Ltd.* (2000), 51 O.R. (3d) 603 (S.C.J.).

[352] *Bow Valley Husky (Bermuda) Ltd. v. Saint John Shipbuilding Ltd.*, [1997] 3 S.C.R. 1210, duty to warn not limited to parties to contract.

[353] *Stewart v. Lepage's Inc.*, [1955] O.R. 937; *Hollis v. Dow Corning*, [1995] 4 S.C.R. 634.

[354] *Ruegger v. Shell Oil Co.*, [1964] 1 O.R. 88, 41 D.L.R. (2d) 183, at p. 191 (*per* Ferguson J.). See also *Fillmore's Valley Nurseries Ltd. v. North America Cyanimid Ltd.* (1958), 14 D.L.R. (2d) 297 (N.S.); *Lambert v. Lastoplex Chemicals Co. Ltd.* (1971), 25 D.L.R. (3d) 121 (S.C.C.).

[355] *Nicholson v. John Deere Ltd., supra*, n. 222.

[356] Manson J. at trial in *O'Fallon v. Inecto Rapid (Canada) Ltd.*, [1940] 4 D.L.R. 276 (B.C.C.A.). plaintiff sensitive to dye. See generally Sone, "Products Liability and The Allergic Consumer" (1976), 24 Chitty's L.J. 114; Rogerson and Trebilcock, "Products Liability and the Allergic Consumer: A Study in the Problems of Framing an Efficient Liability Regime" (1986), 36 U. of T.L.J. 52.

[357] *Rae v. T. Eaton Co. (Maritimes) Ltd.* (1961), 28 D.L.R. (2d) 522, at p. 536 (N.S.).

[358] *Moore v. Cooper Canada Ltd.* (1990), 2 C.C.L.T. (2d) 57 (Ont. H.C.), no warning about neck injuries was required.

[359] See *Lem v. Barotto Sports Ltd.* (1976), 58 D.L.R. (3d) 465; affd 69 D.L.R. (3d) 276 (Alta. C.A.). See also *Allard v. Manahan*, [1974] 3 W.W.R. 588 (B.C.), information about special guard for power tool, which would have prevented the accident, was contained in brochure, but plaintiff did not bother to get one.

[360] *Meilleur v. U.N.I.-Crete Canada Ltd., supra*, n. 320.

[361] *Rothwell v. Raes* (1988), 54 D.L.R. (4th) 193 (H.C.); affd (1990), 76 D.L.R. (4th) 280 (Ont. C.A.); *Baker v. Suzuki Motor Co., supra*, n. 346, at p. 268, no cause shown.

All warnings must be reasonably communicated. To bury the caveat in a brochure accompanying the article will probably not suffice, because, presumably, people rarely read these pamphlets. The caveat should be printed on the container's label and it should be an arresting one.[362] The caution must clearly describe the *specific* danger.[363] For example, language to the effect that a certain weed killer should be kept away from flowers was held to be inadequate where the weed killer's invisible spray floated without any wind for a quarter of a mile and damaged crops.[364] In the same way, a manufacturer of propane gas which relies on the odour of the gas, rather than words, to warn its customers of any leaks will be liable if the odour of the gas is not distinctive enough to alert someone to the danger.[365]

The Supreme Court of Canada has underscored its commitment to explicitness in labelling in the case of *Lambert v. Lastoplex Chemicals Co. Ltd.*[366] The manufacturer of a fast-drying lacquer sealer was found liable for damages from a fire and explosion because of inadequate warning, despite the fact that it had placed three different labels on the container. One of the three labels read: "Caution inflammable! Keep away from open flame!" Another caution, conforming to certain transport regulations stipulated: "Keep away from fire, heat and open-flame lights. . . ." The third warning included the words, "Caution. Inflammable — Do not use near open flame or while smoking. . . ." The plaintiff, an engineer, had read these warnings before he began to lacquer his basement floor. He turned down the thermostat so that his furnace would not go on, but he did not shut off the pilot light. Some fumes caught fire and exploded from contact with the pilot light.

Mr. Justice Laskin (as he then was) decided that none of these cautions was sufficient because they "did not warn against sparks or specifically against leaving pilot lights on in or near the working area". The evidence disclosed that one of the defendant's competitors did issue a warning, *inter alia*, against spark-producing devices and pilot lights. The principle was enunciated by Mr. Justice Laskin as follows:

> Where manufactured products are put on the market for ultimate purchase and use by the general public and carry danger (in this case, by reason of high inflammability), although put to the use for which they are intended, the manufacturer, knowing of their hazardous nature, has a duty to specify the attendant dangers, which it must be taken to appreciate in a detail not known to the ordinary consumer or user. A general warning, as for example, that the

---

[362] *O'Fallon v. Inecto Rapid (Canada) Ltd., supra,* n. 356; but *cf., Holmes v. Ashford,* [1950] 2 All E.R. 76 (C.A.), where warning in pamphlet held sufficient; *Allard v. Manahan, supra,* n. 359.

[363] *Spurling v. Bradshaw,* [1956] 2 All E.R. 121, at p. 125 (C.A.).

[364] *Ruegger v. Shell Oil Co., supra,* n. 354.

[365] *Murphy v. Atlantic Speedy Propane Ltd.*(1979), 103 D.L.R. (3d) 545 (N.S.).

[366] [1972] S.C.R. 569 (*per* Laskin J.); *cf., Law v. Upton Lathing Ltd.,* [1972] 1 O.R. 155, 22 D.L.R. (3d) 407 (C.A.); *Affeldt v. B.D. Wait Co.,* Jan. 7, 1980 (*per* Osler J.), warning about keeping combustible material three feet away from propane heater held inadequate when canvas tent caught fire; *cf., Schmitz v. Stoveld* (1974), 11 O.R. (2d) 17, warning given about pilot light reasonable.

product is inflammable, will not suffice where the likelihood of fire may be increased according to the surroundings in which it may reasonably be expected that the product will be used. The required explicitness of the warning will, of course, vary with the danger likely to be encountered in the ordinary use of the product.[367]

Canadian courts across the country have whole-heartedly embraced *Lambert v. Lastoplex.* For example, in *Meilleur v. U.N.I.-Crete Canada Ltd.*,[368] it was held that, when dealing with a highly corrosive material, warnings of "irritant" properties and cautions that one should seek medical attention if the substance enters the eye are insufficient when the substance can cause blindness and when immediately flushing the eye can greatly minimize the damage. Similarly, in *Smithson v. Saskem Chemicals Ltd.*[369] a plaintiff was severely injured by a violent eruption caused by combining two incompatible drain cleaning compounds. While both products contained the symbol showing they were corrosive, as prescribed by the Hazardous Products Act, and while one of them warned that it must not be used "where other drain chemicals are present" (in the "smallest kind of print used"), this was found to be inadequate.

These principles have been repeated by Mr. Justice LaForest in *Hollis v. Dow Corning,*[370] the breast implant case, to this effect:

> The rationale for the manufacturer's duty to warn can be traced to the "neighbour principle", which lies at the heart of the law of negligence, and was set down in its classic form by Lord Atkin in *Donoghue v. Stevenson*, [1932] A.C. 562 (H.L.). When manufacturers place products into the flow of commerce, they create a relationship of reliance with consumers, who have far less knowledge than the manufacturers concerning the dangers inherent in the use of the products, and are therefore put at risk if the product is not safe. The duty to warn serves to correct the knowledge imbalance between manufacturers and consumers by alerting consumers to any dangers and allowing them to make informed decisions concerning the safe use of the product.
>
> The nature and scope of the manufacturer's duty to warn varies with the level of danger entailed by the ordinary use of the product. Where significant dangers are entailed by the ordinary use of the product, it will rarely be sufficient for manufacturers to give general warnings concerning those dangers; the warnings must be sufficiently detailed to give the consumer a full indication of each of the specific dangers arising from the use of product.

In *Buchan v. Ortho Pharmaceuticals (Canada) Ltd.*,[371] the failure to warn about the danger of stroke being caused by birth control pills was held to be negligent, even though the warning may have complied with the governmentally-mandated text and even though these pills could be obtained only by prescription. In finding Ortho Pharmaceutical liable, the court offered this thorough description of the duty to warn:

---

[367] *Ibid.*, at pp. 574-75.
[368] *Supra*, n. 320.
[369] (1985), 34 C.C.L.T. 195 (Sask. Q.B.).
[370] *Supra*, n. 353, at pp. 653-54.
[371] (1986), 35 C.C.L.T. 1, 25 D.L.R. (4th) 658 (Ont. C.A.).

... it is well settled that a manufacturer of a product has a duty to warn consumers of dangers inherent in the use of its product of which it knows or has reason to know. ...

Once a duty to warn is recognized, it is manifest that the warning must be adequate. It should be communicated clearly and understandably in a manner calculated to inform the user of the nature of the risk and the extent of the danger: it should be in terms commensurate with the gravity of the potential hazard, and it should not be neutralized or negated by collateral efforts on the part of the manufacturer. The nature and extent of any given warning will depend on what is reasonable having regard to all the facts and circumstances relevant to the product in question.[372]

Further, the objective test of causation was held not to apply to products.[373]

The courts have rightly shown no sympathy at all for the manufacturers' complaint that "sales would be prejudicially affected" by clear warnings.[374] Rather, they expressed the desire to "facilitate meaningful consumer choice and promote marketplace honesty by encouraging full disclosure".[375]

A manufacturer is not obligated to give a superfluous warning however. As was recently explained, there is no duty to warn if the danger is "so clearly evident so as to make any warning silly".[376] Consequently, one need not warn that a knife will cut or that a match will burn[377] or that pork must be cooked. As Mr. Justice Galligan has colourfully declared,[378] "a manufacturer of a butcher knife is not under a legal duty to warn consumers that a butcher knife may cut flesh".[379] Nor must the renter of a boat warn of the danger of falling off in the event that a passenger rides on its bow.[380] In other words, there is no requirement to "warn of dangers that would be as apparent to the consumer as to the manufacturer".[381] If a consumer should know about a risk, as a farmer should know about the danger of herbicides, for example, the consumer may be found contributorily negligent, even though the supplier furnished an inadequate warning.[382] But where a manufacturer promotes the safety of a product and does

---

[372] *Ibid.*, at pp. 666-67, D.L.R. (*per* Grange J.).

[373] See also *Hollis v. Dow Corning, supra*, n. 353, objective test does not apply to breast implants.

[374] *Fillmore's Valley Nurseries Ltd. v. North American Cyanimid Ltd., supra*, n. 354, at p. 321.

[375] See *Buchan, supra*, n. 371, at p. 35, C.C.L.T. (*per* Robins J.A.).

[376] See *Tabrizi v. Whallon Machine Inc.* (1996), 29 C.C.L.T. (2d) 176, at p. 189 (B.C.S.C.) (*per* Romilly J.), manufacturer 30% reliable to crushed worker for negligently designed machine and failure to warn.

[377] *Prosser and Keeton on the Law of Torts*, 5th ed. (1984), p. 686.

[378] *Deshane v. Deere & Co.* (1993), 17 C.C.L.T. (2d) 130, at p. 147 (Ont. C.A.), no liability where plaintiff fell into unguarded harvester machine while using it dangerously. Lacourciere J.A., dissenting, felt that there was a duty to warn against known or reasonably knowable dangerous uses. Leave to appeal to S.C.C. was refused, 175 N.R. 321n., 20 C.C.L.T. (2d) 318n.

[379] *Yachetti v. John Duff & Sons Ltd., supra*, n. 338.

[380] See *Schultz v. Leeside Developments* (1978), 6 C.C.L.T. 248 (B.C.C.A.). See also *Thomson v. Cosgrove*, [1998] B.C.J. No. 789, where intoxicated person falls to ground out of hot tub on elevated deck, no liability for failure to warn.

[381] *Moffatt v. Witelson* (1980), 29 O.R. (2d) 7 (*per* Galligan J.), eyeglasses broke during touch-football game; see also *Cominco v. Westinghouse Canada Ltd.* (1981), 127 D.L.R. (3d) 544; vard (1983), 147 D.L.R. (3d) 279 (B.C.C.A.).

[382] *Labrecque v. Saskatchewan Wheat Pool* (1980), 110 D.L.R. (3d) 686 (Sask. C.A.), 50% split.

not warn of its risks, a consumer, even an experienced farmer, will not be denied recovery.[383]

Where the product is a highly technical one that will be used only by experts who have full knowledge of it, and not by the general public, a caution is unnecessary.[384] Thus, a customer need not be warned personally about a hair dye if the hairdresser, who applies it, is forewarned.[385] The decision of *Austin v. 3 M Canada* reaffirmed this principle.[386] It was held that, because it was common knowledge among auto repairers that the use of a disc on a grinder at 8,000 r.p.m.'s was dangerous, there was no need to warn them about this. The discs "carried no danger in their ordinary use in the hands of a reasonably competent auto-repair man". It would, of course, be different if the general public were involved in its use.

It is possible, in certain circumstances, however, for the court to demand that more information be given to experts than to lay consumers. In *Davidson v. Connaught Laboratories*,[387] for example, it was suggested, in a *dictum* that pharmaceutical companies might have to supply doctors with very detailed data about the possible side-effects of a rabies vaccine, whereas patients might not be entitled to as much, because the doctors rely on the companies to furnish complete information in order to assist them in assessing the risk so as to be able to advise their patients wisely.

Where products are not sold to consumers directly but to doctors or other experts who prescribe or use them on consumers, problems arise. It has been held that a warning to the "learned intermediary", as these experts have been described, will suffice. In other words, consumers need not be warned directly as long as the learned intermediary is properly cautioned. This rule applies only where a product is to be used under the supervision of experts or where the consumer would not expect a warning directly. Mr. Justice LaForest explained the rule in *Hollis v. Dow Corning*[388] as follows:

> While the "learned intermediary" rule was originally intended to reflect, through an equitable distribution of tort duties, the tripartite informational relationship between drug manufacturers, physicians and patients, the rationale for the rule is clearly applicable in other contexts. Indeed, the "learned intermediary" rule is less a "rule" than a specific application of the long-established common law principles of intermediate examination and intervening cause developed in *Donoghue v. Stevenson, supra,* and subsequent cases. . . . Generally, the rule is applicable either where a product is highly technical in nature and is intended to be used only under the supervision of experts, or where the nature of the product is such that the consumer will not realistically receive a direct warning from the manufacturer before using

---

[383] *Siemens v. Pfizer C. & G. Inc. et al.* (1988), 51 Man. R. (2d) 252 (C.A.).

[384] *Murphy v. St. Catherines General Hospital* (1964), 41 D.L.R. (2d) 697, at pp. 711-12 (*per* Gale J.), *dictum*; *cf. Lambert, supra,* n. 366.

[385] *Holmes v. Ashford* [1950] 2 All E.R. 76 (C.A.). See also *Schmitz v. Stoveld, supra,* n. 366.

[386] (1974), 7 O.R. (2d) 200, at p. 205. See also *Holt v. PPG Industries* (1983), 25 C.C.L.T. 253 (Alta. Q.B.), product for "industrial printers", not "general public", warning adequate.

[387] (1980), 14 C.C.L.T. 251 (Ont.) (*per* Linden J.).

[388] *Supra,* n. 353, at pp. 659-60.

the product. In such cases, where an intermediate inspection of the product is anticipated or where a consumer is placing primary reliance on the judgment of a "learned intermediary" and not the manufacturer, a warning to the ultimate consumer may not be necessary and the manufacturer may satisfy its duty to warn the ultimate consumer by warning the learned intermediary of the risks inherent in the use of the product.

However, it is important to keep in mind that the "learned intermediary" rule is merely an exception to the general manufacturers duty to warn the consumer. The rule operates to discharge the manufacturer's duty not to the learned intermediary, but to the ultimate consumer, who has a right to full and current information about any risks inherent in the ordinary use of the product. Thus, the rule presumes that the intermediary is "learned", that is to say, fully apprised of the risks associated with the use of the product. Accordingly, the manufacturer can only be said to have discharged its duty to the consumer when the intermediary's knowledge approximates that of the manufacturer. To allow manufacturers to claim the benefit of the rule where they have not fully warned the physician would undermine the policy rationale for the duty to warn, which is to ensure that the consumer is fully informed of all risks. Since the manufacturer is in the best position to know the risks attendant upon the use of its product and is also in the best position to ensure that the product is safe for normal use, the primary duty to give a clear, complete, and current warning must fall on its shoulders.

The scope of this rule was further clarified by the Supreme Court of Canada recently in *Bow Valley*[389] in the following manner:

> ... the rule was an exception to the general rule requiring manufacturers to provide a warning to the ultimate consumers of their product. The exception will generally only apply either where the product is highly technical and is to be used with expert supervision, or where the nature of the product is such that it is unrealistic for the consumer to receive a warning directly from the manufacturer.

It is not necessary for the consumer to prove that the learned intermediary would have imparted the warning to him or her in order to comply with the proof of causation element, for that would require proof of a hypothetical. In a sense, sufficient proof of causation is presumed from the situation. As Mr. Justice LaForest wrote in *Hollis v. Dow Corning*:[390]

> Simply put, I do not think a manufacturer should be able to escape liability for failing to give a warning it was under a duty to give, by simply presenting evidence tending to establish that even if the doctor had been given the warning, he or she would not have passed it on to the patient, let alone putting an onus on the plaintiff to do so. Adopting such a rule would, in some cases, run the risk of leaving the plaintiff with no compensation for her injuries. She would not be able to recover against a doctor who had not been negligent with respect to the information that he or she did have; yet she also would not be able to recover against a manufacturer who, despite having failed in its duty to warn, could escape liability on the basis that, had the doctor been appropriately warned, he or she still would not have passed the information on to the plaintiff. Our tort law should not be held to contemplate such an anomalous result.
>
> As I see it, the plaintiff's claim against the manufacturer should be dealt with in accordance with the following rationale. The ultimate duty of the manufacturer is to warn the plaintiff adequately. For practical reasons, the law permits it to acquit itself of that duty by warning an informed intermediary. Having failed to warn the intermediary, the manufacturer

---

[389] *Supra*, n. 352, at p. 1236.
[390] *Ibid.*, at p. 685, but see Sopinka J. dissenting.

has failed in its duty to warn the plaintiff who ultimately suffered injury by using the product. The fact that the manufacturer would have been absolved had it followed the route of informing the plaintiff through the learned intermediary should not absolve it of its duty to the plaintiff because of the possibility, even the probability, that the learned intermediary would not have advised her had the manufacturer issued it. The learned intermediary rule provides a means by which the manufacturer can discharge its duty to give adequate information of the risks to the plaintiff by informing the intermediary, but if it fails to do so it cannot raise as a defence that the intermediary could have ignored this information.

Moreover, it is the subjective test of causation that is applied here, not the modified objective one applicable to health professionals since *Reibl v. Hughes*. Thus, if the plaintiff can prove that he or she would not have gone ahead with the procedure, whether reasonable or not, he or she is entitled to recover.[391]

In *Hollis v. Dow Corning*, therefore, the plaintiff was allowed to recover against the manufacturer on the basis that its warning to the learned intermediary did not sufficiently reveal the risks of rupture of the breast implant.

In *Buchan v. Ortho Pharmaceutical (Canada) Ltd.*, the trial court determined that the learned intermediary rule does not apply in the case of oral contraceptives.[392] The Ontario Court of Appeal upheld the decision of the court below but relied on the narrower point of the manufacturer's failure to adequately warn the prescribing doctor. However, Justice Lacourcière, writing for the Court of Appeal, stressed that, unlike other prescription drugs, there should also be a duty to warn women directly of the risks involved in the use of prescription contraceptives.[393]

Although the learned intermediary rule may often deprive consumers of adequate information by which to decide whether to risk the use of a product, there are particularly strong policy reasons for avoiding the application of that rule where oral contraceptives are involved.[394] Among other things, contraceptives are not medically necessary; they are, or should be, a matter of choice. Frequently, there is not ongoing supervision by the prescribing doctor and women may not be able to rely on doctors to inform them fully of the risks attendant upon use.

---

[391] See Boivin, "Factual Causation in the Law of Manufacturer Failure to Warn" (1998-99), 30 Ottawa L. Rev. 47.

[392] (1984), 8 D.L.R. (4th) 373 (Ont. H.C.).

[393] (1986), 25 D.L.R. (4th) 658 (Ont. C.A.). See also *Hill v. Searle Laboratories* (1989), 884 F.2d 1064 (8th Cir.); *MacDonald v. Ortho Pharmaceutical Corp.* (1985), 475 N.E.2d 65 (Mass.); cert. denied, 474 U.S. 920; *Stephens v. G. D. Searle & Co.* (1985), 602 F. Supp. 379 (E.D. Mich.); and *Odgers v. Ortho Pharmaceutical Corp.* (1985), 609 F. Supp. 867 (E.D. Mich.). But see *Spychala v. G. D. Searle & Co.* (1988), 705 F. Supp. 1024 (D.N.J.); *Lacy v. G. D. Searle & Co.* (1989), 567 A.2d 398 (Del.); *Humes v. Clinton* (1989), 792 P.2d 1032 (Kan.); *Terhune v. A.H. Robbins Co.* (1978), 577 P.2d 975 (Wash.).

[394] Some courts in the U.S. have distinguished between oral contraceptives and other forms of contraception such as high-copper intra-uterine devices. See *Lacy v. G. D. Searle & Co.*, *supra*, n. 393. But see *Hill v. Searle Laboratories*, *supra*, n. 393. Although contraceptive devices do not raise precisely the same issues as oral contraceptives, the rationale for not applying the learned intermediary rule to cases involving such devices is similarly persuasive.

Another important case is *Rivtow Marine Ltd. v. Washington Iron Works*[395] where the Supreme Court of Canada extended the duty to warn. Manufacturers must not only be vigilant to warn their customers of the dangers of which they know at the time of sale, but they must also take steps to alert them when they discover dangers *after* the product has been sold and distributed (that is, there is a continuing duty to warn).[396] In the words of Mr. Justice Ritchie, speaking for the majority:

> The knowledge of the danger involved in the continued use of these cranes for the purpose for which they were designed carried with it a duty to warn those to whom the cranes had been supplied, and this duty arose at the moment when the respondents or either of them became seized with the knowledge.[397]

Mr. Justice LaForest has reiterated this principle in *Hollis v. Dow Corning*[398] as follows:

> The duty to warn is a continuing duty, requiring manufacturers to warn not only of dangers known at the time of sale but also of dangers discovered after the product has been sold and delivered. . . .

In sum, this duty to warn has opened a very wide door for consumer advocates. It is not an easy task for counsel to prove negligence in the production or design of products. A much simpler approach is for counsel to focus on an inadequate warning. This would enable the courts to base liability on a relatively uncomplicated issue, *i.e.*, whether the warning was specific enough. Naturally a court would look for guidance at whatever legislative warning requirements exist, but it is possible that they will demand more than the standard prescribed in the legislation. We have now seen numerous warning cases and we can expect many more in the coming years.

d) Inherently Dangerous Things

A category of "inherently dangerous articles" or "things dangerous in themselves", for which a stricter standard of care is required, still exists.[399] Devised to avoid the horror of *Winterbottom v. Wright*, this legal concept was an exception to the no-privity rule that enabled courts to hold manufacturers liable for injuries inflicted by poison,[400] guns,[401] gas,[402] or explosives.[403] After *Donoghue v.*

---

[395] (1973), 40 D.L.R. (3d) 530, [1973] 6 W.W.R. 692 (S.C.C.).

[396] *Nicholson v. John Deere Ltd., supra*, n. 222; *Can-Arc Helicopters Ltd. v. Textron Inc., supra*, n. 190.

[397] *Supra*, n. 395, at p. 699, W.W.R. See also *Cominco, supra*, n. 381.

[398] *Supra*, n. 353, at p. 653. This duty may be "triggered by information that became known after the product had been in use," see *Bow Valley Husky (Bermuda) Ltd. v. Saint John Shipbuilding Ltd.* (1995), 126 D.L.R. (4th) 1, at p. 24 (Nfld. C.A.) (*per* Cameron J.A.); affd on this point [1997] 3 S.C.R. 1210.

[399] See Stallybrass, "Dangerous Things and Non-Natural User" (1929), 3 Camb. L.J. 376.

[400] *Thomas v. Winchester* (1852), 6 N.Y. 397.

[401] *Dixon v. Bell* (1816), 5 M. & S. 198, 105 E.R. 1023; *Burfitt v. Kille*, [1939] 2 K.B. 743, [1939] 2 All E.R. 372.

[402] *Dominion Natural Gas Co. v. Collins*, [1909] A.C. 640; *Parry v. Smith* (1879), 4 C.P.D. 325.

[403] *Anglo-Celtic Shipping Co. v. Elliott and Jeffery* (1926), 26 T.L.R. 297.

Stevenson was decided, however, the need for this exception diminished, and over the ensuing decades the courts have recognized this[404] despite the reluctance of some authors to jettison it.[405] Lord Justice Scrutton contributed to the demise of the concept when he complained that he could not "understand the difference between a thing dangerous in itself, as poison, and something not dangerous as a class, but by negligent construction dangerous as a particular thing. The latter, if anything, seems the more dangerous of the two; it is a wolf in sheep's clothing instead of an obvious wolf."[406] The great Lord Atkin agreed that this seemed an "unnatural" distinction and was invalid.[407] Nevertheless, the notion has not been completely discarded.[408]

One legacy of this doctrine of inherently dangerous things is that more care may be required of a producer of dangerous articles, like guns, than is demanded of manufacturers of ordinarily safe things, like butter. Thus, a producer of fireworks,[409] guns,[410] gas furnaces,[411] or dangerous chemicals,[412] may have to conform to a higher standard of care than a manufacturer of other less hazardous products. "This standard of care may be so high that it approximates to or almost becomes strict liability".[413] But this is no special rule; it is consistent with general negligence theory. The burden of taking precautions increases as the probability of harm and the severity of the damage threatened increase.[414] In other words, "Not only the greater risk of injury, but also the risk of greater injury is a relevant factor."[415] Mr. Justice Patterson of the Nova Scotia Supreme Court has expressed   the current Canadian law in *Rae v. T. Eaton Co. (Maritimes) Ltd.*, thus:

---

[404] *Dahlberg v. Naydiuk* (1969), 10 D.L.R. (3d) 319, at p. 325 (Man. C.A.) (*per* Dickson J.A.).

[405] *Salmond and Heuston on The Law of Torts*, 9th ed. (1987), has a separate section on it, though finding it "difficult to support in principle". Even Fleming, *op. cit. supra*, n. 274, has a section on "Inherently Dangerous Chattels", at p. 544.

[406] *Hodge & Sons v. Anglo-American Oil Co.* (1922), 12 Lloyd's L. Rep. 183, at p. 187.

[407] *Donoghue v. Stevenson*, [1932] A.C. 562, at pp. 595-96, quoted by Mr. Justice Ferguson in *Ruegger v. Shell Oil Co.*, [1964] 1 O.R. 88, 41 D.L.R. (2d) 183, at p. 191. See also *Read v. Lyons & Co. Ltd.*, [1947] A.C. 156, at p. 172, [1946] 2 All E.R. 471 (*per* Lord Macmillan).

[408] *Nicholson v. John Deere Ltd.*, *supra*, n. 222, where Smith J. classified a riding mower as inherently dangerous because of its defective design.

[409] *Martin v. T.W. Hand Fireworks Co.* (1963), 37 D.L.R. (2d) 455, at p. 464.

[410] *Dahlberg v. Naydiuk*, *supra*, n. 404, at p. 328.

[411] *Ives v. Clare Brothers Ltd.*, [1971] 1 O.R. 417.

[412] *Pack v. Warner County* (1964), 44 D.L.R. (2d) 215 (Alta. C.A.); *Willis v. F.M.C. Machinery* (1976), 68 D.L.R. (3d) 127 (P.E.I.), herbicide. See also *Schmitz v. Stoveld* (1974), 11 O.R. (2d) 17, at p. 23 (*per* Grossberg C.C.J.).

[413] *Buchan v. Ortho Pharmaceutical (Canada) Ltd.* (1984), 8 D.L.R. (4th) 373, at p. 386 (H.C.); affd (1986), 25 D.L.R. (4th) 658 (Ont. C.A.); see also *Hollis v. Birch* (1990), 50 B.C.L.R. (2d) 344 (C.A.), breast implants.

[414] *Rae v. T. Eaton Co. (Maritimes) Ltd.* (1961), 28 D.L.R. (2d) 522, at p. 528 (N.S.).

[415] Fleming, *op. cit, supra*, n. 274, at p. 128. See also Learned Hand's formula, $B = PL$, in *U.S. v. Carroll Towing Co.* (1947), 159 F.2d 169.

... The test of liability is not whether the product sold was or was not a "dangerous thing", but considering its nature and all relevant circumstances whether there has been a breach of duty by the manufacturer which he owed to the injured person. The duty is to use that due care that a reasonable person should use under all the circumstances. And one of the most important circumstances — and often the controlling circumstance — is the character of the article sold and its capacity to do harm.[416]

Mr. Justice Middleton explained the notion in *Shandloff v. City Dairy Ltd.* in this way:

The lack of care essential to the establishment of such a claim increases according to the danger to the ultimate consumer, and where the thing is in itself dangerous, the care necessary approximates to, and almost becomes, an absolute liability.[417]

Another remnant of the inherently dangerous article theory is that the onus of proof is shifted to the manufacturer and the other defendant. For example, in *Ives v. Clare Brothers Ltd.*,[418] responsibility was attached for a defective gas furnace that caused injury to a homeowner by leakage of gas. Mr. Justice Peter Wright of the Ontario High Court stated:

[O]nce it is established that injury or damages have been caused by the use of natural gas through an installation made, installed or serviced by others, the onus of proving that there is no negligence is on each defendant who made, installed or serviced the installation. In other words, the position of an innocent gas user harmed by the use of gas is analogous to that of a pedestrian under s. 106(1) of the *Highway Traffic Act.*[419]

His Lordship indicated that he was prepared to extend this theory even to ordinary products in these words:

Although I find this a sure ground for determination of legal problems in the use of natural gas, which our legislation and regulations establish to be hazardous, I would not find it unjust or illogical in the modern world of faceless plants and suppliers to apply it to the case of manufacturers and distant powers generally distributing their products in our society. It seems to be a recognition of the position of the lonely hurt citizen in the face of power so great and so remote that the common injured consumer cannot reasonably be expected to discover the secrets and complexities which may have caused him harm. I do not assert that that is the law of products' liability generally, but I shall not be shocked or surprised when higher authority free to do so avers it to be the law.[420]

Both the producers and the service people were unable to "discharge the burden" and, consequently, both were held liable.

It is difficult to tell whether this special category of dangerous articles will eventually disappear or whether it will be expanded to include other products. The concept is similar to the rule of *Rylands v. Fletcher* and it does improve the

---

[416] *Supra*, n. 414, at p. 535, no liability for abnormal use.
[417] [1936] O.R. 579, at p. 590 (C.A.). See also *Ayoub v. Beaupre* (1964), 45 D.L.R. (2d) 411 (S.C.C.) (*per* Spence J.).
[418] *Supra*, n. 411.
[419] *Ibid.*, at p. 420.
[420] *Ibid.*

legal position of the consumer. It would undoubtedly be better to promote product safety without reliance on such an artificial distinction. Nevertheless, absent bolder judicial or legislative approaches, perhaps this device, which permits an indirect response to a social need, is preferable to ordinary negligence principles.

e) Strict Liability in Tort

In 1936, Mr. Justice Riddell, Don Quixote-like, championed a more direct attack upon the problem of liability for defective food products. Without citing any authorities, and without the support of his brethren, Mr. Justice Riddell, in *Shandloff v. City Dairy Ltd.*,[421] declared:

> It is good sense and should be good law, that anyone manufacturing for public consumption an article of food should be held to warrant to the consumer that it is free from hidden defects which are and may be dangerous; and it is no hardship to hold the vendor of food as warranting to the purchaser and consumer in the same way.

His Lordship repeated this "implied warranty" theory five years later, in *Arendale v. Canada Bread Co.*,[422] to the effect that when "one manufactures for human consumption any article, fluid, or solid, he, putting it on the market gives an implied warranty that it contains no deleterious substance".

Mr. Justice Riddell was a lonesome voice crying out in the Canadian wilderness, although this principle has swept across the United States in what has been called the "most rapid and altogether spectacular overturn of an established rule in the entire history of the law of torts".[423] By 1963, the fictional notion of warranty, a "freak hybrid born of the illicit intercourse of tort and contract", was replaced by the more straightforward "strict liability in tort", as had been urged by Dean Prosser.[424] A consumer in the United States must no longer prove negligence to win damages; all the consumer has to show is that the product is "defective".[425] This task is not as simple as might be expected, but it has improved the position of the injured consumer. There are thousands of cases that apply strict liability theory to every sort of product on the market. Not all the problems have been banished; difficulties remain concerning warnings, design defects, side effects and allergic persons, the matter of intermediate inspection, and the treatment of economic loss. Nevertheless, the new basis of

---

[421] *Supra*, n. 417, at p. 581.

[422] [1941] 2 D.L.R. 41 (Ont. C.A.).

[423] See for a detailed description of the development, Prosser, "The Fall of the Citadel (Strict Liability to the Consumer)" (1966), 50 Minn. L. Rev. 791.

[424] *Ibid.*, at p. 800. See also *Greenman v. Yuba Power Products Inc.* (1963), 59 Cal. App. 2d 57, 377 P.2d 897, 27 Cal. Rptr. 697; *Dunham v. Vaughan & Bushnell Mfg. Co.* (1969), 247 N.E.2d 401 (Ill. S.C.); *Barker v. Lull Mfg.* (1978), 143 Cal. Rptr. 225.

[425] See Dobbs, *supra*, n. 5, Chapter 24.

liability has been firmly established in the vast majority of states and, as altered over the years,[426] it appears that it is here to stay.

The policy reasons advanced in the United States in support of strict tort liability are varied. The most common justification is that the injured consumer, who is protected inadequately by the negligence theory, should be assured compensation by no-fault liability. The rationale for shifting accident costs to the producers or other enterprisers is that they are better able to spread them either through insurance or through price increases to their customers, who, after all secure the major benefits of the activity.[427] By exacting a small fee from many, the severity of the economic impact on the injured few is cushioned. This social welfare goal of tort law has become a powerful influence on the inexorable expansion of liability. Another policy justification is that manufacturers, by nation-wide advertising, stimulate reliance upon the safety of their products and they should stand behind them if they prove unsound.[428] To permit the producers to avoid liability by invoking the no-privity rule, while at the same time holding liable the seller who is a mere conduit, does no honour to the law. Besides, needless circuity of action can be avoided by allowing a direct action against the fabricator instead of a series of suits. Furthermore, strict tort liability may deter slipshod working practices which cause accidents. If negligence theory encourages safety measures and reduces faulty conduct, strict liability should promote "super-care". Manufacturers, alert to the diseconomies of accidents, wary of unfavourable publicity for their products, and strategically situated to take drastic measures to cut accidents, may enhance their effort to decrease accidents. More recently, the theory of "market or general deterrence" (as contrasted with specific deterrence which has been described above) has been advanced as a basis for strict liability.[429] Couched in the economic language of better resource allocation, this rationale calls for the ascription of all the accident costs generated by unsound products to the industry producing them. If this were done, the price of the commodity would more accurately reflect its true production cost, enabling society to make more informed decisions on which products to use. Since articles that produce heavy accident expenses will cost more than less risky products, sales of the former should decrease and sales of the latter should increase. Some accident-prone industries may have to close down because of this. Moreover, "unjust enrichment" of these industries will be avoided and a more "just and fair" allocation of the accident losses will be

---

[426] Restatement Third, Torts: Products Liability, 1998 §1 and §2.

[427] See generally Fleming, *The Law of Torts*, 9th ed. (1998); Harper, James and Gray, *The Law of Torts*, 2nd ed. (1986); Ehrenzweig, *Negligence Without Fault* (1951) reprinted in (1966), 54 Cal. L. Rev. 1422; Priest, "The Invention of Enterprise Liability: A Critical History of the Intellectual Foundations of Modern Tort Law" (1985), 14 J. Leg. Stud. 461. See *Beshada v. Johns-Manville Products Corp.* (1982), 447 A.2d 539 (N.J.S.C.), asbestos case.

[428] Shapo, "A Representation Theory of Consumer Protection" (1974), 60 Va. L. Rev. 1113.

[429] Calabresi, *The Costs of Accidents* (1970); Posner, *Economic Analysis of Law*, 3rd ed. (1986).

achieved.[430] Lastly, consumers would acquire a more potent weapon in their struggle to make producers more responsive and humane.[431]

But this American strict tort liability "explosion" has not caused so much as a ripple on our placid Canadian waters, despite the similarity in the products and consumption habits, despite the frequency of American ownership of the manufacturing plants, despite N.A.F.T.A., and despite the encouragement of respected Canadian academics.[432] The policy reasons relied upon by the American courts are no less applicable in this country, but they have not yet influenced our courts, except for one superb statement by Mr. Justice Laskin:

> That liability rests upon a conviction that manufacturers should bear the risks of injury to consumers or users of their products when such products are carelessly manufactured because the manufacturers create the risk in the carrying on of their enterprises and they will be more likely to safeguard the members of the public to whom their products are marketed if they must stand behind them as safe products to consume or to use. They are better able to insure against such risks, and the cost of insurance, as a business expense, can be spread with less pain among the buying public than would be the case if an injured consumer or user was saddled with the entire loss that befalls him.[433]

It is time for the Canadian law of product liability to relieve our injured consumers from the onerous burden of proving fault, and to require our manufacturers to stand behind their defective products, whether they were negligently produced or not.[434] If the courts do not act soon, we can expect the legislatures to fill the vacuum, which they have already done in some provinces.[435]

6. SHODDY PRODUCTS AND PURE ECONOMIC LOSS

It is no longer uncertain whether the duty of care in products liability cases extends to cover pure economic losses resulting from shoddy work, at least where there is danger to safety. In *Rivtow Marine Ltd. v. Washington Iron*

---

[430] Keeton, "Is There a Place for Negligence in Modern Tort Law" (1967), 53 Va. L. Rev. 886, at pp. 892 *et seq.*

[431] Shapo, "Changing Frontiers in Torts: Vistas for the '70s" (1970), 22 Stan. L. Rev. 330; Linden, "Tort Law as Ombudsman" (1973), 51 Can. Bar Rev. 155.

[432] Waddams, *Products Liability*, 3rd ed. (Toronto: Carswell Co., 1993).

[433] *Rivtow Marine Ltd. v. Washington Iron Works* (1973), 40 D.L.R. (3d) 530, at pp. 551-52, [1973] 6 W.W.R. 692 (S.C.C.).

[434] See Waddams, *op. cit. supra*, n. 432; O'Connell, *Ending Insult to Injury: No-fault Insurance for Products and Services* (1975); *cf.*, Stradiotto, "Products Liability in Tort", *Special Lectures on New Developments in the Law of Torts* (1973).

[435] In New Brunswick, strict liability for consumer loss has been enacted for suppliers of consumer products that are unreasonably dangerous because of a "defect in design, material or workmanship", if reasonably foreseeable. See Consumer Product Warranty and Liability Act, S.N.B. 1978, c. C-18.1. See also, in Saskatchewan, Consumer Protection Act, S.S. 1996, c. C-30.1. In Quebec, the U.K. and the European Economic Community there have also been similar developments.

Works,[436] the Supreme Court of Canada allowed recovery for economic losses that resulted when a faulty crane was removed from use to be serviced because of a risk of collapse. The majority in *Rivtow* did not allow recovery for the cost of repairs to the crane but did award damages for the extra monetary loss resulting from the fact that the crane had to be removed from use during a busy period because of the crane supplier's failure to warn immediately upon discovering the defect in the crane.

The dissenting judgment in *Rivtow*, written by Laskin J., went beyond the majority's position. This dissent has been cited with approval in the House of Lords[437] and has now supplanted the majority opinion in Canada.[438] Unlike the majority, Laskin would have allowed recovery for the cost of repairs to the crane; he reasoned that the distinction between actual and potential damage is untenable as a basis for determining whether such repairs are recoverable:[439]

> The case is not one where a manufactured product proves to be merely defective (in short, where it has not met promised expectation), but rather one where by reason of the defect there is a foreseeable risk of physical harm from its use and where the alert avoidance of such harm gives rise to economic loss. Prevention of threatened harm resulting directly in economic loss should not be treated differently from post-injury cure.

The House of Lords in their decision in *Junior Books Ltd. v. The Veitchi Co. Ltd.*[440] referred to the "powerful dissenting judgment by Laskin J." in *Rivtow*. In *Junior Books*, however, the Lords went beyond Laskin's dissenting position by allowing recovery without actual or even potential damage, or danger resulting from the defective product. In this controversial decision, the House of Lords extended tort liability for pure economic loss to a sub-contractor who negligently laid a floor in the plaintiff's factory. Although there was no contract between the sub-contractor and the owner of the premises, Lord Roskill relied heavily on the observation that "the relationship between the parties was as close as it could be short of actual privity of contract".[441] Accordingly, even though there was no additional property damage, and no imminent risk of damage or

---

[436] [1973] 6 W.W.R. 692, 40 D.L.R. (3d) 530 (S.C.C.). This group of cases is in Feldthusen's category four.

[437] See *Anns v. Merton London Borough Council*, [1977] 2 All E.R. 492, at p. 505 (H.L.); *Junior Books Ltd. v. The Veitchi Co. Ltd.*, [1982] 3 All E.R. 201, at pp. 212-13 (H.L.).

[438] In *C.N.R. v. Norsk Pacific SS. Ltd.*, [1992] 1 S.C.R. 1021, a case that further muddied the waters of tort recovery for economic loss, all three opinions devote space to Laskin's dissent in *Rivtow* without rejecting his position. Stevenson J. refers to this dissent as "doubtful authority" but McLachlin J. and LaForest J. (dissenting) treat Laskin's reasons as authoritative. See also, *Fuller v. Ford Motor Co. of Canada* (1978), 22 O.R. (2d) 764 (Co. Ct.); *Ordog v. Dist. of Mission* (1980), 110 D.L.R. (3d) 718 (B.C.S.C.). See also *Winnipeg Condominium Corp. v. Bird Construction*, [1995] 1 S.C.R. 85.

[439] *Supra*, n. 436, at p. 552, D.L.R. Lord Denning made a similar point in *Dutton v. Bognor Regis Urban District Council*, [1972] 1 Q.B. 373 (C.A.). See also, Sir Robin Cooke, "An Impossible Distinction" (1991), 107 L.Q. Rev. 46.

[440] *Supra*, n. 437, at p. 212 (H.L.).

[441] *Ibid.*, at p. 214.

injury, the plaintiff recovered the cost of replacing the defective floor as well as the profits lost during the course of the repairs.

While *Junior Books* has been subsequently disavowed by the House of Lords,[442] the Supreme Court of Canada has not yet been called upon to determine the status of that case in this country. In *City of Kamloops v. Nielsen*,[443] Madam Justice Wilson spoke approvingly of *Junior Books*, commenting that it "carried the law a significant step forward". Some lower courts have followed *Junior Books*,[444] while others have distinguished it.[445] It was left alone by the Supreme Court in *Bird Construction*. It seems, then, that *Junior Books* may still be alive in Canada.[446]

As for the matter of liability for the cost of repairing dangerous structures, the Supreme Court of Canada in *Winnipeg Condominium Corp. No. 36 v. Bird Construction Co.*[447] has unanimously adopted the dissenting view of Laskin J. A subsequent owner of an apartment building sued the original contractor, alleging that the building had structural defects that were dangerous as well as other defects. The pleadings were challenged and the case reached the Supreme Court on the issue of law raised, that is, is a general contractor responsible in tort to a subsequent purchaser for the negligent construction of a building without privity? The Supreme Court unanimously held that those who design or construct a building owe a duty to subsequent purchasers of the building if it was foreseeable that a failure to construct the building carefully would create danger to the health and safety of the occupants. If negligence is established in these circumstances, there is liability for the reasonable cost of repairing the defects to render the building safe. The *D & F Estates Ltd. v. Church Commissioners for England*[448] case was rejected on two bases: (1) it was inconsistent with our law of concurrent liability in contact and tort; and (2) it was inconsistent with *Anns v. Merton*,[449] which our law adopted in the *City of Kamloops* case.

---

[442] *Murphy v. Brentwood District Council*, [1990] 2 All E.R. 908 (H.L.); *D. & F. Estates Ltd. v. Church Commrs for England*, [1988] 2 All E.R. 992 (H.L.); *Department of the Environment v. Thomas Bates & Son (New Towns Commn.)*, [1990] 2 All E.R. 943 (H.L.).

[443] [1984] 2 S.C.R. 2, at p. 32.

[444] *University of Regina v. Pettick* (1986), 38 C.C.L.T. 230 (Sask. Q.B.); affd (1991), 6 C.C.L.T. (2d) 1 (Sask. C.A.); *Strike v. Ciro Roofing Products U.S.A. Inc.* (1988), 46 C.C.L.T. 209 (B.C.S.C.). But see *Buthmann v. Balzer*, [1983] 4 W.W.R. 695 (Alta. Q.B.); leave to appeal to S.C.C. refused, Jan. 31, 1985, preferring *Rivtow* to *Junior Books*.

[445] *Logan Lake (Dist.) v. Rivtow Industries Ltd.* (1990), 71 D.L.R. (4th) 333 (B.C.C.A.); *Zidaric v. Toshiba of Canada Ltd.* (2000), 5 C.C.L.T. (3d) 61 (Ont. S.C.J.); *M. Hasegawa & Co. v. Pepsi Bottling Group (Canada) Co.* (2000), 1 C.C.L.T. (3d) 250, at p. 255 (B.C.S.C.), bottled water with mould not "real and substantial danger" to plaintiff, only "defect in the thing itself".

[446] *Condominium Plan No. 9421710 v. Christenson* (2001), 5 C.C.L.T. (3d) 135 (Alta. Q.B.), refusal to strike out claim for non-dangerous defect.

[447] *Supra*, n. 438. See Chapter 12C., *supra*; see also Rafferty, "Comment" (1996), 34 Alta. L. Rev. 472, reasoning "persuasive" and "defensible".

[448] *Supra*, n. 442.

[449] *Supra*, n. 437.

Writing for the unanimous court, Mr. Justice LaForest refused to follow the House of Lords in its retreat from *Anns* and explained the principle governing cases that deal with shoddy goods, as follows:[450]

> In my view, it is reasonably foreseeable to contractors that, if they design or construct a building negligently and if that building contains latent defects as a result of that negligence, subsequent purchasers of the building may suffer personal injury or damage to other property when those defects manifest themselves. A lack of contractual privity between the contractor and the inhabitants at the time the defect becomes manifest does not make the potential for injury any less foreseeable. Buildings are permanent structures that are commonly inhabited by many different persons over their useful life. By constructing the building negligently, contractors (or any other person responsible for the design and construction of a building) create a foreseeable danger that will threaten not only the original owner, but every inhabitant during the useful life of the building. . . .
>
> In my view, the reasonable likelihood that a defect in a building will cause injury to its inhabitants is also sufficient to ground a contractor's duty in tort to subsequent purchasers of the building for the cost of repairing the defect if that defect is discovered prior to any injury and if it poses a real and substantial danger to the inhabitants of the building. In coming to this conclusion, I adopt the reasoning of Laskin J. in *Rivtow*, which I find highly persuasive. If a contractor can be held liable in tort where he or she constructs a building negligently and, as a result of that negligence, the building causes damage to persons or property, it follows that the contractor should also be held liable in cases where the dangerous defect is discovered and the owner of the building wishes to mitigate the danger by fixing the defect and putting the building back into a non-dangerous state. In both cases, the duty in tort serves to protect the bodily integrity and property interests of the inhabitants of the building.

Further, Mr. Justice LaForest, pursuant to the *Anns* approach, could not see any reason to negate this duty. He explained:[451]

> I conclude, then, that no adequate policy considerations exist to negate a contractor's duty in tort to subsequent purchasers of a building to take reasonable care in constructing the building, and to ensure that the building does not contain defects that pose foreseeable and substantial danger to the health and safety of the occupants. In my view, the Manitoba Court of Appeal erred in deciding that Bird could not, in principle, be held liable in tort to the Condominium Corporation for the reasonable cost of repairing the defect and putting the building back into a non-dangerous state. These costs are recoverable economic loss under the law of tort in Canada.

In addition to the grounds of foresight and logic, Mr. Justice LaForest, following New Zealand, American and Quebec law, felt this rule would act as an "incentive" to mitigate potential losses. In other words, "allowing recovery against contractors in tort for the cost of repairs of dangerous defects thus serves an important preventative function by encouraging socially responsible behaviour".[452]

His Lordship left open the issue of liability for non-dangerous defects, the *Junior Books* situation, which was not raised by the parties, for another case more squarely focussed on this issue.

---

[450] *Supra*, n. 438, at pp. 115-17.

[451] *Ibid*., at p. 129.

[452] *Ibid*., at p. 118.

7. PROBLEMS OF PROOF

A person seeking the aid of the court in a products case must convince the court on the balance of probabilities that the other party was negligent and that that negligence caused the harm complained of. Nothing less will do. This is true whether the basis for liability is defective design, defective manufacture, or failure to warn.[453]

a) Causation

As in any other type of case, if the judge does not believe the plaintiff's story about the cause of injury or that the plaintiff was injured at all, the case will, naturally, be dismissed. For instance where a woman claimed that she was injured by an exploding beer bottle,[454] and where someone complained that his mouth was cut by glass from a soda pop bottle,[455] in the face of medical evidence to the contrary, the actions were dismissed. In *Phillips v. Chrysler Corporation*,[456] the deceased was killed in a collision when the steering mechanism of his 1957 Dodge jammed. Mr. Justice Landreville felt that there was an "enigma" since, although he felt that "definitely something in the apparatus went wrong to cause the steering to jam and freeze," there was no evidence to indicate what it was. There were just "too many unanswered ifs".[457] It is insufficient to demonstrate a "mere possibility" that negligence caused the accident.[458]

In *Snell v. Farrell*,[459] however, Sopinka J. made it clear that a common sense approach to causation should be adopted rather than the rigid approach of the past. He explained that "an inference of causation may be drawn although positive or scientific proof of causation has not been adduced".[460] Other courts have also, on occasion, admitted that "[m]athematical, or strict logical, demonstration is generally impossible",[461] and have found negligence "as a matter of inference" without being able to "lay [the] finger on the exact person in all the chain who is responsible, or to specify what he did wrong".[462] This approach was pushed to the extreme in one case where the court found a stove manufacturer liable when a pot of oil caught fire while on the stove. The plaintiff claimed that she had turned off the element under the pot. Although there was no evidence whatsoever of a defect in the stove, Soper J. determined

---

[453] *Rothwell v. Raes, supra*, n. 361.

[454] *Swan v. Riedle Brewery Ltd.*, [1942] 2 D.L.R. 446, [1942] 1 W.W.R. 577, at p. 584 (Man.).

[455] *Ferstenfeld v. Kik Cola Co.* (1939), 77 Que. S.C. 165.

[456] [1962] O.R. 375, 32 D.L.R. (2d) 347.

[457] *Ibid.*, at p. 359, D.L.R., *res ipsa* not applied, 1 1/2 years had passed and others handled car.

[458] *Ferstenfeld v. Kik Cola Co., supra*, n. 455, at p. 166. See also *Rothwell v. Raes, supra*, n. 361; *Wilsher v. Essex*, [1987] 1 All E.R. 871 (H.L.).

[459] [1990] 2 S.C.R. 311. See Chapter 4, *supra*.

[460] *Ibid.*, at p. 330.

[461] *Grant v. Australian Knitting Mills*, [1936] A.C. 85, at p. 96 (*per* Lord Wright).

[462] *Shandloff v. City Dairy Ltd.*, [1936] O.R. 579, at p. 582 (C.A.).

that "the fire occurred because of some unexplained or inexplicable defect in the stove which the plaintiff need not explain".[463]

There has been a dramatic development in the United States in cases where it is difficult to determine which of several producers caused a loss, known as the market share theory of liability, whereby producers are held liable according to their market share of sales.[464] But, while this theory has been mentioned in several Canadian cases[465] it has not yet been adopted in Canada.[466] Nor has the objective causation theory, which applies in medical cases involving the duty of disclosure, been used in products cases.[467]

b) Inferring Negligence: *Res Ipsa* Expired

Despite indications in *Donoghue v. Stevenson* that it would not apply, Canadian courts in the past asserted their independence and invoked the now defunct doctrine of *res ipsa loquitur* to assist them in the resolution of these disputes.[468] The court occasionally spoke of an "inference" of negligence arising from certain facts without relying expressly on the doctrine of *res ipsa loquitur*,[469] but it was usually invoked by name.[470] *Res ipsa loquitur* was only utilized, however, where the "cause was wholly unknown" and not where the evidence proved, for example, that a can exploded because it was being banged by a child.[471] Normally, *res ipsa loquitur* was relied upon to create an *inference* of negligence where an accident occurred that would not normally happen unless someone was negligent and where the defendant was in control of the conditions giving rise to the accident.[472] This latter requirement was only another way of saying that the finger of guilt must be levelled at the defendant.

The Supreme Court of Canada has now dispatched to the dust bin of history the doctrine of *res ipsa loquitur,* describing it as "expired" in *Fontaine v. British Columbia (Official Administrator).*[473] Although the case dealt with an unexplained auto accident, it is clear that the Latin expression has been abandoned in all situations; but it is also clear that proof of the facts that once led courts to

---

[463] *Osmond v. Sears Canada Inc.* (1988), 220 A.P.R. 75, at p. 78 (Nfld. S.C.).

[464] See *Sindell v. Abbott Laboratories* (1980), 607 P. 2d 924 (Calif. S.C.). See Chapter 4, *supra.*

[465] *Snell v. Farrell,* [1990] 2 S.C.R. 311; *Insurance Corp. of B.C. v. Leland,* [1999] B.C.J. No. 2073; *Valleyview Hotel v. Burns Estate,* [1985] S.J. No. 151; *Gariepy v. Shell Oil,* [2000] O.J. No. 3804.

[466] Except by statute in B.C. to aid in its tobacco litigation, see Tobacco Damages and Health Care Costs Recovery Act, S.B.C. 1997, c. 41, based on U.S. legislation. Declared *ultra vires, JTI-MacDonald Corp. v. British Columbia (Attorney General)* (2000), 184 D.L.R. (4th) 335 (B.C.S.C.).

[467] *Ortho, supra,* n. 371.

[468] *Castle v. Davenport-Campbell Co.,* [1952] O.R. 565, [1952] 3 D.L.R. 540, at p. 546 (C.A.), Chapter 8, *supra.*

[469] *Mathews v. Coca-Cola Co.,* [1944] O.R. 207, [1944] 2 D.L.R. 355 (C.A.).

[470] *Varga v. John Labatt Ltd.,* [1956] O.R. 1007, 6 D.L.R. (2d) 336 (*per* Wells J.).

[471] *Rae v. T. Eaton Co. (Maritimes) Ltd.,* (1961), 28 D.L.R. (2d) 522, at p. 537 (N.S.).

[472] *Interlake Tissue Mills v. Salmon and Beckett,* [1948] O.R. 950, [1949] 1 D.L.R. 207 (C.A.).

[473] [1998] 1 S.C.R. 424. See discussion in Chapter 8.B, *supra.*

infer negligence will continue to do so, but without the use of the Latin phrase. Justice Major explained:[474]

> Whatever value *res ipsa loquitur* may have once provided is gone. Various attempts to apply the so-called doctrine have been more confusing than helpful. Its use has been restricted to cases where the facts permitted an inference of negligence and there was no other reasonable explanation for the accident. Given its limited use it is somewhat meaningless to refer to that use as a doctrine of law.

He concluded by advising that it would be better if the "maxim was treated as expired and no longer used as a separate component of negligence actions". He suggested that henceforth the evidence would be more "sensibly dealt with" if the trier of fact weighed the direct evidence and the circumstantial evidence to determine whether the plaintiff has established a *prima facie* case and, if so, whether the defendant has successfully negated that evidence.

As can be seen, the process of proof in future products cases will not be markedly different than before, except that the mysterious Latin words will be absent from the discussion. This view has been expressed by Justice Mackenzie of the British Columbia Court of Appeal as follows:[475]

> While the Supreme Court was critical of the Latin maxim, the underlying principles governing the use of circumstantial evidence in determining liability for negligence were not modified. The issue becomes simply whether after weighing the whole of the direct and circumstantial evidence, the plaintiff has established a *prima facie* case of negligence against the defendant, and that inference has not been negated by the defendant's evidence. The legal burden of proof, of course, remains on the plaintiff throughout.

The older cases, therefore, may still be useful. In addition, it may be that the treatment of the evidence in the older products cases, that is, to shift the burden of disproof to the defendant, may survive *Fontaine*. Thus, when glass particles emerged from a Coke bottle in *Zeppa v. Coca-Cola Ltd.*,[476] Chief Justice Pickup's statement, in which he did not specifically refer to *res ipsa*, that "there is a *presumption* of negligence on the part of the manufacturer and a *burden on him of disproving negligence on his part to the satisfaction of the jury*", may still be good law. Soon afterwards, the discovery of chlorine in a beer bottle in *Varga v. John Labatt Ltd.*,[477] also raised a presumption which shifted the onus of proof to the defendant. In *Arendale v. Canada Bread Co.*,[478] where glass was found in a loaf of bread, the court had also spoken of an "onus . . . on the defendant to

---

[474] *Ibid.*, at p. 435, para. 26 and 27.

[475] *Marchuk v. Swede Creek Contracting Ltd.*, [1998] B.C.J. No. 2851, at para. 10.

[476] [1955] O.R. 855, at p. 865, [1955] 5 D.L.R. 187, at p. 193 (C.A.). See *supra*, Chapter 8, Section D. 1. See also *Brunski v. Dominion Stores Ltd.* (1981), 20 C.C.L.T. 14 (Ont. H.C.) (*per* Linden J.), onus on both bottler and bottle maker.

[477] *Supra*, n. 470. But see *Hellenius v. Lees*, [1971] 1 O.R. 273, at p. 288 (*per* Laskin J.); affd [1972] S.C.R. 165, 20 D.L.R. (3d) 369; *Phillips v. Ford Motor Co.*, [1971] 2 O.R. 637, 18 D.L.R. (3d) 641, at p. 658 (C.A.) (*per* Schroeder J.A.). See also McPhillips J.A. in *Willis v. Coca-Cola Co.*, [1934] 1 W.W.R. 145, at p. 167 (B.C.C.A.), trial dismissal upheld when court split 2-2.

[478] [1941] 2 D.L.R. 41 (Ont. C.A.).

offer a reasonable explanation" and held the defendant liable because "the evidence falls short of discharging this onerous burden".[479] So too, in *Saddlemire v. Coca-Cola Co.*[480] the court had defined *res ipsa loquitur* as "sufficient evidence to raise a presumption of negligence which must be rebutted by the defendant".

There was even some indication that this development would be extended beyond food products. Mr. Justice Ferguson, in a defective fertilizer case,[481] stated that the mere fact that the accident happened, "raises a presumption of negligence" and places an "onus on the defendant to satisfy the court that the damage was not caused by . . ." the defective product. Unhappily, Mr. Justice Ferguson vacillated somewhat in his reasons, using words like "inference" and "*prima facie*", before stating that the defendant did not show "that the damage is consistent with no negligence on his part . . ."[482] phrasing which accorded less weight to the evidence than a presumption. Similarly, in *Farro v. Nutone Electrical Ltd.*, Mr. Justice Lacourcière of the Ontario Court of Appeal resorted to the language of a "*prima facie* case," and "an inference of negligence" before ruling that the manufacturer was liable for damages following a fire that was ignited by a faulty ceiling fan.[483] Lacourcière J.A. characterized the argument that improper installation might have caused the malfunction of the fan as speculative. He then explained that "to give effect to such a speculative defence would undermine the progressive line of cases which placed liability on the manufacturer of a defective product; this is so even in the case of a latent defect if the manufacturer failed to rebut the onus on it to disprove negligence".[484]

Once a court is satisfied that defective food has caused an injury, defendants will undoubtedly encounter difficulty in exculpating themselves under any word formula. It may not be enough for defendants to prove a process is a safe and modern one,[485] for "even in a system designed to be perfect, the possibility of human error remains".[486] In *Arendale v. Canada Bread Co.*,[487] the defendant was held liable despite evidence that his equipment was "the best and most modern available, designed to safeguard the ingredients entering the finished loaf . . .". On rare occasions courts may be influenced by evidence to the effect that

---

[479] *Ibid.*, at p. 44 (*per* Gillanders J.A.).

[480] [1941] 4 D.L.R. 614, at p. 619 (C.A.).

[481] *Majorcsak v. Na-Churs Plant Food* (1964), 44 D.L.R. (2d) 33, at p. 37, *dictum*; revd as to manufacturer on other grounds 57 D.L.R. (2d) 39. See also *Brad's Transport v. Stevenson* (1974), 7 Nfld. & P.E.I.R. 232, at p. 241 (P.E.I.), jammed steering mechanism. The English courts have moved in this direction, see *Moore v. R. Fox & Sons*, [1956] 1 Q.B. 596.

[482] *Ibid.*, at p. 33.

[483] (1990), 68 D.L.R. (4th) 269 (Ont. C.A.).

[484] *Ibid.*, at p. 275.

[485] *Saddlemire v. Coca-Cola Co.*, [1941] 4 D.L.R. 614, at p. 616 (Ont. C.A.), shows the complexity of the evidence adduced.

[486] Mr. Justice Gillanders in *Mathews v. Coca-Cola Co.*, *supra*, n. 469, at p. 374, D.L.R.

[487] [1941] 2 D.L.R. 41, at pp. 42-43 (Ont. C.A.) (*per* Gillanders J.). See also *Varga v. John Labatt Ltd.*, *supra*, n. 470, where evidence of safe system rejected. *Cf.*, *Willis v. Coca-Cola Co.*, [1934] 1 W.W.R. 145, at p. 148 (B.C.C.A.), where jury absolved defendant on evidence of safe method.

2,000,000 bottles of beer were produced in a year or so without any complaints,[488] but generally they are not so easily impressed.[489] Consequently, while the phrase *res ipsa loquitur* was a valuable aid to claimants in cases where specific evidence was absent or flimsy, similar circumstantial evidence is likely to lead to similar conclusions without the use of the maxim. Lacking the boldness to impose strict liability directly, our courts used *res ipsa loquitur* as a device to move the law in that direction in a roundabout way.[490] This process may continue in a more direct way, even though the maxim is now unavailable to assist.

8. DEFENCES

After demonstrating duty, no intermediate examination, negligence and cause, the plaintiff still is not home free; there may be certain defences such as contributory negligence, voluntary assumption of risk and abnormal use that will cause the plaintiff to be defeated.

a) Contributory Negligence

As indicated in *Shields v. Hobbs Manufacturing Co.*,[491] if, for his or her own protection, a plaintiff does not use reasonable care, recovery may be reduced or even eliminated altogether. As in other areas of tort law, the law helps only those who are deemed worthy of its protection, that is, those who have not contributed to their own injury. The contributory negligence defence is also aimed at deterring carelessness by plaintiffs. This policy survives although its sting has been mollified by contributory negligence legislation. Thus, liability can be divided among a negligent helicopter manufacturer, a company that over stressed the aircraft with overweight loads and the pilots who flew them.[492]

b) *Volenti*

The defence of voluntary assumption of risk or "consent", to use another term, incorporates the philosophy that those who waive their rights do not deserve legal assistance.[493] Thus, when there is an exclusionary clause in a contract, the court will probably honour it[494] unless it violates a fundamental term of the contract.[495] But a contract is not needed at all. Where the plaintiff continued to

---

[488] *Swan v. Riedle Brewery Ltd.*, *supra*, n. 454, at p. 585, D.L.R.

[489] *Grant v. Australian Knitting Mills*, [1936] A.C. 85.

[490] See *Chabot v. Ford Motor Co.*, *supra*, n. 87, truck burst into flames, liability imposed.

[491] *Supra*, n. 320. See also *Lambert v. Lewis*, [1982] A.C. 225 (H.L.), where a defect in a trailer-hitch was discovered, leading to shared liability.

[492] *Forsyth v. Sikorsky Aircraft Corp.*, [2000] B.C.J. No. 813.

[493] *Supra*, Chapter 13.

[494] *Castle v. Davenport-Campbell Co.*, [1952] O.R. 565, [1952] 3 D.L.R. 540 (C.A.), manufacturer held but supplier let off.

[495] Devlin, "The Treatment of Breach of Contract", [1966] Camb. L.J. 192, at p. 208.

drink a Coca-Cola after he realized it had a "disagreeable" odour and taste, the court withheld recovery.[496] Nor was the manufacturer held liable when its fertilizer was mixed with some other material by an independent contractor, with the consent of the plaintiff.[497]

c) Abnormal Use

Another defence used on occasion is that of abnormal use. In *Rae v. T. Eaton Co. (Maritimes) Ltd.*,[498] the manufacturer was absolved of liability for an injury to a child's eye when a can of artificial snow exploded while being banged on concrete, since "in its normal use, or in reasonably foreseeable use, [it] was harmless". It might be otherwise, said the court, if the can fell off a Christmas tree or was dropped from arm's height or from a shelf because this might be expected. In *Yachetti v. John Duff & Sons Ltd.*,[499] the plaintiff tasted some raw pork and contracted trichinosis, but the court dismissed the case on the ground, *inter alia*, that this was an "abnormal use" of pork, which was usually cooked thoroughly before being eaten. Prior cooking would have rendered it harmless. Similarly, where someone drank wood alcohol and died, his family could not recover from the druggist for this reason, among others.[500] Furthermore, where extreme heat was applied directly to a teapot, it was felt that the manufacturer was not negligent because this was not the "purpose for which the teapots were intended nor was it a reasonable use of them".[501] But this is not surprising, for even where strict liability is employed in products cases, this doctrine of abnormal use has been relied upon in absolving manufacturers of liability.[502] Where a plaintiff fell into an unguarded harvester machine while using it dangerously,[503] liability was denied.

Sometimes a manufacturer can be relieved of liability when the consumer is allergic or unusually sensitive to a particular product. This is a complex and confusing issue which has attracted academic attention.[504] There is authority to

---

[496] *Saddlemire v. Coca-Cola Co., supra*, n. 485. See also *Varga v. John Labatt Ltd., supra*, n. 470, where plaintiff with hysteria condition allowed recovery.

[497] *Majorcsak v. Na-Churs Plant Food, supra*, n. 481.

[498] *Supra*, n. 471, at p. 532.

[499] [1943] 1 D.L.R. 194, at p. 202. See also *Griffiths v. Peter Conway Ltd.*, [1939] 1 All E.R. 685 (C.A.), rough suit on sensitive skin not normal use.

[500] *Antoine v. Duncombe* (1906), 8 O.W.R. 719.

[501] *Helfand v. Royal Canadian Art Pottery*, [1970] 1 O.R. 227, at p. 230 (*per* Fraser J.); revd on another point [1970] 2 O.R. 527 (C.A.). See also *Lem v. Barotto Sports Ltd.* (1976), 58 D.L.R. (2d) 465, no liability when hunter injured because he misused shell reloader after receiving proper instruction in its use.

[502] Prosser, "The Fall of the Citadel (Strict Liability to the Consumer)" (1966), 50 Minn. L. Rev. 791, at p. 824.

[503] *Deshane v. Deere & Co., supra*, n. 378.

[504] See generally Rogerson and Trebilcock, *supra*, n. 356; Freedman, *Allergy and Products Liability* (1961); Sone "Products Liability and the Allergic Consumer" (1976), 24 Chitty's L.J. 114; Keeton, "Products Liability: Inadequacy of Information" (1970), 48 Tex. L. Rev. 398.

the effect that allergic consumers may recover in appropriate circumstances,[505] and authority denying compensation, especially where the consumer, aware of a susceptibility, fails to warn the defendant about it.[506]

It would be preferable if abnormal use were not considered to be a separate defence. Despite its attractiveness as a simple case-solver, there is the danger that courts may dismiss a claim on the ground of abnormal use, rather than dealing with the problem as a matter of contributory negligence or voluntary assumption of risk or just plain absence of negligence, which would make more sense. The fact is that there really is no need for a special defence of abnormal use and courts would be wise to avoid it.

9. CLASS ACTIONS

In recent years, headlines have described dramatic class action lawsuits which have been settled or won in the United States, yielding huge amounts to be divided among large groups of consumers injured by defective products. Recently, legislation has been introduced in Ontario[507] and British Columbia[508] facilitating such claims in Canada.[509] The goal of these procedural statutes is to foster judicial economy, access to justice by making uneconomic cases more viable and behavioural modification of wrongdoers.

Canadian consumers have wasted no time in deploying these statutes in products liability cases. Under the new statutes, consumers have attempted to launch class action lawsuits against the manufacturers of silicone breast implants,[510] diet pills which cause heart valve problems,[511] faulty plastic pipes,[512] and defective joint implants,[513] among others with mixed results. While a detailed examination of class actions is beyond the scope of this book, product liability litigation in the 21st century may be transformed in much the same fashion as occurred in the 20th century following *Donoghue v. Stevenson*.

---

[505] *Braun v. Roux Distributing Co.* (1958), 312 S.W. 2d 758 (Mo. S.C.).

[506] *Ingham v. Emes*, [1955] 2 All E.R. 740 (C.A.); *Griffiths v. Peter Conway, supra*, n. 499; *Levi v. Colgate-Palmolive Proprietary Ltd., supra*, n. 167.

[507] Class Proceedings Act, 1992, S.O. 1992, c. 6.

[508] Class Proceedings Act, R.S.B.C. 1996, c. 50.

[509] It should be noted that a form of class action, the representative action, has existed in Canada's common law jurisdictions for many years. Legislation regarding class action also exists in Quebec, has been introduced unsuccessfully in P.E.I., has been studied in Manitoba and is currently being considered by the Federal Court. See Edgell, *supra*, n. 5 at p. 182, n. 17 for more detail about legislative activity across Canada.

[510] *Harrington v. Dow Corning Corp.* (2000), 2 C.C.L.T. (3d) 157 (B.C.C.A.).

[511] *Wilson v. Servier Canada Inc.*, [2000] O.J. No. 3392.

[512] *Gariepy v. Shell Oil Inc.*, [2000] O.J. No. 3804.

[513] *Sawatzky v. Société Chirurgicale Instrumentarium*, [1999] B.C.J. No. 1814, 71 B.C.L.R. (3d) 51 (S.C.).

Chapter 17

Governmental Liability

Tort claims against governments have created difficulties. While there are some who contend that governments should be bound by tort law like anyone else,[1] there are others who urge that governments have "juridical uniqueness" and cannot be subject to the ordinary rules.[2] Neither view has triumphed; a compromise has been reached. A limited immunity from tort liability has been created but only in certain situations over and above the regular no-duty rules that serve to restrain tort law from reviewing certain types of activities.[3] The main basis for this now is judicial respect for separation of powers theory and concern over the capacity of courts to evaluate the conduct of governments. Also part of the reason for this is the mystique surrounding the Crown and its historic position in our system of government.[4] Indeed, it may be that part of the problem is the continuing use of the word "the Crown" or the "the Queen" in our discussion of these issues, rather than the more neutral terms "state", "government" or "administration". In this chapter, in the hope of diminishing the mystery in this area, I shall use the word "government", which fairly describes the administration of the federal, provincial or municipal institutions that are the defendants in these cases.

It is odd that the use of tort law as a technique for reviewing government action is so controversial.[5] After all, nowadays government officials are subject to challenge on constitutional and Charter bases, administrative law grounds, by human rights agencies, by various ombudsmen, by contract actions and even by

---

[1] Hogg and Monahan, *Liability of the Crown*, 3rd ed. (2000), basing themselves on Dicey, *The Law of the Constitution* (1885); Ontario Law Reform Commission, *Report on The Liability of the Crown* (1989); Law Reform Commission of Canada, *The Legal Status of the Federal Administration*, Working Paper 40, (1985).

[2] McLauchlan, "Developments in Administrative Law: The 1989-90 Term" (1991), 2 S.C.L.R. (2d) 33, at p. 44. See also Feldthusen, *Economic Negligence*, 4th ed. (2000), Chapter 6.

[3] See *supra*, Chapter 9.

[4] Lorden, *Crown Law* (Markham: Butterworths, 1990); Dusseault and Borgeat, *Administrative Law*, 2nd ed. (1990), Vol. 5, Crown Liability,

[5] There is less difficulty if the conduct is alleged to be intentional, rather than negligent, see *Nelles v. Ontario*, [1989] 2 S.C.R. 170, 60 D.L.R. (4th) 609; *Roncarelli v. Duplessis*, [1959] S.C.R. 121; see also *Walker v. Ontario* (1997), 40 C.C.L.T. (2d) 197 (Ont. Gen. Div.).

criminal prosecutions. Claims for negligence, however, alarm officialdom, which bemoans their chilling effect, the shortage of funds and opening themselves up to a flood of claims even though fellow professionals in nongovernmental jobs must comply with the rules of tort law.

In recent years, civil actions against governments have become a booming industry both here and abroad. In Canada, suits have been launched against the police,[6] municipalities,[7] federal[8] and provincial[9] Attorneys-General, and against provincial[10] and federal[11] regulatory bodies. In every one of these cases, some right to sue in tort has been recognized by our courts, but inconsistencies and confusion have developed. As doctrines of government liability become more established in each jurisdiction, it seems that the differences among the jurisdictions begin to overwhelm their similarities. Different jurisdictions have different laws of tort, different statutes, different common law traditions, different "Crowns" and different factual contexts[12] to which their laws apply. Increasingly, therefore, reliance on jurisprudence from other jurisdictions is problematic.[13] To better understand the situation, nevertheless, it is necessary to briefly examine the historic background of the law in the United Kingdom, the United States and Canada and the legislation it produced.

A. Historical Perspective and Legislation

The maxim "the King can do no wrong" was the cornerstone of the common law of government immunity. Traditionally, the only way in which a British or Canadian subject could bring a suit against the Crown was by a petition of right.[14] By the mid-nineteenth century, it was clear that this was inadequate. Most early attempts at reform were, at best, only partially successful. The Petition of Right Act of 1860, which simplified the old process and might have heralded a new era of Crown liability, was held to bar tort claims.[15] It was

---

6   *Doe v. Metropolitan Toronto (Municipality) Commrs. of Police* (1990), 5 C.C.L.T. (2d) 77 (Div. Ct.).

7   *City of Kamloops v. Neilsen*, [1984] 2 S.C.R. 2.

8   See *Kealey v. Canada (A.G.)*, [1992] 1 F.C. 195, 46 F.T.R. 107 (F.C.T.D.); 139 N.R. 189 (Fed. C.A.). The action was allowed to proceed as against the government, but the claim was struck against the Attorney General personally. It was found that, where the government is sued, it is not necessary to sue the Attorney General, except in a personal capacity.

9   *Nelles v. Ontario, supra*, n. 5.

10   See *Just v. British Columbia*, [1989] 2 S.C.R. 1228.

11   *Swanson v. Canada* (1991), 124 N.R. 218 (Fed. C.A.).

12   See Cooke, "An Impossible Distinction" (1991), 107 L.Q. Rev. 47, at p. 69.

13   See Fleming, "A Requiem for *Anns*" (1990), 107 L.Q. Rev. 525, at p. 530, for a discussion of "the selective use of foreign authorities" in *Murphy v. Brentwood District Council*, [1990] 2 All E.R. 908 (H.L.).

14   Used federally in Canada until 1971, in conjunction with the Crown Liability Act, see Hogg, *op. cit. supra*, n. 1, p. 8.

15   *Viscount Canterbury v. The Queen* (1843), 12 L.J.Ch. 281 (L.C.); *Tobin v. R* (1864), 2 Mar. L.C. 45, 143 E.R. 1148; *Feather v. R.*. (1865), 6 B. & S. 257, 122 E.R. 1191. The reasoning behind

possible to sue local municipal authorities, but only where they acted under a statutory duty, and not where they exercised, or failed to exercise, a statutory power.[16] By the turn of the century the Crown would nominate a servant (for whose negligence it would have been vicariously liable were it not for Crown immunity) to stand trial in its place and it would pay that servant's damages, if found liable. This helped, but it was not effective in those instances where the responsible servant was unknown, or where the Crown was directly, rather than vicariously, liable.[17] Ideas that the Crown must be subject to the rule of law[18] understandably began to take root.

Early American law adopted a version of the British common law doctrine that the King can do no wrong.[19] This doctrine was expressed as being founded on the "logical and practical ground that there can be no legal right as against the authority on which the right depends".[20] Such an explanation would seem more appropriate to the source of the doctrine, England, than it was to the United States, which had, since its creation, permitted private individuals to challenge legislation on constitutional grounds. As in Britain, the right of an individual to proceed with a civil suit against the United States was dependent on permission, which could be obtained only through the presentation of a private bill in Congress.[21] Government immunity was written into some state constitutions. It usually extended to municipalities, prisons, hospitals, educational institutions, state fairs and commissions for public works.[22] The dual character of municipal corporations (legislative authority and corporation) led to the creation of certain pockets of municipal liability,[23] but, by and large, as in Britain, immunity has been the rule.

---

these cases is now viewed as being based on an error of law. For a fuller treatment see Hogg, *op. cit. supra*, n. 1, at pp. 5-7.

[16] *East Suffolk Rivers Catchment Bd. v. Kent*, [1940] 4 All E.R. 527. The immunity for the exercise of a statutory power, whose use lay within the discretion of the public authority, was not abolished until *Anns v. Merton London Borough Council*, [1978] A.C. 728 (H.L.), and was long confused with the American statutory immunity for discretionary governmental functions, deriving from the American Federal Tort Claims Act, 28 U.S.C.A. §2671.

[17] See *Adams v. Naylor*, [1946] A.C. 543 (H.L.). This case is widely seen as providing the impetus for the passage of the Crown Proceedings Act, 1947. See Fridman, *Torts* (1990), at p. 22.

[18] Dicey, *The Law of the Constitution* (1885).

[19] See *Cohen v. Virginia* (1821), 19 U.S. 264. A second policy ground given was that funds raised through taxation should not be redirected to purposes other than those for which they were collected.

[20] Justice Holmes in *Kawananakoa v. Polyblank* (1907), 205 U.S. 349.

[21] Despite the substantial expense of this process, as well as the need to have the help of a Member of Congress, the number of private bills put before the Congress was so large that this itself provided much of the impetus for reform. See Prosser, Wade, Schwartz, *Cases and Materials on the Law of Torts*, 5th ed. (1988).

[22] Prosser, *ibid.*, at p. 659.

[23] See *Ayala v. Philadelphia Bd. of Public Education* (1973), 453 Pa. 584, but this has not been uniformly followed.

Anticipating comparable British legislation by one year, the United States Congress, in 1946, passed the Federal Tort Claims Act.[24] The Act allowed recovery for damages caused by the tortious conduct of Federal employees "in the same manner and to the same extent as a private individual under like circumstances. . .". Similarities between this Act and the British statute have led some to feel that a "free trade" of jurisprudence in this area is justified,[25] but unfortunately little judicial attention has been paid to the differences between the still largely immune governmental regimes in the United States and the growing scope of liability in much of the Commonwealth.[26] Under the Federal Tort Claims Act, recovery is statutorily barred for damages flowing from what the legislation called the exercise of a "discretionary function or duty. . . whether or not the discretion involved be abused. . .".[27] It will be noted that the American scope of governmental liability is narrower, as it is based on a formulation which excludes discretionary decisions, something that is not found in the Commonwealth statutes. This is often overlooked when American jurisprudence is applied by Commonwealth courts and has been a source of confusion.

The British Crown Proceedings Act was passed in 1947, making the Crown liable in tort, as if it were a person of full age and capacity, for torts committed by its servants or agents.[28] Mirroring this, the Canadian Federal Crown Liability Act (now the Crown Liability and Proceedings Act) was passed in the same year, and now reads:[29]

> The Crown is liable for the damages for which, if it were a person, it would be liable. . . . in respect of a tort committed by a servant of the Crown. . . .[30]

Crown liability statutes were passed by all of the provinces, except Quebec, in the period between 1951 and 1974.[31] All of the provincial Acts, except that of

---

[24]   28 U.S.C.A. §2671 *et ff.* See *Dalehite v. U.S.* (1953), 346 U.S. 15; *Lindgren v. U.S.* (1982), 665 F. 2d 978.

[25]   See Mason J. in *Sutherland Shire Council v. Heyman* (1985), 60 A.L.R. 1, relying on both British and American jurisprudence in reaching his decision.

[26]   Although the British courts are now retreating from the position they took in *Anns*, (through *Murphy*, etc.) other jurisdictions, including Canada, have not been as willing to overturn their established precedents, see *C.N.R. v. Norsk Pacific S.S. Co.* (1992), 91 D.L.R. (4th) 289 (S.C.C.).

[27]   28 U.S.C.A. §2680.

[28]   *Supra,* n. 17, s. 2(1).

[29]   R.S.C. 1985, c. C-50, s. 3(a) [title am. S.C. 1990, c. 8, s. 20; further amended S.C. 2001, c. 4, s. 36]. The Law Reform Commission of Canada has suggested that the statute would benefit from reform on several points, see *The Legal Status of the Federal Administration, supra,* n. 1, at p. 74.

[30]   The Act expressly exempts claims in respect of which a pension or other compensation is payable from the Consolidated Revenue Fund (s. 9, as amended S.C. 2001, c. 4, s. 38) and some other restrictions and exemptions exist, but it does not explicitly refer to the common law immunity of the Crown or the extent to which it still exists. See also s. 8.

[31]   Alta.: Proceedings Against the Crown Act, S.A. 1959, c. 63, now R.S.A. 1980, c. P-18; B.C.: Crown Proceeding Act, S.B.C. 1974, c. 24, now R.S.B.C. 1996, c. 89, s. 289; Man.: Proceedings Against the Crown Act, S.M. 1951, c. 13, now R.S.M. 1987, c. P140; N.B.: Proceedings Against the Crown Act, S.N.B. 1952, c. 176, now R.S.N.B. 1973, c. P-18; Nfld.: Proceedings Against the

British Columbia, were based on a model Act prepared by the Conference of Commissioners on Uniformity of Legislation in Canada,[32] and are similar in their essentials. The British Columbia Act was based on a recommendation of the British Columbia Law Reform Commission.

The model Act,[33] which was adopted by eight provinces, provides for the imposition of liability under s. 5(1) which reads as follows:

> ... the Crown is subject to all those liabilities in tort to which, if it were a person of full age and capacity, it would be subject,
>
> (a) in respect of a tort committed by any of its officers or agents;
> (b) in respect of any breach of those duties that a person owes to his servants or agents by reason of being their employer;
> (c) in respect or any breach of the duties attaching to the ownership, occupation, possession or control of property; and
> (d) under any statute, or under any regulation or by-law made or passed under the authority of any statute.

In Quebec, the Code of Civil Procedure has always granted a more liberal right of action against the provincial and municipal authorities. Article 1011 of the Code provided that "any person having a claim to exercise against the Government of this Province ... may address a petition of right to Her Majesty".[34] In the 1935 case of *R. v. Cliche*,[35] Justice Cannon held that this imposed liability against the provincial Crown, confirming a practice which had been in place for several years. This and other changes obviated the need for the legislative reforms enacted by the other provinces.[36]

The British Columbia Crown Proceedings Act does not deal expressly with tort; it simply provides that the "government is subject to all the liabilities to which it would be liable if it were a person".[37] The British Columbia government is thus fully liable in tort and, like Quebec, it places no particular restrictions on liability.[38]

Municipalities are governed by specific legislative provisions in each province.[39]

Crown Act, S.N. 1973, No. 59, now R.S.N. 1990, c. P-26; N.S.: Proceedings Against the Crown Act, S.N.S. 1951, c. 8; now R.S.N.S. 1989, c. 360; Ont.: Proceedings Against the Crown Act, S.O. 1952, c. 78, now R.S.O. 1990, c. P.27; P.E.I.: Crown Proceedings Act, S.P.E.I. 1973, c. 28, now R.S.P.E.I. 1988, c. C-32; Sask.: Proceedings Against the Crown Act, R.S.S. 1978, c. P-27.

[32] Hogg, *op. cit. supra*, n. 1, at p. 222.

[33] An Act Respecting Proceedings Against the Crown, *Proceedings of 1950* of the Conference of Commissioners on Uniformity of Legislation in Canada, at p. 76.

[34] For a fuller discussion see Dussault and Borgeat, *op. cit. supra*, n. 4, at pp. 17-18.

[35] [1935] S.C.R. 561.

[36] See Peter Hogg, *Constitutional Law in Canada* (1985), at p. 86, and Dussault and Borgeat, *op. cit., supra*, n. 4, at pp. 17-20. See also Arrowsmith, "Governmental Liability in Quebec and the Public Law — Private Law Distinction", [1990] Public Law 481.

[37] R.S.B.C. 1979, c. 86, s. 2(c).

[38] Hogg, *op. cit., supra*, n. 36, at p. 86.

[39] For example, Ontario Municipal Act, R.S.O. 1990, c. M.45, s. 284, specific liability imposed for highway repair.

It seems rather strange that, while governments have abandoned their immunities by legislation, some courts have recently sought to reinstitute them to a degree. It has been held that there is no private duty owed by governments to take care in making their policy decisions, although such a duty is owed for their operational activities. This development might prompt one to observe paradoxically that the rule that "the King can do no wrong" has been changed to "the King can do only little wrongs", the big wrongs still being immune from tort liability.[40] Let us examine the early case law.

B. The Law Before *Just*

There were few problems suing the various governments in tort in the early years following the passage of the Crown liability statutes. Liability was imposed on the federal government in *Grossman and Sun v. R.*[41] where the absence of warning flags around a ditch on an airfield runway resulted in injury and property damage. Where someone drowned as a result of the federal government's failure to replace signs warning boaters about a waterfall[42] liability was imposed. Where a median barrier on a highway was built only 18 inches high, instead of 30 inches as required by department policy,[43] liability was also found against the federal government. There are a number of cases holding various governments liable for giving negligent information, such as incorrect advice about zoning,[44] building permits,[45] licences,[46] or about the cost of heating a room containing an indoor swimming pool.[47]

The sophisticated question of whether governments were liable for conduct beyond ordinary, everyday accidents involving decisions at the higher levels of officialdom surfaced in *Welbridge Holdings Ltd. v. Metropolitan Corp. of Greater Winnipeg.*[48] A by-law passed by a municipality was relied on by a builder who spent money to prepare plans for an apartment building. When the by-law was declared invalid after an attack by some rate-payers, the builder had to abandon his plans, with consequent financial loss. The builder's action against the municipality, on the ground that the loss was suffered as a result of the negligent passage of the by-law, was ultimately dismissed. Mr. Justice Laskin observed that a municipality could incur liability both in contract and in tort during its exercise of "administrative or ministerial, or perhaps better categorized as

---

40 See Jackson J. in *Dalehite v. U.S.*, *supra*, n. 24, at p. 60.
41 [1952] 1 S.C.R. 571.
42 *Hendricks v. R.*, [1970] S.C.R. 237; see also *County of Parkland v. Stetar*, [1975] 2 S.C.R. 884.
43 *Malat v. The Queen* (1980), 14 C.C.L.T. 206.
44 *Windsor Motors v. Powell River (Dist.)* (1969), 4 D.L.R. (3d) 155 (B.C.C.A.).
45 *Gadutsis v. Milne*, [1973] 2 O.R. 503.
46 *Couture v. R.* (1972), 28 D.L.R. (3d) 301; affd [1972] F.C. 1137; affd 2 N.R. 494 (C.A.).
47 *Hodgins v. H.E.P.C. of Twp. of Nepean*, [1972] 3 O.R. 332; revd re no negligence (1976), 10 O.R. (2d) 713; affd [1976] 2 S.C.R. 501.
48 [1971] S.C.R. 957. See also *J.R.S. Holdings v. Maple Ridge* (1981), 122 D.L.R. (3d) 398 (B.C.S.C.), negligent resolution passed.

business powers".[49] However, where a municipality errs while exercising its "legislative capacity" or its "quasi-judicial duty", it is immune from civil liability, even though it acts improperly, in the same way as is a provincial legislature or the Parliament of Canada. No duty of care is owed in such circumstances. Laskin J. (as he then was) explained:

> Moreover, even if the quasi-judicial function be taken in isolation, I cannot agree that the defendant in holding a public hearing as required by statute comes under private tort duty, in bringing it on and in carrying it to a conclusion, to use due care to see that the dictates of natural justice are observed. Its failure in this respect may make its ultimate decision vulnerable, but no right to damages for negligence flows to any adversely affected person, albeit private property values are diminished or expense is incurred without recoverable benefit. If, instead of rezoning the land involved herein to enhance its development value, the defendant had rezoned so as to reduce its value and the owners had sold it thereafter, could it be successfully contended, when the rezoning by-law was declared invalid on the same ground as By-law 177, that the owners were entitled to recoup their losses from the municipality? I think not, because the risk of loss from the exercise of legislative or adjudicative authority is a general public risk and not one for which compensation can be supported on the basis of a private duty of care. The situation is different where a claim for damages for negligence is based on acts done in pursuance or in implementation of legislation or of adjudicative decrees.[50]

This decision recognized that there were certain types of governmental conduct, though not specifically exempted by the Crown Liability Acts, which should not be subject to negligence actions. In other words, there should be no duty owed with regard to them. Thus, because of separation of power theory, the court was, rightly, reluctant to second-guess legislators, recognizing the "awkward vantage point from which [it] assesses public policy decisions with multilateral implications".[51]

Other types of activity were exempted from liability. Judicial decision-making,[52] the exercise of regulatory power by Boards,[53] arbitration decisions,[54] municipalities[55] and professional bodies[56] acting in their quasi-judicial capacities, and negligent interpretation of a statute[57] were immunized. Given their unique governmental and quasi-judicial character, it is not hard to understand why these activities undertaken by these authorities, along with legislative acts, should not be subject to tort law. Beyond them, however, it is harder to determine which governmental authorities should be immune.

---

[49] *Ibid.*, at p. 968.

[50] *Ibid.*, at p. 969-70.

[51] Feldthusen, *op. cit. supra*, n. 2, at p. 284.

[52] *Sirros v. Moore*, [1974] 3 All E.R. 776 (C.A.).

[53] *Everett v. Griffiths*, [1921] 1 A.C. 631 (H.L.).

[54] *Sutcliffe v. Thackrah*, [1974] A.C. 727 (H.L.).

[55] *Bowen v. City of Edmonton (No. 2)* (1977), 4 C.C.L.T. 105 (Alta. C.A.).

[56] *Calvert v. Law Society of Upper Canada* (1981), 32 O.R. (2d) 176 (H.C.); *Edwards v. Law Society of Upper Canada* (2000), 1 C.C.L.T. (3d) 193 (Ont. C.A.); affd 2001 SCC 80, [2001] S.C.J. No. 77.

[57] *Sebastian v. Government of Saskatchewan* (1978), 93 D.L.R. (3d) 154 (Sask. C.A.).

The British courts entered the picture and confused matters for a time.[58] In *Anns v. Merton*,[59] a case that has now been overruled in England[60] but not in Canada,[61] Lord Wilberforce contrasted "operational" functions, for which there could be liability, and "policy" functions, which would be immune from negligence liability. He indicated that there was a "distinction of degree" since many "operational" powers had in them some elements of "discretion". The more "operational" a power may be, the easier it is to impose a duty of care, it was said.

The court went further, however, and held that a municipality had an obligation to *consider* whether it would act under a statutory power and that, if it failed to do so, it might be held liable. If, after due consideration, the municipality chose to adopt a particular policy according to its view of the public interest, however, the courts would refrain from second-guessing that policy decision made as a *bona fide* exercise of its discretion. In arriving at this view, the court relied on an earlier case, *Home Office v. Dorset Yacht Co. Ltd.*,[62] where the House of Lords, in imposing liability, had proudly boasted that "Her Majesty's servants are made of sterner stuff"[63] than the public servants of New York who were exempted from liability because they might be "easily dissuaded from doing their duty"[64] by the fear of civil law suits against them.

The use of the word "discretion" by the House of Lords, which was employed in the United States statute but not in the United Kingdom statute, nor in ours, spawned some unexpected problems, because every government activity beyond the most menial and routine involved some element of discretion or judgment, which invariably invited the argument on behalf of governments that no duty was owed. Discretion was confused with policy decisions. Thus, in *Barratt v. Dist. of North Vancouver*[65] where the plaintiff was injured when his bicycle hit a pothole in the road, liability was denied, since maintaining the roads was a matter of "policy" for the municipality. Similarly, when an elk-feeding program was stopped, causing the elk to feed instead on a farmer's crops,[66] this was found to be a *bona fide* exercise of the Crown's discretion. Failing to warn about the danger of a gas furnace and to enact legislation that required such a warning also could not give rise to liability.[67] The decision to

---

[58]   Until the Supreme Court of Canada sorted things out in *Just v. B.C.*, *infra*, Section C.
[59]   *Supra*, n. 16.
[60]   *Murphy v. Brentwood District Council*, *supra*, n. 13.
[61]   *C.N.R. v. Norsk Pacific*, *supra*, n. 26.
[62]   [1970] 2 All E.R. 294 (*per* Lord Reid), distinguishing *Williams v. New York* (1955), 127 N.E. 2d 545, relying on the U.S. discretion immunity.
[63]   *Ibid.*, at p. 302.
[64]   *Ibid.* The English Courts have recently altered their course, granting very extensive protection to bureaucrats for policy reasons which have been shown to be faulty on a comparative basis, see Markesinis, *Tort Liabillity of Public Authorities* (1999).
[65]   [1980] 2 S.C.R. 418, probably now eclipsed by *Just* case.
[66]   *Diversified Holdings v. R. in right of B.C.* (1983), 23 C.C.L.T. 156 (B.C.C.A.).
[67]   *Kwong v. R.* (1978), 8 C.C.L.T. 1 (Alta. C.A.); affd [1979] 2 S.C.R. 1010, not at operating level; *Mahoney v. R.* (1986), 38 C.C.L.T. 21 (F.C.T.D.), failure to pass crib safety regulations.

release a prisoner who negligently crashed a vehicle was found to be a policy or planning decision and, hence, immune from tort action.[68]

Other cases, however, imposed liability. In *City of Kamloops v. Neilsen,*[69] a municipality which failed to enforce its by-laws in relation to the foundations of a building was found liable on the basis that this was "operational", not "policy". In *Johnson v. Adamson*[70] an allegation that police authorities had failed to take steps to combat racism in the force, which led to a shooting, was allowed to go to trial. Liability was imposed on a municipality that failed to formulate any policy in relation to snow and ice removal in violation of a statute.[71] It was also said that a duty was owed to passengers by security personnel checking baggage for weapons at airports, this apparently being an operational matter.[72]

A complex picture emerged which was difficult to justify and which was widely criticized.[73] A selection of words such as "policy", "planning", "discretionary" were used to describe when a duty was not owed and another set of terms such as "operational", "administrative" and "business" were utilized to determine that a duty was owed, but the meaning of both groups of words remained shadowy. It was time for the Supreme Court of Canada to clarify the situation and it did just that in *Just v. British Columbia.*

C. *Just* And Its Aftermath

A new era of governmental liability dawned in *Just v. British Columbia,*[74] where the Supreme Court of Canada, speaking through Mr. Justice Cory, simplified the law significantly. The plaintiff, Just, and his daughter were driving on a British Columbia highway on their way to a holiday at Whistler when their car was struck by a rock falling from a cliff face. The daughter died as a result of the accident and Just was severely injured. The British Columbia Crown was sued in tort for negligent maintenance of the highway. The trial judge[75] and the Court of Appeal[76] both dismissed the action, holding that the system of highway inspection was one of planning and policy, out of which no duty in tort could arise.

---

[68] *Toews v. MacKenzie* (1980), 109 D.L.R. (2d) 473, at p. 493 (B.C.C.A.).

[69] [1984] 2 S.C.R. 2.

[70] (1981), 18 C.C.L.T. 282 (Ont. C.A.). Leave to appeal to S.C.C. refused 35 O.R. (2d) 64n.

[71] *Dorschell v. City of Cambridge* (1980), 117 D.L.R. (3d) 630 (Ont. C.A.).

[72] *Air India Flight 182 Disaster Claimants v. Air India et al.* (1987), 62 O.R. (2d) 130 (H.C.) (*per* Holland J.).

[73] Bailey and Bowman, "The Policy/Operational Dichotomy — A Cuckoo in the Nest" (1986), 45 Camb. L.J. 430.

[74] [1990] 1 W.W.R. 385 (S.C.C.). See also *Rothfield v. Manolakos*, [1989] 2 S.C.R. 1259, 63 D.L.R. (4th) 449; the Quebec situation is the same, see *Laurentide Motels Ltd. v. Beauport (Ville)*, [1989] 1 S.C.R. 705, where it was decided that once a municipality decided to operate a firefighting service it became an "operational" activity, subject to ordinary fault principles.

[75] [1985] 5 W.W.R. 570, 33 C.C.L.T. 49 (McLachlin J.).

[76] [1987] 2 W.W.R. 231, 40 C.C.L.T. 160 (B.C.C.A.).

Approaching the delicate task of determining whether there was a duty on the Crown in this instance, Mr. Justice Cory warned about restoring government immunity and obliterating the advances in the law. He distinguished between the two types of government activity — "true policy decisions" and "implementation":

> The early governmental immunity from tortious liability became intolerable. This led to the enactment of legislation which in general imposed liability on the Crown for its acts as though it were a person. However, the Crown is not a person and must be free to govern and make true policy decisions without becoming subject to tort liability as a result of those decisions. On the other hand, complete Crown immunity should not be restored by having every government decision designated as one of policy.[77]

He explained further:

> True policy decisions should be exempt from tortious claims so that governments are not restricted in making decisions based upon social, political or economic factors. However, the implementation of those decisions may well be subject to claims in tort.[78]
> ... As a general rule, the traditional tort law duty of care will apply to a government agency in the same way that it will apply to an individual. In determining whether a duty of care exists, the first question to be resolved is whether the parties are in a relationship of sufficient proximity to warrant the imposition of such a duty.[79]

Mr. Justice Cory continued by pointing out some of the hallmarks of a true policy decision, which would be immune from liability:

> The duty of care should apply to a public authority unless there is a valid basis for its exclusion. A true policy decision undertaken by a government agency constitutes such a valid basis for exclusion. What constitutes a policy decision may vary infinitely and may be made at different levels, although usually at a high level.[80]
> ... As a general rule, decisions concerning budgetary allotments for departments or government agencies will be classified as policy decisions.[81]

Thus, immunity from negligence liability should be granted sparingly to Crown agencies;[82] only their "true policy decisions", generally made at higher levels, involving "social, political and economic factors" and "budgetary allotments for departments" are normally exempt.

If the conduct is not immunized, as a "true policy decision", negligence law principles remain applicable. Still needed is a "traditional torts analysis . . . of [the] standard of care required of the government agency . . . in light of all of the surrounding circumstances including, for example, budgetary restraints and the

---

[77] *Supra*, n. 74, at p. 402, [1990] 1 W.W.R.

[78] *Ibid.*, at p. 403.

[79] *Ibid.*, at p. 406.

[80] *Ibid.*, at p. 404.

[81] *Ibid.*, at p. 406.

[82] Bailey and Bowman, *supra*, n. 73, at p. 456, "it should be confined to as narrow a scope as possible".

availability of qualified personnel and equipment".[83] In other words, if a duty is imposed, the actual conduct must still be assessed to see whether it was unreasonable, using the usual indicators of negligence law including regard for available resources.

If the governmental conduct is immune from negligence liability, it should be noted that it is still possible for liability to be imposed, but on another more complex and much narrower basis. It is open to a claimant to prove that a policy decision was made in bad faith and that it was so irrational and unreasonable that it did not constitute a proper exercise of discretion. In such a case liability might be found as in *Kamloops (City) v. Nielsen*.[84] Further, if this hurdle cannot be overcome, and it seldom can be, the government agency can still be held liable if it fails to follow properly the policy it has adopted.

In the result, Mr. Justice Cory concluded that there was a duty owed but that the case had to be sent back for a new trial to see if the proper standard of care was met by the government employees. This is "fair to both the government agency and the litigant", he opined.[85]

Another way of looking at this issue is to say that a government must be entitled to govern free from the restraints of tortious liability. It cannot be a tort for a government to govern.[86] However, when a government is supplying services, that is, doing things for its people other than governing, it should be subject to ordinary negligence principles. Since, in the words of Mr. Justice Cory "the Crown . . . must be free to govern",[87] an immunity is necessary, but it must be limited only to those functions of government that properly can be considered to be "governing" and not extended to the other tasks of government that might be styled "servicing". In other words, governing is normally concerned with large issues, macro decisions, if you will, not routine items, that is, micro decisions.[88] For example, an unemployed person or a business that goes bankrupt cannot be allowed to sue the Crown for the cabinet's negligent management of the economy.[89] Courts are not institutionally suited for such a task; only the ballot box can control this type of conduct.

The *Just* decision has not been without its detractors. Mr. Justice Sopinka felt this was not a time to move the law and wrote a strongly-worded dissent, stating:

---

[83] *Just v. British Columbia, supra,* n. 74, p. 406.

[84] [1984] 2 S.C.R. 2.

[85] *Ibid.,* at p. 408. Liability was imposed at new trial, see (1992), 60 B.C.L.R. (2d) 209 (S.C.); see also *Mochinski v. Trendline Industries Ltd.* (1997), 40 C.C.L.T. (2d) 322 (S.C.C.), rock falling led to liability; see also *Lewis (Guardian ad litem of) v. British Columbia* (1997), 40 C.C.L.T. (2d) 153 (S.C.C.), non-delegable duty to use reasonable care to stop rocks from falling.

[86] See Jackson J. dissenting, in *Dalehite v. U.S., supra,* n. 24, at p. 60.

[87] See *Just v. British Columbia, supra,* n. 74, at p. 402. See also Epstein, Gregory and Kalven, *Cases and Materials on Torts* (1984), at p. 854.

[88] See *Swanson and Peever v. Canada* (1991), 124 N.R. 218, at p. 226 (Fed. C.A.).

[89] See Bailey and Bowman, *supra,* n. 73, at p. 439.

... The expansion of liability by reason of this and other developments in the law of torts has created a crisis in this area of the law leading to demands for the fundamental reappraisal of the tort system itself. The basic premise of adjusting losses on the basis of fault is being subjected to intense criticism.[90]

In stating that the authority "must specifically consider whether to inspect and, if so, the system must be a reasonable one in all the circumstances", my colleague is extending liability beyond what was decided in *Anns v. Merton London Borough Council, Barratt v. North Vancouver* and *Kamloops v. Neilsen*. The system would include the time, manner and technique of inspection. On this analysis it is difficult to determine what aspect of a policy decision would be immune from review.[91]

Commentators have also criticized the inconsistency with prior jurisprudence.[92] One scholar remarked that *Just* had "virtually marginalized" the policy/operation classification.[93] Another article[94] concluded that the end result of the *Just* case was to "confine the true policy decision within very narrow parameters and thus to broaden quite substantially the scope of a public authority's liability in negligence". Professor Klar has warned that *Just* "has significantly extended the potential tort liability of public authorities" and will lead to an "increase in public tort litigation" involving cases which will be "more difficult to litigate . . . and certainly more difficult to try".[95] As might be expected, other scholars have complained that the decision still leaves too large an area of immunity.[96]

Despite these many and sometimes conflicting views, it appears that *Just* is being followed. In *Swanson and Peever v. Canada*[97] an airplane owned by Wapiti Aviation crashed, killing six of the nine passengers. The pilot had been flying in contravention of safety regulations, something that was a common occurrence at Wapiti. Transport Canada knew of Wapiti's past safety violations but took insufficient measures to make them correct their system. A report by one of Transport Canada's inspectors had warned his superiors about Wapiti's "total disregard for regulations, rights of others and safety of passengers" and concluded that if it continued "we are virtually certain to be faced with a fatality".[98] The families of some of the victims sued the Government of Canada, Wapiti having become insolvent. The trial judge found that there was a duty

---

[90] *Just v. British Columbia, supra,* n. 74, at p. 389.

[91] *Ibid.*, at p. 393. See also *Stovin v. Wise,* [1996] 3 All E.R. 801 (H.L.) *per* Lord Hoffman, agreeing with Sopinka J., "inadequate tool".

[92] Rafferty and Saunders, "Developments in Contract and Tort Law: The 1989-90 Term" (1991), 2 S.C.L.R. (2d) 175, at p. 216.

[93] McLauchlan, *supra,* n. 2, at p. 37.

[94] Rafferty and Saunders, *supra,* n. 92, at p. 213.

[95] Klar, "The Supreme Court of Canada: Extending the Liability of Public Authorities" (1990), 28 Alberta L. Rev. 648, at p. 655. See also Galloway, *infra,* n. 96, at p. 135.

[96] Galloway, "The Liability of Government: Just, or Just and Reasonable" (1990), 41 Admin. L.Rev. 133, at p. 152.

[97] (1991), 124 N.R. 218 (Fed. C.A.).

[98] *Ibid.*, at p. 222.

owed to the families and that it had been breached. The Federal Court of Appeal affirmed. Following *Just*, the court reasoned:[99]

> In this case, the trial judge correctly decided that the Crown's response to the complaints and reports was an operational decision, not a policy matter . . . . He later concluded that it was "more than a matter of policy but one of operation". The official making the enforcement decisions was not a high elected official like a Minister or even a Deputy Minister; he was only a regional director. His work involved not policy, planning or governing, but only administering, operations or servicing. The decision had no "polycentric" aspects, nor was there evidence of any lack of resources to permit more rigorous enforcement of the regulations. There were available numerous specific guidelines upon which the court could rely in evaluating the conduct of the decision-maker. This was not a budgetary, macro exercise.
>
> These people were essentially inspectors of airlines, aircraft and pilots, who did not make policy, but rather implemented it; although they certainly had to exercise some discretion and judgment during the course of their work, much like other professional people. . . .

Another case which relied on *Just* was *Brewer Brothers v. Canada (A.G.)*,[100] where several grain producers sued the Government of Canada because the Canadian Grain Commission had negligently allowed a "producer elevator" to operate without having posted adequate bond security, as required by the Canada Grain Act.[101] The plaintiffs, who delivered grain to the "producer elevator", suffered financial losses when the elevator operator's licence was cancelled and it was placed in receivership before paying the plaintiffs. The trial judge held the Government of Canada liable and the Federal Court of Appeal affirmed.

This being a case of economic loss, the analysis was more complex. Mr. Justice Stone explained, however, that the Act was "enacted with a view to protecting those grain producers . . . and cast upon the commission an obligation to be satisfied as to the sufficiency of that security".[102] The evidence, said Mr. Justice Stone, was that the "commission's role in duly administering the licensing and bonding provisions . . . was a cardinal component of the Canadian grain trade. . . . I am satisfied that a relationship of proximity, such as gave rise to a private law duty of care, came into existence".[103]

Mr. Justice Stone, relying on *Just*, explained further that there is "no basis for exempting the [government] from the imposition of liability on the ground that the decisions made were 'policy' decisions. . .".[104] Nor was Justice Stone prepared to say that there was an exemption "from private law liability because its functions were quasi-judicial or analogous to police functions. While it is arguable that certain of the commission's powers might be so characterized, the acts and omissions of which the [plaintiffs] complain are not among them."[105]

---

[99] *Ibid.*, at pp. 226-27.
[100] (1991), 8 C.C.L.T. (2d) 45 (Fed. C.A.).
[101] S.C. 1970-71-72, c. 7 [now R.S.C. 1985, c. G-10].
[102] *Supra*, n. 99, at p. 70.
[103] *Ibid.*, at p. 71.
[104] *Ibid.*, at p. 75.
[105] *Ibid.*

His Lordship then went on to consider whether the expected standard of care had been met in implementing their policy and concluded that it had not.

There have been two recent decisions of the Supreme Court of Canada in which governments have been relieved of liability on the basis of the principles espoused in *Just*. In *Brown v. British Columbia (Minister of Transportation and Highways)*,[106] the plaintiff motorist skidded on an icy road on Vancouver Island. While the court felt that there was a duty owed generally to maintain the road, in this case, the government was exempt from ordinary negligence principles because its decision to adopt a summer schedule of reduced service was one of policy. This decision, said Mr. Justice Cory, involved the "classic policy considerations of financial resources, personnel and, as well, significant negotiations with government unions. It was truly a governmental decision involving social, political and economic factors."[106a] Consequently, as there was neither proof of irrationality or bad faith nor proof of negligence in the operational aspect of the policy decision, no liability was imposed. While the court was unanimous in the result, Mr. Justice Sopinka, in concurring, indicated that he was not happy with "the 'policy/operational' test as the touchstone of liability",[106b] hinting that he would like the court to reconsider its continued usefulness at some future time.

In *Swinamer v. Nova Scotia (Attorney General)*,[107] the second case, the plaintiff was injured by a tree that fell on his truck on a highway maintained in the province. There had been a survey made of trees near the highway that might be a hazard and 200 dead trees — not including the one that hit the plaintiff — were marked. Money was requested to remove these trees over a three-year period. Whereas the court recognized again the duty to maintain the highway, it concluded that the decision to inspect and identify dangerous trees was a preliminary step in the policy-making process. It was, according to Mr. Justice Cory, a "classic example of a policy decision" — that is, one of "setting priorities for the allocation of available funds".[108] "Policy decisions of government must be immune from the application of private law standards of tort liability"[109] he concluded. Since there was no proof of irrationality or bad faith, nor of negligence in relation to the operational aspects of the policy decision, no liability could be found.

While these two cases may appear to some to be "backsliding", they are true to the philosophy of *Just*. It must be noted that the main decisions in both cases were written by Mr. Justice Cory, who was the author of the reasons in *Just*. He certainly did not indicate that he was departing in any way from what he had

---

[106] (1994), 19 C.C.L.T. (2d) 268 (S.C.C.). See also *Holbrook v. Argo Road Maintenance Inc.* (1996), 31 C.C.L.T. (2d) 70 (B.C.S.C.).

[106a] *Ibid.*, at p. 285.

[106b] *Ibid.*, at p. 288.

[107] (1994), 19 C.C.L.T. (2d) 233 (S.C.C.).

[108] *Ibid.*, at p. 249.

[109] *Ibid.*

written earlier, even though there seemed to be some hesitation on various aspects of his reasons by other members of the court. The determinations that the governmental decisions in these two cases were policy ones are certainly justified in the circumstances, even though it might not have been necessary to deal with the duty issue because both cases could have been disposed of on the basis that there was no negligence proven on the facts.

More recent decisions have demonstrated that governments can be held liable for a great variety of their activities. In the field of policing, there has been liability imposed where the police negligently used a gun and a car to block a fleeing fugitive,[110] where a patrolman failed to order the salting of an icy road,[111] where the police failed to provide medical attention to a seriously ill person in their custody,[112] and where they used a woman as "bait" leading to her being raped.[113]

There have been some decisions indicating that governments can be held responsible for abuse of children that were made wards of the Crown,[114] the Court proclaiming that "it is incomprehensible that a lesser expectation follows from assumption of direct care of children than it does for maintenance of highways". When a fire was caused in part by the failure to ensure that a Building Code was obeyed, it was said that there could be liability.[115] Further, governmental inspectors rendered the Crown liable in part when they negligently gave a permit which allowed an illegal water system to be installed, the Court declaring that the Crown has a duty to protect the public from the health hazards of non-potable water.[116]

Another decision which is sure to disturb bureaucrats is *Atlantic Leasing Ltd. v. Newfoundland,*[117] which held the government liable for its negligent delaying of a lease renewal for a museum, which caused economic loss to the plaintiff. This was not a nonfeasance case, the Court explained, as the government had "acted" by declaring its intention to renew and did some work toward that end. The negligence was not in approving the renewal, but in "respect of the procedure employed". Justice Green explained:

---

[110] *Insurance Corp. of British Columbia v. Vancouver (City)* (1997), 38 C.C.L.T. (2d) 271 (B.C.S.C.).

[111] *Roberts v. Morana* (1997), 38 C.C.L.T. (2d) 1 (Ont. Gen. Div.).

[112] *Fortey (Guardian ad litem of) v. Canada (Attorney General)* (1999), 46 C.C.L.T. (2d) 271 (B.C.C.A.).

[113] *Doe v. Metropolitan Toronto (Municipality) Commissioners of Police* (1998), 43 C.C.L.T. (2d) 123 (Ont. Gen. Div.); see also *Odhavji Estate v. Woodhouse* (2001), 3 C.C.L.T. (3d) 226 (Ont. C.A.), shooting.

[114] *B. (K.L.) v. British Columbia* (1998), 41 C.C.L.T. (2d) 107, at p. 145; affd (1999), 46 C.C.L.T. (2d) 237 (B.C.C.A.).

[115] *Wild Rose School Division No. 66 v. Bert Pratch Construction Co.* (1997), 40 C.C.L.T. (2d) 1 (Alta. Q.B.).

[116] *Cook v. Bowen Island Realty Ltd.* (1997), 38 C.C.L.T. (2d) 217 (B.C.S.C.); see also *Ingles v. Tutkaluk Construction Ltd.*, [2000] 1 S.C.R. 298, city partially liable for negligence of inspectors of home renovation.

[117] (1998), 42 C.C.L.T. (2d) 71, at p. 97 (Nfld. C.A.).

Procedural aspects of governmental decision-making may generally be regarded as "operational" where they relate to the process of implementation of other decisions.

There are, of course, decisions denying liability. Where a decision was made by a government agency to stop mass sales of lottery tickets, causing economic loss to the plaintiff, that was held to be a *bona fide* policy decision.[118] Similarly, where an inspector ordered spray to combat bacteria in potatoes causing a lesser crop yield, no liability was imposed because the legislation exempted from liability good faith decisions, which this was.[119] Nor was a provincial regulator of mortgage brokers liable for failing to promptly revoke the licence of a broker who used investors' funds for unauthorized purposes causing financial losses, there being no private duty to do so.[120]

It is now clear that the exclusion of negligence liability for governmental policy decisions derives from the second-stage analysis of the *Anns* test as McLachlin C.J. and Major J. recently explained in *Cooper v. Hobart*:[121]

> . . . In our view, the exclusion of liability for policy decisions is properly regarded as an application of the second stage of the *Anns* test. The exclusion does not relate to the relationship between the parties. Apart from the legal characterization of the government duty as a matter of policy, plaintiffs can and do recover. The exclusion of liability is better viewed as an immunity imposed because of considerations outside the relationship for policy reasons - more precisely, because it is inappropriate for courts to second-guess elected legislators on policy matters. Similar considerations may arise where the decision in question is quasi-judicial (see *Edwards v. Law Society of Upper Canada*, 2001 SCC 80).

These cases demonstrate that courts seem to be having less difficulty with the policy/operational dichotomy in the aftermath of *Just* and are better able to distinguish everyday governmental activities from the decisions relating to governing that must be immune from negligence liability. Although certainly not the most perfect system of government liability that might be devised, the approach of the Canadian judiciary, using ordinary tort principles, is, to quote Mr. Justice Sopinka,[122] "more adaptable to claims against public bodies than initially thought." Even though the Canadian judiciary is not yet ready "to adopt one unifying principle that can be relied on to strike [the appropriate] balance," it has certainly done better than the British and Australian courts.[123]

---

[118] *Reynen v. British Columbia Lottery Corp.* (1997), 37 C.C.L.T. (2d) 221 (B.C.S.C.).

[119] *Lewis v. Prince Edward Island* (1998), 42 C.C.L.T. (2d) 7 (P.E.I. C.A.).

[120] *Cooper v. Hobart,* 2001 SCC 79, 2001 Can. Sup. Ct. LEXIS 81, [2001] S.C.J. No. 76.

[121] *Ibid.*, at para. 38.

[122] "The Liability of Public Authorities: Drawing the Line" (1994), Tort Law Review 123, at pp. 149 and 151.

[123] See *Murphy v. Brentwood District Council*, [1991] A.C. 398; *Rowling v. Takaro Properties Ltd.*, [1988] A.C. 473 (*per* Lord Keith), criticized in Linden, *infra*, n. 132 at p. 542. See also in Australia, *Sutherland Shire Council v. Heyman* (1985), 60 A.L.R. 1.

D. Analysis

There are commentators who have tried to shed some light on this issue by approaching the subject of governmental liability in new ways. Bailey and Bowman in the United Kingdom are critical of the excessive judicial use of the duty of care issue, which they contend is a crude device. They suggest instead that the matter be left to the more subtle "issue of breach". There is "plenty of scope", they say, "within ordinary tort principles for accommodating the policy considerations that might militate against the imposition of a duty of care upon a public authority or against holding an authority to be in breach of duty".[124] In another article, the same authors argue that the "policy/operational dichotomy has proved inadequate for the purpose of identifying the allegedly non-justiciable cases at the preliminary stages, and unhelpful in dealing with them on merits. It merely raises an extra dimension of confusion . . . ." They conclude by saying that if it is to be used "it should be used as sparingly as possible".[125] Mr. Justice Cory's approach in *Just* is entirely consistent with this advice.

Other authors have sought to assist in unravelling the mystery. Professor Stan Makuch[126] offered two factors for courts to consider in determining whether to intrude in order to evaluate government action: one, if the decision is "polycentric" or multi-faceted, that is, a choice between "efficiency and thrift", it should be decided through the "ballot box, not the courts,"[127] and second, if there are "commonly accepted standards" — legislative, custom or other — to guide the courts, they might be more inclined to intrude. A not dissimilar analysis has been offered by Aronson and Whitmore,[128] who explain the phrase "policy decision" as essentially a "political" decision, and "involving considerations of expense, political viability and the competing demands of other governmental projects," rendering the matter "not properly justiciable". Professor David Cohen[129] has listed no fewer than ten factors for courts to consider in making the determination: (1) was there a standard of conduct against which the bureaucrat's behaviour can be judged? (2) was the decision a routine one? (3) was there a great degree of discretion involved in the decision? (4) what type of interest was involved? (5) was the injury deliberate or unintentional? (6) what was the nature of the government activity which was alleged to have been negligent? (7) what was the status of the decision-maker? (8) can the wrong be pinpointed to one party? (9) was there only one victim? (10) did the decision involve resource allocation?

---

[124] "Negligence in the Realms of Public Law", [1984] Public Law 277, at pp. 301 and 307.
[125] "The Policy/Operational Dichotomy — A Cuckoo in the Nest" (1986), 45 Camb. L.J. 430, at pp. 455 and 456.
[126] *Canadian Municipal Planning Law* (1983), at p. 140.
[127] See *Anns, supra*, n. 16 (*per* Lord Wilberforce).
[128] *Public Torts and Contracts* (1988), at p. 70.
[129] "The Public and Private Dimensions of the UFFI Problem" (1984), 8 Can. Bus. L.J. 410.

Professors Hogg and Monahan, in their book *Liability of the Crown*,[130] prefer the word "planning", rather than "policy", to identify those acts which need to be protected. Planning connotes "generality or complexity", which the courts will have difficulty evaluating. The word "operational", they suggest, focuses on the "specific":

> The merit of the word "planning" is that it implies decision-making of a generality and complexity that a court cannot be expected to evaluate, let alone replicate. Whatever language is used, the idea is "to exclude altogether those cases in which the decision under attack is of such a kind that a question whether it has been made negligently is unsuitable for judicial resolution".[131]

This is illuminating, for we are concerned here with differentiating between macro decisions, affecting the welfare of the nation, and micro decisions, which are more limited in their significance. The former are not properly the subject of judicial evaluation, but the latter certainly are.

Others have also entered the fray.[132] For example, Professor Feldthusen believes courts should not substitute their judgment of what is reasonable for that of the government officials who are charged with the responsibility of performing their duty.[133] One might well agree with this as a general principle, and it is certainly in accord with the prevailing public law principles,[134] but, with respect, the *Just* case does not give the courts licence to "substitute their judgment" for that of officials whenever they choose to do so. The *Just* case merely applies the Crown liability legislation, making government liable as if it were a person. In other words, until the legislatures develop a better system, the *Just* case gives government its due, but not more than its due — that is, in its routine functions, it must perform as reasonably as others must, but for important decisions involving governing, it will not be subject to ordinary tort liability.

There is some skepticism about whether government tort liability deters officialdom from negligent conduct. Professor David Cohen, in two major articles,[135] has shown that financial incentives for exercising care based on tort liability are lacking in the current federal administration. He recognizes, however, that "tort claims might be a useful signal of breakdowns in the accountability mechanisms." In other words, "victims of state action have a direct economic incentive to signal the harm which government's activities have

---

[130] *Op. cit. supra*, n. 1, at p. 164.

[131] *Ibid.*, citing from *Rowling v. Takaro Properties Ltd.*, [1988] A.C. 473, at p. 501 (P.C., N.Z.).

[132] Woodall, "Private Law Liability of Public Authorities for Negligent Inspection and Regulation" (1992), 37 McGill L.J. 83; see also P.M. Perell, "Negligence Claims Against Public Authorities" (1994), 16 Adv. Q. 48; Linden, "Tort Liability of Governments for Negligence" (1995), 53 The Advocate 535.

[133] See *supra*, n. 2, at p. 284.

[134] *C.U.P.E., Local 963 v. New Brunswick Liquor Corp.*, [1979] 2 S.C.R. 227.

[135] "Regulating Regulators: The Legal Environment of the State" (1990), 40 U.T.L.J. 213; also Part 7, "Suing the State", *ibid.*, at p. 630.

imposed".[136] He concludes that tort actions may remain "as a default system" until a better legislative solution is found and, thereafter, perhaps as an "alternative" to the new system.[137] Thus, despite its dubious power as a financial deterrent, tort law may serve as an ombudsman in this sphere, as it does in others.[138]

As we review the various attempts at distinguishing the type of government activity which is immune from tortious liability from that which is subject to liability in tort, there are certain recurring matters which emerge as courts seek to unravel this knot. It is clear that at least three questions will be considered in almost every case of government liability: (1) what was the level of the officials involved and in what capacity were they making their decision? (2) what is the nature of the decision and what type of activity is in question? (3) what level of government (federal, provincial or municipal) was involved? While the answers to these questions are rarely determinative, in and of themselves, the questions contribute in a useful way to understanding whether or not the activity in question was a "true policy decision" or an "operational" matter.

1. THE LEVEL OF THE DECISION MAKER

Mr. Justice Cory stated in *Just*:

> In determining what constitutes such a policy decision, it should be borne in mind that such decisions are generally made by persons of a high level of authority in the agency, but may also properly be made by persons of a lower level of authority. The characterization of such a decision rests on the nature of the decision and not on the identity of the actors.[139]

While the level of the official is certainly not conclusive, it is one clue in determining whether there is a duty owed. The courts are properly more willing to hold that a decision is policy-based if it is made by a senior bureaucrat or politician than if it is made by someone more junior.

The issue has not arisen in the context of a torts case, but it would appear that judges, who cannot be compelled to give evidence about how they arrived at their decisions,[140] would likely enjoy a general immunity from all forms of civil suit relating to their judging activities. While administrative and constitutional review may be available against decisions of cabinet ministers,[141] it is doubtful that tortious liability will be imposed for a political decision at this level. Legislators, whether federal, provincial or municipal, are likely to be beyond the reach of negligence law as far as their legislative decisions are concerned. Similar reasoning may apply to deputy ministers, but this does not mean that the

---

[136] *Ibid.*, at p. 269.

[137] *Ibid.*, at p. 660.

[138] See Linden, "Tort Law as Ombudsman" (1973), 51 Can. Bar Rev. 155.

[139] *Supra*, n. 74, at p. 406.

[140] *MacKeigan (J.A.) v. Royal Commn. (Marshall Inquiry)*, [1989] 2 S.C.R. 796.

[141] *Canada (Auditor General) v. Canada (Minister of Energy, Mines and Resources)*, [1989] 2 S.C.R. 49. See also *Operation Dismantle Inc. et al. v. R.*, [1985] 1 S.C.R. 441.

immunity would extend to all the decisions they make. There may be some that are immune and others that are not.

The vast majority of government action is not immune. Those in charge of the implementation or maintenance of transport systems or other government services are subject to a duty in tort.[142] A general guideline which appears to be emerging is that errors in maintenance are likely to be actionable, while errors in overall schemes of maintenance are not, provided the schemes are a reasonable use of the time and money available. Thus, inspectors and regulators of all kinds are generally open to suit,[143] as are the day-to-day activities of officials in federal and provincial institutions such as prisons.[144] This opens a wide area of liability at the provincial and municipal level, where officials devote more time to running the everyday affairs of the city[145] or province[146] and less in policy making and planning. Hence, the proliferation of cases against police commissioners and others in charge of infrastructure maintenance.[147]

The position of the decision-maker is not usually determinative, but it is one of the main factors contributing to an understanding of the activity under question.

2. NATURE OF THE DECISION AND TYPE OF ACTIVITY

As the above cases demonstrate, among the activities which have begun to attract government liability so far are those of inspecting and regulating. As for negligent inspection, the case of *Rothfield v. Manolakos*,[148] released along with *Just*, held a municipality partially liable for faulty inspection of a retaining wall which collapsed. The inspector, who was "armed with all the powers necessary to remedy the situation", failed to inspect the wall properly.[149] In *Mortimer v. Cameron*,[150] a municipality was held partially liable for failing to inspect a stairway for its compliance with building by-laws when a guest at a party, while

---

[142] *Swanson, supra*, n. 97; *Just, supra*, n. 74.

[143] For an early case, see *Mart Steel Corp. v. R.*, [1974] 1 F.C. 45 (T.D.). See also *Rothfield v. Manolakos, supra*, n. 74; *Kamloops, supra*, n. 69, and *Just, supra*, n. 74.

[144] See *MacLean v. R.*, [1973] S.C.R. 2.

[145] *Canada (A.G.) v. Ottawa-Carleton (Regional Municipality)* (1991), 5 O.R. (3d) 11 (C.A.).

[146] *Webster v. New Brunswick* (1976), 15 N.B.R. (2d) 319 (Q.B.), construction of a highway blocking drainage; *Auffrey v. New Brunswick*, [1977] 1 S.C.R. 509, duty to warn of a hidden danger; *Lapierre v. A.G. of Quebec* (1979), 13 C.C.L.T. 1; revd 27 C.C.L.T. 190; affd [1985] 1 S.C.R. 241; *Thorne Riddell Inc. v. R. in Right of Alberta* (1983), 28 Alta. L.R. (2d) 326 (Q.B.).

[147] *Bowman and Pytlik v. Valkenburg and Triangle Homes (1980) Ltd. and R. in Right of B.C.* (1984), 54 B.C.L.R. 139 (S.C.); *Simms v. Metro Toronto* (1976), 14 O.R. (2d) 728 (H.C.J.); appeal to C.A. dismissed 28 O.R. (2d) 606; *O'Rourke v. Schacht* (1974), 55 D.L.R. (3d) 96 (S.C.C.); *Schulze v. R.*, [1974] 1 F.C. 233 (T.D.); *Doe v. Metropolitan Toronto (Municipality) Commrs. of Police, supra*, n. 6.

[148] [1989] 2 S.C.R. 1259.

[149] *Ibid.*, at p. 1274.

[150] (1994), 17 O.R. (3d) 1 (Ont. C.A.).

jostling with another guest, fell from it, injuring himself. There are other negligent inspection cases.[151]

In the negligent regulation area, liability has been imposed against a government agency for failing to see that someone was creditworthy,[152] for negligently supervising the safety of an airline[153] and for failing to warn a regulated investment co-operative about its risky practices.[154] There are negligent licensing cases, as where a fishing licence was cancelled wrongfully,[155] where a building permit was issued negligently,[156] and where approval of a flawed plan to in-fill a mall property caused flooding.[157]

There are also a number of cases dealing with negligent advice given by governments leading to liability, for example, negligent advice about pension rights to an employee,[158] careless advice about whether the plaintiff was authorized to run a radio station,[159] and false information about radioactivity given to a house purchaser.[160] There are other government activities which may attract liability, such as policing,[161] enforcing[162] or prosecuting.[163]

On the other hand, legislative, judicial and quasi-judicial functions appear to be completely immune.[164] A municipality will not be held liable for doing something "ancillary to the exercise of a quasi-judicial function", such as negligently replotting a subdivision before it has proper soil tests,[165] nor will

---

[151] *Givskud v. Kavanaugh* (1994), 147 N.B.R. (2d) 1 (Q.B.), failure to inspect agricultural feed; *Dha v. Ozdoba* (1990), 39 C.L.R. 248 (B.C.S.C.) negligent approval of plans causing house to subside; *cf. Lysack v. Burrard Motor Inn* (1991), 58 B.C.L.R. (2d) 33 (B.C.C.A.), inspection of sidewalk done reasonably.

[152] *Brewer Bros. v. Canada (Attorney General)* (1991), 8 C.C.L.T. (2d) 45 (Fed. C.A.).

[153] *Swanson v. Canada* (1991), 124 N.R. 218 (Fed. C.A.).

[154] *Teacher's Investment & Housing Co-operative (Trustee of) v. Jennings* (1990), 44 B.C.L.R. (2d) 203 (S.C.), affd 56 B.C.L.R. (2d) 145 (C.A.).

[155] *Lapointe v. Canada* (1992), 51 F.T.R. 161; but see *Comeau's Sea Foods v. Canada* (1995), 24 C.C.L.T. (2d) 1 (Fed. C.A.); affd (1997), 31 C.C.L.T. (2d) 236 (S.C.C.).

[156] *Tarjan v. District of Rockyview* (1992), 130 A.R. 181 (Alta. Q.B.), revd on procedural grounds (1993), 13 Alta. L.R. (3d) 220 (C.A.).

[157] *Eagle Forest Products Inc. v. Whitehorn Investments* (1992), 12 M.P.L.R. (2d) 18 (Ont. Gen. Div.).

[158] *Spinks v. Canada*, [1996] 2 F.C. 563 (C.A.).

[159] *Couture v. R.*, [1976] 1 F.C. 515 (T.D.), but *cf. Sebastian v. Saskatchewan* (1978), 93 D.L.R. (3d) 154 (Sask. C.A.).

[160] *Sevidal v. Chopra* (1988), 64 O.R. (2d) 169 (H.C.).

[161] See *Johnson v. Adamson*, *supra*, n. 70, allegation that police authorities failed to take steps to combat alleged racism; *Doe v. Metropolitan Commrs. of Police*, *supra*, n. 6, allegations that the police had not taken adequate steps to warn a woman that she was a potential rape victim, preferring instead to use her as a decoy; *Doern v. Phillips Estate* (1995), 23 C.C.L.T. (2d) 283 (B.C.S.C.); affd (1997), 43 B.C.L.R. (3d) 53 (C.A.), not following pursuit guidelines operational negligence.

[162] *Kamloops v. Nielsen*, *supra*, n. 69.

[163] See *Nelles*, *supra*, n. 5.

[164] See W. Linden, "Municipal Liability for Public Works" (1987), 6 Adv. Soc. J. 21.

[165] *Bowen v. City of Edmonton*, *supra*, n. 55.

liability be imposed for negligently passing a resolution.[166] While some discretionary functions will be found by the courts not to attract liability, for example, where a government elk-feeding program was stopped, causing the elk to feed instead on a farmer's crops,[167] there is nonetheless a clearly established duty to make discretionary decisions in good faith and for no improper purpose.[168] There may also be a duty on government authorities to consider whether they will exercise their discretionary power before they decide not to do so.[169]

Governments have been relieved of liability, where it was found that it was not the duty of a municipality to enforce a by-law, but that of the police,[170] that there was no duty to move earth near a highway even though it blocked the view of motorists,[171] and that a municipality did not have to improve the services for fighting fires.[172] There are other such cases denying liability.[173]

Thus, the courts will examine, in addition to the level of the official, the complexity of the decision, whether it has budgetary and macro effects, whether it has to do with planning and high-level policy making, and whether, in short, it can be fairly described as a decision having to do with "governing".

3. LEVEL OF GOVERNMENT

The courts have been most willing to find the existence of a duty at the municipal level of government. Even prior to the enactment of the federal and provincial Crown liability Acts, the corporate nature of municipalities and similar bodies had traditionally rendered them open to liability. This liability had been imposed by the courts as a matter of course, frequently relying on statutes, with little examination of the underlying issues raised by judicial regulation of governmental practice. Thus, a county was held liable when its warning sign fell and contributed to a collision.[174] In *City of Kamloops v. Nielsen et al.*,[175] liability was imposed on a municipality for negligently failing to inspect the foundations

---

[166] *J.R.S. Holdings Ltd. v. Maple Ridge*, *supra*, n. 48.

[167] *Diversified Holdings Ltd. v. R.*, *supra*, n. 66.

[168] *Roncarelli v. Duplessis*, *supra*, n. 5. Compare this to the wording of the original U.S. statute, which exempted discretionary decisions "whether or not the discretion involved be abused", see *supra*, n. 27.

[169] In *Dorschell v. City of Cambridge*, *supra*, n. 71, liability was imposed on a municipality which had not formulated any policy in relation to snow and ice removal, in contravention of a statutory duty to do so.

[170] *Arsenault v. Charlottetown (City)* (1992), 11 C.C.L.T. (2d) 299 (P.E.I.C.A.). See also *Century Holdings Ltd. v. Delta (Corp.)*, [1994] 5 W.W.R. 229 (B.C.C.A.).

[171] *Stovin*, *supra*, n. 91.

[172] *Riverscourt Farms Ltd. v. Niagara-on-the-Lake (Town)* (1992), 9 C.C.L.T. (2d) 231 (Ont. Gen. Div.).

[173] *Lake v. Callison Outfitters Ltd.* (1991), 7 C.C.L.T. (2d) 274 (B.C.S.C.); *Thornhill v. Martineau* (1987), 39 C.C.L.T. 293 (B.C.S.C.), no liability for traffic control device.

[174] *County of Parkland v. Stetar*, [1975] 2 S.C.R. 884; see also *Earl v. Bourdon* (1975), 65 D.L.R. (3d) 646 (B.C.).

[175] [1984] 5 W.W.R. 1 (S.C.C.) (*per* Wilson J.).

of a building, thus breaching its duty of care.[176] The city's failure to inspect properly could neither be viewed as a policy decision nor as a *bona fide* exercise of discretion and, therefore, was not immune from suit in tort. In *Rothfield v. Manolakos*,[177] a city was found 70 per cent liable for a negligently inspected wall, which collapsed less than a year after it was constructed.

There have been instances, however, where the policy/operational dichotomy has been used to render a municipality immune from suit. In *Barratt v. Dist. of North Vancouver*,[178] a decision that has probably been eclipsed by *Just*, it was found that the decision to inspect municipal roads for potholes was a policy decision. A large pothole had formed causing a bicyclist to fall and be injured; however, the policy of inspection arrived at by the municipality was made after a proper exercise of discretion and, thus, was immune.

Some legislatures, seeking to protect their cash-strapped municipalities, have enacted legislation to immunize them from negligence liability. For example, the *Kamloops (City) v. Nielsen* case led to amendments to the B.C. Municipal Act, relieving all local governmental officials, board members and employees from liability for failing to enforce city by-laws.[179] Far more extensive amendments were enacted in Alberta[180] relieving municipalities from liability in that and many other situations.

Recently we have seen an increase in the instances of liability against provincial governments. The ground-breaking case of *Nelles v. Ontario*,[181] in which it was found that a prosecutor was not immune from actions for malicious prosecution, shows how far the Canadian jurisprudence has diverged from the current British considerations of government immunity. While *Nelles* still leaves the Crown itself immune from the charge of malicious prosecution, the trial was allowed to continue as against the Attorney General. This departure from British jurisprudence was further evidenced by the Supreme Court of Canada in *Just v. British Columbia*,[182] in which British Columbia was found liable for negligently failing to inspect its roadways for falling rocks. The decision in *Just* is consistent with the earlier Canadian jurisprudence, such as *Malat v. the Queen*[183] where a provincial highway department was held liable for placing an 18-inch median on a highway instead of a 30-inch median, which its own policy called for.

---

[176] Justice McIntyre dissenting.

[177] [1989] 2 S.C.R. 1259.

[178] (1980), 114 D.L.R. (3d) 577 (*per* Martland J.).

[179] See Municipal Act (now renamed Local Government Act, S.B.C. 2000, c.7, s.1), R.S.B.C. 1996, c. 323, section 289 which reads:

    289 A municipality or a member of its council, a regional district or a member of its board, or an officer or employee of a municipality or regional district, is not liable for any damages or other loss, including economic loss, sustained by any person, or to the property of any person, as a result of neglect or failure, for any reason, to enforce, by the institution of a civil proceeding or a prosecution, a bylaw under Part 21 or a regulation under section 692(1).

[180] Municipal Government Act, 1994, S.A. 1994, c. M-26.1, part 13.

[181] *Supra*, n. 5. See also *Walker v. Ontario, supra*, n. 5.

[182] See, *supra*, Section C.

[183] *Supra*, n. 43.

At the federal level, recent cases have also shown a trend toward continuing to develop governmental liability.[184] Although the Canadian courts have looked with interest at the recent treatment of the policy/operational dichotomy in British jurisprudence, they have for the most part steered an independent course. The Canadian process has been one of adjusting, rather than changing, the existing jurisprudence by infusing meaning into the policy/operational dichotomy. One might fairly conclude that it has met with considerable success in *Just* and the cases that have followed it.

E. Other Matters

Certain additional problems arise in respect of government liability. So far, our courts have been largely occupied with the issue of duty and its resolution through the policy/operational dichotomy. Questions of standard of care and causation in government liability cases are only starting to surface, but they will become more important in the years ahead.

1. THE STANDARD OF CARE

In *Just*, Mr. Justice Cory reminded us[185] that, even if there is a civil duty owed by the Crown, it is still necessary, in assessing the standard of care required by the government actor in question, to balance the "nature and quantity of the risk . . . in light of all the circumstances including budgetary limits and the personnel and equipment available". Where a decision is made to inspect, the system of inspection must be reasonable and it must be made properly.[186] Clearly, there will be instances where a policy decision has been taken which limits the way in which those implementing the policy in question can fulfil their duties. In these cases, the courts can only scrutinize the way in which the officials carrying out the policy conducted themselves, given the limitations placed on them, whether they be budgetary, equipment, personnel or otherwise. Prior to *Just*, cases[187] were decided on the basis of no duty, where it would have been better to have held no breach of the standard of care. Although the same result might be achieved if these cases were reheard today, the reasoning would be somewhat different. To date, too much attention has been paid to the question of duty at the expense of the question of the standard of care expected, which is, in many ways, a more subtle and more meaningful exercise.[188]

2. CAUSATION

Causation in the case of a government tortfeasor is another issue that has largely gone unexamined. It is clear that the government conduct must not only be

---

[184] See *Swanson v. Canada, supra*, n. 97; *Brewer Brothers v. Canada, supra*, n. 100.

[185] *Supra*, n. 74, at p. 405.

[186] *Indian Towing Co. v. U.S.* (1955), 350 U.S. 61, cited in *Just*, at p. 405.

[187] For example, see *Barratt v. North Vancouver, supra*, n. 178.

[188] See Bailey and Bowman, *supra*, n. 124, at pp. 301 and 307.

negligent, it must also cause the loss. The usual principles of causation will be applied. In *Kamloops*,[189] for example, a city failed to enforce a stop work order issued because a contractor failed to comply with a requirement in the approved plans. The subsequent purchaser of the house sued for damages. Having found that the city owed a duty of care, Madam Justice Wilson went on to examine the issue of negligence. Distinguishing *East Suffolk*, in which the House of Lords had found that a city's inept steps to end flooding had not caused the plaintiff's damages, but had only failed to reduce them, Madam Justice Wilson found that there had been causation:

> This is the case of a duty owed by the City to the plaintiff, a person who met Lord Wilberforce's test of proximity in *Anns*. The City's responsibility as set out in the By-law was to vet the work of the builder and protect the plaintiff against the consequences of any negligence in the performance of it. In those circumstances, it cannot, in my view, be argued that the City's breach of duty was not causative.[190]

It can be seen that ordinary causation principles will be invoked in these cases, as they should be.

F. Conclusion

It is clear that the Canadian trend is toward increased liability for government institutions. This phenomenon is not limited to tort. In Canada, a whole new era of government accountability began with the introduction of the Charter of Rights and Freedoms.[191] Our administrative bodies are subject to increasing requirements that their decisions be made fairly, and free from factual and legal errors. Over the last century there has been a shift away from absolute government immunity toward the recognition that the administration should be held accountable, much like other organizations in society. After all, other professionals must abide by tort law's counsel of caution, even though they would prefer to be left alone. Government officials, who are also professionals, should be treated no differently, except where true policy decisions are involved, that is, where matters of governing are at issue.[192] Statutes have been passed to achieve this, and these Acts have moved us away from the concept of government by a divinely chosen sovereign and toward an administration model which more accurately reflects today's conditions. There is absolutely no reason for courts to protect governments from tort law to a greater extent than they seek to protect themselves.

---

[189] *Supra*, n. 69. See also *Swanson, supra*, n. 97, at pp. 231-34 for a discussion of the causation issue.
[190] *Ibid.*, at p. 15.
[191] Constitution Act, 1982 [en. by Canada Act., 1982 (U.K.), c. 11, s. 1] Pt. I.
[192] Bailey and Bowman, *supra*, n. 125, at p. 438; Aronson and Whitmore, *op. cit. supra*, n. 128, at p. 69.

Chapter 18

Occupiers' Liability

The Canadian common law of occupiers' liability,[1] which is concerned with the tort responsibility of those who control land to those who enter onto their land, was a mess. In this area, perhaps more than in any other part of tort law, rigid rules and formal categories had spawned confusion and injustice.[2] It was understandable in part because "the history of this subject is one of conflict between the general principles of law of negligence and the traditional immunity of landowners".[3]

From this clash, Canadian landowners emerged victoriously more often than not. The trend toward rationalization and generalization in the rest of negligence law made little headway in this area, except for one or two heroic attempts at reform.[4] The courts were unwilling to alter the course of a century of jurisprudence despite its obvious inadequacy for the task. In response to this judicial paralysis, legislatures were forced to undertake major legislative overhauls of the law. The new legislation, however, has not solved all the problems.

This chapter will outline briefly the main contours of the common law in this area. It will then consider several of the legislative schemes that have been enacted in Canada. Finally, it will look at some dramatic judicial reform in Newfoundland.

A. The Common Law

In the last century, the English courts developed three immutable categories of entrants to land: (1) trespassers, (2) licensees, and (3) invitees. To each of these three groups a different standard of care applied.[5] This rigid scheme was embraced

---

[1] Di Castri, Occupiers' Liability (1981); North, Occupiers' Liability (1971).
[2] See *Stuart v. Canada* (1988), 45 C.C.L.T. 290 (F.C.T.D.); [1989] 5 W.W.R. 163, application for reconsideration dismissed.
[3] Bohlen, "The Duty of a Landowner Towards Those Entering His Premises of Their Own Right" (1920), 69 U. Pa. L. Rev. 142, 237, 340, at 237.
[4] *Rowland v. Christian* (1968), 443 P. 2d 561 (Calif.).
[5] *Indermaur v. Dames* (1866), L.R. 1 C.P. 274; affd L.R. 2 C.P. 311 (Ex. Ch.).

without question by Canadian courts[6] and, until recently, had been adhered to ever since, despite a flood of academic criticism.[7] There were suggestions both to increase and to decrease the number of categories. Despite this, the three main categories survived, but with minor variations.

1. WHO IS AN OCCUPIER?

The status of "occupier" is not dependent on ownership of the premises, but rather is based on control over the premises. A person who has the immediate supervision and control of the premises and the power to admit and exclude the entry of others is without doubt an occupier.[8] Thus a tenant in possession is an occupier. However, complete or exclusive control is not necessary.[9] An auctioneer hired to conduct a sale on the vendor's premises may be considered an occupier of those premises.[10] An independent contractor carrying out building or repair work may qualify as an occupier.[11] Moreover, it has become apparent that in many circumstances there may be more than one occupier of premises.[12]

The law of occupiers' liability applies to land, structures on land and moveable structures. Accordingly, it governs the liability of occupiers of elevators,[13] scaffolding,[14] ships,[15] trains,[16] streetcars[17] and other similar things.

---

[6]   *White v. Imperial Optical Co.* (1957), 7 D.L.R. (2d) 471 (Ont. C.A.); revg 6 D.L.R. (2d) 496.

[7]   See Harris, "Some Trends in the Law of Occupiers' Liability" (1963), 41 Can. Bar Rev. 401, reprinted in *Studies in Canadian Tort Law* (1972), p. 250; McDonald and Leigh, "The Law of Occupiers' Liability and the Need for Reform in Canada" (1965), 15 U. of T.L.J. 55; A.L. MacDonald, "Invitees" (1930), 8 Can. Bar Rev. 344; Friedman, "Liability to Visitors of Premises" (1943), 21 Can. Bar Rev. 79; McMahon, "Occupiers' Liability in Canada" (1973), 22 Int'l & Comp. L.Q. 515.

[8]   *MacDonald v. Goderich*, [1949] 3 D.L.R. 788 (Ont. C.A.); *Wheat v. Lacon (E.) & Co.*, [1966] A.C. 552, at p. 578 (*per* Lord Denning).

[9]   *Wheat v. Lacon (E.) & Co., supra*, n. 8, at pp. 578 and 579 (*per* Lord Denning), "if a person has any degree of control over the state of the premises it is enough"; *Couch v. McCann* (1977), 77 D.L.R. (3d) 387 (Ont. C.A.). But see *Trenholm v. Langham & West Insurance Ltd.* (1990), 106 N.B.R. (2d) 181 (Q.B.), where a tenant was not held to be an occupier of the entrance to the premises even though the tenant exercised some control over the entrance, including snow removal and clearing.

[10] *Couch v. McCann, supra*, p. 9.

[11] *Boryszko v. Bd. of Education of Toronto* (1962), 35 D.L.R. (2d) 529 (Ont. C.A.).

[12] *E.g., Couch v McCann, supra*, n. 9; *Boryszko v. Bd. of Education of Toronto, supra*, n. 11; *Finigan v. Calgary* (1967), 62 W.W.R. 115 (Alta. C.A.).

[13] *Haseldine v. Daw*, [1941] 2 K.B. 343 (C.A.); *Hillman v. MacIntosh*, [1959] S.C.R. 384.

[14] *Woodman v. Richardson*, [1937] 3 All E.R. 866 (C.A.).

[15] *King v. Northern Navigation* (1913), 27 O.L.R. 79 (C.A.); *Webber v. Toronto*, [1955] O.W.N. 181.

[16] *Canadian Northern Ry. v. Diplock* (1916), 53 S.C.R. 376; *Nightengale v. Union Colliery Co. of B.C.* (1905), 35 S.C.R. 65.

[17] *Gebbie v. Saskatoon*, [1930] 4 D.L.R. 543 (Sask. C.A.).

2. TRESPASSERS

Trespassers are those who enter premises without the permission of the occupier. Licensees or invitees may subsequently become trespassers by exceeding the scope of their invitations or by overstaying their welcome.[18] The category of trespasser is heterogeneous, and would include both a burglar and a wandering child.

Historically, occupiers have been found liable to trespassers only if they willfully injured them or acted in reckless disregard of their presence.[19] Some attempts have been made to circumvent this rule in cases where its application causes unfairness or hardship. A court may, by some device or other, find that a trespasser, particularly if a child, has an implied licence to be on the premises and, therefore, is owed a duty of protection.[20] In other cases, a generous meaning may be given to the phrase "reckless disregard" or a tenuous distinction drawn between the static condition of premises and current activities conducted upon the premises.[21] In still other cases, a court may find that a particular defendant is not an occupier and, therefore, is not insulated from the higher standard of care which attaches as a result of ordinary negligence principles.[22]

Recently, however, a new line of cases has developed which rejects the use of fictions, and suggests instead a new test which requires the occupier to treat the trespasser with "common humanity".[23] The Supreme Court of Canada adopted this test in the case of *Veinot v. Kerr-Addison Mines Ltd.*[24] In his judgment, Mr. Justice Dickson, speaking for three members of the court, quoted with approval from Denning M.R.'s reasons for judgment in *Pannett v. McGuiness Co. Ltd.* in which Lord Denning suggested four factors for a judge to consider in determin-

---

[18] *Hillen v. I.C.I. (Alkali) Ltd.*, [1936] A.C. 65, at pp. 69-70 (P.C.); *C.P.R. v. McCrindle*, [1956] S.C.R. 473; *Stephens v. Corcoran* (1968), 65 D.L.R. (2d) 407 (Ont.); *Brown v. Wilson* (1975), 66 D.L.R. (3d) 295 (B.C.); *Cullen v. Rice* (1981), 15 C.C.L.T. 180 (Alta. C.A.).

[19] *Robert Addie & Sons (Collieries) v. Dumbreck*, [1929] A.C. 358, at p. 365 (*per* Lord Halisham), at p. 370 (*per* Viscount Dunedin) (H.L.); *Haynes v. C.P.R.* (1972), 31 D.L.R. (3d) 63 (B.C.C.A.); affd (1975), 49 D.L.R. (3d) 480n (S.C.C.); *MacKeigan v. Peake* (1971), 20 D.L.R. (3d) 81 (B.C.C.A.)

[20] *Excelsior Wire Rope Co. Ltd. v. Callan*, [1930] A.C. 404; *Veinot v. Kerr-Addison Mines Ltd.*, [1975] 2 S.C.R. 311. See also *McErlean v. Sarel et al.* (1987), 42 C.C.L.T. 78, at p. 92 (Ont. C.A.), leave to appeal dismissed Feb. 25, 1988, 88 N.R. 204n, where the court found the plaintiff to be a licensee and not a trespasser because "[t]he owner's failure to object to their presence can reasonably be construed as tacit permission to their entry".

[21] See discussion, *infra*, Section 7. Activity Duty.

[22] *Jones v. City of Calgary* (1969), 3 D.L.R. (3d) 455 (Alta.); *Palmer v. City of St. John* (1969), 3 D.L.R. (3d) 649 (N.B.C.A.); *Leadbetter v. The Queen*, [1970] Ex. C.R. 260.

[23] *Herrington v. British Railways Bd.*, [1972] A.C. 877; *Pannett v. McGuiness Co. Ltd.*, [1972] 3 W.L.R. 387 (C.A.); *Southern Portland Cement Ltd. v. Cooper*, [1974] 1 All E.R. 87 (P.C.).

[24] *Supra*, n. 20. The case actually turned by a 5:4 majority on the finding of an implied licence. However, seven of the nine judges expressed an opinion on the issue of the duty owed to a trespasser and adopted the "common humanity" test. Two of the majority judges expressed no opinion on the issue of the duty owed to a trespasser. See also *Eastwick v. New Brunswick* (1987), 45 C.C.L.T. 191 (N.B.Q.B.).

ing whether the occupier is in breach of the duty of common humanity.[25] These are:

(1) the gravity and likelihood of the probable injury;

(2) the character of the intrusion;

(3) the nature of the place where the trespass occurs; and

(4) the knowledge which the defendant has or ought to have of the likelihood of the trespasser being present.

A fifth factor which the courts also consider is the cost to the occupier, relative to financial and other resources, of guarding against the danger.[26] These factors take into account, *inter alia*, the diverse character of the entrants who fall within the category of trespasser. In other words, "a wandering child or a straying adult stands in a different position from a poacher or a burglar. You may expect a child when you may not expect a burglar."[27] Likewise, an open window which may not present a danger to an adult may present a grave peril to a small child.[28]

The occupier's duty of common humanity arises only if the occupier has actual knowledge either of the presence of the trespasser on the premises or of facts which make it likely that the trespasser will come onto the land,[29] and also actual knowledge of facts concerning the condition of the land or of activities carried out on it which are likely to cause injury to a trespasser who is unaware of the danger. The occupier is not under any duty to the trespasser to make inquiries or inspections to ascertain whether or not such facts exist.[30] Furthermore, the duty, when it arises, is limited to taking reasonable steps to enable the trespasser to avoid the danger. Where the likely trespasser is a child, too young to understand or heed a warning, discharging the duty may involve providing reasonable physical obstacles to keep the child away from the danger.[31] In one case, *Laviolette v. Canadian National Railway*,[32] a majority of the New Brunswick Court of Appeal applied the common humanity test to find that the railway

---

[25] *Ibid.*, at p. 317.

[26] *Herrington v. British Railways Bd.*, *supra*, n. 23, at p. 899 (*per* Lord Reid) at p. 920 (*per* Lord Wilberforce), at p. 942 (*per* Lord Diplock); *Veinot v. Kerr-Addison Mines Ltd.*, *supra*, n. 20, at p. 322; *Southern Portland Cement Ltd. v. Cooper, supra*, n . 23, at p. 98; *Pannett v. McGuiness Co. Ltd.*, *supra*, n. 23, at p. 394 (*per* Lord Lawton).

[27] *Pannett v. McGuiness Co. Ltd.*, *supra*, n. 23, at p. 390.

[28] *Harris v. Birkenhead Corp.*, [1976] 1 W.L.R. 279 (C.A.).

[29] *Veinot v. Kerr-Addison Mines Ltd.*, *supra*, n. 20, at p. 341 (*per* Martland J., dissenting, with whom three other judges agreed). Mr. Justice Dickson, with whom two other judges agreed, formulated the test somewhat more objectively, stating at p. 322: "a duty may arise if the owner of land knew of, or from all the surrounding circumstances ought reasonably to have foreseen, the presence of a trespasser".

[30] *Herrington v. British Railways Bd.*, *supra*, n. 23, at p. 909 (*per* Lord Morris of Borthy Gest), at p. 941 (*per* Lord Diplock); *Phillips v. C.N.R.*, [1975] 4 W.W.R. 135 (B.C.C.A.); *Southern Portland Cement Ltd. v. Cooper, supra*, n. 23, at pp. 97, 98.

[31] *Herrington v. British Railways Bd.*, *supra*, n. 23, at p. 941 (*per* Lord Diplock); *Southern Portland Cement Ltd. v. Cooper, supra*, n. 23, at p. 97; *Veinot v. Kerr-Addison Mines Ltd.*, *supra*, n. 20, at pp. 546-47 (*per* Martland J., dissenting).

[32] (1987), 40 C.C.L.T. 138 (N.B.C.A.).

was under a duty to remove an infant plaintiff from its property when employees observed him standing very close to a slow-moving train. An occupier who has created the danger may be expected to take greater measures to safeguard trespassers.[33]

It remains to be seen whether the "common humanity" test will allow the court to reach an equitable compromise "between the demands of humanity and the necessity to avoid placing undue burdens on occupiers".[34] The case law to date is encouraging in its liberal application of the test,[35] even though it is still hard to tell how the duty of common humanity differs from the more onerous duty of reasonable care.

Child trespassers have for a long time presented the courts with a particularly difficult problem. There are still problems with children even after the reforms.[36] It has recently been stated that child trespassers need no longer be classified but should be dealt with by the ordinary law of negligence.[37] It is too early to forecast whether this view will ultimately prevail, although it is a consequence devoutly to be wished by most commentators.

3. LICENSEE OR INVITEE?

Lawful visitors who enter the premises, in circumstances where there is no contractual term relating to their safety, are divided into two categories, "invitees" and "licencees". The distinction between the licensee and the invitee is not always easy to fathom. Generally, a licencee is a person, such as a social guest, who enters the occupier's land with permission but who is not there for any business purpose. The invitee, on the other hand, is a "lawful visitor from whose visit the occupier stands to derive an economic advantage".[38]

---

[33] *Southern Portland Cement Ltd. v. Cooper, supra,* n. 23, at p. 98; *Walker v. Sheffield Bronze Powder Co.* (1977), 77 D.L.R. (3d) 377, at p. 383 (Ont. H.C.J.), "He must match the precautions to the risk."

[34] *Herrington v. British Railways Bd., supra,* n. 23, at p. 920 (*per* Lord Wilberforce).

[35] *Herrington v. British Railways Bd., supra,* n. 23; *Southern Portland Cement Ltd. v. Cooper, supra,* n. 23; *Pannett v. McGuinness Co. Ltd., supra,* n. 23; *Veinot v. Kerr-Addison Mines Ltd., supra,* n. 20; *Hynes v. James A. Garland & Sons Ltd.* (1980), 28 Nfld. & P.E.I.R. 19 (Nfld.); see also *Mitchell v. C.N.R.,* [1975] 1 S.C.R. 592; but *cf., Wade v. C.N.R.,* [1978] 1 S.C.R. 1064, distinguished in *Laviolette v. C.N.R.* (1987), 40 C.C.L.T. 138 (N.B.C.A.).

[36] *Jolley v. Sutton London Borough Council,* [2000] 3 All E.R. 409 (H.L.).

[37] *Walker v. Sheffield Bronze Powder Co., supra,* n. 33, "Too often the occupier shelters behind a policy of insurance rather than a chain link fence". See also *Mitchell v. C.N.R., supra,* n. 35, at pp. 615-16 (*per* Laskin C.J.C., in *passim*). But see *McErlean v. Sarel, supra,* n. 20, holding that the conditions on the premises were not such that young trail bike riders would be unable to recognize and appreciate because of their age.

[38] *Indermaur v. Dames, supra,* n. 5, at pp. 287-88; see also Fleming, *op. cit. supra,* n. 7, at p. 425; Harris, *supra,* n. 7, at p. 403. Some courts have applied a somewhat different test, asking whether the occupier and the entrant share a "*common* interest", a "*common* material interest" or a "*joint* interest". See *Hambourg v. T. Eaton Co. Ltd.,* [1935] S.C.R. 430, at p. 436; *Hillman v. MacIntosh, supra,* n. 13, at p. 390; *Hamelin v. Canada Egg Products Ltd.* (1966), 56 W.W.R. 14, at p. 20 (Sask. C.A.); *Arendale v. Federal Building Corp.* (1962), 35 D.L.R. (2d) 202, at p. 204 (Ont. C.A.).

Thus, a customer who comes into a store with a view to making a purchase qualifies as an invitee.[39] The exact nature and scope of the economic relationship necessary to qualify a visitor as an invitee, however, is somewhat nebulous. An employee's wife attending a social gathering involving only employees and their spouses, at the home of the employer, was considered an invitee of the employer.[40] A friend helping another to clear underbrush from residential property was also held to be an invitee.[41]

On occasion the courts have classified as invitees students at a free public school,[42] visitors to a public library,[43] visitors of patients in hospitals[44] and a person meeting or seeing off a friend at a railroad station,[45] who did not necessarily bring any economic advantage to the occupier. In contrast, visitors in public parks,[46] and public washrooms[47] have been characterized as licencees on the ground that no benefit flows from them to the municipality. Likewise a person attending at a public dump has been classified as a licensee.[48] Many of the cases on this issue are difficult to reconcile and are best understood as contortions of the applicable legal principles for the purpose of achieving what the courts perceive to be an equitable and just result in factual situations that do not easily fit the rigid category system.

---

[39]   *Indermaur v. Dames, supra,* n. 5, at pp. 287-88; *Bednarz v. Burgess,* [1937] O.W.N. 497.

[40]   *Johnston v. Sentineal* (1977), 17 O.R. (2d) 354.

[41]   *Pringle v. Price* (1971), 20 D.L.R. (3d) 229 (B.C.C.A.).

[42]   *Portelance v. Bd. of Trustees, Grantham,* [1962] O.R. 365 (C.A.); *Sombach v. Regina Roman Catholic Separate High School Trustees* (1970), 72 W.W.R. 92; affd [1971] 1 W.W.R. 156 (Sask. C.A.); *Phillips v. Regina Public School Dist. No. 4* (1976), 1 C.C.L.T. 197 (Sask. Q.B.). See also *Griffiths v. St. Clements School,* [1938] 3 All E.R. 537 (K.B.), parents of school children attending exhibit of students' work at school held to be invitees.

[43]   *Nickell v. City of Windsor* (1927), 59 O.L.R. 618 (C.A.).

[44]   *Slade v. Battersea & Putney Hospital,* [1955] 1 W.L.R. 207 (Q.B.), wife visiting husband; *Creighton v. Delisle Union Memorial Hospital Bd.* (1961), 38 W.W.R. (N.S.) 44 (Sask. Q.B.), clergyman visiting patient. See also *Jennings v. Cole,* [1949] 2 All E.R. 191 (K.B.), neighbour coming at the request of husband to sit with his sick wife while he was away at work held to be invitee.

[45]   *Stowell v. Railway Executive,* [1949] 2 K.B. 519; *York v. Canada Atlantic S.S. Co.* (1893), 22 S.C.R. 167; *cf., Spence v. G.T.R.* (1896), 27 O.R. 303 (Div. Ct.), person on railway platform to mail letter held to be a licensee.

[46]   *Coffyne v. Silver Lake Regional Park Authority* (1977), 75 D.L.R. (3d) 300 (Sask. Q.B.); *Palmer v. City of St. John, supra,* n. 22; *Moran v. City of Sault Ste. Marie* (1967), 60 D.L.R. (2d) 14 (Ont.); revd on another point 62 D.L.R. (2d) 452; *Booth v. City of St. Catherines,* [1948] S.C.R. 564, at p. 567 (*per* Kerwin J.), at p. 581 (*per* Estey J.); *Richardson v. Windsor,* [1942] 1 D.L.R. 500 (Ont.); *Moore v. Toronto* (1893), 26 O.R. 59n (Div. Ct.); *Schmidt v. Town of Berlin* (1894), 26 O.R. 54 (Div. Ct.); *cf., Union Estates Ltd. v. Kennedy,* [1940] S.C.R. 625, persons attending free concert at commercial park where no entry was charged were invitees; *Sword v. City of Toronto* (1975), 9 O.R. (2d) 215, child playing at city playground considered to be invitee; *Bundas v. Oyama Regional Park Authority* (1980), 4 Sask. R. 124 (Q.B.), visitor held to be invitee where small fee paid to gain admission.

[47]   *Conlon v. City of St. Catherines,* [1956] O.W.N. 296; *Pearson v. Lambeth Borough Council,* [1950] 2 K.B. 353 (C.A.).

[48]   *Auffrey v. New Brunswick,* [1977] 1 S.C.R. 509.

The relationship between a landlord and persons visiting tenants, with respect to common facilities (*e.g.*, stairs, elevators, and entrances) over which the landlord retains control, has been a matter of some controversy and uncertainty. English courts held that such visitors were licensees, regardless of whether they were social or business guests of the tenant.[49] In Canada, however, with few exceptions,[50] social guests and relatives of residential tenants have been held to be licensees of the landlord,[51] whereas business visitors of tenants in commercial premises have been held to be invitees of the landlord.[52] It has not yet been determined whether business visitors of tenants in residential premises are invitees or licensees of the landlord.[53] Likewise, the status of social guests of commercial tenants *vis à vis* the landlord is an open question.

4. LICENSEES

The occupier's duty to a licensee was traditionally expressed as a duty to prevent damage from concealed dangers or traps of which the occupier has actual knowledge.[54] Traps and concealed dangers are hidden dangers which are not obvious or to be expected under the circumstances.[55] Whether a dangerous condition is a trap or a concealed danger is not always self-evident. For example, what is an obvious danger in daylight may be transformed into a concealed danger after dark.[56]

Knowledge of the concealed danger or trap is a condition precedent to the licensor's ability. However the courts have placed a gloss on the requirement of actual knowledge. In *White v. Imperial Optical Co.*[57] it was held that an occupier must actually know of the physical condition involved, but that once such knowledge is shown, the question is not whether the occupier knew that the

---

[49]   *Fairman v. Perpetual Investment Building Society*, [1923] A.C. 74 (H.L.), guest of residential tenant; *Jacobs v. London County Council*, [1950] A.C. 361 (H.L.), visitor to rented shop injured in forecourt.

[50]   *Lewis v. Toronto General Trusts Corp.*, [1941] 2 W.W.R. 65 (Sask. K.B.), friend of tenant; *Mazur v. Sontowski* (1952), 5 W.W.R. (N.S.) 332 (B.C.), wife of tenant; see also *Power v. Hughes*, [1938] 2 W.W.R. 359 (B.C.C.A.) (*per* O'Halloran J., dissenting).

[51]   *Ottawa v. Monroe*, [1954] S.C.R. 756; *Fraser v. Ronsten Developments Ltd.* (1969), 4 D.L.R. (3d) 475 (Ont.); *Jesmer v. Bert Katz Real Estate Ltd.* (1972), 33 D.L.R. (3d) 662 (Ont. Co. Ct.).

[52]   *Hillman v. MacIntosh*, supra, n. 13; *Arendale v. Federal Building Corp.*, supra, n. 38; *Levy v. Wellington Square Ltd.* (1964), 47 D.L.R. (2d) 567 (Ont. Co. Ct.); *Foster v. Canadian Interurban Properties Ltd.* (1972), 35 D.L.R. (3d) 248 (Sask. Q.B.); *Thorburn v. Badalato* (1974), 47 D.L.R. (3d) 36 (Ont.); *St. Pierre v. Harrison* (1976), 71 D.L.R. (3d) 573 (N.B.C.A.).

[53]   See *Sanders v. Shauer* (1964), 43 D.L.R. (2d) 685 (B.C.), where the plaintiff was held to be an invitee of the defendant motel owner who had let a motel cabin to the plaintiff's employer to be used by the employees while the employer's logging camp was under construction.

[54]   *Hambourg v. T. Eaton Co. Ltd.*, supra, n. 38; *Power v. Hughes*, supra, n. 50; *Fraser v. Ronsten Developments Ltd.*, supra, n. 51; *Hanson v. St. John Horticultural Ass'n*, [1974] S.C.R. 354.

[55]   *MacDonald v. Goderich*, [1948] 4 D.L.R. 569; affd [1979] 3 D.L.R. 788 (Ont. C.A.); *White v. Imperial Optical Co.*, supra, n. 6.

[56]   *Sanders v. Frawley Lake Lumber Co. Ltd.* (1972), 25 D.L.R. (3d) 46 (Ont. C.A.); *Auffrey v. New Brunswick*, [1977] 1 S.C.R. 509.

[57]   *Supra*, n. 6.

condition constituted a concealed danger, but whether the occupier, as a reasonable person, ought to have realized that it constituted a concealed danger.[58] Subsequent cases have modified even the requirement that the occupier must have actual knowledge of the physical condition. It is sufficient if the occupier has actual knowledge that such a condition has existed in the past and may exist again in the future if appropriate preventative steps are not taken. Thus, actual knowledge of the danger will be imputed if the licensor had reason to know of its existence.[59] This has diluted the "actual knowledge" requirement significantly.

More recently there has been a further blurring of the distinction between the standard of care owing to licensees and that owing to invitees. Under the traditional formulation of the obligation, a licensee had no claim if the danger was known to the licensee or obvious. In *Mitchell v. C.N.R.*[60] the Supreme Court of Canada openly abandoned the requirement that the danger be concealed, holding that a licensee's mere knowledge of the danger, falling short of voluntary assumption of risk, does not exonerate the licensor. Such knowledge is, however, still relevant to the issue of contributory negligence.

In a subsequent decision, the Ontario Court of Appeal basing itself on *Mitchell*, reformulated the licensor's responsibility — the licensor must "take reasonable care to avoid foreseeable risk of harm from any unusual danger on the occupier's premises of which the occupier actually has knowledge or of which he ought to have knowledge because he was aware of the circumstances. The licensee's knowledge of the danger goes only to the questions of contributory negligence or *volenti*."[61] Not only was the knowledge required reduced, but the concept of unusual danger was incorporated into the new test as a replacement for the notion of a concealed danger or trap.

As a result of all of this, all that remains of the distinction between the duty owed to an invitee and that owed to a licensee is that, while the invitor is under a duty of reasonable diligence to ascertain the existence of the unusual danger, the licensor is only liable if having knowledge of the facts from which a reasonable person would either infer the existence of the unusual danger or would regard its existence as so highly probable that that person's conduct would be predicated

---

[58] See also *Van Oudenhove v. D'Aoust* (1969), 70 W.W.R. 177 (Alta. C.A.); *Hanson v. St. John Horticultural Ass'n, supra,* n. 54.

[59] *Mantin v. Hamilton* (1969), 11 D.L.R. (3d) 453 (N.B.), defendant did not have knowledge of the precise defect which caused the injury but was aware of the "potential risk"; *Fraser v. Ronsten Developments Ltd., supra,* n. 51, tiles often loose before; *Pearson v. Lambeth Borough Council, supra,* n. 47, at p. 364; *Ellis v. Fulham Borough Council,* [1938] 1 K.B. 212 (C.A.). See also *Hawkins v. Coulsdon & Purley Urban District Council,* [1954] 1 Q.B. 319, at pp. 335-36 (C.A.) (*per* Lord Denning).

[60] *Supra,* n. 35.

[61] *Bartlett v. Weiche Apartments Ltd.* (1974), 7 O.R. (2d) 263, at p. 267 (C.A.) (*per* Jessup J.A.). See also *Alaica v. Toronto* (1976), 14 O.R. (2d) 697 (C.A.); *Whaling v. Ravenhorst* (1977), 16 O.R. (2d) 61 (C.A.); *Davies v. Day* (1977), 2 C.C.L.T. 91 (Ont. C.A.). See also *Evans v. Forsyth* (1978), 21 O.R. (2d) 210; *Urzi v. Bd. of Education for the Borough of North York* (1981), 30 O.R. (2d) 300; *McErlean v. Sarel, supra,* n. 20.

on the assumption that it did in fact exist. Thus the distinction lies in the difference between unusual dangers of which the occupier "ought to know" and those which the occupier merely has "reason to know". The latter does not imply a duty to know.[62]

The occupier's duty to a licensee can usually be discharged by warning the licensee of the danger.[63] However, the warning will not exonerate the occupier if the licensee is not given reasonable time to act on it, or if it is given by means of a sign which is not readily visible.[64] In the case of child licensees, who are usually impervious to warning, the circumstances may require positive physical precautions.

5. INVITEES

The duty that an occupier owes to an invitee was expressed by Willes J. in *Indermaur v. Dames*[65] as follows:

> ... we consider it settled law, that he, using reasonable care on his part for his own safety, is entitled to expect that the occupier shall on his part use reasonable care to prevent damage from unusual danger, which he knows or ought to know; ...

In *Smith v. Provincial Motors Ltd.*[66] it was suggested that, once it is decided that the entrant is an invitee, four additional questions should be asked: First, was there an unusual danger? Second, did the defendant know or have reason to know about it? Third, did the defendant act reasonably? Fourth, did the plaintiff use reasonable care for safety or did the plaintiff voluntarily incur the risk?

The question of what is an unusual danger has been the subject of controversy. Madam Justice Reed has observed that "[w]hen the jurisprudence is reviewed, one finds an inordinate amount of ink spilled, respecting the rules applicable in occupiers' liability cases and, in particular, considerable confusion as to exactly what is meant by the test set out in *Indermaur v. Dames*".[67] Indeed, it has been demonstrated that the concept of unusual danger was introduced into our law by mistake — a misreading of the authorities by Willes J.[68] Nevertheless, the court has clung to the concept to the present day.

The term unusual danger has been held to be a "relative" one, depending upon the kind of premises involved and the class of persons to which the invitee

---

[62] Fleming, *op. cit. supra*, n. 7, at p. 436, quoted with approval in *Nohr v. Anderson* (1968), 69 D.L.R. (2d) 698 (B.C.); *Fraser v. Ronsten Developments Ltd.*, *supra*, n. 51; *cf.*, *Jesmer Bert Katz Real Estate Ltd.*, *supra*, n. 51; and *Graves v. Baxter* (1988), 89 N.S.R. (2d) 19 (S.C.).

[63] *Ashdown v. S. Williams*, [1957] 1 Q.B. 409 (C.A.).

[64] *Whitecourt Transportation Ltd. v. Canadian Kewanee Ltd.*, [1973] 2 W.W.R. 1 (Alta.).

[65] *Supra*, n. 5, at p. 288.

[66] (1962), 32 D.L.R. (2d) 405, at p. 412 (N.S.). See also *Fiddes v. Rayner Construction* (1964), 45 D.L.R. (2d) 367, at p. 373 (N.S.) (*per* Ilsley C.J.).

[67] *Stuart v. Canada*, *supra*, n. 2, at pp. 304-05.

[68] Linden, "A Century of Tort Law in Canada: Whither Unusual Dangers, Products Liability and Automobile Accident Compensation?" (1967), 45 Can. Bar Rev. 831, at pp. 836-40.

belongs.[69] A danger is unusual if it "is not usually found in carrying out the task or fulfilling the function which the invitee has in hand". This is an objective notion rather than a subjective one, so that it is the perspective of the class of which the particular invitee is a member rather than the actual knowledge and experience of the particular invitee[70] which controls. In *Wilkins v. Ryder,*[71] McLellan J. stated that ". . . the test is to consider whether the danger encountered by the oil delivery man of rain on those icy steps and stand . . . was an unusual danger *for an oil delivery man*". [emphasis added]. The trial judge concluded that it was not. The plaintiff's knowledge is not relevant to the question of whether a danger is an unusual one; it is relevant only to the questions of contributory negligence and voluntary assumption of risk.[72]

Dangers such as icy patches,[73] unmarked clear glass panels and doors,[74] wet floors[75] and objects on store floors[76] may be considered "unusual" in some situations but not in others. Also, a running lawnmower,[77] a falling piece of an

---

[69] *Rafuse v. T. Eaton Co.* (1958), 11 D.L.R. (2d) 773 (N.S.); *Fiddes v. Rayner Construction, supra,* n. 66.

[70] *Fiddes v. Rayner Construction, supra,* n. 66 (*per* Ilsley and MacQuarrie JJ.); *Campbell v. Royal Bank,* [1964] S.C.R. 85; *City of Brandon v. Farley,* [1968] S.C.R. 150; *Vyas v. Bd. of Education of Colchester East Hants Dist.* (1989), 65 D.L.R. (4th) 48 (N.S.C.A.); *Stuart v. Canada, supra,* n. 2.

[71] (1995), 165 N.B.R. (2d) 43 (Q.B.).

[72] *Campbell v. Royal Bank, supra,* n. 70; *Mitchell v. C.N.R., supra,* n. 35; *Bartlett v. Weiche Apartments Ltd., supra,* n. 61; *Davies v. Day, supra,* n. 61; *Vyas v. Bd. of Education of Colchester-East Hants Dist., supra,* n. 70.

[73] *Urzi v. Bd. of Education for the Borough of North York, supra,* n. 61; *Phillips v. Regina Public School District No. 4, supra,* n. 42; *Stuckless v. The Queen* (1975), 63 D.L.R. (3d) 345 (Fed. Ct. T.D.); *Bilenky v. Ukrainian Greek Catholic Parish,* [1971] 2 W.W.R. 595 (Man. Q.B.); *Smith v. Provincial Motors Ltd., supra,* n. 66; *Joubert v. Davidner* (1968), 66 W.W.R. 737 (Sask. C.A.); *Levy v. Wellington Square,* [1965] 1 O.R. 289 (Co. Ct.); *cf., Such v. Dominion Stores,* [1963] 1 O.R. 405 (C.A.); *Sanders v. Shauer, supra,* n. 53; *City of Brandon v. Farley, supra,* n. 70; *Foster v. Canadian Interurban Properties Ltd., supra,* n. 52; *Davies v. Day, supra,* n. 61.

[74] *Pajot v. Commonwealth Holiday Inns of Canada Ltd.* (1978), 20 O.R. (2d) 76; *Sombach v. Regina* (1975), 58 D.L.R. (3d) 294 (P.E.I.); *cf., Burke v. Batcules,* [1962] O.R. 697 (C.A.); *Piket v. Monk Office Supply Ltd.* (1968), 64 W.W.R. 63 (B.C.); *Donahoe v. Heritage Properties Ltd.* (1975), 13 N.B.R. (2d) 651.

[75] *Campbell v. Royal Bank, supra,* n. 70; *Tokar v. Town of Selkirk,* [1974] 3 W.W.R. 612 (Man. Q.B.); *Miller v. Unity Union Hospital Bd.* (1974), 54 D.L.R. (3d) 228; affd 55 D.L.R. (3d) 475 (Sask. C.A.); *Davidson v. Morris Drug Store Ltd.* (1980), 42 N.S.R. (2d) 582; *cf., Dankoski v. Orre* (1963), 43 D.L.R. (2d) 747 (B.C.); *Cosgrave v. Busk* (1966), 59 D.L.R. (2d) 425 (Ont. C.A.); *Goldman v. City of Regina* (1967) 63 D.L.R. (2d) 470 (Sask. Q.B.); *Strongman v. Oshawa Holdings Ltd.* (1979), 23 N. & P.E.I.R. 457 (P.E.I.).

[76] *Diederichs v. Metropolitan Stores Ltd.* (1957), 20 W.W.R. 246 (Sask. Q.B.); *MacNeill v. Sobeys Stores Ltd.* (1961), 29 D.L.R. (2d) 761 (N.S.); *Bennett v. Dominion Stores Ltd.* (1961), 30 D.L.R. (2d) 266 (N.S.); *Gartshore v. Stevens* (1967), 64 D.L.R. (2d) 582 (Ont.); *Maimy v. Canada Safeway Ltd.,* [1975] 6 W.W.R. 612 (Sask. Q.B.); *Kennedy v. The Queen* (1980), 116 D.L.R. (3d) 206 (Fed. Ct. T.D.); *cf., Rafuse v. T. Eaton Co., supra,* n. 69; *Eddie v. Hudson's Bay Co.* (1965), 53 D.L.R. (2d) 5 (B.C.); *Desjardins v. Kent's Supermarket Ltd.* (1977), 17 N.B.R. (2d) 219 (Q.B.)

[77] *Whaling v. Ravenhorst* (1977), 2 C.C.L.T. 114 (Ont. C.A.).

elevator,[78] fruit on a supermarket floor,[79] and soapy floors in a shower room[80] have been held to be unusual dangers. Held not to be unusual dangers, however, have been an irregularity on a private walkway,[81] a snow-covered concrete base at a skating rink,[82] the shallow end of a swimming pool,[83] bleachers in a hockey arena,[84] and ice in parking lots in New Brunswick during the winter.[85] This concept is one of the most troublesome in the area and should be abandoned.

An invitor's duty extends both to unusual dangers known to the invitor and those of which the invitor ought to be aware; the invitor must stay acquainted with the state of the property.[86] The invitor's duty is not to prevent unusual dangers but rather to use reasonable care to prevent damages to the invitee from such dangers.[87] What acts will constitute reasonable care on the part of the invitor is a question of fact, depending on the particular circumstances of each case. An adequate warning of the danger will in many circumstances suffice,[88] but some situations may dictate more extensive precautionary measures.[89]

6. CONTRACTUAL ENTRANTS

In addition to the three traditional categories of entrants, the courts have developed a fourth category, that of contractual entrant, who is someone like a college student,[90] or a patron of a hotel, a theatre, a hockey arena[91] or a health club,[92] who has contracted and paid for the right to enter the premises. A

---

[78]   *Sawler v. Franklyn Enterprises Ltd. et al.* (1992), 117 N.S.R. (2d) 316 (T.D.).

[79]   *Grant v. Westfair Foods Ltd.* (1998), 167 Sask. R. 133 (Q.B.).

[80]   *Callow v. British Columbia Distillers Ltd.*, [1972] 4 W.W.R. 614 (B.C.); *Dixon v. Cabot College, infra*, n. 90, wax.

[81]   *Johnston v. Sentineal, supra*, n. 40. See also *Evans v. Forsyth, supra*, n. 61.

[82]   *Alaica v. Toronto, supra*, n. 61.

[83]   *Long v. Owners of Condominium Plan No. 74R40206* (1979), 2 Sask. R. 212 (Q.B.).

[84]   *Starkebaum v. Regina (City)* (1995), 130 Sask. R. 290 (Q.B.).

[85]   *Chiasson v. Conseil Récréatif de Bois-Blanc Inc.* (1995), 157 N.B.R. (2d) 152 (C.A.); *Gadzella v. Hindmarsh Holdings Ltd.* (1998), 164 Sask. R. 64 (Q.B.), snow in October in Saskatchewan.

[86]   *Hillman v. MacIntosh, supra*, n. 13, at pp. 392-93; *Diederichs v. Metropolitan Stores Ltd., supra*, n. 76; *Bennett v. Dominion Stores Ltd., supra*, n. 76; *Snitzer v. Becker Milk Co.* (1976), 75 D.L.R. (3d) 649 (Ont.); *Pringle v. Price*, [1971] 3 W.W.R. 321 (B.C.C.A.).

[87]   *London Graving Dock Co. v. Horton*, [1951] A.C. 737, at p. 745 (*per* Lord Porter); *Fleming v. B.A. Oil Co.* (1952), 7 W.W.R. (N.S.) 135, at p. 138 (*per* McPherson C.J.); *Spelay v. Avalon Studio & Camera Shop Ltd.* (1989), 72 Sask. R. 308 (Q.B.); affd (1990), 86 Sask. R. 80 (C.A.).

[88]   *Indermaur v. Dames, supra*, n. 5; *London Graving Dock Co. v. Horton, supra*, n. 87, at p. 747 (*per* Lord Porter). See *Moore v. New Brunswick Housing Corp.* (1976), 15 N.B.R. (2d) 389 (Q.B.); *Wilson v. Blue Mountain Resorts Ltd.* (1974), 4 O.R. (2d) 713; *Bundas v. Oyama Regional Park Authority, supra*, n. 46.

[89]   See *MacNeill v. Sobeys Stores Ltd., supra*, n. 76.

[90]   *Dixon v. Cabot College*, [1999] N.S. No. 124 (T.D.), even though government paid tuition.

[91]   *Buis v. Centennial Arena Commission* (1994), 136 N.S.R. (2d) 33 (S.C.). *Hauman v. Regina Exhibition Association Ltd.* (1999), 186 Sask. R. 225 (Q.B.), season ticket holder.

[92]   See, for example, *Drodge v. St. John's Young Men's and Women's Christian Assoc.* (1987), 67 Nfld. & P.E.I.R. 57 (Nfld. S.C.), where paying a membership fee placed the person in the position of a contractual entrant.

potential customer of a self-service store is also a contractual entrant.[93] If the contract expressly prescribes the obligations of the occupier in relation to safety, the contractual standard prevails. If, however, the contract is silent on the matter, the law implies a term that the premises are as safe for the purpose as reasonable care and skill on the part of anyone can make them[94] or at least that the premises are reasonably fit for the purpose intended.[95] The occupier is not responsible for defects which could not have been discovered by reasonable care or skill on the part of any person concerned with the construction, alteration, repair or mainte-nance of the premises. But the occupier's liability is the same whether the lack of care is the occupier's own or that of an independent contractor, or whether the negligence occurs before or after the occupier takes possession of the premises.

There is, though, authority for the view that if the entry onto the premises or onto the part of the premises where the injury occurred is only ancillary to the main purpose of the contract (for instance, to attend a physical training class) the duty of the occupier is less exacting. The cases, however, evidence some confusion about what standard of care is required in these circumstances. A number of decisions hold that the less exacting standard entails an obligation on the part of the occupier to personally take reasonable care to see that the premises are in all respects reasonably safe for the purpose. In other words, these decisions apply ordinary negligence principles.[96] But, where the contract is ancillary to the person's entry onto the premises, it is difficult to see why an ordinary negligence standard would be controlling rather than a lesser standard associated with the traditional categories of occupiers' liability. In other words, if a person is not a contractual entrant, why are they not then viewed as an invitee, a licensee, or a trespasser? Indeed, this was the approach taken in *Spelay v. Avalon Studio & Camera Shop Ltd.*[97] where the court found that the use of the premises was entirely incidental to the purpose of the contract. Rather than applying a common negligence standard, the court characterized the plaintiff as an invitee and applied the lower standard of care owed by an invitor.

The duty owed to contractual entrants is higher than that owed to invitees. Responsibility is not limited to "unusual dangers". Furthermore, liability under the "higher" contractual standard applicable where the use of the premises is the

---

[93]   *Minke v. Westfair Properties Ltd.* (1998), 169 Sask. R. 172, (Q.B.); affd [2000] 3 W.W.R. 292 (C.A.).

[94]   *Maclenan v. Segar*, [1917] 2 K.B. 325, at pp. 332-33 (K.B.); *Serediuk v. Posner*, [1928] 1 D.L.R. 648 (Man. C.A.); *Brown v. B. & F. Theatres*, [1947] S.C.R. 486, at pp. 490-91 (*per* Rand J.); *Nelson v. Lithwick*, [1957] O.W.N. 441 (C.A.); *McPhail v. T. & L. Club (Brantford)*, [1968] 2 O.R. 840 (C.A.); *Beaudry v. Fort Cumberland Hotel Ltd.* (1971), 24 D.L.R. (3d) 80 (N.S.C.A.); *Butler v. Scott* (1976), 65 D.L.R. (3d) 692 (N.S.C.A.).

[95]   *Carriss v. Buxton*, [1958] S.C.R. 441, at p. 471 (*per* Cartwright J.).

[96]   *Gillmore v. London County Council*, [1938] 4 All E.R. 331, at p. 333 (K.B.); *Bell v. Travco Hotels Ltd.*, [1953] 1 Q.B. 473 (C.A.); *Protheroe v. Railway Executive*, [1951] 1 K.B. 376; *Sinclair v. Hudson Coal & Fuel Oil Co. Ltd.*, [1966] 2 O.R. 256; *cf. Beaudry v. Fort Cumberland Hotel Ltd.*, *supra*, n. 94; *Finigan v. Calgary* (1967), 62 W.W.R. 115 (Alta. C.A.); *McPhail v. T. and L. Club (Brantford)*, *supra*, n. 94.

[97]   *Supra*, n. 87.

main purpose of the contract, as, for example, in a contract for accommodation, attaches not only for personal negligence on the part of the occupier or occupier's servants but also in respect of dangers created by independent contractors employed in connection with the construction, alteration or repair of the premises and even for defects negligently created before the defendant commenced occupation.

The duty owed to a contractual entrant also requires the exercise of reasonable care by the occupier to supervise and control the conduct of persons whose activities on the premises are likely to endanger the entrant. This aspect of the occupier's duty has been explored in various cases involving injury to a spectator of a sporting event or a theatrical presentation. The occupier's duty is to guard the spectator against dangers, which are reasonably foreseeable.[98] However, the occupier is not responsible for dangers inherent in the particular spectacle which any reasonable spectator can foresee, provided the occupier provides reasonable protection in accordance with the prevailing custom for the spectacle involved notwithstanding that such protection does not eliminate the danger.[99]

7. ACTIVITY DUTY

The field of occupier's liability has been complicated further by an overriding distinction between an "activity duty" and an "occupancy duty", which derives from the misfeasance-nonfeasance dichotomy. If an entrant is injured by "current operations" being carried out by the occupier on the land, as opposed to a defect or danger in the condition of the land, the courts will impose the general duty to use reasonable care.[100] This general duty is owed to all persons lawfully on the premises, but it is unclear whether it is also applicable to trespassers whose presence is known or probable.[101]

---

[98] *Payne v. Maple Leaf Gardens Ltd.*, [1949] O.R. 26 (C.A.); *Reese v. Coleman*, [1979] 4 W.W.R. 58 (Sask. C.A.); *Cox v. Coulson*, [1916] 2 K.B. 177, at p. 187 (C.A.). Also person at zoo, *Maltais-Comeau v. Laliberté* (1986), 36 C.C.L.T. 26 (N.B.Q.B.).

[99] *Klyne v. Town of Indian Head*, [1980] 2 W.W.R. 474 (Sask. C.A.); *Hagerman v. City of Niagara Falls* (1980), 29 O.R. (2d) 609. Nor is a hotel liable for a "random act of vandalism" by an unknown person which injures a guest, see *McTaggart v. Commonwealth Hospitality Ltd.* (1997), 38 C.C.L.T. (2d) 95, at p. 100 (Sask. Q.B.) (*per* Barclay J.).

[100] *Slater v. Clay Cross Co.*, [1956] 2 Q.B. 264 (C.A.); *Videan v. British Transport Commn.*, [1963] 2 Q.B. 650 (C.A.) (*per* Denning and Harman JJ.); *Commr. for Railways v. McDermott*, [1967] 1 A.C. 169 (P.C.); *Van Oudenhove v. D'Aoust*, *supra*, n. 58; *Okanagan Helicopters Ltd. v. Canadian Pacific Ltd.*, [1974] 1 F.C. 465 (Fed. Ct. T.D.); *Graham v. Eastern Woodworkers Ltd.* (1959), 18 D.L.R. (2d) 260, at pp. 267-72 (N.S.C.A.) (*per* McDonald J.); *Willey v. Cambridge Leaseholds Ltd.* (1975), 57 D.L.R. (3d) 550 (P.E.I.C.A.); *C.P.R. Co. v. Kizlyk*, [1944] S.C.R. 98, at p. 106 (*per* Davis J.); *Wade v. C.N.R.*, *supra*, n. 35 (*per* Laskin C.J.C., dissenting); *cf.*, *Herrington British Railways Bd.*, *supra*, n. 23.

[101] See *C.P.R. v. Kizlyk*, *supra*, n. 100, at p. 106 (*per* Davis J.); *Graham v. Eastern Woodworkers Ltd.*, *supra*, n. 100, at pp. 271-72 (*per* Davis J.); *Graham v. Eastern Woodworkers Ltd.*, *supra*, n. 100, at pp. 271-72 (*per* McDonald J.); *cf.*, *Commr. for Railways v. Quinlan*, [1964] A.C. 1054 (P.C.); *Herrington v. British Railways Bd.*, *supra*, n. 23.

B. Statutory and Judicial Reform

Although there were some small improvements in the law, a complete legislative overhaul of the entire field was required.[102] In England, legislation was enacted in 1957 abolishing the distinction between licensees and invitees and holding occupiers to a "common duty of care" to all lawful entrants requiring them to take "such care as in all the circumstances of the case is reasonable to see that the visitor will be reasonably safe in using the premises for the purposes for which he is invited or permitted by the occupier to be there".[103] The Act goes on to give examples of some of the relevant circumstances to be considered.[104] However, the English Act left unaffected the common law which had developed with respect to the duty owed to trespassers.[105] In 1960, Scotland enacted legislation dealing with occupiers' liability which was broader in scope than its English counterpart in that it embraced all entrants to premises, regardless of their former category.[106] New Zealand passed legislation in 1962 which was substantially modelled on the English Act.[107] Legislative and judicial reforms have taken place in Australia.[108] In Canada, six provinces have now enacted occupier's liability legislation,[109] briefly described below.[110] One province, New Brunswick, has recently opted to do away with the law of occupiers' liability altogether, preferring instead a negligence standard.[111] In Newfoundland, the courts have boldly opted to rationalize the legal morass by judicial legislation.[112]

---

[102] *Cf.*, Alexander, "Occupiers' Liability: Alberta Proposes Reform" (1970), 9 Alta. L. Rev. 89, who seems to prefer common law reform.

[103] Occupiers' Liability Act, 1957, 5 & 6 Eliz. 2, c. 31, s. 2, as amended, which applies in England and Wales. Identical legislation was also enacted in Northern Ireland, Occupiers' Liability (Northern Ireland) Act, 1957, 5 & 6 Eliz. 2, c. 25.

[104] *Ibid.*, s. 2(3), (4).

[105] See generally North, *Occupiers' Liability* (1971) and The Law Commission, Working Paper No. 52, *Liability for Damages or Injury to Trespassers and Related Questions of Occupiers' Liability* (1973), which contains various recommendations for bringing trespassers within the ambit of the English Act.

[106] Occupiers' Liability (Scotland) Act, 1960, 8 & 9 Eliz. 2, c. 30.

[107] Occupiers' Liability Act, 1962, N.Z.S. 1962, c. 31. The New Zealand Torts and General Law Reform Committee's *Report on Occupiers' Liability to Trespassers* (1970) recommended certain amendments to the 1962 Act in order to apply it to trespassers as well as lawful entrants, however these recommendations have not been adopted as of yet.

[108] See Fleming, *Torts* (8th ed. 1992), at p. 449.

[109] Alberta Occupiers' Liability Act (R.S.A. 1980, c. O-3), British Columbia (R.S.B.C. 1996, c. 337), Manitoba (R.S.M. 1987, c. O8), Ontario (R.S.O. 1990, c. O.2), P.E.I. (R.S.P.E.I. 1988, c. O-2), and Nova Scotia (S.N.S. 1996, c. 27.)

[110] The Prince Edward Island Occupiers' Liability Act, R.S.P.E.I. 1988, c. O-2, is substantially and structurally similar to the Ontario Act and so has not been separately described. Differences occur, for example, in the definition of "premises" in s. 1 and in the generality of the clause preserving higher obligations imposed by other rules which is found in s. 8. Some other minor differences also exist.

[111] See the New Brunswick Law Reform Act, S.N.B. 1993, c. L-1.2, s. 2, which came into force on June 1, 1994. It states that the "law of occupier's liability is abolished" and that "[a]ny matter which, before the commencement of this section, would have been determined in accordance with the law of occupier's liability shall be determined in accordance with other rules of liability". See *Jones v. Richard* (2000), 226 N.B.R. (2d) 207 (C.A.), "reasonable care to prevent injury".

[112] *Stacey v. Anglican Churches of Canada (Diocesan Synod of Eastern Newfoundland & Labrador)* (1999), 47 C.C.L.T. (2d) 153 (Nfld. C.A.).

1. ALBERTA

The Province of Alberta, following the Report on Occupiers' Liability of the Alberta Institute of Law Research and Reform, was the first Canadian province to bring in legislative reform.[113] The Act defines an "occupier" as a person who is in physical possession of premises or a person who has responsibility for and control over, the condition of premises, the activities conducted on those premises and the persons allowed to enter those premises.[114] This definition is exhaustive and is not intended to be broadened by the common law.[115] Express recognition is given to the possibility of there being more than one occupier.[116] The word "premises" is defined to exclude moveable structures other than staging, scaffolding and similar structures, and trailers used or designed for use as residences, shelters or offices. It also excludes vehicles or vessels other than railway locomotives, railway cars and ships. Poles, standards, pylons and wires used for the purpose of transmission of electric power or communications or transportation of passengers are specifically included in the definition of premises.[117]

The Act provides for a common duty of care in relation to the condition of the premises, activities on the premises and the conduct of third parties on the premises, thus abolishing the "activity duty" — "occupancy duty" dichotomy.[118] The "common duty" is a duty to "take such care as in all the circumstances of the case is reasonable to see that the visitor will be reasonably safe in using the premises for the purposes for which he is invited or permitted by the occupier to be there or is permitted by law to be there".[119] The courts have interpreted this definition as bringing occupiers' liability under the umbrella of the ordinary negligence action, measuring the existence and scope of the duty by the broad standards of foreseeability of harm to the entrant and reasonable conduct.[120] It has been held that one factor in fixing the standard by which it is to be judged

---

[113] The Occupiers' Liability Act, S.A. 1973, c. 79 (now R.S.A. 1980, c. O-3].

[114] See *Reid v. Calgary Board of Education*, [1997] A.J. No. 621, school board not occupier of sidewalk in Alberta, but Ontario and Manitoba definition broader than Alberta's.

[115] In *Reid v. Calgary Board of Education*, [1977] A.J. No. 621, the Alberta Court of Queen's Bench commented that ". . . the definition of occupier in the Ontario and Manitoba statutes is clearly much broader than that contained in the Alberta statute".

[116] The Occupiers' Liability Act, *supra*, n. 113, s. 1(c). In addition, the Federal Crown may be considered an occupier. See *Stuart v. Canada, supra*, n. 2; *Tobler v. Canada (Minister of the Environment)*, [1991] 3 W.W.R. 638 (Fed. Ct. T.D.).

[117] *Ibid.*, s. 1(d).

[118] *Ibid.*, s. 6.

[119] *Ibid.*, s. 5. See *Preston v. Canadian Legion Kingsway Branch No. 175* (1981), 123 D.L.R. (3d) 645 (Alta. C.A.), affirmative duty to use reasonable care imposed.

[120] *Nasser v. Rumford* (1977), 5 Alta. L.R. (2d) 84 (C.A.); *Lyster v. Fortress Mountain Resorts Ltd.* (1978), 6 Alta. L.R. (2d) 388; *Flint v. Edmonton Country Club Ltd.* (1980), 26 A.R. 39 (Q.B.); see *Rai v. Koziar*, [2000] A.J. No. 1390, discussing foreseeability.

whether the occupier has taken "such care as in all the circumstances of the case is reasonable", is the assumption, which the occupier is entitled to make, that a visitor will exercise reasonable care for safety in light of the visitor's own knowledge.[121] This assumption, though, only goes to establishing the required standard of care. The unreasonable actions of a visitor are not relevant to whether an occupier has met that standard of care, although they are relevant for assessing contributory negligence.[122]

The Act stipulates that the common duty is owed to entrants who would previously have been categorized as licensees, invitees and contractual entrants. With the exception of a person whose presence on the premises becomes unlawful after entry and who is taking reasonable steps to leave the premises, the common duty is not owed to trespassers.[123] In *Bossert v. Grover Petroleums*,[124] the court interpreted s. 5 of the Act, which sets out the common duty, rather restrictively, holding that the words "for the purposes for which he is invited" lead to the conclusion that the duty is owed only so long as the visitor stays where expected to stay, doing what is expected to be done. On this reasoning, the occupier was not held liable to the plaintiff who fell down the basement steps in the open rear area of a store while trying to find a clerk she could pay for her purchases. The implication of such a holding would seem to be that, once the visitor wanders from the permitted course, the visitor becomes a trespasser, the logic of which is not overwhelming.

The Act states that an occupier is not under an obligation to discharge the common duty of care to a visitor in respect of "risks willingly accepted by the visitor as his".[125] This provision has been interpreted as preserving the common law defence of *volenti non fit injuria*.[126] In keeping with the narrowing of this defence in the common law and in other jurisdictions,[127] the Alberta Court of Appeal has established two limitations on its use: first, the occupier must show

---

[121] *Epp. v. Ridgetop Builders Ltd.* (1978), 7 C.C.L.T. 291 (Alta. C.A.); *Flint v. Edmonton Country Club, supra,* n. 120.

[122] See *Preston v. Canadian Legion Kingsway Branch No. 175* (1981), 123 D.L.R. (3d) 645 (Alta. C.A.); *Gabrieau v. T. Eaton Co.* (1987), 54 Alta. L.R. (2d) 120 (Q.B.); *Lorenz v. Ed-Mon Developments Ltd.* (1991), 79 Alta. L.R. (2d) 193 (C.A.). A number of cases have determined that the visitor's lack of reasonable care was wholly responsible for the injury suffered and have not determined whether the occupiers met their common duty. See *Epp. v. Ridgetop Builders Ltd, supra,* n. 121; *Meier v. Qualico Developments Ltd. et al.,* [1985] 1 W.W.R. 637 (Alta. C.A.).

[123] The Occupiers' Liability Act, R.S.A. 1980, c. O-3, s. 12(1), setting out lower standard.

[124] (1977), 2 Alta. L.R. (2d) 362 (Dist. Ct.). See also *Laws v. Wright,* [2000] A.J. No. 127, feeding someone else's horse "off limits". But see also *Anderson v. L.J. Ryder Investments Ltd.,* [2000] A.J. No. 268, where "off limits" principle not used since occupier did not enforce it.

[125] The Occupiers' Liability Act, R.S.A. 1980, c. O-3, s. 7.

[126] *Epp v. Ridgetop Builders Ltd., supra,* n. 121. See *Lyster v. Fortress Mountain Resorts Ltd., supra,* n. 120; *Preston v. Canadian Legion of British Empire Service League, Kingsway Branch No. 175* (1981), 29 A.R. 532 (C.A.).

[127] See *Dube v. Labar* (1986), 27 D.L.R. (4th) 653 at p. 658-59 (S.C.C.) and *Waldick v. Malcolm* (1991), 8 C.C.L.T. (2d) 1 (S.C.C.).

that the plaintiff "was aware of the 'virtually certain risk of harm'", and, second, "assumed both the physical and legal risk of entry".[128]

The Act expressly deals with the effect of a warning and provides that a warning without more will not absolve the occupier from liability unless "in all the circumstances the warning is enough to enable the visitor to be reasonably safe".[129]

Except in the case of a person who is empowered or permitted by law to enter premises without the permission of the occupier of those premises (*e.g.*, a firefighter, a police officer with a warrant, a condominium owner[130] or certain statutory inspectors) the liability of an occupier "may be extended, restricted, modified or excluded by express agreement or express notice but no restriction, modification or exclusion of that liability is effective unless reasonable steps were taken to bring it to the attention of the visitor".[131] There were common law decisions recognizing the right of an occupier to limit liability to entrants by means of an exculpatory clause in a contract or a notice posted on the property.[132] These cases indicate that the courts will construe the wording of an exculpatory provision strictly and general disclaimers will not ordinarily suffice.[133] The Act provides that where an occupier is bound by a contract to permit strangers to the contract to enter or use the premises, the liability of the occupier under the Act to the stranger cannot be enlarged, restricted or modified by the contract.[134]

The Act deals with the liability of the occupier for injury caused by the negligence of an independent contractor whom the occupier has engaged, and provides that the occupier will not be liable if the occupier exercised reasonable care in the selection and supervision of the independent contractor and it was reasonable that the work the independent contractor was engaged to do should

---

[128] *Murray v. Bitango* (1996), 40 Alta. L.R. (3d) 110 (C.A.); leave to appeal refused [1996] S.C.C.A. 37.

[129] *Supra*, n. 125, s. 9. See *Nasser v. Rumford* (1977), 2 C.C.L.T. 209, at p. 213; revd on a different point 5 Alta. L.R. (2d) 84 (C.A.); *Laws v. Wright, supra,* n. 124, warning sufficient.

[130] *La Fontaine v. Condominium Plan No. C.D. 1066* (1995), A.J. No. 49 (Q.B.).

[131] *Supra*, n. 125, s. 8. See also *Lyster v. Fortress Mountain Resorts Ltd., supra*, n. 120, where exclusion clause construed *contra proferentem* as not excluding occupiers' liability for negligence.

[132] *Ashdown v. Samuel Williams & Sons Ltd.*, [1957] 1 All E.R. 35 (C.A.); *Richardson v. St. James Ct. Apts. Ltd.* (1963), 38 D.L.R. (2d) 25 (Ont.); affd 40 D.L.R. (2d) 297; *Beauchamp v. Consolidated Paper Corp.* (1961), 29 D.L.R. (2d) 254 (S.C.).

[133] See, for example, *Canada Steamship Lines Ltd. v. R.*, [1952] A.C. 192, and *Lyster v. Fortress Mountain Resorts Ltd., supra*, n. 120. Under statute, the Alberta Court of Appeal reasoned in *Murray v. Bitango, supra*, n. 128 that a defendant could not avoid liability by verbally warning the plaintiff not to use a cattle roping chute without any qualification or explanation. This did not, the court held, constitute putting the chute "off limits", as referred to in *Waldick v. Malcolm, supra*, n. 127.

[134] *Supra*, n. 125, s. 10.

have been undertaken.[135] The latter condition deals with inherently dangerous activities where the mere undertaking of a given type of work in itself creates a substantial risk of harm to persons entering the premises. In such cases Canadian courts have held that an occupier cannot be insulated from liability by retaining an independent contractor.[136] The immunity provided for in this provision of the Act is made subject to any other statute which imposes liability on an occupier for the negligence of the independent contractor.

The Act provides for a separate duty of care with respect to trespassers. An occupier is liable to a trespasser only if the "injury . . . results from the occupier's willful or reckless conduct".[137] In keeping with the traditional common law duty owed to a trespasser, it has been held that the willfulness goes not to the conduct which occasions the injury but to the injury itself. Thus, the duty owed to a trespasser is not to injure the trespasser willfully or recklessly,[138] the same low standard of care as was owed to trespassers at common law prior to the Supreme Court of Canada's decision in *Veinot v. Kerr-Addison*.[139]

A more stringent duty is prescribed with respect to a child trespasser in circumstances where an occupier knows or has reason to know that a child trespasser is on the premises and that the condition of or activities on the premises create a danger of death or serious bodily harm to that child. The occupier owes a duty to the child to take "such care as in all the circumstances of the case is reasonable to see that the child will be reasonably safe from that danger". The age of the child, the ability of the child to appreciate the danger and the burden on the occupier of eliminating the danger or protecting the child as compared to the risk of danger to the child, are all factors to be considered in determining whether duty of care to a child trespasser has been discharged.[140] "Child" is not defined in the Act, but a 16-year-old high school student has been held not to be a child trespasser.[141]

At common law Canadian courts have freely applied the law of occupiers' liability to damaged property.[142] Likewise, the Act expressly provides that the statutory duties of care are applicable to property brought on to the occupier's premises by the entrant regardless of whether the property is owned by the entrant or some other person. The Act specifically provides, however, that the

---

[135] *Supra*, n. 125, s. 11. See also *Popjes v. Otis Canada Inc.* (1995), 171 A.R. 376 (Q.B.), in which the court held that an occupier could not be liable for an accident occurring in its elevator when it had hired a company specializing in elevators to maintain it.

[136] *Savage v. Wilby*, [1954] S.C.R. 376; *Randall's Paints Ltd. v. Tanner*, [1969] 2 O.R. 169; *Custom Ceilings v. S.W. Fleming & Co.* (1970), 12 D.L.R. (3d) 209.

[137] *Supra*, n. 125, s. 12.

[138] *Cullen v. Rice* (1981), 15 C.C.L.T. 180 (Alta. C.A.).

[139] *Supra*, n. 20.

[140] *Supra*, n. 125, s. 13. See *Arnold v. Gillies* (1978), 8 Alta. L.R. (2d) 21 (Dist. Ct.).

[141] *Cullen v. Rice, supra*, n. 138 (Alta. C.A.).

[142] *Grossman v. The King*, [1952] 1 S.C.R. 571; *Redwell Servicing Co. v. Lane Wells Can. Co.* (1955), 16 W.W.R. 615 (Alta. C.A.); *Janes v. Triton Centres* (1969), 4 D.L.R. (3d) 327 (N.S. Co. Ct.).

occupier is not liable to an entrant in respect of loss or damage to property the entrant brings on to the premises if the damage or loss results from the act of a third party. It is further provided that the Act does not apply to or affect any liability of an occupier in respect of personal property arising by virtue of a contract of carriage, a bailment or the Innkeepers Act.[143] Subsection 14(3) of the Act appears to contemplate a direct action against the occupier, under the Act, by a non-entrant whose personal property has been brought on to the premises by an entrant and has suffered damages. It provides that "[w]hen a person in an action under this Act claims damages in respect of the destruction or loss of, or damage to, property of which he is the owner and which was brought on to the occupier's premises, the occupier is entitled to raise any defence to the claim that he would be entitled to raise if the claimant were the visitor or trespasser, as the case may be".[144]

The Act expressly provides that the Contributory Negligence Act and the Tort-Feasors Act apply to actions brought under the Occupiers' Liability Act.[145] This is not surprising, for Canadian courts have in the past utilized contributory negligence legislation to reduce the recovery of plaintiffs in actions founded on occupiers' liability.[146] The Act makes it clear that there will also be contribution between joint tortfeasors where there is more than one occupier of the premises.

The provincial Crown is bound by the Act and is responsible as an occupier of premises.[147] However, neither the Crown nor any municipal corporation is liable as an "occupier" when the premises involved is a highway or private street.[148]

2. BRITISH COLUMBIA

Shortly after the Alberta Act was passed, British Columbia followed suit. A Uniform Occupiers' Liability Act had been prepared by the Conference of Commissioners on Uniformity of Legislation in Canada in 1973[149] and this Act was essentially adopted by the British Columbia legislature.[150]

"Occupier" is given the same definition as in the Alberta Act.[151] "Premises" is defined as including land; non-portable structures; trailers and portable structures designed or used for a residence, business or shelter; ships and vessels;

---

[143] *Supra*, n. 125, s. 14.
[144] See *Drive-Yourself Ltd. v. Burnside* (1959), 59 S.R. (N.S.W.) 390 (C.A.), an Australian common law decision where the plaintiff was the finance company and not the driver of the damaged car.
[145] *Supra*, n. 125, s. 15.
[146] *Whitehead v. North Vancouver*, [1939] 3 D.L.R. 83; *Brown v. B. & F. Theatres*, *supra*, n. 94; see also *Mitchell v. C.N.R.*, *supra*, n. 35.
[147] *Supra*, n. 125, s. 16.
[148] *Ibid.*, s. 4. Other bases of liability, however, may be available.
[149] Consolidation of Uniform Acts, 1973, c. 32.
[150] Occupiers' Liability Act, S.B.C. 1974, c. 60, as amended [now R.S.B.C. 1996, c. 337].
[151] *Ibid.*, s. 1. See *Bennett v. Kailua Estates Ltd.* (1997), 32 C.C.L.T. (2d) 217 (B.C.C.A.), absent manager of bar not occupier; *Braid Estate v. Whistler River Adventures*, [2000] B.C.J. No. 2442, water rafting outfit not occupier of river.

railway locomotives, railway cars, vehicles and aircraft "while not in operation".[152]

The Act establishes a common duty of care, which is defined as "a duty to take that care that in all the circumstances of the case is reasonable to see that a person, and that person's property, on the premises, and property on the premises of a person, whether or not that person personally enters on the premises, will be reasonably safe in using the premises".[153] This standard does not "... create a presumption of negligence against 'the occupier of the premises' whenever a person is injured on the premises".[154] The plaintiff "... must still be able to point to some act (or some failure to act) on the part of the occupier which caused the injury complained of before liability can be established".[155] As with the Alberta statute, there is evidence that this definition may be more restrictively applied than the inclusive definition found in the Ontario Act.[156] The duty applies in relation to the condition of the premises, activities on the premises[157] and the conduct of third parties on the premises.[158] As is the case under the Alberta legislation, the duty is applicable to property damage as well as personal injury.[159] The wording of the section could be interpreted as giving a non-entrant owner of property a direct cause of action against the occupier.

Although a few early cases under the British Columbia legislation interpreted the common duty of care established by the Act as identical to the duty of care owed to an invitee at common law,[160] most of the decisions under the Act have eschewed any reference to the common law tests as an aid in interpreting the statutory duty and have interpreted the common duty of care as embodying the general principles of negligence law.[161] In *Weiss v. Greater Vancouver Y.M.C.A.*[162] the Court of Appeal unequivocally rejected an attempt to resurrect the old specialized duty of care owed to an invitee in the face of the new language of the Act, and declared:

---

[152] *Ibid.*

[153] *Ibid.*, s. 3(1).

[154] *Bauman v. Stein* (1991), 78 D.L.R. (4th) 118, at p. 127 (B.C.C.A.).

[155] *Ibid.*

[156] *Gardner v. Unimet Investments Ltd.* (1996), 19 B.C.L.R. (3d) 196 (C.A.).

[157] See *Wiley v. Tymar Management Inc.*, [1994] B.C.J. No. 3045; affd [1997] B.C.J. No. 770 (C.A.), ladder not "premises".

[158] Occupiers' Liability Act, *supra*, n. 144, s. 3(2).

[159] Robertson v. Stang, [1997] B.C.J. No. 2022 (S.C.), theft from locker led to liability of landlord.

[160] *Hutchinson v. Woodward Stores (Mayfair) Ltd.* (1977), 4 B.C.L.R. 309; *Story v. City of Prince George* (1979), 11 B.C.L.R. 224; *Thomas v. Super-Valu Stores Ltd.* (1978), 9 B.C.L.R. 210.

[161] *Jacobson v. Kinsmen Club of Nanaimo* (1976), 71 D.L.R. (3d) 227 (B.C.); *Roed v. Tahsis Co.* (1977), 4 B.C.L.R. 176; *Lock v. Bouffioux* (1978), 7 B.C.L.R. 184; *Woelbern v. Liberty Leasing of Canada No. 3 Ltd.* (1978), 8 B.C.L.R. 352; *Rheaume v. Gowland and Penticton, Fish, Game & Rifle Club* (1978), 8 B.C.L.R. 93 (S.C.); *Kirk v. Trerise* (1979), 14 B.C.L.R. 310; revd (1981), 7 A.C.W.S. 493 (B.C.C.A.); *Wiebe v. Funk's Supermarket Ltd.* (1980), 19 B.C.L.R. 227; *Duncan v. Braaten* (1980), 21 B.C.L.R. 369; *Rendall v. Ewert*, [1989] 6 W.W.R. 97 (B.C.C.A.).

[162] (1979), 11 B.C.L.R. 112, at p. 118 (C.A.).

In my view, s. 3(1) is comprehensive, in the sense that it fully and clearly imposes a duty on an occupier and defines the standard of care necessary to fulfill that duty. Thus, in my judgment, it is unnecessary to an understanding of the standard prescribed by the subsection to refer to any of the specially formulated standards of care laid down in the common law cases. Indeed, to do so is more likely to mislead than assist in understanding what the subsection says.

The Act provides that the common duty of care established by the Act does not relieve "an occupier of premises of a duty to exercise, in a particular case, a higher standard of care which, in that case, is incumbent on the person because of an enactment or rule of law imposing special standards of care on particular classes of person".[163] In *Stein v. Hudson's Bay Co.*[164] it was argued that the defendant, as an invitor, owed to the plaintiff invitee a higher, common law duty of care which was preserved by s. 3(4) of the Act. The court held that the standard of care an occupier owes to an invitee is no different than the standard of care imposed by s. 3(1) of the Act and, therefore, s. 3(4) was inapplicable. In a subsequent case[165] the Court of Appeal expressly declined to decide or comment upon this issue as it was neither argued nor pleaded in the case on appeal.

The British Columbia Act originally followed the Alberta legislation in providing that an occupier had no duty of care to a person in respect of "risks willingly accepted by that person as his own risks".[166] In 1989, however, the Act was amended to establish a limited duty of care owed by occupiers to persons willingly accepting a risk as their own and to persons trespassing on agricultural land. The Act was further amended in 1998 to include people entering rural and other enumerated premises.[167] In those circumstances, an occupier owes a duty not to create a danger with intent to do harm to the entrants or their property and owes a duty not to act with reckless disregard for the safety of the entrants or their property.[168] Unlike the Alberta Act, the British Columbia legislation does not contain a provision specifically dealing with the effect of a warning. Presumably, however, the fact that a warning was given would be a fact to be considered in determining whether the plaintiff had willingly accepted the risk involved. It would also be an important factor in determining whether an occupier had taken reasonable care in the circumstances.

---

[163] R.S.B.C. 1996, c. 337, s. 3(4). See *Leischner et al. v. West Kootenay Power & Light Co. Ltd.* (1986), 24 D.L.R. (4th) 641 (B.C.C.A.), holding a utility company to a higher standard of care than the ordinary negligence standard.

[164] (1976), 70 D.L.R. (3d) 723 (B.C.).

[165] *Weiss v. Y.M.C.A.*, *supra*, n. 162.

[166] The Occupiers' Liability Act, R.S.B.C., *supra*, n. 150, s. 3(3) [am. S.B.C. 1989, c. 64, s. 31]. This section was recently interpreted as preserving the defence of *volenti non fit injuria*. See *Bains v. Hill* (1992), 68 B.C.L.R. (2d) 193 (C.A.) applying the reasoning in *Waldick v. Malcolm*, [1991] 2 S.C.R. 456, 8 C.C.L.T. (2d) 1, to the British Columbia Act.

[167] *Ibid.*, ss. 3(3), 3.1, 3.2, 3.3 [am. S.B.C. 1998, c. 12, s. 1].

[168] *Smith v. Atson Farms*, [1997] B.C.J. No. 677, no liability when bull injured trespasser because no intent or recklessness.

The Act deals with contracting out of the statutory duty and provides that "if an occupier is permitted by law to extend, restrict, modify or exclude the occupier's duty of care to any person by express agreement, or by express stipulation or notice, the occupier must take reasonable steps to bring that extension, restriction, modification or exclusion to the attention of that person".[169] This general rule is subject to two restrictions. Firstly, an occupier cannot contract out of liability to a person who is a stranger to the contract or a person who is empowered or permitted to enter or use the premises without the consent or permission of the occupier.[170] Secondly, where an occupier is bound by contract to permit persons who are not privy to the contract to enter or use the premises, the duty of care owed to such persons is not affected by anything to the contrary in the contract.[171]

The British Columbia courts have in some cases allowed an occupier to restrict its liability where an exclusionary clause is printed on a ski lift ticket and on signs around the ski hill, finding that these measures constituted "reasonable steps to bring that exclusion ... to the attention of that person".[172] Where, however, a foreign tourist who had never before skied at a North American resort claimed that she was not aware of the exclusionary clause printed on her lift ticket or posted at the mountain, the British Columbia Supreme Court found that this standard was not satisfied.[173] Further, a release of liability signed in exchange for a season's pass at a ski hill is sufficient to restrict the occupier's liability, even where the plaintiff chose not to read the release.[174] In *Karroll v. Silver Star Mountain Resorts Ltd.*[175] McLachlin (then C.J.S.C.) identified three exceptions to the rule that "where a party has signed a written agreement it is immaterial to the question of his liability under it that he has not read it and does not know its contents".[176] These are: first, where *non est factum* is proved; second, where "the agreement has been induced by fraud or misrepresentation"; and third, "[w]here the party seeking to enforce the document knew or had reason to know of the other's mistake as to its terms".[177] As with the exclusion of liability at common law, the effectiveness of the limitation on liability in a

---

[169] *Ibid.*, s. 4(1).

[170] *Ibid.*, s. 4(2).

[171] *Ibid.*, s. 4(3).

[172] *Ibid.*, s. 4(1). See, for example, *Blomberg v. Blackomb Skiing Enterprises Ltd.* (1992), 64 B.C.L.R. (2d) 51 (S.C.); *McQuary v. Big White Ski Resort Ltd.*, [1993] B.C.J. No. 1956.

[173] *Greeven v. Blackomb Skiing Enterprises Ltd.*, (1994) 22 C.C.L.T. (2d) 265 (B.C.S.C.). Esson C.J. distinguished cases in which the exclusion clause had been upheld on the basis that the plaintiffs in those cases "... had skied many times at the same and other mountains and [were] aware, at least in a general way, of the existence of exclusionary clauses".

[174] *Ocsko v. Cypress Bowl Recreations Ltd.* (1992), 74 B.C.L.R. (2d) 159 (C.A.); see also *Mayer v. Big White Ski Resort Ltd.*, [1997] B.C.J. No. 725 (B.C.S.C.); affd [1998] B.C.J. No. 2155.

[175] (1988), 33 B.C.L.R. (2d) 160 (S.C.).

[176] *L'Estrange v. F. Graucob Ltd.*, [1934] 2 K.B. 394 at p. 406.

[177] *Karroll, supra*, n. 175, at p. 164.

particular case depends on whether the negligence alleged fits within the scope of the exclusionary clause.[178]

An occupier is not liable under the Act where damage is caused by the negligence of an independent contractor engaged by the occupier if, in all the circumstances, the occupier exercised reasonable care in the selection and supervision of the independent contractor and it was reasonable that the work the independent contractor was engaged to do should have been undertaken.[179] The Act, however, declares the paramountcy of any other statute imposing liability on an occupier for the negligence of the independent contractor.[180] In *Lewis (Guardian ad litem of) v. British Columbia*,[181] where a rock fell on a motorist it was held that the government's duty to maintain the road was non-delegable and that the Occupier's Liability Act did not limit the Crown's liability.

In contrast to the Alberta Act, the British Columbia Act expressly deals with the liability of landlords towards tenants and other entrants, casting upon landlords, in certain circumstances, the statutory duty of care owed by an occupier. The Act provides that "if premises are occupied or used by virtue of a tenancy under which a landlord is responsible for the maintenance or repair of the premises, it is the duty of the landlord to show toward any person who, or whose property, may be on the premises the same care in respect of risks arising from failure on the landlord's part in carrying out the landlord's responsibility, as is required by this Act to be shown by an occupier of premises toward persons entering on or using the premises".[182] It is further provided that a landlord shall not be deemed to be in default of duty under this provision of the Act unless the landlord's default is such as to be actionable at the suit of the occupier-tenant. This is subject to the overriding provision that nothing in the section shall be construed as relieving a landlord of any duty apart from the section.[183] "Tenancy" is defined quite broadly in the Act.[184]

It is expressly provided that the Act "does not apply to or affect the liability of (a) an employer in respect of his duties to his employee; (b) a person by virtue of a contract for the hire of, or for the carriage for reward of persons or property in, any vehicle, vessel, aircraft, or other means of transport; (c) a person under the Hotel Keepers Act; or (d) a person by virtue of a contract of bailment".[185]

---

[178] *Mayer v. Big White Ski Resort Ltd.* [1977] B.C.J. No. 725, at para. 26. See also *Canada Steamship Lines Ltd. v. R.*, [1952] A.C. 192, and *McGivney v. Rustico Summer Haven (1977) Limited* (1986), 64 Nfld. & P.E.I.R. 358 (C.A.), which dealt with the same question under the P.E.I. legislation.

[179] *Milina v. Bartsch* (1985), 49 B.C.L.R. (2d) 33 (S.C.); affd 49 B.C.L.R. (2d) 99 (C.A.).

[180] The Occupiers' Liability Act, R.S.B.C. 1979, c. 303, s. 5.

[181] [1997] 3 S.C.R. 1145.

[182] *Ibid.*, s. 6(1). See *Blake v. Kensche* (1990), 3 C.C.L.T. (2d) 189 (B.C.S.C.), landlord liable when child fell into well. See also *Zavaglia v. Maq Holdings Ltd.* (1986), 6 B.C.L.R. (2d) 286 (C.A.).

[183] *Ibid.* See *Zavaglia v. Maq Hldg. Ltd.* (1986), 6 B.C.L.R. (2d) 286 (C.A.).

[184] *Ibid.*, s. 1.

[185] *Ibid.*, s. 9.

The Negligence Act is expressly made applicable to any action under the Act.[186]

The provincial Crown is bound by the Act, but public highways, public and private roads and certain other roads, which are occupied by the Crown or a municipality, are specifically exempted.[187] This does not mean that the Crown is not liable for negligent maintenance of highways; it means merely that its liability "must be assessed without regard to the provisions of that Act".[188]

3. ONTARIO

In 1972 the Ontario Law Reform Commission released its Report on Occupiers' Liability recommending the adoption of an occupiers' liability act and suggesting the provisions of a draft act. Its recommendations were accepted by the Ontario government and incorporated in the Occupiers' Liability Act,[189] which came into force on September 8, 1980, along with a companion statute, the Trespass to Property Act.[190] However, the legislature, in response to strong pressure on behalf of agricultural and recreational groups, deviated in a major way from the Commission's draft act, substantially insulating certain landowners from occupiers' liability.[191]

The definition of "occupier" in the Act is similar to the definition found in the Alberta and British Columbia statutes. An occupier "includes, (a) a person who is in physical possession of premises, or (b) a person who has responsibility for and control over the condition of premises or the activities there carried on, or control over persons allowed to enter the premises, despite the fact that there is more than one occupier of the same premises".[192] In contrast to the definitions found in the Alberta and British Columbia Acts, the definition in the Ontario Act is inclusive rather than exhaustive in form. It is much broader than the defini-

---

[186] *Ibid.*, s. 7.

[187] *Ibid.*, s. 8.

[188] See *Lewis (Guardian ad litem of) v. British Columbia*, [1997] 3 S.C.R. 1145, at p. 1170 (*per* Cory J.).

[189] R.S.O. 1980, c. 322 [now R.S.O. 1990, c. O.2]. See Percival, "Occupiers' Liability", Law Society of Upper Canada, *Special Lectures* (1983).

[190] R.S.O. 1980, c. 511 [now R.S.O. 1990, c. T.21].

[191] R.S.O. 1980, c. 322 [now R.S.O. 1990, c. O.2].

[192] *Ibid.*, s. 1(a). In *Olinski v. Johnson* (1997), 32 O.R. (3d) 653, a lacrosse team signed an arena rental contract which provided that the team would "provide policing and/or supervision at all times." The Ontario Court of Appeal held that the team was an "occupier" of not just the playing surface, but also of the corridor leading to a locker room where the plaintiff referees were injured. Furthermore, although an occupier of property adjacent to a public sidewalk is not normally an "occupier" of that sidewalk (*Slumski v. Mutual Life* [1994] O.J. No. 301), in a motion for summary judgment, it was determined that a stadium adjacent to a public sidewalk may be an "occupier" of the public sidewalk when the sidewalk is used exclusively by the stadium's patrons and when the patrons have no alternative but to use the sidewalk in large numbers when exiting the stadium: *Moody v. Toronto (City)* (1996), 31 O.R. (3d) 53 (Ont. Gen. Div.). Dambrot J. disagreed with an earlier case, *Turner v. Windsor (City)* (1984), 46 O.R. (2d) 174 (Co. Ct.), in which Clements Co. Ct. J. held that the definition of "occupier" ought to be read conjunctively so that both control over the condition of the premises and responsibility for the person are required.

tions in the other Acts because of the use of the disjunctive "or" in the second part of the definition, which deals with control, rather than the conjunctive "and" which is used in the other Acts.[193] There are four separate branches to the definition, and meeting the criteria of any one of them is enough to make someone an occupier.[194]

"Premises" is defined as lands and structures and specifically includes water, ships and vessels, trailers and portable structures designed or used for residence, business or shelter, and trains, railway cars, vehicles and aircraft "except while in operation".[195] As a preliminary issue under both the Ontario and British Columbia Acts, courts will have to determine whether the specified vehicles were "in operation" at the relevant time. The rules of the common law and other applicable legislation, rather than occupiers' liability legislation, will apply if it is determined that the vehicles were "in operation".

The Act establishes a common duty of care owed to all entrants to the occupier's premises, regardless of the category the entrant would have fallen into at common law.[196] As Blair J.A. explained:

> The Act replaced with a common statutory duty the complex, arcane and inadequate common-law rules relating to liabilities of occupiers of property to trespassers, licensees and invitees. . . .
>
> It would be contrary to the scheme of the Act to fragment the duty of occupiers by the imposition of arbitrary judge-made rules applicable to different kinds of premises. . . . To do so would be to regress to the categorization of occupiers' liability which characterized the common law. It would also defeat the statutory purpose of establishing a common duty of care.[197]

The duty is defined as "a duty to take such care as in all the circumstances of the case is reasonable to see that persons entering on the premises, and the property brought on the premises by those persons are reasonably safe while on the premises".[198]

The Act "assimilates occupiers' liability with the modern law of negligence. The duty is not absolute, and occupiers are not insurers liable for any damages suffered by persons entering their premises. Their responsibility is only to take 'such care as in all the circumstances of the case is reasonable.'"[199] The words "in all the circumstances of the case" invite an analysis of what constitutes

---

[193] The definition is not so broad, however, as to cover a former property owner who built a hot tub on the property which did not comply with minimum safety requirements, where the former property owner no longer exerted any control over the property: *Ekkebus v. Lauinger* (1994), 22 C.C.L.T. (2d) 148 (Ont. Gen. Div.).

[194] *Lemieux v. Porcupine Snowmobile Club of Timmins Inc.,* [1999] O.J. No. 1779 (C.A.), at para. 5.

[195] Occupiers' Liability Act, *supra*, n. 191, s. 1. Accident on a body of inland water subject to the Act, *Ordon Estate v. Grail,* [1998] 3 S.C.R. 437.

[196] *Ibid.,* ss. 2 and 3(1).

[197] *Waldick v. Malcolm* (1989), 2 C.C.L.T. (2d) 22, at pp. 27 and 31 (Ont. C.A.); affd [1991] 2 S.C.R. 456, 8 C.C.L.T. (2d) 1.

[198] Occupiers' Liability Act, R.S.O. 1990, c. O.2, s. 3(1).

[199] *Waldick v. Malcolm, supra,* n. 197, at p. 30, 2 C.C.L.T. (Ont. C.A.).

reasonable care that is very specific to each situation.[200] This analysis may include a consideration of customary practices. The existence of a customary practice must be established by the person seeking to rely on it and if the practice is unreasonable in itself, or otherwise unacceptable to the court, it will not discharge the duty of care owed by an occupier under the Act.[201]

The common duty of care applies equally to the condition of the premises and activities carried out on the premises.[202] Furthermore, the duty extends to property damage as well as personal injury.[203] It is, however, unclear from the drafting whether the Act applies where a non-entrant sues an occupier in respect of damage to the non-entrant's property which occurred on the premises. The courts have clearly accepted that this Act changes the common law, bringing in a new method of handling these cases.[204]

The duty of reasonable care applies "except in so far as the occupier of premises is free to and does restrict, modify or exclude the occupier's duty".[205] The Act does not elaborate on the means by which the occupier's duty can be modified but it appears that the words "in so far as the occupier of premises is free to" will be interpreted as importing the methods of excluding liability which were recognized at common law, *i.e.*, by agreement or by exhibiting a notice.[206] The Act provides that the occupier must take reasonable steps to bring any restriction, modification or exclusion to the attention of the plaintiff.[207] It further enacts that the duty of care cannot be restricted or excluded by any contract to which the plaintiff is not a party, whether or not the occupier is bound by the

---

[200] *Waldick v. Malcolm, supra*, n. 197. See also *Mortimer v. Cameron* (1994), 17 O.R. (2d) 1, rental property owner's duty to inspect stairway.

[201] *Ibid.*

[202] Occupiers' Liability Act, R.S.O. 1990, c. O.2, s. 3(2). An activity includes apprehension of a shoplifter in a store, see *Pope v. Route 66 Clothing,* [1997] O.J. No. 3211; affd [1998] O.J. No. 5885. Liability for injury resulting from ". . . an activity carried on on the premises" has been resisted by the Ontario courts on a number of occasions: see, for example, *Fitkin Estate (Litigation administrator of) v. Latimer*, [1997] O.J. No. 1449 (C.A.) (Q.L.), residential occupier not responsible for plaintiff who fell into pool from safety railing after consuming alcohol; *Mortimer v. Cameron, supra*, n. 200, tenant not responsible for permanent injury resulting when plaintiff fell through wall after consuming alcohol. In at least one case, however, an Ontario court has found an occupier responsible for activities carried on on the premises where the injury which occurred was foreseeable: see "The Occupier's Responsibility to Protect Guests from Themselves: *Stringer v. Ashley*" (1994), 16 Advocates' Q. 506.

[203] *Ibid.*, ss. 2 and 3(1).

[204] *McCrindle v. Westin Ltd.* (1985), 35 C.C.L.T. 183 (Ont. H.C.) (*per* O'Brien J.).

[205] Occupiers' Liability Act, R.S.O. 1990, c. O.2, s. 3(3).

[206] See *Allison v. Rank City Wall Can. Ltd.* (1984), 6 D.L.R. (4th) 144 (Ont. H.C.), where it was held that restrictions to liability pursuant to s. 3(3) must be specific and must be brought to the attention of the visitor. Smith J. stated that the law as set out in *Canada SS Lines Ltd. v. The King*, [1952] 1 All E.R. 305 (P.C.) should continue to apply. See also *Carson v. Thunder Bay (City of)* (1985), 52 O.R. (2d) 173 (Dist. Ct.) and *Buehl Estate v. Polar Star Enterprises Inc.* (1989), 72 O.R. (2d) 573 (H.C.).

[207] Occupiers' Liability Act, R.S.O. 1990, c. O.2, s. 5(3).

contract to permit such person to enter or use the premises.[208] This provision incorporates the doctrine of privity of contract.[209]

The Act provides that where damage is caused by the negligence of an independent contractor employed by the occupier, "the occupier is not on that account liable if in all the circumstances the occupier had acted reasonably in entrusting the work to the independent contractor, if the occupier had taken such steps, if any, as the occupier reasonably ought in order to be satisfied that the contractor was competent and that the work had been properly done, and if it was reasonable that the work performed by the independent contractor should have been undertaken".[210] Under this provision, unlike the comparable provisions in the Alberta and British Columbia Acts, the occupier must satisfy the court that it was reasonable to engage an independent contractor to do the particular work in the first place. Where the work involves technical expertise which the occupier does not have, it will not be difficult to satisfy this precondition. Both the Ontario and the British Columbia Acts provide that, where damage is sustained as a result of the negligence of an independent contractor and the occupier who engaged the independent contractor is protected from liability by this provision, then any other occupiers of the same premises are likewise exonerated from liability.[211] However, the Act expressly provides that this provision does not apply to a duty which at common law is non-delegable, nor does it affect any other legislation which provides that an occupier is liable for the negligence of an independent contractor.[212] The Act also stipulates that, unless a contract contains an express provision to the contrary, it does not by virtue of the Act, have the effect of making an occupier who has taken reasonable care, liable to a stranger to the contract for dangers due to the faulty execution of work by an independent contractor. This provision was intended to restore the original common law position which appeared to have been modified by some judicial decisions.[213]

Section 4 of the Act, like that of British Columbia, relieves occupiers of certain recreational and rural premises, which are enumerated in subsection (4), of the common duty of care established in section 3(1), and holds them to the much lower standard of care which at common law an occupier owed to trespassers, that is, "a duty to the person to not create a danger with the deliberate intent of doing harm or damage to the person or his or her property and to not act with

---

[208] *Ibid.*, s. 5(1).

[209] It is uncertain whether liability to a stranger can be enlarged by contract. See also s. 4(2), (3) of the Occupiers' Liability Act, R.S.B.C. 1996, c. 337; *cf.*, Occupiers' Liability Act, R.S.A. 1980, c. O-3, s. 10.

[210] The Occupiers' Liability Act, R.S.O. 1990, c. O.2, s. 6(1). See for third party action against elevator installer, *Bouffard v. Canada (A. G.)*, [1998] O.J. No. 1018. See also *Polny v. Cadillac Fairview Corp.,* [1993] O.J. No. 2092.

[211] *Ibid.*, s. 6(2); Occupiers' Liability Act, R.S.B.C. 1979, c. 303, s. 5(3).

[212] *Ibid.*, s. 6(3).

[213] See Ontario Law Reform Commission, *Report on Occupiers' Liability* (1972), pp. 18-19.

reckless disregard of the presence of the person or his or her property".[214] This provision was included for the purpose of protecting the interests of the agricultural community and to promote the availability of land for recreational activities.[215] The Ontario Law Reform Commission's draft Act did not contain this particular section.

Section 4(1) provides that the common duty of care "does not apply in respect of risks willingly assumed by the person who enters on the premises, but in that case the occupier owes a duty to the person to not create a danger with the deliberate intent of doing harm or damage to the person or his or her property and to not act with reckless disregard of the presence of the person or his or her property".[216] This section preserves the defence of *volenti non fit injuria* which requires actual or implied consent by the entrant to accept the risk of injury.[217] Mere knowledge of the risk by the visitor is not sufficient to support this defence.

Section 4 goes on to deem certain entrants to have "willingly assumed all risks". Subsection (2) of s. 4 provides that "a person who is on premises with the intention of committing, or in the commission of, a criminal act shall be deemed to have willingly assumed all risks and is subject to the duty of care set out in subsection (1)". The Act does not define the phrase "criminal act". Accordingly, it is not clear whether this subsection is limited to acts punishable under the Criminal Code or whether it would also extend to acts punishable under other legislation such as the Narcotics Control Act. Subsection (3) sets out three further instances where an entrant will be deemed to have "willingly assumed all risks" and as such is owed only the limited duty of care set out in sub-s. (1). Subsection (3), however, applies only with reference to the particular premises specifically designated in sub-s. (4). Generally speaking, these are rural premises, golf courses not open for playing, marked recreational trails, marked private roads, unopened road allowances and utility rights-of-way.

Subsection (3)(a) of s. 4 provides that only the limited duty of care is owed with respect to the designated premises "where the entry is prohibited under the *Trespass to Property Act*". Sections 3 through 7 of the Trespass to Property Act

---

[214] Under the Motorized Snow Vehicles Act, R.S.O. 1990, c. M.44, s. 22, snowmobilers not paying a fee to use the property and not being provided with accommodation on the property are deemed to have willingly assumed all risks for the purposes of s. 4(1) of the Occupiers' Liability Act. See *Cormack v. Mara (Twp.)* (1989), 59 D.L.R. (4th) 300 (Ont. C.A.). This section of the Motorized Snow Vehicles Act, as it appeared originally, was enacted in response to the Supreme Court of Canada's decision in *Veinot v. Kerr-Addison Mines Ltd.*, *supra*, n. 20; see *Whaley v. Hood*, [1998] O.J. No. 1785, recreational vehicle on private road on rural vacant land, no liability.

[215] Ministry of the Attorney General, *Discussion Paper on Occupiers' Liability and Trespass to Property* (May, 1979), pp. 9-11.

[216] For a comprehensive discussion of this distinction, and the meaning which should be attributed to it, see D.S. Ferguson, "The Battered Burglar: An Analysis of Section 4 and the Position of the Criminal Entrant under the Ontario Occupiers' Liability Act" (1991), 12 Advocates' Q. 257.

[217] *Waldick v. Malcolm*, *supra*, n. 197; *Leblond v. Ottawa Bd. of Education* (1984), 25 A.C.W.S. (2d) 220 (Ont. H.C.) (*per* Catzman J.); *Hewitt v. City of Etobicoke* (1986), 37 A.C.W.S. (2d) 301 (Ont. H.C.).

deal with prohibiting entry on to premises. Entry on certain premises such as gardens, fields or other land under cultivation including lawns, orchards, vineyards and woodlots, or on premises enclosed in a manner that indicates the occupier's intention to keep persons off or to keep persons off or to keep animals on the premises, is automatically prohibited.[218] With respect to other premises, entry can be prohibited by notice to that effect. Such notice can be given orally or in writing, by means of posted signs which are visible in daylight from the approach to points of access, or by means of a marking system set out in the Act.[219] There is a presumption, however, that access for lawful purposes to a door by means apparently provided and used for the purpose of access is not prohibited under the Trespass to Property Act.[220] It should be noted that the methods of giving notice of prohibition under the Trespass to Property Act do not take into account the age or understanding of the prospective entrants. Thus, if the posted prohibition signs substantially comply with the Act,[221] a young child who cannot read or appreciate the significance of a sign will nevertheless be deemed to have willingly assumed all risks of injury if injured on the premises enumerated in sub-s. (4) of the Occupiers' Liability Act.

Subsection (3)(b) of s. 4 of the Occupier's Liability Act provides that entrants to premises enumerated in sub-s. (4) will be deemed to have willingly assumed all risks even where the occupier has posted no notice in respect of entry if the occupier has not otherwise expressly permitted entry. Subsection (3)(c) of s. 4 provides that entrants to the premises enumerated in sub-s. (4) will be deemed to have willingly assumed all risks where the entry is for the purpose of a recreational activity if no fee is paid for the entry or activity and the person is not being provided with living accommodation by the occupier.

The effects of s. 4 are not necessarily benign. It injects an element of uncertainty back into this area. It also makes possible, if the courts are not careful to avoid it, harsh results much like those under the old law. It creates different categories of landowners, who are subject to different obligations and immunities. Similarly, there remain different classes of entrant, some receiving less protection than others. It will surprise no one when efforts are made by counsel to distort the meaning of "reckless disregard" in order to obtain compensation for someone who willingly assumed a risk.[222] In short, problems remain, as they always will, in a humanly administered system of law.

The Ontario Act, like the British Columbia Act, deals with the obligations of a landlord *qua* occupier. If the landlord is responsible for the repair and maintenance of the premises then the landlord owes the common duty of care

---

[218] Trespass to Property Act, R.S.O. 1990, c. T.21, s. 3(1).

[219] *Ibid.*, ss. 3(1) and 5(1).

[220] *Ibid.*

[221] *Ibid.*, s. 5(2).

[222] See *Cormack v. Mara (Twp.)*, *supra*, n. 214, where the court dismissed counsel's submission that the omission of the word "wilful" lessened the burden of proof on snowmobilers to establish the liability of an occupier.

established by the Act to all entrants, and property brought onto the premises by entrants, in respect of dangers arising from the landlord's failure to carry out that responsibility. However, a landlord will not be deemed to have defaulted in the duty toward an entrant unless the landlord's default is such as to be actionable at the suit of the tenant.[223] The term "landlord" is broadly defined.[224]

The Act replaces the common law rules with respect to occupiers' liability.[225] However, any higher liability or any duty to show a higher standard of care which is incumbent upon an occupier by virtue of any enactment or rule or law imposing special liability or standards of care on particular classes of people is expressly preserved. In particular the higher obligation owed by an innkeeper, a common carrier and a bailee are not affected by the Act. Similarly, the Act does not affect rights, duties and liabilities resulting from a master and servant relationship.[226]

The Act binds the provincial Crown, but does not apply to the Crown or any municipal corporation as occupier of a public highway or public road.[227]

The Negligence Act which deals with contributory negligence and contribution between joint tortfeasors is applicable to any cause of action under the Occupiers' Liability Act.[228]

4. MANITOBA

The Manitoba Occupiers' Liability Act[229] originally came into force on October 1, 1983.[230] It is not modelled exclusively on any one of the earlier statutes, but combines the strongest aspects of each of these earlier efforts.

As with the Ontario and Prince Edward Island legislation, an "occupier" is not exhaustively defined but instead "may include" either "a person who is in physical possession of premises" or "a person who has responsibility for, and control over, the condition of premises, the activities conducted on those premises or the persons allowed to enter the premises".[231] As with each of the other statutes, the Manitoba Act specifies that there may be more than one occupier of the same premises.[232] "Premises" are defined in a manner which is

---

[223] Occupiers' Liability Act, R.S.O. 1990, c. O.2, s. 8.

[224] *Ibid.*, s. 8(3).

[225] *Ibid.*, s. 2.

[226] *Ibid.*, s. 9.

[227] *Ibid.*, s. 10.

[228] *Ibid.*, s. 9(3). See for apportionment case, *Leblond v. Ottawa Bd. of Education, supra,* n. 217.

[229] R.S.M. 1987, c. O-8.

[230] It was then re-enacted on February 1, 1988 as part of the Re-enacted Statutes of Manitoba, 1987.

[231] Occupiers' Liability Act, R.S.M. 1987, c. O-8, ss. 1(1). The fact that an occupier has only recently acquired the premises should not afford it an excuse from complying with the duty of care set out in the Act: *Malinoski v. 2727677 Manitoba Inc.* (1996), 113 Man. R. (2d) 175 (C.A.).

[232] *Ibid.*, ss. 1(2).

virtually identical to the British Columbia statute,[233] with the exception that water is also included in the Manitoba definition, as it is in the Ontario statute.[234]

The occupier's duty is specified in subsection 3(1) of the Manitoba Act as "a duty to persons entering on the premises and to any person, whether on or off the premises, whose property is on the premises, to take such care, as in all circumstances of the case, is reasonable to see that the person or property, as the case may be, will be reasonably safe while on the premises". In *Sandberg v. Steer Holdings Ltd.*, the court interpreted subsection 3(1) as imposing a "more onerous" standard than that which existed at common law.[235] Monnin J. stated in that case that "[i]f an occupier has failed to take certain actions which if taken would have prevented injury to a person on the premises, it is incumbent upon the occupier to demonstrate that in the circumstances it was reasonable not to have taken any preventative action".[236] This standard translates into a duty to take ". . . positive steps to protect the safety of entrants".[237] Thus, it is necessary for a bar to protect its patrons from injury as a result of a fight between other intoxicated patrons.[238] The standard does not, however, translate into a standard of perfection.[239]

The occupiers' duty is owed to all categories of entrants, and so does not exclude trespassers. It does not, however, extend to "a person entering on the premises whose property is on the premises in respect of any risks willingly assumed by that person".[240] The legislated standard of care also does not preclude the application of a higher standard of care which may be required by any other Act or rule of law.[241] As has been done in each of the other Acts, the distinction between the duty owed respecting condition of the premises and activities on the premises is abolished.[242]

---

[233] Occupiers' Liability Act, R.S.B.C. 1996, c. 337, s. 1.

[234] *Ibid.*, s. 1. See Ontario Occupiers' Liability Act, R.S.O. 1990, c. O.2, s. 1.

[235] (1987), 45 Man. R. (2d) 264, at p. 268 (Q.B.).

[236] *Ibid.*

[237] *Sto. Domingo Estate v. Kenora (Town)*, [1997] M.J. No. 272, at para. 21 (Q.B.); *Sandberg, supra*, n. 235.

[238] *Pereira v. Airliner Motor (1972) Hotel Ltd.*, [1997] M.J. No. 424 (Q.B.).

[239] *Qually v. Pace Homes Ltd.* (1993), 84 Man. R. (2d) 262 (Q.B.) at p. 266; *Kopen v. 61345 Manitoba Ltd.* (1992), 79 Man. R. (2d) 250 (Q.B.); *Dowbenko Estate v. Westfair Foods Ltd.* (1996), 32 C.C.L.T. (2d) 125 (Man. Q.B.), such care is as ". . . reasonable to see that the person . . . will be reasonably safe while on the premises" does not require constant surveillance of a mat placed in a grocery store vestibule.

[240] *Ibid.*, ss. 3(3). In *Sandberg v. Steer, supra*, n. 235, Monnin J. cautioned against a wide interpretation of this defence. He adopted the statement of Moire J.A. in *Preston v. Canadian Legion, Kingsway Branch No. 175 et al.* (1981), 123 D.L.R. (3d) 645, at p. 649, that "[m]erely because a visitor, upon arrival at the premises, sees that there is a risk in using the premises cannot in my opinion relieve the occupier of the duty placed upon him by the statute".

[241] *Ibid.*, ss. 3(5).

[242] *Ibid.*, ss. 3(2).

Subject to one exception,[243] the Manitoba Act provides for restriction of the occupiers' duty by agreement, stipulation or notice, but only where, "in all the circumstances of the case it is reasonable".[244] In considering whether a restriction is reasonable, the Act specifies that "the circumstances to be considered shall include ... (a) the relationship between the occupier and the person affected; ... (b) the injury or damage suffered and the hazard causing it; ... (c) the scope of the purported restriction, modification or denial; and ... (d) the steps taken to bring the restriction, modification or denial to the attention of the persons affected thereby".[245] The Act also specifies that where an occupier restricts its duty, "... the occupier shall take reasonable steps to bring the restriction, modification or denial to the attention of the person to whom the duty is owed".[246] This is the most comprehensive legislative pronouncement on the use of exclusionary classes, and it essentially follows the case law which has addressed this issue in other jurisdictions.[247] Unlike other Acts, however, the Manitoba Act does not expressly affirm the doctrine of privity of contract.

As in Ontario and P.E.I., the Manitoba statute shields an occupier or occupiers[248] of premises from liability where damage to person or property on the premises has been caused by an independent contractor, so long as "the occupier exercised reasonable care in the selection and supervision of the independent contractor" and "it was reasonable that the work that the independent contractor was engaged to do should have been done".[249] This provision does not, however, limit the liability of an occupier imposed by any other Act for the negligence of independent contractors "engaged by the occupier".[250] The Manitoba statute also establishes, as do the British Columbia, Ontario and P.E.I. statutes, that a landlord who is "responsible for the maintenance or repair of the premises" owes a duty "to persons entering on the premises and to any person, whether on or off the premises whose property is on the premises" which is the same "as is owed by the occupier of the premises".[251]

Section 8 of the Act specifies that the Crown is bound by the Act except where the Crown is the occupier of a public highway, public road, drainage

---

[243] Subsection 4(4) specifies that an occupier shall not be permitted to restrict the duty "... with respect to a person who is empowered or permitted under the law to enter or use the premises without the consent or permission of the occupier".

[244] *Ibid.*, ss. 4(2).

[245] *Ibid.*

[246] *Ibid.*, ss. 4(3).

[247] See, for example, the exclusion of liability cases in British Columbia.

[248] *Ibid.*, ss. 5(3).

[249] *Ibid.*, ss. 5(1).

[250] *Ibid.*, ss. 5(2).

[251] *Ibid.*, ss. 6(1). Subsections (2), (5) and (6) place various conditions on the duty of care owed by the landlord, including its application to subleases, its application to any statutory or contractual lease and to leases existing at the time the Act came into force. Subsection (3) requires that a default be actionable by the occupier of the premises in order for this section to be engaged. Subsection (4) clarifies that this Act does not relieve a landlord of any other duties imposed by other Acts or law.

works or "a river, stream, watercourse, lake or other body of water except those areas thereof that have been specially developed by the Crown for recreational swimming or for the launching and landing of boats".[252] A municipality is exempted from liability where it "is the occupier of a public highway, public road, public walkway or sidewalk".[253] General exceptions are provided for an employer in relation to employees, a person under contract or "carriage for reward" of persons or property in "any vehicle, vessel, aircraft or other means of transportation", any person who fits within The Hotelkeepers Act, or any person whose liability or duty is created "by virtue of bailment".[254]

Unique to the Manitoba legislation, is the fact that the common law rules respecting the duty of care owed by an occupier and the liability of an occupier for breach of that duty are "abolished", with the exception of the common law which determines "who is or is not an occupier for the purposes of this Act".[255] In addition, the Manitoba statute specifies that no duty to take reasonable care is owed towards persons driving, riding in or being towed by an off-road vehicle (*i.e.*, snowmobile) on the premises "without the express or implied consent of the occupier".[256] There is, however, a duty not to "create a danger with deliberate intent of doing harm or damage to the person or the person's property" and a duty "not to act with reckless disregard of the presence of the person or the person's property".[257] An "off-road vehicle" is defined according to The Off-Road Vehicles Act.[258]

5. NOVA SCOTIA

The most recent addition to occupiers' liability legislation in Canada is the Nova Scotia Occupiers' Liability Act,[259] which was assented to December 20, 1996. The statute was preceded by a 1976 study paper by the Nova Scotia Law Reform Commission,[260] and by a discussion paper released by the Nova Scotia Attorney General's office.[261] Some of the proposals set forth in these papers were adopted into the new legislation. In many respects, the statute resembles the legislation already enacted by other provinces. The manner in which the Nova Scotia courts will interpret the legislation has yet to be seen.

To begin, the Nova Scotia statute follows the approach taken in the Ontario legislation by defining an "occupier" to include "a person who is in physical

---

[252] *Ibid.*, ss. 8(2).
[253] *Ibid.*, ss. 9(1).
[254] *Ibid.*, ss. 9(2).
[255] *Ibid.*, s. 2. See also *Sandberg v. Steer Holdings Ltd.*, *supra*, n. 235.
[256] *Ibid.*, ss. 3(4).
[257] *Ibid.*
[258] *Ibid.*, ss. 1(1), am. S.M. 1988-89, c. 13, s. 32.
[259] S.N.S. 1996, c. 27.
[260] Nova Scotia Law Reform Advisory Commission, *Occupiers' Liability Law: A Study Paper*, 1976, prepared by Michael Terry Hertz.
[261] *A Proposal for Reform of Occupiers' Liability in Nova Scotia*, Policy and Planning Branch, Department of Attorney General (1990).

possession of premises" or "a person who has responsibility for, and control over, the conditions of premises, the activities conducted on the premises or the persons allowed to enter the premises".[262] Unlike the Ontario legislation, however, the definition of "occupier" is specifically defined to include "an occupier at common law". This wording may provide Nova Scotia with the broadest definition of "occupier" thus far. "Premises" are defined in a similar manner to the Ontario legislation.[263]

As was suggested in the Attorney General's 1990 Discussion Paper, section 3 provides that the Act replaces the common law rules with respect to determining the duty of care that is owed by an occupier. Subsection 4(1) articulates the duty of an occupier as being ". . . to take such care as in all the circumstances of the case is reasonable to see that each person entering on the premises and the property brought on the premises by that person are reasonably safe while on the premises". As with each of the other Acts, this duty applies in respect of the condition of the premises, activities on the premises and the conduct of third parties on the premises.[264] According to subsection 4(3), whether the duty of care has been satisfied may be determined with reference to "(a) the knowledge that the occupier has or ought to have of the likelihood of persons or property being on the premises; (b) the circumstances of the entry into the premises; (c) the age of the person entering the premises; (d) the ability of the person entering the premises to appreciate the danger; (e) the effort made by the occupier to give warning of the danger concerned or to discourage persons from incurring the risk; and (f) whether the risk is one against which, in all the circumstances of the case, the occupier may reasonably be expected to offer some protection".[265] These enumerated factors appear to replace any distinctions between classes of persons entering on the premises. Despite the draft act contained in the 1976 Law Reform Commission study, no distinction is made between an "intruder" and other entrants.

A lower standard of care is, however, imposed in section 5 ". . . in respect of risks willingly assumed by the person who enters on the premises" and in respect of a person who is on the premises " . . . for the purpose of committing an offence against the person or the right of property contrary to the *Criminal Code* (Canada)" and who is deemed to willingly have assumed the risk. This lower standard requires only that the occupier not "create a danger with the deliberate intent of doing harm or damage to the person or property of that person" and that the occupier not ". . . act with reckless disregard of the presence

---

[262] Occupiers' Liability Act, S.N.S. 1996, c. 27, para. 2(a). As with the other statutes, it is stipulated in para. 2(a) that there may be more than one occupier of the same premises.

[263] Note, however, that while "railway cars" are included in both the Ontario and Nova Scotia definition of "premises", "trains" are not included in the latter. *Ibid.*, para. 2(b).

[264] *Ibid.*, ss. 4(2).

[265] *Ibid.*, ss. 4(3). As with the other Acts, the legislated standard of care owed by an occupier of premises does not, pursuant to ss. 4(4), relieve an occupier from a higher standard of care which may be imposed by some other law.

of the person or property of that person".[266] This is the same lower standard as was set out in the B.C., Ontario and P.E.I. statutes. Pursuant to section 6, persons who enter into "(a) agricultural or forestry land, (b) vacant or undeveloped rural land, (c) forested or wilderness land, (d) [closed] recreational facilities, (e) utility rights-of-way and corridors, (f) highway reservations, (g) [certain mines], (h) private roads . . . and (j) recreational trails" will also be deemed to have willingly assumed the risk and will be subject to the lower standard set out in subsection 5(1).[267]

According to subsection 7(1) of the Nova Scotia Act, an occupier may, by express agreement, express stipulation or notice either "extend or increase the duty . . ." set out in the Act or "restrict, modify or deny" it. The Act lists circumstances which are to be considered in determining the reasonableness of a restriction, modification or denial of the occupier's duty.[268] These circumstances are identical to those set out in subsection 4(2) of the Manitoba legislation. In all other respects, the Nova Scotia modification of liability provision follows existing legislation. Furthermore, an occupier[269] is not liable, pursuant to subsection 8(1), for damage caused by the negligence of an independent contractor where "the occupier exercised reasonable care in the selection of the independent contractor" and "it was reasonable that the work that the independent contractor was engaged to do should have been done". Again, the restriction of liability of an occupier where an independent contractor causes damage in the Nova Scotia legislation follows the Ontario, Manitoba and P.E.I. legislation.

Unlike the B.C., Ontario, P.E.I. and Manitoba statutes, the Nova Scotia Act does not require that a default by a landlord be actionable at the suit of the tenant in order for it to be a default for the purposes of the Act. This may broaden the liability of landlords in Nova Scotia as compared to those in which such a requirement does exist and may also broaden the landlord's liability relative to common law.[270] Instead, subsection 9(1) of the Act simply requires that a landlord who is responsible for the maintenance or repair of premises owe " . . . the same duty to each person entering on the premises as is owed by the occupier of the premises". As with the earlier Acts, the landlord's duty of care is explicitly extended to subleases, a landlord is not relieved of any duties imposed by another law by virtue of the Act and the term "lease" is broadly defined.[271]

---

[266] *Ibid.*, ss. 5(1).

[267] Subsection 6(3) states that the deemed assumption of risk does not apply to persons who enter premises "for a purpose connected with the occupier or any person usually entitled to be on the premises"; to persons who have ". . . paid a fee for the entry or activity of the person on premises. . . ."; are "being provided in exchange for consideration with living accommodation by the occupier" or, are "authorized or permitted by law to enter the premises for other than recreational purposes".

[268] *Ibid.*, ss. 7(2).

[269] Or "occupiers", where there is more than one occupier of the premises: *ibid.*, ss. 8(3).

[270] At common law, before a tenant can sue for injury resulting from a breach of the landlord's covenant to repair, reasonable notice has to be given to the landlord.

[271] S.N.S. 1996, c. 27, ss. 9(2), (3), (4).

Pursuant to section 10, damages arising from a breach of the occupier's duty are subject to the Contributory Negligence Act and the Tortfeasors Act. Limitations on Crown and municipal liability are identical to those set out in section 8 of the Manitoba statute.[272] Finally, sections 5 to 9, which include the assumption of risk and deemed assumption of risk provision, the modification of liability provisions, do not apply to the liability or duties of certain persons as listed in section 13. These persons include an employer in respect of an employee, a person under contract for hire or engaging in carriage for reward of persons or property in a vehicle, vessel, aircraft or other mode of transportation, a person engaged in a bailment, or a person carrying out duties pursuant to the Trails Act.[273]

The proposal contained in the 1976 draft Act to reduce the amount of compensation owed by an individual residential occupier or a small family farm by the amount received by the injured person through other sources in certain cases was not included in the enacted legislation. Furthermore, legislation enacted to address specific kinds of liability prior to the enactment of this Act has been repealed.[274]

6. SASKATCHEWAN

In June, 1980, the Law Reform Commission of Saskatchewan released its report on occupiers' liability[275] recommending the adoption of an occupiers' liability act modelled primarily on the Uniform Act. However, in contrast to the Uniform Act, the Law Reform Commission recommended that the Saskatchewan Act articulate specific factors to be considered in determining whether the common duty of care has been discharged. The suggested provision provides as follows:

> 3.(1) An occupier of premises owes a duty to take such care as in all circumstances of the case is reasonable to see that any person on the premises will be safe in using the premises.
> (2) Without restricting the generality of subsection (1), in determining whether the duty of care under subsection (1) has been discharged consideration shall be given to
> (a) the gravity and likelihood of the probable injury;
> (b) the circumstances of the entry onto the premises;
> (c) the nature of the premises;
> (d) the knowledge which the occupier has or ought to have of the likelihood of persons or property being on the premises;
> (e) the age of the person entering the premises;
> (f) the ability of the person entering the premises to appreciate the danger;

---

[272] *Ibid.*, s. 11 and s. 12.

[273] *Ibid.*, s. 13.

[274] The Occupiers of Land Liability Act, R.S.N.S. 1989, c. 322, is repealed by s. 15 of the Act. The Act provided that there was no duty to anyone driving a motorized vehicle on another's land whether as a trespasser or a licensee, except the "duty not to create a danger with the deliberate intent of doing harm or damage to the trespasser or licensee". This limitation on the duty of an occupier is presumably subsumed into the more general provisions of the new Act.

[275] Law Reform Commission of Saskatchewan, *Tentative Proposals for an Occupier's Liability Act* (1980).

(g)   the burden on the occupier of eliminating the danger or protecting the person entering the premises from the danger as compared to the risk of the danger to the person.

The proposed Act would apply to personal injury and any property damage suffered by the injured person as a result of the same act that caused the personal injury. Property damage which is not collateral to personal injury would continue to be governed by the existing common law rules.

A provision based on s. 4(2) of the Ontario Act dealing with criminal activity was recommended. A person who enters the premises for criminal purposes would be owed a much lower duty of care, that is, a duty not to create dangers with the intent of injuring the entrant or property and not to create dangers with reckless disregard for the presence of the entrant or the entrant's property. The Commission also recommended a provision similar to s. 4(3) of the Ontario Act but narrower in scope than the corresponding Ontario section. A person who enters premises by means of a motor vehicle or in the course of hunting and who enters or uses the premises for a purpose unconnected with the occupier is owed only the lower standard of care applicable to criminal entrants. This provision was designed in light of the particular difficulty faced by farm owners in Saskatchewan because of the large tracts of land that are involved.[276] However, the proposed provision would apply to all premises, not only farms.

The Commission, adopting some of the recommendations contained in the Nova Scotia Study Paper, recommended that there be four limitations on the ability of an occupier to restrict, modify or exclude the common duty of care: (1) reasonable steps must be taken to bring the restriction, modification or exclusion to the attention of the person affected; (2) the restriction, modification or exclusion must be reasonable in all the circumstances; (3) a person who is permitted or empowered by law to enter or use the premises without the permission of the occupier is not bound by any restriction, modification or exclusion; and (4) restrictions, modifications and exclusions contained in notices and documents of admission such as tickets are not effective with respect to death or personal injury.

Under the proposed legislation an occupier would not be liable for damage caused by the negligence of an independent contractor if the occupier exercised reasonable care in the selection of the contractor. However, notwithstanding that these requirements have been met, the occupier is subject to the common law duty of care if the occupier knows or, in all the circumstances, ought to have known, of a dangerous situation created on the premises by an independent contractor.

The suggested provision dealing with landlord and tenant situations follows the recently enacted Nova Scotia legislation insofar as it expressly provides that the entrant can successfully sue the landlord, notwithstanding that the landlord has not had notice of the defect, if the landlord knows or ought to have known of the defect which has caused the injury.

---

[276] *Ibid.*, s. 51.

7. JUDICIAL REFORM: NEWFOUNDLAND

Uniquely in Canada, Newfoundland's Court of Appeal boldly rationalized its occupier's liability law in the 1999 decision *Stacey v. Anglican Churches of Canada*.[277] In a unanimous decision, delivered by Justice Gushue, the Court considered "whether the traditional common law categorizations of lawful visitors to premises as either invitees or licensees should still be regarded as well-grounded law in this province".[278] After summarizing the common law and reviewing the progress of statutory reform in Canada and the Commonwealth, Gushue J.A. refers to a number of cases where a more general duty of care was applied in occupiers' liability cases or where the boundaries between categories of entrants had been blurred. Drawing support from Chief Justice McLachlin's remark[279] that judges should develop or expand the law in areas where it is necessary to keep in step with the "dynamic and evolving fabric of our society", the Court proposed that the following test should henceforth be used for occupiers' liability in Newfoundland:

> An occupier's duty of care to a lawful visitor to his or her premises is to take such care as in all the circumstances is reasonable to see that the visitor will be reasonably safe in using the premises for the purposes for which he or she is invited or permitted by the occupier to be there or is permitted by law to be there.[280]

In a later occupiers' liability case[281] Chief Justice Wells summarized the impact of the *Stacey* decision in the following manner:

> . . . that decision abandoned the traditional approach, of applying descending levels of duty of care, depending on whether the injured person would be classified as an invitee, a licensee or a trespasser, to determine an occupier's liability. In its place the Court applied the simplified standard that had been adopted, either by statute or by common law development, in England and in most jurisdictions in Canada. . . .

Will the Courts of Appeal of the holdout provinces and territories, which have not yet enacted legislation rationalizing occupiers' liability, be brave enough to follow Newfoundland's lead or will they remain "hidebound" and wait for the Legislatures to "free us from those fetters"?[282]

8. SOME COMMON THREADS: EMERGING PRINCIPLES UNDER THE "NEW" OCCUPIERS' LIABILITY REGIMES

Although it is important to consult the unique wording of each statute, and the manner in which such text has been interpreted in the relevant province, one can

---

[277] *Supra,* n. 112, plaintiff injured in cemetery fall denied recovery because reasonable care employed by defendant.

[278] *Ibid.,* at p. 155.

[279] *Bow Valley Husky (Bermuda) Ltd. v. St. John Shipbuilding Ltd.,* [1997] 3 S.C.R. 1210, at p. 1262.

[280] *Supra,* n. 112, at p. 164.

[281] *Empire Co. v. Sheppard,* [2001] N.J. No. 35, at para. 4.

[282] *Stacey, supra,* n. 112, at p. 160.

make some general observations regarding the emerging law of occupiers' liability in Canada.

For example, the heart of all of the statutes, the "occupier's duty" provision,[283] is quite similar — generally requiring occupiers to take such care in all the circumstances to ensure that persons and property entering their premises are reasonably safe. The notion of "reasonableness" in the relevant "circumstances" has been addressed in many cases, and some guiding principles are emerging. In addition, all of the statutes, as well as Newfoundland's *Stacey* decision, incorporate the principles of *volenti* and contributory negligence.[284]

Accordingly, I shall examine briefly some of the case law under the various statutes dealing with the standard of care required of an occupier and a visitor. I shall then focus on cases involving the commonest scenarios in the occupiers' liability field — cases involving "slip and falls" in supermarkets or other stores, or on ice and snow, with a view to identifying some of the factors the courts consider in evaluating an occupier's "reasonableness" under the "circumstances". Finally, I will review some of the developing principles regarding voluntary assumption of risk, and contributory negligence in the occupiers' liability context.

a) The Reasonableness Threshold

The standard of care required of an occupier is one of reasonableness, not perfection.[285] Occupiers are required to take such care as is reasonable in the circumstances to ensure that visitors are reasonably safe on their premises. Occupiers are not expected to be insurers, responsible for all harm that befalls anyone entering their premises,[286] but an affirmative duty — sometimes requiring affirmative action — is imposed on them to take care for the reasonable safety of visitors.[287]

---

[283] See s. 5 of the Alberta Occupiers' Liability Act, R.S.A. 1980, c. O-3; s. 3(1) of the Ontario Occupiers' Liability Act, R.S.O. 1990, c. O.2; s. 3(1) of the British Columbia Occupiers Liability Act, R.S.B.C. 1996, c. 337; s. 3(1) of the P.E.I. Occupiers' Liability Act, R.S.P.E.I. 1988, c. O-2; s. 3(1) of the Manitoba Occupiers' Liability Act, R.S.M. 1987, c. O.8; s. 4(1) of the Nova Scotia Occupiers' Liability Act, S.N.S. 1996, c. 27.

[284] See ss. 7 and 15 of the Alberta Occupiers' Liability Act, R.S.A. 1980, c. O-3; ss. 4 and 9(3) of the Ontario Occupiers' Liability Act, R.S.O. 1990, c. O.2; s. 3(3) of the British Columbia Occupiers Liability Act, R.S.B.C. 1996, c. 337; ss. 4(1) and 8(3) of the P.E.I. Occupiers' Liability Act, R.S.P.E.I. 1988, c. O-2; ss. 3(3) and 7 of the Manitoba Occupiers' Liability Act, R.S.M. 1987, c. O.8; ss. 5(1) and 10 of the Nova Scotia Occupiers' Liability Act, S.N.S. 1996, c. 27 and paragraphs 30 and 31 of *Stacey, supra,* n. 112.

[285] *Carlson v. Canada Safeway Ltd.* (1983), 47 B.C.L.R. 252 (C.A.); *Sulmona v. Seraglio,* [1986] B.C.J. No. 413 (C.A.).

[286] *Roasting v. Blood Band* (1999), 241 A.R. 171, at p. 182 (Q.B.).

[287] *Malcolm v. Waldick, supra,* n. 166; *Preston v. Canadian Legion of British Empire Service League, Kingsway Branch No. 175* (1981), 29 A.R. 532, at p. 536 (C.A.).

As with negligence cases, the notion of foreseeability comes into play here as well.[288] Thus, in *Rai v. Koziar*,[289] when the plaintiff took her husband's gasoline soaked clothing to a laundromat to wash, and an explosion and fire, caused by the fumes, occurred in the washing machine, severely burning the plaintiff, the owner/occupier of the laundromat was not held liable. The risk was not reasonably foreseeable and the premises and washing machines (which, incidentally, did display a warning regarding the dangers of gasoline-soaked clothing) were reasonably safe for the activities customarily carried on there. Similarly, when a ten-year-old boy was killed after falling out of a tree and striking his head on a rock at a city park, the court held that the city was not liable because trees are intended for shade and enjoyment, not climbing. Climbing, it was said, was not foreseeable, not part of the natural and normal use of trees.[290]

Remedial steps taken after a mishap are not generally considered as proof that such steps were required to make the premises safe, but are merely one factor to be considered in whether the premises were reasonably safe.[291] Nor is prior safe use of premises determinative; such use is also merely a relevant factor to consider in the analysis of whether premises or an activity is reasonably safe.[292]

Further, there is a duty to warn about unknown dangers[293] but not about obvious dangers.[294] Accordingly, it is not unreasonable for an occupier of a swimming pool to fail to warn healthy adult visitors not to dive off a high platform if one is not in control of one's own body,[295] nor is it unreasonable to fail to warn that short cuts through steep alleys with loose gravel surfaces might result in a fall,[296] or that falling debris might injure an individual after eastern Canada's severest ice storm in recorded history,[297] nor should an experienced snowmobiler require warning of the danger posed by crossing rail lines on a rail bed when very little snow cover is present.[298]

---

[288] *Rendall v. Ewert* (1989), 38 B.C.L.R. (2d) 1 (C.A.). See *Olinski v. Johnson* (1997), 32 O.R. (3d) 653 (C.A.), where a melée directed at referees that "spontaneously erupted" in a corridor following a lacrosse game was not reasonably foreseeable.

[289] [2000] A.J. No. 1390 (Q.B.).

[290] *Ricard v. Trenton (City)*, [2000] O.J. No. 4700.

[291] *Cahoon v. Wendy's Restaurant of Canada Inc.*, [2000] B.C.J. No. 762 (S.C.).

[292] *Jolley v. Pacific National Exhibition*, [1986] B.C.J. No. 2284; *Crerar v. Dover*, [1984] 3 W.W.R. 236 (B.C.S.C.); *Coleman v. Yen Hoy Enterprises Ltd.*, [2000] B.C.J. No. 403.

[293] *Woods v. Ontario (Ministry of Natural Resources)* (2001), 5 C.C.L.T. (3d) 142 (Ont. S.C.J.), 25% liable for not warning against diving into shallow water.

[294] *Alchimowicz v. Schram*, [1999] O.J. No. 115.

[295] *Fowler v. Ontario (Ministry of Health)*, [1997] O.J. No. 660.

[296] *Oser v. Nelson (City)*, [1997] B.C.J. No. 2809 (S.C.), need not warn an adult without disability of the ordinary risks arising out of the exigencies of everyday life.

[297] *Lebrun v. Ingram*, [2000] O.J. No. 2577.

[298] *Lemieux v. Porcupine Snowmobile Club of Timmins Inc.*, [1999] O.J. No. 1779 (C.A.).

b) Looking Out For One's Own Safety

Along with the requirement that the occupier behave in a reasonable manner, visitors must also behave reasonably by looking out for their own safety. Thus when an adult cyclist was injured when he travelled down a set of stairs that formed part of a detour on a public path, he was denied recovery because he did not slow down on an unknown route which was clearly impacted by construction.[299] Similarly, an adult who knowingly dives into shallow water is foolhardy and should not recover damages,[300] as "a person who knowingly dives into the shallow half of the pool. . . must know that he or she is taking a grave risk".[301] Likewise, when an inebriated college student attending a fraternity party at a hotel pries open the doors and then jumps from a stopped elevator, in an attempt to reach the floor below, but instead plunges down the elevator shaft, he is the author of his own misfortune.[302] Lastly, when a lone workman uses a ladder at premises undergoing renovation without turning on the lights, checking the area, or having someone present to steady it, he cannot recover because he took no care for his own safety in circumstances that required care and caution. There was no evidence that the premises were unsafe.[303]

c) Reasonably Safe In the Circumstances

An important component of the reasonableness inquiry is on examination of all of the relevant circumstances, so that each case must necessarily be decided on its own unique set of facts. One such circumstance is whether premises are rural or urban, as different standards may be applied in these different situations.[304] Local custom may also be part of the relevant circumstances, as is whether the premises are a private home or a public gathering place.[305]

Despite the importance of determining each cased based on its peculiar facts, some fact patterns are common, such as cases arising from falls in supermarkets and on ice. Examining a few of such cases may shed some light on the meaning of reasonably safe in the circumstances.

i) Supermarket Cases

There are dozens of occupiers' liability cases launched each year in Canada by patrons of supermarkets or stores as a result of many injuries sustained by "slip

---

[299] *Whitehead v. Calgary*, [2001] A.J. No. 474.

[300] *McQueen v. Alberta*, [2001] A.J. No. 346.

[301] *Gibney v. Gilliland*, [1992] B.C.J. No. 1496 (C.A.); affd on appeal to S.C.C. without reasons [1994] 1 S.C.R. 157, at para. 5. But see also, *Woods v. Ontario*, [2001] O.J. No. 138, where an adult dove into shallow water without regard to his own safety, and was held 75% responsible for his catastrophic injuries, with the occupier responsible for the remaining 25%.

[302] *Cruikshank v. Delta Hotels Ltd.*, [1998] B.C.J. No. 1742 (S.C.).

[303] *Pogorzelec v. Wincor Properties Ltd.*, [2000] B.C.J. No. 854 (S.C.).

[304] *Waldick v. Malcolm, supra,* n. 166.

[305] *Ibid.*

and falls". Falls have been caused by patrons slipping on an astonishing variety of things such as water,[306] a squished grape,[307] a plum,[308] a loose strawberry,[309] wet lettuce,[310] a banana peel,[311] loose rice,[312] cooking oil,[313] and oriental food sauces,[314] among others.[315] While some store owners are relieved of liability, others have been held responsible for such incidents. Generalizing, it appears that for occupiers to successfully defend themselves, they must demonstrate two things: first, that the store has implemented reasonable policies and procedures of maintenance; and second, that such policies and procedures were actually followed on the day in question.

Accordingly, where it can be shown that although reasonable maintenance policies were in place, such as regularly scheduled sweeps and inspections, if the occupier can lead no evidence that the system was followed on the relevant day, there is liability for a patron's injury.[316] Similarly, if the policies or systems are found lacking, or not reasonable in the circumstances, the occupier will be held liable.[317] Needless to say, the system need not be foolproof; in other words:

> The positive or affirmative duty that is imposed upon the defendant does not extend to the removal of every possible danger. It does not require the defendants to maintain a constant surveillance or look out for potential danger. The defendant meets its duty to take reasonable care if it takes measures that are reasonable in the circumstances.[318]

However, high risk areas, such as produce departments, should have better systems in place[319] than areas with a lower risk of spillage, such as a bakery

---

[306] *Hussein v. Loblaws*, [2000] O.J. No. 2062; *Nikkel v. Westfair Foods Ltd.*, [2001] M.J. No. 30.

[307] *Marché v. Empire Co.*, [2001] N.S.J. No. 133 (C.A.); *Lee v. Loblaws*, [1997] B.C.J. No. 866 (S.C.).

[308] *Garofalo v. Canada Safeway Ltd.*, [1998] O.J. No. 302.

[309] *Evans v. Jim Pattison Industries Ltd.*, [2000] B.C.J. No. 1171.

[310] *Atkins v. Jim Pattison Industries Ltd.*, [1998] B.C.J. No. 3050 (C.A.); *Gryschuk v. Westfair Foods Ltd.*, [1999] B.C.J. No. 302.

[311] *Siovi v. Canada Safeway*, [2001] B.C.J. No. 179.

[312] *Howden v. Westfair Foods*, [2001] M.J. No. 25.

[313] *Lebedynski v. Westfair Foods Ltd.*, [2000] M.J. No. 422.

[314] *Beal v. Canada Safeway Ltd.*, [2000] B.C.J. No. 1665.

[315] *LeClerc v. Westfair Foods Ltd.*, [2000] M.J. No. 372 (C.A.), displayed cans.

[316] *Howden v. Westfair, supra*, n. 312, where the court found a reasonable system of maintenance was in place but no maintenance logs could be produced or evidence led that the system was followed. See also *Lebedynski v. Westfair Foods Ltd., supra*, n. 313; *Hussein v. Loblaws, supra*, n. 306.

[317] *Marché v. Empire Co., supra*, n. 294, where the Trial Judge (affirmed on appeal) found that the systems in place were lacking and not commensurate to the risk of falling grapes. The Judge found that more vigilance was required, including wrapping of grapes to reduce spillage, more regular and scheduled sweepings and inspections.

[318] *Garofalo v. Canada Safeway, supra*, n. 308 at para. 31 (*per* Kozak J.). In that case, the maintenance plan included the requirement that floors be swept every half hour to hour and the log sheets indicated that the floor was swept just 20 minutes prior to the fall. The Court held that it was too onerous to expect more.

[319] This might include positive steps to prevent spillage, such as the way fruits are displayed or wrapped, placing mats on the floor to prevent slipping, erecting warning signs, *etc*. See *Marché, supra*, n. 307.

section, canned food aisle, or a parking lot.[320] Different responses are required for different risks. Similarly, a large store with many employees might be expected to have more elaborate procedures than a small one.[321]

ii) Ice Cases

The leading case under the new legislative regime of occupiers' liability is *Malcolm v. Waldick*.[322] That case involved a plaintiff who was seriously injured when he slipped on an icy driveway leading to a farm house during a social visit. The defendant knew of his driveway's slippery condition but failed to take steps to salt or sand it to improve its condition. The Court held that the defendant breached his duty of care to visitors. Such was the case even though the defendant's neighbours had similarly icy driveways and despite the rural residential locale. Positive action was required by the defendant to make his premises reasonably safe.

Since that case, there have been many more decisions involving ice hazards. Most of these have involved urban locales, where attempts were made, with varying degrees of success, to make premises safe for visitors. A similar picture emerges regarding such cases as with the supermarket cases, that is, the court will look at the reasonableness of the systems and procedures in place to counteract icy conditions and at whether the systems were actually followed in a reasonable manner. As always, the circumstances are very relevant. Thus, where a defendant trailer-park owner worked quite diligently to clear snow from two-and-one-half kilometers of park roadways the day after an unusually heavy snowstorm, in a place where snowstorms of this nature rarely occur, the fact that no official "system" was in place was not fatal. The defendant's actions were entirely reasonable in the circumstances and the plaintiff's injuries from a fall on a patch of ice went uncompensated.[323] Similarly, injuries stemming from a fall on ice at a city-owned parking lot went uncompensated where the city proved that it had been snowing recently, that the lot had been cleared three to five hours prior to the fall and that a reasonable policy of maintenance was demonstrated,[324] as did injuries from a fall on ice in front of a hospital where the hospital had hired reputable contractors to attend to the snow and ice and where the grounds had been inspected that morning.[325] However, it is not reasonable to fail to check pathways for ice at a seniors'

---

[320] See, for example, *Lee v. Loblaws, supra*, n. 307, where a fall occurred in the bakery section (albeit purportedly on a grape) and the case was dismissed because the defendant demonstrated that it had a regular and adequate cleaning system in place; see also *Siovi v. Canada Safeway, supra*, n. 311, where the fall occurred in the parking lot and the Court recognized that more vigilance was reasonable in a produce department than in a parking lot.

[321] *Pignal v. Shoppers Drug Mart*, [1997] O.J. No. 3352; affd (1999), 120 O.A.C. 284 (C.A.).

[322] *Supra*, n. 197.

[323] *Leduc v. Goodwill Investments Ltd.*, [1997] B.C.J. No. 1709 (S.C.).

[324] *Perritt v. Port Moody (City)*, [1997] B.C.J. No. 622 (S.C.).

[325] *Gardiner v. Thunder Bay Regional Hospital*, [1999] O.J. No. 833; affd [2000] O.J. No. 141 (C.A.).

residence when temperatures had been rising over and falling under the freezing mark during the previous day.[326]

d) Voluntary Assumption of Risk

Waldick v. Malcolm[327] is the leading case with respect to voluntary assumption of risk in the occupiers' liability context. That case involved an injury sustained when someone fell on an icy driveway. However, in addition to the defendant having knowledge of the driveway's icy condition, the plaintiff also knew about the driveway's dangerous state, for the fall did not occur upon his entering the premises, but hours later when he traversed the treacherous area to retrieve some cigarettes from his car. The defendant argued that the plaintiff's knowlege of the risk absolved him of his responsibility by virtue of s. 4 of the Ontario Act, which states that the occupier's duty does not apply in respect of risks willingly assumed by a visitor, except when the occupier deliberately creates a danger or acts with reckless disregard for a visitor's safety. The Court determined that the section was simply a codification of the voluntary assumption of risk doctrine, and, as such, the plaintiff must either expressly or by necessary implication consent to the legal risk or waive his legal rights. Justice Iacobucci explained:

> In my view, the legislature's intention in enacting s. 4(1) of the Act was to carve out a very narrow exception to the class of visitors to whom the occupier's statutory duty of care is owed. . . . Rare may be the case where a visitor who enters on premises will fully know of and accept the risks resulting from the occupier's non-compliance with the statute.[328]

This narrow interpretation has been accepted and applied in other jurisdictions, despite minor variations in wording.[329] One Court, in applying *Waldick*, reiterated that "a plaintiff must assume both a physical and legal risk in order to absolve a defendant occupier of liability".[330]

Accordingly, the *volenti* exception will apply only rarely, courts relying more frequently on the contributory negligence doctrine when the plaintiff engages in ill-advised behaviour, not unlike the treatment of these defences in other situations.

e) Contributory Negligence

Plaintiffs in occupiers' liability cases must also have regard for their own safety. Accidents often occur due to a combination of lapses — by the occupier who

---

[326] *Warman v. Kamloops Silver Threads Apt. Society*, [1997] B.C.J. No. 1616. Nor is it reasonable to allow for delay in addressing slippery conditions at a heavily travelled tourist attraction: *Sheikhani v. Ontario (Niagara Parks Commission)*, [1998] O.J. No. 880, 57 O.T.C. 302.

[327] *Supra*, n. 197.

[328] *Ibid.*, at p. 479 [S.C.R.].

[329] See, for example, *Bains v. Hill* (1992), 68 B.C.L.R. (2d) 193 (C.A.).

[330] *Marchand v. New Westminster School District No. 40*, [1997] B.C.J. No. 2889 (S.C.).

fails to provide reasonably safe premises and by visitors who do not exercise caution. In such cases, contributory negligence principles are applicable.

Intoxication is probably the most common example of contributory negligence as a visitor's intoxication may impair his or her balance, perception or judgement, contributing to an injury. Such was the case in *Keenan v. Seardals Ltd.,*[331] where a tavern patron fell down a set of unsafe stairs after consuming a considerable amount of alcohol. The patron was found to be 25 per cent responsible for his injuries. Similarly, a patron at a restaurant who slipped on water on her way to the ladies room was held to be 35 per cent responsible for her injuries, because she had been drinking for several hours and her drunken state contributed to her fall.[332] In another unusual case,[333] the young plaintiff was severely injured when he fell backwards off a private bridge made of wood, while attempting to sit on a side rail like a bench. The occupiers were held 60 per cent responsible for the plaintiff's injuries in failing to provide handrails on the bridge and in allowing the bridge to be used by young people in a manner that could result in tragedy. The plaintiff was held to be 40 per cent responsible for his injuries, because his blood alcohol level was significant enough to impair his balance and perception, contributing to his fall.

Other actions which may constitute contributory negligence include driving too fast,[334] not checking that a work-place is reasonably safe,[335] placing a ladder on a slippery substance (manure),[336] climbing over a high wall and fence to enter the source pool of a hot spring without testing the scalding hot water,[337] and proceeding over hazardous ice that admittedly appeared "impassable" and treacherous to the plaintiff when other options were available.[338]

It should be noted that the apportionment should be done on the basis of the degree of fault, not causation, that is, it is the comparative blameworthiness of the parties which is to be evaluated.[339]

Although all of this legislation already has helped to some degree to simplify and modernize the law of occupiers' liability, it certainly has not eliminated all of the problems associated with this area of the law. Indeed, there may be cases where entrants will be worse off than before and where lawyers and judges will still have considerable difficulty in resolving the disputes. An amazing number of cases are still being litigated, but, hopefully, there are fewer successful appeals launched.

---

[331] [2000] O.J. No. 992.

[332] *Cooper v. Spectra Food Corp.*, [1998] B.C.J. No. 2297 (S.C.).

[333] *Chretien v. Jensen*, [1997] B.C.J. No. 3016 (S.C.); affd [1998] 6 W.W.R. 648 (B.C.C.A.).

[334] *Kennedy v. Waterloo (County) Board of Education*, [1999] O.J. No. 2273, 45 O.R. (3d) 1, 45 C.C.L.T. (2d) 169 (C.A.); application for leave to appeal to S.C.C. dismissed March 23, 2000. Plaintiff was 75% responsible, School Board 25% responsible because position of barriers unsafe.

[335] *Graham v. Lee*, [2001] B.C.J. No. 44 (S.C.), twisted metal near worksite left by plaintiff and co-worker contributed to injury sustained.

[336] *Wiens v. Serene Lea Farms Ltd.*, [2000] B.C.J. No. 1798 (S.C.), Mennonite farmers helping out to build a barn, plaintiff placed his ladder on manure, leading to horrendous fall.

[337] *Cempel v. Harrison Hot Springs Hotel Ltd.*, [1997] B.C.J. No. 2853 (C.A.), young female plaintiff was 40% responsible.

[338] *Cullinane v. Prince George (City)*, [2000] B.C.J. No. 1488 (S.C.).

[339] The B.C. Court of Appeal confirmed this in *Cempel, supra,* n. 337.

Eventually, however, it is hoped that sensible and sensitive statutory interpretation will remove most of the uncertainty and injustice that may remain.[340]

---

[340] Liability of landlord under Occupiers' Liability Act for assault, see *Allison v. Rank City Wall Canada Ltd.* (1984), 45 O.R. (2d) 141 (H.C.J.) (*per* Smith J.). See also *Q. v. Minto Management Ltd.* (1985), 31 C.C.L.T. 158 (Ont. H.C.J.) (*per* Gray J.).

Chapter 19

Defamation

The primary purpose of defamation law is to protect the good reputation of individuals in our society. A good name, which has to be built up painstakingly over many years, is a priceless asset, one that is worthy of the law's protection. As Shakespeare wrote in *Othello*,[1]

> Good name in men and women . . .
> Is the immediate jewel of their souls,
> Who steals my purse steals trash . . .
> But he who filches from me my good name
> Robs me of that which not enriches him
> And makes me poor indeed.

A tort action for libel or slander is available against anyone who filches another's good name, whether by oral word, by written word, or by any other type of conduct. This is desirable because not only does one's reputation have a dignitary value, it also has economic worth, since a person with a poor reputation would encounter difficulty finding and keeping a job. For most people, their good reputation is to be "cherished above all".[2] The goals of such suits, therefore, are to vindicate the stain on one's reputation, to secure compensation for any actual damage done and to deter other acts of defamation by the defendant and by the public generally.

There is another social interest in this area that is prized by our society — freedom of speech. Some argue that, just as the state has no business in the bedrooms of the nation, the law has no business in the pressrooms of the nation. In other words, some contend that there should be no legal restrictions on freedom of expression. This latter view has not prevailed.

Tort law has opted for the preservation of good reputations at the expense of certain aspects of free speech. The conflict between these two vital interests in

---

[1] Act 3, Scene 3.
[2] See Cory J. in *Hill v. Church of Scientology of Toronto*, [1995] 2 S.C.R. 1170, at p. 1175, defamation also "is an invasion of personal privacy" and is an "affront to [a] person's dignity", at p. 1179.

society rages through every defamation case "in which our traditional notions of freedom of expression have collided violently with sympathy for the victim traduced and indignation at the maligning tongue".[3] So the law does enter the pressrooms of the nation, but it does so gingerly and diffidently, ever conscious of the need to permit as much free speech as possible, consistent with due regard for the need to guard reputations from unwarranted attacks. Defamation law is constantly struggling to strike an acceptable balance between freedom of speech, and protection of reputation, both of which we value highly. This tension, along with certain historical factors, has led to the development of some complex legal principles, some difficult procedural issues, and some complicated legislative provisions that are aimed at particular areas of the law.[4]

The problems in this area have been exacerbated by the increased politicization of the public and the demand for greater access to information by the media, as well as the explosion in the technological sophistication of mass communication. The purpose of this chapter is not to explore in any great detail the numerous issues that this raises, but rather to outline the framework of the present state of the law against which they can be viewed.[5]

A. What is Defamatory?

1. THE VARIOUS TESTS

The first and most important matter to be determined in deciding whether liability will be imposed is whether the utterance complained of is defamatory. It should be noted that it is normally a jury that decides this question. The judge, however, performs a screening function to determine whether the words are capable of defamatory meaning.

There is no one universal test that is invariably used here; several different formulae may be utilized by the courts. The classic definition, that was most widely used until recently, declares that libel is that "which is calculated to injure the reputation of another by exposing him to hatred, contempt or ridicule" to which there is sometimes added that the words must cause a person to be "shunned or avoided".[6] This definition, however, is now viewed as too narrow.[7]

---

[3] *Prosser and Keeton on the Law of Torts*, 5th ed. (1984), p. 772. See also Cory J. in *Hill, supra*, n. 2, at p. 1172.

[4] For general texts in the area, see Brown, *The Law of Defamation in Canada*, 2nd ed. (1994); Gatley, *Libel and Slander*, 9th ed. (1998); Duncan and Neill, *Defamation*, 2nd ed. (1983); Carter-Ruck, *Libel and Slander*, 4th ed., (London: Butterworths, 1991); Williams, *The Law of Defamation in Canada* (1976); Eldredge, *The Law of Defamation* (1978); Porter and Potts, *Canadian Libel Practice* (1986).

[5] For a fine article considering some of these problems see Weiler, "Defamation, Enterprise Liability and Freedom of Speech" (1967), 17 U. of T.L.J. 278.

[6] *Parmiter v. Coupland* (1840), 6 M. & W. 105, at p. 108 (*per* Baron Parke); *Youssoupoff v. Metro-Goldwyn-Mayer Pictures Ltd.* (1934), 50 T.L.R. 581 (C.A.).

[7] *Infra*. See *Tournier v. National Provincial & Union Bank of England*, [1924] 1 K.B. 461 (C.A.), at p. 477 (*per* Scrutton L.J.), and at p. 487 (*per* Atkin L.J.); and *Youssoupoff v. Metro-Goldwyn-Mayer Pictures Ltd., supra*, n. 6.

Another test for defamation is a "false statement about a man to his discredit".[8] More recently, a formulation of the test has been expressed to the effect that defamation "tends to lower a person in the estimation of right-thinking members of society generally".[9] A variation of this latter test is offered by Professor Fleming[10] who contends that defamatory words "lower a person in the estimation of his fellows by making them think less of him". Not very different than this is the requirement that the plaintiff has "suffered in social reputation and in the opportunities of receiving respectful consideration from the world".[11] Another helpful test is this:

> A communication is defamatory if it tends so to harm the reputation of another as to lower him in the estimation of the community or to deter third persons from associating or dealing with him.[12]

A skillful interpretation of the various tests for a defamatory communication has been offered by Justice Abella in *Colour Your World Corp. v. Canadian Broadcasting Corp.*[13] as follows:

> A defamatory statement is one which has a tendency to injure the reputation of the person to whom it refers (which tends, that is to say, to lower him [or her] in the estimation of right thinking members of society generally and in particular to cause him [or her] to be regarded with feelings of hatred, contempt, ridicule, fear, dislike, or disesteem. The statement is judged by the standard of an ordinary, right thinking member of society. Hence the test is an objective one. . . . The standard of what constitutes a reasonable or ordinary member of the public is difficult to articulate. It should not be so low as to stifle free expression unduly, nor so high as to imperil the ability to protect the integrity of a person's reputation. The impressions about the content of any broadcast — or written statement — should be assessed from the perspective of someone reasonable, that is, a person who is reasonably thoughtful and informed, rather than someone who is with an overly fragile sensibility. A degree of common sense must be attributed to viewers.

In sum, defamation is the dissemination of information that tarnishes the good name of people,[14] causing their standing in the community to be impaired, or causing them to be pitied.[15]

---

8   *Infra.* See *Scott v. Sampson* (1882), 8 Q.B.D. 491, at p. 503 (*per* Cave J.). See also Scrutton L.J. in *Youssoupoff, supra*, n. 6, at p. 584.

9   *Sim v. Stretch*, [1936] 2 All E.R. 1237, at p. 1240 (*per* Lord Atkin); followed in *Murphy v. La Marsh* (1970), 73 W.W.R. 114; affd [1971] 2 W.W.R. 196 (*per* Wilson C.J.S.C.); leave to appeal refused [1971] S.C.R. ix.

10 Fleming, *The Law of Torts*, 8th ed., p. 581. See also Brown, *op. cit. supra*, n. 4, at p. 38.

11 *Per* Slesser L.J. in *Youssoupoff, supra*, n. 6.

12 *Restatement, Torts, Second*, §559. Copyright 1965 by the American Law Institute. Reprinted with the permission of The American Law Institute.

13 (1998), 156 D.L.R. (4th) 27, at p. 36 (Ont. C.A.); leave to appeal to S.C.C. dismissed (1998), 119 O.A.C. 397n (S.C.C.).

14 *Murphy v. La Marsh, supra*, n. 9.

15 *Morgan v. Lingen* (1863), 8 L.T. (N.S.) 800, insanity; *Youssoupoff, supra*, n. 6, rape; *Katapodis v. Brooklyn Spectator* (1941), 33 N.E. 2d 112 (C.A.), poverty.

Chief Justice Wilson of British Columbia once described some of the things that would amount to defamation, to include:

> a shameful action . . . (he stole my purse), a shameful character (he is dishonest), a shameful course of action (he lives on the avails of prostitution), [or] a shameful condition (he has the pox).[16]

There are many different examples of defamatory words. To say that someone is a liar[17] or a crook[18] or has bribed an M.P.[19] is actionable. An implication of immoral conduct can be defamatory. Thus, when someone said that he knew "five fellows who took [the female plaintiff] behind the church and screwed her", liability was found.[20] So too, it was held defamatory to accuse someone of being a homosexual,[21] of wife-swapping,[22] of molesting a minor,[23] of having a venereal disease,[24] or causing a rise in the illegitimacy and abortion rates.[25] To call someone a drunk, or "hideously ugly"[26] or a traitor is defamatory.[27] To impute an unpopular political belief, such as implying that a person is a Communist,[28] or behaves like a Nazi secret service agent,[29] may be defamatory.

To speak disparagingly of a person's professional capacity can amount to defamation, such as calling a doctor a "quack"[30] or a lawyer a "shyster"[31] or "a thief".[32] Similarly, to say that a professional musician has no aptitude for music or that an accountant has no understanding of accounts is actionable.[33] In one case, a novelist recovered damages against the publishers of a magazine which printed a story under his name, but which he did not write, on the grounds that

---

[16] *Murphy v. La Marsh, supra*, n. 9.

[17] *Penton v. Caldwell* (1945), 70 C.L.R. 219; *Fraser v. Sykes*, [1974] S.C.R. 526, "deception" and "breach of faith".

[18] *Pandolfo v. Bank of Benson* (1921), 273 Fed. 48.

[19] *Hamilton v. Al Fayed*, [1999] 3 All E.R. 317 (C.A.); affd [2000] 2 All E.R. 224 (H.L.).

[20] *French (Elizabeth) v. Smith*, [1923] 3 D.L.R. 904, at p. 906 (*per* Riddell J.).

[21] *Nowark v. Maguire* (1964), 255 N.Y.S. 2d 318; *Buck v. Savage* (1959), 323 S.W. 2d 363, "queer". One day soon this will change.

[22] *Hunter v. Fotheringham*, January 20, 1986.

[23] *Grassi v. WIC Radio Ltd.* (2000), 49 C.C.L.T. (2d) 65 (B.C.S.C.).

[24] *French (Oscar) v. Smith*, [1923] 3 D.L.R. 902.

[25] *Planned Parenthood v. Fedorik* (1982), 135 D.L.R. (3d) 714.

[26] *Berkoff v. Burchill et al.*, [1996] 4 All E.R. 1008 (*per* Neill J.).

[27] *Gouzenko v. Harris* (1976), 1 C.C.L.T. 37 (Ont. H.C.), traitor.

[28] *Dennison v. Sanderson*, [1946] O.R. 601 (C.A.). A thorough catalogue of cases is presented in Brown, *op. cit. supra*, n. 4, at p. 50.

[29] *Boyachyk v. Dukes* (1982), 136 D.L.R. (3d) 28 (Alta. Q.B.); see *Christie v. Geiger* (1986), 38 C.C.L.T. 280 (Alta. C.A.), racist.

[30] *Warren v. Green* (1958), 25 W.W.R. 563.

[31] *Nolan v. Standard Publishing Co.* (1923), 67 Mont. 212, 216 P. 571.

[32] *Botiuk v. Toronto Free Press Publications Ltd.* (1995), 126 D.L.R. (4th) 609 (S.C.C.). Reputation is especially vital for professionals, see *Hill, supra*, n. 2, at p. 1178.

[33] Duncan and Neill, *op. cit. supra*, n. 4, at p. 33.

anyone reading the story would think he was "a mere commonplace scribbler".[34] Where a professional gambler was accused of cheating, the court awarded damages because the accusation was injurious to his professional reputation and would disrupt his source of income.[35] It is forbidden to imply a lack of credit-worthiness, for example, to say that a business person's business had "failed" or that their liabilities were "heavy"[36] or that they did not pay their debts.[37] To say someone is "heartily detested' by their colleagues[38] or overly extravagant[39] may also be actionable.

Charging politicians with making use of secret information for their own profit,[40] or bureaucrats with influencing the course of justice to protect their friends[41] or business persons with "serious abuse of public trust"[42] or selling dangerous goods[43] can be defamatory as well.

A defendant's statement that she felt "uncomfortable" or "naked" when the plaintiff stood close to her, touched her or stared at her, or that the plaintiff perhaps "needed some help" are not, however, defamatory.[44] Rather, they are "merely a subjective expression of how [the defendant] felt when the plaintiff stood close to her and when he touched her".[45]

All of these examples demonstrate that there is no limit on the types of things people say of one another which may amount to defamation; they are ever-changing and know no bounds, as long as the meaning conveyed may hurt the reputation of the person being disparaged in the circumstances of the communication.

2. STANDARD

The standard of measurement in defamation cases is sometimes said to be that of "right-thinking members of society generally".[46] This has been somewhat

---

[34] *Ridge v. The English Illustrated Magazine* (1913), 29 T.L.R. 592. See also *Archbold v. Sweet* (1832), 5 C. & P. 219.

[35] *Caldwell v. McBride* (1988), 45 C.C.L.T. 150 (B.C.S.C.).

[36] *Dominion Telegraph Co. v. Silver and Payne* (1882), 10 S.C.R. 238; see also *Lott v. Drury* (1882), 1 O.R. 577.

[37] *Tran v. Financial Debt Recovery Ltd.* (2000), 2 C.C.L.T. (3d) 270 (Ont. S.C.J.), emotional harm also allowed by Molloy J.

[38] *Murphy v. La Marsh, supra,* n. 9.

[39] *Rapp v. McClelland & Stewart Ltd.* (1981), 34 O.R. (2d) 452, 19 C.C.L.T. 68 (S.C.); *cf., Pearlman v. C.B.C.* (1981), 13 Man. R. (2d) 1 (Q.B.), "slum landlord" fair comment.

[40] *Munro v. Toronto Sun Publishing* (1982), 39 O.R. (2d) 100 (H.C.).

[41] *Vogel v. C.B.C.* (1981), 21 C.C.L.T. 105 (B.C.S.C.).

[42] *Walker v. CFTO* (1987), 39 C.C.L.T. 121 (Ont. C.A.).

[43] *Camporese v. Parton* (1983), 150 D.L.R. (3d) 208 (B.C.S.C.). But alleging that its paint has mercury in it does not defame business, see *Colour Your World Corp. v. Canadian Broadcasting Corp., supra,* n. 13.

[44] *Crandall v. Atlantic School of Theology et al.* (1993), 122 N.S.R. (2d) 359 (N.S.C.A.). (Quote is from trial decision, 120 N.S.R. (2d) 219, at p. 221.)

[45] *Ibid.* (See trial decision at p. 222, 120 N.S.R.).

[46] *Sim v. Stretch,* [1963] 2 All E.R. 1237, at p. 1240 (H.L.) (*per* Lord Atkin).

diluted, however, because a person may be defamed in the eyes of citizens who are not right-thinking at all. Nowadays courts look at what those of "fair average intelligence"[47] would think, or what "ordinary decent folk in the community, taken in general"[48] would feel.

But "liability is not a question of majority vote",[49] so that if a comment would hurt the plaintiff "in the estimation of a substantial and respectable minority" of the community,[50] liability may follow. In other words, it may be that the plaintiff properly values a good reputation amongst a certain segment of society who would think less of the plaintiff even though they might be "wrong-thinking" people if they did.[51]

However, if the views of such a group are so anti-social that their values are unworthy of recognition by the courts, they may be ignored. Thus, it cannot be defamatory to say that someone informed the police about a crime, even though that person may thereafter have been avoided by certain criminal elements.[52] Nor would it be held defamatory if it was said that a member of the Hell's Angels had never killed anyone, even though that member's reputation would be diminished in the eyes of fellow members in that organization.

This issue is usually put to a jury, even though it may be "over-romantic to conceive of juries as champions of freedom of speech".[53]

3. INTERPRETATION

a) Natural and Ordinary Meaning

The words used in a defamatory publication are given their natural and ordinary meaning. Language, however, may be understood by the listener or reader differently from the meaning intended by the speaker or author. Thus, the courts have adopted the test of the meaning which would be reasonably attributed to the words by ordinary sensible people, without special knowledge, who are neither unusually suspicious nor unusually naive.[54]

---

[47] *Slayter v. Daily Telegraph* (1908), 6 C.L.R. 1, at p. 7 (H.C. of Aust.) (*per* Griffith C.J.).

[48] *Gardiner v. John Fairfax & Sons Pty. Ltd.* (1942), 42 S.R. (N.S.W.) 171, at p. 172 (*per* Jordan C.J.).

[49] *Peck v. Tribune Co.* (1909), 214 U.S. 185, at p. 190 (*per* Holmes J.). See also *Quigley v. Creation Ltd.*, [1971] I.R. 269, at p. 272.

[50] *Restatement, Torts, Second*, s. 559, Comment e. Copyright 1965 by The American Law Institute. Reprinted with the permission of The American Law Institute.

[51] *Grant v. Readers Digest Association Inc.* (1945), 151 F. 2d 733 (2nd Cir. C.A.), accusation that a lawyer was the legislative representative of Massachusetts Communist Party.

[52] *Mawe v. Pigott* (1869), I.R. 4 C.L. 54. See also *Byrne v. Deane*, [1937] 1 K.B. 818, golf club member ostracized for telling police about illegal gambling machines; *Berry v. Irish Times Ltd.*, [1973] I.R. 368, Secretary of Department of Justice accused in a placard that he "helped jail Republicans in England". See Brown, *op. cit. supra*, n. 4, at p. 135.

[53] See Lord Cooke in *Reynolds v. Times Newspapers Ltd.*, [1999] 4 All E.R. 609, at p. 646 (H.L.).

[54] See *Lewis v. Daily Telegraph*, [1964] A.C. 234, at p. 259 (*per* Lord Reid).

The natural and ordinary meaning of words includes any inferences or implications which they may reasonably bear. As was explained by Lord Reid:[55]

> There is no doubt that in actions for libel the question is what the words would convey to the ordinary man: it is not one of construction in the legal sense. The ordinary man does not live in an ivory tower and he is not inhibited by a knowledge of the rules of construction. So he can and does not read between the lines in the light of his general knowledge and experience of worldly affairs. . . .
>
> What the ordinary man would infer without special knowledge has generally been called the natural and ordinary meaning of the words. But that expression is rather misleading in that it conceals the fact that there are two elements in it. Sometimes it is not necessary to go beyond the words themselves, as where the plaintiff has been called a thief or a murderer. But more often the sting is not so much in the words themselves as in what the ordinary man will infer from them, and that is also regarded as part of their natural and ordinary meaning.

The meaning intended by the publisher is irrelevant.[56] It does not matter if defamation was unintended, if it exists, or if it was intended, and does not exist.[57] Likewise, the actual understanding of the person reading the statement is not in issue, as the test is the effect on ordinary people.[58] Thus, an action may still lie even though the person reading the words did not believe the imputation against the plaintiff, or knew it to be false.[59] This is subject to the qualification, however, that it may be otherwise if the person hearing the statement is representative of the type of person to whom the words were, or were likely to have been, directed.[60]

The defamatory nature of the words may also arise by reason of the particular characteristic or activity of the plaintiff. Thus, it may be defamatory to call a union member a "scab",[61] but not a general manager or a supervisor. It has also been held to be defamatory to accuse a kosher butcher of selling bacon,[62] or calling a retailer a "price-cutter".[63]

The time and place of an utterance may also make a difference. Thus, depending on the "temper" of the times or the community it may or may not be

---

[55] *Ibid.*, at p. 258. The drawing of inferences in this manner is distinguishable from the law with regard to innuendo which requires reference to extrinsic facts beyond general knowledge. See also *Jones v. Skelton*, [1963] 3 All E.R. 952, at p. 958 (P.C.); *Grubb v. Bristol United Press Ltd.*, [1963] 1 Q.B. 309, at p. 327 (C.A.).

[56] *E. Hulton & Co. v. Jones*, [1910] A.C. 20, at p. 23 (*per* Lord Loreburn L.C.). See also *Johnston v. Ewart* (1893), 24 O.R. 116, at p. 123 (C.A.); *Lever v. George*, [1950] O.R. 115, at p. 116.

[57] *Sadgrove v. Hole*, [1901] 2 K.B. 1.

[58] *Daines and Braddock v. Hartley* (1848), 3 Exch. 200, 154 E.R. 815; *Simmons v. Mitchell* (1880), 6 App. Cas. 156, at p. 163; *Slim v. Daily Telegraph Ltd.*, [1968] 1 All E.R. 497.

[59] See *Morgan v. Odhams Press Ltd.*, [1971] 2 All E.R. 1156, at p. 1163 (H.L.). See also *Hough v. London Express Newspaper Ltd.*, [1940] 2 K.B. 507 (C.A.).

[60] See Duncan and Neill, *op. cit. supra*, n. 4, pp. 13-14.

[61] *Murphy et al. v. Plasterers Union*, [1949] S.A.S.R. 98. See also *Doyle v. International Assn. of Machinists and Aerospace Workers, Loc. 1681* (1991), 110 A.R. 222 (Q.B.).

[62] *Braun v. Armour & Co.* (1930), 173 N.E. 845 (N.Y.C.A.).

[63] *Meyerson v. Hurlburt et al.* (1938), 98 F. 2d 232 (C.A. for D.C.).

defamatory to call someone a Socialist[64] or to refer to a white man as a "coloured gentleman",[65] or, presumably, to describe a woman as a lesbian. As social attitudes change, our view of what is defamatory will reflect those changes; the sooner the better!

b) The Form of the Communication

The form of the communication can be varied. Words are the usual way to defame someone, but there need not be a direct assertion. One can defame "by means of a question, and indirect insinuation, or expression of belief or opinion, or sarcasm or irony".[66] The mode of publication may also have a bearing on the interpretation to be given to the words. Thus, the publication as a whole must be looked at, not just isolated passages. In addition, "the prominence which is given to the words by their position in the newspaper or magazine, or by the emphasis which is provided by the type and heading employed" may be of significance.[67] Similarly, with regard to slander, the meaning of the words may be affected by the speaker's tone of voice or any accompanying gestures or facial expressions. This is particularly so in television defamation, where an impression can be devastatingly conveyed by tone of voice, music, images, *etc.*[68] Thus, seemingly defamatory words may, in fact, be totally innocent, and *vice versa*. As for the latter situation, it has been suggested that this might more properly be considered in terms of legal innuendo.[69] For example, it would not be defamatory if one lawyer jokingly addressed a lawyer friend as "You old shyster, you", whereas it would be if a client called a lawyer an old shyster, because everyone would realize that in the former case the imputation was not meant seriously, while in the latter case it clearly was.

It is also possible to defame someone without the use of words. Thus, it is actionable to print the plaintiff's portrait alongside a picture of a gorilla to indicate a resemblance,[70] or to publish a photograph in an advertisement which, because of blurring, makes it appear that the plaintiff is indecently exposed.[71] So too, in certain circumstances, a cartoonist can defame a person with a drawing. A cartoon showing a politician fiendishly gloating while pulling the wings off a

---

[64] *Slayter v. Daily Telegraph*, *supra*, n. 47, socialist. See also *Braddock v. Bevins*, [1948] 1 K.B. 58 (C.A.), "near-Communist"; *Brannigan v. Seafarers' International Union* (1963), 42 D.L.R. (2d) 249 (B.C.).

[65] *Upton v. Times-Democrat Publishing Co.* (1990), 28 So. 970 (La S.C.).

[66] *Prosser and Keeton, op. cit. supra*, n. 3, at p. 780.

[67] See *English & Scottish Co-operative Properties Mortgage & Investment Society Ltd. v. Odhams Press Ltd.*, [1940] 1 K.B. 440, at p. 452 (C.A.) (*per* Slesser L.J.).

[68] See *Grossman v. CFTO–Television Ltd.* (1982), 39 O.R. (2d) 498, at p. 502 (C.A.).

[69] Duncan and Neill, *op. cit. supra*, n. 4, at p. 15.

[70] *Zbyszko v. N.Y. Am.* (1930), 228 App. Div. 277, 239 N.Y. Supp. 411.

[71] *Burton v. Crowell Publ. Co.* (1936), 82 F. 2d 154 (U.S.C.A., 2nd Cir.).

fly, indicating cruelty, may be defamatory, though this may be fair comment in some circumstances.[72]

The function of the judge in this area is to determine, as a question of law, whether the words, gestures, etc., are capable of bearing a defamatory meaning. It is for the jury to decide what meaning or meanings they, in fact, bear.[73]

c) Innuendo

Words which appear innocent on the surface may be defamatory to certain people who are aware of other facts, not generally known, in relation thereto. The law of defamation recognizes two different situations in this regard: (1) words which have a technical or slang meaning or a meaning which depends on some special knowledge possessed by a limited number of persons only, and (2) ordinary words which may on occasion bear some special meaning other than their natural and ordinary meaning because of some extrinsic facts or circumstances.[74]

These "special meanings" are described as "legal" or "true" innuendos, as distinguishable from the vernacular usage of the term as encompassing reasonable inferences which one may draw from the ordinary and natural meaning of words. The plaintiff must specifically plead a legal innuendo and must prove the underlying facts or circumstances.[75] It is not necessary for the plaintiff to prove that the defendant knew of the special facts which give rise to the innuendo,[76] or that the words were, in fact, published to someone who understood their defamatory sense. It is sufficient to show that there were people who had knowledge of the extrinsic facts and that reasonable persons, with such knowledge, would have understood the words in a defamatory sense.[77]

---

[72] *Vander Zalm v. Times Publishers* (1980), 12 C.C.L.T. 81 (B.C.C.A.); *Mitchell v. Nanaimo District Teachers' Assn.* (1994), 94 B.C.L.R. (2d) 81 (C.A.), cartoon depicting principal as greedy found defamatory.

[73] *Capital and Counties Bank v. Henty* (1882), 7 App. Cas. 741; *Broome v. Agar* (1928), 138 L.T. 698.

[74] Duncan and Neill, *op. cit. supra*, n. 4, at p. 17.

[75] See *Gatley on Libel and Slander*, 9th ed. But see Libel and Slander Act, R.S.O. 1990, c. L.12, s. 19, which provides: "In an action for libel or slander, the plaintiff may aver that the words complained of were used in a defamatory sense, specifying the defamatory sense without any prefatory averment to show how the words were used in that sense, and the averment shall be put in issue by the denial of the alleged libel or slander, and, where the words set forth, with or without the alleged meaning, show a cause of action, the statement of claim is sufficient." At common law each innuendo pleaded gave rise to a distinct cause of action which was subject to a separate verdict. The American jurisprudence distinguishes between the "inducement" which is the facts from which it is said the defamatory meaning arises, and the "innuendo" which establishes the defamatory sense by reference to such facts. See *Prosser and Keeton, op. cit. supra*, n. 3, at p. 780.

[76] *Cassidy v. Daily Mirror Newspapers*, [1929] 2 K.B. 331.

[77] *Hough v. London Express Newspaper Ltd.*, [1940] 2 K.B. 507 (C.A.); *Mark v. Deutsch et al.* (1937), 39 D.L.R. (3d) 568 (Alta.).

The judge must rule on whether the words are capable of bearing the innuendo suggested, but it is the jury which decides whether they in fact do bear such innuendo.[78]

The importance of the proof of the extrinsic facts becomes apparent when one views words or actions that would otherwise appear innocuous. The publication of apparent good news that the plaintiff had given birth to twins was held to be libellous when it was shown that she was married only four weeks before.[79] Likewise, it was defamatory of the real Mrs. X to publish a photograph of another woman as Mrs. X.[80] The displaying of a model of the plaintiff in a wax museum was also defamatory in view of the fact that, although he had been acquitted of a charge of murder, the model was positioned next to the figures of three notorious persons located near the "Chamber of Horrors".[81] And, the unauthorized use of a caricature of the plaintiff, an amateur golfer, to advertise chocolates, was defamatory as it suggested that he accepted money for the advertisement thereby prostituting his amateur status.[82] Using innocent clips of a doctor's own words on T.V. can be made by skillful manipulators to imply wrongdoing by innuendo.[83]

4. IDENTIFICATION

a) Colloquium

It must be pleaded and proved that the defamatory statement was spoken "of and concerning the plaintiff". This is known as the "*colloquium*".[84] Thus, if not specifically identified, the plaintiff must show that reference would reasonably be understood to have been made to the plaintiff.[85] This may require reference to extrinsic facts or circumstances.[86] In one case, even though the plaintiff was the only vendor in the locality selling the product referred to, the "average sensible reader" would not conclude that the statement referred to the plaintiff.[87] A woman was held not to have been sufficiently identified in an obituary which insinuated that her husband committed suicide to avoid her wrath upon discov-

---

[78] *Australian Newspaper Co. v. Bennett*, [1894] A.C. 284, at p. 287 (P.C.) (*per* Lord Herschell L.C.). See also *Ward v. McBride* (1911), 24 O.L.R. 555 (C.A.); *Cassidy v. Daily Mirror, supra*, n. 76, at p. 340.

[79] *Morrison v. John Ritchie & Co.* (1902), 4 F. (Ct. of Sess.) 645. See also, *Bell v. Northern Constitution*, [1943] N.I. 108, false notice of the birth of a son to a man and his housekeeper.

[80] *Cassidy v. Daily Mirror, supra*, n. 76.

[81] *Monson v. Tussauds Ltd.*, [1894] 1 Q.B. 671.

[82] *Tolley v. J.S. Fry & Sons Ltd.*, [1931] A.C. 333 (H.L.).

[83] *Myers v. Canadian Broadcasting Corp.* (1999), 47 C.C.L.T. (2d) 272 (Ont. S.C.J.) (*per* Bellamy J.).

[84] *Prosser and Keeton, op. cit. supra*, n. 3, at p. 783.

[85] *Taylor v. Massey* (1891), 20 O.R. 409 (C.A.); *Syme v. Canavan*, [1918] V.L.R. 540; *Jozwiak v. Sadek*, [1954] 1 All E.R. 3; *Youssoupoff, supra*, n. 6. There is no rule of law that before an article can be said to be defamatory of a person it must contain within itself a "key" or "pointer" to indicate that it is the plaintiff referred to: *Morgan v. Odhams Press, supra*, n. 59.

[86] *Bruce v. Odhams Press Ltd.*, [1936] 1 K.B. 697 (C.A.); *Fraser v. Sykes*, [1971] 1 W.W.R. 246; affd [1971] 3 W.W.R. 161; affd [1973] 5 W.W.R. 484 (S.C.C.).

[87] *Dale's Trad'n Post Ltd. et al. v. Rhodes et al.* (1987), 43 C.C.L.T. 37, at p. 47 (B.C.S.C.).

ering his extramarital affair, because someone glancing at an obituary in a national paper would not appreciate that there had been any reference to her.[88] For the purpose of determining whether it is the plaintiff referred to, it is no defence that the defendant did not know of the existence of the plaintiff,[89] or that he meant to refer to someone else.[90]

b) Group Defamation

The problem of identifying the person defamed is most apparent in cases of group or class defamation. The general test as to whether the words are referable to a particular individual is the same as previously noted, that is, whether ordinary sensible people might reasonably believe that the statement referred to the plaintiff.[91] It obviously will be easier to do so where the group is a small one,[92] but even a member of a large class may have a cause of action in appropriate circumstances. The principles involved with regard to the latter aspect were explained in *Knupffer v. London Express Newspaper*,[93] in which some defamatory things were said of a group called Young Russia, a pro-Nazi organization, of which the plaintiff was a member. There were 2,000 other members in the world, 24 of whom were in Britain. The action was dismissed for reasons which were explained by Lord Atkin:

> I venture to think that it is a mistake to lay down a rule as to libel on a class, and then qualify it with exceptions. The only relevant rule is that in order to be actionable the defamatory words must be understood to be published of and concerning the plaintiff. It is irrelevant that the words are published of two or more persons if they are proved to be published of him, and it is irrelevant that the two or more persons are called by some generic or class name. There can be no law that a defamatory statement made of a firm, or trustees, or the tenants of a particular building is not actionable, if the words would reasonably be understood as published of each member of the firm or each trustee or each tenant. The reason why a libel published of a large or indeterminate number of persons described by some general name generally fails to be actionable is the difficulty of establishing that the plaintiff was, in fact, included in the defamatory statement, for the habit of making unfounded generalizations is ingrained in ill-educated or vulgar minds, or the words are occasionally intended to be a facetious exaggeration. Even in such cases words may be used which enable the plaintiff to prove that the words complained of were intended to be published of each member of the group, or, at any rate, of himself. Too much attention has been paid, I venture to think, in the textbooks and elsewhere to the ruling of Willes J., in 1858 in *Eastwood v. Holmes* [1 F. & F. 347], a case at nisi prius. . . . His words: "it only reflects on a class of persons" are irrelevant

---

[88] See *Allen v. Bailey* (1995), 24 C.C.L.T. (2d) 212 (Ont. Gen. Div.).

[89] *E. Hulton & Co. v. Jones, supra*, n. 56.

[90] *Newstead v. London Express Newspaper Ltd.*, [1940] 1 K.B. 377 (C.A.), two persons with same name. But the defendant may be asked on examination for discovery to whom he meant to refer as this goes to the issue of malice: *Morley v. Patrick* (1910), 21 O.L.R. 240 (Div. Ct.).

[91] *Abraham v. Advocate Co.*, [1946] 2 W.W.R. 181 (P.C.).

[92] See *Albrecht v. Burkholder* (1889), 18 O.R. 287; *Browne et al. v. D.C. Thomson & Co.*, [1912] S.C. 359; *Neiman-Marcus v. Lait* (1952), 13 F.R.D. 311; *Ortenberg v. Plamondon* (1914), 35 C.L.T. 262 (Que.); *Fraser v. Sykes*, [1974] S.C.R. 526.

[93] [1944] A.C. 116 (H.L.). See also *Booth v. B.C.T.V.* (1982), 139 D.L.R. (3d) 88 (B.C.C.A.).

unless they mean "it does not reflect on the plaintiff", and his instance, "All lawyers were thieves" is an excellent instance of the vulgar generalizations to which I have referred. It will be as well for the future for lawyers to concentrate on the question whether the words were published of the plaintiff rather than on the question whether they were spoken of a class. I agree that in the present case the words complained of are, apparently, an unfounded generalization conveying imputations of disgraceful conduct, but not such as could reasonably be understood to be spoken of the appellant.[94]

In addition to the size of the class, other relevant factors to consider as to whether an individual has been defamed include the generality of the charge and its extravagance.[95]

Older authority held "that where defamatory words are spoken impartially in relation to either of two persons", neither of them has a cause of action because it is uncertain which one was aimed at.[96] However, it has been suggested that this "bizarre pedantry" has no place in modern law, since "incontestably a slur is cast on both".[97]

In *Elliott v. Canadian Broadcasting Corporation*[98] a statement of claim was struck out on the ground that it disclosed no reasonable cause of action when it alleged that 25,000 surviving Canadian aircrew who served in World War II were defamed by the documentary "The Valour and the Horror: Death by Moonlight — Bomber Command", and the book *The Valour and the Horror — The Boys of Bomber Command.* Grange J.A. held that there could be no libel where the broadcast was " . . . aimed . . . at the British High Command who ordered the bombing and particularly at its overall Commander . . .".[99] and not at the airmen who were also portrayed in it. Similarly, a reference in the Ottawa Sun to several Ottawa Valley towns, including Pembroke, Ontario, as "bastions of yokeldom", did not sufficiently identify either the Mayor of Pembroke or the residents of the town of Pembroke.[100]

5. WHO MAY BE DEFAMED?

a) Individuals

Only living people can be defamed. Therefore, no action lies at the suit of the estate of deceased persons if defamatory things are said about them, or by their

---

[94] *Ibid.*, at pp. 121-22. See also *Alberta Union of Provincial Employees v. Edmonton Sun* (1986), 39 C.C.L.T. 143 (Q.B.), in which 25 out of a group of 200 prison guards successfully sued where the correctional staff generally was defamed.

[95] Duncan and Neill, *op. cit. supra*, n. 4, p. 30.

[96] *Chomley v. Watson*, [1907] V.L.R. 502, relying on *Falkner v. Cooper* (1666), 124 E.R. 821. But see *Harrison v. Thornborough* (1713), 88 E.R. 691. In *Albrecht v. Burkholder, supra*, n. 92, it was held that in order for one to succeed it was necessary to show that the words were not true of the other as well.

[97] Fleming, *The Law of Torts*, 6th ed. (1983), p. 507. See also Duncan and Neill, *op. cit. supra*, n. 4, at p. 30.

[98] (1995), 25 O.R. (3d) 302 (C.A.); leave to appeal to S.C.C. refused (1996), 131 D.L.R. (4th) vii (S.C.C.).

[99] *Ibid.*, at p. 309.

[100] *McCann v. Ottawa Sun (The)* (1993), 16 O.R. (3d) 672 (Gen. Div.) *(per* Chilcott J.).

friends and relatives for injury to their feelings.[101] However, an imputation against the dead may reflect upon the living, so that an allegation that the deceased was a whore may defame her family because they are personally defamed.[102]

Bankrupts may sue for damages for defamation in their own right as the cause of action does not vest in trustees. This is true also of instances which arise during the currency of the bankruptcy so that any amounts recovered do not form part of the estate.[103]

b) Non-natural Persons

Certain legal entities, other than human beings, may also sue for defamation if the words reflect adversely upon the reputations they have developed. The sting of these statements must relate to the "business character" of the entity suing, not merely to the individuals associated with them.[104] Thus, a corporation may complain of words tending to damage its business interests or goodwill by false imputations of insolvency,[105] or of inefficiency or impropriety[106] in the conduct of its affairs. Similarly, a partnership,[107] a professional association,[108] a municipal corporation,[109] a school board[110] or a trade union,[111] may institute proceedings for defamatory imputations as to its operations.

---

[101] *Broom v. John Ritchie & Co.* (1904), 6 F. (Ct. of Sess.) 942, no recovery for *solatium* by widow and children for newspaper story that husband/father committed suicide. See also *Small v. Globe Printing Co. Ltd.*, [1940] O.W.N. 163. See Symmons, "New Remedies against Libellers of the Dead? A Look at the Recommendation of the Faulks Committee on Defamation" (1980), 18 U.W.O.L. Rev. 521.

[102] Fleming, *op. cit. supra*, n. 10, p. 585. The cases cited in support of this proposition do not deal with defamation of the dead, but rather with whether imputations against one person can reflect on another such as to be actionable by the latter. However, the principle is the same. See *Vicars v. Worth* (1722), 93 E.R. 641; *Hodgkins v. Corbett* (1723), 93 E.R. 690; *Ryalls v. Leader* (1866), L.R. 1 Exch. 296; *Huckle v. Reynolds* (1859), 7 C.B. (N.S.) 114.

[103] See Duncan and Neill, *op. cit. supra*, n. 4, p. 57, and cases cited.

[104] *Metropolitan Saloon Omnibus Co. v. Hawkins* (1859), 4 H. & N. 87, 157 E.R. 769; *Price v. Chicoutimi Pulp Co.* (1915), 23 D.L.R. 116, at p. 122 (S.C.C.) (*per* Idington J.). But see *Manchester v. Williams*, [1891] 1 Q.B. 94, in which it was held that a corporation could not sue with regard to an allegation of "corrupt practices" as it, as distinguished from its individuals, could not be guilty of such charge. See also *Church of Scientology of Toronto v. Globe & Mail Ltd.* (1978), 19 O.R. (2d) 62, wherein it was held that the words complained of, alleging the practice of medicine without a licence, referred not to the plaintiff non-profit corporation but to its members.

[105] *Dominion Telegraph v. Silver*, *supra*, n. 36; *Metropolitan Saloon v. Hawkins*, *supra*, n. 104; *R. v. MacNamara* (1893), 14 L.R. (N.S.W.) 515.

[106] *South Hetton Coal Co. v. North-Eastern News Assoc.*, [1894] 1 Q.B. 133 (C.A.); *Canada Life Assurance Co. v. O'Loane* (1872), 32 U.C.Q.B. 379 (C.A.).

[107] *Le Fanu v. Malcolmson* (1848), 1 H.L. Cas. 637; *Russell v. Webster* (1874), 23 W.R. 59.

[108] *Saskatchewan College of Physicians & Surgeons v. Co-op. Commonwealth Federation Publishing & Printing Co. Ltd.* (1965), 51 D.L.R. (2d) 442 (Sask.).

[109] *Bognor Regis U.D.C. v. Campion*, [1972] 2 Q.B. 169, distinguishing *Manchester v. Williams*, *supra*, n. 104. See also *Prince George v. B.C. Television System Ltd.*, [1979] 2 W.W.R. 404 (B.C.C.A.), *Derbyshire County Council v. Times Newspapers Ltd.*, [1991] 4 All E.R. 795 (Q.B.).

[110] *Windsor Roman Catholic Separate School Bd. v. Southam Inc.* (1984), 46 O.R. (2d) 231 (H.C.).

[111] *Pulp & Paper Workers of Canada v. International Brotherhood of Pulp Sulphite and Paper Mill Workers et al.* (1973), 37 D.L.R. (3d) 687 (B.C.); *National Union of General and Municipal*

Unincorporated associations, other than partnerships, trade unions, and employer's associations, apparently do not have status to in their own right.[112] The members themselves would, of course, be left to pursue their own remedies and would succeed only upon proof that the words complained of had reference to them as individuals.

c) Minority Groups: Hate Propaganda

Defamation law, consequently, offers little protection for minority groups distinguishable by colour, race, religion, or ethnic origin. As a result, it has been left to the legislators to combat this problem. Legislation banning "hate propaganda" has been enacted both federally[113] and provincially in some provinces.[114]

An analysis of this legislation is beyond the scope of this chapter.[115]

Workers v. Gillian et al., [1946] K.B. 81 (C.A.). In *Amalgamated Builders Council v. Herman* (1930), 65 O.L.R. 296, it was held that a trade union did not have status to bring a defamation action, but the recognition of a union as a legal entity appears to have eclipsed this case. *International Brotherhood of Teamsters et al. v. Therien*, [1960] S.C.R. 265.

[112] See Duncan and Neill, *op. cit. supra*, n. 4, at p. 50.

[113] The Criminal Code, R.S.C. 1985, c. C-46, s. 319 provides that: "(1) Every one who, by communicating statements in any public place, incites hatred against any identifiable group [distinguished by colour, race] where such incitement is likely to lead to a breach of the peace. . . . (2) Every one who, by communicating statements, other than in private conversation, wilfully promotes hatred against any identifiable group" is guilty of . . . an offence". It is a defence for the accused to prove that the "statements communicated were true"; or "in good faith, he expressed or attempted to establish by argument an opinion on a religious subject"; or "the statements were relevant to any subject of public interest, the discussion of which was for the public benefit [and he believed] on reasonable grounds [that they were true]" or "in good faith, he intended to point out, for the purpose of removal, matters producing or tending to produce feelings of hatred towards an identifiable group in Canada." See s. 298(1) and *R. v. Georgia Straight Publishing Co.*, [1970] 1 C.C.C. 94 (B.C.). See also Law Reform Commission of Canada. *Hate Propaganda* (Working Paper 50, 1986). See also *R. v. Keegstra*, [1990] 3 S.C.R. 697.

[114] A novel piece of provincial legislation is s. 19(1) of the Manitoba Defamation Act, R.S.M. 1987, c. D20, which provides:

19(1) The publication of a libel against a race or religious creed likely to expose persons belonging to the race, or professing the religious creed, to hatred, contempt or ridicule, and tending to raise unrest or disorder among the people, entitles a person belonging to the race, or professing the religious creed, to sue for an injunction to prevent the continuation and circulation of the libel; and the Court of Queen's Bench may entertain the action.

See *Courchene v. Marlborough Hotel* (1972), 22 D.L.R. (3d) 157, [1972] 1 W.W.R. 449 (Man. C.A.); memo instructing hotel employees not to serve Indian or Metis not defamatory.

[115] For a further discussion of the problem of group defamation, see Riesman, "Democracy and Defamation: Control of Group Libel" (1942), 42 Colum. L. Rev. 727; Fenson, "Group Defamation: Is the Cure too Costly?" (1964), 1 Man. L.S.J. 255; Arthurs, "Hate Propaganda — An Argument Against Attempts to Stop it by Legislation" (1970), 18 Chitty's L.J. 1; Cohen, "The Hate Propaganda Amendments: Reflections on a Controversy" (1971), 9 Alta. L. Rev. 103; Burns, "Defamatory Libel in Canada: A Recent Illustration of a Rare Crime" (1969), 16 Chitty's L.J. 213.

B. Libel or Slander?

Defamation can be divided into the two broad categories of libel and slander. The former has basically been associated with the written word but also extends to pictures,[116] statues,[117] films,[118] television[119] and even conduct implying a defamatory meaning.[120] It is actionable without proof of damage, as general damages are presumed. It may even be the subject of a criminal prosecution.[121]

Slander, on the other hand, is generally conveyed by the spoken word and is not actionable *per se*, so that, no matter how offensive the language used is,[122] an action lies only if special damages are pleaded and proved, subject to certain exceptions.[123]

The basic distinction between libel and slander is in the mode of publication.[124] Sometimes it is suggested that the difference lies in the sense appealed to — if the communication is directed to the sense of sight (or even touch or smell), it is libel; but if it is addressed to the sense of hearing, it is slander.[125] This notion is helpful, but it is not definitive.

A conflict arises in cases where the defamatory matter has been written but it is actually communicated to a third person orally.[126] One rationalization that has

---

[116] *Garbett v. Hazell et al.*, [1943] 2 All E.R. 359 (C.A.).

[117] *Monson v. Tussauds Ltd.*, [1894] 1 Q.B. 671 (C.A.).

[118] *Youssoupoff v. Metro-Goldwyn-Mayer Pictures Ltd.* (1934), 50 T.L.R. 581.

[119] See *Colour Your World Corp. v. Canadian Broadcasting Corp.*, *supra*, n. 13.

[120] For example, see *Eyre v. Garlick* (1878), 42 J.P. 68, hanging the plaintiff in effigy; *Jefferies v. Duncombe* (1809), 103 E.R. 991, placing a red lantern in front of the plaintiff's home to indicate it is a bawdy house.

[121] The Criminal Code, R.S.C. 1985, c. C-46, provides:

> 298(1) A defamatory libel is matter published, without lawful justification or excuse, that is likely to injure the reputation of any person by exposing him to hatred, contempt or ridicule, or that is designed to insult the person of or concerning whom it is published.
>
> (2) A defamatory libel may be expressed directly or by insinuation or irony
>
> (a) in word legibly marked upon any substance, or
>
> (b) by any object signifying a defamatory libel otherwise than by words.

See *R. v. Georgia Straight Publishing Ltd.*, [1970] 1 C.C.C. 94; *R. v. Unwin* (1938), 69 C.C.C. 197. If the publisher knows the libel to be false the penalty can be five years imprisonment: s. 300. Otherwise the publisher is liable to imprisonment for two years: s. 301. Abolition suggested by Law Reform Commission of Canada, *Defamatory Libel* (Working Paper 35, 1984).

[122] *Jones v. Jones*, [1916] 1 K.B. 351; affd [1916] 2 A.C. 481.

[123] See *infra*, Section B, I. Consequences of the Distinction.

[124] See Fleming, *op. cit. supra*, n. 10, at p. 546. J.S. Williams, *The Law of Libel and Slander in Canada*, 2nd ed. (1988), p. 49.

[125] Fleming, *op. cit. supra*, n. 10, at p. 602. But there has been confusion in the application of these principles. In *Gutsole v. Mathers* (1836), 1 M. & W. 495, 150 E.R. 530, it was held that the use of a sign was slander. In contrast, the greeting of an unmarried couple with a charivari which consisted of guns being fired, bells being rung and shouting, according to a local custom with newly married people, was held to be libel in *Varner v. Morton* (1919), 53 N.S.R. 180, 46 D.L.R. 597.

[126] Compare *Meldrum v. Australian Broadcasting Co. Ltd.*, [1932] V.L.R. 425, in which the reading of a script in a radio broadcast was held to be slander, to *Forrester v. Tyrrell* (1893), 9 T.L.R. 257 (C.A.), in which the reading aloud of a defamatory letter at a lodge meeting was held to be a libel.

been advanced is that libel is concerned with the publication of defamatory matters in some permanent form, whereas slander applies to publication in a transient form.[127] Another distinction, which is said to be an intermediate view, is that the categorization depends on the apprehension of the person to whom the publication is made.[128] Thus, if "the hearer understands only that the defamatory matter is spoken, it is slander; but if he understands that the speaker is communicating to him defamatory matter embodied in permanent form, it is libel because it is much the same as if the listener had read it himself."[129]

One can immediately see the problems that might arise in this area by the creation of new methods of communication, such as radio, T.V., computers, etc. Fortunately, most of the early difficulty was resolved by legislation[130] which

---

[127] Fleming, *op. cit. supra*, n. 10, at p. 603; Neill and Duncan and Neill, *op. cit. supra*, n. 4, at p. 4. One area that has caused particular difficulty is the dictation of defamatory matter to a stenographer. In *Ostrowe v. Lee* (1931), 256 N.Y. 505, 175 N.E. 505, Cardozo J. considered this a libel. See also *Langdon-Griffiths v. Smith*, [1957] 1 K.B. 295, minutes of general meeting. But, in *Lawrence v. Finch* (1931), 66 O.L.R. 451, [1931] 1 D.L.R. 689 (C.A.), the view was expressed that the subsequent publication of a transcription would be a slander only. See also *Osborn v. Thomas Boulter & Son*, [1930] 2 K.B. 226. The permanence-transcience dichotomy was apparently at the root of the finding in *Youssoupoff, supra*, n. 118, that both the photographic part as well as the synchronized speech in a film constituted libel. Thus, it is suggested that while it is only slander to utter defamatory words with the intention that they be recorded, once a record has been made, subsequent playing of it would be libel. The *Restatement of Torts*, 2d, para. 568 reads as follows:

(1) Libel consists of the publication of defamatory matter by written or printed words, or by its embodiment in physical form, or by any other form of communication which has the potentially harmful qualities characteristic of written or printed words. (2) Slander consists of the publication of defamatory matter by spoken words, transitory gestures, or by any form of communication other than those stated in Subsection (1). (3) The area of dissemination, the deliberate and premeditated character of its publication, and the persistence of the defamation are factors to be considered in determining whether a publication is a libel rather than a slander. Copyright 1965 by The American Law Institute. Reprinted with the permission of the American Law Institute.

[128] Thus, in *Meldrum, supra*, n. 126, the fact that the audience knew that the statement was being read was offered as a possible explanation for the result in *Forrester, supra*, n. 119. However, this notion was rejected in *Hartmann v. Winchell* (1947), 296 N.Y. 296, 171 A.L.R. 759 (C.A).

[129] Fleming, *op. cit. supra*, n. 10, at p. 547.

[130] See the Libel and Slander Act, R.S.O. 1990, c. L.12, which provides:

1. — (1) In this Act,

"broadcasting" means the dissemination of writing, signs, signals, pictures and sounds of all kinds, intended to be received by the public either directly or through the medium of relay stations, by means of

(a) any form of wireless radioelectric communication utilizing Hertzian waves, including radiotelegraph and radiotelephone, or

(b) cables, wires, fibre-optic linkages or laser beams,

and "broadcast" has a corresponding meaning, ("radiodiffusion . . .", "radiodiffuser . . .")

"newspaper" means a paper containing public news, intelligence, or occurrences, or remarks or observations thereon, or containing only, or principally, advertisements, printed for distribution to the public and published periodically, or in parts or numbers, at least twelve times a year. ("journal")

(2) Any reference to words in this Act shall be construed as including a reference to pictures, visual images, gestures and other methods of signifying meaning.

clearly defined "broadcasting".[131] More significantly, several jurisdictions wisely have actually abolished the distinction altogether,[132] which is something that should be done everywhere.

1. CONSEQUENCES OF THE DISTINCTION

The classification of the conduct is still of importance, despite the statutory reforms, because the procedural rules governing libel and slander may differ. Also, damages are presumed in libel, whereas, in slander, special damage must be proven by a plaintiff. However, there are four types of slander which are actionable *per se*, that is, they are treated in the same way as libel in that damage is presumed and need not be specifically pleaded or proven.

a) Imputation of the Commission of a Crime

Words imputing the commission of a crime are actionable without proof of special damage. Guilt must be alleged, not merely suspicion,[133] and the crime must be a serious one, punishable by a prison term, though it need not necessarily be an indictable offence.[134] A general accusation of criminality is enough; it is, therefore, not necessary to specify a particular crime, although the imputation itself should be unequivocal.[135] Thus, the statement that the plaintiff is a "thief"[136] will suffice, whereas the mere assertion that the plaintiff has the defendant's property will not. Neither will words which suggest only that the plaintiff has a propensity to commit crime be actionable *per se*.[137]

---

2. Defamatory words in a newspaper or in a broadcast shall be deemed to be published and to constitute libel.

[131] See *MacIntyre v. C.B.C.* (1985), 34 C.C.L.T. 243 (N.S.C.A.).

[132] See Defamation Act, R.S.M. 1987, c. D20, ss. 1 and 2; Defamation Act, R.S.A. 1980, c. D-6, ss. 1(b) and 2; Defamation Act, R.S.N.B. 1973, c. D-5, s. 1; Defamation Act, R.S.N. 1990, c. D-3, s. 2(b). Defamation Act, R.S.P.E.I. 1988, c. D-5, s. 1(b); Defamation Act, R.S.N.S. 1989, c. 122, s. 2(b). This is also the case in some states in the U.S., Australia and New Zealand. However, the legislation in some jurisdictions gives no statutory authority to recognize broadcasting as libel. See, for example, Libel and Slander Act, R.S.S. 1978, c. L-14. As a result, resort must still be had to the common law.

[133] *Simmons v. Mitchell* (1880), 6 App. Cas. 156 (P.C.).

[134] *Webb v. Beavan* (1883), 11 Q.B.D. 609; *Hellwig v. Mitchell*, [1910] 1 K.B. 609; *McDonald v. Mulqueen* (1922), 53 O.L.R. 191; *Lever v. George*, [1950] O.R. 115.

[135] *Curtis v. Curtis* (1834), 10 Bing. 477, 131 E.R. 980, "I can transport you"; *Webb v. Beavan, supra*, n. 134; "I will lock you up". But see *Conyd v. Brekelmans*, [1971] 3 W.W.R. 107 (B.C.), wherein the statement that someone would "pocket the money" from a grant was held not to be specific enough to impute the commission of the crime of "obtaining by false pretense". See also *Lever v. George, supra*, n. 134, allegation that plaintiff had a "mysterious fire" not sufficient to impute crime of arson.

[136] *Knowles v. Goldt*, [1951] 1 D.L.R. 458 (Sask. C.A.).

[137] *Dubord v. Lambert*, [1928] 3 D.L.R. 538 (Alta. C.A); *Bureau v. Campbell*, [1928] 3 D.L.R. 907, at p. 913 (Sask. C.A.); affd [1929] 2 D.L.R. 205 (S.C.C.); *Conyd v. Brekelmans, supra*, n. 135.

b) Imputation of a Loathsome Disease

To say that someone is suffering from a contagious or infectious disease is so likely to cause them to be ostracized that it is actionable *per se*.[138] The scope of this exception is confined to the imputation of the most loathsome varieties of disease, such as venereal disease or leprosy. However, a statement that someone suffered from such an infirmity in the past is not treated on the same footing.[139]

c) Imputation of Unchastity to a Woman

To accuse a woman of unchastity was thought so serious that it was actionable *per se*. This exception actually derived from statute rather than the common law.[140] It applies only to women,[141] so that a similar imputation against a man requires him to give proof of special damage.[142] It has been held to be actionable *per se* to call a woman a lesbian,[143] and the same view has been taken of an allegation that a man is a homosexual.[144]

d) Imputation of Unfitness to Practice One's Trade or Profession

Slandering people in relation to their business, trade, profession, office or other employment activity is actionable *per se* because it is clearly calculated to damage them in a pecuniary way.[145] However, this applies only to remunerative activities and not to positions of honour that do not yield financial benefits.[146] In addition, the person being defamed must occupy the office at the time of the publication.[147] At one time, the words had to reflect directly upon the plaintiff's trade or calling.[148] However, this has now been abrogated by statute.[149]

---

138 *French (Oscar) v. Smith* (1923), 53 O.L.R. 28, [1923] 3 D.L.R. 902; *Houseman v. Coulson*, [1948] 2 D.L.R. 62 (Sask.).

139 *Halls v. Mitchell*, [1927] 1 D.L.R. 163 (Ont. C.A.); appeal allowed in part and on other grounds [1928] S.C.R. 125.

140 See The Slander of Women Act, 1891, (U.K.), 54 & 55 Vict., c. 51.

141 *French (Elizabeth) v. Smith* (1923), 53 O.L.R. 31, [1923] 3 D.L.R. 904. Similar provisions to the U.K. Act were enacted but recently repealed in some Canadian provinces.

142 *Hickerson v. Masters* (1921), 226 S.W. 1072 (C.A. of Ky.).

143 *Kerr v. Kennedy*, [1942] 1 K.B. 409.

144 *Nowark v. Maguire* (1964), 255 N.Y.S. 2d 318 (C.A.). Actually, an imputation of homosexuality does not truly fall within this exception and more properly forms a fifth category. See *Prosser and Keeton, op. cit. supra*, n. 3, at p. 793.

145 *Mark v. Deutsch* (1973), 39 D.L.R. (3d) 568 (Alta.), realtor; *Morgenstern v. Oakville Record Star* (1962), 33 D.L.R. (2d) 354 (Ont.), builder; *Warren v. Green* (1959), 15 D.L.R. (2d) 251 (Alta.), doctor; *Ross v. Lamport* (1956), 2 D.L.R. (2d) 225 (S.C.C.), taxi driver.

146 *Gallwey v. Marshall* (1853), 156 E.R. 126; *Alexander v. Jenkins*, [1892] 1 Q.B. 797 (C.A.).

147 *Booth v. Passmore* (1924), 27 O.W.N. 113; *Hicks v. Stephens* (1997), 40 C.C.L.T. (2d) 223 (Ont. Gen. Div.) (*per* Lederman J.), former school trustee alleged to be absent frequently. But see *Gill v. Nesbitt* (1932), 41 O.W.N. 133.

148 *Jones v. Jones*, [1916] 2 A.C. 481 (H.L.); *Hopwood v. Muirson*, [1945] 1 All E.R. 453 (C.A.); *Brockley v. Maxwell*, [1949] 2 D.L.R. 784 (B.C.); *Lawrence v. Finch*, [1931] 1 D.L.R. 689 (Ont. C.A.).

149 See the Libel and Slander Act, R.S.O. 1990, c. L.12, s. 16.

2. SPECIAL DAMAGE

Where special damage must be demonstrated, it is not enough that the plaintiff shows damage to reputation: there must be material or pecuniary loss. For example, where a lawyer proves injury to his practice and career as a result of libel, special damages will be awarded for the business loss.[150] Proof that the plaintiff lost the society of friends or was made ill as a result of the slander, however, has been held not to amount to special damage.[151] However, it may be that once special damage has been proven, general "parasitic" damages for loss of reputation will be recoverable.[152] The special damages awarded must not be too remote; that is, they will be limited to that which one might reasonably have expected to result from the speaking of the words.[153]

C. Publication

A defamatory remark must be communicated to a third person, other than the defamed individual, for it to be actionable. If words are directed at the defamed person, in the presence of others, it must be shown that the other individuals actually heard what was said.[154] It is also necessary for that individual to understand what was said, so that if the offending words were spoken in Greek, in the presence of someone who knows no Greek, no action lies.[155] Dictation to a secretary may constitute publication.[156] So too, handling a telegram message by a telegraph company is publication.[157]

The onus is on the plaintiff to show that the defendant was responsible for the publication, but this may be inferred from the natural and probable conse-

---

[150] *Botiuk v. Toronto Free Press* (1995), 126 D.L.R. (4th) 609, at p. 633 (S.C.C.).

[151] *Allsop v. Allsop* (1860), 5 H. & N. 534, 157 E.R. 1292; *Palmer v. Solmes* (1880), 30 U.C.C.P. 481; *Roberts v. Roberts* (1864), 5 B. & S. 384, 122 E.R. 874. But see, *Davies v. Solomon* (1871), L.R. 7 Q.B. 112, and *Moore v. Meagher* (1807), 127 E.R. 745, wherein the hospitality or assistance of friends was held to be a pecuniary benefit.

[152] Fleming, *op. cit. supra*, n. 10, at p. 607; *Prosser and Keeton, op. cit. supra*, n. 3, at p. 793.

[153] *Lynch v. Knight* (1861), 9 H.L. Cas. 577, at p. 600 (*per* Lord Wensleydale). See also Fleming, *op. cit. supra*, n. 10, at p. 551; *Prosser and Keeton, op. cit. supra*, n. 3, at p. 795, and cases cited.

[154] *Sheffill v. Van Deusen* (1859), 13 Gray (Mass.) 304.

[155] *Economopoulos v. A.G. Pollard Co.* (1914), 105 N.E. 896 (Mass. S.C.).

[156] *Pullman v. Hill & Co.*, [1891] 1 Q.B. 524 (C.A.); *Osborn v. Thomas Boulter & Son*, [1930] 2 K.B. 226; *Lawrence v. Finch*, [1931] 1 D.L.R. 689 (Ont. C.A.). It has been said, however, that this principle is applicable only to "external communications". Thus, it may be that liability will not attach to a corporation where defamatory matter is transmitted "internally" in the ordinary course of business as there is no third party involved, only employees performing a single corporate function. See *Mims v. Metropolitan Life Insurance Co.* (1952), 200 F. 2d 800 (5th Cir.); *Harrison v. Joy Oil Ltd.*, [1938] 4 D.L.R. 360 (Ont. C.A.). See also *Bryanston Finance Ltd. v. DeVries*, [1975] Q.B. 703 (C.A.).

[157] *Dominion Telegraph Co. v. Silver* (1882), 10 S.C.R. 238; *Tobin v. City Bank* (1878), 1 N.S.W.S.C.R.N.S. 267; *Williamson v. Freer* (1874), L.R. 9 C.P. 393; and the mailing of a postcard; *Sadgrove v. Hole*, [1901] 2 K.B. 1 (C.A.).

quences of the utterance.[158] In this regard, some element of fault is required. If defendants intend that someone should hear the defamatory statements, therefore, there will be liability. However, if they did not intend a publication and they could not, by the exercise of reasonable care, have avoided it, they will be exonerated.[159] In fact, this duty of care aspect may even go so far as to impose a positive obligation on a defendant, who is aware of the publication of defamatory matter, and who has the power to remove it, to do so, or be held responsible as a publisher thereof.[160]

Every participant in the publication incurs liability, regardless of the degree of involvement. This includes not only all those who took part in the composition of a libel, but also those responsible for its distribution and dissemination. Further, people may be held liable not only for their own acts, but also when others foreseeably publish or republish their defamatory utterances.[161] Thus, a

---

[158] *McNichol v. Grandy*, [1931] S.C.R. 696, [1932] 1 D.L.R. 225; *Gaskin v. Retail Credit Co.*, [1965] S.C.R. 297. In some circumstances, though, publication will be presumed and it is not necessary to prove publication to any specific individual, for example, where publication takes place in a book, newspaper or broadcast transmitted to the general public. See Duncan and Neill, *op. cit. supra*, n. 4, p. 36.

[159] See *Hall v. Balkind*, [1918] N.Z.L.R. 740, no reason for defendant to think he could be overheard. See also *White v. J. & F. Stone Ltd.*, [1939] 3 All E.R. 507 (C.A.); *Neame v. Yellow Cabs*, [1930] S.A.S.R. 267, trespasser seeing defamatory notice on wall. But see *McNichol v. Grandy*, *supra*, n. 158. With regard to letters being read by a third party, a distinction has been made between postcards and those in a sealed envelope. Compare, *Sadgrove v. Hole*, [1901] 2 K.B. 1 (C.A.) and *Mothersill v. Young* (1897), 18 C.L.T. 5 (Ont. C.A.) to *Huth v. Huth*, [1915] 3 K.B. 32 (C.A.), butler opening letter in breach of duty. In *Hedgepeth v. Coleman* (1922), 111 S.E. 517 (S.C. of N.C.), it was held to be a natural and probable result that a 14-year-old boy who received a letter accusing him of theft would show it to his older brother to seek his advice, and in *Theaker v. Richardson*, [1962] 1 W.L.R. 151 (C.A.), that the husband of the defendant would read a letter written to his wife. But see *Hills v. O'Bryan*, [1949] 2 D.L.R. 716 (B.C.), publication to a friend, her sister and her son of a letter alleging theft from an employer not a reasonable and probable consequence; *Jackson v. Staley* (1885), 9 O.R. 334 (C.A.), no liability where illiterate asked wife to read a defamatory letter to him as there was no knowledge he was illiterate. Other fact situations which have been considered included mistaken mailing: *Fox v. Broderick* (1864), 14 Ir. C.L.R. 453; *Thompson v. Dashwood* (1883), 11 Q.B.D. 43; a letter dropped on the floor; *Weld-Blundell v. Stephens*, [1920] A.C. 956, at p. 971; and a letter left in files to which employees had access: *Edgeworth v. N.Y. Central*, [1936] 2 D.L.R. 577 (Ont. C.A.); *Basse v. Toronto Star Newspaper Ltd.* (1983), 44 O.R. (2d) 64 (H.C.).

[160] *Byrne v. Deane*, [1937] 1 K.B. 818, [1937] 2 All E.R. 204.

[161] Fleming, *op. cit. supra*, n. 10, at p. 537. See *Botiuk v. Toronto Free Press*, *supra*, n. 150, at pp. 625-26. See also *Chinese Cultural Centre of Vancouver et al. v. Holt et al.* (1978), 87 D.L.R. (3d) 744, in which it was held that the publication, in British Columbia, of an article which first appeared in Ontario was a foreseeable result of the original publication and gave rise to a separate cause of action. Some interesting problems arise with regard to so-called "joint publications". For example, publication may be made by an author and a commercial publisher and an action will lie against both as joint tortfeasors. One may then be entitled to contribution or indemnity from the other, depending on the language in the applicable statute. See Williams, *op. cit. supra*, n. 124, pp. 65-66. A defendant may also claim contribution or indemnity from someone not already a party. In *Allan v. Bushnell T.V. Co. Ltd.* (1968), 67 D.L.R. (2d) 499 (Ont. C.A.), the defendant broadcasting company was sued for libel for two telecasts which were based on news supplied by Broadcast

person who gives an interview to a newspaper reporter will be liable for the publication of an accurate account of his statements in the newspaper.[162]

Historically, each communication of a defamatory matter was a separate publication and therefore a separate tort.[163] This was carried to an extreme in *Duke of Brunswick v. Harmer*[164] in which liability was imposed on a newspaper publisher where an agent of the plaintiff purchased a copy of a newspaper, containing an article defamatory of the plaintiff, 17 years after its original publication. The court held that the Statute of Limitations, which provided that an action had to be brought within six years of the date upon which the cause of action arose, was no bar since the recent sale was a distinct and separate publication which gave rise to a separate cause of action. Current authority appears to prefer a "single publication" rule[165] in such situations. Thus, "where large distributions of published matter are involved, the cause of action accrues, for the purpose of the statute of limitations, upon the first publication, when the issue goes into circulation generally".[166]

A publication takes place where the words complained of are heard or read.[167] This is important in resolving any conflict of laws problems[168] as well as with regard to the running of a limitation period.[169]

News Ltd. The Court of Appeal allowed the third party proceedings against Broadcast News to continue, even though the main action sounded in tort and Bushnell's third party action was based on contract, as there was a connection of fact or subject matter between the two causes of action. But see *Atkinson v. A.A. Murphy & Sons Ltd.*, [1974] 2 W.W.R. 367 (Sask.), where it was held that the fact that a letter read over the radio was first published in the newspaper did not give the broadcaster a right over against the newspaper.

[162] *Hay v. Bingham* (1905), 11 O.L.R. 148 (C.A.); *Nixon v. O'Callaghan* (1926), 60 O.L.R. 76, at p. 84 (C.A.); *Douglas v. Tucker*, [1952] 1 S.C.R. 275, at p. 289.

[163] *Restatement of Torts, Second*, para. 578, Comment (b).

[164] (1849), 14 Q.B. 185, 117 E.R. 75.

[165] See *Thomson v. Lambert*, [1938] S.C.R. 253, causes of action limited to one with regard to the publication, distribution and sale of a newspaper in Manitoba and Ontario.

[166] *Hartmann v. Time Inc.* (1946), 64 F. Supp. 671, at p. 679 (Penn D.C.) (*per* Kalodner D.J.). See also *Winrod v. Time Inc.* (1948), 334 Ill. App. 59, 78 N.E. 2d 708 (C.A.); *Ogden v. Association of U.S. Army* (1959), 177 F. Supp. 498 (D.C. of D.C.).

[167] *Jenner v. Sun Oil*, [1952] 2 D.L.R. 526 (Ont.), radio broadcast from New York heard in Ontario; *Bata v. Bata*, [1948] W.N. 366 (C.A.), circular letter sent from Zurich received in London. In *Hubert v. DeCamillis* (1964), 41 D.L.R. (2d) 495 (B.C.), the court held that it had jurisdiction to assess damages not only with regard to mimeographed letters mailed to British Columbia and received there, but also for such letters received in Alberta and Saskatchewan.

[168] *Machado v. Fontes*, [1897] 2 Q.B. 231 (C.A.).

[169] In Canada, several provinces provide by legislation for a short period of limitation in the case of libel in local newspapers or broadcasts. Thus, in Ontario, the Libel and Slander Act, R.S.O. 1990, c. L.12, provides in s. 5(1) that no action for libel in a newspaper or broadcast lies unless the plaintiff, "within six weeks after the alleged libel has come to the plaintiff's knowledge", has given notice in writing specifying the defamatory matter complained of. By the Ontario Act, s. 6, actions for libel in a newspaper or broadcast must be commenced "within three months after the libel has come to the knowledge of the person defamed, but, where such an action is brought within that period, the action may include a claim for any other libel against the plaintiff by the defendant in the same newspaper or the same broadcasting station within a period of one year before the commencement of the action". Section 5(1) and s. 6 apply only to newspapers printed

D. Basis of Liability

Defamation is, in essence, a tort of strict liability. It is the fact of publication alone which is actionable. Liability is in no way dependent on the motive of the defamer,[170] unlike injurious falsehood, in which it is necessary to prove actual malice.[171] Moreover, the intended meaning of the speaker is not relevant. Rather, the test is what meaning would be attributed to the words by a reasonable reader or listener.[172] As a result, a publisher may be found liable for a statement which appears innocent, but which may carry a defamatory imputation. Thus, a wife successfully maintained an action in libel for the publication of a photograph of her husband's "fiancee", even though the husband had authorized it and the newspaper did not know that he was already married.[173]

Similarly, the defendant will not escape responsibility upon proof that what was published was not intended to refer to the plaintiff. "The question is not so much who was aimed at as who was hit".[174] Thus, a defendant was found liable for publishing a defamatory story in which a supposedly fictitious name that was used turned out to be the name of a real person.[175] Likewise, a plaintiff, who had a similar name to a bigamist, recovered when he was erroneously identified as a bigamist.[176] The same principle applies to accidental typographical or similar errors, which have the effect of conveying a meaning, or referring to a person, other than the one intended.[177]

It should be recalled that, despite what has been said above, fault is relevant with regard to responsibility for publication. Professor Fleming has succinctly

---

and published in Ontario and to broadcasts from a station in Ontario (s. 7). See *L'Abbe v. Southam Press Ltd.* (1971), 18 D.L.R. (3d) 410 (Ont.), in which the court ruled that the plaintiff could claim for libels within one year before the commencement of the action, even though he had failed to comply with s. 5(1) with regard to them, provided that this requirement was fulfilled for the specific publication that was the basis of the cause of action. But see *Frisina v. Southam Press* (1980), 30 O.R. (2d) 65.

[170] *Cassidy v. Daily Mirror Newspapers Ltd.*, [1929] 2 K.B. 331, at p. 354 (C.A.).

[171] See Williams, *op. cit. supra*, n. 124, at pp. 25-26. Pursuant to s. 17 of the Libel and Slander Act, R.S.O. 1990, c. L.12, it is not necessary to prove special damages for slander of title, slander of goods or other malicious falsehood. For a review of the historical development of defamation, including its gradual rejection of the requirement of malice, see Veeder, "History and Theory of the Law of Defamation" (1904), 4 Colum. L. Rev. 33.

[172] See Fleming, *op. cit. supra*, n. 10, at p. 595.

[173] *Cassidy v. Daily Mirror, supra*, n. 170. See also *Hough v. London Express*, [1940] 2 K.B. 507, newspaper article indicating that someone other than the plaintiff was the wife of a certain boxer; *Morrison v. John Ritchie & Co.* (1902), 4 F. (Ct. of Sess.) 645, 39 Sc. L.R. 432, false announcement of the birth of twins without knowledge of marriage four weeks earlier.

[174] *Corrigan v. Bobbs-Merrill Co.* (1920), 126 N.E. 260, at p. 262 (N.Y.C.A.) (*per* Pound J.).

[175] *E. Hulton & Co. v. Jones*, [1910] A.C. 20 (H.L.).

[176] *Newstead v. London Express Newspaper Ltd.*, [1940] 1 K.B. 377 (C.A). The proper person was named Henry Newstead, who lived in the same community as the plaintiff Harold Newstead. See also *Lee v. Wilson and Mackinnon* (1953), 51 C.L.R. 276; *Leblanc v. L'Imprimerie Acadienne Ltee.*, [1955] 5 D.L.R. 91 (N.B.).

[177] See Fleming, *op. cit. supra*, n. 10, at p. 541.

summarized the anomalous legal consequence of this requirement of intention or negligence, as follows:

There is no liability for intentionally defamatory matter published accidentally, unlike accidentally defamatory matter published intentionally.[178]

1. INNOCENT DISSEMINATION

As was previously noted, liability for defamation attaches to all those involved in its publication including internet providers.[179] However, a distinction has developed between the "primary participants", such as the writer, newspaper company and the printer, and those who play a secondary role in the distribution system, such as news agents, booksellers, and libraries.[180] This exception has been labeled "innocent dissemination".[181] For example, the defence of innocent dissemination is available to a printing company which printed, bound and then returned an author's book to him, but was not aware of the contents of the book.[182] In *Vizetelly v. Mudie's Select Library*,[183] it was explained

---

[178] *Ibid.*, at p. 599. It has been suggested that a distinction should be drawn between those statements which are defamatory of the plaintiff on their face and those which are innocent on their face and defamatory only by reason of extrinsic facts not reasonably knowable by the plaintiff. See Weiler, "Defamation, Enterprise Liability and Freedom of Speech" (1967), 17 U. of T.L.J. 278, at p. 285. In the U.S. the doctrine of "libel *per quod*' has developed which limits the incidence of liability for libellous statements innocent on their face by requiring proof of special damages. On this subject and suggested alternatives, see Prosser, "Libel *Per Quod*" (1960), 46 Va. L. Rev. 389; Eldredge, "The Spurious Rule of Libel *Per Quod*" (1966), 79 Harv. L. Rev. 733; Prosser, "More Libel *Per Quod*" (1966), 79 Harv. L. Rev. 1629.

[179] See *Godfrey v. Demon Internet Ltd.,* [1999] 4 All E.R. 342 (Q.B.D.).

[180] See Fleming, *op. cit. supra*, n. 10, at p. 542.

[181] *Goldsmith v. Sperrings Ltd.*, [1977] 2 All E.R. 566. See also, *Bottomley v. F.W. Woolworth & Co. Ltd.* (1932), 48 T.L.R. 521 (C.A.); *Balbanoff v. Fossani* (1948), 81 N.Y.S. 2d 732; *Emmens v. Pottle* (1885), 16 Q.B.D. 354; *Sun Life Assurance Co. of Canada v. W.H. Smith & Son* (1933), 150 L.T. 211; *Weldon v. Times Book Club* (1911), 28 T.L.R. 143. The principle was applied in regard to a radio broadcast by those who merely rented the station facilities out to others, since the publication could not have been prevented by the exercise of reasonable care. See *Summit Hotel Co. v. N.B.C.* (1939), 8 A. 2d 302 (Pa.); *Kelly v. Hoffman* (1948), 61 A. 2d 143 (N.J.). See Finlay, "Defamation by Radio" (1941), 19 Can. Bar Rev. 353, at pp. 362-71; Fleming, *op. cit. supra*, n. 10, at p. 543. As to defamation by a telegraph company, see *Dominion Telegraph Co. v. Silver* (1882), 10 S.C.R. 238; *Kahn v. Gt. Northwestern Telegraph Co.* (1930), 39 O.W.N. 11 and 143. See Smith, "Liability of a Telegraph Company for Transmitting a Defamatory Message" (1920), 20 Colum. L. Rev. 30; 369; also 29 Mich. L. Rev. 339; In *Allan v. Bushnell T.V. Co. Ltd.* (1969), 4 D.L.R. (3d) 212, the Ontario Court of Appeal ruled that, in the absence of any relationship analogous to that of principal and agent, a television station is not bound by the malice or gross negligence of a news agency that supplies the station with reports.

[182] *Menear v. Miguna* (1996), 32 C.C.L.T. (2d) 35 (Ont. Gen. Div.); revd (1997), 33 O.R. (3d) 223 (C.A.), case allowed to go to trial on the merits but with "no opinion with respect to the reasons". At trial, Wright J. found in a motion for summary judgment that there was no publication where a printing company neither read nor edited the defamatory manuscript or distributed the book to anyone other than the author and its own employees. Even if it could be said to have published the book, however, Wright J. found that the defence of innocent dissemination would have been available. It has been suggested that the defence may also be available to those involved in the rebroadcasting of television programmes and to Internet servers: R. Harris and P. Bujold, "Annotation to *Menear v. Miguna*" [(1996) 32 C.C.L.T. (2d) 35].

[183] [1900] 2 Q.B. 170 (C.A.) (*per* Romer L.J.).

that someone could escape liability if he could show that he disseminated the work in the ordinary course of his business and:

> ... (1.) that he was innocent of any knowledge of the libel contained in the work dissemi-
> nated by him, (2.) that there was nothing in the work or the circumstances under which it
> came to him or was disseminated by him which ought to have led him to suppose that it con-
> tained a libel, and (3.) that, when the work was disseminated by him, it was not by any negli-
> gence on his part that he did not know that it contained the libel, then, although the
> dissemination of the work by him was prima facie publication of it, he may nevertheless, on
> proof of the before-mentioned facts, be held not to have published it.[184]

The onus of proof of such facts lies on the defendant, and the question of whether or not there has been a "publication" is one for the jury.

2. APOLOGY

Certain jurisdictions have made a specific statutory concession to the media with regard to unintentional defamation. Thus, where a libel is contained in a newspaper or broadcast, the defendant may plead, in mitigation of damages, that it was inserted without actual malice and without gross negligence, and that at the earliest opportunity the defendant made or offered to publish a full apol-ogy.[185] Borins J. has well explained the purpose of this provision in Ontario's Libel and Slander Act to the effect that, "[b]y enacting s. 5(2), the legislature has provided a substitute for general (but not special) damages in actions for defamation based on statements published by a newspaper which its employees reasonably believed to be true and respecting which it has published a suitable and prompt retraction".[186]

E. Defences

1. JUSTIFICATION

Truth is a complete answer to a civil action for defamation, because the wrong is based on the falsity of the imputation. The "law will not permit a man to recover damages in respect of an injury to a character which he either does not, or ought not to possess".[187]

---

[184] *Ibid.*, at p. 180.

[185] See, for example, the Libel and Slander Act, R.S.O. 1990, c. L.12, s. 9. In addition, pursuant to s. 5(2) recovery will be limited to "actual damages" as a result of defamatory material published in error, if it was "published in good faith", "took place in mistake or misapprehension of the facts", and a "full and fair retraction" was made immediately.

[186] See *Murray Alter's Talent Associates Ltd. v. Toronto Star* (1995), 124 D.L.R. (4th) 105, at p. 119 (Ont. Div. Ct.). See also *Kerr v. Conlogue*, [1992] 4 W.W.R. 258 (B.C.S.C.), for a discussion of the British Columbia statute.

[187] *M'Pherson v. Daniels* (1829), 10 B. & C. 263, at p. 272 (*per* Littledale J.). See also Fleming, *op. cit. supra*, n. 10, p. 553. See Brown, *op. cit. supra*, n. 4, at p. 361.

The burden of proving the truth of the statement rests on the defendant, as falsity is presumed in favour of the plaintiff.[188] The defendant must prove not only the truth of the words complained of in their literal sense, but also in their inferential or innuendo meanings.[189] Though the defendant must substantiate all material facts contained in an allegation, it is sufficient, in this regard, that the defendant prove the truth of the substance of the statements. It is not necessary to prove every minute detail.[190] Further, incorrect details which do not aggravate the defamatory statement may be ignored. Thus, to say that a person who was convicted of an offence was fined and imprisoned for three weeks, when, in fact, the sentence was only two weeks, was held to be sufficiently true to be justified.[191] However, where the defamation consists of several distinct allegations, if the defendant fails to justify any component thereof, the plaintiff will be entitled to judgment even though the unproved charge could have caused no appreciable damage in view of the truth of the rest.[192]

It is no justification that one merely repeated a rumour or what one was told by someone else, even if a verbatim account of what was said is given,[193] or it is qualified by an expression of doubt or disbelief,[194] unless the effect of the words in which the statement is couched is such as to remove its defamatory sting.[195]

A rigid hold-over from the common law, with regard to an imputation that the plaintiff has committed a criminal offence, is the requirement that the

---

[188] *Belt v. Lawes* (1882), 51 L.J.Q.B. 359, at p. 361.

[189] *Digby v. Financial News Ltd.*, [1907] 1 K.B. 502, at p. 507 (C.A.); *Hare v. Better Business Bureau*, [1947] 1 D.L.R. 280 (B.C.C.A.). See also *Leonard v. Wharton* (1921), 20 O.W.N. 309 (S.C.C.). As to whether the plaintiff may anticipate the defence of justification or rebut it by way of reply evidence, see *Beevis v. Dawson*, [1957] 1 Q.B. 195 (C.A.).

[190] In *Edwards v. Bell* (1824), 1 Bing. 403, at p. 409, Burrough J. stated that "As much must be justified as meets the sting of the charge. . . ."

[191] *Alexander v. N.E. Rwy.* (1865), 6 B. & S. 340; *Sutherland v. Stopes*, [1925] A.C. 47, at pp. 79-80 (H.L.). But see *Maisel v. Financial Times Ltd.*, [1915] 3 K.B. 336, at p. 339 (C.A.).

[192] Fleming, *op. cit. supra*, n. 10, p. 611. However, justification may be pleaded with regard to parts of a statement if they are severable from the rest: *Clarke v. Taylor* (1836), 2 Bing. N.C. 654; *Plato Films Ltd. v. Speidel*, [1961] A.C. 1090, at p. 1142. The jury would then be instructed to assess damages only for those parts unjustified if they amount to defamation in and of themselves: *Cohen v. Mirror Newspapers Ltd.*, [1971] 1 N.S.W.L.R. 623 (C.A.). The Libel and Slander Act, R.S.O. 1990, c. L.12, s. 22 provides: "In an action for libel or slander for words containing two or more distinct charges against the plaintiff, a defence of justification shall not fail by reason only that the truth of every charge is not proved if the words not proved to be true do not materially injure the plaintiff's reputation having regard to the truth of the remaining charges."

[193] *Watkins v. Hall* (1868), L.R. 3 Q.B. 396; *Macdonald v. Mail Printing Co.* (1900), 32 O.R. 163, at p. 170; revd 2 O.L.R. 278 (C.A.); *Houseman v. Coulson*, [1948] 2 D.L.R. 62; *Douglas v. Tucker*, [1952] 1 S.C.R. 275; *Truth (N.Z.) v. Holloway*, [1960] 1 W.L.R. 997.

[194] *Stubbs Ltd. v. Mazure*, [1920] A.C. 66; *Savige v. News Ltd.*, [1932] S.A.S.R. 240. But see *Stubbs Ltd. v. Russell*, [1913] A.C. 386.

[195] In *Wake v. John Fairfax & Sons Ltd.*, [1973] 1 N.S.W.L.R. 43 (C.A.), it was suggested that the nature and quality of the defamatory publication as well as the purpose of the republication can have a significant bearing on the position of one who reports what another has said.

defendant prove the commission of the offence, not merely the conviction.[196] However, despite earlier authority to the contrary,[197] the standard of proof is the balance of probabilities.[198]

Proof of the conviction may be sufficient where the words imply only that the plaintiff has been found guilty of a crime.[199]

2. ABSOLUTE PRIVILEGE

In some circumstances, on the grounds of public policy, the law grants an absolute protection to certain speakers in order that they may talk freely without fear of liability for defamation. This doctrine of absolute privilege is based on the notion that there are occasions when society's interest is better served by the fullest dissemination of information, regardless of accuracy and regardless of motive, even though this may be at the expense of someone else's reputation. Because of the potential for abuse of such a privilege, the law has been circumspect in granting it, and has interpreted its scope narrowly. In general, it can be said to be restricted to those situations in which it acts as an "aid to the efficient functioning of our governmental institutions: legislative, executive and judicial".[200]

a) Judicial Proceedings

An absolute privilege to speak and write without legal liability for defamation flows to judges,[201] witnesses,[202] advocates,[203] and parties[204] while participating in judicial proceedings. This is because ". . . the law takes the risk of their abusing the occasion and speaking maliciously as well as untruly . . . in order that their duties may be carried on freely and without fear of any action being brought

---

[196] *Goody v. Odhams Press Ltd.*, [1966] 3 All E.R. 369 (C.A.). At common law, a conviction was not even admissible in evidence. However, some jurisdictions have altered this rule by legislation. See Evidence Act, R.S.O. 1990, c. E.23, s. 22.

[197] See *Mays v. Degerness*, [1929] 4 D.L.R. 771 (Sask.); *Meier v.Klotz*, [1928] 4 D.L.R. 4 (Sask. C.A.).

[198] *York et al. v. Okanagan Broadcasters Ltd.*, [1976] 6 W.W.R. 40 (B.C.).

[199] *Mack v. North Hill News Ltd.* (1964), 44 D.L.R. (2d) 147, at p. 156 (Alta.).

[200] Fleming, *op. cit. supra*, n. 10, at p. 615.

[201] *Scott v. Stansfield* (1868), L.R. 3 Exch. 220. See also *Titchmarsh v. Crawford* (1910), 1 O.W.N. 587, police magistrate; *Thomas v. Churton* (1862), 2 B. & S. 475, 121 E.R. 1150, coroner; *Law v. Llewellyn*, [1906] 1 K.B. 487 (C.A.), magistrate.

[202] *Seaman v. Netherclift* (1876), 2 C.P.D. 53. The protection extends equally to evidence which the witness believes to be true and that which is perjured. See *Hargreaves v. Bretherton*, [1959] 1 Q.B. 45. See also *Marinan v. Vibart*, [1963] 1 Q.B. 45 (C.A.), in which it was held that no action could lie for conspiracy of witnesses to make false statements. But see *Roy v. Prior*, [1971] A.C. 470 (H.L.), in which it was held that an action did lie for malicious arrest with regard to the issuance of a bench warrant for the plaintiff, even though the basis upon which it was granted was evidence given in court.

[203] *Munster v. Lamb* (1883), 11 Q.B.D. 588, at p. 607. See also *Cowan v. Landell* (1887), 13 O.R. 13 (C.A.).

[204] *Kennedy v. Hilliard* (1859), 10 Ir. C.L.R. 195.

against them".[205] Pleadings, petitions, affidavits and other documents filed with the courts are protected absolutely.[206]

Utterances arising out of judicial proceedings are so protected, however, only if "relevant" to the issues at bar. Although relevance has been interpreted rather expansively, lest a witness withhold evidence, it likely will not include entirely extraneous matters.[207]

Communications made within the solicitor and client relationship are absolutely privileged, provided that are reasonably related to the preparation of a case for trial, because a solicitor must have full disclosure of all the facts within the client's knowledge.[208] This privilege extends to statements by potential witnesses to persons engaged professionally in preparing evidence to be presented in court,[209] and to reports upon which their testimony is based.[210] However, no absolute privilege will extend to statements made by a client in regard to contemplated proceedings, with the exception of documents necessary for the initiation of judicial proceedings.[211]

A statutory board or tribunal which has, "similar attributes" to a court is included within the absolute privilege.[212] A hearing before the Ontario Workmen's Compensation Board[213] and a Police Act disciplinary hearing[214] were held to be such a judicial proceeding, while a petition to a board of licence commis-

---

[205] *More v. Weaver*, [1928] 2 K.B. 520, at p. 522 (C.A.) (*per* Scrutton L.J.). The privilege has also been extended to the report of an Official Receiver acting in a judicial capacity. See *Bottomley v. Brougham*, [1908] 1 K.B. 584.

[206] See *Hill v. Church of Scientology of Toronto*, *infra*, n. 296; *Taylor-Wright v. CHBC–TV* (2000), 2 C.C.L.T. (3d) 222 (B.C.C.A.), doubting *Hill* concerning an affidavit filed in court, saying qualified privilege only (*per* Esson J.A.). *Razzell v. Edmonton Mint. Ltd.*, [1981] 4 W.W.R. 5 (Alta. Q.B.), pleadings; see also Brown, *supra*, n. 4, at pp. 12-54. But see *Gazette Printing Co. v. Shallow* (1909), 41 S.C.R. 339, absolute privilege does not extend to pleadings between private parties where no judicial action has been taken on them.

[207] *More v. Weaver*, *supra*, n. 205; *Henderson v. Scott* (1892), 24 N.S.R. 232 (C.A.). The situation in some states in the U.S. appears to be more restrictive in that a "good faith" test of reasonable relation or reference to the subject of the inquiry has been adopted. See *Prosser and Keeton*, *op. cit. supra*, n. 3, at pp. 778-79.

[208] *More v. Weaver*, *ibid.*; *Minter v. Priest*, [1930] A.C. 558 (H.L.); *Morgan v. Wallis* (1917), 33 T.L.R. 495, qualified privilege only.

[209] *Watson v. M'Ewan*, [1905] A.C. 480. This principle was applied in *Foran v. Richman* (1976), 10 O.R. (2d) 634 (C.A.), with regard to a letter, sent by a doctor to a solicitor, which contained uncomplimentary remarks about a plaintiff in litigation arising out of a motor vehicle accident. However, the hospital record and the insurance claims forms filled out by the doctor were only qualifiedly privileged.

[210] *Fabian v. Margulies* (1985), 53 O.R. (2d) 380 (CA.), doctor's report absolutely privileged.

[211] *Dashtgard v. Blair* (1990), 4 C.C.L.T. (2d) 284 (Alta. Q.B.).

[212] *Royal Aquarium v. Parkinson*, [1892] 1 Q.B. 431 (C.A.). See also *Lincoln v. Daniels*, [1962] 1 Q.B. 237, at p. 253 (C.A.); *Addis v. Crocker*, [1961] 1 Q.B. 11 (C.A.).

[213] *Halls v. Mitchell*, [1928] S.C.R. 125. See also *Stark v. Auerbach et al.*, [1979] 3 W.W.R. 563 (B.C.).

[214] *Boyachyk v. Dukes* (1982), 136 D.L.R. (3d) 28 (Alta. Q.B.).

sioners regarding a licence application was not.[215] In one case, the court refused to distinguish between the Complaints Committee and the Discipline Committee of the Royal College of Dental Surgeons and thus afforded the former an absolute privilege as a legally recognized tribunal carrying out quasi-judicial functions.[216]

According to the Ontario Libel and Slander Act, this absolute privilege extends, subject to certain exceptions, to reports of judicial proceedings. Thus, in order to be privileged, a report of court proceedings must be "fair and accurate", published or broadcast "contemporaneously with such proceedings" and, where necessary, must contain a "reasonable statement of explanation or contradiction by or on behalf of the plaintiff".[217] At common law, however, as is discussed later in this chapter, fair and accurate reports of public judicial proceedings receive only a qualified privilege, so that if the circumstances of the report do not come under the statutes, the privilege is not absolute but only a qualified one.

b) Parliamentary Proceedings

In order to foster frank and vigorous debate in our democratic institutions, an absolute privilege surrounds all statements by Members of Parliament[218] made on the floor[219] of the House of Commons in the exercise of their duties. Reports of these debates, however, are given only a qualified privilege.[220]

---

[215] *Wilcocks v. Howell* (1884), 5 O.R. 360. In *O'Connor v. Waldron*, [1935] A.C. 76, the Privy Council held that an inquiry under the Combines Investigation Act of Canada was not a "judicial" proceeding. As was explained by Lord Atkin (at p. 81): "The question . . . in every case is whether the tribunal in question has similar attributes to a court of justice or acts in a manner similar to that in which said courts act." Apparently, the fact that the inquiry determined "no rights, nor the guilt or innocence of anyone" was considered determinative, even though the power to summon witnesses and administer oaths existed. See also *Perry v. Heatherington* (1972), 24 D.L.R. (3d) 127 (B.C.), Court of Revision of tax assessments absolutely privileged; *Duquette v. Belanger* (1973), 38 D.L.R. (3d) 613 (F.C.), Public Service Appeal Board proceedings not absolutely privileged: *Trapp v. Mackie*, [1979] 1 W.L.R. 377 (H.L.), local inquiry into dismissal of school rector absolutely privileged; *Voratovic v. Law Society of Upper Canada* (1978), 20 O.R. (2d) 214, investigation, by Law Society, of complaint against solicitor absolutely privileged. For a discussion of the principles involved here, see Duncan and Neill, *op. cit. supra*, n. 4, pp. 85-90.

[216] *Sussman v. Eales* (1985), 33 C.C.L.T. 156 (Ont. H.C.); revd in part (1986), 25 C.P.C. (2d) 7 (C.A.).

[217] See the Libel and Slander Act, R.S.O. 1990, c. L.12, s. 4. See Fleming, *op. cit. supra*, n. 10, p. 559.

[218] *Ex parte Wason* (1869), L.R. 4 Q.B. 573; see *Hamilton v. Al Fayed*, [2000] 2 All E.R. 224 (H.L.), on general scope of privilege.

[219] In *Stopforth v. Goyer* (1978), 20 O.R. (2d) 262; revd on other grounds (1979), 8 C.C.L.T. 172 (Ont. C.A.), it was held that the protection did not extend to defamatory statements made by a Minister, in response to questions by reporters outside the House of Commons, even though the response was, in substance, the same as statements already read in the House.

[220] The Libel and Slander Act, R.S.O. 1990, c. L.12, s. 3(1). This appears to be a codification of the common law.

It appears that the deliberations of municipal councils are not covered by an absolute privilege, but only by a qualified privilege.[221]

c) Executive Communications

There is considerable controversy as to whether absolute privilege protects communications between senior members of the executive arm of government. Although it appears that such a privilege protects Ministers of the Crown,[222] it is not clear how far down the chain it extends.[223]

Likewise, it is uncertain whether there is any limitation on the kind of communication that is privileged in terms of subject matter[224] and the "range of dissemination".[225]

d) Other

There is some further uncertainty as to the nature of the immunity, if any, which attaches to members of the military, police and national security agencies for their secret and less than secret reports about their own members and others. It has been held that no action will lie against senior army or naval officers for defamatory statements contained in reports made by them, in the course of their duty, to a senior officer.[226] However, a report by a police inspector to his superior was held not to be privileged.[227] No case appears to definitively state how middle

---

[221] *Royal Aquarium, supra*, n. 212; *Faminow v. Reid* (1971), 24 D.L.R. (3d) 554 (B.C.); *Edwards v. Gattman*, [1928] 3 D.L.R. 187 (B.C.). See also Gatley, *op. cit. supra*, n. 4, at p. 419.

[222] *Chatterton v. Secretary of State of India*, [1895] 2 Q.B. 189 (C.A.).

[223] *Isaacs (M.) & Sons Ltd. v. Cook*, [1925] 2 K.B. 391, report of High Commissioner of Australia in the U.K. to the Prime Minister of Australia absolutely privileged; *Jackson v. Magrath* (1947), 75 C.L.R. 293, majority view that annual report of Commissioner of Taxation to Federal Treasurer for presentation to Parliament qualifiedly privileged: *Szalatnay-Stacho v. Fink*, [1946] 1 All E.R. 303 (K.B.); affd on other grounds [1946] 2 All E.R. 231 (C.A.), letter from General Prosecutor of Czechoslovakian Military Court to Military Officer of President of Czechoslovakian Government in exile not absolutely privileged. In the last case the view was expressed that absolute privilege did not extend to those below the rank of Minister. But see *Barr v. Mateo* (1959), 360 U.S. 564, in which it was held that the privilege would include subordinate officers while acting within the "outer perimeter of their line of duty" (*per* Harlan J., at p. 575).

[224] See Fleming, *op. cit. supra*, n. 10, at p. 616. The question involved here is what can be considered to be an "act of state'. It is suggested that, given the expanding role of government, greater latitude must be given here so as to include, for example, commercial matters. See *Peerless Bakery Ltd. v. Watt*, [1955] N.Z.L.R. 339 (C.A.); *Isaacs v. Cook, supra*, n. 223.

[225] The privilege apparently also extends to communications from a high officer of State to another party who is not, as long as they are made in execution of the former's official capacity: *Peerless Bakery, supra*, n. 224, pp. 352-54. See generally Becht, "The Absolute Privilege of the Executive in Defamation" (1962), 15 Vand. L. Rev. 1127. See also Veedeer, "Absolute Immunity in Defamation: Legislative and Executive Proceedings" (1910), 10 Colum. L. Rev. 131.

[226] *Dawkins v. Lord Paulet* (1869), L.R. 5 Q.B. 94; *Dawkins v. Lord Rokeby* (1873), L.R. 8 Q.B. 255; affd (1875), L.R. 7 H.L. 744. But the *ratio* of these decisions may be that cases involving questions of military discipline and duty are not cognizable by a court of law. See Duncan and Neill, *op. cit. supra*, n. 4, at p. 95. However, the question still appears to be open: *Fraser v. Balfour* (1918), 34 T.L.R. 502 (H.L.).

[227] *Gibbons v. Duffell* (1932), 47 C.L.R. 520. See also *Merricks v. Nott-Bower*, [1965] 1 Q.B. 57 (C.A.).

and lower ranks are to be treated.[228] It is also open to question whether the secret service or any other intelligence gathering agency should be treated like the armed forces or the police.[229]

The common law protects communications between husband and wife with an absolute immunity.[230] Whether this proposition is supported on the technical grounds of want of publication, because of the fiction that the husband and wife are one person, or on grounds of social policy, the rule is well embedded in the law and reflects a healthy respect for the sanctity of confidentiality in the marital relationship. The privilege, of course, does not protect the publication of a defamatory utterance to one spouse about the other.[231]

3. QUALIFIED PRIVILEGE

Qualified privilege is a conditional immunity that attaches to certain occasions deemed to be of a lesser importance than those absolutely privileged. Here, certain communications for certain specified purposes are excused from liability for defamation, if made without malice.

This privilege is said to arise "where the person who makes [the] communication has an interest or a duty, legal, social, or moral, to make it to the person to whom it is made, and the person to whom it is so made has a corresponding interest or duty to receive it".[232] Another general description is that a publication is privileged when it is "fairly made by a person in the discharge of a public or private duty, whether legal or moral, or in the conduct of his own affairs, in matters where his interest is concerned".[233]

Thus, a qualified privilege will be found to exist where "the common convenience and welfare of society" demands it.[234] On these occasions, a person is permitted to say something that might otherwise be actionable.[235] However, as the word "qualified" indicates, the extent of the privilege is limited. It must not be abused by using it for a purpose unrelated to the interest for which the privilege is afforded. Further, only those statements which are relevant to the privileged communication are protected;[236] irrelevant information cannot be imparted in this way.

---

[228] *Dictum* of Denning M.R. in *Richards v. Naum*, [1966] 3 All E.R. 812, at p. 814 (C.A.). However, it would appear that, on the basis of *Gibbons, supra*, n. 227, *a fortiori*, no absolute privilege could attach with regard to a police officer of middle or lower rank. The same may also be said of such military officers on the basis of the result in *Szalatnay-Stacho, supra*, n. 223.

[229] *Richards v. Naum, ibid.*

[230] *Wennhak v. Morgan* (1888), 20 Q.B.D. 635.

[231] *Wenman v. Ash* (1853), 138 E.R. 1432; *Theaker v. Richardson*, [1962] 1 All E.R. 229.

[232] *Adam v. Ward*, [1917] A.C. 309, at p. 334 (*per* Lord Atkinson). Adopted in *McLoughlin v. Kutasy*, [1979] 2 S.C.R. 311. See Brown, *op. cit. supra*, n. 4, at p. 465.

[233] *Toogood v. Spyring* (1834), 1 Cr. M. & R. 181, 149 E.R. 1044, at pp. 1049-50 (*per* Parke B.).

[234] *Halls v. Mitchell*, [1928] 2 D.L.R. 97 (S.C.C.); *Muller v. Canada*, [1991] F.C.J. No. 966, R.C.M.P. files attracted qualified privilege.

[235] See *Banks v. Globe & Mail Ltd.* (1961), 28 D.L.R. (2d) 343, at p. 350 (S.C.C.) (*per* Cartwright J.), quoting from *Gatley on Libel and Slander*, 5th ed., at pp. 322-23.

[236] *Oana v. Maxwell Constr. Co. Ltd.* (1957), 8 D.L.R. (2d) 377, at p. 380 (B.C.), credit information greater than requested privilege; *Snapp v. McLeod*, [1926] 2 D.L.R. 1083 (Ont. C.A.), mention of name of other person privileged as relevant to main communication.

The trial judge determines as a matter of law whether an occasion is privileged.[237] If so found, and there is no evidence of malice, the action must be dismissed. If there is no privilege, or if there is evidence of malice,[238] or if the privilege has been exceeded,[239] the case must then go to the jury. The distinction has been said to be between what is a "privileged occasion" and what is a "privileged communication" — the judge decides the former, the jury the latter.[240]

There are four main areas where a qualified privilege has been recognized:

a) Protection of one's own interest.

b) Common interest or mutual concern.

c) Moral or legal duty to protect another's interest.

d) Public interest.

a) Protection of One's Own Interest

If people have legitimate "interests" which they wish to protect by making statements, they may do so under a qualified privilege. The interest must belong to the individual; "something more is necessary than the mere fact that the words are being addressed to a matter of public interest".[241] The privilege has been said to be akin to self-defence[242] and, thus, may attach to a reply to an imputation against one's own personal reputation,[243] to a businessperson's defence of proprietary interests,[244] or even to an employee's response to aspersions cast on an employer.[245]

---

[237] *Stuart v. Bell*, [1891] 2 Q.B. 341, at p. 343; *Wade & Wells Co. Ltd. v. Laing* (1957), 11 D.L.R. (2d) 276 (B.C.C.A.); *Savidant v. Day*, [1933] 4 D.L.R. 456 (P.E.I.C.A.).

[238] *Taylor et al. v. Despard et al.*, [1956] O.R. 963, at p. 978 (C.A.); *Sun Life Assurance Co. v. Dalrymple*, [1965] S.C.R. 302, at pp. 309-10. The judge must determine if there is sufficient evidence to raise a probabilty of malice before leaving it to the jury: *Davies v. Davies Ltd. v. Kott* (1979), 9 C.C.L.T. 249 (S.C.C.).

[239] *Telegraph Newspaper v. Bedford* (1934), 50 C.L.R. 632. If the facts which relate to whether or not the privilege exists are in dispute the jury must pass on them before the judge can rule: *Hebditch v. MacIlwaine*, [1894] 2 Q.B. 54, at p. 58; *Adam v. Ward, supra*, n. 232, at p. 318.

[240] See *Pullman v. Hill & Co.*, [1891] 1 Q.B. 524, at p. 529 (C.A.).

[241] *Littleton v. Hamilton* (1974), 47 D.L.R. (3d) 663 (Ont. C.A.); leave to appeal refused 47 D.L.R. (3d) 663n, at p. 665 (*per* Dubin J.A.).

[242] Fleming, *op. cit. supra*, n. 10, at p. 567.

[243] See *Nixon v. O'Callaghan, supra*, n. 162; *Falk v. Smith*, [1941] O.R. 17 (C.A.); *Turner v. M.-G.-M. Pictures Ltd.*, [1950] 1 All E.R. 449 (H.L.).

[244] *Netupsky v. Craig*, [1973] S.C.R. 55, 28 D.L.R. (3d) 742; *Wooding v. Little* (1982), 24 C.C.L.T. 37 (B.C.S.C.) (*per* McKenzie J.). In *Pleau v. Simpsons-Sears Ltd.* (1976), 15 O.R. (2d) 436, 75 D.L.R. (3d) 747 (C.A.), the plaintiff's wallet was stolen and, shortly thereafter, forged cheques began appearing in his name. The court held that, by posting notices to its employees to detain the plaintiff and call security if he presented a cheque, the defendant was properly protecting its interest in safeguarding against loss from the passing of bad cheques. A qualified privilege is also said to exist with regard to inquiries about someone with whom the inquirer is contemplating a business relationship. See *Jackson v. Hopperton* (1864), 16 C.B. (N.S.) 829; *London Assoc. for the Protection of Trade v. Greenlands*, [1916] 2 A.C. 15 (H.L.); *Oana v. Maxwell Constr., supra*, n. 236. But see *Macintosh v. Dun*, [1908] A.C. 390 (P.C.).

[245] *Penton v. Calwell* (1945), 70 C.L.R. 219. See also *Sun Life Assurance v. Dalrymple, supra*, n. 238.

Because the privilege is similar to self-defence, it is limited to those words which are reasonably necessary to meet the original attack.[246] The response must be confined to information that is reasonably related to the refutation[247] — one cannot abuse the occasion to completely destroy another's reputation.[248] Some latitude is allowed, however, so that if a third person's character is besmirched incidentally, in defence of one's own reputation, the privilege is still available to the publisher.[249]

The privilege protects the communications so long as they are made only to those who have an interest or duty in receiving them, but the law has not "restricted the right within any narrow limits".[250] The class of recipients and the means whereby a reply may be made are directly related to the nature of the original communication. Thus, if an individual's character or conduct was the subject matter of comment in the press, the individual may be justified in communicating a response to the general public by that medium.[251]

b) Common Interest or Mutual Concern

A privilege will arise with regard to communications between parties on a subject in which the speaker and the recipient both have a common legitimate interest.[252] "Interest" is used in the sense of the purposeful acquisition of knowledge, as opposed to mere curiosity or news-gathering.[253] The question of protection has, therefore, commonly arisen in the context of the activities of what might be called special interest groups. Thus, a privilege has been granted to communications published in papers devoted to particular organizations,[254]

---

[246] *Turner v. M.-G.-M.*, *supra*, n. 243. See also *Botiuk v. Toronto Free Press*, *supra*, n. 150, at p. 628.

[247] *Kinney v. Fisher* (1921), 62 S.C.R. 546.

[248] *Douglas v. Tucker*, [1952] 1 D.L.R. 657 (S.C.C.). In *Pleau v. Simpsons-Sears*, *supra*, n. 244, the notices were posted near the cash registers and were visible by customers. In fact, the plaintiff was informed of this by one of his friends who saw one of the notices. The court considered whether or not such publicity was "incommensurate to the occasion". The majority held that the number and size of the notices were such as not to exceed the privilege. Brooke J.A., in dissent, was of the view that the employees could have been as effectively informed in a less conspicuous manner. See also *Tench v. Gr. Western Rwy.* (1873), 33 U.C.Q.B. 8.

[249] *Loveday v. Sun Newspaper* (1938), 59 C.L.R. 503; *Mowlds v. Ferguson* (1940), 64 C.L.R. 206.

[250] *Toogood v. Spyring*, *supra*, n. 233, at p. 1050, E.R. The duty to receive the communication may be legal, moral or social. See *White v. J. & F. Stone Ltd.*, [1939] 2 K.B. 827 (C.A.).

[251] Fleming, *op. cit. supra*, n. 10, at p. 625.

[252] *Harrison v. Bush* (1855), 119 E.R. 509, at pp. 511-12. See also *Robertson v. Boddington* (1925), 56 O.L.R. 409; *Clark v. Duncan* (1923), 53 O.L.R. 287 (C.A.); *Quillinan v. Stuart* (1917), 38 O.L.R. 623 (C.A.); *Schultz v. Porter et al.* (1979), 9 Alta. L.R. (2d) 381.

[253] *Howe v. Lees* (1910), 11 C.L.R. 361, at p. 398.

[254] In *Bereman v. Power Publishing Co.* (1933), 27 P. 2d 749 (S.C. of Cal.), an article in the official publication of the Colorado State Federation of Labour accusing the plaintiff and others of turning traitor to the union was held privileged. See also *Doyle v. International Assn. of Machinists*, *supra*, n. 56, in which a union publication referring to "a new-hired scab" would have been extended qualified privilege but for a finding of malice. But see *Hebert v. Jackson*, [1950] O.R. 799 (C.A.), in which an allegation was made in an editorial in a union periodical that the plain-

discussion by church members of church affairs,[255] a complaint about a doctor by interns to a Hospital Education Committee,[256] complaints by tenants to the landlord with regard to third parties on the rented premises,[257] and meetings of the members of a lodge, social club or fraternity.[258] The privilege is lost, of course, if the utterance goes beyond the interests of the group or is communicated to a non-member.[259]

More often than not, the common interest is a business or pecuniary one. In such circumstances, people may discuss amongst themselves matters of mutual economic concern in a privileged setting. Shareholders and directors,[260] for example, are privileged to exchange information about employees and customers without attracting tort liability, unless they are malicious. Members of professional associations[261] or unions[262] may discuss matters of joint concern. It was held that lawyers, defending actions for different clients being sued by the same plaintiff, regarding the same subject matter, were privileged to exchange information.[263] Similarly, creditors for the same debtor have a qualified privilege to consult together in the furtherance of their common interest.[264]

A common interest may, however, also arise outside the business or pecuniary context. In *N. (R.) v. S. (S.L.)*,[265] the Nova Scotia Supreme Court found that statements made by two sisters regarding sexual abuse by their father were protected by a qualified privilege arising out of a common interest in communicating this information to each other, for the purpose of protecting their own children, and to a friend and a psychiatrist, in order to gain support and seek treatment.

---

tiff, who had been expelled from the union, was "an unscrupulous individual" was held not privileged although the news article reporting the expulsion was. In *Chapman v. Lord Ellesmere et al.*, [1932] 2 K.B. 431, it was held that the publication of the Jockey Club, of a notice of the plaintiff's suspension, in its own racing periodical, was privileged. However, several newspapers which had printed the story were not so protected because there was "no general interest to the public or duty owed to the public to publish matters which concern a section of the public only". But see Libel and Slander Act, R.S.O. 1990, c. L.12, s. 2(4).

[255] *Slocinski v. Radwan* (1929), 144 Atl. 787 (N.H.).

[256] *MacArthur v. Meuser* (1997), 35 C.C.L.T. (2d) 197 (Ont. Gen. Div.).

[257] *Toogood v. Spyring, supra*, n. 233.

[258] *Hayden v. Hasbrouck* (1912), 84 Atl. 1087 (R.I.), organization of women's clubs.

[259] See, for example, *Guise v. Kouvelis* (1947), 74 C.L.R. 102, member of Greek club accusing non-member of cheating at cards.

[260] *Telegraph Newspaper v. Bedford* (1934), 50 C.L.R. 632; *Watt v. Longsdon*, [1930] 1 K.B. 130. But see *Lawless v. Anglo-Egyptian Cotton Co.* (1869), L.R. 4 Q.B. 262; *Bryanston Finance v. DeVries, supra*, n. 156.

[261] *Thompson v. Amos* (1949), 23 A.L.J. 98, special district synod of Methodist ministers; *Allbutt v. The General Council of Medical Education and Registration* (1889), 23 Q.B.D. 400, minutes of council of medical practitioners.

[262] *Hanly v. Pisces Productions*, [1980] 1 W.W.R. 369 (B.C.S.C.).

[263] See *Spielberg v. A. Kuhn & Bros.* (1911), 116 Pac. 1027 (Utah).

[264] *Smith Bros. & Co. v. W.C. Agee & Co.* (1912), 50 So. 647 (Ala.).

[265] (1993), 120 N.S.R. (2d) 228 (S.C.).

In Britain, there was once recognized a common interest among voters in elections to communicate under the protection of a qualified privilege,[266] but this has now been abrogated by statute.[267] The Canadian law apparently never did recognize such a privilege.[268]

c) Moral or Legal Duty to Protect Another's Interest

A qualified privilege may be enjoyed by someone who makes a statement in the discharge of a public or private duty, whether legal, moral or social. Again, the recipient must have a reciprocal interest in receiving it.[269] It should be emphasized that the protection here is fairly narrow because it is the duty aspect which is controlling. It is not sufficient, therefore, that the information would be something that the recipient would like to know.[270] Neither is it to be confused with the right to report truthfully and comment fairly on matters of public interest.[271] Furthermore, the existence of the duty does not protect statements which unnecessarily defame the plaintiff.[272]

Whether the duty exists depends on actual facts and not on the belief of the publisher.[273] There will likely be little difficulty in determining whether a legal duty exists.[274] As for a moral or social duty, this has been said to mean "a duty recognized

---

[266] *Braddock v. Bevins*, [1948] 1 K.B. 580 (C.A.).

[267] The Defamation Act, 1952, 15 & 16 Geo. 6 & 1 Eliz. 2, c. 66, s. 10 provides: "A defamatory statement published by or on behalf of a candidate in any election to a local government authority or to Parliament shall not be deemed to be published on a privileged occasion on the ground that it is material to a question in issue in the election, whether or not the person by whom it is published is qualified to vote at the election."

[268] *Bureau v. Campbell*, [1928] 3 D.L.R. 907 (Sask. C.A.); *Douglas v. Tucker, supra*, n. 248; *Globe & Mail Ltd. v. Boland* (1960), 22 D.L.R. (2d) 277 (S.C.C.). See also *Jones v. Bennett*, [1969] S.C.R. 277, 2 D.L.R. (3d) 291. But see *Parlett v. Robinson, infra*, n. 287; *Stopforth v. Goyer, infra*, n. 286.

[269] *Cockayne v. Hodgkisson* (1933), 5 C. & P. 543, at p. 548, 172 E.R. 1091, at p. 1093; *Pullman v. Hill & Co., supra*, n. 240, at p. 528.

[270] *Watt v. Longsdon*, [1930] 1 K.B. 130 (C.A.), a stranger not privileged to make disclosures to wife about morals and integrity of husband.

[271] *Globe & Mail Ltd. v. Boland, supra*, n. 268, at pp. 280-81; *Banks v. Globe & Mail Ltd.* (1961), 28 D.L.R. (2d) 343, at p. 349 (S.C.C.); *Littleton v. Hamilton* (1974), 47 D.L.R. (3d) 663, at pp. 664-65 (Ont. C.A.). See *infra*, Section E.3.(d).

[272] *Botiuk v. Toronto Free Press* (1995), 126 D.L.R. (4th) 609, at p. 628 (S.C.C.).

[273] *Beach v. Freeson*, [1972] 1 Q.B. 14, at p. 25, wherein the *obiter dictum* of Scrutton L.J., in *Watt v. Longsdon, supra*, n. 270, at p. 146, to the contrary was rejected and the judgment of Lord Esher M.R., in *Hebditch v. MacIlwaine, supra*, n. 239, at p. 59, was applied.

[274] The duty may be imposed by statute: *Lacarte v. Bd. of Education of Toronto*, [1959] S.C.R. 465, duty to disclose reasons for dismissal of teacher pursuant to The Teachers' Board of Reference Act, 1946 (Ont.), c. 97, s. 2; *Fisher v. Ramkin* (1972), 27 D.L.R. (3d) 746, duty of company representative of joint standing committee to report reasons for dismissal of employee pursuant to collective agreement and Labour Relations Act, R.S.B.C. 1960, c. 205, s. 22(1) (rep. & sub. 1963, c. 20, s. 3); or by contractual obligations: *Oana v. Maxwell Constr. Co. Ltd., supra*, n. 236, Dunn & Bradstreet report provided for subscriber; or arise as an incident to one's employment or the holding of an office: *Maass v. Seelheim*, [1936] 4 D.L.R. 267, at p. 271 (Man.

by . . . people of ordinary intelligence and moral principle, but at the same time not a duty enforceable by legal proceedings, whether civil or criminal".[275]

One of the leading cases with regard to public duty is *Adam v. Ward*,[276] in which a Member of Parliament made certain charges against a senior army officer. The Army Council made an official investigation, exonerated the officer, and, incidentally, made remarks defamatory of the Member of Parliament. The Council's report was found to be privileged since it had been made in the discharge of a public duty. Although the Council released the information to the public press, this was held not to be an abuse, having regard to the fact that the accusation had been made in the Parliament.

Courts are more inclined to find a qualified privilege where statements are made in response to specific inquiries than when they are volunteered, since this tends to indicate the significance with which the recipient regards the information. For example, if previous employers give character references regarding discharged employees, at the request of a prospective employer, they are more likely to be protected than if they volunteer the information.[277] Similarly, a businessperson who comments on the financial standing of a buyer at the request of another stands in a better position than if the comments were unsolicited.[278] In a somewhat different context, a police officer who responds to a mother's request for information on a police investigation involving her son by disclosing to her information reported to the police regarding her son's criminal activities is protected by a qualified privilege.[279]

An inquiry is not always required, however. Certain relationships generate a duty to inform even without any request to do so. For example, defamatory statements by a father to his daughter about a prospective husband are privileged because of his moral obligation as a father.[280] An employer may also tell an employee certain things related to work.[281]

Mercantile agencies that collect and sell credit information for profit to their customers were denied qualified privilege on the ground that it was not in the public interest to protect those who trade for profit in the characters of other

---

Q.B.); *Edgeworth v. N.Y. Central*, [1936] 2 D.L.R. 577 (Ont. C.A.) (*per* dissent of Fisher J.A., at p. 582); see also *Sapiro v. Leader Publishing Co. Ltd.*, [1926] 3 D.L.R. 68, at p. 71 (Sask. C.A.).

[275] *Stuart v. Bell*, [1891] 2 Q.B. 341, at p. 350 (C.A.) (*per* Lindley L.J.).

[276] [1917] A.C. 309.

[277] *Jackson v. Hopperton* (1864), 16 C.B. (N.S.) 829, but malice destroyed privilege; *Anderson v. Smythe*, [1935] 4 D.L.R. 72 (B.C.C.A.). Information given to investigation of teacher's conduct by fellow workers subject to qualified privilege, *Haight-Smith v. Neden* (2000), 2 C.C.L.T. (3d) 148 (B.C.S.C.).

[278] *Robshaw v. Smith* (1878), 38 L.T. 423.

[279] *Chrispen v. Novak*, [1995] 5 W.W.R. 752 (Sask. Q.B.).

[280] *Bordeaux v. Jobs* (1913), 6 Alta L.R. 440, at p. 443. See also *Todd v. Hawkins* (1837), 8 C. & P. 88, 173 E.R. 411.

[281] *Cooke v. Wildes* (1855), 5 E. & B. 328. Thus, in *Clarke v. Austin et al.* (1974), 51 D.L.R. (3d) 598 (B.C.), it was held that a report by an employee to his superior, that he thought he saw a customer shoplift an item, was qualifiedly privileged. In contrast, in *Risk v. Zellers Ltd.* (1977), 27 N.S.R. (2d) 532, there was no privilege attaching to a store manager's statement to a third party that a certain item properly belonged to the store.

people.[282] However, this much-criticized view was subsequently modified to furnish a qualified privilege to credit reports by a mutual trade protective society, which was a co-operative service, rather than a business run for profit.[283] Those who rely on the reports of such agencies are equally protected if a privilege originally existed.[284]

d) Public Interest

Absent the defence of fair comment, there was authority which said that there was no claim of privilege with regard to a defamatory publication on the basis that it was in the public interest. Thus, "the *right* which the publisher of a newspaper has, in common with all Her Majesty's subjects, to report truthfully and comment fairly upon matters of public interest" was not to be confused with "a *duty* of the sort which gives rise to an occasion of qualified privilege".[285]

There has recently been a shift in judicial attitude toward statements made in the public interest. It now appears that public officials may have a qualified privilege to communicate with the electorate about matters of public interest if they do so in good faith. For example, in *Stopforth v. Goyer*,[286] the Ontario Court of Appeal held that a Minister of the Crown had a public duty to inform the electorate about why a civil servant had been demoted and that the electorate had a corresponding interest in hearing the Minister's comments and, hence, there was a qualified privilege to do so. Similarly, in *Parlett v. Robinson*[287] the British Columbia Court of Appeal held that a Member of Parliament could claim a qualified privilege to communicate "to the world" through the media about his own profit. The court, in dismissing the action, explained that he had a

---

[282] *MacIntosh v. Dun*, [1908] A.C. 390. See also *Gillett v. Nissen Volkswagen Ltd. et al.*, [1975] 3 W.W.R. 520 (Alta.). But see *Todd v. Dun* (1888), 15 O.A.R. 85; *Robinson v. Dun* (1897), 24 O.A.R. 287.

[283] *London Assoc. for the Protection of Trade v. Greenlands*, *supra*, n. 244. See also *Howe v. Lees* (1910), 11 C.L.R. 361; *Harper v. Hamilton Retail Grocers Assoc.* (1900), 32 O.R. 295 (C.A.); J.M. Sharp, *Credit Reporting and Privacy* (1970). This appears to be the position in the U.S. as well. See Prosser and Keeton, *op.cit. supra*, n. 3, at p. 790.

[284] *Oana v. Maxwell Constr.*, *supra*, n. 236. See generally Consumer Reporting Act, R.S.O. 1990, c. C.33.

[285] *Globe & Mail Ltd. v. Boland*, [1960] S.C.R. 203, at p. 207 (*per* Cartwright C.J.C.). The court was concerned with whether an editorial accusing the plaintiff, a candidate in a federal election, of "shabby tactics" by suggesting that the Liberals were "soft on Communism" was defamatory. The trial judge held that the occasion was one of qualified privilege. The Court of Appeal allowed the appeal and ordered a new trial. The Supreme Court of Canada concurred in this result. For an account of the second trial and subsequent appeal ordering a third trial see *Boland v. Globe & Mail Ltd.*, [1961] O.R. 712, 29 D.L.R. (2d) 401. See also *Banks v. Globe & Mail*, [1961] S.C.R. 474, statements in the newspaper concerning director of labour union which had called a strike affecting eight Canadian-owned vessels; *Jones v. Bennett* (1968), 2 D.L.R. (3d) 291 (S.C.C.), public meeting of party supporters at which Premier justified suspension of a member of provincial commission.

[286] (1979), 8 C.C.L.T. 172 (Ont. C.A.).

[287] (1986), 37 C.C.L.T. 281 (B.C.C.A.). See also *Baumann v. Turner* (1993), 82 B.C.L.R. (2d) 362 (C.A.).

"duty to ventilate the matter" and the Canadian electorate had a *"bona fide interest"* in it. This development is a welcome move toward more openness in this area, something that should continue in the era of the Charter.

A privilege is also recognized, in the interest of the general public, for individuals who report crimes to the police,[288] who warn the public about a dangerous product[289] or who complain about the conduct of public officers to their superiors,[290] or to their Members of Parliament.[291] So too, statements made to public authorities with regard to matters over which they have jurisdiction are qualifiedly privileged.[292] This would include an allegation of wrongdoing made against an Indian band chief or councillor to the Minister of Indian Affairs.[293] But one is not so privileged to write defamatory remarks about someone in a book documenting the history of a well-known organization, merely because the public would be interested in such an account, since there were no "valid social reasons" to do so.[294]

A qualified privilege extends to the "publication without malice of a fair and accurate report" of judicial proceedings by the press.[295] Cory J. stated in *Hill v. Church of Scientology* that "[t]he rationale behind this rule is that the public has a right to be informed about all aspects of proceedings to which it has the right of access".[296] Historically, the privilege did not extend to ". . . a report on pleadings or other documents which [have] not been filed with the court or referred to in open court".[297] In *Hill v. Scientology*, however, the notice of motion containing the allegations read out by Morris Manning had not actually been filed with the court prior to the press conference. Despite this, Cory J. held that the privilege ought not be defeated by such a "technicality". In support, he reasoned that ". . . Morris Manning had every intention of initiating the contempt action in accordance with the prevailing rules".[298] L'Heureux Dube J.

---

[288] *Foltz v. Moore McCormack Lines Inc.* (1951), 189 F. 2d 537 (U.S.C.A., 2nd Cir.). But see *Lowther v. Baxter* (1890), 22 N.S.R. 372 (C.A.); letter to justice of the peace accusing plaintiff of theft and cheating not privileged as was not in the context of a judicial proceeding.

[289] *Camporese v. Parton, supra,* n. 43.

[290] *Nuyen v. Slater* (1964), 127 N.W. 2d 369 (Mich.); *Goodwin v. Graves* (1904), 4 O.W.R. 449, at p. 473. Likewise a teacher can be reported to a school board in a privileged context: *Segall v. Piazza* (1965), 260 N.Y.S. 2d 543.

[291] *R. v. Rule,* [1937] 2 K.B. 375 (C.A.).

[292] *Wilcocks v. Howell* (1884), 5 O.R. 360 (C.A.), petition to licence commissioners seeking denial of tavern licence to plaintiff; *Latta v. Fargey* (1906), 9 O.W.R. 231, 661 (C.A.), complaint to cheese inspector about the plaintiff, a cheesemaker.

[293] *Westbank Indian Band v. Tomat* (1992), 63 B.C.L.R. (2d) 273 (C.A.).

[294] *Littleton v. Hamilton, supra,* n. 271 (book called the "Children's Crusade" about the Company of Young Canadians).

[295] See Fleming, *op. cit. supra,* n. 10, at p. 559.

[296] *Hill v. Church of Scientology of Toronto,* [1995] 2 S.C.R. 1130 at p. 1191. See also *Edmonton Journal v. Alberta (Attorney General),* [1989] 2 S.C.R. 1326, at p. 1339, in which Cory J. held that ". . . members of the public have a right to information pertaining to public institutions and particularly the courts. Here the press plays a fundamentally important role."

[297] *Ibid.,* at p. 1191. See *Gazette Printing Co. v. Shallow* (1909), 41 S.C.R. 339.

[298] *Ibid.,* at p. 1193.

disagreed with this position, finding instead that the traditional rule ought to stand.[299] It remains to be seen how this ambiguity in the scope of the qualified privilege will be resolved. Despite this, it is clear that the privilege does not protect conduct which exceeds ". . . the legitimate purposes of the occasion".[300] In *Hill v. Church of Scientology of Toronto*, Cory J. found that Morris Manning, Scientology's lawyer, exceeded the legitimate purpose of a press conference by reading out a notice of motion which contained a very scathing attack on the plaintiff lawyer's credibility on the steps of Osgoode Hall without checking whether there was any truth to the allegations.[301]

However, the British Columbia Court of Appeal has held that there was no defence of qualified privilege for a newspaper which reported that the appellant was a "terrorist official" because neither the appellant nor the party with which he was associated posed a threat to the public which gave rise to a duty to report.[302]

It appears that a defendant may be held liable for mistakenly reporting defamatory information to the wrong authority even if honestly and reasonably believing that it was the proper agency to receive it.[303] There is, however, authority to the contrary which is to be preferred.[304]

e) Malice

Malice will defeat the defence of qualified privilege (as well as fair comment) in any of the above four situations. It may also be taken into account in the assessment of damages.

---

[299] *Ibid.*, at pp. 1215-1216. See also *Mack v. North Hill News* (1964), 44 D.L.R. (2d) 147, at p. 163 (Alta. T.D.).

[300] *Ibid.*, at p. 1193.

[301] *Ibid.* Although Cory J. declined at p. 1193 to find that Manning's conduct constituted "actual malice", he did find him to have been "high-handed and careless".

[302] *Moises v. Canadian Newspaper Co.* (1996), 30 C.C.L.T. (2d) 145 (B.C.C.A.); leave to appeal to S.C.C. refused (1997), 208 N.R. 320n (S.C.C.).

[303] *Hebditch v. MacIlwaine*, [1894] 2 Q.B. 54 (C.A.), ratepayer complaining of election irregularities to wrong body; *DeBuse v. McCarthy*, [1942] 1 K.B. 156, town clerk sending notice of borough council agenda and report to be discussed to public libraries. See also *Beach v. Freeson*, *supra*, n. 273.

[304] In *McIntire v. McBean* (1856), 13 U.C.Q.B. 534, parents who complained to the wrong authority about a teacher's moral character were excused from liability since it was found commendable to do this as long as the information was "well-founded, or that they had good reason to believe it was, and that they acted in sincerity and good faith, not maliciously and without just cause or excuse". Similarly, in *Kerr v. Davidson* (1873), 9 N.S.R. 354, it was held that a privilege exists if a communication is made to a person "not in fact having such interest or duty, but who might reasonably be and is supposed by the party making the communication to have such an interest or duty". Some jurisdictions have dealt with the hardship created by the rule in *Hebditch* by statute. See Fleming, *op. cit. supra*, n. 10, at p. 596. The U.S. has apparently adopted the approach that a privilege will attach if the matter is published to anyone who reasonably appears to have a duty, interest or authority in receiving it. See *Prosser and Keeton, op. cit., supra*, n. 3, at p. 793, and cases cited.

Malice should be distinguished from the concept of excess or abuse of privilege, although the latter may be evidence of the former. Excess of privilege is a matter for the determination of the trial judge, whereas the question of whether the defendant has acted "maliciously" is for the jury to decide.[305] Once the judge rules that the occasion is privileged, the onus of proof of malice shifts to the plaintiff.[306] If there is no evidence of malice, the defendant is entitled to a non-suit.[307]

Malice should not be restricted to the notion of spite or ill-will, for it also encompasses any indirect motive not connected with the purpose for which the privilege was given by law.[308] For example, a mother's desire to win a custody dispute is an indirect motive which will defeat a qualified privilege which would otherwise extend to the distribution of reports alleging sexual and physical abuse by the children's father and new wife.[309]

Evidence of malice may be expressed or implied, that is, it may be embodied in the statement itself,[310] or depend upon proof of extrinsic facts.[311] As to the language of the statement, it has been suggested that the test is whether the words employed were "utterly beyond and disproportionate to the facts".[312] Approached from the other direction, the question is whether, given the facts as they appeared to the defendant at the time of the publication, the terms used were "such as the defendant might have honestly and *bona fide* employed in the circumstances".[313]

Extrinsic evidence of malice may include personal animosity, but this would likely be insufficient in and of itself. It must be coupled with proof that the defendant had an improper purpose in mind and was motivated to make the defamatory remark because of the existence of the antagonism.[314]

Legal malice can also be demonstrated by proof that the publisher did not have a genuine belief in the truth of the statement, as one who knowingly asserts a falsehood clearly is using an otherwise privileged occasion for a dishonest and improper purpose.[315] But, while lack of an honest belief or "reckless disregard

---

[305] *Adam v. Ward, supra*, n. 232, at p. 321 (*per* Earl Loreburn).

[306] *Clark v. Molyneux* (1877), 3 Q.B.D. 237; *Jenoure v. Delmege*, [1891] A.C. 73 (P.C.); *Netupsky v. Craig, supra*, n. 244.

[307] *Dewe v. Waterbury* (1881), 6 S.C.R. 143.

[308] *Jerome v. Anderson* (1964), 44 D.L.R. (2d) 516 (S.C.C.); *Sun Life Assurance Co. v. Dalrymple, supra*, n. 238.

[309] *G. (R.) v. Christison* (1996), 31 C.C.L.T. (2d) 263 (Sask. Q.B.).

[310] *Edmonson v. Birch & Co. Ltd.*, [1907] 1 K.B. 371, at p. 381; *Laughton v. Bishop of Sodor and Man* (1872), L.R. 4 P.C. 495, at p. 505. See also *Wlodek v. Kosko* (1976), 56 D.L.R. (3d) 187 (Ont. C.A.); appeal dismissed 65 D.L.R. (3d) 383 (S.C.C.).

[311] Fleming, *op. cit. supra*, n. 10, at p. 635.

[312] *Sun Life v. Dalrymple, supra*, n. 238, at p. 310.

[313] *Ogders on Libel and Slander*, 6th ed., at p. 292. See *McLoughlin v. Kutasy* (1979), 8 C.C.L.T. 105, at p. 114 (S.C.C.).

[314] Fleming, *op. cit. supra*, n. 10, at p. 637.

[315] *Stewart v. Biggs*, [1928] N.Z.L.R. 673. See also *English v. Lamb* (1900), 32 O.R. 73; *Green v. Miller* (1901), 31 S.C.R. 177 and 33 S.C.R. 193. Normally the onus is on the plaintiff to show

for the truth",[316] will prove malice, an honest belief will not necessarily negate malice.[317] Reckless indifference is treated in the same manner,[318] although one is entitled to honestly hold an unreasonable view.[319]

Agents through whom a person publishes a privileged communication are themselves protected by the privilege.[320] It does not follow, however, although there is earlier authority to the contrary,[321] that the malice of one participant in a defamatory publication will defeat the privilege pleaded by another.[322] Similarly, a joint publisher has an independent right to claim privilege.[323] In so far as employees and agents are concerned, the principle of *respondeat superior* applies to statements made within the scope of the employment or agency.[324] But, the converse does not obtain, so that, even where the principals do not claim privilege, those further down the chain of participation or dissemination may still be protected.[325]

f) Excess of Privilege

If the words complained of are clearly outside the scope of the privilege, liability will attach.[326] This will be so where the defendant makes imputations against the plaintiff which are unwarranted by the circumstances,[327] or the publication is unjustifiably wide or excessive.[328] However, the inclusion of extraneous material does not necessarily negate the privilege with regard to the rest.[329]

---

that the defendant did not believe the statement to be true. However, this appears not to be the case with regard to obviously irrelevant matter. See *Horrocks v. Lowe*, [1975] A.C. 135 (H.L.).

[316] *McLoughlin v. Kutasy*, [1979] 2 S.C.R. 311, at p. 321.

[317] *Christie v. Westcom Radio Group Ltd.* (1990), 5 C.C.L.T. (2d) 301 (B.C.C.A.).

[318] *Horrocks v. Lowe, supra*, n. 315. See also *Leverman v. Campbell Sharp Ltd.* (1987), 40 C.C.L.T. 75 (C.A.), explaining that carelessness in forming an honest belief does not vitiate the defence of qualified privilege, but that carelessness in the publication of the statement so that it does not express the honest belief or shows the honest belief was never formed, removes that defence.

[319] *Korach v. Moore* (1991), 76 D.L.R. (4th) 506 (Ont. C.A.).

[320] *Baker v. Carrick*, [1894] 1 Q.B. 838 (C.A.).

[321] *Smith v. Streatfeild*, [1913] 3 K.B. 764.

[322] *Egger v. Viscount Chelmsford*, [1965] 1 Q.B. 248 (C.A.); *Riddick v. Thames Bd. Mills Ltd.*, [1977] 3 All E.R. 677.

[323] *Langdon-Griffiths v. Smith*, [1957] 1 K.B. 295; *Meekins v. Henson*, [1964] 1 Q.B. 472.

[324] *Egger v. Viscount Chelmsford, supra*, n. 322; *Sun Life v. Dalrymple, supra*, n. 238; *Webb v. Bloch* (1928), 41 C.L.R. 331.

[325] *Egger v. Viscount Chelmsford, supra*, n. 322.

[326] *Knapp v. McLeod*, [1926] 2 D.L.R. 1083 (Ont. C.A.).

[327] Thus, it is not ordinarily permissible for the defendant to resort to the press for the communication of privileged information. "The method of publication must never exceed what is reasonably appropriate for protecting the particular interest which the defendant is entitled to assert": Fleming, *op. cit. supra*, n. 10, at p. 548, citing *Chapman v. Lord Ellesmere*, [1932] 2 K.B. 431. See also *Douglas v. Tucker, supra*, n. 248; *Globe & Mail Ltd. v. Boland*, [1960] S.C.R. 203; *Pleau v. Simpsons-Sears, supra*, n. 244; *Daniel v. Mt. Allison University* (1976), 15 N.B.R. (2d) 373. An unnecessary attack on the character of another to defend one's own character does not come under the privilege, see *Botiuk v. Toronto Free Press, supra*, n. 272, at p. 628.

[328] *Adam v. Ward, supra*, n. 232, at p. 329 (*per* Lord Dunedin) and, at p. 340 (*per* Lord Atkinson).

[329] *Dunford Publicity Studios Ltd. v. News Media Ownership Ltd. et al.*, [1971] N.Z.L.R. 961, at p. 968.

4. FAIR COMMENT

Fair comment on matters of public concern or interest is protected from liability for defamation provided it is based on fact. In other words, it must be a comment, not an imputation of fact.[330] These matters fall within two main categories; first, those in which the public has a legitimate interest, such as government activity, political debate, proposals by public figures, and public affairs generally; second, works of art displayed in public, such as theatrical performances, music and literature. In a democratic and culturally vibrant society, a discussion of these matters must be unfettered. In the case of the former, the public has an interest by reason of the nature of the subject matter. With regard to the latter, the objects of the comment have voluntarily submitted their deeds to public scrutiny.

Fair comment must be based on fact. The facts must be included in the communication, or they must be indicated with sufficient clarity to lay a proper foundation for the comment being made.[331]

A comment is not protected if it appears to be an allegation of fact. For the defence to hold, the ordinary unprejudiced reader must take the remarks to be a comment based on facts.[332] Thus, if the "sting of the words complained of do not appear to be comment at all", the defence will fail.[333] In other words, to say that someone did something dishonourable is a fact, whereas to say that someone did a particular thing and that that was dishonourable is a statement of fact and a comment.[334] The latter is permitted, but not the former.

It is a question of fact for the jury to decide whether the communication is fact or comment, unless the judge withdraws the question from them on the basis that the words complained of are not reasonably capable of being regarded as comment.[335]

Unless the facts upon which the comment is based are true and undistorted, the comment cannot be "fair". The defendant must "get his facts right" in order to win the protection of the defence. It will not suffice that the defendant

---

[330] *Reynolds v. Times Newspapers Ltd., supra,* n. 53.

[331] *Kemsley v. Foot,* [1952] A.C. 345, at p. 357 (H.L.) (*per* Lord Porter).

[332] *Clarke v. Norton,* [1910] V.L.R. 494, at p. 501. See *Christie v. Geiger* (1986), 38 C.C.L.T. 280, at p. 285 (Alta. C.A.) (*per* McLung J.A.).

[333] *Jones v. Bennett, supra,* n. 268, at p. 285, S.C.R. (*per* Cartwright C.J.C.).

[334] There is no comprehensive statement in the case law as to how to distinguish between a statement of fact and a statement which represents an inference drawn by the commentator. Prefatory words such as "in my opinion", "in other words", or "it appears" are not decisive, but may be some indication that the succeeding words are comment. See generally, Duncan and Neill, *op. cit. supra,* n. 4, at pp. 67-8. Compare *Dakhyl v. Labouchere,* [1908] 2 K.B. 325n (H.L.) to *Smith's Newspapers v. Becker* (1932), 47 C.L.R. 279. See also *Turner v. M-G-M, supra,* n. 243, at p. 474. But see *London Artists Ltd. v. Littler,* [1969] 2 Q.B. 375, at p. 392.

[335] *Jones v. Skelton,* [1963] 1 W.L.R. 1362, at p. 1379; *Bulletin Co. v. Sheppard* (1917), 55 S.C.R. 454.

reasonably believed them to be true.[336] For example, in *Barltrop v. C.B.C.*[337] the radio show "As It Happens" broadcast some information about a doctor who was alleged to have "sold" his evidence, which was said to be contrary to public health, to an inquiry. Because the facts upon which the comment were based, suggesting that the plaintiff was professionaly dishonest, were false, the comments were, therefore, not mere expressions of opinion on proven facts, and the defence of fair comment failed.

There is an exception to the requirement of accurate facts. If facts are erroneously asserted on a privileged occasion, such as in Parliament or in a court of law, and if a commentator relies on these alleged but mistaken facts in making a comment based on them, there will be no liability, even though the facts are inaccurate, as long as the comment is a fair one.[338] The commentator will, however, have to show that the report of the occasion on which the privileged statements were made was fair and accurate.[339]

At common law, the defendant had to prove that *all* the facts mentioned were true in order to use this defence. It was said that if the defendant "fails to justify one, even if it be comparatively unimportant, he fails in his defence".[340] This rule, however, has been modified by statute.[341]

Although the comment must be fair, this does not necessarily mean that it must be reasonable.[342] Unreasonable individuals are allowed to express their unreasonable views. The test for the jury is whether they might reasonably regard the opinion as one that no fair-minded person could possibly have promulgated. The jury must not substitute its own opinion on the subject.[343] In other words, as long as the comment is not actuated by malice and represents a legitimate opinion honestly held by the speaker, it will be protected.[344]

---

[336] See *Douglas v. Stephenson* (1898), 29 O.R. 616; affd (1899), 26 O.A.R. 26; *Price v. Chicoutimi Pulp Co.* (1915), 51 S.C.R. 179.

[337] (1978), 86 D.L.R. (3d) 61 (N.S.C.A.). See also *Holt v. Sun Publishing Co.* (1978), 83 D.L.R. (3d) 761 (B.C.); *England v. C.B.C.*, [1979] 3 W.W.R. 193 (N.W.T.).

[338] *Mangena v. Wright*, [1909] 2 K.B. 958, at p. 977, comment on excerpt from Parliamentary paper; *Grech v. Odhams Press*, [1958] 2 Q.B. 275, at p. 285 (C.A.), comment on report of judicial proceedings. See also *Cook v. Alexander*, [1974] Q.B. 279, at p. 288 (C.A.).

[339] *Brent Walker Group plc. v. Time Out Ltd.*, [1991] 2 All E.R. 753 (C.A.).

[340] *Kemsley v. Foot, supra*, n. 331, at pp. 357-58.

[341] Libel and Slander Act, R.S.O. 1990, c. L.12, s. 23, states: "In an action for libel or slander for words consisting partly of allegations of fact and partly of expression of opinion, a defence of fair comment shall not fail by reason only that the truth of every allegation of fact is not proved if the expression of opinion is fair comment having regard to such of the facts alleged or referred to in the words complained of as are proved."

[342] The limits of the right of comment are said to be very wide. See *Stopes v. Sutherland* (1924), House of Lords, Printed Cases, 375; revd [1925] A.C. 47 (H.L.) (*per* Lord Hewart C.J.).

[343] *McQuire v. Western Morning News*, [1903] 2 K.B. 100, at p. 109 (C.A.).

[344] See also *Reynolds, supra*, n. 53, at p. 615, "honest belief".

Newspapers have no special rights in this regard. In *Cherneskey v. Armadale Publishers*,[345] two law students wrote a letter to the editor, which the Saskatoon Star-Phoenix published, complaining about the racist attitude of a local alderman. He sued the newspaper for libel. The law students did not give evidence at the trial and the newspaper staff testified that they did not agree with the contents of the letter. The trial judge withheld from the jury the defence of fair comment; this was reversed by the Saskatchewan Court of Appeal; the Supreme Court of Canada affirmed the trial judge, with Dickson, Spence and Estey JJ. dissenting.

Mr. Justice Ritchie, for the majority, reaffirmed the traditional scope of the defence, saying:

> . . . each publisher in relying on the defence of fair comment is in exactly the same position as the original writer. . . .
> . . . the newspaper and its editor cannot sustain a defence of fair comment when it has been proved that the words used in the letter are not an honest expression of their opinion and there is no evidence as to the honest belief of the writers.[346]

Dickson J., dissenting, disagreed fundamentally, espressing his concern about how this would muzzle the press in relation to letters to the editor as follows:

> It does not require any great preception to envisage the effect of such a rule upon the position of a newspaper in the publication of letters to the editor. An editor receiving a letter containing matter which might be defamatory would have a defence of fair comment if he shared the views expressed, but defenceless if he did not hold those views. As the columns devoted to letters to the editor are intended to stimulate uninhibited debate on every public issue, the editor's task would be an unenviable one if he were limited to publishing only those letters with which he agreed. He would be engaged in a sort of censorship, antithetical to a free press. One can readily draw a distinction between editorial comment or articles, which may be taken to represent the paper's point of view, and letters to the editor in which the personal opinion of the paper is, or should be, irrelevant. No one believes that a newspaper shares the views of every hostile reader who takes it to task in a letter to the editor for error of omission or commission, or that it yields assent to the views of every person who feels impelled to make his feelings known in a letter to the editor. Newspapers do not adopt as their own the opinions voiced in such letters, nor should they be expected to. . . .[347]

---

[345] (1978), 90 D.L.R. (3d) 321 (S.C.C.). See Doody, Comment (1980), 58 Can. Bar Rev. 174; Klar, "The Defence of 'Fair Comment'" (1979), 8 C.C.L.T. 149; McLaren, "The Defamation Action and Municipal Politics" (1980), 29 U.N.B.L.J. 123.

[346] *Ibid.*, at p. 336. See also *Slim v. Daily Telegraph*, [1968] 2 Q.B. 157, at p. 170, where Denning M.R., though holding the defendants liable because of false facts, had this to say:
> [T]he right of fair comment is one of the essential elements which go to make up our freedom of speech. We must ever maintain this right intact. It must not be whittled down by legal refinements. When a citizen is troubled by things going wrong, he should be free to 'write to the newspaper'; and the newspaper should be free to publish his letter. It is often the only way to get things put right. The matter must, of course, be one of public interest. The writer must get his facts right, and he must honestly state his real opinion. But that being done, both he and the newspaper should be clear of any liability. They should not be deterred by fear of libel actions.
See also *Lyon v. Daily Telegraph*, [1943] 1 K.B. 746 (C.A.).

[347] *Ibid.*, at p. 343.

It was his view that it was not only the right, but the duty of the press to promote the free flow and exchange of new and different ideas in a democratic society. He preferred to adopt a new, more liberal test, promulgated by Duncan and Neill:

(a)   the comment must be on a matter of public interest;
(b)   the comment must be based on fact;
(c)   the comment, though it can include inferences of fact, must be recognisable as comment;
(d)   the comment must satisfy the following *objective* test: could any man honestly express that opinion on the proved facts?
(e)   even though the comment satisfies the objective test the defence can be defeated *if the plaintiff proves that the defendant was actuated by express malice.*[348]

The decision in this case caused a public outcry which led to legislative reform in some jurisdictions. For example, Ontario enacted the following:

Where the defendant publishes defamatory matter that is an opinion expressed by another person, a defence of fair comment by the defendant shall not fail for the reason only that the defendant or the person who expressed the opinion, or both, did not hold the opinion, if a person could honestly hold the opinion.[349]

It seems that this section would enable the media to escape liability in circumstances such as *Cherneskey* as long as a person, not necessarily the publisher, could honestly hold the opinion expressed. In *Telnikoff v. Matusevitch*[350] the House of Lords expressed its preference for the position of Dickson J. relieving the defendant of the onus of proving honest belief. The House of Lords did not, however, limit this holding to situations involving newspapers.

Comments directed at public officials should bear only on their official conduct or fitness for office.[351] Likewise, criticism of artists should not descend to a personal attack.[352] It has been held that, where comments imputed dishonesty or other dishonourable conduct or motives, it was necessary either to prove the correctness of the allegation or that it was a reasonable inference which one could draw from the facts on which the comment was made.[353] However, it has been suggested that this

---

[348]   *Ibid.*, at p. 346.
[349]   See S.O. 1980, c. 35, s. 2, now s. 24 of the Libel and Slander Act, R.S.O. 1990, c. L.12.
[350]   [1991] 4 All E.R. 2 (H.L.).
[351]   *Manitoba Free Press Co. v. Martin* (1892), 21 S.C.R. 578; *Vander Zalm v. Times Publishers et al.* (1980), 12 C.C.L.T. 81 (B.C.C.A.). But see *Brown v. Orde* (1912), 3 O.W.N. 1230, leave to appeal denied (1912), 3 O.W.N. 1312, wherein it was suggested that the inference of incompetence in personal affairs might reflect on the capacity to hold public office since unfitness in that regard "arises from the general character and reputation and business standing of the plaintiff".
[352]   *Merivale v. Carson* (1887), 20 Q.B. 275, at p. 280; *McQuire v. Western Morning News, supra,* n. 343. With regard to criticism of artistic works, see generally, Duncan and Neill, *op. cit. supra,* n. 4, at pp. 70-1.
[353]   *Campbell v. Spottiswoode* (1863), 32 L.J.Q.B. 185; *Dakhyl v. Labouchere, supra,* n. 334; *Hunt v. Star Newspaper Co. Ltd.*, [1908] 2 K.B. 309, at p. 320. See also *Bulletin Co. v. Sheppard, supra,* n. 335.

approach, based on a test of reasonableness, runs counter to the whole concept of the defence of fair comment.[354] It is submitted that the better approach is to view the defence as available, where there is an imputation of dishonesty or dishonourable conduct or motives, if such is put forward as an expression of opinion.[355]

The test to be applied as to the meaning of the comment is that which the words can reasonably bear and not the intention of the defendant.[356] However, such intention is relevant to the question of whether the author was actuated by malice.[357]

The burden of proof of fair comment is on the defendant. Once established, the onus shifts to the plaintiff to prove malice defeating the defence.

5. OTHER DEFENCES

Consent will be a defence in circumstances where it can be said that the plaintiff instigated, procured or invited the publication of the defamatory words.[358] The defence, however, is narrowly construed and must be given for each publication separatley. Thus, agreeing to discuss on a radio programme certain information that is defamatory of oneself does not indicate consent to defamatory comment on the programme afterwards.[359]

Partial defences, said to go to mitigation of damages only include evidence that the plaintiff already had a bad reputation and "provocation".[360]

---

[354] See Duncan and Neill, *op. cit. supra*, n. 4, at p. 74.

[355] See *Silkin v. Beaverbrook Newspapers Ltd.*, [1958] 2 All E.R. 516; *Broadway Approvals Ltd. v. Odhams Press Ltd.*, [1965] 2 All E.R. 523 (C.A.); *O'Shaughnessy v. Mirror Newspapers Ltd.* (1970), 45 A.L.J.R. 59, at p. 60.

[356] *Merivale v. Carson, supra*, n. 352, at p. 281.

[357] *Thomas v. Bradbury, Agnew & Co. Ltd.*, [1906] 2 K.B. 627 (C.A.); *Adams v. Sunday Pictorial Newspapers (1920) Ltd.*, [1951] 1 K.B. 354, at pp. 359-60; *Lyon v. Daily Telegraph, supra*, n. 346.

[358] See *Jones v. Brooks* (1974), 45 D.L.R. (3d) 413, [1974] 2 W.W.R. 729 (Sask.); *Rudd v. Cameron* (1912), 26 O.L.R. 154; affd 27 O.L.R. 327 (C.A.); *Collerton v. Maclean*, [1962] N.Z.L.R. 1045. *Hanly v. Pisces, supra*, n. 262. The issue commonly arises where the plaintiff hires private investigators to check out stories that defamatory things are being said about the plaintiff. The defence has been dealt with in terms of qualified privilege: *Lupee v. Hogan* (1920), 47 N.B.R. 492 (C.A.); *Loveday v. Sun Newspaper* (1938), 59 C.L.R. 503, at pp. 523-25. It has also been treated as akin to the principle of *volenti non fit injuria*; *Chapman v. Lord Ellesmere*, [1932] 2 K.B. 431, at p. 465 (C.A.) (*per* Slesser L.J.); *Jones v. Brooks, supra*, n. 358.

[359] *Syms v. Warren* (1976), 71 D.L.R. (3d) 558 (Man.). See also *Cook v. Ward* (1830), 6 Bing. 409, 130 E.R. 1338, ludicrous story about himself, which plaintiff told to friends, published in news-paper. But see *Sharman v. C. Scmidt & Sons* (1963), 216 F. Supp. 401, consent to use plaintiff's picture in advertising held to include beer advertisements.

[360] See *Prosser and Keeton, op. cit. supra*, n. 3, at p. 847.

Other partial defences are available by statute. These include apology,[361] and retraction.[362] The statute also mandates compliance with certain notice requirements, failing which, no action will lie.[363]

6. THE CHARTER

Generally, the Canadian Charter of Rights and Freedoms[364] will be an infrequent visitor to defamation litigation, for it does not apply to a defamation action between private litigants.[365] Subsection 32(1) restricts its application to the actions of legislative, executive and administrative arms of government.[366] As a result, although the Charter will obviously govern the various defamation statutes,[367] it can only influence the common law of defamation in one of two ways. First, it may be directly applicable. ". . . . in so far as the common law is the basis of some governmental action which, it is alleged, infringes a guaranteed right or freedom".[368] In the context of defamation law, it appears that something more than the presence of a government figure, either speaking in an official capacity or being referred to in an official capacity, may be required in order to run afoul of the Charter.[369] A defamation action launched by a Crown

---

[361] At common law, apology was no defence, but went to the issue of mitigation of damages. This has been codified. See the Libel and Slander Act, R.S.O. 1990, c. L. 12, s. 20. As to the proper nature of an apology, see *Thompson v. NL Broadcasting Ltd.* (1976), 1 C.C.L.T. 278 (B.C.). A more limited defence is available to newspapers and broadcasters. See the Libel and Slander Act, R.S.O. 1990, c. L.12, s. 9.

[362] This defence is limited to newspapers and broadcasters. See the Libel and Slander Act. R.S.O. 1990, c. L.12, s. 5(2). The requirements of the statute must be strictly complied with. See Williams, *op. cit. supra*, n. 124, at pp. 110-13.

[363] See the Libel and Slander Act, R.S.O. 1990, c. L.12, s. 5(1). The notice is to be treated as a condition precedent to the bringing of an action. Its purpose is "to enable the defendant to correct or withdraw statements; to apologize for having published them; to mitigate or limit damages if an action is commenced and if the statements are found to be defamatory": *Barber v. Lupton* (1970), 9 D.L.R. (3d) 635, at p. 636 (Man.) (*per* Hall J.). See also *Redmond v. Stacey* (1918), 14 O.W.N. 73; *Burwell v. London Free Press* (1895), 27 O.R. 6. But see *Canadian Plasmapheresis Centres Ltd. v. C.B.C.* (1975), 8 O.R. (2d) 55.

[364] Constitution Act, 1982 [en. by Canada Act, 1982 (U.K.), c. 11, s. 1] Pt. I.

[365] See *Pangilinan v. Chaves* (1988), 47 C.R.R. 371 (Man. C.A.).

[366] *Dolphin Delivery Ltd. v. R.W.D.S.U., Local 580*, [1986] 2 S.C.R. 573, at p. 598 (*per* McIntyre J.).

[367] Since many of the defamation statutes across Canada essentially codify the common law, it remains uncertain what the effect will be of striking down a provision of a statute for which there is a similar common law rule.

[368] *Dolphin Delivery Ltd. v. R.W.D.S.U., Local 580, supra*, n. 366, at p. 599. For a discussion of what constitutes a sufficient government nexus in another context, see *McKinney v. University of Guelph*, [1990] 3 S.C.R. 229; *Harrison v. University of British Columbia*, [1990] 3 S.C.R. 451 and *Stoffman v. Vancouver General Hospital*, [1990] 3 S.C.R. 483.

[369] In *Coates v. Citizen (The)* (1988), 44 C.C.L.T. 286 (N.S.T.D.), the court dismissed the argument that, because the comments complained of referred to Coates, the Minister of National Defense at the time, acting in his official capacity, there was a sufficient government nexus to attract the Charter. Compare the American case *New York Times v. Sullivan* (1964), 376 U.S. 254, where the common law of libel was reviewed under the First Amendment in an action involving a public official at Alabama.

Attorney in response to an attack on his personal integrity will also be insufficient to establish a government nexus. In *Hill v. Church of Scientology of Toronto*, Cory J. held that "[t]he appellants impugned the character and competence and integrity of Casey Hill, himself, and not that of the government. He, in turn, responded by instituting legal proceedings in his own capacity".[370] Second, the Charter may be used by judges to shape the common law of defamation even where it is raised by private litigants in order to ensure that it develops "in a manner consistent with *Charter*-principles".[371] Cory J. emphasized, however, that ". . . *Charter* rights do not exist in the absence of state action. The most that the private litigant can do is argue that the common law is inconsistent with *Charter values*".[372] Despite this, even where it is not expressly raised, the existence of the Charter will exert a subtle influence on the future development of the common law of defamation by indirectly affecting its spirit.

In *Coates v. Citizen (The)*,[373] a Charter challenge based on the freedom of the press guarantee in s. 2(b) and the right to liberty in s. 7 was launched by *The Citizen* newspaper against the Nova Scotia Defamation Act.[374] The Nova Scotia Supreme Court concluded that, although "the laws of defamation are imperfect and in some aspects convoluted,"[375] they are "the citizens' defence against the awesome power of the printed word".[376] Accordingly, the court found the Defamation Act to be consistent with the Charter. In a later case, the Supreme Court of Canada declared that the protection afforded to defamatory statements by subsection 2(b) of the Charter is not strong. As Cory J. explained in *Hill v. Church of Scientology of Toronto*,[377] defamatory statements are only ". . . very tenuously related to the core values which underlie s. 2(*b*).". This is because they are ". . . inimical to the search for truth" and ". . . harmful to the interests of a free and democratic society".[378]

---

[370] *Hill, supra*, n. 296, at p. 1162.

[371] *Ibid.*, at p. 1165. In *Dolphin Delivery, supra*, n. 366, at p. 603, McIntyre J. confirmed that ". . . the question whether the judiciary ought to apply and develop the principles of the common law in a manner consistent with the fundamental values enshrined in the Constitution" should be answered in the affirmative. See also *R. v. Swain*, [1991] 1 S.C.R. 933 and *R. v. Salituro*, [1991] 3 S.C.R. 654. But see *Bank of British Columbia v. Canadian Broadcasting Corp.* (1995), 25 C.C.L.T. (2d) 229 (B.C.C.A.), in which Hutcheon J.A. expressed doubt about the ability to distinguish meaningfully between Charter rights and Charter values and so refused to consider the effect of s. 2(b) on the common law defence of privilege where there was no government action.

[372] *Ibid.*, at p. 1170. See also *Moises v. Canadian Newspaper Co.* (1996), 30 C.C.L.T. (2d) 145 (B.C.C.A.), in which the court held that s. 2(b) of the Charter did not require that the common law defence of qualified privilege for reports of proceedings be extended to the publication of statements on matters of public interest; leave to appeal to S.C.C. refused (1997), 208 N.R. 320n (S.C.C.).

[373] (1988), 44 C.C.L.T. 286 (N.S.T.D.).

[374] R.S.N.S. 1967, c. 72.

[375] *Supra*, n. 373, at p. 311.

[376] *Ibid.*, at p. 312 (*per* Richard J.).

[377] *Supra*, n. 296, at p. 1174.

[378] *Ibid.*

In rejecting *The Citizen*'s challenge to the Defamation Act, the Nova Scotia Supreme Court commented on the constitutional dimensions of American defamation jurisprudence. Prior to 1964, the protection of free speech and the freedom of the press guaranteed in the Constitution of the United States were held not to protect libelous statements. In that year, the case of *New York Times v. Sullivan* changed the landscape of American defamation law.[379] Under the *"New York Times* rule", as it has evolved, the equivalent of a qualified privilege based on the First Amendment is granted to those who criticize public figures, immunizing those critics from liability unless the public figure can prove actual malice in the publication of the defamatory falsehood. In this setting, actual malice consists of knowledge that the statement is false, or reckless disregard for whether it is false, and should not be confused with bad motive, ill will or spite.[380] Citing a stronger Canadian concern for the personal reputation of our public servants, the Nova Scotia Supreme Court expressly rejected the American approach.[381]

Similarly, in *Hill v. Church of Scientology of Toronto* it was argued that the actual malice rule ought to be adopted into the common law in order to make it consistent with Charter values. This position was firmly rejected by the Supreme Court. Cory J. stated[382]

The law of defamation is essentially aimed at the prohibition of the publication of injurious false statements. It is the means by which the individual may protect his or her reputation which may well be the most distinguishing feature of his or her character, personality and, perhaps, identity. I simply cannot see that the law of defamation is unduly restrictive or inhibiting. Surely it is not requiring too much of individuals that they ascertain the truth of the allegations they publish. The law of defamation provides for the defences of their fair comment and of qualified privilege in appropriate cases. Those who publish statements should assume a reasonable level of responsibility.

The Supreme Court of Canada also appears to have distanced itself from the American jurisprudence in its recent decision in *R. v. Keegstra*.[383] In that case, the Supreme Court had the opportunity to measure the wilful promotion of

---

[379] *New York Times v. Sullivan* (1964), 376 U.S. 254.

[380] See Prosser and Keeton, *supra*, n. 3, at p. 821. For a sample of the criticism which the actual malice rule has generated in the United States, see "The End of *New York Times v. Sullivan*: Reflections on *Masson v. New Yorker Magazine*", [1991] Sup. Ct. Rev. 1, in which L. Bollinger wrote at p. 6 that a ". . . major omission in the *New York Times v. Sullivan* analysis is any consideration of how libelous remarks can damage public discourse and undermine the very values that animated the court to protect them . . . in the first place". See also Tingley, "Reputation, Freedom of Expression and Defamation" (1999), 37 Alta. L.R. 620.

[381] *Coates v. The Citizen*, *supra*, n. 373.

[382] *Ibid.*, at p. 1187.

[383] [1990] 3 S.C.R. 697. The Supreme Court of Canada's willingness to recognize the limits of free speech dates back to 1938, when, in *Reference re Alberta Legislation*, [1938] S.C.R. 100, at p. 133, it stated that ". . . freedom of discussion means . . . 'freedom governed by law'". See also *R. v. Butler*, [1992] 1 S.C.R. 452, pornography laws do not violate Charter; M.D. Lepofsky, "Making Sense of the Libel Chill Debate: Do Libel Laws 'Chill' the Exercise of Freedom of Expression?" (1994), 4 N.J.C.L. 169.

hatred provision of the criminal defamation laws against the Charter. In a four to three decision, the court determined that s. 319(2) of the Criminal Code violates the freedom of expression guarantee of the Charter. However, that section of the Code was upheld under s. 1 as a reasonable limit on freedom of expression. The court also held that s. 319(3)(a), outlining the defences to s. 319(2), violates the presumption of innocence guarantee in s. 11(d) of the Charter, but upheld that reverse onus provision of the Criminal Code under s. 1. Of course, the reasoning in *R. v. Keegstra* is not directly relevant to civil defamation cases in which the Charter is invoked, but it does give some insight into how the court views the balance between promoting free speech and protecting people's reputations. Apparently, the former will not be allowed to trump the latter.

7. SOME DAMAGE ISSUES: GENERAL DAMAGES, THE CAP, AGGRAVATED DAMAGES, PUNITIVE DAMAGES AND INJUNCTIONS

Where there has been libel, general damages are presumed to follow "at large", that is, without the need to provide specific injury. Such damages are determined by the jury.[384] In *Hill v. Church of Scientology of Toronto*, Cory J. wrote that "[i]t is members of the community in which the defamed person lives who will be best able to assess the damages. The jury, as representative of that community should be free to make an assessment of damages which will provide the plaintiff with a sum of money that clearly demonstrates to the community the vindication of the plaintiff's reputation".[385] In other words, general damages are intended to compensate the plaintiff for the injury suffered to his or her reputation as a result of the defamation. The extent to which damages are awarded may, however, depend upon the context in which the defamation occurred.[386] In assessing general damages, it has been held that ". . . there is little to be gained from a detailed comparison of libel awards" as "each libel case is unique".[387] Where there are joint tortfeasors, they will be jointly and severally liable for these damages.[388]

The issue of whether or not there ought to be a limit or "cap" on damages in defamation cases has been raised in several jurisdictions, with different results.

---

[384] *Ley v. Hamilton* (1935), 153 L.T. 384 (H.L.), *Hill v. Church of Scientology of Toronto*, [1995] 2 S.C.R. 1130, at p. 1196.

[385] *Hill, supra*, n. 384, at p. 1196.

[386] In *Westbank Indian Band v. Tomat* (1992), 63 B.C.L.R. (2d) 290, Wood J.A. (Hinds J.A. concurring) advocated restraint in assessing damages for defamatory statements made in the political context. He stated at p. 291 that "[t]he rhetoric of modern political debate is replete with extravagant hyperbole, partisan viewpoints and inaccuracy. The result is that any libel which occurs in such a context is likely to be undertaken for what it is, and thus to a considerable extent deprived of what would otherwise be its sting." On the basis of these reasons, Wood J.A. also advocated extreme caution in imposing punitive damages where a defamatory statement was made in the political context.

[387] *Hill, supra*, n. 384, at p. 1205. See also *Botiuk v. Toronto Free Press, supra*, n. 272, at p. 632.

[388] *Ibid.*, at p. 1200; *Gatley on Libel and Slander*, 9th ed. (1998), at p. 600.

In Canada, the Supreme Court has rejected the imposition of a limit on general damages for defamation, as was imposed in personal injury cases,[389] in part because the purpose served by such damages in the defamation context is quite different. In defamation cases, unlike personal injury, ". . . special damages for pecuniary loss are rarely claimed and often exceedingly difficult to prove. Rather, the whole basis for recovery for loss of reputation usually lies in the general damages award".[390] Furthermore, in contrast to general damages for personal injury cases, damage awards in defamation cases have been both modest and relatively consistent.[391] In both Australia and England, however, it has been held that reference to awards made in personal injury cases may serve as a useful tool in controlling the size of defamation awards.[392]

Aggravated damages are to be awarded in defamation cases, as in other cases, where ". . . the defendants' conduct has been particularly high-handed or oppressive, thereby increasing the plaintiff's humiliation and anxiety arising from the libellous statement".[393] In order to satisfy this standard, "actual malice" must be proved, either through evidence intrinsic to the statement or evidence which surrounds the publication of the statement.[394] Factors relevant to the assessment of aggravated damages include: whether an apology was subsequently offered;[395] whether the statement was withdrawn; whether there was repetition of the libel; whether the defendant attempted to prevent the plaintiff

---

[389] General damages were limited to $100,000 (now $250,000) in personal injury cases in a trilogy of Supreme Court decisions: *Andrews v. Grand & Toy Alberta Ltd.*, [1978] 2 S.C.R. 229; *Arnold v. Teno*, [1978] 2 S.C.R. 287; and *Thornton v. Prince George School District No. 57*, [1978] 2 S.C.R. 267.

[390] *Hill, supra*, n. 384, at p. 1198.

[391] Cory J. cited the following statistics on damage awards in *Hill v. Church of Scientology of Toronto, supra*, n. 384, at p. 1198: from 1987 to 1991, 27 libel judgments were reported with an average award of $30,000; from 1992 to 1995, 24 libel judgments were reported with an average award of less than $20,000.

[392] In *Carson v. John Fairfax & Sons Ltd.*, (1993), 113 A.L.R. 577, a slim 4-3 majority decided in favour of referring to damages made in personal injury cases. The English Court of Appeal reached a similar conclusion in *John v. MGN Ltd.*, [1996] 3 W.L.R. 593, at p. 614 that "[I]t is . . . offensive to public opinion, and rightly so, that a defamation plaintiff should recover damages for injury to reputation greater, perhaps by a significant factor, than if that same plaintiff had been rendered a helpless cripple or an insensate vegetable. The time has in our view come that judges, and counsel, should be free to draw the attention of juries to these comparisons".

[393] *Hill, supra*, n. 384, at p. 1205. See also *Walker v. CFTO Ltd.* (1987), 59 O.R. (2d) 104 (C.A.).

[394] *Ibid.*, at p. 1206. While evidence of carelessness will not generally be sufficient to make a finding of actual malice, a higher standard may be applied to a lawyer, ". . . who must be presumed to be reasonably familiar with both the law of libel and the legal consequences flowing from the signing of a document": *Botiuk, supra*, n. 272, at p. 631. As a result, Cory J. concluded in *Botiuk* at p. 631 that ". . . actions which might be characterized as careless behaviour in a lay person could well become reckless behaviour in a lawyer with all the resulting legal consequences of reckless behaviour".

[395] The mitigation of damages by way of an apology is explicitly set out in some provincial legislation. See, for example, R.S.O. 1990, c. L.12, s. 9(1). See also s. 5(1). These sections were discussed in *Murray Alter's Talent Associates Ltd. v. Toronto Star* (1995), 124 D.L.R. (4th) 105 (Ont. Div. Ct.).

from bringing the action; whether the defendant subjected the plaintiff to a "hostile cross-examination"; the manner in which the defendant conducted its defence; and, finally, the defendant's conduct at the time of the defamatory publication.[396] Evidence that the defendant ". . . clearly aimed at obtaining the widest possible publicity in circumstances that were the most adverse possible to the plaintiff" may, according to Cory J., justify aggravated damages on this latter indicia.[397] Where aggravated damages are awarded, joint tortfeasors will not be jointly and severally liable, as with general damages. Instead, aggravated damages ". . . arise from the misconduct of the particular defendant against whom they are awarded".[398]

As with all punitive damage awards, punitive damages in the defamation context are awarded in order to punish the defendant and to deter others from acting in a similar manner. As a result, ". . . punitive damages should only be awarded in those circumstances where the combined award of general and aggravated damages would be insufficient to achieve the goal of punishment and deterrence".[399] For example, $800,000 punitive damages were awarded against the Church of Scientology in *Hill v. Church of Scientology of Toronto*, in addition to the award of $800,000 for general and aggravated damages, because there was ". . . insidious, pernicious and persistent malice" evident in the actions of Church of Scientology which could not adequately be punished or deterred through general and aggravated damages alone.[400]

In only the rarest and clearest of cases, an injunction may be awarded to restrain the publication of a libel,[401] because of the need to "protect free speech and unimpeded expression of opinion."[402] Nevertheless, where the words on a picket sign, "Abortion Butcher Sent to Jail", were found to be absolutely false, an interlocutory injunction was issued. It is, however, only where the words complained of are so "manifestly defamatory that only jury verdict to the contrary would be considered perverse", that an injunction should be issued in advance of trial.[403]

In conclusion, defamation law is available to assist individuals whose reputations have been besmirched by improper methods. Other remedies are available but they are often inappropriate. For example, a criminal prosecution may be too harsh a weapon. On the other hand, a slap on the wrist by a press council may be too lenient. A defamation action, though certainly cumbersome and expensive,

---

[396] *Hill, supra*, n. 384, at p. 1206.
[397] *Ibid.*
[398] *Ibid.*, at p. 1208. See also *Egger v. Chelmsford*, [1965] 1 W.B. 248 (C.A.).
[399] *Ibid.* See also *Rookes v. Barnard*, [1964] A.C. 1129.
[400] *Ibid.*, at p. 1211. See also *Vogel v. C.B.C.*, *supra*, n. 41, in which punitive damages were awarded against members of the media.
[401] See *Ontario (Attorney-General) v. Dieleman* (1994), 117 D.L.R. (4th) 449 (*per* Adams J.) (Ont. Gen. Div.).
[402] See Stark J. in *Canada Metal Co. v. Canadian Broadcasting Corp.* (1975), 55 D.L.R. (3d) 42 (Ont. Div. Ct.).
[403] *Rapp v. McClelland and Stewart Ltd.* (1981), 19 C.C.L.T. 68 (Ont. H.C.).

may offer the best blend of deterrence and compensation, without unduly inhibiting free speech. That is, undoubtedly, why the defamation action has survived and will continue to flourish, despite its many obvious shortcomings.[404] Just like other areas of tort law, it just happens to serve our society and therefore is worthy of preservation until something better can be found.

---

[404] A major blueprint for reform has been offered by Forer, *A Chilling Effect* (1987); see also Smolla, *Suing the Press* (1986); Franklin, "Winners and Losers and Why", [1980] A.B.F. Res. J. 457, empirical study of defamation cases showing 86% of appeals by defendants successful in U.S.

Chapter 20

The Civil Law of Delict in Quebec[1]

Tort law operates differently in the province of Quebec. Whereas nine provinces and the three territories of Canada are governed by the common law regime of torts, drawn mostly from English sources, the province of Quebec belongs to the romanist and civilian tradition derived mostly from French law. This tradition is based principally upon a codified body of law expressed as a series of general rules or propositions which are interpreted and applied by the courts with reference to past jurisprudence and scholarly doctrine. This chapter is designed to introduce, if only in a cursory manner, Quebec's law of delict, as tort law is called there, to students and practitioners in the common law jurisdictions of Canada and elsewhere who are not familiar with the civil law's approach to issues of delictual or "extra-contractual" liability.

The first Civil Code of Quebec (then known as the Civil Code of Lower Canada) came into force in 1866. Its main source of inspiration was the French Civil Code of 1804,[2] as well as the corresponding French jurisprudence that had been decided for more than 50 years. Yet, the Quebec codifiers did not hesitate to depart from the French solutions where they felt it was necessary to reflect their own national culture and tradition.[3]

The Civil Code of Lower Canada originally contained only four articles dealing with extra-contractual or delictual liability, namely, arts. 1053 to 1056 C.C.L.C. Five more sections were added over the years.[4] The cornerstone

---

[1] This chapter is based principally upon a book and monograph prepared by the Honourable Mr. Justice Jean-Louis Baudouin of the Quebec Court of Appeal. Mr. Justice Baudouin is the recognized authority on contractual and extra-contractual liability in Quebec civil law. He is also a professor at the Faculty of Law of the University of Montreal; see Baudouin and Deslauriers, *La responsabilité civile*, 5th ed. (Cowansville, Que.: Yvon Blais, 1998).

[2] Also known as the Napoleonic Code.

[3] See Brierley, "Quebec's Civil Law Codification Viewed and Reviewed" (1968), 14 McGill L.J. 521; Association Henri Capitant, *Droit québecois et droit français: communauté, autonomie, concordance* (Cowansville, Que.: Yvon Blais, 1993).

[4] Arts. 1054.1 (re: liability of tutors and curators); 1056a. and d. (prohibiting civil actions with the adoption of workers' compensation and automobile accident compensation legislation); 1056b.

provisions framing the law of delict in the original Civil Code were arts. 1053, 1054 and 1055 C.C.L.C., dealing respectively with the general principles of liability for one's own fault, liability for the faults of others (*e.g.*, children, students, employees), liability for things under one's care, and liability of pet owners and building owners. These sections were drawn directly from French sources but were not identical to the corresponding sections of the Napoleonic Code. Indeed, these provisions were interpreted differently by Quebec courts, which, in a number of cases, chose to depart markedly from French jurisprudence.

On January 1, 1994, the new Civil Code, known as the Civil Code of Quebec, came into force, replacing the old Civil Code of Lower Canada. Sections 1457 to 1481 C.C.Q. now deal with civil liability. By and large, the 1994 Civil Code codifies the basic solutions arrived at by the jurisprudence under the old Code and does not depart significantly from the previous tradition.[5] It innovates, however, in codifying a number of rules that, under the previous regime, were exclusively jurisprudential[6] and in adding entirely new rules to the existing body of law.[7]

The civil liability provisions of the new Civil Code maintain the general structure established by the corresponding provisions of the old Code. In this way, the Quebec system of civil liability can be best divided into two broad categories. The first category is the general regime, which includes the liability resulting from one's own fault, from damages caused by others for whom one can be held accountable, and for damages caused by things under one's care. The second category includes an increasing corpus of civil liabilities that are governed by specific statutes which, most of the time, have done away with the notion of fault and adopted a system of compensation based on the notion of risk or absolute liability. The rest of this chapter will concentrate on the first of these two categories, namely, the general regime of delictual liability and the basic conditions necessary for its imposition.

A. General Conditions for Delictual Liability

There are four basic conditions to the existence of civil liability in Quebec law. First, the defendant must be endowed with mental capacity. Second, the defendant must be at fault. Third, that fault must have brought about a harm or a loss. Fourth, there must be a sufficient causal connection between the fault of the defendant and the harm or loss caused to the plaintiff. These basic conditions

---

(protecting the rights of accident victims); and 1056c. (re: legal interest payable on the final award of damages).

5   Brierley, "The Revival of Quebec's Distinct Culture: The New Civil Code of Quebec" (1992), 42 U.T.L.J. 484.

6   *E.g.*, arts. 1478 to 1481 C.C.Q., regarding the apportionment of liability.

7   *E.g.*, art. 1471 C.C.Q., regarding the exception, in some cases, of "good samaritans" from liability.

are expressed in art. 1457 C.C.Q., which is the first and foundational provision in the Code's chapter on civil liability. It reads:

> **1457.** Every person has a duty to abide by the rules of conduct which lie upon him, according to the circumstances, usage or law, so as not to cause injury to another.
>
> Where he is endowed with reason and fails in this duty, he is responsible for any injury he causes to another person and is liable to reparation for the injury, whether it be bodily, moral or material in nature.
>
> He is also liable, in certain cases, to reparation for injury caused to another by the act or fault of another person or by the act of things in his custody.

1. CAPACITY

It is a basic principle in Quebec law that civil liability can only be imposed on persons who have the capacity to know and understand the consequences of their acts or omissions and who are able to discern right from wrong. The phrase "[w]here he is endowed with reason" in art. 1457 C.C.Q. clearly states the principle that mental capacity is a condition precedent to the existence of civil liability.

Determining the existence of capacity becomes an issue with respect to three categories of persons: underage children, mentally handicapped persons, and moral persons or organizations. The inability to commit a fault can result from incapacity related to tender age or derived from a mental condition that prevents the defendant from properly distinguishing right from wrong or from foreseeing the normal consequences of one's acts or omissions. However, in the case of incapacity resulting from a mental condition, the law will not excuse persons who have voluntarily or by negligence brought about their own incapacity by, for example, coming under the influence of alcohol or illegal drugs. In such cases, liability will be imposed on the theory that such behaviour is in itself a fault.

Unlike the criminal law, Quebec civil law does not impose a "bright line" rule stipulating the age at which a child automatically becomes open to civil liability. Rather, civil courts have been left to determine capacity on a case-by-case basis. By and large, courts have generally regarded the transition period to full capacity as taking place at age seven or eight. However, this guideline will vary with the particular circumstances of each case, and the court will consider the intelligence and maturity of the child, his or her degree of education and, for comparative purposes, the behaviour of a child of the same age and under the same circumstances who would have conducted him or herself in a reasonably prudent and diligent manner.[8] The same rules apply to mentally handicapped persons. In such cases, incapacity remains a question of fact that does not depend upon a previous judicial finding of incapacity.

---

[8]   Kasirer, "The Infant as Bon Père de Famille: Objectively Wrongful Conduct in the Civil Law Tradition" (1992), Am. J. Comp. L. 343.

Should a person be found not to possess the requisite capacity to attract civil liability, the victim will be left without compensation and the loss suffered will be considered to have been caused by a fortuitous event. Of course, leaving victims without legal recourse is a socially undesirable state of affairs. For this reason, arts. 1459 and 1460 C.C.Q. impose vicarious liability on parents and those who assume a duty of supervision or education of children (*e.g.*, teachers, educators and guardians). However, such liability is subject to certain precise conditions being met. Similarly, art. 1461 C.C.Q. imposes vicarious liability on tutors or guardians of mentally handicapped persons, but such liability is limited to instances where an intentional fault or gross negligence on their part can be proven. In any event, a third person cannot be found liable for the act or omission of a person not endowed with reason if the latter's conduct would not otherwise be considered wrongful.[9] Articles 1459 to 1461 C.C.Q. establish three of the special regimes for civil liability in the Code, which will be discussed later in the chapter.

"Moral persons" or organizations such as corporations, partnerships, trade unions or associations do not, of course, have a will of their own. They can only act through their legal representatives. Nonetheless, they can be held liable in the same manner and under the same conditions as a physical person. Their regime of liability, however, is best characterized as a regime of liability for others in that they are accountable for the damage caused by their representatives, agents or directors acting for them. For example, administrators ("mandataries") under arts. 300, 311, 321, 2160 and 2164 C.C.Q. will by their acts render a corporation civilly liable.[10] Though denied legal personality in the nineteenth century, trade unions can now also be sued for their tortious acts and those of their members. Indeed, losses flowing from illegal strikes have given rise to an abundant jurisprudence.[11]

Historically Quebec had held that both the federal and provincial governments were totally immune from liability. With respect to the liability of the Crown in right of Canada, the position, like in the rest of Canada, has evolved towards greater government accountability, as has been described in Chapter 17. The liability of the Crown in right of Quebec, however, is somewhat different. Article 1376 C.C.Q. has effectively done away with the general rule of Crown immunity, stating as it does that the Code's rules on obligations "apply to the State and its bodies, and to all other legal persons established in the public interest, subject to any other rules of law which may be applicable to them". This general openness to civil liability is buttressed by art. 1464 C.C.Q., which provides that an agent or servant of the State or of a Crown corporation contin-

---

[9] Art. 1462 C.C.Q.
[10] Baudouin and Deslauriers, *supra*, n. 1, at ¶92-93.
[11] See, *e.g.*, *West Island Teachers' Association v. Nantel*, [1988] R.J.Q. 1569 (C.A.); *Quebec (Public Curator) v. Syndicat national des employés de l'Hôpital St-Ferdinand*, [1996] 3 S.C.R. 211.

ues to act in the performance of his or her duties even where he or she performs an illegal or unauthorized act or an act outside of his or her competence.

2. FAULT

Liability cannot be imposed without a finding of fault. Indeed, the system of civil liability in Quebec is premised on the concept of fault. Not unlike the common law notion of negligence, fault can be understood as arising from the breach of a duty imposed by law. Such duty can be based in a specific legislative text or in the more general standard of good behaviour prescribed by art. 1457 C.C.Q., namely, that "(e)very person has a duty to abide by the rules of conduct which lie upon him, according to the circumstances, usage or law, so as not to cause injury to another". The wording of art. 1457 C.C.Q. makes it clear that allegedly wrongful conduct will crystallize into a fault where it falls short of the conduct expected of a normally prudent and reasonable person acting under identical circumstances. In this way, fault can also be understood as the transgression or violation of a minimum norm of behaviour accepted by law in human relationships. This standard model of good conduct, when not flowing from a legislative norm, is a judicial construct which is always evolving, making the notion of fault a flexible and adaptable one that has been able to reflect prevailing social, cultural and economic contexts and developments.[12]

Though fault remains the cornerstone of civil liability in Quebec, certain statutory regimes are based on different rationales such as the theory of risk or strict liability.[13] For example, an employer will be responsible for work accidents suffered by his or her employees, without the necessity of fault being proven on his or her part, simply because the employer derives financial profit from the economic activity of his or her workers. Fault has also been displaced in the compensation scheme for traffic accidents. That scheme proceeds on the basis that automobiles represent a serious and known risk in modern society. Therefore, it is socially desirable that victim compensation not be left to the uncertainties of judicial evaluation of the conduct of alleged tortfeasors. Rather, the economic burden should be borne by the community as a whole.

a) The Classification of Fault

Articles 1457 and 1458 C.C.Q. codify the rule that contractual and extra-contractual fault are but two different illustrations of the same concept. On the one hand, parties to a contract are at fault should they fail to perform an explicit or implicit obligation which they have agreed to under the contract. On the other hand, individuals will be liable civilly if they fail to behave as a normally prudent and diligent person would have behaved in identical circumstances. In the first case, the liability stems from the failure to perform a duty voluntarily

---

[12] Baudouin and Deslauriers, *supra*, n. 1, at ¶125ff.
[13] L. Josserand, *De la responsabilité du fait des choses inanimées* (Paris: Rousseau, 1897).

assumed, while in the second case, the liability results from the failure to act in conformity with a legislative or jurisprudential standard. However, the contractual and extra-contractual regimes of fault are not interchangeable. Article 1458 C.C.Q. specifically prevents a party to a contract from avoiding the application of the contractual regime and opting for the delictual rules, even if they are more favourable. However, it remains for the courts to clearly distinguish between those duties that should reasonably be qualified as duties implicitly resulting from the contract and those duties said to derive from the general duty imposed by law to repair the harm caused to another by one's fault.

Unlike the traditional common law, which is reluctant to impose liability unless there exists a positive duty to act, the Quebec civilian system has always taken the view that fault can result both from an action or an omission (for instance, the failure to help someone in danger).[14] This position flows logically from the approach of comparing an alleged tortfeasor's conduct (whether active or passive) against that of a reasonable person in the circumstances. The paramountcy of compensating victims for the damage they have suffered means that the intentional or unintentional character of the impugned act or omission is immaterial and does not enter the analysis at the stage of determining the existence of fault. However, the intentional nature of the fault may have some impact at the stage of determining damages, particularly punitive damages. From a purely practical point of view, a plaintiff who proves that a fault is intentional will not, as a rule, have to prove causality between the fault and the loss suffered; such causality will be presumed. Moreover, in certain exceptional cases, for public policy reasons, the Code limits the liability of principals to damages arising from their intentional acts. This is the case for tutors, curators or guardians with respect to damages caused by legally incapable adults in their custody (art. 1461 C.C.Q.) and for the "good samaritan" who injures another in coming to their aid (art. 1471 C.C.Q.).

Unlike the Roman law, Quebec law has not distinguished between different degrees of fault (*culpa levis, culpa levissima, culpa lata*). However, the notion of "gross negligence" ("faute lourde"), involving the total and wanton disregard for others, is recognized both in the Code and the case law, and such notion gives rise to important legal effects. For instance, contractual limitations of liability are unenforceable in cases of gross negligence. Similarly, liability insurance for damage caused by ordinary faults does not extend to cover intentional or gross faults.

Finally, let us consider the effect of a breach of a statutory duty. The breach of a statutory duty in Quebec law will in principle be considered a civil fault giving rise to liability as long as all of the other necessary elements of civil liability are present. In other words, the breach of statutory duty must be causally connected to the damage suffered by the plaintiff. If this were not the

---

[14]   Quebec Charter of Human Rights and Freedoms, R.S.Q., c. C-12, art. 2; S. Rogers-Magnet, "The Right to Emergency Medical Assistance in Quebec" (1980), 40 R. du B. 373.

case, liability could automatically be imposed in inappropriate circumstances such as where a participant in a car accident does not possess a driver's licence required by statute. The failure to obtain a licence is not causally connected to the accident itself. Rather, the fault lies in the ability of the driver, and reference must therefore be made to the standard of conduct expected of a reasonably prudent driver under similar circumstances. Conversely, meeting a minimum statutory standard set out by the legislator will not confer absolute immunity from liability since the particular circumstances may, of course, call for a higher standard of conduct.

b) The Standard of Care

As has been seen, determining the existence of fault requires courts to compare the conduct of a defendant to an abstract model, *i.e.*, the reasonably prudent and diligent person.[15] The jurisprudential standard of reference is the ordinary citizen, not the person who possesses the highest possible degree of education, intelligence and skill. This standard will always be applied in the context of the specific facts of the case such that the impugned conduct of a physician will be compared to that of the reasonably diligent physician in the same specialty and acting in the same circumstances.

c) Excuses and Justifications

There are a limited number of excuses and justifications which, if successfully invoked, will excuse an act otherwise determined to be a "fault" or mitigate the liability normally flowing from such conduct. Self-defence, a classic criminal law justification, is also recognized in civil law in that a person is allowed to use reasonable force to avoid personal or property damage. The standard required by civil courts, however, will be less strict than that imposed at criminal law.[16] Provocation may also, in certain circumstances, be considered as a mitigating factor in order to justify the imposition of divided liability between the defendant and the victim.

Actions taken to uphold the law will, in principle, be an excuse or justification for an act that would otherwise have the appearance of a fault. This is the case, for instance, of a police officer arresting a suspect and causing him or her some damage in the process. However, the use of unnecessary force by a police officer in carrying out an otherwise legal arrest would not be justified, as the officer must nevertheless comply with the standard of conduct expected from a reasonably prudent and diligent police officer in the circumstances. Obeying a superior's legitimate orders is a related justification for an otherwise wrongful

---

[15] This abstraction was referred to in the older jurisprudence as the "bon père de famille".

[16] *Di Perna v. Courval*, [1994] R.R.A. 506 (Sup. Ct.); *Coulombe-Vaillancourt v. Dumont*, [1994] R.R.A. 292 (Sup. Ct.).

act. This justification does not apply, however, where the order being obeyed is itself illegal or if, while obeying such order, the defendant commits a fault.

There are a number of additional justifications that warrant mention. Necessity has been recognized in the jurisprudence as a justification for an otherwise wrongful act. Though rarely applicable in civil matters, the doctrine of necessity can be invoked where a person deliberately causes some kind of damage in order to prevent the occurrence of a much larger damage. In this way, a fire brigade could invoke the justification of necessity where it decided to demolish an individual's house in order to contain the spread of a fire.[17] The act of rescuing another has also been recognized in the jurisprudence as meriting some limited protection. As a general proposition, damage caused by the awkward or clumsy acts of a rescuer will not give rise to liability unless he or she has acted in a reckless manner.[18]

Finally, assumption of the risk and the victim's consent may also serve to exonerate persons from the normal legal consequences of their actions. Of course, any assumption of the risk or giving of consent must be clearly discernable on the evidence. Moreover, the acceptable scope of consent is likely limited by public order. As to the assumption of risk, the author of the damage will only be exonerated for the harm normally associated with the risks known and assumed by the victim. There will be no justification for harm caused by aggravating circumstances flowing from a defendant's fault. The Civil Code also provides a number of rules governing the exemption from liability which need not be canvassed in this chapter.[19]

d) Abuse of Rights

The Code also contemplates situations where a right may be exercised in a manner that can attract liability. Art. 7 C.C.Q. states:

> **7.** No right may be exercised with the intent of injuring another or in an excessive and unreasonable manner which is contrary to the requirements of good faith.

The abuse-of-right theory has been the object of intense doctrinal and jurisprudential debate in Quebec.[20] It is not yet clear whether the doctrine of abuse of rights is merely a specific illustration of the notion of fault in the exercise of a subjective right or rather a separate notion referring to cases where the exercise of a right, although done in a perfectly legal manner, produces antisocial effects.

For the limited purposes of this chapter, it will suffice to outline the application of the abuse of rights doctrine with respect to two different types of rights: property rights and procedural/judicial rights. Insofar as property rights are

---

[17]   *Mahoney v. Cité de Québec* (1901), 10 B.R. 378.

[18]   Baudouin and Deslauriers, *supra*, n. 1, at ¶163.

[19]   See arts. 1470-1477 C.C.Q.

[20]   A detailed examination of this debate is beyond the scope of this chapter; however, a good overview is found in Baudouin and Deslauriers, *supra*, n. 1, at ¶166ff.

concerned, courts will qualify as abusive any conduct that deliberately seeks to deprive one's neighbour of the normal use and enjoyment of his or her property. The example *par excellence* of such conduct is the erection of an unseemly fence for the sole purpose of destroying a neighbour's view from his or her property.[21] It should be noted, however, that courts have applied the abuse of rights doctrine in cases where no intentional fault could be discerned from a defendant's conduct but where the mere exercise of his or her property rights caused undue or unusual damages to third persons. This is the case, for example, of polluting industries which hold the necessary licences or permits to emit such pollutants and which even do their best to diminish the inconvenience to their neighbours.[22] The standard applied in such cases does not appear to be the classic standard of fault, but rather some other standard of antisocial behaviour in the exercise of a right. Indeed, this interpretation is consonant with art. 976 C.C.Q., which states that:

976. Neighbours shall suffer the normal neighbourhood annoyances that are not beyond the limit of tolerance they owe each other, according to the nature or location of their land or local custom.

In these cases, it is no defence for the defendant to have had the necessary administrative authorizations and licences. Nor is the fact that the defendant was established on his or her property prior to the plaintiff becoming a neighbour considered a bar to injunctive relief or damages.

Quebec courts have also long recognized the application of abuse of rights theory in cases where procedural or judicial rights have been exercised without discrimination, without reasonable or probable cause, in a negligent or malicious manner, or in bad faith. For example, there exists in Quebec a large body of jurisprudence holding various people responsible for malicious, imprudent or simply negligent arrests or seizures of property. The simple fact that, before acting, the defendant sought legal advice is no excuse, and, in certain cases, lawyers have also been held personally liable for abusive or dilatory proceedings.[23] Of course, the dismissal of an action will not necessarily give rise to an action in damages for malicious prosecution. There must be conclusive evidence demonstrating that the commencement of the action was, in the first place, a fault.

Under the old Civil Code of Lower Canada, courts had been reluctant to apply the abuse-of-rights doctrine to contractual matters. However, by the 1950s they began to recognize that a subjective right voluntarily given to a contracting party could, in certain circumstances, be exercised abusively and give rise to liability.[24] This position was formally adopted by the Supreme Court in *Houle v.*

---

[21]   See, *e.g.*, *Brodeur v. Choinière*, [1945] C.S. 334.

[22]   *Drysdale v. Dugas* (1894), 26 S.C.R. 20; *Canada Paper Co. v. Brown* (1922), 63 S.C.R. 243.

[23]   *Juneau v. Taillefer*, [1992] R.J.Q. 2550 (Sup. Ct.).

[24]   *Quaker Oats Co. of Canada v. Côté*, [1949] K.B. 389.

National Bank of Canada,[25] and the new Civil Code of Quebec includes a series of rules concerning the unconscionability of contracts. Abuse of rights in contractual matters is now the law.

3. DAMAGE

The existence of a loss or harm is the third general requirement for the imposition of civil liability. Even acts of gross negligence will not give rise to liability if no damage is suffered as a consequence thereof. Nor is there a relationship between the degree or magnitude of fault and recoverable damages. Indeed, even a modest fault can engender significant damages. As long as the fault causes the loss or harm, the amount of such loss will, as a general rule, be recoverable. However, as at common law, Quebec civil law imposes principled limits to recoverable damages. These limits contain recoverable damages to those that are certain, directly related to the fault committed and suffered in the course of lawful activity.

Art. 1607 C.C.Q. codifies the rule that only direct damages are compensable. Those that qualify as too remote will not, therefore, be recoverable. The difficulty of distinguishing direct from remote damages has been reflected in the jurisprudence.[26] It is now well settled, however, that direct damages are not only those caused to the immediate victim, but also those suffered by third parties that result from the same negligent act. For instance, courts have awarded damages for loss of *consortium* and *servitium* where a spouse has been injured and for shock suffered by family members of an accident victim. Similarly, an insurer who has paid an insured under a civil liability insurance policy has a right of action against the tortfeasor under art. 2472 C.C.Q. while a victim is given the option of suing the insured, the insurer or both in accordance with art. 2501 C.C.Q.

The second limit on recoverable damages is that they must be certain. In practice, courts require that the occurrence of the damage, in the past or in the future, is reasonably certain under the circumstances. In this way, damages are allowed to compensate future physical incapacity where expert medical evidence is adduced. Compensation for "loss of chance", however, has given rise to jurisprudential controversies in legal and medical malpractice cases.[27] A client or patient will be compensated for his or her loss if, due to the fault of the lawyer or physician, the possibility has been lost of bringing a potentially victorious claim before the courts or of recovering one's health. Naturally, the determining factor in such cases will be the probability of the claim's success or of the medical recovery absent the fault of the lawyer or physician.

Recoverable damages are further limited to those that are suffered in the course of lawful activity. Any loss suffered during the conduct of illicit activity

---

[25] [1990] 3 S.C.R. 122.
[26] *Regent Taxi & Transport Co. v. Congrégation des Petits Fréres de Marie*, [1929] S.C.R. 650.
[27] See Baudouin and Deslauriers, *supra*, n. 1, at ¶243-246.

will not be compensated. In a similar vein, the law will not, as a matter of public order, recognize certain "damages" as being compensable. This is the case, for example, of a child's claim for wrongful life where his or her parents had undertaken sterilization procedures so as not to have any more children. Coming into the world, by itself, is not a prejudice.[28] However, parents can, in certain circumstances, receive compensation for the additional financial burden caused by the birth of an unwanted child.[29]

Once a victim is acknowledged to have suffered a compensable loss, it remains for the court to determine how and to what extent reparation should be made by the defendant. In this respect, the nature of compensation in Quebec civil law is as complex as it is at common law. The general assessment of damages is regulated by arts. 1611ff. C.C.Q. and is designed to compensate the actual loss suffered by the victim, including all direct damages. Compensation should put the aggrieved party in the same position as he or she would have been in had the delict not been committed. Of course, the assessment of non-pecuniary or "moral" damages, as they are called in Quebec, will never be straightforward, and the award of punitive damages in special circumstances also requires a degree of judgment on the part of the court.

Indeed, Quebec civil law has increasingly recognized the potential application of punitive damages where it once viewed such awards as limited to a few specific statutorily described circumstances.[30] The increased acceptance of punitive damages came in 1970 with adoption of the Quebec Charter of Rights and Freedoms, which specifically allows for the award of punitive damages in cases where a Charter right has been violated by an illicit and intentional act.[31] The Supreme Court has since confirmed the requirement of wilful intent such that gross negligence or a wanton disregard for the rights of others will not suffice to trigger an award of punitive damages.[32] Though the Civil Code lacks a general provision mandating the award of punitive damages, it does contain a number of articles that make such damages available in specific circumstances.[33] In assessing punitive damages, Quebec courts have by and large followed the guidelines set forth by art. 1621 C.C.Q., namely, that attention should given to the gravity of the defendant's fault, the defendant's financial situation, the amount of non-punitive damages already owing by the defendant, the fact that the payment of damages may be wholly or partly assumed by a third party and all other salient circumstances. It should be noted that the punitive awards

---

[28] *Cataford v. Moreau*, [1978] C.S. 933.

[29] *Engstrom v. Courteau*, [1986] R.J.Q. 3048 (C.S.); *Faucher-Grenier v. Laurence*, [1987] R.J.Q. 1109 (C.S.); *Suite v. Cooke*, [1993] R.J.Q. 514 (C.S.); affd [1995] R.J.Q. 2765 (C.A.).

[30] Baudouin and Deslauriers, *supra*, n. 1, at ¶253ff.

[31] R.S.Q., c. C-12, art. 49. See Dallaire, *Les dommages exemplaires sous le régime des chartes* (Montreal: Wilson & Lafleur, 1995).

[32] *Quebec (Public Curator) v. Syndicat national des employees de l'Hôpital St-Ferdinand, supra*, n. 11.

[33] *E.g.*, arts. 1899, 1902 & 1968 C.C.Q.

granted by Quebec courts are substantially lower than those granted by U.S. or other Canadian courts.

4. CAUSATION

The final requirement for civil liability is causation; that is, the defendant's fault must have a sufficient causal link to the loss suffered by the plaintiff. Despite a formidable and contentious corpus of scholarly theories of causation, Quebec courts have adopted a strictly practical approach to causation, steadfastly refusing to involve themselves in doctrinal controversies and discussions on the subject. Treating the issue of causation as a purely factual one, courts tend to rely most often on the notion of "adequate causation", coupled sometimes with a reasonable expectation test. As a general rule, the plaintiff's loss must be the direct, logical and immediate consequence of the defendant's fault. Similarly, if the damages sustained by the defendant were reasonably foreseeable in the circumstances under which the fault was committed, causality will be proven.

Matters become more complicated when the causal connection between the fault and the damage is interrupted by one or more intervening events. Such events may include a subsequent fault of a third party, the fault of the victim or the occurrence of a fortuitous event. Where the victim or a third party commits an intervening fault that outweighs the defendant's fault, the defendant will be exonerated from liability. Given the difficulty in weighing faults, the situation will often resolve itself by an apportionment of liability. In the case of an intervening fortuitous event, or "an act of God", the defendant will in principle be exonerated. However, probably for reasons of equity and in order not to deprive the victim of some form of compensation, courts have often held defendants liable on some basis or other.

Proof of the causal connection between the fault committed and the damage suffered will generally rest on the plaintiff's shoulders. However, the plaintiff will often benefit from legal and factual presumptions that will facilitate discharging the burden of proof.[34] If it can be demonstrated that, as a general rule, damages identical to those suffered by the plaintiff occur where the same type of fault committed by the defendant is involved, causation will be taken to be conclusively proven.

Causation also plays an important role in determining the appropriate apportionment of liability for damages resulting from the combination of several different acts. Where damage results from faults committed by a third party and the victim himself or herself, the latter can only recover the proportion of the total damage which is directly related to the fault of the third party. This limitation flows from the principle that plaintiffs must assume the economic consequences of their own fault, which itself is buttressed by art. 1479 C.C.Q.'s codification of the long-standing rule that victims must take all reasonable means to mitigate their losses. It is notable that Quebec courts have refused to

---

[34] See arts. 2846ff. C.C.Q.

adopt the old common law doctrine of contributory negligence, according to which victims were not entitled to compensation if their own fault contributed in any degree to the realization of the damage.[35] Instead, art. 1478 C.C.Q. clearly states that liability for damage caused by several persons will be shared by them according to the relative seriousness of the faults of each. However, Quebec courts do often apply the principle, familiar to the common law, of *volenti non fit injuria* whereby victims must accept the risks born of voluntarily exposing themselves to dangerous activities.[36]

B. Liability for the Acts or Faults of Others

The Civil Code recognizes certain situations in which liability will be imposed for the acts or omissions of others. The vicarious liability regimes set out at arts. 1459, 1460, 1461, and 1463 C.C.Q. are expressly contemplated by art. 1457, which, in addition to setting out the general duty of care owed to others, states that people are "also liable, in certain cases, to reparation for injury caused to another by the act or fault of another person. . . . " Vicarious liability is traditionally supported on two principal grounds. The first is the social policy concern that victims should not, in general, be left without any form of compensation. The second is the legal rationale that persons subject to vicarious liability assume towards the authors of potentially negligent acts a position of control and, therefore, a duty of adequate supervision so as to avoid causing injury to others. Accordingly, the codified regimes of vicarious liability seek to render more financially responsible debtors such as parents, educators, guardians and employers accountable for the acts of those persons under their authority and supervision.

1. PARENTS, EDUCATORS AND GUARDIANS

Article 1459 C.C.Q. imposes on individuals with parental authority vicarious liability for the damages caused by the faults or wrongful acts of their minor children. Specifically, the provision states:

> **1459.** A person having parental authority is liable to reparation for injury caused to another by the act or fault of the minor under his authority, unless he proves that he himself did not commit any fault with regard to the custody, supervision or education of the minor.
>
> A person deprived of parental authority is liable in the same manner, if the act or fault of the minor is related to the education he has given to him.

Article 1459 C.C.Q. codifies the jurisprudential rule[37] extending victim compensation to those cases where the defendant child, due to his or her young age

---

[35] As discussed in Chapter 13, contributory negligence is no longer a complete bar to recovery in common law jurisdictions of Canada.

[36] Giroux, "L'acceptation des risques" (1968), 9, C. de D. 65.

[37] *Laverdure v. Bélanger*, [1975] C.S. 612; affd on appeal October 21, 1977, Que. C.A.; leave to appeal rejected December 19, 1977, S.C.C.

or lack of mental capacity, is legally incapable of being found at fault. Of course, where children are endowed with reason, they can still be sued and remain personally responsible for the loss they have caused. In practice, however, the usually impecunious nature of minor children dissuades plaintiffs from taking them to court.

Imposing vicarious liability on parents provides plaintiffs with the necessary recourse to fuller compensation by creating against parents a presumption of fault in the custody, supervision or education of their minor children. The regime of parental responsibility is, therefore, premised on the existence of a link between a child's bad behaviour and a parent's negligence in educating and supervising the child. A presumption of fault will be triggered against the parent where the plaintiff can establish the filiation of the child, the minor age of the child at the time the damage was caused and the existence of a fault or wrongful act on the part of the child which caused damage to the plaintiff. If the plaintiff succeeds in triggering the presumption, parents will only be exonerated if they can demonstrate that they provided the child with a good education and that their supervision was adequate in the circumstances. In assessing rebuttal evidence offered by parents, courts will take account of all relevant factors including the age, social milieu and temper of the child as well as the education provided by the parents, their tolerance for the use by the child of dangerous things and the foreseeability of the child's behaviour given the parental knowledge of the child's past conduct. Every case is determined on its own merits and according to its own particular circumstances.[38]

Under art. 1460 C.C.Q., persons who do not have parental authority over children, but who are entrusted with their custody, supervision or education are similarly responsible for the damage caused by them. That provision reads as follows:

> **1460.** A person who, without having parental authority, is entrusted, by delegation or otherwise, with the custody, supervision, or education of a minor is liable, in the same manner as the person having parental authority, to reparation for injury caused by the act or fault of the minor.
>
> Where he is acting gratuitously or for reward, however, he is not liable unless it is proved that he has committed a fault.

Article 1460 C.C.Q. applies to a relatively broad cross-section of people, from teachers and coaches to camp counsellors and friends or family members. Though buttressing the alternate recourse afforded to plaintiffs by the parental liability regime, art. 1460 C.C.Q. is unique in restricting the liability of supervisors and educators acting gratuitously or for simple reward (*e.g.*, babysitters) to instances where such persons themselves committed a fault in the supervision or education of the minor. In all other cases, art. 1460 C.C.Q. operates in the same

---

[38] Boucher, "Minorité et responsabilité: essai de sociologie juridique" (1967), R.J.T. 432; Desrosiers, "La responsabilité de la mère pour le préjudice causé par son enfant" (1995), 36 C. de D. 61.

manner as art. 1459 C.C.Q. by requiring the plaintiff to prove the fault or act of the child causing damage, the minor age of the child and the status of the defendant as supervisor or educator of the child in order to establish against the defendant a rebuttable presumption of fault with respect to the supervision or education of the minor in his or her care.

It is noteworthy that arts. 1459 and 1460 C.C.Q. both target the negligent custody, supervision and education of minors, and it will therefore be difficult in some cases to determine who of the parent or educator/supervisor should ultimately be held responsible for a minor's conduct. For instance, harm caused by a child in the schoolyard can be attributable to a deficient upbringing on the part of the parents or to a lack of proper supervision by the school authorities or to both.

In the case of harm suffered as a result of acts by a person of full age who is not endowed with reason, the Code is less generous to potential plaintiffs. Art. 1461 governs that scenario and reads as follows:

> **1461.** Any person who, as tutor or curator or in any other quality, has custody of a person of full age who is not endowed with reason, is not liable to reparation for injury caused by any act of the person of full age, except where he is himself guilty of a deliberate or gross fault in exercising custody.

The limitation of liability to those cases of deliberate or gross fault on the part of the tutor or curator is an innovation of the 1994 Civil Code. The elimination of the old rule imposing vicarious liability in circumstances of ordinary negligence in the exercise of custody was thought necessary in order to promote voluntary tutorship or guardianship by family members.

2. EMPLOYERS

The Code also provides for a regime of vicarious liability vis-à-vis employers. Art. 1463 C.C.Q. establishes this regime in the following terms:

> **1463.** The principal is liable to reparation for injury caused by the fault of his agents and servants in the performance of their duties; nevertheless, he retains his recourses against them.

Unlike the rebuttable presumptions of fault imposed by the vicarious liability regimes applying to parents, educators and guardians, a strict liability approach has been adopted in art. 1463 C.C.Q. to address the issue of employer responsibility for the faults of his or her employees. This approach precludes the employer from exonerating him or herself by proving that an adequate level of supervision was maintained over employees. Rather, the only way an employer can deflect liability is to prove that the plaintiff has failed to establish one of the conditions necessary to trigger the strict liability regime: that the employee committed a fault causing prejudice to the plaintiff, that an employment relationship existed between the employee-tortfeasor and the employer-defendant, and that the fault was committed in the performance of the employee's duties.

While proving the existence of fault on the part of the employee is a relatively straightforward exercise, the latter two requirements for triggering an employer's strict liability have given rise to some difficulties in practice. The existence of an employment relationship will generally be found where the agent, servant or employee acted for the benefit of another within a context of subordination. The subordination of the employee to the employer must be manifested by the latter's direct and specific power of control. Among other things, courts will pay close attention to the nature of the contractual relationship, if any, between the alleged employer and employee to determine the existence of the requisite degree of control. Accordingly, contracts of employment or of mandate — but rarely contracts with independent contractors[39] — tend to include provisions for the direct control of the employee, agent or servant. Similarly, professionals cannot be held to be agents or employees of an institution because administrators do not have the expertise or authority to tell them how to treat their clients. This is particularly true in the case of health professionals working out of hospitals.[40]

The condition that the damage be caused during the performance of the employee's duties can also raise difficulties. As long as the fault is committed within the general framework of the employee's duties, the employer will find it very difficult to escape liability. For example, the fact that the fault amounts to a criminal act like assault will not by itself exonerate the employer.[41] Nor will the transgression of an express order discharge the employer from liability unless the employee has clearly stepped outside the performance of his or her duties. In this respect, disobedience as to the manner of performing a certain task will not *per se* take the employee outside of the scope of his or her duties.[42] In fact, a merely temporal connection between the employee's fault and the employment schedule will set up a rebuttable presumption that the injury to the plaintiff was caused in the performance of the employee's duties.[43] The only instance where the employer will escape vicarious liability is where the damage is caused by the employee totally outside the general scope of his or her functions. One jurisprudential illustration of this rule is the case of the angry bus driver who, after he has discharged his driving duties, violently assaults a former passenger who had caused a disturbance while riding on the driver's bus earlier in the day.[44]

---

[39] *Kerr v. Atlantic & North-West Railway* (1895), 25 S.C.R. 197; *Quebec Asbestos Corp. v. Couture*, [1929] S.C.R. 166.

[40] Ménard and D. Martin, *La responsabilité médicale pour la faute d'autrui* (Cowansville: Yvon Blais, 1992); Chalifoux, "Vers une nouvelle relation commettant-préposé" (1984), 44 R. du B. 815.

[41] *Hudson's Bay Co. v. Vaillancourt*, [1923] S.C.R. 414.

[42] *Zambon Co. v. Schrijvershof*, [1961] S.C.R. 291; *Hreha v. Gordon Vacuum Cleaners Inc.*, [1964] S.C. 316.

[43] *Trans-Quebec Helicopters Ltd. v. Estate of David Lee*, [1980] C.A. 596.

[44] *Cie de transport provincial v. Fortin*, [1956] S.C.R. 258.

The rationale for imposing a strict liability regime against employers is two-fold. First, as with the case of prejudice caused by minors, the legislator has sought to secure for plaintiffs a better chance of full compensation by allowing suit to be taken against the employer, who is likely more solvent than the individual employee. That the employer derives an economic benefit from the labour of his or employees helps to justify the social policy decision to impose strict vicarious liability. Second, the imposition of strict vicarious liability can be defended on the basis that employers should be taken to assume the risk of negligent employee conduct. By using the services of employees to perform what he or she should perform alone, the employer magnifies the risk of harm to others and therefore should properly assume responsibility for any harm that materializes from that risk.

C. Liability for Things Under One's Care

Like the common law, Quebec civil law recognizes a brand of the *res ipsa loquitur* doctrine. Though perhaps less controversial in the civil law than in the common law,[45] the doctrine developed for much the same reason in the two legal traditions. An effective regime of liability for damages caused by things under one's care was of considerable importance in the late nineteenth century, as such a regime was the only basis of compensation for labour accidents prior to the Workman's Compensation Act of 1909. It was often impossible for victims of work accidents to establish the cause of their injuries in order to relate them back to a fault on the part of the employer. The socially deplorable conse-quences of this state of affairs led courts to develop a new regime of liability out of the language contained in art. 1054 of the old Civil Code of Lower Canada, which read in part as follows:

> **1054.** He is responsible not only for the damage caused by his own fault, but also for that caused by the fault of persons under his control and by things he has under his care.

In forging this new regime, the courts read into the language of art. 1054 C.C.L.C. a presumption of fault against the custodian of the thing causing damage to another.[46] In other words, if the damage was caused by the autono-mous act of a thing, its guardian was presumed to be at fault and could only escape liability by showing that he or she acted in a prudent and diligent manner under the particular circumstances of the case.

---

[45] See Chapter 8, *infra*.

[46] The notion of presumptive fault as the cornerstone of the regime was first propounded by Anglin J. in *Shawinigan Carbide Co. v. Doucet* (1909), 42 S.C.R. 281 and was cemented in *Montreal (City) v. Watt and Scott Ltd.* (1930), 48 B.R. 295. See Crépeau, "Liability for Damage Caused by Things from the Civil Law Point of View" (1962), 40 Can. Bar Rev. 222.

1. GENERAL REGIME

This jurisprudential solution was formally entrenched by art. 1465 C.C.Q., which provides:

> **1465.** A person entrusted with the custody of a thing is liable to reparation for injury resulting from the autonomous act of the thing, unless he proves that he is not at fault.

Though no definition of "thing" exists in the Code, courts have interpreted the term broadly to include moveables[47] (chattels), immovables[48] (real property), with the possible exception of buildings,[49] and even incorporeal things such as electricity, steam, chemical emanations and gases. In order for the act of the thing to be "autonomous", the thing must have caused the damage by itself and not as a mere extension of normal human activity. Therefore, a loaded gun that falls off a table and injures someone is an autonomous act, but a gun fired by a person does the bidding of the shooter and does not act autonomously. Furthermore, the act of the thing will not be autonomous unless it plays an active or dynamic role in the creation of the damage. In this way, an icy pathway only passively causes a person to slip and fall, whereas icicles falling from a roof actively cause injury to a passerby. Finally, the thing must be in the custody or care of the defendant in order for the plaintiff to benefit from the presumption of fault. Custody exists where an individual has the power of, control, direction and surveillance of the thing. While custody and ownership often coincide, the law requires custody in fact rather than in any abstract sense. Accordingly, liability for damage caused by the autonomous act of something that has been stolen will rest not with the owner but the thief, who has immediate control of the thing. The control must also be exercised for the benefit of the actual controller such that an employee with actual custody of an object that causes damage to another will not attract liability because the control is exercised for the benefit of his or her employer. In this instance, the abstract control of the employer is sufficient to bring him or her within the scope of art. 1465 C.C.Q.'s presumption.

Once the plaintiff has established that the damage suffered was caused by a dynamic and autonomous act of something that was under the care of the defendant at the relevant time, the burden of proof is shifted to the defendant. This burden will be discharged if the defendant can prove that the damage was caused by a fortuitous act, the fault of a third party for whom he or she cannot be held responsible or the fault of the plaintiff. In practice, art. 1465 C.C.Q.'s

---

[47]   Article 905 C.C.Q. defines movables as "[t]hings which can be moved either by themselves or by an extrinsic force. . . ." See also arts. 906-907 C.C.Q.

[48]   Article 900 C.C.Q. provides the basic definition of immovables as "[l]and, and any constructions and works of a permanent nature located thereon and forming an integral part thereof. . . ." See also arts. 901-903 C.C.Q.

[49]   Article 1467 C.C.Q. provides a special regime for damage caused by buildings, but this regime only applies if the damage is attributable to a lack of repair or defect in construction. See discussion in the next section, below.

presumption of fault will require the defendant to prove conclusively the exact cause of the loss. The necessary standard of care is that of the normally prudent and diligent person in identical circumstances. Courts will pay particularly close attention to any knowledge the guardian may have had regarding the dangerous, defective or abnormal nature of the thing in his or her custody.

2. DAMAGE CAUSED BY BUILDINGS

Buildings are excluded from the general regime of art. 1465 C.C.Q. and are treated under a special regime found at art. 1467 C.C.Q., which imposes liability on owners of buildings that cause damage to others. Art. 1467 C.C.Q. reads as follows:

> **1467.** The owner of an immovable, without prejudice to his liability as custodian, is liable to reparation for injury caused by its ruin, even partial, where this has resulted from lack of repair or from a defect of construction.

It is clear from the wording of the provision that only owners are made liable, not persons like lessees who have actual control of a building from time to time. However, mere possessors — as well as owners — remain liable as custodians for damage caused for reasons other than the full or partial ruin of the immovable (*i.e.*, dynamic autonomous acts). Art. 1467 C.C.Q. singles out the owner for special treatment only for damages resulting from a lack of repair or defect in construction. The use of the general term "immovable" in the art. 1467 C.C.Q. is a codification of past jurisprudence which gave a large and liberal interpretation of the term "building" as used in the predecessor regime under the old Code.[50] Indeed, damage caused by staircases, balconies, walls, roofs and sprinklers had all been held to fall under the regime applicable to buildings.

A critical distinction between the regimes in arts. 1465 and 1467 C.C.Q. is that under the latter provision the plaintiff must conclusively show that the ruin or collapse of the building was due to a lack of repair or a defect in construction. Therefore, the plaintiff invoking art. 1467 C.C.Q. does not enjoy the preferential treatment with respect to causation that is accorded to victims seeking compensation under art. 1465 C.C.Q. In relating the damage to a defect in construction or a lack of repair, the plaintiff must keep in mind the purpose for a which a building and its parts are designed to be used. Accordingly, a window screen that gives way when someone leans against it is not defective because it is not intended to be subjected to unusual force.[51] The duty of the building owner is therefore limited to ensuring that the building is constructed and maintained in such a way as to make it solid and safe for the type of regular use for which it is intended. The burden of proving that this duty has been infringed rests entirely on the plaintiff.

---

[50] 1055 C.C.L.C.
[51] *Rubis v. Gray Rocks Inn Ltd.*, [1982] 1 S.C.R. 452.

However, once that burden is discharged, the owner is foreclosed from arguing his or her diligence, good faith or lack of knowledge as to the defect or lack of repair. Instead, the owner must successfully plead a fortuitous event, the fault of a third person for whom he or she cannot be held responsible or the fault of the victim. If the owner is ultimately held liable, he or she may pursue the actual builder, architect or maintenance person in warranty. Owners may also seek to limit or exclude their liability vis-à-vis their contractual counterparts such as lessees. In any event, however, an owner will never be able to escape liability for moral or bodily injury and liability arising from his or her gross negligence.[52]

3. DAMAGE CAUSED BY ANIMALS

Like buildings, animals also qualify as "things" yet are governed by a special regime for liability arising out of the damage they cause. Art. 1466 C.C.Q. sets out this regime in the terms that follow:

> **1466.** The owner of an animal is liable to reparation for injury it has caused, whether the animal was under his custody or that of a third person, or had strayed or escaped.
>
> A person making use of the animal is, together with the owner, also liable during that time.

The legal basis for the owner's liability is the care, custody and control of the animal, but the underlying theory is that owners or possessors of animals create a risk for others and therefore must compensate their victims should the risk materialize. In distinction to the general regime of liability for things in one's care, art. 1466 C.C.Q. applies both to the legal caretaker or custodian of the animal and to the person who in fact exercised control of the animal at the time the damage was caused. An example of this parallel liability is the case of damages caused by a dog while under the control of a veterinarian.

Art. 1466 C.C.Q. is most frequently applied to cases involving domesticated animals, but courts have also held defendants liable for the conduct of wild animals over which they in fact exercised a certain amount of control. Though the harm suffered by the plaintiff must have been caused by the act or conduct of the animal, no physical contact with the victim is necessary for the imposition of liability. Indeed, an owner whose pet frightens or startles a victim into a state of nervous shock will be held liable.

The regime of liability for damage caused by animals is unique in establishing a presumption of liability that cannot be overturned by proving the absence of fault on the part of the owner or handler. The only means of exoneration is to prove the damage was caused by a fortuitous event, the fault of the victim or the fault of a third person for whom the defendant cannot, in law, be held responsible.

---

[52] See art. 1474 C.C.Q.

Index

Index